NTA UGC NET/JRF/SET

PAPER - 2

Home Science

NTA UGC NET/JRF/SET

PAPER - 2

Home Science

Author

Nandini Sharma, Kanika Khandelwal
Renu Kulshreshtha, Monika Majumdar

ARIHANT PUBLICATION (INDIA) LIMITED

卐 **Administrative & Production Offices**

Regd. Office

'Ramchhaya' 4577/15, Agarwal Road, Darya Ganj, New Delhi -110002
Tele: 011- 47630600, 43518550

卐 **Head Office**

Kalindi, TP Nagar, Meerut (UP) - 250002
Tel: 0121-7156203, 7156204

卐 **Sales & Support Offices**

Agra, Ahmedabad, Bengaluru, Bareilly, Chennai, Delhi, Guwahati, Hyderabad, Jaipur, Jhansi, Kolkata, Lucknow, Nagpur & Pune.

卐 **PRICE** ₹675.00

卐 **PO No. :** TXT-59-T068432-12-25

Published by Arihant Publications (India) Ltd.

For further information about the books published by Arihant, log on to www.arihantbooks.com or e-mail at info@arihantbooks.com

PREFACE

NET (National Eligibility Test) determines eligibility for lectureship and for award of Junior Research Fellowship (JRF) for Indian nationals in order to ensure minimum standards for the entrants in the teaching profession and research. This test is conducted in Humanities (including languages), Social Sciences, Forensic Science, Environmental Sciences, Computer Science and Applications and Electronic Science.

UGC NET Tutor for Computer Science & Applications has been designed to help the students get away with their initial qualms and hiccups about the NET. In the course of preparation of this book, we have followed the pattern and syllabus of the examination for the maximum benefit of the aspirants, difficulty level of the questions has also been kept in mind.

Salient Features of the Book

- Only book in the market which has complete and exhaustive theory exactly on the UGC NET pattern and difficulty level.
- For complete understanding all units have been divided into individual chapters with sufficient number of Multlple Choice Questions.
- Separate study material have been given According to the Latest Syllabus.
- Previous Years' UGC NET questions have been covered chapterwise.

We are thankful to Arihant Publications (India) Limited for giving us this opportunity to make such a book, which will help the students to get 100% success. Any suggestion for the enhancement of the quality of this book is most welcome.

Author

CONTENTS

SYLLABUS

Applicabe from June 2019, Examination

UNIT-I FOOD SCIENCE AND FOOD SERVICE MANAGEMENT

- Food science and nutrition.
- Properties of food — physical and chemical properties
- Quality evaluation of foods — objectives and subjective.
- Effects of cooking and processing techniques on nutritional components and other physical parameters, food preservation and application.
- Food pigments and additives.
- Food standards, microbiological safety of food, HACCP, food packaging.
- Perspectives of food service — menu planning, food cost analysis.
- New product development — nano technology.
- Food service management of institutional level — hospital, educational institutions, social and special institutions.
- Research methods — fundamental issues, concept, need relevance, scope and ethics in research.

UNIT-II NUTRITION AND DIETETICS

- Food groups — balanced diet, food pyramid, macro and micro nutrition.
- Nutrients — role of nutrients in the body, nutrient deficiencies and requirements for Indians.
- Public health nutrition
- Nutrition through life span — physiological changes, growth and development from conception to adolescence, nutritional needs and dietary guidelines for adequate nutrition through life cycle, nutrition concerns.
- Community nutrition, sports nutrition, nutrition in emergencies and disasters.
- Nutritional assessment-methods and techniques.
- Nutritional intervention — national nutrition policies and programmes, food and nutrition security.
- Clinical and therapeutic nutrition.
- Diet counseling and management.
- Research methods — research designs, principles and purpose of research.

UNIT-III TEXTILES

- Textile terminologies — fibre, yarn, weave, fabric etc., classification of fibres, yarns and weaves, Identification of fibres and weaves.
- Manufacturing process of major natural and manmade fibres, properties and their end uses.
- Different methods of fabric construction — woven, knitted and non woven fabrics, their properties and end uses.
- Textiles finishes — classification, processing and purposes of finishes.
- Dyeing and printing — classification, method of block printing, tie and dye, batik, roller printing, screen printing, discharge, heat transfer printing and digitized printing.

- Traditional textiles of India — embroidered textiles, printed textiles, woven textiles, dyed textiles of various regions in India. Identification on the basis of fibre content, technique, motif, colour and designed.
- Textile Testing and quality control — need of testing, sampling method, techniques of testing fibres, yarn, fabrics and garments. Testing of colour — fastness, shrinkage, pilling and GSM of fabrics.
- Textile and environment — banned dyes, eco-friendly textiles, contamination and effluent treatment, Eco-label and eco marks.
- Recent developments in textiles and apparels — nano textiles, technical textiles, occupational clothing, zero waste designing, up cycling and recycling.
- Research methods — types of research, descriptive, survey, historical, qualitative, quantitative, analytical and
action research.

UNIT-IV APPAREL DESIGNING

- Body measurements — procedure, need, figure types and anthropometry.
- Equipments and tools used for manufacturing garments — advancements and attachments used for sewing machine. Types of machines used and their parts.
- Elements and principles of design and its application to apparel. Illustrations and parts of garments.
- Fashion-Terminologies, fashion cycle, fashion theories, fashion adoption, fashion forecasting and factors
affecting fashion.
- Pattern making — drafting, draping and flat pattern making techniques, pattern alteration and dart manipulation techniques.
- Apparel manufacturing — terminology used, seams, techniques and machines used, process of fabric to apparel manufacture.
- Apparel Quality testing — Quality standards and specification, Quality parameters and defects of fabrics
and garments.
- Care and maintenance of clothing-principles of washing, laundry agents, storage techniques case labels
and symbols.
- Selection of clothing for different age groups. Selection of fabrics for different and uses.
- Research methods — hypothesis testing, types and scope.

UNIT-V RESOURCE MANAGEMENT AND CONSUMER ISSUES

- Management — concept, approaches, management of time, energy, money, space, motivating factors, motivation theories, decision making.
- Functions of management — planning, supervision, controlling, organising, evaluation, family life cycle-stages, availability and use of resources.
- Resources — classification, characteristics, factors affecting use, resource conservation, time management, work simplification techniques, classes of change, fatigue and its management.
- Management of natural resources — land, forest, water, air, water harvesting, municipal solid waste management, concept of sustainable development, SDGs.
- Money management — family income, types, supplementation, budgeting, household accounts, family savings and investment, tax implications.

- Human resource management — functions, need, human resource development-challenges, functions, manpower planning, training need assessment, training methodologies, training evaluation.
- Consumer — definition, role, rights and responsibilities, consumer behavior, consumer problems, education
and empowerment.
- Consumer protection — consumer organisation, cooperatives, alternative redressal, standardisation, standard marks, quality control, buying aids, consumer legislation.
- Entrepreneurship — concept, process, barriers, entrepreneurial motivation, challenges, enterprise setting, project planning and appraisal, enterprise management.
- Research methods — sampling techniques, types of sampling, sampling procedures, probability and non
probability sampling.

UNIT-VI HOUSING AND INTERIOR DESIGN

- Design fundamentals — elements of art, principles of design, principles of composition.
- Colour — dimensions of colour, psychological effects of colour, colour schemes, factors affecting use of colour.
- Space planning and design — housing need and important, principles of planning spaces, types of house plans, economy in construction, planning for different income groups.
- Building regulations — norms and standards, zoning, housing for special groups and areas, housing finance.
- Housing and environment — building materials- impact on environment, green rating systems, energy efficiency in buildings, energy auditing, indices of indoor comfort.
- Energy as a resource — conventional and non-conventional sources, renewable /non-renewable energy, energy management, national efforts on energy conservation.
- Product design — design thinking process, diffusion and innovation, design communication, ergonomic considerations.
- Ergonomics — significance, scope, anthropometry, man, machine, environment relationship, factors affecting physiological cost of work, body mechanics, functional design of work place, time and motion
study, energy studies.
- Furniture and furnishing — historical perspectives, architectural styles, contemporary tends, wall finishes, window and window treatments.
- Research methods-selection and preparation of tools for data collection-questionnaire, interview, observation, measuring scales, ranking and measurement, reliability and validity of tools

UNIT-VII CHILD/HUMAN DEVELOPMENT

- Principles of growth and development, care during pregnancy and pre-natal and neonatal development.
- Theories of human development and behaviour.
- Early childhood care and education – activities to promote holistic development.
- Influence of family, peers, school, community and culture on personality development.
- Children and persons with special needs, care and support, special education, prevention of disabilities, rehabilitation.

- Children at risk — child labour, street children, children of destitute, orphans, child abuse and trafficking.
- Adolescence and youth: changes, challenges and programs to promote optimal development.
- Adulthood, characteristics, changing roles and responsibilities in early and middle adulthood.
- Ageing — physical and psychological changes and care needs.
- Research methods — types of variables and their selection.

UNIT-VIII FAMILY STUDIES

- Dynamics of marriage and family relationships.
- Family welfare — approaches, programmes and challenges, role in national development.
- Domestic violence, marital disharmony, conflict, resolution of conflict.
- Parent education, positive parenting, community education.
- Family disorganisation, single parent families.
- Family studies — family in crisis, family therapy, initiatives for child development.
- Human rights, rights of children, rights of women, status of women, gender roles.
- Guidance and counseling — across life span and for care givers.
- Health and well being across life span development.
- Research methods — data collection and classification, coding, tabulation, inferential and descriptive statistics.

UNIT-IX COMMUNICATION FOR DEVELOPMENT

- Basics of communication — nature, characteristics, functions, process, models, elements, principles, barriers, perception, persuasion and empathy, types of communication, levels (settings) of communication transactions, process of listening.
- Communication systems and communication theories — human interaction theories, mass communication theories, message design theories, communication systems, culture and communication.
- Concept of development — theories, models, measurement and indicators of development.
- Concept of development — communication models and approaches, diffusion and innovation, mass media,
social marketing.
- Role of communication in development- need and importance, development journalism, writing for development-print, radio, television and internet.
- Concerns of development communication — gender, health, environment, sustainability, human rights, population, literacy, rural and tribal development.
- Advocacy and behavior change communication — concept, theories, models, approaches, application and challenges.
- Traditional, modern and new media for development — folk forms of songs, art, dance, theatre, puppetry, advertisement, cinema, ICTs for development — community radio, participatory video, social media and mobile phones.

- Organisation/agencies/institutes working for development communication-international/national/state and local.
- Research methods — analysis of data through parametric and non parametric tests.

UNIT-X EXTENSION MANAGEMENT AND COMMUNITY DEVELOPMENT

- Historical perspectives of extension — genesis of extension education and extension systems in India and other countries, objectives of extension education and extension service, philosophy and principles of extension programme development.
- Programme management — need assessment, situation analysis, planning, organization, implementation, monitoring and evaluation.
- Extension methods and materials — interpersonal, small and large group methods, audiovisual aids-need, importance, planning, classification, preparation and field testing, use and evaluation of audio-visual materials.
- Curriculum development and planning for extension education and development activities, Bloom's taxonomy of educational objectives and learning.
- Non-Formal, adult and lifelong education — historical perspectives, concept, theories, approaches, scope, methods and materials used, challenges of implementation and evaluation, issues to be addressed.
- Training, skill development and capacity building for human resource development-methods of training, entrepreneurship development.
- Community development — perspectives, approaches, community organization, leadership, support structures for community development, Panchayati raj institutions, NGOs and community based organisations.
- People's participation and stakeholders' perspectives, Participatory Learning and Action-methods and techniques.
- Development programmes in India for urban, rural and tribal population groups- programmes for nutrition, health, education, wage and self employment, women's development, skill development, sanitation and infrastructure.
- Research methods — scientific report writing, presentation of data, interpretation and discussion.

Solved Papers 2024-23

Home Science (Paper-2)

Solved Paper, August 2024

General Instructions

1. There are total one hundred questions in this paper. Each question carries 2 marks.
2. All questions are compulsory.

---

1. Arrange the steps of Extension Program Planning in sequence.

A. Situation analysis

B. Need assessment

C. Determining objectives

D. Development of plan of work

E. Evaluation of progress

Choose the correct answer from the options given below.

(1) D, C, A, B, E (2) A, E, C, D, B
(3) B, A, C, E, D (4) A, B, C, D, E

2. World Diabetes Day is celebrated on

(1) 12th November (2) 13th November
(3) 14th November (4) 15th November

3. The three enzymes produced by the pancreas which continue breaking down proteins into simpler substances

A. Amylase B. Trypsin

C. Hydrochloric Acid D. Chymotrypsin

E. Carboxypeptidases

Choose the correct answer from the options given below.

(1) C, D and E (2) A, B and C
(3) A, B and D (4) B, D and E

4. The process of learning appropriate social behaviour chiefly by observing and imitating is known as

(1) cognitive learning
(2) reinforcement
(3) conditioning
(4) observational learning

5. The fatty acids known to be essential for complete human nutrition are

A. Linoleic acid

B. Alpha - linolenic

C. Sterols

D. Docosahexaenoic Acid

E. Transfatty Acid

Choose the correct answer from the options given below.

(1) A, B, C (2) B, C, D
(3) A, B ,D (4) C, D, E

6. In 1973, Henry Mintzberg provided one of the first comprehensive studies on.

(1) scientific management
(2) the nature of managerial work
(3) styles of leadership
(4) the wealth of nations

7. Culture possesses specific characteristics that shape it

A. culture in transferred

B. culture is common sense

C. culture is permanent and rewarding

D. culture is an adaptable category

E. culture in shared among members of the society

Choose the correct answer from the options given below.

(1) A, C, D, E (2) B, A, C and E
(3) A, B, C, D (4) A, B, D and E

8. Arrange the absorption and metabolism of iodine in correct sequence.

A. Iodide

B. Tri-iodothyronine (T_3)

C. Dietary Iodide

D. Iodine

E. Thyroxine (T_4)

Choose the correct answer from the options given below.

(1) A, B, C, D, E (2) C, A, D, E, B
(3) C, D, A, B, E (4) C, B, D, E, A

9. Arrange the steps of effective listening.

A. Don't ask questions to grab attention, empathise with the speaker.

B. Be open minded and create a mental picture of what the speaker is saying.

C. Give genuine feedback, both verbal and non-verbal.

D. Don't respond in haste, be patient, and wait for your turn.

E. Establish eye contact and observe the body language of the speaker.

Choose the correct answer from the options given below.

(1) B, E, D, A, C (2) E, D, C, A, B
(3) B, C, E, D, A (4) E, B, D, A, C

10. The single cell which divides again and again and is the beginning of life is

(1) DNA (2) Autosome
(3) Zygote (4) Chromosome

11. Well planned accent lighting puts the focus on

(1) lighting source (2) lighting fixture
(3) on desired objects (4) on work surfaces

12. Arrange the sequence of Erickson's stages of psychosocial development.

A. Initiative *v/s* Guilt

B. Generativity *v/s* Stagnation

C. Identity *v/s* Role Diffusion

D. Ego Integrity *v/s* Despair

E. Trust *v/s* Mistrust

Choose the correct answer from the options given below.

(1) E, A, C, B, D (2) A, C, E, B, D
(3) C, E, D, B, A (4) B, E, A, D, C

13. Dimensions of well-being during middle adulthood are

A. Self-acceptance

B. Autonomy

C. Grief and resentment

D. Midlife crises

E. Personal growth

Choose the correct answer from the options given below.

(1) A, C, E (2) A, B, E
(3) C, D, E (4) B, C, E

14. Which of the following is not the part of components of Investment Portfolio ?

(1) Financial investments
(2) Cash funds
(3) Defensive investments
(4) Aggressive investments

15. Match List-I with List-II.

	List-I		List-II
A.	Alkaline-ash diet	I.	Celiac disease
B.	Low purine diet	II.	Cystine calculi
C.	Moderate to low fat diet	III.	Obesity
D.	Low calorie diet	IV.	Gout

Codes

	A	B	C	D		A	B	C	D
(1)	I	II	III	IV	(2)	IV	I	II	III
(3)	II	IV	I	III	(4)	II	I	IV	III

16. One of the reasons due to which extension programs fail is

(1) commitment to goals
(2) recognition of limiting factors
(3) authoritarian management
(4) use of strategies for change

17. Identify the leadership styles from the following.

A. Laissez-fair B. Autocratic
C. Interactive D. Democratic
E. Bureaucratic

Choose the correct answer from the options given below.

(1) B, C, D (2) A, B, D
(3) A, B, C (4) B, D, E

18. Match List-I with List-II.

List-I (Novelty Yarns)		List-I (Structures)
A. Flock yarn	I.	Short thick pile yarn with soft velvety appearance
B. Chenille yarn	II.	Single yarn in which small tufts of fibers are inserted at regular intervals.
C. Core-spun yarn	III.	Base is heavy and coarse yarn. The effect yarn is curled up around the base and is held by the binder yarn.
D. Loop yarn	IV.	Base yarn is completely covered or wrapped by another yarn

Codes

	A	B	C	D
(1)	I	II	III	IV
(2)	II	I	IV	III
(3)	IV	III	I	II
(4)	III	IV	II	I

19. Arrange the steps in the manufacture of Cellulose Xanthate solution.

A. Ripening of viscose and filtration for the removal of foreign particles

B. Deaeration

C. Reaction with carbon disulphide for conversion to alkali-soluble cellulose xanthate and dissolution in dilute alkali

D. Reaction with strong alkali, known as steeping and shredding into small crumbs or lumps

E. Ageing of alkali cellulose for lowering the degree of polymerisation.

Choose the correct answer from the options given below.

(1) D, E, C, A, B
(2) C, D, E, B, A
(3) B, C, D, E, A
(4) A, B, C, D, E

20. Match List-I with List-II.

List-I (Kitchen Zones)		List-II (Items Stored)
A. Consumable Zone	I.	Knife, cutting board and gadgets
B. Cleaning Zone	II.	Pots, lids and other utensils
C. Preparation Zone	III.	Sink, dishwasher and supplies
D. Cooking Zone	IV.	Spices, sugar, tea, coffee and oil

Codes

	A	B	C	D
(1)	III	IV	II	I
(2)	IV	III	I	II
(3)	I	III	IV	II
(4)	II	III	IV	I

21. Match List-I with List-II.

List-I (Types of Pockets)		List-II (Characteristics)
A. Flap pocket	I.	The opening is visible like a slot and can be finished with a rectangular piece of fabric standing upwards from the pocket edge
B. Welt pocket	II.	The opening is covered with flap, which can be left open or buttoned down
C. Bound pocket	III.	It is applied on the face (right) side of the garment and can be made in any number of shapes
D. Patch pocket	IV.	It looks similar to a large bound button hole with two pleats of fabric meeting at the centre of the opening

Codes

	A	B	C	D
(1)	I	II	III	IV
(2)	II	I	IV	III
(3)	III	II	I	IV
(4)	IV	III	II	I

22. Among the following cryogenic liquids, which liquified gas has an extremely low boiling point ?

(1) Freon
(2) Liquid Nitrogen
(3) Liquid Carbon Dioxide
(4) Liquid Helium

23. Mention the common changes in motor abilities experienced by elderly.

A. Reduced income and entertainment

B. Decline in mascular strength

C. Decrease in speed in skilled movements

D. Reduced reasoning and memory skills

E. Delay in leaning of new skills

Choose the correct answer from the options given below.

(1) B, C and E
(2) A, B and E
(3) B, C and D
(4) C, D and E

24. Match List-I with List-II.

List-I (Type of Risks)	List-II (Uncertainty of Future Returns)
A. Financial risk	I. Investor psychology
B. Market risk	II. Capital market
C. Purchasing power risk	III. Financial capacity
D. Political and social risk	IV. Price level

Codes

	A	B	C	D
(1)	III	IV	I	II
(2)	II	III	IV	I
(3)	IV	I	III	II
(4)	III	I	IV	II

25. All persons throughout life, as indicated by the recommended dietary allowances need

(1) the same nutrients in varying amounts
(2) the same amount of nutrients in any state of health
(3) the same nutrients at any stage in the same amounts
(4) different nutrients in mixed amounts

26. A group of genetic disorders of haemoglobin synthesis which result from a defective rate of synthesis of one or more of the globin chains, but there is no defect in the amino acid structure of globin chains.

(1) Methemoglobinemias (2) Thallasemias
(3) Agammaglobinemias (4) Aminoaciduria

27. Changes in performance of work in the interest of work simplification can be grouped into three classes. Select the changes from the least to the most important in sequence.

A. Product
B. Body positions and motions and sequence of work
C. Tools, equipments, and work arrangement
D. Energy spent on activities
E. Time spent on performing activities

Choose the correct answer from the options given below.

(1) D, E, C (2) B, C, A
(3) A, D, C (4) A, D, E

28. Identify the advantages of individual contact method.

A. Helps in teaching complex practices to the community
B. Helps in building rapport with the community
C. Helps in gaining first-hand knowledge from the community
D. Help in selection of state and national level leaders
E. Helps in maintaining social norms and rituals

Choose the correct answer from the options given below.

(1) A, B, C (2) A, C, D
(3) B, C, D (4) B, D, E

29. In static continuous exertions

(1) blood flow is irregular
(2) blood flow is fast
(3) blood flow is normal
(4) blood flow is diminished

30. Which one of the following is not a category of adopters ?

(1) Early suggestors (2) Early adoptors
(3) Early majority (4) Late majority

31. Identify the PLA methods.

A. Resource map
B. Bar graph
C. Transact walk
D. Folk songs
E. Key informant interviews

Choose the correct answer from the options given below

(1) B, C, D, E (2) C, D, A, B
(3) A, C, D, E (4) D, E, A, B

32. Arrange the stages of group development in sequence.

A. Performing B. Norming
C. Forming D. Adjourning
E. Storming

Choose the correct answer from the options given below.

(1) E, A, B, D, C
(2) C, A, B, D, E
(3) C, E, B, A, D
(4) A, B, E, C, D

33. Following are the properties of hydrophobic fabric.

A. It does not absorb perspiration.
B. It tends to have a static build-up.
C. It has better wrinkle recovery.
D. It accepts dyes and finishes more readily.
E. Stain can be easily removed from it.

Choose the correct answer from the options given below.

(1) A, B and C
(2) B, C and E
(3) C, D and E
(4) D, C and A

34. Arrange the steps involved in staff employment in an organisation.

A. Orientation

B. Selection and placement

C. Advertising

D. Recruiting

E. Training

Choose the correct answer from the options given below.

(1) C, A, B, E, D (2) C, D, B, A, E
(3) C, D, A, B, E (4) C, B, A, D, E

35. Which type of packaging method is used for extending the life of food products by changing the atmosphere surrounding the food inside the package?

(1) Aseptic packaging
(2) Shrink wrap packaging
(3) Modified atmospheric packaging
(4) CPET packaging

36. According to the nature of personnel involved which one of the following is not a type of channel in communication ?

(1) Personal localite
(2) Impersonal localite
(3) Personal cosmopolite
(4) Impersonal cosmopolite

37. Identify limitations of Mass Media.

A. Very little scope for personal contact with audience

B. Generalised recommendations hinder application of messages by individuals

C. Difficulty in getting feedback from audience

D. Reinforces previous learning of the audience

E. Large number of people may communicate within a short period of time

Choose the correct answer from the options given below.

(1) C, D and E (2) C, A and B
(3) A, E and C (4) D, E and A

38. Which of the following are primary properties of textile fibers ?

A. Tenacity B. Cohesiveness
C. Luster D. Uniformity

Choose the correct answer from the options given below.

(1) B and D (2) A, B and C
(3) B, C and D (4) C and D

39. Arrange the processing of linen in correct sequence.

A. Harvesting B. Drawing
C. Retting D. Spinning
E. Rippling

Choose the correct answer from the options given below.

(1) A, C, E, D, B (2) A, E, C, B, D
(3) B, A, D, C, E (4) A, B, C, D, E

40. Match List-I with List-II.

List-I (Name of the Theorists)	List-II (Name of the Theories)
A. Urie Bronfenbrenner	I. Psychosocial Theory
B. Jean Piajet	II. Sociocultural Theory
C. Erick Erickson	III. Bioecological Theory
D. Levs Vygotsky	IV. Cognitive Development Theory

Codes

	A	B	C	D
(1)	I	II	IV	III
(2)	II	IV	I	III
(3)	I	II	III	IV
(4)	III	IV	I	II

41. Match List-I with List-II.

List-I (Fiber)	List-II [(Microscopic Characteristics)(Longitudinal View)]
A. Cotton	I. Presence of cross markings and nodes
B. Viscose	II. Flattened, collapsed, spirally twisted tube with a rough surface and convolutions
C. Wool	III. Uniform diameter with striations running parallel to fiber axis
D. Flax	IV. Irregular and roughly cylindrical prominent scale margins.

Codes

	A	B	C	D
(1)	II	III	IV	I
(2)	IV	III	I	II
(3)	III	IV	I	II
(4)	II	I	IV	III

42. Types of belts included under 'Tie Belt' category.

A. Spaghetti

B. Straight tie ups

C. Bias belt

D. Contour belt

E. Rever belt

Choose the correct answer from the options given below.

(1) A, B and C
(2) B, C and E
(3) C, D and E
(4) D, C and A

43. Steps to be followed in sequence for planning and creating new designs.

A. Make a plan

B. Set the goal

C. Carry out the plan

D. Examine the relevant outside influences

E. Evaluate

Choose the correct answer from the options given below.

(1) D, A, E, C, B (2) C, E, B, D, A
(3) B, D, A, C, E (4) A, B, C, D, E

44. Generous bustline, shapely waist, pronounced hips are the characteristics of

(1) round body type (2) pear body type
(3) diamond body type (4) hourglass body type

45. The main characteristics of exceptional children are

A. deviant and different from children of their age

B. deviation may fall on positive or negative side of exceptionality

C. require special provision in education and adjustment

D. usually get social acceptance

E. have high self-esteem and confidence

Choose the correct answer from the options given below.

(1) A, D and E (2) B, C and D
(3) C, D and E (4) A, B and C

46. Match List-I with List-II.

	List-I (Programmes)		List-II (Beneficiary)
A.	National IDD Control Programme	I.	Below Poverty Line families
B.	Antyodaya Anna Yojana	II.	Drought affected States/UT
C.	Mid-Day Meal Programme	III.	Entire population
D.	Food for Work programme	IV.	Primary school children

Codes

	A	B	C	D		A	B	C	D
(1)	III	IV	II	I	(2)	I	II	III	IV
(3)	IV	III	II	I	(4)	III	I	IV	II

47. When we eat meal some compounds do not get metabolised, they instead become special molecules called

(1) ligands (2) metabolomes
(3) proteomics (4) genomes

48. In which textile finishing process, the surface fibres are burned off to produce smooth surface ?

(1) Raising (2) Singeing
(3) Calendaring (4) Sanforising

49. The management function of management by objectives under Policy and Planning Techniques used in Management of Public Organisations is

(1) Policy making
(2) Planning and decision making
(3) Planning and controlling
(4) Planning, decision making and controlling

50. Match List-I with List-II.

	List-I (Types of Radio Programmes)		List-II (Salient Features)
A.	Newsreel	I.	Talk among people and about people involved in news or events
B.	Interview	II.	Radio plays of short duration or in series
C.	Documentary	III.	Eye witness accounts, extracts of speeches, talks, and interviews
D.	Radio Drama	IV.	A short story of a person, group, organisation or situation

Codes

	A	B	C	D		A	B	C	D
(1)	III	I	IV	II	(2)	I	III	II	IV
(3)	IV	I	III	II	(4)	I	III	IV	II

51. Which of the following is the characteristic motif of the Kullu shawls ?

(1) Kalash (2) Swastika
(3) Panbhat (4) Chinar leaf

52. Due to the fibrous surface, threads made from spun yarn possess following properties

A. Highly elastic properties

B. Good sewing performance

C. Good dimensional stability

D. Good stitch locking properties

Choose the correct answer from the options given below.

(1) B and C (2) B, D and A
(3) A, B and C (4) B, C and D

53. According to Kohlberg which level of moral reasoning is based on the person's own moral standards ?

(1) Conventional (2) Pre-conventional
(3) Beginning (4) Post-conventional

54. Match List-I with List-II.

	List-I (Cost)		List-II (Examples)
A.	Hidden cost	I.	Payroll payments
B.	Semi-Variable Overhead cost	II.	Pilferage in delivery points
C.	Food cost	III.	Loss due to repair and maintenance
D.	Labour cost	IV.	Loss due to spillage

Codes

	A	B	C	D
(1)	IV	III	II	I
(2)	IV	III	I	II
(3)	III	II	IV	I
(4)	II	I	IV	III

55. Fabrics prepared by two layers of fabrics combined onto one fabric with foam

(1) bonded fabric (2) laminated fabric
(3) coated fabric (4) poromeric fabric

56. Walk-in bathtubs can be good options for those with

(1) limited mobility
(2) individual user
(3) average adult with good of motion
(4) individual using a wheelchair

57. Match List-I with List-II.

	List-I (Type of Plays)		List-II (Meanings)
A.	Functional play	I.	Play involving use of materials or objects to draw or make something
B.	Symbolic play	II.	Play involving repetitive motor activity
C.	Constructive play	III.	Play involving social interactions, physical activity and rules
D.	Formal games	IV.	Play involving creating settings, characteristics and scripts

Codes

	A	B	C	D
(1)	IV	I	II	III
(2)	II	IV	I	III
(3)	III	I	II	IV
(4)	I	IV	III	II

58. As per classification of mental retardation based on what IQ score, a person is considered as profoundly mentally retarded ?

(1) 50 (2) 20 (3) 35 (4) 70

59. Arrange the stages of language development during infancy.

A. Intonation B. Crying
C. Babbling D. Echolalia
E. Cooing

Choose the correct answer from the options given below.

(1) A, C, B, E and D
(2) D, E, A, C and B
(3) B, E, C, D and A
(4) C, D, A, B and E

60. Match List-I with List-II.

	List-I (Types of Barriers in Communications)		List-II (Examples)
A.	Physical and Mechanical Barrier	I.	Incorrect translation
B.	Language Barrier	II.	Distance
C.	Socio-Psychological Barrier	III.	Rules and Regulations
D.	Organisational Barrier	IV.	Resistance to change

Codes

	A	B	C	D
(1)	II	III	I	IV
(2)	I	IV	II	III
(3)	I	II	III	IV
(4)	II	I	IV	III

61. Which one of the following is not a technique for noise reduction at source ?

(1) Use of quiet machines
(2) Endose noisy machines
(3) Using ear-plugs or muffs
(4) Regular maintenance of machines

62. The genetic endowment inherited from a persons biological parents at conception is

(1) environment (2) heredity
(3) maturation (4) conception

63. The three sewing machine parts which together constitute the drop feed mechanism are

(1) needle, thread take-up lever, presser foot
(2) presser foot, throat plate, feed dog
(3) needle bar, spool, feed dog
(4) bobbin, needle, throat plate

64. The public provident fund account deposits are qualified for income tax rebate under

(1) Section 80 L of IT Act
(2) Section 80 DD of IT Act
(3) Section 80 CCA of IT Act
(4) Section 88 of IT Act

65. Which one of the following is not a criteria for effective learning ?
(1) Learning should be general in nature
(2) Learning should engage maximum number of the senses of the learner
(3) Learning should be challenging
(4) Learning should result in functional understanding

66. Which one of the following is not a non-projected visual aid ?
(1) Chalk board (2) Bulletin board
(3) Flip chart (4) Puppet show

67. Utensil to keep food hot without actually boiling by standing the dish containing the food in a large pan filled with water which is kept just below boiling point is called
(1) casserole (2) hot case
(3) steamer (4) bain- Marie

68. Match List-I with List-II.

List-I (Types of Researches)		List-II (Meanings)
A. Action Research	I.	Research is designed to provide data to support a theory through its application
B. Applied Research	II.	Research is designed to solve problems through the application of scientific method
C. Experimental Research	III.	Research is designed to study, understand and explain events that occurred in past
D. Historical Research	IV.	Research is designed with independent and dependent variables to study cause and effect

Codes

	A	B	C	D
(1)	I	III	IV	II
(2)	II	I	IV	III
(3)	I	IV	II	III
(4)	III	I	IV	II

69. The first step in extension teaching is
(1) interest (2) satisfaction
(3) action (4) attention

70. Assessment of nuritional status through direct method is done by
A. anthropometry
B. vital health statistics
C. clinical examination
D. radiological examination
E. biochemical estimation
Choose the correct answer from the options given below.
(1) A, B, C, E (2) A, C, D, E
(3) B, C, D, E (4) D, C, B, A

71. Arrange the correct sequence of stages of pre-natal development.
A. Fetal stage B. Germinal stage
C. Embryonic stage D. Conception stage
E. Delivery stage
Choose the correct answer from the options given below
(1) B, C, E, A, D (2) D, B, C, A, E
(3) A, B, C, D, E (4) E, D, B, A, C

72. Arrange in sequence the five phases that constitute Strategic Human Resource Management process.
A. HR strategy formulation
B. Identify HR strategies
C. Scan the environment
D. Monitor and evaluate HR strategies
E. Identify the sources of competitive advantage
Choose the correct answer from the options given below.
(1) B, A, D, E, C
(2) C, E, B, A, D
(3) A, E, C, B, D
(4) C, B, A, D, E

73. Match List-I with List-II.

List-I (Techniques of Work Simplifications)		List-II (Descriptions)
A. Micromotion Film Analysis	I.	Step-by-step description of the worker performing entire task
B. Process Chart	II.	Pin and String Method
C. Operation Chart	III.	Photographic Device
D. Pathway/ Flow Chart	IV.	One particular step is studied in a whole process

Codes

	A	B	C	D
(1)	II	IV		III
(2)	III	I	IV	II
(3)	III	IV	I	II
(4)	I	II	III	IV

74. Which one is the property of Hemicellulose ?
(1) Indigestible and insoluble in water
(2) Indigestible but soluble in water
(3) On hydrolysis yields galacturonic acid and small amounts of galactose and arabinose
(4) Highly fermented by colonic bacteria

75. Which one of the following is not a group method of communication ?
(1) Result demonstration
(2) Exhibition
(3) Field day
(4) Study tour

76. Match List-I with List-II.

List-I (Stages of Group Developments)		List-II (Purposes)
A. Forming	I.	Learning to work with each other and co-exist
B. Storming	II.	Getting in action as a cohesive group.
C. Norming	III.	Getting to know about each other
D. Performing	IV.	Challenging each other

Codes

	A	B	C	D		A	B	C	D
(1)	II	III	IV	I	(2)	II	IV	I	III
(3)	III	IV	I	II	(4)	III	I	II	IV

77. Which of the following is not the 'probability method' of sampling ?
(1) Systematic sampling (2) Stratified sampling
(3) Cluster sampling (4) Quota sampling

78. In research, ... means simply taking things for granted so that the situation is simplified for logical procedures.
(1) hypothesis (2) assumptions
(3) tenability (4) postulate

79. The functions of a family therapist are
A. acts as a collaborator for the whole family
B. expresses empathic comments
C. demonstrates a caring attitude
D. designs a rating scale
E. gives birth control advice
Choose the correct answer from the options given below:
(1) C, D, E
(2) A, B, E
(3) A, B, C
(4) B, D, E

80. The natural colourants used in food are
A. Annatto B. Carmosine
C. Indigo carmine D. Betalaines
E. Anthocyanins
Choose the correct answer from the options given below.
(1) B, C and D (2) A, D and E
(3) A, C and D (4) B, C and E

81. Arrange the steps of designing a chart in sequence.
A. Divide content into headings and subheadings
B. Research the topic from credible sources
C. Prepare a draft layout with text and visuals
D. Identify visuals and colour scheme
E. Design the final layout with text and visuals
Choose the correct answer from the options given below.
(1) C, A, E, D, B (2) D, A, C, E, B
(3) B, A, D, C, E (4) B, C, A, E, D

82. The first step of any parent education program is to find similarities between a group of parents by developing which one of the following?
(1) Communication (2) Eye contact
(3) Therapy (4) Rapport

83. The period from conception to implantation of the embryo is called
(1) Conception stage (2) Embryonic stage
(3) Fetal stage (4) Germinal stage

84. Arrange the process of job analysis in sequence.
A. Job specification
B. Job description
C. Strategic choices
D. Process information
E. Gather information
Choose the correct answer from the options given below.
(1) A, B, C, E, D (2) B, D, A, C, E
(3) C, E, D, B, A (4) D, A, C, E, B

85. For maximum usefulness, market segments must exhibit the following characteristics.
A. Measurability B. Substantiality
C. Action ability D. Dependability
E. Accessibility
Choose the correct answer from the options given below.
(1) A, B, C and D
(2) B, D, E and A
(3) A, B, C and E
(4) D, E, C and B

86. The traditional textile which is mordant and resist block printed on both sides (of the fabric) with geometrical motifs with a strong grid pattern in the shades of blue and red.

(1) Ajrakh (2) Sanganeri
(3) Rogan (4) Bagh

87. Which of the following is not a characteristic of extension education ?

(1) Heterogenous learners
(2) Choice of subject matter is with learners
(3) Fixed curriculum
(4) Teaching with the help of local leaders

88. Which part of the body develops more quickly than any other organ in early childhood ?

(1) Limbs (2) Head circumference
(3) Brain (4) Heart

89. Arrange the following steps in order which provide a useful procedural guideline regarding research.

A. Extensive literature survey
B. Formulating the research problem
C. Analysis of data
D. Collecting data
E. Interpretation and report writing

Choose the correct answer from the options given below.

(1) B, D, C, A, E (2) A, B, C, D, E
(3) B, A, D, C, E (4) B, E, C, A, D

90. In resolving industrial disputes, collective bargaining has been viewed from three perspectives ;

A. as a change in contract language
B. as a peace treaty between the conflicting parties
C. as a system of industrial jurisprudence
D. as a process of company policy
E. as a process of social change

Choose the correct answer from the options given below.

(1) A, B and C (2) B, E and A
(3) E, B and C (4) E, A and C

Directions (Q. Nos. 91-95) *Read the passage carefully and answer the questions that follows.*

Rusa Manjhi was a woman Panchayat worker of the Lahiripur Gram Panchayat in the Sunderbans of West Bengal. She showcased the success of women power in rural development in the 1980s. Rusa choose to be a Panchayat functionary as she knew it was the right forum to plan programmes for women, address their needs and have them believe in taking hold on their lives. Earlier, women in the Sunderbans had to depend entirely on the earnings of their men, most of whom were engaged in fishing or collecting honey from the wild. The Panchayat Samitis in early 1980s introduced schemes Like DWCRA, TRYSEM and ICDS in the region, This lead to the participation of women, espeçially the neo-literate and illiterate women, in entrepreneurial programmes. Change was also apparent in the growth of social awareness about womens rights. Women came forward to fight their own battles regarding wife-beating, dowry, desertion and bigamy. Often husbands did not agree with wives becoming self-sufficient. However, the women did not give up on their dream of self-empowerment.

91. The main earnings of the men in the Sunderbans was from

(1) agriculture (2) floriculture
(3) fishing (4) hunting

92. Which Development Program was not introduced in the Sunderbans ?

(1) DWCRA
(2) TRYSEM
(3) ICDS
(4) Sukanya Samridhi Yojana

93. Which one of the following PLA technique will be most suitable to locate and identify families engaged in fishing ?

(1) Resource inventory (2) Transect walk
(3) Venn diagram (4) Resource map

94. To which state did Rusa Manjhi belong ?

(1) Jharkhand
(2) West Bengal
(3) Orissa
(4) Assam

95. What role did Rusa choose?

(1) DWCRA functionary
(2) Panchayat functionary
(3) ICDS functionary
(4) TRYSEM functionary

Directions (Q. Nos. 96-100) *Read the passage carefully and answer the questions that follows.*

FM Radio stations, satellite radioa dn television channels are major avenues for the growth of the music industry. Much of the programming on FM radio channels, like AIR's Vividh Bharti, is dideicated to music, primarily to film music, This is equally true of round-the-clock music channels of television. But besides the dedicate music channels, telvision programming on all 'General Enternainment Channels' in the various Indian languages includes several mucis based geners. 'Talent Hunt' programmes focused on singing, dancing and acting are based largely on Indian film music, One of the channels organised a Talent Hunt programme called 'Pospstars' which involved the nationawide search for a five member all-girl band of singers called 'Viva', the winning band of girls reeased two albums. In a similar vein a music project called, 'The Underground' was condcuted by Saregama India in Mubai, Delhi and Kolkata in 1980 to select 30 music performers (Bands, Artistes and DJs).

96. AIR's 'Vividh Bharati' is dedicated primarily to
(1) news (2) film music
(3) talent hunt (4) documentary

97. 'Popstar' Talent Hunt Programme involved the national wide search fora five member band of singers that included
(1) all girls
(2) all women
(3) all boys
(4) all men

98. The full form of GEC is
(1) Generic Electric Channels
(2) Generic Editing Channels
(3) General Entertainment Channels
(4) General Educational Channels

99. In which one of the following cities, Saregama Production did not introduce a music project ?
(1) Delhi (2) Mumbai
(3) Chennai (4) Kolkata

100. Which of the following is not a music based programme ?
(1) Talent Hunt
(2) The Underground
(3) Popstar
(4) Shark Tank

ANSWERS

1 (4)	2 (3)	3 (4)	4 (4)	5 (3)	6 (2)	7 (1)	8 (2)	9 (4)	10 (3)
11 (3)	12 (1)	13 (2)	14 (1)	15 (3)	16 (3)	17 (2)	18 (2)	19 (1)	20 (2)
21 (2)	22 (4)	23 (1)	24 (4)	25 (1)	26 (2)	27 (2)	28 (1)	29 (4)	30 (1)
31 (3)	32 (3)	33 (1)	34 (2)	35 (3)	36 (2)	37 (2)	38 (1)	39 (2)	40 (4)
41 (1)	42 (1)	43 (3)	44 (4)	45 (4)	46 (4)	47 (1&2)	48 (2)	49 (3)	50 (1)
51 (2)	52 (4)	53 (4)	54 (1)	55 (2)	56 (1)	57 (2)	58 (2)	59 (3)	60 (4)
61 (3)	62 (2)	63 (2)	64 (3)	65 (1)	66 (4)	67 (4)	68 (2)	69 (4)	70 (2)
71 (2)	72 (2)	73 (2)	74 (1)	75 (2)	76 (3)	77 (4)	78 (2)	79 (3)	80 (2)
81 (3)	82 (4)	83 (4)	84 (3)	85 (3)	86 (1)	87 (3)	88 (3)	89 (3)	90 (3)
91 (3)	92 (4)	93 (4)	94 (2)	95 (2)	96 (2)	97 (1)	98 (3)	99 (3)	100 (4)

Home Science (Paper-2)

Solved Paper, December 2023

General Instructions

1. There are total one hundred questions in this paper. Each question carries 2 marks.
2. All questions are compulsory.

---

1. Which of the following digital dashboard is an integral part of overall POSHAN 2.0 Abhiyaan?

(1) POSHAN Tracker (2) Open Data Kit
(3) ICDS CAS (4) POSHAN Drishti

2. Which of the following hormone is not a counter regulatory hormone of insulin?

(1) Glucagon (2) Cortisol
(3) Growth hormone (4) Anti diuretic hormone

3. Which of the following derivatives of chlorophyll is stable during canning and the green colour is retained?

(1) Pheophytin (2) Pyropheophytin
(3) Chlorophyllides (4) Chlorophyll 'a'

4. Who are the beneficiaries of WIFS Programme ?

(1) Pregnant and lactating women
(2) Children below 6 years of age
(3) School going adolescent girls and boys and out of school adolescent girls
(4) Only adolescent girls

5. Which of the following is a new logo introduced by FSSAI in September 2021 for Vegan foods ?

(1) A green colour filled circle inside a square with green outline.
(2) A brown colour filled triangle inside a square with brown outline.
(3) Green colour 'V' inscribed in middle of a square box with a small plant on top of it and vegan written at the bottom.
(4) A green colour filled triangle inside a square with green outline.

6. As per the nutrient requirements for Indians 2020 (latest RDAs), what is the requirement of Vitamin C for lactating women in the period of first 6 months of lactation?

(1) 65 mg (2) 80 mg
(3) 115 mg (4) 60 mg

7. Which of the following is used to keep food warm over long period ?

(1) Bratte pan
(2) Microwave oven
(3) Bain marie
(4) Electric tandoor

8. National Handloom Day is celebrated on

(1) 5th August (2) 7th August
(3) 8th August (4) 7th September

9. Jacquard loom is used for making

(1) lightweight fabrics
(2) plain weave
(3) complex patterned weave
(4) twill weave

10. Which one of the following is not a principle of flat pattern making?
(1) Principle of dart manipulation
(2) Principle of drafting
(3) Principle of added fullness
(4) Principle of body contouring

11. The diagonal joining of two edges at corners is called
(1) mitring (2) edging
(3) binding (4) banding

12. Which one of the following is a fabric tunnel?
(1) Placket (2) Facing (3) Casing (4) Binding

13. Out of India's agricultural Gross Domestic Products cotton contributes
(1) 40 % (2) 30 % (3) 20 % (4) 10 %

14. Traditional Pipli work of Odisha is a type of
(1) mirror work (2) cut work
(3) applique work (4) zari work

15. According to Mundell, 'change in product' is
(1) highest class of change.
(2) intermediate class of change.
(3) lowest class of change.
(4) not considered as an option in work simplification.

16. Micro inverters are used when
(1) a part of solar panel system is temporarily blocked from sunlight.
(2) the solar panel system gets abundance of sunlight in all parts.
(3) panels are fitted with waterproof components only.
(4) panels are made of polythene only.

17. Articulation Index is a technique used to give indications about
(1) air quality (2) illumination levels
(3) noise levels (4) humidity levels

18. Bivalent evaluative reactions are
(1) satisfactory and control reactions.
(2) unsatisfactory and control reactions.
(3) mixture of satisfactory and unsatisfactory reactions.
(4) control reactions.

19. GRIHA stands for
(1) Green Ranking for Integrated Housing Assessment.
(2) Green Rating for Integrated Habitat Assessment.
(3) Green Rating for International Housing Analysis.
(4) Green Ranking for International Habitat Analysis.

20. As suggested by Miller, TOTE is the basic pattern for
(1) feedback unit (2) output unit
(3) through put unit (4) input unit

21. Diagonal lines in interiors suggest
(1) repose (2) stability and alertness
(3) relaxation and rest (4) dynamism

22. A child can hold a glass of water before he/she could button the shirt. This example holds true for which one of the following principles of development?
(1) Cephalocaudal (2) Proximodistal
(3) Random (4) Fixed

23. Which of the following is the most appropriate activity for a 5 year-old child?
(1) Squeeze toy (2) Board games
(3) Play-dough play (4) Computer games

24. During adolescence, the formation of small groups with about 5-7 members, who are either close or good friends are called
(1) Crowds (2) Liaisons
(3) Cliques (4) Isolates

25. REBT in counselling is an acronym for
(1) Reactive Emotional Behaviour Therapy
(2) Reactive Emotive Behaviour Therapy
(3) Rational Emotional Behaviour Therapy
(4) Rational Emotive Behaviour Therapy

26. A parent putting his arm on the child's shoulder in a comforting way and saying 'you know, you should not have done that. Let's talk about how you can handle the situation better next time', is said to practice
(1) Authoritative parenting style
(2) Authoritarian parenting style
(3) Neglectful parenting style
(4) Indulgent parenting style

27. Which of the following intervention would calm an agitated old person with Alzheimer's disease?
(1) Involve the agitated person in group activities
(2) Hold the hand gently/put an arm around the waist of the agitated person
(3) Turn the light off and make the agitated person sleep
(4) Switch on the TV/Play a radio for the agitated person

28. Sara feels angry each time she sees her father showing affection to her mother. According to Freud, what is this behaviour referred to as?
(1) Castration anxiety (2) Oedipus complex
(3) Inferiority complex (4) Electra complex

29. When communication enhances the interaction of learner, it is

(1) physiological (2) psychological
(3) artistic (4) transient

30. Which of the method is not a method of group contact?

(1) Field trip
(2) Conference
(3) Farm and home visit
(4) Demonstration

31. Radio is a media for

(1) mass communication
(2) official communication
(3) group communication
(4) interpersonal communication

32. Sarvodaya Scheme was started by

(1) RN Tagore
(2) Mahatma Gandhi
(3) Acharya Vinoba Bhave
(4) Sewa Ram Phule

33. The National Service Scheme was launched in the country in the year

(1) 1949 (2) 1959
(3) 1969 (4) 1979

34. Through this the organism learns to make various responses to a wide variety of stimulus situation

(1) Learning (2) Conditioning
(3) Behaving (4) Motivating

35. SPEAKER→SPEECH→AUDIENCE, model of communication process is

(1) J. Paul Legons' Model
(2) Aristotle's Model
(3) Berlo' Model
(4) Westley and Machean's Model

36. Type I error is when one is

(1) rejecting null hypothesis when it is true.
(2) accepting null hypothesis when it is true.
(3) rejecting null hypothesis when it is not true.
(4) accepting null hypothesis when it is not true.

37. For any normal distribution approximately, how much of the observations in the population fall within one (1) standard, above and below mean?

(1) One-fourths (2) One-thirds
(3) Half (4) Two-thirds

38. One of the following is not a characteristic of good sampling design, when it

(1) gives representative sample.
(2) does not control systematic bias.
(3) results in small sampling error.
(4) is viable in context of funds available.

39. The usefulness of the test is closely relating to measures of known validity, is

(1) content validity
(2) concurrent validity
(3) predictive validity
(4) criterion related validity

40. The questionnaire format, where the questions are uniform throughout, with all the questions being at one level, is called

(1) Diamond format (2) Funnel format
(3) Box format (4) Mixed format

41. Which of the following changes occur due to denaturation of protein?

A. Peptide bonds of the protein are readily available for hydrolysis
B. Solubility of protein increases
C. The viscosity decreases
D. Solubility of protein decreases
E. Biological properties such as catalytic, hormonal are lost

Choose the correct answer from the options given below.

(1) A, B and C (2) A, C and D
(3) A, D and E (4) B, C and E

42. Which of the following are correct ways to ensure food safety in institutional feeding?

A. Safety education of staff
B. Safety engineering
C. Enforcement of safety regulations
D. Providing maternity leave to female staff
E. Installation of new equipments

Choose the correct answer from the options given below.

(1) A, B and C only
(2) C, D and E only
(3) B, C and D only
(4) A, C and D only

43. Which of the following are important functions of food packaging?

A. To preserve the quality and freshness of food products
B. To enhance the taste of food products
C. To provide information about the food products to the consumers
D. To promote the food product
E. To enhance the nutritional quality of food product

Choose the correct answer from the options given below.

(1) A, B and C (2) B, C and D
(3) C, D and E (4) A, C and D

44. Which of the following are few causative factors for ascites in liver diseases?

A. Hypoalbuminemia
B. Retention of potassium by kidneys
C. Renal retention of sodium and fluid
D. Portal hypertension
E. Hyperalbuminemia

Choose the correct answer from the options given below.

(1) A, B and C (2) A, C and D
(3) C, D and E (4) B, C and D

45. Examples of condensation polymerisation are

A. acrylic B. modacrylic
C. nylon D. elastomers
E. polyester

Choose the correct answer from the options given below.

(1) A, B and C (2) C, D and E
(3) B, C and D (4) A, D and E

46. Post-washing steps in laundry are

A. scrubbing B. rinsing
C. whitening D. stiffening
E. kneading

Choose the correct answer from the options given below.

(1) B, C and D (2) A, B and C
(3) A, C and D (4) C, D and E

47. Select the correct statements.

A. Custom-made stitching method badly affects customer satisfaction due to poor fit.
B. In custom-made stitching method, the consumer gets a good fit in the garment.
C. Getting the right garment fit is an easy task in the ready-to-wear apparel industry.
D. Custom-made tailoring method uses individual measurements.
E. Each company has its own measurements chart which reflects its common standards in the market.

Choose the correct answer from the options given below.

(1) B, C and D (2) A, D and E
(3) A, B and C (4) B, D and E

48. Stitches used in 'Kasuti embroidery' are

A. Gavanti
B. Murgi
C. Murri
D. Methi
E. Taipachi

Choose the correct answer from the options given below.

(1) A, B and D (2) A, B and C
(3) C, D and E (4) B, D and E

49. Work zone in residential building consists of

A. kitchen B. drawing room
C. laundry area D. lawn
E. kid's room

Choose the correct answer from the options given below.

(1) A and B (2) A and C
(3) B and D (4) A and D

50. Factors affecting use of anthropometric data in designing include

A. static and dynamic anthropometry
B. nature of anthropometric measurements
C. changes over time
D. reference population
E. sequence of use of parts of the equipment

Choose the correct answer from the options given below.

(1) A, B, D and E (2) B, C, D and E
(3) A, B, C and E (4) A, B, C and D

51. Window treatments containingsheers are

A. Glass curtain B. Bamboo shades
C. Shoji screen D. Sash curtain
E. Quilt shade

Choose the correct answer from the options given below.

(1) A and D (2) B and C
(3) B and E (4) A and E

52. Symptoms of boredom fatigue include

A. slow passage of time
B. loss of interest in the activity
C. aversion from work
D. frustration due to lack of capacity to perform
E. time running too fast

Choose the correct answer from the options given below.

(1) A, D and E (2) A, B and C
(3) B, D and E (4) C, D and E

53. In performing which of the following tasks, a child with a fine impairment will have greater difficulty?

A. Drawing a picture
B. Holding a ball
C. Stringing beads
D. Carrying a book
E. Stenciling letters

Choose the correct answer from the options given below.

(1) A, C and E (2) A, B and E
(3) A, D and E (4) A, B and D

54. Which of the following strategies do not lead to marital happiness?

A. Remake your spouse
B. Open communication
C. Respectful consideration for each other
D. Exercise coercive power
E. Insist on your rights

Choose the correct answer from the options given below.

(1) A, D and E (2) A, B and E
(3) B, C and E (4) B, D and E

55. Select the statements which indicate the advantages of joint family.

A. Children learn good mannerisms and etiquette
B. Children learn the traits sharing and caring
C. Children learn to be rigid
D. Children learn to be moody

Choose the correct answer from the options given below.

(1) A, B and D (2) A, C and E
(3) A, B and E (4) B, C and D

56. Counselling and guidance are not synonymous terms. Which of the following explains this fact?

A. All counselling is guidance but all guidance is not counselling.
B. Counselling is a higher order technical career, but guidance can be provided by a person who has sufficient information about the topic of concern.
C. Counselling is giving advice, but guidance is to assist.
D. Counselling is curative and guidance is preventive.
E. Counselling is preventive and guidance is curative.

Choose the correct answer from the options given below.

(1) B, C and D (2) A, B and E
(3) A, C and E (4) A, B and D

57. Which of the following are characteristics and features of communication?

A. It involves the exchange of ideas, facts and opinions.
B. It is a continuous process.
C. It is verbal and non-verbal.
D. It is synchronous and asynchronous in nature.
E. It is always verbal.

Choose the correct answer from the options given below.

(1) A, D and E (2) B, C and E
(3) A, B and E (4) A, B and C

58. Below is given a list of teaching methods and approaches. Which among them are individualised approaches?

A. Demonstration method
B. Modular approach based learning
C. Programmed learning method
D. Personalised teaching
E. Collaborative method

Choose the correct answer from the options given below.

(1) A, B and C (2) B, C and D
(3) C, D and E (4) A, C and E

59. Learning is more likely to occur if the learning experiences are

A. repeated with meaning
B. unrelated
C. intense and vivid
D. annoying
E. generalised

Choose the correct answer from the options given below.

(1) A and B (2) B and C
(3) A and C (4) C and D

60. Which of the following programmes of extension were launched in India before independence of the country?

A. Gurgaon Experiment
B. Community Development Programme
C. Indian Village Services
D. Integrated Rural Development Programme
E. Shanti Niketan Project

Choose the correct answer from the options given below.

(1) A, B and C (2) B, C and D
(3) A, B and E (4) A, C and E

61. Which of the following are probability sampling?

A. Cluster sampling
B. Quota sampling
C. Multiphase sampling
D. Stratified random sampling
E. Snowball sampling

Choose the correct answer from the options given below.

(1) A, C and D
(2) B, C and D
(3) C, D and E
(4) A, D and E

62. Match List-I with List-II.

List-I (Chemical Compounds)	List-II (Purposes)
A. Sodium nitrite	I. Thickeners
B. Calcium silicate	II. Preservative
C. Gelatin	III. Curing agent
D. Benzoic acid	IV. Anticaking agent

Codes

	A	B	C	D		A	B	C	D
(1)	IV	I	III	II	(2)	I	II	III	IV
(3)	III	IV	I	II	(4)	III	IV	II	I

63. Match List-I with List-II.

List-I (Parameter Lengths)	List-II (Nutrition Status)
A. Weight for height/length <–3sd of WHO standards in children below 3 years of age	I. Underweight
B. Height for age <–2sd of WHO standards in children below 3 years of age	II. Stunting
C. Weight for age <–2sd of WHO standards in children below 3 years of age	III. Severe wasting
D. Weight for height <– 2sd of WHO growth standards in children below 3 years of age	IV. Moderate wasting

Codes

	A	B	C	D		A	B	C	D
(1)	IV	II	III	I	(2)	III	II	I	IV
(3)	III	II	IV	I	(4)	II	III	I	IV

64. Match the yarn count systems in List-I with unit in List-II.

List-I (Numbering Systems)	List-II (Units)
A. Denier	I. Weight in grams per 10,000 meters
B. Tex	II. Weight in grams per 9,000 meters
C. Milli Tex (mtex)	III Weight in grams per 1,000 meters
D. Deci Tex (dtex)	IV. Weight in milligrams per 1,000 meters

Codes

	A	B	C	D		A	B	C	D
(1)	III	I	IV	II	(2)	II	IV	I	III
(3)	II	III	IV	I	(4)	III	I	II	IV

65. Match List-I with List-II.

List-I (Garment Construction Techniques)	List-II (Descriptions)
A. Godet	I. Short flare attached to the waist of garment
B. Gusset	II. Panels in the garment
C. Peplum	III. Triangular piece attached at the hemline
D. Gores	IV. Piece attached at sleeve

Codes

	A	B	C	D		A	B	C	D
(1)	III	IV	I	II	(2)	III	II	IV	I
(3)	I	II	III	IV	(4)	II	III	I	IV

66. Match List-I with List-II.

List-I (Indoor Climate Conditions)	List-II (Comfort Zone Specifications)
A. Air temperature in °C	I. 70
B. Rate of air movement in m/s	II. 15.6-20.0
C. Radiant temperature	III. 0.15
D. Air humidity in %	IV. 16.7-20.2

Codes

	A	B	C	D		A	B	C	D
(1)	IV	III	II	I	(2)	IV	I	III	II
(3)	II	III	IV	I	(4)	II	I	IV	III

67. Match List-I with List-II.

List-I (Parameters of Planning)	List-II (Details)
A. Reality in sequence	I. Range of acceptable order of tasks
B. Flexibility of sequence	II. Degree of specified order within or among tasks
C. Complexity in sequence	III. Feasibility of order within or among tasks
D. Clarity in sequence	IV. Degree of interrelationship between persons and tasks

Codes

	A	B	C	D
(1)	I	III	IV	II
(2)	III	II	IV	I
(3)	III	I	IV	II
(4)	I	II	IV	III

68. Match the domains of development (List-I) with sub-domains (List-II).

List-I (Domains)	List-II (Sub-domains)
A. Physical	I. Honesty
B. Cognitive	II. Attachment
C. Emotional	III. Brain
D. Social	IV. Creativity

Codes

	A	B	C	D
(1)	III	I	II	IV
(2)	III	II	I	IV
(3)	II	III	IV	I
(4)	III	IV	I	II

69. Match the stages of cognitive development in List-I as proposed by Jean Piaget with its unique characteristics in List-II.

List-I (Stages of Cognitive Developments)	List-II (Unique Characteristics)
A. Sensorimotor	I. Emergence of symbolic functions
B. Preoperational	II. Application of logic
C. Concrete operational	III. Hypothetic deductive reasoning
D. Formal operational	IV. Exploration through sense organs

Codes

	A	B	C	D
(1)	I	II	IV	III
(2)	IV	I	II	III
(3)	IV	II	III	I
(4)	I	IV	II	III

70. Match List-I with List-II.

List-II (Teaching Learning Methods)	List-II (Situations Appropriate)
A. Lecturing	I. Working in groups
B. Project Method	II. Small steps with feedback
C. Heuristic Method	III. Economical and time saving
D. Programmed learning	IV. Use of problem solving experience based and discovery based learning for students

Codes

	A	B	C	D
(1)	III	I	II	IV
(2)	III	I	IV	II
(3)	II	III	IV	I
(4)	I	III	II	IV

71. Match List-I with List-II.

List-I (Audio Visuals Aids)	List-II (Classification)
A. Video	I. Audio aid
B. Slide	II. Projected audio visual aid
C. Chart	III. Projected visual aid
D. Tape recorder	IV. Non-projected visual aid

Codes

	A	B	C	D
(1)	I	II	III	IV
(2)	II	III	IV	I
(3)	IV	I	III	II
(4)	III	I	II	IV

72. Match List-I with List-II.

List-I (Tests)	List-II (Descriptions)
A. z-test	I. Used for judging the significance of difference between means of two samples
B. t-test	II. Used for comparing variance of two independent samples
C. x^2-test	III. Used for judging the significance of several statistical measures particularly mean
D. F-test	IV. Used for comparing a sample variance to a theoretical population variance.

Codes

	A	B	C	D
(1)	III	I	IV	II
(2)	III	I	II	IV
(3)	I	II	III	IV
(4)	IV	III	II	I

73. Arrange the following ocular signs of vitamin A deficiency in the stage of appearance from earliest to late stage of deficiency.

A. Keratomalacia
B. Bitot's spot
C. Night blindness
D. Conjuctival xerosis
E. Corneal xerosis

Choose the correct answer from the options given below.

(1) C, D, B, E, A
(2) C, B, A, D, E
(3) B, A, D, E, A
(4) D, A, B, C, E

74. Arrange the following phases of microbial growth curve in correct sequence.

A. Logarithmic or exponential phase
B. Negative acceleration
C. Lag phase
D. Positive acceleration
E. Maximum stationary phase

Choose the correct answer from the options given below.

(1) C, D, E, B, A (2) C, D, A, B, E
(3) A, B, E, D, C (4) B, C , D, E, A

75. Arrange the following stages of Kalamkari in sequence.

A. Fabric is immersed in a solution of cow dung.
B. The iron acetate solution is filled in for solid space or as out line.
C. Mordanting by applying alum solution.
D. All the portions that are not to be blued are covered with wax and after wax is removed by boiling the cloth in water.
E. The clothe is treated in myrobalam solution.

Choose the correct answer from the options given below.

(1) B, C, D, A, E (2) E, B, A, C, D
(3) A, C, D, B, E (4) A, E, B, C, D

76. Arrange the following fibres in order of their strength from higher to lower (Tenacity under dry condition).

A. Acetate B. Cotton
C. Acrylic D. Wool
E. Flax

Choose the correct answer from the options given below.

(1) B, E, C, A, D (2) B, E, A, C, D
(3) E, C, D, B, A (4) E, B, C, D, A

77. Arrange the stages of work curve in sequence.

A. Plateau of greatest production
B. Warming up
C. Rest period
D. Peak load
E. Decline in output

Choose the correct answer from the options given below.

(1) B, A, E, C, D (2) B, D, A, C, E
(3) A, B, E, C, D (4) B, A, C, E, D

78. Arrange the steps of entrepreneurial process in sequence

A. Company formation/execution
B. Growth
C. Brainstorming and exploration
D. Idea generation
E. Opportunity evaluation

Choose the correct answer from the options given below.

(1) B,C, E, D, A (2) C, B, D, A, E
(3) C, D, E, A, B (4) A, D, C, E, B

79. Arrange the following in the order of life span development.

A. Adolescence B. Senescence
C. Infancy D. Prenatal period
E. Childhood

Choose the correct answer from the options given below.

(1) B, D, C, E, A (2) C, E, A, B, D
(3) D, C, E, B, A (4) D, C, E, A, B

80. Sequence the stages of Kubler-Ross's five stage model of grief.

A. Denial B. Acceptance
C. Bargaining D. Anger
E. Depression

Choose the correct answer from the options given below.

(1) A, C, D, E, B (2) A, E, D, C, B
(3) A, C, E, D, B (4) A, D, C, E, B

81. Arrange the steps of presentation of experiential learning cycle in sequence.

A. Determining the experimental phase of work
B. Plan the process and activity of the work
C. Determine the generalisation
D. Determine the application of activity planned
E. Evaluation of learning cycle

Choose the correct answer from the options given below.

(1) A, B, C, E, D (2) C, B, D, A, E
(3) A, B, C, D, E (4) C, B, A, D, E

82. Find the correct order for plan of work.

A. Determining need and defining the problem
B. Collecting and analysing the data
C. Selection of problem and determining the priorities
D. Planning and carrying out plan of work
E. Checking evaluation and reviews the programme and reconsider the new plans

Choose the correct answer from the options given below.

(1) A, B, C, D, E (2) A, C, B, E, D
(3) B, A, C, D, E (4) E, C, A, B, D

83. The sequential procedures of developing likert scale is

A. estimate reliability after administration on large group
B. retain and drop selected items
C. collecting large number of statements relevant to the research problem
D. identify items with high discriminatory power
E. conduct trial test

Choose the correct answer from the options given below.

(1) A, B, C, D, E (2) C, E, D, B, A
(3) A, D, E, B, C (4) E, D, C, A, B

84. Arrange the steps of the observation process in sequence.

A. Research design
B. Selection of area
C. Report writing
D. Collection and analysis of data
E. Formulation of topic

Choose the correct answer from the options given below.

(1) B, D, E, A, C (2) B, A, D, E, C
(3) B, E, A, D, C (4) B, E, D, A, C

85. Given below two statements, one is labelled as Assertion (A) and the other is labelled as Reason (R).

Assertion (A) Post menopausal women are at three times the risk of developing cardiovascular diseases than premenopausal women.

Reason (R) Women in reproductive age including premenopausal women have female sex hormones specially estrogen which protects against cardiovascular diseases. Estrogen relaxes the arteries and promotes good cholesterol. Estrogen declines as the menopause approaches.

In the light of the above statements, choose the correct answer from the options given below.

(1) Both A and R are true and R is the correct explanation of A.
(2) Both A and R are true, but R is not the correct explanation of A.
(3) A is true, but R is false.
(4) A is false, but R is true.

86. Given below are two statements, one is labelled as Assertion (A) and the other is labelled as Reason (R).

Assertion (A) Adopting eco-friendly methods and bio-degradable substance for dying and printing processes in textile and garment making can save the resources of the nature and reduce chemical landfill in a big way.

Reason (R) Bio-degradable dyes do not require heavy metals,amines and inorganic salts. Hence, they do not easily get decomposed without leaving any landfill in the environment.

In the light of the above statements, choose the correct answer from the options given below.

(1) Both A and R are true and R is the correct explanation of A.
(2) Both A and R are true, but R is not the correct explanation of A.
(3) A is true, but R is false.
(4) A is false, but R is true.

87. Given below are two statements, one is labelled as Assertion (A) and the other is labelled as Reason (R).

Assertion (A) Degree of flexibility in work organisation can be used to take advantage of variability in planning and executing work.

Reason (R) Variety of social, cognitive and physical features in different domains can be observed in different individuals and same individual over time.

In the light of the above statements, choose the correct answer from the options given below.

(1) Both A and R are true and R is the correct explanation of A.
(2) Both A and R are true, but R is not the correct explanation of A.
(3) A is true, but R is false.
(4) A is false, but R is true.

88. Given below are two statements, one is labelled as Assertion (A) and the other is labelled as Reason (R).

Assertion (A) A teacher is said to follow the vygotskian principle in setting-up a pretend grocery store and allowing the children to take on different roles such as cashiers, customers and store managers.

Reason (R) A child's cognitive development and learning ability are guided and mediated by their social interactions.

In the light of the above statements, choose the correct answer from the options given below.

(1) Both A and R are true and R is the correct explanation of A.
(2) Both A and R are true, but R is not the correct explanation of A.
(3) A is true, but R is false.
(4) A is false, but R is true.

89. Given below are two statements, one is labelled as Assertion (A) and the other is labelled as Reason (R).

Assertion (A) The effectiveness of audio visual aids rely upon the skill of the user.

Reason (R) The audio visual aids are selected on the basis of the criteria used for teaching and learning.

In the light of the above statements, choose the correct answer from the options given below.

(1) Both A and R are true and R is the correct explanation of A.
(2) Both A and R are true, but R is not the correct explanation of A.
(3) A is true, but R is false.
(4) A is false, but R is true.

90. Given below are two statements, one is labelled as Assertion (A) and the other is labelled as Reason (R).

Assertion (A) Applied research is more important than pure research in contributing to human welfare.

Reason (R) Pure researches are conducted in laboratories whereas applied researches are conducted field.

In the light of the above statements, choose the correct answer from the options given below.

(1) Both A and R are true and R is the correct explanation of A.
(2) Both A and R are true, but R is not the correct explanation of A.
(3) A is true, but R is false.
(4) A is false, but R is true.

Directions (Q. Nos. 91-95) *Read the passage carefully and answer the questions that follows.*

The fast fashion industry has evolved into an even faster-paced phenomenon called ultra-fast fashion largely influenced by the interplay between micro trends and social media.

The unsustainable nature of this fast and furious fashion has led to adverse effects such as climate change, depletion of natural resources, loss of biodiversity. Fashion, evidenced as the world's second most polluting sector, emits a staggering amount of carbon dioxide, accounting for up to 10 percent of global emissions, surpassing even the combined emissions from international flights and shipping. Not only that, but it also ranks as the second largest consumer of the worlds water supply. Disturbingly speaking, more than two billion animals are subjected to cruelty within the global fashion industry each year for the production of wool, fur and leather products. As a result, fashion has suffered accumulated unpayable debts to the environment. These toxic debts are a consequence of a myriad of factors, encompassing overproduction, overconsumption, waste, etc. In light of this pressing issue, how has this multibillion-dollar industry initiated measures to address this alarming situation ?

It was found that, out of staggering 100 billions tones of garments manufactures annually 92 million tonnes eventually find their way into landfills.

If this concerning trend persists, experts predict that the volume of waste generated by the fast fashion industry could skyrocket to shocking 134 million tonnes per year by the conclusion of the decade. According to projections, the global emissions produced by the apparel industry are expected to surge by 50 per cent by the year 2030. This alarming increase in carbon footprint highlights the significant impact of the industry on climate change and underscores the urgent need for sustainable and environmentally conscious practices within the fashion sector. In a quest for sustainability, experts are exploring novel eco-friendly materials like fungus, algae, shell waste and others. Concurrently, they are also spearheading groundbreaking recycling techniques, aiming to revolutionise resource management and promote a circular economy.

91. Ultra-fast fashion is

(1) microtrend
(2) eco-friendly fashion
(3) sustainable fashion
(4) faster-paced phenomenon

92. Out of 100 billion tonnes of garments manufacture annually how many tonnes find their way into landfills ?

(1) 82% (2) 90%
(3) 92% (4) 93%

93. Among world's most polluting sectors, fashion is ranked

(1) top most (2) 2nd most
(3) 3rd most (4) 4th most

94. Global emissions produced by the apparel industry are expected to surge by the year 2023 to

(1) 20% (2) 30%
(3) 40% (4) 50%

95. In a quest for sustainability experts are exploring novel eco-friendly materials like

A. leather B. fur
C. fungus D. algae
E. shell waste

Choose the correct answer from the options given below.

(1) C, D and E
(2) A, B and C
(3) B, C and D
(4) A, D and E

Directions (Q. Nos. 96-100) *Read the passage carefully and answer the questions that follows.*

Biomechanics or Kinesiology is the study of human movement including the interaction between the human and equipment. Primarily these studies are broken down into two broad areas : Kinetics (the study of forces acting on the body) and kinematics (the study of movements of the body). Biomechanics uses techniques including mathematical modelling, computer simulations and measurements to enhance performance and reduce injury. It can be applied to a wide variety of activities in order to identify optimal movement patterns to improve activity-specific techniques, analyse muscular recruitment and loading to determine the safest method of performing a particular task/ movement, assist in developing proper movement habits which can be maintained long-term (maximising performance and minimising injury risk) and analyse equipment. Biomechanical testing can take place in the lab or in the field. Testing methodology is determined based on the problem that needs to be answered and in consultation with an expert. Some typical biomechanical testing methods are 3D analysis is appropriate for activities involving complex body movements and were very accurate, detailed information is needed. Typically 3D analysis is done using high speed 3D motion analysis system in a lab, force plate analysis is typically used for walking, running and landing activities and used inconjuction with 3D motion useful for determining impact, breaking and propulsive forces, calculation joint kinetics, and weight transfer in dynamic activities, high speed video analysis is done with the help of high speed cameras, such as photron, that can operate upto 1000 Hz. It is very useful for qualitative analysis of high speed movements and impacts, EMG is used for measuring muscle activity, often combined with 3D motion analysis and force plate testing. It is only used for higher level analysis and accelerometers, gyroscopes, and lasers are used to determine the technical characteristics of the worker's motion.

96. Photron can operate upto

(1) 10,000 Hz (2) 10,500 Hz
(3) 1,000 Hz (4) 3,000 Hz

97. Biomechanical testing can be done in

(1) lab only
(2) field only
(3) computerised systems only
(4) Both lab and field

98. To determine weight transfer in dynamic activities, one should use

(1) EMG
(2) Gyroscope
(3) Lasers
(4) Force plate analysis

99. A qualitative analysis of high speed movements and impacts can be done by

(1) High speed video analysis
(2) EMG
(3) Gyroscope
(4) Lasers

100. The study of human movement including the interaction between the human and equipment covers

(1) consideration of only the forces action on the body.
(2) consideration of only the movements of the body.
(3) both kinetics and kinematics.
(4) consideration of potential energy only.

ANSWERS

1 (1)	2 (4)	3 (3)	4 (3)	5 (3)	6 (3)	7 (3)	8 (2)	9 (3)	10 (2)
11 (1)	12 (3)	13 (2)	14 (3)	15 (1)	16 (1)	17 (3)	18 (3)	19 (2)	20 (1)
21 (4)	22 (2)	23 (3)	24 (3)	25 (4)	26 (1)	27 (2)	28 (4)	29 (2)	30 (3)
31 (1)	32 (2)	33 (3)	34 (2)	35 (2)	36 (1)	37 (4)	38 (2)	39 (2)	40 (3)
41 (3)	42 (1)	43 (4)	44 (2)	45 (2)	46 (1)	47 (4)	48 (1)	49 (2)	50 (4)
51 (1)	52 (2)	53 (1)	54 (1)	55 (*)	56 (4)	57 (4)	58 (2)	59 (3)	60 (4)
61 (1)	62 (3)	63 (2)	64 (3)	65 (1)	66 (3)	67 (3)	68 (4)	69 (2)	70 (2)
71 (2)	72 (1)	73 (1)	74 (2)	75 (4)	76 (4)	77 (1)	78 (3)	79 (4)	80 (4)
81 (3)	82 (3)	83 (2)	84 (3)	85 (1)	86 (3)	87 (1)	88 (1)	89 (2)	90 (2)
91 (4)	92 (3)	93 (2)	94 (4)	95 (1)	96 (3)	97 (4)	98 (4)	99 (1)	100 (3)

Solved Paper

2022

Home Science (Paper-2)

Solved Paper, October 2022

General Instructions

1. There are total one hundred questions in this paper. Each question carries 2 marks.
2. All questions are compulsory.

---

1. Which food service system produces food at a central unit and distributes processed food to other smaller units.

(1) Conventional (2) Assembly line
(3) Commissary (4) Cook and Chill

2. Which of the following governs the selection of needle?

(1) Type of thread (2) Type of fabric
(3) Stitch length (4) Tension of thread

3. The term 'Therbligs' was given by

(1) Prang (2) Gilbreth
(3) Denmann W Ross (4) Mundell

4. International Literacy day is celebrated on

(1) 6th March (2) 8th May
(3) 8th September (4) 8th November

5. The process of assessing the progress of a project based on pre-determined indicators of the programme is called

(1) Feedback (2) Feed Forward
(3) Monitoring (4) Planning

6. Chi-square test is used

(1) When there are only two groups for comparison
(2) When the data is in frequencies
(3) To check accuracy of data
(4) When there are three or more groups for comparison

7. Given below are two statements, one is labelled as Assertion (A) and the other is labelled as Reason (R).

Assertion (A) Brocade, Huckaback, Jacquard and Tapestry can be classified under same category.

Reason (R) All can be made on the Jacquard loom.

Codes

(1) Both A and R are false.
(2) Both A and R are true.
(3) A is true, but R is false.
(4) A is false, but R is true.

8. Which of the following foods do not contain gluten and is acceptable for patients with celiac disease to consume?

I. Wheat flour II. Rice flour
III. Gram flour IV. Corn flour

Codes

(1) II, III, IV (2) I, II, III
(3) III, IV, I (4) IV, I, II

9. In a pattern, darts can be replaced by

I. Tucks II. Gather
III. Style line IV. Control seam

Codes

(1) I and II (2) II and III
(3) II and IV (4) III and IV

10. Development is a product of
I. Heredity and Environment
II. Learning and Maturation
III. Learning and Training
IV. Learning through observation
Codes
(1) I, II and III
(2) I and II
(3) II, III and IV
(4) I and IV

11. Given below are two statements, one is labelled as Assertion (A) and the other is labelled as Reason (R).
Assertion (A) Browning in condensed milk occurs due to Millard reaction.
Reason (R) It is due to reaction between reducing Sugar and fat.
Codes
(1) Both A and R are true.
(2) Both A and R are false.
(3) A is true, but R is false.
(4) A is false, but R is true.

12. Steps to be followed in applying Participatory Rural Appraisal (PRA) techniques
I. Build up personal rapport with villagers.
II. Identify villagers who are willing to share their experiences.
III. Setting the climate for discussion.
IV. Meet the villagers.
V. Select suitable place for interview.
VI. Show full interest and enthusiasm.
Codes
(1) I, IV, II, V, III, VI
(2) IV, V, III, I, VI, II
(3) IV, I, II, VI, III, V
(4) V, VI, I, IV, III, II

13. The tool of Management that does not deal with personnel
I. Organisation chart
II. Production schedule
III. Job description
IV. Job specification
V. Budget
VI. Communication
Codes
(1) I and II
(2) II and V
(3) V and III
(4) VI and II

14. Match the types of indicators given in List I with their explanation given in List II.

List I	List II
A. Direct indicators	I. Set to be measured within a time frame
B. Formative indicators	II. Measure magnitude of change
C. Summative indicators	III. Used when expected change is not directly observable
D. Quantitative indicators	IV. Relate to precise and comprehensive change
E. Process indicators	V. Measure performance at the end
	VI. Measure qualitative data

Codes

	A	B	C	D	E
(1)	II	I	IV	III	V
(2)	IV	V	I	II	VI
(3)	IV	I	V	II	VI
(4)	II	V	I	III	IV

15. A consumer passes through five stages in buying decision process. Arrange the sequence of decision making steps in correct order.
I. Information search
II. Problem recognition
III. Purchase decision
IV. Post purchase behaviour
V. Evaluation of alternatives
Codes
(1) III, IV, V, II, I
(2) I, III, V, IV, II
(3) II, I, V, IV, III
(4) V, IV, II, III, I

16. Indicate the correct sequence of activities in the Home Management process.
(1) Planning, organisation, feedback, implementation.
(2) Planning, organisation, implementation, feedback.
(3) Planning, implementation, organisation, feedback.
(4) Planning, feedback, organisation, implementation.

17. Given below are two statements, one is labelled as Assertion (A) and the other is labelled as Reason (R).
Assertion (A) Home Management is not an all-encompassing concept compared to decision making or problem solving.
Reason (R) Home Management does not consider the totality of managerial functioning.

Codes

(1) A is false, but R is true.
(2) A is true, but R is false.
(3) Both A and R are true, but R is not the complete explanation of A.
(4) Both A and R are false.

18. Match the foods in List I to its pigments in List II.

List I (Food)	List II (Pigments)
A. Beet root	I. Flavones
B. Carrot	II. Betalin
C. Onions	III. Chlorophyll
D. Spinach	IV. Carotenoids

Codes

	A	B	C	D
(1)	I	II	III	IV
(2)	II	IV	I	III
(3)	III	II	IV	I
(4)	IV	III	I	II

19. Which of the following features can be studied through Mapping while conducting PLAS?

(1) Natural Resources
(2) Priority Patterns
(3) Conflict Resolutions
(4) Problem Solving

20. According to Lawrence Kohlbergs theory, the development of moral reasoning takes place in six stages. Arrange these stages in sequence.

I. Universal Ethical principles
II. Authority and maintaining social order
III. Interpersonal Accord and Conformity
IV. Social Contract
V. Self-Interest
VI. Obedience and Punishment

Choose the correct answer from the options given below.

(1) I, II, III, IV, V, VI
(2) II, IV, I, VI, V, III
(3) VI, V, III, II, IV, I
(4) III, II, IV, V, VI, I

21. Given below are two statements, one is labelled as Assertion (A) and the other is labelled as Reason (R).

Assertion (A) Communication serves to construct as well as reflect family relationships.

Reason (R) Family member spend so much time with each other, they use and understand communication shortcuts and Idiosyncrasies that may elude an outsider.

In light of the above statements, choose the correct answer from the options given below.

(1) Both A and R are true and R is the correct explanation of A.
(2) Both A and R are true, but R is not the correct explanation of A.
(3) A is true, but R is false.
(4) A is false, but R is true.

22. Common elements between BCC and Advocacy are

I. both rely on persuasion techniques.
II. both seek to bring in behaviour change.
III. both need strategic planning.
IV. both use only intrapersonal communication
V. both can work only with people at the grassroots.

Choose the correct answer from the options given below.

(1) II, III and V (2) I, II and III
(3) III, IV and V (4) I, III and V

23. Which of the following can be used for outdoor publicity?

I. Flash cards II. Bill boards
III. Kiosks IV. Banners
V. Flip charts

Choose the correct answer from the options given below.

(1) I, II and III (2) II, III and IV
(3) III, IV and V (4) I, III and V

24. Given below are two statements, one is labelled as Assertion (A) and the other is labelled as Reason (R).

Assertion (A) Energy requirements during lactation are higher than during pregnancy.

Reason (R) As the turnover of iron is greater during lactation because of milk secretion.

Codes

(1) Both A and R are true.
(2) Both A and R are false.
(3) A is true, but R is false.
(4) A is false, but R is true.

25. Arrange in sequence the development of milestones during infancy.

I. Social smile
II. Sits without support
III. Turns from prone to supine
IV. Pulls to standing
V. Climbs stairs

Codes

(1) I, III, II, IV, V (2) III, IV, I, II, V

(3) V, II, III, I, IV (4) III, I, V, II, IV

26. Match the active ingredient of foods in List I related to cancer prevention with their sources in List II.

List I	List II
A. Phytochemical	I. Tomatoes
B. Alpha Lipoic acid	II. Green tea
C. Flavonoids	III. Potatoes
D. Glutathione	IV. Turmeric
E. Selenium	V. Broccoli
	VI. Sea foods
	VII. Asparagus

Codes

	A	B	C	D	E		A	B	C	D	E
(1)	I	V	II	VI	IV	(2)	V	I	IV	VII	II
(3)	I	III	VII	VI	IV	(4)	V	III	II	VII	VI

27. A healthy diet in humans does not include which one of the following?

(1) Preparation of food and storage methods that preserve nutrients from oxidation, heat or leaching.

(2) Provides all the nutrients in required amounts and proper proportions.

(3) Causes deficiency related diseases.

(4) Provides non-nutrients such as dietary fibre, antioxidants and phytochemicals.

28. Which of the following is incorrect?

(1) Packages designed for uniform shipping cannot be loaded into mixed shopping.

(2) Waste prevention is the most sought after option and disposal the least sought after.

(3) Shrink wraps is one of the forms of packing used.

(4) None of the above

29. Deliberate manipulation of people's beliefs, values and behaviour through words, gestures, images is known as

(1) Publicity (2) Propaganda

(3) Persuasion (4) Perception

30. Match the glands with their respective hormones.

List I	List II
A. α cells pancreas	I. Adrenal corticoid steroid
B. Adrenal cortex	II. Insulin
C. β cells pancreas	III. Prolactin
D. Pituitary	IV. Glucagon

Codes

	A	B	C	D		A	B	C	D
(1)	IV	I	II	III	(2)	I	II	III	IV
(3)	IV	III	I	II	(4)	II	I	III	IV

31. Match the catering unit with the right type of method of service. Catering Unit Method of Service.

List I	List II
A. Cafeteria	I. Centralised
B. Hospital	II. Scramble
C. Railways	III. Buffet
D. Conference Hall	IV. Plated service

Codes

	A	B	C	D		A	B	C	D
(1)	I	II	III	IV	(2)	II	I	IV	III
(3)	III	IV	I	II	(4)	IV	III	II	I

32. Match the following diseases in List I with 'foods involved' in List II.

List I	List II
A. E Coli infection	I. Tuna and shrimp
B. Gastroenteritus	II. Cream-filled pastry
C. Bacillary dysentry	III. Cheese
D. Arizona infection	IV. Cereal product

Codes

	A	B	C	D		A	B	C	D
(1)	III	IV	I	II	(2)	III	II	I	IV
(3)	III	I	II	IV	(4)	II	IV	III	I

33. Which of the following is not correct about ISO?

I. It is a worldwide, non-governmental federation of national standard bodies.

II. It coordinates and promotes codex activities in India.

III. Its mission is to develop standardisation.

IV. Its objective is to help in the smooth, free and fair flow of trade practices.

Codes

(1) I, II and III (2) II and IV

(3) II, III and IV (4) III and IV

34. Which of the following tests are not used the routine quality of food products?

I. Objective method

II. Ranking for intensity test

III. Difference test

IV. Scoring for intensity test

Codes

(1) I, II, III (2) II, III, IV

(3) I, II, ,IV (4) I, III, IV

35. Which of the following methods of printing are currently practiced largely in the Indian textile industry?

I. Screen Printing
II. Digital
III. Roller Printing
IV. Block Printing

Codes
(1) II, III and IV (2) I, II and III
(3) I, III and IV (4) I, II and IV

36. Match the fashion terms given in List I with their meanings given in List II.

List I	List II
A. Classic	I. Exclusive custom fitted clothing
B. Fad	II. Ready to wear
C. Haut couture	III. Last through ages
D. Pret-aporteriv	IV. Short lived craze

Codes

	A	B	C	D
(1)	I	II	III	IV
(2)	III	IV	I	II
(3)	II	III	IV	I
(4)	IV	I	II	III

37. Why is it essential to maintain standards in food quality.

I. Food helps in existence of all beings.
II. Food can be consumed in its contaminated form.
III. Adulterated food is beneficial to health.
IV. To enhance nutritional quality of food.

Codes
(1) I and II (2) III and II
(3) I and IV (4) II and III

38. What are the qualifications to be appointed as the member of the consumer Dispute Redressal Forum/Commission?

I. Not less than 35 year of age.
II. Posses a bachelor's degree from a recognised university.
III. Be persons of ability, integrity and good reputation.

Codes
(1) I and II (2) I and III
(3) II and III (4) I, II and III

39. PCPNDT Act was enacted to prevent
(1) Child Labour
(2) Sex Selective Abortions
(3) Domestic Violence
(4) Dowry

40. Match List I with List II.

List I	List II
A. Human Resources	I. Interrelated
B. Resources	II. Recurring
C. Routine decisions	III. Golden oblong
D. Proportion	IV. Intangible

Codes

	A	B	C	D
(1)	IV	I	II	III
(2)	IV	I	III	II
(3)	I	II	III	IV
(4)	II	IV	I	III

41. Match List I with List II.

List I (Right)	List II (Features)
A. Right to Safety	I. Consumers should not be forced to select a product.
B. Right to Education	II. Consumers to be informed about the quality, purity and standards of goods.
C. Right to be Informed	III. To make sure that the consumers have information programmes enable them to make purchasing decisions.
D. Right to Choose	IV. Ensure that consumers have a way to demand justice from those who can harm them.

Codes

	A	B	C	D
(1)	IV	III	II	I
(2)	IV	I	II	III
(3)	I	II	III	IV
(4)	III	II	I	IV

42. Which of the following statement(s) is/are correct with regard to tax efficiency?

Statement I Investment should be made in those investments which lead to tax savings.

Statement II It is the most important factor sound investing.

Codes
(1) Statement I is correct.
(2) Statement II is correct.
(3) Both the statements are correct.
(4) Neither I nor II statements are correct.

43. Consider the following statement(s) is/are correct with regard to money management.

Statement I Money management is an essential part of debt free life-style.

Statement II It is a broad term involves incorporates services and solutions across the entire investment.

Codes
(1) Statement I is correct.
(2) Statement II is correct.
(3) Both the statements I and II are correct.
(4) Neither statements I nor II are correct.

44. Match List I with List II.

List I	List II
A. Project schedule development	I. Specifying budgeted cost to be incurred at the completion of project.
B. Budget planning	II. Listing the entire schedule of activities.
C. Quality planning	III. Who will do what work at which time
D. Resource planning	IV. Assessing quality criteria used for project.

Codes

	A	B	C	D		A	B	C	D
(1)	II	I	IV	III	(2)	IV	III	II	I
(3)	I	II	III	IV	(4)	II	IV	I	III

45. Which the following characteristic(s) is/are helpful in manpower planning?
(1) Employee development
(2) Finding out the deficiencies in existing manpower
(3) Overall planning process of organisation
(4) All of the above

46. The consumer education is important because it
(1) helps consumers to understand their rights.
(2) provides complete information of marketing conditions.
(3) familiarises the consumer with various standards and standardisation marks.
(4) All of the above

47. Match List I with List II.

List I	List II
A. Psychological needs	I. Fulfilment of capacities
B. Self-esteem needs	II. Freedom from danger, job security, health care etc.
C. Self-actualisation needs	III. Recognition by others/feeling of achievement
D. Need for safety and security	IV. Food, clothing and shelter

Codes

	A	B	C	D		A	B	C	D
(1)	IV	III	I	II	(2)	II	III	I	IV
(3)	I	II	III	IV	(4)	IV	III	II	I

48. Arrange in order of sequence the functions of FSSAI
I. Lay guidelines for accreditation of certification bodies.
II. Framing of regulations.
III. Collect and collate data.
IV. Provide training programme
V. Promote general awareness about food standards.

Codes
(1) II, I, V, IV, III (2) II, V, III, I, IV
(3) V, I, II, III, IV (4) III, IV, V, II, I

49. What is 'Carryover Principle'?
(1) Additives added in raw materials are not present in final products.
(2) Antioxidant added to oil is present in all oil based products made from it.
(3) Both 1 and 2
(4) Neither 1 nor 2

50. Which is not an objective of building's bylaws?
(1) Allow disciplined and systematic growth of buildings and towns and prevent haphazard development.
(2) Protect safety of public against fire, house, health, hazards and structural failures.
(3) They provide health, safety and comfort to the people who live in buildings.
(4) Renovation of old buildings without any charge by the government.

51. Bibliography given in a research report
I. makes the report authentic.
II. helps those interested in further research and in studying the problem from another angle.
Which of the statement(s) given above is/are correct?
(1) Only I (2) Only II
(3) Both I and II (4) None of these

52. Following are the provisions of PWDVA.
I. Civil law
II. Non-protection of women
III. It does not penalise criminally
IV. It was enforced on 26th October, 2006
V. It does not define domestic violence
Codes
(1) I, III and IV (2) I, II and V
(3) II, III and IV (4) I, II and IV

53. A person shall be disqualified for appointment as a member of the Consumer Dispute Redressal forum/commission, if he/she
I. has been convicted and sentenced to imprisonment for an offence which involves moral turpitude.
II. is an undischarged insolvent.
III. is of unsound mind and stands so declared by a competent court.
IV. has been removed or dismissed from the service of the government or a body corporate owned or controlled by the government.

V. has such financial or other interest as is likely to affect prejudicially, the discharge by him of his functions as a member.

Codes

(1) I and III (2) I, II and IV
(3) II, IV and V (4) All of these

54. Match List I with List II.

List I	List II
A. Process chart	I. It is similar to process chart.
B. Multiman chart	II. It helps pinpoint all movements that can be reduced or eliminated.
C. Operation chart	III. It is also called identical chart
D. Pathway chart	IV. In it some signs and symbols are alloted to the movement of activity.

Codes

	A	B	C	D		A	B	C	D
(1)	I	II	III	IV	(2)	IV	III	II	I
(3)	IV	III	I	II	(4)	II	IV	III	I

55. Given below are two statements labelled as Assertion A and Reason R. In the context of the two statements, which one of the following is correct?

Assertion (A) After Independence, many libraries were established for expansion of adult education.

Reason (R) National Fundamental Education Center established in the year 1956.

Codes

(1) A is true, but R is false.
(2) R is true, but A is false.
(3) Both A and R are true and R is the correct explanation of A.
(4) Both A and R are true, but R is not the correct explanation of A.

56. Which of the following is related to programme management?

I. Planning II. Organisation
III. Evaluation IV. Entertainment

Codes

(1) Only I (2) Only II
(3) I, II and III (4) III and IV

57. 'Integrated Subsidised Housing Scheme for Industrial Workers and Economically Weaker Sections is meant for which purpose?

(1) To provide open developed plots, two named single or multi-storied houses on rental basis, subject to certain ceilings.
(2) It provided a subsidy.
(3) It aimed at re-building or improving houses in rural areas.
(4) It was initiated by Ministry of Textiles.

58. Curriculum is all the learning which is planned and guided by the school, whether, it is carried on in groups or individually, inside or outside the school. According to this definition, what are the inter-related components?

I. Curriculum objective
II. Curriculum evaluation
III. Knowledge
IV. Learning experience

Codes

(1) I, II and III (2) I, II, III and IV
(3) I and II (4) I and IV

59. Match List I with List II.

List I	List II
A. National Small Industries Extension Training Institute	I. Rajasthan
B. National Institute of Entrepreneurship and Small Business Development	II. Guwahati
C. Indian Institute of Entrepreneurship	III. Noida
D. Entrepreneurship and Management Development	IV. Hyderabad

Codes

	A	B	C	D		A	B	C	D
(1)	I	II	III	IV	(2)	IV	III	II	I
(3)	IV	I	II	III	(4)	III	II	I	IV

60. Which of the following options is not the factor that hinders with human resource planning process?

(1) Time horizons
(2) Unite the perspectives of line and staff managers
(3) Environmental uncertainities
(4) Type and quality of forecasting information

61. The following are the characteristics of informal education.

I. It does not contain Pre-scheduled courses.
II. It has both theory and experiment.
III. Teaching work is need and problem oriented.
IV. It is very important to follow the rules.

Codes

(1) I and II (2) II and III
(3) I and III (4) III and IV

62. Consider the following statements.

I. Research design will help identifying the importance of each step in the whole scheme of things.
II. The design help in making the research known as to why is he studying the issue and what type of data will be needed, how data will be found.

III. A research design will always helps us in knowing successive stages.

IV. Design will also help in finding out what total time the study is likely to take and what time each step in the study is likely to consume.

Which of the statement(s) given above is/are correct?

(1) I and II (2) II and III
(3) I, II and III (4) All of these

63. The safety of the principal amount can be ensured by

(1) owing securities in both government and private sectors.
(2) owing shares and bonds in different companies.
(3) investing in companies in different geographical zones.
(4) All of the above

64. Consider the following statements

I. Interpretation leads to the establishment of explanatory concepts that can serve as a guide for future research studies. It opens new avenue of intellectual adventure and stimulates the quest for more knowledge.

II. They can better explain only through interpretation why these findings are, what they are and can make others to understand the real significance of these research findings.

Which of the statements given above is/are correct?

(1) Both I and II (2) Only I
(3) Only II (4) None of these

65. Consider the following statement(s). Which is/are true with regard to Green Rating System?

Statement I It provides economic benefits.
Statement II Environmental aspirations.

Codes

(1) Only statement I is true.
(2) Only statement II is true.
(3) Both the statements are true.
(4) Neither statement I nor II is true.

66. Which of the following is the benefit of need assessment?

(1) Assessment makes training department more accountable
(2) Higher training costs
(3) Loss of business
(4) Increased overtime working

67. Arrange in sequence the following levels of bloom's Taxonomy.

I. To apply II. To create
III. To understand IV. To remember

Codes

(1) IV, III, I, II (2) I, II, IV, III
(3) IV, II, I, III (4) I, II, III, IV

68. Which is not a building bylaws characteristics?

(1) The rules must be specific, clear and the language of the rules should be grammatically correct.
(2) Terms used should be defined clearly, so that there must be one and only one meaning of the term.
(3) Due to some special conditions and requirements, some bylaws differ from the by laws of other places.
(4) No modification is allowed if required.

69. Match description given in List I with the terms given in List II.

List I	List II
A. A device for transmitting information to some machine	I. Hertz (Hz)
B. Measurement of intensity of sound	II. Control
C. A study of human motion and its physical aspects	III. Biomechanics state of a system
D. Measurement of frequency of sound	IV. Decibel (dB)

Codes

	A	B	C	D		A	B	C	D
(1)	III	II	IV	I	(2)	II	III	IV	I
(3)	II	IV	III	I	(4)	IV	II	III	I

70. Consider the following statements.

I. The purpose of research is not well served unless the findings are made known to others.

II. Writing report is the last step in a research study requires a set of skills.

Which of the statement(s) given above is/are correct?

(1) Only II (2) Only I
(3) Both I and II (4) None of these

71. Give the correct sequence in the processing of textiles.

I. Bleaching
II. Mercerisation
III. Scouring
IV. Singing
V. Desizing

Codes

(1) IV, V, II, III, I (2) IV, V, III, I, II
(3) V, III, II, I, IV (4) I, II, III, V, IV

72. Match List I with List II.

List I	List II
A. Shyama Prasad Mukherjee Rurban Mission	I. 16th August, 2015
B. Pradnan Mantri Gram Sadak Yojana	II. 25th December, 2000
C. Deendayal Upadhyaya Antyodaya Yojana	III. 25th September, 2014
D. Ayushman Bharat	IV. 23rd September, 2018

Codes

	A	B	C	D
(1)	I	II	III	IV
(2)	II	I	III	IV
(3)	III	I	IV	II
(4)	IV	III	II	I

73. What is the role of a food control system?

I. To enforce adoption of food standards.
II. To implement food standards.
III. To inspect food.
IV. To allow food to be contaminated.

Codes

(1) I, III and IV (2) II, III and IV
(3) I, II and III (4) IV, I and II

74. Which of the following are the objectives of the Consumer Protection Council?

I. The right to be protected against the marketing of goods and services, which are hazardous to life and property.
II. The right to be informed about the quality, quantity, potency, purity, standard and price of goods or services so as to protect the consumer against unfair trade practices.
III. The right to seek redressal against unfair trade practices or restrictive trade practices or unscrupulous exploitation of consumers.
IV. The right to consumer education.

Codes

(1) I, II and IV (2) I, II and III
(3) I, III and IV (4) I, II, III and IV

75. Give the correct sequence of 'Kanil' shawl weaving.

I. Drawing of design pattern
II. Threading of warp onto the loom
III. Weaving of shawl in long strips
IV. Winding of thread
V. Combing and spinning of fibers
VI. Collection and sorting of fleece
VII. Joining together of fragments of shawl
VIII. Washing and dyeing

Codes

(1) II, III, IV, V, VI, I, VII, VIII
(2) VI, V, VIII, IV, II, I, III, VII
(3) VI, VII, VIII, I, II, III, IV, V
(4) I, II, IV, III, VI, V, VII, VIII

76. Suppose you need to deactivate the enzymes in sliced potatoes that cause browning to occur. Which processing method is specifically designed for this purpose?

(1) Blanching (2) Bleaching
(3) Pasteurization (4) Retorting

77. Which of the following is a form of misdescription?

(1) Incorrect origin
(2) Incorrect quantitative description
(3) Extending the food
(4) All of the above

78. Match List I with List II.

List I	List II
A. Rehabilitation of Juvenile in India	I. 1960
B. Probation Act	II. 3 to 7 years
C. Children Act	III. 1850
D. Reform House	IV. 1958

Codes

	A	B	C	D
(1)	I	III	IV	II
(2)	II	I	III	IV
(3)	III	IV	I	II
(4)	III	II	I	IV

79. The word .... on a label means that a product contains no amount of, or only trivial or 'physiologically inconsequential' amount of, one or more of these components: fat, saturated fat, cholesterol, sodium, sugar and calories.

(1) low (2) lean
(3) free (4) reduced

80. The buildings bylaws apply to the building where

(1) the building is newly erected.
(2) the whole or any part of the building is demolished.
(3) where the occupancy of the building is charged.
(4) All of the above

81. Match List I with List II.

List I	List II
A. Scarlet fever, septic sore throat	I. Salmonella typhi
B. Typhoid fever	II. Escherichia coli
C. Colitis	III. Staphylococcus aureus
D. Bacillary dysentery	IV. Streptococcus pyogenes
E. Gastroenteritis	V. Shigella sonnei

Codes

	A	B	C	D	E
(1)	II	III	V	I	IV
(2)	I	II	III	IV	V
(3)	V	I	II	IV	III
(4)	IV	I	II	V	III

82. Research reports should be reviewed in the light of

I. investigator bias

II. cultural context

III. methodological factor

Select the correct answer using the codes given below.

(1) I and III (2) Only I

(3) Only III (4) All of these

83. Principle of leadership are

I. Specific Goal Target

II. Humanistic Approach

III. Personalised Principle

IV. Path Oriented Approach

Codes

(1) I, II and IV (2) II, III and IV

(3) I, III and IV (4) I, II, III and IV

84. Arrange the following in correct order.

I. Heritage City Development and Augmentation Yojana

II. Jawaharlal Nehru National Urban Renewal Mission (JNNURM)

III. Swarna Jayanti Shahari Rozgar Yojana

Codes

(1) I, III, II (2) I, II, III

(3) III, II, I (4) III, I, II

85. Which of the following statement is not correct about employment?

(1) Child labour is not allowed in India.

(2) MGNREGA is a big scheme in India.

(3) Wage is same throughout India.

(4) According to 7th Pay Commission, ₹ 18000 is the minimum monthly salary.

86. Which of the following is a non-formal education assessment challenge?

I. Missing Performance Record

II. Lack of Time

III. Lack of Scientific Method

IV. Lack of Monitoring by teacher or students

Codes

(1) I, III and IV (2) I, II and IV

(3) II, III and I (4) I, II, III and IV

87. Match List I with List II.

List I	List II
A. Manmade fibres	I. Accept dyes and finishes more readily
B. High lustre, low lustre	II. May be pure white
C. Fibres with good moisture regain	III. Rayon and cotton
D. Low wet strength, high wet strength	IV. The percentage of return from elongation to the original length
E. Elastic recovery	V. Silk and cotton

Codes

	A	B	C	D	E
(1)	IV	I	II	III	V
(2)	V	IV	III	I	II
(3)	II	V	I	III	IV
(4)	I	II	V	IV	III

88. Match List I with List II.

List I	List II
A. Asset Based Approach	I. People are motivated to use local resources.
B. External Agent Approach	II. People work as representatives of the whole community.
C. Multiple Approach	III. Best approach for community development programme.
D. Inner Resource Approach	IV. Based on capabilities and available resources.

Codes

	A	B	C	D
(1)	I	II	III	IV
(2)	II	III	IV	I
(3)	IV	III	II	I
(4)	IV	II	I	III

89. "Human Resource Development is fostering long-term work related learning capacity at individual, group and organisation level." Who said this?

(1) Watkins (2) Leonard Nadler

(3) MC Farland (4) RC Davis

90. What is the intention behind programme management?

I. Managing several related projects

II. Improving an organisation performance

III. Doing social work

Codes

(1) Only I (2) I and II

(3) I, II and III (4) None of these

Direction *(Q. Nos. 91-95) Read this passage given below and answer the questions that follow.*

The hypothesis that is being tested can be used to predict the way the data should point. The hypothesis may state that the experimental group will perform better than the control group. By confronting the hypothesis with the dependent variable values of the two groups, the experimenter can determine whether the hypothesis accurately predicted the results. But it is difficult to tell, simply by looking at unorganised data, whether the (dependent variable) values for one group are higher or lower than the values for the second group. Therefore, the data must be organised numerically to yield numbers that will provide an answer. For example, we may complete average scores and find that the experimental group has a higher mean (say, 100) than the control group (say, 99). Although, there is a difference between the groups, it is very small and we must ask whether it is 'real' or only a 'chance' difference. If we conduct the experiment again, would we obtain similar results?

If it is a 'real', reliable difference the experimental group should obtain a higher mean than the control group almost every time the experiment is repeated. If there is no reliable difference between the two groups, we would expect to find each group receiving the higher score half of the time. To tell whether the difference between the two groups in a single experiment is reliable, rather than simply due to random fluctuations (chance), the experimenter resorts to a statical test. The particular statistical tests used will be determined by the type of data obtained and the design of the experiment. On the basis of such tests, it can be determined whether the difference between me to groups is likely to be 'real' (statistically reliable) or merely 'accidental' (due only to chance). If the difference between the dependent variable values of the groups is statistically reliable, the difference is very probably not due to random fluctuation. It is therefore concluded that the independent variable is effective in influencing the dependant variable (promoting that the extraneous variables have been properly controlled).

91. Based on the passage, which one of the following is the correct hypothesis?

(1) Performance of experimental group will be less than control group.

(2) There will be no difference in the performance of experimental and control groups.

(3) Performance of experimental group will be better than control group.

(4) Performance of control group will be better than experimental group.

92. Statistical tests could be used, if the data are

(1) unorganised (2) organised

(3) normal (4) variable

93. The reliable difference between two groups could be obtained, if we use

(1) norms (2) validity

(3) statistical test (4) reliability

94. Statistically reliable difference is known as

(1) chance difference

(2) hypothesised difference

(3) random difference

(4) real difference

95. Arrange the following concepts in which they appeared in the passage.

I. Reliable difference II. Hypothesis

III. Statistical test IV. Random fluctuation

Codes

(1) III, IV, II, I (2) II, I, III, IV

(3) I, II, III, IV (4) IV, III, I, II

Direction *(Q. Nos. 96-100) Read the passage given below and answer the questions that follow.*

At birth, the average baby's brain is about a quarter of the size of the average adult brain. Incredibly, it doubles in size in the first year. It keeps growing to about 80% of adult size by age 3 and 90% nearly full grown by age 5.

The brain is the command center of the human body. It receives signals from the body's sensory organs and output information to the muscles. It is responsible for all body functions. A newborn baby has all of the brain cells (neurons) they'll have for the rest of their life, but it's the connections between these cells that really make the brain work.

Brain connections enable us to move, think, communicate and do just about everything. The early childhood years are crucial for making these connections. At least one million new neural connections (synapses) are made every second, more than at any other time in life.

Brain development builds on itself, as connections eventually link with each other in more complex ways. This enables the child to move and speak and think in more complex ways. The early years are the best opportunity for a child's brain to develop the connections they need to be healthy, capable, successful adults. The connections needed for many important, higher level abilities like motivation, self-regulation, problem-solving and communication are formed in these early years or not formed. It's much harder for these essential brain connections to be formed later in life.

Starting from birth, children develop brain connections through their everyday experiences. They are built though positive interactions with their parents and care givers and by using their senses to interact with the world. A young child's daily experiences determine which brain connections develop and which will last for a lifetime. The amount and quality of care, stimulation and interaction they receive in their early years make all the difference. A child's relationships with the adults in their life are the most important influences on their brain development. Loving relationships with responsive, dependable adults are essential to a child's healthy development. These relationships begin at home, with parents and family, but also include child care providers, teachers and other members of the community.

From birth, young children serve up invitations to engage with their parents and other adult caregivers. Babies do it by cooing, smiling and crying.

Toddlers communicate their needs and interests more directly. Each of these little invitations is an opportunity for caregiver to be responsive to the child's needs.

96. Which of the following statement(s) is/are correct about the brain of the human body?

(1) It is the command centre of the human body.

(2) Brain connections enable us to move, think, communicate and do everything.

(3) It receives signals from the body's sensory organs and output information to the muscles.

(4) All of the above

97. The growth of brain of a baby

(1) at the birth is about the quarter of the size of adult brain.

(2) triples in size in the first year.

(3) keeps growing to about 80 percent of the adult size by the age of 5 years.

(4) grows 90% by the age of 12 years.

98. Consider the following statement(s) is/are correct with regard to child's brain.

Statement I Children developed brain connections through their everyday experiences.

Statement II A young child's daily experiences determine which brain connections develop and which will last for a lifetime.

Codes

(1) Statement I is correct.

(2) Statement II is correct.

(3) Both the statements I and II are correct.

(4) Neither statement I nor II is correct.

99. Which among the following is essential for child's healthy development?

(1) Loving relationship with adults.

(2) The responsive adults.

(3) Not responding for child's essential social and psychological needs.

(4) Both 1 and 2

100. How do toddlers communicate?

(1) They communicate their needs and interest more directly.

(2) They communicate through gestures.

(3) They do it by cooing, smiling or crying.

(4) All of the above

ANSWERS

1 *(3)*	2 *(2)*	3 *(2)*	4 *(3)*	5 *(3)*	6 *(2)*	7 *(1)*	8 *(1)*	9 *(3)*	10 *(2)*
11 *(3)*	12 *(3)*	13 *(2)*	14 *(3)*	15 *(3)*	16 *(2)*	17 *(4)*	18 *(2)*	19 *(1)*	20 *(3)*
21 *(1)*	22 *(2)*	23 *(2)*	24 *(3)*	25 *(1)*	26 *(4)*	27 *(3)*	28 *(4)*	29 *(2)*	30 *(1)*
31 *(2)*	32 *(1)*	33 *(2)*	34 *(2)*	35 *(3)*	36 *(2)*	37 *(3)*	38 *(3)*	39 *(2)*	40 *(1)*
41 *(1)*	42 *(1)*	43 *(3)*	44 *(1)*	45 *(4)*	46 *(4)*	47 *(1)*	48 *(1)*	49 *(2)*	50 *(4)*
51 *(3)*	52 *(1)*	53 *(4)*	54 *(3)*	55 *(4)*	56 *(3)*	57 *(1)*	58 *(2)*	59 *(2)*	60 *(2)*
61 *(3)*	62 *(4)*	63 *(4)*	64 *(4)*	65 *(3)*	66 *(1)*	67 *(1)*	68 *(4)*	69 *(3)*	70 *(3)*
71 *(2)*	72 *(1)*	73 *(3)*	74 *(4)*	75 *(2)*	76 *(4)*	77 *(4)*	78 *(3)*	79 *(2)*	80 *(4)*
81 *(4)*	82 *(3)*	83 *(1)*	84 *(3)*	85 *(3)*	86 *(4)*	87 *(3)*	88 *(3)*	89 *(1)*	90 *(2)*
91 *(3)*	92 *(2)*	93 *(3)*	94 *(4)*	95 *(2)*	96 *(3)*	97 *(4)*	98 *(1)*	99 *(3)*	100 *(4)*

Solved Paper

2021

Home Science (Paper-2)
Solved Paper, December 2021

General Instructions

1. There are total one hundred questions in this paper. Each question carries 2 marks.
2. All questions are compulsory.

---

1. When was the POSHAN abhiyaan launched?
(a) 8th March, 2018
(b) 26th January, 2018
(c) 1st May, 2018
(d) 30th April, 2018

2. What are Sequestrants?
(a) They are added to keep the food stable
(b) Form a complex ion with metals like copper, iron etc.
(c) Added for colour
(d) They keep the food oxidised

3. Vitamin D_3 is also known as
(a) Retinol (b) Cholecalciferol
(c) Tocopherol (d) Ergocalciferol

4. When the food is directly given in the veins, it is called ?
(a) Parenteral nutrition
(b) Enteral nutrition
(c) Nasogastric nutrition
(d) Saline nutrition

5. The time and temperature used for the pasteurisation of milk is
(a) 72° C/15 min (b) 72° C/15 sec
(c) 72° C/30 min (d) 72° C/30 sec

6. In order to pursue the research, which of the following is pre required?
(a) Developing a research design
(b) Formulating a research question
(c) Deciding about the data analysis procedure
(d) Formulating a research hypothesis

7. Any two immisicible liquid when mixed together form an
(a) Aerosol (b) Emulsion
(c) Gel (d) Sol

8. Symptoms of thiamin deficiency are
1. Peripheral neuropathy
2. Photophobia
3. Cardiomegaly
4. Koilonychia
5. Tachycardia

Choose the correct answer from the options given below
(a) 1, 2 and 4
(b) 3, 4 and 5
(c) 1, 3 and 5
(d) 2, 4 and 5

9. Proteins present in milk are
1. Lactalbumins 2. Lactoglobulins
3. Casein 4. Ovalbumin
5. Myosin

Choose the correct answer from the options given below
(a) 1, 2 and 3
(b) 1, 3 and 5
(c) 2, 3 and 4
(d) 3, 4 and 5

10. Identify the names of essential fatty acids.

1. Linoleic
2. Butyric
3. Linolenic
4. Myristic
5. Arachidonic

Choose the correct answer from the options given below

(a) 1, 3 and 4
(b) 3, 4 and 5
(c) 1, 3 and 5
(d) 2, 4 and 5

11. Major symptoms of diabetes are

1. Polyuria
2. Glossitis
3. Acidosis
4. Techycardia
5. Nocturia

Choose the correct answer from the options given below

(a) 1, 2 and 4
(b) 1, 3 and 5
(c) 1, 2 and 5
(d) 1, 3 and 4

12. Match List I with List II.

List I (Food additives)	List II (Functions)
A. Yeast	1. Emulsifier
B. Soy lecithin	2. Antioxidant
C. Butylated hydroxyltoluene	3. Bleaching agent
D. Benzoyl peroxide	4. Preservative
E. Calcium sorbate	5. Leavening

Choose the correct answer from the options given below

	A	B	C	D	E
(a)	2	3	1	4	5
(b)	5	1	3	4	2
(c)	5	1	2	3	4
(d)	5	1	2	4	3

13. Match List I with List II.

List I (Biochemical test)	List II (Nutritional deficiency diseases)
A. Serum albumin	1. Vitamin A deficiency
B. Haemoglobin	2. Goitre
C. Urinary iodine	3. Kwashirkar
D. Serum retinol	4. Anaemia

Choose the correct answer from the options given below

	A	B	C	D
(a)	4	1	3	2
(b)	3	1	2	4
(c)	2	3	4	1
(d)	3	4	2	1

14. Match List I with List II.

List I (Vitamins)	List II (Functions)
A. Vitamin B12	1. Protection of PUFA from oxidative damage
B. Vitamin A	2. Role in carbohydrate metabolism
C. Vitamin E	3. Role in formation of normal RBC
D. Thiamin	4. Integrity of epithelial tissues

Choose the correct answer from the options given below

	A	B	C	D
(a)	3	4	2	1
(b)	3	1	2	4
(c)	2	1	3	4
(d)	3	4	1	2

15. Arrange the stages of new food product development:

1. Idea generation
2. Product development
3. Screening
4. Commercialisation
5. Concept development

Choose the correct answer from the options given below

(a) 1, 3, 4, 2, 5
(b) 1, 3, 2, 4, 5
(c) 1, 3, 5, 2, 4
(d) 1, 2, 5, 3, 4

16. Given below are two statements, one is labelled as Assertion (A) and the other is labelled as Reason (R).

Assertion (A) Calcium requirements during lactation are higher than during pregnancy.

Reason (R) As lactating women lose bone mass during breast feeding because less estrogen hormone is produced.

In light of the above statements, choose the correct answer from the options given below

(a) Both (A) and (R) are true and (R) is the correct explanation of (A)
(b) Both (A) and (R) are true, but (R) is not the correct explanation of (A)
(c) (A) is true, but (R) is false
(d) (A) is false, but (R) is true

17. By mistake you have over blued your clothes, which of the following reagents you would use to rectify the fault?

(a) Acetic acid
(b) Borax
(c) Sodium chloride
(d) Oxalic acid

18. Which of the following apparel production systems is based on teamwork and shared responsibility for quantity and quality of output?

(a) Progressive bundle system
(b) Unit production system
(c) Modular production system
(d) Customised production system

19. Light fastness ratings are in the range of

(a) 1-5 (b) 1-6
(c) 1-7 (d) 1-8

20. Which of the following is a knit fabric that uses fine worsted yarns?

(a) Inlay (b) Zephyr
(c) Intarsia (d) Shaker

21. For making a dress with kasuti embroidery, which of the following motifs will you use?

(a) Gopuram (b) Tulsi Vrindavan
(c) Nandi (d) Chokla

22. Reactive dyes form the following bonds with the fiber

(a) Ionic (b) Hydrogen
(c) Van-der-waals forces (d) Covalent

23. Which of the following is not an advantage of plasma technology?

(a) Increases abrasion resistance
(b) Increases dyeing speed
(c) Assists bio-scouring
(d) Gives liquid repellency

24. Shifting of darts from one place to other changes the

1. Fit of the garment
2. Amount of dart control
3. Shape of the pattern
4. Design of the garment

Choose the correct answer from the options given below

(a) 1 and 2 (b) 2 and 3
(c) 3 and 4 (d) 1 and 4

25. For making a dress for yourself in a plain-woven fabric, which of the following fabrics will you use?

1. Percale 2. Flannel
3. Burlap 4. Chino
5. Moleskin

Choose the correct answer from the options given below

(a) 1, 2 and 3 (b) 2, 3 and 4
(c) 3, 4 and 5 (d) 1, 2 and 4

26. Which of the following factors favour fashion?

1. Advertising
2. Transportation and communication
3. Political Instability
4. Sumptuary laws
5. An economy of abundance

Choose the correct answer from the options given below

(a) 1, 2 and 3 (b) 2, 3 and 4
(c) 3, 4 and 5 (d) 1, 2 and 5

27. Which of the following are examples of condensation polymer?

1. Acrylic 2. Modacrylic
3. Polyester 4. Nylon

Choose the correct answer from the options given below

(a) 1 and 2 (b) 2 and 3
(c) 3 and 4 (d) 1 and 4

28. Given below are two statements, one is labelled as Assertion (A) and the other labelled as Reason (R)

Assertion (A) Overweight people look heavier in stiff fabrics.

Reason (R) These fabrics stand away from the body creating an illusion of additional thickness.

In light of the above statements, choose the most appropriate answer from the options given below

(a) Both (A) and (R) are correct and (R) is the correct explanation of (A)
(b) Both (A) and (R) are incorrect
(c) (A) is correct, but (R) is not correct
(d) (A) is not correct, but R is correct

29. Match List I with List II.

List I (Figure types)	List II (Description)
A. Ideal Type	1. Curves diagonally outwards from waist to hip
B. Square shaped	2. Curves outward abruptly from waist and rounds sharply inwards
C. Heart Shaped	3. Curves outward gradually from waist and round over hip bone
D. Diamond Shaped	4. Curves outward abruptly from waist and falls straight to hips

Choose the correct answer from the options given below

	A	B	C	D		A	B	C	D
(a)	3	4	2	1	(b)	1	4	2	3
(c)	3	2	1	4	(d)	4	1	3	2

30. Match List I with List II.

List I (Colour problems)	List II (Description)
A. Frosting	1. Weak areas in a fabric resulting from chemical damage
B. Tendering	2. Horizontal off shade band across fabric
C. Barre	3. Same colour appears different under different light sources
D. Metamerism	4. Change of colour due to localised abrasive wear
	5 Unintentional shade variation within a piece of fabric

Choose the correct answer from the options given below

	A	B	C	D		A	B	C	D
(a)	4	1	2	3	(b)	1	5	2	3
(c)	3	2	1	5	(d)	4	1	3	2

31. Give the correct sequence of cotton spinning system.

1. Drawing
2. Carding
3. Blending
4. Roving
5. Spinning
6. Picking

Choose the correct answer from the options given below

(a) 1, 2, 4, 5, 3, 6 (b) 3, 1, 4, 2, 6, 5
(c) 3, 6, 2, 1, 4, 5 (d) 3, 1, 2, 4, 6, 5

32. Give the correct sequence of converting the waist dart of the bodice into two french darts.

1. Trace the front bodice
2. Locate the position and draw the lines for the number of French darts required
3. Cut on the French dart lines
4. Close the waist dart
5. Shorten the darts and connect the end of the dart lines to the apex
6. Draw the line for the French dart
7. Distribute the dart control equally

Choose the correct answer from the options given below

(a) 1, 2, 4, 5, 7, 3, 6 (b) 3, 1, 4, 2, 6, 7, 5
(c) 2, 1, 4, 5, 6, 7, 3 (d) 1, 6, 2, 5, 3, 4, 7

33. A comorbid means

(a) a disorder or condition that may co-occur with another disorder or condition.
(b) absence of diseases or medical conditions.
(c) a cognitive impairment can shorten lifespan.
(d) a condition can appear independently and have a detrimental effect on performance.

34. A fifth-grade student with Autism Spectrum Disorder (ASD) attends a general education class full time with support from a special education teacher. Which of the following would be the most effective way for the Individualised Education Program (IEP) team to integrate social skills training into the general academic curriculum for this student?

(a) Incorporate individual counselling services into the student's IEP
(b) Establish clear expectations for appropriate classroom behaviour
(c) Assign the student a one-on-one aide to model appropriate behaviour.
(d) Include peer-to-peer supports in the general education class as part of the student's IEP

35. Ethological theory of attachment was proposed by

(a) Jean Piaget (b) Pavlov
(c) Erik Erikson (d) Bowlby

36. A special education teacher is participating in a three-year revaluation of a high school student with an intellectual disability. As part of an assessment, the teacher accompanies the student to a store and asks the student to locate and purchase an item. This is an example of which of the following types of assessments?

(a) Ecological (b) Portfolio
(c) Authentic (d) Interview

37. One of the reasons for using drugs by the Adolescents is

(a) Pleasurable feelings
(b) Thrill of doing something illegal
(c) Parental Pressure
(d) Escape from everyday life

38. Compared to younger adults, middle aged adults who lose their jobs

(a) Tend to stay unemployed longer and have fewer opportunities for gratifying work as they age.
(b) Tend to find jobs quickly because of their skills but find it difficult to stay employed.
(c) Find it difficult to get new jobs, but once employed have a stable work history.
(d) Are less likely to become depressed , which makes it easier for them to obtain employment.

39. What is the focus of younger preschoolers and older preschoolers respectively when they indulge in play?

(a) Shared activities; trust and shared interest
(b) Trust and shared interest; Shared activities
(c) Parallel play; Solitary play
(d) Communicative play; non-verbal play

40. One of the reading readiness skills is the development of comprehension that includes

1. Ability to arrange a picture story with events in the correct sequence
2. Ability to tell some personal experience
3. Ability to write his or her name
4. Ability to answer questions about a story which has been read and tell it in simple words

Choose the correct answer from the options given below

(a) 1, 2, 3 and 4
(b) 2, 3 and 4
(c) 1, 2 and 4
(d) 2, 3 and 1

41. Egocentric thoughts can involve

1. The lack of awareness that others see things from a different physical perspective.
2. The inability to present their own perspectives to others.
3. Failure to realise that others may hold thoughts, feelings and points of view that differ from theirs.
4. Being intentionally selfish and inconsiderate.

Choose the correct answer from the options given below

(a) 1 and 2 (b) 1 and 3
(c) 2 and 3 (d) 2 and 4

42. The major principles that govern growth are

1. Cephalocaudal Principle
2. Proximodistal Principle
3. Principle of Hierarchical Integration
4. Principle of the independence of systems

Choose the correct answer from the options given below

(a) 1, 2, 3 and 4 (b) 1, 2 and 3
(c) 1 and 2 (d) 3 and 4

43. Which type of speech is used in the example : Like other 2 year old, Arjun can say, "Ma bye, bye" and "ball broken"; Which type of speech is used in the example: When 9-month-old Radha's mother talks to her, she uses short, simple sentences, repetitive words, and higher pitches.

1. Holophrastic 2. Telegraphic
3. Interpretive 4. Infant-directed

Choose the correct answer from the options given below

(a) 1 and 4 (b) 1 and 3
(c) 2 and 3 (d) 2 and 4

44. Match List I with List II.

List I (Basic Virtue)	List II (Erikson's Psychosocial Stages)
A. Hope	1. Autonomy vs. Shame
B. Will	2. Initiative vs. Guilt
C. Purpose	3. Trust vs. Mistrust
D. Competency	4. Identity vs. Role Confusion
E. Fidelity	5. Industry vs. Inferiority

Choose the correct answer from the options given below

	A	B	C	D	E
(a)	3	1	2	5	4
(b)	1	3	2	5	4
(c)	2	1	3	4	5
(d)	3	2	1	4	5

45. Match List I with List II.

List I (Description of prenatal development)	List II (Labels)
A. This stage lasts from 8 weeks until birth and involves the differentiation of major organs	1. Embryonic
B. From 2 to 8 weeks following fertilisation, when the major organs and basic anatomy begin developing	2. Germinal
C. The first and shortest stage, where the zygote begins to divide and grow in complexity during the first 2 weeks following conception	3. Fetal

Choose the correct answer from the options given below

	A	B	C		A	B	C
(a)	1	3	2	(b)	3	1	2
(c)	2	1	3	(d)	3	2	1

46. Arrange the four phases of Adult Development as given by Cohen in sequence.

1. Encore
2. Liberation
3. Midlife Re-evaluation
4. Summing Up

Choose the correct answer from the options given below

(a) 1, 2, 3, 4 (b) 2, 4, 1, 3
(c) 1, 2, 4, 3 (d) 3, 2, 4, 1

47. According to Lawrence Kohlberg's theory, the development of moral reasoning takes place in six stages. Arrange these stages in sequence.

1. Universal Ethical principles
2. Authority and maintaining social order
3. Interpersonal Accord and Conformity
4. Social Contract
5. Self-interest
6. Obedience and Punishment

Choose the correct answer from the options given below

(a) 1, 2, 3, 4, 5, 6
(b) 2, 4, 1, 6, 5, 3
(c) 6, 5, 3, 2, 4, 1
(d) 3, 2, 4, 5, 6, 1

48. Given below are two statements, one is labelled as Assertion (A) and the other is labelled as Reason (R).

Assertion (A) Communication serves to construct as well as reflect family relationships.

Reason (R) Family member spend so much time with each other, they use and understand communication shortcuts and idiosyncrasies that may elude an outsider.

In light of the above statements, choose the correct answer from the options given below

(a) Both (A) and (R) are true and (R) is the correct explanation of (A)
(b) Both (A) and (R) are true, but (R) is not the correct explanation of (A)
(c) (A) is true, but (R) is false
(d) (A) is false, but (R) is true

49. Muster rolls are prepared under the programme

(a) SGSY (b) MDM
(c) NHM (d) MGNREGA

50. Which one of the following is not a component of the services offered under ICDS?

(a) Immunisation
(b) Referral Services
(c) Formal Education
(d) Supplementary Nutrition

51. Licence to operate Community Radio stations is granted by

(a) State Governments
(b) Ministry of Information and Broadcasting
(c) Prasar Bharti Corporation
(d) Department of Telecommunications

52. International Literacy day is celebrated on

(a) 8th March
(b) 8th May
(c) 8th September
(d) 8th November

53. PCPNDT Act was enacted to prevent

(a) Child Labour
(b) Sex Selective Abortions
(c) Domestic Violence
(d) Dowry

54. The process of assessing the progress of a project based on pre-determined indicators of the programme is called

(a) Feedback (b) Feed Forward
(c) Monitoring (d) Planning

55. Which of the following features can be studied through 'Mapping' while conducting PLAs?

(a) Natural Resources
(b) Priority Patterns
(c) Conflict Resolutions
(d) Problem Solving

56. Common elements between BCC and Advocacy are

1. Both rely on persuasion techniques
2. Both seek to bring in behaviour change
3. Both need strategic planning
4. Both use only intrapersonal communication
5. Both can work only with people at the grassroots

Choose the correct answer from the options given below

(a) 2, 3 and 5
(b) 1, 2 and 3
(c) 3, 4 and 5
(d) 1, 3 and 5

57. Which of the following can be used for outdoor publicity?

1. Flash Cards 2. Bill Boards
3. Kiosks 4. Banners
5. Flip Charts

Choose the correct answer from the options given below

(a) 1, 2 and 3 (b) 2, 3 and 4
(c) 3, 4 and 5 (d) 1, 3 and 5

58. The communication process is always

1. Systematic
2. Transactional
3. Universal
4. Functional
5. Interactional

Choose the correct answer from the options given below

(a) 1, 2 and 3
(b) 1, 3 and 4
(c) 2, 3 and 4
(d) 1, 3 and 5

59. The major functions of KVKs in Extension are

1. Organising vocational training for rural youth
2. Organising training for farmers
3. Providing loans to farmers
4. Providing labour for farming activities
5. Conducting research for new farming technologies

Choose the correct answer from the options given below

(a) 1, 2 and 3
(b) 1, 2 and 4
(c) 1, 2 and 5
(d) 2, 3 and 4

60. Match List I with List II.

List I (Theories of Mass Communication)	List II (Characteristic features of theories)
A. Authoritarian Theory	1. Media assist in the growth of society
B. Liberatarian Theory	2. Media are responsible
C. Social Responsibility Theory	3. Media are free
D. Development media Theory	4. Media are controlled
	5. Media are agents of government

Choose the correct answer from the options given below

	A	B	C	D		A	B	C	D
(a)	2	3	4	5	(b)	3	2	4	5
(c)	4	3	2	1	(d)	5	3	2	1

61. Match List I and List II.

List I (Adopter categories)	List II (Estimated distribution in population)
A. Innovators	1. 13.5%
B. Early Adopters	2. 2.5%
C. Early Majority	3. 16%
D. Laggards	4. 34%
	5. 44%

Choose the correct answer from the options given below

	A	B	C	D		A	B	C	D
(a)	2	4	5	1	(b)	2	1	4	3
(c)	3	1	2	4	(d)	3	4	2	5

62. Arrange the following terms in the increasing order of complexity as per the Bloom's Taxonomy of Objectives.

1. Creating
2. Applying
3. Understanding
4. Evaluating
5. Analysing

Choose the correct answer from the options given below

(a) 1, 3, 4, 5, 2
(b) 2, 4, 5, 1, 3
(c) 3, 2, 5, 4, 1
(d) 4, 5, 2, 3, 1

63. Arrange the steps of Programme Planning in a sequential order.

1. Identify the Problem
2. Analyse Situation
3. Collection of facts
4. Develop a plan of work
5. Decide on the objectives

Choose the correct answer from the options given below

(a) 1, 2, 3, 4, 5
(b) 2, 3, 4, 5, 1
(c) 3, 2, 1, 5, 4
(d) 4, 2, 3, 1, 5

64. Given below are two statements, one is labelled as Assertion (A) and the other is labelled as Reason (R).

Assertion (A) Strategy for behaviour change must include providing communication that might trigger individuals to make decisions.

Reason (R) Internal and external factors may serve as cues to action.

In light of the above statements, choose the most appropriate answer from the options given below

(a) Both (A) and (R) are correct and (R) is the correct explanation of (A)
(b) Both (A) and (R) are correct, but (R) is NOT the correct explanation of (A)
(c) (A) is correct, but (R) is not correct
(d) (A) is not correct, but (R) is correct

65. Which one of the following is not the characteristic of scientific research?

(a) Precision
(b) Objectivity
(c) Systematisation
(d) Speculation

66. Identify the pure research problem from the following.

(a) Vocational interests of adolescent girls
(b) Role of ICT's in empowering rural women
(c) Estimating time and energy consumption in use of solar cooker
(d) Entrepreneurial activities of rural woman

67. The crucial weakness encountered in laboratory experiment is

(a) Control
(b) Manipulation
(c) Accuracy
(d) Time

68. The parametric tests are used when

(a) Variables are qualitative
(b) Distribution is normal
(c) Data is skewed
(d) Observations are independent

69. Which data collection tool is appropriate for the study of job satisfaction of KVK professionals ?

(a) Interview
(b) Aptitude Test
(c) Questionnaire
(d) Interest inventories

70. The advantages of using probability sampling are

1. Perfect control on extraneous variables
2. Convenient when sample is very small
3. Absence of sampling biasness
4. Lesser degree of judgement
5. Faster and cost effective

Choose the correct answer from the options given below

(a) 1, 3 and 4 (b) 2, 4 and 5
(c) 1, 4 and 5 (d) 3, 4 and 5

71. Match List I with List II.

List I (Variables)	List II (Characteristics)
A. Experimental	1. Cannot be altered by researcher
B. Organismic	2. Uncontrolled but have significant effect on dependent variable
C. Assigned	3. Manipulated
D. Dependent	4. Measurable, can't be manipulated
	5. Is the presumed cause of dependent variable

Choose the correct answer from the options given below

	A	B	C	D		A	B	C	D
(a)	2	1	4	3	(b)	4	5	3	1
(c)	5	3	2	4	(d)	3	1	4	5

72. The sequential steps of constructing Thurstone Equal Appearing Interval attitude scale are

1. Collection and Editing of items
2. Calculating Scale and Q values
3. Finalisation of items
4. Sorting items on different continuum
5. Administration

Choose the correct answer from the options given below

(a) 1, 3, 4, 5 (b) 1, 4, 2, 3
(c) 3, 1, 4, 2 (d) 4, 2, 3, 5

73. What is the correct sequence of statistical analysis of data?

1. Gathering 2. Analysing
3. Organising 4. Interpreting

Choose the correct answer from the options given below

(a) 2, 1, 3, 4 (b) 1, 3, 2, 4
(c) 1, 2, 4, 3 (d) 3, 1, 2, 4

74. Given below are two statements, one is labelled as Assertion (A) and the other is labelled as Reason (R).

Assertion (A) Statistics is the servant (not master) of logic rather than an end of research.

Reason (R) Careful collection and logical analysis of data contributes more to the search of truth than statistics.

In light of the above statements, choose the correct answer from the options given below

(a) Both (A) and (R) are true and (R) is the correct explanation of (A)
(b) Both (A) and (R) are true, but (R) is not the correct explanation of (A)
(c) (A) is true, but (R) is false
(d) (A) is false, but (R) is true

75. Per minute calorie consumption for moderate activities is

(a) 1.4–2.0 calories
(b) 1.5–2.5 calories
(c) 2.0–3.5 calories
(d) 3.0–4.5 calories

76. What type of adaptation it is where humans exhibit the capacity of being moulded?

(a) Genetic (b) Plasticity
(c) Acclamatisation (d) Behavioural adaptation

77. Quarternary Purple is

(a) $3B + 3Y + 2R$ (b) $2R + 2B + 2Y$
(c) $3Y + 3R + 2B$ (d) $3R + 3B + 2Y$

78. The general guidelines of work height for the task where there is frequent use of eyes and infrequent use of hands are

(a) 2-8 cms below eye level
(b) 3-10 cms below eye level
(c) 5-10 cms below eye level
(d) 8-12 cms below eye level

79. The group of commodities listed in the essential commodities act is

(a) Iron, Steel, Petroleum, Aluminium
(b) Coal, Steel, Cotton, Plastic
(c) Paper, Drugs, Brass, Steel
(d) Coal, Cotton textile, Iron, Petroleum products

80. Which colour combinations are used in achromatic colour schemes?

(a) Value variation of neutral colours
(b) Secondary colours
(c) Primary colours
(d) Opposite colours

81. Project size is decided by

(a) Government
(b) Financial institutions
(c) Project formulation team
(d) Project engineer

82. Identify from the list the values of working environment.

1. Punctuality
2. Creativity
3. Variety in work
4. Economic reward
5. Flexibility

Choose the correct answer from the options given below

(a) 1, 2 and 3 (b) 2, 4 and 5
(c) 2, 3 and 4 (d) 1, 3 and 5

83. The expected standards of a consumer education material are

1. Accuracy 2. Completeness
3. Commercial 4. Objectivity
5. Discriminatory

Choose the correct answer from the options given below

(a) 1, 3 and 4 (b) 1, 2 and 4
(c) 1, 4 and 5 (d) 2, 4 and 5

84. From the list given below which are the indicators of static work

1. Increased muscle blood flow
2. Sustained muscle contraction
3. Increased muscle oxygen consumption
4. Oxygen independent energy production
5. Glycogen and blood sugar is used to produce energy

Choose the correct answer from the options given below

(a) 1, 2 and 3 (b) 2, 3 and 5
(c) 2, 4 and 5 (d) 1, 2 and 4

85. From the styles given below which of the following styles are part of Late Georgian Style.

1. Adam 2. William and Marry
3. Happle White 4. Chippendale
5. Shearton

Choose the correct answer from the options given below

(a) 2, 3, 4 and 5 (b) 1, 3, 4 and 5
(c) 1, 2, 4 and 5 (d) 1, 2, 3 and 4

86. Match List I with List II.

List I (Project appraisal dimensions)	List II (Activity)
A. Economic appraisal	1. Suitability is examined
B. Technical appraisal	2. Determines financial viability
C. Organisational appraisal	3. Scale of project and the process adopted
D. Managerial appraisal	4. Adequacy and competencies are scrutinized
E. Operational appraisal	5. Indicates priority use
F. Financial appraisal	6. Capability of project is judged

Choose the correct answer from the options given below

	A	B	C	D	E	F
(a)	1	2	6	5	4	3
(b)	5	3	1	4	6	2
(c)	3	6	4	2	5	1
(d)	3	1	5	2	6	4

87. Match List I with List II.

List I	List II
A. EL Nino	1. An interaction where one organism beneficially affects second organism
B. Greenhouse effect	2. A practice/process that tends to 'long term change' in land to non-forest uses
C. Desertification	3. The progressive warming of the earth's atmospheric temperature due to insulating effect of CO_2 and other similar gases
D. Deforestation	4. A periodic rise in temperature of the Eastern Pacific
E. Commensalism	5. Degrading a once fertile land

Choose the correct answer from the options given below

	A	B	C	D	E
(a)	1	2	3	5	4
(b)	3	1	4	2	5
(c)	3	1	5	2	4
(d)	4	3	5	2	1

88. Arrange the steps of organisation process in sequence.

1. Delegating the work
2. Grouping activities
3. Delegation of authority
4. Identifying and classifying the activities
5. Coordination

Choose the correct answer from the options given below

(a) 4, 2, 3, 1, 5
(b) 1, 2, 3, 4, 5
(c) 2, 1, 4, 3, 5
(d) 4, 3, 1, 2, 5

89. Arrange the steps of buying process in sequence.

1. Evaluate the product
2. Exchange product with money
3. Find the product
4. Recognise the need
5. Develop interest in the product

Choose the correct answer from the options given below

(a) 2, 1, 3, 4, 5 (b) 4, 3, 5, 1, 2
(c) 4, 5, 3, 1, 2 (d) 1, 4, 3, 2, 5

90. Given below are two statements, one is labelled as Assertion (A) and the other is labelled as Reason (R).

Assertion (A) The colour of ripe watermelon is higher in strength as compared to colour of strawberry ice cream.

Reason (R) The colours at normal value as in watermelon are always in their pure form and thus are full intensity colours.

In light of the above statements, choose the most appropriate answer from the options given below

(a) Both (A) and (R) are correct and (R) is the correct explanation of (A)
(b) Both (A) and (R) are correct, but (R) is not the correct explanation of (A)
(c) (A) is correct, but (R) is not correct
(d) (A) is not correct, but (R) is correct

Directions (Q. Nos. 91-95) *Read the passage carefully and answer the question that follows :*

After ratification of the 'United Nations' Convention on the Rights of the Child (UNCRC) in 1992, India changed its law on juvenile to ensure that every person below the age of 18 years of age, who is in need of care and protection, is entitled to receive it from the state. The National Commission for Protection of Child Rights (NCRC) was set up in March 2007 under the Commission for Protection of Child Rights Act, 2005.

The constitution of India guarantees all the children certain rights which include: (i) Right to free and compulsory elementary education for all children between the age group of 6-14 years. (ii) Right to be protected from any hazardous employment till the age of 14 years (iii) Right to be protected from being abused and forced by economic necessity to enter occupation unsuited to their age or strength (iv) Right to equal opportunities and facilities to develop in a healthy manner.

However, despite having so many legal instruments the children in India are still not secured. Several indicators are showing how the Child Rights are being violated in different parts of our country whose plausible social and economic consequences would be more dangerous. Child Abuse is another dangerous part of erosion which silently kills the potential and development spurt of many children. We still live in a tabooed society in our country, where no proper sex education is provided to the children. Children get molested and abused but due to ignorance, they fail to protest and keep on becoming victim of exploitation for long.

91. Which is one of the dangerous things done to the children that silently kills the potential and development spurt of many children?

(a) Child rights (b) Child abuse
(c) Sex education (d) Child protection

92. This is not the right of a child

(a) Right to free and compulsory elementary education for all children between the age group 6-14 years.
(b) Right to be protected from being abused and forced by economic necessity to enter occupation unsuited to their age or strength.
(c) Right to be protected from any hazardous employment till the age of 16 years.
(d) Right to equal opportunities and facilities to develop in a healthy manner.

93. Child abuse occurs in India but is not reported and children fail to protest because

(a) Children are not vulnerable
(b) Children are ignorant
(c) Child rights are being violated
(d) Children don't have any right

94. The full form of UNCRC is

(a) United Nations Child Rights Commission
(b) United Nations Convention on the Rights of the Child
(c) Union of Nations for Child Rights Convention
(d) United Nations for Child Resource Commission

95. Right to free and compulsory elementary education for all children covers the children between the age group of

(a) 3-6 years (b) 3-18 years
(c) 6-14 years (d) 6-18 years

Directions (Q, Nos. 96-100) *Read the passage carefully and answer the question that follows :*

New technology does not remove the need to employ systematic approach to Communication for Development. Well-designed mobile content is often informed by local tastes so that people can identify with the content. The content needs to be 'sticky' so that the user wants to return to it again and again. It could be conveniently used by frontline social workers, easily understood by the masses and easy to recall.

Creative techniques are used to make educational content engaging and entertaining. '*Mobile kunji*', an innovative audio visual job aid developed by BBC Media Action for use by front line health workers is one such example, that features an empathetic yet authoritative female doctor character, Dr. Anita, who speaks to rural families. She is designed to be both trusted and respected by community health workers and families alike.

The audio message from the doctor is followed by rhyming couplets, punctuated by drum beats and the sound of a stringed instrument, which function as a mnemonic for key health messages. This rhyme is about preparing for delivery: "Keep three phone numbers in mind: Hospital, transportation and community health worker. To keep tension at bay: Plan as we say!"

The audio message is motivating health workers too. A nurse midwife in Samastipur, Bihar was surprised that someone was giving such an expert advice in her local language, 'even though she is a doctor and educated, she was speaking in Bhojpuri!', another community health worker summed up, 'I have learned how to explain things in simple and easy language. Now, I can explain the content to the beneficiaries in the same' way". Localised content is thus crucial for achieving resonance with users. However, it's much harder to take context-specific content to scale across disparate geographical regions.

96. Making the content 'sticky' means
(a) Pasting it on the walls in public places
(b) Making it complex enough to be understood by the doctors only
(c) User wants to return to it again and again
(d) The message should be abstract

97. '*Mobile kunji*' is an innovative audio visual job aid developed by
(a) All India Radio
(b) Bihar State Government
(c) Women and Child Welfare Department
(d) BBC Media Action

98. Which three numbers are needed to be kept in mind?
(a) Hospital, BLO and medical store
(b) Hospital, transportation and community health worker
(c) Doctor, Neighbourer and BLO
(d) Sarpanch, transportation and ward member

99. *Mobile Kunji* has a potential to be used as
1. Capacity building tool for the health workers
2. Tool to educate health workers
3. Tool to inform only health workers
4. Tool to inform people directly
5. Tool to educate masses only

Choose the correct answer from the options given below
(a) 1, 2, and 3
(b) 2, 3 and 4
(c) 1, 2 and 4
(d) 1, 3 and 4

100. The characteristic features of context specific content for communication are
1. It cannot be scaled up
2. It cannot be used in all states
3. It will be equally valid in all states
4. It can be scaled up easily
5. It is very powerful for behaviour change communication

Choose the correct answer from the options given below
(a) 1, 2 and 3
(b) 1, 2 and 4
(c) 2, 3 and 4
(d) 1, 2, and 5

ANSWERS

1	(a)	2	(b)	3	(b)	4	(a)	5	(b)	6	(b)	7	(b)	8	(c)	9	(a)	10	(c)
11	(b)	12	(c)	13	(d)	14	(d)	15	(c)	16	(a)	17	(a)	18	(c)	19	(a,d)	20	(b)
21	(a)	22	(d)	23	(c)	24	(c)	25	(a)	26	(d)	27	(c)	28	(a)	29	(a)	30	(a)
31	(c)	32	(d)	33	(a)	34	(d)	35	(d)	36	(c)	37	(a)	38	(a)	39	(a)	40	(c)
41	(b)	42	(a)	43	(d)	44	(a)	45	(b)	46	(d)	47	(c)	48	(b)	49	(d)	50	(c)
51	(b)	52	(c)	53	(b)	54	(c)	55	(a)	56	(b)	57	(b)	58	(b)	59	(c)	60	(d)
61	(b)	62	(c)	63	(c)	64	(a)	65	(d)	66	(c)	67	(a)	68	(b)	69	(c)	70	(a)
71	(*)	72	(b)	73	(b)	74	(c)	75	(c)	76	(b)	77	(d)	78	(c)	79	(d)	80	(a)
81	(c)	82	(d)	83	(b)	84	(d)	85	(b)	86	(b)	87	(d)	88	(a)	89	(b)	90	(a)
91	(b)	92	(*)	93	(b)	94	(b)	95	(c)	96	(c)	97	(d)	98	(b)	99	(c)	100	(d)

Home Science (Paper-2)
Solved Paper, November 2020

General Instructions

1. There are total one hundred questions in this paper. Each question carries 2 marks.
2. All questions are compulsory.

1. The emulsifying property of mayonnaise is attributed to
(a) Bromolein (b) Lecithin
(c) Pepsin (d) Ovaglobulin

2. The preservative used in yellow coloured fruit squash is
(a) Sodium benzoate
(b) Potassium peroxide
(c) Potassium metabisulphite
(d) Sodium mono glutamate

3. The delivery of hot cooked midday meals in an urban city is done by
(a) Centralised service
(b) Commissary system
(c) Cook and chill method
(d) Bulk decentralised mode

4. One of the methods for recipe adjustment is by
(a) Prime method (b) Factor method
(c) Process charting (d) PERT

5. Nutrition labelling has become mandatory even in the absence of nutrition claim in the following country.
(a) Japan (b) South Africa
(c) India (d) Singapore

6. The community intervention programme launched by the Union Health Ministry for youth both rural and urban, poor and affluent is
(a) NFSM (b) SABLA
(c) RKSK (d) NGCP

7. The major sign of ARF is
(a) increased serum creatinin level.
(b) elevated blood cholestrol.
(c) decreased blood pressure.
(d) decreased bone mass density.

8. Which of the following instruments is used for estimation of colour values?
(a) Crockmeter
(b) Laundro meter
(c) Pad steam range
(d) Spectrophotometer

9. The applique work in Bihar is known as ....
(a) Khatwa (b) Kanbi
(c) Rabari work (d) Jhik-tiki

10. In which of the following places Warp-ikat is not produced?
(a) Patan (b) Tanjore
(c) Kanchipuram (d) Surat

11. Which of the following is the most lustrous weave?
(a) Sateen (b) Swivel
(c) Jaquard (d) Dobby

12. Which of the following is the primary property of a fibre?
(a) Cohesiveness (b) Density
(c) Lustre (d) Resiliency

13. Which of the following is not a Dart equivalent?
(a) Style line (b) Princess line
(c) Gathers (d) Dart tuck

14. Starch paste is used in removing which of the following stains?
(a) Iodine (b) Ink
(c) Rust (d) Grass

15. Management process is
(a) long (b) continuous
(c) intermittent (d) an end in itself

16. Sensitivity to problem is
(a) creativity (b) awareness
(c) intelligence (d) knowledge

17. The flow of goods and services in a family at a particular time.
(a) Money income (b) Real income
(c) Psychic income (d) Physical income

18. One of the internal constraints in implementation of a project is
(a) improper feasibility report
(b) government policy
(c) documents desired by financial institutions
(d) licencing

19. The low cost material hollow gypsum board and blocks are used for
(a) roofs (b) foundations
(c) interior walls (d) floor

20. Expenditure for celebrating Deepawali is
(a) planned expenditure
(b) semifixed expenditure
(c) uncontrolled expenditure
(d) extra expenditure

21. Which one of the following groups are organic resources?
(a) Plants, water, fossil fuel
(b) Fossil, fuel, plants, animals
(c) Animals, air, water
(d) Air, plants, Minerals

22. The formation of a connection between parents and the newborn in the period soon after birth is called
(a) attachment (b) connection
(c) bonding (d) love

23. The theory that holds that behaviour is strongly influenced by biology and evolution is referred to as
(a) the Ecological Theory
(b) the Eterological Theory
(c) Erikson's Epigenetic Theory
(d) Darwin's Theory

24. In the New Education Policy 2019, one of the new elements is
(a) inclusion of early childhood education.
(b) provision of father's education.
(c) focus on adolescent education.
(d) introduction of adult education.

25. Children with average intelligence who have difficulty in reading, writing and mathematics are likely to have
(a) low intelligence quotient.
(b) lack of interest in studies.
(c) learning disability.
(d) low emotional intelligence.

26. The third stage in Erick Erickson's Theory of human development is called
(a) Autonomy versus shame and doubt
(b) Trust versus mistrust
(c) Identity versus identity confusion
(d) Initiative versus guilt

27. The basic premise of the Prohibition of Child Marriage Act, 2006 is that
(a) a child can be married only after 15 years of age.
(b) making a child go through marriage is an offence.
(c) a girl or a boy is a minor upto 18 years of age.
(d) a girl is a minor upto 18 years and a boy is a minor upto 21 years.

28. Which of the following statements does not describe a matriarchal family?
(a) Authority vests in the woman head of the family.
(b) Marriage relation are transient. The husband is sometimes a casual visitor.
(c) Descent is through the mother.
(d) Property is transferred through the mother.

29. The term used to refer to a person who controls or selects the content that reaches an audience is known as
(a) Watchman (b) Gatekeeper
(c) House keeper (d) Guard

30. Which of the following models of development emphasised that the modernisation could be achieved by increased productivity, economic growth and industralisation?
(a) The new paradigm of development.
(b) Interdependent model of development.
(c) Dominant paradigm of development model.
(d) Basic needs model of development.

31. Which of the following is not a group approach for communication and extension?
(a) Workshop (b) Home visits
(c) Training (d) Demonstration

32. In communication, the interpretation of body language, posture and movement is termed as
(a) Proxemics (b) Paralanguage
(c) Kinesics (d) Chronemics

33. Who was the ancient Greek philosopher who wrote the book 'Rhetoric' describing the role of persuasion in public speaking?
(a) Alexander (b) Aristotle
(c) Plato (d) Devito

34. The art and science of helping adults learn is called
(a) Pedagogy (b) Sociology
(c) Anthropology (d) Andragogy

35. Panchayati Raj institutions in India are important expressions of people's participation in local self governance through
(a) domination (b) Centralisation
(c) Decentralisation (d) Demonitisation

36. Which of the following scale represents the least powerful and lowest level of measurement?
(a) Ordinal scale (b) Interval scale
(c) Nominal scale (d) Ratio scale

37. Study of nutritional status of children born in 2010 in a village would be an example of
(a) Emperical study (b) Cohort study
(c) Trend study (d) Intervention study

38. Sampling error associated with random sampling can be determined by the following formula (Where *S*-sample standard deviation ; *n*-sample size).
(a) $\frac{S}{\sqrt{n-1}}$ (b) $\frac{S}{S\sqrt{n-1}}$
(c) $\frac{S-n}{S\sqrt{n+1}}$ (d) $\frac{S+n}{\sqrt{n+1}}$

39. Which of the following tests is most suitable for studying association between income level of mothers and their buying practices for infant wear?
(a) T-test (b) Chi-Square Test
(c) ANOVA (d) Pearson's *r*

40. Which of the following is not an advantage of fixed response question in questionnaries?
(a) Facilitate completion of the questionnarie.
(b) Easy to score and code.
(c) Useful where there is little or no information about the sample.
(d) No writing is required by respondants.

41. Antimicrobial properties can be attributed to the following species.
1. Asafoetida 2. Aniseed
3. Mace 4. Turmeric
5. Clove
Choose the most appropriate answer from the options given below.
(a) 3, 4 and 5 only (b) 1, 2 and 5 only
(c) 1, 3 and 4 only (d) 1, 2 and 3 only

42. Records to be maintained in the dietary department of a hospital to deliver diets to patients are
1. Requisition slip (wards)
2. Work schedule
3. Production schedule
4. Menu tally
5. Cash book
Choose the most appropriate answer from the options given below.
(a) 1, 4 and 5 only (b) 1, 3 and 4 only
(c) 1, 2 and 3 only (d) 2, 4 and 5 only

43. Adequate zinc is needed for
1. cellular growth
2. immune function
3. blood clotting
4. reproduction
5. muscle contraction
Choose the most appropriate answer from the options given below.
(a) 1, 2 and 3 only (b) 2, 4 and 5 only
(c) 1, 2 and 4 only (d) 2, 3 and 5 only

44. Emerging lipid risk factors for CVD are
1. elevated Lipo protein (a).
2. low apolioprotein A-1.
3. impaired glucose level.
4. high total cholestrol HDL cholestrol ratio.
5. inflammory markers.
Choose the most appropriate answer from the options given below.
(a) 2, 3 and 4 only
(b) 2, 1 and 5 only
(c) 1, 3 and 5 only
(d) 1, 2 and 4 only

45. Which of the following pockets come under the category of slashed pockets?
1. Kangaroo
2. Welt
3. Flap
4. Bound
Choose the correct answer from the options given below.
(a) 2, 3 and 4 only (b) 3, 4 and 1 only
(c) 1, 2 and 3 only (d) 1, 2 and 4 only

46. Which of the following are distinct styles in Kathiawar Embroidery?
1. Moti Bharat
2. Sindhi Taropa
3. Abla Bharat
4. Chalak-Tiki
Choose the correct answer from the options given below.
(a) 2, 3 and 4 only (b) 1, 2 and 3 only
(c) 1, 2 and 4 only (d) 1, 3 and 4 only

47. Which of the following parts of machine needle fit into the needle bar?

1. Shank 2. Blade
3. Butt 4. Scarf

Choose the correct answer from the options given below.

(a) 1 and 2 only (b) 2 and 3 only
(c) 3 and 4 only (d) 1 and 3 only

48. Which of the following properties are imparted in a fabric by nanotechnology?

1. Stain and wrinkle resistance
2. Flame retardance
3. Anti-microbial
4. Water resistance

Choose the correct answer from the options given below.

(a) 3, 4 and 1 only (b) 4, 1 and 2 only
(c) 1, 2 and 3 only (d) 2, 3 and 4 only

49. Which of the following fibers can be confirmed by their microscopic appearance?

1. Cotton 2. Wool
3. Silk 4. Nylon
5. Flax

Choose the correct answer from the options given below.

(a) 1, 2 and 3 only (b) 1, 2 and 5 only
(c) 2, 3 and 4 only (d) 5, 4 and 2 only

50. What are the objectives of Consumer Movement from among the options given below?

1. Product safety
2. Price cut
3. Solution to consumer problems
4. Providing consumer information
5. Formulations of rules

Choose the correct answer from the options given below.

(a) 1, 2 and 3 only (b) 1, 3 and 4 only
(c) 2, 3 and 4 only (d) 3, 4 and 5 only

51. What are the characteristics of hard wood as per the list given below?

1. These are equally strong across and along fibre.
2. They resist transverse loading shock and vibrations.
3. These are light in weight and colour.
4. These have more moisture content.

Choose the correct answer from the options given below.

(a) 1 and 2 only (b) 2 and 3 only
(c) 3 and 4 only (d) 1 and 4 on ly

52. From among the list given identify the features that enhance the visual weight of element and attract attention.

1. Regular shapes 2. Bright colours
3. Matching textures 4. Large dimensions
5. Elaborate details

Choose the correct answer from the options given below.

(a) 1, 3, 4 only (b) 1, 2, 4 only
(c) 3, 4, 5 only (d) 2, 4, 5 only

53. From the list given below indicate the features of traditional standard.

1. Rigid 2. Stable
3. Flexible 4. Socially acceptable
5. Modern

Choose the correct answer from the options given below.

(a) 2, 3, 4 only (b) 1, 3, 4 only
(c) 1, 2, 4 only (d) 3, 4, 5 only

54. From among the following items choose the objectives of aesthetic planning.

1. Expressiveness 2. Cost-effectiveness
3. Beauty 4. Functionally
5. Variety

Choose the correct answer from the options given below.

(a) 3, 4, 5 only (b) 2, 3, 4 only
(c) 1, 2, 4 only (d) 1, 3, 4 only

55. The most common psychological features of the Alzheimer's disease are

1. gradual loss of memory.
2. bad temperament.
3. difficulty in comprehension.
4. difficulty with speech production.
5. difficulty in walking.

Choose the correct answer from the options given below.

(a) 1, 2, 3 only (b) 1, 3, 4 only
(c) 2, 3, 5 only (d) 2, 4, 5 only

56. In case of children with disability dietary intervention is advisable because

1. they need more nutrition than other children of their age.
2. they tend to have poor appetite.
3. they may not be able to chew regular food.
4. they need to be reinforced with food to manage their behaviour.
5. nutritional aspects may be overlooked by parents.

Choose the correct answer from the options given below.

(a) 1, 2, 5 only (b) 2, 4, 5 only
(c) 2, 3, 5 only (d) 1, 3, 4 only

57. Emotional competence includes skills such as
1. being able to mimic others emotions.
2. being aware of one's emotional states.
3. being sensitive to other's emotions.
4. using the vocabulary of emotion terms.
5. not having any negative emotions.

Choose the most appropriate answer from the options given below.

(a) 1, 2, 3 only (b) 2, 3, 5 only
(c) 3, 4, 5 only (d) 2, 3, 4 only

58. The formation of the self from childhood to adolescence involves processes such as
1. Self-concept
2. Personality development
3. Selfishness
4. Self-esteem
5. Self-awareness

Choose the most appropriate answer from the options given below.

(a) 1, 2, 3 only (b) 2, 3, 4 only
(c) 1, 4, 5 only (d) (3), (4), (5) only

59. Which of the following are the components of ICDS?
1. Formal Education
2. Antenatal Services
3. Referral Service
4. Supplomentary Nutrition
5. Immunisation

Choose the correct answer from the options given below.

(a) 2, 3, 4, 5 only (b) 1, 2, 4, 5 only
(c) 1, 2, 3, 5 only (d) 1, 2, 3, 4 only

60. Which of the following schemes are for rural upliftment?
1. SSY 2. MGNREGA
3. PMGSY 4. DDUGKY
5. ICDS

Choose the correct answer from the options given below.

(a) 1, 2, 4 only (b) 2, 3, 5 only
(c) 2, 3, 4 only (d) 1, 3, 5 only

61. Which of the following are advocacy techniques useful in influencing policy?
1. Interviewing 2. Lobbying
3. Research 4. Negotiating
5. Campaigning

Choose the correct answer from the options given below.

(a) 2, 4, 3 only (b) 1, 2, 3 only
(c) 3, 4, 5 only (d) 2, 4, 5, only

62. Which of the following are 3 dimentional visual aids?
1. Specimen
2. Model
3. Powerpoint Presentation
4. Puppets
5. Objects

Choose the correct answer from the options given below.

(a) 1, 2, 3, 4 only
(b) 2, 3, 4, 5 only
(c) 1, 3, 4, 5 only
(d) 1, 2, 4, 5 only

63. The following are characteristics of Non-Parametric Tests : They
1. do not suppose any particular distribution.
2. are quick and easy to use.
3. cannot be applied to nominal and ordinal scales.
4. can be used when measurements are not very accurate.
5. make assumption about homogeneity of variance.

Choose the correct answer from the options given below.

(a) 1, 3, 4 only (b) 1, 2, 4 only
(c) 5, 2, 3 only (d) 2, 4, 5 only

64. Which of the following are types of case studies?
1. Observational
2. Historical
3. Dimensional
4. Situational
5. Experimental

Choose the correct answer from the options given below.

(a) 1, 2, 5 only (b) 3, 4, 5 only
(c) 2, 3, 4 only (d) 1, 2, 4 only

65. Which of the following data collection tools are most suitable for a research study on assessment of preference of adolescents for choice of career with a sample size of 40?
1. Semi-structured interview
2. Focussed group discussion
3. Participant observation
4. Non-participant observation
5. Projective techniques

Choose the correct answer from the options given below.

(a) 5, 3, 1 only (b) 1, 2, 5 only
(c) 3, 4, 2 only (d) 5, 4, 1 only

66. Match List I with List II.

List I (Process)	List II (Food Item)
A. Gelatinisation	1. Ice-cream
B. Carmelisation	2. Boiled rice
C. Pasteurisation	3. Chapati
D. Dextrinisation	4. Peanut brittle
E. Homogenisation	5. Custard
	6. Milk

Choose the correct answer from the options given below.

	A	B	C	D	E		A	B	C	D	E
(a)	2	4	1	6	5	(b)	2	4	3	5	6
(c)	4	3	1	2	5	(d)	2	4	6	3	1

67. Match List I with List II.

List I (Diets)	List II (Disease)
A. Dash	1. Gout
B. Gluten free	2. Diabetes mellitus
C. Low uric acid	3. Celiac
D. Carbohydrate counting	4. Hepatitis
E. High CHO, high protein moderate fat diet	5. Hypertension

Choose the correct answer from the options given below.

	A	B	C	D	E		A	B	C	D	E
(a)	1	2	4	3	5	(b)	2	1	4	3	5
(c)	5	3	1	2	4	(d)	3	4	2	5	1

68. Match List I with List II.

List I (Finishes)	List II (Purpose)
A. Carbonising	1. Sets the weave and eliminate shrinkage
B. Crabbing	2. Develops permanent sheer
C. Decating	3. Burns off vegetable impurities
D. Fulling	4. Imparts crease resistance
	5. Makes the fabric more compact and soft

Choose the correct answer from the options given below.

	A	B	C	D		A	B	C	D
(a)	3	1	2	4	(b)	3	1	2	5
(c)	3	2	1	5	(d)	4	3	1	2

69. Match List I with List II.

List I (Textures)	List II (Effect on Person)
A. Shiny textures	1. Do not enlarge the body and are suitable for all body types
B. Dull textures	2. Make the person appear thinner
C. Soft and clingy fabrics	3. Make the person appear larger
D. Stiff bulky fabrics	4. Reveal body irregularities
	5. Hide body irregularities and add weight to the body

Choose the correct answer from the options given below.

	A	B	C	D		A	B	C	D
(a)	3	1	4	5	(b)	2	3	4	5
(c)	1	2	3	4	(d)	4	3	2	1

70. Match List I with List II.

List I	List II
A. Mental Effort	1. Reach, Rising, Lifting, Holding, Caring
B. Visual Effort	2. Thinking, Reasoning, Planning, Decision Making, Worrying, Talking
C. Manual Effort	3. Walking, Moving, Standing
D. Torsal Effort	4. Looking, Reaching, matching, Adjustment to Distance
E. Pedal Effort	5. Bending, Leaning, Turning, Stooping, Sitting, Gardening

Choose the correct answer from the options given below.

	A	B	C	D	E
(a)	1	2	3	4	5
(b)	2	3	4	5	1
(c)	2	4	1	5	3
(d)	3	2	4	1	5

71. Match List I with List II.

List I (Polluting Agents)	List II (Category)
A. Carbon mono oxide	1. Volatile organic chemical
B. Benzene	2. Respirable particulate
C. Asbestos	3. Radio-nuclides
D. Fungi	4. Combution products
	5. Biologics and bio-aerosoal

Choose the correct answer from the options given below.

	A	B	C	D		A	B	C	D
(a)	2	3	5	4	(b)	1	2	3	4
(c)	3	2	1	5	(d)	4	1	2	5

72. Match List I with List II.

List I	List II
A. Vygotsky	1. Social-learning theory
B. Piaget	2. Socio cultural cognitive theory
C. Lorenz	3. Ecological theory
D. Bronfenbrenner	4. Ethological theory
	5. Cognitive development theory

Choose the correct answer from the options given below.

	A	B	C	D		A	B	C	D
(a)	2	5	3	1	(b)	5	2	3	1
(c)	5	3	1	4	(d)	2	5	4	3

73. Match List I with List II.

List I	List II
A. Morphologpy	1. System of meaningful units involved in word formation
B. Syntax	2. System that involves the meaning of words and sentences
C. Pragmatics	3. The way words are combined to form acceptable phrases and sentences
D. Semantics	4. Sound system of a language
	5. System of using appropriate conversation and how to use language in context

Choose the correct answer from the options given below.

	A	B	C	D		A	B	C	D
(a)	1	5	3	2	(b)	1	3	5	2
(c)	5	3	2	1	(d)	4	2	5	3

74. Match List I with List II.

List I (Types of Training)	List II (Description)
A. Job training	1. Training to introduce a new employee to the organisatin's mission, vision, philosophy and structure
B. Pre-service training	2. Training given to keep an employee updated with latest knowledge for a job
C. In-service training	3. A special training given to an employee to do a particular new task
D. Orientation training	4. Training undertaken by a person before joining a job

Choose the correct answer from the options given below.

	A	B	C	D		A	B	C	D
(a)	4	3	2	1	(b)	1	3	2	4
(c)	3	4	1	2	(d)	2	4	1	3

75. Match List I with List II.

List I (Space Zones for Communication)	List II (Distance)
A. Social space	1. Extends within 18 inches (one and a half feet) of a communicator
B. Public space	2. Starts from 12 feet and may extend upto 25 feet or to the range of eye sight and hearing of a communicator
C. Intimate space	3. Extends within a radius of 18 inches (one and a half feet) to 4 feet of a communicator
D. Personal space	4. Extends within a radius of 4 feet to 12 feet of a communicator

Choose the correct answer from the options given below.

	A	B	C	D		A	B	C	D
(a)	4	3	1	2	(b)	3	2	4	1
(c)	4	2	1	3	(d)	1	3	2	4

76. Arrange the steps of chocolate making in the correct sequence.

1. Refining
2. Cocoa liquor
3. Tempering
4. Addition of milk, sugar, fat
5. Enrobing
6. Conching

Choose the correct answer from the options given below.

(a) 1, 4, 3, 2, 5, 6 (b) 2, 4, 1, 6, 3, 5
(c) 1, 3, 6, 4, 5, 2 (d) 2, 3, 6, 1, 5, 4

77. Put in the correct sequence the steps in planning the food plan.

1. Check if the meals planned give satiety and is within income.
2. Indicate number of exchanges.
3. Include meat and pulse for protein.
4. List dishes served in each meal.
5. Note energy and protein requirement.

Choose the correct answer from the options given below.

(a) 1, 2, 4, 3, 5 (b) 2, 4, 3, 1, 5
(c) 5, 2, 3, 4, 1 (d) 5, 3, 4, 1, 2

78. Give the correct sequence of apparel production in a apparel industry.

1. Production pattern and grading
2. Costing and scheduling
3. Assembly
4. Marker making
5. Cutting

Choose the correct answer from the options given below.

(a) 2, 1, 4, 5, 3 (b) 2, 1, 5, 4, 3
(c) 1, 2, 3, 5, 4 (d) 3, 4, 5, 2, 1

79. Give the correct sequence of manufacturing acrylic fiber.

1. Dissolving
2. Filtering
3. Spinning
4. Polymerisation
5. Stretching

Choose the correct answer from the options given below.

(a) 4, 1, 2, 3, 5 (b) 1, 2, 3, 4, 5
(c) 1, 4, 2, 3, 5 (d) 4, 2, 3, 5, 1

80. Arrange the steps of flower arrangement in correct sequence.

1. Cut the stalks of flowers in the desired length.
2. Arrange the flowers in order of length in container.
3. Collect all the required material.
4. Add water in the container.
5. Anchor pin/stem holder firmly in the container.

Choose the correct answer from the options given below.

(a) 1, 4, 2, 3, 5 (b) 2, 1, 3, 4, 5
(c) 1, 3, 5, 4, 2 (d) 3, 1, 5, 2, 4

81. Arrange the following stages of moral development in the correct order.

1. Social order maintaining
2. Instrumental purpose
3. Heteronomous morality
4. Social contract orientation
5. Universal ethical principles

Choose the correct answer from the options given below.

(a) 3, 1, 2, 4, 5 (b) 1, 2, 3, 4, 5
(c) 1, 3, 2, 5, 4 (d) 3, 2, 1, 4, 5

82. Arrange the following reflexes in the correct order of their disappearance.

1. Stepping 2. Moro
3. Rooting 4. Babinski
5. Palmer grasp

Choose the correct answer from the options given below.

(a) 1, 2, 5, 4, 3 (b) 2, 1, 3, 4, 5
(c) 3, 1, 5, 2, 4 (d) 4, 1, 2, 3, 5

83. The stages of 'development' of a relationship as given by mark Knapp are

1. Integrating 2. Bonding
3. Experimenting 4. Initiating
5. Intensifying

Choose the correct answer from the options given below.

(a) 1, 2, 3, 5, 4 (b) 3, 2, 5, 2, 1
(c) 4, 3, 5, 1, 2 (d) 4, 5, 3, 1, 2

84. What is the correct order of the 5 elements of communication in the Shannon and Weaver's model?

1. Transmitter 2. Receiver
3. Information source 4. Channel
5. Destination

Choose the correct answer from the options given below.

(a) 1, 2, 4, 5, 3 (b) 3, 1, 2, 5, 4
(c) 3, 1, 4, 2, 5 (d) 1, 2, 3, 5, 4

85. Steps for executing Action Research are

1. fact finding
2. formulation of problem.
3. selection of research procedure and implementation.
4. review of literature.
5. brain storming and generation of hypothesis.

Choose the correct answer from the options given below.

(a) 5, 2, 4, 1, 3 (b) 1, 5, 2, 4, 3
(c) 4, 1, 2, 5, 3 (d) 2, 1, 4, 5, 3

86. Given below are two statements. One is labelled as Assertion (A) and the other is labelled as Reason (R).

Assertion (A) Vitamin C supplementation may help to alleviate side effects of chemotherapy.

Reason (R) Vitamin C has shown to promote the cytotoxic effect of antineoplastic agents from killing tumor cells.

In the light of the above two statements, choose the correct answer from the options given below.

(a) Both A and R are true and R is the correct explanation of A
(b) Both A and R are true, but R is not the correct explanation of A
(c) A is true, but R is false
(d) A is false, but R is true

87. Given below are two statements. One is labelled as Assertion (A) and the other is labelled as Reason (R).

Assertion (A) Cap height measurement is crucial for the hand and fit of the sleeve.

Reason (R) More the cap height more difficult is the lift of the arm and lesser the cap height more comfortable is the left of the arms.

In the light of the above two statements, choose the most appropriate answer from the options given below.

(a) Both A and R are true and R is the correct explanation of A
(b) Both A and R are true, but R is not the correct explanation of A
(c) A is true, but R is false
(d) A is false, but R is true

88. Given below are two statements. One is labelled as Assertion (A) and the other is labelled as Reason (R).

Assertion (A) A room with dark coloured walls will require more light sources to get reflective light levels.

Reason (R) The illumination in a room with dark colour walls will be distributed farther and more evenly as the light is reflected from surface to surface.

In the light of the above two statements, choose the correct answer from the options given below.

(a) Both A and R are true and R is the correct explanation of A
(b) Both A and R are true, but R is not the correct explanation of A
(c) A is true, but R is false
(d) A is false, but R is true

89. Given below are two statements. One is labelled as Assertion (A) and the other is labelled as Reason (R).

Assertion (A) Socialisation refers to "the process of inducting the individual into the social and cultural world: of making him a particular member in society ands its various groups."

Reason (R) Through socialisation children and adolescents learn ways of their everyday lives and acquire skills of social interaction with the family, with their peer group and other social groups.

In the light of the above two statements, choose the correct answer from the options given below.

(a) Both A and R are true and R is the correct explanation of A
(b) Both A and R are true, but R is not the correct explanation of A
(c) A is true, but R is false
(d) A is false, but R is true

90. Given below are two statements. One is labelled as Assertion (A) and the other is labelled as Reason (R).

Assertion (A) Technical problems are related to the interpretation of meaning by the receiver as compared to the intended meaning of the sender.

Reason (R) Semantic barriers are related to speech and language.

In the light of the above two statements, choose the correct answer from the options given below.

(a) Both A and R are true and R is the correct explanation of A
(b) Both A and R are true, but R is not the correct explanation of A
(c) A is true, but R is false
(d) A is false, but R is true

Directions *(Q. Nos. 91-95) Read the following paragraph and answer the five questions which as follows :*

India has only 3% of the world's land resources and 5% of the world's water resources. Yet India is the second largest food producer in the world and second in production of fruits and vegetables. On the contrary, Indian Medical Council in 2015 reports that 12-13% of the population in India die due to non-availability of nutritious food : and 25% of Indians go to bed without food. Why is there such discrepency in India? The reasons may be clubbed under three broad classifications First, production of food crops that do not satisfy nutritional needs (nutritional unavailability), Second, healthy foods are beyond purchasing power of the poor (unaffordablity) Third, week supply chain and failure of government intervention that still prevents dissection to exercise their right to food (nutritional inaccessability). Our food production has reached the capacity to provide one third of the population with adequate food grains under NFSM. But to ensure nutritional security we have to focus on existing agricultural methodologies. We have to shift cropping pattern from cereals to nutrients based one that promotes horticulture, coarse grains, pulses, millets, Horticulture production has doubled over the years according to NNM.

An Indian has access to only 2455 Kcal/day which is much lower than 3000 Kcal of European countries. FAO/WHO recommends atleast 400 gms of fruits and vegetables per day Indians cannot even manage to get half of the daily target. Government should promote domestic nutrition needs by Government ensuring quality seeds, promotion of integrated pest and disease management encourage peri-urban vegetable farming and roof gardens to grow vegetables. School premesis that raise vegetable and greens will have nutritional impact.

Recent increase in the minimum support price of pulses and their inclusion in National Food Security Mission is a welcome step. Organic farming should be put forward as an alternative better farming practice. As nutrient dense food is expensive, so food fortification can help it to reach the poor. Non-availability of nutritious food leads directly to poor quality life, loss of productivity, poor mental development, increased health cost and decreased school days. The demographic divide now is turning into demographic liability.

91. If fruits and vegetable production, India stands

(a) 1st (b) 2nd (c) 5th (d) 10th

92. According of Indian Medical Council, Report 2015 the persons who die due to the non-availability of food are (in per cent).

(a) 10 (b) 13 (c) 20 (d) 24

93. Measures that encourages pulse production are

1. shifting to nutrient dence crop.
2. minimum support price for pulses.
3. inclusion in the National Food Security Mission.
4. encouraging more calorie consumption.
5. recommending consumption of 400 g fruits.

Choose the most appropriate answer from the options given below.

(a) 1, 2, 5 only (b) 3, 4, 5 only
(c) 1, 2, 3 only (d) 3, 1, 5 only

94. Measures to ensure nutrition security are

1. shift from cereal to nutrient dense cropping pattern
2. food fortification
3. good quality seeds
4. providing packed foods
5. peri-urban vegetable gardens

Choose the most appropriate answer from the options given below.

(a) 1, 3, 4, 5 only (b) 1, 2, 4, 5 only
(c) 2, 3, 1, 4 only (d) 1, 2, 3, 5 only

95. Non-availability of nutritive foods lead to
1. poor quality of life
2. low productivity
3. poor mental development
4. more health cost
5. unemployment
6. low literacy rate

Choose the most appropriate answer from the options given below.
(a) 1, 2, 4, 3 only (b) 2, 3, 1, 5 only
(c) 2, 5, 4, 6 only (d) 1, 3, 5, 6 only

Directions *(Q. Nos. 96-100) Read the following paragraph and answer the five questions which as follow :*

Research around the world shows that child labour and poverty are intimately linked. However, it is also known that the specific circumstances of child labour are influenced by many other factor. Thus, parental illiteracy, non-accessibility of schools, social and cultural milieu and ineffective enforcement of legal provisions pertaining to child labour are some of the significant cause of child labour. However, no cause can justify the existence of child labour.

There is complete loss of invaluable childhood with near permanent damage to social development. Lack of education forces children into the worst employment prospects as adults. Although the labour of young children of both sexes is exploited, the plight of the girl child's labourer is worse off. She is a child, a girl, and a labourer. She faces discrimination on all counts–in almost all areas–rural and urban. Girl child labour is prevalent in the following areas.

- Household work
- Agriculture work
- Bonded labour
- Domestic service

96. Which two of the following options refer to the factors linked to child labour as stated in the paragraph?
1. Parent's Education
2. The Indian Justice System
3. Mother's attitude
4. Child's lack of interest in the schooling

Choose the most appropriate answer from the options given below.
(a) 1 and 4 (b) 2 and 3 (c) 1 and 2 (d) 1 and 3

97. What harm does child labour cause to children? From among the following options which one is incorrect with reference to the paragraph?
1. The children become delinquent.
2. The children do not develop social skills.
3. The children are not able to find quality jobs as adults.
4. Child labours are rejected by society.

Choose the most appropriate answer from the options given below.
(a) 1 and 2 only (b) 1 and 3 only
(c) 3 and 4 only (d) 2 and 3 only

98. The plight of girl child labour is worse than that of the boy child because
1. she is a labourer.
2. she is a child.
3. she is girl.
4. she is weaker then a boy.
5. she does not go to school.

Choose the correct answer from the options given below.
(a) 1, 2, 3 only (b) 1, 3, 5 only
(c) 2, 3, 5 only (d) 1, 2, 5 only

99. Which are the areas of labour in which the girl children are found to be employed?
1. House hold work
2. Agricultural work
3. Tuitions to school going children
4. Bonded labour
5. Sanitation worker

Choose the correct answer from the options given below.
(a) 1, 2, 5 only (b) 1, 2, 4 only
(c) 2, 3, 4 only (d) 3, 4, 5 only

100. The girl child is engaged for labour usually in
(a) tea shops (b) railways
(c) factories (d) domestic work

ANSWERS

1	(b)	2	(a)	3	(d)	4	(b)	5	(c)	6	(c)	7	(a)	8	(d)	9	(a)	10	(d)
11	(a)	12	(a)	13	(a)	14	(a)	15	(b)	16	(b)	17	(b)	18	(a)	19	(c)	20	(d)
21	(b)	22	(c)	23	(d)	24	(a)	25	(c)	26	(d)	27	(d)	28	(b)	29	(b)	30	(c)
31	(b)	32	(c)	33	(b)	34	(d)	35	(c)	36	(c)	37	(b)	38	(a)	39	(b)	40	(c)
41	(c)	42	(b)	43	(b)	44	(d)	45	(a)	46	(b)	47	(d)	48	(c)	49	(c)	50	(b)
51	(a)	52	(d)	53	(c)	54	(d)	55	(b)	56	(c)	57	(d)	58	(c)	59	(a)	60	(c)
61	(d)	62	(d)	63	(b)	64	(d)	65	(b)	66	(d)	67	(c)	68	(b)	69	(a)	70	(c)
71	(d)	72	(d)	73	(b)	74	(a)	75	(c)	76	(b)	77	(c)	78	(a)	79	(a)	80	(d)
81	(d)	82	(c)	83	(c)	84	(c)	85	(d)	86	(c)	87	(a)	88	(c)	89	(a)	90	(d)
91	(b)	92	(b)	93	(c)	94	(d)	95	(a)	96	(c)	97	(d)	98	(a)	99	(b)	100	(d)

Home Science (Paper-2)

Solved Paper, June 2019

General Instructions

1. There are total one hundred questions in this paper. Each question carries 2 marks.
2. All questions are compulsory.

---

1. The conversion ratio of beta carotene to vitamin A (retinol) recommended by ICMR (2010) is

(a) 1 : 1 (b) 1 : 2 (c) 1 : 4 (d) 1 : 8

2. An ideal quality fat for good health is the one which maintains $n-6/n-3$ ratio of

(a) 5 – 10 (b) 10 – 12 (c) 0.8 – 1.0 (d) 2 – 3

3. A diet rich in BCAA is given for which disease condition?

(a) Chronic kidney disease (b) Hepatic encephalopathy
(c) Crohn's disease (d) Diverticular disease

4. Government establishments such as hospitals, home for elderly generally adopt which of the following methods for purchasing of food and material?

(a) Auction buying (b) Negotiated buying
(c) Blanket order purchase (d) Formal buying

5. Foods, supplements provided to athletes with the aim to improve sports performance are called

(a) health foods (b) therapeutic foods
(c) ergogenic aids (d) nutraceuticals

6. The food cost in any food service establishment whatever its size varies between

(a) 40–60 per cent
(b) 20–30 per cent
(c) 55–75 per cent
(d) more than 75 per cent

7. Which of the following diseases is transmitted through fecal-oral route?

(a) Tuberculosis (b) Trachoma
(c) Typhoid (d) Taeniasis

8. GRAS refers to

(a) generally recognised as supplement.
(b) generally recognised as safe.
(c) generally recognised as superior.
(d) generally recognised as starter.

9. The loss of moisture from the gel results in a condition, called

(a) dextrinisation (b) retrogradation
(c) marbling (d) syneresis

10. Braising combines two methods of cooking. Tick the correct option from the list given.

(a) blanching-cum-roasting (b) stewing-cum-poaching
(c) roasting-cum-frying (d) sauteing-cum-toasting

11. The core of all food preparation and service activity in a food service unit is

(a) purchasing (b) menu
(c) production (d) work scheduling

12. Which of the following machine beds is commonly used for stitching small, curved or pieces that are awkward in shape?

(a) Flat (b) Cylinder
(c) Feed off the arm (d) Oval

13. Which of the following reagents is used for removing the grass stain?

(a) Oxalic acid (b) Methylated spirit
(c) Sodium hydrosulphite (d) Broax

14. Which printing method will you suggest to your friend for printing a sheet on both sides simultaneously?

(a) Screen (b) Duplex (c) Photographic (d) Transfer

15. Which of the following is not a Kasuti stitch?
(a) Gavanti (b) Phanda (c) Menthi (d) Murgi

16. Which of the following fibres can be confirmed by the microscopic test?
(a) Cotton (b) Polyester (c) Silk (d) Nylon

17. Which of the following parts of sewing machine has serrated edges?
(a) Presser foot (b) Feed dog
(c) Throat plate (d) Oscillating hook

18. Which of the following is the most appropriate for achieving good quality scalloped hemline of a dress?
(a) Bias facing (b) Binding
(c) Band (d) Shaped facing

19. Which of the following is the secondary property of fibres?
(a) Uniformity (b) Density
(c) Cohesiveness (d) Tensile strength

20. Which of the following lines creates shapes representing unity and variety?
(a) Diagonal lines (b) Zigzag lines
(c) Transitional lines (d) Contrasting lines

21. Hallmark certification is awarded by
(a) BIS (b) ISO
(c) ISI (d) BEE

22. Which of the following is the most energy efficient lamp?
(a) Halogen lamp (b) Fluorescent lamp
(c) Light emitting diode lamp (d) Sodium vapour lamp

23. Reducing material use, minimising toxic dispersion, recycling for protection of environment is referred to as
(a) energy conservation (b) eco-efficiency
(c) energy efficiency (d) material efficiency

24. Which one is the paper and pencil technique of charting time and motion study?
(a) Micro motion analysis (b) Process chart
(c) Cycle graph (d) Chronocycle graph

25. Which of the following are intrapersonal human resources?
(a) Parks, school, public, transport
(b) Skills, attitudes, knowledge
(c) Air, space, temperature
(d) Car, house, furniture

26. International norms specified for various activities keeping in mind the equipment and user requirement (Edited by Baiche and Walliman, 2006) are referred to as
(a) international space standards
(b) neufert Architect's Data
(c) Building standards
(d) space standards

27. A pregnant woman was informed that her fertilised ovum was growing in an area other than the uterus. The condition is called
(a) RH incompatibility (b) Invitro fertilisation
(c) Surrogacy (d) Ectopic pregnancy

28. Harlow's famous attachment studies were conducted using which animals/birds?
(a) Pigeons (b) Rats
(c) Rabbits (d) Monkeys

29. Marcia's term for adolescents who have made a commitment but have not experienced a crisis is
(a) identity achievement (b) identity diffusion
(c) identity foreclosure (d) identity moratorium

30. The childline service is a 24-hour free phone service that can be accessed by dialing
(a) 1081 (b) 100 (c) 1099 (d) 1098

31. Levinson proposed a model of adult development in his book, entitled.
(a) passages (b) seasons of a man's life
(c) adaptation of life (d) how we age

32. Disorders or disease not associated with the biological aging process is
(a) Bulimia (b) Presbycusis
(c) Macular disease (d) Dementia

33. The practice of marriage within the boundaries of kin group, clan lineage, village and social class is known as
(a) exogamy (b) endogamy
(c) hypogamy (d) hypergamy

34. A couple would like to adopt a child. They need to register online with the organisation, called
(a) SARA (b) DCCW (c) CARA (d) SAA

35. The elements present the Aristotle's model of communication are
(a) speaker, speech, audience (b) source, signal, destination
(c) sender, encoder, decoder (d) sender, decoder, feedback

36. 'Putting the last first' is the guiding philosophy of people-centric development, proposed by
(a) Paul Leagans (b) Everett Rogers
(c) Spencer Hatch (d) Robert Chambers

37. Which of the following is an example of organised social-change initiative?
(a) Self-help group (b) Youth club
(c) Dairy co-operative (d) Religious discourse

38. A pamphlet announcing launch of coaching classes in your colony in an example of
(a) verbal channel (b) localite channel
(c) cosmopolite channel (d) implicit channel

39. Noble Laureate Mohammad Yunus is acclaimed for his work on
(a) cooperatives (b) dairy development
(c) promotion of literacy (d) micro-credit

40. Protection of Women from Domestic Violence Act was passed in the year

(a) 2001 (b) 2005 (c) 2010 (d) 2015

41. Which of the following statements is not true about folk media?

(a) Folk media are indigenous equivalents of mass media.
(b) Folk media include plays, dances and songs.
(c) Folk media are used purely for entertainment.
(d) Folk media are used during fairs and festivals.

42. Income is .... scale of measurement.

(a) nominal (b) ordinal (c) ratio (d) interval

43. In retrospective research studies which of the following types of research methodology is used?

(a) Observational (b) Historical
(c) Quantitative (d) Action

44. Regression analysis is of particular interest

(a) for testing the difference between means of 2 groups.
(b) for testing the difference among more than 3 different groups.
(c) for testing the association between 2 variables.
(d) for identifying risk factors in any causal factor analysis.

45. Type-I error ind drawing statistical inference while testing the null hypothesis is

(a) reject $_0$ when it is true. (b) accept $_0$ when it is false.
(c) accept $_0$ when it is true. (d) reject $_0$ when it is false.

46. Difference between the mean of researcher's sample and the mean of the population of the sample is known as

(a) confidence interval (b) sampling error
(c) significance level (d) standard deviation

47. In an experimental study

(a) researcher collects information on attributes of interest, but not influences the events.
(b) researcher influences events and investigates the effects of intervention.
(c) researcher collects data forwards in time from the start of the study.
(d) researcher collects data referring to past events.

48. Which is the most appropriate test of significance to test the association between mother's education and children's school attainment?

(a) Kruskal-Wallis Test (b) Chi-Square Test
(c) *F*-Test (d) *t*-Test

49. Which of the following lists present the section of a research report in the correct order?

(a) Title Page, Title, Abstract, Introduction, Method, Results, Discussion, Conclusion, Appendices, Reference.
(b) Title Page, abstract, Title, Introduction, Method, Results, Discussion, Conclusion, Appendices, Reference.
(c) Title Page, Abstract, Title, Introduction, Method, Result, Discussion, Conclusion, Reference, Appendices.
(d) Title Page, Abstract, Title, Introduction, Method, Results, Conclusion, Discussion, Reference, Appendices.

50. Arrange the following foods in the increasing order of Glycemic Index (GI).

1. Popcorn 2. Orange
3. Barley 4. Whole wheat bread
5. Milk (Full fat)

Select the most appropriate option.

(a) 4, 1, 3, 2, 5 (b) 2, 4, 5, 3, 1
(c) 3, 5, 2, 1, 4 (d) 2, 1, 4, 5, 3

51. Which of the following is not a symptom of metabolic syndrome?

1. Ischaemia 2. Osteoporosis
3. Dyslipidemia 4. Insulin resistance
5. Obesity 6. Thrombosis

Select the most appropriate option.

(a) 1, 3 and 6 (b) 3, 4 and 5
(c) 2, 5 and 6 (d) 1, 2 and 6

52. Children 6-59 months suffering from SAM should fulfill which of the following three criteria?

1. Weight for height < –3SD
2. Height for age < –3SD
3. MUAC < 115 mm
4. MUAC < 125 mm
5. Bilateral oedema
6. No oedema

Select the most appropriate option.

(a) 1, 2 and 3 (b) 3, 4 and 5
(c) 2, 4 and 6 (d) 1, 3 and 5

53. Which of the following are weft knit structures?

1. Purl 2. Rib
3. Interlock 4. Tricot
5. Raschel

Select the most appropriate option.

(a) 1, 2 and 3 (b) 1, 3 and 4
(c) 3, 4 and 5 (d) 2, 4 and 5

54. Which of the following body landmarks have to be located for taking measurements for a saree blouse?

1. Apex
2. Armpit level
3. Biceps
4. Highest shoulder point
5. Lowest shoulder point

Select the most appropriate option.

(a) 1, 2 and 3 (b) 1, 3 and 4
(c) 1, 4 and 5 (d) 2, 3 and 4

55. Which of the following are set-in sleeves?

1. Bishop 2. Tulip
3. Lantern 4. Cartwheel
5. Basic dolman 6. Raglan

Select the most suitable option.

(a) 1, 2, 3, 4 (b) 1, 3, 4, 5 (c) 1, 4, 5, 6 (d) 2, 3, 5, 6

56. Which of the following could maximise the use of family resources?
1. Careful selection of goals
2. Positive attitude
3. Family heritage
4. Media functions
5. Alternative uses of resources

Select the most appropriate option.
(a) 2, 3 and 5 (b) 1, 4 and 5 (c) 1, 2 and 5 (d) 3, 4 and 5

57. Identify the air related legal provisions in India.
1. Air Act, 1981
2. Wildlife (Protection) Amendment Act, 2002
3. Motor Vehicle Act, 1939
4. The Factories Act, 1948
5. Forest Dwellers (Rights) Act, 2006

Select the most appropriate option.
(a) 1, 3 and 4 (b) 2, 3 and 5 (c) 1, 3 and 5 (d) 2, 3 and 4

58. Which among the following are green building materials?
1. Commercial boards 2. Plastic boards
3. Pozzolanic materials 4. Cement
5. Bamboo board

Select the most appropriate option.
(a) 1, 3 and 5 (b) 1, 2 and 3 (c) 2, 3 and 4 (d) 3, 4 and 5

59. Structuring interior space involves analysis of the following.
1. Number of occupants
2. Minimal space required for activities
3. Relationship of difference spaces with one another
4. Rendering plans
5. Income of occupants

Select the most appropriate option.
(a) 1, 3 and 4 (b) 2, 3 and 5 (c) 3, 4 and 5 (d) 1, 2 and 3

60. There is sufficient research evidence to show that consumption of food high on sugar may lead to the following in children.
1. hyperactivity 2. aggression
3. inattentiveness 4. lying
5. skin infection

Select the most appropriate option.
(a) 1, 2 and 4 (b) 1, 2 and 3 (c) 1, 3 and 5 (d) 3, 4 and 5

61. A school teacher notices that one of his students is regularly copying incorrectly from the board. What assessment will he recommend to the parents?
1. Vision 2. Reflexes
3. Intellectual functioning
4. Dyslexia
5. Allergies

Select the most suitable option.
(a) 1, 2 and 3 (b) 2, 3 and 4 (c) 1, 3 and 4 (d) 2, 4 and 5

62. Which criteria are used in legislations for treating juveniles differently from young adults?
1. Physical development
2. Economic development
3. Intellectual development
4. Socio-emotional development

Select the most suitable option.
(a) 1, 2 and 3 (b) 1, 2 and 4
(c) 1, 3 and 4 (d) 2, 3 and 4

63. Use of ICTs for development is limited in India because of
1. Poor telecom infrastructure
2. Illiteracy of people
3. Large geographical area
4. Large population of the country

Select the most suitable option.
(a) 1 and 2 (b) 2 and 3 (c) 3 and 4 (d) 1 and 4

64. Advocacy' is
1. an independent persuasion activity.
2. dependent on a planned strategy.
3. to highlight priority issue before decision-makers.
4. a surrogate activity to meet political leaders.

Select the most appropriate option.
(a) 1 and 2 (b) 2 and 3 (c) 2 and 4 (d) 1 and 4

65. A non-formal educator develops a lesson plan for each session to
1. identify local leaders.
2. adopt definite objective/(s).
3. present material in a logical sequence.
4. evaluate the learning outcomes.
5. to do cost-benefit analysis.

Select the most appropriate option.
(a) 1, 2 and 3 (b) 1, 2 and 4 (c) 1, 2 and 5 (d) 2, 3 and 4

66. Which of the following are important for maintaining credibility of news?
1. Precision 2. Accuracy
3. Timeliness 4. Tangibility
5. Reliability

Select the most suitable option.
(a) 1, 2, 3, 4 (b) 1, 3, 4, 5
(c) 1, 2, 3, 5 (d) 1, 2, 4, 5

67. Determination of sample size in research is based on
1. Type of statistical test
2. Desired confidence level
3. Estimated standard deviation
4. and
5. Degree of precision required

Select the most appropriate option.
(a) 1, 2 and5 (b) 2, 3 and 5
(c) 2, 3 and 4 (d) 2, 4 and 5

68. Which of the following are the general ethical principles according to APA?

1. Beneficence and non-malficence
2. Patriotic
3. Conformity
4. Credibility
5. Justice
6. Integrity
7. Respect

Select the most appropriate option.

(a) 1, 4, 5, 6 (b) 1, 4, 5, 7 (c) 1, 3, 4, 5 (d) 1, 2, 3, 7

69. Assertion (A) Undernourished mothers can successfully breast feed.

Reason (R) Quality and quantity of breastmilk may not be affected in serve malnutrition.

Select the most appropriate option.

(a) Both A and R are true and R is the correct explanation of A
(b) Both A and R are true, but R is not the correct explanation of A
(c) A is true, but R is false
(d) A is false but R is true

70. Assertion (A) Nanotechnology can be applied in the manufacture of antistatic garments.

Reason (R) Nanotechnology develops an antistatic membrane on the garment which protects the wearer from electrostatic charges.

Select the most appropriate option

(a) Both A and R are true and R is the correct explanation of A
(b) Both A and R are true, but R is not the correct explanation of A
(c) A is true, but R is false
(d) A is false, but R is true

71. Assertion (A) Counterfeit and know off are same type of products.

Reason (R) They are both imitations of the original, but do not carry the labels and trademarks of the original.

Select the most appropriate option

(a) Both A and R are true and R is the correct explanation of A
(b) Both A and R are true, but R is not the correct explanation of A
(c) A is true, but R is false
(d) A is false, but R is true

72. Assertion (A) Cotton are dyed with reactive dyes without creating any polluted effluents.

Reason (R) Reactive dye reacts with the fiber molecule by addition or substitution.

(a) Both A and R are true and R is the correct explanation of A
(b) Both A and R are true, but R is not the correct explanation of A
(c) A is true, but R is false
(d) A is false but R is true

73. Assertion (A) Innovation is same as creativity.

Reason (R) Creativity is the ability to generate new ideas and innovation refers to social application of the creative idea.

Select the most appropriate option

(a) Both A and R are true and R is the correct explanation of A
(b) Both A and R are true, but R is not the correct explanation of A
(c) A is true, but R is false
(d) A is false, but R is true

74. Assertion (A) Bay windows project outward from the face line of the wall of a building.

Reason (R) It is introduced with a view to provide an increased floor area to allow more seating.

Select the most appropriate option

(a) Both A and R are true and R is the correct explanation of A
(b) Both A and R are true, but R is not the correct explanation of A
(c) A is true, but R is false
(d) A is false but R is true

75. Assertion (A) Warmth of sun' rays is advantageous during evening time.

Reason (R) Evening air contains moisture which absorbs the heat and allows the light.

Select the most appropriate option

(a) Both A and R are true and R is the correct explanation of A
(b) Both A and R are true, but R is not the correct explanation of A
(c) A is true, but R is false
(d) A is false, but R is true

76. Assertion (A) : Alternating physically active and quiet activities is developmentally appropriate for children in preschools.

Reason (R) Young children's attention span is short and energy levels high; therefore they require periodic change in activity.

Select the most appropriate option

(a) Both A and R are true and R is the correct explanation of A
(b) Both A and R are true, but R is not the correct explanation of A
(c) A is true, but R is false
(d) A is false, but R is true

77. Assertion (A) Ratifying international conventions has impacted legislations, policies and programmes for women and children.

Reason (R) Non-compliance with the article in the conventions leads to punitive measures against the transgressing state.

Select the most suitable option

(a) Both A and R are true and R is the correct explanation of A

(b) Both A and R are true, but R is not the correct explanation of A
(c) A is true, but R is false
(d) A is false, but R is true

78. **Assertion** (A) A Harvard longitudinal study done on well-being proves that getting a good education is the most important variable for life satisfaction.

Reason (R) Academic achievement is positively correlated with success in life.

Select the most suitable option
(a) Both A and R are true and R is the correct explanation of A
(b) Both A and R are true, but R is not the correct explanation of A
(c) A is true, but R is false
(d) A is false, but R is true

79. **Assertion** (A) The modernisation paradigm of development advocates for a change in the mindsets of individuals in poor countries.

Reason (R) Modernisation required people to be guided by their cultures and traditions rather than by outside pressures.

Select the most appropriate option
(a) Both A and R are true and R is the correct explanation of A
(b) Both A and R are true, but R is not the correct explanation of A
(c) A is true, but R is false
(d) A is false, but R is true

80. Given are the seven principles of HACCP. Arrange them in the correct sequences.
1. Establish verification procedure
2. Determine the critical control point
3. Establish correction action
4. Conduct a hazard analysis
5. Establish record keeping and documentation procedures
6. Establish critical limit
7. Establish monitoring procedures

Select the appropriate sequence of the principles.
(a) 2, 6, 1, 4, 5, 7, 3 (b) 4, 2, 6, 7, 3, 1, 5
(c) 6, 3, 5, 1, 4, 7, 2 (d) 4, 1, 3, 6, 5, 2, 7

81. Arrange the steps involved in the preparation of cotton fabric in the correct sequence.
1. Scouring 2. Desizing 3. Tentering 4. Bleaching
5. Calendaring 6. Singeing 7. Mercerising

Choose the most appropriate option.
(a) 1, 2, 4, 3, 7, 5, 6 (b) 6, 2, 1, 4, 7, 3, 5
(c) 6, 2, 4, 1, 7, 3, 5 (d) 1, 2, 3, 5, 4, 6, 7

82. Arrange the following steps of controlling in sequential order.
1. Establishing standards
2. Measuring performance
3. Comparing performance with standards
4. Detecting deviation
5. Taking corrective action

Select the most appropriate option.
(a) 3, 4, 1, 2, 5 (b) 2, 1, 5, 4, 3
(c) 1, 2, 3, 4, 5 (d) 4, 3, 5, 2, 1

83. Arrange the reproductive process in sequence.
1. Fetal period
2. Spermatogenesis and oogenesis
3. Embryonic period 4. Fertilisation
5. Ovulation 6. Germinal period

Select the most suitable option.
(a) 2, 5, 4, 6, 3, 1 (b) 2, 5, 4, 3, 6, 1
(c) 2, 4, 5, 6, 3, 1 (d) 5, 2, 4, 6, 1, 3

84. Arrange the following 'learning experiences' in decreasing order of 'learning' as per Edgar Dale's cone of experience
1. Watch videos
2. Attend an exhibition
3. Participate in hands on workshop
4. Design and conduct collaborative lessons
5. Watch a demonstration
6. Hear a radio programme

Choose the most appropriate option.
(a) 1, 2, 5, 3, 4, 6 (b) 2, 3, 5, 4, 6, 1
(c) 3, 4, 2, 1, 6, 5 (d) 4, 3, 5, 2, 1, 6

85. Arrange the following development campaigns/programmes in the chronological order of their inception.
1. Swachh Bharat Abhiyan
2. Beti Bachao Beti Padhao Abhiyan
3. Sarva Shiksha Abhiyan
4. Anaemia Mukt Bharat Abhiyan

Choose the most appropriate option
(a) 2, 3, 4, 1 (b) 1, 2, 3, 4
(c) 4, 3, 2, 1 (d) 3, 1, 2, 4

86. Match List I with List II.

	List I		List II
A.	0–6 month infant	1.	75
B.	Moderately active adult male	2.	118
C.	16–17 year old boy	3.	82
D.	Child 4–6 years	4.	35
E.	Infant 6–12 months	5.	92
		6.	55
		7.	25

Choose the most appropriate option.

	A	B	C	D	E
(a)	2	4	3	4	7
(b)	5	4	6	1	3
(c)	7	3	1	6	4
(d)	3	7	4	5	2

87. Match List I with List II.

	List I		List II
A.	Food allergy	1.	Heavy metal
B.	Food poisoning	2.	Trichinella
C.	Food spoilage	3.	Aflatoxin
D.	Food infection	4.	Curdled milk
E.	Food Contamination	5.	Metanil yellow
		6.	Hepatitis A
		7.	Botulism
		8.	Tree nut

Choose the most appropriate option

	A	B	C	D	E
(a)	4	6	1	5	8
(b)	5	3	2	8	4
(c)	8	7	4	6	1
(d)	3	2	1	6	5

88. Match List I with List II

	List I		List II
A.	Antistatic	1.	Provides lustre
B.	Water repellent	2.	Environmental protection
C.	Slip resistance	3.	Creates texture
D.	Gigging	4.	Alters durability
		5.	Protective finish
		6.	Provides comfort and safety

Choose the most suitable option.

	A	B	C	D
(a)	1	3	4	3
(b)	6	5	4	3
(c)	3	4	5	6
(d)	2	3	5	6

89. Match List I with List II.

	List I		List II
A.	Billiard cloth	1.	Interlining
B.	Burlap	2.	Towels
C.	China silk	3.	Bagging
D.	Huck	4.	Lingerie
		5.	Table covering

Choose the most suitable option

	A	B	C	D
(a)	1	2	4	3
(b)	5	2	3	4
(c)	5	3	4	2
(d)	5	1	3	2

90. Match List I with List II

	List I		List II
A.	Classical Management Theory	1.	New man
B.	Human Relations Theory	2.	Simon
C.	Neo-classical Management Theory	3.	Max Weber
D.	Modern Management Theory	4.	Edgar Henry Schein
E.	Decision Theory	5.	McGregor
		6.	P. R. Lawrence

Choose the most appropriate option

	A	B	C	D	E
(a)	3	4	5	6	2
(b)	1	2	3	4	5
(c)	2	3	1	6	4
(d)	6	5	3	1	2

91. Match List I with List II.

	List I		List II
A.	Soft floor	1.	Rubber flooring
B.	Rug	2.	Area rug
C.	Hard floor	3.	Carpet
D.	Sound proof	4.	Marble
		5.	Wooden flooring

Choose the most appropriate option.

	A	B	C	D
(a)	3	2	4	1
(b)	1	3	4	5
(c)	2	1	3	4
(d)	5	3	1	2

92. Match List I with List II

	List I		List II
A.	Article 21 A	1.	Employment of children
B.	Article 23	2.	Free and compulsory education
C.	Article 24	3.	Prohibition of traffic in human beings
D.	Article 45	4.	Early childhood care and education
		5.	Raising standard of living

Choose the most appropriate option

	A	B	C	D
(a)	2	3	1	4
(b)	2	3	1	5
(c)	1	5	2	4
(d)	3	1	3	4

93. Match List I with List II.

	List I		List II
A.	Infancy	1.	Mitosis
B.	Preschool years	2.	Object permanence
C.	Middle childhood	3.	Centration
D.	Adolescence	4.	Concrete operations
		5.	Psychosocial moratorium

Choose the most suitable option

	A	B	C	D
(a)	2	3	4	5
(b)	1	3	4	5
(c)	2	4	1	5
(d)	2	3	4	1

94. Match List I with List II.

	List I		List II
A.	Enculturation	1.	Fixed notions about cultures
B.	Ethnocentricism	2.	Process of learning about other cultures
C.	Stereotyping	3.	Transmission of family values
D.	Acculturation	4.	Undermining other cultures
		5.	Eulogizing other cultures

Choose the most appropriate option.

	A	B	C	D
(a)	4	5	3	1
(b)	3	4	1	2
(c)	2	5	1	4
(d)	4	5	2	3

95. Match List I with List II

	List I		List II
A.	WHO	1.	Protection of displaced people
B.	FAO	2.	Protection of children
C.	UNESCO	3.	Public health
D.	UNHCR	4.	Preservation of World Culture Heritage
E.	UNICEF	5.	Protection of women
		6.	Protection of hunger

Choose the most appropriate option

	A	B	C	D	E
(a)	3	1	4	5	2
(b)	3	5	4	6	2
(c)	3	6	4	1	2
(d)	3	4	6	5	2

Direction *(Q.Nos. 96-100) Read the following paragraph and answer the five questions which as follows.*

The Janani Suraksha Yojana (JSY) is one of the flagship components of the National Rural Health Mission, and the key strategy to enable women to access institutional deliveries and thereby effect reduction in material mortality.

The rationale is that institutional deliveries would help the pregnant women access a team of skilled birth attendants more reliably and it would also improve her access to emergency obstetric care and this in turn would lead to reduced material and neonatal mortality.

The cove strategies envisaged to realise the objective include access to health care at household level through local women in age group of 25-40 years known as ASHA. As per National Guidelines, all pregnant women in rural areas, who deliver in a health facility are eligible for cash transfers.

The amount is given at or immediately after the delivery and is meant to defray the expenses–both visible (drugs, supplies, transport) and invisible cost (cost of accompanying attendant, informal, gifts/fee to hospital staff, cost of food).

96.* Match List I with List II.

	List I		List II
A.	Physical	1.	Co-acting dayds
B.	Physiological	2.	Hearing impairment
C.	Psychological	3.	Screeching of cars
D.	Semantic	4.	Differences in meanings assigned
		5.	Biases and Prejudices

Choose the most appropriate option

	A	B	C	D		A	B	C	D
(a)	3	2	5	4	(b)	2	3	4	1
(c)	2	5	1	4	(d)	4	2	3	1

97. What is the role of ASHA?

(a) Access to health care of pregnant women at household level.
(b) To provide cash transfer.
(c) To provide antenatal care.
(d) To provide supplementary care.

98. Cash transfers to women in JSY are to cover which of the following visible costs during delivery?

(a) Cost of accompanying attendant
(b) Drugs supply
(c) Fee to hospital staff (d) Cost of food

99. Following are the components of JSY.

1. To encourage hospital deliveries.
2. Improved access to obstetric care.
3. Cash transfer.
4. To encourage home deliveries

Select the most appropriate option.

(a) 2, 3 and 4 (b) 1, 2 and 4 (c) 1, 2 and 3 (d) 1, 3 and 4

100. What are the rationale of providing care to pregnant women under JSY?

1. Access to institutional deliveries
2. To reduce material mortality
3. To reduce neo-natal mortality
4. To provide cash benefit before delivery

Select the most appropriate option

(a) 1, 2 and 4 (b) 1, 3 and 4 (c) 2, 3 and 4 (d) 1, 2 and 3

ANSWERS

1 (d)	2 (a)	3 (b)	4 (d)	5 (c)	6 (a)	7 (c)	8 (b)	9 (d)	10 (c)
11 (b)	12 (b)	13 (b)	14 (b)	15 (b)	16 (a)	17 (b)	18 (d)	19 (b)	20 (c)
21 (a)	22 (c)	23 (b)	24 (b)	25 (b)	26 (b)	27 (d)	28 (d)	29 (c)	30 (d)
31 (b)	32 (a)	33 (b)	34 (c)	35 (a)	36 (d)	37 (d)	38 (b)	39 (d)	40 (b)
41 (c)	42 (c)	43 (b)	44 (d)	45 (a)	46 (b)	47 (b)	48 (b)	49 (c)	50 (c)
51 (d)	52 (d)	53 (a)	54 (c)	55 (a)	56 (c)	57 (a)	58 (a)	59 (d)	60 (b)
61 (c)	62 (c)	63 (a)	64 (b)	65 (d)	66 (c)	67 (b)	68 (b)	69 (c)	70 (a)
71 (b)	72 (d)	73 (a)	74 (a)	75 (d)	76 (a)	77 (a)	78 (b)	79 (a)	80 (b)
81 (b)	82 (c)	83 (a)	84 (d)	85 (d)	86 (c)	87 (c)	88 (b)	89 (c)	90 (a)
91 (a)	92 (a)	93 (a)	94 (b)	95 (c)	96 (*)	97 (a)	98 (b)	99 (c)	100 (d)

* Answer not given in official answer key.

UNIT I

Food Science

Food science is an important science playing a key role in a vast industry and the well-being of humanity. As an applied science, it is devoted to the study of food which studies about technical aspects of food. Food science allows us to make the best use of our food resources and minimum waste.

Food and Food Science

Food is any substance consumed to provide nutritional support for an organism. It is usually of plant or animal origin and contains essential nutrients such as carbohydrates, fats, proteins, vitamins or minerals. The substance is ingested by an organism and assimilated by the organism's cells to provide energy, maintain life or stimulate growth. In short, food is the raw material from which our body is made. Intake of the right kind and amount of food can ensure good nutrition and health, which may be evident in our appearance, efficiency and emotional well-being.

Food comprises of protein, carbohydrate and fat i.e. used in the body of an organism to sustain growth, repair, carry on vital processes to furnish energy. It may be in the form of solid or liquid. Food is essential because it contains substances, which perform important functions in our body.

These essential substances are known as nutrients. The non-nutrients include colouring and flavouring substances in food. Therefore, we can also say that food is a complex mixture of nutrients and non-nutrients.

Study of food science includes understanding the nutritive value of different foods and methods of preserving them during cooking.

Definitions of Food Science

The various definitions with regard to food science are given as :

- Food Science is the study of the physical, biological and chemical make up of food; and the concepts underlying food processing.
- Food Science is the science of nature devoted to the study of food. It is often confused with 'Food Technology'.

- According to the **Institute of Food Technologists**, "Food Science is the discipline in which the engineering, biological and physical sciences are used to study the nature of foods, causes of deterioration, the principles underlying food processing and the improvement of foods for the consuming public."
- According to **Norman N Potter and Joseph Hotchkiss** "It is the application of basic sciences and engineering to study the physical, chemical and biochemical nature of foods and the principles of food processing."

  Therefore, Food Science brings together multiple scientific disciplines, It incorporates concepts from fields such as Chemistry, Physics, Physiology, Microbiology and Biochemistry.
- Food Science also deals with such charges and reactions which occur due to environmental conditions such as heat, cold, light and air to which foods are subjected during cooking.

Physical and Chemical Properties of Food

The physical and chemical properties of food and food products have central roles in biotechnology, pharmaceutical and food industries. Understanding these properties is essential for engineers and scientists to tackle the numerous issues in food processing, including preservation, storage, distribution and consumption.

Physical Properties of Food

The physical attributes of food consist of size and shape, volume and density and porosity. Physical property is a characteristic of matter that is not associated with a change in its chemical composition.

Size and Shape

Size and shape are important physical attributes of food that are used in screening, grading and quality control of food. Size can be determined using the projected area method. In this method, three characteristic dimensions are defined :

- Major diameter which is the longest dimension of the maximum projected area.
- Intermediate diameter, which is the minimum diameter of the maximum projected area or the maximum diameter of the minimum projected area.
- Minor diameter, which is the shortest dimension of the minimum projected area.

Size is important in screening solids to separate foreign materials, in grading of fruits and vegetables and evaluating the quality of food materials.

In fluid flow, heat and mass transfer calculations, it is necessary to know the size of the sample. Size of the particulate food is also critical.

For example, particle size of powdered milk must be large enough to prevent agglomeration, but small enough to allow rapid dissolution during reconstitution.

Volume and Density

Volume is another important physical property of food which affects consumer acceptance.

Volume can be calculated from the measured dimension or by using various methods such as liquid, gas or solid displacement methods and image processing. Volume measurement methods can also be used for measuring the density of solids. Volume/density can be expressed in different forms such as solid, apparent and bulk volume/ density depending on pores.

Porosity

Porosity is a physical property characterising the texture and the quality of dry and intermediate moisture foods.

Pores may be in three different forms :

- Closed pores that are closed from all sides.
- Blind pores in which one end is closed.
- Flow-through pores that are open at both ends so that flow can take place.

Chemical Properties of Food

The change of one type of matter into another type (or the inability to change) is a chemical property. Examples of chemical properties include flammability, toxicity, acidity, reactivity (many types) and heat or combustion. For example, iron combines with oxygen in the presence of water to form rust. A chemical change always produces one or more types of matter that differ from the matter present before the change.

Common chemical properties analysed in foods include the following :

- pH-Acidity
- Fat content
- Fat and oil quality
- Protein analysis

pH-Acidity

The pH is an indicator of the amount of acid or base present in a food. For canned foods, a pH of 4.6 or lower would prevent microorganisms such as **'Clostridium Botulinum'** to grow if proper sterilisation time and temperature are used.

The pH also affects flavour, colour and texture. The pH is measured using a pH meter. Here are some examples of the pH ranges for different food products.

pH for Various Food Products

Description	pH Range	Examples of Food Products
Alkaline	7.0 - 9.6	Egg white
Neutral	7.0 - 6.5	Milk and chicken
Low acid	6.5 - 5.3	Bacon, canned vegetables, and fresh meat
Medium Acid	5.3 - 4.5	Canned soup, soft cheese and pickled cucumbers
Acid	4.5 - 3.7	Mayonnaise, yogurt and orange juice
High Acid	< 3.7	Pickles and canned sauerkraut

The pH scale ranges from 0-14. A pH of O is extremely acid. A pH of 14 is extremely alkaline.

Fat and Oil Quality

The fat and oil quality depends on the composition of the product, size of the product, type of processing and type of oil used. Higher fat products are more susceptible to rancidity.

Rancidity is measured by the peroxide value and TBA test.

'Rancidity' refers to spoilage of food in a way that it becomes unsafe for consumption. Oils can be susceptible to rancidity because their chemistry can make them exceptionally susceptible to oxygen damage. This type of rancidity is called oxidative rancidity.

During this process, oxygen molecules interact with the structure of oil and damage its natural structure to change its odour, taste and safety for consumption.

Fat Content

It is measured using equipment that can evaluate solid and semi-solid foods. An example is the Foss-Let instrument. Analysis can take 5-8 minutes to complete.

Protein Analysis

Protein is measured by Kjeldahl Method.

Common Food Poisoning Bacteria, their Food Sources and Symptoms

Bacterias	Most Likely Food Sources	Symptoms
Campylobacter	Raw poultry and meat, unpasteurised milk	Fever, headache, diarrhoea
Salmonella	Raw meat, poultry and eggs, raw unwashed vegetables, unpasteurised milk and dairy products	Fever, diarrhoea, vomiting, abdominal pain.
Listeria monocytogenes	Raw milk, meat, poultry, cheeses (soft, mould-ripened variety), salad vegetables.	Flu-like symptoms, meningitis, septicemia and in pregnant women-abortion and miscarriage.

Functional Properties of Food

Functional properties describe how ingredients behave during preparation and cooking, how they affect the finished food product in terms of how it looks, tastes and feels. Functional properties include :

- Dextrinisation
- Caramelisation
- Flavour
- Preserving
- Jellying
- Denaturation
- Coagulation
- Gluten formation
- Shortening
- Plasticity
- Aeration
- Flakiness
- Retention of moisture
- Sensory attributes

Food Preparation

Food unites us all, across cultures and across time. Human beings generally prepare their food before eating it, both out of necessity and to enhance its flavour. Food preparation is a broad topic involving all steps that occur between obtaining raw ingredients and consumption of food. It generally involves the selection, measurement and combining of raw ingredients in an ordered fashion/procedure to achieve a desired product. This is called preparation of food, which may or may not include cooking.

Cleaning

Food preparation involves the entire spectrum of events from obtaining to eating food. Most of the food that is available in raw form is not best to eat as it is. Therefore, the first step, in food preparation is cleaning the raw food. It is important to clean natural fruits, vegetables, grains and meat. Meat can contain harmful bacteria if not cleaned properly. Most food products that are consumed today are not only grown commercially but treated with pesticides or other chemicals to ensure the survival of crop. These chemicals should be washed off before consumption. Additionally, dust, natural bacteria and trace chemicals from insects or birds can be found on organic produce.

Cooking

Once the ingredients are clean, the next stage in food preparation is cooking. There are many methods of cooking which include baking, roasting, frying, grilling, boiling, steaming, barbecuing, smoking and braising. Microwaving is a very recent innovation. Various methods use differing levels of heat and moisture and vary in cooking time. Food is heated in order to kill bacteria, enhance flavours and create texture.

Cooking can be classified as :

- Dry-heat cooking
- Moist-heat cooking

Dry-Heat Cooking This form of cooking involves applying heat to something without liquid. Roasting, broiling, grilling and pan-frying are all forms of dry-heat cooking.

Moist-Heat Cooking This kind of cooking uses steam or liquid as part of the cooking process and includes techniques like steaming, boiling or poaching. Thus, cooking is the process of producing safe, nourishing, flavourful, satisfying, delicious and edible food by preparing and combining ingredients and (in most cases) applying heat. It is a means of processing food, without which many foods would be unfit for human consumption.

Precautions to be taken While Cooking

Raw foods such as meat, fish and eggs may harbour food poisoning bacteria, which if consumed are likely to cause illness. The optimum temperature for the multiplication of most food poisoning bacteria is between 5-63°C whilst, at temperature over 70°C most bacterias are killed. Below 5°C, most food poisoning bacteria can only multiply slowly or not at all. Most cooking methods, if performed properly, will heat food to over 70°C. Applying such a temperature for a carefully calculated time period (along with correct food preparation and storage procedures) will prevent many food borne illnesses. The three most common food poisoning bacterias that affect over 3,80,000 European Union (EU) citizens every year are :

- Campylobacter
- Salmonella
- Listeria monocytogenes

Types of Cooking

The fundamental types of cooking are listed below :

Frying

Frying is the cooking of food in oil or fat. Foods that have been fried have a characteristic crisp texture, because oils and fats can reach higher cooking temperature than water. This results in the food being seared.

Note 'Sear' means to quickly fry the food at a high temperature to retains its juices and flavour.

Common types of foods that are fried include battered or breaded fish or vegetables, crisps, chips and doughnuts. There are different types of frying, which vary by the amount of fat/oil required, cooking time and type of cooking pan used. They are :

Stir Frying A frying pan is used to cook foods at a very high temperature, in a thin layer of fat. The food is fried very quickly, during which time it is stirred continuously to prevent the food from burning.

Deep Frying A large deep pan or deep fat fryer is half filled with fat and heated. Food is immersed in the fat for a few minutes, then removed from the fat and drained.

Shallow Frying A large shallow pan is filled with a layer of fat deep enough to cover about one-third of each piece of food to be fried. The fat is heated prior to the food being added to the pan, as in deep frying. After cooking for a few minutes, the food is removed from the pan and drained.

Baking

Baking is the process of cooking food in the dry heat of an oven. During baking, moisture within the food is converted to steam, which combines with the dry heat of the oven to cook the food. Common types of foods that are baked include : bread, cakes, jacket potatoes and pastries.

Boiling

Boiling is the cooking of food in a liquid (e.g., water, milk or stock), which is at boiling point. Common types of foods that are boiled include vegetables, rice and pasta.

Blanching

Blanching is very similar to boiling and involves immersing food into a boiling liquid for a very short period of time. It is then removed and plunged into ice water to stop the cooking process. Common types of food that are blanched include vegetables and fruits.

Simmering

Simmering is a cooking method, similar to boiling, where the food is cooked in a liquid, which is held below boiling point. The simmering point of most liquids is between 85-90°C and is a gentler, slower method of cooking, as compared to boiling. Common types of foods that are simmered include vegetables, soups and sauces.

Poaching

Poaching is a cooking technique similar to simmering except that the temperature of the liquid, in which the food is cooked, is slightly cooler than simmering point. The temperature is around 70°-85°C. This makes poaching an ideal method of cooking fragile foods such as eggs and fish.

Grilling

Grilling is the cooking of food using direct, dry heat. There are several sources of dry heat that may be used for grilling, such as charcoal, wood, gas or electric heated grills. Common types of food that are grilled include fish, meat, vegetables and bread.

Steaming

Steaming is the cooking of foods by steam. Steam is generated by boiling water, which evaporates and carries the heat to the food. Typical foods that are cooked by steaming include vegetables and fish.

Roasting

Roasting is the cooking of food using dry heat. This may include cooking in an oven or over an open flame. Normally, the food is placed in a roasting pan or rotated on a spit to ensure an even application of heat. Foods that are typically cooked by roasting are meat and vegetables.

Effects of Cooking and Processing Techniques

Heating causes a complex series of physical and chemical changes to occur. These changes vary depending on the type of food being cooked and the method used to cook it. The changes may be advantageous e.g. improving the flavour, texture and colour of food; or disadvantageous e.g. reducing the nutrient value of food or generation of undesirable compounds. Following are the main physical and chemical changes that occur during the cooking of foods :

Flavour

After cooking and processing, flavour of the food is affected in the following ways :

Caramelisation

It produces desirable flavours and colours in food products like coffee, confectionery, dark beer and products. Caramelisation reaction occurs when foods containing a high concentration of carbohydrates are cooked at high temperatures using dry heat e.g. roasting peanuts.

- As the food is heated, sucrose in the food melts and starts to boil. Caramelisation temperature is the temperature at which this process occurs. It is generally between 110°-180°C (depending on the types of carbohydrate present in the food).
- Once the caramelisation temperature has been reached, sucrose begins to decompose into monomer molecules, glucose and fructose.
- A series of complex chemical reactions occur between the molecules which ultimately generate flavour compounds.
- One of the most important flavour compound produced is diacetyl. Diacetyl is generated during the initial stage of caramelisation and has a butterscotch flavour.
- Other important flavour compounds produced are furans hydroxymethylfurfural and hydroxyacetylfuran, maltol from disaccharides, hydroxymaltol from monosaccharides. These together give the sweet, slightly burnt flavour of the caramelisation reaction.
- The flavours generated during caramelisation vary on the type of carbohydrate undergoing the reaction.
- In general, there is a decrease in sweetness and increase in burnt, bitter taste in all caramelisation reactions as temperature is increased.
- Cooking methods that result in caramelisation are roasting, grilling, baking and frying.

Maillard Reaction

It is a chemical reaction between an amino acid and sugar such as glucose, fructose or lactose. Heat is required to cause a cascade of chemical changes that result in the formation of a range of flavour and colour compounds.

This reaction is responsible for producing many sulphur containing compounds which contribute to the savoury, meaty, and flavour characteristics of cooked meat. Foods that contain both protein and carbohydrate undergo the maillard reaction, e.g. meat, biscuits, bread, coffee and nuts. The cooking methods that may result in the Maillard Reaction are frying, baking, grilling and roasting.

Starch Degradation

When foods containing starch are cooked, the heat can break the glycosidic bonds linking the glucose units together and breakup the polysaccharides to release glucose monosaccharides. This imparts a natural sweetness to cooked food. Polysaccharide starch is present in all plant seeds and tubers e.g. pasta, rice, bread, potatoes, oats, and wheat. It is a common form of carbohydrate, composed of several thousand glucose units linked together by glycosidic bonds. Cooking methods that result in starch degradation are boiling, baking, roasting, frying, grilling and steaming.

Colour

After cooking and processing, colour of the food is affected in the following ways :

Caramelisation

It is one of the most important type of browning process in foods. Molecules known as caramels are generated during this reaction. Caramels can be divided into three groups :

- Caramelans
- Coramelens
- Caramelins

These compounds are responsible for the characteristics brown colour of caramelised foods. The colour of the caramel depends on the type of carbohydrate undergoing reaction, the colour becomes darker as temperature is increased. Types of food that contain high concentration of carbohydrate are beer, coffee, peanuts and confectionery that undergo caramelisation. Cooking methods that result in caramelisation are roasting, grilling, baking and frying.

Maillard Reaction

It is one of the most important type of browning process in food, producing brown colour compounds known as melanoidins. Melanoidins give many foods their characteristic colouring e.g. coffee, bread and meat. Foods that undergo Maillard Reaction contain both protein and carbohydrate such as meat, biscuits, bre d, coffee and nuts. Cooking methods resulting in this rεaction are frying, baking, grilling and roasting.

Loss of Pigmentation

The main foods containing pigments which are prone to losing pigmentation during cooking are fruits and vegetables. There are three families of pigments found in fruit and vegetable plants, which vary depending on the ripening stage of the plant and the cooking method :

- Chlorophyll: Green pigment.
- Carotenoids: Yellow pigment to deep red.
- Flavonoids: Yellow or red/blue pigment.
- Anthocyanin: Red, blue or purple pigments according to pH.
- Anthoxanthin: White pigment.

Foods Containing Chlorophyll

Chlorophyll is responsible for photosynthesis and can be found in cabbage, broccoli, kiwi fruit and green apples. It is a fat soluble pigment and may leach from fruit and vegetables if cooked in a medium containing fat e.g. stir frying. As foods containing chlorophyll are heated, the pigment becomes deficient of air, resulting in the appearance of a bright green colour. As cooking continues, acids in the cells of the fruit or vegetable are released and cause a chain reaction that results in the following conversions :

- Chlorophyll to pheophytin (grey-green coloured pigment).
- Chlorophyll to phenophytin (olive-green coloured pigment).

Overtime, chlorophyll degrades to yellow colour. Long cooking methods with a fatty cooking medium will have a detrimental effect on the concentration and intensity of chlorophyll pigment contained in fruits and vegetables.

Food Containing Carotenoid Pigment

Carotenoids are fat soluble colourants. Cooking methods that involve the use of fats may cause leaching of the pigment. Fruits and vegetables containing carotenoid pigments are lemons, oranges, strawberries, peppers, carrots and sweet potatoes. Carotenoids also undergo oxidation when carotenoid cells come in direct contact with air and react with oxygen molecules.

This reaction leads to degradation of pigment. Cooking methods, which expose fruits and vegetables containing carotenoids to the atmosphere for long period of time. For example, boiling without a lid, will cause pigment depletion resulting in paler coloured food.

Foods Containing Anthocyanins and Anthoxanthin

Anthocyanins are found in fruits and vegetables such as blueberries, cherries and red plums, red potatoes and aubergines. Anthoxanthins are found in apples, cauliflower, onions and potatoes. Both these pigments are water soluble and leach into cooking water during soaking or prolonged heating. Cooking methods that avoid water such as stir frying will minimise the loss of these flavonoids during heating.

Food types that may undergo pigment loss are fruits and vegetables. The cooking methods resulting in pigment loss are boiling, frying, grilling, steaming and roasting.

Texture

After cooking and processing, texture of the food is affected in the following ways :

Protein Denaturation

Foods that contain proteins are meat, fish, eggs, vegetables, nuts and pulses. During cooking, the heat causes proteins to vibrate violently resulting in the breakage of the weak hydrogen bonds holding the amino acid strands in place. The denaturation of protein molecules in foods causes a substantial change to the texture of the product. For example, eggwhite is composed of two key proteins : ovotransferrin and ovalbumin. As the eggwhite is heated, ovotransferrin begins to denature first, entangling and forming new bonds with ovalbumin.

As the temperature rises, ovalbumin starts to denature to form new bonds with ovotransferrin till rearrangement of protein molecules is complete. This results in the change of a runny, fluid texture to a rigid and firm texture. Conversely, protein denaturisation can cause formation of soft textures e.g. meat.

Foods containing protein e.g. meat, fish, eggs and pulses undergo protein denaturation. Cooking methods resulting in this kind of denaturation are boiling, frying, grilling, roasting, steaming, and baking.

Use of Oil and Phytochemicals in Diet

Oil and phytochemicals also affect our diet. Their effects are discussed as follows :

Cooking Oil

For health benefits, the ideal cooking oil should contain high amount of monounsaturated and polyunsaturated fats, with low or no saturated fat and trans fat and a smoke point higher than the cooking temperature.

Suitable Cooking Uses of Fats and Oils

Fats and Oils	Cooking Uses	Types of Fats
Almond oil	Sauteing, Stir fry	Monounsaturated
Butter	Baking, cooking	Saturated
Butter (Ghee), Clarified	Frying, sauteing	Saturated
Canola oil (Rape seed oil)	Good all-purpose oil. Salad dressing and cooking	Monounsaturated
Coconut oil	Coatings, confectionery, shortening	Saturated
Corn oil	Frying, salad dressing, shortening.	Polyunsaturated
Cotton seed oil	Margarine, salad dressing, shortening, frying,	Polyunsaturated
Grape seed oil	Sauteing, Frying, Salad dressing	Polyunsaturated
Hazelnut oil	Salad dressing, marinades, baked foods	Monounsaturated
Lard	Baking, Frying	Saturated
Palm oil	Cooking, Flavouring	Saturated
Peanut oil	Frying, Cooking, Salad dressing	Monounsaturated
Sesame oil	Cooking, Salad dressing	Polyunsaturated
Shortening, vegetable	Baking, frying	Saturated
Sunflower oil	Cooking, margarine, salad dressing, Sautening.	Polyunsaturated
Vegetable oil	Cooking, salad dressing	Polyunsaturated
Walnut oil	Sauteing, pan frying, searing, deep frying, stir frying, grilling, boiling	Monounsaturated

Phytochemicals as Part of Diet

Phytochemicals are chemicals found in plants that protect plants against bacteria, viruses and fungi. Eating large amounts of brightly coloured fruits and vegetables (yellow, orange, red, green, white, blue, purple), whole grains/cereals and beans containing phytochemicals may decrease the risk of developing certain cancers as well as diabetes, hypertension and heart disease.

The action of phytochemicals varies by colour and type of food. They may act as antioxidants or nutrient protectors, or prevent carcinogens (Cancer causing agents) from forming.

Sources of Phytochemicals

Following is a partial test of phytochemicals found in foods :

- **Allicin** is found in onions and garlic. Allicin blocks or eliminates certain toxins from bacteria and viruses.
- **Anthocyanins** are found in red and blue fruits (such as raspberries and blueberries) and vegetables. They help to slow the ageing process, protect against heart disease and tumours, prevent blood clots and fight inflammation and allergies.
- **Biflavonoids** are found in citrus fruits.
- **Carotenoids** are found in dark yellow, orange and deep green fruits and vegetables such as tomatoes, parsley, oranges, pink grapefruit and spinach.
- **Flavonoids** are found in the fruits, vegetables, wine, green tea, onions, apples, kale and beans.
- **Indoles** are found in broccoli, cabbage, kale, brussel sprouts and turnips (also known as 'cruciferous' vegetables). They contain sulphur and activate agents that destroy cancer causing chemicals.
- **Isoflavones** are found in soyabeans and soyabean products.
- **Lignin** are found in flaxseed and whole grain products.
- **Lutein** is found in leafy green vegetables. It may prevent mascular degeneration and cataracts as well as reduce the risk of heart disease and breast cancer.

Note 'Macular degeneration' is the leading cause of severe, irreversible vision loss in people over 60. It occurs when the small central portion of the retina, known as the macula, deteriorates. The retina is the light sensing nerve tissue at the back of the eye.

- **Lycopene** is found primarily in tomato products. When cooked, it appears to reduce the risk for cancer and heart attacks.
- **Phenolics** are found in citrus fruits, fruit juices, cereals, legumes and oilseeds. It is thought to be extremely powerful and is studied for a variety of health benefits including slowing the ageing process, protecting against heart disease and tumours, fighting inflammation, allergies and blood clots.

Foods High in Phytochemicals

Phytochemicals cannot be found in supplements and are only present in food. Following are some foods high in phytochemicals : (There is no recommended dietary allowance for phytochemicals).

- Broccoli
- Berries
- Soynuts
- Pears
- Turnips
- Celery
- Soya beans
- Carrots
- Spinach
- Olives
- Tomatoes
- Lentils
- Cantaloupe
- Garlic
- Onions
- Apricots
- Apples
- Cabbage
- Green tea

Effect of Cooking on Phytochemicals Content of Vegetables

Cooking induces many chemical and physical modification in foods; among these the phytochemical content can change. Changes in phytochemicals upon cooking may result from two opposite phenomenas :

- Thermal degradation, which reduces their concentration.
- A matrix softening effect, which increases the extractability of phytochemicals, resulting in a higher concentration with respect to the raw material. The final effect of cooking on phytochemical concentration depends on the processing parameters, the structure of food matrix and the chemical nature of the specific compound.
- Steaming will ensure better preservation/ extraction yield of phenols and glucosinolates than do other cooking methods. Steamed issues are not in direct contact with the cooking material (water or oil) e.g. in idli and dhokla, so leaching of soluble compounds into water is minimised and thermal degradation is limited. Carotenoids showed a different behaviour. A positive effect on extraction and solubilisation of carotenes were reported after severe processing.

Food Processing

Food processing is a set of methods and techniques used to transform raw food ingredients into consumable food. The primary goal was to enlarge the life of a foodstuff by acting as a preservative.

As per **Ministry of Food Processing of India**, "the process of value addition to the agriculture or horticulture product by various methods like grading, sorting and packing is known as 'food processing'. It is a technique of manufacturing and preserving food substances in an effective manner with a view to enhance their shelf life; improve quality and to make it more useful. It covers a wide range of products from sub-sectors comprising agriculture, horticulture, plantation, animal husbandry and fisheries. Food processing industry comprises of three segments based on levels of processing :

- Primary processing of food comprises of sorting, grading and packaging of fruits and vegetables, milk, rice, spices, etc.
- Secondary processing of food comprises of reshaping of food for ease of consumption. It includes flour, oil cakes, tea leaf, beverages powder, etc.
- Tertiary processing of food or value added food segment includes processed fruits and vegetables, juices, jam and jelly, etc.

Disadvantages of Processed Food

More distant a food product is from its natural form, the less it retains its healthful nutritional properties.

- Vitamins evaporate, minerals are leached and fibre is non-existent.
- Decrease in nutrients has led to enrichment and fortification, but these add only a small number of nutrients back to a product.
- Some preservatives that are used to increase shelf life of products have adverse side effects on some or all human population.
- Additives are used to make food more platable and attractive.

Preservation

One of the oldest form of food processing, dating back to BC, was the salting of meats as a means of preservation. Sugar was introduced much later as a preservative for fruit and thus the jam was born. Keeping food cold, either underground or by using ice was an effective and ancient method of preservation until the ascent of ice boxes and recently electrical refrigeration.

Food Preservation

Food preservation is the process of treating and handling food to stop or slow down food spoilage, loss of quality, edibility or nutritional value, allowing for longer food storage. Preservation involves preventing growth of bacteria, fungi (such as yeast) and other micro organisms as well as retarding the oxidation of fats which cause rancidity.

Preserving Fruits

Fruits can be preserved by turning them into jam. It involves boiling (to reduce the fruit's moisture content and to kill bacteria,yeasts, etc.), sugaring to prevent their regrowth, sealing within an airtight jar (to prevent recontamination). Maintaining or creating nutritional value, texture and flavour are important aspects of food preservation.

Following are some techniques of food preservation :

Drying Drying is one of the most ancient techniques of food preservation. It reduces water activity sufficiently to prevent bacterial growth.

Refrigeration Food is preserved by slowing down the growth and reproduction of microorganisms. The introduction of commercial and domestic refrigerators improved the storage of fresh fruits, vegetables and dairy products for longer period of time, especially during summer season.

Freezing It is one of the most commonly used processes commercially and domestically for preserving a wide range of food e.g. potato waffles are stored in the freezer. Cold stores provide large volume, long-term storage for strategic food stocks held in case of national emergency in many countries.

Vacuum Packing It stores food in a vacuum environment, usually in an air tight bag or bottle. The vacuum environment strips bacteria of oxygen needed for survival, slowing spoilage of food. It is used to store nuts, to reduce loss of flavour from oxidation.

Salting Salting or curing draws moisture from meat through a process of osmosis. Meat is cured with salt or sugar. Nitrates and nitrites are often used to cure meat. This contributes to the characteristic pink colour and inhibits 'clostridium botulinum'.

Sugaring It is used to preserve fruits such as apples, pears, peaches, apricots and plums. The preserved material is cooked in sugar to the point of crystallisation and the resultant product is stored dry.

Smoking It is used to lengthen the shelf life of perishable food items. This effect is achieved by exposing the food to smoke from burning plant materials such as wood. It is one of the oldest food preservation method.

Pickling It is a method of preserving food in an edible anti-microbial liquid. Pickling can be categorised into chemical pickling and fermentation pickling.

Canning and Bottling Canning involves cooking food, sealing it in sterile cans or jars. The containers are boiled to kill weaken remaining bacteria. This is sterilisation. It was invented by **Nicolas Appert**. High acid fruits like strawberries require no preservatives to can/bottle and only a short boiling cycle. Marginal fruits such as tomatoes require longer boiling and addition of other acidic elements. Low acid foods, such as vegetables and meats require pressure canning. Food preserved by canning or bottling is at immediate risk to spoilage, once the can or bottle has been opened.

Food Pigments and Additives

Food Pigment It is any colour pigment or dye or substance that imparts colour when added to food or drink. They come in many forms consisting of liquids, powders, gels and pastes. Food colouring is used both in commercial food production and in domestic cooking.

Additives is any substance not normally consumed as food in itself and not normally used as a characteristic ingredient of food, whether or not it has nutritive value. It has to be added. There are many types of food additives; preservatives, sweetners, firming agents, anti-caking agents, etc.

Purpose of Food Colouring

People associate certain colours with certain flavours as the colour of food can influence the perceived flavour in anything from candy to wine.

The aim is to simulate a colour that is perceived by the customer as natural such as adding red colouring to glace cherries (which would otherwise be beige). Sometimes it is for effect, like the green Ketchup that Heinz launched in 1999.

Colour additives are used in foods for the following reasons :

- To make food more attractive, appealing, appetising and informative.
- To offset colour loss due to exposure to light, air, extreme temperature, moisture and storage conditions.
- To correct natural variations in colour.
- To enhance colours that occur naturally.
- To provide colour to colourless and 'fun' foods.
- To allow consumers to identify products on sight, like candy flavours or medicine dosages.

Colours Exempted from Certification

These colours include pigments derived from natural sources such as vegetables, minerals or animals. Nature derived colour additives are typically more expensive than certified colours and may add unintended flavours to foods. Example of exempted colour includes :

- Annatto
- Beet extract
- Caramel
- Beta-carotene
- Turmeric
- Grape skin extract

This list contains substances which may have synthetic origins, such as nature identical beta-carotene.

Most of the countries have their own regulations and list of food colours which are generally approved as in United States and European Union.

United States

In US, FD and C numbers are given to approved synthetic food dyes that do not exist in nature.

The following seven artificial colourings are generally permitted in food :

- FD and C Blue No. 1 — Brilliant Blue
- FD and C Blue No. 2 — Indigotine
- FD and C Green No. 3 — ast Green
- FD and C Red No. 3 — Erythrosine
- FD and C Red No. 40 — Allura Red AC
- FD and C Yellow No. 5 — Tartrazine
- FD and C Yellow No. 6 — Sunset Yellow FCF

European Union

In the European Union, E numbers are used for all additives, both synthetic and natural, that are approved in food applications. The food colours are known by E numbers that begin with 1 such as E 100 (turmeric) or E 161 b(lutein).

The safety of food colours and other food additives in the EU is evaluated by the, 'European Food Safety Authority'. Any changes have to be implemented into their national laws within a given time frame.

In Non-EU Member States, food additives are regulated by their national authorities which try to harmonise with the laws adopted by the EU.

Most other countries have their own regulations and list of food colours which can be used in various applications, including maximum daily intake limits.

Permitted Colourants in EU

- E 104 — Quinoline Yellow
- E 122 — Carmoisine
- E 124 — Ponceau 4R
- E 131 — Patent Blue
- E 142 — Green S

In India , as per the **Food Safety and Standard Act, 2006,** the following eight artificial colourings are generally permitted in food :

Colours	Common Names	INS No.	Chemical Classes
Red	Ponceau 4R	124	Azo
	Carmoisine	122	Azo
	Erythrosine	127	Xanthene
Yellow	Tartrazine	102	Pyrazolone
	Sunset Yellow FCF	110	AZO
Blue	Indigo Carmine	132	Indigoid
	Brilliant Blue FCF	133	Triaryl methane
Green	Fast Green FCF	143	Triaryl methane

Natural Food Colours

These refer to the dyes obtained from vegetables, animals or minerals, capable of colouring food, drugs or cosmetics. These are obtained using only naturally available products. They are usually extracted from natural things like seeds, fruits, vegetables, leaves, insects, algae, etc.

Benefits of Using Natural Food Colours

These are safe to use as food additives. Since, they are natural derivatives, they are free from any harmful side effects. They might be harmful to those who suffer from certain allergies and intolerances. But, such allergies are usually individual problems and do not generalise. Natural food colours are popular food additives that can be found in everyday consumption products.

Natural Food Dyes

The four main categories of plant pigments grown to colour food products are :

- Carotenoids (E160, E161, E164)
- Chlorophyllin (E140, E141)
- Anthocyanins (E163)
- Betanin (E162)

Other colorants or specialised derivatives of these core groups include :

- Annatto (E 160b), a reddish-orange dye made from the seeds of the 'achiote.
- Caramel colouring (E 150 a-d), made from caramelised sugar.
- Carmine (E 120), a red dye derived from the cochineal insect 'Dactylopius Coccus'.
- Elderberry juice (E 163).
- Lycopene (E 160 d).
- Paprika (E 160 c).
- Turmeric (E 100).

Blue colours are specially rare. One feasible blue dye currently in use is derived from 'spirulina'.

New Product Development: Nanotechnology

Nanotechnology has the potential of application in the food industry and processing as new tools for pathogen detection, disease treatment, delivery systems, food, packaging and delivery of bioactive compounds to target sites. The application of Nanotechnology in food systems will provide new methods to improve safety and the nutritional value of food products.

Meaning of Nanotechnology

Nanotechnology is a science, engineering and technology conducted at the nano scale, which is about 1 to 100 nanometers. One nanometre is (one) billionth of a metre of 10^{-9} of a metre. For example :

- There are 25,400,000 nanometers in an inch.
- A sheet of newspaper is about 100,000 nanometers thick.
- On a comparative scale, if a marble were a nanometer, then one meter would be the size of the Earth.

Nano Science and Nanotechnology are the study and application of extremely small things and can be used across all the other science fields such as chemistry, biology, physics, materials science and engineering. It involves the ability to see and control individual atoms and molecules. Everything on Earth is made up of atoms . The food we eat, the clothes we wear, the buildings and houses we live in and our own body. But something as small as an atom is impossible to see with the naked eye. The microscopes needed to see things at the nano scale were invented recently, about 30 years ago.

Physicist **Richard Feynman** is considered the 'Father of Nanotechnology'. Professor **Norio Taniguchi** coined the term 'Nanotechnology'. Today's scientists and engineers are finding a wide variety of ways to deliberately make materials at the nano scale to take advantage of their enhanced properties such as higher strength, lighter weight, increased control of light spectrum and greater chemical reactivity than their larger scale counter parts.

Development of New Products Nanotechnology

Over the past few decades, the evolution of a number of new science disciplines and technologies has revolutionised the food sector. Most notable among these are biotechnology, cognitive sciences, Information Technology (IT) and more recently, Nanotechnology. Nanotechnology is an enabling technology that has opened up new avenues of R and D in a number of fields, including medicine, cosmetics, agriculture and food and is being used as a means to understand how physiochemical characteristics of nanosized substances can change the structure, texture and quality of food stuffs.

Food Packaging

Food packaging is the enclosing of food to protect it from damage, contamination, spoilage, pest attacks and tampering during transport, storage and retail sale. The package is often labelled with information such as amount of the content, ingredients, nutritional content, cooking instructions (if relevant) and shelf life. The package needs to be designed and selected in a manner that there are no adverse interactions between it and the food. Packaging types include bags, bottles, cans, cartons and trays.

Functions of Food Packaging

Food packaging serves many important functions, which may be as follows :

Containment For items that are granulated, paper-based packages are the best, with a sealing system to prevent infiltration of moisture into the product. Other products are packaged using metal cans, plastic bags and bottles and glass containers. Another factor in containment is packaging durability. The packaged food has to survive transport from the food processing facility to the supermarket to the consumer's home.

Protection The packaging must protect the food from :

- biological agents such as rats, insects and microbes.
- mechanical damage, such as product abrasion, compressive forces and vibrations.
- from chemical degradation, such as oxidation, moisture transfer and ultraviolet light.

Communication Packaged food must be identified for consumer use, with label, text and graphics. It can use special shapes for the package, such as Coca Cola bottle or a can. Other food package shapes include potato chip bags. These packages detail nutritional information and whether it is safe to put the packaged food through a microwave process.

Environmental Issues To protect the environment, we must be willing to reuse or recycle the packaging or reduce the size of packaging.

Package Safety Before using a particular type of package for food, researchers must ensure that it is safe to use that packaging for the food being considered and there are no adverse interactions between the package and the food. This includes any metal contamination issues from a can to the food product or any plastic contamination from a bottle to the food product.

Product Access The packaging must be such that the product is readily accessible when the consumer is ready to use it.

Special Techniques for Packaging

Special techniques for packaging are :

Vacuum Packaging or Inert Atmosphere Packaging Oxygen in the air tends to reduce the shelf life of food by the process known as oxidation. To prevent this process, some foods are packaged at reduced pressure Partial vacuum) or using an inert gas (such as nitrogen) to replace oxygen.

Bags-in-Boxes These are used for soft drink syrups, other liquid products and meat products.

Wine Box This is a type of box designed for storage of wine.

EXAM BASED QUESTIONS

1 Food comprises of any material or substance which consists of

(a) protein (b) carbohydrate
(c) fat (d) All of the above

2 Food is a .... commodity.

(a) global (b) local
(c) national (d) state

3 Which of the following is not a functional property of food?

(a) Frothing ability (b) Elasticity
(c) Water retention (d) Anti-caking agent

4 Which of the following cannot be characterised as food property?

(a) Structure of food product
(b) Nutritional value of food product
(c) Acceptability of food product
(d) Grilling of food product

5 Which one of the following is not the definition of Food Science?

(a) The application of basic sciences and engineering to study the physical, chemical and biochemical nature of foods and the principles of food processing.
(b) The study of the physical, biological and chemical make up of food and the concepts underlying food processing.
(c) The science of nature devoted to the study of food.
(d) The science that interprets the interaction of nutrients and other substances in food.

6 Food authenticity means

(a) the food should match the description.
(b) the food should taste good.
(c) food should be cheap.
(d) None of the above

7 How many certified colour additives have been approved for use in the United States?

(a) Nine (b) Ten
(c) Eight (d) Seven

8 Foods that are sterilised by irradiation can be stored for .... without refrigeration.

(a) years (b) weeks
(c) months (d) days

9 Reducing the volume and weight of a product saves .... during processing.

(a) time (b) money
(c) energy (d) flavour

10 Which vitamin is used most commonly to control browning in fruits by enzymes?

(a) Vitamin K (b) Vitamin B
(c) Vitamin C (d) Vitamin D

11 .... implies a person eats but does not receive the amount of nutrients to keep the body healthy.

(a) Undernutrition (b) Hunger
(c) Malnutrition (d) Starvation

12 Sugars and sugary foods provide a valuable and inexpensive source of

(a) fat (b) dessert
(c) energy (d) carbohydrates

13 One of the most common physical test performed on fats is a determination of the .... point.

(a) boiling (b) melting
(c) cooling (d) separating

14 Ingredients on a food label are listed in .... order, based on weight.

(a) descending (b) alphabetical
(c) ascending (d) chronological

15 One well known substitute for a milk product is

(a) cheese (b) powdered milk
(c) dried milk (d) margarine

16 The basic foundation of baked products is usually flour and

(a) sugar (b) liquid
(c) eggs (d) leavening

17 .... is a soft cheese like food made by curdling fresh soya milk with a coagulant.

(a) Tempeh (b) Yogurt
(c) Tofu (d) Cheddar

18 Starch potato begins to .... at a lower temperature than corn starch.

(a) burn (b) smell
(c) gelatinize (d) separate

19 .... flour has been used for many products as a substitute flour for individuals with an allergy to wheat flour.

(a) Cake (b) Bread
(c) Rice (d) Soy

20 .... makes a food acidic or sour.

(a) Flavouring (b) Colouring
(c) Texturing (d) Acidulant

21 Monoglycerides and diglycerides are used as .... in a variety of foods.

(a) emulsifiers (b) calories
(c) flavours (d) colours

22 Fruits and vegetables get their characteristic colour from

(a) pigment (b) sunshine
(c) sugar (d) osmosis

23 The word ...... on a label means that a product contains no amount of, or only trivial or 'physiologically inconsequential' amounts of, one or more of these components : fat, saturated fat, cholesterol, sodium, sugar and calories.
(a) low (b) lean
(c) free (d) reduced

24 .... like onions and garlic are enlargements above the roots.
(a) Roots (b) Bulbs
(c) Tubers (d) Stems

25 Of the microorganisms, ... are the greatest threat to food safety.
(a) viruses (b) fungi
(c) parasites (d) bacteria

26 Suppose you need to deactivate the enzymes in sliced potatoes that cause browning to occur. Which processing method is specifically designed for this purpose?
(a) Blanching (b) Bleaching
(c) Pasteurization (d) Retorting
(e) Belching

27 'GMO' stands for
(a) Genetically Modified Organism
(b) Grass Mouldy Oranges
(c) Genetically Manufactured Oranges
(d) Genetically Malfunctioning Organisms

28 Fermentation is stopped by pasteurising and
(a) cooling (b) stirrting
(c) heating (d) settling

29 .... help in maintaining/controlling acidic/alkaline changes during food processing and hence maintain flavour and stability.
(a) Buffering agents (b) Sequestrants
(c) Anti-caking agents (d) Anti-foaming agents

30 Which of the following is a form of misdescription?
(a) Incorrect origin
(b) Incorrect quantitative description
(c) Extending the food
(d) All of the above

31 Which of the following need not be in the same vision of field?
(a) Product name (b) Quantity
(c) Date mark (d) Place of origin

32 It is legal for a label to say 'this product cures xyz disease'.
(a) True (b) False
(c) Both (a) and (b) (d) None of these

33 A substance intentionally added that preserves flavour and improves the taste is called
(a) food additive
(b) food adulterant
(c) food contaminant
(d) food material

34 What is 'Carryover Principle'?
(a) Additives added in raw materials are not present in final products.
(b) Antioxidant added to oil is present in all oil based products made from it.
(c) Both (a) and (b)
(d) Neither (a) nor (b)

35 Which of the following is a must in food labelling?
(a) Name
(b) Standard specification
(c) Place of origin
(d) All of the above

36 Which of the following is incorrect?
(a) Packages designed for uniform shipping cannot be loaded into mixed shopping.
(b) Waste prevention is the most sought after option and disposal the least sought after.
(c) Shrink wraps is one of the forms of packing used.
(d) None of the above

37 The prefix 'nano' comes from
(a) French word 'meaning billion'.
(b) Greek word 'meaning dwarf'.
(c) Spanish word 'meaning particle'.
(d) Latin word meaning 'invisible'.

38 Which of these condiments is unique due to the nano scale interactions between its ingredients?
(a) Ketchup (b) Mustard
(c) Mayonnaise (d) All of thess

39 The term 'Nanotechnology' was coined by
(a) Richard Feynman (b) Edward Jennings
(c) Norio Taniguchi (d) Albert Einstein

40 1 nanometre = ... cm.
(a) 10^{-9} (b) 10^{-8} (c) 10^{-7} (d) 10^{-6}

41 A healthy diet in humans does not include which one of the following ?
(a) Preparation of food and storage methods that preserve nutrients from oxidation, heat or leaching.
(b) Provides all the nutrients in required amounts and proper proportions.
(c) Causes deficiency related diseases.
(d) Provides non-nutrients such as dietary fibre, antioxidants and phytochemicals.

42 Which of the following spices is not rich in antioxidants?
(a) Cumin (b) Cloves
(c) Red chilly powder (d) Turmeric

43 Which of the following chain reactions produce free radicals damaging the cells of organisms?
(a) Catabolism (b) Oxidation
(c) Reduction (d) Anabolism

44 Which of the following is an example of overlapping antioxidant?
(a) Vitamin E (b) Glutathione
(c) Vitamin C (d) Thiol

45 What does 'Calorie' of a food signify?
(a) The physical and chemical changes that occur during preparation of food.
(b) It is a measurement of the amount of energy stored in that food.
(c) People who exercise need more energy to walk, think and breathe.
(d) It is the amount of heat required to cook that particular food.

46 Which of the cooking methods preserves vitamins and nutrients?
(a) Cooking (b) Frying in oil
(c) Steaming (d) Broiling

47 Which of the following processes improved the safety of milk and milk products?
(a) Preservation (b) Pasteurisation
(c) Packaging (d) Using additives

48 Which of the following is incorrect about additives?
(a) It is not normally consumed as food.
(b) It is not a characteristic ingredient of food.
(c) It is never added to food.
(d) Preservatives and sweeteners are food additives.

49 A diet high in saturated fats can be linked to which of the following?
(a) Kidney failure
(b) Bulimia
(c) Anorexia
(d) Cardiovascular disease

50 In developing countries, the time before .... is most difficult for meeting nutritional needs of the people.
(a) planting (b) harvest
(c) evicting (d) spring

51 Nanotechnology in other words is
(a) carbon engineering (b) atomic engineering
(c) small technology (d) microphysics

52 A substance needed by the body for growth, energy, repair and maintenance is called
(a) nutrient (b) carbohydrate
(c) calorie (d) fatty acid

53 All of the following are nutrients found in food except
(a) plasma (b) proteins
(c) carbohydrates (d) vitamins

54 Which one of the following is not a pathogen?
(a) Virus (b) Bacterium
(c) Fungus (d) Phytochemical

55 Which of the following is not a function of food additive?
(a) To maintain product consistency
(b) To maintain nutritive value
(c) Controlling acidity/alkalinity
(d) None of the above

56 Which dye has been obtained from 'Dactylopius Coccus'?
(a) Caramel (b) Red
(c) Reddish-orange (d) Pink

57 Which of the following functions is/are not included in packaging?
(a) Communication
(b) Environmental issues
(c) Product access
(d) Flavour enhancement

58 Which of the following is irrelevant to Nanotechnology?
(a) It has the potential of application in the food industry.
(b) It will provide new methods to improve nutritional value of food products.
(c) It is the study and application of extremely small things.
(d) It is an enabling technology that has not opened up new avenues of.

59 Fermentation is the ...... form of food preservation.
(a) oldest (b) best
(c) newest (d) cheapert

60 Microwave radiation is often called ...... radiation.
(a) ionising (b) electrical
(c) non-ionising (d) magnetic

61 Is it true or false that toxins can be produced by certain bacteria outside the body, in the food we eat, but never by bacteria once they are inside the GI tract.
(a) True (b) False
(c) Bath (a) and (b) (d) None of these

62 In terms of additives, ... include both natural and synthetic colourants.
(a) flavours (b) colours
(c) gums (d) sweeteners

63 Which of the following can be attributed to food preparation?
1. It is a broad topic involving all steps from obtaining raw ingredients to consuming food.
2. It is about cooking food.
3. The temperature is around 70-85°C in poaching.
4. A sheet of newspaper is about 100,000 nanometres thick.

Codes
(a) 1, 2 and 3 (b) 1, 3 and 4
(c) 2, 3 and 4 (d) 1, 2 and 4

64 Ideal cooking oil include which of the following ?
1. It must contain high amounts of monounsaturated fats.
2. It must have a smoke point higher than the cooking temperature.
3. It should not have any trans fat.
4. It must contain high amount of saturated fats.

Codes

(a) 2, 3 and 4 (b) 1, 2 and 3
(c) 3, 4 and 1 (d) 1, 2 and 4

65 **Which of the following smoking point are correct?**

1. Extra light olive oil = 242°C
2. Walnut oil = 204°C
3. Butter = 177°C
4. Coconut oil = 216°C

Codes

(a) 1, 3, 4 (b) 3, 4, 2
(c) 1, 2, 3 (d) 4, 2, 1

66 **Poaching is used to cook which of the following foods ?**

1. Eggs 2. Fish
3. Dhokla 4. Soup

Codes

(a) 1 and 2 (b) 3 and 4
(c) 1 and 4 (d) 2 and 3

67 **Which of the following can be attributed to Maillard Reaction?**

1. Foods that undergo Maillard Reaction contain both protein and carbohydrates.
2. It is a chemical reaction between an amino acid and glucose or fructose.
3. This reaction results in a flavour of food.
4. It is a techingue of preserving fruit

Codes

(a) 1, 2 and 4 (b) 2, 3 and 4
(c) 1, 2 and 3 (d) 4, 1 and 3

68 **Arrange the following food products in increasing order of their pH range.**

1. Egg white 2. Pickle
3. Soft cheese 4. Yogurt
5. Milk

Codes

(a) 2, 4, 3, 5, 1 (b) 1, 5, 2, 3, 4
(c) 5, 1, 2, 4, 3 (d) 4, 3, 1, 2, 5

69 **Arrange the following works of 'Food Chemistry' in increasing years of occurrence.**

1. 'Elements of Agricultural Chemistry' was published.
2. Isolation of malic acid from apples.
3. Formation of Society of Public Analysts.
4. Establishment of Food Chemistry Division by Institute of Food Technologists.

Codes

(a) 4, 3, 1, 2 (b) 2, 1, 3, 4
(c) 3, 1, 2, 4 (d) 1, 2, 3, 4

70 **Arrange in correct sequence the processes involved in food technology.**

1. Preservation 2. Selection
3. Use of safe food 4. Distribution
5. Packaging

Codes

(a) 5, 2, 1, 3, 4 (b) 4, 3, 2, 1, 5
(c) 1, 2, 3, 5, 4 (d) 2, 1, 5, 4, 3

71 **Who developed the process of canning?**

(a) Nicolas Appert (b) Louis Pasteur
(c) Norman Borlaug (d) Walter Hesse

72 **Which of the following pairs is/are correctly matched?**

1. Food technology – Study of food
2. Food processing – Sorting
3. Functional property – Calorie
4. Phytochemicals – Animal origin

Codes

(a) Only 3 (b) Only 2
(c) None of these (d) All of these

73 **Match the following.**

List I	List II
A. Phytochemicals	1. Cereal group
B. Pathogens	2. Minerals
C. Millets	3. Vitamin E
D. Oilseeds	4. Disease producing
	5. Flavones

Codes

	A	B	C	D		A	B	C	D
(a)	2	3	4	1	(b)	3	4	1	2
(c)	4	1	2	5	(d)	5	4	1	2

74 **Match the following.**

List I	List II
A. E 104	1. Green S
B. E 122	2. Ponceau 4R
C. E 124	3. Patent Blue
D. E 131	4. Quinolino yollow
	5. Carmoisine

Codes

	A	B	C	D		A	B	C	D
(a)	3	2	4	1	(b)	4	5	2	3
(c)	5	1	4	2	(d)	2	3	1	5

75 **Match the following.**

List I	List II
A. FD & C Blue No. 1	1. Erythrosine
B. FD & C Yellow No. 5	2. Indigotine
C. FD & C Red No. 3	3. Brilliant Blue
D. FD & C Blue No. 2	4. Tartrazine
	5. Sunset Yellow

Codes

	A	B	C	D		A	B	C	D
(a)	4	3	2	1	(b)	3	4	1	2
(c)	5	3	1	2	(d)	3	5	1	2

76 **Package serves the purpose of**

1. protection of merchandise.
2. details nutritional information.
3. protecting environment.
4. certification by a regulatory authority.

Codes

(a) 1, 2 and 4 (b) 1, 2 and 3
(c) 2, 3 and 4 (d) 1, 3 and 4

77 Match the following.

List I	List II
A. Chlorophyll	1. Yellow pigment
B. Carotenoid	2. Red/blue
C. Anthocyanin	3. White
D. Anthoxanthin	4. Green pigment

Codes

	A	B	C	D		A	B	C	D
(a)	4	1	2	3	(b)	1	3	2	4
(c)	2	3	1	4	(d)	3	2	1	4

78 Match the following.

List I	List II
A. Fat content	1. Potential for Hydrogen
B. Rancidity	2. Kjeldahl method
C. pH	3. Foss-Let instrument
D. Protein analysis	4. TBA test

Codes

	A	B	C	D		A	B	C	D
(a)	3	4	1	2	(b)	2	1	4	2
(c)	2	3	4	1	(d)	4	1	2	3

79 Match the following .

List I	List II
A. Non-nutrients	1. Water
B. Macro nutrients	2. Minerals
C. Micro nutrients	3. Carbohydrates
D. Nutrients	4. Dietary fibre

Codes

	A	B	C	D		A	B	C	D
(a)	4	3	2	1	(b)	2	1	3	4
(c)	3	4	1	2	(d)	4	1	2	3

80 Match the following .

List I	List II
A. Copper	1. Sensory analysis
B. Lactic acid	2. Winter green odour
C. Food colouring	3. Tart taste
D. Methyl salicyclate	4. Dietary supplement

Codes

	A	B	C	D		A	B	C	D
(a)	2	1	4	3	(b)	3	1	4	2
(c)	4	3	1	2	(d)	1	3	2	4

81 Match the following .

List I	List II
A. Protein sensitivity	1. Bio-chemical catalysts
B. Vitamin C	2. Fat soluble
C. Vitamin E	3. Water soluble
D. Enzymes	4. Food allergy

Codes

	A	B	C	D
(a)	3	4	1	2
(b)	4	3	2	1
(c)	2	1	3	4
(d)	1	4	2	3

82 Match the following.

List I	List II
A. Rheology	1. Thermal degradation
B. Phytochemicals	2. Atoms
C. Nanotechnology	3. Value addition
D. Food processing	4. Deformation of water

Codes

	A	B	C	D		A	B	C	D
(a)	2	3	4	1	(b)	3	1	4	2
(c)	4	2	1	3	(d)	4	1	2	3

83 Match the following.

List I	List II
A. FD & C Blue No. 1	1. Indigotine
B. E 100	2. Lutein
C. E 161 b	3. Turmeric
D. FD & C Blue No. 2	4. Brilliant Blue

Codes

	A	B	C	D		A	B	C	D
(a)	4	3	2	1	(b)	1	3	4	2
(c)	4	3	1	2	(d)	1	2	3	4

84 Match the following.

List I	List II
A. Indoles	1. Green tea
B. Isoflavones	2. Pink grape fruit
C. Flavonoids	3. Broccoli
D. Carotenoids	4. Soyabean products

Codes

	A	B	C	D		A	B	C	D
(a)	3	4	1	2	(b)	2	3	1	4
(c)	1	4	2	3	(d)	4	1	2	3

85 Match the following.

List I	List II
A. Sieve analysis	1. Pycnometer
B. Fluid flow	2. Image processing
C. Porosity	3. Particle diameter
D. Volume	4. Size of sample

Codes

	A	B	C	D		A	B	C	D
(a)	3	4	1	2	(b)	2	1	4	3
(c)	3	1	2	4	(d)	2	1	4	3

86 Match the following.

List I	List II
A. Coal Wilhelm Scheele	1. Father of nanotechnology
B. Richard Feynman	2. Isolation of malic acid from apples
C. Food Chemistry	3. Scientific approach to food
D. JG Wallerius	4. Single grain experiment

Codes

	A	B	C	D		A	B	C	D
(a)	2	4	1	3	(b)	2	1	4	3
(c)	3	4	2	1	(d)	4	1	3	2

87 Match the following.

List I	List II
A. WHO	1. Nanotechnology
B. MOSPI	2. Generally recognised as safe
C. AgNPs	3. World Health Organisation
D. GRAS	4. Food processing

Codes

	A	B	C	D		A	B	C	D
(a)	3	4	1	2	(b)	2	1	4	3
(c)	3	4	2	1	(d)	1	3	2	4

88 Arrange the functions of packaging in their correct order.

1. Containment　2. Environmental issue
3. Communication　4. Protection
5. Product access

Codes

(a) 4, 5, 1, 2, 3　(b) 5, 2, 3, 4, 1
(c) 1, 4, 3, 2, 5　(d) 3, 4, 1, 5, 2

89 Arrange in sequence the following processes involved in nutrition.

1. Assimilation　2. Bio synthesis
3. Food intake　4. Excretion
5. Absorption

Codes

(a) 3, 5, 1, 2, 4　(b) 4, 1, 2, 3, 5
(c) 2, 3, 4, 5, 1　(d) 1, 5, 2, 3, 4

90 Match the following.

List I	List II
A. Baking	1. Ice water
B. Blanching	2. Fragile food
C. Poaching	3. Browning process
D. Caramelisation	4. Dry heat

Codes

	A	B	C	D		A	B	C	D
(a)	2	3	4	1	(b)	4	1	3	2
(c)	1	2	3	4	(d)	4	3	2	1

Directions (Q. Nos. 91-101) *In the questions given below are two statements labelled as Assertion (A) and Reason (R). In the context of the two statements, which one of the following is correct?*

Codes

(a) Both A and R are true and R is the correct explanation of A.
(b) A is true, but R is not the correct explanation of A.
(c) A is true, but R is false.
(d) A is false, but R is true.

91 **Assertion** (A) All health conscious consumers eat more raw food.
Reason (R) Fruits and vegetables should be thoroughly washed before eating.

92 **Assertion** (A) Food science is often confused with food technology.
Reason (R) Food technology is the application of food science to selection, preservation, processing, packaging, distribution and use of safe food.

93 **Assertion** (A) Calorie is not a unit of energy.
Reason (R) The SI unit of energy is Joule (J).

94 **Assertion** (A) Men generally need more calories than women.
Reason (R) A person's specific daily calorie intake may vary according to their age, gender and physical activity level.

95 **Assertion** (A) A functional property of food is determined by physical, chemical and organoleptic properties.
Reason (R) Organoleptic properties are not associated with the senses of taste, sight, smell and touch.

96 **Assertion** (A) Nano technology is not science, engineering and technology conducted at the nano scale.
Reason (R) One nanometer is one billionth of a meter.

97 **Assertion** (A) Preserving food substances enhance their shelf life.
Reason (R) Food processing is a set of techniques used to transform raw food ingredients into consumable food.

98 **Assertion** (A) Anything that people can safely eat is described as edible.
Reason (R) The word 'edible' comes from the Latin word 'edere', meaning 'to eat'.

99 **Assertion** (A) Food is heated in order to kill bacteria and enhance flavours.
Reason (R) Microwaving is a very recent innovation.

100 **Assertion** (A) Natural food colours are safe to use as food additives.
Reason (R) Since, these are natural derivatives, they are free from any harmful side effects.

101 **Assertion** (A) 'Package safety' is an important function of food packaging.
Reason (R) There must be adverse reactions between the food and its package.

102 **Statement I** Simmering is a cooking method similar to boiling.
Statement II In this method, the food is cooked in a liquid which is held below boiling point.
Which of the above statement(s) is/are true?

(a) Only statement I is true
(b) Only statement II is true
(c) Both the statements, I and II are true
(d) Neither statement I nor statement II is true

103 **Statement I** Nano technology has the potential of application in the food industry and processing.
Statement II It is an enabling technology which opened new avenues of research and development.
Which of the above statement(s) is/are true?

(a) Statement I is true　(b) Statement II is true
(c) Both the statements, I and II are true.
(d) Neither statement I nor statement II is true

104 **Statement I** Drying is one of the most modern technique of food preservation.

Statement II In this method, the food is preserved by slowing down the growth and reproduction of microorganisms.

Which of the above statement(s) is/are true?

(a) Only statement I is true
(b) Only statement II is true
(c) Both the statements, I and II are true
(d) Neither statement I nor statement II is true

Directions (Q. Nos. 105-109) *Read the passage carefully and answer the questions that follow.*

Microwaves are a form of 'electromagnetic' radiation; i.e., they are waves of electrical and magnetic energy moving together through space. Electromagnetic radiation spans a broad spectrum from very long radio waves to very short gamma rays. The human eye can only detect a small portion of this spectrum called visible light. A radio detects a different portion of the spectrum and an X-ray machine uses yet another portion.

Visible light, microwaves and Radio Frequency (RF) radiation are forms of non-ionising radiation. Non-ionising radiation does not have enough energy to knock electrons out of atoms. X-rays are a form of ionising radiation. Exposure to ionising radiation can alter atoms and molecules and cause damage to cells in organic matter.

Microwaves are used to detect speeding cars and to send telephone and television communications. Industry uses microwaves to dry and cure plywood, to cure rubber and resins, to raise bread and doughnuts and to cook potato chips. But, the most common use of microwave energy is in microwave ovens. Microwaves have three characteristics that allow them to be used in cooking: they are reflected by metal; they pass through glass, paper, plastic and similar materials and they are absorbed by foods.

Microwaves are produced inside the oven by an electron tube called a magnetron. The microwaves are reflected within the metal interior of the oven where they are absorbed by food.

Microwaves cause water molecules in food to vibrate, producing heat that cooks the food. That's why foods that are high in water content, like fresh vegetables, can be cooked more quickly than other foods. The microwave energy is changed to heat as it is absorbed by food and does not make food 'radioactive' or 'contaminated'.

Although, heat is produced directly in the food, microwave ovens do not cook food from the 'inside out'. When thick foods are cooked, the outer layers are heated and cooked primarily by microwaves while the inside is cooked mainly by the conduction of heat from the hot outer layers.

Microwave cooking can be more energy efficient than conventional cooking because foods cook faster and the energy heats only the food, not the whole oven compartment. Microwave cooking does not reduce the nutritional value of foods any more than conventional cooking. Infact, foods cooked in a microwave oven may keep more of their vitamins and minerals because microwave ovens can cook more quickly and without adding water. Glass, paper, ceramic or plastic containers are used in microwave cooking because microwaves pass through these materials. Although, such containers cannot be heated by microwaves, they can become hot from the heat of the food cooking inside.

Some plastic containers should not be used in a microwave oven because they can be melted by the heat of the food inside. Generally, metal pans or aluminum foil should not be used in a microwave oven, as the microwaves are reflected off these materials causing the food to cook unevenly and possibly damaging the oven.

105 **Which of the following is not non-ionising radiation?**

(a) Visible light (b) Microwave
(c) Radio frequency (d) X-ray

106 **Waves of electrical and magnetic energy are known as**

(a) electromagnetic radiation (b) microwaves
(c) X-rays (d) gamma rays

107 **Why are microwave ovens used for cooking food?**

1. Microwave ovens cook fresh vegetables faster than other foods.
2. Microwave energy is not reflected by metal.
3. Microwave ovens do not cook food from inside out.
4. The energy inside a microwave oven heats only the food.

Codes

(a) 2, 3 and 4 (b) 1, 2 and 3
(c) 1, 3 and 4 (d) 1, 2 and 4

108 **Why is microwave cooking preferred more than conventional cooking?**

1. Cooks slowly, without adding water.
2. Cooks quickly, energy heating only food.
3. Food retain vitamins and minerals when cooked in microwave oven.
4. Microwave energy does not contaminate food.

Codes

(a) 1, 2 and 3 (b) 2, 3 and 4 (c) 1, 3 and 4 (d) 1, 2 and 4

109 **Cooking food 'inside out' means**

1. the outer layers of food is not cooked at all.
2. the outer layers of food is cooked by microwave.
3. the inside layers of food is cooked by conduction of heat from outer layers
4. thick food is cooked .

Codes

(a) 1, 2 and 3 (b) 2, 3 and 4 (c) 1, 2 and 4 (d) 4, 2 and 1

PREVIOUS YEARS' QUESTIONS

June 2018

1 Egg is used in cookery as

1. sequestrant 2. stabiliser
3. emulsifier 4. clarifier
5. tenderiser

Codes

(a) 1, 2 and 3 (b) 3, 4 and 5 (c) 2, 3 and 4 (d) 1, 2 and 5

2 **Assertion** (A) Green leafy vegetables should be cooked in open pan to retain its green colour.

Reason (R) The formation of dark green colour is brought about by the reaction of iron and sulphur present in it which forms Ferrous Sulphide.

Codes

(a) Both A and R are true
(b) Both A and R are false
(c) A is true, but R is false
(d) A is false, but R is true

3 Match the following.

List I (Tests)	List II (Chemical Compounds)
A. Fehling's test	1. Nitrogen
B. Seliwanoff's test	2. Free fatty acids
C. Kjeldahl's test	3. Ketose sugar
D. Xanthoproteic test	4. Aromatic amino acids
E. Nitroprusside test	5. Reducing sugar
	6. Distinguish between mono and di saccharides
	7. Sulphur containing amino acids

Codes

	A	B	C	D	E
(a)	5	3	1	4	7
(b)	6	5	1	2	7
(c)	5	6	1	7	4
(d)	5	2	1	6	7

4 Match the following.

List I (Active Ingredients of Foods)	List II (Sources of Cancer Prevention)
A. Phytochemical	1. Tomatoes
B. Alpha Lipoic acid	2. Green tea
C. Flavonoids	3. Potatoes
D. Glutathione	4. Turmeric
E. Selenium	5. Broccoli
	6. Sea foods
	7. Asparagus

Codes

	A	B	C	D	E
(a)	1	5	2	6	4
(b)	5	1	4	7	2
(c)	1	3	7	6	4
(d)	5	3	2	7	6

5 Match the following.

List I (Organisms)	List II (Foods)
A. Salmonella	1. Raw vegetables and salad
B. Streptococcus	2. Low acid canned foods
C. Clostridium botulinum	3. Dehydrate vegetables
D. Taenia Solium	4. Egg and meat products
E. Shigella	5. Pork and its products
	6. Cream and dairy products

Codes

	A	B	C	D	E
(a)	3	4	2	1	5
(b)	4	6	2	5	1
(c)	4	1	3	5	2
(d)	3	5	2	6	1

November 2017

6 Crystallisation of sugar occurs in

(a) Chenna Murki (b) Peanut Brittle
(c) Guava Jelly (d) Lemon Squash

7 **Assertion** (A) Cooking foods by moist heat methods like boiling increases the glycemic effect of foods.

Reason (R) Moist heat reduces the particle size of the food.

Codes

(a) Both A and R are true
(b) Both A and R are false
(c) A is true, but R is false
(d) A is false, but R is true

8 **Assertion** (A) Flavour potentiators are used to enhance the flavour of the food.

Reason (R) They exert their action of flavour enhancement by adding their own distinctive flavour.

Codes

(a) Both A and R are true
(b) A is true, but R is false
(c) Both A and R are false
(d) A is false, but R is true

9 **Assertion** (A) Addition of Soda Bicarbonate during cooking of green vegetables makes them bright green.

Reason (R) The pigment 'chlorophyll' changes to pheophytins in alkaline medium.

Codes

(a) Both A and R are true
(b) A is true, but R is false
(c) A is false, but R is true
(d) Both A and R are false

10 Match the following.

List I (Laboratory Tests)	List II (Chemical Compounds)
A. Ninhydrin test	1. Cholesterol
B. Benedict's test	2. Free fatty acids
C. Kjeldahl's test	3. Reducing sugars
D. Iodine value	4. Ascorbic acid
E. 2, 6 dichlorophenol indophenol test	5. Amino acid
	6. Nitrogen
	7. Unsaturation of fats

Codes

	A	B	C	D	E
(a)	6	3	1	2	7
(b)	2	3	4	7	1
(c)	5	3	6	7	4
(d)	6	3	1	2	4

January 2017

11 Following are the properties of egg.

1. Binding
2. Browning
3. Emulsifying
4. Fermenting
5. Thickening
6. Leavening

Codes

(a) 2, 3, 4, 6 (b) 1, 2, 5, 6
(c) 1, 3, 5, 6 (d) 3, 4, 5, 6

12 **Assertion** (A) Mayonnaise is considered as a permanent emulsion.

Reason (R) Sugar, salt and acids are used as stabiliser in mayonnaise.

Codes

(a) Both A and R are true
(b) Both A and R are false
(c) A is true, but R is false
(d) A is false, but R is true

13 Match the following.

List I (Organisms Causing Food Spoilage)	List II (Modes of Transmission)
A. Taenia solium	1. Milk and milk products
B. Clostridium botulinum	2. Eggs and meat products
C. Staphylococcus aureus	3. Pork and its products
D. Streptococcus	4. Cream filled foods
E. Salmonella	5. Frozen vegetables
	6. Pickles
	7. Canned protein foods

Codes

	A	B	C	D	E
(a)	3	7	5	2	6
(b)	2	7	4	1	2
(c)	1	6	4	1	5
(d)	5	3	1	2	4

July 2016

14 The degree of unsaturation in fats is estimated by which method?

(a) Acid value (b) Saponification
(c) Benedict's method (d) Iodine value

15 Following foods have low glycemic index.

1. Cornflakes
2. Rajmah
3. White bread
4. Oats
5. Apple

Codes

(a) 1, 2 and 5 (b) 2, 4 and 5
(c) 1, 3 and 4 (d) 2, 3 and 5

16 Match the following.

List I (Nutrients)	List II (Methods of Estimation)
A. Monosaccharides	1. Microkjeldahl method
B. Ketose sugars	2. Iodine value
C. Amino acids	3. Fehlings test
D. Proteins	4. Dichlorophenol indophenol titration
E. Ascorbic acid	5. Seliwanoff's test
	6. Ninhydrin test

Codes

	A	B	C	D	E
(a)	3	5	6	1	4
(b)	3	6	2	1	5
(c)	3	2	1	6	4
(d)	3	5	4	1	4

December 2015

17 Following are the moist heat methods of cooking.

1. Simmering
2. Broiling
3. Stewing
4. Steaming
5. Sauteing

Select the correct answer using the codes given below .

(a) 1, 2 and 4 (b) 1, 3 and 4
(c) 3, 4 and 5 (d) 2, 4 and 5

18 **Assertion** (A) Consumption of foods rich in antioxidants can lower the risk of carcinogenesis.

Reason (R) Antioxidants neutralise the free radicals circulating in blood stream.

Codes

(a) Both A and R are true
(b) Both A and R are false
(c) A is true, but R is false
(d) A is false, but R is true

19 Match the following.

List I (Active Ingredients)	List II (Food Sources)
A. Selenium	1. Garlic
B. Flavonoids	2. Tomato
C. Glutathione	3. Sea food
D. Vitamin E	4. Spinach
E. Alpha lipoic acid	5. Almonds
	6. Asparagus

Codes

	A	B	C	D	E
(a)	3	1	6	5	4
(b)	5	1	4	2	6
(c)	3	2	6	1	4
(d)	4	3	5	1	6

June 2015

20 Following food is the richest source of ω - 3 fatty acids.
(a) Coconut (b) Flax seed
(c) Olives (d) Ground nut

21 Following foods have Glycemic Index less than 50%.
1. Soya bean 2. White wheat bread
3. Apple 4. Boiled rice
5. Methi
Select the correct answer using the codes given below.
(a) 1, 2 and 5 (b) 2, 3 and 4
(c) 1, 3 and 4 (d) 1, 3 and 5

22 Match the following.

List I (Active Components)	List II (Food Sources)
A. Lycopene	1. Cloves
B. Flavonoids	2. Turmeric
C. Selenium	3. Sea foods
D. Vitamin E	4. Garlic
E. Coumarin	5. Tomatoes
	6. Wheat germ

Codes

	A	B	C	D	E
(a)	5	1	4	3	2
(b)	5	1	6	4	2
(c)	3	6	1	5	2
(d)	5	4	3	6	2

23 The anti-nutritional factors present in foods of plant origin are
1. phytochemicals 2. trypsin inhibitor
3. tannins 4. antioxidants
5. phytates
Codes
(a) 2, 3 and 5 (b) 2, 3 and 4
(c) 3, 4 and 5 (d) 1, 2 and 4

24 Arrange in correct sequence the processing steps involved in manufacturing of 'black tea'.
1. Withering 2. Rolling
3. Drying 4. Fermentation
5. Blending 6. Grading
Codes
(a) 2, 3, 1, 4, 6, 5 (b) 1, 2, 4, 3, 6, 5
(c) 1, 2, 3, 4, 5, 6 (d) 2, 1, 4, 5, 3, 6

December 2014

25 Which of the following microorganisms are responsible for causing food poisoning?
1. Clostridium botulinum
2. Trichinella spiralis
3. Ascaris lumbricoides
4. Staphylococus aureus
Select the correct answer using the codes given below.
(a) 1 and 2 (b) 2 and 4
(c) 1 and 4 (d) 3 and 4

26 **Assertion** (A) Foods that provide additional health promoting benefits beyond their well-established functions of nutrients contained in them are called functional foods.
Reason (R) Bio active ingredients like probiotic, flavonoids and phytosterols possess health promoting effect.
Codes
(a) A is true, but R is false
(b) Both A and R are false
(c) A is false, but R is true
(d) Both A and R are true and R is the correct explanation of A

27 Arrange the foods in decreasing order as per their fibre content.
1. Wheat 2. Bengal gram whole
3. Banana 4. Cheeku (Sapota)
5. Methi
Codes
(a) 2, 1, 4, 3, 5 (b) 2, 1, 5, 3, 4
(c) 1, 2, 4, 5, 3 (d) 2, 1, 4, 5, 3

June 2014

28 In the preparation of paneer from milk, the pH at which case in precipitate is
(a) pH 6.5 (b) pH 4.6
(c) pH 7.5 (d) pH 3.0

29 Factors responsible for browning of cut fruits are
1. oxygen 2. phenolic compounds
3. enzymes 4. optimum pH
Codes
(a) 1, 2 and 3 (b) 2, 3 and 4
(c) 1, 3 and 4 (d) All of these

30 Match the following.

List I	List II
A. Dextrinisation	1. Mayonnaise
B. Gelatinisation	2. Peeled potatoes
C. Coagulation	3. Kneeding of dough
D. Emulsification	4. Toasted bread
E. Enzymatic browning	5. Preparation of paneer
	6. Preparation of white sauce

Codes

	A	B	C	D	E
(a)	4	3	6	1	5
(b)	3	5	6	1	2
(c)	5	4	3	1	2
(d)	4	6	5	1	2

31 Which of the following methods of cooking food use moist heat?
1. Poaching 2. Broiling
3. Sauteing 4. Stewing
5. Braising
Codes
(a) 1, 2 and 4 (b) 1, 3 and 4
(c) 1, 4 and 5 (d) 1, 2 and 3

32 Which of the following foods are rich source of omega-3 fatty acid?

1. Walnuts
2. Fish
3. Butter
4. Egg

Codes

(a) 1 and 2 (b) 2 and 4
(c) 3 and 4 (d) 1 and 3

33 **Assertion** (A) Holding temperatures of foods must be carefully watched to prevent them from coming within the danger zones of 10°C to 62°C.

Reason (R) Higher holding temperatures than necessary, are not advisable because they affect the quality of food.

Codes

(a) A is false, but R is true
(b) A is true, but R is false
(c) Both A and R are true and R is the correct explanation of A
(d) Both A and R are true, but R is not the correct explanation of A

ANSWERS

Exam Based Questions

1 (d)	2 (a)	3 (b)	4 (c)	5 (d)	6 (a)	7 (d)	8 (a)	9 (b)	10 (b)
11 (c)	12 (b)	13 (c)	14 (a)	15 (d)	16 (c)	17 (b)	18 (b)	19 (b)	20 (d)
21 (a)	22 (a)	23 (b)	24 (b)	25 (a)	26 (a)	27 (a)	28 (a)	29 (a)	30 (d)
31 (d)	32 (b)	33 (a)	34 (b)	35 (a)	36 (d)	37 (b)	38 (c)	39 (c)	40 (c)
41 (c)	42 (c)	43 (b)	44 (b)	45 (b)	46 (c)	47 (b)	48 (c)	49 (d)	50 (b)
51 (b)	52 (a)	53 (a)	54 (d)	55 (d)	56 (b)	57 (d)	58 (d)	59 (a)	60 (b)
61 (b)	62 (b)	63 (a)	64 (b)	65 (c)	66 (a)	67 (c)	68 (d)	69 (b)	70 (d)
71 (a)	72 (d)	73 (d)	74 (b)	75 (b)	76 (b)	77 (a)	78 (a)	79 (a)	80 (c)
81 (b)	82 (d)	83 (d)	84 (a)	85 (a)	86 (b)	87 (a)	88 (c)	89 (a)	90 (a)
91 (d)	92 (a)	93 (d)	94 (a)	95 (c)	96 (d)	97 (a)	98 (b)	99 (b)	100 (a)
101 (c)	102 (c)	103 (c)	104 (d)	105 (d)	106 (a)	107 (c)	108 (b)	109 (b)	

Previous Years' Questions

1 (c)	2 (c)	3 (a)	4 (d)	5 (b)	6 (a)	7 (a)	8 (b)	9 (b)	10 (c)
11 (c)	12 (c)	13 (b)	14 (a)	15 (b)	16 (a)	17 (b)	18 (a)	19 (a)	20 (b)
21 (d)	22 (d)	23 (a)	24 (b)	25 (c)	26 (d)	27 (d)	28 (b)	29 (d)	30 (d)
31 (c)	32 (a)	33 (d)							

Food Quality, Safety and Standards

The food quality and safety are very important in the modern times. To ensure that the food processing environment is as clean as possible in order to produce safest possible food for the consumers. To ensure food quality and safety food standards are set in India and in other countries too.

Food Quality

The quality of food that a human being consumes is of immense importance as food plays a very vital role in the growth, development and existence of an individual. Contamination of food during manufacturing process will be harmful to an individual when he/she consumes it.

Therefore, quality of food must be monitored daily to ensure that it meets the required quality standards. Manufacturing units must monitor their raw materials, work in progress and finished products. Now and improved storage facilities should be developed to discourage spoilage and destruction. Quality includes both external and internal factors of food item. External factors include size, shape, colour and consistency while internal factors are its physical and chemical compositions.

Quality refers to the degree of excellence of a food. It includes all the characteristics that make the food acceptable.

Evaluation of Food Quality

To evaluate the means to critically examine or assess the purity of food. Hence, quality of food can be evaluated by two methods :

- Sensory/Subjective Method of Evaluating Food
- Objective Method of Evaluating Food

In this Chapter

Sensory/Subjective Method of Evaluating Food

When the quality of food is assessed by means of human sensory organs such as eyes (sight), nose (smell), tongue (taste), skin (feel), it is called sensory evaluation.

Following characteristics of food can be analysed this way :

Appearance and Texture This includes size, shape, colour and texture of food. For example, idli is solid round, white colour, soft and spongy, and has pores on its surface.

Taste and Flavour Food must be tasty and delicious for it to be palatable and readily consumed and to satisfy an individual's hunger.

Consistency This characteristic of food signifies whether it is in solid or liquid form. Semi-solid food includes curd, custard pudding and various chutneys, etc.

Types of Tests for Sensory Evaluations

Food scientists and sensory specialists have classified tests as :

- consumer-oriented (affective)
- product-oriented (analytical)

Consumer-Oriented or Affective Tests

These evaluate the preference or degree of liking for food products by customers. These tests are conducted using untrained consumers in their panel. Preference, acceptance and hedonic (degree of liking) tests are consumer-oriented. Hedonic tests are used to measure indirectly the preference for food products while in preference and acceptance tests, panelists can indicate their liking directly.

Product-Oriented Tests

These are conducted in food testing laboratories using trained laboratory panels. The following tests are included in this category :

- difference tests
- scoring for intensity tests
- ranking for intensity tests
- descriptive analysis tests

Difference Tests These determine whether two samples can be distinguished from each other by sensory analysis. Difference tests are used to determine a noticeable changes in the appearance, flavour, texture of food during storage, change in processing method or while altering its ingredient. The triangle test is the most common type of difference test used to determine perceptible differences between two samples of food.

In Ranking for Intensity Tests The trained panelists rank coded samples from most intense (very strong) to least intense (weak) specific characteristic of food. For example, the seed coat toughness of beans was compared under different conditions of temperature and humidity for three months.

In Scoring for Intensity Tests The perceived (visible) intensity (strength) of specific characteristic of food (For example, hardness of bean seed coat) is coded from low intensity to high (strong) intensity in a food sample. The hardness of beans was compared by cooking five times.

In Descriptive Analysis Tests Panelists score the intensity of multiple characteristics in a sample, instead of single characteristic, such as appearance, odour, flavour, texture and after taste. It is similar to scoring intensity test in which the coding of sample is from low to high intensity.

Objective Method of Evaluating Food Quality

The objective test only measures one characteristic of food rather than its overall quality. This characteristic must have a major effect on quality. Objective methods are used to test routine quality of food products with the help of physical and chemical techniques. These tests identify contaminants present in food, faulty processing methods used, deterioration and rancidity in food. These tests must be correlated with sensory testing to measure overall acceptability of a food product.

Comparison of Sensory and Objective Evaluation

Sensory Evaluation	Objective Evaluation
Expensive and time consuming.	Inexpensive and efficient.
Gives judgement of overall acceptability of product.	Measures only one aspect of food.
Required for research and development.	Essential for routine quality control of food products.
Uses individuals.	Uses equipment.
Results may vary.	Results are repeatable.
Involves human sensory organs.	Uses physical and chemical techniques.
Determines human sensitivity to changes in ingredients, processing or packaging.	Need to find a technique appropriate for the food being tested.

Food Standards

A food standard is a document providing specifications and guidelines to ensure that materials and processes used to manufacture food are deemed fit for consumption; and meet minimum specifications for quality and safety. Standardisation is, therefore, a process of ensuring uniformity in products and services by use of appropriate standards. These guidelines are known as food standards. Food standards are a set of criteria that food must follow in order to be fit for human consumption. It covers aspects such as composition, appearance, freshness, permissible additives and maximum bacterial content.

As a result of these standards, food must be free from contamination and adulteration. It helps to safeguard the health of consumers. It ensures confidence within the population, in the food system. It communicates product quality and safety to consumers.

Aims and objectives of Food Standards are :

- To protect the health of consumers by reducing food related risks.
- To support public health by maintaining and enhancing nutritional quality of food.
- To ensure supply of hygienic, high grade, unadulterated food to all.

Types of Standards

There are four levels of standards which are well coordinated :

Company Standards These are prepared by a company for its own use.

Regional Standards These are prepared by regional groups under similar geographical area or climate.

National Standards These are issued by the national standards body.

International Standards These are published by international bodies like ISO (The International Organisation for Standardisation).

- CAC (Codex Alimentarius Commission)
- (WTO) World Trade Organisation

Food Standards Regulations in India

FSSAI, Fruit and Vegetable Product Order and Voluntary Product Certification are Food Standards Regulations in India. Their description is given below:

FSSAI

The FSSAI (Food Safety and Standards Authority of India) was established under the Food Safety and Standards Act, 2006. The Act is a consolidating statute related to food safety and regulation in India. The FSSAI has been created for laying down science based standards for articles of food and to control their manufacture, storage, allotment, sale and import to make sure availability of safe and decent food for human consumption. All entities involved in manufacturing, storing, transportation or selling of food products are required to obtain FSSAI registration and comply with FSSAI regulations. Thus, FSSAI is responsible for protecting and promoting public health through regulations and supervision of food safety.

Advantages of FSSAI

This Act has provisions for those regulations that were not specified in PFA.

- Maintenance of hygienic conditions in and around manufacturing premises.
- Assessing and managing factors, in a scientific manner risky to human health.
- This Act also reflects an international shift in food laws from compositional or vertical standards to safety or horizontal standards.

List of Bans Imposed by FSSAI

The FSSAI have been executing a few changes to promote higher standards in food quality in India. These bans have been enforced in light of a legitimate concern for overall population health and sanitation. The following seven imperative bans have been enforced by FSSAI on the food industry :

- Ban on plastic and newspaper in food packaging.
- Ban on stapler pins in tea bags.
- Ban on carbide for artificial ripening of fruits.
- Ban on 'non-veg' silver leaf in Indian desserts (also known as Chandi-ka-vark).
- Ban on toulene printing in food packages.
- Ban on business-listing on unregistered FBOs (Food Business Operators) on e-commerce sites.
- Ban on health supplements as medicines.

Fruit and Vegetable Product Order

The orders to ensure quality of foods are Fruit Products Order, Meat Products Control Order and Vegetable Oil Control Order, Milk and Milk Product Order, etc. Their description is given below :

Fruit Products Order

FPO came under the Essential Commodities Act in the year 1955. Under the provisions of FPO, it is obligatory to obtain a licence for manufacturing fruit products. This act has laid down hygienic and sanitary requirements for setting-up factories to manufacture the fruit products which include :

- suitable location.
- minimum fly-proof requirement and adequate storage space.
- construction and maintenance of factory premises.
- worker's amenities and personal hygiene.

Packing fruits and vegetables of a below standard prescribed by this order is an offence, punishable by law. This mark is a certification mark mandatory on all processed fruit products sold in India such as packaged fruit beverages, fruit jams, crushes and squashes, dehydrated fruit products, and fruit extracts, following the Food Safety and Standards Act, 2006. The FPO standards are concerned with the standards required for maintaining the quality of fruits and vegetables and products manufactured from them.

The FPO also specifies the conditions of hygiene and sanitation required to be maintained by the manufacturer of F and V products. The specification for labelling of packaging of these products has been laid down.

Meat Products Control Order (MPCO)

According to the provisions of this order, it is illegal to transport meat unless, it has been prepared and processed and should carry the mark of inspection. It provides means to :

- detect and destroy meat of diseased animals.
- ensure that the preparation and handling of meat and meat products should be conducted in a clean and sanitised manner.
- prevent the use of harmful substances in meat products.
- see that every piece of meat is inspected before sale to ensure wholesomeness.
- This standard relates to the quality of meat products manufactured for sale. Quality refers to the health of the animal being slaughtered under hygienic conditions and the microbial quality of meat.

Vegetable Oil Control Order (VOCO)

This specifies the standards desired for edible oil and hydrogenated fat to be marketed. The Directorate of Vanaspati, Vegetable Oils and Fats holds the responsibility for implementation of the standards of quality of the vegetable oil product mainly at the manufacturing stage.

Milk and Milk Product Order (MMPO)

The MMPO provides for setting up of an advisory board to advise the government on production, sale, purchase and distribution of milk. The main objective of the order is to maintain and increase the supply of liquid milk of required quality. It also regulates the production, processing and distribution of milk and milk products.

Voluntary Product Certification

The voluntary grading and marking schemes include the following :

BIS Mark The BIS (Bureau of Indian Standards) standardises consumer goods including food products, running a voluntary and mandatory certification scheme called 'ISI' mark for processed goods. The products include infant foods packaged drinking water. This mark ensures that the product confirms to the Indian standards mentioned by Indian Standard Institute. It was formerly known as Indian Standards Institution (ISI).

AGMARK Standards It is a voluntary scheme of certification. These standards are formulated on the physical and chemical characteristics of food, both natural as well as those acquired during processing.

Products graded under AGMARK include vegetable oils, ghee, milk products gur, eggs, groundnuts, potatoes, fruits, pulses and spices. These standards ensure accurate weights and correct selling practices. It mainly certifies raw and processed agricultural products for safeguarding health of consumers.

ECOMARK This system launched by the BIS in 1991 was introduced to preserve the environment from pollutants. The mark ensures the consumer that products do not produce hazardous waste materials, which are biodegradable and can be recycled. Food items covered include edible oil, tea, coffee, beverages, infant food, processed foods alongwith food additives, preservatives and packaging materials.

C *Vegetarian and Non-vegetarian Mark*

In 2006, Food Safety and Standards (Packaging and Labelling) Act was passed which implemented packaging regulations in India. According to the law, vegetarian packaged food should be identified by green symbol and non-vegetarian packaged food with a brown or red symbol. It is mandatory for all manufacture since 2011.

International Organisations and Agreements in Food Standards

There have been several international organisations that have played an active role in enhancing food safety, quality and facilitating research. The three major organisations are as follows :

Codex Alimentarius Commission (CAC) It is the most important international body for developments associated with food standards. Its main objective is to establish international standards to protect consumer health and facilitate food and agricultural trade.

CAC publishes a document called 'Codex Alimentarius' meaning 'Food Code'. This document is a collection of internationally adopted food standards, to ensure fair practices in food trade. Different countries use codex standards to develop their national standards.

'Codex India' is the National Codex Contact Point (NCCP) for India. It coordinates and promotes codex activities in India with the National Codex Committee, and is located at the Directorate General of Health Services (DGHS).

International Organisation for Standardisation (ISO) It is a world wide, non-governmental federation of national standards bodies. Its mission is to develop standardisation, to facilitate international exchange of goods and services and other related activities.

The work done by ISO results in international agreements that are published as International Standards. ISO 9000 is an international reference for quality requirements, which is concerned with 'Quality Management'. The adoption of these standards is voluntary.

Difference between Codex and ISO

Codex	ISO
Used to develop national regulations.	Voluntary
Slow to change	Standards are reviewed every five years
Describe minimal acceptable practices	Describe current standard industrial practices

World Trade Organisation (WTO) It was established in 1955 and covers goods, services and intellectual properties. Its main objective is to help in the smooth, free and fair flow of trade practices.

Food Control System

A strong food control system is required to enforce adoption and implementation of food standards. An effective food control system must consists of :

- Food Inspection
- Analytical Capability

Food Inspection This kind of inspection verifies conformity of products to standards regarding production, processing, handling, storage and distribution. Food inspectors are appointed by government or municipal authorities to investigate the status of quality conformation to standards in the laboratory.

Analytical Capability There is need for well-equipped laboratories to carry out food analysis and detect food contaminants, biotoxins, food borne viruses and pathogenic bacteria.

Food Adulteration

Adulteration of food is defined as "the addition or subtraction of any substance to or from food so that the natural composition and quality of food substances is affected." Adulteration can be deliberate by either removing substances from food or varying the existing natural properties of food intentionally. Adulteration can also be unintentional due to ignorance, carelessness or lack of amenities for maintaining food quality.

The Prevention of Food Adulteration Act, 1954 (PFA, 1954) was enacted by the Government of India to prevent adulteration of food. The Act has undergone over 200 amendments. All food products manufactured and sold in India or imported and exported have to meet requirements under this Act.

Prevention of Food Adulteration Act

It is also known as PFA Act, 1954 is related to food sold and food adulterant. The prohibited practices under this law are as follows :

- A mixture of inferior or cheap substances.
- Extraction of certain quality ingredients from the food.
- Preparing and packing under unsanitary conditions.
- Sale of insect-infested food.
- Obtaining food from a diseased animal.
- Incorporation of poisonous component.
- Use of colouring matter or preservatives other than approved ones.
- Sale of sub-standard products which may be injurious to health.

Process for Checking Food Adulteration

The implementation and enforcement of Food Safety and Standards Act, 2006 rests with State Governments. Random samples of food items are drawn by the state food safety officers and sent to laboratories recognised by the FSSAI for analysis. In cases, where samples are found to contain adulterants, action is taken as per the provisions of FSSAI Act.

Food Safety Management System

A food hazard can enter the food at any stage of the food chain. Therefore, adequate control throughout the food chain is essential. Food safety and quality management system can be optimised through the following :

- Good Manufacturing Practices (GMP)
- Good Handling Practices (GHP)
- Hazard Analysis Critical Control Points (HACCP)

GMP

These practices are part of quality assurance by manufactures to minimise or eliminate contamination and false labelling to ensure the safety of their products. GMP is an effective business tool to improve and refine performance by the manufacturers.

GHP

This is a comprehensive approach from farm to consumer to identify and minimise risk of contamination. It ensures that people handling food must have good hygiene practices. To protect themselves, multinational food manufactures, retailers and grocers are asking their suppliers to implement a food safety management system.

The Global Food Safety Initiative (GFSI) has bench marked a number of Food Safety Management Systems Certification Programmes, all of which are HACCP marked. Some of the Certification Programmes are SQF, FSSC 2000, BRC, IFS, etc. Their description is given below :

SQF (Safe Quality Food) It is a rigorous and credible food safety and quality program recognised by retailers, brand owners, and food service providers worldwide.

FSSC 22000 The Food Safety System Certification 22000 offers a complete certification scheme for auditing and Certification of Food Safety Management Systems. This scheme is widely accepted by Accreditation Bodies worldwide and supported by important stakeholders like Food Drink Europe (FDE) and Grocery Manufacturers Association (GMA).

BRC (British Retail Consortium) It campaigns for the retail industry and is recognised for its powerful campaigning. It is a provider of in-depth retail information.

IFS (International Featured Standards) The IFS Food Standard is a GFSI recognised standard for auditing food manufacturers. The focus is on food safety and the quality of processes and products. It concerns food processing companies and companies that pack loose food products.

HACCP

HACCP stands for Hazard Analysis and Critical Control Point. Awareness of food-borne illness is increasing and concern throughout the industry is driving the use of HACCP and HACCP based certification programs. HACCP is an internationally recognised system for reducing the risk of safety hazards in food, including the analysis and control of biological, chemical and physical hazards from raw material production, procurement and handling.

It spans the manufacturing, distribution and consumption areas of the finished product. A HACCP system requires that potential hazards are identified and controlled at specific points in the process. HACCP plans are prepared for each process or product, and identify possible hazards and control to make sure that these are eliminated or controlled to ensure acceptable levels in the food products.

Seven Principles of HACCP

The seven principles of HACCP are detailed as :

Conduct a Hazard Analysis Here evaluation of processes and identification of hazards can be introduced. Hazards can be :

- physical (metal contamination)
- chemical (contamination by toxins)
- biological (contamination by bacteria or virus)

Then an evaluation of the hazards by an expert is done. This evaluation is a determination of the degree of risk to the user from the identified hazard. Then critical control points are identified. Critical control points are points where the hazard must be controlled or it will present a risk to the end user.

Identify the Critical Control Points A Critical Control Point (CCP) is a point, step or procedure at which control can be applied and a food safety hazard can be prevented, eliminated or reduced to acceptable levels. The HACCP team will use a CCP decision tree to help identify the critical control points in the process. A critical control point may control more than one food safety hazard or in some cases more than one CCP is needed to control a single hazard. The number of CCPs needed depends on the processing steps and the control needed to assure food safety.

Establish Critical Limit A Critical Limit (CL) is the maximum and/or minimum value to which a biological, chemical or physical parameter must be controlled at a CCP to prevent, eliminate or reduce to an acceptable level the occurrence of a food safety hazard. The critical limit is usually a measure such as time, temperature, water activity (aw), pH weight or some other measures that are based on scientific literature and/or regulatory standards.

Monitor CCP The HACCP team will describe monitoring procedures for the measurement of the critical limit at each critical control point. Monitoring procedures should describe how the measurement will be taken, when the measurement is taken, who is responsible for the measurement and how frequently the measurement is taken during production.

Establish Corrective Action Corrective actions are the procedures that are followed when a deviation in a critical limit occurs. The HACCP team will identify the steps that will be taken to prevent potentially hazardous food from entering the food chain and the steps that are needed to correct the process. This usually includes identification of the problems and the steps taken to assure that the problem will not occur again.

Verification Those activities, other than monitoring, that determine the validity of the HACCP plan and that the system is operating according to the plan. The HACCP team may identify activities such as auditing of CCPs, record review, prior shipment review, instrument calibration and product testing as part of the verification activities.

Record Keeping A key component of the HACCP plan is recording information that can be used to prove that the food was produced safely. The records also need to include information about the HACCP plan. Record should include information on the HACCP team, product description, flow diagrams, the hazard analysis, the CCPs identified, critical limits, monitoring systems, corrective actions, record keeping procedures, and verification procedures.

Other Programmes of HACCP

The application of HACCP does not stand alone in a food processing facility. The plan must be built on other safety food programmes. Good Manufacturing Practices (GMPs) that are practiced by the processing facility will support HACCP plan and will address food safety and food quality issues that are not critical for the reduction of food safety hazards. Sanitation Standard Operating Procedures (SSOPs) are required in federally inspected meat and poultry operations, and address procedures for clean facilities, equipments and personal that are necessary for all products produced in a facility.

Microbiological Safety of Food

Food fulfils all our nutritional requirements, but it can also be a carrier of microorganisms and other substances, which can cause harm to our body. Food, that we need for our living, growth and maintenance also provide material for the growth of microorganisms which can cause great harm to us.

Therefore, it is very important that through all the stages of producing, handling, storage, preparation and serving, food is kept safe from such contamination.

The microbiology of the main raw product is important. Excessive mold mycelium in the raw fruit which is indicative of the presence of rotten parts may lead to condemnation of the canned or frozen product.

Large number of the modusic bacteria in raw milk may yield a pasteurised milk that will not meet the bacterial standards for numbers as estimated by the standards plate count method. Large numbers of bacteria on vegetables or in fruits may indicate inferiority of the frozen products.

There are chances for microorganisms to grow in a food product during handling and processing of the plant. To reduce contamination with microorganisms and to obtain good keeping quantity of the product, the raw materials should be examined, the equipment contacting the food should be adequately cleaned, samitised and tested, the preserving process should be checked and packaging and storage should be checked.

There are more than 400 different viruses that cause disease in humans. AIDS (Acquired Immune Deficiency Syndrome) is a disease caused by a virus called HIV (Human Immuno Deficiency Virus).

Categories of Food Contaminants

Food contaminants can be grouped into two categories :

- Contamination due to microorganisms.
- Contamination due to chemicals.

Food contamination due to microorganisms have already been discussed in the chapter. A little detail of chemical contaminants is given below :

Substances that are not supposed to be present in food and can cause injury to human health are called as contaminants. Pesticides are example of chemical contaminant. Pesticides get accumulated in our bodies with the food we eat and can cause abnormalities in the functioning of vital organs and body systems such as the kidney, circulatory system (blood) and brain. Besides pesticides, chemicals that may reach into food from packaging material or trace amounts of lubricants that can get into the food from processing machinery are unintentional contaminants in our food. Some of the major chemical contaminants and their health hazards are given in the following table:

Major Chemical Contaminants of the Food

Contaminant	Foods Involved	Health Effects
Poly Chlorinated Biphenyls (PCBs)	Fish, milk, poultry, eggs, meat, processed and packaged food	Eye inflamation, severe skin problems, hair loss, reproductive problems, liver damage, male sterility, learning problems and other abnormalities in children, if mothers are exposed to PCBs
Mercury	Fish from polluted water, seeds treated with mercury fungicides, plants grown close to polluted water, milk from cattle grazing on contaminated plants	Severe abdominal pains with nausea, vomiting, diarrhoea, damage to kidney and liver, damage to brain and central nervous system, loss of concentration, loss of vision, paralysis and emotional disturbances
Cadmium	Aquatic plants and animals, food stuffs from soil where sewage and industrial wastes are dumped or treated with phosphate fertilizers, processed foods and cigarettes (one cigarette may have 2 micro grams of cadmium, 10% of which may be inhaled as smoke	Kidney stones, increased excretion in urine of calcium and amino acids (from proteins) kidney damage and multiple fractures
Lead	Water, liver and kidney of animals agricultural produce from orchards treated with a pesticide lead arsenate or from places close to roads with heavy traffic, canned food especially acidic food, canned milk and milk products	Nausea, sleeplessness, constipation, fatigue, abdominal pain, anaemia, abortions, still births, neonatal deaths, irreversible changes in the kidneys and brain, paralysis, convulsions, mental disorders and permanent retardation in children

Microbiology

The study of microorganisms, that inhibit, create or contaminate food is called food microbiology. The focus of this study is on the detection and analysis of food borne illness, its causes, identifying disease causing microbes, measures to control them and also how to make the best use of them. Microbiology is related to different fields such as development of pharmaceutical products, food and dairy products and other industrial applications.

Food Borne Diseases

Food borne diseases include those diseases resulting from the consumption of any solid food or milk, water or other beverage. Food borne diseases may be due to bacterial contamination of food, because of mycotoxins or viruses and also because of parasitic worms like round or flatworms, protozoa and flukes and from the consumption of food contaminated with toxic substances. Foods consumed raw are the possible sources of pathogens. Fresh fruits or vegetables, may carry pathogens from a diseased handler to a healthy consumer. Foods may be contaminated with microorganisms from food handlers, food utensils, air, soil and water, from the animals from which meat or milk is obtained and other agents such as flies, roaches and rodents. The carriers of microorganisms could also be the people, who handle foods after pasteurisation, cooking or other processing *e.g.* cooks and helpers in the kitchen, waiters in the eating place, sellers of unwrapped foods such as candies, ice-creams, sandwiches, baked goods and frozen desserts.

Most of the diseases transmitted by pathogenic organisms are intestinal or respiratory. Some of the intestinal diseases are typhoid and paratyphoid fevers, bacillary and ameobic dysentries and cholera. Diseases of the throat and respiratory tract are tuberculosis, scarlet fever, diphtheria and septic sore throat. All food borne diseases are subdivided into poisonings and infections. Food poisonings can be the result of either chemical poisonings or the ingestion of a toxicant (intoxication). A bacterial food intoxication refers to food borne illnesses caused by the presence of a bacterial toxin formed in the food. A bacterial food infection refers to food borne illnesses caused by the entrance of bacteria into the body through ingestion of contaminated foods and the reactions of the body to their presence or to their metabolites.

Agents of Food Borne Diseases

Description of some common agents of food borne diseases is given below :

Bacteria

Bacteria are the simplest of creatures that are considered alive. Bacteria are everywhere. They are in the bread, the soil that plants growing and even inside of man and woman. They are very simple cells that fall under the heading prokaryotic. That means they do not have an organised nucleus. Bacteria are small single cells whose purpose in life is to replicate. Food infections caused by bacteria can be divided into two types :

- Those in which the food does not support growth of the pathogens, but merely carries them. e.g. pathogens causing tuberculosis, diphtheria, dysenteries, typhoid fever, cholera, infections hepatitis, Q-fever, etc.
- Those in which the food can serve as a culture medium for growth of the pathogens to numbers that will increase the likelihood of infection of the consumer of the food. *e.g.* Salmonella spp, Vibrio Para Haemoly- ticerss and Enteropathogenic Escherichia Coli.

Food Borne Diseases Caused by Bacteria

Some food borne diseases with their etiologic agents, 'bacteria' are given below :

Enteropathogenic Escherichia Coli (EEC)

E coli is generally regarded as part of the normal flora of the human intestinal tract and that of many animals. Serotypes of E coli, which have been implicated in human diarrheal diseases or food poisonings have been designated as Enteropathogenic Escherichia Coli (EEC). The foods which are highly contaminated or inadequately preserved or refrigerated allow the growth of such bacteria.

Salmonellosis It is the most frequently occurring bacterial food infection caused by salmonella typhi and salmonella stanleyville.

Botulism It is a disease caused by the ingestion of food containing the neurotoxin produced by Clostridium Botulinum.

Staphylococcus Food Intoxication It is one of the most commonly occurring food poisonings, caused by the ingestion of the enterotoxin formed in food during growth of certain strains of staphylococcus aurens. The toxin is termed as *enterotoxin,* because it causes gastro- enteritis or inflammation of the living of the intestinal tract.

Campylobacter

C Jejum and C coli are most frequently associated with acute gastro-enteritis in humans. Campylobacter are widespread in foods of animal origin. Other bacterial food-borne infections include :

- Streptococcus faecalis
- Shigellosis
- Bacillus cereus
- Vibrio parahaemolyticus infection
- Aeromonas hydrophilia

Non-bacterial food borne poisonings, infections and intoxications, some of the food borne diseases are not caused by bacteria or their toxins. They are caused from mycotoxins, viruses, parasitic worms or protozoa or from the consumption of food contaminated with toxic substances.

Mycotoxins

They are the fungal metabolites and are highly toxic to many animals and human beings. Mycotoxins can cause chronic as well as acute diseases in humans when ingested from contaminated foods. The diseases includes gastrointestinal disturbances, problems in immune system and reproductive system and cancers and tumors of different organs. Mycotoxins occur mainly in cereal grains (barley, maize, rye, wheat), coffee, dairy products, fruits, nuts and spices. Different mycotoxins are Fungi, Aflatoxin, Patulin, Ochratoxin, Luteoskyrin, Sterigmatocystin, Penicillic acid, Roquefor tine, etc.

Viruses

Viruses are ultramicroscopic in size and able to pass through most bacterial filters. Viruses are able to infect people, animals and plants. Some of the diseases caused by viruses in humans are as follows :

- Inflectious Hepatitis
- Encephalitis
- Measles
- Mumps
- Small Pox
- Yellow Fever

Viruses Implicated In Food-Borne Outbreaks

Illness	Causative Agent	Foods Usually Involved	Signs and Symptoms	Measures to Prevent Spread by Food
Poliomyelitis	Poliovirus types I, II, III	Milk, possibly other beverages and prepared foods	Fever, vomiting, headache pain in muscle groups, paralysis	Personal cleanliness, adequate heating of foods, disinfection of water prevention of contact of flies with foods
Infectious hepatitis	Infectious hepatitis virus (or viruses)	Milk and other beverages, shellfish (raw oysters and clams), specific toods served as part of a meal, such as potato salad	Jaundice in approximately one-half of cases, loss of appetite, gastro-intestinal disturbance	Cooking of shellfish; checking personnel handling, food, adequate heating of milk and foods adequate heating
Acute non-bacterial gastroenteritis	Coxsackie and ECHO viruses; viral agents as yet unidentified	Possibly food-borne, but as yet this mode of transmission is unestablished	Fever, constitutional symptoms, headache, abdominal pain, vomiting and diarrhoea	Probably the same as for poliomyelitis

Enteric Viruses

Food and waterborne viruses contribute to a substantial number of illnesses throughout the world.

Among those most commonly known are hepatitis A virus, rotavirus, astrovirus, enteric adenovirus, hepatitis E virus and the human calliciviruses consisting of the noroviruses and the sapporo viruses.

This diverse group is transmitted by the fecal-oral route, often by ingestion of contaminated water and food.

Yeast

Microorganisms like yeast causes fermentation in food products. Yeast is often used in preparing foods like bread, dhoklas and idlis, but if the fermentation is more, then after a certain point, it causes spoilage of food.

Spoilage depends upon the extent to which alcohol is produced due to fermentation fruit juice, tomato sauce, sqashes, etc., spoil easily due to yeast fermentation.

Moulds

Moulds are minute plants which grow on warm, damp and dark places, preferably on all kinds of foods. They look ugly when growing on food. For example, the black hairy growth of moulds on bread or grey fuzzy growth on cheese.

They do not however produce harmful substances. Quite often when the growth is slight you can remove and the rest of the food without any risk.

But there are few moulds that do produce toxic materials known as mycotoxins. Aflatoxins produced by moulds growing on groundnuts is one example.

Characteristics of Some Food Borne Diseases

Disease	Etiologic Agent	Incubation Period, Signs and Symptoms	Foods Involved	Control Measures
Vibrio parahaemolyticus infection	*V parahaemolyticus*	2-48 hours, usually 12 hours, abdominal pain, diarrhoea (watery stools containing blood and mucus), usually nausea and vomiting, mild fever, chills, headache, prostration, recovery within 2-5 days	Raw foods of marine origin, saltwater fish, shellfish, crustacea, and fish products	Cook foods thoroughly, chill foods rapidly in small quantities, prevent cross contamination from saltwater fish, sanitise equipment, avoid using seawater for rinsing foods to be eaten raw or for cleaning
Enteropathogenic Escherichle coli infection	*E coli; both enterotoxigenic and invasive straline cause illness*	8-24 hours, mean 11 hours (invasive type), 8-44 hours mean 26 hours (enterotoxigenic type), invasive illness, fever chills, headache, myalgia, abdominal cramps, profuse, watery diarrhea, similar to shigellosis, enterotoxigenic illness diarrhea (rice-water stools), vomiting, dehydration, shock, similar to cholera	Coffee substitute, salmon, cheese	Chill foods rapidly in small quantities, cook foods thoroughly, practice personal hygiene; prepare foods in sanitary manner, protect and treat water; dispose of sewage in sanitary manner
Bacillus cereus	*Diarrheal, syndrome, diarrheagenic toxin*	8-16 hours or 1.5-5 hours, nausea, abdominal cramps, watery diarrhoea, some vomiting	Custards, cereal products, puddings, sauces, meat loaf	Chill foods rapidly in small quantities, hold hot foods at 65 °C or above, practice personal hygiene, process and prepare food in sanitary manner, reheat leftover foods to 71.1°C
Gastroenteritis	*Emetic Syndrome, emetic toxin*	Incubation period 1-6 hours, 2-5 most common, with nausea and vomiting predominant, similar to staphylococcal intoxication), short duration, 1 day or less	Fried rice, mashed potatoes, vegetable sprouts	
Shigellosis (bacillary dysentery)	Shigella sonnei, S flexneri, S dysenteriae, S boydii	1-7 days usually less than 4 days, extremely variable, mild to severe symptoms, abdominal cramps, fever, chills, diarrhoea, watery stools (frequently containing blood, mucus or pus), tenesmus, headache, lassitude, prostration, nausea, dehydration	Moist, mixed foods, milk, beans, potato, tuna, shrimp, turkey and macaroni salads, apple cider and poi	Practice personal hygiene, chill foods rapidly in small quantities, prepare food in sanitary manner, cook foods thoroughly, protect and treat water, dispose of sewage in sanitary manner, control flies
Yersininsis	Yarsinia pseudotuberculosis, Y enterocolitica	24-36 hours and longer abdominal pain suggesting acute appendicitis, fever, headache, malaise, anoexia, diarrhoea, vomiting, nausea, chills, pharyngities, leukocytosis, erythema nodosum	Pork and other meats, raw milk or any contaminated raw or leftover food	Cook foods thoroughly, protect foods from contamination, control rodents
Arizona infection	Arizona hinshaw	2-46 hours, usually 24 hours, abdominal pain, diarrhea, nausea, chills, headache, weakness, fever lasts a few days	Turkey, chicken, cream-filled pastry, ice-cream, custard containing eggs	Chill foods rapidly in small quantities, cook foods thoroughly, prevent faecal contamination, avoid cross contamination from raw to cooked foods, sanitise equipment, reheat leftover foods thoroughly
Beta-hemolytic streptococcal infections (scarlet fever, septic sore throat)	Streptococcus pyogenes	1-3 days, sore and red throat, pain in swallowing, tonsillitis, high fever, headache, nausea, vomiting, malaise, rhinorrhea, occasionally a rash occurs	Milk, ice-cream, eggs, steamed lobster, potato salad, egg, salad, custard and pudding, foods usually contain eggs or milk	Chill foods rapidly in small quantities, practice personal hygiene, cook foods thoroughly, pasteurise milk, exclude workers with respiratory illness or skin lesions

EXAM BASED QUESTIONS

1 Which of the following are the internal factors of food quality?
(a) Consistency
(b) Physical and chemical compositions
(c) Size
(d) Shape and colour

2 Which method evaluates the external features of food?
(a) Subjective evaluation method
(b) Objective method
(c) Both (a) and (b)
(d) None of the above

3 Consistency of food refers to
(a) its thickness viscosity (b) its taste
(c) its odour (d) its colour

4 Hedonic tests are associated with
(a) affective tests
(b) analytical tests
(c) scoring for intensity tests
(d) difference tests

5 Which of the following tests are used to differentiate perceptible appearance of two samples using sensory analysis?
(a) Triangle test (b) Objective evaluation test
(c) Descriptive analysis test (d) Scoring for intensity test

6 In which of the following tests, multiple characteristics of a sample are analysed?
(a) Objective method (b) Descriptive analysis test
(c) Difference test (d) Scoring for intensity test

7 Which of the following is not a definition of food quality?
(a) It is the quality characteristics of food that is acceptable to consumers.
(b) It is an important food manufacturing requirement.
(c) It deals with product traceability.
(d) It is the addition or subtraction of any substance from food.

8 The FSSAI was formed in
(a) August 2012 (b) August 2010
(c) August 2011 (d) November 2011

9 Which of the Act is not under FSSAI Act?
(a) Prevention of Food Adulteration Act, 1954.
(b) Milk and Milk Products Order, 1992.
(c) Fruit Products Order, 1955.
(d) AGMARK

10 AGMARK head office is located at
(a) New Delhi (b) Faridabad (c) Chandigarh (d) Panipat

11 The implementation and enforcement of Food Safety and Standards Act, 2006 rests with …… .
(a) Central Government (b) State Government
(c) The traders (d) The scientists

12 Full form of ISO is
(a) International Space Organisation
(b) Indian Space Organisation
(c) International Organisation for Standardisation
(d) International Standardisation Organisation

13 Full form of CAC is
(a) Codex Commission Alimentarius
(b) Codex Alimentarius Committee
(c) Codex Alimentarius Commission
(d) Alimentarius Committee for Codex

14 The signs of spoilage apparent in canning can be
(a) microorganisms
(b) flat sour and hydrogen swell
(c) metallic salts and discolourations
(d) All of the above

15 Which of the following is not true about Clostridium Botulinum?
(a) Improperly canned food is contaminated by this bacteria.
(b) Honey is contaminated by this bacteria.
(c) This bacteria attacks children who do not have a normal immune system.
(d) Low acid vegetables are affected by this bacteria.

16 PFA stands for
(a) Association for Prevention of Food Adulteration.
(b) Act for Prevention of Food Adulteration.
(c) Prevention of Food Adulteration Association.
(d) Prevention of Food Adulteration Act.

17 Which of the following marks is compulsory for Indian F and V products?
(a) FPO (b) ECOMARK (c) VOCO (d) GFSI

18 Which of the following marks was introduced in 1991 to identify biodegradable products?
(a) ISO (b) ECOMARK (c) FSSAI (d) SQF

19 Which of the following international bodies is concerned with 'Quality Management' ?
(a) CAC (b) ISO (c) WTO (d) HACCP

20 What is the meaning of 'Codex Alimentarius'?
(a) A system of codes
(b) Food code
(c) Food standards
(d) A document published by ISO

21 The causal agent of human disease botulism can be classified under
(a) bacterial toxin (b) viral toxin
(c) mycotoxin (d) chemical toxin

22 The 'FSSAI' stands for ……
(a) The Food Standards and Safety Authority of India.
(b) The Food Safety and Standards Authority of India.
(c) The Food Standards and Security Authority of India.
(d) The Food Safety and Standards Association of India.

23 **Which one of the following is not true for the FSSAI?**
(a) It lays down science based standards for articles of food.
(b) It regulates the manufacture, storage, distribution and sale of food articles.
(c) It is an internationally recognised system for reducing the risk of safety hazards in food.
(d) It ensures availability of safe and wholesome food for human consumption.

24 **The FSSAI has its head-office at**
(a) Chennai (b) Mumbai
(c) Kolkata (d) New Delhi

25 **Which one of the following is not a regional office of FSSAI?**
(a) Cochin (b) Guwahati
(c) Ahmedabad (d) Delhi

26 **Reasons for testing food quality are**
1. It affects a person's health.
2. It affects a person's mental strength.
3. It does not affect a person's nutritional status.
4. It improves the appearance of food.
5. It improves the nutritional value of food.
6. It does not effect taste of food.

Codes
(a) 1, 2, 4, 5 (b) 1, 3, 4, 6
(c) 1, 3, 4, 5 (d) 1, 2, 5, 6

27 **Which of the following are a part of 'objective measurement' of food quality testing?**
1. It measures overall quality of product.
2. There in no need to change existing product in case of new product development.
3. It includes all types of instrumental analysis.
4. The test results should be correlated with sensory testing of similar product.
5. The test must be appropriate for the food product being tested.

Codes
(a) 3, 4, 5 (b) 3, 2, 5
(c) 3, 1, 5 (d) 4, 1, 5

28 **Which of the following are included in the seven imperative bans enforced by FSSAI?**
1. Stapler pins for tea bags.
2. 'Non-veg' silver leaf in Indian desserts.
3. Ban on medicines.
4. Ban on health supplements as medicines.
5. Ban on carbide for artificial ripening of fruits.

Codes
(a) 1, 3, 4, 5 (b) 2, 3, 4, 5
(c) 1, 2, 4, 5 (d) 1, 2, 3, 4

29 **Which of the following are included under flavour of food?**
1. Odour 2. Colour
3. Taste 4. Mouth feel

Codes
(a) 1, 2, 3 (b) 2, 3, 4 (c) 1, 2, 4 (d) 1, 3, 4

30 **Which one of the following refers to microbial contamination of food?**
1. Accidental introduction of microbes.
2. Food poisoning occurs before eating food contaminated by bacteria.
3. Bacteria cannot be seen, smelled or tasted.
4. Microbes include yeast, fungi and virus.

Codes
(a) 1, 2, 3 (b) 2, 3, 4 (c) 1, 3, 4 (d) 1, 2, 4

31 **Which of the following are part of High Pressure Processing (HPP)?**
1. Help in new development of product.
2. A new processing method.
3. A cold pasteurisation technique.
4. It is part of traditional thermal and chemical treatment.

Codes
(a) 1, 2, 4 (b) 1, 2, 3 (c) 1, 3, 4 (d) 2, 3, 4

32 **Consider the following statement**
1. A bacterial food intoxication refers to food borne illnesses caused by the presence of a bacterial toxin formed in the food.
2. A bacterial food infection refers to food borne illnesses caused by the entrance of bacteria into the body through ingestion of contaminated foods and the reaction of the body to their presence or to their metabolites.

Which of the statements given above is/are correct?
(a) Only 1 (b) Only 2
(c) Both 1 and 2 (d) None of these

33 **Consider the following statements**
1. The Indian Standard Institution is now called Bureau of Indian Standards.
2. Bureau of Indian Standards operates the ISI Certification Marks Act, 1952.

Which of the statements given above is/are correct?
(a) Only 1 (b) Only 2
(c) Both 1 and 2 (d) None of these

34 **Arrange in order of sequence the principles of HACCP**
1. Identify critical control points.
2. Record keeping.
3. Verification.
4. Conduct a hazard analysis.
5. Establish critical limits.

Codes
(a) 4, 1, 5, 3, 2 (b) 4, 3, 2, 1, 5
(c) 4, 1, 5, 3, 1 (d) 1, 5, 4, 2, 3

35 **Which of the following microorganisms cause food borne intoxication?**
1. Staphylococcus aureus. 2. E coli.
3. Clostridium botulinum. 4. Listeria monocytogenes.
5. Salmonella.

Select the correct answer using the codes given below
(a) 1 and 2 (b) 1 and 3 (c) 3 and 4 (d) 4 and 5

36 Arrange in order of sequence the functions of FSSAI

1. Lay guidelines for accreditation of certification bodies.
2. Framing of regulations.
3. Collect and collate data.
4. Provide training programmes.
5. Promote general awareness about food standards.

Codes

(a) 2, 1, 5, 4, 3 (b) 2, 5, 3, 1, 4
(c) 5, 1, 2, 3, 4 (d) 3, 4, 5, 2, 1

37 Which of the following tests are not used to test the routine quality of food products?

1. Objective method.
2. Ranking for intensity test.
3. Difference test.
4. Scoring for intensity test.

Codes

(a) 1, 2, 3 (b) 2, 3, 4 (c) 1, 2, 4 (d) 1, 3, 4

38 Why is it essential to maintain standards in food quality?

1. Food helps in existence of all beings.
2. Food can be consumed in its contaminated form.
3. Adulterated food is beneficial to health.
4. To enhance nutritional quality of food.

Codes

(a) 1 and 2 (b) 3 and 2
(c) 1 and 4 (d) 2 and 3

39 Which of the following is not correct about ISO?

1. It is a worldwide, non-governmental federation of national standard bodies.
2. It coordinates and promotes codex activities in India.
3. Its mission is to develop standardisation.
4. Its objective is to help in the smooth, free and fair flow of trade practices.

Codes

(a) 1, 2 and 3 (b) 2 and 4
(c) 2, 3 and 4 (d) 3 and 4

40 What is the role of a food control system?

1. To enforce adoption of food standards.
2. To implement food standards.
3. To inspect food.
4. To allow food to be contaminated.

Codes

(a) 1, 3, 4 (b) 2, 3, 4 (c) 1, 2, 3 (d) 4, 1, 2

41 Match the following.

List I	List II
A. Campylobacter	1. Poor hygiene
B. Shigellosis	2. Improperly canned food
C. Botulism	3. Poisonous mushrooms
D. Cryptosporidosis	4. Raw or uncooked chicken

Codes

	A	B	C	D
(a)	4	1	2	3
(b)	1	3	2	4
(c)	2	3	4	1
(d)	4	2	1	3

42 Match the following.

List I	List II
A. FPO	1. Agricultural produce
B. AGMARK	2. Edible oil
C. VOCO	3. Meat products
D. MPO	4. Processed fruit products

Codes

	A	B	C	D
(a)	4	2	1	3
(b)	3	4	1	2
(c)	3	2	1	4
(d)	4	1	2	3.

43 Match the following.

List I	List II
A. Scarlet fever, septic sore throat	1. Salmonella typhi
B. Typhoid fever	2. Escherichia coli
C. Colitis	3. Staphylococcus aureus
D. Bacillary dysentery	4. Streptococcus pyogenes
E. Gastroenteritis	5. Shigella sonnei

Codes

	A	B	C	D	E
(a)	2	3	5	1	4
(b)	1	2	3	4	5
(c)	5	1	2	4	3
(d)	4	1	2	5	3

44 Match the following.

List I (Contaminants)	List II (Health Effects)
A. Mercury	1. Sleeplessness
B. Cadmium	2. Loss of concentration
C. Lead	3. Eye inflamation
D. Poly Chlorinated Biphenyls (PCBs)	4. Kidney damage

Codes

	A	B	C	D
(a)	4	1	3	2
(b)	2	4	1	3
(c)	1	2	3	4
(d)	3	2	4	1

45 Match the following.

List I (Mycotoxin)	List II (Foods form which isolated)
A. Aflatoxin	1. Apple juice
B. Patulin	2. Barley
C. Penicillic acid	3. Blue cheese
D. Roquefortine	4. Dried beans

Codes

	A	B	C	D
(a)	2	1	4	3
(b)	2	1	3	4
(c)	2	3	4	1
(d)	4	3	2	1

46 Match the following diseases in List I with 'foods involved' in List II.

List I	List II
A. E Coli infection	1. Tuna and shrimp
B. Gastroenteritus	2. Cream-filled pastry
C. Bacillary dysentry	3. Cheese
D. Arizona infection	4. Cereal product

Codes

	A	B	C	D
(a)	3	4	1	2
(b)	3	2	1	4
(c)	3	1	2	4
(d)	2	4	3	1

47 Match the following.

List I	List II
A. Product oriented	1. Routine test
B. Consumer oriented	2. Triangle test
C. Difference test	3. Affective
D. Objected evaluation	4. Analytical

Codes

	A	B	C	D		A	B	C	D
(a)	4	3	2	1	(b)	4	1	2	3
(c)	3	1	2	4	(d)	3	4	1	2

48 Match the following.

List I	List II
A. Yeast	1. Fermentation
B. Moulds	2. Mycotoxin
C. AIDS	3. HIV
D. Fungi	4. Damp places

Codes

	A	B	C	D		A	B	C	D
(a)	2	1	4	3	(b)	2	3	4	1
(c)	3	4	1	2	(d)	3	1	2	4

Directions (Q. Nos. 49-66) *In the questions given below are two statemeats labelled as Assertion (A) and Reason (R). In the context of the two statements, which one of the following is correct?*

Codes

(a) Both A and R are correct.
(b) Both A and R are incorrect.
(c) A is correct and R is incorrect.
(d) A is incorrect and R is correct.

49 **Assertion** (A) The study of microorganism that inhibit create or contaminate food is called microbiology.

Reason (R) The focus of this study is on the detection and analysis of food borne illness.

50 **Assertion** (A) Food products are highly susceptible to microbial contamination.

Reason (R) Ethyl carbonate and biogenic amines may be produced as by-products of fermentation.

51 **Assertion** (A) Some food standards have been formulated.

Reason (R) These standards lay down the minimum standards for all types of food.

52 **Assertion** (A) The Indian Standard Institution is now called Bureau of Indian Standards.

Reason (R) It covers most of the consumer goods like utensils, cosmetics, electrical equipments and processed food products.

53 **Assertion** (A) Food borne diseases may be due to bacterial contamination of food.

Reason (R) Mycotoxins or viruses and also because of parasitic worms like round or flatworms, protozoa and flukes and from the consumption of food contaminated with toxic substances.

54 **Assertion** (A) Different sensory tests are employed for food evaluation.

Reason (R) To know consumer preference is one of the reasons for testing or evaluating food quality.

55 **Assertion** (A) Making water into beer made it safe to drink.

Reason (R) Fermentation can make food healthier and safer to consume.

56 **Assertion** (A) Products that produce hazardous materials are good for the environment.

Reason (R) Such products help to preserve the environment from harmful pollutants.

57 **Assertion** (A) Probiotics provide numerous health benefits.

Reason (R) These are live bacteria found in certain foods.

58 **Assertion** (A) Food fulfils all our nutritional requirements, but it can also be a carrier of microorganism and other substances which can cause harm to our body.

Reason (R) Therefore, it is very important that through all stages of producing handling storage preparation and serving food is kept safe from such contaminators.

59 **Assertion** (A) Pasteurisation in milk is done to destroy the microbes.

Reason (R) It is tested for the presence of lactic acid in milk.

60 **Assertion** (A) Most food borne is preventable.

Reason (R) Hygienic care should be taken to maintain cleanliness while preparing food.

61 **Assertion** (A) Quality is ultimate criterion of desirability of a food product.

Reason (R) Food quality can be evaluated by only subjective method.

62 **Assertion** (A) Sensory properties are not at all vital.

Reason (R) They are not apparent to consumers.

63 **Assertion** (A) Food scientists and specialists have incorporated various tests to evaluate quality of food.

Reason (R) These tests only check the physical properties of food like shape, size and colour.

64 **Assertion** (A) Food standards help to safeguard the health of consumers.

Reason (R) Company standards are prepared by a company for its own use.

65 **Assertion** (A) Chemicals may reach food from packaging material or processing machinery.

Reason (R) These substances are not supposed to be present in food and can cause injury to human health.

66 Assertion (A) There are voluntary grading and marking schemes to certify food products.
Reason (R) AGMARK certifies only processed agricultural products to safeguard health of consumers.

Directions (Q. Nos. 67-71) *Read the following passage carefully, and answer the following questions.*

The type of food we eat has both immediate and long-term effect on us, at all the three levels- the body, the mind and the spirit. Food which is Tamasik (i.e. stale or leftover) in nature is bound to generate stress as it tends to upset the normal functioning of the human body. Taking hot tea or milk or steaming hot food, whenever available, must be preferred. Excessive use of spices also disturbs one's usually calm attitude.

Further, it is a mistaken belief that smoking or drinking, even in moderation, relieves stress. Simple meals with one or two food items, rather than too many lavish dishes, are advisable. Thus, a vegetarian diet is preferable. Although it is customary to serve fruits with food, it is not the right thing to do. This is because different kind of digestive secretions is produced by the stomach for variant foods.

Mixing up too many varieties of food items at one meal creates unavoidable problems for the digestive system. In fact, any one type of fruit, preferably taken in the morning, is better. On average, we eat almost three to four times the quantity of food than we actually need. A lot of body's energy is used up for digesting the excess food. It is said that after a particular level of food intake, the food actually eats one up'. It is always good to eat less than your 'full-stomach' capacity. Besides, never eat food unless you are really hungry. In fact, skipping an odd meal is always good if the stomach is upset. There are varying views on the benefits of fasting, but we will not discuss them here.

However, giving a break to one's stomach, at least once a week, by having only fruit or milk, etc. May be worth trying. While a little bit of water taken with meals is all right, drinking too much water with food is not advisable. Water, taken an hour or so before or after meals, is good for digestion.

One's diet must be balanced with all the required nutrients for healthy living. Also remember, an excess of everything is bad. Related to the problem of stress, excessive intake of salt is. Too much of sugar, fried food and chillies are not good either.

Overindulgence and excessive craving for a particular taste/type of food generates Rajasik (aggressive) or at worst, Tamasik (dull) tendencies. An even more important aspect of the relationship between food and stress lies not so much in what or how much we eat but how the food is taken.

For example, food eaten in a great hurry or in a state of anger or any other negative state of mind is bound to induce stress. How the food is served is also very important. Finding faults with food while it is being eaten is the worst habit. It is better not to eat the food you do not like. It is good to have regular food habits.

Work aholics who do not find time to eat food at proper mealtimes are inviting stomach ulcers. One must try to enjoy one's food, and therefore, eating at the so-called lunch/dinner meetings is highly inadvisable. Every morsel of food should be enjoyed with a totally peaceful state of mind. Food and discussions should not be mixed. Prayer is perhaps 'the best method for energising the food' and it will do some definite additional well at no extra cost.

67 Which part of the body is affected most by our diet?
(a) Body only
(b) Mind only
(c) Sprit only
(d) Body, mind and sprit

68 How is a simple meal beneficial to health?
(a) It is easier to eat.
(b) It takes less time to cook.
(c) It is easily digestible.
(d) Because we eat more than we require.

69 What effect does Tamasik food have on our body?
(a) It makes us feel lethargic.
(b) It makes us feel energetic.
(c) It generates stress.
(d) It relieves stress.

70 Which of the following must not be avoided for healthy living?
(a) A balanced diet
(b) Excess salt in food
(c) Fried food and chillies
(d) Sugar intake

71 How does one's attitude affect intake of food?
(a) It is considered bad manners.
(b) It energises the food to be eaten.
(c) It enables one to fast.
(d) It results in more lunch/dinner meetings.

PREVIOUS YEARS' QUESTIONS

June 2018

1 Fermentation is used in the production of
1. Ketchup.
2. Wine.
3. Cocoa powder.
4. Marmalade.
5. Cheese.

Codes
(a) 1, 3, 4
(b) 2, 3, 5
(c) 1, 2, 3
(d) 3, 4, 5

2 Assertion (A) Food safety plan serves as an operational tool.

Reason (R) HACCP is a stand alone safety for food service unit.

Codes

(a) Both A and R are correct.
(b) Both A and R are incorrect.
(c) A is correct and R is incorrect.
(d) A is incorrect and R is correct.

November 2017

3 Assertion (A) Prebiotics help in regulating gastrointestinal functions.

Reason (R) Prebiotics get fermented in the colon, where they stimulate the growth and activity of healthy bacteria.

Codes

(a) Both A and R are correct.
(b) Both A and R are incorrect.
(c) A is correct, but R is incorrect.
(d) A is incorrect, but R is correct.

4 Match the following.

List I	List II
A. ECO MARK	1. Product certification
B. HALL MARK	2. Agricultural marketing
C. ISI MARK	3. Honesty
D. AGMARK	4. Environment friendly products
	5. Jewellery

Codes

	A	B	C	D		A	B	C	D
(a)	4	5	1	2	(b)	4	5	3	2
(c)	4	5	1	3	(d)	4	3	5	1

January 2017

5 Food Safety and Standards Act was implemented in the year.

(a) 2008 (b) 2006 (c) 2000 (d) 2010

6 Assertion (A) Dietary interventions with probiotics are recommended in diarrhoea patients.

Reason (R) Foods high in probiotics alter the gut micro flora.

Codes

(a) Both A and R are correct.
(b) A is correct and R is incorrect.
(c) A is incorrect and R is correct.
(d) Both A and R are incorrect.

7 Match the following.

List I	List II
A. CPA	1. 1969
B. MRTP	2. 1986
C. The Agricultural Produce Act	3. 1955
D. The Essential Commodities Act	4. 1937
	5. 1980

Codes

	A	B	C	D		A	B	C	D
(a)	2	1	4	3	(b)	3	5	1	2
(c)	1	4	2	5	(d)	5	3	1	2

July 2016

8 Match the following.

List I	List II
A. Agricultural marketing	1. ISI MARK
B. Environment friendly products	2. HALL MARK
C. Product certification	3. AGMARK
D. Gold Jewellery	4. TRADEMARK
	5. ECO MARK

Codes

	A	B	C	D		A	B	C	D
(a)	1	2	4	5	(b)	4	1	3	2
(c)	5	4	1	2	(d)	3	5	1	2

9 Match the following.

List I	List II
A. Micro encapsulation	1. Crinkled look
B. Antimicrobial	2. Perfumed lingerie
C. Nanotechnology	3. Combats foul odour of perspiration
D. Water proofing	4. Shower curtains
	5. Self cleaning clothes

Codes

	A	B	C	D		A	B	C	D
(a)	1	2	4	5	(b)	2	3	5	4
(c)	3	1	2	4	(d)	4	1	3	2

December 2015

10 Expanded form of FSSAI is

(a) Food Safety and Sanitation Authority of India.
(b) Food Security and Standards Authority of India.
(c) Food Standards and Safety Authority of India.
(d) Food Safety and Standards Authority of India.

11 Give the correct sequence of steps involved in the HACCP system.

1. Developing criteria for control and prevention.
2. Monitoring each critical control point.
3. Identifying critical control points.
4. Identifying and assessing hazards.
5. Taking immediate corrective action.

Codes

(a) 3, 4, 2, 1, 5 (c) 3, 4, 1, 2, 5 (b) 4, 1, 3, 2, 5 (d) 4, 3, 1, 2, 5

12 Arrange the following Acts in the ascending order of their years of enactment.

1. Environmental Protection Act.
2. MRTP. 3. PFA.
4. ISI Certification Marks Act. 5. Air Pollution Act.

Codes

(a) 4, 3, 2, 5, 1 (c) 2, 3, 1, 4, 5 (b) 4, 2, 3, 1, 5 (d) 1, 2, 3, 4, 5

13 Match the following.

List I (Quality marks)	List II (Their respective applications)
A. ECOMARK	1. Product certification
B. HALLMARK	2. Agricultural marketing
C. ISI MARK	3. Land identification
D. AGMARK	4. Environmental friendly products
	5. Organisational standards
	6. Jewellery

Codes

	A	B	C	D		A	B	C	D
(a)	4	3	1	2	(b)	4	6	1	2
(c)	1	4	6	3	(d)	4	5	1	2

June 2015

14 Give the right sequence for establishing HACCP.

1. Establish the critical points.
2. Establish the correct action.
3. Identify the critical control point.
4. Establish effective record keeping.
5. Identify hazard and assess the severity and risk.
6. Establish procedure to verify that system.
7. Establish procedure to monitor CCP.

Codes

(a) 1, 3, 4, 6, 5, 2, 7 (b) 2, 6, 4, 1, 3, 7, 5
(c) 5, 3, 1, 7, 2, 4, 6 (d) 5, 6, 4, 2, 3, 1, 7

December 2014

15 Match the following.

List I	List II
A. Consumer Protection Act	1. 1937
B. The Essential Commodities Act	2. 1976
C. The Drugs and Cosmetics Act	3. 1986
D. The (AGMARK) Agricultural Product Act	4. 1955
E. The Standards of Weight and Measures Act	5. 1940
	6. 1952

Codes

	A	B	C	D	E		A	B	C	D	E
(a)	6	4	5	1	3	(b)	1	4	5	6	2
(c)	2	6	1	5	3	(d)	3	4	5	1	2

16 Full form of FSSAI is

(a) Food Security and Standards Association of India.
(b) Food Security and Safety Authority of India.
(c) Food Safety and Standards Association of India.
(d) Food Safety and Standards Authority of India.

17 Arrange the following steps of the HACCP system in the correct sequence.

1. Identifying critical control points.
2. Developing criteria for control and prevention.
3. Identification and assessment of hazards.
4. Taking corrective action.
5. Monitoring each critical control point.

Codes

(a) 3, 1, 2, 5, 4 (b) 1, 2, 3, 5, 4
(c) 3, 2, 1, 4, 5 (d) 2, 1, 3, 5, 4

18 Match the following.

List I (Food items)	List II (Items used for food adulteration)
A. Curd	1. Sand
B. Ghee	2. Water
C. Cereals	3. Talc
D. Flour	4. Blotting paper
	5. Starch

Codes

	A	B	C	D		A	B	C	D
(a)	4	5	1	3	(b)	1	5	2	4
(c)	2	4	1	3	(d)	4	3	2	1

June 2014

19 HACCP is a preventive programme for hygienic control and food safety. Arrange the following steps of the HACCP system in their correct sequence.

1. Identifying critical control points.
2. Monitoring each critical control point.
3. Developing criteria for control and prevention.
4. Identification and assessment of hazards.
5. Taking immediate corrective action.

Codes

(a) 3, 1, 2, 5, 4 (b) 4, 1, 3, 2, 5
(c) 3, 1, 2, 4, 5 (d) 4, 3, 1, 2, 5

ANSWERS

Exam Based Questions

1 (b)	2 (a)	3 (a)	4 (a)	5 (a)	6 (b)	7 (d)	8 (c)	9 (d)	10 (b)
11 (b)	12 (c)	13 (c)	14 (d)	15 (c)	16 (d)	17 (a)	18 (b)	19 (b)	20 (b)
21 (a)	22 (b)	23 (c)	24 (d)	25 (c)	26 (a)	27 (a)	28 (c)	29 (d)	30 (c)
31 (b)	32 (c)	33 (c)	34 (a)	35 (a)	36 (a)	37 (b)	38 (c)	39 (b)	40 (c)
41 (a)	42 (d)	43 (d)	44 (b)	45 (a)	46 (a)	47 (a)	48 (b)	49 (c)	50 (a)
51 (a)	52 (b)	53 (b)	54 (a)	55 (a)	56 (b)	57 (a)	58 (b)	59 (c)	60 (a)
61 (c)	62 (b)	63 (b)	64 (c)	65 (c)	66 (b)	67 (d)	68 (c)	69 (c)	70 (a)
71 (b)									

Previous Years' Questions

1 (b)	2 (c)	3 (a)	4 (a)	5 (b)	6 (a)	7 (a)	8 (d)	9 (b)	10 (d)
11 (d)	12 (a)	13 (b)	14 (c)	15 (d)	16 (d)	17 (a)	18 (c)	19 (b)	

Food Service Management

Food service or catering industry is gaining popularity as this industry is constantly shifting to reflect the ever changing needs of the people and institutions. Nowadays people want healthy and nutritious food and this requires proper management at different levels i.e. menu planning, cost control, transporting or selling prepared foods. Thus, food service management plays important role in this industry.

Food Serving Industry

Food service or catering industry defines those businesses, institutions and companies responsible for any meal prepared outside home. This industry includes restaurants, schools, hospitals cafeterias, catering operations, etc. The food service industry encompasses all of the activities, services and business functions involved in preparing and serving food to people eating away from home.

Food service is the industry related to making, transporting or selling prepared foods to restaurants, hospitals, schools and lodging establishments.

Food service managers are responsible for the daily operation of restaurants or other establishments that prepare and serve food and beverages. They direct staff to ensure that customers are satisfied with their dining experience and they manage the business to ensure that it is profitable.

In this Chapter

Perspectives of Food Service

Menu planning and food cost analysis are the perspectives of food service. Their description is given below

Menu Planning

A menu is a list of food dishes, which includes meals, snacks or beverages for production in catering fields.

There must be sequential flow of production from its raw material to finished product.

Food management is the ability to manage (menu planning service) activities so that work flows smoothly to the point where the meal reaches the customer, and gives them physical, physiological and emotional satisfaction.

Menu planning is the 'heart' of any food service organisation, upon which all further activity is centred. The menu determines the food or ingredients to be purchased, the equipment needed and the personnel required. When food has to be bought, prepared and served in large quantities to people of varying tastes and requirements. The success of a food service organisation is dependent on its menu.

The goal of the menu is to maximise resources to produce highest quality products having greatest financial return.

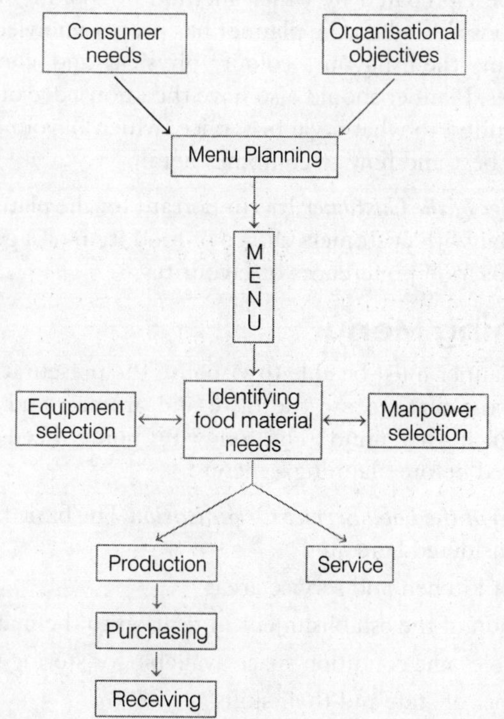

Flow chart of typical operation in a food service establishment

Functions of Menu Planning

Important functions of menu planning are :

- It provides and authorise production of meals in the kitchen.
- It helps to prepare shopping list of food and ingredients for use in the meals.
- It introduces interesting food combinations to customers.
- It also provides the knowledge of foods eaten in different states, countries and cultures.
- It provides means of developing good eating habits in people.
- It serves as a control and spells out the monetary prerequisites for purchasing food, hiring personnel and using appropriate equipment for production and service.

Advantages of Menu Planning

Advantages of menu planning are :

- Planning meals help to determine requirements accurately.
- An ability to provide appetising, nourishing and attractive meals to customers at a fair price. This is only possible, if the meals are planned in advance, so that price advantage can be obtained by buying seasonal food and in quantities which carry discounts.
- Time and effort spent on haphazard ordering. Shopping and receiving of food materials is saved to greater extent.
- Time and effort spent in preparation and cooking is also minimised because ingredients needed for subsequent meals are known in advance.
- Carefully planned menus save and cut down on waste through excessive leftovers.
- Planned menus help to note favourite dishes and those which did not sell too well in the past. It also tend to offer a wider choice of dishes because seasonal varieties of foods can be introduced in advance.
- Advance planning removes a lot of anxiety for the planner and enables clear-cut instructions to be given to staff.
- Meal planning helps in the accurate calculation of food costs and inclusion of items that can be profitably sold.

Types of Menu

Menus can be planned for commercial operations such as restaurants or for welfare operations. The objective of welfare operations is to provide nutritionally adequate, reasonably priced meals for the target groups and to foster good eating habits. Menus are basically of three types :

- A la carte
- Table d' hote
- A combination of the two

A la Carte Menu

This menu is basically a choice menu and generally offers choice of dishes or items to customers under different food categories such as starters, soups, main dishes, side dishes, salads, desserts, sandwiches, snacks, etc.

The advantage of a la carte menu is that customers can choose the items as per his own needs, moods and pocket.

Table d'hote Menu

Table d'hote means table of the host. This menu is a set menu in which a number of dishes are planned by the host and food served at a set price. A typical table d'hote menu is served in India in the form of thali meals in some establishments and on trains.

Combination Menu

This menu combines the tela carte and table d'hote menu. For example, A la carte menu offers a combination of riceslash breads, vegetables, potatoes in the entree dish price. On the other hand the table d'hote menu offers an option of the whole meal or a choice of individually priced appetisers or dessert from the menu.

Menu Display

The menu can perform its rightful function only if the customer can see and read it clearly on or before entering a food service establishment. Menus may be displayed in many ways :

- Plastic letters can be used on menu board for writing the dish name. These can easily be re-arranged to change the name of dishes in day-to-day life. Such type of display is neat and clear. Its effect can be enhanced by using contrasts in colour such as white on black or red on white boards.
- In small kiosks, canteens or mobile catering vans, menus are displayed on black boards written out with chalk.
- In coffee shops and cafeterias where a number of customers handle the menu to make their selections printed or neatly typed menus may be inserted in plastic cases and displayed.
- Printed booklets placed in attractive waterproof folders are a method of presenting menus to customers in restaurants offering extensive choices.
- In hostels or other institutions typed menus are displayed on notice boards outside diving areas.
- Menus must be written in a form that is simple, legible and attractive to draw the customer's attention.
- Names of dishes should be clearly understood. Descriptions should follow unfamiliar names so that customer knows what to order.

Knowledge and Skills Required for Planning Menu

The success of a food service establishment depends on those who plan the menus. Good menu planning requires a lot of skills. Usually, it is the management or the owner of the establishment who determines the menu. Other sources may include the cook/chefs or the customers.

The person responsible for planning a menu must be creative and imaginative, and must have wide knowledge of food. He/she must have the ability to work within the confines of the budget. Individuals responsible for planning menus must have the following skills :

Wide Knowledge of Foods It involves knowledge about different varieties of foods such as their seasonal availability, nutritional and anti-nutritional factors and the presence of toxic elements present in certain food varieties, the edible portion obtained from each food colour, taste and flavour differences and how they can best be combined for meals acceptability and cost factors.

Knowledge of Food Presenting Menu planner can introduce a variety of form and colour in menus to attract the customers. Colour, taste, texture, flavour and appearance of meal can be presented in such a way which catch the eye of the customer.

Knowledge of Different Method of Preparing and Serving of Food It is important for the menu planner to know, which food is best prepared by which method of cooking. It can only be possible when the planner has proper knowledge of food item, their flavour, colour, physical and chemical properties. Planner should also have the knowledge of what food is suited to what style of service, which flavour blend together best and how to combine them.

Knowledge of the Customer It is important for the planner to be familiar with customers choice of food item or a general idea of his food preferences or favourites.

Planning Menu

Menu planner must be able to visualise the presentation of food on the plate, sense the taste and aromas, and judge texture in his/her mind. The following points need to be considered before planning a menu :

Situation of the Food Service Organisation The basic factors to be considered here are :

- Size of kitchen and service areas
- Location of the establishment in relation to the market.
- In wholesome condition space available for storing food
- Number of staff and their skills
- Service areas and equipment available in kitchen

The Customer Customers are likely to be of varying ages, activities, occupations, physiological status and backgrounds. They would belong to various religious and cultural backgrounds, some having rigid religious belief and habits. Various requirements of customers form the basis for menu planning.

Food Cost Analysis

Food cost analysis is the first step in creating a restaurant budget. It can act as an important tool to monitor business costs to ensure higher profit margins. Once the menu has been planned, the next operation involved in any food service organisation in procurement or purchasing of raw material.

Food Purchasing

Purchasing for a food service establishment is an important and primary step in the production of quality finished food product, that is acceptable to customers. The person in charge of purchasing should have an understanding of the external market, and factors that affect menu production.

Food service purchasing requires knowledge of terminology, specifications, processing requirements and a thorough objective and subjective assessment of quality. Purchasing food for an establishment is a series of activities from knowing what to buy and for what end use. The person responsible for placing the orders for food on behalf of his customers must know the following :

How various commodities are marketed and handled?

- Food and food products available in markets undergo a constant change.
- Newer varieties of fresh fruits and vegetables are researched to improve size, colour, texture and flavour.
- Apart from the different forms and varieties grown, fresh food is available in forms as desired by a consumer. *e.g.* meat can be purchased as chops, boneless, leg of mutton for roast, mince, etc. Fish may be bought whole or fitteted as required.

What food and food products are available in the market in particular seasons?

- The manner in which foods are brought from the farms or factories to the markets provides a good index to their nutritional and keeping qualities. Fresh foods which have to be transported long distances reach the customer after a lapse of a few days.
- It is therefore, important to know what handling procedures are followed before placing orders for foods.
- Appearances should not be the only characteristic on which to base one's decisions regarding food purchasing.

Prevailing prices and fluctuations occuring from time to time in wholesale and retail markets.

Prices of food items change from season to season because of some reasons such as factory closures, customer demand, droughts and so on.

A knowledge of these is essential for a food buyer to buy the cheapest and best products. Suppliers tend to offer products which are most profitable to them within their conditions of supply and the best quality may never reach an establishment unless the suppliers is aware of the buyer's knowledge.

Quantities to be bought of each commodity at a time buying qualities will depend on a number of factors :

- Degree of perish ability of the food and thus its keeping quality.
- Frequency of deliveries possible.
- Rate of use in the menus of establishments.
- Amount of storage space available and the types of storages necessary for different foods.
- Suppliers and their terms of supply agree to fixed prices on a range of items over a period of time and have no objections to supply immediately on demand.
- What quality is best suited for using in the production of meals.
- How must food costs be controlled at the purchasing point.
- Relative quality of different foods : Different types of food, perishable, semi and non-perishables require different temperature storage, if food quality is to be maintained and loss through deterioration must be prevented.
- Communication of requirements to the supplier to ensure that the right quality is received in the right form and at the right time.

Purchasing Activity

Purchasing food for an establishment is not a single activity involving exchange of money for food in a market, but a series of activities leading to preparation food.

Purchasing is the process of getting the right product at a right price. Food must be purchased from an approved reputable supplier. For suppliers to be considered so, they must meet the following criteria :

- They have been inspected and can show an inspection report.
- They must meet all applicable local, state and federal laws.

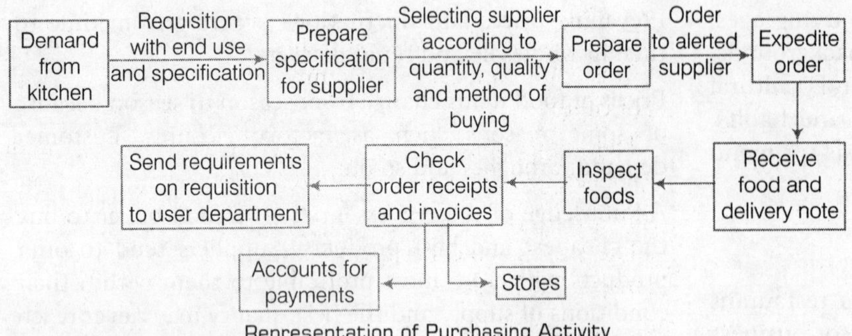

Representation of Purchasing Activity

Food Buyer

An institutional buyer spends a lot of money on behalf of the establishment and for customers. Qualities of food buyer should be :

- A food buyer should have high moral and ethical value, so that he is not influenced by suppliers in any way.
- He should have a quality of objectivity in his judgement in terms of price and service.
- He should be loyal towards the institution through devotion to duty, sense of justice.
- He should be loyal to in terms of being able to recognise good quality food that is free from adulteration and contamination.
- A food buyer should have the skill in identifying markets and establishing good relations with people around.
- He should accept food brands that are marked by standardising agencies approving their quality such as ISI, FPO or AG MARK in India.

Functions of a Food Buyer

The buyer has certain functions attributed by the food service unit which include :

- To keep records of specifications for each types of dish on the menu developed with the help of those who prepare the meals.
- Using perishable foods within two days of purchase if used fresh.
- Ability to store foods in a manner that will enhance or maintain their qualities.
- Rotating use of packaged foods, so that order packages are used first.
- Formulating specifications for food items.

Food Production

Many food service units follow various principles for production of food. It is based on number of people to be served or type of occasion such as festival, wedding or for a patient who is ill. These require special rules for producing food in a particular manner ensuring taste, flavour and contentment of customers. Food production encompasses the preparation of a large variety of items ranging from appetisers to curries, roasts, sandwiches, snacks salads, vegetables and beverages. For each type of item, certain skills are needed and different methods of processing are required to produce final product.

Food production system are of three types :

Conventional Food System In this food is produced totally from raw ingredients processed on the premises prior to service. Most small catering establishment and institutional kitchens follow this system in India.

Convenience System In this method of food production some of the food and ingredients used are bought pre-prepared or pre portioned from the markets. Some of the items like soups, noodles, marinated chicken, tandoori items require only finishing at the time of service, while others may be completely ready to serve not requiring processing at all.

Ready Food System In this the production of food is done continuously everyday. The ready food system works on the lines of a factory production system where foods are prepared, packed, freezer stored and transported to the points of use.

Receiving and Storage of Food

Receiving means the food materials have been ordered for supplying and their handling at the time of delivery. Precautions are necessary to use at this stage because these ensure that the food is not damaged or discarded due to careless handling, spillage, cross contamination and incorrects weights.

It is always good to follow the procedure that involves in the receipt of goods. Each category of food requires separate treatment before it is accepted for storage.

Delivery Procedure

- The supplier gets an order in writing stating the date on which supplies are required.
- He passes it on to his stores department or purchasing officers.
- The order is then noted to be kept ready for delivery on the specified date.
- It is transported to the buyer's stores for receiving.
- Goods are delivered along with two copies of the delivery chalan, one signed by the buyer and returned to the supplier, which help in confirmation of goods received and the second is retained by the buyer for counter checking the bill or invoice when it is received from the supplier for payment.

Receiving Procedure

- Delivery note is checked with copy of the placed order .
- Count, weight or volume are checked to tally with the amounts of various items on the delivery note.
- The quality of all ingredients are checked with the specifications given to the supplier.
- Any acceptable items should be returned with the person bringing the delivery.
- Check the quality and quality certification of delivered food *i.e.* ISI, AGMARK, FPO brand name, ingredient label, grade verification.
- For canned products, packaging date, expiry date, batch number should be checked any sign of bulging, damage, leakage, undesirable odour, discolouration should be checked.
- For milk and milk products check for any signs of spoilage-rancid odours in butter, sourness in curd, curdling in milk.

After receiving the food, items are stored carefully.

Storage

Principle of store keeping is to know what is where is, when it is needed by the user department. The following points should be kept in mind while storing food items :

- All items received and checked should be appropriately stored to prevent deterioration of quality and pilferage.
- Those items that need room temperature storage should be sorted out and perishables should be immediately stored at the right temperature, if they are not to be used immediately.
- Item such as cereals, pulses, condiments, spices, bottled and packed items can be safely stored at room temperature.
- All commodities will retain its quality only, if they stored in a clean place in a proper manner.
- The store room should be well ventilated to allow air circulation and reduce humidity.
- Appropriate storage space in the form of racks and airtight containers should be provided in the store.
- The store should be systematically maintained that is place for everything and everything in its place. This enables optimum utilisation of the storage space and also facilitates easy location of the items.
- The placement of commodities should follow First-In-First-Out policy (FIFO) *i.e.* the older commodity should be placed in front of the shelf so, that they are used earlier.
- Good purchasing system ensures that the next lot arrives before the first lot is completely exhausted.
- Items that come in paper packets or sachets once opened, should be transferred to air tights containers to ensure the retention of its quality.
- Proper label for each container should be ensured. This helps to locate the commodity without any waste of time.
- The store room should be preferably kept locked and opened only for issue to safeguard the commodities from pilferage.
- The store should be kept clean and free from rodents, insects and pests.

Food Cost Control

Control is a process by which managers regulate the action of people in order to achieve goals. It is important in the area of food because of the possibility of loss in every stage.

Control may be exercised in many ways through selection of techniques and devices suitable for each establishment. *e.g.* observing and correcting employee actions, preparing performance records, reports and budgets.

Two of the main causes of excessive costs in an establishments are inefficiency and waste. The process by which cost are regulated and excessive expenditure guarded against is known as cost control. It is a continuous process at every stage of the catering cycle.

The food costs in any catering management depends on the nature of the organisation. The variability in costs due to different prices and qualities purchased and used food is subject to losses in many different ways as it passes through the production and service cycle.

Method of Controlling Food Costs

- Ordering perishable foods in quantities for immediate use in preparation and service.
- Ordering semi or non-perishables in quantities, which can be turned over fast enough to prevent spoilage.
- Closed supervision and regular checks at strategic points in the catering cycle.
- Using modular equipment for storage, preparation and service, so that portions are not lost in transferring food from one piece of equipment to another.
- Offering incentive scheme to staff for achieving sales targets at established gross profit margins.
- Developing lists of customers favourites through kitchen, services and sales analysis.
- Forecasting the quantities of each menu item that will sell, so that excess leftovers are avoided.
- Developing staff initiative and creativity by initiating their participation in forecasting and planning activities.
- Using standardised simple recipes from which portions can be clearly indentified.
- Substituting low cost ingredients for those which are very expensive out of stock or rarely used.

Food Service Management of Institutional Level

Management thinking has undergone a number of changes in the last few decades resulting in adoption of new techniques of managing food services of institutions and catering to their needs at various levels.

Food Service Management is the art of providing food and beverages esthetically and scientifically to a large number of people, in a satisfactory and cost effective way.

It requires a professional approach along with special skills, knowledge and vigilance at each and every stage in food service operation. Food service in dusty may also be referred to as 'Catering industry'.

Institutional food service can be defined as entities that provide meals at institutions including schools, colleges and universities, hospitals, correctional facilities, public and private cafeterias, nursing homes, day-care and senior centres.

Food Service Establishments

These establishments are places set up to plan, prepare and serve food to a large number of people from different regions, cultural backgrounds and various socio-economic levels of society. The food is prepared and served in quantities larger than is done in homes. These food service institutions vary from small to very large establishments.

Types of Food Service Establishments

Food service establishments fall into two categories :

- Commercial Establishments
- Non-Commercial Establishments (welfare)

Commercial Establishments

These are set up with a profit motive, where the customer is willing to pay for the food, service and comfort received.

Examples of commercial catering establishments are :

- Mid-days meals in schools
- School food services
- Industrial canteens (when employers provide free or subsidised food to employees
- Institutions school and college hostels, working women's hostels
- Special needs e.g. hospitals old age homes, nursing homes
- Orphanages
- Creches
- Prisons

Commercial establishments are of two types :

Contract Catering Services These operate on behalf of people who wish to celebrate an event according to their own menu; in a hired hall in the community centre, in their houses or any other venue of their choice. The arrangements are made by caterers, according to the menu decided by the host. In these establishments, food services make more than 25 per cent profit.

Semi-Commercial Services These include establishments that do not have very high costs of staff such as roadside establishments or vendors. These places do not spend money on furniture or decoration to attract customers, thereby lowering their total cost of operation. Therefore, they charge less from customers, making profits within 15-25 percent.

Non-Commercial Establishments

Such establishments have been set up with a social objective and provide non-commercial services. Food preparation and services in these establishments are only a complimentary part of their care giving aspect. These institutions, however, carry on activities that will enhance their income or charge a fee for services rendered from those who can afford to pay. These establishments cover their expenses through government grants or public donations, and do not aim at profits from sale of food and services. Financially, they are said to break even, though they may charge private ward patients in hospitals.

Examples of commercial catering establishments are :

- Small to large hotels, restaurants, dhabas, cafe
- Expensive luxury restaurants, spas, speciality restaurants
- Guest houses, Holiday camps
- Fast food joints/take away (quick service restaurants)
- Coffee shops, speciality food services e.g. ice-cream parlours, pizza shops.
- Food services in cinema halls, theaters, malls
- Chain catering organisations.
- Travel services on sea land, air e.g. flight kitchen

Role of Food Service Management at Institutional Level

Food service and catering has evolved into an expanding industry with changes in the socio-economic status of society. There is presently a greater demand for food outside home which is delicious, hygienic, healthy and aesthetically served. Scientific and technological advancement has enabled mass production of food with longer shelf life and greatly improved quality and safety standards. Use of computers has contributed tremendously for maintaining records, accounting systems, on line ordering of food, information about equipment manufactured in different parts of the world and recipes for various preparations. Food needs to be provided to people of all ages, in all walks of life and at any time in a day. Food is provided at the work place and at institutions providing care for different target groups such as hospitals, old age homes, orphanages and hostels. Other institutions where food is routinely provided are school/college/office, prisons, feeding programmes undertaken by the government or voluntary sector to improve the health and nutrition of specific groups.

Food Service in Hospitals

Food services ensuring food safety, should be of prime importance in hospitals because their patients are at a higher risk of developing food-borne illness due to weak immune systems. It has been suggested that food and nutritional care quality in a hospital must be evaluated and deemed fit to enhance the efficacy of its services. Hospital food standards can form a part of the overall service quality standards along with other supportive services. This requires development of guidelines and qualification as well as assessment of food services on a regular basis.

Hospital food service departments have policies and procedures that address food safety such as :

- recording a food's final cooking temperature
- monitoring refrigeration temperatures
- monitoring temperature of food before and after service
- cleaning and sanitising procedures for equipment
- monitoring temperature in dish washing machines

Measures followed at the kitchen in health facilities :

- Hygiene measures of food items at the receiving location of kitchen
- Hygiene measures of food items at the storage location
- Hygiene measures to be followed while preparing food
- General cleaning
- Cleaning of refrigerators weekly
- Personal hygiene in the kitchen
- Pest control
- Medical check-up and health of food handlers
- Method of disposal of kitchen waste

Dietary Services in Healthcare Institutions

A well balanced diet plays an important role in a patients's treatment and recovery. The dietary services department in a healthcare unit makes every effort to provide patients with nutritious and appetising meals that are prepared according to the physician's orders.

Improvement by Hospital Food Service

- It can improve patient's satisfaction score.
- It can reduce cost of food production.
- It can cut down on food waste.
- It can boost staff productivity.
- It will be able to improve hospital's reputation.

Importance of Nutrition on Healthcare Facilities

More healthcare institutions have been committed to improve the nutritional profile of food served to patients, guests and staff. This is a part of an overall strategy to show that nutrition can be associated with delicious food while meeting new standards on health. Food service directors associate better nutrition in their institutions with reduced readmissions, thereby setting a good example and lowering costs through improved patient discharge outcome.

Food Service in Educational Institutions

A canteen in a school or college is a place where food is to be served and eaten, where different snack and drink products are sold. A school or college utilises a canteen to meet the food and nutritional needs of its students in order for them to have the energy to accomplish their tasks for the day.

The establishment and operation of canteens in educational institutions enables the students, faculty and the institution personnel to buy nutritious, hygienic and healthy food at affordable prices during working hours.

Food services provided at school or college have a considerable influence on the development of children's long-term eating habits, food preferences and attitudes towards food. By promoting and encouraging healthier food choices during childhood, it is anticipated that healthy eating habits will be carried through to adulthood. It may help to prevent chronic diseases later in life. The food services must promote a balanced healthy eating pattern rather than focusing on weight management.

Food Service in Social Institutions

Social institutions are a complex set of social norms, beliefs, values and role relationships that arise to satisfy the needs of society. Types of social institutions include :

- Informal social institutions such as family and religion based.
- Formal social institutions such as low and education based institutions e.g. corporates, multinational companies and other offices.

Food Service in a Family

It may be referred to as 'Family Style Meal Service'. This service allows participants to eat together and to make food choices based on individual appetites and food preferences. It promotes learning at mealtime, helping participants to develop a positive attitude towards nutritious food and good eating habits. They help in clearing the table, setting places and cleaning up after the meal.

Family style meal service operates as follows :

- All required meal components are placed on the table at the same time.
- Participants may serve themselves from serving dishes that are on the table.
- Adults, supervising the meal, help those who are unable to serve themselves, especially children and old people.
- Participants are allowed to make a choice in selection and size of serving.
- A supervising adult is seated at each table to inculcate good eating habits in children. Children should not be encouraged to waste food by taking small portions of food initially. They may be allowed to opt for more food if necessary.

Food Service in Context of Religion

Food patterns have changed globally due to migration and globalisation. Religious practitioners, having migrated to countries without religious dietary laws, adjusted their food pattern to local food habits.

Food behaviours have been influenced by socio-economical, socio-cultural and religious factors. India's food regulatory body FSSAI plans to implement Food Safety Management System (FSMS) to ensure quality of food in places of worship in the following ways :

- By standardising prasad ingredients and manufacturing process to improve its shelf life and safety.
- Vendors to be trained in food safety and hygiene; persuaded to apply for licence.
- Encourages self-audit to ensure that ingredients used in prasad are safe.
- Food handlers are trained in good manufacturing practices; to be educated about personal hygiene and usage of protective clothing, such as aprons and gloves.
- Introduces rotational system for food stock to ensure first expired, first out, strengthens documentation and record keeping, so that stock can be traced.
- Mandates management of wastes, such as flowers, fruits and vegetables , in a way that food quality is not affected.

Food Service in Corporate Entities, Multinational Companies and Other Offices

The humble office canteen is undergoing a vast sea-change as employees spend most of their time at work and need to eat at least one two meals there. In order to motivate the workforce, companies are investing heavily to hire professional caterers to lay out a lavish spread at meal times. This has opened up lucrative opportunities for catering companies. The companies that have been voted as best work places around the globe, are those that have a very active food programme.

Consequently, corporates have started to view food as a value proposition and not an expense to ensure availability of high quality food to its employees, the companies :

- Offer food ranges from local to global cuisines
- Offer fresh fruit and salad stations
- allow employees to personalise their meals with choice of toppings and condiments
- food facilities are regularly inspected for hygiene and safety of food
- Interact with culinary specialists from different regions to decide and plan menu
- Have a dedicated food team.

Food Service in Special Institutions

A special institution is one which caters to students with special educational needs due to learning difficulties, physical disabilities or behavioural problems. Such schools may be specifically designed, staffed and resourced to provide appropriate education for children with additional needs. Children with disabilities generally function better on a specialised diet.

This specialised diet may consist of meals that are free from allergens and dyes and include the following :

- Information from healthcare provider including diagnosis, child's allergen and reaction history
- Strategies to prevent exposure to allergens in classroom, while eating and playing
- Emergency action plan
- Hand-washing before and after consuming handling food
- Keep eating area separate from learning playing area
- Wash tables and chairs and any other eating area with approved cleaner before each meal and snack
- General training to be given on food allergies to all staff of such centres
- In-depth training for staff with frequent contact of children with food allergies

In these centres, children and older adults gain access to wholesome and nutritions food that contributes to the wildness and development of young children, and sustenance of older adults and chronically impaired disabled persons. A vast majority of these centres provide meals that are free or at a discounted price. Homeless children residing at a participating homeless shelter are considered eligible for meals served by that shelter.

EXAM BASED QUESTIONS

1 Which one of the following means the same as food service?
(a) Catering (b) Transporting
(c) Courier service (d) Dining

2 Role of food service manager does not include
(a) daily operation of restaurants
(b) customer satisfaction in a restaurant
(c) run profitable food business
(d) ensures that restaurant runs into losses

3 Which of the following is not 'heart' of a food service organisation?
(a) Menu planning
(b) Old and disabled people
(c) Food
(d) Equipment needed

4 Which of the following is not a benefit of a carefully planned menu?
(a) Cut down expenses
(b) Accurate calculation of food costs
(c) Provides unappetising meals
(d) Time and effort is minimised

5 Which of the following means 'Table of the host' menu?
(a) Table d'hote menu (b) A la carte menu
(c) Combination menu (d) Buffet

6 Which menu allows the customers to choose items as per his/her liking?
(a) A la carte (b) Table d'hote
(c) Combination menu (d) Buffet

7 A prison would most likely utilise which type of menu?
(a) Table d'hote (b) Cycle
(c) A la carte (d) Degustation

8 When planning a menu, what considerations need to be taken into account?
(a) Clientele (b) Location
(c) Season (d) All of these

9 A table d'hote menu can be described as
(a) A set menu for a set price
(b) Individually priced items with a choice in each course
(c) Individually priced items with a set number of courses
(d) Similar to a degustation menu

10 Breakfast menus appear as
(a) A la carte, set or buffet styles
(b) Buffet style
(c) A la carte style
(d) In hotels

11 A standard recipe card sets out costs for?
(a) A la carte menu (b) A function menu
(c) A cycle menu (d) A menu item

12 Which of the following is an example of an internal factor influencing decisions to change a menu?
(a) Consumer demand (b) Menu mix
(c) Supply levels (d) Competition

13 The corporate management team of a theme restaurant chain recently evaluated the chain's menu items and identified several puzzles. Which of the following would be reasonable strategies for the management team to adopt in relation to these items?
(a) Decrease prices
(b) Place the items in more visible locations on the menu.
(c) Shift demand to these items by using suggestive selling techniques
(d) All of the above are reasonable strategies

14 In relation to the food servicing purchasing cycle, which of the following positions is generally responsible for completing an issue requisition when items are needed in food production areas?
(a) Chef (b) Purchasing agent
(c) Receiving agent (d) Storeroom clerk

15 Subsidised pricing is followed in
(a) restaurant (b) fast food unit
(c) air catering (d) industrial canteen

16 In relation to the purchasing function, the term quality refers to
(a) highest price
(b) popularity of a menu item
(c) suitability for intended use
(d) greatest value

17 Ownership of product is transferred from the supplier to the food and beverage operation when the receiving employee signs the
(a) delivery notice
(b) daily receiving report
(c) purchase order
(d) standard purchase specification sheet

18 To help make the receiving function secure and efficient, the physical transfer of food and beverage products to the storage area should be the responsibility of
(a) supplier delivery personnel
(b) assigned staff from the property
(c) the food and beverage controller
(d) None of the above

19 Which of the following statements is/are correct?
(a) Self-service is an informed style of service.
(b) It is an arrangement which requires customers to come to the counter to serve themselves.
(c) The amount of food handling in such service is considerably reduced which increases safety of food for consumption.
(d) All of the above

20 A la carte menu is used in
(a) railway catering (b) mid-day meals
(c) college hostel (d) office canteen

21 Which of the following food service control points links receiving and issuing functions?
(a) Storing (b) Issuing
(c) Purchasing (d) Accounting

22 The first step in preparing to welcome guests to a food service establishment is
(a) hiring service staff
(b) purchasing supplies
(c) designing the menu
(d) creating recipes

23 Food suppliers are often called
(a) Peddlers (b) Purveyors
(c) Providers (d) Distributors

24 Lodging properties use food and beverage service for all but which of the following marketing purposes?
(a) Creating new business opportunities
(b) Creating a desired public image
(c) Increasing operating profitability
(d) Attracting desired business

25 A method of service, where food is displayed and the guests have to help themselves is termed as
(a) banquet (b) buffet
(c) counter service (d) cafeteria service

26 In addition to professionally planned menus, a properly designed and equipped kitchen, well trained employees, and effective preparation and production systems, high quality food and service depend on
(a) cost and portion control
(b) direction and over right
(c) rhythm, timing and flow
(d) organisation and execution

27 Which of the following statements is/are correct?
(a) In a canteen, lunch room or cafeteria, the menu would probably be displayed as a list of items with prices on a board.
(b) In institutions like hostels and hospitals, menus are charted out for a week or ten days in advance.
(c) In these institutional menus, it is not the practice to indicate prices or portions because these establishments are generally non-profit making.
(d) All of the above

28 This type of menu is similar to those found in early restaurants and provides little, if any, choice.
(a) Cuisine (b) A la carte
(c) Ristorante (d) Table d'hote

29 table d'hote is a
(a) meal comprised of main dish and sweet
(b) set menu, sold at an inclusive price
(c) list of all the available dishes each individually priced
(d) sequence of dishes in categories from soup to sweet

30 The term A la carte means
(a) a set menu without any alternatives or beverages
(b) a carte du jour menu inclusive of coffee and service charge
(c) a series of dishes as chosen by a customer and cooked to order
(d) a prix-fixe menu with several choices on each course

31 Selection of equipments in catering management must be guided by
(a) simplicity of construction
(b) ease with which it can be operated using existing skills of catering staff
(c) hygiene and safety of both equipment and its environment factors
(d) All of the above

32 Consider the following statements.
1. To ensure a healthy environment, it is necessary to guarantee clean drinking water should be provided.
2. Proper washing and toilet facilities are essential.
Which of the statements given above is/are correct?
(a) Only 1 (b) Only 2
(c) Both 1 and 2 (d) None of these

33 Fast food restaurants are able to keep prices low because
(a) they have fewer seats than other restaurants.
(b) they do not need to train staff, and the work is easy.
(c) they use poor quality food products.
(d) they use a limited mean and provide no table service.

34 If a restaurant makes you feel as though you have been transported in time and place and offers you entertainment with your meal, it might be called a (an)
(a) haute cuisine restaurant (b) specially restaurant
(c) theme restaurant (d) ethnic restaurant

35 What is the main difference between commercial food services and non-commercial food services?
(a) Non-commercial food services are not permanent, whereas commercial food services are full service restaurants.
(b) The size of the establishment and the clientele differ.
(c) Non-commercial food services are found in businesses whose focus is not food.
(d) In commercial food services, the same company owns and manages the restaurant, and in non-commercial food services, one person owns the restaurant and another company manages it.

36 A speciality restaurant
(a) serves food from a special culturelity (for example, Indian)
(b) serves one kind of food (for example, Pizza)
(c) serves only trendy, eclectic boods
(d) serves a special target market (for example, tourists)

37 The most sophisticated style and extremely formal service is
(a) waiter service (b) self-service
(c) room service (d) banquet service

38 The most common methods of food service may be classified as
(a) waiter service (b) self service
(c) vending (d) All of these

39 Which of the following statements is/are correct?
(a) In conventional food system the food is produced totally from raw ingredients processed on the premises prior to service.
(b) In convenience food system some of the food and ingredients are brought prepared or from the markets.
(c) The ready food system involves preparation of food into ready portions of individual food items or cooked dishes which are sealed and chilled, frozen and stored for use when required.
(d) All of the above

40 Codes for food handlers are
1. neat and clean working cloth.
2. wash kitchen utensils and equipments once in week.
3. wash hands before touching the food.
4. can smoke in kitchen of service areas.
Select the correct answer using the codes given below
(a) 1 and 2 (b) 1 and 4
(c) 1 and 3 (d) All of these

41 Meal planning is important for
1. planning of food budget.
2. nutritional adequacy.
3. variety in diet.
4. efficient utilisation of resources.
Select the correct answer using the codes given below
(a) 1, 2, 3 and 4 (b) 1 and 2
(c) 2 and 3 (d) 1 and 3

42 Work can be simplified by viewing the kitchen and its activities from different aspects like
1. work area
2. worker's area of reach
3. work space
4. equipment, materials and supplies
Select the correct answer using the codes given below
(a) 1 and 2 (b) 2, 3 and 4
(c) 3, 4 and 5 (d) All of these

43 Important attributes for a food buyer must include
1. objectivity in judgement regarding price and service
2. loyalty to customers and institution
3. accepting food brands without ISI, FPO or AGMARK in India.
4. accepting and purchasing adulterated food ingredients
Select the correct answer using the codes given below
(a) 1, 2, 3 (b) 1 and 2
(c) 2, 3, 4 (d) 1, 2, 3, 4

44 Purchasing activity for food includes
1. activity involving exchange of money only
2. series of activities
3. receipt of demand from kitchen
4. selecting supplier according to quantity and quality of food stuff required
Select the correct answer using codes given below
(a) 1 and 4 (b) 2, 3, 4
(c) 2 and 3 (d) 1, 3, 4

45 Convenience food system allows
1. preparation of food from raw ingredients prior to serving customers.
2. freezer storage and transportation to user point.
3. allows purchase of pre prepared food items.
4. finishing at the time of service e.g. soups and noodles, pizza.
Select the correct answer using codes given below
(a) 1 and 4 (b) 2 and 3
(c) 3 and 4 (d) 2 and 4

46 Which of the following are optimum storage procedures for safety of food?
1. All ingredients should be kept on the floor.
2. Perishable and non-perishable items should be stored together.
3. Items should be transferred to air tight containers from packets.
4. Containers should be properly labelled.
(a) 1 and 2 (b) 2 and 3
(c) 4 and 1 (d) 3 and 4

47 Which of the following statements is/are correct?
1. Semi-commercial services include establishments that do not have high investment on staff, e.g. roadside eatery.
2. Contract catering services operate on behalf of people who hire a hall, of their choice, to celebrate an event.
Select the correct answer
(a) Only 1 (b) Only 2
(c) Both 1 and 2 (d) None of these

48 Which of the following statements is/are correct?
1. Food service industry requires professional approach and special skills and knowledge; while catering does not require any aesthetic or scientific knowledge about food industry.
2. Industrial canteens, where employees are entitled to subsidised food, is part of welfare catering.
Select the correct answer
(a) Only 1
(b) Only 2
(c) Both 1 and 2
(d) None of the above

49 **Which of the following statements is/are correct?**
1. There is no adult supervision at a 'Family Style Meal Service'.
2. Food is not served in hospitals where patients are at a higher risk of developing food borne illness.

Select the correct answer
(a) Only 1 (b) Only 2
(c) Both 1 and 2 (d) None of these

50 **Arrange in the right sequence the steps taken in planning a physical facility for food service unit.**
1. Planning team 2. Menu analysis
3. Architectural features 4. Prospectus
5. Budget 6. Feasibility study

Codes
(a) 1, 2, 4, 3, 6, 5 (b) 1, 6, 3, 4, 5, 2
(c) 4, 1, 6, 2, 3, 5 (d) 6, 5, 4, 3, 2, 1

51 **Arrange in the right sequence the steps taken for purchasing activity in food service industry.**
1. Inspect foods 2. Prepare order
3. Accounts for payments
4. Demand from kitchen
5. Prepare specification for supplies
6. Selecting supplies according to quantity and quality

Codes
(a) 1, 2, 6, 5, 4, 3 (b) 3, 1, 2, 4, 6, 5
(c) 4, 6, 5, 2, 1, 3 (d) 3, 5, 4, 6, 1, 2

52 **Arrange in the right sequence the steps taken in food management.**
1. Storage 2. Service
3. Preparation 4. Receiving
5. Packing 6. Menu planning

Codes
(a) 1, 4, 6, 3, 5, 2 (b) 4, 1, 6, 2, 3, 5
(c) 6, 4, 1, 2, 3, 5 (d) 6, 4, 1, 3, 5, 2

53 **Consider the following statements.**
1. Hygiene and sanitation play a role in promoting and protecting health and well-being of people for whom food is prepared.
2. Safety implies the concern for providing, conditions at work which will protect people from inflection and injury.

Which of the statements given above is/are correct?
(a) Only 1 (b) Only 2
(c) Both 1 and 2 (d) None of these

54 **Which of the following statements is correct?**
1. Purchasing good food materials is the basis for preparing and serving meals that are acceptable to the consumer.
2. Food purchasing is a difficult, but challenging task and needs to be based on certain established principles.

Select the correct answer using the codes given below
(a) Only 1 (b) Only 2
(c) Both 1 and 2 (d) None of these

55 **Consider the following statements.**
1. Menu planning helps to determine requirement accurately, money and time to be spent.
2. It, however, has not impact on saving the wasting food.

Which of the statements given above is/are correct?
(a) Only 1 (b) Only 2
(c) Both 1 and 2 (d) None of these

56 **Which of the following statements is/are correct?**
1. It is important to achieve reduction of food waste and duplication of procurement time and effort which can result from sudden menu changes or production policy shifts.
2. Purchasing in charge need to have a thorough knowledge of the market environment and the purchasing policies of those offering similar goods and services to their customers.

Select the correct answer using the codes given below
(a) Only 1 (b) Only 2
(c) Both 1 and 2 (d) None of these

57 **Match the following.**

List I (Food Standards)	List II (Descriptions)
A. The PFA standard	1. Concerned with physical and chemical characteristics of food, both natural and acquired during processing
B. The FPO standard	2. Lay down the minimum standards for all types of foods
C. The AGMARK standards	3. Indicates conformity to laid down standards
D. Indian standards	4. Concerned with the standards required for maintaining quality of fruits, vegetables and any products manufactured from them

Codes

	A	B	C	D		A	B	C	D
(a)	3	2	4	1	(b)	1	2	3	4
(c)	2	4	1	3	(d)	4	3	2	1

58 **Match the following.**

List I	List II
A. Cyclic menu	1. Menu of the day
B. A-La-carte menu	2. Set menu
C. Table d' hote menu	3. Choice of dishes
D. Dujour menu	4. Menu rotated at definite interval

Codes

	A	B	C	D
(a)	4	3	2	1
(b)	1	2	3	4
(c)	2	1	3	4
(d)	3	4	2	1

59 Match the following.

List I	List II
A. Food is completely prepared and portioned in kitchen. Food is arranged in platter.	1. American service style
B. Customer selects food from menu card, prepared food is served in the crockery placed on table.	2. Banquet service style
C. A much elaborated style where final finishing is given on the table	3. Russian service style
D. Large number of people are served together by a team of waiters .	4. French service style

Codes

	A	B	C	D		A	B	C	D
(a)	2	3	1	4	(b)	4	1	2	3
(c)	2	4	3	1	(d)	3	1	4	2

60 Match the following.

List I	List II
A. Egg and butter toast	1. Soup
B. Fruit cream	2. Snack
C. Rasam	3. Dessert
D. Grilled sandwich	4. Breakfast

Codes

	A	B	C	D
(a)	1	4	2	3
(b)	3	1	4	2
(c)	4	3	1	2
(d)	4	2	3	1

61 Match the following.

List I	List II
A. Hospital	1. Table service
B. Cafeteria	2. Counter service
C. Hotel	3. Pantry service
D. Hostel	4. Banquet
E. Railways	5. Centralised

Codes

	A	B	C	D	E
(a)	1	3	4	5	2
(b)	2	4	1	5	3
(c)	5	2	4	1	3
(d)	4	1	3	2	5

62 Match the following.

List I	List II
A. Tomato onion	1. Bread
B. Naan	2. Fruit
C. Peach	3. Snack
D. Biscuit	4. Salad

Codes

	A	B	C	D
(a)	4	1	2	3
(b)	2	3	4	1
(c)	3	1	2	4
(d)	4	3	1	2

63 Match the following.

List I	List II
A. Patients	1. Educational institution
B. Children without guardians	2. Special institution
C. Children with autism	3. Hospitals
D. Students	4. Orphanages

Codes

	A	B	C	D		A	B	C	D
(a)	3	4	2	1	(b)	2	4	1	3
(c)	1	2	4	3	(d)	2	3	4	1

64 Arrange the correct order of food consumption during the day.

(a) milk shake, spinach dal, eggs butter toast, (yogurt) chappati rice.

(b) egg and butter toast, (yogurt) chappati rice, milk shake, spinach dal.

(c) spinach dal, milk shake, egg and butter toast, (yogurt) chappati rice.

(d) (yogurt) chappati rice, milk shake, spinach dal, egg and butter toast.

65 Arrange the correct order of catering personnel according to seniority

(a) Manager, Utility worker, Cook, Supervisor

(b) Manager, Cook, Supervisor, Utility worker

(c) Manager, Supervisor, Cook, Utility worker

(d) Manager, Utility worker, Supervisor, Cook

Directions (Q. Nos. 66-72) *In the questions given below are two statements labelled as Assertion (A) and (R). In the context of the two statements, which one of the following is correct?*

Codes

(a) Both A and R true and R is the correct explanation of A

(b) A is true but R is not the correct explanation of A

(c) A is true but R is false

(d) A is false but R is true

66 **Assertion** (A) Menu is stated to be the heart of food service unit.

Reason (R) It is an essential control which determines the food to be purchased, personnel and equipment needed.

67 **Assertion** (A) The success of a food service operation, depends heavily on the menu planning of the establishment.

Reason (R) Menu serves many functions and forms the care of all other activities in a food service establishment.

68 **Assertion** (A) The menu is the heart of the entire food establishment on which all activities are centered.

Reason (R) The menu determines the materials to be purchased equipments to be used, current food trends and even the style of lead rship and workman's compensation.

69 Assertion (A) Providing a clean, safe food service facility is basic to achieving a successful operation and strategic to health and well-being of both employees and customer.

Reason (R) Sanitation and safety are closely related environmental factors to be considered, while planning the layout and physical facility of food service unit.

70 Assertion (A) Food service has evolved into an expanding industry with change in the socio-economic status of society.

Reason (R) Demand for food prepared outside home has increased with more women taking up jobs.

71 Assertion (A) Scientific and technological advancement has greatly improved quality and safety standards in food production.

Reason (R) Use of computers has contributed tremendously for standardising operations.

72 Assertion (A) Thali meals served on trains and in some establishments is an example of Table d'hote menu.

Reason (R) A table d'hote menu is planned by the host and served at a set price.

Directions (Q. Nos. 73-77) *Read the following passage and answer the questions that follow.*

Food Service Management is a process of managing the food service operation, a place where a traveler can get food and accommodation. Food and drinks provided in a good ambience, aesthetically for a cost- 'effective price to the satisfaction of a customer is the basic objective of a food service operation. Safe and tasty food.with quality served in a hygienic environment is important. People eating outside are increasing day by day and customers look for food which is healthy and safe. Food service management is needed whether a food service operation is small, medium or large.

The scope and prospects for food service management are that you can become an entrepreneur in running a food. service operation successfully. Manage to run a food service operation. Establish linkages with corporates and industries to provide food (on contract basis": Manage food services in 'hospitals like dietaries and canteens. Set up food preservation and bakery units.

Establish a snack bar/kiosk with nutritious foods like salads, fresh juices and herbal drinks. Become a teacher in schools and in colleges.Become an event manager to meet the needs of food and beverages for various events. Develop food products and become a food designer. Work in airline, railway and ship catering services. Design and develop new cuisines. Create employment opportunities for many and provide good and healthy food to the community. There are some general etiquettes needs to be followed in Food Service Operation such as: Receive the guests with smile as soon as they enter the restaurant. Wish them good morning, good afternoon, good evening, and good night based on the time of the day. Help the ladies to sit by pulling the chair. Serve water as soon as guests are seated. Present the menu card. Help the children below 5 years with babysitting chairs. Take orders of food from the guest, who will pay the bill. Inform the guest the time required to serve the food.

Serve preplated food from right handside and if not preplated to serve individual items from left hand side. Be attentive to guest's tables. Fulfill the requirements of the customers quickly. Clear the used or soiled- plates from the right side of the customer. Present the bill.

Accompany.the guest to the door politely and send them off. Then clear and reset the table. While serving keep do not interrupt when the guests are taking food. Do not over hear conversation. Do not argue with the guests even though they may be wrong. Do not touch hair or nose, mouth while in service. Do not solicit for tips. So, it can be said, the scope ofthe food service management is unlimited.

73 Food service management is needed whether the food service operation being

(a) small (b) medium
(c) large (d) All of these

74 Which of the following statements is/are true regarding food service operation?

Statement I Food and services should be proided in ambience.

Statement II Provide cost effective price food to the satisfaction of the customers.

(a) Statement I is true.
(b) Statement II is true.
(c) Both the statements I and II are true.
(d) Neither statements I nor II are true.

75 Which of the following are the prospects of food service management?

(a) Can be an entrepreneur in running food service operation.
(b) Can become a teacher in schools and colleges.
(c) Can set-up independent restaurants.
(d) All of the above

76 Which of the following etiquettes needs to followed in food service operation?

(a) Receive guests with smile.
(b) Argue with the guests, if they are wrong.
(c) Fulfil the requirements of the customers quickly.
(d) Both (a) and (c)

77 Which of the following things one should not do while serving food?

(a) Hear the conversation of the guests.
(b) Interrupt the customers when they are taking food.
(c) Do not solicit for tips.
(d) Present the menu card only, if asked by the customer.

PREVIOUS YEARS' QUESTIONS

July 2018

1 Food cost increase in a restaurant can be attributed to

1. Raw material bought off season.
2. Specification not precise.
3. Kitchen being automised.
4. Maintenance of Food Standards.
5. Storage temperature not maintained.

Codes

(a) 2, 4, 5 (b) 1, 2, 5 (c) 1, 2, 3 (d) 3, 4, 5

November 2017

2 A guest relation programme adopted in a restaurant should include

1. anticipate customer need
2. never admit mistakes
3. do not specify the time of delivery
4. use pleasant and reassuring words
5. observe customer behaviour

Codes

(a) 1, 2 and 4 (b) 3, 4 and 5
(c) 1, 4 and 5 (d) 1, 2 and 3

3 Arrange in the correct sequence the steps involved in food production in a commissary system

1. Rapid Chill 2. Production 3. Portioning
4. Hold refrigerated raw material
5. Reheat 6. Cold hold 7. Service

Codes

(a) 1, 3, 4, 5, 2, 6, 7 (b) 4, 2, 1, 3, 6, 5, 7
(c) 4, 1, 2, 3, 9, 5, 7 (d) 4, 2, 1, 3, 9, 7, 5

4 Quick service restaurants offer the nutritive value of their menus on

(a) menu card (b) fisplay board
(c) website (d) emails

5 Match the institutions in List I with type of service in List II.

List I	List II
A. Restaurant	1. Decentralised
B. Airports	2. Tray service
C. Malls	3. Table service
D. Hospital	4. Food court
E. Cafeteria	5. Fork Buffet
F. Trains	6. Vending
	7. Plated service

Codes

	A	B	C	D	E	F
(a)	3	6	4	1	2	7
(b)	3	6	1	5	6	7
(c)	6	2	5	7	3	1
(d)	1	2	3	4	6	5

January 2017

6 Which of the following is concerned with the functions of management?

(a) Henri Fayol (b) Taylor
(c) Gilbreth (d) Elton Mayo

7 Assertion (A) A cycle menu is a selective menu.

Reason (R) It is rotated at definite intervals.

Codes

(a) Both A and R are correct
(b) A is incorrect and R is correct
(c) A is correct and R is incorrect
(d) Both A and R are incorrect

8 Which method is used for recipe adjustment?

(a) Mark up (b) Percentage
(c) Prime (d) BARS

9 Arrange the steps involved in bulk purchasing of food in the correct sequence.

1. Estimate quantities
2. Identify amounts to be purchased
3. Determine standards
4. Market research for vendors
5. Identify needs
6. Develop purchase order
7. Select and negotiate with vendors

Codes

(a) 5, 3, 1, 2, 6, 4, 7
(b) 1, 2, 7, 6, 4, 5, 3
(c) 1, 3, 4, 5, 1, 7, 6
(d) 4, 1, 3, 2, 6, 7, 5

July 2016

10 Arrange the mechanics at waiter service in the correct sequence

1. Clearing
2. Receiving customers and taking order
3. Serving
4. Preparation of service boys, sideboards and table
5. Sending off the customer

Codes

(a) 2, 3, 5, 1, 4 (b) 4, 2, 3, 1, 5
(c) 1, 2, 3, 4, 5 (d) 2, 3, 5, 4,

11 Match the type of menu in List I with its characteristic in List II.

List I	List II
A. A la carte menu	1. Menu of the day
B. Single use menu	2. Menu rotated at definite time intervals
C. Table d'hote menu	3. Complete meal at a fixed price
D. Du jour menu	4. Food items are priced separately
E.	5. Menu planned for a certain day or event and not repeated exactly in same form

Codes

	A	B	C	D		A	B	C	D
(a)	3	1	5	4	(b)	4	1	3	5
(c)	5	4	3	2	(d)	4	5	3	1

12 Arrange the steps of flow of food for a conventional food service system in the correct sequence.

1. Production
2. Storage
3. Holding
4. Receiving
5. Service

Codes

(a) 4, 2, 1, 3, 5 (b) 1, 3. 2, 4, 5
(c) 4, 1, 3, 5, 2 (d) 1, 2, 4, 3, 5

13 Arrange the following as per the Maslow's theory of hierarchy of needs for motivation.

1. Safety and security
2. Social needs - friendship and family
3. Physiological needs - air and water
4. Self actualisation - creativity and problem solving
5. Self esteem - confidence and achievement

Codes

(a) 3, 2, 1, 4, 5 (b) 3, 1, 2, 5, 4
(c) 3, 1, 4, 5, 2 (d) 3, 2, 5, 4, 1

December 2015

14 Which of the following is not a characteristic of A la carte menu?

(a) It is a choice menu.
(b) Each dish is priced separately.
(c) Food is kept in fully prepared form and can be served immediately.
(d) Customers pay for the dishes they order.

15 **Assertion** (A) Planning menus helps to provide meals to customers at a reasonable price.

Reason (R) Price advantage can be obtained by buying seasonal foods and in quantities which carry discounts.

Codes

(a) A is correct, but R is incorrect
(b) A is incorrect, but R is correct
(c) Both A and R are correct
(d) Both A and R are incorrect

16 Arrange the steps to be taken while purchasing equipment for food service establishments in the correct sequence.

1. Set guidelines/specifications for purchase of these items.
2. Estimate the expenditure by obtaining prices of these items from different sources.
3. Assess the need.
4. Select after careful consideration ensuring that the equipment satisfy the required specification.
5. Decide on the list of equipments to be purchased.

Codes

(a) 3, 2, 1, 5, 4 (b) 3, 5, 2, 1, 4
(c) 5, 3, 2, 4, 1 (d) 5, 1, 2, 3, 4

17 **Assertion** (A) Preparing a production schedule helps in controlling the activities in the hotel kitchen.

Reason (R) Production scheduling involves setting a time-table for implementing various activities that need to be completed in order to achieve the objectives.

Codes.

(a) A is incorrect, but R is correct
(b) A is correct, but R is incorrect
(c) Both A and R are incorrect
(d) Both A and R are correct

18 Give the correct sequence of steps involved in the process of receiving the supplies in a food service establishment.

1. Quality of ingredients are checked with specifications given to supplier.
2. Counts, weights or volume are checked to tally with amounts of various items on the delivery note.
3. Unacceptable items are returned with the person executing the delivery along with a note on delivery challan stating the items returned.
4. Delivery note is checked with copy of the order placed.
5. Delivery challan is countersigned by the receiving authority and the deliverer of supplies.

Codes

(a) 2, 4, 1, 3, 5 (b) 4, 2, 1, 3, 5
(c) 1, 4, 2, 5, 3 (d) 2, 1, 4, 5, 3

June 2015

19 A la carte menu is

(a) served on a particular day as special
(b) limited choice of fixed price
(c) choices of items listed with its price
(d) series of dishes repeated after a period of time

20 **Assertion** (A) Commissary service has a large centralised production unit with satellite units located separately where food is finally prepared and served.

Reason (R) This type of system uses frozen and chilled food, does large volume purchase, has large labour force and equipment and minimal transport.

Codes

(a) A is partially correct and R is correct
(b) Both A and R are correct
(c) A is correct and R is partially correct
(d) Both A and R are incorrect

21 Arrange in sequence the steps involved in the planning process of management.

1. Formulating possible course of action
2. Setting priorities
3. Obtaining relevant information
4. Organising
5. Recognition of the fact that a problem exists
6. Selecting the best course

Codes

(a) 1, 2, 3, 4, 6, 5 (b) 5, 3, 1, 4, 2, 6
(c) 5, 3, 1, 2, 6, 4 (d) 5, 2, 4, 3, 1, 6

December 2014

22 A menu where food items are priced separately is called

(a) Table d'hote (b) Du Jour
(c) Set menu (d) A la carte

23 Give the correct sequence of steps in buying non-perishable foods for food service institutions.

1. Develop purchase order
2. Write specifications
3. Award contract
4. Issue bid request

Codes

(a) 1, 2, 4, 3 (b) 2, 1, 4, 3
(c) 4, 2, 1, 3 (d) 2, 4, 1, 3

24 The most sophisticated and extremely formal style of service is

(a) waiter service (b) self service
(c) room service (d) banquet service

25 Match the following.

List I (Cost components)	List II (Their examples)
A. Food costs	1. Equipment repair
B. Labour costs	2. Electricity
C. Overhead costs	3. Raw materials
D. Maintenance costs	4. Employee uniforms

Codes

	A	B	C	D
(a)	3	4	2	1
(b)	3	1	4	2
(c)	3	4	1	2
(d)	4	3	2	1

ANSWERS

Exam Based Questions

1 (d)	2 (d)	3 (b)	4 (c)	5 (a)	6 (a)	7 (b)	8 (d)	9 (d)	10 (a)
11 (d)	12 (b)	13 (d)	14 (a)	15 (d)	16 (c)	17 (a)	18 (b)	19 (d)	20 (d)
21 (a)	22 (c)	23 (b)	24 (c)	25 (b)	26 (c)	27 (d)	28 (a)	29 (b)	30 (c)
31 (d)	32 (c)	33 (d)	34 (c)	35 (c)	36 (b)	37 (a)	38 (d)	39 (b)	40 (c)
41 (a)	42 (d)	43 (b)	44 (b)	45 (c)	46 (d)	47 (c)	48 (b)	49 (d)	50 (c)
51 (c)	52 (d)	53 (b)	54 (c)	55 (c)	56 (b)	57 (b)	58 (b)	59 (d)	60 (c)
61 (c)	62 (a)	63 (c)	64 (c)	65 (a)	66 (d)	67 (c)	68 (c)	69 (a)	70 (a)
71 (b)	72 (c)	73 (d)	74 (c)	75 (d)	76 (d)	77 (c)			

Previous Years' Questions

1 (b)	2 (c)	3 (b)	4 (c)	5 (a)	6 (a)	7 (b)	8 (b)	9 (a)	10 (b)
11 (d)	12 (a)	13 (b)	14 (c)	15 (c)	16 (b)	17 (d)	18 (b)	19 (c)	20 (c)
21 (c)	22 (d)	23 (b)	24 (d)	25 (a)					

UNIT II

CHAPTER 04 Food Groups and Nutrition

Food is a basic part of our existence and food with essential and required nutrients is most beneficial for our body. Awareness of different food groups can help us to decide a balanced nutritive diet. Our food choices affect our health so, we must choose a diet which is healthy, nutritive and useful for our body. Not consuming a balanced healthy diet can result in Malnutrition and other diseases.

Food plays a crucial role in our lives. It is termed as life giver as one cannot exist without food. After air and water, food is the utmost important thing for survival. With nutritive and nourishing components, food influences the health of an individual.

It refers to any substance of plant or animal origin that are edible and functions to nourish the body of an individual. It generates energy after the process of ingestion, digestion and absorption, such that it is utilised by the body for its various functions.

Consumption of the variety of foods in correct and balanced proportion makes up a healthy body. These substances keep a person alive, also aid the growth and development, regulate the body processes and boost the immune system that protects the body from diseases.

Food Groups

To get the maximum benefit of food, it is essential to take a diet that contains the essential and required nutrients in adequate amount. It is important to include different types of food in diet, as one food item may not contain the required nutritional value of all nutrients. Also, it is important to know that all food items cannot be included in the diet at one time. Thus, food has been categorised into food groups.

A food group then is a collection of foods that share similar nutritional properties. A selection of different food items from each food group leads to a healthy body.

In this Chapter

- *Food Groups*
  - *Balance Diet*
  - *Food Pyramid*
- *Nutrition and Nutrients*
- *Nutritional Deficiencies*
- *Nutritional Requirement for Indians*

Classification of Food Groups

Depending upon the nutritive value, food can be classified into different groups like 'Basic four', 'Basic five', 'Basic seven' etc. These food groups can be used to plan a diet, so that the nutritional requirements can be met.

Basic Four Food Groups

Food at a very basic level can be divided into four groups which are shown in the table given below :

Groups	Nutrients
Cereals, millets and pulses	Energy, protein and B Vitamins
Vegetables and fruits	Vitamins, minerals and fibre
Milk, milk products and animal foods	Protein, calcium and B Vitamins
Oils, fats, nuts and oilseeds	Energy and protein

Basic Five Food Groups

The Indian Council of Medical Research (ICMR) has classified food items into the basic five food groups which are as follows :

Groups	Nutrients
Cereals, grains and products like rice, wheat, ragi, maize, bajra, jowar and rice flakes.	Energy, protein, invisible fat, thiamine, riboflavin, folic acid, calcium, iron and fibre.
Pulses and legumes like Bengal gram, black gram, cowpea, rajma and soyabeans.	Energy, protein, invisible fat, thiamine, riboflavin, folic acid, calcium, iron and fibre.
Milk and meat products.	Protein, fat, riboflavin, calcium, protein and fat.
Fruits and vegetables like mango, guava, tomato, papaya, orange, sweet lime and water melon.	Carotenoids, Vitamin C, riboflavin, folic acid, iron and fibre.
Green leafy vegetables like spinach, drumstick, fenugreek and coriander leaves and other like carrots, onion, brinjal, ladyfinger, beans, capsicum, cauliflower and drumstick.	Riboflavin, folic acid, calcium, fibre, iron and carotenoids. Carotenoids, folic acid, calcium and fibre.
Fats and sugars like butter, ghee, hydrogenated fat, cooking oils, sugar and jaggery.	Energy, essential fatty acids and fat soluble vitamins. Energy and iron.

Basic Seven Food Groups

After diversifying and expanding the basic four food groups, food can further be divided into seven food groups. The classification is shown in the table given below :

Groups	Nutrients
Green and yellow vegetables	Carotenoids, ascorbic acid and iron
Oranges, grape fruits, tomatoes and raw cabbage	Ascorbic acid, carbohydrates
Potatoes and other vegetables and fruits	Vitamins, minerals and fibre
Milk and milk products	Calcium, phosphorus, protein and vitamins
Meat, poultry, fish and eggs	Protein, phosphorus, iron and B-vitamins
Bread, flour and cereals	Thiamine, niacin, riboflavin, iron, carbohydrate and fibre
Butter or fortified margarine	Vitamin A and fat

General Classification of the Food Items into Food Groups

Food is classified into various food groups. They are discussed below :

Dairy Milk and milk products are categorised into the group of dairy. As rich in calcium, products like yoghurt, cheese, ice-cream, pudding, etc., they come under the category of dairy.

Fruits This category of food group is at most time categorised with vegetables. As a seperate group, it contains carbohydrates as well as some important vitamins and minerals.

Grains, Beans and Legumes Categorised as cereals, this category is often the largest category in nutrition guides. They are rich source of starch.

Meat/Protein Food Protein rich food products, such as meat, fish, eggs, nuts, etc., come under this category of food groups. The food items in this group uses the protein to maintain, build and repair the muscles and bones of the body.

Vegetables Second to the largest category of grains, vegetables are rich in Vitamin A and C, folate, iron and magnesium. The food items in this group provides/enriches the body with phyto nutrients.

Some Other Food Groups Confections, beverages and the herbs and spices are called food accesson. Essential in the cooking of food items, these groups contain certain important nutrients. However, their nutritive value is very low to essentially consider them as seperate food groups.

Classification of Food Based on Functionality

Food products can be classified on their functionality as well. These classifications are :

Energy Yielding Foods Food products that are rich in carbohydrates and fats come under this group. The products are used by the body to produce energy. Food items like cereals, pulses, oil, butter, ghee, etc., are parts of energy yielding food.

Body Building Foods Foods that are rich sources of protein are body building foods. Milk, meat, eggs, fish, pulses, oilseeds and nuts are good sources of proteins.

Protective Foods Foods rich in vitamins and minerals come under this group. The food in this group functions to protect us from all health problems and diseases. Water, milk, egg, fruits, vegetables, etc. come under protective food.

Balanced Diet

A balanced diet is one which provides all the nutrients in required amount and proper proportion. It can easily be achieved through a blend of the four basic food groups. The quantities of food needed to meet the nutrient requirements vary with age, gender, physiological status and physical activity. A balanced diet should provide around 50-60% of total calories from carbohydrates, preferably from complex carbohydrates, about 10-15% from proteins and 20-30% from both visible and invisible fat.

In addition, a balanced diet should provide other non-nutrients such as dietary fibres, antioxidants and photochemical which provide positive health benefits. Antioxidants such as vitamins C and E, beta-carotene, riboflavin and selenium protect the human body from free radical damage.

A balanced diet should be one based on eating a variety of different foods and eating foods that have not been processed. This means trying natural unprocessed foods. People should eat 5 portions or more of fruits and vegetables a day. This reduces the amount of processed food they eat. They should drink at least 2 litres of water a day. They should maintain a balance between the amount of carbs, fats and proteins they consume. People should reduce the amount of table salt they have (below 6 gm) and amount of sugar in their diet.

Benefits of Eating a Balanced Diet

Important benefits of balanced diet are :

Provides Perfect Concentration The balanced diet makes mind healthy and mind works more actively. It also increases the focus and concentration. By taking breakfast before starting day contains the enough amount of energy that would be enough to make you concentrated throughout your day.

Helps Body to Lose Store Fat In balanced diet, people drink water instead of soda and eat fruit salad instead of chips. Thus, people leave junk food and take healthy, clean and unprocessed food. This automatically reduces body weight

Makes Body Strong and Active Balanced diet makes body strong that helps to fight against the virus and another types of diseases. A healthy diet contains low saturated fat that prevents the body from many cancers. It also recommends to take some healthy steps like to quit smoking or drinking can also lower the risk of many diseases.

Provides Boost of Energy The balanced diet provides perfect boost of energy that means it provides enough energy that promotes body to do more activities like exercise or any other activity that make people more active and energetic .

Provides Longer Life Span Balanced diet increases lifespan as one lives an active life. It will lower the risk of some diseases.

Reduction of Inflammation The balanced diet encourages the body to reduce inflammation as it provides the food that has more bases and makes body acidity low so that one have less inflammation. The best anti-inflammatory ingredient is garlic that helps to reduce inflammation in body.

Induces Peaceful Sleep After balanced diet mind and body are relaxed. This help in perfect sleep. This helps body to gain more stability and activeness throughout hectic day.

Balanced Diet for Adults—Sedentary/Moderate/Heavy Activity (Number of Portions)

Food Groups	Portion (gm)	Types of Work					
		Sedentary		Moderate		Heavy	
		Man	Woman	Man	Woman	Man	Woman
Cereals and millets	30	14	10	16	12	23	16
Pulses	30	2	2	3	2.5	3	3
Milk	100 ml	3	3	3	3	3	3
Roots and tubers	100	2	1	2	1	2	2
Green leafy vegetables	100	1	1	1	1	1	1
Other vegetables	100	1	1	1	1	1	1
Fruits	100	1	1	1	1	1	1
Sugar	5	5	4	8	5	11	9
Fats and oils (visible)	5	4	4	7	6	11	8

Balanced Diet for Infants, Children and Adolescents (Number of Portions)

Food Groups	Portion (gm)	Infants 6-12 months	Years						
			1-3	4-6	7-9	10-12		13-18	
						Girls	Boys	Girls	Boys
Cereals and millets	30	1.5	4	7	9	9	11	10	14
Pulses	30	0.5	1	1.5	2	2	2	2	2
Milk (ml)	100	5	5	5	5	5	5	5	5
Roots and tubers	100	0.5	0.5	1	1	1	1	1	2
Green leafy vegetables	100	0.25	0.5	0.5	1	1	1	1	1
Other vegetables	100	0.25	0.5	0.5	1	1	1	1	1
Fruits	100	1	1	1	1	1	1	1	1
Sugar	5	5	5	6	6	6	7	6	7
Fats/Oils (visible)	5	2	4	5	5	5	5	5	5

Source *National Institute of Nutrition, Hyderabad.*

Food Pyramid

The food pyramid is designed to make healthy eating easier. Healthy eating is about getting the correct amount of nutrients i.e., proteins, fats, carbohydrates, vitamins and minerals, that one needs to maintain good health.

Foods that contain the same type of nutrients are grouped together on each of the shelves of the food pyramid. This gives a choice of different foods from which to choose for a healthy diet. Following the food pyramid as a guide helps to get the right balance of nutritious foods within calorie range. Studies show that when we take in too many calories from foods and drinks high in fat, sugar and salt, on the top shelf of the food pyramid, they provide very little of the essential vitamins and minerals our body needs. Limiting these is essential for healthy eating. The food pyramid was a recognisable nutrition tool that was introduced by the United States Department of Agriculture (USDA) in 1992. It was shaped like a pyramid to suggest that a person should eat more foods from the bottom of the pyramid and fewer foods from the top of the Pyramid.

The food pyramid guidelines for healthy living are :

- Balancing diet with physical activity.
- Eating a variety of foods.
- Eating plenty of vegetables, fruits and grain products.
- Eating foods low in fat, saturated fat and cholesterol.
- Eating sweets in moderation.
- Eating salt in moderation.
- Limiting intake of alcohol.

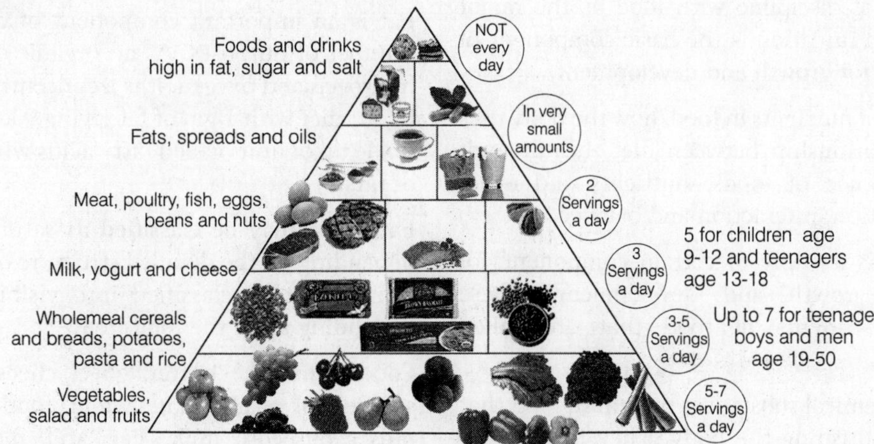

Food Pyramid

Food Pyramid Published by WHO and FAO

In 2002, the World Health Organisation (WHO) in conjunction with the Food and Agriculture Organisation (FAO), published guidelines that can be effectively represented in a food pyramid.

This pyramid was related to the objectives that worked to prevent obesity, improper nutrition, chronic diseases and dental cavities.

The given below table is explaining the quantity of intake in either percentage, grams or milligrams :

Dietary Factors	2002 Joint WHO/FAO Expert Consultation Recommendations
Total fat	15-30%
Saturated fatty acids (SFAs)	< 10%
Poly Unsaturated Fatty acids (PUFAs)	6-10%
n-6 PUFAs	5-8%
n-3 PUFAs	1-2%
Trans Fatty Acids	< 1%
Mono Unsaturated Fatty Acids (MUFAs)	By difference
Total carbohydrate	55-75%
Free sugars	< 10%
Complex carbohydrate	No recommendation
Protein	10-15%
Cholesterol	< 300 mg/day
Sodium chloride (Sodium)	< 5 g/day (< 2 g/day)
Fruits and vegetables	≥ 400 g/day
Total dietary fiber	From foods
NSP	From foods

Nutrition and Nutrients

Nutrition is a scientific discipline with food as the major focus of interest. Good nutrition is the basic component of health and is essential for growth and development.

Nutrition is the study of nutrients in food, how the body uses nutrients and the relationship between diet, health and disease. It is the science of foods, nutrients and other substances, of their action, interaction and balance.

Nutrition is defined as a study of certain components of food, essential for growth and development. These components are constituents of food that are called nutrients.

Nutrients are those chemical substances present in food that are responsible for nourishing the body. They help in the nourishment and health of the body.

Kinds of Nutrients

Nutrients can be divided into two categories macro nutrients and micro nutrients. Both these categories are equally essential in required amount to aid growth and development.

Macronutrients

Macronutrients are those nutrients that are required by the body in large amount. Present in large quantities in food, macronutrients provide structural, material and energy to the body. They are the body's source of fat and energy that fuel the life processes. They include carbohydrates, proteins, fats and amino acids.

Carbohydrates

Carbohydrates are sugars or polymers of sugar, such as starch that can be broken down to form simple sugars (glucose) by hydrolysis. With a general formula $(CH_2O)n$, it is the cheapest and the preferred source of energy for the body.

Carbohydrates can be classified into three categories i,e, mono saccharides, disaccharides and poly saccharides, depending on the number of sugars they contain. Mono saccharides contain one, disaccharides contain two and poly saccharides contain three or more units of sugar.

Functions of Carbohydrates

- They provide energy i.e. 1gm of carbohydrate gives 4 caloric worth of energy.
- By being the preferred source of energy, carbohydrates spare protein for other body functions, specially tissue building.
- By its fibres, it facilitates the excretion of intestinal waste.

Fats

Fat is an important component of our diet and serves a number of purposes. As an organic compound of carbon, hydrogen and oxygen, it is a concentrated source of energy in our diet with 1 gm of fat giving 9 kcal of energy. Fats are made up of units called fatty acids which decide the nature of fats.

Fats then may be classified as saturated or unsaturated, depending on the detailed structure of the fatty acids. Fats can further be classified into visible and invisible fats, depending upon the food item.

Food items like butter, ghee, cheese, oil, etc., are rich sources of visible fat, while food items like cereals, pulses, oilseeds, milk, egg and meats are sources of invisible fat.

Functions of Fat

- It provides concentrated source of energy that is stored in our body for future use.
- It also performs the protein sharing action.
- It helps in absorption of fat soluble vitamins.
- It helps to maintain body temperature.
- It acts as a cushion to vital organs.
- It helps in growth of tissues.

Essential Fatty Acids

Most fatty acids are non-essential, as the body can produce them whenever required. However, there are source of fatty acids that need to be taken as a part of our diet. The essential fatty acids like omega-3 and omega-6 perform certain essential functions, especially for metabolism and maintenance of healthy skin.

Proper types of fats are found in peanut, cotton seed, corn and sunflower oil that are rich in the essential fatty acids and therefore must be added to the diet.

Lipids

Lipids are heterogeneous group of compounds related to fatty acids and includes fats, oils, waxes and other related substances. Generally, oily in nature and hydrophobic, they are soluble only in non-polar solvents, such as chloroform, ether, benzene, etc.

Proteins

The word 'protein' means 'to take the first place' as suggested by Mulder in 1838. It was described as the substance without which life is not possible. Being a complex nitrogenous substance, it constitutes over half the dry weight of most organisms. It is made up of smaller units called amino acids, protein contain carbon, hydrogen, oxygen, nitrogen and usually sulphur. The food products that are source of proteins include meat and poultry products along with milk, milk products and cereals.

Essential to the building, maintenance and repair of body tissues, protein is also a major component of our immune system and hormones. It also provides energy whenever it is required Moreover it also help in the clotting of blood.

Amino Acids

As amino acids are the building block of proteins, it is essential to understand that out of the 22 amino acids that form protein, 8 amino acids are essential amino acids. It means that the 8 amino acids need to be taken as it is not produced in the body, while the rest can be produced when needed.

Micronutrients

Other important nutrients which are present in small quantities in foods, but are essential for our body are called micro nutrients. These include minerals and vitamins that are required by our body in small quantity. If these micro nutrients are not eaten in required amount, they result in deficiency diseases.

Vitamins

Vitamins are nutrients that are essential for growth and are found in less quantity in our body. They do not produce energy but are essential catalyst in various major processes and functions of the body. As they cannot be produced by our organs, they need to be supplied through the diet.

Vitamins essentially can be divided into two categories i.e. fat soluble vitamins and water soluble vitamins. The fat soluble vitamins are vitamin A, E, D and K that dissolve in fat and not in water. The water soluble vitamins, as the name suggests are soluble in water and include vitamin of B group and vitamin C.

Vitamin A It is essential for normal vision, normal skeletal and teeth development and for healthy working of organs as well as skin. It is found richly in green leafy vegetables. Milk and its products as well as yellow and orange fruits and vegetables also make up the rich sources of vitamin A.

Vitamin D It is necessary for formation of strong teeth and healthy bones. It helps in proper absorption of certain essential minerals like calcium and phosphorus in the body. A rich source of vitamin D is the sunlight. Food products like eggs, fish liver oil, milk, butter, ghee, etc., also provide vitamin D.

Vitamin E The primary role of vitamin E is to act as an anti-oxidant. It not only saves vitamin A from oxidation, but also plays an important role in the formation of the RBCs in the bone marrow. Many vegetables, nuts, legumes, cereals and eggs are rich sources of vitamin E.

Vitamin K The important role of vitamin K is that it is necessary for the clotting of blood. It is mainly found in plants. Thus, plant products including green leafy vegetables, cereals, fruits and an animal produce, pork liver are good sources of vitamin K.

Vitamin B Complex The vitamin B complex, initially discovered as a single vitamin, is actually a group of compounds to which we designate the name. The various compounds are discussed below :

- **Vitamin B1 or Thiamine** Vitamin B1 teams up with an enzyme to form a co-enzyme that acts as a catalyst for the oxidation process. Seperately it is also essential for the maintenance of a good appetite and normal digestion. It is present in all natural foods. Some rich sources include whole grain, cereals, pulses, oilseeds and nuts.

- **Vitamin B2 or Riboflavin** Just like thiamine, riboflavin also forms a co-enzyme to help in tissue oxidation with the release of the energy and thus, helps in protein, fat and carbohydrate metabolism. Good sources of this vitamin include milk, meat, eggs and dried yeast.
- **Niacin or Nicotinic Acid** Niacin is rapidly converted to nicotinamide to aid metabolism for carbohydrates, fats and proteins. It also helps in the normal functioning of skin, intestinal tract and the nervous system. Poultry, meat, fish and peanuts and some good sources of niacin.
- **Vitamin B6 or Pyridoxine** Pyridoxine acts as a co-enzyme for a large number of enzyme systems associated with amino acid metabolism. Meat, poultry and fish are rich sources of vitamin B6 or pyridoxine.
- **Folic Acid Group** 'Folion' is a generic term for several compounds, having the activity of folic acid. This group is required for the synthesis of the DNA, normal production of Red Blood Cells and the oxidation of amino acid phenylalanine to tyrosine. Deep green leafy vegetables and cereals are good sources of folic acid group.
- **Vitamin B12 or Cyanocobalamin** As the only cobalt contain substances, it is an essential vitamin needed for maintaining health. It helps in the synthesis of nucleic acid and nucleo proteins and is essential for maturation of the red blood cells. The only source of this vitamin is food of animal origin.
- **Vitamin C or Ascorbic Acid** Most easily destroyable of all vitamins, vitamin C is required for the formation and maintenance of collagen, a cementing material that holds the cells of the body together.

  It also plays an important role in the production of tissues and for the metabolism of a previously formed scar. Fruits, especially citrus fruits along with some vegetables are rich sources of ascorbic acid.

Minerals

Minerals may be defined as those elements which remain largely as ash when plant and animals are burnt. The human body is made up of 19 minerals that make up the 4% of the body weight.

These minerals are derived from the food we eat because they are present in minute amount. These minerals are referred to as trace elements or micro nutrients.

Some essential nutrients that are required by the body include calcium, phosphorus, iron, iodine, sodium, potassium, zinc and chloride.

Minerals are important for body in various ways. They are required to form organic compounds, such as phosphoproteins, haemoglobin, etc., as well as the hard skeletal structures. They are required for the constitution of enzymes and to maintain water balance. They are also essential as they help in proper functioning of the nervous system along with many other functions.

Calcium

Calcium together with phosphorus and other elements gives rigidity to bones and teeth. A common electrolyte, approximately 1200 gm of calcium is present in the body. A part from giving rigidity to the bones and teeth, calcium acts as a catalyst for the conversion of prothrombin to thrombin. It also activates the permeability of the cell mebrane and plays a major role in the transmission of nerve impulses.

Milk and milk products are excellent sources of calcium, while certain green leafy vegetables also give a good amount of calcium.

Phosphorus

Accounting for one-fourth of the total mineral element present in the body, organic form of phosphorus is found in soft tissues. Phosphorus is found richly in milk and meat products. Cereals and flours, specially whole grains are also rich sources of phosphorus. Phosphorus is one mineral that performs several functions in the body. They are as follows :

- Its combination with calcium provides rigidity to the bones and teeth.
- The phosphorus containing lipoproteins facilitate the transport of fat.
- It is a constituent of nucleoproteins, the basic genetic material.
- Phosphorus are constituents of cell membranes in regulating the transport of solutes.
- Phosphorus captures and stores vital energy in the cells of many tissues.
- Inorganic phosphorus found in body fluids that acts as an important buffer system in the regulation of body neutrality.

Magnesium

Magnesium is found in very less quantity in the body, i.e. 20-35gm. Of about 60% of this mineral are found on the surface of the bones in the form of carbonates and phosphates.

Magnesium is essential for the release of energy and bone mineralization. It is also required for normal metabolism of calcium and phosphorus and for activation of enzymes that are responsible for break down of glycogen. Flour, cereals, dry beans, peas, nuts and green leafy vegetables along with dairy products excluding butter are some good sources of magnesium.

Potassium

An adult body contains about 250 gm of potassium out of which 97% is found in the intra cellular fluid. Potassium within a cell maintains the osmotic pressure and fluid balance. It is required for the synthesis of proteins and sometimes is bound with a phosphate to aid the conversion of glucose to glycogen. It is widely found in meat, poultry, fish, fruits, vegetables and whole grain like cereals. Banana, potatoes, tomatoes, carrots, orange juice and grapefruit juice are some rich sources of potassium.

Sodium

Sodium is found in extra cellular fluids, bones and in some intra cellular fluids. Of about 120 gm sodium, about 50% is found in extra cellular fluids, 40% in bones and about 10% or less in intra cellular fluids. Sodium is required for maintenance of normal osmotic pressure and water balance, along with maintaining the permeability of the cell membrane.

Salt i.e. sodium chloride is an essential source of sodium, while it is also found in animal products and certain vegetables including spinach, celery, fenugreek and beet greens.

Chlorine

It is found entirely as a chloride ion, most of 100 gm of chloride ion found in body is entirely in extra cellular fluids. It also regulates osmotic pressure, water balance and acid base balance. It functions as an activator of gastric enzymes as well as of salivary amylase.

Iron

It is an important mineral that is found in the body. Iron requirements differ for a male and a female. An adult male requires about 3-5 gm of iron while a female needs 2-3gm.

It is an essential requirement for haemoglobin that transports oxygen to the various parts of the body. It facilitates the complete oxidation of carbohydrates, fats and proteins.

It plays an important role in maintenance of brain and is also a vital part of enzymes and substances that aid metabolism. Lean meats, deep green leafy vegetables and whole grain cereals are good sources of iron. Jaggery, eggs and organ meats are also rich sources of iron.

Iodine

About one-third i.e. 25 to 50% of iodine found in the body is found in thyroid gland. The only known function of iodine is as a constituent of thyroglobulin, a protein complex of several iodine containing compounds.

It is essential as it regulates growth, rate of oxidation with the cells and aids the functioning of nervous and muscle tissues, circulating activity and the metabolism of all nutrients.

It is supplied by food and water; variations are wide depending upon the iodine content of the soil. Soils found in coastal areas are enriched with iodine, while in hilly areas there is a deficiency of iodine.

Fluorine

Flourine occurs in the body as a calcium salt in the bones and teeth. Being not necessary for life, flourine is essential for dental cavities. The main source of fluorine is drinking water, while it can be traced in good amount in certain food items like shell fish, cheese, etc.

Zinc

Zinc is one mineral that is found in traces in all body tissues, making up 2 to 3 gm. in the body. It is found essentially in insulin and various other enzymes found in the body.

Meat, shell fish, Eggs, legumes seeds, nuts, dairy products and whole grains are good source of zinc.

Water

Apart from the macro and micro nutrients essential for the healthy development of body, water is also an essential element required second to oxygen. One can live without food but not without water.

Making upto 70% of the body weight, water acts as a structural component and as a cushion of all the cells. It is a medium of all body fluids and a carrier of all nutrients and waste.

It acts as a body lubricant and also helps in maintaining the body temperature. It is found in almost every food product and also can be ingested through the different beverages.

Process of Nutrition

The process of nutrition is a complex and tedious process which undergoes a number of processes, so that the nutrients are absorbed and assimilated. It can be understood as given below :

Ingestion In this process, food stuffs are taken inside the body. This process is called ingestion.

Digestion After food is taken inside the body, it starts breaking into simpler and simpler molecules by digestion.

Absorbption As digestion begins, the nutrients found in food are absorbed in the small intestine. An essential part of this process is the presence of small structure, named villis in the small intestine.

Assimilation The absorbed food is brought to various cells through the blood to form and release cellular energy. This energy produced is then utilised by the body and the process involved is called assimilation.

Egestion The last phase of nutritional process is the removal of all waste and toxic substances from the body. This process of expulsion is known as egestion.

Role of Nutrition

Our food choices each day affect our health for not only the present but also in the future. Good nutrition is an important part of leading a healthy lifestyle. Combined with physical activity, your diet can help you to reach and maintain a healthy mind and body, along side reducing the risk of any disease.

Good nutrition can :

- reduce the risk of some disease, including heart disease, diabetes, stroke, some cancers and osteoporosis.
- reduce high blood pressure.
- lower high cholestrol.
- improve your well-being.
- improve your ability to fight off illness.
- improve your ability to recover.
- increase energy level.

For a proper functioning of all parts of the body, both nutrients and physical activities are essential. Our body to maintain, it burns all extra calories even when one is not performing any strenous activity. For such purpose, nutritional science defines basal/basic **metabolic rate**.

Nutritional Deficiency

Nutritional deficiency is an inadequate supply of essential nutrients (as vitamins and minerals) in the diet. Nutritional deficiency occurs when the body does not absorb on get nutrients from food.

Deficiency can lead to a variety of health problems. These can include digestion problem, skin disorders, stunted bone growth and even dementia.

Terms Associated with Nutritional Deficiency

Malnutrition Malnutrition is a state of health which arises from incomplete nutrition. This lack of nutrition results from inadequate food and ill-balanced diet and results in health problems.

Inadequate diet can be due to both excess or less amount of food than the required amount.

Overnutrition A nutrient excess diet can lead to overnutrition, when the diet contains excess of nutrients required for normal growth, development and metabolism.

It can result in serious health problems including obesity and vitamin and mineral poisoning.

Undernutrition Undernutrition stands for the diet which is deficient both in quality and quantity. In other term, the food which does not provide essential nutrients for the proper maintenance of health. Such condition leads to deficiency diseases.

Deficiency Diseases

Diseases that occur due to the lack of nutrients, over a long period are called deficiency diseases. Lack of food leading to either malnutrition or starvation gives rise to these diseases.

The various deficiency diseases are discussed below :

Protein Deficiency Diseases

Protein Energy Malnutrition (PEM) is a form of malnutrition that is defined as a range of pathological conditions arising from lack of protein and energy.

Basically, it can be categorised into three types which include :

Kwashiorkor Kwashiorkor is a form of severe protein malnutrition. In this deficiency disease, the person's body retains fluid in the lower legs causing it to swell. It also results in a bulging abdomen, an enlarged liver, thinning of hair, loss of teeth and various skin problems. Its symptoms are :

- Loss of appetite
- Loss of energy
- Irritability
- Skin pigmentation

Marasmus Another disease resulting from severe malnutrition or the deficiency of energy, marasmus usually occurs in children. It is different from kwashiorkor as it is an energy deficiency disease, while kwashiorkor is a protein deficiency one. Some symptoms of marasmus are :

- Loss of muscle mass
- Anemia
- Dehydration
- Skin infections
- Abdominal problems
- Unusal body temperature

Marasmus Kwashiorkor The most severe form of malnutrition, this deficiency disease is a marked protein and calorie deficiency. Symptoms include that of both marasmus and kwashiorkor.

Calcium Deficiency Diseases

A deficiency of calcium in the diet results in the reduction in calcification of bones and teeth. Due to this deficiency many problems in the skeletal system occur.

Most common problems are :

Osteoporosis It is a deficiency disease in which bones weaken, increasing the risk of a broken bone. Without any symptom, this disease can lead to fractures typically of vertebral column, rib, hip and wrist.

Rickets Rickets is a condition that results in weak or soft bones in children. Symptoms of this disease include bowed legs, stunted growth, bone pain, large forehead and sleeping problems.

Tetany Tetany is a medical sign consisting of the involuntary seizure of muscles or muscles contraction. This disease is characterised by contraction of distal muscle of the hands and limbs.

Iron Deficiency Diseases

Iron deficiency is a state in which a body lacks enough iron to supply its needs. This lack if prolonged can lead to iron deficiency anaemia.

Anaemia It is a decrease in the number of the red blood cells or the amount of haemoglobin in the blood. As it develops slowly, the disease can adapt and can go unrecognized for sometime. It symptoms are :

- Fatigue
- Light headedness
- Irritability
- Breathlessness
- Poor appetite
- Brittle nails, etc.

Iodine Deficiency Diseases

Iodine deficiency is a lack of the trace element, iodine, an essential nutrient in the diet. Its deficiency can result in Goiter. A low amount of thyroxin in the blood gives rise to the thyroid stimulating hormone, which aids growth and development. If this hormone is produced in low quantity, it affects the functioning of the thyroid gland. This malfunction leads to the swelling of the gland.

The symptoms of goiter include :

- Breathlessness
- Hairfall
- Tremors
- Nervousness
- Increased blood pressure
- High heat intolerance

Vitamin A Deficiency Diseases

Vitamin A deficiency or VAD is a lack of vitamin A in humans, most common in poor and developing countries. The most common VAD is night blindness in which a person cannot see in dim light or dusk. This problem is followed by various other eye problems such as the dryness of cornea, conjunctival xerosis and xerophthalmia to finally lead to irreversible blindness.

Another disease called the toad's skin disease is a result of lack of vitamin A. In this disease, the skin goes dry and scaly.

Vitamin D Deficiency Diseases

Vitamin D just like calcium is essential for bones. Deficiency of this vitamin leads to osteoporosis and rickets in children.

Vitamin E Deficiency Diseases

Lack of vitamin E leads to the break down of the red blood cells as haemolysis. This breakdown finally leads to anaemia.

Vitamin C Deficiency Diseases

Deficiency of vitamin C or the ascorbic acid results in the disease called scurvy.

Its symptoms include :

- Discomfort, uneasiness or pain
- Fatigue
- Roughness of skin
- Gum disease
- Loosening of teeth
- Poor wound healing
- Bleeding from skin

Vitamin B1 Deficiency Diseases

Deficiency of vitamin B or thiamine can lead to severe and a chronic disease known as beri-beri, existing in three forms i.e. wet, dry and infantile. Its symptoms vary widely. In wet beri-beri, the cardiovascular system is affected, while in dry beri-beri, the nervous system is affected.

Some common symptoms of beri-beri include :

- Weight loss.
- Impaired sensory perceptions.
- Weakness and pain in the limbs.
- Irregular heart rate.
- Swelling of bodily tissues.

Vitamin B1 Deficiency Diseases

Deficiency of vitamin B_2 results in ariboflavinosis. There are no specific symptoms of this disease. However, some commonly seen symptoms include :

- Cracks on both sides of the lips.
- Crack on the lips that go red.
- Sourness of the tongue.
- Redness and burning sensation in the eyes.

Niacin Deficiency Diseases

Niacin or vitamin B_3 deficiency leads to pellagra which affects the gastrointestinal tract, the skin and the nervous system.

Some symptoms of pellagra include :

- Inflamed skin
- Diarrhoea
- Mouth sores
- Sensitivity to sunlight
- Hair loss
- Swelling
- Tongue inflammation, etc.

Nutritional Requirement for Indians

The nutritional requirement of a person differs for all individual based on their age and size. For the Indian context, this nutrient requirement is set and revised by the Indian Council of Medical Research. With their Recommended Dietary Allowances (RDAs), It seeks to guide the population and provide policy directions regarding the nutritional requirement of Indians.

Recommended Dietary Allowances (RDAs)

It is the amount of nutrients to be consumed by people to meet the requirement of the body. The requirement for a particular nutrient is the minimum amount that is required to prevent symptoms of deficiency and to maintain the satisfactory level.

The three important points to remember about Recommended Dietary Intakes are :

- They are set high enough to meet the needs of almost all healthy people.
- They do not apply to people who are suffering from a disease, which influences the nutrient needs.
- Recommended dietary intake for adults are based on sex, age, body size and activity level.

Salient Features of RDAs

- RDAs also known as Recommended Dietary Allowances is measured/expressed in kilocalorie (Kcal), gram (gm), milligram (mg) or microgram (µg).
- The RDAs for adults depend upon the activity level.
- RDAs for thiamine, riboflavin and niacin are dependent on RDAs for energy.
- RDAs for protein are based on body weight.
- RDAs for energy and protein are given as additional intake for pregnancy and lactation.
- The referred man and woman in the table were the Indian adults whose ages lie between 20-39 yrs for males and 18-29 yrs for females.
- The fat energy, according to the table should be 15% of the total energy to ensure essential consumption of fatty acids and fat soluble vitamins.
- Energy requirement depends on the level of activity that are sedentary workers, moderate workers and heavy workers.
- RDAs for energy, protein, iron, thiamine, riboflavin and niacin are expressed per kg body weight.
- RDAs for vitamins require intake of proper vitamins to keep the body healthy.

EXAM BASED QUESTIONS

1 Food generates energy after the process of
(a) digestion (b) ingestion
(c) absorption (d) All of these

2 Food helps in
(a) bringing people together (b) making people fight
(c) making people lazy (d) making people energetic

3 Which nutrient(s) is/are called body fuel(s)?
(a) Carbohydrates (b) Fats
(c) Both (a) and (b) (d) None of these

4 Which nutrient aids in growth and repair of body?
(a) Carbohydrate (b) Protein
(c) Fat (d) Vitamin

5 Vitamins and minerals help in ....
(a) protection (b) repair
(c) giving energy (d) maintenance of health

6 What does oils, nuts and oil seeds give us?
(a) Energy and protein (b) Vitamin B
(c) Calcium (d) Mineral

7 Ascorbic acid is found in
(a) potatoes (b) oranges
(c) milk product (d) poultry

8 Pulses and legumes are good sources of ......
(a) protein (b) iron
(c) calcium (d) All of these

9 Milk products are rich in which nutrient?
(a) Calcium (b) Carbohydrate
(c) Vitamin (d) Phosphorus

10 Which is/are energy yielding food item(s)?
(a) cereals (b) pulses
(c) ghee (d) All of these

11 Milk, meat, eggs, fish and pulses are good sources of
(a) carbohydrates (b) vitamins
(c) protein (d) fat

12 Fruits and vegetables are
(a) energy giving foods (b) body protective foods
(c) body building foods (d) All of these

13 Example(s) of energy yielding food is/are
(a) meat (b) yams
(c) pulses (d) Both (b) and (c)

14 Nutrition is essential for
(a) growth (b) to promote overall health
(c) Both (a) and (b) (d) None of these

15 Macro nutrient includes ......
(a) carbohydrates (b) proteins
(c) amino acids (d) All of these

16 Carbohydrates are made up of
(a) sugar (b) salt (c) acid (d) base

17 How much energy does 1 gm of carbohydrate gives?
(a) 14 calorie (b) 5 calorie
(c) 4 calorie (d) 15 calorie

18 Fats are made up of units of
(a) sugar (b) fatty acid
(c) amino acids (d) All of these

19 Which of the following is a source of invisible fats?
(a) Cereals (b) Pulses
(c) Eggs (d) All of these

20 What kind of fatty acids, omega-3 and omega-6 are ?
(a) Essential fatty acids
(b) Non-essential fatty acids
(c) Saturated fatty acids
(d) Unsaturated fatty acids

21 Who suggested the word 'Protein'?
(a) Hulder (b) Mulder
(c) Holder (d) Molder

22 How many amino acids are essential amino acids?
(a) 7 (b) 5 (c) 8 (d) 6

23 Which vitamin is essential for vision?
(a) Vitamin D (b) Vitamin A
(c) Vitamin E (d) Vitamin K

24 Vitamin D helps in absorption of
(a) calcium (b) phosphorus
(c) Both (a) and (b) (d) None of these

25 What is the role of vitamin K?
(a) Anti-oxidant (b) Anti-inflamatory
(c) Clotting of blood (d) Formation of bone

26 Which of the following acts as co-enzyme?
(a) Thiamine (b) Riboflavin
(c) Both (a) and (b) (d) None of these

27 .... is required for synthesis of DNA.
(a) Niacin (b) Follic acid
(c) Pyridoxine (d) Cyanocobalamine

28 How much calcium is present in the body?
(a) 1200 gm (b)1500 gm
(c) 1300 gm (d) 1400 gm

29 ...... plays a role in facilitating the transport of fat.
(a) Calcium (b) Phosphorus
(c) Magnesium (d) Potassium

30 What is the function of potassium within a cell?
(a) Osmotic pressure (b) Fluid balance
(c) Both (a) and (b) (d) None of these

31 What is the daily requirement of iron in case of females?
(a) 2-3 gm (b) 3-5 gm
(c) 5-6 gm (d) 1-2 gm

32 Iodine is found in human body in
(a) pancreas (b) thyroid
(c) pineal (d) duedenum

33 Which mineral is found in insulin?
(a) Zinc (b) Chlorine
(c) Iodine (d) Potassium

34 It is the term, used to signify amount of heat released so that our body can function. What is it?
(a) Calorie (b) Vitamins
(c) Joules (d) Minerals

35 What is the full form of BRM?
(a) Basal Metabolic Rate (b) Basal Mortalities Rate
(c) Basal Maternity Rate (d) None of these

36 Which of the following affect(s) BMR?
(a) Sex (b) Weight
(c) Age (d) All of these

37 Where was first food pyramid published?
(a) USA (b) Britain (c) Sweden (d) Chile

38 What were the objectives to release food pyramid in 2002?
(a) Prevent obesity (b) Improper nutrition
(c) Chronic diseases (d) All of these

39 ……… is a state of health that arises from incomplete nutrition.
(a) Malnutrition (b) Overnutrition
(c) Undernutrition (d) Deficiency

40 What are different types of PEM?
(a) Kwashiorkor (b) Marasmus
(c) Marasmic Kwashiorkor (d) All of these

41 Which part of body swells in kwashiorkor?
(a) Abdomen (b) Arms (c) Legs (d) Neck

42 Marasmus occurs in
(a) adults (b) children
(c) women only (d) elderly people

43 Calcium deficiency affects the
(a) skeletal system (b) circulatory system
(c) nervous system (d) All of these

44 Calcium deficiency can lead to
(a) osteoporosis (b) rickets
(c) tetany (d) All of these

45 What does iodine deficiency cause?
(a) Anaemia (b) Tetany
(c) Goiter (d) None of these

46 Which disease is caused by vitamin A deficiency?
(a) Night blindness
(b) Toad skin disease
(c) Both (a) and (b)
(d) None of these

47 Scurvy is caused by deficiency of which vitamin?
(a) Vitamin D (b) Vitamin E
(c) Vitamin C (d) Vitamin K

48 Common symptom of beri-beri includes
(a) weight loss
(b) weakness and pain in limb
(c) irregular heart rate
(d) All of the above

49 Niacin deficiency causes
(a) pellagra (b) scurvy
(c) osteoporosis (d) beri-beri

50 RDI is based on
(a) sex (b) age
(c) body size (d) All of these

51 Consider the following statements.
1. Nutrition intake cannot be linked to cultural and psychological implications.
2. Nutrition is concerned with social and economic implications of a person.

Which of the statement(s) given above is/are correct?
(a) Only 1
(b) Only 2
(c) Both 1 and 2
(d) Neither 1 nor 2

52 Which of the following statements is/are correct?
1. The energy requirement increases when an individual has fever.
2. In cold climate, the BMR rises while in warm weather, it comes down.

Select the correct answer using the codes given below
(a) Only 1
(b) Only 2
(c) Both 1 and 2
(d) Neither 1 nor 2

53 Consider the following statements.
1. Milk is known as complete food.
2. It helps to add vitamin A and vitamin D to the diet.

Which of the statement(s) given is/are correct?
(a) Only 1
(b) Only 3
(c) Both 1 and 2
(d) Neither 1 nor 2

54 Which of the following can be included within food?
1. Energy
2. Growth repair
3. Maintenance

Select the correct answer using the codes given below
(a) 1 and 2 (b) Only 3
(c) All of these (d) None of these

55 Cereals provide
1. energy 2. iodine
3. vitamin A 4. protein
Find out the correct combination according to codes.
(a) 1, 2 and 3 (b) 1 and 4
(c) 2 and 3 (d) 1 and 3

56 Consider the following statements.
1. A pregnant woman requires more calories than a general adult woman.
2. A pregnant woman requires lesser amount of calcium than a general adult woman.
Which of the statement(s) given above is/are correct?
(a) Only 1 (b) Only 2
(c) Both 1 and 2 (d) Neither 1 nor 2

57 Consider the following statements.
1. BMR increases with age and reaches highest in old age.
2. Physical illness does not affect BMR.
Which of the statements given above is/are correct?
(a) Only 1 (b) Only 2
(c) Both 1 and 2 (d) Neither 1 nor 2

58 Multi-purpose foods are
1. specially prepared 2. nutritious
3. cheap 4. healthy
Select the correct answer using the codes given below
(a) 1 and 2 (b) 3 and 4
(c) All of these (d) None of these

59 The term 'food' means
1. removing hunger 2. renewing strength
3. getting satisfied 4. nourishing body
Select the correct answer using the codes given below
(a) 2, 3 and 4 (b) 1 and 3
(c) None of these (d) All of these

60 Consider the following statements.
1. Enzymes act as catalyst in digestion process.
2. Body secretes different chemicals to digest food.
Which of the statements given above is/are correct?
(a) Only 1 (b) Only 2
(c) Both 1 and 2 (d) Neither 1 nor 2

61 Consider the following statements.
1. BMR decreases while performing physical exercises.
2. Starvation increases BMR.
Which of the statements given above is/are correct?
(a) Only 1 (b) Only 2
(c) Both 1 and 2 (d) Neither 1 nor 2

62 Consider the following statements.
1. A balanced diet should have maximum amount of carbohydrates and fats.
2. A balanced diet should have adequate amount of roughage.
Which of the statements given above is/are correct?
(a) Only 1 (b) Only 2
(c) Both 1 and 2 (d) Neither 1 nor 2

63 Which of the following statements is/are correct?
1. Root vegetables do not suffer much loss of nutrients by either wet or dry methods of cooking skin prevents leaching.
2. If soda (sodium-bicarbonate) is added to pulses to facilitate cooking or to preserve the colour, most of thiamine is destroyed.
Select the correct answer using the codes given below
(a) Only 1 (b) Both 1 and 2
(c) Only 2 (d) Neither 1 nor 2

64 Oral fluids do not include
1. Fruit punch 2. Whey water
Select the correct answer using the codes given below
(a) Only 1
(b) Only 2
(c) Both 1 and 2
(d) Neither 1 nor 2

65 Consider the following statements.
1. RDIs are set high enough to meet the needs of almost all healthy people.
2. RDIs are also applicable for people suffering from diseases.
Which of the statements given above is/are correct?
(a) Only 1 (b) Only 2
(c) Both 1 and 2 (d) Neither 1 nor 2

66 Arrange in sequence the phases of fat absorption.
(a) Mucosal uptake, Esterification, Emulsification, Chylomicron formation
(b) Esterification, Emulsification, Chylomicron formations, Mucosal uptake
(c) Emulsification, Chylomicron formation, Esterification, Mucosal uptake
(d) Chylomicron formation, Mucosal uptake, Emulsification, Esterification

67 Arrange the following in the sequence.
1. Distribute total amount of calorie required, decided between meals.
2. Check day's diet inclusion of specific food groups in the amount decided.
3. Identify the individual and his/her specific requirements.
4. Decide number of meals to be consumed.
Codes
(a) 3, 4, 1, 2 (b) 3, 1, 4, 2
(c) 1, 2, 3, 4 (d) 2, 3, 1, 4

68 Arrange the following in correct sequence.
1. Juices are secreted from digestive organs glands.
2. Food intake from the mouth.
3. Enzymes break down the food.
4. Food passes through oesophagus.
Codes
(a) 1, 2, 3, 4 (b) 2, 3, 1, 4
(c) 2, 1, 4, 3 (d) 2, 4, 1, 3

69 Arrange the following oils in increasing percentage of poly unsaturated fatty acids.

1. Olive oil 2. Groundnut oil
3. Coconut oil 4. Mustard oil
5. Sunflower oil 6. Soyabean oil

Codes

(a) 1, 2, 3, 4, 5, 6 (b) 3, 2, 1, 4, 5, 6
(c) 3, 1, 2, 4, 6, 5 (d) 3, 1, 4, 6, 5, 2

70 Match the following.

List I	List II
A. Vitamin C	1. By atmospheric oxidation
B. Vitamin C destruction	2. Present in fresh fruits and vegetables
C. Sprouted pulses	3. Three times more Vitamin C
D. Sprouted green gram	4. Richest source of Vitamin C
E. Amla	5. Vitamin C in enhanced

Codes

	A	B	C	D	E		A	B	C	D	E
(a)	2	1	5	3	4	(b)	3	2	4	1	5
(c)	5	3	2	4	1	(d)	1	4	5	2	3

71 Match the following.

List I	List II
A. Papaya	1. Iron
B. Orange	2. Calcium
C. Dates	3. Vitamin C
D. Ragi	4. Vitamin A

Codes

	A	B	C	D		A	B	C	D
(a)	1	2	3	4	(b)	2	3	4	1
(c)	4	3	1	2	(d)	3	2	4	1

72 Match the following.

List I (RDI Components)	List II (Determinant Factors)
A. Energy	1. Retinol
B. Vitamin A	2. Activity level
C. Protein	3. Per kg body weight
D. For infants	4. Body weight

Codes

	A	B	C	D		A	B	C	D
(a)	2	1	4	3	(b)	2	3	1	4
(c)	2	4	3	1	(d)	3	2	1	4

73 Match the following.

List I (Components)	List II (Requirements)
A. Calcium (for adults)	1. 20 mg/1000 kcal
B. Fat soluable vitamins	2. 1000-1200 mg
C. Calcium (for pregnant women)	3. 600 mg/day
D. Iron	4. 800 µg

Codes

	A	B	C	D		A	B	C	D
(a)	3	2	4	1	(b)	3	4	1	2
(c)	3	4	2	1	(d)	3	2	1	4

74 Match the following.

List I	List II
A. Dates	1. Potassium
B. Mango	2. Calcium
C. Ragi	3. Vitamin A
D. Mushroom	4. Iron
E. Banana	5. Protein

Codes

	A	B	C	D	E		A	B	C	D	E
(a)	2	3	1	4	5	(b)	1	2	4	3	5
(c)	4	3	2	5	1	(d)	3	2	1	4	5

75 Match the following.

List I	List II
A. Carbohydrates	1. Rigidity to bones
B. Amino acids	2. Synthesis of proteins
C. Phosphorous	3. Building block of proteins
D. Potassium	4. Facilitates excretion

Codes

	A	B	C	D		A	B	C	D
(a)	4	3	1	2	(b)	1	3	2	4
(c)	3	2	4	1	(d)	2	4	3	1

76 Match the following.

List I	List II
A. Energy giving	1. Proteins
B. Regulation and maintenance	2. Vitamins and minerals
C. Body building	3. Carbohydrates
D. Protective food	4. Water

Codes

	A	B	C	D		A	B	C	D
(a)	1	2	4	3	(b)	3	4	1	2
(c)	2	3	4	1	(d)	4	1	3	2

77 Match the following.

List I	List II
A. Green and yellow vegetables	1. Calcium, phosphorus, proteins and vitamins
B. Milk and milk products	2. Ascorbic acid
C. Bread, flour and cereals	3. Carotenoids, ascorbic acid and iron
D. Oranges, grapefruit, tomatoes and raw cabbage	4. Thiamine, niacin, riboflavin, iron, carbohydrates and fibre

Codes

	A	B	C	D		A	B	C	D
(a)	2	4	1	3	(b)	1	2	4	3
(c)	4	1	3	2	(d)	3	1	4	2

78 Match the following.

List I	List II
A. Roots	1. Cabbage and spinach
B. Leaves and stems	2. Mushroom
C. Flower	3. Beet root, carrot, radish, sweet potato and turnip
D. Fungus	4. Broccoli and cauliflower

Codes

	A	B	C	D		A	B	C	D
(a)	3	1	4	2	(b)	4	3	2	1
(c)	2	4	1	3	(d)	1	2	3	4

79 Match the following.

List I (Components)	List II (Requirements)
A. Maganese	1. 50-20 µg/day
B. Copper	2. 400 g/day
C. Anti-oxidants	3. 2-5 mg/day
D. Chromium	4. 2 mg/day

Codes

	A	B	C	D
(a)	4	3	2	1
(b)	3	4	2	1
(c)	3	4	1	2
(d)	4	2	1	3

80 Match the following.

List I	List II
A. Fruits are generally	1. Contain carotene
B. Yellow fruits like mango and papaya	2. Rich in carbohydrates
C. Dried fruits like dates and raisins	3. Rich in iron
D. Banana	4. Good sources of Vitamin C
E. Jaggery is	5. Sources of iron

Codes

	A	B	C	D	E
(a)	4	1	5	2	3
(b)	1	2	5	4	3
(c)	2	3	4	1	5
(d)	5	4	3	2	1

Directions (Q. Nos. 81-95) *In the questions given below are two statements, labelled as Assertion (A) and Reason (R). Into context of the two statements, which one of the following is correct?*

Codes

(a) Both A and R are true, but R is the correct explanation of A
(b) A is true, but R is not the correct explanation of A
(c) A is true, but R is false
(d) A is false, but R is true

81 **Assertion** (A) Males have higher BMR than females.
Reason (R) Males perform more physical work than females.

82 **Assertion** (A) A balanced diet should have variety and should not be completely different from the habitual diet of a person.
Reason (R) Habitual diet often consists of high amount of carbohydrates, fats and proteins.

83 **Assertion** (A) Macro nutrients provide structural materials and energy to the body.
Reason (R) Macronutrients are required by the body in large quantity.

84 **Assertion** (A) Energy giving function of the body is performed mainly by vitamins.
Reason (R) The energy released by burning of these two nutrients in the body is helpful in performing the various activities.

85 **Assertion** (A) Foods needed for growth and repair of body cells and tissues are called body building foods.
Reason (R) Foods such as pulses, oilseeds and nuts are rich in fat, but may not contain all the essential amino acids.

86 **Assertion** (A) A balanced diet should have adequate roughage.
Reason (R) Roughage is very important in digestion process.

87 **Assertion** (A) Calorie intake should be correct and should balance energy expenditure.
Reason (R) Excess of calorie helps to work faster and better.

88 **Assertion** (A) Health of a person is influenced by the quality of foods eaten.
Reason (R) Health is also influenced by body's ability to utilise these foods to meet the need.

89 **Assertion** (A) The basal metabolic rate decreases gradually, once adulthood is attained.
Reason (R) Energy degree rise in temperature results in 12% increases in the BMR.

90 **Assertion** (A) Nutrient requirements differ with the size and age of individual.
Reason (R) A person of specified age and size is labelled as reference.

91 **Assertion** (A) Plant foods usually contain insufficient quantities of four essential amino acids.
Reason (R) Plant foods may supplement one another, since they are not lacking in the same amino acids.

92 **Assertion** (A) RDAs is the minimum amount of a nutrient to be actually consumed to meet the requirement of the body.
Reason (R) It is required to prevent symptoms of deficiency and maintain satisfactory level of nutrients.

93 **Assertion** (A) Energy requirements of an adult man and woman are based on reference man and reference woman.
Reason (R) During adulthood, nutrients are required for the purpose of energy, for replacement of worn out tissues and maintenance of body functions.

94 **Assertion** (A) A balanced diet, suitable to individuals should never be generallised.
Reason (R) People have their own dietery subjected to their own taste, region and income.

95 Assertion (A) Prominent food possessing anti-oxidant properties are green leafy vegetables, fruits like amla and guava, plam oil and sunflower oil and spices like turmeric and cloves.

Reason (R) Some nutrients like carotenoids, ascorbic acid and tocopherols possess anti-oxidant properties.

Directions (Q. Nos. 96-100) *Read the passage given below and answer the questions that follow, based on your understanding of the passage.*

Research to determine the appropriate amount of nutrients for health began in the 1940s because men were being rejected from the military during World War II due to the effects of poor nutrition on their health. The first Food and Nutrition Board was formed to evaluate the nutritional intakes of large populations. Since then, the Food and Nutrition Board has undergone many changes and published comprehensive guidelines on nutrition for both maintenance of good health and disease prevention.

The latest and most comprehensive nutrition recommendations are contained in the so called Dietary Reference Intakes (DRIs). DRIs were created in 1997 and have changed the way that diets are evaluated. The primary goal of these guidelines was not only to prevent nutrient deficiencies, but also to reduce the risk of chronic diseases such as cancer, cardiovascular disease, diabetes and osteoporosis. DRIs have been set for macro nutrients (carbohydrates, proteins, and fats), micro nutrients (vitamins and minerals), electrolytes and water, the role of alcohol in health and disease and bio-active compounds such as phytoestrogens and phytochemicals. There are four types of DRI reference values and they are :

Estimated Average Requirements (EARs) The nutrient intake that is estimated to meet the needs of 50% of the individuals in a given gender and age group.

Recommended Dietary Allowances (RDAs) These tend to be the most well known guidelines. They were set for the nutrient intake that is sufficient to meet the needs of nearly all individuals (about 97%) in a given gender and age group. Many people often incorrectly refer to these as the recommended 'daily' allowances and believe that it is their goal to reach the RDA, each day. It was not meant to be used as a guide for an individual's daily needs. The RDAs were established to be used in setting standards for food assistance programs, for interpreting food record consumption of population and for establishing guidelines for nutrition labels.

Adequate Intakes (Als) The nutrients for which there is not enough information to establish an EAR.

Tolerable Upper Limits (Upper Levels or ULs) A nutrient's maximum level of daily intake that is unlikely to cause adverse health effects in nearly all individuals (97% to 98%) of the population.

96 When was first Food and Nutritional board set up?

(a) During World War I
(b) During world War II
(c) Renaissance
(d) All of these

97 When was DRI created?

(a) In 1988
(b) In 1997
(c) In 1999
(d) In 1988

98 What is the primary goal of DRI?

(a) To prevent nutrient deficiency
(b) To prevent chronic disease
(c) Both (a) and (b)
(d) Neither (a) nor (b)

99 These were set up for nutrient intake that is sufficient for nearly all individuals.

(a) EARs (b) RDAs
(c) AIs (d) ULs

100 Tolerable upper limits include?

(a) minimum level of daily intake by an individual
(b) maximum level of daily inlake by an individual
(c) maximum intake of vtamins
(d) None of the above

PREVIOUS YEARS' QUESTIONS

July 2018

1 During fevers with every 1°F increase in body temperature, the Basal Metabolic Rate changes by

(a) 7% increase (b) 7% decrease
(c) 5% increase (d) 5% decrease

2 Recommended Dietary Allowance of Iron (ICMR, 2010) for a 15 year old girl is

(a) 32 mg/day (b) 27 mg/day
(c) 35 mg/day (s) 28 mg/day

3 Following nutrients are required for an efficient immune response.

1. Vitamin A 2. Zinc
3. Calcium 4. Protein
5. Thiamine

Codes

(a) 1, 2 and 5 (b) 2, 3 and 4
(c) 1, 2 and 4 (e) 2, 3 and 5

4 Following are the symptoms of ascorbic acid deficiency.

1. Gingivitis 2. Delayed wound healing
3. Angular stomatitis 4. Petechial haemorrhage
5. Tachycardia

Codes

(a) 1, 2 and 3 (b) 2, 4 and 5
(c) 3, 4 and 5 (d) 1, 2 and 4

5 Match the following.

List I (Nutrients)	List II (Deficiency Symptoms)
A. Folic acid	1. Tetany
B. Zinc	2. Microcytic anaemia
C. Calcium	3. Cheilosis
D. Iodine	4. Koilonychia
E. Riboflavin	5. Megaloblastic anaemia
	6. Hypogeusia
	7. Impaired mental function

Codes

	A	B	C	D	E
(a)	5	4	1	7	3
(b)	2	4	1	7	3
(c)	5	7	4	6	3
(d)	2	6	1	4	3

November 2017

6 Following are the symptoms of niacin deficiency.

1. Diarrhoea 2. Dermatitis
3. Cretinism 4. Dementia
5. Koilonychia

Codes

(a) 1, 2 and 3 (b) 1, 2 and 4
(c) 2, 3 and 4 (d) 2, 3 and 5

7 Arrange the following food items in increasing order of their iron content per 100g of food.

1. Soya flour 2. Spinach
3. Bajra 4. Ground nuts
5. Jaggery

Codes

(a) 2, 4, 5, 3, 1 (b) 5, 2, 3, 4, 1
(c) 2, 4, 5, 1, 3 (d) 2, 5, 3, 4, 1

8 Match the following.

List I (Nutrients)	List II (Deficiency Symptoms)
A. Cynocobalamine	1. Tetany
B. Thiamine	2. Petechial ha emorrhage
C. Ascorbic acid	3. Pernicious anaemia
D. Iron	4. Hypogeusia
E. Zinc	5. Muscle weakness
	6. Hypochromic Microcytic anaemia
	7. Cretenism

Codes

	A	B	C	D	E
(a)	3	1	7	6	4
(b)	6	5	1	3	2
(c)	3	1	2	6	7
(d)	3	5	2	6	4

9 Ascorbic acid is essential for maintaining the following functions in the body.

1. Collagen formation 2. Acts as a co-enzyme
3. Blood clotting 4. Acts as an anti-oxidant
5. Acts as a reducing agent

Codes

(a) 1, 2 and 4 (b) 1, 4 and 5
(c) 2, 3 and 5 (d) 3, 4 and 5

10 RDA of vitamin A for 10 years old boy as per ICMR, 2010 is ....

(a) 400 µg retinol (b) 350 µg retinol
(c) 600 µg retinol (d) 950 µg retinol

January 2017

11 Match the following.

List I (Nutrients)	List II (Deficiency Symptoms)
A. Folic Acid	1. Tetany
B. Iron	2. Angular stomatitis
C. Niacin	3. Oedema
D. Calcium	4. Megaloblastic anaemia
E. Riboflavin	5. Castle's necklace
	6. Hypochromic microcytic anaemia
	7. Neuropathy

Codes

	A	B	C	D	E
(a)	4	1	7	2	3
(b)	4	6	5	1	2
(c)	6	4	7	3	2
(d)	6	3	5	1	7

July 2016

12 Arrange in correct sequence the progression of the development of eye symptoms due to Vitamin A deficiency.
1. Conjunctival xerosis
2. Corneal xerosis
3. Night blindness
4. Corneal scar
5. Keratomalacia

Codes
(a) 3, 1, 2, 5, 4 (b) 3, 1, 2, 4, 5
(c) 1, 3, 2, 5, 4 (d) 3, 2, 1, 4, 5

13 Following are the disorders due to iodine deficiency.
1. Mental retardation
2. Cretinism
3. Tetany
4. Hypothyroidism
5. Dermatitis

Codes
(a) 1, 2 and 5 (b) 1, 2 and 4
(d) 2, 3 and 4 (d) 2, 4 and 5

14 Following are the symptoms of ascorbic acid deficiency.
1. Symmetrical dermatitis
2. Gingivitis
3. Oedema
4. Delayed wound healing
5. Petechial haemorrhage

Codes
(a) 1, 2 and 4 (b) 2, 4 and 5 (c) 2, 3 and 4 (d) 2, 3 and 5

July 2016

15 Iodine deficiency disorders include the following.
1. Abortion
2. Impaired coordination
3. Impaired skeletal growth
4. Low haemoglobin level
5. Mental retardation

Codes
(a) 1, 3 and 4 (b) 2, 3 and 5 (c) 1, 2 and 5 (d) 3, 4 and 5

16 Match the following.

List I (Nutrients)	List II (Deficiency Disorders)
A. Riboflavin	1. Hypogeusia
B. Ascorbic acid	2. Neural tube defects
C. Zinc	3. Dermatitis
D. Folic acid	4. Glossitis
E. Iodine	5. Gingivitis
	6. Cretinism

Codes

	A	B	C	D	E		A	B	C	D	E
(a)	4	5	1	2	6	(b)	4	3	2	5	6
(c)	3	5	1	4	6	(d)	4	5	1	2	3

17 Match the following.

List I (Nutrients)	List II (Functions)
A. Iron	1. Normal taste acuity
B. Calcium	2. Vision in dark
C. Iodine	3. Haemoglobin synthesis
D. Zinc	4. Stability of teeth enamel
E. Fluorine	5. Bone mineralisation
	6. Brain development

Codes

	A	B	C	D	E		A	B	C	D	E
(a)	3	1	5	2	4	(b)	3	5	6	1	4
(c)	3	5	6	4	2	(d)	3	5	4	2	1

December 2015

18 Match the following.

List I (Nutrients)	List II (Functions)
A. Thiamine	1. DNA-RNA synthesis
B. Pyridoxine	2. Transfer of single carbon unit
C. Riboflavin	3. Carbohydrate metabolism
D. Folic acid	4. Hydroxylation of amino acids
E. Ascorbic acid	5. Oxidation-reduction reaction
	6. Transamination reaction

Codes

	A	B	C	D	E		A	B	C	D	E
(a)	3	1	5	6	4	(b)	1	6	2	3	4
(c)	3	6	5	2	4	(d)	3	4	5	6	1

19 Following are the disorders of vitamin D deficiency.
1. Osteomalacia
2. Rickety rosary
3. Bow legs
4. Koilonychia

Select the correct answer using the codes given below
(a) 2, 3 and 4 (b) 1, 2 and 3
(c) 1,3 and 4 (d) 1,2 and 4

20 RDA of vitamin D for adults as given by ICMR, 2010 is
(a) 25. μg/day (b) 5 μg/day
(c) 10 μg/day (d) 50 μg/day

June 2015

21 The active form of vitamin D is
(a) ergosterol (b) ergocalciferol
(c) cholecalciferol (d) dihydroxy cholecalciferol

22 Following are the disorders of vitamin A deficiency.
1. Xeropthalmia
2. Night blindness
3. Osteoporosis
4. Cretinism
5. Keratomalacia

Select the correct answer using the codes given below
(a) 2, 4 and 5 (b) 1, 3 and 4
(c) 1, 2 and 5 (d) 1, 3 and 5

23 Following are the functions of vitamin A.
1. Vision
2. Co-enzyme
3. Immune response
4. DNA synthesis
5. Maintenance of differentiated epithelia

Select the correct answer using the codes given below.
(a) 1, 3 and 5 (b) 1, 2 and 3 (c) 3, 4 and 5 (d) 2, 4 and 5

December 2014

24 Major function of zinc in the human body is
(a) haemoglobin synthesis (b) DNA and RNA synthesis
(c) bone health (d) vision

25 Iodine deficiency disorders include the following
1. Goitre
2. Still birth
3. Osteoporosis
4. Mental retardation

Select the correct answer using codes given below

(a) 1, 2 and 3 (b) 1, 2 and 4
(c) 1, 3 and 4 (d) 2, 3 and 4

26 Following factors enhance the bio availability of iron in the diet.

1. Dietary fiber 2. Ascorbic acid
3. Animal protein 4. Phytate

Select correct answer using the codes given below

a) 2 and 3 (b) 1 and 2
(c) 3 and 4 (d) 1 and 4

27 Match the following.

List I (Nutrients)	List II (Deficiency Symptoms)
A. Protein	1. Dementia
B. Folic acid	2. Osteoporosis
C. Thiamin	3. Glossitis
D. Vitamin D	4. Microcytic anaemia
E. Riboflavin	5. Macrocytic anaemia
	6. Neuropathy
	7. Flaky paint dermatosis

Codes

	A	B	C	D	E
(a)	7	5	6	2	3
(b)	1	5	3	2	7
(c)	7	4	6	2	3
(d)	1	2	3	5	7

June 2014

28 Match the following.

List I (Deficiency Diseases)	List II (Symptoms)
A. Xerophthalmia	1. Glossitis
B. Beri- Beri	2. Koilonychia
C. Ariboflavinosis	3. Bow legs
D. Pellagra	4. Keratomalacia
E. Anaemia	5. Petechial haemorrhages
F. Rickets	6. Diarrhea and dementia
G. Scurvy	7. Neuropathy

Codes

	A	B	C	D	E	F	G
(a)	1	2	3	4	5	6	7
(b)	2	4	7	5	3	1	6
(c)	4	5	7	6	3	1	2
(d)	4	7	1	6	2	3	5

29 **Assertion** (A) Ascorbic acid and iron in the meal should be in 2 : 1 ratio.

Reason (R) Desirable level of ascorbic acid in a meal improves iron absorption among Indians on a vegetarian diet.

Codes

(a) A is false, but R is true
(b) A is true, but R is false
(c) A is true, but R is not the correct explanation of A
(d) A is true and R is the correct explanation of A

30 Which of the following are essential amino acids?

1. Tryptophan 2. Valine
3. Lysine 4. Leucine
5. Serine 6. Alanine

Codes

(a) 1, 2, 3 and 4 (b) 1, 3, 4 and 5
(c) 5, 4, 2 and 1 (d) 3, 4, 5 and 6

31 Arrange the following foods in decreasing order of Vitamin B_{12} content.

1. Liver 2. Fish
3. Mutton 4. Milk

Codes

(a) 1, 2, 3, 4 (b) 2, 3, 4, 1
(c) 3, 1, 2, 4 (d) 4, 2, 1, 3

32 Daily zinc requirement of an adult man is

(a) 12 mg (b) 8 mg
(c) 350 mg (d) 600 mg

ANSWERS

Exam Based Questions

1 (d)	2 (d)	3 (c)	4 (b)	5 (a)	6 (a)	7 (b)	8 (d)	9 (a)	10 (d)
11 (c)	12 (b)	13 (d)	14 (c)	15 (d)	16 (a)	17 (c)	18 (b)	19 (d)	20 (d)
21 (b)	22 (c)	23 (b)	24 (c)	25 (c)	26 (c)	27 (b)	28 (a)	29 (b)	30 (c)
31 (a)	32 (b)	33 (a)	34 (a)	35 (a)	36 (d)	37 (c)	38 (d)	39 (a)	40 (d)
41 (c)	42 (b)	43 (a)	44 (d)	45 (c)	46 (c)	47 (c)	48 (d)	49 (a)	50 (d)
51 (d)	52 (c)	53 (c)	54 (a)	55 (b)	56 (a)	57 (d)	58 (c)	59 (d)	60 (c)
61 (d)	62 (b)	63 (b)	64 (b)	65 (a)	66 (c)	67 (a)	68 (d)	69 (c)	70 (a)
71 (c)	72 (a)	73 (b)	74 (c)	75 (a)	76 (b)	77 (d)	78 (a)	79 (b)	80 (a)
81 (a)	82 (c)	83 (b)	84 (d)	85 (c)	86 (a)	87 (b)	88 (c)	89 (b)	90 (b)
91 (b)	92 (d)	93 (b)	94 (d)	95 (a)	96 (b)	97 (b)	98 (c)	99 (b)	100 (b)

Previous Years' Questions

1 (a)	2 (b)	3 (c)	4 (d)	5 (a)	6 (b)	7 (a)	8 (b)	9 (b)	10 (c)
11 (b)	12 (a)	13 (b)	14 (b)	15 (c)	16 (a)	17 (b)	18 (c)	19 (b)	20 (c)
21 (d)	22 (c)	23 (a)	24 (b)	25 (b)	26 (a)	27 (a)	28 (d)	29 (d)	30 (a)
31 (a)	32 (b)								

Public Health Nutrition

The public health nutrition programmes train individuals to promote health and reduce the risk of chronic diseases and obesity through educational and environmental approaches. It is important to understand that nutrition problems in developing as well as developed countries can not be solved in the laboratory or clinic alone.

Public Health

The rapidly changing global trends in the area of food consumption patterns, lifestyles and environment have a tremendous impact on the nutrition and health profiles of the communities. Though, today consumer is much better informed about various issues relating to his health, the information explosion also adds to confusion in making the right choices and staying clear of misinformation and misconceptions.

Therein, emerges the need for professionals with sound knowledge to ensure proper nutrition and positive health of the people they serve. This need is being felt more acutely in the current health scenario prevailing all over the world, though the specific issues may vary from country to country.

Nutrition

Nutrition may be defined as the science of food and its relationship to health. Nutrients are required for body growth, development and maintenance. Good nutrition means "maintaining a nutritional status that enables us to grow well and enjoy good health". The subject of nutrition is very extensive. Nutrient requirement can be defined as the minimum amount of the absorbed nutrient that is necessary for maintaining the normal and physiological functions of the body.

In this Chapter

Public Nutrition

Public nutrition is concerned with improving nutrition of population, both poor and industrialised countries, linking with community, public health nutrition and complementary disciplines.

Concept of Public Nutrition

It is widely quoted among applied nutrition professional that "Nutrition is not a discipline to be studied; it is a problem to be solved". Solving nutrition problems requires multi-disciplinary cooperation. It is important to understand that nutrition problems in developing as well as developed countries cannot be solved in the laboratory or clinic alone. The skills and knowledge needed to address these constraints are quite different from those of the laboratory scientist. They require a different kind of training associated with the science of nutrition.

In 1996, letter to 'The American Journal of Clinical Nutrition', **Mason** and others suggested the name 'public nutrition' to define a new field, encompassing the range of factors known to influence nutrition in population including diet and health, social, cultural and behavioural factors and the economic and political context. Public health and nutrition would focus on problem-solving in a real world setting, making it by definition, an applied field of study whose success is measured in terms of effectiveness in improving nutritional conditions.

Scope of Public Nutrition

Nutritional status is important as a determinant and correlate with health status and as a maker of individual welfare. A consequence of nutrition as the focus of a programme and policy specialisation may be that solutions are often linked to food, failing to integrate health concerns such as immunisation, environmental sanitation, disease prevention and treatment. The field of public nutrition is unique in requiring at least some understanding of the entire range such as of determinants of nutritional outcomes. The study of these basic determinants extends into areas of economics, agricultural policy, health science and the social sciences as well as public policy and management.

Public nutrition is an applied and very vast field. It includes many activities, which are as follows:

- An understanding and raising awareness of the nature, causes and consequences of nutrition problems in society.
- Epidemiology, including monitoring, surveillance and evaluation.
- Nutritional requirements and dietary guidelines for population.
- Community nutrition and community based programmes.
- Public education, especially nutrition education for behavioural change.
- Programmes and interventions and their design, planning, management and evaluation.
- Timely monitoring and prevention and mitigation of emergencies, including use of emergency food aid.
- Advocacy and linkage with population and environmental concerns.
- Public policies and programmes relevant to nutrition in several sectors *e.g.*, economic development, health, agriculture and education.

Nutritional Requirements of Different Groups

The nutritional requirements of the human body change as we move through different life stages. It is very important to take into account the extra demands placed on your body by these changes. The nutrient requirements during the four main stages of the human lifecycle vary considerably what infants and children require is different from what adults and the elderly need. In order to estimate nutritional requirements of individuals or groups, we need to consider the following factors :

Physical Activity Whether a person is engaged in heavy physical activity.

Body Size and Composition The general build of a person or group.

Climate Whether a person or group is living in hot or cold climate.

Physiological States Such as pregnancy and lactation.

Based on these factors, nutritional requirements in the different segments of the population can be classified into four groups:

Nutritional and Food Requirements for Infants

Infant's first year is the time of most rapid growth. Healthy child doubles his birth weight (3.2 kg) by 6 months and his weight becomes 3 times by the time the child is 1 year old. The normal birth length of child, 50 to 55 cm increases by another 23 to 25 cm during the first year. With increase in length the body proportions also change.

Nutritional Requirements

As growth during infancy is very rapid, dietary adaptation is required during early infancy. Much of the nutrient requirements are by breast feeding and the RDA (Recommended Dietary Allowances) of an infant is based on composition of breast milk. The RDA of ICMR is for infants.

Recommended Dietary Allowances (Revised in 2010) for Infants 0-6 and 6-12 Months

	Infants (0-6 months)	**Infants** (6-12 months)
Body weight	5.4 kg	8.4 kg
Net Energy	92 kcal/kg/day	80 kcal/kg/day
Protein	1.16 g/kg/day	1.69 g/kg/day
Visible fat	–	19 g/day
Calcium	500	500
Iron	46 µg/kg/day	46 µg/kg/day
Vitamin A (Retinol)	350 µg/day	350 µg/day
Vitamin A (β-carotene)	–	2800 µg/day
Thiamine	0.2 mg/day	0.3 mg/day
Riboflavin	0.3 mg/day	0.4 mg/day
Niacin equivalent	710 µg/day	650 µg/day
Pyridoxine	0.1 mg/day	0.4 mg/day
Ascorbic Acid	25 mg/day	25 mg/day
Dietary folate	25 µg/day	25 µg/day
Vitamin B_{12}	0.2	0.2
Magnesium	30	45
Zinc	–	–

Food Requirements

The word 'nutrition' is derived from 'nutricus', which means to suckle at the breast'. Breast milk is the natural food for the infant. Successful breast feeding is an important child rearing skill to be learnt and practiced.

Colostrum

During the first 2 or 3 days watery and yellowish fluid that comes from the mammary gland differs from the regular milk and is called colostrum. It is secreted in small quantity of about 10-40 ml.

It is rich in protein. The total fat content of colostrum is less than mature milk. The concentration of lactose is also less.

The levels of niacin pantothenic acid, biotin and riboflavin are also low. Vitamin C is secreted at about the same level as in mature milk. Zinc content of colostrum is 20 mg/1 whereas mature milk has 2.6 mg/1.

The composition of colostrum is given in table Colostrum contains an interfer on like substance, which possesses strong antiviral activity. Colostrum contains B_{12} binding protein, which renders B_{12}. It also contains anti-bodies against viral diseases such as small pox, polio, measles and influenza.

Enzymes like lysozyme, peroxidase and xanthine oxidase that promote cell maturation are found to be more in colostrum.

Composition of Colostrum

Nutrients	Amount	Nutrients	Amount
Energy (kcal)	58	Protein (g)	2.7
Fat (g)	2.9	Lactose (g)	5.3
Calcium (mg)	31	Carotene I (U)	186
Phosphorus (mg)	14	Vitamin AI (U)	296
Iron (mg)	0.09		

Comparison of Human Milk with Cow's and Buffalo's Milk

Nutrients	Human's Milk	Cow's Milk (values per 100 g)	Buffalo's Milk
Water (g)	88	87.5	81
Energy (kcal)	65	67	117
Protein (g)	1.1	3.2	4.3
Carbohydrate (g)	7.4	4.4	5
Fat (g)	3.4	4.1	6.5
Calcium (mg)	28	120	210
Phosphorus (mg)	11	90	130
Iron (mg)	–	0.2	0.2
Carotene (mcg)	137	174	160
Thiamine (mg)	0.02	0.05	0.04
Riboflavin (mg)	0.02	0.19	0.1
Vitamin C (mg)	3	2	1
Caseinogen and Lactalbumin Ratio	1.2	3.1	–

Artificial Feeding

Though no milk can be a real substitute for mother's milk, sometimes it is needed to give artificial feeding.

Circumstances under which artificial feeding is essential are:

- The mother is suffering from serious illness, fever or infection.
- Another pregnancy intervenes during lactation.
- The child is too weak to nurse or cannot be because of harelip or cleft palate.
- Breast milk has completely stopped or insufficient for a child.
- Mother is not able to feed the child.
- The mother is on anti-coagulants, steroids and radio active drugs.
- Death of the mother.

Feeding Problems

Unfeeding is suggested by restlessness and crying and by failure to gain weight adequately. Despite complete emplying of the breast or bottle under feeding may also result from the infant's failure to take a sufficient quantity of food even when offered. Constipation, failure to sleep, irritability and excess crying can result due to under feeding.

Supplementary Foods

Liquid supplementary foods like fresh fruit juice of orange, tomato, sweet lime grapes, etc. and cod liver oil

Mashed supplementary foods like starch rich cereals, and vegetables like potato cooked and mashed. Green leafy vegetables cooked and mashed.

Solid supplementary foods like carrot, cucumber, cooked rice, piece of roti, toast, biscuit, etc. It will help the infant to chew and exercise his gums.

Pre-Term Baby

The pre-term babies are those who are born before 37 weeks of gestation. Low birth weight babies are born with a birth weight of less than 2500 g. The incidence of low birth weight babies in India is 30%. The pre-term is at a disadvantage in many aspects of nutrition.

The problems faced pre-term babies are poor sucking and shallowing reflexes, relatively high caloric requirement with small stomach capacity, poor gag reflex and incompetent cardio oesophageal sphincter leading to aspiration, decreased absorption of essential nutrients.

Weaving

The term 'weaving' comes from the word 'werrian', which 'means to accustom'. Weaving begins from the moment when supplementary food starts and continues till the child is taken off the breast completely. Solid food added to an infant's diet is called **beikost**. There is an increase in activities of the enzymes at the time of weaving.

The first solid foods are normally introduced at 5-6 months. The foods given are cereals, milk or cereal per day preparation such as suji halwa, rice-milk, upma, rice-dal, khichdi, bread, rice flakes, poha, etc are given to the child. Fruits such as ripe banana, mango, papaya, which are soft and pulpy are also given.

Nutritional and Food Requirements for Pre-School Children (1-6 years)

The growth in the years between 1 to 6 is generally slower than in the first year of life, but continues gradually. Activity also increases, markedly during the second year of life as the child starts moving. Development of a full dentition by about the age of 2 years also increases the range of foods that can safely be eaten by the child.

Recommended Dietary Allowances for Pre-School Children

	Children (1-3 years)	Children (4-6 years)
Body weight (kg)	12.9	18.0
Net energy (kcal/day)	1060	1350
Protein (gm/day)	16.7	20.1
Visible fat (gm/day)	27	25
Calcium (mg/day)	600	600
Iron (mg/day)	.9	13
Vitamin A Retinol (µg/day)	400	400
Vitamin A β-carotene (µg/day)	3200	3200
Thiamine (mg/day)	0.5	0.7
Riboflavin (mg/day)	0.6	0.8
Niacin (equivalent mg/day)	8	11
Pyridoxine (mg/day)	0.9	0.9
Ascorbic acid (mg/day)	40	40
Dietary folate (µg/day)	80	100
Vitamin B_{12} (µg/day)	0.2-1.0	0.2-1.0
Magnesium (mg/day)	50	70
Zinc (mg/day)	5	7

Dietary Guidelines for Pre-School Children

- The diet should be adequate in quantity and quality of different nutrients in addition to the amount of milk recommended. The pre-school child should have 2 small servings of protein-rich foods.
- Proper elimination is usually maintained by a daily diet of fruits, vegetables and whole grain products.
- Their food intake will improve if the food is interesting and attractive.
- Food should be slightly seasoned, so that they taste better and the child takes it well.
- Child should never be forced to eat more than he can take.
- Regularity of meal times is essential.
- Beverages like tea and coffee should be restricted as they overstimulate the system.
- The child should never be hurried, while taking the food.
- Different cooking methods and new attractive combinations encourage the child to eat more.
- The diet should include a variety of foods.

Nutritional and Food Requirements for School Children (7-15 years)

The school age period has been called the latent time of growth. The rate of growth slow down and body changes occur gradually. The slowed rate of growth during this period results in a gradual decline in the food requirement per unit of body weight.

Recommended Dietary Allowances for School Children

	Boys (7-9 years)	Girls (7-9 years)	Boys (10-12 years)	Girls (10-12 years)	Boys (13-15 years)	Girls (13-15 years)
Body weight (kg)	25.1	25.1	34.3	35.0	47.6	46.6
Net energy (kcal/day)	1690	1690	2190	2010	2750	2330
Protein (gm/day)	29.5	29.5	39.9	40.4	54.3	51.9
Visible fat (gm/day)	30	30	35	35	45	40
Calcium (mg/day)	600	600	800	800	800	800
Iron (mg/day)	16	16	21	27	32	27
Vitamin A Retinol (μg/day)	600	600	600	600	600	600
Vitamin A (β-carotene μg/day)	4800	4800	4800	4800	4800	4800
Thiamine (mg/day)	0.8	0.8	1.1	1.0	1.4	1.2
Riboflavin (mg/day)	1.0	1.0	1.3	1.2	1.6	1.4
Niacin Equivalent (mg/day)	13	13	15	13	16	14
Pyridoxine (mg/day)	1.6	1.6	1.6	1.6	2.0	2.0
Ascorbic acid (mg/day)	40	40	40	40	40	40
Dietary folate (μg/day)	120	120	140	140	150	150
Vitamin B_{12} (μg/day)	0.2-1.0	0.2-1.0	0.2-1.0	0.2-1.0	0.2-1.0	0.2-1.0
Magnesium (mg/day)	100	100	120	160	165	210
Zinc (mg/day)	8	8	9	9	11	11

Dietary Guidelines for School Children

- Nutritional requirement should meet their increasing activity and growth and special requirements because of sickness or injury.
- Children are generally restless and do not like to spend too much time at the table of eating.
- Children also tend to be bored with foods easily. So, menus need to provide variety in colour, texture, taste and flavour.
- The climatic and weather conditions are important consideration too.
- Children have varying appetites and often prefer snacky meals at frequent intervals to a few large one.
- New foods are likely to be accepted if it is given in a form, which can be easily handled and they should be offered at regular intervals until the child learns to accept it.
- The young child should be encouraged to eat with the rest of the family as he is ready to take the family meals and also because the interactions between family members are a part of normal development.
- If the child does not like salads, they can be incorporated in recipes like sandwiches.

Nutritional and Food Requirements for Adolescents

The period of transition from childhood to adulthood is called adolescence with accelerated physical, bio-chemical and emotional development. It is during this period that the final growth spurt occurs.

There are many body changes, which result due to the influence of hormones. The growth spurt of the boys is slower than that of the girls. The growth spurt signalling the onset of a critical body composition of 10% body fat. However, 22% of body fat is required to maintain regular ovulation. Greatest nutrient need for boys is between 12-15 years and for girls is 10-13 years. Both males and females are influenced by the adequacy of zinc status. They attain their adult stature between 18-20 years, but bone mass continues to increase upto the age of 25 years. With the preformed growth of adolescence, there is increased demand for energy, protein, minerals and vitamins.

The dimensional changes and changes in maturational timing over the generations are called secular changes. The term 'secular' referring to successive periods of time. The secular trend refers to average age of puberty decreasing over time. The puberty is starting earlier for boys and girls now than it did a hundred years ago. Magnitude of secular trend in stature, which may approximate 1 cm/decade, and the inverse secular trend in menarcheal timing, which may approximately 0.2 yr/decade. Adolescent anorexia may lead to diminution of the secular trend.

Recommended Dietary Allowances for Adolescents

	Boys (13-15 years)	Girls (13-15 years)	Boys (16-17 years)	Girls (16-17 years)
Body Weight (kg)	47.6	46.6	55.4	52.1
Net Energy (kcal/day)	2750	2330	3020	2440
Protein (g/day)	51.3	51.9	61.5	55.5
Visible fat (gm/day)	45	40	50	35
Calcium (mg/day)	800	800	800	800
Iron (mg/day)	32	27	28	26
Vitamin A Retinol (μg/day)	600	600	600	600
Vitamin A β-carotene (mg/day)	4800	4800	4800	4800
Thiamine (mg/day)	1.4	1.2	1.5	1.0
Riboflavin (mg/day)	1.6	1.4	1.8	1.2
Niacin equivalent (mg/day)	16	14	17	14
Pyridoxine (mg/day)	2.0	2.0	2.0	2.0
Ascorbic acid (mg/day)	40	40	40	40
Dietary folate (μg/day)	150	150	200	200
Vitamin B_{12} (μg/day)	0.2-1.0	0.2-1.0	0.2-1.0	0.2-1.0
Magnesium (mg/day)	165	210	195	235
Zinc (mg/day)	11	11	12	12

Dietary Guidelines for Adolescents

- Adequate well-balanced nutritious foods should be taken to prevent obesity under nutrition.
- An adolescent girl should take enough calcium rich foods in her diet to increase bone density, which delays the onset of osteoporosis.
- No meal of the day should be missed.
- Avoid empty caloric foods such as carbonated beverages.
- Iron rich foods may be included in the diet to prevent anaemia.

Nutritional and Food Requirements for Expectant Mother

Adequate nutrition, before and during pregnancy has greater potential for a long term health impact than it does at any other time. Maternal health is a complex, influenced by various genetic, social and economic factors, infections and environmental conditions, many of which may affect the foetal growth.

Physiological adaptations result in improved utilisation of nutrients either through increased absorption, decreased excretion or alternations in metabolism.

A woman who has been well nourished before her pregnancy, she has reserves of several nutrients. Due to this, the needs of the growing foetus can be met without affecting her health. Infants, who are well nourished in the womb have an enhanced chance of entering life in good physical and mental health.

The effects of undernutrition during reproduction will vary depending upon the nutrients involved, the length of time it is lacking and the stage of gestation at which it occurs.

A women whose diet is adequate before pregnancy is usually able to bear a full term viable infant, without extensive modification of her diet. Mother's diet should produce adequate nutrients, so that maternal stores do not get depleted and produce sufficient milk to nourish her child after birth.

Recommended Dietary Allowances for Expectant Mother

RDA for Pregnant Woman	Amount
Body weight (kg)	55
Net Energy (kcal/day)	+350
Protein (gm/day)	82.2
Visible fat (gm/day)	30
Calcium (mg/day)	1200
Iron (mg/day)	35
Vitamin A Retinol (μg/day)	800
Vitamin A β-carotene (μg/day)	6400
Thiamine (mg/day)	+0.2
Riboflavin (mg/day)	+0.3
Niacin equivalent (mg/day)	+2
Pyridoxine (mg/day)	2.5
Ascorbic acid (mg/day)	60
Dietary folate (μg/day)	500
Vitamin B_{12} (μg/day)	1.2
Magnesium (mg/day)	310
Zinc (mg/day)	12

Dietary Guidelines for Expectant Mother

- Small and frequent feedings should be taken. Avoid fasting or missing any meal.
- More fibre should be included in the diet to prevent constipation, which is a common problem during pregnancy. 5-6 servings of fruits and vegetables should be included in the daily diet.
- Diet should be rich in calcium to prevent osteomalacia. Calcium supplement may also be taken.
- Iron rich foods should be taken to prevent anaemia and to build up iron stores in the foetal body. Iron supplements may be taken.
- Diet should contain optimum amount of sodium. In case of oedema or hypertension, sodium is restricted.
- Inclusion of green leafy vegetables ensures minerals like calcium and iron.
- Plenty of water should be taken to keep your system running.
- Fatty rich foods, fried foods, excessive seasoning and strongly flavoured vegetables may be restricted in case of nausea and gastric distress.
- Fluids should be taken between meals, rather than along with the meals.
- Adequate amount of calories should be taken, so that enough fat is deposited during pregnancy which is required for lactation.

Nutritional and Food Requirements for Lactating Women

The nutritional link between the mother and the child continues even after birth. The new born baby depends for some period solely on breast milk for his existence.

Recommended Dietary Allowances for Lactating Women

	Lactating Women (0-6 months)	Lactating Women (6-12 months)
Body weight (kg)	55	55
Net Energy (kcal/day)	+600	+520
Protein (gm/day)	77.9	70.2
Visible fat (gm/day)	30	30
Calcium (mg/day)	1200	1200
Iron (mg/day)	25	25
Vitamin A retinol (μg/day)	950	950
Vitamin A β-carotene (μg/day)	7600	7600
Thiamine (mg/day)	+0.3	+0.2
Riboflavin (mg/day)	+0.4	+0.3
Niacin equivalent (mg/day)	+4	+3
Pyridoxine (mg/day)	2.5	2.5
Ascorbic Acid (mg/day)	80	80
Dietary folate (μg/day)	300	300
Vitamin B_{12} (μg/day)	1.5	1.5
Magnesium (mg/day)	310	310
Zinc (mg/day)	12	12

Dietary Guidelines for Lactating Women

- Nutritional requirements are maximum during lactation, compared to any other age group in a women's life. Hence, the diet should be balanced and meet the requirement. Number of meals can be increased.
- The diet can include lactogogues, which stimulate the production of milk. Garlic, milk, almonds and garden cress seeds are considered to increase the milk production in certain regions of India. Some also believe foods of animal origin like goat's meat, fish and mutton increase the secretion of breast milk.
- Weight gain beyond the desirable body size, should be avoided. When the baby is weaved, the mother must reduce her food intake in order that obesity may be avoided.
- It is better to control constipation by inclusion in the diet of raw and cooked fruits and vegetables, whole grains and an adequate amount of water than by use of laxatives.
- No food need to be withheld from the mother, unless it causes distress to the infant. Tomatoes, onions, members of cabbage family, chocolate, spices and condiments may cause gastric distress or loose stools in the infant.
- If the mother loses rapid weight loss while breast feeding, her calorie intake is to be increased.

Successful lactation is dependent not only upon an adequate diet, but also upon sufficient rest for the mother, freedom from anxiety and a desire to nurse the baby.

Nutritional and Food Requirements for Adults

Man needs a wide range of nutrients to perform various functions in the body and to lead a healthy life. During adulthood, nutrients are required for the purpose of energy for replacement of wornout tissues and their maintenance of body functions. Though, there is no growth during adulthood, protein is required for the replacement of wornout tissues. The nutritional requirement of other age groups is sometimes extrapolated from adult's requirements.

Satiety Value A meal with good satiety value is the meal which satisfies the hunger for a reasonable longer time. Carbohydrates have low satiety value as compared to proteins and fats.

Fatty foods like halwa and puree provide greater satisfaction. Proteins take a long time to get digested in the alimentary canal and hence, provide considerable satiety value.

Importance of Flexibility in Meal Planning It is very important to allow a certain amount of flexibility, while planning a meal for your family. For example, you planned to cook matar panner curry, if the paneer is not available, it can be substituted by nutrinuggets.

Socio-cultural and Religious Factors Affecting Meal Planning Meals should be planned according to social custom. Non-vegetarian foods are often avoided due to religious, socio and cultural consideration in Hindu. Whereas, Muslims take non-vegetarian food, North Indians like to eat more chappati, whereas South Indians eat dosa, idli, etc. Some special dishes are prepared on religious festivals like Diwali, Holi, Dusshera, etc.

Nutritional and Food Requirements During Old Age

Old age is best defined as the age of retirement i.e., 60 years and above. Improvement in healthcare technology has resulted in increased life expectancy. The number of persons in old age has increased. In India, the elderly constitute about 10% of the total population.

Changes in Organs Or Functions with Ageing that may Influence Nutrient Requirements

Organs/Functions	Changes	Effect on Nutrition
Taste and smell	• Decreased taste buds and papillae on tongue. • Decrease in taste and olfactory nerve endings.	• Loss of ability to detect salt and sweet. • Decreased palatability causing poor food intake. • Decreased sensory stimulation that may impair metabolic processes.
Salivary glands	• Decrease in salivary secretion causes feeling of dry mouth, xerostomia.	• Difficulty in chewing and swallowing makes them to avoid certain foods like crunchy, dry and sticky foods.
Teeth	• Loss of teeth and wearing dentures.	• Decreased consumption of meats and fresh fruits and vegetables. In turn, this can result in inadequate intake of energy, iron and vitamins, particularly Vitamin C, folate and beta-carotene.
Gastric function and emptying	• Decreased secretion of hydrochloric acid, intrinsic factor and pepsin. • > 60 years of age rapid rate of emptying of liquids. • Increased proximal small bowel pH and bacterial overgrowth in bowel. • Decreased calcium absorption.	• Decreased bioavailability of minerals, vitamins and proteins. • Decreased absorption of protein bound Vitamin B_{12} and folate. • Increase in bacterial folate synthesis to counteract mal-absorption. • Poor Vitamin D nutriture.
Small intestine	• Decreased secretion of lactose. • *Constipation* prolonged recto sigmoid transit.	• Can be a risk factor for developing osteoporosis.
Liver and biliary function	• Decreased size and blood flow. • Minor structural and bio-chemical changes. • Gall bladder becomes sluggish in releasing bile. • Activity of drug, matabolising enzymes reduced.	• Rate of albumin synthesis may be decreased. • Susceptible to gallstones. • Drug dosages may need to be lower.
Metabolic function	• Impaired glucose tolerance. • Decreased metabolic rate due to changes in body composition and reduction in physical activity. • Body protein level decreases.	• Requires dietary modifications, exercise and oral pharmacologic agents. • Requirement of energy decreases. • Activity decreases.

Dietary Guidelines During Old Age

- Empty calorie foods should be taken and calorie dense food should be avoided.
- Foods rich in protein, vitamin and mineral should be included.
- Vegetables and fruits are good sources of antioxidants. A minimum of 5 servings should be taken.
- Fat promotes weight gain. Fat particularly saturated fat should be limited.
- Gas forming foods like sulphur containing vegetables and certain type of pulses have to be avoided.
- Soft well cooked foods are preferred.
- Fried and concentrated foods should be avoided.
- Caffeine containing beverages should be limited, otherwise may suffer from insomina.
- High fibre diet including greens and whole grains are to be included in the diet.
- Easily digestible steamed foods like idlies and idiyappam can be parts of the diet.
- Plenty of fluids and semi-solid foods should be taken.
- Excess salt intake should be avoided.
- 2-3 servings of low fat milk should be included in the diet.
- Tobacco, chewing, smoking and betel leaves should be avoided. Chewing are the habits which may affect consumption of food in the elderly person.

Healthcare

Health is a fundamental human right. Thus, it is imperative for the state to assume responsibility for the health of its people.

The most widely accepted definition of health is the one given by **World Health Organisation** (WHO) (1948) in the Preamble to its Constitution. "Health is a state of complete physical, mental and social well being and not merely absence of disease or infirmity".

Health care involves much more than just medical care. It can be defined as "Multitude of services provided to individuals or communities by agents of health services or professions, for the purpose of promoting, maintaining, monitoring or resorting health."

Levels of Healthcare

Health care services are usually delivered at three levels. These are at primary care, secondary care and tertiary care levels.

Primary Level Care This is the first level of contact of an individual, the family and the community with the national health system. It is possible to deal with most of the health problems of the community effectively at this level. In India, these services are provided through a network of Primary Health Centres (PHCs) and their Sub-Centres (SCs) spread all over the country.

The functionaries involved in dispensing these services include the multi-purpose health workers, village health guides and Trained Birth Attendants (TBAs or Dais).

Secondary Level Care More complex health problems of the community are resolved at the secondary level care through the district hospitals and the community health centres. The latter are upgraded primary health centres, which provide a variety of specialist facilities at the block level. The community health centres also act as the first referral level. This implies that patients can be directed to the next level of health care facility without first going to the district level hospital.

Tertiary Level Care This is the highest level of health care available to the community for dealing with their most complex health problems, which cannot be solved at the primary and secondary level. The institutions involved in providing the requisite facilities and care include medical college and hospitals, All India Institutes, regional hospitals, specialised hospitals and other apex institutions. These institutes have highly specialised health personnel who dispense their services.

Primary Health Care

The international conference on Primary Health Care held at Alma Ata, USSR, 1978, focused universal attention on the concept of primary health care as the most effective means of achieving an acceptable level of health for maximum number of people in the community.

It has been defined as "Essential health care based on practical, scientifically sound and socially acceptable methods and technology made universally accessible to individuals and family in the community through their full participation and at a cost that the community and the country can afford to maintain at every stage of their development in the spirit of self-determination."

Thus, defined primary healthcare becomes a practical approach to provide essential health care at affordable cost to all the members of the community with their full participation. The basic tenets of primary health care rest on equitable distribution of resources, inter-sectoral co-ordination, appropriate technology and community participation. Though, all factors are responsible for successful implementation of primary health care activities, community participation is perhaps the crucial determinant of success of any developmental programme.

It is the process by which the individuals and families assume responsibility for their own health and welfare and for those of the community and develop the capacity for contributing to their community's development.

The declaration of Alma-Ata stated that primary health care includes at least:

- education about prevailing health problems and methods of preventing and controlling them.
- promotion of food supply and proper nutrition.
- an adequate supply of safe water and basic sanitation.
- maternal and child health care, including family planning.
- prevention and control of endemic diseases.
- appropriate treatment of common diseases and injuries.
- provision of essential drugs.

Health Care Delivery

The challenge that exists today in many countries is to reach the whole population with adequate health care services and to ensure their utilisation. Rising costs in the maintenance of large hospitals and their failure to meet the total health needs of the community have led many countries to seek alternative models of health care delivery with a view to provide health care services that are reasonably inexpensive and have the basic essentials required by the population.

Health System in India

The country is divided into 29 states and 7 union territories for the purpose of administration. These are further divided into smaller administrative units called the districts, which are 729 in number at present. Within the districts, there are many smaller demarcated units. One of them is the community development block.

The main links in the health system comprise the centre, state, district, block and the village. Since, health is a state subject in India, the states have a considerable amount of independence in the delivery of health services to their people. Thus, each state has developed its own system of health care delivery. The centre is responsible for policy-making, planning, guiding, assisting, evaluating and coordinating the work of State Health Ministers. Thus, it ensures universal coverage of the country with health services.

Health System at the Centre Level

At the national or centre level, the health system comprises of :

- Union Ministry of Health and Family Welfare is headed by a Cabinet Minister and a Minister of State, which are political appointments. The minister is assisted by the secretory in the Department of Health and Family Welfare and specially mentioned in the Union List as the sole responsibility of the centre as well as those mentioned in the concurrent list, which are the joint responsibility of both the centre and the states.
- The Director General (DG) of health services acts as the principle advisor to the Union Government in all matters pertaining to medical and public health area. Two additional Director Generals and several Deputy Director Generals assist the DG in performing various tasks. Further, the directorate has three bureaus namely Bureau of Health Planning, Central Bureau of Health Intelligence and Central Health Education Bureau, which have specified roles.
- Central Council of Health comprises all the State Health Ministers, under the chairmanship of the Union Health Minister.

Health System at the State Level

Like the Centre, Minister of Health and Family Welfare is head of the Ministry and the secretary, at the state level Ministry, is the bureaucratic head. The State Health Directorate, likewise has a Director of Health Services, who is the chief technical advisor to the state government on all natures pertaining to health. Also, all states have a family planning bureau, which is instrumental in the implementation of the Family Welfare Programme. In addition, there are many specific health programmes, which come under the State Health Directorate.

Health System at the District Level

There are six types of administrative areas namely sub-divisions, tehsils, community, development blocks, municipalities and corporations, villages and panchyats in a district. Collector is the administrative head in each district. Most districts are divided into two or more sub-divisions, each in charge of an assistant collector or sub-collector.

The office of the Chief Medical Officer (CMO) of a district serves as the nerve centre to integrate all state financed health activities in the rural areas. The CMO is assisted by superintendent for the district hospital, a District Health Officer, a District Family Planning Office and others in the field of malaria, TB, leprosy, school health, etc.

Voluntary Health Agencies in India

- Indian Red Cross Society
- Hind Kusth Nivaran Sangh
- Indian Council for Child Welfare
- Tuberculosis Association of India
- Bharat Sevak Samaj
- Central Social Welfare Board
- The Kasturba Memorial Fund
- The All Indian Blind Relief Society
- Professional bodies
- International agencies

Health System at the Block Level

A block is generally the unit of rural planning and development, under the charge of a Block Development Officer.

Health System at the Sub-Centre Level

A PHC in a block may not be able to cover the entire population, so within the block sub-centres are located to provide health care facilities or services to smaller population. There is a male and female multi-purpose health worker posted at each sub-centre.

The services provided at present include mother and child health care, family planning and immunisation. It is proposed to enlarge these to include facilities for intrauterine devices insertions and simple laboratory investigations, like routine examination of urine for sugar and albumin.

Health System at the Village Level

There are three functionaries at the village level, who are responsible for taking care of the health needs of the community.

These are Village Health Guide, Local Dais and Anganwadi Worker

Village Health Guide This scheme was launched on 2nd October, 1977 as a part of the Rural Health Scheme. The village health guide is not a government functionary, but a volunteer chosen from the community, preferably a woman, who serves as a link between the community and the formal health system. The village health guide is capable of taking care of simple medical ailments of mothers and child health, including family welfare, health education and sanitation.

Local Dais Under the Rural Health Scheme, an extensive training programme has been undertaken by the government to train all Traditional Birth Attendants (TBAs/Dais) in the country to improve their knowledge and skills relating to maternal and child health. Thus, every village should have an access to the services of a trained birth attendant. This will ensure that home deliveries, which are still a norm in the rural area, will be performed under safe and hygienic conditions, which will reduce maternal and infant mortality.

Anganwadi Worker Under the ICDS scheme, there is an aganwadi worker for a population of 1000. She is also an honorary part time worker selected from the community, who is responsible for a package of services delivered at the anganwadi. These include supplementary nutrition, health checkups, immunisations, non-formal pre-school education, nutrition, health education and referral services. The beneficiaries include children below 6 years, pregnant, nursing mothers and women in the age group of 15-45 years. Along with the village health guide, she constitutes the major link of the community with the health services.

Health Service Delivery System in India

It shows linkage between various functionaries and health institutions at various levels within the state.

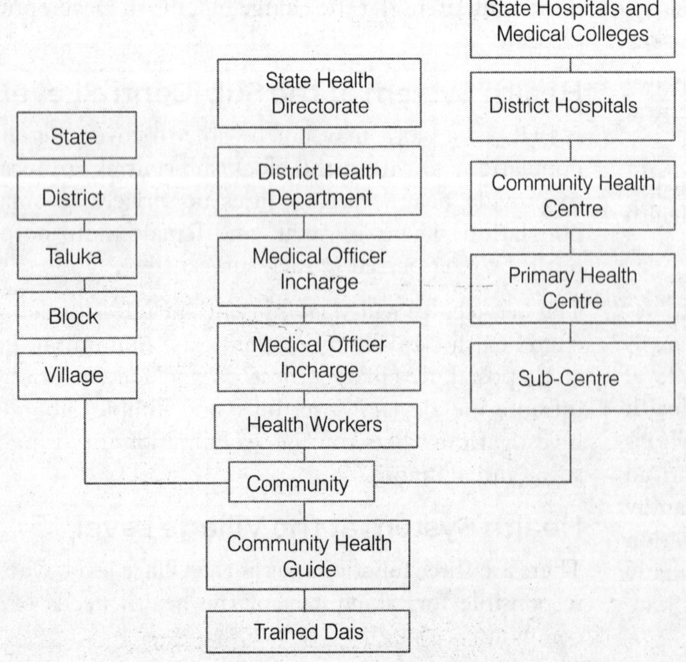

Linkage Between Functionaries and Health Institutions

Role of Public Health Nutritionist in Health Care Delivery

Nutrition is an important but it is not the only determinant of health of an individual. The root cause of many health problems of the community can be traced to facility of nutrition. It could be lack, excess or an imbalance of certain nutrients in the diet, which compromise the nutritional status leading to health problems. Hence, nutrition can be viewed as a subset of the health. Since, attainment of health for all is a universal goal public nutrition has to be an integral part of any strategy designed to achieve this goal.

Primary health care becomes the major approach to achieve an acceptable level of health for maximum number of people in the community. It has already been stated that the promotion of food supply and proper nutrition is one of the eight basic essential services included in the primary health care. Thus, we can conclude that public nutrition is an essential component of health and health care. The continuing changes in the health scenario of nations across the world, present varied and newer challenges to the public nutrition professional, who is intimately involved with providing nutrition support in all health care activities. The shift in accent on health promotion from the earlier one, primarily on prevention and cure has added more responsibilities to all those engaged in health care of the community.

Today, much of the ill health is related to lifestyle and environmental factors, whereas a lot of illness could be attributed to the causation of germs, when the first movement for public health began.

Though, the latter has been contained in the developed and less successfully in the developing nations, the former situation continues to be of concern in the public health arena.

The public nutritionist equipped with the knowledge of food, nutrition and health is eminently suited to participate in all the strategies of health promotion, required to combat this situation.

In Indian context, where under nutrition is extensively present in the pre-school children and pregnant and nursing mothers on the one hand and the threat from lifestyle related health diseases like obesity and degenerative heart diseases show alarming trends on the other hand the role of public nutritionist assumes tremendous importance along with responsibility.

Functions of public Health Nutritionist

A public nutritionist can perform the following:

- In the hospital based setup, he/she is a part of the team delivering, therapeutic and rehabilitative services to the patient.
- He/She is responsible for food service management nutritional care of the patients, including diet counselling and imparting nutrition education to various categories of medical personnel.
- The Directorate General of Health Services has recommended the appointment of atleast an assistant dietitian for every 100 bed hospital with progressive increase in their numbers as the hospital beds increase.
- There is a role for the public nutritionist in the national health setup at the centre as the Nutrition Advisor and Research Officer. At the state level, they can function as the State Nutrition Officers.
- The public nutritionist can make a significant contribution in all the programmes of development undertaken by voluntary and non-government organisations.
- At the international level, organisations like WHO; FAO and UNICEF provide opportunities for public nutritionists for policy-making, planning and implementation of stages.

Objectives of Public Health Nutritionist

Objectives of Public health nutritionists are :

- Improve nutrition and health outcomes of different communities and families.
- Change in consumer behaviour towards increased consumption of a diversified diet of vegetables and fruits with implications for obesity and diet related diseases.
- Guarantee food security to provide essential nutrition, especially for mother and child.
- To know the organic and functional alterations of the individual and their relationship to the nutritional aspect.
- To provide correct information to buyers and consumers of food items.
- To provide adequate information regarding nutrition to the whole community.

EXAM BASED QUESTIONS

1 "Health is a state of complete physical, mental and social being and not merely an absence of disease or infirmity". This statement was given by
(a) UNESCO (b) WHO
(c) Health Ministry of India (d) Governmnt of India

2 Public nutrition is concerned with nutrition in
(a) poor countries (b) industrialised countries
(c) Both (a) and (b) (d) None of these

3 Who was the first person to suggest the word 'public nutrition'?
(a) Mason (b) David
(c) Codey (d) None of these

4 What activities are included in public nutrition?
(a) Monitoring, surveillance and evaluation
(b) Nutritional requirement and dietery guidelines
(c) Community nutrition and community based programmes
(d) All of the above

5 What is the birth weight of new born child?
(a) 3.2 kg (b) 2.2 kg (c) 3.8 kg (d) 4.1 kg

6 Which is the most required nutrient for an infant?
(a) Protein (b) Energy (c) Iron (d) Riboflavin

7 What are infants fed?
(a) Whey water (b) Lentil/pulses
(c) Breast milk (d) Leafy vegetables

8 Colostrum is
(a) a light yellow colour liquid, produced by lactating mother
(b) produced within 24 to 48 hours after delivery
(c) not a complete milk, it has more of protein and Vitamin A
(d) All of the above

9 Which of the following statement(s) is/are correct?
(a) Mother milk has lactalbumin protein, which is easily digestible than casein
(b) Maternal diet is reflected in the milk by fat and fatty acid content
(c) Linoleic acid content amount over 10% of the total fatty acid present in human milk
(d) All of the above

10 Breast feeding prolongs the period of natural immunity to viral infection(s) like
(a) mumps and measles
(b) roliv
(c) some kinds of pneumonia and diarrhoeas
(d) All of the above

11 What is the weight of pre-term baby?
(a) Less than 2500 g (b) 2500-.3000 g
(c) 3000g-4000 g (d) More than 2500 g

12 The process of getting accustomed to food other than breast milk is called
(a) accustoming (b) weaving
(c) habituating (d) All of these

13 When is first solid food introduced to baby?
(a) After 3-4 months (b) After 1-2 months
(c) After 5-6 months (d) After 4-5 months

14 What suplementory food can be given to infant?
(a) Juice (b) Cereal
(c) Carrot (cooked) (d) All of these

15 Recommended dietary allowances for 0-6 months old infant for protein is
(a) 1g/kg body weight (b) 1.5 g/kg body weight
(c) 1.65 g/kg body weight (d) 2.05 g/kg body weight

16 What is the ideal body weight of children of 4-6 years of age?
(a) 18 kg (b) 20 kg (c) 10 kg (d) 15 kg

17 Why is the food seasoned?
(a) To make it taste better
(b) To enhance its nutritive value
(c) To make it look better
(d) None of the above

18 .... over stimulates the system of a child.
(a) Tea (b) Coffee
(c) Both (a) and (b) (d) None of these

19 What is the RDA of calcium for children of 7-8 years age?
(a) 800 (b) 600 (c) 700 (d) 500

20 What can be changed in food to make it interesting?
(a) Colour (b) Texture
(c) Taste (d) All of these

21 How can vegetables be fed to children other than cooking?
(a) Salad (b) Sandwiches
(c) Both (a) and (b) (d) None of these

22 How much body fat is required by adolescence girl to maintain regular ovulation?
(a) 23% (b) 22% (c) 20% (d) 25%

23 Young girl should have calcium to delay
(a) osteoporosis (b) osteomalacia
(c) rickets (d) None of these

24 Which of the following statement(s) is/are incorrect?
(a) A poor diet during pregnancy is a major cause of the high death rate of woman and infant.
(b) Hemoglobin blood content of non-pregnant woman is about 13 to 14.1.
(c) A pregnant woman must eat 2 times a day.
(d) None of the above

25 Additional requirement for protein, iron and folic acid for pregnant women over non-pregnant women are
(a) 10g, 30mg and 100 µg (b) 15g, 38mg and 400 µg
(c) 15g, 8mg and 300 µg (d) 20g, 10mg and 500 µg

26 Which of the following statement(s) is/are correct?
(a) In pregnancy, estrogen production along with progesterone stimulate the growth of mammary gland and inhibits the lactogenic function of the pituitary gland until the birth of the infant.
(b) In pregnancy, there is increased intake of fat because energy gets converted into milk.
(c) Well nourished mother secretes about 850 ml of milk per day.
(d) All of the above

27 Which group of population is most affected by anaemia.
(a) Pre-school children (b) Pregnant women
(c) Non-pregnant woman (d) Men

28 Additional energy and protein requirement during pregnancy is
(a) 700 kcals and 30g (b) 300 kcals and 15g
(c) 350 kcals and 15g (d) 300 kcals and 30g

29 Bottle feeding results in increased infant sickness and mortality because of
(a) use of milk substitutes of poor nutrient content
(b) insanitary preparation and poor handling of bottles and milk formula
(c) ignorance of the basic rules of sanitation
(d) All of the above

30 Mortality rate for artificially fed infants is more in the lower economic group due to
(a) lack of facilities for making the formula
(b) lack of refrigeration
(c) lack of water for cleaning
(d) All of the above

31 How much energy is required by heavy worker pregnant mother?
(a) 2175 (b) 2525 (c) 3225 (d) 3125

32 What does lactogogues do?
(a) Stimulate milk production
(b) Provide nutrients to mother
(c) Give multi-vitamin to child
(d) All of the above

33 Which of the following food should be avoided by lactating mother?
(a) Tomatoes (b) Cabbage family
(c) Spices (d) All of these

34 Which of the following have low satiety value?
(a) Fat (b) Protein
(c) Carbohydrate (d) All of these

35 Why does protein provide satiety value?
(a) It takes long time to digest in alimentary canal
(b) It is tasty to eat
(c) It get stored in tissues
(d) None of the above

36 Vegetarian foods are eaten by
(a) Muslims (b) Hindus
(c) Christians (d) All of these

37 How much protein does an adult man requires?
(a) 60 g/day (b) 40 g/day (c) 55 g/day (d) 65 g/day

38 Xerostonia in old age occurs in
(a) tongue (b) teeth
(c) salivary gland (d) intestine

39 Loss of teeth in old age results in
(a) less consumption of meat and fruit
(b) osteoporosis
(c) Both (a) and (b)
(d) Neither (a) nor (b)

40 What kind of change(s) occur(s) in liver and biliary, in case of old age?
(a) Decrease in size and blood flow
(b) Structure and bio-chemical changes
(c) Activity of drug metabolising enzyme reduced
(d) All of the above

41 What is the effect on nutrition, when metabolic function gets disrupted in old age?
(a) Requirement of energy decreases
(b) Activity decreases
(c) Both (a) and (b)
(d) Neither (a) nor (b)

42 What is/are the level(s) of health care?
(a) Primary level care (b) Secondary level care
(c) Tertiary level care (d) All of these

43 What does 'TBA' stands for?
(a) Trained Birth Attendant (b) Taught Baby Attendant
(c) Trained Baby Attendant (d) Taught Birth Army

44 What comes under secondary level care?
(a) District hospitals
(b) Community Health Centres
(c) Both (a) and (b)
(d) Neither (a) nor (b)

45 Where was International Conference on Primary Health Care held?
(a) Alma Ata (b) Germany
(c) Chile (d) Tokyo

46 Which of the following is primary health care as declared in Alma Ata?
(a) Promotion of food supply and proper nutrition
(b) Prevention and control of endemic disease
(c) Provision of essential drugs
(d) All of the above

47 How many administrative areas are under a district?
(a) 7 (b) 6 (c) 8 (d) 5

48 What is the global prevalence of obesity in adult men and woman?
(a) 11% of men; 15% of women
(b) 6% of men; 20% of women
(c) 27% of men; 34% of women
(d) 45% of men; 36% of women

49 Insufficient food intake could be due to
(a) missed meals
(b) poor health practices
(c) poor schedule
(d) All of the above

50 The supplementary nutrition provided to pre-schooler at ICDS should provide
(a) 350 calories and 10 gram protein
(b) 300 calories and 10 gram protein
(c) 600 calories and 16 gram protein
(d) 300 calories and 8 gram protein

51 Which of the following statement(s) is/are correct?
1. Infants fed on fresh milk should be given fruit juice in small quantities for Vitamin C.
2. Vitamin D is obtained from liver, liver-oils, egg yolk, milk and exposure to sunlight.
3. Osteomalacia's first symptom is pain in the bones that may occur during pregnancy.

Codes
(a) Only 1 (b) Only 2
(c) None of these (d) All of these

52 Consider the following statements.
1. Adequate well balanced nutritions food should be taken to prevent obesity under nutrition.
2. An adolescent girl should take enough calcium and rich foods in her diet to increase bone density, which delays the onset of osteoporosis.

Which of the statement(s) given above is/are correct?
(a) Only 1 (b) Only 2
(c) Both 1 and 2 (d) None of these

53 More thyroid activity is indicated in the pregnant woman when
1. iodine in the blood decreases in the first two weeks after delivery.
2. rise of blood iodine in beginning of the second month of pregnancy.

Codes
(a) Only 1 (b) Only 2
(c) Both 1 and 2 (d) Neither 1 nor 2

54 A cycle menu contains
1. menu rotated at definite interval
2. a seven days' menu.
3. set menu
4. menu of the day

Codes
(a) 1, 2 and 3 (b) 1 and 2
(c) 2 and 3 (d) 1 and 3

55 The nutritional status of the family members depends on
1. the time and energy at the disposal of the housewife.
2. the knowledge of the housewife on nutrition.
3. the efficiency of the housewife to work and serve food.

Codes
(a) 1, 2 and 3 (b) 2 and 3
(c) 1 and 2 (d) 1 and 3

56 Multi-purpose foods are especially prepared for
1. school going children 2. infants

Codes
(a) Only 1 (b) Only 2
(c) Both 1 and 2 (d) None of these

57 The term 'food' means that
1. nourishes the body 2. removes hunger
3. gives satisfaction 4. renews strength

Codes
(a) 1 and 2 (b) 3 and 4
(c) 3, 4 and 1 (d) All of these

58 Consider the following statements.
1. The International Conference on Primary Healthcare was held at Alma-Ata USSR, 1978.
2. It has been defined as essential healthcare is based on practical, scientifically sound.

Which of the statement(s) given above is/are correct?
(a) Both 1 and 2 (b) Only 2
(c) Only 2 (d) Neither 1 nor 2

59 Which of the following statement(s) is/are correct?
1. Folic acid deficiency results in certain types of anaemia, especially in infants and pregnant women.
2. Only animal foods like milk, meat and liver contain Vitamin B_{12}.

Codes
(a) Both 1 and 2 (b) Only 1
(c) Only 2 (d) Neither 1 nor 2

60 Consider the role of aanganwadi worker.
1. She is honorary part time worker selected for a community.
2. She is a paid nurse who helps in providing health care.
3. Along with the village health guide, she constitutes the major link of the community with the health service.

Select the correct answer using the codes given below.
(a) Only 1 and 2 (b) Only 1 and 3
(c) Only 3 (d) All of them

61 Consider the following statements.
1. Village health guide is a volunteer choosen from the community.
2. At primary health centre, the services provided are mother and child health care, family planning and immunisation.
3. In villages, there are still untrained dais who are undertaking deliveries at homes.

(a) Only 3 (b) 1, 2 and 3 (c) 1 and 2 (d) Only 1

62 For a successful outcome of the nutrition programme for the community, the sequentional order of steps to be taken.
1. Implementation 2. Mobilising resources
3. Monitoring and evaluation 4. Prioritise problem
5. Identify target 6. Setting objectives

Codes
(a) 5, 4, 6, 2, 1, 3 (b) 1, 4, 5, 6, 2, 3
(c) 4, 5, 6, 1, 2, 3 (d) 4, 6, 5, 2, 3, 1

63 The sequence of functions in any health care system will be ....
(a) Provision of health services, resources, management, arrangement of resources into health programs
(b) Resources, provision of health services, management, arrangement of resources into health programs
(c) Resources, management, arrangement of resources into health programs, provision of health services
(d) Resources, provision of health services, management, arrangement of resources into health programs

64 Arrange the correct order of catering personnel, according to seniority.
(a) Manager, utility worker, cook, supervisor
(b) Manager, cook, supervisor, utility worker
(c) Manager, supervisor, cook, utility worker
(d) Manager, utility worker, supervisor, cook

65 Identify the correct order of Food Supplementation Programme, launched by Government of India.
(a) ICDS, SNP, ANP, MDMP (b) SNP, MDMP, ANP, ICDS
(c) ANP, MDMP, SNP, ICDS (d) ANP, SNP, ICDS, MDMP

66 Match the following.

List I (RDA for Pregnant Women)	List II (mg/day)
A. Protein	1. 35 mg
B. Zinc	2. 310 mg
C. Magnesium	3. 12 mg
D. Iron	4. 82.2 mg

Codes

	A	B	C	D		A	B	C	D
(a)	4	3	2	1	(b)	1	2	3	4
(c)	3	1	2	4	(d)	2	4	1	3

67 Match the following.

List I	List II
A. Baine Marie	1. Personnel
B. FIFO	2. Purchase
C. Invoice	3. Menu
D. Orientation	4. Storage
	5. Equipment

Codes

	A	B	C	D		A	B	C	D
(a)	5	4	2	1	(b)	4	3	2	5
(c)	1	2	3	4	(d)	5	1	2	4

68 Match the following.

List I	List II
A. Amino acids	1. Are the bricks with which tissue protein milk is built and replaced
B. Amino acid make up of protein	2. Resembles that of the tissues the greater its value
C. Essential amino acids	3. Cannot be synthesised by the body
D. Proteins of whole egg human	4. Taken as a standard for comparison

Codes

	A	B	C	D		A	B	C	D
(a)	1	2	3	4	(b)	4	3	2	1
(c)	3	4	1	2	(d)	2	1	4	3

69 Match the following.

List I (Changes in Organ Function with Ageing)	List II (Effect on Nutrition)
A. Decreased taste buds	1. Poor Vitamin D
B. Decreased calcium absorption	2. Requirement of energy decrease
C. Impaired glucose tolerance	3. Can be a risk factor for developing osteoporosis
D. Decreased secretion of lactose	4. Loss of ability to detect salt and sweet

Codes

	A	B	C	D		A	B	C	D
(a)	4	1	2	3	(b)	3	4	1	2
(c)	2	3	1	4	(d)	1	2	3	4

70 Match the following.

List I	List II
A. Well balanced diet	1. Are in general and are more expensive than deficient ones
B. If funds do not permit	2. Give butter and skimmed milk reconstitute from skimmed milk power to children. It is cheaper
C. Milled rice eaters	3. Need protective foods like pulses, milk, green vegetables, fruits, etc
D. Growth of the fotus, placenta and maternal tissues	4. Save a high metabolic activity

Codes

	A	B	C	D		A	B	C	D
(a)	1	2	3	4	(b)	4	3	2	1
(c)	2	4	1	3	(d)	3	4	1	2

71 Match the following.

List I	List II
A. Milk	1. Vitamin A lost during cooking
B. Butter, ghee	2. 50 IU of Vitamin D perounce
C. Government regulation	3. Provide fatty acids indeic, linolenic, rachidonic acid
D. Manufactures in Vanaspati	4. Vanaspati should contain 700 IU added vitamin A perounce
E. Vegetable oils	5. Best source of animal protein for growing children

Codes

	A	B	C	D	E		A	B	C	D	E
(a)	5	1	4	2	3	(b)	1	2	4	5	3
(c)	1	2	3	4	5	(d)	5	4	3	1	2

72 Match the following.

List I	List II
A. Requirement of folic acid in an adult	1. Phrynoderma
B. A measure to calculate Vitamin A in the meal	2. Athenoslerosis
C. Deficiency of fatty acids	3. 3y per kg body weight
D. Access amount of cholesterol leads to	4. Retinol + β Carotene × 0.25

Codes

	A	B	C	D		A	B	C	D
(a)	3	4	2	1	(b)	4	3	2	1
(c)	4	3	1	2	(d)	3	4	1	2

73 Match the following.

List I	List II
A. Convulsions in infants	1. Inadequate intake of Vitamin B_6
B. Milk effective in preventing pellagra	2. Because of its richness in trypto phanm
C. Vitamin B_6	3. Pyridoxal, pyridoxamine and pyridoxine
D. Vitamin B_6 is required	4. For conversion of tryptophan to nicotinic acid and metabolism of essential fatty acids
E. Niacin equivalent	5. In the assessment of the value of a food stuff as a source of nicotinic acid, take into account the tryptophan content

Codes

	A	B	C	D	E		A	B	C	D	E
(a)	1	2	3	4	5	(b)	5	4	3	2	1
(c)	4	5	2	3	1	(d)	1	3	2	4	5

74 Match the following.

List I	List II
A. For infants, children and pregnant and nursing mothers	1. Significant amount of thiamine
B. 70% of the calories in a diet	2. Can be from carbohydrates
C. Par-boiled rice	3. Supply about 217 of total protein from animal foods
D. The allowance for calories protien B complex	4. Good supplementary value to cereal diet
E. Pulse protien is rich in lysine	5. Increased or decreased depending on body weight

Codes

	A	B	C	D	E		A	B	C	D	E
(a)	3	2	5	1	4	(b)	3	2	1	5	4
(c)	4	5	2	3	1	(d)	3	2	1	4	5

75 Match the following.

List I	List II
A. Babies feed on breast milk	1. Less likely to develop cousti patrim and allergies
B. A baby	2. Increased infant sickness and mortality
C. Bottle feeding realtsin	3. 5-6 months of age
D. Breast feeding discontinued	4. Doubles its birth weight between 4-6 months and triples by end of 10-12 months
E. First solid feed	5. When mother suffers from chronic illness and infant is weak

Codes

	A	B	C	D	E
(a)	1	4	2	5	3
(b)	1	5	2	4	3
(c)	4	5	2	1	3
(d)	5	4	3	2	1

Directions (Q. Nos. 76-85) *In the questions given below are two statements labelled as Assertion (A) and Reason (R). In the context of the two statements, which one of the following is correct?*

Codes

(a) Both A and R are true and R is the correct explanation of A
(b) A is true, but R is not the correct explanation of A
(c) A is true, but R is false
(d) A is false, but R is true

76 **Assertion** (A) The most widely accepted definition of health is the one given by WHO (1948) in the Preamble of its Constitution.
Reason (R) Health is a state of complete physical, mental and social well being and not merely and absence of disease or infirmity.

77 **Assertion** (A) The International Conference on Primary Health Care held at Alma Ata USSR, 1978.
Reason (R) It focused universal attention on the concept of primary health care as the most effective means of achieving an acceptable level of health for maximum number of people in the community.

78 **Assertion** (A) Protein value of cereals can be improved by addition of pulses and leafy vegetables.
Reason (R) Pulses and leafy vegetables have rich Iron component.

79 **Assertion** (A) Providing a clean and safe food service facility is basic for achieving a successful operation and strategic to heath and well being of both employees and customers.
Reason (R) Sanitation and safety are closely related environmental factors to be considered, while planning the layout and physical facility of food service unit.

80 **Assertion** (A) Nutritional requirements of human body change during different life stages.
Reason (R) Nutrition is required at all stages of life.

81 **Assertion** (A) Supplementation of food can improve partitioning muscle to fat ration in your body.
Reason (R) It is less effective and a number of studies have been inconclusive.

82 **Assertion** (A) Energy requirements during lactation is higher than during pregnancy.
Reason (R) As the turn over of iron is greater during lactation because of milk secretion.

83 **Assertion** (A) Large food service institutions use formal competitive bid buying.
Reason (R) Here the purchaser goes to the whole sale market and bids the price.

84 **Assertion** (A) Nutrition problem is not a discipline to be studied, it is a problem to be solved.
Reason (R) Solving nutrition problems require multi-disciplinary cooperation.

85 **Assertion** (A) Pre-term babies are born after 37 week of gestation.
Reason (R) Pre-term babies are low weight babies.

Directions (Q. Nos. 86-90) *Read the following passage and answer the questions.*

In India, 84% of all health care expenditure is out of pocket. This places a great number of families at risk of falling into poverty due to high health expenses. Millions of children are at risk of becoming malnourished. Every third child in India is malnourished. Infant and child mortality rates still remain very high. They are lowest among marginalised groups, such as Scheduled castes and tribes and females. Discrimination in food based schemes and in society, in general leads to starvation and deaths among women and children of the Scheduled Castes and Scheduled Tribes. Muslim children have the highest rate of stunting and second highest rate of being underweight. There are almost no services or programmes for children with mental health issues. Children with disabilities, HIV/AIDS and mental disorders are stigmatised and hence, have little access to health facilities. India has one of the poorest health records in the world with the highest TB prevalence, every 3 out of 4 children have anaemia and polio eradication is actually back sliding. With varying social sector budgets, health indicators differ greatly across the country.

Kerala is best off with only 21% stunted children. Uttar Pradesh has the worst record with 46% of the children being under developed. Girls are at a higher risk of not being able to access health care. The mental health budget remains at 1% of the total health budget. According to UNICEF, in India over 2 million children die every year from preventable diseases. IMR in India is 63 deaths for every 1000 live births. Of these, 47% of the deaths occur within the first week after birth. Measles is the largest cause of death among children which can be prevented by a vaccine. Tetanus in newborns remains a major problem in Uttar Pradesh, Madhya Pradesh, Rajasthan, West Bengal and Assam.

Breastfeeding is the first crucial step for ensuring good health in infants. According to NFHS-3 data, 24.5% of new mothers initiated breast feeding in the hour after birth, 46.4% breastfed exclusively the first 6 months and 56.7% nursed beyond 6 months with the introduction of complementary food.

This results in more than 50% the child population below 5 years being underweight, 44.9% of the children under 3 year are stunted and 22.9% of children under 3 years are wasted. Less than 50% of children receive complete immunisation during infancy. This number has been dropping significantly over the years, indicating a problem with the Universal Immunisation Programme.

86 Which of the following is/are marginalised group(s)?
(a) Schedule Castes (b) Schedule Tribes
(c) Females (d) All of these

87 Muslim children has a highest rate of
(a) stunting (b) malnourishment
(c) starvation (d) under weight

88 Which state has the lowest record for stunted growth?
(a) Uttar Pradesh (b) West Bengal
(c) Kerala (d) Madhya Pradesh

89 How much is the mental health budget?
(a) 10% (b) 1% (c) 50% (d) 5%

90 Which is the major disease affecting Uttar Pradesh, Madhya Pradesh, Rajasthan, West Bengal and Assam?
(a) Measles (b) HIV
(c) Anaemia (d) Tetanus

PREVIOUS YEARS' QUESTIONS

July 2018

Directions (Q. No 1-4) *Read the passage given below and answer the following questions.*

Given the evidence we have, that early and exclusive breastfeeding for the first 6 months can contribute substantially to enhance child survival and good complementary feeding can contribute to reduction in stunting, it becomes imperative that action on early nutrition must be taken. A pilot project provides useful model to set up delivery mechanism. It used, both community based and facility based strategies for promotion of optimal Infant and Young Child Feeding (IYCF). The IYCF practices skilled counselling, better supervision and monitoring with the aim of reaching out to all pregnant and lactating women, to contribute to the nutrition and health status of their children under 2 years of age. A base line, pre-intervention evaluation was done to document feeding practices. The implementation included building capacity at the grassroots and support system at the block and district level. This was achieved through engaging 48 local graduate women mentors, 8 in each of the 6 blocks.

These 'mentors' were trained as trainers with knowledge and skills of counselling on feeding practices. They were also asked to further train a team of 3-4 'village level counsellors' among Anganwadi Workers, ASHA, Dai (Traditional Birth Attendant) or a link mother from the same village, who formed a 'Mother Support Group'. These did home visiting and facility based counselling to provide education to mothers and families on breast feeding and complementary feeding. They used 'counselling guides' received along with their training, for the purpose of counselling.

They also used IEC Approach and materials, like pamphlets and posters. The village level counsellors help and support mothers with feeding difficulties and referred them to block level counselling centres, if they were not able to solve their problems. The post intervention evaluation showed significant improvement in four feeding practices, namely reduction in pre-lacteal feeding from 44.4%to 28.3%,increase in initiation of breastfeeding within 1 hour of birth from 39.2%to 57.9%, exclusive breastfeeding for the first 6 months from 6.85%to 24.9% and introduction of complementary foods along with continued breast feeding between 6-9 months from 4.6% to 35.8%.

1 Which research design was used in the pilot project?
(a) Descriptive (b) Exploratory
(c) Experimental (d) Survey

2 The use of training a few mentors to train village level workers is called
(a) Counselling guides (b) Training of trainers
(c) Mother's support group (d) Village level counsellors

3 Why was action early nutrition intervention important?
1. To promote child survival
2. To reduce malnutrition among children
3. To achieve global targets of child feeding programmes
4. To reduce stunting among children

Codes
(a) 1, 2 and 3 (b) 1, 2 and 4 (c) 1, 3 and 4 (d) 2, 3 and 4

4 Why was it important to know baseline pre-intervention figures for key behaviours related to IYCF?
1. To measure gain in knowledge
2. To assess change in skills
3. To know the priorities of intervention
4. To assess change in attitude towards breast feeding

Codes
(a) 1, 2 and 3 (b) 1, 3 and 4 (c) 2, 3 and 4 (d) 1, 2 and 4

5 **Assertion** (A) Public health nutrition programmes should create more open spaces for physical activity to promote fitness.

Reason (R) Overweight and obesity are major pre-disposing factors for developing non-communicable diseases.

Codes
(a) Both A and R are false (b) Both A and R are true
(c) A is false, but R is true (d) A is true, but R is false

6 **Assertion** (A) To assess malnutrition levels in population during famines, the most widely accepted practice is to assess it in children ages 6 to 59 months.

Reason (R) In times of food shortages, the young children are the first to develop signs of malnutrition.

Codes
(a) Both A and R are true (b) Both A and R are false
(c) A is true, but R is false (d) R is false, but A is true

November 2017

7 Following agencies provide data for nutrition monitoring in India.
1. NFHS 2. CPWD 3. NSSO
4. FSSAI 5. CBHI

Codes
(a) 1, 2 and 3 (b) 1, 3 and 5
(c) 3, 4 and 5 (d) 2, 3 and 5

8 RDA of Energy (ICMR, 2010) for a moderately active pregnant woman is
(a) 2250 kcal (b) 2320 kcal
(c) 2580 kcal (d) 2850 kcal

9 **Assertion** (A) Including oats and its products in the diet, helps in reducing the risk of cardio-vascular diseases in population.

Reason (R) B-glucan helps in normalising the lipid profile.

Codes
(a) Both A and R are true (b) Both A and R are false
(c) A is true, but R is false (d) A is false , but R is true

January 2017

10 As per ICMR (2010), the RDA of Thiamin for a moderately active man is
(a) 1.2 mg/day (b) 1.4 mg/day
(c) 1.1 mg/day (d) 1.5 mg/day

11 Match the following.

List I (Physiological Groups)	List II (RDA of Energy ICMR 2010)
A. Sedentary working man	1. 3020 kcals/day
B. Moderately working woman	2. 2250 kcals/day
C. 13 years old girl	3. 2230 kcals/day
D. 16 years old boy	4. 2750 kcals/day
E. Sedentary working pregnant woman	5. 2320 kcals/day
	6. 2330 kcals/day

Codes

	A	B	C	D	E
(a)	6	4	5	1	2
(b)	2	3	5	4	1
(c)	5	3	6	1	4
(d)	5	3	6	1	2

July 2016

12 **Assertion** (A) The first outward sign of puberty is the rapid gain in height and weight.

Reason (R) The secretion of insulin and cortisol stimulates the growth spurt.

Codes

(a) Both A and R are true (b) Both A and R are false
(c) A is true, but R is false (d) R is true A is false

13 Match the following.

	List I (Category/Age)		List II (RDA of Energy)
A.	Moderate working pregnant woman	1.	2190 kcals
B.	2 years old child	2.	2320 kcals
C.	12 years old boy	3.	2440 kcals
D.	16 years old girl	4.	1060 kcals
E.	Sedentary man	5	2850 kcals
		6.	2580 kcals

Codes

	A	B	C	D	E		A	B	C	D	E
(a)	6	4	1	3	2	(b)	5	4	3	1	6
(c)	2	4	1	3	5	(d)	6	4	5	1	2

14 **Assertion** (A) Exclusive breast feeding for first 6 months protects the infant from infectious diseases.

Reason (R) Breast milk provides certain anti-bodies which develop natural immunity in the infant.

Codes

(a) Both A and R are true (b) Both A and R false
(c) A is true, but R is false (d) A is false , but R is ture

15 RDA of thiamin (ICMR, 2010) for a modertely active man is

(a) 1.2 mg/day (b) 1.4 mg/day
(c) 1.5 mg/day (d) 1.7 mg/day

16 Haemoglobin level below which a pregnant woman is considered anaemic is

(a) 12 g / dl of blood (b) 11 g / dl of blood
(c) 11.5 g/ dl of blood (d) 10 g / dl of blood

December 2015

17 The RDA of Vitamin A for pregnant women given by ICMR (2010) is

(a) 600 μg/day (b) 800 μg/day
(c) 950 μg/day (d) 400 μg/day

18 **Assertion** (A) The colostrum secreted in the first few days of lactation helps to build up immunity in the infant.

Reason (R) Colostrum is rich in Gamma Globulins and Vitamin A.

Codes

(a) A is true, but R is false (b) A is false, but R is true
(c) Both A and R are true (d) Both A and R are false

June 2015

19 The RDA of Zinc for 16-17 years old girl is

(a) 12 mg/day (b) 11 mg/day
(c) 8 mg/day (d) 10 mg/day

20 Match the following.

	List I (Physiological Groups)		List II (RDA of Protein, ICMR 2010)
A.	5 years old girl	1.	29.5 g/day
B.	9 years old boy	2.	60 g/day
C.	16 years old girl	3.	20.1 g/day
D.	Adult male	4.	78 g/day
E.	Pregnant woman	5	68 g/day
		6.	55.5 g/day

Codes

	A	B	C	D	E		A	B	C	D	E
(a)	3	1	6	2	4	(b)	3	2	6	1	4
(c)	3	1	2	4	5	(d)	3	1	6	4	5

ANSWERS

Exam Based Questions

1 (b)	2 (c)	3 (a)	4 (d)	5 (a)	6 (b)	7 (c)	8 (d)	9 (d)	10 (d)
11 (a)	12 (b)	13 (c)	14 (d)	15 (d)	16 (a)	17 (a)	18 (c)	19 (b)	20 (d)
21 (c)	22 (b)	23 (a)	24 (c)	25 (c)	26 (b)	27 (a)	28 (b)	29 (d)	30 (d)
31 (c)	32 (a)	33 (d)	34 (c)	35 (a)	36 (b)	37 (a)	38 (c)	39 (a)	40 (d)
41 (c)	42 (d)	43 (a)	44 (c)	45 (a)	46 (d)	47 (b)	48 (a)	49 (d)	50 (d)
51 (d)	52 (c)	53 (c)	54 (c)	55 (a)	56 (c)	57 (d)	58 (a)	59 (a)	60 (b)
61 (b)	62 (a)	63 (c)	64 (c)	65 (d)	66 (a)	67 (a)	68 (a)	69 (b)	70 (a)
71 (a)	72 (c)	73 (a)	74 (b)	75 (a)	76 (b)	77 (b)	78 (b)	79 (c)	80 (b)
81 (b)	82 (c)	83 (c)	84 (a)	85 (d)	86 (d)	87 (a)	88 (c)	89 (b)	90 (d)

Previous Years' Questions

1 (c)	2 (c)	3 (b)	4 (d)	5 (d)	6 (a)	7 (b)	8 (c)	9 (a)	10 (b)
11 (d)	12 (c)	13 (a)	14 (a)	15 (b)	16 (b)	17 (b)	18 (c)	19 (a)	20 (a)

Nutrition Through Different Stages

Nutrition is required at every stage of growth in human beings. The individual's needs for nutrients and energy change over the life span. During body's growth period need of nutrients is greatest. Significant phases of growth are infancy, adolescence and pregnancy. In the area of nutrition, community nutrition plays an important role in educating individuals and groups so that they adopt healthy eating habits.

An individual's needs for nutrients and energy change over the life span. For example, while a typical adult woman may need only 6.7 mg of calcium per pound of body weight, a 9 months old infant needs 27mg of calcium per pound of body weight. It is during a body's growth periods that the need of nutrients is greatest. These occur during pregnancy, infancy, adolescence, adulthood and old age. Once the growth period stops, energy need and need of certain nutrients decline. Social, psychological, economic and leisure roles influence person's food choice across the life span. For example, during the teenage years, the teenagers are concerned with body image. On the other hand, adults are more likely to be influenced by their health needs.

Nutrition Through Life Span

Life span of an individual can be divided into stages such as foetus, infancy, adolescence and old age. Description of physiological changes, growth, development nutritional needs and dietary guidelines is given below :

Physiological Changes of Pregnant Women

Maternal physiological changes in pregnancy are the adaptation during pregnancy that a woman's body undergoes to accommodate the growing embryo or foetus. These physiological changes include behavioural (brain), cardiovascular (heart and blood

In this Chapter

vessels), hematologic (blood), metabolic, renal, posture and respiratory changes. There is increase in blood sugar, breathing and cardiac output are all expected to change to allow pregnant woman's body to facilitate the proper growth and development of the foetus during the pregnancy. Physiological changes occur in pregnancy to nurture the developing foetus and prepare the mother for labour and delivery. Some of these changes influence normal biochemical values while others may mimic symptoms of medical disease.

Physiological changes during pregnancy are :

- Plasma volume increases progressively throughout normal pregnancy. Most of this 50% increase occurs by 34 weeks' gestation and is proportional to the birth weight of baby.
- Because the expansion in plasma volume is greater than the increase in red blood cell mass, there is a fall in haemoglobin concentration and red blood cell count.
- The platelet count tends to fall progressively during normal pregnancy although it usually remains within normal limits.
- There is a 10 to 20 fold increase in folate (iron) requirements and a two fold increase in the requirement for vitamin B_{12}.
- Changes in the coagulation system during pregnancy produce a physiological hyper coagulable state. The concentration of certain clotting factors are increased.
- Fibrinogen levels rise significantly by upto 50% and fibrinolytic activity is decreased.
- Changes in the cardiovascular system in pregnancy are profound and begin early. By eight (8) weeks' gestation, the cardiac output has already increased by 20%. The heart rate increases but generally not above 100 beat per minute.
- The primary event is probably peripheral vasodilatation. It leads to a 25-30% fall in systematic vascular resistance, and to compensate for this, cardiac output increases by around 40% during pregnancy. This is achieved by an increase in heart rate.
- All of these cardiovascular adaptations can lead to common complaints, such as palpitations, decreased exercise tolerance and dizziness.
- The average weight gained by healthy first time pregnant woman, eating without restrictions is 12.5 kg. This weight gain represents two major components i.e. the products of conception: foetus, amniotic fluid and the placenta and maternal accretion of tissues; expansion of blood and extracellular fluid, enlargement of uterus and mammary glands.

Nutritional Concerns for Pregnant Women

- Eat more food during pregnancy both in quality and quantity.
- Eat more whole grains, sprouted grams and fermented foods.
- Eat plenty of fruits and green leafy vegetables.
- Do not consume alcohol and tobacco. It is harmful for the health of mother as well as child.
- Take medicines only when prescribed by doctor.
- Take iron, folate and calcium supplements regularly as prescribed by the doctor.
- Green leafy vegetables, legumes, nuts, etc., are good sources of folic acid.
- No 'crash dieting', as this can have a negative impact on the baby.
- No 'eating for two', as this will lead to unnecessary weight gain. A healthy pregnancy only requires about an extra 1,400 to 1,900 kilojoules a day during the second and third trimester, which is equivalent to a glass of milk or a sandwich.
- Accommodate cravings, but don't let them replace more nutritious foods.
- Nutrients for which there are increased requirements during pregnancy include folate, iron, vitamin B12 and iodine.
- Pregnant women are advised to avoid foods that are associated with increased risk of the Listeria bacteria (such as soft cheese and cold seafood) and to be careful with foods that are more likely to contain mercury (such as certain fish, shell fish or flake). Listeria can seriously affect the growing baby.
- Being physically active has many benefits. If the mother is active and fit and is experiencing a normal pregnancy, she can remain physically active during her pregnancy. Otherwise, consult the doctor for advice.
- Drink plenty of fluids.

Physiological Changes During Lactation

Lactation is an important feature of female mammals. Lactation is under endocrine control. The two main hormones involved are prolactin and oxytocin.

Colostrum is the first milk a breast fed baby receives. It contains higher amounts of White Blood Cells and antibodies than mature milk.

Some of the physiological changes during lactation are as follows :

- Lactogenesis or the process of changes to the mammary glands to begin producing milk, begins during the late stages of pregnancy. The delivery of the placenta and the resulting dramatic reduction in progesterone, estrogen and human placental lactogen levels stimulate milk production.
- Galactopoiesis is the maintenance of milk production. This state requires prolactin and oxytocin.
- Oxytocin released from the posterior pituitary results from neural impulses reaching the hypothalamus caused by sucking of the nursing infant.
- Circulating oxytocin causes contraction of myoepithelial cells that surround mammary alveoli and ducts forcing milk into the ducts of the nipple so that it can be removed by the infant.
- Continuation of lactation and associated hyperprolactinemia inhibit ovarian activity by suppressing the pulsatile release of luteinizing hormone and by interfering with the secretion of gonadotropin releasing hormone.

Nutritional Concerns for Lactating Women

- Drink water, milk and fruit juices as needed.
- You need to eat more than usual to replenish energy that is lost through breastfeeding.
- Energy is essential, so eat regularly to increase your food intake and meet all your nutritional needs.
- Keep your intake of empty calorie foods to the minimum and eat more nutrient-dense foods.
- Plan your meals well and use the food pyramid as a guide in selecting your daily foods. Include plenty of fresh fruits, vegetables, milk and milk products, fish, poultry, nuts, whole grains, parboiled rice, beans and lentils.

Food to Avoid While Breastfeeding

- Chocolate, spices (cinnamon, garlic, curry and chili pepper), citrus fruits and their juices, like oranges, lemons, limes and grapefruit, strawberries, Kiwifruit, pineapple, etc should be avoided while breastfeeding.
- The 'gassy' veggies (onion, cabbage, garlic, cauliflower, broccoli, cucumbers and peppers) fruits with a laxative effect, such as cherries and prunes. A daily cup or two of coffee is fine, but too much caffeine can interfere with the baby's sleep or make him fussy. Caffeine is also found in some sodas, teas and over the counter medicines.

Physiological Changes During Infancy

During this time, tremendous growth, coordination and mental development occur. Another characteristic of infancy is the development of deciduous teeth. Deciduous teeth (also known as milk teeth, baby teeth or primary teeth).

They are the first set of teeth in the growth development of humans and many other animals. They develop during the embryonic stage of development and erupt *i.e.* become visible in the mouth during infancy. They are usually lost and replaced by permanent teeth, but in the absence of permanent replacements, they can remain functional for many years.

Deciduous teeth starts to form during the embryo phase of pregnancy. By the time, the embryo is eight weeks old, there are ten areas on the upper and lower arches that will eventually become the deciduous dentition. These teeth will continue to form until they erupt in the mouth. In the deciduous dentition, there are a total of twenty teeth *i.e.* five per quadrant and ten per arch. In most babies, the eruption of these teeth begins at the age of 6 months and continues until 25 to 33 months of age. The permanent teeth replacements develop from the same tooth bud as the deciduous teeth; this provides a guide for permanent teeth eruption. The roots of deciduous teeth provide an opening for the permanent teeth to erupt through. These teeth are also needed in the development of a child's ability to speak and chew their food correctly.

Changes in Body Size during Infancy

- The infant body will grow more rapidly than at any time after birth during the first 2 years.
- By the end of the first year its length will be 50% greater than it was at birth and by 2 years of age it will be 75% greater.
- A baby's birth weight will double by 5 months of age, triple by 1 year and quadruple at 2 years. These height and weight gains occur in little growth spurts, according to researches.
- According to researches, an average child will grow 2.5 inches in height and 5-7 pounds a year. However, the rate at which the height and weight increases, decreases with each additional year and depends on the gender.
- Growth first year follows the cephalocaudal and proximodistal patterns as follows :
  - **Cephalocaudal development** refers to growth and development that occur from the head down. It consists of development starting at the top of the body and working its way down *i.e.* from the head to the feet. What this means is that the development of the head and brain tends to be more advanced (in the sense that it occurs first) than the rest of the body. This pattern is largely complete by the beginning of adulthood, though of course other aspects of development continues throughout life.

- **Proximodistal development** occurs from the centre or core of the body in an outward direction. It consists in the tendency for growth to start at the center of the body and work its way outward, toward the extremities.
  This is called the proximodistal pattern. Thus, the spine develops first in the uterus, followed by the extremities and finally the fingers and toes.

Nutritional Concern for Infants

- Do not give your baby honey before 1 year of age. Honey may contain bacteria that can cause botulism in babies.
- Avoid cow's milk before age 1, since it does not have all of the nutrients that babies need and babies cannot digest it.
- Unpasteurised drinks or foods (such as juices, milk, yogurts or cheeses) may put your child at risk for an E-coli infection. E-coli is a harmful bacteria that can cause severe diarrhoea.
- Certain foods that can cause choking, such as hard candy, popcorn, whole nuts, and grapes (unless they are cut into small pieces). Don't give your child these foods before age 3.
- Natural juice of fruits like sweet lime or apples can be given after 8 or 9 months.
- Most babies can have peanut products when they are about 6 months of age.
- Babies who have mild to moderate eczema have a higher risk of food allergies.

Physiological Changes in Adolescents

Puberty is different for everyone, each of our bodies takes its own natural course.Many of these changes are caused by hormones, special signaling chemicals that are produced by glands in our bodies and that give directions to our cells to do particular things.

Female

Puberty is caused by alterations in brain functions that result is increased secretion by the hypothalamus of Gonadotropin Releasing Hormone (GnRH). Increased levels of GnRH stimulate secretion of pituitary gonadotropins FSH and LH which cause follicle development and estrogen secretion.

Estrogen is responsible for accessory sex organs and secondary sex characteristics. Menarche, the first menstrual cycle, occurs at about 12.5 years of age as a result of the release of FSH.

Changes to the Female Body

Growth and Shape It is normal to experience a growth spurt as part of puberty. This will usually happen before one gets her first period. One will also notice other changes to her body shape, such as more curves or wider hips.

Breasts Breast development usually marks the beginning of the puberty. Fully developed breasts come in all shapes and sizes.

Skin Many teenagers will notice that as they go through puberty their skin becomes oily and pimples start to appear on the face and body.

Vaginal Discharge As one goes through puberty, the body will start to produce a whitish vaginal discharge. It is normal and it helps to clean and moisten the vagina.

Body Hair Pubic hair usually starts to appear on the genitals after the breasts start growing. One will also notice hair growing in the underarms and on the legs.

Menstruation Starting of menstruation (also referred to as period) is a natural and normal part of female puberty.

Sweat and Body Odour The body's sweat glands become more active during puberty, which can mean an increase in body odour.

Male

GnRH secretion from the hypothalamus results in an increase in pituitary gonadotropins secretion of LH / ICSH and FSH. The pituitary gonadotropins stimulate the seminiferous tubules and testosterone secretion. Testosterone causes changes in the accessory reproductive organs, secondary sex characteristics and male sex drive.

Changes to the Male Body

Growth and Shape Most of the growth spurt happens towards the end of puberty. One will also notice other changes to his body shape, such as more muscle development and larger shoulders.

Penis and Testicles As one transition to an adult, one will notice growth of his testicles, as well as enlargement of penis. This usually marks the beginning of puberty.

Body Hair Pubic hair usually appears on the genitals after the growth of the penis and testicles. After that, underarm hair begins to grow and later on, hair might start to grow on the face and chest as well.

Voice During puberty, boy's larynx will grow and it might stick out in the neck area, this is called the Adam's apple. When the larynx grows, it will cause a deepening of the voice. This usually happens in the beginning of puberty.

Skin Many teenagers will notice that as they go through puberty their skin becomes oily and pimples start to appear on the face and body.

Ejaculation About a year after the penis starts growing, most boys will experience their first ejaculation, a release of sperm and other liquids from inside the male reproductive tract that comes out through the penis.

Sweat and Body Odour The body's sweat glands become more active during puberty, which can mean an increase in body odour.

Nutritional Concern for Adolescents

- Eat 3 meals a day, with healthy snacks.
- Increase fiber in the diet and decrease the use of salt.
- Drink water. Try to avoid drinks that are high in sugar. Fruit juice can have a lot of calories, so limit teen's intake. Whole fruit is always a better choice.
- Eat balanced meals.
- When cooking for the teen, try to bake or broil instead of fry.
- Make sure the teen takes only proper sugar intake.
- Eat fruits or vegetables for a snack.
- Decrease the use of butter and heavy gravies.
- Eat more chicken and fish. Limit red meat intake and choose lean cuts when possible.
- Provide regular daily meal times with social interaction. Demonstrate healthy eating behaviour.
- Involving teens in selecting and preparing foods and teach them to make healthy choices by giving them the chance to select foods based on their nutritional value.
- Select foods with nutrients such as proteins calcium, magnesium, potassium and fiber.
- Parents are encouraged to limit a teen's screen time to less than 2 hours daily. Instead encourage activities that call for more movement.
- Teens need at least 60 minutes of moderate to vigorous physical activity on most days for good health and fitness and for healthy weight during growth.
- To prevent dehydration, encourage teens to drink fluid regularly during physical activity and drink several glasses of water or other fluid after the physical activity is completed.

Physiological Changes During Adulthood

By the time we reach early adulthood, our physical maturation is complete, although our height and weight may increase slightly. In early adulthood, our physical abilities are at their peak including muscle strength, reaction time, sensory abilities and cardiac functioning.

The ageing process, although not overt, begins during early adulthood. Around the age of 30, many changes begin to occur in different parts of the body. For example, the lens of the eye start to stiffen and thicken, resulting in changes in vision (usually affecting the ability to focus on close objects). Sensitivity to sound decreases; this happens twice as quickly for men as for women. Hair can start to thin and become gray around the age of 35, although this may happen earlier for some individuals and later for others.

The skin becomes drier and wrinkles start to appear by the end of early adulthood. The immune system becomes less adept at fighting off illness and reproductive capacity starts to decline. After 40, the ageing process becomes more apparent.

Around the age of 60, the eyes lose their ability to adjust to objects at varying distances, known as presbyopia. Most people between the ages of 40 and 60 will need some form of corrective lenses for vision deficits. Middle-aged adults are also at higher risk than younger adults for certain eye problems, such as glaucoma. Hearing also further declines. Skin continues to dry out and is prone to more wrinkling, particularly on the sensitive face area. Age spots and blood vessels become more apparent as the skin continues to dry and get thinner.

The muscle-to-fat ratio for both men and women also changes throughout middle adulthood, with an accumulation of fat in the stomach area. Women experience a gradual decline in fertility as they approach the onset of menopause, the end of the menstrual cycle around 50 years old. This process involves hormonal changes and may last anywhere from six months to five years. Because of the shifting hormone levels, women going through menopause often experience a range of other symptoms, such as anxiety, poor memory, inability to concentrate, depressive mood, irritability, mood swings and less interest in sexual activity.

Nutritional Concern for Adults

- Enjoy the wide variety of foods. Human body needs more than 40 different nutrients for good health and no single food can supply them all. That's why consumption of a wide variety of foods is necessary for good health.
- Breakfast is particularly important as it helps kick starts the body by supplying energy after the all night fast. Breakfast also appears to help control weight.
- Balancing your food intake means getting enough, but not too much of each type of nutrient. If portion sizes are kept reasonable there is no need to eliminate favourite foods. Any food can fit into a healthy lifestyle by remembering **moderation** and balance. Moderate amounts of all foods can help ensure that energy (calories) intake is controlled and that excessive amounts of any one food or food component are not eaten.

- A healthy **weight** varies between individuals and depends on many factors including gender, height, age and heredity. Excess body fat results when more calories are eaten than are needed. Those extra calories can come from any source *i.e.* protein, fat, carbohydrate or alcohol, but fat is the most concentrated source of calories.
- Physical activity is a good way of increasing the energy (calories) expended and it can also lead to feelings of well-being.
- Don't forget to have fruits and vegetables. Numerous studies have shown an association between the intake of these foods and a decreased risk of cardiovascular disease and certain cancers. An increased intake of fruits and vegetables has also been associated with decreased blood pressure.
- Base the diet on foods rich in carbohydrates.Most dietary guidelines recommend a daily diet in which at least 55% of the total calories come from carbohydrates. This means making more than half of our daily food.
- Drink plenty of fluids.Adults need to drink at least 1.5 litres of fluid daily, even more if its hot or they are physically active.

  Plain water is a good source of liquid but variety can be both pleasant and healthy. Alternative sources are juices, soft drinks, tea, coffee and milk.
- Balance the salt intake. Salt (NaCl) is made up of sodium and chloride. Sodium is a nutrient and is present naturally in many foods. Sodium and chloride are important in helping the body to maintain fluid balance and to regulate blood pressure.

  However, for some people it can increase blood pressure. Reducing the amount of salt in the diet of those who are sensitive to salt may reduce the risk of high blood pressure. The relationship between salt intake and blood pressure is still unclear and individuals should consult their doctor for advice.

Physiological Changes During Old Age

Physiological changes occur with ageing in all organ systems. Energy reserves dwindle and body cells decay. There is decrease in muscle mass also.

During old age, body systems and organs, such as the heart and lungs become less efficient. Immune system also loses its capacity to guard the body.

Certain neurological disorders also occur during old age as the capacity of the brain to transmit signals and communicate reduces.

Ageing Changes in the Male Reproductive System

- It may include changes in testicular tissue, sperm production and erectile function. These changes usually occur gradually.
- It occurs primarily in the testes. Testicular tissue mass decreases. The level of the male sex hormone, testosterone stays the same or decreases gradually. There may be problems getting an erection.
- The tubes that carry sperm may become less elastic (a process called sclerosis). The testes continue to produce sperm, but the rate of sperm cell production slows.
- The prostate gland enlarges with age as some of the prostate tissue is replaced with a scar like tissue. This condition, called Benign Prostatic Hypertrophy (BPH), affects about 50% of men.

Ageing Changes in the Female Reproductive System

- Menopause is a normal part of a woman's ageing process.
- With menopause :
  - the ovaries stop making the hormones estrogen and progesterone.
  - the ovaries also stop releasing eggs (ova). After menopause, you can no longer become pregnant.
  - menstrual periods stop.
- As hormone levels fall, other changes occur in the reproductive system, including :
  - vaginal walls become thinner, drier, less elastic and possibly irritated.
  - the external genital tissue decreases and thins and can become irritated.
- Other common changes include :
  - Menopause symptoms such as hot flashes, moodiness, headache and trouble sleeping.
  - Increased risk of bone loss (osteoporosis). Osteoporosis is a skeletal disease resulting in bone loss and changes in the bone quality that leads to diminished bone strength and an increased risk to sustain fractures. It can be prevented and treated using a number of different drugs and lifestyle modifications including proper diet, exercise and hormone replacement therapy.

Cumulative Changes in Adults Around 65

- Hearing impairment among older adults is often moderate or mild, yet it is widespread.
- Visual changes among ageing adults include problems with reading speed, seeing in dim light, reading small print and locating objects.

- The amount of time it takes to respond to features in the environment, once they are detected is typically slower among older adults.
- The proportion of older adults needing assistance with everyday activities increases with age.
- The performance of many organs, such as the heart, kidneys, brain, or lungs show a gradual decline over the life span. Part of this decline is due to a loss of cells from these organs, with resultant reduction in the reserve capacities of the individual. Furthermore, the cells remaining in the elderly individual may not perform as well as those in the young. Certain cellular enzymes may be less active and thus more time may be required to carry out chemical reactions. Ultimately the cell may die.
- Cognitive changes, which are associated with mental processes such as sensation and perception, memory, intelligence, language, thought and problem-solving, occur among ageing adults.
- Because it may take older adults more time to encode, store and retrieve information, the rate at which new information is learned can be slower among ageing adults and older adults often have a greater need for repetition of new information. Although, it may take older adults longer to input and retrieve new information, daily occupational and social functioning among those over age 65 is not impaired.

Nutritional Concern for Older Adults

- Balance food intake with physical activity. The more active the older people are, the more food they need. Keep an eye on meal portion size, if you are less active choose smaller serving sizes and add plenty of vegetables, salad and fruits.
- Include a carbohydrate food at each meal. Choose high fibre options whenever you can.
- Aim for five servings of fruits and vegetables each day. These are packed with important nutrients to help you stay healthy. Remember these can be fresh, frozen, tinned or dried. Colour is important, have a mixture of different coloured fruits and vegetables each day, such as apples, oranges, bananas, spinach, cabbage, carrots, sweet potatoes, broccoli, cauliflower, peppers, sweet corn, etc.
- Protein foods help to make new cells and keep your muscles healthy. Stay fit and strong by eating a variety of protein rich foods each day. Great sources include lean meat, poultry and fish. Salmon, sardines, trout, fresh tuna and kippers are packed with heart healthy omega 3 fats. Eating beans, eggs and nuts are a simple way of boosting the protein in your diet.
- Keep your bones healthy by having three servings of low fat dairy foods (milk, yoghurt or cheese) each day. Dairy foods with added calcium and vitamin D are even better. Look out for these in the supermarket as fortified foods.
- Choose heart healthy fats. This includes monounsaturated and polyunsaturated fats.
- Use less salt. Too much salt in the diet can contribute to high blood pressure, which in turn can lead to stroke or heart disease.
- Limit amount of foods high in 'empty calories' like biscuits, cakes, savoury snacks (crisps and peanuts), sweets, confectionary, etc. These foods are rich in calories, fat, sugar and salt, so remember not too much and not too often.
- Stay hydrated. Among other things, dehydration causes tiredness, dizziness and constipation. Get plenty of fluids (water, fruit cordials, juices, milk, etc.) on board each day. As a general guide, about 8 glasses a day should be adequate.
- Alcohol should be enjoyed in moderation. The recommendations are no more than 11 standard drinks a week for women or 17 standard drinks a week for men with a number of alcohol free days in the week.

Community Nutrition

Community nutrition is the process of helping individuals and groups develop healthy eating habits in order to promote wellness and prevent disease.

The goal of community nutrition is to educate individuals and group so that they adopt healthy eating habits. Dieticians and nutritionist work with many other healthcare professional in promoting improved community nutrition. Community nutrition focuses on all age groups. The group targeted range from babies to pregnant women to older adults.

For example, a young pregnant woman may not realise how her poor eating habit affect her developing foetus. Older adult may loose interest in eating due to loneliness, inability to prepare meals or physical condition, such as difficulty in chewing.

Obesity is an issue for many age groups. This may be due to lack of physical education programmes in schools and an overly busy lifestyle for adults. The accessibility and convenience often prompts people to make unhealthy food choices.

Community nutrition programmes attempt to change attitude, so that a diet rich in fruits, vegetables and whole grains is taken more often. Community nutrition emphasises a lifetime of routine healthy eating.

Community nutrition programmes are administered by organisations, such as public health agencies, public schools, residential facilities for the elderly hospitals, social service organisations and healthcare systems.

Healthcare professionals may develop a community nutrition project aimed at group, such as new immigrant or elderly. They may implement an existing project, such as Food Distribution Programme.

Community nutrition addresses health conditions, such as obesity and economic conditions, such as poverty, which limits access to healthy food, lack of nutritional information and cultural traditions that promote unhealthy eating. Community nutrition programmes strive to improve eating habits through food banks that distribute food as needed.

The anticipated outcome of community nutrition programmes is that participant will eat healthy food on a regular basis. Improved health is another anticipated result. Some positive outcomes are related to educational efforts. Others are due to change in behaviour.

Community nutrition programmes may fail because of inadequate funding, programme cancellation, poor participation, cultural barriers between programme personnel and client, lack of consistent access to healthy food and lack of desire on the part of individual to change.

Sports Nutrition

Water is the most important nutrient for athletes. Athletes should stay hydrated and avoid overheating, drink plenty of fluids before, during and after sports or exercise. When you workout or compete especially in hot weather, one should replace the amount of water lost in sweat by drinking the same amount of fluid.

The athlete should keep in mind the following:

- Drink small amount of water frequently.
- Drink cool beverages to lower the core body temperature and reduce sweating.
- Track the sweat loss; for every pound of water lost through sweat, drink one or two glasses of water.

A balanced diet is another key to sports nutrition. Eating the right combination of fuel from carbohydrates, proteins and fats gives the energy for top performance.

Elements of Balanced Diet for a Sportsperson

The elements of balanced diet for a sportsperson are :

Carbohydrates

Carbohydrates provide about 60% to 70% of daily calories. Human body converts the sugar and starches in carbohydrates into energy (glucose) or stores it in liver and muscle tissues. This gives endurance and power for high intensity, short duration activities if a body runs out of carbohydrates fuel during exercise, it will burn fat and protein exercise, it will burn fat and protein for energy causing performance level to drop. This may happen if one starts exercising without enough stored muscle glycogen.

Proteins

Proteins provide 12%–15% of the daily calories. Protein gives the body the power to build new tissues and fluids among other things. Human body cannot store extra protein so it burns it for energy or converts it to fat.

Protein requirement of a sportsperson are :

Level of Fitness Physically active people need more protein than those who do not exercise, and body builder.

Endurance Athletes and body builder often burn protein for fuels.

Total Daily Calories Body burns more protein if one does not consume enough calories to maintain body weight.

Carbohydrate Intake Body will use protein for energy if one exercises with low levels of muscle glycogen or if he/she does repeated training session without eating more carbohydrates.

Fats

Fats should not provide more than 20% to 30% of daily calories. Saturated fats come from animal-based foods while unsaturated fats are found in vegetable product, such as corn oil.

Human body needs small amount of fat for certain critical functions and as an alternative energy source to glucose. Eating too much fat, however is associated with heart disease and other major health problems.

Body's capacity of using fat depends on intensity and duration of exercise. For example, when one rests or does moderate exercise, body uses carbohydrates as fuel source. If the body uses up its glycogen supply the fat is burned for energy.

Nutrition Before Competition

Athletes eat several days before, an endurance activity affects performance. The food eaten on the morning of a sports competition can ward off hunger, keep blood sugar level adequate and aid hydration. Athletes should avoid eating high protein/high fat foods on the day of an event, since this can put stress on kidney and take a long time to digest.

Some general rules to be followed by an athelete before an event :

- Eat a meal high in carbohydrates.
- Eat solid foods 3-4 hours before an event. Drink liquid 2-3 hours before an event.
- Choose easily digestable food.
- Avoid sugary foods and drinks within 1 hour of the event.
- Drink enough fluid to ensure hydration.

Nutrition in Emergencies and Disaster

The nature of humanitarian crisis is rapidly changing. More people are in need of support and for longer periods. Malnutrition is common consequence of emergencies, impacting women and young children. Those affected often have poor nutritional status prior to the crisis which is then worsened as disaster strips communities of their infrastructure, livelihood and social structures.

Malnutrition in Emergencies

Not all disasters produce food shortage, which are so severe as to have a critical impact on the nutritional status of the affected population. The nature of food and nutrition problems depends on the type of disaster, its duration, the size of the area affected and the nutritional status of the population prior to disaster.

Earthquakes usually have little effect on long-term food supplies. In contrast hurricanes, floods and tsunami directly affect the availability of food by ravaging crops, killing livestock and domestic animals and destroying stored food.

Any type of disaster will disorganise transportation systems, communications and social and economical routines. Thus, even though food stores may exist, the population may not have access to them.

Purpose of Food Aid

Main purpose of food aid is **prevention of malnutrition in the population affected by disaster.** It is necessary to plan for the treatment and management of cases of malnutrition that existed prior to the disaster or which have become acute, and will become evident during aid operation.

The steps to follow in order to ensure an effective food aid programme are :

- Estimate the quantity of food available.
- Calculate the dietary needs of the affected population.
- Determine the food quantity in accordance with the characteristic of the population and estimated duration of the effect of disaster.

After disaster occurs, immediately provide food where the need is urgent or appears to be, as in isolated population institution, hospitals, refugee camps, etc. Make an initial estimate of food needs of the affected population taking into account its demographic characteristic.

Identify food stocks, transportation, storage and distribution. Monitor the food and nutrition situation closely, so that the supply and rationing of food can be modified in keeping with changing conditions.

Proper Management of Food Supplies

The objective is to ensure safety and prevent the transmission of disease through food. It is necessary to inspect the food received, identify and discard damaged supplies and confirm that containers or grain shacks are in good conditions. Discard tins that are bulging, broken or rusted and reject products whose expiration date has passed.

Store food by its date of entry so that it can be distributed First In First Out basis. As an immediate measure to disaster, provide any population that is or appears to be at high nutritional risk with 3-4 kg of food per person per week.

The important thing is to provide sufficient energy even if its not a balanced diet. For a short period of time, 1700 kcal daily will prevent severe deterioration of the nutritional status and famine.

EXAM BASED QUESTIONS

1 How much calcium does an adult woman need?
(a) 8.4 mg (b) 6.7 mg (c) 9.5 mg (d) 4.6 mg

2 Into how many stages the life span of an individual can be divided?
(a) Foetus (b) Infancy
(c) Adolescence and old age (d) All of these

3 Which is the growth period that require more nutrient?
(a) Infancy (b) Pregnancy
(c) Adolescence (d) All of these

4 What do/does increase(s) during pregnancy?
(a) Blood sugar (b) Cardiac output
(c) Both (a) and (b) (d) None of these

5 Which hormone increases immediately after implantation of the ovum?
(a) Adrenaline (b) Serotonine
(c) HCG (d) FSH

6 What stimulates mammary gland growth?
(a) Placental lactogen (b) Prolatin
(c) Both (a) and (b) (d) None of these

7 Which is called the hormone of pregnancy?
(a) Progesterone (b) Estrogen
(c) Prolactin (d) None of these

8 What is the function of estrogen in pregnancy?
(a) Stimulation of uterine growth
(b) Uterine blood flow
(c) Promotion of breast development
(d) All of the above

9 How much does blood volume increase in case of pregnancy?
(a) 40-50% (b) 50-60%
(c) 35-40% (d) 30-45%

10 When does cardiac output peaks in pregnant woman?
(a) During first trimester (b) After conception
(c) During fourth trimester (d) During third trimester

11 All the cardiovascular adaptation can lead to ....
(a) palpitation
(b) dizziness
(c) decreased exercise tolerance
(d) All of the above

12 How much average weight does first time pregnant woman gains?
(a) 10 kg (b) 11.2 kg
(c) 12.5 kg (d) 12.2 kg

13 Elevated level of prolactin results in
(a) parturation (b) ovulation
(c) fertilisation (d) copulation

14 What is colostrum rich in?
(a) Lactoferrin (b) Immunoglobin A
(c) Both (a) and (b) (d) None of these

15 How much milk can infant get from his mother by 3 months of lactation?
(a) 750 ml (b) 250 ml (c) 50 ml (d) 500 ml

16 Which nutrient(s) is/are required by pregnant lady?
(a) Folate (b) Iron
(c) Iodine (d) All of these

17 Which food bacteria should be avoided by pregnant lady?
(a) Listeria (b) E-coli (c) Bacillus (d) Vibrio

18 Which food should be avoided by lactating mother?
(a) Chocolate (b) Citrus fruits
(c) Both (a) and (b) (d) None of these

19 What interferes with baby's sleep and makes him fussy?
(a) Caffeine (b) Sweets (c) Alcohol (d) Salt

20 What is the first set of teeth called?
(a) Morning teeth (b) Pre-teeth
(c) Deciduous teeth (d) None of these

21 When does the eruption of deciduous teeth begin in a child?
(a) After six months (b) After seven months
(c) After five months (d) After four months

22 Which of the following is/are the characteristic(s) of cephalocaudal development?
(a) It consists of development that starting at the top down of the body and working its way down.
(b) It occurs from the centre or core of the body in an outward direction.
(c) In this, the pattern is largely completed by the beginning of adulthood.
(d) Both (a) and (c)

23 What contains bacteria that can cause botulism in babies?
(a) Apple (b) Honey (c) Potato (d) Pulses

24 What does e-coli cause?
(a) Diarrhoea (b) Fever
(c) Sore throat (d) Polio

25 Increased level of GnRH stimulates secretion of ....
(a) FSH (b) LH
(c) Both (a) and (b) (d) None of these

26 .... is responsible for accessory sex organ and secondary sex characteristics, in females.
(a) Estrogen (b) Progesterone
(c) Adrenaline (d) Prolactin

27 **Release of FSH leads to**
(a) pregnancy (b) menarche
(c) menopause (d) All of these

28 **What marks the starting of puberty in females?**
(a) Menarch
(b) Body hair
(c) Development of breasts
(d) Vaginal discharge

29 **The adolescents' nutritional food should consist of**
(a) balanced diet that contains proteins, calcium, magnesium, carbohydrates and fibre
(b) fruits and vegetables for a snack
(c) eat baked or boiled food instead of fried
(d) All of the above

30 **What change(s) does a boy in adolescence show(s)?**
(a) Change in growth
(b) Appearance of body hair
(c) Change in voice
(d) All of the above

31 **Which nutrient(s) is/are required for adolescent?**
(a) Calcium (b) Magnesium
(c) Potassium (d) All of these

32 **What is the type of physiological change that takes place during adulthood around the age of 30?**
(a) The lens of the eye start to stiffen and thicken.
(b) Skin becomes drier and wrinkle starts to appear.
(c) Age spots and blood vessels become more apparent as the skin continues to dry and get thinner.
(d) The immune system becomes less adapt at fighting of illness and reproductive capacity starts to decline.

33 **The condition of eyes, loosing the ability to adjust object at varying distance is known as**
(a) presbyopia (b) glaucoma
(c) cataract (d) eye degeneration

34 **Diet of adult should be rich in**
(a) fats (b) proteins
(c) carbohydrates (d) vitamins

35 **Why breakfast is important for human beings?**
(a) It breaks overnight fasting period.
(b) It replenishes yours' supply of glucose.
(c) It also helps to control weight.
(d) All of the above

36 **Where do changes occur in male reproductive system during old age?**
(a) Testicular tissue (b) Sperm production
(c) Erectile function (d) All of these

37 **What is the process of end of menstrual period called?**
(a) Menopause (b) Menarche
(c) Menoend (d) None of these

38 **What is/are the symptom(s) of menopause?**
(a) Hot flashes (b) Woodiness
(c) Headache (d) All of these

39 **What cumulative changes are seen in adult around the age of 65?**
(a) Hair start to thin and become gray.
(b) Hearing impairment is often moderate or mild
(c) Certain cellular enzymes may be less active and more time is required to carry out chemical reactions
(d) Both (b) and (c)

40 **Which is/are the heart healthy fat?**
(a) Monounsaturated fat (b) Polyunsaturated fat
(c) Both (a) and (b) (d) None of these

41 **All of the following are characteristic of cholesterol except**
(a) it is used for making estrogen and testosterone
(b) it is incorporated into cell membranes
(c) it is converted to bile
(d) it is an essential nutrient

42 **Whom do community nutrient targets?**
(a) All age groups (b) Only woman
(c) Older people (d) Pregnant lady

43 **Where are community nutrition programmes administered?**
(a) Public health agencies (b) Public schools
(c) Social service organisations (d) All of these

44 **Which is the most important nutrient for athletes?**
(a) Water (b) Vitamin
(c) Carbohydrate (d) Protein

45 **What should athletes avoid before any event?**
(a) Sugary food (b) Sugary drink
(c) Both (a) and (b) (d) None of these

46 **What is/are the common cause of food emergency?**
(a) Malnutrition (b) Over population
(c) Both (a) and (b) (d) None of these

47 **What step(s) needs to be followed to ensure an effective Food Aid Programme?**
(a) Calculate the dietary needs of the affected population
(b) Estimate the quantity of food available
(c) Determine the food quantity in accordance with the characteristics of the population
(d) All of the above

Directions (Q. Nos. 48-59) *Which of the statements is true?*

48 **Statement I** Body of infant grows more rapidly at any time after birth during first 2 years.
Statement II By the end of 2 years of age, length of baby will be 75% greater.
(a) Only I (b) Only II
(c) Both (a) and (b) (d) None of these

49 **Statement I** Old people should not have milk product.
Statement II Old people should have 5 service of fruits and vegetables per day.
(a) Only I (b) Only II
(c) Both (a) and (b) (d) None of these

50 Statement I Human body cannot store extra protein.

Statement II Protein is the most required nutrient of the body.

(a) Only I (b) Only II
(c) Both (a) and (b) (d) None of these

51 Statement I There is a change in body shape in puberty.

Statement II Menarche occurs at about 12.5 years of age.

(a) Only I (b) Only II
(c) Both (a) and (b) (d) None of these

52 Statement I HCG increases immediately upon start of pregnancy.

Statement II HCG is detected in urine after a month.

(a) Only I (b) Only II
(c) Both (a) and (b) (d) None of these

53 Statement I The deciduous dentition appears 2 months after the baby is born.

Statement II Deciduous dentitions are permanent teeth.

(a) Only I (b) Only II
(c) Both (a) and (b) (d) None of these

54 Statement I Adult needs to drink 1.5 litre of fluid daily.

Statement II Salt intake should be balanced in adults.

(a) Only I (b) Only II
(c) Both (a) and (b) (d) None of these

55 Statement I Individual's need for nutrient changes over the life span.

Statement II Less nutrients are needed during the growth phase.

(a) Only I (b) Only II
(c) Both (a) and (b) (d) None of these

56 Statement I There is no increase in blood volume during pregnancy.

Statement II Estrogen changes plasma protein level in pregnant woman.

(a) Only I (b) Only II
(c) Both (a) and (b) (d) None of these

57 Statement I Larynx in boys is also known as Adam's apple.

Statement II Larynx causes deepening of voice.

(a) Only I (b) Only II
(c) Both (a) and (b) (d) None of these

58 Statement I Estrogen promotes lobular development of breast.

Statement II It is also responsible for inhibition of milk secretion during pregnancy.

(a) Only I (b) Only II
(c) Both (a) and (b) (d) None of these

59 Statement I A pregnant woman needs folate, iron, vitamin B12 and iodine.

Statement II A first time pregnant woman can gain 480 kg of weight.

(a) Only I (b) Only II
(c) Both (a) and (b) (d) None of these

60 Arrange the following in sequential order.

1. Determine the food ration
2. Estimate the quantity of food available
3. Calculate dietary need of affected population

(a) 1, 2, 3 (b) 2, 3, 1 (c) 3, 2, 1 (d) 3, 1, 2

61 Arrange the following order on the basis of priority by an athlete.

1. Fat 2. Protein
3. Carbohydrate 4. Water

(a) 4, 3, 2, 1 (b) 1, 2, 3, 4 (c) 3, 4, 1, 2 (d) 1, 4, 3, 2

62 Match the following.

List I (Hormones)	List II (Applications)
A. HcG	1. Stimulates maternal respiration
B. Prolactin	2. Maintains corpus luteum function
C. Progesterone	3. Stimulation of uterine growth
D. Estrogen	4. Promotes mammary gland growth

Codes

	A	B	C	D		A	B	C	D
(a)	1	2	3	4	(b)	4	2	3	1
(c)	2	4	1	3	(d)	1	4	3	2

63 Match the following.

List I	List II
A. Pregnant women	1. Eat three meals a day
B. Lactating women	2. Avoid food having listeria
C. Infants	3. Avoid chocolate and spices
D. Adolescents	4. Avoid cow milk before the age of 1

Codes

	A	B	C	D		A	B	C	D
(a)	2	3	4	1	(b)	1	2	3	4
(c)	4	3	1	2	(d)	3	1	4	2

64 Match the following.

List I	List II
A. Skin	1. Whitish discharge in female
B. Vaginal discharge	2. Deepening of voice in boys
C. Body hair	3. Becomes oily
D. Voice	4. Hair in pubic region

Codes

	A	B	C	D		A	B	C	D
(a)	1	3	4	2	(b)	3	2	1	4
(c)	4	3	2	1	(d)	3	1	4	2

65 Match the following.

List I	List II
A. Age of 30	1. Hair thins and becomes gray
B. Age of 35	2. Decrease in immunity
C. Age of 40	3. Decreased hearing and wrinkling of skin
D. Age of 60	4. Lens stiffens and problem in focusing

Codes

	A	B	C	D		A	B	C	D
(a)	4	1	2	3	(b)	4	3	2	1
(c)	1	4	2	3	(d)	3	4	2	1

66 Match the following.

List I	List II
A. Testicular tissue	1. Menstrual period stops
B. Sclerosis	2. Testicular tissue mass decreases
C. Menopause	3. Risk of bone loss
D. Osteoporosis	4. Tube carrying sperm becomes less elastic

Codes

	A	B	C	D		A	B	C	D
(a)	1	3	4	2	(b)	2	4	1	3
(c)	2	3	4	1	(d)	1	2	4	3

67 Match the following.

List I	List II
A. Community nutrition	1. Water is the most important nutrient
B. Sports nutrition	2. Prevention of malnutrition
C. Nutrition in emergencies	3. Develops healthy eating habit

Codes

	A	B	C		A	B	C
(a)	3	2	1	(b)	1	2	3
(c)	3	1	2	(d)	1	3	2

Directions (Q. No. 68-81) *Given below are two statements, one labelled as Assertion A and other labelled as Reason R. Following are the codes given, choose the correct code.*

Codes

(a) Both A and R are true (b) Both A and R are false
(c) A is true, but R is false (d) A is false, but R is true

68 **Assertion** (A) Immediately after delivery colostrum is released from mother's breast.

Reason (R) It is thick and straw coloured.

69 **Assertion** (A) Cardiovascular adaptation during pregnancy leads to palpitation and dizziness.

Reason (R) Estrogen has a vasodilatory effect.

70 **Assertion** (A) Cephalocaudal development refers to growth of dentition.

Reason (R) Permanent teeth are also known as deciduous teeth.

71 **Assertion** (A) Babies should be given honey from early years.

Reason (R) Unpasteurised drinks must not be given to babies.

72 **Assertion** (A) Adult should include fruits and vegetables in diet.

Reason (R) Large quantity of salt is good for an adult's health.

73 **Assertion** (A) End of menstruation is known as menopause.

Reason (R) It involves lots of hormonal changes.

74 **Assertion** (A) Presbyopia is a common hearing problem in adults.

Reason (R) It occurs after 65 years of age.

75 **Assertion** (A) Dieticians and nutritionist work to promote community nutrition.

Reason (R) Community nutrition focuses on all age groups.

76 **Assertion** (A) Carbohydrate provides 60-70% of daily calories to athletes.

Reason (R) Carbohydrates are stored as fats.

77 **Assertion** (A) Community nutrition also works for immigrant or elderly.

Reason (R) Existing project is applied to them.

78 **Assertion** (A) All disasters cause a food shortage.

Reason (R) The nature of food shortage depends on the type of disaster.

79 **Assertion** (A) Puberty is caused by GnRH hormone.

Reason (R) GnRH hormone stimulates pituitary gland.

80 **Assertion** (A) Growth spurt in men occurs before puberty.

Reason (R) Growth of testicles marks is the starting of puberty in males.

81 **Assertion** (A) Community Nutrition Programme may fail due to inadequate funding.

Reason (R) Community Nutrition Programme is a programme led by General Public.

Directions (Q. Nos. 82-86) *Read the passage and give answer to following questions.*

While specific nutrition interventions (like micronutrient supplementation, micronutrient fortification and biofortification) can transform lives and improve the health of entire populations, their obvious limitation is that with each intervention, only a small part of the overall problem is being addressed: for example vitamin A supplements solve the specific problem of vitamin A deficiency.

To make further progress, households will need to change their food practice. This means behavioural change, which is considerably more complex than micronutrient supplements or fortification. A key opportunity to try to encourage these changes comes during pregnancy. Undernutrition in infants is extremely difficult, to reverse. The key message to impart to pregnant women is about improving diet, breastfeeding, complementary feeding of infants and young children and identifying inadequate growth and weight gain in babies.

A research by Sne Horton et al. finds that nutrition education is an order of magnitude more expensive than micronutrient supplements and micronutrient fortification but its cost-effectiveness is on par with many other attractive health investments.

82 How specific nutrition intervention is limited in its use?
(a) It does not address the poor
(b) Only a small part of overall problem is addressed
(c) Overall health is neglected
(d) Both (b) and (c)

83 What does the author mean by 'behavioural change' in the area of public nutrition?
(a) People buy specific micronutrients
(b) Change their food habits
(c) Change in lifestyle and sleep pattern
(d) None of the above

84 What is extremely difficult to reverse in infants?
(a) Mal nutrition (b) Undernutrition
(c) Health (d) All of these

85 How an infant's nutritional needs can be fulfilled?
(a) Others improving their diets
(b) Breastfeeding
(c) Complement feeding of infants
(d) All of the above

86 What is the most attractive health investment according to a research?
(a) Nutrition (b) Nutrition education
(c) Supply of micronutrients (d) Increasing people's health

PREVIOUS YEARS' QUESTIONS

July 2018

1 **Assertion** (A) Public Health Nutrition programmes should create more open spaces for physical activity to promote fitness.
Reason (R) Overweight and obesity are major predisposing factors for developing non-communicable diseases.
Codes
(a) Both A and R are incorrect.
(b) A is correct and R is incorrect.
(c) A is incorrect but R is correct.
(d) Both A and R are correct.

July 2015, 2017

2 **Assertion** (A) The colostrum secreted in the first few days of lactation helps build up immunity in the infant.
Reason (R) Colostrum is rich in gamma globulins and vitamin A.
(a) A is correct, but R is incorrect.
(b) A is incorrect, but R is correct.
(c) Both A and R are correct.
(d) Both A and R are incorrect.

July 2016

3 **Assertion** (A) The first outward sign of puberty is the rapid gain in height and weight.
Reason (R) The secretion of insulin and certisol stimulates the growth spurt.
(a) Both A and R are true. (b) Both A and R are false.
(c) A is true, but R is false. (d) R is true, but A is false.

4 **Assertion** (A) Exclusive breastfeeding for first six months protects the infant from infectious diseases.
Reason (R) Breast milk provides certain antibodies which develop natural immunity in the infant.
Codes
(a) Both A and R are correct.
(b) Both A and R incorrect.
(d) A is correct and R is incorrect.
(d) A is incorrect and R is correct.

ANSWERS

Exam Based Questions

1 (b)	2 (d)	3 (d)	4 (c)	5 (c)	6 (c)	7 (a)	8 (d)	9 (c)	10 (d)
11 (d)	12 (c)	13 (a)	14 (c)	15 (a)	16 (d)	17 (a)	18 (c)	19 (a)	20 (c)
21 (a)	22 (d)	23 (b)	24 (a)	25 (c)	26 (a)	27 (b)	28 (c)	29 (d)	30 (d)
31 (d)	32 (a)	33 (c)	34 (c)	35 (d)	36 (d)	37 (a)	38 (d)	39 (d)	40 (d)
41 (a)	42 (a)	43 (d)	44 (a)	45 (c)	46 (a)	47 (d)	48 (c)	49 (b)	50 (a)
51 (c)	52 (a)	53 (d)	54 (c)	55 (a)	56 (b)	57 (c)	58 (d)	59 (a)	60 (b)
61 (a)	62 (c)	63 (a)	64 (d)	65 (a)	66 (b)	67 (c)	68 (a)	69 (c)	70 (b)
71 (d)	72 (c)	73 (a)	74 (b)	75 (a)	76 (c)	77 (a)	78 (d)	79 (a)	80 (d)
81 (c)	82 (d)	83 (b)	84 (b)	85 (d)	86 (b)				

Previous Years' Questions

1 (d)	2 (c)	3 (c)	4 (c)

Clinical & Therapeutic Nutrition and Dietetics

Clinical Nutrition incorporates primarily the scientific fields of nutrition and dietetics. Therapeutic nutrition is the provision of nutrients to maintain or restore optimal nutrition and health. Different diets are prescribed under different medical conditions for the patients. Normal diet of a patient can be modified for therapeutic purposes. A dietician plays a major role in providing healthy and nutritive diet to the patient as per specifications.

Clinical and Therapeutic Nutrition

Clinical nutrition focuses on the nutritional management of individual or group of individual with established disease condition. It deals with issues such as altered nutritional requirement associated with the disease, disease severity and malnutrition. Therapeutic nutrition is the provision of nutrients to maintain and/or restore optimal nutrition and health. Designed as dietary supplements, therapeutic diets compensate for the lack of nutrients in the food intake of an individual. These diets are made from a mixture of carbohydrates and proteins embedded in a lipid matrix along with vitamins and minerals.

Importance of Therapeutic Diet

A therapeutic diet is a special diet plan that is crafted to cater to the nutritional needs of a patient. This special diet may be prescribed by a dietician or a physician for the following reasons :

- To sustain, correct or restore nutritional value in the patient's diet.
- To increase calories to enable weight gain.
- To decrease calories to enable weight loss.
- To control diabetes by balancing the carbohydrate, protein and lipid levels.
- To facilitate dialysis for kidney failed patients.
- To exclude foods due to food intolerance like gluten-sensitivity.

In this Chapter

- To avoid foods due to food allergies like peanut or milk allergies.
- To increase the protein content.
- To decrease sodium content.

Objectives of Therapeutic Diet

The objectives of therapeutic diet are as follows :

- To give a diet in keeping with the ability of body to metabolise certain food *e.g.*, as in diabetes.
- To give relief to a particular organ. For instance, fat content is reduced in diseases of gall bladder.
- To give a high protein diet.
- To treat or to prevent oedema by restricting salt as an cardiac and renal (kidney disease).
- To treat chronic malnutrition.
- To make digestion easier by exclusion or removal of irritating substances or those, which delay the emptying time of the stomach such as fibre, spices, fixed foods as in certain disease.

Diet Therapy

Diet therapy means the use of diet (food and drink) not only in the care of sick, but also in the prevention of disease and maintenance of health. It is concerned with the use of food as an agent in affecting recovery from illness.

The diet may have to be modified depending upon the disease, the severity of the nutrition status of the patient as well as the metabolic changes involved.

Normal Diet

Normal diet is defined as one, which consists of any and all foods eaten by the person in good health. It is planned by keeping the basic food group in mind, so that optimum amount of all the nutritions provided. As there is no restriction of any kind of food, this diet is nutritionally adequate.

The term 'normal diet' refers to the diet, which provides all the nutrients to the body, that are necessary for growth, maintenance and the optimum functioning of organ system *i.e.* the right quantity and proportion are in relation to each other.

All food that are eaten by the person in normal health. Food to be used in restricted amount are fatty food items like rich cakes, pasteries, halwas, etc, fried food, too many spices or pickles pakoras, poories, parathas.

Advantages of normal diet are :

- Nutrition balance is based on three food groups pattern.
- Easy in planning and preparation.
- Easy to evaluate and modify, accordingly if necessary.

Modification of Normal Diet for Therapeutic Purposes

The normal diet may be subjected to the following modification :

- Change in the calories contents.
- Change in the consistency, mostly in the fluid and soft diet.
- Variation in the amount of one or more nutrients *e.g.*, high or low protein diet or it may be no protein diet.
- Variation in the fibre content of the diet.
- Inclusion of food, blend (very low spices and salt) in the taste.
- Addition or inclusion of any specific food *e.g.*, allergic condition or the time interval between the feeding as in gastric ulcer.

When the normal diet is used as the basis for planning therapeutic diet, it is easy to see what the effect of addition of specific food, may have on the nutrient value e.g. if the individual with lactose intolerance also allergic to milk. It becomes immediately apparant that some other means must be sorted to provide protein, calcium and riboflavin.

Types of Diet

Two types of diet are provided to the patient who comes to the hospital. They are : (i) General Diet (ii) Modified Diet.

General Diet

It is divided into two types :

Full Diet/Whole Diet

This is a normal diet, which provides all the nutrients in slightly higher amount than recommended for a healthy sedentary worker. It can also be used for an adult patient admitted to a hospital. In this, no dietary modification are done. This is also known as regular or general diet. This is a well balanced and nutritious diet. The following foods should be avoided by formulating the diet :

- All cereals
- Fried food
- Too much of spices
- Diet chart for full diet

Diet Chart for Full Diet

Food Stuff	Vegetarian	Non-Vegetarian
Cereal	400 gm	400 gm
Pulses	70	50
Green-leafy vegetables	50	50
Other vegetables	100	100
Roots and tuber	100	100
Fruits	100	100
Milk	400	200
Flesh food	–	100
Sugar	20	20
Oil for cooking	20	20

This diet proved calories = 2.450

Protein = 77

Retinol = 800 mg

Thiamine = 9 mg

Riboflavin = 1.4 mg

Calcium = 1.1 mg

Iron = 43 mg

Half Diet

This diet provides nutrients required for children upto the age of 10 years. The following food should be avoided by formulating the diet :

- All cereals
- Too much of spices
- Fried foods

Diet Chart for Half Diet

Food Stuff	Vegetarian	Non-Vegetarian
Cereals	25 gm	25 gm
Pulses	60 gm	40 gm
Green-leafy vegetables	25 gm	25 gm
Other vegetables	75 gm	75 gm
Roots and tubers	75 gm	75 gm
Fruits	100 gm	100 gm
Milk	400 ml	300 ml
Flesh food	–	50 gm
Sugar	30 gm	30 gm
Oil for cooking	20 ml	25 ml

This diet provides calories = 1800

Protein = 55 gm

Calcium = 927

Iron = 29

Retinol = 520

Thiamine = 1.3

Riboflavin = 1.1

Modified Diet

Types of modified diet are :

- Soft diet, fluid diet
- Blend diet
- Low calories diet
- Low protein diet
- Low fat diet
- Low cholestrol diet
- Low sodium diet
- High calories diet

Soft Diet

This diet is soft in texture and consists of liquid and semi-solid foods. It is an intermediate step between full and liquid diet. It is indicated in certain post operation cases in acute infection in some condition and cardiac disease. It is low in residue and readily digested. Little or no spices and condiments are used in the preparation of diet. Usually, they are only used on a daily basis for a short time instead of long time. The nutritive value of soft diet is low consequently.

Diet Chart for Soft Diet

Soft Diet	Sample Diet
Food stuff	200
Rice	70
Green gram dal	100
Cucumber	100
Potato/onion	200
Orange, sweet	–
Lime, banana	–
Milk	–
Egg	400
Paneer, cheese	2
Sugar	30
Oil	20

This diet provides calories = 2000

Protein = 64

Calcium = 89

Iron = 19.5

Retinol = 78.5

Thiamine = 1.4

Riboflavin = 1.1 mg

Fluid Diet

This is used, when the patient is unable to digest the solid foods. The nutrition adequacy will depend on the type of food given to the patient. The fluid diet may be :

Clear Fluid Diet The clear fluid diet is given to the patient, when they are actually ill and **have marked influence of food**. For example, nausea, vomiting, acute diarrhoea, etc. It consists of clear fluids only *i.e.* is light tea without milk, clear soups, dal water, carbonated beverages, glucose, electrolyte solution, H_2O and strained food juices. The diet provides only fluids and electrolytes *i.e.* certain water soluble vitamins and certain minerals. Clear fluid diet is one which is fully liquid, but any of the part should not be visible in that *e.g.*, rice, H_2O, dal and hot milk as such contain fat (but thin in appearance).

Full Liquid Diet It is a liquid diet, which is nutritionally adequate, if planned properly and can contribute for a longer period of time. Then ingredients are near to the normal diet. It's indicated for those patients who cannot swallow or tolerate solid foods.

Blend Diet

This is a diet, which is non-irritating, chemically blend and inhibit gastric secretion. It can be used for the patient of GIT. This can be brought by slight changes and reduction in fibre and fat contents. It can be used for various GIT diseases, like diarrhoea. In this, the ordinary food item, which cannot be swallowed are blended to make them liquid which can pass through nasogastic tube, H_2O is added to make the volume 1500 ml, gives 1500 calories and 50g protein.

The following food stuff should be avoided, while formulating the diet :

- All bran, coarse cereals
- Skin and seed of foods
- Raw vegetables like cabbage, beans, lady finger,etc.
- Spices and condiments
- Fried foods
- Strong beverages
- Pickle and chutney
- Tender coconut water
- Chocolate pudding and similar
- Meat extracts and soups

Low Calories Diet

This diet provides low calories and the total energy requirement of the day. It is used in the obese patient, hypertension, heart patient, obesity inducing foods like concentrated sweet, fried food, dry fruits, nuts, alcoholic drinks, cream and excess of fat should be avoided, while in formulating the diet.

Low Protein Diet

It is used for patient with acute chronic renal failures and also in hepatic and encephalopathy patient.

Low Fat Diet

It is a normal diet modified to reduce fat content for approximately 30 gm/day. It may be used in treatment of diseases with intolerence to fat such as a gall bladder, liver and pancreatic diseases or in condition of steatorrhea.

The following food should be avoided in such diet :

- High fat food like nuts and seed
- Fried food
- Free fat and cream, etc.

Diet Chart for Low Protein Diet

Food Stuff	Vegetarian	Non-vegetarian
Cereal	200	250
Pulses	100	75
Cow milk	–	100
Milk powder	50	–
Curd (Cow milk)	200	–
Green leafy vegetables	100	100
Other vegetables	100	100
Potato	50	50
Sugar	50	50
Banana	75	75
Orange	100	100
Ghee or oil	17	15
Chicken fish	–	100
Egg	–	1

This diet provides calories = 2100 k/cal

Protein = 75 gm

Fat = 30 gm

C H O = 385 gm

Low Cholesterol Diet

This diet is used for the treatment of patient with high cholesterol level and patient with coronary heart disease. The high cholesterol source is in the food like egg yolk, liver, red meat should be avoided, in addition to this total fat content should be reduced in which the ratio of poly saturated mono unsaturated and saturated fatty acid should be 1 : 1 : 1. In general, ghee and oil should be used in 1 : 1 proportion. It can help in lowering plasma, cholesterol calories and protein plasma can be changed as per individual needs.

The following foods should be avoided while formulating the diet :

- Butter, hydrogenated fat and lard
- Coconut and coconut oil
- Food cooked with these fats
- Fatty meat, visible fat, meat savage, etc.
- Whole milk with cream
- Chocolate and ice-cream
- Cheese
- Organ meats like liver, kidney, brain, etc.
- Egg more than one or at most 2/week

Diet Chart for Low Cholesterol Diet

Food Stuff	Amount
Cereals	300
Pulses	50
Green leafy vegetables	50
Other vegetables	100
Root and tubers	100
Fruits	100
Skimmed milk	400
Sugar	30
Oil	20

This diet provides calories = 2400

Protein = 70 gm

Fat = 55 gm

C H O = 400 gm

Low Sodium Diet

This is a normal diet with low sodium content and use in condition, where there is hypertension, in oedema nephrite, in congestive heart failure, etc. It can be salt free diet or moderate salt restriction diet and accordingly 1-2 gm of salt may be allowed. The food prepared in this diet is cooked without extra salt and high sodium foods are avoided in this.

The following food should be avoided while formulating the diet :

- Salt in cooking or in table
- Sea fish
- Salted meat
- Salted dry fish, liver, etc.
- Salted butter/ cheese

All foods in which salt or baking soda has been added in cooking pickle or chutneys.

Diet Chart for Sodium Diet

Food Stuff	Vegetarian	Non-vegetarian
Rice	250	300
Dal	100	75
Fruits	200	200
Vegetables	200	200
Potatoes	100	125
Milk	600	200
Oil	30	30
Sugar	–	50
Meat/fish	–	50
Egg	–	1

This diet provides calories = 2000

Protein = 70 gm

Sodium = 0.5 gm

High Calorie Diet

High calories diet are in the form of concentrated CHO or fat, so that the bulk of the diet is not used much. It should not be used for the patient for hypertension, etc.

Diet Chart for High Calories Diet

Food Stuff	Vegetarian	Non-vegetarian
Cereals	250	300
Pulses	100	50
Roots and tubers	50	75
Other vegetables	50	50
Green leafy vegetables	100	100
Bread	60	60
Butter	10	20
Milk	75	300
Curd	100	–
Sugar	50	50
Ghee and oil	30	35

Diet Counselling and Management

Diet counselling is an ongoing process in which a health professional, usually a registered dietician, works with an individual to assess his/her usual dietary intake and identify areas where change is needed. The diet counsellor provides information, educational material support and follow up to help the individual make and maintain the necessary dietary changes. The goal of diet counselling is to help a person make and maintain dietary changes. For a person with mental disorder, dietary changes may be needed to promote healthier eating, to adopt a therapeutic diet, or to avoid nutrient drug interactions. Diet counselling is an integral part of treatment for persons with eating disorder or chemical dependencies.

The diet counsellor and the individual work together to assess current eating patterns and identify areas which need change. Registered dieticians have met certain education and experience standard and are well qualified to provide nutrition counselling. But, nurses, physicians and health educators also provide nutrition counselling.

Steps in Diet Counselling and Management

Assessing Dietary Habits

Dietary counselling begins with an interview in which counsellor asks questions about a person's typical food intake. Diet counsellor use different methods to assess typical food intake.

The 24 hours recall method is a listing of all the foods and beverages, a person consumed within the previous 24 hours period. The dietician may ask the person to recall the first thing he/she ate or drank in the previous morning. The dietician then records the estimated amount of all the foods and beverages, the person consumed in the rest of the day. The 24 hours food recall can be used to provide an estimate of energy and nutrient intake. However, people tend to over or underestimate the intake of certain food and food intake on one day may not accurately represent typical food intake.

A food frequency questionnaire can sometimes provide more accurate picture of person's typical eating patterns. For example, the dietician may ask a person that how many servings of dairy products, fruits, vegetables, grains , cereals, meats or fat he/she consumes in a typical day, week or month.

Daily food records are also useful in assessing food intake. An individual keeps a written record of the amount of all foods and beverages consumed over a given period of time. The dietician can then use the food records to analyse actual energy and nutrient intake.

Identifying Changes Needed

- The initial dietary assessment and interview provide the basis of identifying behaviour that needs to be changed.
- Sometimes, a person already has a good idea of what dietary changes are needed, but may require help in making the changes.
- Other times, the dietician can help to educate a person on the health effect of different dietary choices.
- The dietician and the individual work together to identify areas where change is needed. They prioritise changes and solve problems as to how to make the changes.
- Making dietary change is a gradual process. An individual may start with one or two easier dietary changes in the first few weeks and gradually make additional or more difficult changes over several weeks or months.
- In making dietary changes, each individual's situation and background must be carefully considered.
- Factors that affect food decisions include an individual's ethnic background, religion, group affiliation, socio-economic status and world view.

Identifying Barriers to Change

Once the needed changes have been identified, the individual and dietician must think through potential problems that may arise. For example, changing eating behaviour may mean involving purchasing different foods, planning ahead for social events or bringing special foods to work. Some common barriers to changing eating habit include :

- Inconvenience
- Social gathering
- Food preferences
- Lack of knowledge or time
- Cost

Setting Goals

The dietician and client set behaviour oriented goals together. Goals should focus on the behaviour needed to achieve the desired dietary change, not an absolute value, such as achieving a certain body weight.

Maintaining Changes

- The challenge for the individual lies not in making the initial dietary changes, but in maintaining them over the long term.
- Self monitoring, realistic expectation and continued follow-ups can help a person to maintain dietary changes.
- Self-monitoring involves regularly checking eating habits against desired goals and keeping track of eating behaviour.
- Individual and dietician should not expect a perfect dietary compliance as slips can occur inevitably. The goal is to keep small slips, such as eating few extra cookies, from becoming big slips, like total abandonment of dietary change.
- The dietician can help to identify situation relapse and plan ways to handle the situation ahead of time.
- Diet counselling is an ongoing process that can take months or years.

Role of Dietician in Diet Counselling and Management

One who plans, supervises and prepares therapeutic or other diet for individual or other group in hospital, institution and other establishment of workers in particular sector is known as dietician. Dietician gives instruction in selection and proper preparation of food, according to dietic principles.

A dietician, also called a nutritionist, is a healthcare professional, who is responsible for making sure, that food is nutritious and that people understand how and what to eat. This can be done in a group setting or in one-on-one consultations. Dietitians may work full or part time in a hospital, clinic or wellness center to fulfill their responsibilities.

Types of Dieticians

Administrative dietician and consultant dieticians are two main types of dieticians. Their description is given below :

Administrative Dietician

- She/he is a member of management team and affects the nutritional care of group, therapeutic and management of food service system.
- She/he plans, develops, controls and evaluates food service system.
- Develops short and long range department plan and progress consistent and organisation policies.
- Manages and control resources and recommend budget programme.
- Coordinates and integrates clinical and administrative aspects of dietetics to provide quality nutritional care.
- Establishes and maintains standard of food production and service, sanitation, safety and security.
- Plans, conducts and evaluates organisation and In-Service Educational Programme.
- Develops menu pattern and evaluates client acceptance.

- Develops specification for procurement of food, equipment and supplies.
- Administrate personal policies as established by the department and organisation.
- Plans layout designs and determine equipments required for new or renovative food store facilities.

Consultant Dietician

- He/She is a nutrition expert that uses food to maximise the health and well-being of individuals in assisted living facilities.
- Maintains effective verbal and written communication and public relation *i.e.* inter and intra-departmentally.
- Interprets and evaluates, utilises current searches relaled to nutritional care.
- Provides guidance and evaluation of the job performance of the dietic personnel.
- Consults with the healthcare team and with the nutrition care of client.
- Recommends and monitors standard for sanitation, safety and security in food service.
- Plans, organises and conducts orientation and In-Service Education Programme for food service.
- Develops budget proposal and recommends procedure for cost controls.

Code of Ethics for Dietician

Dietic practitioner voluntarily develop a code of ethics. Dietic practitioner provides professional services and obligation of the ethic principle to self-client society and profession.

Code of ethics for dietician is as follows :

- He does not discriminate other individuals on basis of religion, sex, age and national origin.
- He fulfils professional commitment in good faith.
- He conducts himself/herself with honesty, integrity and fairness.
- He maintains confidentiality of information.
- He practices dietetics based on scientific principle and current information.
- He recognises an exercise, professional judgement within the limits of his qualification and seeks counsel and makes referral as appropriate.
- He provides sufficient information to enable clients to make their own decision.
- The Dietician should be aware of estimated energy requirement. The average dietary energy intake that maintains energy balance in a healthy person of a given age, gender, weight, height and activity level.

Aims and Objectives of Dietician

Aims and objectives of dietician are as follows :

- To discuss important advances and problems in dietic, nutrition and other relevant sciences and to adopt measures for the advancement and popularisation of dietetics nutrition and other relevant science.
- To promote knowledge of dietetics and nutrition through discussion. To encourage the spirit of active pursuit of knowledge and original scientific research.
- To support and project the status and interest of the member of the association and work for their general welfare.
- To encourage the study of dietetics, nutrition and other science relating to human health and raise funds to institute for the purpose of scholarship, prizes, awards and travel grants.
- To invite scientist of eminence in India/abroad to deliver lectures and to participate in the scientific deliberation of the association.
- To create public opinion in favour of the aims and objects of the association through its publication holdings, seminars, conferences and press campaigns.
- To perform many other acts that may assist in conducting or be necessary for the fulfilment of the aims and objectives of the association.

Non-Compliance to Dietary Advice of a Dietician

Large number of patients fail to adhere to advice on diet, exercise and blood glucose monitoring leading to risk of complication. Some of the possible reasons for non-compliance are :

- Resistance to changing a diet.
- Competing time and energy demand.
- Lack of relevant education.
- Diet therapy is infrequently prescribed.
- The changes required are life long, so life styles need to be changed.
- The impact of nutrition counselling is not dramatic and those who do not have patience stop complying.
- Festivals and party occasions may disturb the schedule.
- Patients are not referred for nutritional counselling.

Feeding

The act of giving food to a person or an animal is known as feeding. Artificial methods of feeding a patient are some of the most controversial interventions available, along with other forms of prolonging or supporting life that would not continue without doing something to assist the patient.

Methods of Feeding

A lot of problems are faced while feeding so the following factors should be kept in mind :

Environment for Meal A favourable environment is made, while having a meal. Such as environment can be made by making and surrounding areas clean and orderly arranged. Having proper ventilation and facilities should be provided.

Cooperation of Patient Patient's cooperation is very important as non-cooperative patients are difficult to treat. Patients should be given the meals, when he is ready for meals.

Presentation of Food Presentation of tray, in which food is served is of good importance, since more appealing is the food , the better is the therapeutic diet of a patient.

There should be variation in colour, texture and flavour. Tray size should be such, which can be easily handled by the patient.Food should be served on time.

Types of Feeding

Taking food orally is the general method of food acceptance, when the patient is conscious and can eat, digest and absorb food. In illness, when the patient is unable to eat or he is unconscious then mode of feeding differs, when the patient is unable to chew or swallow because of deformity of mouth/throat, unconsciousness, paralysis of throat muscles, then there are other methods of feeding that are introduced.

Types of feeding are :

Tube Feeding

Tube feeding may be required for a short period or for an indefinite time as the circumstances may be. It is used after the surgery of mouth or gastrostomy intestinal tract or in case of severe burns, ordinarily. Nasogastric tube feeding is given, but if the oesophagus is blocked then the patient is fed through a tube inserted into the stomach through the abdominal wall.

Conditions of tube feeding are as follows :

- Babies who have low birth weight and cannot suck.
- Those who are under nourished and cannot take or retain food taken, orally.
- Persistent anorexia patients, who need forced feeding.
- After certain types of surgery.
- Patients with severe mal-absorption.
- Patients who cannot absorb or digest food.
- Semi-conscious or unconscious patients or any other condition, which prevents intake of sufficient food.

Importance of tube feeding is stated in the points below :

- Necessary nutrients can be provided in required amount through tube feeding.
- The food given through tube feeding is easily and quickly digested and assimilated.
- By this method, without vomiting fluid can be administered to the patient.
- This method is cheaper than the other artificial methods of feeding.
- In this method, all types of food administered provide a calorie per mili litre of fluid.
- By this method, such foods and medicines can be administered easily to the patients, which cannot be sterilised.

Nasogastric Tube Feeding

In this, a plastic tube of 3-4 mm in diameter lubricated with olive oil or paraffin is pushed from the nasopharyngeal passage upto the stomach. If the patient feels uncomfortable then a solution of procaine is sprayed and the tube is again slipped slowly, when the tube is inserted into the nose and reaches to the pharynx and patient will tend to cough. At this stage, patient should be asked to swallow the tube, so that it may enter the oesophagus. After this, tube can be easily pushed into the stomach. It is essential to make sure that the tube has passed into the oesophagus and not the trachea.

This can be ascertained by the tube reaches about 8" in the body of the patient, coughs a little by which it is concluded that a tube has reached upto the pharynx with drawing a sample of gastric content after the tube has reached the stomach. The tube can be left in position for 4-5 days, it is desirable that the tube is withdrawn once in 2 days washed and boiled and inserted into the stomach.

Diets of tube feeding are :

Blendarised Feeding Such type of feeding is given to the patient, when feeding is administered for a long time. Any food, which is liquidified in high speed blend, can be used in such type of feeding.

Planned Feeding Generally, a planned diet is preferred over tube feeding as in this quantity of nutrients remain constant and it can be quickly prepared.

Gastrostomy Feeding

Such type of feeding is used when digestive system is affected due to injury, surgery, cancer, etc. In that case, nasogastric feeding is impossible and, so that through surgery a tube is attached to the stomach, which comes outside through which the patient can be fed.

In that case following nutrients are given and feeds can be used depending on the condition of patient :

1. Cow's milk – 2 l
2. Fats as in liquid form – 100 ml
3. Lactose (phosphoral) – 60 gm

Jejunostomy Feeding

The method of jejunostomy feeding is used, when the alimentary canal/stomach is highly affected or has developed cancer or any part of the digestive tract is removed.

In this method, also by surgery an opening is created in the jejunium (intestinal part), through which a tube is introduced and it is through this tube a patient is fed. It is a difficult method to feed the patient as in this ,digestive juice in the salivary glands and stomach are lacking due to which patient may experience vomiting and nausea, hunger cramps in the stomach, etc.

Rectal Feeding

In some special type of deformities of GIT, the essential nutrients, especially minerals like Ca, K, etc. are made to reach the body through a tube, which enter the body through the rectum. In such type of feeding Ca and K bi-carbonate or 1 tsp of salt dissolved in 1tsp of H_2O can be given in 5 tsp tea. Glucose can also be given. Such type of feeding can be administered only in a hospital, under the guidance of doctors and dieticians and nutrition at home.

Intravenous Feeding

It is used, when the patient's stomach needs to be provided complete rest or when tube feeding is not possible, either because the patient is unconscious or is unable to accept the tube in his body, Intravenous, as the name suggests means through the veins. Thus, in this method, the nutrients are injected in the veins of the body, where the food is directly mixed with the blood and assimilated.

Special Feeding Method

Oral feeding is the best for the nourishment of a patient, but in the following condition it is not possible to give :

- Those who can't be persuaded to eat
- Short bowel syndrome
- After surgery
- Babies with very low birth weight
- Patient with neurological or renal disorders or who have continued fever or diabetes.
- Those who cannot digest or absorb.
- Semi-conscious and unconscious patients
- Those who are under-nourished or are at risk of becoming so.

Diet in Different Medical Conditions

Description of necessary diet in different medical conditions is given below :

Diet After Surgery

No matter how big or small, surgery can always have a significant impact on your health. The way you look after your body after surgery can be just as important as the procedure itself. It can also make a big difference to the success of the healing process. Surgery takes a big toll on the body. Speedy and effective postsurgery recovery requires catering to its special nutrition needs, while it is still in a relatively weakened state and during a period, when it is most susceptible to postoperative diseases and ailments. Proper nutrition can help to boost your immune system, so that it can resist those threats.

Importance of Diet After Surgery

- Surgery causes considerable increase in the nutritional requirement of an individual, as a result of loss of blood, consequently the circulating blood volume and the concentration of serum protein haemoglobin and electrolytes are reduced.
- Further, the food intake usually is inadequate and restricted for a few days prior to the operation.
- The dietary deficiency will cause loss in body weight and delay in healing of wound.

Nutritional Requirement After Surgery

The nutritional requirement after surgery and injury are briefly discussed below :

Calories Since, the patient will be at rest in bed, their calories requirement will be slightly less than those of sedentary person.

- Since, a majority of individual would suffer loss of body weight due to surgery.
- The weight loss has to be made up by the calories intake.
- Hence, the calories intake 8 about $1\frac{1}{2}$ times, of the actual requirement is desirable.

Protein Since, the patient who has undergone surgical treatment will be out of nitrogen balance.

- The protein intake from the diet should be about twice the daily requirement e.g., about 100-120 gm daily.
- The protein should be of high nutritive value and derived from milk, egg and meat.

CHO It should provide atleast 50% of calories in the diet.

- The CHO should consist of starch and glucose.

- **Fat** The fat intake should be kept at about 10% in the diet.
- The fat provides about 20% of the calories requirements
- About 1/2% of fat consist of vegetable oil, rich in EFA and vitamins.

Minerals Loss of sodium and potassium occur due to break down of tissue proteins.

- Further, deficiency of Na and Cl ions may occur due to loss of these elements in vomiting, perspiration, etc.
- Since, blood loss is likely to occur iron deficiency and anemia may develop and iron salt should be administered along with ascorbic acid, folic acid and vitamin B_{12}.

H_2O Balance The H_2O balance is upset after surgery.

- Due to the loss of H_2O from the body and haemorrhage.
- The H_2O loss should be made up by parental fluids until satisfactory oral intake is ensured.

Feeding the Patient After Surgery

- During the first 24-48 hours after the surgical operation, fluid or food should not be given orally as it may lead to vomiting and some of the fluid or vomiting may be drawn to the lungs.
- During the period, the fluid and electrolyte balances are maintained by administering them paranterally.
- Glucose and amino-acid, with and some time fat emulsion will have to be administered intravenously.
- If oral feeding cannot be done after 48 hours or 72 hours.
- Tube feeding should be instituted.

Diet After Total Gastrostomy

When the stomach is removed, the organ which serves as the reservoir of food is lost and hence the patient will have to be fed small amount of food at frequent intervals. Due to gastric secretion, the absorption of iron is low and the vitamin B_{12} is not absorbed hence, vitamin B_{12} has to be given by injection.

The oral feeding of the graded is indicated below :

- **3rd Day** 30ml of glucose, H_2O and fruit juice once in 30 minutes .
- **4th Day** 50-100 ml of milk containing glucose to be given hourly.
- **8th Day** onwards milk, egg, small amount of bread and fruits to be given once in 2 hours.

Diet After Operation of Mouth

- Minor operation of mouth, like extraction of tooth formation of dentures, etc., may lead to nutrition inadequacy due to one or the other complication.
- For 1 or 2 days, after the extraction of teeth, it may be necessary to restrict the fluid diet.
- Soft food, which require little chewing may be used for 2 or 3 weeks.
- In cases of major operation of mouth, a fluid diet orally or by tube feeding may be given to the patient for a week or 15 days.
- Similarly, in operation of oesophagus, tube feeding is practiced, in which a tube is inserted from the mouth to the stomach and the patient is fed through it.

Diet After Burns

- Huge protein salt and fluid loss occur through the badly burnt region of the body.
- Due to which nutritional requirement are greatly high.

Diet in Fever

Fever is an elevation in body temperature above the normal, which may occur due to exogenous and endogenous factors.

Causes of fever are :

- **Endogenous Factor** Antigen-antibody reaction, malignancy and graft rejections
- **Exogenous Factor** Bacteria or fungi

Types of fever are :

- **Short Duration Fever** Colds, tonsillitis, influenza and typhoid
- **Chronic Fever** Tuberculosis
- **Intermittent Fever** Malaria

Dietary Suggestions in Fever

Some general dietary suggestions for fever are given below :

Energy The caloric requirement may be increased as much as 50%, if the temperature is high and the tissue destruction is great. Restlessness also increases the caloric requirement.

Protein About 100 g protein or more is prescribed for the adult, when fever is prolonged. This will be most efficiently utilised, when the calorie intake is liberal.

Carbohydrates Glycogen stores are replenished by a liberal intake of carbohydrate. Glucose, which is less sweet and readily absorbed into the blood stream is preferred.

Fats The energy intake may be rapidly increased through the judicious use of fats, but fried foods and rich pastries may retard digestion unduly.

Minerals A sufficient intake of sodium chloride is accomp' ·d by the use of salty broth and soups and by liberal sp ·aklings of salt on food. Fruit juices and milk are relatively good sources of this element.

Vitamins Fevers apparently increase the requirement for vitamin A and ascorbic acid just as the B-complex vitamins are needed at increased levels, proportionate to the increase in calories.

Oral therapy with antibiotics and drugs interfere with synthesis of some B-complex vitamins by intestinal bacteria.

Fluid The fluid intake must be liberal to compensate for the losses from the sweat and to permit adequate volume of urine for excreting the wastes. Daily 2500-5000 ml is necessary, including beverages, soups, fruit juices and water.

Interval of Feeding Small quantities of food at intervals of 2 to 3 hours will permit adequate nutrition without overtaking the digestive system. At time with improvements, many patients consume more food if given three meals and bed time feeding.

Diet in Typhoid

Typhoid is an infectious disease with an acute fever of short duration and occurs only in humans. *Salmonella typhi* causes typhoid, *Salmonella schottmulleri* causes paratyphoid. Faeces and urine of the patients or carriers of the disease are the source of infection.

The infection is often passed on through contaminated food and drinking water. It is more prevalent in places where hand washing is less frequent.

A high calorie, high protein, high carbohydrate, low fat, high fluid, low fibre and bland diet is suggested for typhoid patients.

Dietary Suggestions for Typhoid

- The general principles of dietary treatment of fever is followed for typhoid also. At first, clear fluid diet is given followed by full fluid and soft diet. In liquid diets, the patient may not meet high caloric and high protein requirements. As the patient is improving, soft diet can be given.
- Food to be included are fruit juices with glucose, coconut water, barley water, milk, milk shakes. If there is no diarrhoea custards, thin dal, curries, eggs, baked fish, minced meat, curd, cottage cheese, cereals, steamed vegetable juices, milk puddings and vegetable puree can be given.
- Food to be avoided are butter, ghee, vegetable oil, no irritating fibre foods, chilies and other spices, rich pastures, fried foods, pudding and cream sou .

Diet in Tuberculosis

Tuberculosis is an infectious disease caused by the acillus mycobacterium tuberculosis. It affects the lungs most often, but may also be localised in other organs, such as the lymph nodes or kidneys or it may be generalised. A high calorie, high protein, high vitaminised and mineralised, high fluid soft diet is recommended.

Dietary Suggestions in Tuberculosis

- Since, patients have poor appetite, food must be appetising and patient's likes and dislikes must be considered.
- During the acute stage, a high-calorie fluid and soft diet are prescribed followed by high calorie soft regular diet.
- Initially, small quantities of fluid diet should be given once in 3 hours. When the fever comes down, the interval can be increased to every 4 hours.
- For meeting the protein requirement, good quality protein like eggs should be included.
- Fatty foods, highly fibrous foods and very spicy foods, which are hard to digest should be avoided.
- As the patient progresses, normal, attractive and palatable food should be given. The patient should come back to ideal weight.

Diet in Obesity

Obesity is a state, in which there is a generalised accumulation of excess adipose tissue in the body, leading to more than 20% of the desirable weight. Obesity invites disability disease and premature death. Excess body weight is a hindrance, leading to breathlessness on moderate exertion and predisposes a person to diseases like atherosclerosis, high blood pressure, stroke, diabetes, gall bladder diseases and osteoarthritis of weight bearing joints and varicose veins.

Dietary Suggestions in Obesity

- The patient should be convinced that there is no other way of reducing weight, except by consuming less calories than needed by the body.
- Body wraps and any kind of massage of both cannot bring reduction of weight. No single food or drug can reduce weight.
- The diet should be adequate in all other nutrients except kilo calories should be high in fibre.
- Maintaining weight is life long process. Hence, after 40 one should know appreciating low calorie foods and rejecting heavy sweets should become natural way of life.
- Modification of normal diet is the best of planning good reducing diet. A diet that promises to allow to cast as much as one wants is almost certainly made up of foods that are so impalatable that one will not want even in small amount. The diet should not include new and peculiar foods.
- The ideal way of reducing weight is not reducing calories, but also spending more calories. Exercise reduces body fat and increases muscle mass, bungs down blood pressure, blood sugar, blood cholesterol, reduces stress and improves feeling of well being.
- Obesity patient should be encouraged to eat 'improcessed' foods. They should limit fat, sucrose and alcohol.

Diet in the Under Weight Condition

Half the Indian rural population is under weight with upto quarters being so classified in deprived communities.

Dietary Suggestions in Under Weight Condition

A high calorie, high proteins and high fat diet with liberal vitamin intake is recommended. But before going into the diet, the first step is to determine and eliminate the cause for under eating. Then a balanced diet should be planned based on the following requirements :

Energy The calorie requirements vary depending upon the activities. For increasing weight, the total caloric intake should be in excess of the energy requirement. An additional 500 Kcals per day is recommended. The increase should be gradual over 1 or 2 weeks, otherwise digestive disturbances may occur.

Proteins Instead of 1g protein, over 1.2g per kg is recommended for tissue building. Good quality protein is completely utilised by the body and as far as possible best protein sources must be liberally included in the initial stage.

Fats Even though fat content is increased, easily digestible fats are to be included. Fried and fatty foods are not recommended as they may cause diarrhoea. Fatty food should not be taken at the beginning of a meal as they reduce appetite. High calorie fatty foods such as cream, butter, margarine and oils help to increase the weight.

Carbohydrates High carbohydrate sources must form the basis of the diet. Leafy vegetables should be restricted and preference to be given to potato and yam. Dried fruits, sweets, nuts, desserts, jam, jelly, cereals, cereal products and non-vegetarian foods are rich source of energy and can be liberally included in the diet. The number of meals should be increased. Two feeds incorporating soups, juices or sweets in between major meals improve the nutritive value of the diet. Easily digestible foods should be given. Porridge, cutlets, desserts, potato chips, high protein drinks like milk, malted milk and badam kheer can be included. Thick soups are easily digestible and highly nutritious items.

Vitamins and Minerals With a liberal diet there is no need for extra vitamin and mineral supplement.

Fluids Fluids should not be taken before or with a meal, but only after a meal, so that food intake is not reduced. Enough fluids must be taken, so as to avoid constipation.

Exercise and Bowels Regular outdoor exercise helps to stimulate over appetite, emotional well being is essential to have a good appetite. Constipation may reduce the appetite, so the bowel movements should be regulated with adequate fluids, exercise and fruits. Synthetic drinks, soft drinks, alcohol, a erated drinks, too much of tea and coffee reduce appetite and should be avoided.

Diet in Cardiovascular System Diseases

Heart disease affects people of all ages, but is most frequent in middle age and is most often caused by atherosclerosis. Disease of the heart may affect the pericardium, myocardium or endocardium. In addition, the blood vessels within the heart, leaving the heart or the heart valves may be diseased. A heart attack and a stroke are by no means always fatal. Some can go back to their old activities, some remain invalid and some are handicapped. In arteriosclerosis, the walls of small arteries become thickened to ageing or due to hypertension.

Dietary Suggestions in Cardiovascular Diseases

- Patient should maintain slightly lower than the standard weight. Accordingly, total calories should be restricted.
- The diet should be rich in fibre by including foods like raw salads, fruits, green leafy vegetables and whole grains.
- Five servings of fruit and vegetables should be included in the diet, not only to meet the nutritional requirement, but also to meet antioxidants and fibre.
- Vegetable oils rich in poly unsaturated fatty acids like safflower and sunflower oil should be included in the suggested combinations.
- Inclusion of fish in the diet is beneficial as they contain omega-3 fatty acids.
- Concentrated foods like sweets, chocolates, cakes, pasteries, ice-creams and fried foods should be restricted or preferably avoided.
- Foods giving only empty calories, like carbohydrate, beverages, alcohol, sugar and sago are totally avoided.
- Small quantities of almonds can be consumed to bring down the cholesterol level. High amount of nuts and oil seeds increase the calories and fat content in the diet.
- Egg yolk contains cholesterol. Hence, eggs should be restricted to 2-3 eggs/week. Cholesterol containing foods should be limited in the diet.
- Instead of whole milk, skimmed milk can be used.
- Coconut should be avoided in the diet as it contains high amount of saturated fatty acids and concentrated source of energy.
- Coffee and tea can be taken in moderation. Excess amount of caffeine increases the heart rate.
- To restrict sugar intake, artificial sweeteners can be included in the diet.

- Animal foods like meat and pork, which contain high amount of saturated fat should be avoided. Shrimps and crabs have less amount of fat and can be included in the diet. All sea foods are rich in sodium. Hence, hypertensive patients should avoid these foods.
- Foods that have hypocholesterolmic effects, like soyabean, fenugreek, garlic, onion and turmeric should be included in the diet.
- If the patient is suffering from hypertension, sodium should be restricted.
- Vegetable oils in combination should be included.
- Alcohol intake should be limited.
- Constipation should be prevented by including plenty of water and fibre in the diet.
- Heavy meals should be avoided. Small and frequent meals are preferred.
- Antioxidant supplement can be given.

Diet in Hypertension

Every individual has blood pressure, which is necessary to move blood through arteries and to provide oxygen to the tissues of the body. Hypertension is elevated blood pressure. WHO defines hypertension as a condition, in which systolic pressure exceeds 160 mm hg and diastolic pressure exceeds 95 mm hg or more therapy should be initiated with drugs as well as diet. High blood pressure is not a disease, but only a symptom indicating that some underlying disease is progressing.

Types of Hypertension

Three major types of hypertension which is given below :

Mild Hypertension Diastolic pressure is 90 to 104 mm hg in this form. Treatment is based on weight loss, sodium restriction and behavioural techniques.

Moderate Hypertension Diastolic pressure is 105 to 119 mm hg with moderate hypertension. Nutritional therapy is supported by drugs such as beta blockers.

Severe Hypertension Diastolic pressure is 120 to 130 mm hg and above. A part from giving treatment for moderate hypertension, peripheral vasodilators are given. Diet therapy revolves around potassium replacement in the use of and nutritional support for weight management and sodium modification.

Dietary Suggestions in Hypertension

For the patient of hypertension following food products should not be used :

- Salt in cooking or at the table
- Salt preserved foods like pickles and canned foods
- Highly salted foods, such as potato chips
- Spices and condiments, such as ketchup sauce
- Cheese, peanut butter and salted butter
- Frozen peas
- Shell fish and dry fish
- Regular baking powder and sodium metal bisulphite ajinomoto.
- Prepared mixes.
- For restricting sodium less than 500mg low sodium vegetables should be chosen, apart from the above restrictions.

Diet in Gastrointestinal Diseases

Digestive disorders are among the most common problems in health care. Approximately, 30% to 40% of adults claim to have frequent indigestion. Dietary habits and specific food types can play a significant role in the onset, treatment and prevention of many GI disorders.

Dietary Suggestions for Gastrointestinal Diseases

- Whether a patient is on bland diet or regular diet, he needs to know which foods are needed for a nutritionally adequate diet and the importance of including these daily.
- He should select food from a wide variety of foods, omitting those foods known to be distressing to the patient.
- Moderate use of seasonings are permitted.
- Regularity of meal times is essential. The patient gets benefitted by small and frequent meals.
- In between meals, protein rich snacks should be taken.
- Moderate amount of food should be eaten. Heavy meals should be avoided. Volume of any food, sufficient to exert antral pressure against the stomach wall stimulates gastic secretion through the gastrin mechanism.
- The diet should be planned in consultation with patient, taking into consideration his preferences, cultural pattern and economic status.
- Meals should be eaten in a relaxed atmosphere and should forget personal or family problems while eating.
- A short rest before and after meals may be conducive to greater enjoyment of meal.
- Food should be eaten slowly and chewed null. Hold one eat is more important than what one eats because fast eating provokes gastric feeding reflex.
- Dairy products like milk, cream, butter, mild cheese and (egg not fried) steamed fish, rice, rice flakes, puffed rice, well cooked cereal, semolina cooked green leafy vegetables, custards, malted drinks and cooked pulses (if they are not causing gas formation) should be included in diet.

- Alcohol, strong tea, coffee, cola, beverages, gravies, pickles, spices chillies, curries, condiments, all fried foods, pastries, cakes, heavy sweets, like halwa, barfi, raw and unripe fruits, raw vegetables like cucumber, onions, radish and tomatoes should be avoided in diet.

Diet in Diabetes Mellitus

Diabetes Mellitus is a chronic metabolic disorder that prevents the body to utilise glucose completely or partially. It is characterised by raised glucose concentration in the blood and alterations in carbohydrate, protein and fat metabolism. This can be due to failure in the formulation of insulin or liberation or action.

Dietary Suggestions for Diabetes Mellitus

- Daily energy intake must be estimated after considering such factors as age, sex, actual weight in relation to desirable weight, activity and occupation. Adequate calories for the existing weight, gradually raised for the expected weight, due to allowance of activity. 1000 calories for age 1 and + 100 kcal for each additional year of age for young diabetics should be given. Diet low in calories and high in fibre should be suggested for obese diabetes.
- An obese middle aged or elderly person can have 1000-1600 kcal and elderly and not overweight can have 1400-1800 kcal and an active young person can have 1800-3000 kcal. The total intake of calories is more important for a diabetic than the exact proportions of protein, fat and carbohydrate in the diet. A diabetic should maintain standard body weight or slightly lower.
- Dietary calories should be 60-70% from carbohydrates, 15-20% from protein and 15-25% from fat. The minimum amount of carbohydrates should be 100g to prevent ketosis.
- Simple sugar should be restricted, since they are easily absorbed and have a high glycaemic index. Avoid glycaemic peaks.
- Insulin is adjusted depending upon the need. Calorie distribution is adjusted according to the type of insulin.
- Fat with high poly unsaturated fatty acids like vegetable oil is preferred (Sunflower oil, corn oil and gingelly oil) than animal fat and hydrogenated fat, which contain more saturated fatty acids. Fish and chicken are preferred than meat and egg. Turmeric, bengalgram, onion and garlic have cholesterol lowering effect. Avoid atherogenic diet.
- High protein intake helps to increase insulin production and promotes satiety.
- Vitamins and minerals are supplemented to meet daily requirement (especially fat soluble vitamins).
- Whole wheat is preferred to rice because it contains 'ascarbose', which allows carbohydrate to be absorbed slowly.
- Timely intake of between meal snacks should be stressed to avoid hypoglycaemia. Three main meals and three between meal snacks can be taken.
- Food exchange lists should be followed to prevent hypo and hyperglycaemia. The exchange systems should be followed to avoid monotony, dietary constancy and flexibility.
- Complex carbohydrates and fibre should be included in the diet. 25-40 g of dietary fibre can be included for each 1000 kcal consumed.
- Influence of chew count, glycaemic indices, type and form of food in altering the blood sugar level should be recognised.
- The water soluble fibre has greatest hypoglycaemic and hypocholesterolemic effect. The diet should include legumes, whole grain and fenugreek seeds.
- Patients should avoid fasting and feasting.
- Regulating of meals is needed for persons taking insulin. Meals should be spaced to consider with the availability of insulin.
- If insulin or an oral hypoglycaemic agent is not required, marked obesity is not present or hyperglycaemic is relatively mild, it may not be necessary for the patient to follow such accurate diets.
- Sodium intake is to be no more than 6g daily. Sodium is restricted to 3g in hypertensive patients.
- Instead of simple sugar, artificial sweeteners may be suggested.

Suggested Diet Chart for Diabetic Patient

Foods to be Avoided	Foods to be Eatern in Moderation	Foods Permitted
Simple sugars like glucose, honey, syrup, sweets, dried fruits, cake, candy, fried foods, alcohol, nuts, jaggery, and sweetened juices.	Fats, cereals, pulses, meat, egg, nuts roots, fruits and artificial sweetener.	Green leafy vegetables, fruits except banana, lemon, clear soups, onion, mint, spices, salads, plain coffee or tea, skimmed and butter milk and spices.

Diet in Cancer

Cancer, known medically as a malignant neoplaism, is a broad group of diseases involving unregulated cell growth. In cancer, cells divide and grow uncontrollably, forming malignant tumors and invade nearby parts of the body. Cancer is a term, used to sugar malignant neoplasms or turnovers. Neoplasia means cells in a tissue proliferate without the normal control on growth.

In the malignant neoplarm, the cells spread to adjacent tissues and interferes with the function and often has undesirable systematic effects. Benign turnover represents the accumulation of cells which have been transferred to reproduce in abnormal numbers, but under circumstance where they remain within the tissue of origins.

Classification of cancer is as follows :

- Tissue or cell of origin
- Carcinoma endoderm or ectoderm
- Sarcoma mesoderm.
- Leukaemia white blood cells
- Lymphoma monocytte, macrophage

Seven danger signals of cancer are :

- A sore that does not heal.
- Change in the colour of a wart or mole.
- Chronic indigestion or difficulty in swallowing or early satiety.
- A lump or thickening in the breast or any part of the body.
- Abnormal bleeding or discharge from any body opening.
- Change in normal bowel habits.
- Persistent hoarseness of voice.

Some Side Effects of Cancer Therapy and Suggested Dietary Management

Nausea and Vomiting Clear, cold and carbonated beverages with added polycose; slipping beverages slowly through a straw, small, frequent meals low in fat dry crackers or toast before arising tart or salt foods liquids 30 to 60 minutes before eating.

Dry Mouth Drinking at least 2 quarts of liquid daily. High calorie beverage are preferable to mater. Sauces and gravies broth to moisten foods and to make them easier to swallow. Chewing sugar free gum or sugar free candy to stimulate salivation (Artificial saliva).

Taste Alterations Experimenting with different flavours and seasonings substitution of other protein for red meats.

Loss of Appetite Small, frequent feeding, high calorie, high protein snacks and beverages.

Sore Mouth and Throat Soft, non-acid foods blended or liquified foods and beverage at room temperature using straw with liquids.

Swallowing Problem Avoiding highly seasoned foods. Liquid feedings or pureed foods, frequent feedings. Tube feeding adding butter and sauces to foods. Finally chopped foods.

Nutritional Assessment in the Clinical Setting

Nutritional assessment is used to decide the nutritional status of the patient. Nutritional assessment includes anthropometric, clinical, dietary and laboratory measurements.

Anthropometric The measurement includes height, weight, BMI, triceps skinfold and sometime other skinfold.

Body Mass Index It is a value derived from mass and height of a person. It is a measure of body fat based on height and weight that applied to men and women. BMI have been developed for use in judging the health status of the person.

$$BMI = \frac{\text{wt. in kg.}}{\text{Ht. in metre}^2}$$

Adults	BMI
Normal	19 - 24
Obesity grade I	25 - 29
Obesity grade II	30 - 40
Obesity grade III	> 40

Skinfold measurement helps to assess the energy reserves in the form of fat. An average of three of their values are used to compare with a set of normal values.

Midarm Circumference gives an indication of body protein reserves and helps to detect protein malnutrition.

Dietary Assessment is an essential basis for dietary counselling. There are several methods used, which include 24 hours recall, food frequency list, a food diary, diet history and observation at meal times.

These helps in evaluation of the food intake to detect possible deficiency.

Laboratory Assessment involves whole blood, blood serum and blood plasma analysis; sometimes urine analysis is done to determine the level or the excretion rate of the nutrient or their metabolites.

Clinical Assessment includes examination of eyes, teeth, gums, tongue, skin and hair to observe symptoms of nutritional deficiency. It is quick but subjective and not specific.

EXAM BASED QUESTIONS

1 Clinical nutrition focuses on individual/group with established
(a) disease (b) poverty
(c) disaster survivor (d) All of these

2 How much calories should healthy adult take in full diet?
(a) 2000 (b) 2450
(c) 2500 (d) 2400

3 Half diet is recommended for
(a) children (b) women
(c) men (d) old people

4 The nutritive value of soft diet is
(a) high (b) low
(c) equal (d) None of these

5 Whom do we serve low protein diet?
(a) People having chronic renal failure
(b) Encephalopathy patient
(c) Both (a) and (b)
(d) None of the above

6 How much is the protein consumption in case of soft diet?
(a) 64 mg (b) 66 mg
(c) 65 mg (d) 63 mg

7 Clear fluid diet is given to patient suffering from
(a) nausea (b) vomiting
(c) diarrhoea (d) all of these

8 For which disease blended diet is given?
(a) Cardiovascular (b) urinary tract
(c) GIT (d) muscular

9 What should be avoided in low fat diet?
(a) High fat food like nuts and seed
(b) Fried food
(c) Fat free and cream
(d) All of the above

10 Which diet is given to patient with coronary heart disease?
(a) Low cholestrol diet (b) Low sodium diet
(c) Low protein diet (d) Blend diet

11 What is avoided while formulating low cholestrol diet?
(a) Coconut (b) Whole milk
(c) Cheese (d) All of these

12 Low sodium diet means
(a) salt free diet (b) moderate salt restriction
(c) Both (a) and (b) (d) None of these

13 High calories diet have concentrated amount of ....
(a) carbohydrate (b) protein
(c) salt (d) vitamin

14 Who helps in monitoring the dietary intake of individual?
(a) Dietician (b) Doctors
(c) Nurses (d) Vet

15 What procedure do diet counsellor follow to help individual to make dietary changes?
(a) Provides information (b) Educational support
(c) Follow-up (d) All of these

16 Which is a method of assessing dietary intake by listing all food consumed in previous 24-hours period?
(a) Pre-eating habit (b) 24 hours recall
(c) 24 hours diary (d) None of these

17 .... gives better result of person's dietary intake than 24-hours recall.
(a) Food frequency questionnaire
(b) Food record
(c) Food diary
(d) All of the above

18 What is/are the factor(s) affecting food intake?
(a) Ethnic background (b) Religion
(c) Socio-economic status (d) All of the above

19 Which is the common barrier to dietary changes?
(a) Food preferences (b) Social gathering
(c) Both(a)and(b) (d) Nono of thoso

20 How do dietician give consultation?
(a) In group (b) One-on-one
(c) Both (a) and (b) (d) None of these

21 What is/are the function(s) of administrative dietician?
(a) To plan, develop, control and evaluate food service system
(b) To develop short and long range department plan
(c) Manage and control resource and recommend budget programme
(d) All of the above

22 What is/are the reason(s) for non-compliance to dietary advice?
(a) Resistance to changing a diet
(b) Lack of relevant education
(c) Both (a) and (b)
(d) None of the above

23 What helps the food to be presented well?
(a) Variation in colour, texture and flavour
(b) Appropriate tray size
(c) Food served on time
(d) All of the above

24 What is the diameter of tube used in nasogastric tube feeding?
(a) 5 - 6 mm (b) 3 - 4 mm (c) 10 - 12 mm (d) 5 - 10 mm

25 **The tube is lubricated using what?**
(a) Olive oil (b) Kerosene
(c) Local anaesthesia (d) None of these

26 **What kind of feeding is done when digestive system is affected?**
(a) Narogastric feeding (b) Rectal feeding
(c) Gastronomy feeding (d) Jejunostomy feeding

27 **Which of the following is made to feel in rectal feeding?**
(a) Ca (b) K
(c) Both (a) and (b) (d) None of these

28 **Where is the nutrient injected in case of intravenous feeding?**
(a) Veins (b) Artery (c) Nerves (d) Muscles

29 **How much protein is required after surgery?**
(a) 100-120 gm (b) 200-220 gm
(c) 250-260 gm (d) 150-160 gm

30 **What does CHO consist of in case of surgery patient?**
(a) Starch (b) Glucose
(c) Both (a) and (b) (d) None of these

31 **Which mineral should be provided to the patient after surgery?**
(a) Iron (b) Ascorbic acid
(c) Vitamine B_{12} (d) All of these

32 **What kind of diet is given just after the extraction of teeth?**
(a) Tube feeding (b) Fluid diet
(c) Soft diet (d) None of these

33 **What is/are the cause(s) of fever?**
(a) Antigen antibody reaction
(b) Graft rejection
(c) Bacteria/fungi
(d) All of the above

34 **Which form of carbohydrate should be taken during fever?**
(a) Fructose (b) Glucose (c) Sucrose (d) Surolose

35 **What should be the interval between food consumption during fever?**
(a) 2-3 hours (b) 5-6 hours (c) 4-5 hours (d) 1-2 hours

36 **Salmonella typhi causes which disease?**
(a) Cholera (b) Tuberculosis
(c) Jaundice (d) Typhoid

37 **Which food should be avoided during typhoid?**
(a) Butter and ghee (b) Spices
(c) Fried food (d) All of these

38 **Which part of body is affected by tuberculosis?**
(a) Lungs (b) Muscles
(c) Bones (d) None of these

39 **There is accumulation excess adipose tissue in case of**
(a) obesity (b) malnutrition
(c) tuberculosis (d) All of these

40 **How one can get rid of obesity?**
(a) Lower the intake of calories
(b) Exercising
(c) Both (a) and (b)
(d) None of the above

41 **How much additional calories are recommended for an under weight person?**
(a) 150 kcal (b) 500 kcal (c) 200 kcal (d) 1000 kcal

42 **What can help to bring down the cholestrol level?**
(a) Sunflower oil (b) Sweets
(c) Almonds (d) Eggs

43 **What is the value for diastole and systole value for hypertension, according to WHO?**
(a) > 95 mm hg, > 160 mm hg
(b) > 100 mm hg, > 150 mm hg
(c) > 105 mm hg, > 180 mm hg
(d) > 90 mm hg, > 140 mm hg

44 **Which food should be included in G1 disease?**
(a) Butter (b) Steamed fish
(c) Rice (d) All of these

45 **Which factor affects the calorie intake in case of diabetic patient?**
(a) Age (b) Sex
(c) Weight (d) All of these

46 **What kind of food can be given to cancer patient with altered taste?**
(a) Experimenting with different flavours
(b) Change in consistency of diet
(c) Serve carbonated drink
(d) None of the above

47 **Anthropometric measurement includes**
(a) BMI (b) skinfold
(c) Both (a) and (b) (d) None of these

48 **What is the formula to calculate BMI?**
(a) $\frac{(\text{Wt. in kg})^2}{\text{Ht. in metre}}$ (b) $\frac{\text{Wt. in kg}}{(\text{Ht. in metre})^2}$
(c) $\frac{(\text{Ht. in metre})^2}{\text{Wt. in kg}}$ (d) $\frac{\text{Ht. in metre}}{(\text{Wt. in kg})^2}$

49 **What does midarm circumference measures?**
(a) Body fat (b) Energy reserve
(c) Protein reserve (d) Muscle strength

50 **Which method is used for dietary assessment?**
(a) 24-hours recall (b) Food frequency list
(c) Food diary (d) All of these

51 **Laboratory assessment includes**
(a) blood test (b) urine test
(c) Both (a) and (b) (d) None of these

52 **Arrange in the correct sequence, the symptoms of diabetes as they appear with advancement of disease.**
1. Dehydration 2. Glycosuria
3. Polyurea 4. Ketosis
5. Hyperglycemia 6. Diabetic coma

Codes

(a) 5, 3, 2, 4, 1 and 6 (b) 5, 2, 3, 1, 4 and 6
(c) 2, 1, 3, 5, 6 and 4 (d) 3, 2, 1, 4, 5 and 6

53 Match the following.

List I	List II
A. Clear liquid diet	1. Clear fluid diet
B. Tea, lemon, cereal extracts, strained fruit juices, carbonated beverages, dal extract and fat free	2. In heart disease
C. Avoid foods, which produce gas like cabbage beans and peas.	3. Common heart diseases
D. Heart disease occurs	4. Replaces the fluids lost by the body preventing dehydration
E. Arrhythmia, ischemic and chronic valvular are	5. Heredity, diabetes, fat abnormalities, cigrette smoking, lack of exercise, and emotionally stressful life.

Codes

	A	B	C	D	E		A	B	C	D	E
(a)	4	1	2	5	3	(b)	3	2	1	4	5
(c)	5	4	3	1	2	(d)	2	3	4	5	1

54 Match the following.

List I	List II
A. Clear Liquid diet	1. Rest, drugs and fuid diet
B. Acute cholecystitis	2. Triples this birth weight end of 10-12 months
C. Infant	3. Septic throat
D. Staphylococci causes	4. Replaces the fluids lost by the body preventing dehydration

Codes

	A	B	C	D		A	B	C	D
(a)	4	3	2	1	(b)	2	4	1	3
(c)	4	1	2	3	(d)	1	3	4	2

55 Match the following.

List I	List II
A. Nephrosis	1. Pancreas
B. Diabetes	2. Kidney
C. Arteriosclerosis	3. Intestine
D. Coeliac disease	4. Blood vessels
	5. Heart

Codes

	A	B	C	D		A	B	C	D
(a)	3	5	2	4	(b)	1	2	3	4
(c)	2	1	5	3	(d)	2	1	4	3

56 For a healthy heart, the following group of food should be

List I	List II
A. Fried vegetable chips, banana chips and potato cutlets.	1. Preferred
B. White bread, maida, biscuit, coffee, cola soft drinks	2. Taken in moderate quantity
C. Wheat, rice, sprouted dal, butter milk and fresh fruits	3. Avoided

Codes

	A	B	C		A	B	C
(a)	1	2	3	(b)	3	2	1
(c)	2	3	1	(d)	1	3	2

57 Match the following.

List I	List II
A. Mechanical soft	1. Soft diet
B. Soft diet	2. For fevers, post operation and intolerance to solid foods
C. Food easy to chew and easy to digest	3. For those without teeth
D. Liquid diet	4. Food liquid at 37°C
E. Full fluid diet	5. Patients of acute infections, gastrointestinal disturbances and recovery from surgery

Codes

	A	B	C	D	E		A	B	C	D	E
(a)	3	5	1	2	4	(b)	5	2	3	4	1
(c)	5	4	3	2	1	(d)	1	2	5	3	4

58 Match the following.

List I	List II
A. Full diet	1. Calories-1500
B. Half diet	2. Cereal-400 gm
C. Soft diet	3. Protein-55 gm
D. Blend diet	4. Calories-2000

Codes

	A	B	C	D		A	B	C	D
(a)	1	2	3	4	(b)	2	3	4	1
(c)	3	4	2	1	(d)	2	1	3	4

59 Match the following.

List I	List II
A. Myocardium	1. Fat deposition in the lumen of an artery
B. Atherosclerosis	2. Myocardium infraction
C. Hypertension	3. Significant narrowing of lumen of coronary artery
D. Angina pectoris	4. Heart muscle
	5. Diastolic/Systolic

Codes

	A	B	C	D		A	B	C	D
(a)	4	1	5	3	(b)	1	2	3	4
(c)	5	4	2	3	(d)	4	2	3	5

60 Given the correct sequence of Iron Deficiency Anaemia (IDA).

1. Fall in serum ferritin level.
2. Decrease in sustainable iron in bone marrow.
3. Fall in hemoglobin level.
4. Exhaustion of body iron reserves.

Codes

(a) 1, 2, 3 and 4 (b) 4, 2, 1 and 3
(c) 2, 3, 4 and 1 (d) 3, 4, 2 and 1

Directions (Q. Nos. 61-75) *Below given are two statements, one labelled as Assertion (A) and other labelled as Reason (R). Following are the codes given below. Select the correct code for the following.*

Codes
(a) A is false, but R is true
(b) Both A and R are true
(c) Both A and R are false
(d) A is true, but R is false

61 **Assertion** (A) Bulimia nervosa is defined by little eating or reduced intake of food over a long period of time.

Reason (R) Little eating is used to describe the consumption of food that is much smaller than most people would eat during a similar period of time.

62 **Assertion** (A) Consumption of plenty of fruits and vegetables protects individuals from certain cancers.

Reason (R) The antioxidants present in fruits and vegetables help in removal of free radicals.

63 **Assertion** (A) High salt and low potassium intakes are risk factors for developing hypertension.

Reason (R) Consuming plenty of fruits and vegetables are recommended for hypertension.

64 **Assertion** (A) Hypertension is a risk factor for Coronary Heart Disease (CHD).

Reason (R) High blood pressure leads to raised cholesterol level.

65 **Assertion** (A) Acute Renal failure means the kidneys have failed suddenly.

Reason (R) Various toxins or severe blood loss or trauma affect kidney functioning.

66 **Assertion** (A) Obesity and heart disease result in excessive energy intake and reduced physical activity.

Reason (R) Sedentary life style and availability of high energy density foods lead to degenerative disease.

67 **Assertion** (A) Fish plays a protective role in heart disease.

Reason (R) It is attributed to the presence of long chained omega 6 poly saturated fatty acid.

68 **Assertion** (A) Iron absorption is enhanced by the co-ingestion of Vitamin C.

Reason (R) Ascorbic acid reduces ferric to ferrous ion and it also binds the ferrous form.

69 **Assertion** (A) The diabetic patient presents with symptoms of polyurea, polydypsia and nocturia.

Reason (R) Deficiency of insulin in the diabetic patient's body leads to hyperglycemia, which leads to glycosuria.

70 **Assertion** (A) Full diet is a normal diet, which provide all the nutrients in slightly higher amount then recommended for a healthy dietary.

Reason (R) It can be used for an adult patient admitted to a hospital.

71 **Assertion** (A) Gastrostomy feeding is used, when digestive system is affected due to injury, surgery and cancer.

Reason (R) In this method also, by surgery an opening is created in the jejunum through which a tube is introduced and it is through this tube, patient is fed.

72 **Assertion** (A) Fat is not digested in the stomach.

Reason (R) The presence of fat in the diet delays the emptying of the food from the stomach.

73 **Assertion** (A) Certain foods like pulses show marked result of heat treatment.

Reason (R) They contain substances, which hinder digestion of protein by the enzyme trypsin.

74 **Assertion** (A) Fats and carbohydrates are the main sources of body energy.

Reason (R) They produce the energy to warm the body and to enable it to do muscular work.

75 **Assertion** (A) Diet therapy is use of appropriate foods as a tool in the recovery from illness.

Reason (R) In most illnesses, the patient's diet complements the medical or surgical or surgical treatment.

76 Consider the following statements.

1. Soft diet in consistency, easy to chew, low in cellulose and unflavoured basically for gastro intestinal tract disorder, infection and for people without teeth is soft diet.
2. Steroids are produced in greater amount in pregnancy, so that water and sodium are retained in the body.

Which of the statements given above is/are correct?

(a) Only 1 (b) Only 2
(c) Both 1 and 2 (d) Neither 1 nor 2

Directions (Q.Nos. 77-91) *Consider the following statements and state which of the following in each are true?*

Codes
(a) Only I (b) Only II
(c) Both I and II (d) Neither I nor II

77 **Statement I** Lower blood pressure comparatively.

Statement II Decreased insulin secretion.

78 **Statement I** Glucose is the sole form of energy for brain and nervous tissues.

Statement II Caramel is known as animal starch.

79 **Statement I** Low cholesterol diet is used for the treatment of patients with high cholesterol level and patient with coronary heart diseases.

Statement II Low sodium diet provides low calories and the total energy requirement of the day.

80 **Statement I** Soft diet is a diet, which is non-irritating, chemically blend and inhibit gastic secretion.

Statement II Blend diet is soft in texture and consist of liquid and semi-solid foods.

81 **Statement I** Fatty acids which are unsaturated and those saturated acids, which have less than 12 carbon atoms are liquids at room temperature.

Statement II Saturated fatty acids containing 14 or more than fourteen carbon atoms are semi liquids at room temperature.

82 **Statement I** Typhoid increased intake regarding typnoid of water and fluid to replace loss due to dehydration.

Statement II Increase intake of vitamins and minerals.

83 **Statement I** Liver glycogen is available as a source of energy.

Statement II About 500 gm of glycogen is found in the body as reserve.

84 **Statement I** Protein content of a diet can be increased addition of skimmed milk, soup of mashed dal in soup and beverges and strained grained meat or fish broths.

Statement II To enhance the energy content of the diet, add cream to milk butter oil to cereal gruels and dal soups to juice milk, etc.

85 **Statement I** Overweight is associated with ailment of diabetes, kidneys, heart and circulatory system.

Statement II Insufficient food intake could be due to messed meals poor health practice and poor schedule.

86 **Statement I** To given relief to a particular organ for instance fat content is reduce in diseases of gall bladder is objective of therapeutic diet.

Statement II The principles of therapeutic diet is the diet should be well balanced with respect to micro and macro nutrient.

87 **Statement I** Extensive observations have shown that consumption of diets, in which fats supply is more than 30% of the calories may result in increase of blood cholesterol.

Statement II The percentage contribution of calories in the diet by fat should be 15-20%.

88 Which of the following statements is/are correct?

(a) When we feel cold, the heat production increases due to shivering or muscular exercise.
(b) The adipose tissue prevents the loss of heat, thus produced.
(c) Thicker the adipose layers, more effective is the body blanket.
(d) All of the above

89 Which of the following statement(s) is/are correct?

(a) Blood pressure is associated with palpitation, headache and giddyness
(b) Obesity, stress and food habits are liked with blood pressure
(c) The increase in nutritional intake depends on the rate of growth during infancy, childhood and adolescence
(d) All of the above

90 State which is/are true.

(a) Soft diet is soft in texture and consists of liquid and semi-solid foods.
(b) Blend diet is given to the patients, when they are actually ill and have marked influence to food
(c) Fluid diet is a diet with non-irritating chemically blend and inhibit gastric secretion
(d) Half diet provides low calories and the total energy requirement of the day

Directions (Q. Nos. 91-95) *Read the passage and answer the following questions.*

Diet therapy is a branch of dietetics concerned with the use of food for therapeutic purpose. Diet therapy is a broad term used for the practical application of nutrition as a preventive or corrective treatment of a disease. It concerns with recovery from illness by giving good diet and prevention of disease. It may involve the modification of the existing dietary life style to promote optimum health. For example, a dietitian or a nutrition counsellor may prescribe a diet therapy to an obese person to improve health. The therapy may involve including foods (such as fats, sugars etc.) that may make the condition worse. Basically the therapy promotes a balanced selection of foods vital for good health. The principles of diet therapy are to

- maintain good nutritional status
- correct deficiencies or disease, if any
- provide rest to the body
- help metabolise the nutrients and
- make changes in body weight, when necessary.

Diet therapy may include prescribing specialised dietary regimes or meal plans. The specialised diet regimens or meal plans are called therapeutic diets. Therapeutic diet refers to a meal plan that controls the intake of certain foods or nutrients. They are adaptation of the normal, regular diet.

91 Diet therapy is concerned with

(a) use of food for pleasure
(b) use of food for complete relaxation
(c) use of food for recovery from illness and prevention of illness
(d) All of the above

92 The phrase 'optimum health' means

(a) more focus on mental health.
(b) more focus on emotional health.
(c) ability to adapt to and manage life experiences and challenges.
(d) None of the above

93 Some principles of diet therapy are
(a) correct deficiencies or diseases, if any
(b) help in reducing weight
(c) maintain good nutritional status
(d) Both (a) and (c)

94 The therapeutic diet refers to
(a) a diet which controls intake of certain foods or nutrients.
(b) liquid diet
(c) protein diet
(c) only soft diet

95 What will be a suitable title of the given passage?
(a) Optimum health, need of the day
(b) Diet therapy, its uses
(c) Nutrition and meal plan
(d) Prevention of diseases

PREVIOUS YEARS' QUESTIONS

July 2018

1 Following are anthropometric methods for assessment of nutrition status.
1. Haemoglobin estimation 2. MUAC
3. Waist-hip ratio
4. Urinary iodine measurement
5. Body Mass Index

Codes
(a) 1, 2 and 5 (b) 2, 3 and 4
(c) 1, 4 and 5 (d) 2, 3 and 5

2 Following are the symptoms of diabetes mellitus.
1. Polyuria 2. Polydypsia
3. Hypoglycemia 4. Hyperglycemia
5. Hypophagia

Codes
(a) 1, 2 and 3 (b) 1, 2 and 5
(c) 1, 2 and 4 (d) 2, 3 and 4

November 2017

3 Which of the following food is not allowed in a clear fluid diet?
(a) Black tea
(b) Milk
(c) Coconut water
(d) Carbonated beverage

4 Match the follwing.

List I (Diseases)	List II (Symptoms)
A. Diabetes	1. Peyer's patches
B. Chronic renal failure	2. Large, pale and foul smelling stools
C. Infective hepatitis	3. Portal hypertension
D. Typhoid	4. Anorexia and dark coloured urine
E. Coeliac disease	5. Uremia and azotemia
	6. Polyuria and polydipsia

Codes

	A	B	C	D	E
(a)	6	5	4	1	2
(b)	1	5	4	6	3
(c)	6	1	5	2	3
(d)	4	3	5	1	2

5 Which of the following are retrospective methods of diet assessment?
1. 24 hours dietary recall
2. Duplicate sample method
3. Food frequency questionnaire
4. Weighment method
5. Food balance sheets

Codes
(a) 1, 2 and 3 (b) 1, 3 and 5
(c) 2, 3 and 4 (d) 1, 3 and 4

January 2017

6 **Assertion** (A) Diet induced thermogenesis is lower in diets that contain very high amount of fats.

Reason (R) The process of digestion, absorption and metabolism of fats utilises more energy compared to carbohydrates.

Codes
(a) Both A and R are true (b) A is false and R is true
(c) A is true and R is false (d) Both A and R are false

7 Which of the following is not a method of dietary survey?
(a) Food frequency questionnaire
(b) 24 hours recall
(c) BMI
(d) Food weighment

8 Arrange the following steps involved in conducting 24 hours dietary recall in correct sequence.
1. Convert the amount of food and beverages, consumed into amount of raw foods.
2. Standardise the recipes.
3. Preparation and pre-testing of questionnaire.
4. Compare energy and nutrient intake with RDA.
5. Collect information on all foods and beverages eaten by respondent in previous 24 hours, using standardised equipment.
6. Calculate energy and nutrients using food composition tables.

Codes
(a) 2, 5, 3, 1, 6, 4 (b) 5, 2, 3, 1, 6, 4
(c) 3, 5, 2, 1, 6, 4 (d) 3, 5, 1, 2, 6, 4

9 **Assertion** (A) Complex carbohydrates are recommended in diabetic diets.

Reason (R) The complex carbohydrates have a low Glycemic Index.

Codes

(a) Both A and R are true (b) A is true R is false
(c) A is false and R is true (d) Both A and R are false

July 2016

10 Following measurements are made in anthropometry assessment of individuals.

1. Weight 2. Blood pressure
3. Height 4. Hemoglobin
5. MUAC 6. Waist circumference

Codes

(a) 1, 3, 5 and 6 (b) 1, 2, 3 and 6
(c) 1, 3, 4 and 6 (d) 1, 4, 5 and 6

December 2015

11 Arrange the following in correct sequence, the steps in conducting a 24 hours dietary recall.

1. Comparing the intakes of energy and nutrients with RDA.
2. Listing all the foods and beverages consumed in previous 24 hours.
3. Calculating the energy and nutrient content of raw foods.
4. Converting cooked food into amount of raw ingredients.

Codes

(a) 1, 4, 2 and 3 (b) 2, 4, 3 and 1
(c) 3, 2, 4 and 1 (d) 2, 1, 4 and 3

12 Arrange the following in correct sequence, the metabolic changes occurring in uncontrolled diabetes mellitus patient.

1. Glycosuria 2. Dehydration
3. Hyperglycemia 4. Anuria
5. Peripheral circulatory failure

Codes

(a) 3, 1, 5, 2 and 4 (b) 1, 3, 2, 5 and 4
(c) 3, 1, 2, 5 and 4 (d) 3, 1, 2, 4 and 5

13 Match the following.

List I (Diabetes Conditions)	List II (Diagnostic Criterias)
A. Diabetes mellitus	1. SBP > 140 mm Hg
B. Hypertension	2. DBP < 80 m Hg
C. Atherosclerosis	3. HbAlc > 7%
D. Anaemia	4. Total cholesterol > 200 mg/dl
	5. Hb > 120 mg/dl
	6. HDL cholestrol > 60 mg/dl

Codes

	A	B	C	D		A	B	C	D
(a)	5	2	4	3	(b)	3	1	4	5
(c)	2	1	6	3	(d)	3	2	6	5

June 2015

14 The following are the methods of nutritional assessment using anthropometry.

1. Skinfold thickness
2. 24 hours dietary recall
3. Mid upperarm circumference
4. Blood pressure
5. Waist-hip ratio

Codes

(a) 1, 2 and 3 (b) 1, 3 and 4 (c) 2, 3 and 5 (d) 1, 3 and 5

15 **Assertion** (A) Persons with BMI between 18-25 kg/m^2 are classified as obese.

Reason (R) Reduced physical activity and high intake of junk foods lead to obesity.

Codes

(a) Both A and R are true (b) Both A and R are false
(c) A is false and R is true (d) A is true, but R is false

Deccember 2014

16 Following are the methods of conduction dietary survey.

1. HPLC 2. 24 hours recall
3. FFQ 4. Diet history

Codes

(a) 2, 3 and 4 (b) 1, 2 and 4
(c) 1, 3 and 4 (d) 1, 2 and 3

ANSWERS

Exam Based Questions

1 (a)	2 (b)	3 (a)	4 (b)	5 (c)	6 (a)	7 (d)	8 (c)	9 (d)	10 (a)
11 (d)	12 (c)	13 (a)	14 (a)	15 (d)	16 (b)	17 (a)	18 (d)	19 (c)	20 (c)
21 (d)	22 (c)	23 (d)	24 (b)	25 (a)	26 (c)	27 (c)	28 (a)	29 (a)	30 (c)
31 (d)	32 (b)	33 (d)	34 (b)	35 (a)	36 (d)	37 (d)	38 (a)	39 (a)	40 (c)
41 (b)	42 (c)	43 (a)	44 (d)	45 (d)	46 (a)	47 (c)	48 (b)	49 (c)	50 (d)
51 (c)	52 (b)	53 (a)	54 (c)	55 (d)	56 (b)	57 (a)	58 (b)	59 (a)	60 (d)
61 (b)	62 (b)	63 (b)	64 (d)	65 (b)	66 (c)	67 (d)	68 (b)	69 (a)	70 (b)
71 (a)	72 (d)	73 (d)	74 (d)	75 (b)	76 (c)	77 (c)	78 (c)	79 (a)	80 (d)
81 (a)	82 (c)	83 (a)	84 (d)	85 (c)	86 (a)	87 (d)	88 (a)	89 (c)	90 (c)
91 (d)	92 (c)	93 (d)	94 (a)	95 (b)					

Previous Years' Questions

1 (d)	2 (c)	3 (b)	4 (a)	5 (b)	6 (b)	7 (c)	8 (c)	9 (a)	10 (a)
11 (b)	12 (c)	13 (b)	14 (d)	15 (c)	16 (a)				

Nutritional Assessment and Intervention

Nutrition is one of the basic components of life. A nutrition assessment is an indept evaluation of both objective and subjective data related to an individual's food and nutrient intake, lifestyle and medical history. The nutrition intervention is purposefully planned action intended to positively change a nutrition related behaviour, environmental condition or aspect of health status for an individual, target group or the community at large.

Nutritional Assessment

Nutritional assessment is the systematic process of collecting and interpreting information. This is a process to make decision about the nature and cause of nutrition related health issue that affects an individual.

Structured assessment path enables health professional to carry out a quality nutritional assessment in order to identify those who need nutritional intervention and to improve clinical decision making, using a person centred approach. The process promotes consistent quality of practice, is user friendly and allow effective monitoring of patient.

Methods of Nutritional Assessment

Nutrition is assessed by two methods–direct and indirect. The direct method deals with the individual and measure objective criteria. In direct assessment, we measure certain indicators on representative sample of community to determine the nutritional status of the community. In other words, we can directly take measurements like body weight or clinically examine or estimate haemoglobin level of certain group of individuals. The indirect method uses the community indices that reflect the community's nutritional status/needs.

In this Chapter

These include three categories such as :

- Ecological variables including crop production.
- Economic factors i.e. per capcta income, population density and social habits.
- Vital health statistics of particularly infants and under 5 years mortality and fertility indicies.

Techniques of Nutritional Assessment

There are four techniques of nutritional assessment as described below :

Anthropometry

It is the measurement of body height, weight and proportions. It is an essential component of clinical examination of infants, children and pregnant women. These measurement are compared to the reference data of the same age and sex group, in order to evaluate the nutritional states. The measurement indicate the nutritional status in general still, they are not used to identify specific nutritional deficiencies. They are used to evaluate both under and over nutrition. The measured values reflect the current nutritional status and don't differentiate between acute and chronic changes.

Anthropometric measurement include :

- Body Mass Index (BMI)
- Mid-arm circumference
- Skinfold thickness
- Head circumference
- Head/chest ratio
- Hip/waist ratio

Biochemical Method

The blood tests conducted within a nutrition assessment are interpreted in conjunction with a clinical examination, previous medical history and current medication. Biochemical tests measure level of chemical substance present in the blood. Functional tests measures the function of vital organs such as kidney or liver. The tests are useful in detecting early changes in body metabolism and nutrition before the appearance of overt clinical signs. It is precise, accurate and reproducible.

Clinical Assessment

It is an essential feature of all nutritional surveys. It is the simplest and most practical method of ascertaining the nutritional status of a group of individuals. It utilises a number of physical signs (specific and non-specific), that are known to be associated with malnutrition and deficiency of vitamins and micronutrient.

Symptoms that occur due to low nutritional status include :

- altered bowel movement
- upper gastrointestinal upset
- early satiety
- dysphagia
- lethargy

Example of diseases which can be detected by clinical assessment :

- Xeropthalmia (Vitamin A deficiency)
- Beri Beri (Vitamin B deficiency)
- Scurvy (Vitamin C deficiency)
- Ricket (Vitamin D deficiency)
- PEM (Protein energy malnutrition)
- Anaemia (Iron deficiency)
- Osteoporosis (Calcium deficiency)
- Goitre (Iodine deficiency)

Dietary Assessment

An estimation of the total daily calorie intake, as well as overall quality of diet should be assessed. Asking the patient about their daily dietary intake, will help understand pattern of eating, portion sizes, cooking methods and type of food and drink taken.

Dietary intake in humans is assessed by five different methods. These are :

(i) 24 hour dietary recall
(ii) Food frequency questionnaire
(iii) Dietary history since early life
(iv) Food dairy technique
(v) Observed food consumption

Nutritional Interventions

Diet is one of the most important and modifiable life style determinant of human health. Undernutrition and overnutrition play a role in morbidity and mortality.

Therefore, nutritional intervention are needed to reduce morbidity and mortality through dietary changes. They can be implemented at an individual, local or national level through policy by different organisations.

National Nutrition, Policies and Programmes

Some of the national nutrition policies and programmes are given below :

National Nutrition Week (2019)

It was celebrated from September 1-7, 2019 to aware the people about important tips of their health and well-being. The objective of the National Nutrition Week is to enhance the nutritional practice awareness among people of the community, through seminars, discussions, timely education, road shows and many other campaigns.

National Nutrition Mission (NNM)

It was commenced from 2017-18 by the Government of India. The NNM as an apex body, under the Ministry of Women and Child Development supervise, monitor, fix targets and guide nutrition related interventions all over the ministries. It is setup with a vision to ensure attainment of Malnutrition free India by 2022.

Poshan Abhiyan

It is a flagship programme of the Ministry of Women and Child Development. The programme aimed at improving the nutritional status of children from 0-6 years, adolescent girls, pregnant women and lactating mothers during the three years beginning from 2017-18.

Mothers' Absolute Affection (MAA)

It is a nationwide programme for promoting breastfeeding. The programme launched in 2016, seeks to create an enabling environment to ensure that mothers' husbands and families receive adequate information and support for promoting breastfeeding. It has been named MAA to signify the support a lactating mother requires from family members and at health facilities to breastfeed successfully. The chief components of the programme are community awareness generation, strengthening inter-personal communication through ASHA, skilled support for breastfeeding at delivery points in public health facilities and monitoring and award/recognition. It is an intensified programme to enhance optimal breastfeeding practices in the country.

Mission Indradhanush

It was launched by the Ministry of Health and Family Welfare in 2014. The scheme seeks to drive towards full immunisation coverage of India by 2020. Mission Indradhanush depicts seven colours of the rainbow which aims to cover all those children who are either unvaccinated or are partially vaccinated against seven vaccine preventable diseases.

The diseases are diptheria, whooping cough, tetanus, polio, tuberculosis, measles and Hepatitis B. WHO, UNICEF, Rotarty International are the donor partners for Mission Indradhanush. It is a systematic immunisation drive throuh a catch up campaign mode aiming to cover all the children who have left out or missed out for immunisation. To further intensify the immunisation programme, Prime Minister Shri Narendra Modi launched the intensifed Mission Indradhanush on October 8, 2017. Through this programme, the government aims to reach each and every child upto two years and pregnant woman who have been left uncovered under the routine immunisation programme.

Rashtriya Kishore Swasthaya Karyakram

It was launched in January, 2014. The key objective of this programme is adolescent participation and leadership.

The programme envisions enabling all adolescents in India to realise their full potential by making informed and responsible decisions related to their health and well-being and by accessing the services and support they need to do so.

The National Policy for Children 2013, provides a strong foundation for addressing the immediate and the underlying determinants of under nutrition through both direct and indirect interventions.

The 12th Five Year Plan reinforced the commitment to preventing and reducing child undernutrition. As per 2014 policy which was reinforced by the PMO, mandating NITI Aayog to examine the data on undernutrition and prepare a specific strategy for poor performing states/districts.

A wide spectrum of national programmes contribute to improved nutrition outcomes addressing both the immediate and the underlying determinants of undernutrition through nutrition specific and nutrition sensitive interventions. These include Jnani Suraksha Yojana, Matriva Sahyog Yojana, and the National Rural Livelihood Mission.

Vision 2022

According to this, the National Nutrition Strategy is committed to ensuring that every child, adolescent girl and woman attain optimal nutritional status especially those from most vulnerable communities. The focus is on preventing and reducing undernutrition across the life cycle-as early as possible, especially in the first three years of life.

National Food Security Mission (NFSM)

The National Development Council (NDC) on 29th May, 2007 adopted a centrally sponsored scheme, 'National Food Security Mission' (NFSM), was launched in October 2007. The Mission met with an overwhelming success and achieved the targeted additional production of rice, wheat and pulses. The Mission is being continued during 12th Five Year Plan.

Objectives of the mission are :

- Increasing production of rice, wheat, pulses and coarse cereals through area expansion and productivity enhancement in a sustainable manner in the identified districts of the country.
- Restoring soil fertility and productivity at the individual farm level.
- Enhancing farm level economy (i.e. farm profits) to restore confidence amongst the farmers.

Strategy of the Mission

To achieve the above objectives, the mission has adopted following strategies :

- Focus on low productivity and high potential districts including cultivation of food grain crops in rain-fed areas.
- Implementation of cropping system centric interventions in a mission mode approach through active engagement of all the stakeholders at various levels.
- Agro-climatic zone wise planning and cluster approach for crop productivity enhancement.
- Focus on pulse production through utilisation of rice fallow, rice bunds and intercropping of pulses with coarse cereals, oilseeds and commercial crops (sugarcane, cotton, jute).
- Promotion and extension of improved technologies i.e., seed, Integrated Nutrient Management (INM) including micronutrients, soil amendments, Integrated Pest Management (IPM), input use efficiency and resource conservation technologies along with capacity building of the farmers/extension functionaries.
- Close monitoring of flow of funds to ensure timely reach of interventions to the target beneficiaries.
- Integration of various proposed interventions and targets with the district plan of each identified district.
- Constant monitoring and concurrent evaluation by the implementing agencies for assessing the impact of the interventions for a result oriented approach.

Rashtriya Krishi Vikas Yojana (RKVY)

Concerned by the slow growth in the agriculture and allied sectors, the National Development Council (NDC), in its meeting held on 29th May, 2007 resolved that Rashtriya Krishi Vikas Yojana (RKVY) be launched. The NDC resolved that agricultural development strategies must be reoriented to meet the needs of farmers and called upon the Central and State governments to evolve a strategy to rejuvenate agriculture.

The Department of Agriculture, in compliance of the above resolution has prepared the guidelines for the RKVY scheme, to be known as National Agriculture Development Programme (RKVY).

Objectives of the RKVY are :

- To incentivise the states that increase their investment in agriculture and allied sectors
- To provide flexibility and autonomy to the states in planning and executing programmes for agriculture
- To ensure the preparation of Agriculture Plans for the districts and states
- To achieve the goal of reducing the yield gaps in important crops
- To maximise returns to the farmers
- To address the agriculture and allied sectors in an integrated manner

Areas of focus under the RKVY

- Integrated development of food crops, including coarse cereals, minor millets and pulses
- Agriculture Mechanisation and Soil Health and Productivity
- Development of rainfed farming systems
- Integrated pest management and organic and bio-fertilisers
- Promoting extension services
- Horticulture and sericulture
- Animal husbandry, dairying and fisheries
- Study tours of farmers
- Innovative schemes

Pradhanmantri Fasal Beema Yojana

The New Crop Insurance Scheme is in line with One Nation One scheme theme. It incorporates the best features of all previous schemes and at the same time, all previous shortcomings /weaknesses have been removed. The PMFBY will replace the existing two schemes National Agricultural Insurance Scheme as well as the Modified NAIS.

Objectives of the scheme are :

- To provide insurance coverage and financial support to the farmers in the event of failure of any of the notified crop as a result of natural calamities, pests and diseases.
- To stabilise the income of farmers to ensure their continuance in farming.
- To encourage farmers to adopt innovative and modern agricultural practices.
- To ensure flow of credit to the agriculture sector.

Highlights of the Scheme

- The use of technology will be encouraged to a great extent. Smart phones will be used to capture and upload data of crop cutting to reduce the delays in claim payment to farmers. Remote sensing will be used to reduce the number of crop cutting experiments.
- PMFBY is a replacement scheme of NAIS / MNAIS, there will be exemption from service tax liability of all the services involved in the implementation of the scheme. It is estimated that the new scheme will ensure about 75-80 per cent of subsidy for the farmers in insurance premium.

- Farmers in the notified area who possess a Crop Loan account/KCC account (called as Loanee Farmers) to whom credit limit is sanctioned/renewed for the notified crop during the crop season and such other farmers whom the government may decide to include from time to time.

Mid day Meal Programme (MDM)

The Midday Meal Programme is a school meal programme started by Government of India in 2001. The programme was designed to improve the nutritional status of school age children nationwide.

Under this every child in every Government and Government aided primary school was to be served a prepared midday meal. It was with a minimum content of 300 calories of energy and 8-12 grams protein per day for a minimum of 200 days.

This programme was further extended to cover not only children studying in Government; Government aided and local body schools but also children studying in Education Guarantee Scheme and Alternative and Innovation Education Centres.

In September 2004, the scheme was revised to provide central assistance for cooking cost of ₹ 1 per school day. In 2006, it was further revised to enhance cooking cost to ₹ 1.80 per child/school day for states in North Eastern Region and ₹ 1.50 per child/school day for other states/UTs.

In October 2007, the Midday Meal Programme was extended to cover children of upper primary classes (Class VI-VIII) studying in 3, 479 Educationally Backward Blocks and the name of the scheme was changed from National Programme of Nutritional support to primary education to 'National Programme' Midday Meal in schools. The nutritional norm for upper primary was fixed at 700 calories and 20 grams of protein.

The programme from 2008 was extended to all areas across the country.

Wheat Based Nutrition Programme (WNP)

It was a centrally sponsored programme introduced in 1986, but now transferred to the state sector. This programme follows the norms of SNP or of the nutrition component of the ICDs.

The central assistance of the programme consist of free wheat and supportive cost for other ingredients, cooking transport, etc. This programme aimed at improving the nutritional status of children below 6 years of age and expectant/lactating women. The scheme consists of two components namely the centrally sponsored component and state funded component.

Development of Women and Children in Rural Areas (DWCRA)

Development of Women and Children in Rural Areas (DWCRA) was launched as a sub scheme of Integrated Rural Development Programme (IRDP) during the year 1982-83 in 50 districts. It subsequently extended to cover all the districts in the country by 1994-95. This initiative was taken by the ministry and the programme 'Development of women and children in rural areas. DWCRA with exclusive focus on economic empowerment of women provides all these inputs by considering women as critical to development. The basic unit under DWCRA is a group of 10-15 poor women who have come together to help each other in order to use their collective strength to break social bonds that have denied them income generating and self-fulfilling opportunities.

The group size may be smaller in difficult terrain and far-flung areas. One woman amongst the members functions as the group organiser who helps in the choice of activity, procurement of raw material, marketing of products. Before undertaking the activities women were made aware of the objectives and benefits of group. Studies have been conducted to compare food and nutrition intake of DWCRA beneficiary families and non-DWCRA families. The per capita income were more among DWCRA families. Thus, the per capita expenditure on food item was more among the DWCRA families. The intake of cereals, pulse, green leafy vegetables animal foods and milk was more among DWCRA families.

Integrated Child Development Service (ICDS)

It was launched by the Government of India in 1975. The ICDS scheme is one of the world's largest and most, unique programmes for early childhood development. Its aim is to provide nutritional support, healthcare and pre-school education for children under 6 (and for pregnant or lactating mothers) in order to reduce the incidence of mortality, malnutrition and school dropout.

Under the ICDS scheme, children under 6 and pregnant or lactating mothers can access four main services :

Supplementary Nutrition Vitamin A tablets, food grains and rice, and fortified food packages are available for children and mothers who are showing signs of malnourishment. Weight-for-age growth cards should be maintained for all children under six years of age-children below the age of 3 should be weighed once a month and children aged 3-6 should be weighed quarterly.

Immunisations Children should be given full vaccinations against six preventable diseases : poliomyelitis, diphtheria, pertussis, tetanus, tuberculosis and measles. Pregnant women should receive a vaccination against tetanus that reduces maternal and neonatal mortality.

Health Check-ups Various health services should be provided for children including treatment of diarrhoea, de-worming and distribution of simple medicines (along with weight and height monitoring, and immunisations). Ante-natal and post-natal check-ups should be provided for pregnant women and new mothers.

Referral Services If, after a health check-ups, children or mothers are in need of medical attention they should be referred to the Primary Health Centre or Sub-centre. Severely malnourished children should be referred to Nutrition Rehabilitation Centres (NRCs) and young children with disabilities should be referred to specialists.

Balwadi Nutrition Programme

Bal (children) wadi (home or centre) Nutrition Programme is a contemporary of SNP and is being implemented since 1970-71 by the Central Social Welfare Board and national level non-governmental voluntary organisations, namely, Indian Council for Child Welfare, Harijan Sevak Sangh, Bhartiya Adimjati Sevak Sangh and Kasturba National Memorial Trust.

This segment of nutrition programme is thus implemented essentially by Non-governmental Organisations. The Central Social Welfare Board, which is a semi-government umbrella organisation in the field of social work, gives in turn, grants-in-aid to voluntary organisations to run the programme and so do the other four national level voluntary organisations, which also extend assistance to various voluntary organisations beside running some centres directly.

The programme aims to supply about one-third of the calorie and half of the protein requirements of the pre-school child as measure to improve nutritional and health status. Its beneficiaries are pre-school children between the age of 3 to 5 years. Priority is given to children belonging to low income group.

The supplementary nutrition consisting 300 calories and 10 grams of protein per child per day is given for 770 days a year. Apart from nutritional supplementation, the activities for social and emotional development are undertaken at balwadis.

Special Nutrition Programme (SNP)

The Special Nutrition Programme (SNP) was launched in 1970-71 by the Ministry of Social Welfare, Government of India. It was initially launched as a central programme but was transferred to the state sector during the Fifth Five Year Plan. During the sixth and seventh Five Year Plans, steps were taken to convert the SNP centres on the pattern of ICDS Scheme by strengthening them with health and other inputs. At present 22.87 million beneficiaries are covered by the scheme. The objective of the programme is to improve the nutrition of pre-school children, pregnant and lactating mothers of poor socio-economic groups in urban slums, tribal areas and drought prone rural areas.

The activities of the programme include :

- To provide supplementary nutrition.
- To provide health care services including supply of Vitamin A solution and iron and folic acid tablets.

The supplementary nutrition is provided to children in 6-7 months, to provide 300 calories and log protein per child per day. The severely malnourished children are provided 600 calories and 20 grams protein/day. Iron and folic acid tablets and Vitamin A solution are also provided.

The pregnant and lactating mothers receive supplementary nutrition containing 600 calories and 20 grams protein per day. Iron and folic acid tablets are also provided.

Applied Nutrition Programme

This programme was first implemented in Odisha and Andhra Pradesh in 1962. By 1973, the whole country was covered by the scheme. This programme uptill now is the best conceived nutrition programme but it could not achieve the desired results due to management failure. It was a centrally sponsored scheme but now is implemented by the states.

The ANP is a non-expandable, low priority programm as compared to other nutrition programmes implemente by the states. The programme aimed at the approac of self-reliance to be developed at community/ individual l vel.

Organisations Involved in Nutritional Intervention

Many organisations have been formed to fight malnutrition. These are given below :

UNICEF

UNICEF, acronym of United Nations Children's Fund, formerly (1946-53) United Nations International Children's Emergency Fund, special programme of the United Nations (UN) devoted to aiding national efforts to improve the health, nutrition, education, and general welfare of children.

UNICEF was created in 1946 to provide relief to children in countries devastated by World War II. After 1950 the fund directed its efforts toward general programmes for the improvement of children's welfare, particularly in less-developed countries and in various emergency situations. The organisation's broader mission was reflected in the name it adopted in 1953, the United Nations Children's Fund.

UNICEF Programmes in India

UNICEF has been working in India since 1949. The largest UN organisation in the country, UNICEF is fully committed to work with the Government of India to ensure that each child born in this vast and complex country gets the best start in life, thrives and develops to his or her full potential.

Nutrition UNICEF is trying to improve the nutritional and health status as well as the social development of young children. In India poor people are unable to provide good stuff to the kids. Due to this problem, children are catching more diseases which are incurable. The poor cannot meet the expenditure towards diseased children.

Through ICDS nutrition food served for children and mothers. In all villages Anganwadi helpers are appointed to observe the people. They are trained to extend their services throughout the clock. Thus, in India UNICEF rendered good welfare service in this aspect.

Health and Immunisation In 1990 many of the young children were immunised against six major childhood diseases, those are Diphtheria, Tuberculosis, whopping Cough, Tetanus, polio and Measles. UNICEF fought for reduction of diseases of child survival. UNICEF does its best extent to eradicate all the diseases of children and put endeavors to protect the children from all the dreads.

Water and Sanitation UNICEF played key role in providing water supplies in rural areas through hand pumps. It promoted especially hygiene, sanitation and safe water.

WHO

The World Health Organissation (WHO) was created in 1948 by member states of the United Nations (UN) as a specialised agency with a broad mandate for health. The WHO is the world's leading health organisation. Its policies and programmes have a far-reaching impact on the status of international public health. Its constitution defines itself as "the directing and coordinating authority on international health work," WHO aims at "the attainment by all peoples of the highest possible standard of health." Its mission is to improve people's lives, to reduce the burdens of disease and poverty, and to provide access to responsive health care for all people.

Nutrition Guidelines by WHO

Given are some of the dietary guidelines by WHO :

- A healthy diet helps to protect against malnutrition in all its forms, as well as Non-Communicable Diseases (NCDs). Such as diabetes, heart disease, stroke and cancer.
- Unhealthy diet and lack of physical activity are leading global risks to health.
- Healthy dietary practices start early in life breastfeeding. It fosters, healthy growth and improves cognitive development, and may have longer term health benefits such as reducing the risk of becoming overweight or obese and developing NCDs later in life.
- Energy intake (calories) should be in balance with energy expenditure. To avoid unhealthy weight gain, total fat should not exceed 30% of total energy intake. Intake of saturated fats should be less than 10% of total energy intake, and intake of trans-fats less than 1% of total energy intake.
- Limiting intake of free sugars to less than 10% of total energy intake is part of a healthy diet. A further reduction to less than 5% of total energy intake is suggested for additional health benefits.
- Keeping salt intake to less than 5 grams per day (equivalent to sodium intake of less than 2 grams per day) helps to prevent hypertension, and reduces the risk of heart disease and stroke in the adult population.

CARE

Cooperative for Assistance and Relief Everywhere (CARE) was established in 1945. It is based on over 70 years of poverty-fighting and humanitarian action experience. It tackles the underlying causes of poverty and social injustice. The motto is to bring lasting change to the lives of poor and vulnerable people.

CARE prioritises three ways of addressing the main underlying causes of poverty and social injustice that we encounter all around the world: gender inequality; poor governance and unequal power relations; and humanitarian crises and climate change. They address these underlying causes of poverty and social injustice by strengthening gender equality and women's voice, promoting inclusive governance, and increasing resilience.

CARE in India

CARE has been working in India for over 68 years, focusing on alleviating poverty and social exclusion. They do this through well-planned and comprehensive programmes in health, education, livelihoods and disaster preparedness and response. They also focus on generating and sharing knowledge with diverse stakeholders to influence sustainable impact at scale. Our overall goal is the empowerment of women and girls from poor and marginalised communities, leading to improvement in their lives and livelihoods.

CARE India's interventions in the health sector works to improve access to quality health services for the poor and marginalised communities. By identifying the root causes of healthcare challenges, CARE India works at the individual, community and systemic levels to develop innovative solutions and help implement quality healthcare services.

To work with community groups and government, CARE use cross-cutting strategies to improve the health and nutrition status of the poorest and excluded groups, particularly women and children. CARE India builds the capacities of healthcare service providers and officials of the Integrated Child Development Services (ICDS), to create impact at scale.

CARE India's projects include improving the quality of services for maternal and reproductive health, child health and nutrition, and early identification and treatment of communicable diseases such Tuberculosis (TB), kala azar, pneumonia, diarrhoea and HIV. The aim of the health interventions is to strengthen and promote comprehensive health for women and girls, and create a positive and enabling environment for accessing quality healthcare services.

CFTRI

Central Food Technological Research Institute (CFTRI) is one of the largest R and D institutions devoted to Food Science and Technology under Council of Scientific and Industrial Research (CSIR), Ministry of Science and Technology, Government of India, New Delhi. Established in the year 1950, the institute is also an associated institution of United Nations University, Tokyo.

The Institute has been focusing on the development of technologies beneficial to farmers and growers and ultimately the society as a whole. The present scenario in the country is very vibrant with rising capital investment in food industry which is expanding at a rapid pace due to demands in rural, semiurban and urban markets for processed foods with a focus on traditional as well as eco-friendly technologies along with underutilised agro-produce for value addition.

Role of Anganwadi in Nutrition Intervention

The name anganwadi worker is derived from the Indian word-angan, which means the court yard (a central area in and around the house where most of the social activities of the household takes place). The anganwadi worker and helper are the basic functionaries of the ICDS who run the anganwadi centre.

They implement the ICDS scheme in coordination with the functionaries of the health, education, rural development and other departments. Their services also include the health and nutrition of pregnant women, nursing mothers, and adolescent girls.

Anganwadi workers are India's primary tool against the menace of child malnourishment, infant mortality, and lack of child education, community health problems and in curing preventable diseases. They provide services to villagers, poor families and sick people across the country helping them access healthcare services, immunisation, healthy food, hygiene, and provide healthy learning environment for infants, toddlers and children.

Role of Anganwadi Workers

The anganwadis are engaged to provide the following formal services to the areas under their cover :

- Immunisation of all children less than 6 years of age
- Immunisation against tetanus for all the expectant mothers
- Supplementary nutrition to children below 6 years of age
- Supplementary nutrition to women who are pregnant and nursing, especially epically. from the low income group
- Nutrition, health education and health check-ups to all women in the age group of 15- 45 years
- Antenatal care of expectant mothers
- Postnatal care of nursing mothers
- Caring for newborn babies
- Caring for all children under 6 years of age
- Referral of serious cases of malnutrition or illness to hospitals, upgraded PHCs/ Community Health Services of district hospitals
- Non-formal pre-school education to children of 3-5 years of age.

Nutrition in Anganwadi

Rice/Wheat or Ragi based nutritious food are served in anganwadi centres. Over 500 calories energy is given to the beneficiary's diet. This contains carbohydrates protein, fat and vegetable. Common menu is applicable to all project is prepared and food items are limited to 2-3 varieties.

Nutritional Awareness

To spread the information about the nutrition, awareness is necessary. What to eat and how to eat, what not to eat, these question can be easily solved by nutritional awareness. This can be done through the following :

Community

Nutritional awareness can be promoted by organising seminars, workshops, debates, discussions and through practical demonstrations. Professionals other than researcher like teachers, socialites, local doctors and experienced persons can give advice to the whole community.

Television, Radio and Film

Television, film, radio are good medium for spreading nutrition awareness. These are good medium to make and show nutritious dishes with readily available inexpensive material. Nutritious food preparation for young children are also shown in the programmes. Programmes related to talks by expert regarding nutritious food is also telecasted. The ways to construct kitchen garden can be shown, so that the house wives can plant a kitchen garden and use fresh vegetables. Many people can be influenced/ motivated by these and many more initiatives. Therefore, media is the best way to spread nutrition awareness.

Institutions, Programmes and Organisations

Nutrition awareness can also be disseminated by various institutions and their programmes. Apart from voluntary organisation applied nutrition programme, supplementary programme, school lunch programme are also spreading nutrition awareness to the people. Along with national institutions, international institutions are also spreading these programmes to the people. International institution like FAO, WHO, CARE, UNICEF etc., are running programmes to raise the health and nutritional level of the people. While distributing nutritious food to the people all these organisation create nutritional awareness.

Education

Nutrition awareness can be created by giving nutritional science a place in the courses of colleges and schools. So that the young generation know about nutrition related problem from the start. They won't be affected by them in the future. It is very important to have nutritional education, so that future generation can be strong and nurturing.

Newspapers and Phamplets

These are methods to provide theoretical information but they can also provide nutritional awareness. It is considered to be a means of public relation, through newspapers, there is an increase in nutrition related knowledge in homes and communities and nutritional awareness is well spread.

Innovation in Nutrition

Innovation in nutrition are :

Fructooligosaccharides The Institute has developed a process for the production of fructooligosaccharides (FOS), a class of prebiotics. The unique features of the process are utilisation of sucrose, a widely available substrate and Aspergillus oryzes (GRAS). The institute holds various patents and products involving FOS, besides successful transfer of the process to the industry.

Spirulina Alleviation of Protein Malnutrition Biomass from alga sources are known for their applications in food and other non-food items. Their outdoor cultivation with enhanced attributes has been standardised in the laboratory. These include spirulina with enriched iron content of high bioavailability; Dunaliella as a rich source of betacarotene, Haematococcus pluvialis as a source of astaxanthin and Botryococcus brauii for hydrocarbon source. A few of these have been transferred to industries.

Bottled Sugarcane Juice India offers itself a potential market for soft beverages and fruit based beverages. A process has been developed for the preservation of sugarcane juice as a bottled beverage. The beverage, being natural, possesses a lot of medicinal and curative properties and it is calorific and nutritive.

Technology Protocols for Export of Fruits The Institute has standardised pre and post-harvest technology protocols for the export of fresh mangoes, bananas and pomegranate by surface transport.

Energy Food Energy Food developed by the Institute is a ready-to-eat supplementary food based on cereals, legumes and defatted protein-rich oilseed meals. The mixture is fortified with vitamins and minerals. The product is useful as a weaning/nutrition food for children and pregnant women.

Food and Nutrition Security

Food and Nutrition Security are :

Food Security, as defined by the United Nation's Committee on World Food Security, means that all people, at all times have physical, social and economic access to sufficient, safe and nutritious food that meets their food preferences and dietary needs for an active and healthy life. The three component of food security-availability, (having sufficient quantities of appropriate food available), utilisation (having adequate dietary intake and the ability to absorb and use nutrients in the body), and access (having adequate income or other resources to access food).

Nutrition Security is a situation when all people are able to consume necessary and sufficient quality of food at all time. In order to live life in an active and healthy way, it is important to have variety and availability of nutrient in food. Simultaneously there should be complete cleanliness of environment and adequate health related services. India has moved away from dependence on food aid to become a net food exporter. In 2016, the government launched a number of programmes to double farmers' incomes by 2022.

These seek to remove bottlenecks for greater agricultural productivity, especially in rain-fed areas. They include: The National Food Security Mission, Rashtriya Krishi Vikas Yojana (RKVY), and Pradhan Mantri Fasal Bima Yojana.

EXAM BASED QUESTIONS

1 Nutritional assessment is a systematic process of
(a) collecting information
(b) interpreting information
(c) Both (a) and (b)
(d) None of the above

2 Which of the following are techniques of nutrition assessment?
(a) Antropometry (b) Biochemical method
(c) Clinical assessment (d) All of these

3 Anthropometry is the measure of body
(a) temperature (b) weight
(c) activity (d) None of these

4 What does anthropometric method evaluates?
(a) Under nutrition (b) Over nutrition
(c) Both (a) and (b) (d) None of these

5 Different type of anthropometric measurement include
(a) BMI (b) skinfold thickness
(c) head circumference (d) All of these

6 Functional test measures
(a) height
(b) function of vital organ
(c) chemical present in blood
(d) hormone levels

7 Which of the following diseases can be detected by clinical assessment?
(a) Anaemia (b) Goitre
(c) Scurvy (d) All of these

8 24 hour dietary recall is a measure to assess through
(a) dietary assessment (b) clinical assessment
(c) biochemical assessment (d) anthropometry

9 What is/are the step(s) taken in community level to make people aware about nutrition?
(a) Speech (b) Direct contact
(c) Both (a) and (b) (d) None of these

10 Which of the following is telecasted for nutritional awareness?
(a) Programmes showing food making with readily aware material
(b) Food for young children
(c) Talks by expert regarding nutritions food
(d) All of the above

11 Which of the following programmes help in nutritional awareness of people?
(a) Applied nutrition programme
(b) Supplementary programme
(c) School lunch programme
(d) All of the above

12 It is very important to have nutritional education so that future generation can be ......
(a) strong (b) nurturing
(c) Both (a) and (b) (d) None of these

13 the National Nutrition Mission which is celebrated from September 1-7, 2019 was aimed to
(a) provide supplementory nutrition
(b) provide healthcare services
(c) to make people aware about important tips of their health and well-being
(d) Both (a) and (b)

14 The National Nutrition Mission is setup with a vision to ensure attainment of malnutrition free India by the year
(a) 2021 (b) 2022
(c) 2025 (d) 2023

15 Mothers' Absolute Affection Programme launched in 2016 has which of the following chief components?
(a) Community awareness generation
(b) Strengthening interpersonal communication through ASHA
(c) Monitoring and award/recognition
(d) All of the above

16 The main characteristics of Mission Indradhanush include
(a) It seeks to drive towards full immunisation coverage of India by 2020.
(b) It depicts seven colours of the rainbow.
(c) It covers all those children who are either unvaccinated or partially vaccinated against seven preventable diseases.
(d) All of the above

17 What are the key principles of the Rashtriya Kishore Swasthaya Karyakram?
(a) Adolescent participation and leadership
(b) Equity and inclusion
(c) Mental health and concerns of adolescents
(d) All of the above

18 When was DWCRA launched?
(a) 1982-83 (b) 1994-97
(c) 1991-93 (d) 1989-90

19 What is the main focus of DWCRA?
(a) Meeting of basic needs (b) Empowerment of women
(c) Sustainable living (d) None of these

20 How many women constitute basic unit of DWCRA?
(a) 5-10 (b) 2-4
(c) 10-15 (d) 15-25

21 What are the approaches by DWCRA?
(a) Provide income generating assets
(b) Make rural women understand role of hygiene
(c) Organising women into groups
(d) All of the above

22 When was ICDS launched?
(a) 1965 (b) 1975
(c) 1985 (d) 1995

23 What are the services provided under ICDS?
(a) Supplementary Nutrition
(b) Nutrition and health education
(c) Immunisation
(d) All of above

24 When was Special Nutrition Programme (SNP) launched?
(a) 1970-1971 (b) 1972-1973
(c) 1980-1981 (d) 1982-1983

25 22.87 million beneficiaries are covered under which scheme?
(a) Anganwadi
(b) Special Nutrition Programme
(c) DWCRA
(d) ICDS

26 Balwadi Nutrition Programme is basically implemented by whom?
(a) NGO (b) Central Government
(c) State Government (d) All of these

27 Which age group benefits from Balwadi Nutrition Programme?
(a) 5-10 years (b) 3-5 years
(c) 4-7 years (d) 10-15 years

28 What is the role of anganwadi worker?
(a) Immunisation of children
(b) Supplementary nutrition
(c) Antenatal care of mother
(d) All of the above

29 How many anganwadi worker is in single anganwadi?
(a) One (b) Two
(c) Three (d) Four

30 When was UNICEF launched?
(a) 1950 (b) 1934 (c) 1946 (d) 1951

31 Which are the diseases against which children were immunised by UNICEF India?
(a) Diptheria (b) Tuberculosis
(c) Tetanus (d) All of these

32 UNICEF has employed ……… to check on nutrition status in India.
(a) ICDS (b) ANMS
(c) Both (a) and (b) (d) None of these

33 What is the broad mandate of WHO?
(a) Health (b) Poverty
(c) Nutrition (d) All of above

34 When was Universal Declaration of Human Rights launched?
(a) 1968 (b) 1958
(c) 1938 (d) 1948

35 How many articles address the issue of nutrition in convention on the Right of the Child?
(a) Three (b) Two
(c) Four (d) Five

36 What is/are the main goal of CARE?
(a) Poverty fighting (b) Humanitarian action
(c) Both (a) and (b) (d) None of these

37 What is/are the objective(s) of CARE?
(a) Strengthening Gender Equality
(b) Inclusive Governance
(c) Resilence
(d) All of the above

38 CFTRI comes under which organisation?
(a) CSIR (b) UGC
(c) UNESCO (d) WHO

39 Which of the following functionaries, the ICDS workers coordinate to implement the scheme of ICDS?
(a) Health
(b) Rural development and other departments
(c) Education
(d) All of the above

40 When was CFTRI established?
(a) 1947 (b) 1950 (c) 1952 (d) 1954

41 CFTRI is associated which which institute?
(a) United Nation University, Tokyo
(b) Oxford University, London
(c) Indian Institute of technology, Delhi
(d) None of the above

42 What does virgin coconut oil contain?
(a) Lauric acid (b) Vitamin E
(c) Both (a) and (b) (d) None of these

43 What are the component of food security?
(a) Availability (b) Utilisation
(c) Accessebility (d) All of these

44 When was NFSM launched?
(a) October 2007 (b) August 2007
(c) May 2007 (d) December 2007

45 Production of which of the following comes under NFSM?
(a) Rice, wheat, cereal
(b) Vegetables
(c) Fruits
(d) Biologically modified food item

46 Which areas are under focus of RKVY?
(a) Soil Health and Productivity
(b) Horticulture
(c) Animal Husbandry, Dairying and Fisheries
(d) All of the above

47 Choose the correct statement
(a) The NFSM had over whelming success when it was launched.
(b) There has been an increase in production of rice, wheat, pulses and cereals.
(c) Both (a) and (b)
(d) None of the above

Directions (Q. Nos. 42-50) *Choose the corret option of the statements given above the options.*

48 Consider the following statements
1. SNP was launched by Ministry of Social welfare, Government of India.
2. Its objective is to improve nutritional status pregnant women only.
(a) Only 1 (b) Only 2
(c) Both 1 and 2 (d) None of these

49 Consider the following statements
1. UNICEF is trying to help working male.
2. UNICEF has immunised children against 6 major childhood disease.
(a) Only 1 (b) Only 2
(c) 1 and 2 (d) None of these

50 Consider the following statements
1. Clinical Assessment utilises numbers of physical sign that are associated with nutrition.
2. Xerophthalamia, beri-beri, rickets are the disease which can be detected by clinical assessment.
(a) Only 1 (b) Only 2
(c) Both 1 and 2 (d) None of these

51 Consider the following statements
1. Nutrition can not be spread by TV, radio or film.
2. TV promote bad health.
(a) Only 1 (b) Only 2
(c) Both 1 and 2 (d) None of these

52 Consider the following statements
1. DWCRA was launched by IRDP
2. A single woman can appeal for loan from DWCRA.
(a) Only 1
(b) Only 2
(c) 1 and 2
(d) None of the above

53 Consider the following statements
1. Food security means that all people at all times have physical, social, and economic access to food.
2. Nutrition security means that the community is disease free.
(a) Only 1 (b) Only 2
(c) 1 and 2 (d) None of these

54 Consider the following statements
1. CARE works on poverty fighting and humanitarian actions.
2. CARE works with community and government.
(a) Only 1 (b) Only 2
(c) 1 and 2 (d) None of these

55 Consider the following statements
1. Anthropometry is the measurement of body height, weight and proportion.
2. Anthropometry can help in detecting diseases.
(a) Only 1 (b) Only 2
(c) 1 and 2 (d) None of these

56 Consider the following statements
1. Organisation works to eleminate poverty not to spread nutritional awareness.
2. Nutritional awareness can be spread by educating young children about it.
(a) Only 1 (b) Only 2
(c) 1 and 2 (d) None of these

57 Match the following.

List I	List II
A. DWCRA	1. Integrated child development service
B. ICDS	2. Development of women and children in rural area.
C. CFTRI	3. Special nutrition programme
D. SNP	4. Central food technological research institute

Codes

	A	B	C	D		A	B	C	D
(a)	2	1	4	3	(b)	1	2	4	3
(c)	2	1	3	4	(d)	4	3	1	2

58 Match the following.

List I	List II
A. Xerophthalmia	1. Iodine deficiency
B. Anaemia	2. Vitamin C Deficiency
C. Scurvy	3. Vitamin A Deficiency
D. Goitre	4. Iron Deficiency

Codes

	A	B	C	D		A	B	C	D
(a)	4	1	2	3	(b)	3	4	2	1
(c)	2	3	1	4	(d)	4	1	3	2

59 Match the following.

List I	List II
A. ICDS	1. 1948
B. SNP	2. 1975
C. UNICEF	3. 1970
D. WHO	4. 1949

Codes

	A	B	C	D		A	B	C	D
(a)	3	2	1	4	(b)	4	2	3	1
(c)	2	3	4	1	(d)	3	2	1	4

60 Match the following.

List I	List II
A. Anthropometry	1. 24 hour recall
B. Biochemical Method	2. BMI
C. Clinical Assessment	3. Level of chemical in blood
D. Dietary Assessment	4. Symptoms like altered bowl movement

Codes

	A	B	C	D		A	B	C	D
(a)	2	3	4	1	(b)	4	2	1	3
(c)	3	1	2	4	(d)	4	1	3	2

61 Match the following.

List I	List II
A. DWCRA	1. Supplementary nutrition, immunisation, health checkup
B. ICDS	2. Increase in production of rice, wheat, pulses and cereal
C. NFSM	3. Give loan to farmer.
D. RKVY	4. Group of women gets resources

Codes

	A	B	C	D		A	B	C	D
(a)	1	2	3	4	(b)	4	1	2	3
(c)	4	3	1	2	(d)	1	2	4	3

Directions (Q. Nos. 62-71) *Given below are two statements, one labelled as Assertion (A) and the other labelled as Reason (R). Following are the codes given below.*

(a) Both A and R are true
(b) Both A and R are false
(c) A is true, but R is false
(d) A is false, but R is true

62 **Assertion** (A) NFSM was launched by National Development Council.
Reason (R) The mission failed in intial stages.

63 **Assertion** (A) RKVY works for malnourished children.
Reason (R) RKVY was launched on May 2007.

64 **Assertion** (A) PMFBY replaced NAIS.
Reason (R) PMFBY provide insurance coverage.

65 **Assertion** (A) Biochemical method is measurement of height, weight and proportion.
Reason (R) Biochemical test are useful in detecting early changes in body metabolism.

66 **Assertion** (A) Dietary Assessment is estimate of total daily calorie intake.
Reason (R) Food frequency questionnaire can be used in dietary assessment.

67 **Assertion** (A) Nutritional awareness can be promoted by organising seminars.
Reason (R) Professionals can also help in nutritional awareness.

68 **Assertion** (A) Newspapers are not a good way to spread nutritional awareness.
Reason (R) Nutrition should not be taught at school level.

69 **Assertion** (A) Balwadi Nutrition Programme was launched by Central Social Welfare Board.
Reason (R) The programme aims to help adolescent girls.

70 **Assertion** (A) Anganwadi workers are basic functionaries of DWCRA.
Reason (R) Their services include health and nutrition of pregnant women.

71 **Assertion** (A) WHO was created by UN.
Reason (R) WHO fights against malnutrition in all its forms.

Directions (Q. Nos. 72-76) *Read the following passage and answer the questions.*

Good nutrition is an important part of leading a healthy lifestyle. Combined with physical activity, your diet can help you to reach and maintain a healthy weight, reduce your risk of chronic diseases (like heart disease and cancer), and promote your overall health. Nutrition is the study of nutrients in food, how the body uses nutrients, and the relationship between diet, health, and disease.

Proper nutrition means that you are receiving enough foods and supplements for the body to function at optimal capacity. It is important to remember that no single nutrient or activity can maintain optimal health and well-being, although it has been proven that some nutrients are more important than others. All of the nutrients are necessary in different amounts along with exercise to maintain proper health.

There are six main types of nutrients used to maintain body health. They are carbohydrates, fats, proteins, vitamins, minerals, and water. They all must be in balance for the body to function properly. There are also five major food groups. The groups are fats and oils, fruits and vegetables, dairy products, grains, and meats. Exercise is also an important part of nutrition. Exercise helps tone and maintain muscle tissue and ensure that the body's organs stay in good condition. Healthy eating without exercise-will not result in good nutrition and a healthy body - neither will exercise without nutrition. The most important thing about exercise is that it be practiced regularly and that it be practiced in accompaniment with a healthy diet. It is also desirable to practice more than one sports as different sports exercise different areas of the body.

Carbohydrates, proteins, and fats are the sources of energy for the body. The contained energy is expressed in calories. There are nine calories per gram in fat and there are about four calories per gram in proteins and carbohydrates. Carbohydrates are the main source of energy for the body. This energy is mostly used for muscle movement and digestion of food. Some sources of carbohydrates are grains, fruits, vegetables, and anything else that grows out of the ground. The energy in carbohydrates is almost instantly digested. Results in quick rise in blood sugar which is usually followed by a drop in blood sugar which is interpreted by the body as a craving for more sugars.

Low sugar may also result in fatigue, dizziness, nervousness, and headache. However, not all carbohydrates do this. Most fruits, vegetables, legumes, and whole grains are digested more slowly. Fats, which are lipids, are the source of energy that is the most concentrated. Fats produce more than twice the amount of energy that is in carbohydrates or proteins. Besides having a high concentration of energy, fat acts as a carrier for the fat soluble vitamins, A, D, E, and K. Also, by helping in the absorption of vitamin D, fats help make calcium available to various body tissues, in particular, the bones and teeth. Another function of fat is to convert carotene to vitamin A.

Fat also helps keep organs in place by surrounding them in a layer of fat. Fat also surrounds the body in a layer that preserves body temperature and keeps us warm. One other function of fat is to slow the production of hydrochloric acid thereby slowing down digestion and making food last.

72 Which of the following statement(s) is/are correct about the nutrients in consumption in our daily lives?
(a) They help building all parts of the muscle, bone teeth and blood.
(b) They help in keeping the body in good working order.
(c) They are helpful in producing energy.
(d) All of the above

73 Which of the following main nutrients are used to maintain a body health?
(a) Carbohydrates, fats, proteins
(b) Proteins, vitamins, minerals
(c) Carbohydrates, fats, proteins, minerals, vitamins water
(d) Carbohydrates, fats, water, proteins, minerals

74 **Statement I** Exercise is an important part of nutrition.

Statement II It helps maintain muscle tissues and ensure that the body's organs stay in good condition.
(a) Statement I is correct.
(b) Statement II is incorrect.
(c) Both the statements I and II are correct.
(d) Neither statement I nor statement II is correct.

75 There are .... calories per gram in fat.
(a) four (b) nine (c) six (d) three

76 Which of the following statements about the fat is/are correct?
(a) Fats produce more than twice the amount of energy that is in carbohydrates or proteins.
(b) Fat acts as a carrier for the fat soluble vitamins A, D, E and K.
(c) Fat surrounds the body in a layer that preserves body temperatures and keeps us warm.
(d) All of the above

PREVIOUS YEARS' QUESTIONS

July 2018

1 **Assertion** (A) Public Health Nutrition Programmes should create more open spaces for physical activity to promote fitness.

Reason (R) Overweight and obesity are major predisposing factors for developing non-communicable diseases.

Codes
(a) Both A and R are incorrect
(b) A is correct and R is incorrect
(c) A is incorrect and R is correct
(d) Both A and R are correct

2 **Assertion** (A) To assess malnutrition levels in population during famines the most widely accepted practice is to assess it in children ages 6 to 59 months.

Reason (R) In times of food shortages, the young children are the first to develop signs of malnutrition
(a) Both A and R are correct
(b) Both A and R are incorrect
(c) A is correct and R is incorrect
(d) A is incorrect and R is correct

3 Following are anthropometric methods for assessment of nutrition status.
1. Haemoglobin estimation
2. MUAC
3. Waist hip ratio
4. Urinary iodine measurement
5. Body mass index

Codes
(a) 1, 2 and 5
(b) 2, 3 and 4
(c) 1, 4 and 5
(d) 2, 3 and 5

November 2017

4 Following agencies provide data for nutrition monitoring in India.
1. NFHS 2. CPWD
3. NSSO 4. FSSAI
5. CBHI

Codes
(a) 1, 2 and 3
(b) 1, 3 and 5
(c) 3, 4 and 5
(d) 2, 3 and 5

July 2016

5 Iodine deficiency disorders include the following.
1. Abortion
2. Impaired coordination
3. Impaired skeletal growth
4. Low Haemoglobin level
5. Mental Retardation

Codes
(a) 1, 3 and 4 (b) 2, 3 and 5 (c) 1, 2 and 5 (d) 3, 4 and 5

December 2015

6 Which of the following is not a method of Nutritional Status Assessment by anthropometry?
(a) MUAC (b) Blood Pressure
(c) Height (d) Waist Circumference

June 2015

7 The following are the methods of nutritional assessment using anthropometry.
1. Skin fold thickness
2. 24 hours dietary recall
3. Mid Upper Arm Circumference
4. Blood Pressure
5. Waist Hip Ratio

Codes
(a) 1, 2 and 3 (b) 1, 3 and 4
(c) 2, 3 and 5 (d) 1, 3 and 5

June 2014

8 Following are non-conventional novel food developed for nutrition security.
1. Leaf Protein Concentrate
2. Fermented foods
3. Spirulina
4. Textured Soy Protein
5. Amylase Rich Food

Codes
(a) 2, 5 and 1 (b) 1, 2, 3 and 4
(c) 4, 3 and 2 (d) 1, 3 and 4

9 Components of the National Anaemia Programme are
1. promotion of regular consumption of iron rich foods.
2. providing 60 mg iron and 500 mg folic acid for 100 days to a pregnant woman.
3. identification and treatment of severely anaemic women.
4. providing 300 kcal as supplementary nutrition to children 1-6 years.
5. improve the nutrition and health status of adolescent girls.

Codes
(a) 1, 2 and 5 (b) 1, 2 and 4
(c) 1, 2 and 3 (d) 1, 3 and 4

June 2014

10 Match the development programmes from List I with its development issues from List II.

List I	List II
A. NRHM	1. Education
B. ICDS	2. Health
C. MGNREGA	3. Employment
D. DPEP	4. Nutrition
	5. Environment

Codes

	A	B	C	D		A	B	C	D
(a)	1	3	4	2	(b)	5	4	3	2
(c)	2	4	3	1	(d)	2	4	3	5

ANSWERS

Exam Based Questions

1 (c)	2 (d)	3 (b)	4 (c)	5 (d)	6 (b)	7 (d)	8 (a)	9 (c)	10 (d)
11 (d)	12 (c)	13 (c)	14 (b)	15 (d)	16 (d)	17 (d)	18 (a)	19 (b)	20 (c)
21 (d)	22 (b)	23 (d)	24 (a)	25 (b)	26 (a)	27 (b)	28 (d)	29 (a)	30 (c)
31 (d)	32 (c)	33 (a)	34 (d)	35 (b)	36 (c)	37 (d)	38 (a)	39 (d)	40 (b)
41 (a)	42 (c)	43 (d)	44 (a)	45 (a)	46 (d)	47 (c)	48 (a)	49 (b)	50 (c)
51 (d)	52 (a)	53 (a)	54 (c)	55 (a)	56 (b)	57 (a)	58 (d)	59 (c)	60 (a)
61 (b)	62 (c)	63 (d)	64 (a)	65 (d)	66 (a)	67 (a)	68 (a)	69 (b)	70 (c)
71 (a)	72 (d)	73 (c)	74 (c)	75 (b)	76 (d)				

Previous Years' Questions

1 (d)	2 (a)	3 (d)	4 (b)	5 (b)	6 (b)	7 (d)	8 (d)	9 (c)	10 (c)

Textile and Its Manufacturing Process

Textile fibre which is used for yarn and fabric production should have some properties. Generally physical, chemical and structural properties are important to know the textile fibre. Due to their complexity and diversity, understanding the structure of textile fibres is of key importance.

The primary needs of human beings are food, clothing and shelter. Textile serves the clothing requirement of every individual. They add much to our comfort, appearance and happiness by their exceptional versatility. In the recent years, there has been a growing demand for our textiles and clothing.

Each of our Five Year Plans presents a picture of continuous evolution in our basic economic, social and political scenario. Over the past few decades, a new textile world has emerged. New fabrics, new fibres and new finishes make new demands for understanding and evaluation. Modern production methods overcome some of the old difficulties in making fibres into fabrics.

Fibres

A 'fibre' is defined as any product capable of being woven or made into a fabric. A fibre can be defined as a pliable hair-like strand that is very small in diameter in relation to its length. Fibres are fundamental units or the building blocks used in the making of textile yarns and fabrics.

Textile fibre has some characteristics, which differ between fibre to textile fibre. Textile fibre can be spun into a yarn or made into a fabric by various methods including weaving, knitting, braiding, felting and twisting.

In this Chapter

The essential requirements for fibres to be spun into yarn include a length of atleast 5 millimetres, flexibility, cohesiveness and sufficient strength. Other important properties include elasticity, fineness, uniformity, durability and luster.

Textile is a type of material composed of natural or synthetic fibres. Types of textiles include animal-based material such as wool or silk, plant-based material such as linen, cotton and synthetic material such as polyester and rayon textile are often associated with the production of clothing.

The word textile was originally used to define a woven fabric and the process involved in weaving. Textile refers to any material made of interlacing fibres or yarns. Yarn is produced by spinning raw fibres of wool, flax, cotton or other material to produce long strands.

History of Fibres

The history of fibres is as old as human civilisation. Traces of natural fibres have been located to ancient civilisations all over the globe for thousand years.

The usage of fibre was limited by natural fibres such as flax, cotton, silk, wool and plant fibres for different applications. Fibres can be divided into natural fibres and man-made fibres or chemical fibres. Flax is considered to be the oldest and the most used natural fibre since ancient times.

A unit of matter, which is capable of being spun into a yarn by various methods including weaving, knitting, braiding, felting, twisting or webbing and which is the basic structural element of textile products. It is a smallest textile component, which is microscopic hair-like substance that may be man-made or natural.

Properties of Fibres

Fibres are like vitamins, in that you are customising characteristics to get a certain result in your fabric. It sounds complicated, but it is really simple to the consumer. Some basic fibre properties applicable to the home saving consumer include :

Natural Cellulose Fibres Cotton and Flax are examples of natural cellulose fibres. These have good absorbency and are a good conductor of heat. They wrinkle easily and pack tightly. They are heavy fibres very flammable and printed easily.

Natural Protein Fibres (wool) These fibres have an animal origin and they resist wrinkling. They are hygroscopic and comfortable in cool, damp climate, but weaker as they shrink. Natural protein fibres are harmed by dry heat. They are flame resistant and dye well.

Synthetic Fibres These are fibres made from chemicals. They are heat sensitive and they melt easily. They are resistant to moths and fungi, low absorbency and are abrasion-resistant. Synthetic fibres are strong and easy to care for. They are less expensive and readily available.

Properties Essential to Make a Fibre Each fibre has particular properties which help us to decide, which particular fibre should be used to suite a particular requirement. Certain fibre properties increase its value and desirability in its intended end-use, but are not necessary properties essential to make a fibre. Thus, it is very essential to know the individual aspects and specific properties of each kind of fibre.

Fibre Properties for Specific Requirements Utility of fibre are broadly categorised into two different uses, one is apparel or domestic use and the other is industrial use. In order to be used in each of these categories the fibre has to meet some specific requirements.

Primary Properties of Fibre

Primary properties of fibre are following :

High Length to Width Ratio Fibres must be considerably longer than they are wide to permit processing into yarns and fabrics. This quality is referred to as a high length to width or length to breadth ratio.

Tenacity Strength varies among different kinds of fibres. It must always be sufficient to withstand chemical and machine processing of the fibres as well as to provide durability in the end product.

Flexibility Fibres must be bendable, pliable or flexible, if they are to be made into yarns and fabrics that can be creased that have the quality of drapability and the capacity to move with the body and that permit freedom of movement.

Spinning Quality or Cohesiveness Cohesiveness is the ability of the fibres to stick together during fibre arranging or yarn manufacturing process. Without cohesiveness or spinning quality fibres would not hold together properly.

Uniformity For the processing of yarns, it is important that fibres be similar in length and width in spinning quality and in flexibility. Uniformity will produce even yarn and ultimately provide fabrics of uniform appearance.

Secondary Properties of Fibre

Following are the secondary properties of fibre :

Physical Shape In addition to the high length and breadth ratio the shape of a fibre includes such factors as average length, surfaces, contours, surface irregularities and cross sections. They are responsible for certain differences in yarn and fabric properties.

Specific Gravity The specific gravity of a fibre indicates the density relative to that of water. The density of water 4°C temperature is 1. Fabrics composed of fibres such as nylon or acrylic (with low density), provided all other factors are identical. The fibres with a specific gravity of less than 1 will float on water.

Luster It refers to the glass or shine that a fibre possesses. It depends upon the amount of light reflected by a fibre and determines the fibre's natural brightness or dullness. Among natural fibres, silk inherently has a high luster, cotton has a low luster, in manufactured fibres it is possible to control the degree of luster, either raising it or reducing it by means of added pigments or other modifying processes.

Moisture Regain and Moisture Absorption Most textile fibres have a certain amount of water as an internal part of their structure. This water is called **'Moisture regain'** and is expressed as a percentage of the weight of the moisture- free fibre. The following table provides an evaluative view on the properties of some common textile fibres :

Classification of Fibres

There are two broad classification of fibre shown below :

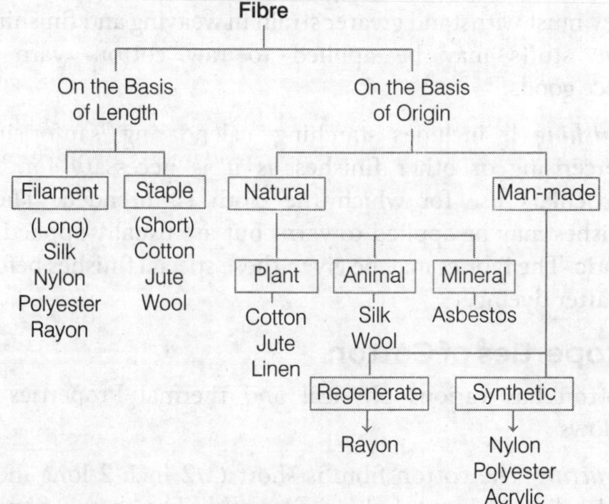

On the Basis of Length

A fibre can be described as any substance natural or manufactured that is suitable for being processed into a fabric. Fibre properties include length (staple or filament), size and surface contour. These properties affect the end use such as serviceability, aesthetics, durability, comfort, retention and care.

To create a fabric, fibres are spun into yarns and then woven into fabric. Through these processes a fabric's characteristics can be manipulated through blending and other methods. Look through a microscope and the secret to any fabric is beneath the surface.

Filament Fibres

All fibres having a practically unlimited or infinite length are called filaments. Filament fibres are continuous (long) fibre. It may be natural like silk or synthetic like nylon. Filament fibres are measured in yards or meters.

Silk, in filament form is ruled from cocoons. Man-made fibres of a chemical composition, liquid nature are forced through spinners, hardened and produced into continuous filament strands of a determined length. When filament fibres are planned to be cut into staple fibres a large spinnerets with many openings are used.

The filament fibres are grouped into a bundle referred to as a low and then cut into the desired staple length. Line or low man-made fibres are manufactured in continuous strands of any desired length. The tones may be cut into staple lengths or flocks based on specific end use.

Staple Fibres

Any fibre with a practically limited or finite length is called 'staple fibre'. These are small length fibre like cotton, wool, jute, etc, it may be natural (cotton) or man-made (viscose rayon, polyester). The length of the fibre varies within fibre of the same source and also between varieties obtained from different sources. Staple fibres are measured in inches or centimeters.

Staple fibre include almost all natural fibres except silk. Silk is a natural filament fibre and may be cut up to form short staple fibres. Staple fibres must be spun or twisted together to make a long continuous strand of yarn. They may also be used in their staple form to produce non-woven or felted fabrics. Staple is fibre of cotton wool or ramie, etc., of no more than a few inches long.

On the Basis of Origin

Fibres are classified on the basis of their origin. It can be natural or man-made . Those fibres which are obtained from the natural origin directly or indirectly referred to as natural fibres. Whereas, man-made are those which are made by man according to requirement. They are of two types :

Man-made Fibres Man-made fibres are those fibres which are developed by man. Their chemical composition, structure and properties are changed during manufacturing process. e.g. rayon, nylon, polyster, etc.

Natural Fibres Natural fibres include cotton, linen, flax, wool (any form of animal hair including human hair, not just sheep wool as most associate with wool) and various other minor novelty fibres such as hemp and spun corn. These fibres you can pick up and spin right into a fabric.

Natural Fibres

Natural origin fibres are sub-classified into three different categories i.e., cellulosic fibres derived from plants, protein fibres derived form animals and minerals fibres.

Cellulosic Plant Fibres

Cotton, linen and jute are main examples of cellulosic fibres.

The description of their manufacturing process, properties and uses is given below :

Cotton

Cotton is obtained by plant source and it is classified as a natural material as it is obtained from the cellulose seed fibre. Staple fibre measuring 10- 65mm in length and white to beige in colour in its natural state. It is composed basically of a substance called cellulose. As cotton occupies 50% of the consumption of fibres by weight in the world it is called as the king of all fibres.

Cotton is the fabric for every home and is the most widely produced of textile fabrics today. It has now been proved that India was the first country to manufacture cotton. Among the recent findings at Mohenjo-Daro were a few scrapes of cotton sticking to the side of a silver vase. Cotton is the white downy covering of the seed grown in the pods.

The cotton plant grown in the tropics needs a climate with 6 months of summer weather to blossom and produce pods.

Manufacturing Process of Cotton

The manufacturing process of cotton involves following steps :

Preparation The fibres are first removed from seeds in a gin. This process is called ginning. Every bit of the cotton fibre is used in the manufacture. The fibre mass is then compressed into bales and shipped into spinning mills.

The short ends left on the seeds after the longer fabric. Fibres have been removed, are used in the production of rayon, plastics, dynamite and many other by products, which are then used in the production of seed oil, hydrogenated fats, soaps and cosmetics.

Forming the Laps In the step dirt from cotton fibre is removed and fibres are made into a soft roll or lap. Then several laps are combined into one.

Carding These fibres are drawn together to form a loose rope called sliver.

Doubling Slivers are combined here for uniformity.

Combing This process is continuation and refinement of carding process. All cotton yarns for fabrics are carded but not all are combed. Yarns that are combed are finer even and free from all woody stalk of the plant. They are used for finer quality fabrics such as voile and organdie. Fabrics made from these fabrics are expensive too. The slivers are called carded slivers.

Drawing The slivers is then combined, smoothened and stretched. The slivers may be drawn reduced further in size and given a slight twist by a process called roving in which the slivers is passed through rollers and wound on to bobbins set into spindles. It is done in a speed frame.

Roving The bobbins are placed on the roving frame where further drawing and twisting takes place until the cotton stock is about a pencil lead in diameter.

Spinning Done on the spinning frame where the stock passes through sets of high speed rollers and gives the yarn of desired thickness.

Weaving and Dying The yarn is then knitted or woven in any one of the variety of weaves and structures. Warp yarn are usually more strongly twisted than filling yarn since they must withstand greater strain in weaving and finishing. Dye stuffs may be applied to raw cotton, yarn or piece goods.

Finishing It includes starching, calendaring, sanforising, mercerising or other finishes as it is necessary for the particulars use for which the cloth is intended. These finishes may be applied to yarns but are usually applied to fabric. The fabrics may be given these special finishes before or after dyeing.

Properties of Cotton

Cotton has various physical and thermal Properties as follows :

Structure The cotton fibre is short (1/2 inch-2 long inch) and cylindrical or tubular as it grows. The cotton fibre is essentially cellulose consisting of carbon, hydrogen and oxygen. Bleached cotton is almost pure cellulose raw cotton contains about 5% of impurities.

Strength Cotton fibre is relatively strong which is due to the intricate structure and 70% crystalline.

Elasticity Cotton is relatively inelastic because of its crystalline polymer system and for this reason cotton textile wrinkle and crease readily.

Hygroscopic Moisture Cotton does not hold moisture so well as wool or silk but absorbs it and so feels damp much more quickly. It also rapidly spreads throughout the material.

Electrical Property The hygroscopic nature ordinarily prevents cotton textile materials from developing static electricity.

Absorbency As cotton has cellulose it is a good absorbent of fibre.

Drap Ability Cotton does not have good body to drape well in shape. The type of construction of the fabric may improve this property.

Resilience Cotton wrinkles easily some wrinkle resistant finishes may reduce this property.

Cleanliness and Wash Ability Though cotton absorbs dust due to its rough nature. It can be washed easily in the hot water and strong soaps without damaging the fibre.

Lustre The natural cotton has no pronounced lustre. This can be improved by the mercerisation finish of the cotton (that is sodium hydroxide treatment).

Shrinkage The fibre itself does not shrink but cotton fibre which has been stretched in the finishing process tends to relax back creating shrinkage.

Heat Conductivity Cotton is the better conductor of heat than wool or silk but not as good as rayon.

Uses of Cotton

Important end needs of cotton are as follows :

Home Furnishing Towels are most common as it is high in absorbency, wide range of colours, washability and durability. Sheets and pillow cases are mostly blends of cotton with polyester or made of pure cotton.

Drapes, curtains and upholstery fabrics are made of cotton and its blends. Since, cotton can be auto claved at high temperatures, absorbency, washability and low static build up are important factors for use of cotton in hospitals.

Wide Range of Wearing Apparels Many apparels are made of cotton like blouses, shirts, dresses, napkins, sheets, bedspreads, etc.

Linen

Linen is a highly absorbant and strong fibre. It is obtained from the stalk or stem of the *Liman lesistatissimuni.* Flax for fibre is pulled by hand or by mechanical pullers to keep the roots intact, for the fibres extend below ground surface.

Manufacturing Process of Linen

The manufacturing process of linen involves following steps :

Reting For obtaining fibres from the stalk, one must remove the outer woody portion. This process is known as retting.

Retting can be accomplished by several procedures as follows :

- **Dew Retting** It involves exposing the fibres to the action of dew and sunlight. This requires four to six weeks.
- **Pool Retting** The flax is packed in sheaves and immersed in pools of stagnant water. It requires two-four weeks.
- **Tank Retting** The fibre is stacked in large tanks and covered with warm water. It requires few days.
- **Chemical Retting** It requires the fibres to be stacked in tank and covered with a chemical solution which will ret the fibre in a few hours.

Passing Through Fluted pillars After retting, flax is passed between fluted pillars. These rollers help breaking the woody covering into small particles.

Sotching After this scotching process takes place i.e. the other covering is sparated from the spinable fibres.

Combing Once scotching is complete, the flax fibres are hackled or combed. This combing helps in separating the short fibres called two, from long fibres called line.

Spinning After this, the flax fibres are drawn out into yarn and twist is imparted.

The spinning of flax fibres is of two types :

- Dry spinning
- Wet spinning

Wet spinning is considered to give the best quality yarn.

Properties of Linen

Linen is comfortable, good strength, twice as strong as cotton, hand-washable or dry-cleanable, crisp hand tailors, well absorbent of dyes and prints, well light weight to heavy weight, no static or pilling problems, fair abrasion resistant etc.

The physical properties of linen are as follows :

Tensile Strength Linen is a strong fibre. It has a tenacity of 5.5 to 6.5 gm/den. The strength is greater than cotton fiber.

Elongation at Break Linen does not stretch easily. It has an elongation at break of 2.7 to 3.5 %.

Colour The colour of linen fiber is yellowish to grey.

Length 18 to 30 inch in length.

Lusture It is brighter than cotton fiber and it is slightly silky.

Elastic Recovery Linen fibre has not enough elastic recovery properties like cotton fibre.

Specific Gravity Specific gravity of linen fiber is 1.50.

Moisture Regain (MR %) Standard moisture regain is 10 to 12%.

Resiliency Very poor

Effect of Heat Linen has an excellent resistance to degradation by heat. It is less affected than cotton fibre by the heat.

Effect of Sun Light Linen fibre is not affected by the sun light as others fibre. It has enough ability to protect sun light.

Uses of Linen

Important end uses of linen are as follows :

Tablecloths Linen has been used as a tablecloth in households for several years now. It is preferred over cotton or other fabrics as it proves to be more durable. It is able to absorb water very quickly and does not get damaged by any liquid spills easily which makes it an ideal choice.

Napkins Just like tablecloth, napkins are able to soak up spills on the dinner table easily and effectively. The spills and wetness does not damage the cloth making them an ideal choice for use of clearing up after a meal.

Clothing Linen clothing is a popular choice, especially in warm climate countries. Its construction is lightweight and it allows for air to pass through, which gives the user a cooling effect in hot weather. Also, as it is easily able to absorb moisture, it can absorb the sweat off the users skin very fast, providing a very cooling effect. It is commonly used in the manufacture of shirts, t-shirts, pants and even dresses.

Decoration Linen has a very nice texture which allows for it to be used in decorating of homes. One could take any unwanted linen that is meant to be disposed and make decorative items out of it. Using linen that has different colours and design could add to the decorative element. Not only as coasters but the unwanted material can even be used as tablecloths or floor mats.

Cleaning and Storage of Linens Proper care of household linens is important no matter what purpose they serve. If a linen cloth is used as a tablecloth or napkin, it may frequently encounter stains from foods, drinks or even oils. Stains that occur from regular foods or drinks can be easily rinsed off immediately, however stains that occur from red wines or berries are usually more stubborn and difficult to get rid off. Washing the cloth on hot water may help to get rid of these stains.

Jute

Jute fibre is a natural fibre. It is one of the most affordable natural fibres and is second only to cotton in amount produced and variety of uses of vegetable fibres. It is harder than other textile fibres. It is environment friendly. Normally jute are used for sacking, burlap, and twine as a backing material for tufted carpets. Jute is a long staple fibre. It is widely used natural fibre after cotton. This fibre is hard and stiff used for all types of packaging materials and also some home textile manufacturing. This fiber is varied by its length, fineness, colour and strength. Jute fibre contains small amount of impurities.

Manufacturing Process of Jute

Manufacturing process of jute involves following steps :

Selection/Batching As jute grown in different areas varies in strength, colour and fineness, the first step in preparing the fibre is 'batching', consisting of blending the various fibers to obtain uniformity in strength and colour to give the precise quality of yarn for spinning.

This involves the opening of various qualities of bales. These are then examined, sorted and mixed to form various batches.

Softening In the first mechanical operation in the mill, the jute is fed into a softener in which the jute, treated with an emulsion oil and water, passes between sets of heavy spiral fluted rollers. This process renders the fiber thoroughly pliant and removes any barky portions adhering to the fibre. The piled jute is cut in order to remove the roots.

Carding The fibres are then carded in machines, known as breaker cards and finisher cards, which reduces the average length of the fibres by teasing and combing and deliver them in the form of a long continuous ribbon, 5″ or 6″ in width, called sliver.

Drawing The carded jute is next fed into drawing machines in three stages through the first, second and third drawing frames which draw out and attenuate the sliver, parallelise the fibres, and by means of a doubling process, produce a smoother, more even sliver.

However, in case of sacking weft, the passage through, drawing frame is only done twice i.e, through first and second drawing frames.

Spinning The last operation in the preparing department is spinning, a process which imparts a slight twist to the sliver and delivers the material on to bobbins in the form of rove, a loose yarn ready for spinning. The spinning machinery known as silver spinning, an extra drawing operation delivers a crimped sliver, which can be fed direct to the sliver spinning form. Spinning frames convert the rove to finished yarn.

Beaming After spinning, the yarns are wound into the form required spools for warp yarn and cops for weft yarn - for subsequent processing. Jute yarn is processed much like other textile fibers, the yarn itself being dressed (i.e, sized or starched), before being passed on to the warp beam ready for weaving.

Weaving Jute fabrics are of simple construction and are woven on a variety of looms. Woven fabrics are inspected, damped and calendared to produce the desired smoothness of finish.

Sewing The woven cloth is then folded in the desired length, packed in bales by hydraulic press, covered with gunny cloth for protection and stored in godowns (warehouses) to await shipment. Where jute goods are sold in the form of bags, the woven cloth is cut to the required size and then hemmed, sewn and hand stitched. These bags are folded and packed in bales. All such goods are then stored in the finished goods godown and are dispatched as per the delivery schedule.

Properties of Jute

Properties of jute are as follows :

- Jute fibre is 100% bio-degradable and recyclable and thus environment friendly.
- Jute is a natural fibre with golden and silky shine. Hence called **The Golden Fibre**.
- Jute is the cheapest vegetable fibre procured from the bast or skin of the plant's stem.
- It is the second most important vegetable fibre after cotton, in terms of usage, global consumption, production, and availability.
- It has high tensile strength, low extensibility, and ensures better breathability of fabrics. Therefore, jute is very suitable in agricultural commodity and bulk packaging.
- It helps to make best quality industrial yarn, fabric, net, and sacks. It is one of the most versatile natural fibres that has been used in raw materials for packaging, textiles, non-textile, construction, and agricultural sectors. Bulking of yarn results in a reduced breaking tenacity and an increased breaking extensibility when blended as a ternary blend.
- Jute is one of the most versatile natural fibres that has been used in raw materials for packaging, textiles, non-textile, and agricultural sectors.

Uses of Jute

Important end uses of jute are as follows :

- Jute is used chiefly to make cloth for wrapping and to make sacks and coarse cloth.
- The fibres are also woven into curtains, chair coverings, carpets, area rugs, hessian cloth, and backing for linoleum.
- While jute is being replaced by synthetic materials in many of these uses, some uses take advantage of jute's biodegradable nature, where synthetics would be unsuitable.
- Jute butts, the coarse ends of the plants, are used to make inexpensive cloth.
- Traditionally, jute was used in traditional textile machineries as textile fibres having cellulose (vegetable fibre content) and lignin (wood fibre content). But, the major breakthrough came when the automobile, pulp and paper, the furniture and bedding industries started using jute and its allied fibres with their non-woven and composite technology to manufacture non-wovens, technical textiles, and composites.
- Jute can be used to create a number of fabrics such as Hessian cloth, sacking, scrim, Carpet Backing Cloth (CBC), and canvas.
- Hessian, lighter than sacking, is used for bags, wrappers, wall coverings, upholstery, and home furnishings.
- Sacking, a fabric made of heavy jute fibres, has its use in the name.

Other Cellulosic Fibres

Ramie and Hemp are also other important cellulosic fibres but are lesser used than cotton, linen and jute. Their description is given below :

Ramie

It is a bast fibre and has been cultivated for hundreds of years in China and Formosa. It is commonly known as **'China gauss'**. It is a member of a netcle family as is a perennial shrub that can be cut several times a season after the necessary preliminary growth.

After cutting the ramie stalks are decorticated by either hand or machine. Decortication consists of peeling away on bealing the bark to free the bast fibre. Fibres are then dried in the sun for bleaching. Later on, the fibres are degummed in caustic soda to remove pectins and waxes. Finally, they are washed and dried. Ramie fabrics sometimes resemble fine lines on they can be heavy and coarse like canvas.

Hemp

Hemp was much used by the people of Asia. It is a tough plant and grows in climates where temperatures are warm or hot. The processing of hemp is very similar to that of flex. It begins with retting i.e. loosening the outer covering followed by stripping or scotching to obtain the usable fibres. The final step is of drawing and spinning of fibres into yarns. The fibre is dark tan or brown and is difficult to bleach. It can be dyed bright and dark colours. Shorten fibres are used for some domestic fabrics especially in under developed countries. Longer hemp fibres are used in industrial yarns and fabrics, i.e. canvas, twiner, sacking and ropes. The process of hemp manufacturing is same as flux/linen. Being stronger then linen or jute, it is ideal for twine, ropes, cables, carpets, canvas, ship cordage and sailcloth as it is not weakened on rotten by water. Today, even fine fabrics are made from hemp.

Protein (Animal) Fibres

Protein fibres are formed by natural animal sources through condensation of a amino acids to form repeating polyamide units with various substituents on a carbon atom. In general, protein fibres are fibres of moderate strength, resiliency and elasticity. They have excellent moisture absorbency and transport characteristics. They do not build up a static charge. Example of some of these fibres are wool, silk, mohair, cashmere llama, alpaca and Vicuna.

Wool

Wool is one of the first fibres to be converted into fabric. Wool fibre grows from skin of sheep. It is composed of protein known as keratin. It is crimp and has scales on its surface depending upon the breed of sheep. The natural protein fibre consists of amino acids.

Wool has 19 amino acids, keratin, protein and other organic acids. Man uses wool as clothing in the very early stages of human history. The primitive man has used it in the form of skin of certain animals to protect as well as to decorate his body. Man then discovered the use of hair of sheep after interlocking and twisting them together under pressure and thus hair of sheep were used in making fabrics The interlocking of woolen fabrics is known as '**felting**'.

Manufacturing Process of Wool

Manufacturing process of wool involves following steps :

Shearing Sheep are generally shorn of their fleeces in spring but the time of shearing differs in different parts of the world. Machine clippers remove the fleece faster and closer than hand clippers. Superior wool variety comes from the sides and shoulders where it grows longer, finer and softer is treated as good quality fleece. Wool from the chest, belly and shanks is treated as a second fleece.

Preparation An average about 8 pounds of fleece is made from one sheep. Then the fibers are packed in bags or bales. The raw wool or newly sheared fleece is called Grease wool because it contains the natural oil of the sheep. When Grease wool is washed, it loses from 20 to 80% of its original weight. The grease known as yolk is widely used in the pharmaceutical industries for lanolin compounds.

Sorting and Grading Skilled workers do wool sorting. Each grade is determined by type, length, fineness, elasticity and strength. Separating of fibre by touch and sight.

Scouring Washing of raw wool is an alkaline solution is known as scouring. The wool is treated with warm water, soap, mild solution of soda ash or other alkali to remove dirt in the fibres. If the raw wool is not sufficiently clear of vegetable, substance after scouring is put through the carbonising bath.

The fibres are then put through a dilute solution of sulphuric or hydrochloric acid which destroys any vegetable. This process is called as carbonising and resultant wool is called 'extract'. To remove the Grease and dirt in raw wool it is put through a series of naphtha balls followed by clear water to remove the naphtha. This is called naphtalation. This process improves the dye up take property of wool.

Garnetting Recycled wool fibres are obtained by separately reducing the unused and used fibrous mass by a picking and shredding process called garnetting.

Drying Wool is not allowed to become absolutely dry usually about 12 to 16% of moisture is left in wool to condition it for subsequent handling.

Oiling As wool is un manageable after scouring the fibre is usually treated with various oils including animals, vegetable, mineral or a blend of these to keep it from being becoming brittle lubricate it for the spinning operation.

Dyeing If the wool to be dyed in raw stock it is dyed at this stage. Some wool fabrics piece dyed, some are yarn or skin dyed and some are top dyed.

Blending Wool of different grades or pure wool fibres and other textile fibers may be blended mixed together at this point. All the information should be present on the labels.

Carding The carding process introduces the classification of woolen yarns and worsted yarns. It makes the fibre parallel and some amount of dirt is removed due to straightening of fibres. Fibres are used for the worsted yarn are more straightened than the wool yarns.

Gelling and Combing The carded wool which is to be made into worsted yarn is put through gelling and combing operations. The gelling process removes the shorter staple and straightens the fibre. This process removes short fibres from 1 to 4 inch length places the long fibre as parallel as possible and further cleans the fibre by removing any remaining loose impurities.

Drawing It is an advanced operation for worsted yarns which doubles and redoubles slivers of wool fibres. The process draws, drafts, twists and winds the stock making slivers more compact and thinning them into slubbers.

Roving This is the final stage before spinning roving is actually a light twisting operation to hold thin slubbers intact.

Spinning In the spinning operation, the wool roving is drawn out and twisted into yarn. Woolen yarns are chiefly spun on the mule-spinning machine are worsted yarns are spun on any kind of spinning machine mule, ring, cap or flyer.

Properties of Wool

Properties of wool are as follows :

Strength It is stronger than silk. When wet wool looses about 25% of its strength. Longer the fibre the greater will be the strength of yarn.

Resiliency Wool is highly resilient and comes to its original shape when hanged after wrinkled or created.

Stretchability Wool is highly elastic. It is about 10 to 30% stretched when dry and 40 to 50% when wet upon receiving pressure upon drying it readily regains its original dimensions.

Shrink Ability Wool is resistant shrinkage. However long exposure to moisture may cause shrinkage.

Effect of Friction Friction will soften the wool fibre especially when wet and thus is advantageous in maintaining smooth, soft texture of fabrics.

Crimps Wool fibre is more or less wavy and has twists. This waviness termed as 'crimp'. Finer the wool the more will be the crimps in it. Merino wool has 30 crimps per inch while coarse wool has one or two.

Effect of Moisture Wool is the most hygroscopic in nature. It can absorb up to 50% of its weight and carry upto 20% weight, without giving the feeling of being wet. Upon drying it losses moisture slowly preventing rapid evaporation thus avoiding chilling feel to the user. It absorbs perspiration after violent exercise and guards the body against sudden change in temperature.

Heat Conductivity Wool fibre is a part of poor conductor of heat and therefore the fabrics made from the fibre are considered most suitable as winter wear.

Felting Wool fibres interlock and contract when exposed to heat, moisture, and pressure. The scale like exterior of the fibres contributes of felting. The fibres get softened in weak alkaline solutions due to expansion of scales at their free edges, with friction and pressure they again interlock to form a felt. This property is used in making felts for hats, shoes, floor-coverings and sound proofing purposes.

Effect of Heat Low heat has no effect but strong heat weakens the fibre and destroys the colour of the fibre.

Uses of Wool

Important end uses of wool are follows :

- The majority of wool (72.8%) is used in apparel, home furnishing account for (15-45%) industrial uses (6 to 7%) and exports (5%), wool account for (3.3%)of all fibres for apparel.
- The most important use of wool is for apparel coats, jackets, suits, dresses, shirts, slacks made from woven fabrics of varying weights and knitted fabrics. All these give the warmth garments and with goods tailored look.
- In the home furnishing area the major use of wool is in carpets and rugs where wool is used more, coven to the carpets and warm in the rugs.
- Blends of different synthetic fibres with wool for suiting materials are increasingly important. This result in fabrics that are more appropriate in warmer conditions.

Silk

Silk is considered as 'Queen of all textile fibres' as it has beauty and elegance and good properties of performance. Silk is the natural protein fiber obtained from silk worm cocoons. Japan is known for producing best variety of silk. India produces different varieties of silk and is famous for hand woven silk textiles.

There is a tremendous silk production increase in recent years. The production of silk is called Sericulture. To obtain quality and quantity of silk rearing conditions are controlled carefully throughout the life cycle of silk moth.

These are two types of silk mulberry or cultivated silk and wild silk. Cultivated silk is creamy silk white or yellowish white in colour. White wild silk colour range from brownish to golden yellow in colour.

Production of Silk

Silk worms feed on mulberry tree leaves and therefore for rearing them, the growing of mulberry trees is the first essential step. These are grown by the agriculturists.

Silk worms have a short life of only about two months and during which these pass through the following four stages :

1. Egg
2. Worm or larvae
3. Pupa and
4. Moths.

Silk moth and eggs

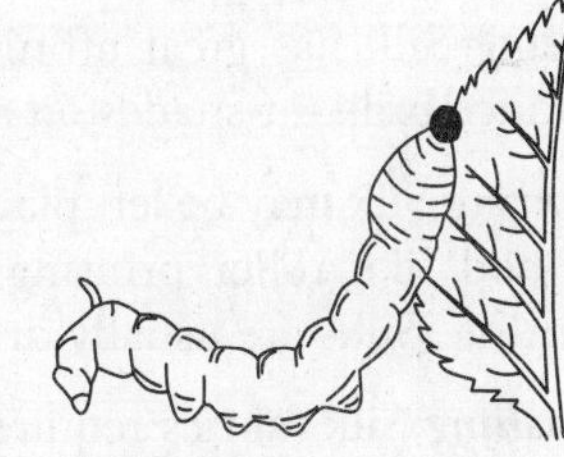

Area of Italian Bombyx mori silk worm moth

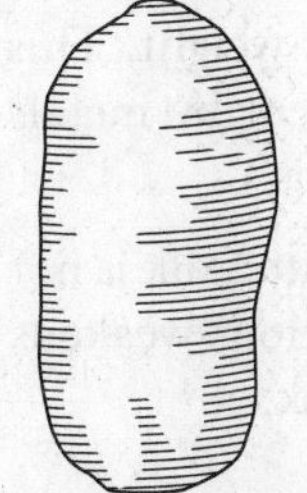

Cocoon of Bombyx mori

Male Bombyx mori or mulberry-feeding silk worm moth

Manufacturing Process of Silk

Manufacturing process of silk involves following steps :

Reeling The process of unwinding the filament from the cocoon is called reeling. The care and skill in the reeling operation prevents defects in the raw silk. As the filament of single cocoon is too fine for commercial use, three to ten strands are usually reeled at a time to produce the desired diameter of raw silk thread. Several cocoons are placed in hot water to soften the gum and the surfaces are brushed lightly to find the ends the filaments. These ends are collected, threaded through a guide and wound on to a wheel called 'reel'.

Throwing As the fibres are combined and pulled on to the reel, twist can be inserted to hold the filaments together. This is called as throwing and the resulting yarn is 'thrown yarn'. This yarn later goes to weaving or knitting industry based the type of yarn produced.

Spinning Short ends of silk fibres from the outer and inner edges of the cocoons and from broken cocoons are spun into yarns in a manner similar to that used for cotton. This is called spun silk.

Degumming Sericin or gum up to 30% of the weight of the silk fibre. It is not usually removed until after the cloth is woven because serves as warp sizing that protects the yarns from mechanical injury during weaving. Sericin remains on the fibre during reeling and throwing before finishing, the gum is removed by boiling the fabric in soap and water. The presence of gum and sericin increases the tendency for the silk to water spots on fabrics when ironed.

Bleaching Silk thread is treated with hydrogen peroxide.

Dyeing Silk has great affinity for the dyes. Acid dyes produce brilliant shades on silk.

Printing Silk may be left plain or may be printed by any method like roller printing, screen printing or block printing. Silks are usually dried and then printed.

Finishing Silk fabrics require very few finishes because they have natural lustre, softness and drapability.

Weighting of Silk When silk is boiled to remove the excess of natural gum or sericin it looses weight. This loss of weight is replaced through treatment by metals like tin, aluminium, etc., in water solutions.

These are not removed by washing. Weighted silk is not durable because sunlight and perspiration weakens fibres. Heavy weighting causes silk to crack.

Properties of Silk

Properties of silk are as follows :

Strength Silk is the strongest natural fibre. It has a tenacity of 2.4 to 5.1 grams per denier. Moreover smoothness of the silk filament yarn reduces the problem of wear from abrasion. The strength of the spun silk yarns depends on the length of silk staple.

Shape and Appearance Silk filaments are very fine and long. They frequently measure about 1000 to 1300 yards in length. The width of the silk is from 9 to 11 microns.

Elasticity It is an elastic fibre and its elasticity varies. Silk fibre may be stretched from 17 to 15 its original length before breaking. Cultivated degummed silk viewed longitudinally under a microscopic, resembles a smooth transparent rod under microscope. Silk in the gum has rough irregular surface. Wild silk tend to be quite uneven and is some what dark. It may have longitudinal striations.

Resilience Silk retains the shape and resists wrinkling rather well. This is more in fabrics made from pure silk rather than spun silk or weighted silk.

Drapabilty Silk has a pliability and suppleness that aided by its elasticity and resilience gives it excellent drapability.

Heat Conductivity Since silk is a protein fibre. It is a non-conductor of heat like wool. Hence, it is used for winter apparel.

Absorbency The good absorbtive property of silk also contributes to its effect in warmer atmosphere. Silk generally absorbs about 11% of its weight in moisture which makes silk for easy dying and printing.

Cleanliness and Wash Ability Silk is hygienic material because its smooth surface does not attract dirt. It can also be easily cleaned by mild soaps and dry cleaning.

Shrinkage Due to the filament in length, smooth surface silk have normal shrinkage which can be easily restored by ironing at moderate heat and damp conditions.

Effect of Light Continuous exposure to light weakens silk faster then either cotton or wool.

Uses of Silk

Important end uses of silk are as follows :

- Silk is an expensive luxuary fabric used for making different garments. Silk is used primarily in apparel and home furnishing items because of its appearance and cost.
- Silk is extremely versatile and can be used to create a variety of fabrics from sheer chiffons to heavy beautiful brocades and velvets.

- Silk has absorbency due to which it is appropriate for warm weather wear. Because of its low conductivity, it is used for cold weather wear, also in furnishing, silk is often blended with other fibres to add soft luster for furnishing fabric.
- Occasionally, expensive handmade rugs are made from silk.

Mohair

Mohair is a very resilient hair fibre obtained from the angora goat. The two primary classifications for mohair are the finer kid mohair and the coarser adult mohair. In many respects, mohair resembles wool in structure and possesses properties including the characteristic scale structure of the fiber. The average length of mohair fibres is longer than wool.

Cashmere

Cashmere is the fine, soft inner coat of down obtained from the cashmere goat found on the inner plateaus of Asia. In many ways, the properties of cashmere resemble those of wool, but cashmere fibres are extremely fine and soft compared to wool. Cashmere is used in luxury applications where a soft, warm, fine fiber with beautiful drape is desired.

Llama, Alpaca and Vicuna

These fibres come from a group of related animals found in South America. They are fine fibers that are white to tan and brown in colour. They are longer than most wool fibers and generally stronger, with a finer scale structure. They are generally used only in the expensive luxury items of textiles and apparel.

Mineral Fibres

They are the inorganic materials shaped in to fibres and are mainly used in the fire proof fabrics. Asbestos is the example of mineral fibre.

Mineral fibres are fire proof, resistant to acids and are used for industrial purposes. The common feature of these fibres is their inorganic or metallic composition and tendency to be heat resistant and non-flammable, with the exception of polymercoated metallic fibers.

Asbestos

Asbestos is a naturally occurring mineral that can be pulled into a fluffy consistency. Asbestos fibers are soft and flexible yet resistant to heat, electricity and corrosion. These qualities make the mineral useful, but they also make asbestos exposure highly toxic. Pure asbestos is an effective insulator, and it can be used in cloth, paper, cement, plastic and other materials to make them stronger. But when someone inhales or ingests asbestos dust, the mineral fibres can become forever trapped in their body.

Over decades, trapped asbestos fibres can cause inflammation, scarring and eventually genetic damage to the body's cells. A rare and aggressive cancer called mesothelioma is almost exclusively caused by asbestos exposure. Asbestos also causes other forms of cancer as well as progressive lung disease. Microscopic asbestos fibers cannot be seen, smelled or tasted, and it is unsafe to sniff a substance suspected of being asbestos. To detect asbestos, a sample of questionable material must be sent to a lab for testing.

Although, it has low strength, asbestos fibre does not deteriorate in normal usage, and it is not attacked by insects or micro-organisms. Asbestos is used in fireproof clothing, conveyor belts, brake linings, gaskets, industrial packings, electrical windings, insulations, and soundproofing materials.

Inhaled asbestos fibers have been shown to be a serious health hazard, and it has been removed from the textiles market.

Man-Made Fibres

Man-made fibres are types that come from cellulose and protein such as **Rayon** and **Acetate**.

Common man-made fibres include polyester, microfibres and nylon. Special use fibres are less common, but people may not realise that they come into contact with them on a daily basis. Surprisingly fibres such as rubber are used in spandex, Metal such as stainless steel is used in carpets and other metals such as silver and gold are woven into fabrics. Man-made fibres are categorised as regenerated and synthetic fibres.

Regenerated Fibres

Regenerated synthetic textile fibres are called those fibres which are made up of naturally long chain polymer structure, which are modified and partially degraded by chemical process. e.g. Rayon.

Rayon

Rayon was the first manufactured fibre in 1949 and is also known as *artificial silk* since, it was developed to mimic the costly silk fabrics of the time. Many people consider Rayon a natural fibre, but technically, it is not. Rayon is spun from naturally occurring polymers that replicates a natural fibre.

Manufacture of Rayon

All types of rayon are made from cellulose. There are four main procedures by which cellulose is transformed into rayon. They are :

- The nitrocellulose process
- The cuprammonium process
- The viscose process
- The cellulose acetate process

The general principles of rayon yarn production involve the following steps:

- To treat cellulose chemically for rendering from it a liquid
- Force the liquid through fine holes
- To change from liquid stream into solid cellulose filaments

Viscose Process

The largest production of rayon today is manufactured by this process. The cost is low.

This is discovered in 1892 in England. In this process Spruce, a type of tree chips are used. Spruce logs are reduced to wood pulp and purified for cellulose base. Wood pulp is treated with caustic soda to form alkali cellulose.

It is treated with carbon disulphide to form cellulose xanthate. This is dissolved in dilute caustic soda solution. A reddish or orange liquid is formed. This liquid is filtered and then kept for ageing until a thick fluid is formed which is called 'Viscose'. This fluid is forced through fine jets into a dilute solution of sulphuric acid. In this way, cellulose is regenerated into continuous fibres.

Properties of Rayon

Strength The tensile strength of viscose rayon is greater than that of wool but is only half as great as silk. Viscose rayon is also weaker than cotton and its strength is reduced from 40 to 70 percent when wet. Yet, it produces fairly durable, economical and serviceable fabric whose smoothness of surface favourably withstands with friction of wear.

Elasticity Viscose rayon has greater elasticity than cotton but less than wool and silk. While viscose rayon fabrics have some inherent extensibility, undue strain might cause them to sag or even burst.

Resilience Viscose rayon lacks the resilience. It should be remembered that the resistance of a fabric to creasing depends on the kind of yarn, weave and finishing process.

Drapability Viscose rayon possesses a marked quality of drapability because it is relatively heavy weight fabric.

Heat Conductivity Viscose rayon is a good conductor of heat and is therefore appropriate for summer clothing like cotton.

Absorbency Viscose rayon is one of the most absorbent of all textiles. It is more absorbent than cotton or linen, but less than wool and silk.

Reaction to Bleaches Household bleaches containing sodium hypochlorite, sodium perborate or hydrogen peroxide may be safely used.

Shrinkage Viscose rayon fabrics tend to shrink more than cotton fabrics. Spun Viscose rayon fabrics shrink more, which can be given a shrink resistant finish, such as Sanforset.

Effect of Heat Viscose rayon is pure cellulose fiber which burns as cotton. When ironing, only moderately hot temperature must be used.

Uses of Rayon

Apparel Accessories, blouses, dresses, jackets, lingreie, sport shirt, sportwear, suit, ties, work clothes.

Home Furnishing Bed spreads, blankets, curtains, draperies, sheets, slipcovers, table clothes, upholstery.

Industrial Uses Industrial products, medical products, non-woven products.

Other Uses Feminine hygine products.

It is used in industrial wiper, medical supplies, including bandages, diapers, sanitary napkin and tampons in non-woven fabrics.

Synthetic Fibres

Synthetic fibers are a subset of the larger area of textile. They are man-made fibres composed of chemicals . They are generally based on polymers and are stronger than natural and regenerated fibres. e.g. Polyester, nylon, acrylic, etc.

Polyester

Polyester fibre is the long chain polymer produced from elements derived from coal, air, water and petroleum. Polyester is a thermoplastic fibre and has good strength. It melts in flame and forms a grey hard non-crushable bead. It is an easy care fabric and can be easily washed. Polyester fibre looks like a smooth, glass rod similar to Nylon. If delustered it shows black spotted appearance. The length, width, shape and luster of the polyester fibres are controlled during manufacture to suit a specific end use. It is mostly blended with other fibres to improve its absorbency and to lower static electricity.

Method of Manufacture

Generally, each company produces its own variety of polyester though there are modifications under specific trademarks. PET (Principle raw material is ethylene diamine and terepthalic acid) obtained from petroleum and PCDT polyester.

Spinning of Fibre

The molten polymer is rigourously maintained at airtight condition, as oxygen will affect its stability. The viscous melt is extruded through spinneret, and the filaments are subsequently drawn into desired polyester fibre. Variations in production process depends on desired end results. The holes of spinneret may be round or modified to be trilobal, pentagonal, hexagonal or octagonal shapes so as achieve specific effects such a greater cushioning and insulative properties. Other properties may be obtained with the aid of specific additives given to the spinning solution.

Upon extrusion of spinneret, the polyester filament does not have all the desired characteristics because of random arrangement of polymer molecules. The fibres are therefore drawn or elongated with the aid of godet wheels. The temperature conditions and the extent to which the fibres are drawn to 5 times their original length.

Properties of Polyester

Shape and Appearance These fibres are generally round and uniform : The fibre is partially transparent and white to slightly off-white in colour.

Strength The PET polyesters are in general, stronger. Polyester is found in industrial uses and the highly durable fabrics.

Elasticity Polyester fibres do not have high degree of elasticity. In general, polyester fibre is characterised as having a high degree of stretch resistance, which means that polyester fabrics are not likely to stretch out of shape too easily.

Resilience Polyester fibres have high degree of resilience. Not only does a polyester fabric resist wrinkling when dry, it also resists wrinkling when wet.

Drapability Fabrics of polyester filament have satisfactory draping quality. Polyester spun yarn is flexible and softer, thereby draping quality is improved.

Heat Conductivity Fabrics of polyester filament are good conductors of heat. Polyester staple does not provide greater insulation in the yarns and fabrics. One of the reason for apparel greater warmth of polyester is its low absorbency.

Absorbency Polyester is one of the least absorbent fibres. This low absorbency has important advantages- they will dry very fast, suited for water repellent purposes, such as rain wear and they do not stain easily.

Dimensional Stability If the polyester is properly heat set, it will not shrink, nor stretch when subjected to boiling water, boiling cleaning solvents or ironing temperatures that are lower than heat setting temperatures.

Shrinkage Polyester fabrics shrink as much as 20% during wet-finishing operations and they are generally heat set in later treatments. They have excellent dimensional stability.

Cleanliness and Washability Since, polyester fibres are generally smooth, has low absorbency, many stains lie on surface, and are easily washed, by hand or machine but oil stains are very hard to remove.

Uses of Polyester

- The most important uses of the polyester is in 'woven fabrics'. The blended fabrics are attractive, durable and comfortable, retain their appearance will and easy care.
- The first use of staple polyester was in tropical suiting for men's summer suits.
- Polyester and polyester blends are also used in home furnishings, sheets, blankets, bed spreads, curtains that match bed spreads, mattress ticking, table clothes.
- Other most important use where it is used in a fibre fill.
- It is used in pillows, comforters, bedspreads, other quilted households, and apparels, winter jackets, etc.

Nylon

The invention of nylon in 1931 created a revolution because it was the first non-cellulose fibre made directly from petrochemicals or coal. The first commercial production of nylon was in 1939 for women's hosiery. Some of the characteristics of nylon include abrasion resistance, washability, resistance to oil and most chemicals, low moisture absorbency, resistance to mildew, mold, and moths, etc. It is used for making swimmer, ski apparel, raincoats, swimwears, etc.

Acrylic

Acrylic fibers are made from acrylonitrile, a petrochemical. The combination of acrylonitrile with small amounts of other chemicals improves the ability of the fiber to absorb dyes. Acrylic fibres are unique among synthetic fibres because of they have an uneven surface. Some characteristics of acrylic include wool-like feel, softness and warmth, shape retention, quick drying, resistance to moths, sunlight, oil and chemicals, etc. It is used for making sweaters, socks, sportswear, blankets, etc.

Identification of Fibres

A number of methods are available for characterisation of the structural physical and chemical properties of fibres. Various methods are used for fibre identification like microscopic methods, solubility, heating, burning method density and staining, etc., while the end-use property characterisation methods involve use of laboratory techniques, which are adapted to simulate actual conditions of average wear on the textile or that can predict performance in end-use.

The knowledge of identifying the textile fibres helps a producer of garments to identify the type of fibre and the care to be taken in maintaining the fabrics made of particular type of fibre. This is important factor for labelling of the garments, which includes specifying the fibre content in the garment. There are different tests, which could be used for the identification of the textile fibres such as burning test, microscopic test, solubility test, optical test, density test, etc.

A number of interesting developments that have taken place in the textile industry have made process of identification more complex. Few of the methods of identifying the textile fibres are discussed below:

Feeling Test

It is a subjective test and can only be performed by one with skill in this art acquired after handling many different fabrics over a period of time-this refines the individual's perception, *e.g.* when he feels fabrics through his fingers, the warmth in the finger is retained, when the fibre is wool, but is conducted away when touching fibres like cotton, linen or rayon, the fabrics thus feel cold to touch. Cotton is cool to touch and feels soft and inelastic.

Burning Tests

The fibres being chemically different, they show different burning characteristics, which can be used to identify them.

The burning test is a relatively simple test as all that is needed is a flame and a keen observer, who should carefully watch and note down the observations made (a) when approaching the flame, (b) on the burning behaviour inside the flame. (c) during removal from the flame, (d) relating to the smell emitted and (e) on the residue life behind after the fibre has burnt out. These tests are useful and simple to perform and also provide ready identification under certain circumstances :

Microscopic Identification Positive identification of many natural fibres is possible using the microscope.

Solubility The chemical structure of polymers in a fibre determines the fibre's basic solubility characteristics.

Heating and Burning Characteristics The reaction of fibres to heat from an open flame is a useful guide in identification of fibres.

Density or Specific Gravity Fibre density may be used as an aid in fibre identification.

Staining Fibres have differing dyeing characteristics and affinities dependent on the chemical and morphological structure of the fibre.

Visual Inspection

Inspection of a fabric for appearance and hand is always the first step in fibre identification. Manufactured fibres can be made into fabrics that resemble natural fibre, fabrics and natural fibres can be changed by finishes.

Experience in using and feeling fabrics develops the ability to do a better job of verification by inspection. Look for the following things when inspecting a fabric :

- Length of fibre. Any fibre can be made into staple length but not all can be filament length.
- Lustre on lack of lustre.

Microscope Test

A knowledge of fibre structure, obtained by seeing the fibres under the microscope and observing some of the difference among fibres in each group, is of help in understanding fibre and fabric behaviour.

Directions for using microscope :

- Clean the lens, slide and cover glass.
- Place a drop of water on the slide.
- Untwist a yarn and place the loosened fibres on the slide. Cover with the cover glass and press down to eliminate air bubbles.
- Place the slide on the stage of the microscope and focus. The fibres should be well loosened, such as to enable focusing on a single fibre.
- If the fabric contains more than one kind of fibre, test each. Be sure to check warp and filling yarns.
- Observe both cross sectionally and longitudinally.

Solubility Test

Some fibres look very similar under the microscope and a solvent test may be needed to complete identification. Solubility test is very useful in fibre identification. Solubility test may be done on a slide under the microscope so that the results could easily and definitely be observed.

Introduction to Yarn

Yarn plays an important role in the fabric manufacturing process, since a majority of the textile materials is constructed with yarns. Yarn is a generic term for a continuous stand of textile or filaments or material in a form suitable for knitting, weaving or otherwise intertwining to form a textile fabric.

In short, yarn is the generic name for an assemblage of fibres that is laid or twisted together. Yarns are also used for products such as sewing and embroidery thread, string and rope. Yarns are produced in various size, texture and also vary in other characteristics. Performance end use and fabric care are affected by these yarn characteristics.

Yarn is used when the assemblage of fibres is used in the construction of fabric. Yarn is a generic term for a continuous strand of textiles fibres, filaments or material in a form suitable for knitting weaving or otherwise intertwinity to form a textile fabric. Yarn occurs in the following forms :

- A number of fibres twisted together.
- A number of filaments laid together without twist.
- A number of filaments laid together with more on less twist.
- A single filaments.
- One or more strips made by lengthwise division of sheet of material such as natural or synthetic polymer, a paper or a metal foil.

Yarn Processing Methods

Yarn processing methods for spun yarns are very different from those of filament yarns.

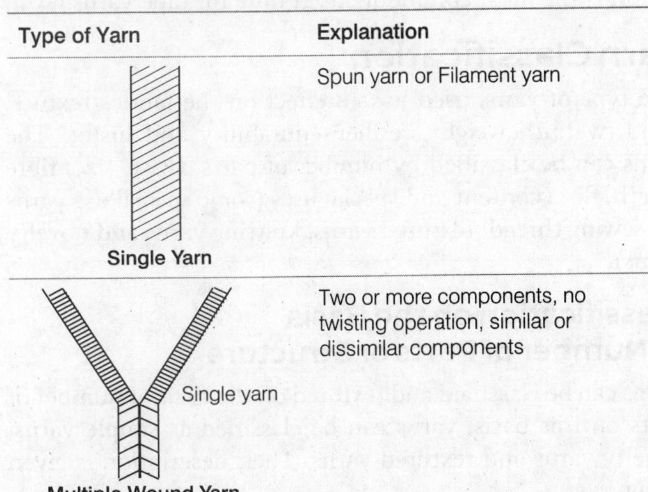

Type of Yarn	Explanation
Single Yarn	Spun yarn or Filament yarn
Multiple Wound Yarn	Two or more components, no twisting operation, similar or dissimilar components

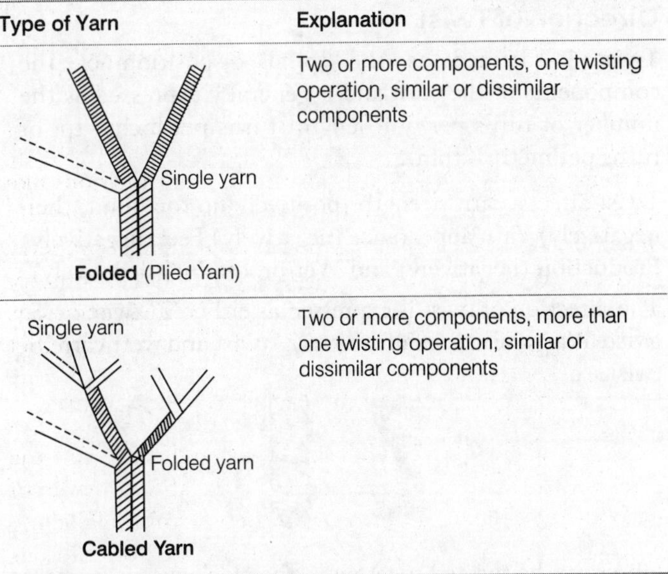

Type of Yarn	Explanation
Folded (Plied Yarn)	Two or more components, one twisting operation, similar or dissimilar components
Cabled Yarn	Two or more components, more than one twisting operation, similar or dissimilar components

Factors Affecting Yarn

Two important things in spinning of yarn that will later on affect the fineness and strength of the fabric woven are :

Yarn Twist

Yarns (especially spun yarns) are twisted to hold the fibres together. The number of twists per unit length is used to measure twist.

Yarn twist can be broadly divided by number of twists : none or very low, low, average and high twist.

Some of the common uses for yarns with different twists are given below :

- Filament yarns used for smooth fabrics have no or very low twist.
- Yarns used for napping, bulky sweaters and pile in towels have low twist.
- Most spun yarns used for woven fabrics have average twist.
- Crepe yarns used for plain and crepe weave fabrics have high twist.

Yarn twist impacts the yarn's appearance, fineness, strength and absorption :

- To a point, the fineness and strength increase with an increase in twist, but excessive twist causes yarn strength to decrease.
- Absorption decreases with an increase in twist, however, in hydrophobic fibres, even yarns with little or no twist may not have good absorption.
- In high twist yarns such as crepe, the twist increases the elasticity of the yarns, thus giving the fabric a lively suppleness.

Direction of Twist

Twist is defined as the spiral disposition of the components of the yarn and is generally expressed as the number of turns per unit length (turns per inch – tpi or turns per metre – tpm).

Twist affects–yarn strength (positively up to a limit, then negatively) Yarn appearance (negatively) Feel (negatively) Production (negatively) and Wet-processing (negatively)

The direction of twist is expressed as either 'Z' twist or 'S' twist. Warp yarns, usually, have 'Z' twist and weft yarn 'S' twist.

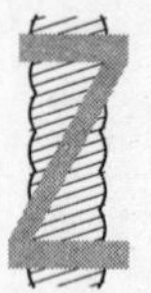
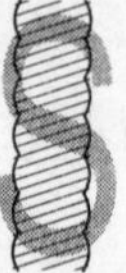

Fibres can be twisted together in the clockwise or counter clockwise direction to form yarns. Yarns are twisted in the clockwise direction for 'S' twist, and counter clockwise for 'Z' twist. The 'Z' twist is employed in a majority of the spun yarns used for fabric construction.

Yarn Count

Yarn count is also known as yarn number. Count is a numerical value, which express the coarseness or fineness (diameter) of the yarn and also indicate the relationship between length and weight of that yarn.

This is not to be confused with the number of yarns in an inch of fabric called thread count. In a counting system, we count how many lengths called a hank, (weigh one pound).

Thus, if there are 10 hanks of cotton yarn that weigh one pound, this is 10s yarn. Each of the hanks is 840 yards long, so the total length of the yarn is 8400 yards. So, if it is a coarser yarn, it will take fewer hanks and less length to make up a pound. On the other hand, the higher the number, the finer the yarn.

It takes more of the finer yarns to make up one pound :

- If the cotton count is 1, then 840 yards × 1 weighs one pound.
- If the cotton count is 2, then 840 yards × 2 weighs one pound.

The length of a hank depends upon the spinning system :

- Cotton system : 1 hank = 840 yards
- Worsted system : 1 hank = 560 yards
- Woollen cut system : 1 hank = 300 yards
- Woollen run system : 1 hank = 1600 yards

Types of Yarn

Spun/Staple yarns and filament yarns are two main types of yarns. Their description is given below :

Spun/Staple Yarns

These are composed of short staple fibres, or long filament fibres that have been cut into short staple fibres. Spun yarns may contain fibres of the same type or a blend of different fibres. The spinning method used to manufacture the yarn affects properties such as uniformity and strength. Finer, smoother, better quality cotton yarns known as **combed cotton yarns**, are produced by combing the fibres prior to spinning. A similar process is used to manufacture fine quality worsted wool yarns.

Filament Yarns

Majority of the filament yarns are extruded yarns that are made of natural extruded fibres or manufactured fibres extruded through the spinneret. These yarns fibres can be broadly divided into :

Monofilament Yarn It is made from a single, relatively thicker filament fibre. Transparent sewing thread, metallic yarns, bare elastic and fishing lines are examples of monofilament yarns. Silk is too fine to be used as a monofilament yarns.

Multifilament Yarn It is made from multiple filament fibres. Continuous filament fibre length requires little or no twisting to hold the multifilament yarn together.

Some filament yarns are produced by slitting or splitting polymer films. Olefin is the most commonly used fibre for tape yarns. Some example, are metallic coated yarn is made by slitting a metallic foil laminated between plastic films. Tape yarns is made by slitting or splitting polymer films. Olefin is the most commonly used fibre for tape yarns.

Yarn Classification

The type of yarns used has an effect on the fabrics texture, hand, warmth weight, resilient durability and luster. The yarns can be classified by number of parts, twist, size, fibre length, fibre content and special uses (some special use yarns are sewing thread, textured yarns, knitting yarns and novelty yarns).

Classification on the Basis of Number of Parts or Structure

Yarns can be classified and textured on the basis of number of parts on this basis, yarns can be classified as simple yarns, novelty yarns and textured yarns. Their description is given below :

Simple Yarns

Yarns that are even in size, have an equal number of turns or twists per inch through their length and are relatively smooth and uniform are called **simple yarns**.

In general, simple yarns tend to produce smooth flat fabrics. Simple yarns are classified as single, ply cord and double yarns. They must be made of staple fibres or filament fibres.

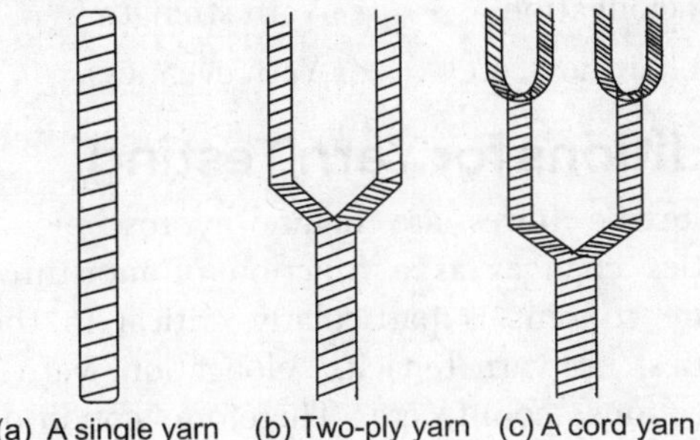

They are characterised by uniform size and regular surface.

They can be broadly divided into :

Single Yarn It is the simplest type of yarn. It is commonly produced by twisting together staple or filament fibres.

Ply Yarns They are produced by twisting two or more single yarns. Each strand of single yarn is referred to as a ply. Thus, four single yarns twisted together would form a four-ply yarn.

Cord Yarns They are produced by twisting two or more ply yarns.

Double Yarns They are produced by twisting two or more cord yarns.

Novelty or Speciality or Complex Yarns

Novelty or complex yarns are made basically for their appearance value. They differ from simple yarns in that their structure is characterised by regularities in size, twist and effect. In short, novelty yarns may be defined as yarns that are irregular at regular intervals.

Novelty yarns are made on twisters has special attachment for giving different plies (parts) of yarns and thus, allow loose, curled, twisted or looped in the yarns. Slub and flakes of colour are also introduced into the yarn by special attachments. Novelty yarns may be made up of staple fibres or filament and fabrics made from them are used mostly upholstery fabrics, draperies, etc.

A typical novelty yarn has three basic parts. The ground or foundation or core, the fancy or effect, the binder.

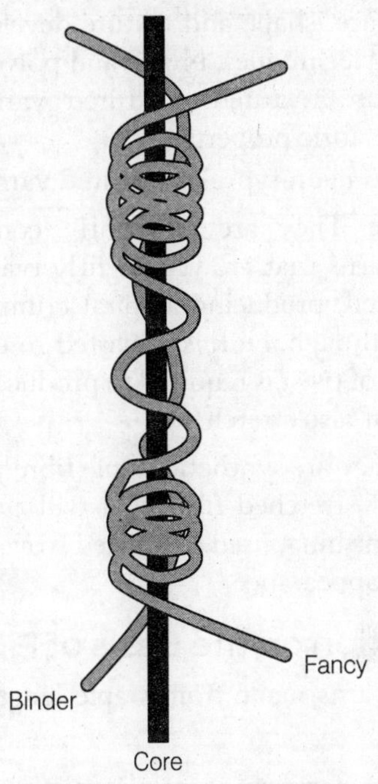

Basic parts of a novelty yarn

Types of novelty yarns are :

Slub Yarns It can be either single or ply yarns. These yarns are characterised by the soft bulky area that is spun at regular or irregular intervals.

Flock/Flake Yarns have small tufts of different coloured fibres added at intervals. These tufts can be easily pulled out. Flock/Flake yarns are generally single yarns.

Spiral and Corkscrew Yarns They are ply yarns in which one ply is soft and thick and the other is fine.

Boucle and Loop Yarns They are ply yarns that use three sets of yarns : base or core yarn, effect yarn and tie yarn. The effect yarn is looped around the base or core yarn and tied with a binder yarn.

Nub, Knot and Spot Yarns They are ply yarns in which the effect yarn is twisted around the base yarn to produce a thicker area or a bump.

Chenille Yarns They are pile yarns that are often made by slitting leno weave fabrics into narrow strips in the warp direction.

Textured Yarns

These yarns are made of fully drawn filament fibres with a changed surface, shape and texture developed by using the new spinning techniques. Nylon and polyester are two main fibres that are textured. Textured yarns provide many variations in fabric properties.

There are two main types of textured yarns :

Stretch Yarn They are frequently continuous filament man-made yarns that are very tightly twisted, heat-set and then untwisted, producing a spiral crimp giving a springy character. Although, bulk is imparted in the process, a very high amount of twist is required to produce yarn that has not only bulk, but also stretch.

Bulk Yarn They are synthetic staple fibre yarns containing a proportion of stretched fibre that will contract and crimp during wet finishing, used in knitted woven fabrics for a full well-covered appearance.

Classification on the Basis of Fibre Length

Spun Yarn Yarns made from staple length fibre are called spun yarn.

Filament Yarn Yarns made from continuous length fibres are called filament yarns continuous filament is made by a chemical spinning process. Filaments Yarns can be classified as :

- **Mono Filament Yarns** Yarns made from one filament.
- **Multi Filament Yarns** Yarns made from more than one filament.

Smooth Filament Yarns Regular or conventional filament yarns are smooth and silk like. Their smooth nature gives them more luster then spun yarns.

Textured Filament Yarns Textured is a general term for any continuous filament yarn, whose smooth straight fibres have been displaced from their closely packed, parallel position by the introduction of some form of crimp, curl, loop or coil. In the process of texturing, the filament yarn is geometrically modified or altered to change its surface characteristics. The properties of bulk cover and elasticity or stretch are improved. Textured yarns are commonly classified as follow :

- Stretch textured yarn
- Bulk textured yarn
- Set modified stretch textured yarn

Classification on the Basis of Fibre Content

Blended Yarn It is an intimate mixture of staple fibres of different composition, length, diameter or colour spun together into a yarn.

Combination Yarn It has two unlike fibre strands twisted together as a ply. In case of ply or novelty yarn each ply may be of different fibre.

Identification of Yarns

Yarn occupies the intermediate position in the manufacture of fabric from raw material. Yarn result are therefore, essential, both for estimating the quality of raw material and for controlling the quality of fabric produced.

The important characteristics of yarn being tested are :

- Yarn twist
- Linear density/Yarn Count
- Yarn elongation
- Yarn strength
- Yarn hairiness, etc
- Yarn evenness

Conditions for Yarn Testing

Some textile fibres are highly hydroscopic and their properties changes as a function of moisture content. Moisture content is particularly critical in the case of properties, i.e. yarn tenacity, elongation, yarn evenness, imperfections, count, etc. Therefore, conditioning and testing must be carried out under constant standard atmospheric conditions.

The standard atmosphere for textile testing involves a temperature of $20° \pm 2°$ c and $65 \pm 2\%$ Rh. In tropical regions, maintaining a temperature of $27° \pm 2°$ c and $65 \pm 2\%$ Rh is legitimate. Prior to testing, the samples must be conditioned under constant standard atmospheric to attain the moisture equilibrium.

The other points to be kept in mind of testing the yarns are as follows :

Linear Density /Yarn Count

The fineness of the yarn is usually expressed in terms of its linear density or count. There are a number of systems and units for expressing yarn fineness known as **direct system** and **indirect systems.**

The direct and indirect systems of expressing yarn counts includes. English count (Ne), Metric count (Nm) French count (Nf), Tex, Denier.

- For the determination of the count of yarn, it is necessary to determine the weight of a known length of the yarn. For taking out known lengths of yarns, a wrap-reel is used.
- Another factor which determines the length of yarn taken for testing is the type of balance used. Some balances like quadrant balance and Beesley's balance have been specially designed to indicate the yarn count.
- One of the most important requirements for a spinner is to maintain the average count and count variation within control. After reeling the appropriate length of yarn, the yarn is conditioned in the standard atmosphere for testing before its weight is determined.

Yarn Strength and Elongation

- Breaking strength, elongation, elastic modulus, resistance abrasion, etc., are some important factors which will represent the performance of the yarn during actual use or further processing.
- Strength testing is broadly classified into two methods :
  - Single end strength testing
  - Skein strength or lea strength
- During routine testing, both the breaking load and extension of yarn at break are usually recorded for assessing the yarn quality.
- Two types of strengths can be determined for a yarn :
  - Tensile strength-load is applied gradually
  - Ballistic strength-applying load under rapids impact conditions

Introduction of Weaves

Weaves are named according to the system or design followed in interfacing wrap and weft yarns. The basic weaves used in fabric construction are plain, twill and satin weaven. Weaving is probably the oldest out which was used originally for making baskets and mats. Today, we know that all fabrics are made by weaving. A woven fabric consists of two sets of yarns which are interlaced at right angles to each other to produce a compact construction.

To construct a woven fabric one sets of yarns are fitted on the loom. This set is called warp yarns and run parallel to the length of the fabric being woven. Another yarn is then interlaced with these yarns.

Basic Weave Patterns

Some of the common weave patterns are discussed below :

Plain Weave

Simplest weave requiring a two harness loom, formed by yarns at right angles whereby each warp yarn interlaces with each weft yarn properties: least expensive to produce, reversible unless surface design, wrinkles more, firm and wears well, less absorbent, abrasion resistant, used as background for printing/ embroidery.

Pattern of Plain Weave

Rib Weave

Rib effect is produced by using heavy yarns in the filling direction or by more warp than filling yarns per inch.

Basket Weave

Basket weave is made by treating two or more yarns as one in either the warp or weft or both the directions and interlacing them in plain weave. It is not as firm as plain weave, have more yarn slippage, shrinks easily. In this each weft passes alternately over and under each warp in a square pattern. The fabric is symmetrical, with good stability and reasonable porosity. It has a flat surface and is easy to manufacture. Good for printing and embroidering.

Twill Weave

In twill weave, each warp or weft yarn floats across two or more weft or warp yarns with a progression of interlacing by one to the right to left, from left to right or a combination. Soil resistant, softer and pliable, good wrinkle recovery, durable and wears well. Following harness are required in twill weave :

- Right Hand Twill-diagonals run upwards to the right.
- Left Hand Twill-diagonals run upwards to the left.
- Balanced Twill-same number of warp pass over filling yarns. It is reversible $2 \times 2, 4 \times 4$.
- Unbalanced Twill-have uneven number of warp or filling yarn. It has a right or wrong.
- Denim Broken Twill-combines right or left had twills.
- Herring bone Twill-a series of inverted V's are formed commonly used in suiting fabrics.
- Twill Angles- according to the angles of the diagonal line, Regular Twill.

- Reclining Twill-with smaller angles, Step Twill-with larger angles.

Twill weaves are characterised by diagonal lines from one selvedge to another. More ends per inch and picks per inch then plain weave consequently more cloth thickness.

The number of wefts the warp goes over and then under are used to identify the interlacing pattern. So, 2/1 is used to describe a fabric in which the warp yarns go over 2 and under 1 weft yarn, and the weaver is referred to be as '2 up 1 down'.

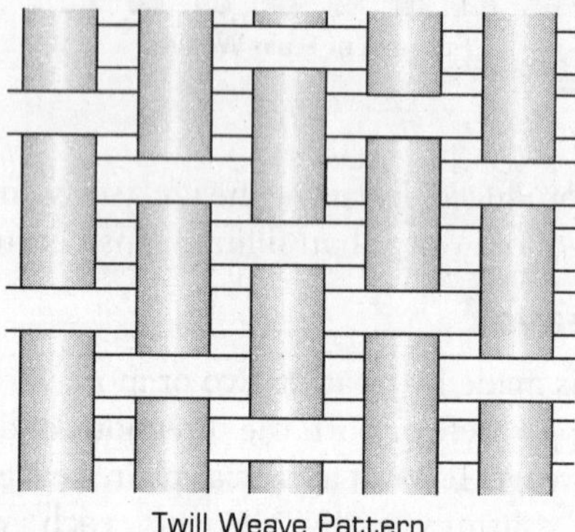
Twill Weave Pattern

Satin Weave

Each warp/filling yarn floats over 4 filling/warp yarns and interlaces with 5 filling/warp yarn, with progression of interlacing by 2 to right or left (warp faced/weft faced) haster (long floats) firm, durable (yarns packed closely together)pliable, wrinkle resistant, yarn slippage. Satin is warp faced. Satin is weft faced. 5 harness are required for Satin weave.

Stain Weave

Compound/Complex/Novelty Weave

In the complex weaves, we have various distinctions. They are as follows :

Dobby Weave

Small figured designs (floral or geometrical) woven repeatedly throughout the fabric, produced by a combination of two or more basic weaves, using a dobby attachment on the loom. Weaving pattern controlled by a plastic tape with punched holes that control the raising and lowering of warp yarns.

Jacquard Weave

Highly intricate large designs using coloured yarns and multi-weaves produced on loom with jacquard attachment incorporates all three basis weaves and their combination. Each warp yarn is controlled separately by punched cards that are laced together in continuous strip.

Surface Figure/Extra Yarn Weaves

Extra warp or weft yarn introduced in fabric to produce designs at regular intervals. Between 2 motifs, extra yarn floats across back of fabric clipped/unclipped spot-embroidery like design are achieved through either extra warp or weft yarn. Long floats on the back, when cut is called clipped spot and when uncut-unclipped spot.

Pique

Lightweight to heavy weight cotton fabric with a raised woven design lengthwise waves or cords on the face of fabric (formed by extra warp yarns) that are held in place by cross wise weft floats on the back of fabric. Extra warp yarns (stuffer yarn) do not show on face of fabric. They are not inter woven, but laid under the cords to emphasise quilted effect.

Double Cloth

They are made with 3, 4 or 5 sets of yarn. Two fabrics are woven together on the same loom, one above the other and laced together with an extra set of warp or weft yarns called binder yarns (5 sets of yarns).

Pile fabrics are commonly prepared by this method produces a variety of fabrics, reversible, stable may have different colour or design on the two sides. Used for upholstery, drapery and heavy apparels.

Textile Terminology

In the textile industry, we came across various, terms that need to be understand in much details. These are as follows :

Abrasion Resistance	This is the ability of a fibre to withstand the rubbing or abrasion it gets in everyday use. Inherent toughness natural pliability and smooth filament surfaces are fibre characteristics that contribute to abrasion resistance.
Absorbancy	This the ability of a fabric to take up moisture from the air understandard condition of temperature and humidity. The ability of fibre to absorb moisture is directly related to washability, dyeing, shrinkage, absorption of wet finishes, comfort on humid days. Staple fibres hold more water than filament fibres.
Antique Satin	Fabric with horizontal (weft) slubs that imitate spun shantung silk evident on one side with a satin weave on the other. Typically, 60% rayon (face yarn) and 40% acetate (back yarn).
Batik	Process of printing where areas are opaqued with wax. In succeeding dye baths, the fabric is waxed to retain each colour. The crinkled effect is the result of cracking the wax, allowing the dark dyes to create fine veined lines. Primitive or ethnic patterns from Indonesia and Africa are often used. Batik look designs are sometimes created through silk-screening or roller printing.
Batiste	Most commonly made today in cotton, but may be made of many other fibres, very fine and sheer. In cotton, a sheer, fine, combed mercerised muslin. In wool, smooth, finer than challis.
Battenberg Lace	Coarse form of lace from linen braid or tape and linen thread, assembled together to form various designs.
Bengaline	A sturdy warp-faced fabric with pronounced crosswise ribs, larger than faille, smaller than ottoman. Filling is not very discernable on back or face of goods.
Boucle'	Knitted or woven textile, medium to heavy weight. Boucle yarns give a tightly curled, bumpy surface texture. Boucle yarns are novelty yarns that are looped in the fabric.
Broadcloth	Tightly woven lustrous cotton or blend with fine imbedded crosswise ribs that resemble poplin, but with finer ribs. Highly napped, weave is not visible. Has 'up and down'.
Brocade	A multi-use, formal jacquard weave with supplemental warp or weft woven to give an embroidered design. This construction is used to give an embossed effect. The background is often satin weave. The face of the fabric is easily distinguished from the back, as the fabric does not reverse, and floater threads cross the back in a random way.
Burn-out	A method of printing a design into a semi-sheer fabric. Often a mixed cotton and polyester fabric is printed with acid to dissolve the cotton in planned designs.
Calico	Cotton or cotton blend fabric usually printed in small all over multicolour floral patterns or 'country/pioneer' patterns. It is often used in quilting, where the 100% calico is preferred.
Canvas	Versatile medium to heavy weight cotton fabric in a plain or twill weave.
Challis	One of the softest fabrics made. Usually plain weave with printed floral pattern. Very good drape. Originally made from wool. Has a slight nap to create softness.
Chambray	Light weight cotton or blended fabric in a plain weave. It has the look of a lightweight 'denim', but is not a twill weave. Like denim, the warp and weft threads are different colours the warp is white with a solid coloured weft. The yarns used are slightly stubbed in both the warp and weft directions.
Chiffon	Very light, transparent fabric in plain weave, gauze-like. Excellent drape. Crepe yarns. Sheerer than georgette.
China Silk	A soft, semi-sheer, plain weave fabric used for dress linings and scarves. Original is 100% silk, but now is also made in polyester.
Corduroy medium or Wide Wale	A pile weave cotton or blend with a corded pile that is heavy and fairly durable. Originally known as cor du roi, or the fabric of the kind, it was used for pantaloons for the king's servants in France. Lengthwise cords are named according to the width.
Corduroy-Pinwale	A pile weave cotton or blend wit a corded pile that is heave and fairly durable. Lengthwise cards are named according to the width pinwale is very narrow, while wide-wale is broad.
Crimp	This refers to the waves or bends that occur along the length of the fibre. Wool has natural crimp. Manufactured fibres may be given a permanent crimp. Fibre crimp increases cohesive, resilienc[illegible] [illegible]d resistance to abrasion.
Crepe	Fabrics characterised by a crinkly surface obtained primarily by hig[illegible] [illegible]wist yarns. They are known for good drape. May be made from many different fibres.
Crepe Back Satin	Fabric constructed with a crepe texture on one side and a satin-like sheen on the other. A satin weave with crepe filling yarns.
Damask	A formal, satin based jacquard fabric with a reversible pattern. The patterns are often historic in nature and go back into Renaissance times. Floral and leafy patterns are reversible, so a design will change in colour from front to back. Damask patterns can be made in sheeny formal fibres or in cottons or linens.

Denim	Cotton or blend, twill weave fabric, which is heavy and durable. The warp threads are coloured and the weft thread is white. The name comes from its historic roots, having begun in Nimes, France. Hence, 'di Nimes' where denim was used for the ship's sails.
Denim-stretch	Traditional denim look with added stretch yarns such as lycra.
Dupioni Silk	Silk made from two cocoons that have nested together. In spinning, the double thread is not separated giving it a unique thick and thin appearance. Heavier slubs and texture than true shantung.
Elasticity	It means the ability of a stretched material to return immediately to its original size.
Electrical Conductivity	This is related to the build up of static electricity charges on a fabric. A good conductor doesn't build up static electricity.
Felt	A woven or non-woven textile consisting of wool, and perhaps hair and cotton fibres, compressed using moisture, heat, pressure, and agitation. In woven, it is achieved by interlocking the natural serration of the wool on the surface through heat, moisture, steam, pressure, and hammering. Heavy felts are termed 'Melton'. Felt comes in many weights, from light craft weight felt to heavy 'hat' and interlining felts.
Flannel	Any fabric that is woven then brushed to achieve a soft nap. Types include cotton, flannelette, outing (for outerwear), French (finely twilled), Melton (cotton and/or wool), and suede (two sided nap, trimmed and pressed.)
Fleece Knit	Cotton and polyester and acrylic blends, top to bottom weight. Knit fleece is a circular weft knit, plain stitch with thicker, soft-twist yarn laid in the back, later napped to give a soft, fuzzy surface.
Fur (faux)	Synthetic pile fabric intended to look like real animal fur
Flammability	This refers to the case of ignition and the speed and length of burning flame. Non-flammable fibres will not burn. Finish can be added to make the fibres non-flammable.
Gabardine	Steep-pitch twill fabric woven with natural or synthetic yarns. Has more warp than filling yarns. The surface has obvious diagonal ribs that are tightly woven of fine lustrous yarns. Woven in wool, this fabric is fine and lightweight. It makes beautiful suits and clothing.
Gauze	A loosely woven, lightweight, very thin, sheer or semi-sheer fabric, usually with a wrinkled look.
Georgette	Heavy, sheer crepe made of yarn twisted both ways in the weave. Usually made with the same yarn in both warp and weft.
Interfacing (non-facing)	Non-woven fabric intended for interior of garment to add body and stiffness.
Jacquard (dress weight)	A textile woven on the Jacquard loom. Selected threads raise, forming the intricate pattern by the progression of interlacing yarns. Today, the loom is computer operated. 'Spot prints', the earliest type of design, included bee, star or rose motifs.
Lace	A machine/hand made, needle constructed fabric using natural/synthetic yarns.
Linen	Light to medium weight, a firm fabric in balanced plain weave. 'Linen' has slubs in both the warp and weft yarns. Traditionally used in informal table linens. 'Linen' is a generic name for flax fibre. To be called linen, fabric should be 100% flax, or at least 50% if a blend.
Loft	It is a term used in relation to compressional resiliency. When a pressure is put on a fabric, if it springs back to its original thickness, it is maintaining its loft.
Lustue	It is the shine, sheen or brightness of a fabric caused by reflection of light. Smooth fibres reflect more light than rough or serrated fibres. Round fibres reflect more light than flat fibres.
Madras	Plain weave cotton, usually uneven. Multi-coloured light weight plaid with white filling. One of the oldest fabrics in the cotton trade.
Moire'	Moire' is faille, which has been calendered (rolled through heavy drums) to produce the distinctive 'watermark' pattern. This fabric is highly versatile, somewhat formal and of light to medium weight.
Muslin	Thin cotton cloth with a plain balanced weave. It is the base for numerous cotton fabrics. It may be natural (unbleached) or bleached, dyed, or printed.
Net	A mesh fabric made in geometric shapes. Holes of empty space between fibres.
Organdy	Sheerest of the cotton cloths made. An acid finish gives it its crispness and stiffness. It wrinkles badly. Related to lawn and batiste. Very light and thin, but very stiff.
Organza	Usually a very thin, transparent, crisp, stiff silk (also in polyester). Withstands repeated launderings retaining its stiffness.
Pile Fabric	This fabric has a third dimension, using an extra warp or weft set woven or knotted into the fabric to produce a deep surface texture. Examples of pile include velvet, terry cloth, and corduroy.

Pinstripe	Narrow stripes woven parallel to the selvedge. Found frequently in mens suits.
Pique'	A type of weave with raised cords, stripes or geometric patterns. The rib or cord usually runs lengthwise in the face of the goods. Types of pique' include birds eye (diaper cloth), dimity (sheer), pinwale pique (warp ribs), embossed pique (design pressed into the face of fabric), and waffle pique' (three dimensional patterns).
Plasticity	It is the property of fibre which enables the user to shape its semi-permanence or permanence by moisture, heat and pressure.
Pliability	It is the ease of bending ad shaping. Pliable fibres are easily twisted to make yarns. They make fabrics that resist spltling when folded or creased many times in the same place.
Resiliency	It is the ability of a fabric to recover over a period of time from deformation such as stretching, compressing bending or twisting.
Rib Knit	Knitted fabric with pronounced straight, raised cord. Ribs usually running lengthwise.
Sateen	Strong, lustrous medium to heavy weight spun yarn (cotton) satin weave.
Satin	Strong, high shine and lustrous medium to heavy weight fabric made with filament yarns with a satin weave (floats in either warp or weft).
Seersucker	A crinkled surface in all-over, spaced stripes that is permanently woven into a cotton or blend fabric. The puckers are woven in by loosening or relaxing some.
Suede Cloth	A light to medium weight synthetic knit or woven with a brushed nap that imitates genuine suede.
Taffeta	A plain balanced weave in light weights, of natural or synthetic fibres. Weft threads are slightly larger than warp, creating a fine horizontal rib. Types of taffeta include Moire', antique taffeta, and paper taffeta (this often has a very crisp finish, or is a plaid).
Tapestry	A plain weave technique used to produce complex hand-woven European pictorial tapestries. These are now most often jacquard woven with multiple warps and wefts. Today the term covers a large category of patterned floral or pictorial textiles.
Terry	The medium pile weave used in robes and beachwear. Loops may be cut for plush or velour type texture, or left uncut as looped pile. Good quality absorbent cotton makes the most luxurious terry towels.
Tulle	Very fine lightweight, machine-made net in, which small mesh effects are seen. Used in bridal veils, dress goods, and formal wear.
Tweed	A rough, irregular soft and flexible, shaggy woolen named for the Tweed river, which separates England from Scotland. Characterised by nubs of different colours. Made of a two and two twill weave, right or left hand in structure. Also, loosely applied to 'tweedy', heathery fabrics.
Twill	A type of weave with a pattern of diagonal parallel ribs. This is done by passing the weft thread over one or more warp threads and then under two or more warp threads and so on, with a 'step' or offset between rows to create the characteristic diagonal pattern.
Velvet	Woven pile fabric with a soft, yet sturdy, face. Natural, synthetic and blend fibres are used, usually silk and rayon.
Velvet - Panne'	Flat velvet pile, where nap is pressed in one direction to create a pattern, knit or woven.
Velveteen	A filling pile cloth known as, cotton velvet, this low pile fabric is strong, can be laundered and tailors rather well.
Vinyl	Vinyl is a synthetic fabric. It consists of an extruded polyvinyl chloride, which has been 'flowed' onto a woven, knitted or non-woven base cloth. Vinyl is a medium to heavy weight fabric that often imitates leather.
Voile	Very fine sheer fabric in balanced, plain weave. Usually made of manufactured fibre filament, or cotton. Cotton type uses fine, high-twist, combed yarn for smoothness. Voile has excellent drapability, a crisp body and lustrous appearance.
Wool Jersey Knit (Jersey rib)	Single weft knit made from wool. The face of the fabric shows vertical lines. Used for women's soft suiting. Made popular in the 1920's and 30's by designer Coco Chanel.
Wicking	This refers to the conduction of moisture along the fibre on through the fabric. The property is related to surface wetting and is not the same as absorbency. Apart from the above mentioned terms, there are few other most important terms of clothing textiles i.e. fibre, yarn, weaves. Lets begin with fibre.

EXAM BASED QUESTIONS

1 What is the aim of textile industry?
(a) To serve the clothing requirements.
(b) To provide shelter to the people.
(c) To promote happiness among people.
(d) To bring in social revolution.

2 What is the term used for printing process where areas are opaqued with wax?
(a) Brocade (b) Block
(c) Batik (d) None of these

3 Which among the following fibres looks like animal fur?
(a) Flax (b) Faux
(c) Crepe (d) Velvet

4 Which property of fibre, helps in recovering over the period of time?
(a) Pliability (b) Wicking
(c) Elasticity (d) Resiliency

5 Tenacity of a fibre is directly related to
(a) polymer orientation and strength
(b) length of polymer
(c) interpolymer forces of attraction
(d) All of the above

6 The fibre which has a mineral origin is
(a) asbestos (b) silk
(c) flax (d) acrylic

7 The fibre that will float on water is
(a) nylon (b) polyester
(c) acrylic (d) poly propylene

8 Fibres can be found in
(a) hot air balloons (b) sails
(c) tennis ball fuzz (d) All of these

9 Which of the following statements is/are correct?
(a) Short fibres are called denim.
(b) Man-made fibres absorb water easily.
(c) Grease and oil stains are difficult to remove in nylon garments.
(d) None of the above

10 Staple fibres are short fibres, the length ranges from
(a) 1/2-40 cms (b) 1-20 cms
(c) 1-40 cms (d) None of these

11 Filament fibres are long continuous strands, the length runs into thousands of meters. e.g.,
(a) nylon (b) silk
(c) polyester (d) All of these

12 Man-made filament fibre is converted into staple length in
(a) synthetic fabrics (b) mixed fabrics
(c) blended fabrics (d) None of these

13 Synthetic textile fibres are
(a) more durable and absorbent
(b) more durable and smooth
(c) less toxic and eco-friendly
(d) less smooth and weak

14 Staple fibres are cut from filaments extruded in large bundles. It is called
(a) monofilament (b) tow
(c) multifilament (d) None of these

15 Man-made filament fibre is converted into staple length in
(a) synthetic fabric (b) blended fabric
(c) mixed fabric (d) None of these

16 Which of the following is true of plant fibre?
(a) Vegetable fibre is made of cellulose.
(b) Cotton has 91% cellulose and lines has 70% cellulose.
(c) Its chemical composition is carbon dioxide, hydrogen and oxygen.
(d) All of the above

17 Cotton, linen, silk and wool are examples of
(a) synthetic fibres (b) natural fibres
(c) blended fibres (d) man-made fibres

18 Cotton is stronger when it is wet. This is because of
(a) the presence of water, which promotes a more uniform distribution of stresses across and along the cellulose layer
(b) its being hydrophilic in nature
(c) its crystalling fibre arrangement
(d) All of the above

19 Flax and cotton does not show pilling because of
(a) static, which is nil (b) short length fibre
(c) hydrophillic fibre (d) None of these

20 Which of the following best describes the appearance of cotton fibre?
(a) A flattened tape (b) Bamboo
(c) A smooth tube (d) Scaled

21 Why cotton towel is used by the people?
(a) Because of the softness
(b) Because of absorbency
(c) Because of durability
(d) Because of elasticity

22 Linen is called the bast fibre because it is
(a) present in woody part of stem
(b) present in branches
(c) present in leaf of the plant
(d) None of the above

23 In the manufacturing of linen, the process of removing other woody portion is called
(a) shrinking (b) retting
(c) lusture (d) cleaning

24 What are the ways through which spinning of linen is done?
(a) Dry spinning (b) Wet spinning
(c) Only (b) (d) Both (a) and (b)

25 Which among the following fibre doesn't have pilling problem?
(a) Wool (b) Jute (c) Cotton (d) Linen

26 What is the status of linen cloth resilience?
(a) High (b) Low
(c) Very Poor (d) Can't say

27 Jute is called as
(a) silver fibre (b) copper fibre
(c) golden fibre (d) aluminium fibre

28 Which among the following is not a part of jute manufacturing process?
(a) Drawing (b) Carding (c) Spinning (d) Beaming

29 Which among the following is the property of jute?
(a) Expensive (b) 100% bio degradable
(c) Low tensile strength (d) High extensibility

30 Which fibre is known as China grass?
(a) Ramie (b) Hemp (c) Jute (d) Nylon

31 Which fibre has same manufacturing process as Hemp?
(a) Flax (b) Linen
(c) Only (a) (d) Both (a) and (b)

32 What makes wool fibre strong?
(a) Overlapping scales (b) Smooth fibre surface
(c) Varying lengths (d) None of these

33 Which fibre is marked as 'Queen of all textile fibres'?
(a) Silk (b) Crepe (c) Linen (d) Jute

34 Mohair has very good resistance power and has a high degree of
(a) lustre
(b) resiliency
(c) adaptability to other yarns
(d) All of the above

35 Which of the following is a synthetic fibre?
(a) Polyester (b) Viscose rayon
(c) Flax (d) Wool

36 The non-technical test for fibre identification includes
(a) chemical test (b) microscope test
(c) burning test (d) solvent test

37 Polyester dissolved in
(a) hot phenol (b) meta cresol
(c) conc HCL (d) formic acid

38 The methods used to test water repellency of fabric are
(a) static absorption test (b) dynamic absorption test
(c) bundesmann test (d) All of these

39 These stiff plastics soften in hot water and are molded before they cool and stiffen
(a) plaster bandage (b) thermo plastics
(c) fibre glass (d) sculptural arts coatings

40 What test is performed to check the appearance of the fibre?
(a) Feeling test (b) Burning test
(c) Density test (d) Visual inspection

41 Lower twisted yarns are
(a) softer, bulkier, used for weft yarns or knitting
(b) blended with another type of fibre
(c) single, ply, cable, core, spun, fancy
(d) promoting, advertising and selling a product

42 Novelty yarns produce
(a) fabrics with interesting and decorative surface effects
(b) core spun threads
(c) provide greater cover and opacity
(d) better insulation

43 Disadvantage of textured yarns is
(a) they have deliberate irregularities throughout like bumps, knots, curls
(b) poor abrasion resistance
(c) regenerated viscose
(d) synthetic polyester

44 Advantage of textured yarns is
(a) made from a core filament yarn, with two spun yarns twisted around it
(b) safe environment, comfort and well being of factory workers
(c) higher stretch and bulk, better insulation
(d) not very durable and susceptible to abrasion and wear

45 Novelty yarns are used for decoration. Examples of novelty yarns include
(a) raschel, tricot and lace
(b) woollen, staple and boucle
(c) slub, boucle and core spun
(d) None of the above

46 What is the feature of twist yarn?
(a) Low strength (b) High strength
(c) Medium strength (d) None of these

47 Which two different methods of spinning are used to create yarns?
(a) Staple spinning and Extrusion spinning.
(b) Carded spinning and Combed spinning.
(c) Worsted spinning and Combed spinning.
(d) Extrusion spinning and Twisting.

48 Which of the following statements is/are correct?
(a) Novelty yarns are usually ply yarns, but they are not used to add strength to the fabric.
(b) Novelty yarns add interest to plain weave fabrics at lower cost than, if effects were obtained from weave.
(c) Novelty yarn effects are permanent.
(d) All of the above

49 The yarn passage in a winding machine is
(a) unwinding zone, clearing zone, tensioning zone, winding zone
(b) unwinding zone, winding zone, clearing zone, tensioning zone
(c) unwinding zone, tensioning zone, winding zone, clearing zone
(d) unwinding zone, tensioning and clearing zone, winding zone

50 The dirty oily looking spots on the warp or filling yarns or on packaged-dye yarn. It means
(a) water spots (b) scrimp
(c) soiled filling (d) mixed filling

51 Which of the following factors contribute to yarn slippage?
(a) Smoothness of the yarns
(b) Loosely woven construction
(c) Poor finish
(d) All of the above

52 Among the following yarn types the specific volume is highest for
(a) spun rayon (b) cotton (c) worsted (d) woollen

53 To produce a soft and flexible yarn, one needs
(a) fine fibres and high twist
(b) coarse fibres and high twist
(c) fine fibres and low twist
(d) coarse fibres and low twist

54 Staple spun yarns are
(a) smooth and have poor elasticity
(b) strong and durable
(c) lusturous and resilient
(d) elastic and absorbent

55 What are bicomponent yarns?
(a) Two different yarns plied together.
(b) Yarns consisting of two different natural fibres.
(c) Yarns consisting of fibres of two different colours.
(d) Yarns consisting simultaneously of fibres made from two polymers extruded.

56 For a light weight and fine fabric you require
(a) single strand yarn (b) ply yarn
(c) cord yarn (d) any yarn

57 Which of the following is not a direct system of yarn numbering?
(a) Cotton count (b) Denier
(c) Metric count (d) Tex

58 Fineness of a yarn depends on
(a) length of yarn (b) weight of yarn
(c) twist given to the yarn (d) nature of yarn

59 Novelty yarns are made primarily for ...... which has three basic parts.
(a) texture (b) appearance
(c) decoration (d) strength

60 What are all these i.e. Basket, plain, it twill and satin?
(a) Weaves (b) Fibres (c) Materials (d) Limings

61 Weaver can be created by
(a) Cam (b) Jacquard
(c) Dobby (d) All of these

62 Which twill weave material is used for expensive suits and outer wear?
(a) Gabardine (b) Linen
(c) Velour (d) Pellon

Directions (Q. Nos. 63-76) *In the questions given below are two statements labelled as Assertion (A) and Reason (R). In the context of the two statements, which one of the following is correct?*

Codes
(a) Both A and R are true and R is the correct explanation of A
(b) Both A and R are true, but R is not the correct explanation of A.
(c) A is true, but R is false
(d) A is false, but R is true

63 **Assertion** (A) Spinning quality or cohesiveness of a fibre influences year fineness, fabric thickness, snagging or pilling of surface textures, appearance, fabric or textile product durability.
Reason (R) Cohesiveness is the ability of fibres to stick together during fibre arranging or yarn manufacturing process.

64 **Assertion** (A) Both silk and cotton have high lustre.
Reason (R) Both are natural protein fibres.

65 **Assertion** (A) Fibres with good moisture regain accept dyes and finishes more readily than fibres with low regain.
Reason (R) Fibres with no regain with wash and dry quickly.

66 **Assertion** (A) Fibres must be bendable, pliable or flexible.
Reason (R) If the fibres are to be made into yarns or fabrics that can be creased, that have the quality of drapability and the capacity to move with the body.

67 **Assertion** (A) Rayon garments under go progressive shrinkage.
Reason (R) Hence, care has to be taken, while drying and ironing.

68 **Assertion** (A) Inspection of a fabric for appearance and hand is always the first step in fibre identification.
Reason (R) Manufactured fibres can be made into fabrics that ensemble natural fibre fabrics.

69 **Assertion** (A) Yarn appearance and evenness are influenced by short fibres protruding form the surface of the yarn.
Reason (R) Yarn appearance and evenness test is carried out by conducting subjective assessment and by instrumental methods.

70 **Assertion** (A) Twist is the measure of the spiral turns given it a yarn in order to hold the constituent fibres or thread together.

Reason (R) The amount of twist is measured by the number of turns per meter.

71 **Assertion** (A) By passing the filling yarn over and under a different number of warp yarns, different designs in weaving can be created.

Reason (R) Filling yarns run along the width wise grain or weft.

72 **Assertion** (A) Decorative weaves are also called as fancy, figure and design weaves.

Reason (R) Dobby weave, Jacquard designs and Leno weaves are the examples of decorative weaves.

73 **Assertion** (A) Plain weaves is the least expensive and most commonly used weaves for both thick and sheer fabrics.

Reason (R) The plain or has a surface finish, it has no right or wrong side.

74 **Assertion** (A) Basket, ribbed, twill and satin are all basic weaves.

Reason (R) In all these weaves, third set of yarn is used.

75 **Assertion** (A) To identify the polyester fibre, it is important to negate the presence of nylon and acrylic by dissolving in hot phenol and concentrated nitric acid.

Reason (R) Polyester is insoluble in both hot phenol and concentrated nitric acid.

76 **Assertion** (A) Fabrics can be made fluffy with slub yarns.

Reason (R) Use of slub yarns makes fabrics abrasion resistant.

77 Which of the following statements is/are correct?

1. Jute and Hemp are bast fibres and have to be obtained after retting.
2. Hemp and jute are coarser fibres and are mostly used for making gunny bags and ropes.
3. Jute fibre is weak in dry state.
4. In moist environment, jute takes up 23% moisture. In dry environment it has 6% moisture.

Select the correct answer using the codes given below

(a) 1 and 2 (b) 3 and 4
(e) 1, 2 and 3 (d) All of these

78 Each fibre whether natural or man-made, filament or staple has characteristics, which affect the properties of the fabric. These properties is/are

1. Appearance or look
2. Texture of feel
3. Strength
4. Moisture absorbancy and warmth

Select the correct answer using the codes given below

(a) 1 and 2 (b) 3 and 4
(c) 1, 2 and 3 (d) All of these

79 Primary fibre properties includes

1. high length to breadth ratio
2. flexibility and tenacity
3. spinning quality and cohesiveness
4. uniformity

Select the correct answer using the codes given below

(a) 1 and 2 (b) 3 and 4
(c) 1,2 and 3 (d) All of these

80 Which of the following statements is/are correct?

1. The physical structure of asbestos makes it very difficult to open into yarns because it lacks in length and cohesiveness.
2. Asbestos is used for padding for laundry presses, belting for conveying hot materials, brake-lining and in clothes such as gloves and aprons.
3. Asbestos fibres are $3/8^{11}$ to $3/4^{11}$ in length.
4. Asbestos occurs as veins or strips in rocks.

Select the correct answer using the codes given below

(a) 1 and 2 (b) 3 and 4
(c) 1, 2 and 3 (d) All of these

81 Primary fibre properties include

1. high length to breadth ratio
2. flexibility and tenacity
3. spinning quality and tenacity
4. uniformity

Select the correct answer using the codes given below

(a) 1 and 2 (b) 1 and 4
(c) All of these (d) 1, 2 and 3

82 The properties which make wool a popular fibre

1. warmth
2. resiliency
3. feeling
4. easily damaged by moths and alkalis

Select the correct answer using the codes given below

(a) 1 and 2 (b) 3 and 4
(c) 1, 2 and 3 (d) All of these

83 The properties of silk which makes it a queen of the fibres include

1. smoothness 2. soft lustre 3. resiliency 4. cost

Select the correct answer using the codes given below

(a) 1 and 2 (b) 3 and 4
(e) 1, 2 and 3 (d) All of these

84 Like cotton fabrics man-made fibre cloth is made by produces in

1. Cottage Industry
2. Handloom Weaves
3. Large Spinning and Weaving Mills
4. Power Looms

Select the correct answer using the codes given below

(a) 1 and 2 (b) 2 and 3
(c) 1, 2 and 3 (d) All of these

85 **Which of the followings statements is/are correct?**

1. Yarn used for weaving or knitting may either be in the form of continuous filaments or in the firm of staple-short fibres.
2. Filaments are smoother and more regular and lustrous than the twisted yarns.
3. The properties of the yarn may add or impair the quality of the fabric.

Select the correct answer using the codes given below.
(a) Only1 (b) 1 and 2 (c) 1 and 3 (d) All of these

86 **Arrange the correct sequence of weaving operations.**

1. Drawing 2. Looming and Weaving
3. Warp and Weft Winding 4. Denting
5. Warping and Sizing

Codes
(a) 5, 4, 1, 3, 2 (b) 3, 5, 1, 4, 2
(c) 1, 4, 5, 2, 3 (d) 1, 4, 2, 3, 5

87 **Arrange the correct sequence in weaving a fabric.**

1. Shedding 2. Picking 3.Let off 4. Beat up

Codes
(a) 1, 4, 3, 2 (b) 2, 3, 4, 1 (c) 3, 1, 2, 4 (d) 4, 2, 1, 3

88 **Arrange the correct sequence of weaving process.**

1. Shedding 2. Picking 3.Take up 4. Beating

Codes
(a) 1, 2, 3, 4 (b) 4, 3, 2, 1 (c) 2, 3, 4, 1 (d) 1, 2, 3, 4

89 **Chemical finishes exclusively given to cotton to increase lustre, strength and dye ability are**

1. fulling 2. crabbing
3. bleaching 4. mercirisation

Select the correct answer using the codes given below
(a) 1 and 2 (b) 2 and 3 (c) 3 and 4 (d) 1 and 4

90 **Asbestos yarns can be used in fabrics of various structure like**

1. asbestos curtains 2. clothing for fire fighting
3. fire smothering blankets
4. protective milts for cooking

Select the correct answer using the codes given below
(a) 1 and 2 (b) 3 and 4
(c) 1, 2 and 3 (d) All of these

91 **Which of the following statements is/ are correct?**

1. Uniform silk yarns are more suitable for weaving on high speed looms than hand reeled silk yarns.
2. Reeling or unwinding the filament from the cocoon is done in an establishment called a filature.
3. Doupion silk comes from two silk worms who spin their cocoon together.
4. Reeled silk or Gandhi Ashram silk is a long continuous filament 300-1600 yards in length.

Selects the correct answer using the codes given below
(a) 1 and 2 (b) 3 and 4 (c) 1, 2 and 3 (d) All of these

92 **Which of the following statements is/are correct?**

1. Vicuna is one of the softest fibres in the world.
2. Vicuna fibre can be obtained only by killing the animals.
3. Chrysolite is the asbestos, most often found in textile, because of several properties making it specially adaptable to fabrics.
4. Yarn of asbestos may be plain, they may have a core of wire glass or nylon filament that may be piles or cords

Select the correct answer using the codes given below
(a) 1 and 2 (b) 3 and 4
(c) 1, 2 and 3 (d) None of these

93 **Which statement is true regarding the yarn quality parameters which include many tests?**

1. Appearance and evenness of yarn
2. Strength of yarn
3. Count of yarn of yarn number
4. Twist of yarn

Select the correct answer using the codes given below
(a) 1, 2 and 3 (b) 2, 3 and 4
(c) 1, 2 and 4 (d) All of these

94 **The prominent properties of asbestos fibre includes**

1. fireproof 2. acid resistant
3. low pliability 4. white greyish colour

Select the correct answer using the codes given below
(a) 1 and 2 (b) 3 and 4
(c) 1, 2 and 3 (d) All of these

95 **Match the following.**

List I	List II
A. Cotton	1. Plant stem
B. Pineapple	2. Seed hair
C. Flax	3. Plant leaf
D. Coir	4. Fruit husk

Codes

	A	B	C	D		A	B	C	D
(a)	2	3	1	4	(b)	1	2	4	3
(c)	3	4	2	1	(d)	4	1	3	2

96 **Match the following.**

List I	List II
A. Wool	1. Glass rod structures
B. Linen	2. Scales
C. Silk	3. Convolutions
D. Cotton	4. Nodes

Codes

	A	B	C	D		A	B	C	D
(a)	2	4	1	3	(b)	1	2	3	4
(c)	3	1	4	2	(d)	4	3	2	1

97 **Match the following.**

List I	List II
A. Linen	1. Naturally flame resistant
B. Nylon	2. Bast fibre
C. Silk	3. Seed fibre
D. Wool	4. Used to make high end fabrics
E. Cotton	5. Made of polymides containing carbon, oxygen, nitrogen and hydrogen

Codes

	A	B	C	D	E		A	B	C	D	E
(a)	2	5	4	1	3	(b)	1	2	3	4	5
(c)	5	4	3	2	1	(d)	2	4	5	3	1

98 Match the following.

List I	List II
A. Polyamide fibre	1. Filament
B. Yarn number	2. Nylon
C. Pile weave	3. Count
D. Strand of long fibres	4. Velvet

Codes

	A	B	C	D		A	B	C	D
(a)	1	2	3	4	(b)	2	1	3	4
(c)	4	2	3	1	(d)	2	3	4	1

99 Match the following.

List I	List II
A. Plain weave	1. A weave with three sets of yarn warp 60 inch to weft
B. Basket weave	2. Weft interlaced wit warp to form diagonal ridges in fabric
C. Triaxial weave	3. Simplest and least expensive weave
D. Twill weave	4. Variation of plain weave of 2 weft 2 warp

Codes

	A	B	C	D		A	B	C	D
(a)	1	2	3	4	(b)	2	3	4	1
(c)	3	4	1	2	(d)	4	1	2	3

100 Match the following.

List I	List II
A. Staining	1. Glass and metallic fibres, provide lustre and textural interest
B. Mineral fibres	2. Formally called artificial silk, soft, drapable, high lustre, less expensive than silk
C. Rayon	3. The stain seeps into the woods, still can see the grain of the wood
D. FFE	4. Fixtures, furnishings and equipment
E. Hand	5. A term used to describe the feel of a fabric to the touch

Codes

	A	B	C	D	E		A	B	C	D	E
(a)	1	2	3	4	5	(b)	5	4	3	2	1
(c)	3	1	2	4	5	(d)	3	2	1	4	5

Directions (Q. Nos. 101-105) *Read the following passage and answer the questions that follow.*

Fibres form a class of hair-like materials that occur as continuous filaments or in discrete elongated pieces, similar to pieces of thread. They are two types: natural fibres and man-made or synthetic fibers. Natural fibres may be obtained from plant, animal, and mineral sources. Those from plant sources include cotton, flax, hemp, sisal, jute, and coconut. Fibres from animal Sources include silk, wool. and mohoir. Those from mineral sources include asbestos and metal fibers.

Many natural fibres can be spun into filaments, thread or rope. Some can be matted into sheets to make products such as paper or felt. Others can be used as components of composite materials. In recent years, natural fibres are being increasingly used in the textile, building , plastics, and automotive industries.

After World War II, there was an enormous rise in the production of synthetic fibres, and the use of natural fibres significantly decreased. Recently, with rising oil prices and environmental considerations, there has been a revival of the use of natural fibres in the textile, building, plastics, and automotive industries. This interest is reinforced by economic developmental perspectives on the agro-industrial market and local productions, with emphasis on economic development and independence versus the use of imported materials.

101 What do you mean by fibre?

(a) Fibre is like a thread
(b) Fibre is the class of hair-like material
(c) Fibre is a discrete elongated piecl
(d) All of the above

102 What are the two types of fibres?

1. Natural Fibres
2. Animal Fibres
3. Man-made Fibres
4. Mineral Fibres

Codes

(a) Only 2 (b) 1 and 4
(c) 1 and 3 (d) None of these

103 Match the following.

List I	List II
A. Natural Fibres	1. Mohair
B. Plant Sources	2. Cotton, flax, hemp
C. Animal Sources	3. Mineral sources

Codes

	A	B	C		A	B	C
(a)	1	2	3	(b)	3	1	2
(c)	3	2	1	(d)	2	1	3

104 Where natural fibres are used?

1. Textile
2. Building
3. Plastics
4. Automotive industry

Codes

(a) 1 and 2 (b) 3 and 4
(c) All of these (d) None of these

105 What leads to the use of synthetic fibres?

(a) Decline in natural fibres
(b) Rise of World War II
(c) Rise of oil and environmental conditions
(d) None of the above

PREVIOUS YEARS' QUESTIONS

July 2018

1 Which of the following are twill weave fabrics?

1. Chino
2. Chambray
3. Monk's cloth
4. Drill
5. Broad cloth

Codes

(a) 1, 2 and 3 (b) 2, 4 and 5
(c) 1, 4 and 5 (d) 1, 3 and 4

2 **Assertion** (A) The grain in a woven fabric can be identified by the degree of stretch along the yarns.

Reason (R) Warp yarns stretch more in comparison to weft yarns.

Codes

(a) Both (A) and (R) are correct
(b) Both (A) and (R) are incorrect
(c) (A) is incorrect but (R) is correct
(d) (A) is correct but (R) is incorrect

November 2017

3 **Assertion** (A) Maintenance of fabrics made from low twisted yarns is easier for the consumer.

Reason (R) Low twisted yarns shed soil easily since there is less space between the fibres for soil to settle.

Codes

(a) A is correct, but R is incorrect
(b) A is incorrect, but R is correct
(c) Both A and R are incorrect
(d) Both A and R are correct

4 Which of the following are leaf fibres?

1. Kapok
2. Ramie
3. Pina
4. Abaca

Codes

(a) 1 and 2 (b) 2 and 3
(c) 3 and 4 (d) 1 and 4

5 Which of the following fibres can be confirmed by performing microscopic test?

(a) Wool (b) Silk
(c) Nylon (d) Acrylic

January 2017

6 Which of the following fibres have good resiliency?

1. Wool
2. Polyester
3. Rayon
4. Cotton

Codes

(a) 1 and 3 (b) 3 and 4
(c) 1 and 2 (d) 1 and 4

July 2016

7 Give the correct sequence of making nylon.

1. Formation of chips
2. Polymerisation
3. Lubrication and crimping
4. Spinning
5. Drawing

Codes

(a) 2, 1, 4, 5 and 3 (b) 1, 2, 5, 4 and 3
(c) 3, 2, 1, 5 and 4 (d) 1, 3, 2, 4 and 5

8 Which of the following fibres when taken away from flame continue burning with an after glow?

1. Cotton
2. Rayon
3. Silk
4. Nylon

Codes

(a) 1 and 2 (b) 2 and 3
(c) 3 and 4 (d) 1 and 4

9 Which of the following is not a primary property of a fibre?

(a) Strength (b) Flexibility
(c) Cohesiveness (d) Density

December 2015

10 Bulky yarns are made by

1. modification in chemical spinning.
2. varying the cross-sectional shape of fibres.
3. varying the pressure of extrusion through spinneret.
4. addition of bubbles using air duct.

Select the correct answer using the codes given below

(a) 1 and 2 (b) 2 and 3
(c) 3 and 4 (d) 2 and 4

11 Which of the following are regenerated cellulosic fibres?

1. Rayon
2. Lyocell
3. Azlon
4. Alpace

Select the correct answer using the codes given below

(a) 1 and 4 (b) 1 and 2
(c) 2 and 3 (d) 1 and 3

12 Match the following.

List I (Fibres)	List II (Components)
A. Rayon	1. PVC
B. Polyester	2. Polyurethane
C. Carbon	3. Copper sulphate
D. Nylon	4. Acrylonitrile
E. Wool	5. Terephthalic acid
	6. Cystene
	7. Caprolactum

Codes

	A	B	C	D	E		A	B	C	D	E
(a)	3	7	6	5	2	(b)	2	1	3	6	4
(c)	1	2	5	4	3	(d)	3	5	1	7	4

13 Give the correct sequence of manufacturing wool.

1. Shearing
2. Carding
3. Combing
4. Carbonising
5. Grading

Codes

(a) 1, 4, 5, 3, 2 (b) 2, 3 4, 5, 1
(c) 1, 5, 4, 2, 3 (d) 3, 4, 5, 2, 1

June 2015

14 **Assertion** (A) Terry Towel is the most absorbant fabric structure.

Reason (R) It is a cut pile hence more surface area to absorb water.

Codes

(a) Both A and R are correct
(b) Both A and R are incorrect
(c) A is correct, but R is incorrect
(d) A is incorrect, but R is correct

15 Give the correct sequence for manufacturing of Rayon.

1. Shredding
2. Dissolving
3. Xanthation
4. Ageing
5. Steeping
6. Spinning

Codes

(a) 1, 2, 3, 4, 5, 6 (b) 5, 1, 4, 3, 2, 6
(c) 2, 3, 4, 5, 1, 6 (d) 5, 2, 4,3 1, 6

ANSWERS

Exam Based Questions

1 (a)	2 (c)	3 (b)	4 (d)	5 (d)	6 (a)	7 (d)	8 (d)	9 (d)	10 (c)
11 (d)	12 (c)	13 (b)	14 (b)	15 (b)	16 (c)	17 (b)	18 (a)	19 (b)	20 (a)
21 (b)	22 (a)	23 (b)	24 (d)	25 (d)	26 (c)	27 (c)	28 (c)	29 (b)	30 (a)
31 (d)	32 (a)	33 (a)	34 (d)	35 (a)	36 (c)	37 (a)	38 (d)	39 (b)	40 (d)
41 (a)	42 (a)	43 (b)	44 (c)	45 (c)	46 (a)	47 (b)	48 (d)	49 (d)	50 (c)
51 (d)	52 (d)	53 (c)	54 (d)	55 (d)	56 (b)	57 (c)	58 (a)	59 (b)	60 (a)
61 (d)	62 (a)	63 (b)	64 (c)	65 (a)	66 (a)	67 (d)	68 (b)	69 (b)	70 (c)
71 (c)	72 (c)	73 (a)	74 (c)	75 (a)	76 (b)	77 (d)	78 (d)	79 (d)	80 (d)
81 (c)	82 (a)	83 (d)	84 (d)	85 (d)	86 (b)	87 (b)	88 (d)	89 (c)	90 (d)
91 (d)	92 (d)	93 (d)	94 (c)	95 (a)	96 (a)	97 (a)	98 (d)	99 (c)	100 (d)
101 (d)	102 (c)	103 (c)	104 (c)	105 (b)					

Previous Years' Questions

1 (b)	2 (a)	3 (c)	4 (c)	5 (a)	6 (c)	7 (a)	8 (a)	9 (d)	10 (d)
11 (b)	12 (d)	13 (c)	14 (c)	15 (b)					

Fabric : Construction and Textiles Finishing

Fabrics are formed by weaving, knitting, knotting or pressing fibres together. Fabric construction and textile finishing are important processes of textile industry. In this, conversion of yarns and sometime fibres take place.

Fabrics

Fabrics are manufactured from various raw materials, which are available from natural or artificially generated or mix fibres. Fabrics can be classified based on the origin of fibres, its process and its end usage. Different types of fabrics are :

Natural Fabrics

Natural fabrics are those fabrics which are created from the fibres of animals' coats, the cocoons of silk worms and plants' seeds, leaves and stems. It is breathable and never cause rashes apart from being soft and durable. Natural fabric is the best choice for everyone. It does not change colour from UV light and there is no warming until the material looses its tensile strength.

There are different types of natural fabrics as given below :

Cotton Fabric

The fabric which is believed to be most smoothing and safe is called as cotton fabric. Immense use of cotton fabric for infant's dresses or beddings is a live testimony of its softness and skin friendliness.

Cotton fabric has a distinctive feature that it adjusts easily with climatic requirements. That's why it is called all season fabric. It is warm in winter season and cold in summer season.

In this Chapter

- *Fabrics*
- *Fabric Construction*
  - *Woven Fabrics*
  - *Knitted Fabrics*
  - *Non-Woven Fabrics*
- *Textile Finishing*
  - *Classification of Finishes*
  - *Various Finishing Processes*
  - *Process of Textile Finishing*
- *Dyeing and Printing*

Silk Fabric

Silk counts to the strongest natural fabric in the world. It is known for its softness, luster, beauty and luxurious look. It is one of the highest grade fabric providing comfort to the wearer in all types of weather. Today, there are different varieties of silk available in the market like chiffon, georgette, organza, chepe de chine, Duponi Noil Pongee, Tussar, etc. Because of its sheer variety of designs, weaving and quality, Indian silk textiles are popular worldwide.

Linen Fabric

Linen is known as the King of Natural Fabrics. It is extensively used for apparel making and home furnishing. Linen, being a natural fibre is considered to be safe for all types of skin. Linen fabric is also suggested for sensitive skin as its natural properties make it resistant of allergies.

Jute Fabric

Being among the strong and durable fabrics, jute fabric is ideally being used as bags or sacks for packing since ages. The jute fabric is much sought item for fashionable clothes, home furnishing and fashion accessories Bangladesh counts to be the largest cultivator of jute fabric and is the manufacture of carpets, linoleum, cordage and twines. Sometimes, it is used as webbing to cover inner springs of the auto seats and sometimes as fashion accessory for fashion garments, tapestrics, soft luggage, etc.

Leather Fabric

Leather fabric is not affected by surrounding temperature and is comfortable for both hot and cold. Adding a classic luxury, pleasant to touch and comfortable, leather fabric is soft, elastic and firm. Leather fabric is blessed with the quality of absorbing water vapour without loosing dryness and retaining to the original.

Wool Fabric

Soft, strong and very durable wool fabric provides warmth and attractive appearance. It is the fabric, which does not wrinkle easily and it is resistant to dirt, wear and tear. It is also having the quality of not burning when put over the flame, it only smolder. Felt made of wool fabric is used as covers for piano hammers.

It is also used in absorbing odours and noise in machinery and stereo speakers. Wool fabric is equipped with different characteristics like warm, resists to wrinkle, wear and tear, it is light weight and durable which also absorbs moisture. It have been largely used in blankets and carpets. Every wardrobe contains garment made of woollen fabric.

Ramie Fabric

Ramie fabric have characteristics like moisture absorption and air permeability. These are valued as a summer fabric, not harmed by mild acid and are resistant to alkali.

Hemp Fabric

Highly versatile hemp fabric is used in countless number of products like shoes, furniture, apparel, accessories and home furnishing. Hemp fabric is a fabric which is commonly known for its warmth, softness and durability. Providing beautiful lusture, hemp fabric is best for making apparel fabric withstand water better than any other textile product. It is obtained from stem of the plant. The finest hemp fabric is produced in Italy. Acting as a great choice for comfortable work clothes, home decoration etc. It is also used in the manufacturing of clothing, curtains, draperies, upholstery, bedspreads, table linens, sheets, dish towels, canvas, etc.

Synthetic/Man-made Fabrics

Synthetic fabrics are made from fibres which are either completely made from inorganic materials or organic materials combined with chemicals. They have numerous properties with the purpose for which it is produced and finished. Some are light weight with ultra sheer, while others are moisture picking and fast drying. Few are very luxurious to imitate some other natural fabrics and some are very strong and tough.

The fabrics given below are the types of synthetic fibres :

Georgette Fabric

Georgette is a sheer and strong silk like clothing fabric that often comes with a dull, creped surface. In simple words, it is a sheer lightweight fabric that provides utmost comfort. It is usually made out of silk or polyester. As compared to chiffon, it is opaque and slightly heavy.

Velvet Fabric

Velvet is one of the smoothest and softest amidst all the other kinds of fabrics. Velvets are specially manufactured and processed because of their distinctive properties. Velvet fabrics are used in variety of appliances like clothing including trousers, shirts and many more. Also, velvet fabric is used in bed sheets, covers, curtains, etc. Velvet fabric is not less than silk in any assessments whether be glossiness or be the unending glaze. Velvet fabric, due to its high class looks and price viability has made it the most preferred fabric.

In modern times, velvet fabrics are availed in the multifarious designs and colours. And also are stronger and elastic than the previous times. The velvet fabric needs less maintenance and can be easily washed and dried. Use of modern innovations in the composition of the velvet fabrics have made it more easily accessible to the common masses.

Polyester Fabric

Polyester is a type of fabric which is not found naturally. It is man-made. It is widely used in various applications and is very much in demand in the markets. It has various qualities due to those it is so popular, like wrinkle resistance and springing back into its smooth shape. It is very strong and soft as well.

It can also be mixed with other fabrics to make a strong and durable fabric or to achieve any other motive. For example, in upholstery, polyester is generally blended with wool to eliminate crushing and reduce fading. There are various uses of polyester fabric like it is used in curtains, draperies, floor coverings, throw rugs, bedding and as a cushioning or insulating material.

Nylon Fabric

The word 'nylon' is derived from the New York and London. Nylon is yet another form of synthetic fibre *i.e.,* commonly used amidst the masses. Fabric composed of nylon called nylon fibre is used in variety of forms like clothing sheets, covers and many other domestic and industrial appliances. Nylon fabric is preferred amidst all other fabrics as it is really strong and has a strong ability of stretchiness. High elasticity of nylon fabric makes it prime use in luggage, baggage, wallets and many more.

They are easy to maintain as it gets cleaned and dried without any special effort. They are availed in the latest forms that are much more stiff and lighter in weight.

It is highly durable, long lasting and resistant to wear and tear. Nylon is the 'polymer of amide', termed as 'polyamide' extracted from the petroleum.

Nylon is an easy product to manufacture as it needs less time and also lesser attention. That is indeed makes nylon fabric a nice product to trade and make money. The increasing use and popularity of nylon fabric have made the finest product to trade.

Polypropylene Fabric

Polypropylene fabric is especially meant for winter season, because the only layer of 100% polypropylene rib knit generally stays dry and due to this feature it keeps one's body warmer.

A high quality light weight polypropylene fabric is preferred in winter season because it allows user to perform any moderate activity in cold weather at ease. It basically consists of hydrophobic, which relinquishes any possibility of moisture in such fabric and further it pushes the moisture vapour away from the skin. Entailing a large number of features, polypropylene can simply be termed 'stunning' in each and every aspect.

Satin Fabric

Satin fabric is also said to be the most elegant fabrics. The reason behind is its astonishing looks and smooth surface. It is used in loads of apparels and many other things. Especially for women, satin fabric is used in variety of apparels like blouse, panties, gowns and many more clothing.

Also, satin fabric is used for bed sheets, curtains and many other decorative purposes. The glossiness of the satin fabric really makes the material high class. At top of that, satin fabric is availed in multifarious colour options like black, red, green, purple, blue, etc.

Satin fabric generally composed of silk or rayon and that's why it is so smooth. Also, satin fabrics are availed in various weights and normally are very light. It is very delicate and are manufactured with a great deal of care and attention. Satin fabrics need a fine setup of manufacturing and processing unit as each and every strand of the satin fabric must be well knitted.

Satin fabric huge demand amidst the masses is not a new thing as has been the most demanded fabric since a long time. In the present too, with the innovative designed apparels, satin fabric usability range has expanded like never before.

Acrylic Fabric

Acrylic fabric is a kind of synthetic fibre that is artificially manufactured. It can also be referred as the imitation of wool. It is used to make loads of apparels and many other things.

The main use of the acrylic fabric is in outfits like shirts and many other ladies outfits. It is used in seats of chairs and sofas as well. They are known for their stiffness and ability of wear and tear resistance. It also does not lose the glaze for a longer period of time.

Rayon Fabric

Rayon fabric is basically that synthetic textile fibre, which is obtained by forcing a cellulose solution through fine spinnerets. In other words, rayon fabric is a final result of solidifying filaments.

Rayon is a unique type of fabric that cannot be termed either a synthetic fabric or natural one. The process of making rayon is quite distinct through which natural raw supplies are transformed to make it practical.

Rayon is a fabric that can be woven or knit further ensuring a versatile use. The efficiency of rayon fabric is comparatively much higher than taffeta or other cotton fabric.

It is economical too. Apart from this, its soft texture makes rayon one of the most lovable fabrics. Rayon fabric is widely used in making of number of apparels and home furnishing items.

Physical Properties of Fabrics

Physical properties are the static physical dimensions of fabrics. The following physical properties are used to define the static physical dimensions of strand fabrics :

Fibre or Filament Type, size, length.

Yarn Diameter, twist, weight or size, count, fibre content for mixed yarns, ply.

Weight Ounces per squared or yards per pound.

Thickness Vertical depth.

Fabric Structure Woven or knitted fabrics

Woven Fabrics Weave type, wale and course count per inch.

Knitted Fabrics Knit type, wale and course count per inch.

Finishes Chemicals such as resins, starches, waxes and mechanical effects such as calendaring and mapping applied to the woven fabric to yield or enhance style durability and utility values.

Fabric width The length of the filling or course.

Colour Hue, value and intensity (degree of brilliance).

Fabric Density Weight per unit of volume.

Surface Contour The geometric dimension of the surface plane.

Fabric Construction

Fabrics can be made or constructed by using a number of techniques as given below :

Woven Fabrics

Woven fabrics are made by using two or more sets of yarn interlaced at right angles to each other. Much variety is produced by weaving. Woven fabrics are generally more durable. They can be easily cut into different shapes and are excellent for producing style in garments.

Types of Woven Fabrics

Given below are the types of woven fabrics :

Buckram It is a stiff coated fabric made from a light weight loosely woven fabric, impregnated with adhesives and fillers, bands, button closers, etc., in garments. They are also used as reinforcements for hand bags and articles.

Cambric It a light weight fabric woven in plain weave and produced with a stiff finish. It is suitable for women's dresses and children's dresses that require crispness.

Casement It is a medium weight cotton fabric made of closely packed thick warp yarns. Generally, it is used for curtains, table linen, upholstery and rarely used for dresses.

Cheese Cloth It is popular light weight sheer fabric having open weave. It has a low count fabric consisting of carded yarns. Originally, it was used for wrapping cheese or meat and hence the named 'cheese cloth'. It is neither strong nor durable.

Chiffon These fabrics are sheer, light weight fabrics made of hard twisted yarns. Originally, these are made in silk fabrics, but today they are made from rayon or polyester. The fabric encounter with the problem of shrinkage.

Chintz It is a medium weight, plain woven cotton yarn. It is often given a glazed finish, which may be temporary or semi- permanent glazed. Chintz are available in solid colour as well as printed with floral prints.

Corduroy It is a cut pile fabric available in solid colour. The cut pile fibres are seen in the form of ribs on the surface.

Crepe A silk fabric is originally characterised by a crinkle, puckered surface formed by highly twisted yarns in the warp or weft or both.

Denim Traditionally, it was a yarn dyed, warp faced cotton twill fabric warp is usually coloured and weft is white. This fabric is made of two weights for sports wear and overalls.

Georgette It is a sheer light weight fabric, woven in plain weave. It has characteristic rough texture produced by hard twisted ply, yarn both in warp and weft. Originally, it was made in silk, but today it is produced in rayon and polyester too.

Khadi It is a term used for a wide variety of fabrics that are hand spun and hand woven. They are produced in mainly one cotton fibre, blends of two or more fibres.

Lawn It is a fine sheet, light weight, crisp fabric either made in cotton or linen.

Mulmul It is an Indian term generally applied to fine cotton fabric slightly heavier, than muslin.

Muslin It is a light weight open cloth of plain weave. It may be used as grey or bleached and dyed. It is used as household textiles and dress materials.

Poplin It is a medium weight cotton fabric having a fine weft rib. It is generally used for shirting, dresses and upholstery.

Velvet It is a wrap cut pile fabric, originally made from silk. It is also produced in rayon. The dense cut pile make it very soft and lustrous. It is also produced with special high twisted yarns, which are single or ply yarns. Based on the yarns used and twist given, they are named as semi-voiles (single yarns 1 × 1) full voiles. (ply yarn 2 × 2) or half voiles (double in warp and single in weft 2 × 1).

Properties of Woven Fabrics

Tensile Strength It implies the behaviour of the fabric under different loads applied.

Extensibility It is the ability of the fabric to extend under load.

Tear Strength A hole has been made in the fabric because it has been pulled sharply.

Abrasion Resistance Resistance of the fabric against the surface friction.

Crease Resistance Crease are irregular lines that appear on cloth when it has been crushed.

Pilling Resistance Hairs on the surface of a fabric tend to collect into little balls (pills) and if the fibres are strong, these balls do not break off, this spoils the appearance of the fabric.

End Uses of Woven Fabrics

Woven fabrics are widely available; you can purchase a huge range of woven fabric online in a variety of weaves and finishes. Because there are three different types of woven fabrics, there is a huge variety of uses for this kind of material, including clothing, soft furnishings and industrial platform.

Clothing made from woven fabrics are made to be sturdy. They cannot be stretched and don't overly shrink, so woven materials have great deal of longevity. Many heavy duty fabrics are made from weaves, thanks to their strength and durability.

Woven fabrics offer a crisp and distinguished look and can add structure to an outfit making it appear more luxurious and high end.

Knitted Fabrics

Knitting is the construction of an elastic, porous fabric, created by interlocking yarns by means of needles. Knitted fabrics can be made much more quickly and easily than woven fabrics at comparatively less cost. Knitted fabrics are generally light in weight, comfortable in wear even during travel. But, yet require little care to keep their neat appearance. The tendency of knits to resist wrinkling is another factor to boost up their popularity.

Knitted fabrics are used for designing active clothing such as sports clothing. Their elastic nature permits for abundant physical activity. Knitted fabrics are produced by two general methods i.e. warp knitting and weft knitting. They are made as flat or tabular fabrics depending on the end use. Tubular fabrics may not have any seams at the sides whereas flat fabrics are treated just like woven fabrics.

Types of Knitted Fabrics

Following are the types of knitted fabrics :

Jersey Knit These fabrics are weft knitted and are characterised by distinct, but flat vertical lines on the face and dominant horizontal ribs on the reverse side.

Rib Knit These fabrics are made by using rib stitch with two sets of needles. These fabrics are used where stretch is desired as they show excellent degree of elasticity. Rib knits are warm to wear.

Double Knit Double knits are produced by the interlock stitch. The fabrics is riblike in appearance on both the sides. Decorative fabrics are also produced by jacquard attachment. These fabrics show good dimensional stability and are easy to cut and sew. Double knits are commonly made from polyester, acrylic or wool fibres. They are used as durable apparels.

Properties of Knitted Fabrics

Stitches density knitted fabrics is the number of loops or stitches per inch. Stitch density is the next important parameter to be set in knitting and represents the total number of needle loops in the given area. Stitch density is the product of loop per inch and wales per inch. It is measured in units of loops per square inch or cm.

Stitches Length Stitch length (or loop length) is the key factor to determine and maintain quality of the knitted fabrics.

Heales The fabric that has both more wales and courses will have better recovery from stretching, while that with fewer wales and courses will be less rigid, stretch more easily, fit the body contour better with poor recovery. A knit fabric is defined according to the number of courses per inch followed by the number of wales per inch. Each wale is formed by a different knitting needles which knit that wale throughout the length of the fabric.

Uses of Knitted Fabrics

Knitted fabrics are versatile and are used to create not only clothing, but certain home furnishings as well. It is made from interlocking stitches.

Knits are available in five different categories :

- **Stable Double Knits** They don't have a lot of stretch.
- **Single Knits** They are light weight.
- **Tentured Knits** Such as velour cloth.
- **Two Way Stretch Knits** They have lot of stretch.
- **Ribbing Knits** They are furnishing garments like the necklines of T-shirts.

Clothing It is the most popular item to make with knits because of the many varieties of knit fabrics available. Use jersey, which is single knit makes the clothing soft and fluid. On the other hand, double knits are used to create jackets, coats and pants. Interlock knits are suitable for evening wear and lingerie. Tricot is perfect for active wear such as bathing suits. Sweater knits can be used to make tops, sweater dresses and shirts.

Curtains Although, knits are mainly considered for clothing, stable knits are an excellent choice for curtains. Knits are made of strong fabrics that are able to retain their original shape easier, which allows the fabric to drape well, especially when tiebacks are used.

Blankets, Towels and Pillows As knit stretches, only certain types can be used for blankets, towels and pillows. Fleece knits, which are easy to sew, can be used to make blankets. Stretch terry cloth, which is bulky, is perfect for use in beach, bath and hand towels, where complicated seams are unnecessary. Raschel knits, which are soft and lofty, are suitable for projects such as throw and decorative pillows, where bulky seams are not a concern.

Non-Woven Fabrics

Non-woven fabrics do not depend on the interlacing of yarn for internal cohesion. Intrinsically, they have neither an organised geometrical structure. They are essentially the result of the relationship between one single fibre and another. This provides non-woven fabrics with characteristics of their own, with new or better properties and therefore, opens them up to other applications.

Non-woven fabrics are around us and one uses them everyday, often without knowing. Non-wovens can be made absorbent breathable, drapeable, flame resistant, heat sealable, light, limit-free, moldable, soft, stable, stiff, tear resistant, water repellent, but not all the properties mentioned can be combined in a single non-woven, particularly those that are contradictory.

Type of Non-Woven Fabric : Felt

To manufacture Felt, it is necessary to use fibres that will interlock and shrink when heat, moisture and pressure are applied to form a solid fabric mass. Felt is also made by combining rayon or other manufactured fibres with wool. However, to produce acceptable felt, at least 50% of the fibre content must from fibres other than wool, particularly synthetics that are produced by the needle punch method rather than the felting process.

Properties of Non-Woven Fabrics

- It is made in a wide range of weights.
- These fabrics are neither strong nor fray.
- They can be moulded into different shapes.
- Non-woven fabrics are made from recycled fibres and are soluble.
- It can be made to soften with heat and act like a glue.
- It will also take on some of the properties of the fibre used in the web leg-wool felt is warm and insulating, polyester wadding is light weight and elastic.

Uses of Non-Woven Fabrics

Personal Care and ***Hygiene*** As in baby diapers, feminine hygiene products, adult incontinence items, dry and wet pads, but also nursing pads and nasal strips.

Health Care Like operation drapes, gowns and packs, face masks dressings and swabs, ostomy bag liners.

Clothing Interlinings, insulation and protection clothing, industrial work wear, chemical defence suits, shoe components, etc.

Home Wipes and dusters, tea and coffee bags, fabric softeners, food wraps, filters, bed and table linen, etc.

Automotive Boot liners , shelf trim, oil and cabin air filters, moulded bonnet liners, heat shield, air bags, tapes, decorative fabrics, etc.

Construction Roofing, thermal and noise insulation house wrap, understanding, drainage, etc.

Geotextiles Asphalt overlay, soil stabilisation, drainage, sedimentation and erosion control, etc.

Filtration Air and gas, HVAC, HEPA, ULPA filters.

Industrial Cable insulation, abrasives, reinforced plastics battery separators, satellite dishes, artificial leather, air conditioning, coating.

Agriculture Home furnishing, leisure and travel, school, office, etc.

Textile Finishing

Textile finishing is a process used in manufacturing of fibre, fabric or clothing. In order to impart the required functional properties to the fibre or fabric, it is customary to subject material of different type of physical and chemical treatments. For example, wash and wear finish for a cotton fabric is necessary to make it crease free or wrinkle free.

Textile finishing is a very diversified sector due to the processed raw materials, manufacturing techniques and finalised products. Trends in fashions cause a continuous change in colouring and functional finishing.

Textile finishing gives a textile its final commercial character with regard to appearance, shine, handle, drape, fullness, usability, etc. Nearly all textiles are finished. When finishing takes place in a wet state, it is called wet finishing and in a dry state, it is called dry finishing.

Purposes of Textile Finishing

- To improve the attractiveness and service ability of the textile materials.
- To accentuate/inhabit some natural characteristics on the textile materials such as softening, brightening, de-lustering, etc.
- To change the surface characteristics of textile materials.
- To impart new characteristics/properties of textile materials such as flame retardant, water repellent or water proof finishes.
- To increase life and durability of textile materials.
- To set the fabric, so that it can be maintained by the shape and structure.
- To set the chemicals into the textile materials.
- To meet up specific end uses.

Classification of Finishing

Finishing can be classified into following themes :

- Aesthetic finishes and functional finishes.
- Chemical and mechanical finishes.
- Permanent durable, semi-durable and temporary finishes.

Finishing processes are categorised in several ways :

On the Basis of Degree of Permanence On this basis, finishes are classified as permanent, durable, semi-durable and temporary finish.

- A **permanent finish** generally involves a chemical process that changes the fibre's structure, so that it will not alter subsequently throughout the fibre life of the fabric.
- A **durable finish** may last through out the life, but its effectiveness diminishes (or finishes).
- A **semi-durable finish** will last through several laundering or dry cleaning.
- A **temporary finish** will be removed or substantially reduced when the fabric is laundered or dry cleaned.

On the Basis of Designing and Sales Purpose On this basis, finishes are classified as aesthetic and functional.

On the Basis of Textile Processing On this basis, finishes are classified as chemical and mechanical.

Finishing Processes

Tentering

To bring a fabric to the right width, it is passed through a 20-90 ft long tentering machine. The cloth is carried through the machine to moving chains, pins or clips one on each side, which grip the selvedge formally.

Tentering is an important and necessary operation because the fabric has been pulled in length during bleaching, drying and is therefore, generally narrower than the required finished width. During the operation the clip chains diverge from the entry end about one quarter or slightly less than the length of the machine. As the cloth is carried forward, gripped on either side it is gradually widened. In order that this stretching may take place easily, the cloth is slightly passed through a hot air chamber to dry and set its width.

Calendering

It is essentially an ironing process. Most of fabrics (and yarn too) become stiff, board like when wet and dried under tension. Running a fabric through a calender removes the stiffness and makes it quite soft. At the same time, calendering flatters the fabric and makes it more lustrous. The process consists of applying a lot of pressure by passing the cloth through the nips of heavily weighted. Rayon fabrics are not calendered as heavily as cotton or linen, but silk fabrics often required fairly heavy calendering.

Some calenders use waxy substances to give added luster in addition to friction treatment by steam heated pressure bowls. Calendering flatters and closes the thread of the fabric to give it required smooth fall and appearance. The finish depend chiefly on pressure, temperature and moisture.

Sanforising

After weaving or knitting the interlaced threads of a fibre are in a state of strain. They are stretched. Therefore, freshly made fabrics are not stable, they are larger than they would be if the strain were relieved. Calendering and other finishing process further stretch a cloth. Furnishing fabrics are sometimes deliberately stretched.

Modern fabrics and garments must only be null-finished, they should not shrink on washing or least shrink on washing or at least shrink only within reasonable limits.

Therefore, the fabric undergoes a process called sanforising, by which its stretch is closed up without spoiling the finish. It is contracted in length by passing the punched cloth between a blanket and a large steam, heated metal cylinder.

Schreinering

It is an inexpensive method of imparting luster to low priced cottons. The fabric is pressed between steal rollers engraved with fine lines, giving it between 125 and 600 diagonal ridges per inch. When light reflects off these ridges the fabrics. But, the luster is not permanent because the imprinted ridges reduce the tendency of the fabrics to cling. If the fabric has also been mercerised, the additional schreinering produces a luster like that of silk.

Moirning

A watery more effect (from the French mattered watered) is sometimes given to cotton fabric on a calendering machine. Fine lines on the rollers produce the effect. The luster is caused by the divergent reflection of light on the lines of the design.

Weighting

Sometimes, fabrics are weighted to give them additional body. The weight and body of the silk fabric is increased by immersing it in a solution containing metabolic salts. The salts penetrate the yarns and become a permanent part of the fabric, but cannot be detected by handling. However, if excessive metallic salts, penetrated the yarn and become the permanent part of the fabric than it will eventually weakened. Only lone grade woollen fabrics are weighted. Magnesium Chloride makes a woollen fabric absorb more moisture by increasing its weight.

Embossing

This process produce raised figures or designs in relief on the surfaces of fabrics by passing the cloth through resin and then pressing in the design with engraved rollers. The designs may be large floral or geometric and of one or more colour. The colour and resin can be added at the range time. The process can be applied to all types of fabrics except wool.

The finish made of this permanent, when applied to fabrics made of natural fibre or synthetic, non-thermoplastic fibres, except with certain chemical resin. To pressure the embossed finish of such fabrics, they should be washed in lukewarm water with a mild soap, never bleached. Ironed on the wrong side while damp.

Process of Textile Finishing

After the process of cleaning clothes get creased and used to be straight to look like new finishing. This process used to straighter the clothes so that, the appearance is attractive and neat. There are some finishes given to the clothes to the laundry.

It is essential that the fabrics contain sufficient amount of moisture, so that it is pliable enough to be pulled into shape during the process of finishing.

Fabrics like cotton and linen are damped before finishing. In cases of silk and wool, where the sprinkle does not spread evenly, these should be left half dried for finishing. Following are the methods of finishing :

Ironing This process consists of running a hot iron backward and forward along selvage thread of the clothes with pressure. The heat of iron and the pressure is controlled according to the texture and the nature of the fabric. For example, silks are not ironed and a fine muslin cloth does not need much pressure to smoothen the surface cotton and linen are ironed with a hot iron.

Pressing This process consists of placing a hot iron on the creased portion of the material and then lifting it up. The operation is continued till the crease disappear. It differs from ironing because in that it is not a continuous running of ironing on the surface of clothes. Pressing is used for finishing woollen and fabrics with a texture, such as georgette and crepe.

Mangling It is used only in cases of rough article such as threads, jhalars, laces, etc., where the surface is excepted to be neat, but not very smooth. The article immediately after washing before drying is pressed through a mangle several times and them put to dry. This process helps to straighter the threads.

Calendering It is used in commercial laundry to finish pieces of cotton and linen such as table cloth, curtain, bed sheet, etc. Drying and finishing is done in some process. The straight piece of articles are passed through heated metal rollers, which continuously rotate. The process dry up the moisture and the pressure caused by the radiation, iron out the material.

Steaming It consists of allowing the steam to pass through the surface of the fabric clothes with a pile surface. The passing of steam through the pile surface of the fabric on the wrong side helps to raise and freshen the pile. The heat of iron convert moisture in the cloth into the steam, which escapes through the fabric through are sufficient pressure to straighten the surface of the cloth. The steam kettle brings about a similar result.

Dyeing and Printing

Dyeing and printing are processes employed in the conversion of raw textile fibres into finished goods that add much to the appearance of textile fabrics.

Dyeing

Most forms of textile materials can be dyed at almost any stage. Quality woollen goods are frequently dyed in the form of loose fibre, but top dyeing or cheese dyeing is favoured in treating worsteds.

Manufacturers prefer piece dyeing, which allows stocking of white goods, reducing the risk of being overstocked with cloth dyed in colours that have not been ordered.

The dye used, depends on the type of material and the specific requirements to be met. For some purposes, higher light fastness is essential, but for others it may be inconsequential.

Factors considered in dye selection include fastness to light, reaction to washing and rubbing and the cost of the dyeing process. Effective preparation of the material for dyeing is essential.

Dyeing Process

It is process of colouring fibres, yarns or fabrics with either natural or synthetic dyes. Dyeing is an ancient art which predates written records. It was practised during the Bronze age in Europe.

Primitive dyeing techniques included sticking plants to fabric or rubbing crushed pigments into cloth. The methods became more sophisticated with time and techniques using natural dyes from crushed fruits, berries and other plants, which were boiled into the fabric and gave light and water fastness (resistance), were developed.

The property of colour fastness depends upon two factors i.e. selection of proper dye according to the textile material to be dyed and selection of the method for dyeing the fiber, yarn or fabric.

Some major types of dyes used dyeing processes are discussed below :

Acid Dyes

Acid dyes are seldom used on cotton or linen as this process requires a mordant. They are widely used on nylon when high wash fastness is required. In some cases, even higher wash fastness can be obtained by after treatment with fixatives.

Natural Dyes

Natural dyes are obtained from plants and minerals. Most of the natural dyes are from plant sources such as roots, bark, leaves, berries, etc. These are eco-friendly and yield to excellant wash and light fastness.

Basic Cationic Dyes

Basic dyes are water-soluble and are mainly used to dye acrylic fibres. They are mostly used with a mordant. A mordant is a chemical agent which is used to set dyes on fabrics by forming an insoluble compound with the dye.

Synthetic Dyes

Synthetic dyes are classified based upon their chemical composition and the method of their application in the dyeing process.

Mordant Dyes

The mordant or chrome dyes are acidic in character. Sodium or Potassium Bichromate is used with them in the dye, before or after the process of dyeing is completed. This is done for getting the binding action of the chrome. They are mostly used for wool which gets a good colour fastness after treatment with mordant dyes. They are also used for cotton, linen, silk, rayon and nylon but are less effective for them.

Vat Dyes

Vat dyes are insoluble in water and cannot dye fibres directly. Indigo is the original vat dye. These dyes are the fastest for cotton, linen and rayon. They are used with mordants to dye other fabrics such as wool, nylon, polyesters, acrylics and modacrylics.

Reactive Dyes

Reactive dyes react with fibre molecules to form a chemical compound. These dyes are either applied from alkaline solution or from neutral solutions which are then alkalised in a separate process. Reactive dyes were originally used for cellulose fibres only but now their various types are used for wool, silk, nylon, acrylics and their blends as well.

Dyeing Techniques

Direct printing, gel dyeing, tie and die, etc., are most commonly used dyeing techniques.

Gel Dyeing

Passing a wet spun fibre that is in the gel state (not yet at full crystallinity or orientation) through a dye bath containing dye with affinity for the fibre. This process provides good accessibility of the dye sites.

Direct Printing

It is the most common approach to apply a colour pattern onto a fabric. If done on coloured fabric, it is known as overprinting. The desired pattern is produced by pressing dye on the fabric in a paste form. Most pigment printing is done without thickeners because the mixing up of resins, solvents and water produce thickening anyway.

Tie and Dye

Tie and dye is an ancient method of pattern making on cloth. It is a resist technique, where the cloth is knotted or tied and covered before the actual dying is done.

The parts tied and covered with a thread will not absorb a dye and will retain the actual colour of the cloth. Tie and dye is a craft, which has been in practice in many parts of the world from earliest times.

In this method of colouring fabric, dyeing is used to colour parts of fabric. A mordant, usually Methalium oxide is used to act as a fixing agent for the dye stuffs.The mordant is painted on cloth in the desired pattern areas and the cloth is immersed in a path of dye solution.

The dye only becomes fixed on the fabric is those areas, where the mordant has been painted because the mordant reacts with the dye stuff making it insoluble to washing and fast to light.

Different mordant will react with a dye to give different colours and this means that a cloth painted with several mordants can be passed through one dye bath and rinsed off to give a pattern of many colours.

Equipments used for Tie and Dye

- Large containers for dyeing process and few small bowls to prepare the dye.
- Buckets for rinsing the material.
- Rubber gloves to keep hands clean and to ensure safety.
- Big vessel and soap flakes to wash the material after dyeing.
- A stove for heating and boiling the dye.
- An apron to prevent dye patches on cloth.
- Newspaper to protect table from dye colour.
- Measuring spoons to measure dye.
- A pair of tongs for holding cloth.

Dyeing Process

Direct dyes are the simplest and easy to use and have variety of colours to choose from. They are usually in powder form. Enamel and copper vessels are best suited for this purpose.

Process of Dyeing

- Heat sufficient amount of water in the vessel.
- Add hot dry paste to the boiling water in dye bath and stir.
- Add a spoonful of common salt in the dye bath as it fasten the colour.
- Squeeze the cloth in the dye bath. Keep stirring it.
- Take out cloth and rinse it in water, soapy solution and again play it in water till the last rinse show no colour.
- Let the material be completely dried in shade before opening it.
- Now, remove the threads with a pair of scissors. Iron the cloth flat after drying.

Pattern of Tie and Dye

- To get the stripped effect, the material is gathered horizontally or folded diagonally and tied with isolated strings.
- To get a circular design, the material is held from the centre and pleated like an umbrella.
- To achieve bandies or spots, the threads are tied inside for the purpose.
- Marbling is one of the easiest technique, in which the cloth is crumpled together and then tied all around giving an abstract pattern.
- In another pattern, the cloth is simply gathered horizontally and knotted at several or few places. It gives an interesting effect.
- In one type, the cloth is pleated with large pleats horizontally and then the long strip achieved is folded from one corner to give a triangle and this procedure is continued till a triangle is achieved, which three corners are tied. This is called triangular folding.
- In one of the pattern, we draw a design on the cloth and then draw lines of design and finally stretch the threads to knit tightly. This secures the lines to draw. This method is called stitching method.
- Twisting involves gathering the cloth together diagonally or horizontally and then twisting the length of this and further turning it to make both ends meet. This is then tied at several places.
- In another pattern, all corners are tied with thread at the centre by gathering.
- Diamonds are obtained by pleating the cloth and then tying the thread in a criss-cross manner, throughout. All these designs and many other give interesting effects and can be dipped in different colours to add to their beauty.

Technique for Tie and Dye

Preliminary washing and treating of the cloth should be done to remove all the traces of the starch. Keep varying types of agents to get different effects. Forming pattern is the first stage. It is done according to the effects, which are required. The cloth is tied as per designs desired.

Printing

Printing is a process for reproducing text and images, typically with ink on paper using a printing press. It is often carried out as a large scale industrial process and is an essential part of publishing and transaction printing.

The earliest form of printing was woodblock printing, with existing examples from China, dating to before AD 220 and Egypt to the 4th century. Later, developments in printing include the movable type, first developed by **Bi Sheng** in China. And later the printing press, which is more efficient printing process for Western languages with their more limited alphabet, developed by **Johannes Gutenberg** in the 15th Century.

Types of Printing

Some important types of printing are given below :

Batik Printing

Batik is originally a 'Japanese', which refers to the whole range of activities of drawing, painting and writing. It uses a simple principle of a mechanical resist. Traditionally it is done either on pure silk or cotton. After the usual pre-treatment process of degumming or bleaching, the fabric can be taken for printing the fabric should be stretched over the batik frame. Stretching the fabric over the frame has the additional advantage of allowing the user to check the penetration of the wax. Matter wax is applied for getting the resistance.

The wax should be at the temperature between 50-60°C. Wax used for batik can be paraffin wax or bees wax and the combination of two types melted together.

Paraffin wax is hard and brittle and results in more cracks. If used alone, it is quiet likely that the wax will chip off from the cloth and it has very poor adhesion, which gives cracks very easily. For these specific reasons, artists use pure bees wax. The waxing combination of bees and paraffin wax are quite popular and the combination can vary from 50:50 to a ratio of three parts of paraffin to one part of bees wax.

Screen Printing

Screen printing is the method of applying colour, design and it is done either by hand or by photographic method. The fabric to be printed is spread out on a long table. Screen is prepared for each colour of the design. At the time, when this procedure was developed, silk was used. A lacquer matting closes all areas of design except the area, on which one of the colour of the design is to be printed. For example, if a red rose with green leaf is to be printed, one screen is to be made that closes off all, but the red rose area and another is made green leaf area. Design is transferred to the screen often by photo chemical in which the design for each colour is made separately.

Thus, screen is coated with photo sensitive material that will have to close the dye. The screen has contact with the photo graphic plate behind, which the screen has to be placed. Exposed areas of the screen are changed chemically, so that they can be washed out and unexposed areas remain opaque. Further, opaque areas are reinforced by a layer of lacquer. The printer takes the screen, which is mounted on frame and places it in correct position above all fabric. The dye is coated on back of screen by squeeze, which is made to run across the screen, through open areas of screen on to the fabric. To colour the next session of fabric the screen is further moved along the fabric.

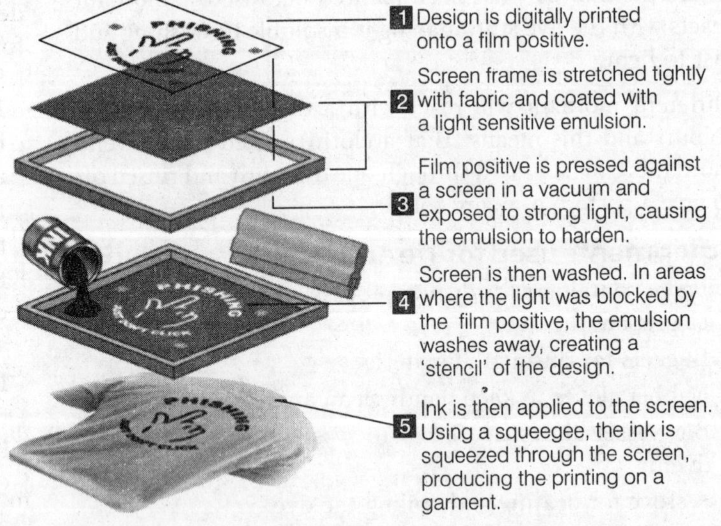

Process of Screen Printing

Stencil Printing

Stencil printing is one of the resist process of textile design. The resist in this case being the stencil itself, which prevents the paints from spreading beyond the margin of the cut out pattern. Stencil can be made out of heavy wax paper, card board or metal. Metal stencils are the most durable and are used for commercial work.

Sprinkle small pieces of paraffin wax on the surface, cover it with another similar sheet of paper and run a moderately hot iron overall, separate the two top sheets. This provides two sheets of stencil paper.

Repeat the process, if more wax is needed. When the paint is applied around the outside of the pattern, the stencil is said to be negative stencil and when it is applied to the inside of the cut out opening, the stencil is said to be the positive stencil.

Block Printing

Block printing appears to be the most ancient printing. Some experts design a date of 200 BC to printing. The Russia Block that is used in printing textile have been recovered from Egyptian graves of the 4th Century AD. This is the simplest printing technique and requires limited technology. A block of material (usually wood) has a design drawn on a flat side, the design covered by cutting the spaces between the areas that form the pattern, thus placing the design in raised position.

Sometimes, during printing the block is tapped with a metal to assure complete contact of a block with the fabric. In order to make the best possible, print the dye had to be in a viscous form.

Otherwise, the insized area would have been filled in by a watery dye substance and the block would not have carried sufficient dye to make a clear image.

Printing wooden blocks may be used to apply colourant directly to a fabric or to apply a resist. Some 2000 years ago, block printing were used in India and China. In Europe, block printing is thought to have originated in the Middle Ages and there is evidence of early block. Printed linen fabric was produced in Germany between 900 and 1300 AD. Printed with pigments and with details painted on by hand, these early designs were often of animals enclosed in circular shapes.

Roller Printing

Roller printing was developed in 1785. Thousands yards of coloured designed fabrics are produced in an hour by the method of printing. In this printing, several copper cylinders or rollers are engraved with design. Engraving the design on the rollers is a hard and careful work lasting many days, but actual printing by this method takes very little time.

The roller is as wide as the cloth. The number of rollers required depend on the number of colours used in the design. One roller prints one colour only.

The roller printing machine comprises of a large central cylinder around which passes the fabric to be printed, this cylinder rotates with the moving fabric.

Number of colour printing rollers, carrying different colours, press against the fabric and the central cylinder. Thus, if there are five colours in the design, there are five colour printing rollers.

Each of these rollers is made to copper and engraved with the respective design. Furnished rollers which move at intervals, containing the colour or dye are placed close to the design rollers. The dye is absorbed by the brush, like surface and transferred to the design engraved rollers.

Discharge Printing

This type of printing is suitable for fabrics with dull backgrounds. The fabric is first dyed. A discharge paste which contains chemicals to remove the colour is then printed on the fabric, to produce a white pattern on a ground colour. This print is done on materials like cotton and rayon.

Heat Transfer Printing

Transfer printing technique involves the transfer of a design from one medium to another. The most common form used is heat transfer printing in which the design is printed initially on to a special paper, using conventional printing machinery. The paper is then placed in close contact with the fabric and heated when the dyes sublime and transfer to the fabric through the vapour phase.

Digital Printing

Digital printing describes the process of transferring a document on a personal computer or other digital storage device to a printing substrate by means of a device that accepts tent and graphic output. As with other digital processes, information is reduced to binary code or digitised to facilitate its stage and reproduction. Digital printing has steadily replaced lithography in many markets, especially at the consumer and business level, as a result of its substantially lower production costs.

The following peripherals are capable of digital printing :

- Inkjet printer
- Laser printer
- Multi-functional peripheral printer

EXAM BASED QUESTIONS

1 What is true with regard to fabric?
(a) Fabric is only manmade.
(b) Fabrics are only used for making clothes.
(c) Fabrics are first industry to benefit from energy produced from steam engine.
(d) All of the above

2 How many types of fabrics are available in the market?
(a) Natural fabrics
(b) Artificial or man made fabrics
(c) Mix fabrics
(d) All of the above

3 What do you mean by natural fabrics?
(a) They are made from animal coats, silk worms and plant leaves, steams, etc.
(b) They are man-made
(c) They don't protect us from UV light.
(d) They are very scarce.

4 What are the factors that could affect the fabric durability?
(a) Finishes (b) Yarn structure
(c) Fibre content (d) All of these

5 Which fabric is referred as luxurious, beautiful, highly comfortable and soft?
(a) Silk (b) Wool
(c) Cotton (d) Linen

6 What is linen fabric?
(a) King fabric (b) Woven fabric
(c) Knitted fabric (d) Elastic fabric

7 Who is marked as the biggest cultivator of Jute?
(a) India (b) Pakistan
(c) Bangladesh (d) Afghanistan

8 Which fabric is suitable for both hot and cold climatic conditions?
(a) Cotton (b) Jute
(c) Linen (d) Leather

9 What do you mean by synthetic fibres?
(a) They are natural
(b) They are best to wear
(c) They are dull
(d) They are madeup of chemicals

10 What is the property of Georgette?
(a) Opaque (b) Slightly heavy
(c) Only (a) (d) Both (a) and (b)

11 ……… is performed on pattern requiring a solid ground, usually dark shades and extremely tight registration of peg objects to the background.
(a) Block printing (b) Discharge printing
(c) Carpet printing (d) Stencil printing

12 Different fibres in a blend are dyed to different values of the same, have
(a) tone-on-tone (b) union dyeing
(c) cross dyeing (d) batch dyeing

13 One of the latest method of dyeing fabric is in the form of rope. Two ends are joined up together and the fabric moves in dye liquor is known as
(a) beam dyeing (b) jig dyeing
(c) winch dyeing (d) jet dyeing

14 Choose the option which is not used for yarn dyeing?
(a) Jet dyeing (b) Beam dyeing
(c) Skein dyeing (d) Package dyeing

15 Sulphur dyes are basically used for
(a) silk (b) stone and acid wash
(c) air oxidation (d) None of these

16 Fabric is first treated with dye and then treated with mordant. It means
(a) after chrome (b) scouring
(c) chrome mordant (d) metachrome

17 Garment dyeing is not a very popular way of dyeing as
(a) garment may loose shape
(b) dye is patchy
(c) there is serving thread problem
(d) All of the above

18 Which of the following fibres is the most difficult to dye?
(a) Cotton (b) Nylon
(c) Polyester (d) Viscose rayon

19 Slim set point needles are used for
(a) woven fabric with medium packed yarn
(b) woven fabric with very tightly packed yarn
(c) knits or delicate fabrics with loosely packed yarns
(d) woven fabric with loosely packed yarn

20 When all the elements of design are nicely related the design has
(a) unity (b) discriminity
(c) proportion (d) emphasis

21 Which of the following textile properties are most desirable for Olympic swim wear?
(a) Absorption and reduced drag
(b) Comfort and durability
(c) Maximum stretch and durability
(d) Maximum stretch and reduced drag

22 Series of loops that intersect horizontally in a fabric are called as
(a) courses (b) wales
(c) warp (d) weft

23 Which of the following finishing techniques is most appropriate for a fabric to be used on the seats in a movie theatre?
(a) Mildew proof and calendered
(b) Non-pilling and water repellent
(c) Sanforised and antistatic
(d) Soil-resistant and fire-retardant

24 The weft yarns go under and over two or more warp yarns at regular intervals, creating a diagonal pattern. This kind of weave is called as
(a) plain weave (b) twill weave
(c) leno weave (d) None of these

25 This twill weave material is used for expensive suits and outer wear
(a) gabardine (b) linen
(c) velour (d) pellon

26 Weaves can be created on
(a) cam (b) dobby
(c) jacquard (d) All of these

27 It is a type of warp knitting
(a) interlock (b) tricot
(c) float jacquard (d) rib-knit

28 Which of the following fabrics is a knitted fabric?
(a) Chiffon (b) Seersucker
(c) Jacquard (d) Jersey

29 Basket, pile, twill and satin are all types of
(a) weaves (b) fibres
(c) materials (d) draps

30 A chemical finish, exclusively given to cotton to increase lustre, strength and dye ability is
(a) fulling (b) crabbing
(c) bleaching (d) mercerisation

31 Shiny and Lustrous fabrics reflect light and emphasise
(a) body contours (b) quality
(c) drapability (d) None of these

32 Acid dyes are so called because
(a) they are dyed in acidic conditions.
(b) they are applied on fabrics, which have affinity for acids.
(c) their content is acidic.
(d) All of the above

33 Dye auxiliaries include
(a) swelling agents (b) dispersing agents
(c) antifoaming agents (d) All of these

34 Satin, twill and plain are
(a) types of weaves (b) types of fabrics
(c) types of fibres (d) types of knits

35 Dye is applied to fabric via
(a) hot water (b) steam
(c) dry heat (d) All of these

36 Weaving, knitting, felting and knotting are all means of making
(a) fabrics (b) fibres
(c) threads (d) knits

37 The word 'textiles' comes from Latin word 'textile' which means
(a) weave (b) textile (c) fabric (d) stitches

38 A fabric used for outerwear in plain or twill weave in wool or as a mixture is of light to medium weight and is raised from one or both sides is
(a) flannel (b) cheriot
(c) tweed (d) afgalaine

39 Which dyeing method you would propose for dyeing 45×100 woven corduroy with direct dyes, under low cost, covering dead cotton also?
(a) Transfer (b) Continuous
(c) Beck (d) Package

40 Acid dyes have good affinity for
(a) cotton (b) wool
(c) rayon (d) polyester

41 Lock knit fabric is basically a
(a) warp knitted fabric
(b) weft knitted circular fabric
(c) weft knitted flat fabric
(d) braided fabric

42 Natural dyes are
(a) more eco-friendly and non-allergic
(b) light and wash fast
(c) fixed with mordants which are eco-friendly
(d) less costly and are sufficiently available

Directions (Q. Nos. 43-48) *In the questions given below are two statements, labelled as Assertion (A) and Reason (R). In the context of the two statements, which one of the following is correct?*

Codes
(a) Both A and R are true and R is the correct explanation of A
(b) Both A and R are true, but R is not the correct explanation of A
(c) A is true,but R is false
(d) A is false,but R is true

43 **Assertion** (A) The shrinkage test may be carried out either by immersion of the fabric in water for a specified period or by subjecting it to washing treatment at various temperatures.

Reason (R) The extent of shrinkage of fabric depends on fabric weave, tension during weaving and finishing treatment given to the fabric.

44 **Assertion** (A) Tie and dye is an ancient method of pattern-making on cloth.

Reason (R) Tie and dye is an ancient method of pattern-making cloth.

45 **Assertion** (A) Screen printing is the method of applying colour, design and it is done either by hand or photographic method.

Reason (R) The fabric to be printed is spread out on a long table.

46 **Assertion** (A) The first non-woven fabrics from manufactured fibres were produced in 1942.

Reason (R) All non-woven fabrics are made directly from fibres.

47 **Assertion** (A) The finishes given to the fabrics to get different properties like durability, anti-crease property, wash and wear, water repellency, etc. must be identified.

Reason (R) Some of the chemicals used for finishing of the fabrics like formaldehyde, penta-chlora phenol, etc. are harmful for the body.

48 **Assertion** (A) Surface designing includes printing.

Reason (R) Printing is a form of applying colour all over the fabric.

49 Indian designers and producers have come up with attractive jute

1. carpets
2. handbags and footwear
3. garments
4. blankets

Codes

(a) 1 and 2 (b) 1 and 4
(c) 1, 2, 3 and 4 (d) 1, 2 and 3

50 The main characteristics of Dobby weave are

1. small figure like dots
2. geometric designs
3. floral designs
4. two or more basic weaves

Codes

(a) 1 and 2 (b) 1 and 4
(c) 1, 2, 3 and 4 (d) 1, 2 and 3

51 The clothing used for undergarments should possess the qualities of

1. softness
2. wash ability
3. porous
4. flexibility

Codes

(a) 1, 2, 3 and 4 (b) 1, 2 and 3
(c) 1 and 2 (d) 3 and 4

52 While, choosing household textiles like towel, linen, etc. one should look for

1. quality
2. washability
3. absorbency
4. durability and softness

Codes

(a) 1 and 2 (b) 1 and 4
(c) 1, 2 and 3 (d) All of these

53 Factors to be considered while choosing men's wear are

1. quality
2. light weight
3. durability
4. appearance requirement

Codes

(a) 1 and 2 (b) 1 and 4
(c) 1, 2 and 3 (d) All of these

54 Which of the following statements are correct?

1. In scouring, proteins are hydrolysed into soluble products.
2. Knitted fabrics are scoured under wild processing conditions.
3. Hydrogen peroxide is universal bleaching agent.

Codes

(a) 1and 2 (b) 2 and 3 (c) 1 and 3 (d) All of these

55 Sewing thread require final finishing as

1. a protective coating against abrasion.
2. the appearance and characteristics desired in final seam.
3. the frictional characteristics required for satisfactory sewing.
4. protection against heat generated during sewing.

Codes

(a) 1 and 2 (b) 3 and 4 (c) 3 and 4 (d) All of these

56 Which of the following statements is/are correct?

1. Felt is made from wool or mixed wool. Matt is dampened and heated and pressure applied to it the wool fibres entangled and form dense material felt.
2. Knitted fabrics can be stretched more than woven fabrics, so can used for rests under weavers socks.

Codes

(a) 1 and 2 (b) Only1
(c) Only 2 (d) None of these

57 Which of the following methods of printing are currently practised largely in the Indian textile industry?

1. Screen printing
2. Digital printing
3. Roller printing
4. Block printing

Codes

(a) 2, 3, and 4 (b) 1, 2 and 3
(c) 1, 3 and 4 (d) 1, 2 and 4

58 Which of the following build self-confidence and sense of security in clothing?

1. Quality
2. Style
3. Neat and clean
4. Colour

Codes

(a) 1 and 2 (b) 1 and 4
(c) 1, 2 and 3 (d) All of these

59 Which of the following senses help in the selection of clothing?

1. Sight
2. Touch
3. Smell
4. Hear

Codes

(a) 1, 2, 3 and 4 (b) 1, 2 and 3
(c) 1 and 2 (d) 1 and 4

60 Arrange the following in correct sequence in preparation of fabric for clothing construction.

1. Blocking
2. Shrinking
3. Pressing
4. Straightening

Codes

(a) 1, 2, 3, 4 (b) 2, 4, 1, 3
(c) 4, 1, 2, 3 (d) 3, 4, 1, 2

61 Consider the following statements regarding the inspection of a fabric.
1. Length of any fibre can be made into staple length, but not all can be filament length.
2. Body, textile, hand, soft to hard, rough to smooth, warm to cool or stiff to flexible.
3. Lustre or lack of lustre.

Which of the statements given above is/are correct?
(a) 1 and 2 (b) 2 and 3
(c) 1 and 3 (d) All of these

62 The correct sequence for preparation of fabric for cutting is
(a) Blocking, straightening, marking, pressing
(b) Pressing, blocking, straightening, marking
(c) Straightening, blocking, pressing, marking
(d) Marking, pressing, straightening, blocking

63 Identify the most suitable fabric for lace and curtains.
(a) Cotton fibre, monofilament yarn, double knit.
(b) Polyester fibre, high twist yarn, sateen weave
(c) Polyester fibre, multi filament yarn, Raschel knit
(d) Viscose rayon, staple spun yarn, Jaçquard weave

64 Which of the following are all principles of dyeing?
(a) Absorption, wetting-out, abrasion
(b) Agitation, migration, fixation
(c) Migration,abrasion, wetting out
(d) Decoration, absorption, fixation

65 Match the following.

List I	List II
A. Knits	1. Open work
B. Wovens	2. Web structure
C. Felt	3. Warps and wefts
D. Lace	4. Wales and courses

Codes

	A	B	C	D		A	B	C	D
(a)	1	4	3	2	(b)	2	1	4	3
(c)	3	2	1	4	(d)	4	3	2	1

66 Match the following.

List I	List II
A. Manmade fibres	1. Accept dyes and finishes more readily
B. High lustre, low lustre	2. May be pure white
C. Fibres with good moisture regain	3. Rayon and cotton
D. Low wet strength, high wet strength	4. The percentage of return from elongation to the original length
E. Elastic recovery	5. Silk and cotton

Codes

	A	B	C	D	E
(a)	4	1	2	3	5
(b)	5	4	3	1	2
(c)	2	5	1	3	4
(d)	1	2	5	4	3

67 Match the following.

List I	List II
A. Wet spinning	1. Changing the size and number of holes in the spinnet
B. Dry spinning	2. Nylon, Polyester
C. Melt spinning	3. Acrylic
D. The fineness of the fibre in manmade fibres altered	4. Rayon

Codes

	A	B	C	D		A	B	C	D
(a)	4	1	3	2	(b)	1	2	3	4
(c)	4	3	2	1	(d)	4	2	1	3

Directions (Q. Nos. 68-71) *Read the following passage and answer the questions that follow.*

Fabric construction involves the conversion of yarns and sometime fibres into a fabric having characteristics determined by the materials and methods employed. Most fabrics are presently produced by some methods of interlacing, such as weaving of knitting. Weaving , currently the major method of fabric production includes the basic weaves plain or tabby, twill and satin and the fancy weaves, including pile, jacquard, dobby, and gauze.

Knitted fabrics are rapidly increasing in importance and include weft types and the warp types, raschel and tricot. Other interlaced fabrics include net, lace and braid. Non-woven fabrics are gaining importance and include materials produced by felthing and bonding. Laminating processes are also increasing in importance and fairly recent developments include needle weaving and the seving-knitting process.

68 What do you mean by the construction of fabric?
(a) For the conversion of yarn
(b) Leads to the change in the current fibre
(c) Only (a)
(d) Both (a) and (b)

69 What is the common method of fabric construction?
(a) Weaving (b) Knitting
(c) Sewing (d) All of these

70 Match the following

List I	List II
A. Fabric construction	1. Net, lace and braid
B. Fancy weavers	2. Felting and bonding
C. Interlaced fabrics	3. Weaving or knitting
D. Non-woven	4. Dobby and jacquard

Codes

	A	B	C	D		A	B	C	D
(a)	3	4	1	2	(b)	1	2	3	4
(c)	3	1	4	2	(d)	4	3	2	1

71 In which of the fabric construction process we use sewing knitting process?
(a) Non-woven fabric (b) Lamination process
(c) Woven fabric (d) Knitted fabric

PREVIOUS YEARS' QUESTIONS

January 2017

1 **Assertion** (A) Acid dyes are suitable for wool and silk.

Reason (R) Acid dyes form ionic bonds with the amino groups found in wool and silk.

Codes

(a) A is true, but R is false
(b) A is false, but R is true
(c) Both A and R are false
(d) Both A and R are true

2 **Assertion** (A) Microscopic test is a confirmatory test for man-made fibres.

Reason (R) Manmade fibres have their distinct characteristic microscopic appearance.

Codes

(a) Both A and R are true
(b) Both A and R are false
(c) A is true, but R is false
(d) A is false, but R is true

3 Which to the following are components of a dye?

1. Auxochrome 2. Chromophore
3. Pigment 4. Ink

Codes

(a) 1 and 3 (b) 2 and 4 (c) 1 and 2 (d) 2 and 3

July 2016

4 **Assertion** (A) While removing blood stain, heat must be avoided.

Reason (R) Heat coagulates the protein and fixes the stain on the fabric.

Codes

(a) Both A and R are true
(b) Both A and R are false
(c) A is true, but R is false
(d) A is false, but R is true

5 Which of the following dyes is cationic in nature?

(a) Acid
(b) Disperse
(c) Basic
(d) Direct

6 **Assertion** (A) Textured yarns are not prone to snagging.

Reason (R) Lesser surface area is available to contact rough or sharp objects.

Codes

(a) Both A and R are false
(b) Both A and R are true
(c) A is true, but R is false
(d) A is false, but R is true

ANSWERS

Exam Based Questions

1 (c)	2 (d)	3 (a)	4 (d)	5 (a)	6 (a)	7 (c)	8 (d)	9 (d)	10 (d)
11 (b)	12 (a)	13 (d)	14 (a)	15 (b)	16 (a)	17 (d)	18 (b)	19 (b)	20 (a)
21 (c)	22 (d)	23 (d)	24 (b)	25 (a)	26 (d)	27 (b)	28 (d)	29 (a)	30 (d)
31 (a)	32 (c)	33 (b)	34 (a)	35 (d)	36 (a)	37 (a)	38 (a)	39 (c)	40 (b)
41 (a)	42 (c)	43 (a)	44 (c)	45 (c)	46 (b)	47 (a)	48 (c)	49 (c)	50 (c)
51 (a)	52 (d)	53 (b)	54 (b)	55 (d)	56 (a)	57 (a)	58 (d)	59 (b)	60 (c)
61 (d)	62 (b)	63 (c)	64 (b)	65 (d)	66 (c)	67 (c)	68 (d)	69 (d)	70 (a)
71 (b)									

Previous Years' Questions

1 (d)	2 (b)	3 (c)	4 (a)	5 (c)	6 (a)

Textile Testing and Environmental Control

Textile testing and quality control are very important work or process in each department of export oriented industry. In every department of textile industry, quality is maintained of each material. In the process of textile manufacturing and testing, environment is affected to a great extent. Thus, environmental control has become important field in textile industry.

Textile Testing and Quality Control

Textile testing means checking the quality, suitability of raw material and selection of material. It is an important part of textile production, distribution and consumption. Though, it is an expensive business but essential too. There are some reasons for textile testing; such as checking raw materials, monitoring production, assessing the final product, investigation of faulty material, product development and research.

Quality control is a process by which entities review the quality of all products in an industry. It refers to ways of ensuring the quality of a service or product. Actually quality control is a system for verifying and maintaining a desired level of quality in an existing product or service by careful planning, use of proper equipment, continued inspection and corrective action as required.

Need of Textile Testing

Due to following reasons, textile testing is needed :

Checking Raw Materials The production cycle as far as testing is concerned starts with the delivery of raw material. If the raw material is incorrect or sub-standard then it is impossible to produce the required quality of final product. The textile industry consists of a number of separate processes such as natural fibre production, man-made fibre entrusion, wool scouring, yarn spinning, weaving, dyeing and finishing.

The processes are very often carried out in separate establishments, therefore what is considered to be a raw material depends on the stage in processing at which the testing take place.

In this Chapter

Monitoring Production Production monitoring involves testing samples taken from the production line, is known as quality control. Its aim is to maintain, within known tolerances, certain specified properties of the product at the level at which they have been set. A quality product for these purposes is defined as one whose properties meet or exceeds the set specifications. Besides the need to carry out the tests correctly, successful monitoring of production also requires the careful design of appropriate sampling procedures and the use of statistical analysis to make sense of the results.

Assessing the Final Product In this process the bulk production is examined before delivery to the customer to see if it meets the specifications. By its nature this takes place after the material has been produced. It is therefore too late to alter the production conditions. In some cases selected samples are tested and in other cases all the material is checked and steps are taken to rectify faults. For instance, some qualities of fabric are inspected for faulty places which are mended by skilled operatives; this is a normal part of the process and the material would be dispatched as first quality.

Investigation of Faulty Material If faulty material is discovered either at final inspection or through a customer complaint, it is important that the cause is isolated. This enables steps to be taken to eliminate faulty production in future and to provide a better quality product. Investigations of faults can also involve the determination of which party is responsible for faulty material in the case of a dispute between supplier and a user, especially where processes such as finishing have been undertaken by outside companies. Work of this nature is often contracted out to independent laboratories who are then able to give an unbiased opinion.

Product Development and Research The textile industry is changing all over time, bringing modified materials or different methods of production. Before any modified product reaches the market place, it is necessary to test the material and check that the properties have been improved or have not been degraded by faster production. In this way an improved product on a lower-cost product with the same properties can be provided for the customer. A large organisation will often have a separate department to carry out research and development; otherwise it is a part of the normal duties of the testing department.

Textile Sampling Method

Sampling is the process by which a sample is collected from a large number of materials. By the sampling we know the perfect characteristics of desired clothes. Sampling increases the quality of clothing and reduces the cost. In textile industry, sampling is essential for export quality product. Textile sampling depends on few factors such as the form of the material, amount of material available, nature of the test etc.

Need for Sampling Method

Textile testing is destructive in nature, i.e. the materials used for testing go as waste after testing and hence it is not desirable to test all of the material. As textile production is always huge and bulk it is impossible to test all the final output from a production process. Thus, only representative samples of the material are tested, sampling saves time and cost.

Various Sampling Techniques of Testing Fibres

Description of various sampling techniques of testing fibres is given below :

Zoning Sampling Technique Zoning is used for selecting samples from raw cotton or wool or other loose fibre where the properties may vary considerably from place to place. A handful of fibres is taken at random from each of at least 40 widely spaced places (zones) throughout the bulk of the consignment and is treated as follows.

If the bulk of the material is not homogeneous, a number of sub-samples must be taken at random from different places in the bulk. The number of sub-samples depends upon the degress of heterogeneity of the bulk and may be found by experiment.

Each handful is divided into two parts and one half of it is discarded at random; the retained half is again divided into two and half of the discarded. This process is repeated until about nine × fibres that lead to only handful fibre left. Each handful is treated in a similar manner and the fibres that remain are placed together to give a correctly sized test sample containing in fibres. The method is shown in fig below. It is important that the whole sample must be tested.

Core Sampling Techniques The core sampling technique is used for assessing the proportion of foreign matter, the waste percentage, and the moisture content in the compressed unopened bales of raw wool or cotton. A tube with a sharpened tip is forced into the bale and a core of wool or cotton is withdrawn. The technique was first used as core boring in which the tube was rotated by a transportable electric drill. It was then developed further to facilitate the cores to be cut by pressing the tube into the bale by hand.

Random Sampling Techniques The random sampling technique is the most widely used technique. It can be applied in both fibre and yarn testing. The steps involved are as follows :

- Determine the size of the population
- Determine the sample size
- Prepare a random numbers table

- Determine the number of each item in a sample
- Collect the sample

The following types of random sampling are used in the industry :

- **Stratified Random Sampling** This is done by dividing the population into several mutually exclusive regions.
- **Cluster Sampling** This is done by subdividing the population into groups or clusters and taking a sample from each.
- **Selected Sampling** In this type, the samples are collected from one part of the population.
- **Systematic Sampling** This is performed systematically at a regular interval.
- **Acceptance Sampling** This is used to accept the incoming raw material or for quality assurance of outgoing consign- ments.

Testing of Fibres and Fabrics

There are two methods that are used for identifying different fibres :

1. Non-technical tests
2. Technical tests

Non-Technical Tests

It includes Feeling test and Burn test. These are discussed below :

Feeling Test

Feeling test involves touching a fabric and feeling the fabric to know its component fibres. *e.g.,* wool fabrics will feel warm when touched because the heat generated by wool, which is a non-conductor of heat, will remain in the touched area itself. On the other hand, the fabrics made up of plant fibre such as cotton fabrics, linen fabrics and even rayon fabrics that are made from the cellulose of wood pulp or cotton fibre, feel cool to touch.

As they are conductors of heat, the heat generated by the finger passes off making the fabric cold. However, it requires a long experience of handling different fabrics over a period of time for such skillful perception. Also, it is difficult to examine and compare the fabrics made of different fibre contents with the feeling test.

Burn Test

It involves burning a sample of fabric and observing the various characteristics shown by it after burning in order to determine its fibre content.

The burning test is more efficient than the feeling test, but it also has its limitations. *e.g.,* fabrics made of biconstituent fibre, that are combination of two different textile polymers, cannot be identified with this test.

The following chart provides a more clear view about the burn test of different fibres e.g.

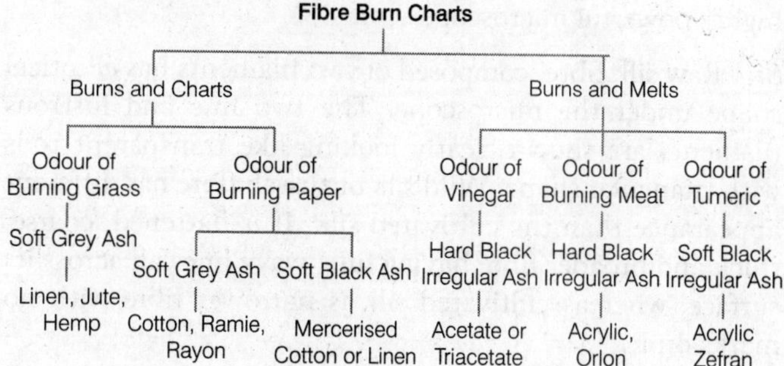

Technical Tests

The technical tests for fibre identification done with the help of laboratory equipments are for more reliable than the non-technical tests. However, technical knowledge and skill, particularly, while handling chemicals, are the basic requirements for conducting these tests. Technical tests include microscope test and chemical testing. These are discussed below :

Microscope Test

Microscope test is very effective for testing the natural fabrics. Difficulties can be faced, while testing the synthetic fabrics as many of them have similar appearence. Many finishing processes like mercerising and delustering, change the appearance of fibres under microscope.

Apart from it, dark coloured fabrics also cannot be tested with microscope as light cannot pass through dark substances. For such fabrics, either the textile dyes have to be removed by stripping, bleaching etc., or they have to be chemically tested.

Microscope Test for Natural Fibres

Natural fibres have their own peculiar structures spots, lines and other marks that help, identifying them.

Following are some examples of natural fibres and how they look like under a microscope :

Cotton Under a microscope, it looks like flat spirally twisted ribbon like tube with rough granular surface. Mercerised cotton doesn't have swollen, straight, smooth surface. It is round with a shining surface.

Linen Linen fibre, under a microscope, looks like having multiple sided cylindrical filaments with fine pointed edges. The filaments show nodes at intervals. It infact, looks like a bamboo stick having joints that results into a little unevenness.

Wool It has irregular, roughly cylindrical, multi cellular structure with tapered ends. Under a microscope, three basic layers are shown. These are epidermis (outer layer), cortex (middle layer) and medulla (inner layer). Medulla is seen only in coarse and medium wool fibres and that too under a highly powerful microscope.

Silk Raw silk fibre, composed of two filaments has elliptical shape under the microscope. The two fine and lustrous filaments are shown clearly looking like transparent rods with triangular shape. Wild silk or tussah fibre has different appearance than the cultivated silk. It is flattened, coarse, thick and broader fibre having fine, wavy lines all across its surface, whereas cultivated silk is narrower fibre with no marks on it.

Microscope Test for Man-made Fibres

Man-made fibres are difficult to identify through microscope because of similar appearance of many fibres. However, their certain distinguishable characteristics under a microscope are mentioned below :

Rayon It has uniform diameter with glass like shine. If delustered, then rayon fibre shows marks similar to pepper, when viewed cross-sectionally . Viscose fibre of rayon looks irregular, when viewed cross-sectionally.

Acetate This looks lesser irregular than viscose rayon when viewed cross-sectionally. It has indentations that look like occasional marks when viewed longitudinally.

Nylon There are many variants of nylon fibre. However, generally it appears fine, round, smooth and translucent. Sometimes, it has shiny appearance. If it looks dull, it will also be dotted under the microscope.

Aramid If viewed longitudinally, aramid fibre looks smooth and straight. If viewed cross sectionally it may be round or like peanut's shape.

Polyester Generally, polyester fibre is smooth and straight. It looks round cross-sectionally. However, with various finishing processes, its appearance changes in context of texture and luster.

Spandex These fibre have the outstanding characteristic of appearing like groups of fibres fused together. However, different variants of spandex show different characteristics too. The lycra fibre looks like fused multifilaments cross-sectionally. Individual fibres are dotted and in shape like that of dog-bone. If viewed longitudinally, they appear straight.

Poly Propylene When viewed cross-sectionally, poly propylene fibre looks some what round, but it looks straight and smooth when viewed longitudinally.

Glass The glass fibre looks smooth, round, translucent shiny and flexible.

Chemical Testing

Chemical tests for fibre identification can only be conducted in well-equipped laboratories. There are two primary methods to conduct chemical testing i.e., the stain and the solvent.

The Stain Method Stain technique uses acid on different fabrics to identify their fibre contents. Most of the fibres have two colour reactions when treated with stain. A fibre stained with dilute acetic acid it turns to a specific colour. The same fibre when stained with mild alkali like soda carbonate turns to a different colour again specific to that fibre only.

Acetate changes to light green colour, when acetic acid is used and turns orange when dilute carbonate of soda is used. Similarly, nylon turns beige in one and bright red in other. As double testing is done in this method, it is sometimes referred to as double-barreled stain identification.

The Solvent Method Various solvents are used in this method to distinguish one kind of fibre from another. However, there is no single solvent or chemical that can be used on all fibres. It becomes difficult to use solvent methods in view of fibres that have similar chemical characteristics. When more fibres are mixed to produce the blended fabric, then also it becomes tough to identify the fibres with the help of solvent method. In order to have accurate results, the fabric has to be cleaned thoroughly and the finishing chemicals should also be removed completely. The fabric has to be unraveled, yarns have to be untwisted and the fibres have to be put in the solutions in a loose condition as possible.

If wool or silk fibre has to be eliminated from a blended fabric then strong alkalies can be used because animal particles are destroyed in it. 5% of caustic soda or sodium hydroxide is used in water. The action of the chemical is hastened by boiling the solution before immersing the sample fabric in it.

The wool or silk fibre gets completely dissolved in it. The plant fibres remain unaffected. Dilute acids destroy plant fibres. A drop of sulphuric acid, if put on the sample fabric of cotton, linen or rayon then the fabric gets charred at the spot.

Methenamine Test

A standard flammability test used to measure flame retardancy of traditional textiles and nonwovens. In a controlled environment, the methenamine tablet is ignited on the test sample and the amount of charring and burn is measured.

Testing of Yarns

Yarn occupies the intermediate position in the manufacture of fabric from raw material. Yarn results are therefore, essential, both for estimating the quality of raw material and for controlling the quality of fabric produced.

The important characteristics of yarn being tested are :

- Yarn twist
- Linear density/Yarn count
- Yarn strength
- Yarn elongation
- Yarn evenness
- Yarn hairiness etc

Conditions for Yarn Testing

Some textile fibres are highly hydroscopic and their properties change as a function of moisture content. Moisture content is particularly critical in the case of properties, *i.e.* yarn tenacity, elongation, yarn evenness, imperfections, count etc. Therefore, conditioning and testing must be carried out under constant standard atmospheric conditions. The standard atmosphere for textile testing involves a temperature of 20°± 2° and 65 ±2% Rh. In tropical regions, maintaining a temperature of 27°±2° Celcius and 65 ±2% Rh is legitimate. Prior to testing, the samples must be conditioned under Constant standard atmospheric to attain the moisture equilibrium.

The other points to be kept in mind while testing the yarns are as follows :

Yarn Twist

Twist is defined as the spiral disposition of the components of yarn, which is generally expressed as the number of turns per unit length of yarn, *e.g.* turns per inch. Twist is essential to keep the component fibres together in a yarn.

The strength, dyeing, finishing properties, the feel of the finished product etc., are all dependent on the twist of the yarn.

With increase in twist, the yarn strength increases first, reaches a maximum and then decreases.

Depending on the end use, two or more single yarns are twisted together to form **plied yarns** or **folded yarns** and a number of plied yarns twisted together to form **cabled yarn**. Among the plied yarns, the most commonly used are the doubled yarns, where in two single yarns of identical twists are twisted together in a direction opposite to that of the single yarns.

For cabled and plied yarns, the direction of twist and number of turns per unit length of the resultant yarn as well as of each component have to be determined for a detailed analysis.

Direction of twist is expressed as 'S'-twist or 'Z' -twist. Direction depends upon the direction of rotation of the twisting element.

'Twist take-up' is defined as,"The decrease in length of yarn on twisting, expressed, as a percentage of the length of yarn before twisting."

Linear Density /Yarn Count

The fineness of the yarn is usually expressed in terms of its linear density or count. There are a number of systems and units for expressing yarn fineness known as **direct system** and **indirect systems.**

The direct and indirect systems of expressing yarn counts include English count (Ne), Metric count (Nm) French count (Nf), Tex, Denier.

For the determination of the count of yarn, it is necessary to determine the weight of a known length of the yarn. For taking out known lengths of yarns, a wrap-reel is used.

Another factor which determines the length of yarn taken for testing is the type of balance used. Some balances like Quadrant balance and Beesley's balance have been specially designed to indicate the yarn count. One of the most important requirements for a spinner is to maintain the average count and count variation within control. After reeling the appropriate length of yarn, the yarn is conditioned in the standard atmosphere for testing before its weight is determined.

Yarn Strength and Elongation

- Breaking strength, elongation, elastic modulus, resistance abrasion etc., are some important factors which will represent the performance of the yarn during actual use or further processing.
- Strength testing is broadly classified into two methods :
  - Single end strength testing
  - Skein strength
- During routine testing, both the breaking load and extension of yarn at break are usually recorded for assessing the yarn quality.
- Two types of strengths can be determined for a yarn :
  - Tensile strength - load is applied gradually
  - Ballistic strength - applying load under rapids impact conditions

Testing of Colour Fastness

Colour fastness is one of the important factors in case of buyers demand. The outstandingly important property of a dyed material is the fastness of the shade of colour. Colour fastness refers to the resistance of colour to fade or bleed of a dyed or printed textile materials to various types of influences e.g. water, light, rubbing, washing, perspiration etc., to which they are normally exposed in textile manufacturing and in daily use.

Factors Affecting the Colour Fastness Properties

- The chemical nature of the fibre. For example, cellulosic fibres dyed with reactive or vat dyes will show good fastness properties. Protein fibres dyed with acid mordant and reactive dyes will achieve good fastness properties and so on. That is to say compatibility of dye with the fibre is very important.
- The molecular structure of a dye molecule, if the dye molecule is larger in size, it will be tightly entrapped inside the inter-polymer chain space of a fibre. Thus, the fastness will be better.
- The manner in which the dye is bonded to the fibre or the physical form present.
- The presence of other chemicals in the material.
- The amount of dye present in the fibre i.e. depth of shade. A deep shade will be less faster than a pale or light shade.
- The actual conditions prevailing during exposure.

Method of Testing Colour Fastness

The conditions and the requirements of fabric processing and uses are very different. Most of the current test methods are simulated according to the working environment and conditions, so the testing methods of colour fastness are very extensive.

Most commonly used tests are wash resistance, light resistance, friction resistance, sweat resistance, ironing resistance, water resistance and so on. The testing items are mainly determined according to the final use of the product and the product standard. For example, the wool textile product stand stipulates that the light fastness must be tested, and the knitted underwear, of course, has to be tested for perspiration fastness.

Standards of Colour Fastness

- AATCC (American Association of Textile Chemists and Colourists) technical mannual : It describes 66 members of different colour fastness tests.
- SDC (Society of Dyers and Colourists): In 1927, SDC (Europe) made fastness test committee.
- ISO (International Organisation for Standardisation): In 1947, ISO made colour sub committee.
- ISO also grades the fastness:
  - For light fastness : 1 ~ 8
  - For other fastness : 1 ~ 5

Testing For Shrinkage

Shrinkage is the process in which a fabric becomes smaller than its original size, usually through the process of laundary. Cotton fabric suffers from two main disadvantages of shrinking and creasing during subsequent washing. There are two types i.e., length wise and width wise of shrinkage occurs during washing. Due to high tension during preparation of fabric which results in excess stretch in yarn. This type of shrinkage is known as London shrinkage i.e. swelling of fibres for fibre structure.

Working Procedure for Testing Shrinkage

The sample which is done with shrinkage test, spread on table. Then, a glass template put on sample fabric which is of square size. There are six marks on glass template and distance between two marks is 35 cm. Making the sample fabric by unchangeable marker. Then sample is sewn by hand sewing machine. Sample is ready for washing. Simply wash the fabric at 60°C temperature for 90 minutes. After washing the fabric, take it out. Dry the sample as per any of the method. It can either be line dry or flat dry or tumble dry. To find the dimensional change read the shrinkage/stretch on 3 points on the wrap side and 3 points on weft side. Get the mean value of wrap-wise and weft wise readings to get the accurate shrinkage or stretch.

Testing from Pilling

A garment is considered to be serviceable when it is fit for its particular end use. It is a fabric surface fault characterised by little pills of entangled fibre clinging to the cloth surface and giving the garment an unsightly appearance. Formed by rubbing action on loose fibres that are present on the fabric surface. Even stronger component in the blend aggravated its seriousness. Higher breaking strength and lower bending stiffness results more pill. Low twist factor, higher hairiness, and loose fabric structure results easy and large pills.

Measurement of Fabric Pilling

Measurement of fabric pilling is done by objective and subjective methods.

Objective Method Counting the number of pills or by removing them. Time consuming, also does not take into account the degree of colour contrast with the ground.

Subjective Method By comparing it with either standard sample or with photograph or by the use of a written scale of severity.

Pilling Resistance Test

This method is intended for the determination of the resistance of textiles of all kinds in all forms to the action of an applied resistive force. This causes pilling in the tested fabrics

Apparatus for the Test

- Pilling tester
- Metal plates 4 inch diameter and 1 inch thick
- Standard for assessing the pilling grade

Working Procedure of the Test

A piece of fabric measuring 10 × 10 inch is sewn to a firm fit when placed round a rubber tube. The out end of the fabrics is covered by cellophane tape and metal plates are placed on the tester. Run the tester for 300 cycles. Remove the sample and compare the sample with standard scale.

Standard

Pilling Standard 3-4 gray scale matching

GSM Test

Fabric GSM means **Gram per Square Metre** of a knit, woven or non-woven fabric. It is essential to know the weight of the fabric before manufacturing and after getting the finished fabric. It needs to measure the weight of the fabric to be sure about the finished weight of the fabric. This test can be carried out in different ways but it is very easy to know the weight of the fabric by cutting the fabric with the GSM cutter.

Working Procedure of GSM Test

- For measuring with Quadrant balance, at first we should cut the fabric sample according to the template area. By this way we cut 10 woven samples and 10 knitted samples.
- Now weigh these samples in pounds by quadrant balance according to 100 yards scale.
- By this way we get the weight in pound per 100 square yards fabric.
- For Measuring GSM, we should cut the fabric sample by GSM cutter. By this way cut 10 woven samples and 10 knitted samples.
- Now weigh these samples by electric balance in grams.
- By this way we get the weight in gram per one square metre fabric.
- Now find out the average of these found weights.
- For woven fabrics find out the weight per running yards assuming the loom width 48 inches.

Quality and Quality Control

The term quality refers to the excellence of a product. When we say the quality of a product is good, we mean that the product is good for the purpose for which it has been made.

Quality Control

It is the synthetic and regular control of the variable, which affect the quality of a product. It consists of quality planning, data collection, data analysis and implementation and is applicable to all phases of product life-cycle, design, manufacturing, delivery and installation, operation and maintenance.

It is seen that 90% defects found in textiles and clothing, are due to inadequate preparation of fabric (cloth) during processing, that is, before dyeing and are noticed after dyeing cycle is over or printing process is over. Production of good quality fabric requires efficient and continuous online monitoring of production process.

The following diagram depicts the problems experienced in clothing :

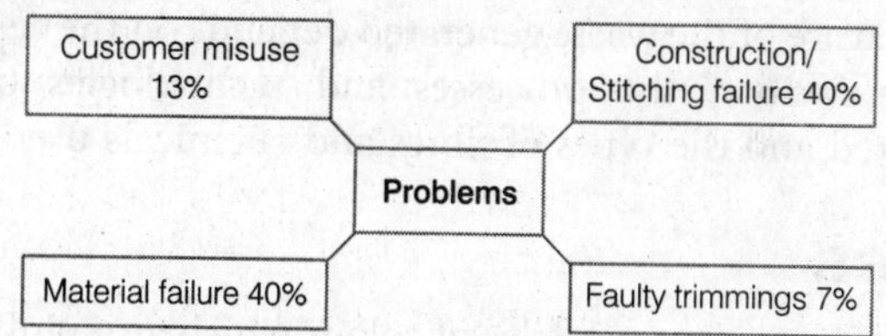

Main Quality Problems Experienced in Apparel

Objectives of Quality Control

- To produce required quality product.
- To fulfill the customer's demand.
- To reduce the production cost.
- To reduce wastage.
- To earn maximum profit at minimum cost.

Importance of Quality Control and Research Institutes

In response to ever changing consumer demands for high quality, textile testing helps to minimise risk and protect the interest of both manufacturers and consumers. Most of the countries require fibre indentification labels indicating the fibre type and percentage of fibre components.

Major European and United States textile product buyers view their textile products from an ecological standpoint. Eco testing targets environmental protection and consumer health and safety.

Eco testing includes :

- Banned Azo colorants and Ozone depleting chemicals.
- Heavy metal, pesticide residues and fungicides such as dimethyl fumorate.
- Formaldehyde content.
- Eco textile certification.

Textile and Environment

Textile processing industry is characterised not only by the large volume of water required for various unit operations but also by the variety of chemicals used for various processes. There is a long sequence of wet processing stages requiring inputs of water, chemicals, energy and generating wastes at each stage.

The other feature of this industry, which is a backbone of fashion garment, is large variation in demand of type, pattern and colour combination of fabric resulting into significant fluctuation in waste generation volume and load. Textile processing generates many waste streams, including liquid, gaseous and solid wastes, some of which may be hazardous.

The nature of the waste generated depends on the type of textile facility, the processes and technologies being operated and the types of fibres and chemicals used.

Dyes

Dyes are very fine particles of colour which are soluble in water. With the help of heat and chemical processes clothes are dyed. They have the quality of pigmentation and assimilation. Due to this colour of fabric, they hold in every corner of the cloth. But not all colours have the ability to dye with the fibrees of all classes. The textile dyeing method is chosen according to the type of fibre and their resemblance to colours, because not all fibres have the same uniformity towards all colours. As different pigments have different reactions of sunlight, washing method, soap used and worker.

Banned Dyes

- Banned dyes are also obtained from some special ants, fishes, moths, etc.
- Dark red colour is obtained from an insect called cochineal.
- Purple colour is obtained from a special type of fish found in the mediterranean sea. Similarly, crimson, scarlet, orange dyes are obtained from insects called cactus.
- Crimson, orange, scarlet, etc., are made from this liquid juice, the colours obtained from the animal world are more expensive, because they have to be killed first to get the colour, the second biggest danger is the elimination (extinction) of their race.
- One of the best options for other types of fibre dyes, sulfur dyes, are dyes and vat dyes. The Institute of Dyes and expertise ecology safety and toxicity studies on Human Health and environment has been established.

Eco-Friendly Textiles

Any textile product, which is produced in eco-friendly manner and processed under eco-friendly limits, is known as eco-friendly textiles. It is also known as sustainable fashion, eco fashion and ecotech.

Materials be considered as 'Eco-friendly' on the basis of various factors :

- Renewability of products.
- Ecological footprints of resources.
- Determining the eco friendliness of a product.

Eco-Friendly Fibres

The description of eco-friendly fibres is given below :

Bamboo It is a regenerated cellulosic fibre produced from bamboo pulp. It is a hardy, highly renewable grass which is generally grown with few chemical inputs. The main factor which makes it consider as an eco-friendly fibre is its renewable property. It has natural anti- bacterial properties and the fabric breathes. Bamboo has a wider application due to its comfort, soft, lustre and absorbency.

Organic Cotton More than 25 percent of the world's pesticides are used in conventional cotton production whereas organic cotton is more eco-friendly than the traditional method as it uses no pesticides,insecticides during the growing cycle. But, it is more labour intensive and furthermore fields must be free of chemicals for three years before the crop can be certified organic. Another recent promising trend is the production of coloured cotton or natural dyes which can further reduce the amount of chemicals used.

Hemp The most potential eco-friendly fibre is hemp. The ecological footprint is considered to be low in hemp fibres when compared to other fibres. It is rapidly renewable, requires little or no pesticides, grows without fertiliser, requires minimum attention and doesn't deplete soil nutrients. So it is easy to harvest. It is a long fibre which is long lasting.

Soy Cashmere/Silk This fabric is made from soy protein fibre left over after processing soybeans into food. The liquefied proteins are extruded into fibres which are then spun and used like other fibres. The high protein content makes it receptive to natural dyes. So, they can create their own colours.

Wool It is renewable, fire-resistant and doesn't need chemical inputs. Organic wool is increasingly becoming available as it is produced using sustainable farming practice. Wool is a very useful textile with many important properties that make it hugely attractive. One of the major benefits of wool is that it can absorb moisture well by drawing moisture into the core of its fibres. A recent innovation in the world of wool is a product created in New Zealand, a place well-known for its sheep, called Wojo.

Eco-Labels

Eco-labelling is becoming a differentiating factor on a worldwide scale in retail markets for textile and apparel purchase. Consumers are becoming increasingly concerned with the adverse impacts of industrial pollution on the environment and their health, resulting mounting pressure on textile, fashion industry to adopt more eco-friendly, chemicals and manufacturing processes.

Environmental concerns raised by production systems have been recognised since the late 1960s and attempts to move towards more sustainable and environmental friendly approaches have been through a range of regulatory measures from green taxes to strict banning of harmful products.

Eco-Mark

Eco-mark is issued by the **Bureau of Indian Standards (BIS)** as a certification mark for the products which are ecologically safe conforming to the standards prescribed by the BIS. The scheme first saw its application in 1991. It is voluntary in nature and helps in identifying eco-friendly products in the market. The mark is being issued in around 16 categories like food, medicine, chemicals, electronic goods, paper, lubricating oils, packing materials etc. The eco-mark scheme falls under the ambit of Ministry of Environment, forest and climate change.

Objective of Eco-Mark Scheme

- Encourage all citizens to use and buy products which are environment-friendly.
- Reward and promote genuine initiatives by companies to reduce the adverse environmental impact on their products.
- Provide incentives for manufacturers and importers to control the ill-effects of their products on the environment.
- Improve the overall quality of the environment and promote sustainable management of resources in India.

Contamination and Effluent Treatment

Industrial revolution has played an important role in increasing environmental pollution. In this context, textile/textile industry is the largest industry in terms of production and labour efficiency as compared to other industries. The fibre industry is classified into cotton, woolen and synthetic industry.

In this industry, the use of lubricants, oily substances, water, dyes and various other chemical substances are used during the production process. As a result, various types of waste from these industries such as water waste, solid waste organic matter and chemical wastes of various colours are extracted, which cause damage to the environment in various forms. Thus, the flow of wastes in the form of liquid/solid from the textile industry leads to increase in water, air and soil pollution. Due to which various animals, flora and whole human community is harmed. Some of the major pollutants of textile industry are as follows :

- Colours
- Poisonous metals
- Organic materials
- Detached solids
- Residual chlorine
- Suspended solids

Characteristics of Effluent

Effluents are divided into three groups - physical, chemical and biological. Physical characteristics include temperature, pH, colour, odour etc. Chemical characteristics include the nature of the amount of various functional and inorganic compounds, while biological characteristics include different types of microbes.

Treatment of Textile

Influence production of textiles includes spinning (yarn to fiber), weaving (textile to yarn), chemical (wet) processing and garment manufacturing. The majority of water consumption (72%) is in chemical (wet) processing of textiles. In addition to the extensive amount of water and dyes in wet processing of textiles, a variety of inorganic and organic chemicals, detergents, soaps and finishing chemicals are included to aid the dyeing process to provide the desired properties to dyed textile products. Additionally, natural impurities (wax, protein and pigments) and other impurities used in processing (spinning oil, chemicals in cotton textiles and oil stains etc.) are given during bleaching operations.

There are different types of Effluent Treatment Plants (ETPs) and they vary in texture, the quantity and quality of the effluent, manufacturing operations. And the amount of money available for maintenance and the amount of land available varies. There are three areas for treatment; such as - physical, chemical and biological. These systems are commonly used in the same ETP. There are generally four levels of effluent treatment which are the following :

- Initial large concrete; such as - Rags, Sticks, Grit and Grease removal. Its removal may cause damage to equipment or an operational problem.
- Removal of primary floating and sustainable materials i.e. suspended, solids and organic matter (physical and chemical) Industries.
- Removal of secondary bio-degradable organic matter and suspended solids (organic dyes and chemicals) .
- Removal of tertiary residual suspended solids/soluble solids (physical, chemical and biological).

EXAM BASED QUESTIONS

1 Where textile testing and quality control is important?
(a) Cotton Industry
(b) Import Industry
(c) Export Industry
(d) Research Industry

2 What will be the outcome of qualified fibre?
(a) Yarn
(b) Fabric
(c) Diversified fibre
(d) Raw material

3 What are the major reasons for textile testing?
(a) Production and distribution
(b) Production, selection and consumption
(c) Selection, production and distribution
(d) Production, distribution and consumption

4 What do you mean by Quality Control?
(a) Checking the production through raw material
(b) Process by which entities review the quality of the product in the industry
(c) Monitoring the production of any product
(d) None of these

5 What is the first step for production cycle?
(a) Delivery of raw material
(b) Availability of resources
(c) Manpower
(d) Proper infrastructure

6 What are the reasons due to which final product is not produced?
(a) Unavailability of equipments
(b) Material is incorrect or sub-standard
(c) Lack of natural fibres
(d) Problem in weaving and dyeing

7 What is the name of the process in which quality control is the priority at every level?
(a) Preserving output
(b) Promoting goods
(c) Monitoring production
(d) Proper use of equipments

8 What can be done for getting the best desired output?
(a) Appropriate sampling
(b) Statistical Analysis
(c) Both (a) and (b)
(d) Only (b)

9 What is the stage of final assessment?
(a) When the material was produced.
(b) When the raw material arrives.
(c) When machinery was decided.
(d) When processing starts.

10 Why the investigation procedure is done by independent laboratories?
(a) Because they are cheap
(b) Because they provide huge labour
(c) Because they give unbiased result
(d) All of these

11 What are the benefits of conducting research?
(a) To decide the raw material
(b) To decide which route one should follow
(c) To provide job opportunities
(d) To provide better equipments

12 What is said about the property of raw material?
(a) Raw material is a relative term.
(b) Raw material is indifferent.
(c) Raw material is least important.
(d) Raw material is waste of time and money.

13 What is the need of sampling in textile industry?
(a) In the production of export quality products
(b) In gaining varied knowledge
(c) To increase cost
(d) Decrease quality of production

14 What are the basis of textile sampling?
(a) Form of the material
(b) Amount of the available material
(c) Nature of test
(d) All of these

15 What is nature of sampling?
(a) Destructive (b) Inductive
(c) Useful (d) Useless

16 What is the key characteristic of performing sampling?
(a) Reduce labour (b) Save time and cost
(c) High biasness (d) Irrelevant production

17 What is zoning sampling technique?
(a) Method for selecting samples from raw cotton, wool or other fibres
(b) Method of doing quality control
(c) Method of handling bulk material
(d) Method of placing bulk fibres on the place

18 Why core sampling technique is used?
(a) To make best fibre
(b) To assess the proportion of foreign matter
(c) To expand the raw material
(d) To press the fibre from tubes

19 Which technique is widely used for both fibre and yarn?
(a) Stratified sampling (b) Cluster sampling
(c) Random sampling (d) None of these

20 Which type of sampling is systematically at a regular interval?
(a) Acceptance sampling (b) Systematic sampling
(c) Cluster sampling (d) Core sampling

21 What among the following is said to be the non-technical test for fibres?
(a) Feeling test (b) Chemical test
(c) Microscope test (d) All of these

22 What is said to be the characteristics of technical test?
(a) Chemical test (b) Microscope test
(c) Both (a) and (b) (d) None of these

23 In the non-technical test what are the limitations of burning test?
(a) Light colour
(b) Odour of burning fibre
(c) Non-technical yarn
(d) Irrelivant quality

24 What is the basic characteristic of technical test?
(a) Involve equipments
(b) Contain chemicals
(c) Involves technical knowledge and skills
(d) Microscopically small

25 Which kind of fabric cannot be tested with microscope?
(a) Woolen (b) Dark Colour
(c) Light Colour (d) Linen

26 What is the image of cotton in the microscope?
(a) Straight yarn
(b) Flat twisted yarn
(c) Spirally twisted ribbon
(d) Basic fabric

27 Which fibre is viewed cross sectionally?
(a) Rayon
(b) Viscose fibre
(c) Cultivated silk fibre
(d) Medulla fibre

28 Which of the following statements is/are correct?
(a) Moisture content refers to the physical ability to hold a certain quantity of water.
(b) Moisture content of fibre varies depending upon the type of and nature of the fibre.
(c) The amount of moisture absorbed by a textile material can be determined by drying it to a constant mass and expressing the difference in weight as a percent.
(d) All of the above

29 Which of the following statements is/are correct?
(a) The pH of the fabric indicates the condition of the fabric, whether it is alkaline or acidic.
(b) The ideal pH is neutral, i.e. 7 in the scale of 0 to 14.
(c) Depending on the nature of the fibre, finishes are given either in the alkaline medium or acidic medium.
(d) All of the above

30 What is the result of the immersion of the fabric in water for a specified period to test dimensional changes?
(a) potential shrinkage
(b) laundering
(c) relaxation shrinkage
(d) resist shrinkage

31 Which of the following correctly shows that percentage of water resistance of the fibres in ascending order?
(a) Nylon, Cotton, Silk, Acetate Rayon
(b) Acetate Rayon, Nylon, Silk, Cotton
(c) Nylon, Acetate Rayon, Cotton, Silk
(d) Nylon, Silk, Acetate Rayon, Cotton

32 The fabric quality characteristics determined may be classified into which of the following categories?
(a) Constructional characteristics
(b) Analytical characteristics
(c) Performance characteristics
(d) All of the above

33 What do you mean by colour fastness?
(a) Refers to resistance of colour
(b) Refers to fadeness of colour
(c) Refers to washing of clothes
(d) Refers to lightening of colours

34 Shrinkage of cotton fabrics can be reduced by
(a) mercerisation process
(b) sanforisation process
(c) felting process
(d) calendering process

35 What is the result of pilling?
(a) Fabric colour
(b) Fabric construction of yarn
(c) Fabric surface have a fault characteristic
(d) Fabrics have strong blend

36 What does 'GSM' stands for?
(a) Graphic Per Square Metre
(b) Gram Per Sequencial Metre
(c) Gram Per Square Metre
(d) Gram Per Metre Square

37 What do you mean by dyes?
(a) Dyes are coloured powder
(b) Dyes are fine particles which are soluble in water
(c) Dyes are patterned fabric
(d) Dyes are the product of cellulose fibre

38 Eco testing of fibres and fabrics includes
(a) formaldehyde content
(b) eco textile certification
(c) Presence of heavy metals and pesticides
(d) All of the above

39 Which among the following is not eco-friendly fibres?
(a) Jute (b) Hemp
(c) Wool (d) Silk

40 Which organisation issue Eco-mark?
(a) National Testing Agency
(b) Food Security India Limited
(c) Indian Standardised Formulation
(d) Bureau of Indian Standards

41 What happens in textile testing?
1. Production of yarn
2. Quality and suitability of raw material
3. Selection of material
4. Dispatching of raw material

Codes
(a) 1 and 3 (b) 2 and 4
(c) 2 and 3 (d) 1, 2 and 4

42 Guides for judging quality can include
1. Handle 2. Fibre yarn
3. Weave 4. Finish

Codes
(a) 1 and 2 (b) 1 and 4
(c) 1, 2, 3 and 4 (d) 1, 2 and 3

43 The general methods of determining fabric is by
1. Unravelling the cloth
2. Use of pick glass
3. Medical pick counter
4. Fabric projector

Codes
(a) 1 and 2 (b) 1 and 4
(c) 1, 2 and 4 (d) 1, 2, 3 and 4

44 India designs and produces have come up with attractive jute
1. Carpets
2. Handbags, footwear
3. Garments
4. Blankets

Codes
(a) 1 and 2 (b) 1 and 2
(c) 3 and 4 (d) All of these

45 What are the ways to check quality?
1. Use of proper resources
2. Proper planning
3. Continued inspection
4. Corrective action

Codes
(a) 1 and 4 (b) 2 and 3
(c) 1 and 2 (d) All of these

46 Which of the following statements is/are correct?
1. In pile weave an extra set of warp or filling yarns interlaced with the ground warp and filling cut ends are produced on the surface of the fabric.
2. In lappet weave extra threads creats design over predetermined portion

Select the correct answer using the codes given below
(a) 1 and 2 (b) Only 1
(c) Only 2 (d) None of the above

47 Which of the following statements is/are correct?
1. Dense fabrics.
2. Cloth with felted surface.
3. Determines the weights of warp and weft.

Select the correct answer using the codes given below
(a) 1 and 2
(b) Only 1
(c) Only 2
(d) All of the above

48 When a weaver selects a yarn for a fabric, he looks for such characteristics properties as
1. elasticity, twist
2. evenness and cleanliness
3. thickness
4. strength

Select the correct answer using the codes given below
(a) 1, 2, 3 and 4 (b) 1, 2 and 3
(c) 1 and 3 (d) 1 and 2

49 The general methods of determining fabric is by
1. fabric projector
2. medical pick counter
3. use of pick glass
4. unravelling

Select the correct answer using the codes given below
(a) 1 and 2 (b) 2 and 3
(c) 1, 2 and 3 (d) All of these

50 What are the three basic layers of wool under microscope?
1. Epidermis 2. Viscose
3. Cortex 4. Medulla

Codes
(a) 1 and 3
(b) 2 and 4
(c) 1, 3 and 4
(d) All of these

51 Match of following.

List I	List II
A. Man made fibres	1. Accept dyes and finishes more readily
B. High Lustre, Low-Lustre	2. May be pure white
C. Fibres with good moisture regain	3. Rayon, cotton
D. Low wet strength, high wet strength	4. The percentage of return from elongation to the original length
E. Elastic recovery	5. Silk, cotton

Codes

	A	B	C	D	E
(a)	1	2	5	4	3
(b)	2	5	1	3	4
(c)	4	1	2	3	5
(d)	5	4	3	1	2

52 Match of following.

List I	List II
A. Worsted yarns	1. Suitable for knit blankets, soft fabric casual dress material
B. Woollen yarns	2. Tailor use for suiting
C. More firmly woven, do not sag	3. Woollen yarn
D. Tensile strength relatively low	4. Worsted yarn
E. It has protein called keratin and layers-cuticle, cortex, medulla	5. Wool

Codes

	A	B	C	D	E
(a)	4	3	2	5	1
(b)	1	2	5	4	3
(c)	2	1	4	3	5
(d)	1	2	3	5	4

53 Match of following.

List I	List II
A. Wale	1. Series of loops extending cross wise
B. Weft	2. Longitudinal yarns
C. Warp	3. Crosswise yarns
D. Courses	4. Coloums of loops parallel to length

Codes

	A	B	C	D		A	B	C	D
(a)	1	4	3	2	(b)	2	1	4	3
(c)	4	3	2	1	(d)	3	2	1	4

54 Match of following.

List I	List II
A. Seer-sucker	1. Loops on the surface
B. Satin	2. Puckered effect
C. Terry-towelling	3. Smooth lustrous face and dull back
D. Velvet	4. Short soft thick cut pile

Codes

	A	B	C	D		A	B	C	D
(a)	1	4	2	3	(b)	3	2	4	1
(c)	2	3	1	4	(d)	4	1	3	2

55 Match of following.

List I	List II
A. Silk-worm	1. The basic building block of fabric
B. Acetate	2. Made by reacting hydrocarbonic acid with dihydric alcohol
C. Fibre	3. Artificial wool
D. Dupont	4. Caterpiller
E. Polyester	5. Manufacturer of synthetic fibres

Codes

	A	B	C	D	E
(a)	1	2	3	4	5
(b)	3	4	2	5	1
(c)	4	3	1	5	2
(d)	2	1	5	4	3

Directions (Q. Nos. 56-68) *In the questions given below are two statements labelled as Assertion (A) and Reason (R). In the context of the two statements, which one of the following is correct?*

Codes

(a) Both A and R are true and R is the correct explanation of A
(b) Both A and R are true, but R is not the correct explanation of A
(c) A is true, R is false
(d) A is false, R is true

56 **Assertion** (A) Pilling is reduced by increasing the nylon filament denier.

Reason (R) Pilling is a fabric - surface fault characteristics by little 'pills' of entangled fibre clinging to the cloth surface.

57 **Assertion** (A) Colour fastness to perspiration is an important test which is carried out in the laboratory.

Reason (R) It involves different chemicals which give the effect of human perspiration either acidic or alkaline.

58 **Assertion** (A) It is not often possible to given illusion of texture through use of appropriate colour.

Reason (R) The roughness or smoothness of material affects its capacity to reflect or absorb light.

59 **Assertion** (A) Quality monitor performed at management level and takes place of regular intervals.

Reason (R) A Random sample of the latest production is taken from the finished goods who use and collectively appraised with discussion on the overall quality.

60 **Assertion** (A) Microscope test is a knowledge of fibre structure, obtained by seeing the fibres under the microscope and observing some of the difference.

Reason (R) If the fabric contains more than one kind of fibre test each.

61 **Assertion** (A) Inspection of a fabric for appearance and hand is always the first step in fibre identification.

Reason (R) Manufactured fibres can be made into fabrics that resemble natural fibre fabrics can be changed by finishes.

62 **Assertion** (A) Twist is defined as the spiral disposition of the components of the yarn and is generally expressed as the number of turns per unit length (turns per inch - tpi or turns per metres - tpm).

Reason (R) Yarn strength and yarn appearance is not affected by yarn twist.

63 Assertion (A) In order to have accurate results, the fabric has to be cleaned throughly and the finishing chemicals should also the removed completely.

Reason (R) The fabric has to be unraveled, yarns have to be untwisted and the fibres have to be put in the fibres loose a condition as possible.

64 Assertion (A) Stain techniques uses acid on different fabrics to identify reactions when treated with stain.

Reason (R) A fibre stained with dilute acetic acid it turns to a specific colour.

65 Assertion (A) Dyed yarns can be used in the wrap and filling to make attractive checks and stripes.

Reason (R) Interesting surface effects can be achieved without changing the weave, but by using yarns of different size.

66 Assertion (A) Mercerised cotton doesn't have natural twist.

Reason (R) The finishing process makes them swollen, straight, smooth and round with a shining surface.

67 Assertion (A) In chemical testing of fibres, acetate changes to light green colour when acetic acid is used a turns orange when dilute carbonate of soda is used.

Reason (R) Most of the fibres have two colour reactions, when treated with stain.

68 Assertion (A) Colour fastness of fabric/yarn depends on the nature and depth of shade of dye staff.

Reason (R) It also depends on the nature of fibre and method of dyeing or printing employed.

Directions (Q. Nos. 69-72) *Read the passage given below and answer the questions that follows.*

The textile industry is considered as the most ecologically harmful industry in the world. The Eco-problems in textile industry occur during some production processes and are carried forward right to the finished product. In the production process like bleaching and then dyeing, the subsequent fabric makes a toxin that swells into our ecosystem. Therefore, the need for eco-textiles is felt. Green textiles refer to clothing and other accessories that are designed to use the organic and recycled material.

Every textile item releases effluents that are harmful to the environment. The traditional textile industry consumes large amounts of earth's natural resources and pollutes the environment as their production and processing involve Chemical Intensive Applications, therefore, the need for green textiles. During the production process controlling pollution is as vital as making a product free from the toxic effect.

The utilisation of rayon for clothing has added to the fast depleting forests and opened the door to the development of natural sustainable fibres like Organic Cotton, Hemp, and Bamboo fibres.

Petroleum-based products are harmful to the environment. In order to safeguard our environment from these effects, an integrated pollution control approach is needed. Fabrics made in an eco-friendly way can substitute normal products.

Green textiles refer to clothing and other accessories that are designed to use organic and recycled materials, less packaging and more energy-efficient manufacturing. Reducing the environmental impact throughout the life-cycle of a fabric item or using lower impact products can contribute actively to improve the situation. In general, there are four major environmental key factors associated with the making of textiles: water, energy, pollution, and use of non-renewable resources.

69 Which industry is regarded as ecologically harmful industry?
(a) Automobile Industry
(b) Textile Industry
(c) Kitchen Industry
(d) Fire cracker Industry

70 Which is the solution of harm caused by the textile industry?
(a) Green textile
(b) Eco-labels
(c) Eco-marks
(d) Non-acidic textile

71 Which among the following contribute to the development of natural sustainable fibres?
1. Organic cotton
2. Hemp
3. Bamboo
4. Wool

Codes
(a) 1 and 2
(b) 2 and 4
(c) 1, 2 and 3
(d) All of the above

72 What does green textiles refers to in clothing and other accessories?
(a) Designed to use organic and recycled materials.
(b) Less packaging will be needed.
(c) Move energy-efficient manufacturing
(d) All of the above

PREVIOUS YEARS' QUESTIONS

July 2018

1 Match the dyes given in List I with their characteristics given in List II

List I	List II
A. Disperse dye	1. Contain a functional group to improve solubility in alcohols
B. Direct dye	2. Applied from acid bath
C. Azoic dye	3. Water-soluble dyes and substantive to cellulose and protein fibres
D. Metallised dye	4. Dye developed with in textile from chemical reactions
	5. Only slightly soluble in water and diffuses into most thermoplastic fibres

Code

	A	B	C	D
(a)	1	2	4	5
(b)	3	1	5	4
(c)	5	3	4	2
(d)	2	4	3	1

2 **Assertion** (A) Acid dyes are suitable for wool and silk.

Reason (R) Acid dyes form ionic bonds with the hydroxy groups found in wool and silk.

Code

(a) Both A and R are correct
(b) Both A and R are incorrect
(c) A is correct but R is incorrect
(d) A is incorrect but R is correct

November 2017

3 **Assertion** (A) Disperse dyes connot be used in transfer printing.

Reason (R) Disperse dyes do not sublime when heated to high temperature.

Codes

(a) Both A and R are incorrect
(b) Both A and R are correct
(c) A is correct, R is incorrect
(d) A is incorrect, R is correct

January 2017

4 Assertion (A) The most suitable method of printion with disperse dyes is transfer printing.

Reason (R) Disperse dyes sublime when hearted to high temperature.

Codes

(a) Both A and R are incorrect
(b) Both A and R are correct
(c) A is correct, but R is incorrect
(d) A is incorrect, but R is correct

July 2016

5 Wrinkle resistant fabrics are made environment friendly and cost dffective by the use of

(a) formaldehyde
(b) citric acid
(c) xylitol
(d) cross linking citric acid and xylitol

ANSWERS

Exam Based Questions

1 (c)	2 (a)	3 (d)	4 (b)	5 (a)	6 (b)	7 (c)	8 (c)	9 (a)	10 (c)
11 (b)	12 (a)	13 (a)	14 (d)	15 (a)	16 (b)	17 (a)	18 (b)	19 (c)	20 (b)
21 (a)	22 (c)	23 (b)	24 (c)	25 (b)	26 (c)	27 (b)	28 (d)	29 (d)	30 (c)
31 (c)	32 (d)	33 (a)	34 (b)	35 (c)	36 (c)	37 (b)	38 (d)	39 (a)	40 (d)
41 (c)	42 (c)	43 (d)	44 (d)	45 (d)	46 (a)	47 (d)	48 (a)	49 (d)	50 (d)
51 (b)	52 (c)	53 (c)	54 (c)	55 (c)	56 (b)	57 (a)	58 (a)	59 (b)	60 (b)
61 (b)	22 (c)	63 (a)	64 (b)	65 (b)	66 (a)	67 (a)	68 (b)	69 (b)	70 (a)
71 (c)	72 (d)								

Previous Years Questions

1 (c)	2 (c)	3 (a)	4 (a)	5 (d)

CHAPTER 12

Indian Textile and Recent Developments

India has the rich textile history. Every part of the country is contributing to some type of embroided or printed textile. In the recent years, the great change in the textile industry was seen and now things are shifting towards technology while keeping preservation of resources in mind.

Traditional Textile of India

The traditional textile of India is varied and rich. India has an old tradition of textile and is traced back to the Indus Valley Civilisation. The people of Indian Valley Civilisation used homespun cotton for weaving their garments. Indian textiles had a great market in number of countries. India enjoyed a flourishing trade with the outside world on account of its textile products. There was a great demand for Indian textile products in the Roman Empire. Indian silk was popular in Rome in the early centuries of the Christian era. Cotton products, originating from India has been found in many Middle East countries.

As far as literacy information about Indian textiles are concerned, the Rig Veda refers to weaving in ancient period. Ramayana and Mahabharata also speak of a variety of fabrics of those times. The Ramayana refers to the rich stuff worn by the aristocracy on one hand and simple clothes by commoners.

Murals and sculptures, belonging to ancient period also bear testimony to the great tradition of textiles in India. The past traditions of textiles and handlooms can still be seen amongst the motifs, patterns, designs and the old techniques of weaving, still used by the Indian weavers.

Silk fabrics from South India were exported to Indonesia during the 13th century. India also exports printed cotton fabric to European countries and the far East before the coming of the Europeans to India. Indian textiles were so popular that most of the European trade companies began to trade in cotton and other textile materials.

In this Chapter

The Indian textile industry is divided broadly into four parts :

- Embroidered textiles
- Printed textiles
- Woven textiles
- Dyed textiles

Embroidered Textiles

An embroidered textile of India is the result of the passion of womenfolk to express their creativity and ornament their apparel and household textiles. Primarily a feminine art, young girls learned the craft from their mothers and older women in the family.

The artistic expressions of the embroiderer are skillfully created on fabric with a simple tool, needle or a hook needle known as awl or tambour.

Different embroidery styles have developed regionally in India that has a distinct identity of their own. Cotton, silk, woolen thread or gold/silver is used to embroider on various media, from cotton, silk, woolen fabric to velvet and leather.

Besides thread, pieces of fabric, beads, mirrors, shells, coins, precious stones and sequins are also used for embellishing the fabric. With the passage of time, a variety of embroidery designs have been created by artisans from their own imagination. The Indian embroideries can be classified on the basis of the technique of production or as per the region of production.

Indian embroideries are classified on the basis of region as follows :

- **Northern India**
  - Kashida from Kashmir
  - Phulkari from Punjab
  - Chamba rumal from Himachal Pradesh
- **Western India**
  - Embroidery from Gujarat
  - Parsi embroidery
- **Central India**
  - Chikankari from Uttar Pradesh
  - Phool Patti ka Kaam from Uttar Pradesh
  - Zardozi from Uttar Pradesh
- **Southern India**
  - Kasuti from Karnataka
  - Lambadi from Andhra Pradesh
- **Eastern India**
  - Kantha from West Bengal
  - Sujani from Bihar
  - Pipli applique from Odisha

Northern India

The embroidery styles or prevalent in originated. North Indian region are as follows :

Kashida

- Kashida is an embroidery style from Kashmir that is practised by men folk of the region.
- The base material for Kashida is cotton, wool or silk in a variety of colours like white, blue, yellow, purple, red, green and black. The embroidery threads used to execute Kashida on wool, silk or cotton depending on the product to be embroidered. The main stitches employed for Kashida are darning stitch, stem stitch, satin stitch and chain stitch.
- The motifs used in Kashida depict the natural elements which includes the rich flora and fauna of the region of Kashmir. Typical motifs are birds like magpie, kingfisher; flowers, butterflies, maple leaves, almonds, cherries, grapes and plums. A popular motif seen on embroidered shawls is derived from the cypress cone.
- There are three styles of embroidery followed in Kashmir :
  - **Sozni** is intricate embroidery that uses stitch like fly stitch, stem stitch and darning stitch.

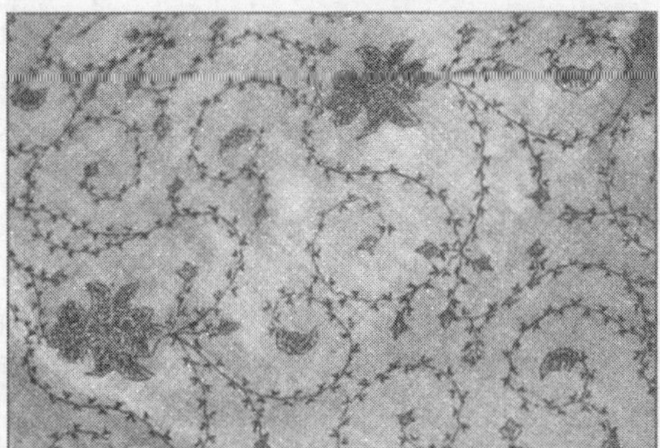

Sozni Style of Embroidery

  - The **aari style**, also called **Zalakdozi** employs hook or aari to fill-in motifs with chain stitch.

Zari Thread

- The Zari thread is laid on the fabric along a pattern and is held in place with another thread.

Zalakdozi Style of Embroidery

- Kashmiri embroidery is primarily done on shawls and regional garments like phiran. Kashida is also used to decorate household items like bed covers, cushion covers, lampshades, bags and other accessories.

Phulkari

- Phulkari is an embroidery style that originated in Punjab. It is used and embroidered in different parts of Punjab namely Jalandhar, Amritsar, Ludhiana, Bhatinda and Patiala etc. The needle work is widely practised by the women of Punjab and holds significance in a life of a woman, from her marriage till her final abode to heaven.
- The base material to execute Phulkari is handspun and handwoven Khaddar that is dyed in red, rust, brown, blue and darker shades. Soft untwisted silk thread 'Pat' is used for the embroidery. The basic stitch employed for Phulkari is darning stitch, which is done from the reverse side of the fabric. The stitches follow the weave and a beautiful effect is created on the fabric by changing the direction of the stitches.
- The motifs used in Phulkari are inspired by objects of everyday use like rolling pin, sword, flowers, vegetables, birds, animals, etc. They are generally geometrical and stylised. Usually, one motif is left unembroidered or is embroidered in a different colour. This motif is called 'nazarbuti' which is considered to ward off the evil eye.
- The two embroidery styles prevalent in Punjab are Bagh and Phulkari.
  - **Bagh** is a fully embroidered wrap that is used for special occasions.

Bagh Embroidery

  - **Phulkari** is simple and lightly embroidered for everyday use.

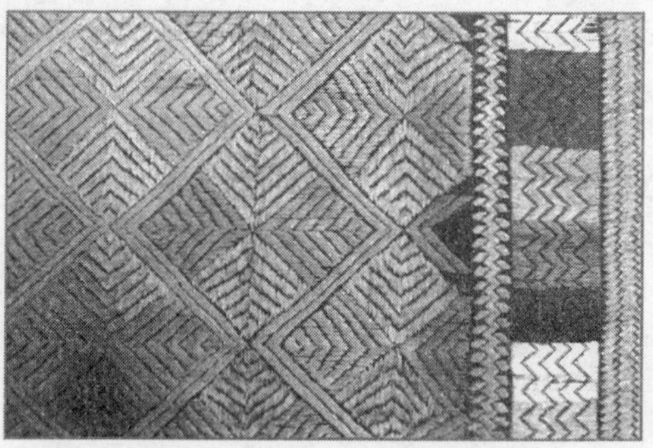

Phulkari Embroidery

- Phulkari is an important part of the bridal trousseau and is worn as a veil or wrap by women on special occasions like Karva Chauth, a festival celebrated in North India for longevity of husbands. Phulkari is being done on bed linen and apparel like tops, tunics and skirts.

Chamba Rumal

- Chamba rumal, an embroidery from Himachal Pradesh. This embroidery being practised in Pathankot, Chamba and other remote villages of Himachal Pradesh in Buddhist literature and the Jataka tales. Chamba was known for the most picturesque needle work.
- The embroidery is executed on two types of unbleached cotton cloth: lightweight, delicate muslin or handspun, hand-woven, coarser khaddar. Untwisted, dyed silk threads 'Pat' in bright colours like red, yellow, green, blue, crimson and purple are used for the embroidery. The embroidery uses double satin stitch which simultaneously fills in the motif on both sides of the fabric, making it reversible.
- The motifs used are inspired from Pahari paintings depicting Lord Krishna and his playful antics. The embroidery also depicts the flora and fauna of the Himalayan region. Typical motifs include: tiger, goat, deer, horse, peacock, parrot; flowers, shrubs and plants, willow and cypress trees and musical instruments like sitar, tabla, veena, tanpura, etc.
- The embroidery is executed on a square piece of cloth. The motifs are arranged on the rumal in order to portray scenes from Lord Krishna's life. There are floral borders on all four sides of the rumal.
- Traditionally, the rumal was used as a cover for food prasad offered to Gods and Goddesses. It was also a custom to gift embroidered rumals at the time of weddings. Nowadays, the Chamba embroidery is done on fabrics like silk, polyester or terrycot and made into blouses, caps, slippers, cushion covers, etc. Embroidered silk wall hangings are also exported from Himachal Pradesh.

Part of Chamba Rumal

Western India

The embroidery styles originated or prevalent in Western India are as follows :

Embroidery from Gujarat

- The embroidery of Gujarat is colourful and vibrant practised by different communities of the state. The most popular embroidery styles originate from Kutch and Kathiawar region of Gujarat.
- The embroidery is done with multi-coloured threads, usually cotton or silk embroidery threads. There is also use of mirrors that are fixed on the fabric with an embroidery stitch. Another technique used in Gujarat is applique where scraps of fabric are cut into a form and stitched onto the base fabric.
- The motifs used in Gujarati embroidery are mostly taken from flora and fauna. Some typical motifs are flowers, creepers, trees, peacocks, parrots and elephants. Besides flowers and animals, human figures in different poses like dancing women and men are also seen in some styles of Gujarati embroidery.
- There are different embroidery styles carried out by tribal communities of Gujarat, which are as follows :
  - **Mochi Bharat** The embroidery style from Kutch is practised by the mochis of shoemakers. The ari or the hook is used to embroider designs with chain stitch.

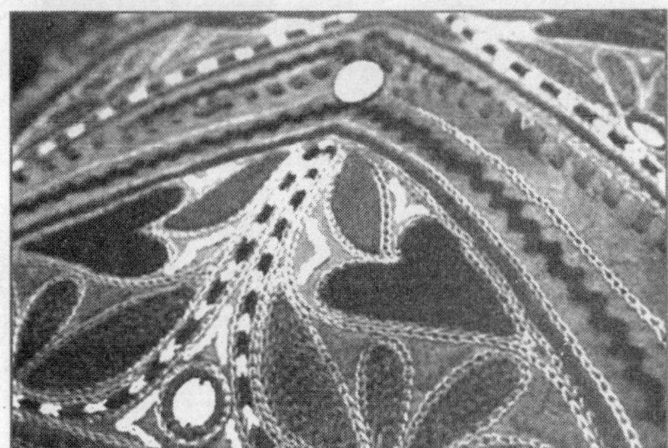

Mochi Bharat

  - **Soof Bharat** The embroidery is executed with untwisted silk floss and geometric patterns are created using the darning stitch.

Soof Bharat

  - **Abhla Bharat** The embroidery style is defined by the use of mirror work along with other embroidery stitches to create designs on fabric.

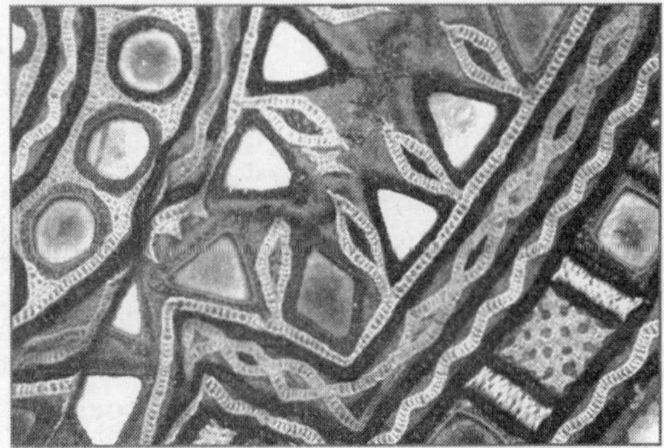

Abhla Bharat

- A range of embroidered articles are produced in various regions of Gujarat. Some examples are quilts, doorway hangings, pouches, bags, ghagra, choli, wedding costumes, animal trappings, etc.

Parsi Embroidery

- Parsi embroidery is practised by the Parsi community. The Parsi embroidery is an interesting mix of Eastern and Western cultures, imbibing from Persian, Chinese, Indian and European influences.
- The base material for Parsi embroidery is silk fabric in bright red, purple, blue, magenta and black colour. The embroidery is done with silk threads in light pastel colours like off-white, pink and cream. Besides the satin stitch, French knots are used that imparts texture to the fabric, resembling small beads fixed on the fabric.
- The motifs are derived from Persian, Chinese, Indian and European cultures. The range of motifs from nature includes flowers like chrysanthemum, peony, lily and lotus; foliage like cherry, weeping willow and pine; birds like crane and peacock and butterflies.

- The Parsi gara is an embroidered sari that has heavily embellished borders on all its four sides.
- The Parsi embroidery is done on garas (sari) and jhablas. Though the embroidery is becoming extinct, attempts are being made to revive the craft and produce fast selling products like scarves, bags and other accessories.

Parsi Embroidery Depicting Birds and Floral Motifs

Central India

The embroidery styles originated prevalent in from central India are of follows:

Chikankari

- Chikankari is white work embroidery practised in Lucknow, Uttar Pradesh. It is believed that Nur Jahan, wife of Mughal emperor Jahangir embroidered a cap for her husband and hence popularised this craft of white embroidery.
- The embroidery is done on fine white cotton fabric with untwisted white cotton or silk thread.
- There are three types of stitches used in chikankari :
  - Flat stitches like stem stitch and herringbone stitch,
  - Raised stitches like bullion and French knots
  - Pulled thread work or jali.
- The motifs are inspired from nature's flora including flowers, creepers and lace, like patterns.
- A common style present in each piece of Chikankari is the shadow work. To create the light and shade effect, herringbone stitch is executed from the wrong side of the fabric which creates shadow of lighter colour on the right side and at the same imparts an outline to the motif.
- Traditionally, the embroidery was done mainly for male garments such as kurta, bandi, choga, etc., for summer wear. Presently, Chikankari is being explored for apparel as well as home products on different fabrics like crepe silks, chiffons, georgettes and cotton polyester blends. Besides the traditional white on white embroidery, the contemporary chikankari has a wider colour palette, from pastels to bright colours.

Contemporary Chikankari

Phool Patti ka kaam

- 'Phool Patti ka Kaam' is traditional applique style embroidery practised in Uttar Pradesh, chiefly Aligarh and Rampur. The embroidery is executed by Muslim women, who work from their homes.
- The applique is done on fine white cotton fabric. Traditionally, applique is done in two ways :
  - 'Badi Patti ka Kaam', small pieces of white fabric cut into floral forms are stitched onto the white fabric, creating the light and shade effect. The detailing of the motifs is done with stem stitch.
  - 'Choti Patti ka Kaam', small pieces of cloth are folded into diamond shapes and used as petals or leaves in the motifs, along with stem stitch work.
- The motifs used in 'Phool Patti ka Kaam' are flowers and leaves. The floral forms are geometric in nature.
- 'Phool Patti ka Kaam' was traditionally done on dupattas and saris. Nowadays, the applique is also done on home furnishings like curtains, table linen and cushion covers using other colours besides white.

Phool Patti Ka Kaam

Zardozi

- Zardozi is a gold and silver embroidery which is practised in Lucknow, Agra, Varanasi, Bareilly, Bhopal, Delhi and Chennai. The craft flourished under the patronage of the Mughal courts.
- The embroidery is done on different fabrics like velvet, satin and silk with a variety of zari threads and materials like badla (the untwisted wire), salma (stiff finely twisted

circular wire) gijai (twisted metallic wire), dabka (zig-zag coiled wire), sitara (small circular disc), pearls and coloured beads. The different stitches used in Zardozi are chain stitch, stem stitch and satin stitch. The fabric to be embroidered is first stretched on a rectangular wooden frame supported on two tripods called a karchob, a hook or an awl is used to execute the embroidery.

- The motifs used are mainly floral and geometrical. Some popular motifs are creepers, flowering bush, floral scrolls and intricate jali patterns.
- There are two embroidery styles namely :
  - **Karchobi**, the fabric is clamped on wooden frame and elaborately embroidered to create decorative home furnishings and ornate apparel.
  - **Kamdani** is lighter embroidery done on apparel like dupattas and scarves without clamping the fabric on any frame.
- Zardozi was traditionally done to ornament wall hangings, bed covers, cushion covers, curtains, palanquin covers, trappings for elephants, bullocks and horses, canopies, shoes, jackets, purses, boxes, etc. The embroidery continues to be one of the most favoured ornamentation for decoration of apparel such as lehenga choli, sari, etc. Presently, Zardozi is also explored on different types of base material like jute to develop trendy products like bags and decorative fashion accessories.

Zardozi Embroidery

Southern India

The embroidery styles originated or prevalent in Southern India are as follows:

Kasuti

- Kasuti embroidery is practised in Karnataka. The embroidery considered as an auspicious craft, is executed by women. The embroidery is done on hand-woven cloth of darker colour usually black with cotton threads in different colours like red, orange, purple, green, yellow and blue.
- Four basic stitches are used :
  - Gavanti, double running stitch that creates the same effect on both sides of fabric;
  - Murgi, zig-zag running stitch that works in stepwise manner;
  - Negi, simple running stitch that produces a weave-like effect .
  - Menthi, cross stitch that gives a heavier appearance. The embroidery threads used are drawn from the old silk sari borders.
- The motifs are inspired from religion, architecture, flora and fauna and objects of daily use. Some examples are star shaped designs, chariot and palanquin for deity, tulsi pot holder, cradle, sacred bull, deer, elephant, peacock, horse and lotus.
- The embroidery uses a combination of horizontal, vertical and diagonal stitches. The motifs are not traced on the fabric and the embroidery is executed by counting the yarns on the base material.
- Traditionally, the embroidery was done on Ilkal sari and other apparel items like women's blouse and children's bonnets. Presently, Kasuti embroidery is also done on home products like cushion covers, bed covers, curtains and accessories like handbags, mobile pouches, belts, etc.

Kasuti Embrodiery Depicting Tulsi Pot Holder and Elephant Motifs

Lambadi Embroidery

- Lambadi embroidery is practised by the lambadas or lambanis, the Banjaras of Bellary and Bijapur in Karnataka and Hyderabad in Andhra Pradesh. The colourful embroidery was done by the women to decorate their costumes, namely phetia or skirt and kanchali or blous
- The embroidery is done on hand-woven cloth in dark blue or red colour. The embroidery is done with colourful threads using basic stitches like herringbone stitch, chevron stitch, cross stitch and running stitch, combined with applique. The embroidery is further embellished with mirrors, cowrie shells, beads, coins and silver trinkets.

- The motifs are mainly geometrical with gird like patterns.
- The embroidery uses a combination of stitches and applique, along with mirror work and other embellishments like cowrie shells and coins.
- Lambani women embroidered their garments and other utility products like pouches and bags. Nowadays, the embroidery is done on a variety of products like cushion covers, bed covers, wall hangings, garments and accessories like bags, headbands, waist belts, etc.

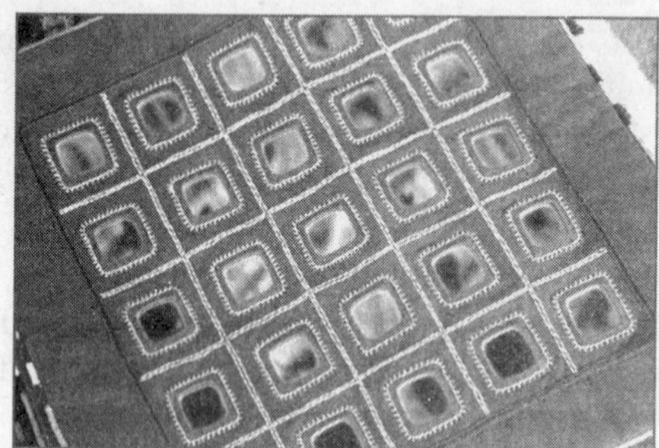

Lambadi Embroidery

Eastern India

The embroidery styles originated or prevalent in Eastern India are as follows:

Kantha

- Kantha is an embroidery style that originated in West Bengal. In the past, it was used to transform old, used fabric into an embroidered textile.
- The embroidery is executed on layers of old white cotton saris that are stitched together with simple running stitch in white thread. The motifs are traced and embroidered using different coloured threads. The embroidery threads used are drawn from the old sari borders.
- The motifs used in Kantha are lotus flowers, floral scrolls, tree of life, creepers; animal and bird forms; fish, sea-monsters, mermaids, ships, submarine scenes; domestic articles like mirrors, pitcher, nut cracker, umbrella, musical instruments and human figures like Gods and Goddesses, horse man, fisher woman, etc.
- Different embroidery layouts are followed in Kantha. Some examples are a central motif and tree of life on all four corners, motifs arranged in panels or a big central panel and smaller motifs placed around.
- Kanthas were mainly used as quilts and also offered to special guests to sit or sleep on it. It was presented to the bride and groom as well as used to wrap valuables and gifts. Other uses of Kantha include bags for keeping money and book cover. Nowadays, Kantha embroidery is done on single layer of white or coloured fabric base using contemporary motifs. The product range includes stoles, dupattas, saris and suit materials.

Kantha Embridery

Sujani

- Sujani is an embroidery style practised in parts of Bihar, namely Muzaffarpur, Bhusra, Madhubani and Patna. Similar to Kantha, the embroidery was traditionally done on layers of old saris and converted into a quilt. In the past, Sujanis or embroidered quilts were made on the arrival of a new born.
- The embroidery is carried out on layers of old white cotton saris that are stitched together with simple running stitch in white thread. The motifs are filled-in with rows of running stitch in coloured threads drawn from the old sari borders. The outlines of the motifs are defined with chain stitch.
- The motifs used in Sujani are drawn from daily life and the natural surroundings. Some examples are flowers, plants, elephants, birds, fishes, Gods and Goddesses. The contemporary Sujanis are also portraying social concerns like female foeticide, women empowerment, girl child education and domestic violence.
- The embroidery layout is such that each piece of Sujani tells a story. The motifs are simpler and bolder in comparison to the Kantha embroidery.
- Traditionally, Sujanis were used as baby wraps. Presently, the women artisans are doing sujani embroidery on different products like bed covers, cushion covers, wall panels, stoles, dupattas and fashion accessories.

Sujani Embroidery

Pipli Applique

- Pipli applique is a traditional craft from Odisha that gets its name from its place of origin. Pipli is a small town in Odisha, where the applique embroidery is practised by artisans called Darjis. It is believed that the appliqued textiles were initially made to decorate the idols in Lord Jagannath temple of Puri, Odisha.
- The appliqué is done using pieces of fabric that are cut into specific shapes and stitched on a base fabric. The raw edges of the applied motif are finished with a row of chain stitch. The other stitches used for applique are stem stitch and blanket stitch.
- The motifs in Pipli work are mainly geometric, abstract and stylised inspired from flora and fauna and mythology. Typical motifs are flowers, birds, animals, fishes and deities of the Lord Jagannath Temple.
- The Pipli applique is easily identified by its vibrant colours. Fabric pieces in bright colours are cut in a particular shape and applied on a contrasting coloured base material.
- Traditionally, Pipli products were used to decorate the royal kingdoms and the Jagannath Temple of Puri. Even today, big sized appliqued canopies are used for deities during religious processions. Presently, a range of contemporary Pipli products are available including garden umbrellas, wall hangings, lampshades, home furnishings like cushion covers, bed covers and fashion accessories like bags and pouches.

Pipli Applique

Dyed Textile

Dyed textile is a process in which colour is transferred to a finished textile or textile material to add permanent and long lasting colour. It can be done by hand or by machine. Dyes can come as powders, crystals, pastes or liquid dispersions and they dissolve completely in solution. When the textile and the dye come into contact, the textile is completely saturated by the dye and colored. Dyeing can be done at any stage of the manufacturing process. It involves the change in the crystal structure of substance.

Bandhani, Bandhaj, Lehariya, Ikat, Patola and Bandhas are most popular dyed textiles techniques. Their description is given below:

Bandhani

- Bandhani, derived from the word 'bandha' which means to tie, are tie-dyed textiles primarily from Rajasthan and Gujarat. Tie-dye is a resist dyeing technique in which pre-determined areas on the fabric are tied tightly with thread to protect them from the colour followed by dyeing and removal of threads to reveal an interesting pattern on fabric.
- The tie-dye from Gujarat called Bandhani is regarded for its fine resist dots and intricate designs. Traditionally, the tie-dye is done on silk, cotton and wool. The motifs created by outlining with tiny dots are animal and human figures, flowers, plants and trees.
- The products range varies from odhanis, saris, shawls to stitched garments like kurta and skirts. Gharcholu, Chandrokhani, Aba or Abo are social bandhani textiles from Gujarat. The major centres of special bandhani in Gujarat are Jamnagar, Bhavnagar, Rajkot and Porbandar.

Bhandhani of Gujarat

Bandhej

- The tie-dyed textiles produced in Rajasthan are known as bandhej and are similar to the bandhani of Gujarat in terms of production process. Besides the fine resist dots, other types of shapes seen in bandhej are tiny boxes called dabbi, sweetmeats termed laddu and cowrie shells named kori.
- The tie-dye motifs range from very simple to complex forms including geometric and floral designs. The colourful textile that is considered auspicious is also offered to Goddesses on special occasions.
- The finest bandhej is made in Sikar and Bikaner in Rajasthan.

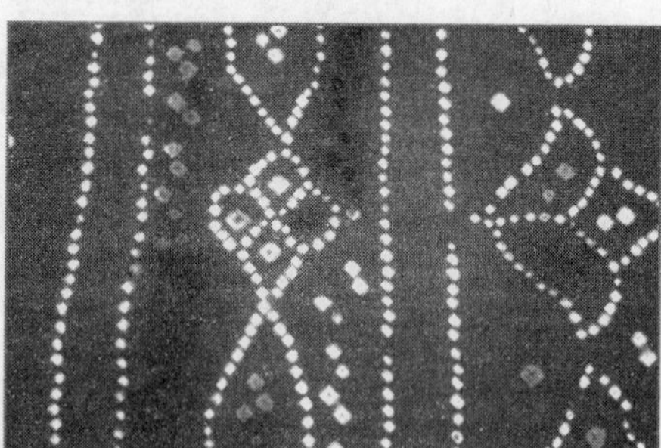

Bandhej from Rajasthan

Lehariya

- Another category of tie-dyed fabrics which are very popular from Rajasthan are **lehariya**. The patterns are diagonal or zig-zag lines created by wrap resist technique.
- Fine cotton or silk fabric is diagonally rolled into a tight rope and tied with thread at regular intervals to obtain stripes on dyeing. The fabric when opened fully shows diagonal white and varied light coloured lines on a darker background.
- Lehariya fabrics are used as head cloth or safa by men worn on special occasions like festivals and weddings. The finest lehariya is made in Jodhpur, Udaipur, Barmer and Jaipur.

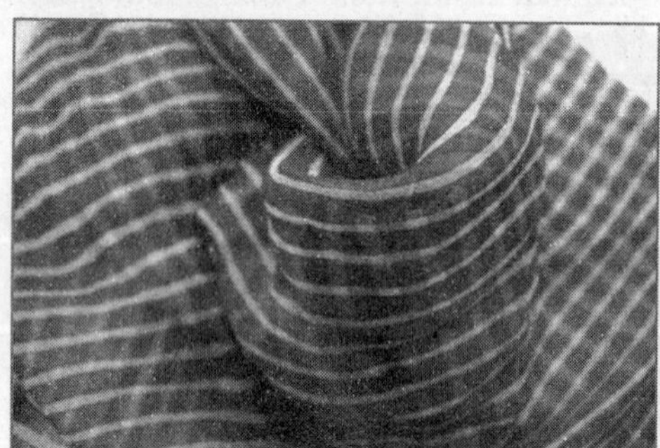

Lehariya from Rajasthan

Ikat

- The term 'Ikat' is derived from the Malay-Indonesian word 'Mangikat' that means to bind or knot. It is a yarn resist technique wherein the yarns are tie-dyed and on weaving a pattern is created on the surface of the fabric. An Ikat textile can be identified from the typical hazy patterning on fabric due to the resist dyeing of the yarns prior to weaving.

Ikat can be classified into three categories :

- **Single Ikat** There are two kinds of single Ikat, namely Warp Ikat and Weft Ikat. As the name suggests, in Warp Ikat, the warp yarns are tie-dyed and woven with plain solid coloured weft yarns and similarly in Weft Ikat, the weft yarns are tie-dyed and woven with plain warp yarns.
- **Double Ikat** In Double Ikat, both warp and weft yarns are tie-dyed according to a pre-determined pattern and then woven to create clear designs on fabric.
- **Combined Ikat** In Combined Ikat, both warp and weft yarns are tie- dyed but they are present in selected areas of a textile, to create interesting patterns.

- The main production centres of Ikat in India are **Gujarat, Odisha** and **Andhra Pradesh**.
- The Ikat of each region known by different names can be identified from the motifs and the patterns achieved on weaving the tie-dyed yarns. The Ikat textiles of India can be classified on the basis of region as follows :
  - Patola of Gujarat
  - Bandhas of Odisha

Patola of Gujarat

- The Double ikat weaving tradition of Gujarat is called 'Patola'. The textile is produced by the weavers of the Salvi community using expensive silk yarns.
- In the past, Patolas were manufactured in Patan, Khambat, Surat, Porbander, Ahmedabad and Baroda in Gujarat.
- In India, Patola saris are considered to be auspicious and are thus, worn on very special occasions like weddings and festivals. In the past, the textile was also used as temple hangings and offered to the divinity.
- The process of producing the Double Ikat Patola fabrics is very time consuming and labour intensive. The design is planned very carefully since both warp and weft yarns are tie-dyed repeatedly in order to introduce more than one colour. Due to the perfect alignment of the warp and weft, the motifs formed have defined outlines in comparison to the hazy outlines seen in Single Ikats.
- Patola textiles use intense colours like bright red, golden yellow, green, dark blue, reddish brown, etc. The distinctive Patola motifs are flowers, jewels, elephants, birds and dancing women for the Hindu and Jain communities.
- The Muslim community restricts themselves to abstract designs. The Patola designs are named as Kunjar Popat Bhat (elephant - Parrot), Nari Kunjar Popat Bhat (lady - Elephant - Parrot), Navratan Bhat (Jewel Mosaic), Phool Wali Bhat (Floral), Chabri Bhat (Basket of flowers), etc.
- The expensive Patola saris are prized possession of every Indian woman, reserved for ceremonial wear. Due to the high cost, the Patola sari attracts very limited clientele and also cheap imitations manufactured by Ikat weavers of Pochampalli, has affected its sales. Thus, the number of artisans practising the craft has drastically declined over a period of time.

Patola Print of Gujarat

Bandhas

- The Ikat textiles called 'bandhas' are produced in **Odisha.** Mostly, bandhas are Single Ikats or Combined Ikats, woven by specific weaver groups like Mehars and Patras. Cotton and Silk Ikats are manufactured in Cuttack, Nuapatna, Sonepur, Bargarh and Sambalpur.
- The bandhas of Odisha are characterised by curved forms with hazy outlines. The distinct hazy lines are created since only one set of yarns in the fabric are tie-dyed. Mainly Weft Ikat is done in Odisha. Some popular motifs are shankha or conch shell, swastika, creepers, flowers like lotus, intertwined snake, fish, tortoise and elephant.
- The bandha weavers of Odisha are known for the usage of striking colour combinations and delicate and intricate patterns. The Ikat saris of Odisha are the popular attire of the local women and are also preferred by the modern women of India. Besides the cotton and silk Ikat saris, the other products woven by the weavers are yardage, stoles, scarves and dupattas.
- A well-known example of the Ikat sari from Odisha is 'Saktapar' sari. This sari is traditionally the pride of the region, with the Double Ikat checker board pattern and extra weft brocaded border of rudraksha, bead and fish. The sari is characterised by its typical end piece, pallu comprising of bands of floral and figurative Ikat motifs, divided by narrow woven patterned lines.

Bandhas of Odisha

Printed Textiles

Printed textile is the process of applying colour of fabric in definite patterns or designs. In printed fabrics, the colour is blended with the fibre, so as to resist washing and friction. Printed textile is related to dyeing but in dyeing property the whole fabric is uniformly covered with one colour, whereas in printing one on more colours are applied to it in certain parts only.

In printing, wooden blocks, stencils, engraved plates, rollers, etc., can be used to place colours on the fabric. The printing process does involve several stages in order to prepare the fabric and printing paste and to fix the impression permanently on the fabric.

Popular examples of tranditional printed textiles in India are Bangru prints from Rajasthan, Sanganer Prints from Rajasthan and Kalamkari from Andhra Pradesh, etc. Their description are given below :

Bagru Prints from Rajasthan

- Bagru is a small village in Rajasthan, which is known for its mud-resist block prints.
- In Bagru, the printer first processes the raw material which is mainly cotton. The fabric is then printed with mordants in paste form. The printing is done by using outline and filling blocks. The mud resist paste is used to resist the penetration of dyes, mainly vegetable dyes on cotton fabric as per the design. After dyeing, the fabric is thoroughly washed at the river. The mud resist paste is washed off exposing printed motifs on white background surrounded by the base colour. Hence, the resulting effect of dark and deep background with light coloured prints is achieved by resisting and mordanting.
- The motifs are inspired by the 17th century Persian motifs and are classified into the following five categories :
  - Single motifs like flowers, leaves and buds. Some examples are suraj ka phool, chakri, anguthi and gende ka phool.
  - Entwined tendrils that include all over jaal of leaves, flowers and buds.
  - Trellis patterns include jaalis from the Mughal period.
  - Figurative designs that include animal and human figures such as elephant, deer, lion, peacock, dancing women, warrior men, etc.
  - Geometric designs include waves (lehariya), chess (chaupad), Fortress wall projections (kangura), lines (dhariya), dots (bindi), etc.

- The brightly coloured block printed fabrics from Bagru are used for apparel as well as home furnishings such as quilts, bed spreads, cushions and curtains.

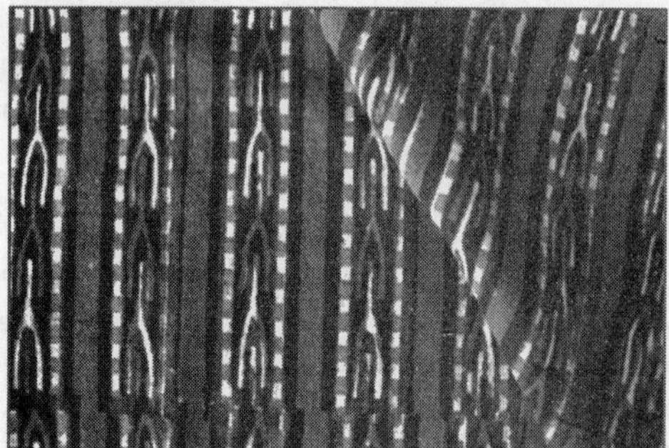

Bagru Prints from Rajasthan

Sanganer Prints from Rajasthan

- Sanganer on the outskirts of Jaipur is a large centre for printing on fabrics. Many block printing and screen printing units are located here.
- The technique used by the printers in Sanganer is much simpler than Bagru. The bright vibrant colours are printed on white, off white or light colour background. Firstly, the outlines are printed with fine blocks and then varied colours are filled in with a set of blocks. For each colour, a separate block is required.
- The motifs seen in Sanganer prints are same as the ones used in Bagru.
- The block printing is done mainly for products such as saris, dupattas, salwar- kameez sets, bed covers, curtains, scarves, and yardage for appare land home.

Sanganer Prints from Rajasthan

Kalamkari from Andhra Pradesh

- Andhra Pradesh is famous for many of its textile crafts, one of which is Kalamkari, which means 'pen-craft'. This style of printing was practised in Coastal Deccan and many other places. Kalamkari, the dye painted and printed exquisite textile symbolically named after the technique of its making, 'kalam/qualam' meaning pen and 'kari' meaning art, has been prevalent in several parts of Southern India since ancient times.
- Srikalahasti, Masulipatnam, Polavaram and Pedana in Andhra Pradesh have been the major centres of this craft.
- The main tool used in Kalamkari is an improvised brush known as 'kalam'. It is made up of bamboo stick which has a pointed edge like a pen. The kalam is dipped in dye, the ball of wool absorbs the dye which is pressed while drawing. This maintains constant flow of the dye to the tip for continuous drawing.
- Natural dyes used in Kalamkari are colours extracted from plants, roots, leaves and similar vegetable matter, combined with minerals like iron, and mordants like alum which help in fixing the colour on to the fabric.
- The art of Kalamkari under the patronage of Mughals in Coromandal and Golconda provinces branched out into two schools.
- Blue, ochre yellow, red and black are the main colours used in Kalamkari.
  - blue is associated with Lord Krishna and also other Gods.
  - yellow is used to show female bodies and also gold ornaments in deeper ochre shade.
  - green colour is used to depict Lord Hanuman.
  - red colour depicts demons and bad characters.
- The fabrics printed at Masulipatnam are used as furnishings such as bed-spreads, curtains, table cloths, etc apart from apparel like kurtas, saris and dupattas.

Kalamkari from Andhra Pradesh

Woven Textile

The richness and diversity of India's woven textiles are talked about for the last two thousand years in the global market. Foreigners, local travelers and writers have described the textures, quality and the designs of Indian fabrics in great detail.

Amongst the earliest woollen textiles are the 'Kani' shawls of Kashmir, woven with Pashmina goat fleece. Their sophisticated and sensitive designs were in high demand. Varanasi had an ancient tradition of weaving fine cotton fabrics, but is now world famous for the rich silks known as 'Kinkhab' and 'Tanchoi'. 'Kinkhab' was a heavy gold or silver brocaded fabric, often used for robes or furnishing.

The famous light weight patterned fabrics '**Jamdani**' was woven in Dhaka in Bengal, now in Bangladesh. These fabrics were so delicate and fine that they would be invisible on wet grass. Gujarat was considered the main centre for silk and brocade weaving in India. Surat, Jamnagar and Ahmedabad were the other important weaving centres for brocades.

In the Deccan, the 'Paithani' weavers in Maharashtra used interlock tapestry technique to pattern the elaborate ornamentation. Down South, arni and dharmavaram produced rich coloured silk saris. Heavy Kanjeevaram saris are still an integral part of every Indian women's wardrobe. They are made in silk and have motifs inspired by the temple architecture and sculptures of the region.

In addition to handlooms, the mill and the power loom sector has also contributed to the booming textile industry. But, the tradition of handloom cloth manufacturing in India is still flourishing and is still very much appreciated by the younger generation and the visitors to the sub-continent.

Categorisation of weaving styles on the basis of end product is as follows :

Saris

- Banaras brocades
- Baluchari, Jamdani
- Paithani
- Kanjeevaram
- Chanderi, Maheshwari

Shawls

- Kashmir shawl
- Kullu and Kinnaur
- Wraps of North-East

Floor Coverings

- Carpets

Saris

Description of popular styles of saris heoven in different parts of India is as follows :

Banaras Brocades

- Banarasi brocade saris are from Varanasi/Banaras, a small town in the state of Uttar Pradesh. The brocaded fabrics from Banaras are considered to be one of the finest saris in India and are known for their gold and silver brocade or 'zari'. These saris are made up of finely woven silk, decorated with intricate design.
- The designs are produced by warp and weft threads of different colours and materials, suitably woven. Extra warp/weft or both are woven into the fabric. Pattern is woven with or without attachments like jacquard or dobby attachment or by jala weaving. It can be silk on silk, cotton on cotton, silk on cotton or zari on silk. The brocade designs are made with extra yarns other than the ground threads.
- These extra or supplementary yarns are usually inserted in weft wise direction in Banaras brocades. When these extra yarns are picked from selvedge to the other end, the yarns appear on the face of the fabric in the design portion and as floats on the back of the fabric in the remaining portion.
- A very special technique often seen in Banaras is the 'Minakari'. In this technique, a motif is woven with an additional colour which stands out and resembles the enamelling in jewellery. The additional coloured yarns are slightly untwisted and hence appear raised.
  The most commonly used motifs are :
  - Chrysanthemum buta
  - Keri (paisley) buta
  - Ganga jamuni style (half gold and half silver zari)
  - Ari jhari (diagonal stripes)
  - Latifa buta
- The designs are extremely fine and delicate. They have a strong Mughal influence. Motifs like intertwining floral and foliage (Jaal), paisley in a creeper (Kalka bel) and hunting scene (shikargah pattern) are often seen.
- These textiles were popular items of export to European countries. Traditionally, Banarasi brocades were used during Mughal period as fabrics for royal coats, achkans and jamas. Courts and palaces were adorned with brocade curtains, fabric fans, bolsters and foot stools, upholstered with brocades. Brocade saris, dupattas and dress fabric were worn by women on special occasions, mainly on weddings and festivities.

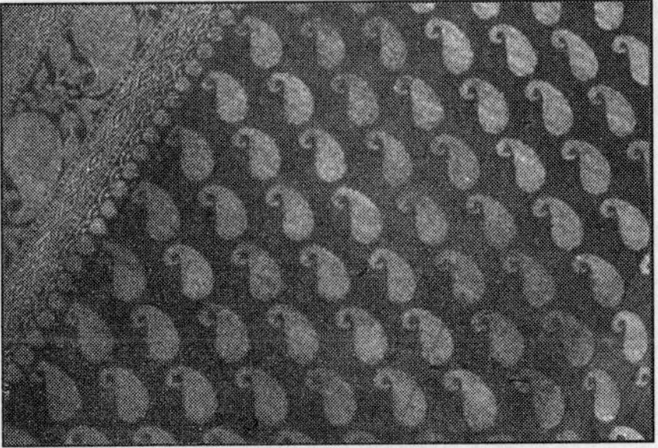

Banaras Brocades

Jamdani Saris

- The Jamdani saris are from West Bengal. These are sheer, delicate saris woven in Phulia, Nadia and Shantipur villages. These are made in combination of cotton with cotton, cotton with silk and silk with silk. The technique of interlocking the extra weft yarns for creating motifs in the fabric is used in Jamdani saris. These are woven on traditional handlooms.
- Floral geometric creepers, paisleys and leeves are the most common motifs in the Jamdani saris.

Jamdani Saris

Paithani Saris

- Paithani saris are woven in Paithan and Yevla villages of Aurangabad in Maharashtra. Paithani saris are heavy silk saris which are preferred for wedding trousseau and festive wear.
- The intricate motifs are woven by interlock twill tapestry weaving technique on traditional handlooms. Bright jewel tones such as emerald green, ruby red and yellow coloured silk yarns were used, however mid-night blue coloured saris were most preferred. The interlocking technique created geometric angular forms out of patterns which were floral, paisleys, parrots, peacocks and lotus flowers.

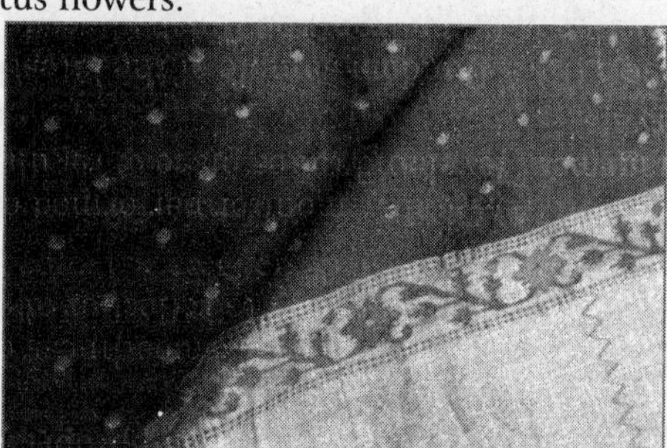

Paithani Saris

Kanjeevaram Saris

- These saris hail from the town of Kanchipuram in Tamil Nadu. It is considered to be one of the most expensive saris in the world and thus, used for all special occasions. The sari is woven in pure mulberry silk and gold zari on hand operated pit looms.
- The colours most commonly used are mustard, deep green, maroon, aubergine, etc. The motif imagery is drawn from the nature and forms of temple architecture. Some examples are peacock, parrot, rosary beads, bird's eye, kalash, mythical creatures, temple designs, scenes from Ramayana, Mahabharata and Bhagwad Gita, etc.

Kanjeevaram Saris

Chanderi Saris

- Chanderi, near Gwalior, in Madhya Pradesh is renowned for its woven saris appropriate for summer wear. The craft is practised by Muslim Ansari weavers. The sari is woven in a blend of cotton and degummed silk.
- It is diaphanous and is woven in pastel colours with small buties and a narrow gold border. The pallu generally has fine lines in zari yarn. The motifs are very simple.

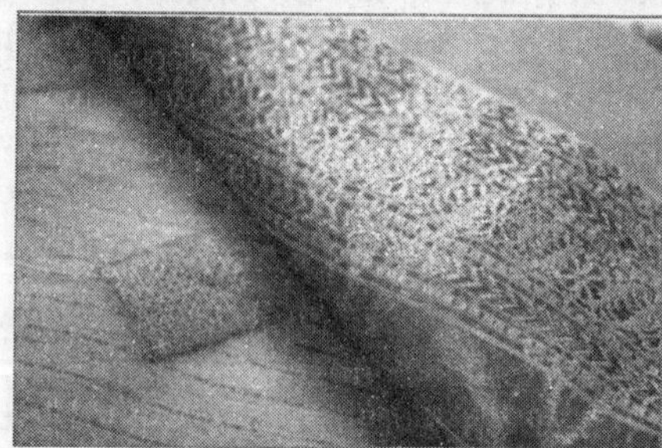

Chanderi Saris

Shawls

Description of popular styles of shawls women in different parts of India is as follows:

Kashmiri Shawls

- The Kashmiri shawls have remained as one of the most cherished acquisitions in the world since centuries. The English word 'Shawl' is derived from Persian word 'Shal', meaning a woven woollen fabric, which is draped across the shoulder to provide protection against the cold.
- Three districts of Kashmir valley, viz Srinagar, Ganderbal and Budgaon are famous for Pashmina shawl making. Shawl is prepared from material like woollen fleece, Pashmina, Shatoosh and Angora wool. Pashmina considered as the king of fibres derived its name from Persian word, Pashm meaning soft gold. It is famous for its softness, warmth, fineness and desirable aesthetic value.

- On the basis of production techniques, the Kashmiri shawl can be categorised into two main types *i.e.* the loom woven or Kani shawls and the needle embroidered or sozni shawls.
- The motifs are inspired from beauty of nature. Some examples are mango or kairi, almond or badam, chinar leaf, apple blossom, tulip, lily flower, cherries, plum; birds like parrot, woodpeeker, magpie ,etc.
- Pashmina fleece colours range from beige, grey and brown to black. However, the fabric adapts itself beautifully to dyeing and colouring. Rich colours are most commonly seen on kani shawls like yellow (zard) , white (sufed), black (mushki), blue (ferozi), purple (uda), crimson (gulnar) and scarlet (kirmiz).
- The shawl or shoulder mantle has been in existence in India in a variety of forms since ancient times. It was worn and used as a warm protective garment against biting cold.
- Unrivalled for its light weight, in earlier times people folded these shawls into four folds and draped them. Nowadays, they are generally worn as stoles without folds or are merely thrown over the shoulder.

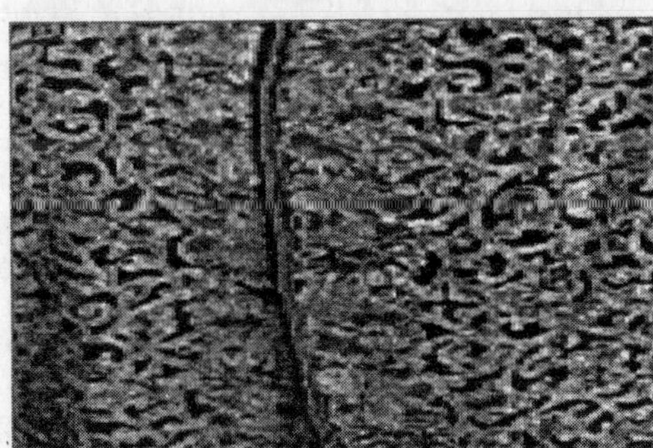

Kashmir Shawls

Kullu and Kinnauri Shawls

- Kullu and Kinnauri in Himachal Pradesh are also known for good quality woollen shawls. The traditional colours used for the base of the shawls are red, maroon, black, brown and off-white. Bright colours are inserted in extra weft on borders of the shawl. Geometric motifs inspired from nature are made into beautiful and colourful borders.
- Kinnauri shawls are known for their labour intensive skillful weaving. These shawls are heavily embellished with motifs and are treasured by the women of Himachal Pradesh. These are draped by the women in two peculiar ways. Heavy silver jewellery is then worn along with it to give it a festive look.

Wraps of North-East

- North Eastern India comprises of both tribal and non-tribal population. Textile weaving is done by women in these states. There are more than 38 tribes in North-East of India and each of them have their own distinctive design, colour combination and a different design for special occasions.
- The design and colour, which varies not only between the tribes but also sometimes between clans of the same tribe and between different villages, records the wearer's position in society. Shawls and wraps were originally made of cotton and the use of wool came much later. The colors used were mainly black, dark blue, red and yellow.

Floor Coverings: Carpets

- A carpet is a textile floor covering which consists of an upper layer of 'pile', which is attached to a backing. The pile is either made from wool or a manmade fibre such as nylon or polyester and usually consists of twisted tufts which are often heat-treated to maintain their structure. Carpets can be from wall to wall or smaller in size, such as area rugs.
- Carpet weaving in India can be traced to the beginning of the Mughal empire, wherein under the patronage of the Mughals, Indian craftsmen adopted Persian techniques and designs. Akbar, a Mughal emperor, introduced the art of carpet weaving to India, during his reign.
- The Mughal emperors patronised Persian carpets for their royal courts and palaces. The carpets woven in India showed the classic Persian style of fine knotting. The Indian carpets are known for their designs with attention to detail and presentation of realistic attributes. In India, carpet industry uses wool, silk, acrylic and jute.

Carpets

Recent Developments in Textile and Apparels

The world is realizing a very fast change not only in electronic but also in textile The recent developments are as follows :

Nano Textiles

Nano textiles can be produced by a variety of methods. The key difference among them is whether synthetic nano particles are integrated into the fibres or the textiles, or are applied as a coating on the surface and whether nano particles are added to the nanoscale fibres or coating.

However, information about manufacturing methods, the nanomaterials themselves and the quantities used, as well as the 'life cycle' of the 'nano-treated' textile for scale is largely unavailable to the consumer. The present dossier, therefore clarifies nano-textile manufacturing processes and application areas and gives an overview about the potential effects on the environment and health. Many questions remain unanswered, however, there is a need for considerably more research not only for product development but also into the usefulness and risks associated with nano-textiles.

Technical Textiles

Technical textiles are the products manufactured for non-aesthetic purposes. They are used for automotive applications, medical usages, crop protection, protective clothing, etc. It means textile materials and products manufactured primarily for their technical and performance properties rather than their aesthetic or decorative characteristics.

Major Segments of Technical Textiles

Technical textiles are functional fabrics that have applications across various industries including automobiles, civil engineering and construction, agriculture, healthcare, industrial safety, personal protection, etc. The technical textile is broadly grouped under the following 12 segments based on the functional applicability :

Name	Description
Agrotech	Agriculture, horticulture and forestry
Buildtech	Building and construction
Cloth tech	Technical components of shoes and clothing
Geotech	Geotextiles and civil engineering
Hometech	Components of furniture, household textiles and floor coverings
Indutech	Filtration, cleaning and other industrial
Medtech	Hygiene and medical
Mobitech	Automobiles, shipping, railways and aerospace
Oekotech	Environmental protection
Pactech	Packaging
Protech	Personal and property protection
Sportech	Sport and Leisure

Technical textile markets are usually more application specific and demanding altogether different types of production strategies. The strict adherence to the product specification and quality standards are the prime requirements to enter in this field.

Usually, there is a need for special dialogue between the producers and the users. The users need products with specific performance and functional requirement. Therefore, the producers must peep into requirements and provide the same in the products to the satisfaction of the users.

Occupational Clothing

Occupational clothing is associated with a specific profession/occupation. It satisfies specific guidelines of employer.

Since the second half of the twentieth century, the character of occupational clothing has changed significantly. Within a company, uniform dress, which is comfortable, fashionable, and clean, has been shown to improve working performance of employees by increasing their motivation and their identification with their company and fellow workers. A good-looking professional uniform attracts new customers and produces the image of trustworthiness and economic achievement.

For example, Fast food companies, such as McDonald's, which cater mainly to young people, frequently dress their employees in cheerful colourful and casual-looking uniforms that correspond to the tastes and lifestyles of children and teenagers.

By the end of the twentieth and the beginning of the twenty-first century, an increasing section of the fashion industry was specialising in the production of corporate wear.

Today the industry offers a wide variety of clothes ranging from simple standard items, such as T-shirts and sweaters individualised by embroideries and corporate colours, to complete corporate fashion lines. When a large organisation decides to introduce new uniforms it usually follows a long procedure.

Well-known designers are hired to work very closely with the executive management in order to develop a unique design that communicates the company's corporate image. Before ordering new uniforms, prudent companies find out their employees' wishes and expectations and have them test sample garments to determine whether the uniforms can fulfil the requirements of practical function, quality, and comfort.

At the same time, corporate fashion is spreading to more types of companies. Besides airlines, railways, and postal services, which continue a long tradition, a wide variety of service industries make increasing use of corporate wear, such as grocery stores, shopping malls, department stores, entertainment parks, restaurants, hotels, hospitals, and cleaning companies.

Zero Waste Design

Zero waste simply means a product or process that eliminates waste materials. The term can be applied to many different industries and can even encompass a 'way of life'. Within the fashion industry, a zero waste garment is systematically designed to avoid and eliminate wasting materials, so that no textiles are disposed off.

The concept of zero waste is one where everything is reused and nothing is discarded. It is the antithesis of the 'Build, Buy and Bury' Model a one way ticket from raw material to factory, to user, then landfill. The circular economy has the potential to completely transform the way in which businesses operate and resource intensive industries like fashion are at the heart of the debate.

Waste is a major contributor to global warming, solid waste landfills are the single largest man-made source of methane gas in the United States. Methane is a powerful greenhouse gas that is 23 times more effective at trapping heat in the atmosphere than the most prevalent greenhouse gas, carbon dioxide.

Zero waste is all about addressing waste as a primary root cause of global warming. A zero waste strategy supports all three of the generally accepted goals of sustainability economic well being, environmental protection and social well being.

Upcycling and Recycling

Recycling and upcycling play a major role in the sustainability criteria of economic, environmental and social dimensions. They underwrite a Closed Loop Model which funds the notion of 'for all forever' in a globe of finite resources.

For the fashion sector, recycling contributes to elimination of waste through reuse of materials and finished garments, conservation of the environment in particular reduction in landfill and pollution through redirection of waste to alternative uses and preservation of natural resources including water and nature through a model in which the same materials can be used over and over again.

Upcycling is a process, where waste or useless products are converted into new materials or products of equal or better quality or a higher environmental value. The goal of upcycling is to prevent the wasting of potentially useful materials by making use of the existing ones. Recycling requires energy and resources to gather, sort and process the waste only to make something else out of it.

EXAM BASED QUESTIONS

1 Where we can trace the tradition of Indian textile?
(a) British era (b) Mughal era
(c) Harappa civilisation (d) Indus Valley civilisation

2 Which fabric was used by the people of Indus Valley civilisation?
(a) Jute (b) Cotton
(c) Wool (d) Silk

3 Which country is said to be the major importer of Indian silk?
(a) Britain (b) South East Asia
(c) Rome (d) Europe

4 Which Indian text informs us about the weaving technique?
(a) Rig Veda (b) Sama Veda
(c) Yajur Veda (d) Atharva Veda

5 Which cloth is worn by aristocrats in Ramayana?
(a) Cotton (b) Silk
(c) Wool (d) Hemp

6 Which country is said to be the major importer of silk fabric?
(a) Sri Lanka (b) Myanmar
(c) Indonesia (d) China

7 How the artistic expression of the embroider is skillfully created on fabric?
(a) Through creativity (b) Through awl or tambour
(c) Through golden thread (d) Through children

8 How various embroidery designs are created?
(a) By creativity (b) By imagination
(c) By teaching (d) By skills

9 Which is said to be the famous embroidery of Kashmir?
(a) Phulkari (b) Chamber
(c) Kasuti (d) Kashida

10 Which region is famous for Zardozi embroidery?
(a) Andhra Pradesh (b) West Bengal
(c) Uttar Pradesh (d) Bihar

11 Who were the main practicer of Kashida embroidery?
(a) Women folk (b) Men folk
(c) Both (a) and (b) (d) Neither (a) nor (b)

12 What are motifs?
(a) Design or pattern of something
(b) Colour of the thread
(c) Neddle for weaving
(d) Embroidery threads

13 What is the style of an embroidery that uses fabric where stiches are like fly stitch, stem stitch and darning stitch?
(a) Sozni (b) Zalakdozi
(c) Zaui (d) All of these

14 What is the base material for Phulkari embroidery?
(a) Handspun and handwoven Khaddar
(b) Cotton and silk
(c) Woven and knitted wool
(d) Longitudinal fibre

15 Which thread is used for Phulkari embroidery?
(a) Handspun (b) Twisted woolen thread
(c) Untwisted silk thread (d) None of these

16 What are the two most prevalant embroidery styles of Punjab?
(a) Pashmina, and Bagh (b) Bagh, and Phulkari
(c) Pat, and Chamba Rumal (d) Phulkari and Chikankari

17 What is the symbolisation of Chamba rumal?
(a) Chamba rumal is geometrically styled.
(b) Chamba rumal is most picturesque needle work.
(c) Chamba rumal is done on bed linen.
(d) Chamba rumal is used as a veil.

18 Which among the following is true with respect to Chamba rumal?
(a) It is from Andhra Pradesh
(b) Motif of this depicts Lord Krishna's life
(c) Divided into two types, : Bagh and Phulkan
(d) Wore on the occasion of Karva Chauth

19 What is the major significance of embroidery from Gujarat?
(a) Mirrors on the fabric with an embroidery stitch
(b) Picturesque drawing of mountains
(c) Shows the life of Lord Krishna
(d) All of the above

20 What is the basic material for Parsi embroidery?
(a) Cotton (b) Jute (c) Wool (d) Silk

21 What is the region where Chikankari is practised?
(a) Uttarakhand (b) Uttar Pradesh
(c) Andhra Pradesh (d) Bihar

22 Who first practised this art of Chikankari?
(a) Fatima Begum (b) Jahangir
(c) Raziya Sultan (d) Nur Jahan

23 Which among the following is not the feature of Chikankari?
(a) It happens on white cotton fabric.
(b) It includes flora patterns.
(c) It is a shadow work.
(d) It is used only as a veil.

24 What is applique work?
(a) Fabric secured onto a base fabric by embroidery stitches.
(b) A surface decoration using the application of print paste.
(c) The application of wax as a resist method to colour fabric.
(d) A decorative design applied by the interlacing of different coloured yarns.

25 What is the major motifs on 'Phool Patti Ka Kaam'?
(a) Flora (b) Fauna (c) Sitara (d) Pearls

26 What is the key feature of Zardozi work?
(a) White embroidery
(b) Jute embroidery
(c) Gold and silver embroidery
(d) All of the above

27 Which among the following is the Zardozi style of embroidery?
(a) Karchobi (b) Kamdani
(c) Both (a) and (b) (d) Only (b)

28 What is Kasuti embroidery?
(a) Kasuti embroidery is done on white fabric.
(b) Kasuti is considered as an auspicious craft.
(c) Kasuti is made up of wool.
(d) Kasuti embroidery only have elephants.

29 What is the famous embroidery of Andhra Pradesh?
(a) Phulkari (b) Sujani
(c) Lambadi (d) Kasuti

30 Which embroidery tells story in its work?
(a) Sujani (b) Kathan
(c) Soof Bharat (d) Chamba Rumal

31 What marked the origin of Pipli applique?
(a) Quilt for newly wedded
(b) Clothes for newly born
(c) Decorative materials for the idol of Jagannath
(d) Shows story of Lord Krishna

32 What do you mean by 'dyed textile'?
(a) Process in which colour is transfered to finished textile.
(b) Process where fibre is transformed to yarn.
(c) Process where threads are coloured.
(d) Process where weaving is done.

33 What do you mean by word 'Bandha' ?
(a) Tie (b) Dye
(c) Tie Dye (d) All of these

34 Which among the following is the textile of Rajasthan?
(a) Bandhej (b) Bandhani
(c) Zaukan (d) Zardozi

35 What are the regions where finest 'Bandhej' is produced?
(a) Bikaner (b) Sikar
(c) Both (a) and (b) (d) Only (b)

36 What is the pattern of 'Lehariya print'?
(a) Mirrors (b) Fine dots
(c) Tiney boxes (d) Diagonal lines

37 What is the etymological meaning of the word 'Ikat'?
(a) It is derived from the word 'Magikat' which means thread.
(b) It is derived from the word 'Kagikat' which means knot.
(c) It is derived from the word 'Magikat' which means bind or knot.
(d) It means coloured thread.

38 What is called about the doubt 'Ikat' weaving tradition of Gujarat?
(a) Pat (b) Patola
(c) Patiyala (d) Phulkari

39 Where the Ikat textile called 'Bandhas is produced?
(a) Odisha (b) Jharkhand
(c) West Bengal (d) Andhra Pradesh

40 What is the popular sari from Odisha which is an example of 'Ikat'?
(a) Silk Sari (b) Madhubani Sari
(c) Ikat Sari (d) Saktapar Sari

41 What is printed textile?
(a) It is applying of colours in the fabric.
(b) It is spreading colours in the thread.
(c) It is applying colours in the definite pattern.
(d) All of the above

42 What is called about mud resistant block print?
(a) Bandhej Print (b) Printed lines
(c) Bangar Prints (d) Bagru Prints

43 What do you mean by 'Kalamkari'?
(a) Stencil Printing
(b) Pen Craft
(c) Sanganeur print
(d) Block-pen printing

44 What does one mean by 'Kalam' and 'Kari'?
(a) Pencil Work (b) Stencil Art
(c) Pen Art (d) Pencil Art

45 How does 'Kalam' made up of?
(a) Bamboo stick (b) Feather
(c) Wooden piece (d) Coloured threads

46 What is the earliest form of woolen textile?
(a) Jamdani (b) Paithani
(c) Kinkhab (d) Kani

47 What is the special technique often used in Banaras Brocade?
(a) Zari (b) Zardozi
(c) Minakari (d) Pashmina

48 Which saree is said to be the most expensive?
(a) Jamdani (b) Kani
(c) Kanjeevaram (d) Pashmina

49 What does the word 'Shawl' mean?
(a) Drapper (b) Cloth
(c) Woollen fabric (d) Woven woollen fabric

50 What is nano textile?
(a) Nano textile comprises of nano particles
(b) Nano textile have small equipments
(c) Nano textile is based on recycled material
(d) Nano textile has non-fabrics

51 What do you mean by technical textiles?
(a) They have scientific formula to do things.
(b) Things is this have functional fabrics
(c) They have performance based properties.
(d) The hold non-aesthetic properties

52 Why upcycling and recycling are important criteria for growth?
(a) It helps in production.
(b) It helps in manufacturing process.
(c) It helps in sustainable development.
(d) It helps in fashion sector.

53 Which among the following are the embroidery style of Eastern India?
1. Pausi embroidery
2. Sujani
3. Kantha
4. Chamba rumal

Codes
(a) 1 and 3 (b) 3 and 4
(c) 2 and 3 (d) All of these

54 Which among the following is a kind of Gujarat embroidery?
1. Mochi Bharat
2. Soof Bharat
3. Alpha Bharat
4. Abhla Bharat

Codes
(a) 1 and 3 (b) 2 and 3
(c) 1, 2 and 4 (d) None of these

55 Which among the following is the part of Indian textile industry?
1. Embroidered textile
2. Printed textile
3. Non-woven textile
4. Dyed textile

Codes
(a) 1 and 3 (b) 1, 2 and 4
(c) 2, 3 and 4 (d) All of these

56 Which among the following is Uttar Pradesh embroidery?
1. Kasuti
2. Chikankari
3. Phool Patti Ka Kaam
4. Zardozi

Codes
(a) 1 and 3 (b) 2 and 3
(c) 2, 3 and 4 (d) All of these

57 Chikankari though done on the white muslin background, now is done on
1. voile or 2 by 2
2. mulmul or organdy
3. chiffon or georgettes
4. net

Codes
(a) 1 and 2 (b) 2 and 4
(c) All of these (d) 1, 2 and 3

58 Which of the following statement(s) is/are correct?
1. Kutch embroidery is from Gujarat.
2. Bandhini word comes from Sanskrit word Bandha and Bandhana which means tieing.
3. The textile labelling regulations in various countries constrain trade and industry to display information, about the raw materials on their products.
4. In clothing fibre content, information must be provided in sewn-in-labels.

Codes
(a) 1 and 2 (b) 3 and 4
(c) 1, 2 and 3 (d) All of these

59 Which of the following is/are the characteristic(s) of Kanjivaram sarees?
1. Korvai i.e., solid contrast border.
2. Pelni *i.e.* Palla in contrast warp yarn.
3. Motives inspired by temples.
4. Only in green colour.

Codes
(a) 1 and 2 (b) 3 and 4
(c) 1, 2 and 3 (d) All of these

60 Which among the following comes under Embroidered textile?
1. Bandhani
2. Lehariya
3. Phulkari
4. Sujani

Codes
(a) 1 and 3 (b) 2 and 4
(c) 1 and 2 (d) 3 and 4

61 Match the following.

List I	List II
A. Kashida	1. Punjab
B. Phulkari	2. Himachal Pradesh
C. Chamba Rumal	3. Kashmir
D. Chikankari	4. Uttar Pradesh

Codes

	A	B	C	D		A	B	C	D
(a)	1	2	3	4	(b)	2	1	3	4
(c)	3	1	2	4	(d)	4	3	2	1

62 Match the following.

List I	List II
A. Simple and lightly embroidered for everyday use	1. Mochi Bharat
B. Kutch embroidery done by mochis	2. Abhla Bharat
C. Embroidery executed with untwisted silk	3. Soof Bharat
D. Use of mirror work	4. Phulkari

Codes

	A	B	C	D		A	B	C	D
(a)	1	2	3	4	(b)	4	1	3	2
(c)	4	3	2	1	(d)	1	2	4	3

63 Match the following.

List I	List II
A. Banaras brocades	1. Kanchipuram
B. Jamdani	2. Varanasi
C. Kanjeevaram	3. Gwalior
D. Chanderi	4. West Bengal

Codes

	A	B	C	D		A	B	C	D
(a)	1	2	3	4	(b)	2	3	4	1
(c)	4	1	2	3	(d)	2	4	1	3

64 Match the following.

List I	List II
A. Gavanti stitch	1. Stiches that provide weaving like effect.
B. Murgi stitch	2. Stiches that give same effect on both sides.
C. Negi stitch	3. Stiches that work in stepwise manner.
D. Menthi stitch	4. Stiches that give heavy appearance.

Codes

	A	B	C	D		A	B	C	D
(a)	2	3	1	4	(b)	1	2	3	4
(c)	4	3	2	1	(d)	3	2	1	4

Directions (Q. Nos. 65-70) *Given below are two statements, one labelled as Assertion (A) and other labelled as Reason (R) codes are given below. Select the correct code for the following*

Codes
(a) Both A and R are true and R is the correct explanation of A
(b) Both A and R are true but R is not the correct explanation of A
(c) A is true, R is false
(d) A is false, R is true

65 **Assertion** (A) Traditional textile of India is vast.
Reason (R) It is spreaded in the country only.

66 **Assertion** (A) Embroidered textile is the result of women folk.
Reason (R) They learn the craft from their mothers and older women in the family.

67 **Assertion** (A) Kashida embroidery depicts the natural elements.
Reason (R) In Kashida embroidery, we have pictures of flora and fauna of the region of Kashmir.

68 **Assertion** (A) Zardozi was traditionally done to ornament wall hangings.
Reason (R) Zardozi is flourished in Mughal court.

69 **Assertion** (A) Bandhani is tie dye textile technique.
Reason (R) This technique pre-determines the areas on the fabric which are tied tightly with thread to protect from the colour.

70 **Assertion** (A) 'Kani' shawls from Kashmir is the earliest woolen textile.
Reason (R) It is made with Pashmina goat fleece.

PREVIOUS YEARS' QUESTIONS

July 2018

1 Which of the following are major properties of activewear that are of interest today ?
1. Thermal insulation
2. Stretch with full recovery
3. Moisture transfer
4. Water resistance
5. Flame retardant

Codes
(a) 2, 3, 4, 5 (b) 1, 2, 4, 5
(c) 1, 2, 3, 5 (d) 1, 2, 3, 4

2 Which of the following are Ikat centres in India?
1. Chirala 2. Sambalpur 3. Mandvi
4. Ajanta 5. Bhuj

Codes
(a) 2, 3, 4, 5 (b) 1, 2, 3, 4 (c) 1, 2, 3, 5 (d) 1, 3, 4, 5

3 Give the correct sequence of 'Kani' shawl weaving.
1. Drawing of design pattern
2. Threading of warp onto the loom
3. Weaving of shawl in long strips
4. Winding of thread
5. Combing and spinning of fibers
6. Collection and sorting of fleece
7. Joining together of fragments of shawl
8. Washing and dyening

Codes
(a) 2, 3, 4, 5, 6, 1, 7, 8 (b) 6, 5, 8, 4, 2, 1, 3, 7
(c) 6, 7, 8, 1, 2, 3, 4, 5 (d) 1, 2, 4, 3, 6, 5, 7, 8

November 2017

4 Match the finishes given in ListI with their purpose given in ListII

List I	List II
A. Singeing	1. Increases the lustre of the fabric
B. Scouring	2. provides smooth surface
C. Tentering	3. Removal of desizing products, pectin and wax from wool
D. Calendering	4. Mechanical straightening process
	5. Burning of the raised fiber ends

Codes

	A	B	C	D		A	B	C	D
(a)	5	2	3	4	(b)	1	2	4	3
(c)	2	5	1	4	(d)	5	3	4	2

5 Give the correct sequence for the conventional ring spinning process
1. Picking
2. Combing
3. Opening cleaning and blending
4. Carding
5. Spinning
6. Roving
7. Drawing and drafting

Codes
(a) 3, 5, 4, 7, 6, 2, 1 (b) 3, 5, 7, 4, 2, 6, 1
(c) 1, 2, 3, 4, 5, 6, 7 (d) 2, 3, 4, 5, 6, 7, 1

January 2017

6 Give the correct sequence of making kanthas.
1. Collection of coloured and while threads from the border.
2. Forming a lay of fabrice and stitching it together.
3. Washing of fabric with gram flour.
4. Compatmentalisation of the surface
5. Tearing off the coloured borders and making the fabrics uniform in size.
6. Filling in between spaces.
7. Filling the compartments with the required design.

Codes
(a) 1, 3, 2, 4, 6, 7, 5 (b) 5, 6, 4, 3, 2, 1, 7
(c) 3, 5, 1, 4, 7, 6, 2 (d) 3, 5, 1, 2, 4, 7, 5

7 Which of the following are styles of printing?
1. Direct 2. Resist
3. Discharge 4. Transfer

Codes
(a) 2, 3 and 4 (b) 3, 4 and 1 (c) 1, 2 and 3 (d) 1, 2 and 4

8 Which of the following are types of Phulkari?
1.Chope 2. Til patra
3. Saloo 4. Bayton
5. Durjani

Codes
(a) 1, 2 and 3 (b) 2, 3 and 4
(c) 3, 4 and 1 (d) 4, 1 and 2

9 Assertion (A) Threadless bonding and welding offers a tangible alternative solution to the sewing of microfiber textiles.
Reason (R) This technology has the ability to produce narrow lap seams which are less bulky.

Codes
(a) Both A and R are incorrect
(b) Both A and R are correct
(c) A is correct, but R is incorrect
(d) A is incorrect, but R is correct

ANSWERS

Exam Based Questions

1 (d)	2 (b)	3 (c)	4 (a)	5 (a)	6 (c)	7 (b)	8 (b)	9 (d)	10 (c)
11 (b)	12 (a)	13 (a)	14 (a)	15 (c)	16 (b)	17 (b)	18 (b)	19 (a)	20 (d)
21 (b)	22 (d)	23 (d)	24 (a)	25 (b)	26 (c)	27 (c)	28 (b)	29 (c)	30 (a)
31 (c)	32 (a)	33 (a)	34 (a)	35 (c)	36 (d)	37 (c)	38 (b)	39 (a)	40 (d)
41 (c)	42 (d)	43 (b)	44 (c)	45 (a)	46 (d)	47 (c)	48 (c)	49 (d)	50 (a)
51 (c)	52 (c)	53 (c)	54 (c)	55 (b)	56 (c)	57 (c)	58 (d)	59 (c)	60 (d)
61 (c)	62 (b)	63 (c)	64 (a)	65 (c)	66 (a)	67 (a)	68 (b)	69 (a)	70 (a)

Previous Years' Questions

1 (d)	2 (b)	3 (b)	4 (d)	5 (c)	6 (d)	7 (c)	8 (a)	9 (b)

UNIT IV

Body Measurements and Equipments

A well grommed appearance is admired by everyone. Clothes play a prominent role in appearance of a person. The body shape of the person varies due to which there is a requirement of different equipments for taking the measurement of the body.

Measurements

The most crucial and essential step in garment construction is taking body measurements. The fit of a garment depends on the accuracy of body measurements. A well fitted garment enhances the look of the person and adds to the personality of the weaver.

The measurements needed for garment making depend not only on the style and type of the garment but also on the age and sex of the user. The only tool required for measurement is a measuring tape. We should use a good quality tape for measurements. A torn/damaged or stretchy tape will give incorrect measurements.

Procedure of Taking Body Measurements

Procedure of taking body measurements for most of the garments is same; only sleeve, skirt, pant measurements vary. Procedure of taking measurements is discussed below :

Neck This is a round measurement taken around the base or the largest part of the neck. Pass the tape around the neck, over the collar bone in the front and the base of the neck, at the back. This measurement gives the neck width and is needed for a close fitting collar.

Shoulder This point can be located by feeling for the end of the flat bone at the end of the shoulder or by raising the arm until a dimple appears at the end of the shoulder and feeling for the shoulder bone in this depression. The distance between the base of the neck and the end of the shoulder gives this measurement.

Shoulder Width/Back Width Measure from one end of the shoulder bone to the other at about 4" below the back neck.

In this Chapter

High Chest Measurement This measurement will help in getting a close fit under the armpit, eliminating the wrinkles. Place the tape straight under the armpits in the front and across back to get the measurement. Take care to keep the tape parallel to the floor, both at the front and at the back.

Bust Measure around the fullest part of the bust with the tape held parallel to the floor. Do not let the tape to sag at the back. The tape should be tight enough so that it does not slip and loose enough for one finger to pass through.

Waist It is essential to locate the natural waist first, in order to take this measurement. The natural waistline is located above the hip bone in the narrowest part of the body. A cord tied at the waist will facilitate in taking this measurement. Measure around the cord with the tape held parallel to the floor.

High Hip At around 3" below the waistline, hold the tape around the hip to get the measurement.

Hip Measure around the fullest part of the hip (7" from the waistline) with the tape held parallel to the floor.

Armscye/Armhole Measure by passing the tape under the armpit and around the armhole.

Front Waist Length Measure down from the highest part of the neck over the fullest part of the bust to the waist.

Shoulder to Bust Measure down from the highest part of the neck to the tip of the bust. This is also called bust point height. This is useful in locating the bust point while drafting a blouse.

Distance Between Bust Points A horizontal measurement that measures the distance between the bust points, useful for dart placement in blouse drafting. It is known as bust point width.

Back Waist Length Measure down from the highest part of the neck over the centre back to the waistline.

Front Neck Depth Measure across from the highest part of the neck diagonally towards the centre front.

Back Neck Depth Measure across from the highest part of the neck diagonally towards the centre back.

Sleeve Measurements

Upper Arm Measure around the fullest part of the biceps with one finger underneath the tape.

Lower Arm Measure around the bottom or at the lower edge of the sleeve.

Elbow Measure around the elbow of the arm.

Wrist Take a round measurement at the wrist level of the arm.

Sleeve Length The length of the sleeve varies from one style to another. For short sleeves, measure down the arm from the tip of the shoulder to the desired level. For full length sleeve, bend the arm slightly at a 90° angle and measure from the tip of the shoulder, down to the elbow and then on to the wrist.

Skirt Measurements

Waist to Hip Measure from waist down to the fullest part of the hip.

Skirt Length Measure from waistline down to the desired length as per the garment design.

Pant Measurements

Pant Length Measure from waistline down to the desired length of the pant.

Inseam Distance from the innermost part of the thigh to the ankle or the length of the pant.

Leg Circumference

- **Thigh** Measure around the fullest part of the thigh.
- **Knee** Measure from the waist to the knee.
- **Calf** Measure around the calf muscle.
- **Ankle** Measure around the ankle.

Crotch Depth After sitting on a hard flat surface, measure down from the waist to the flat surface along the side seam.

Crotch Length Measure from front waistline to the back waistline by passing the tape in between the legs.

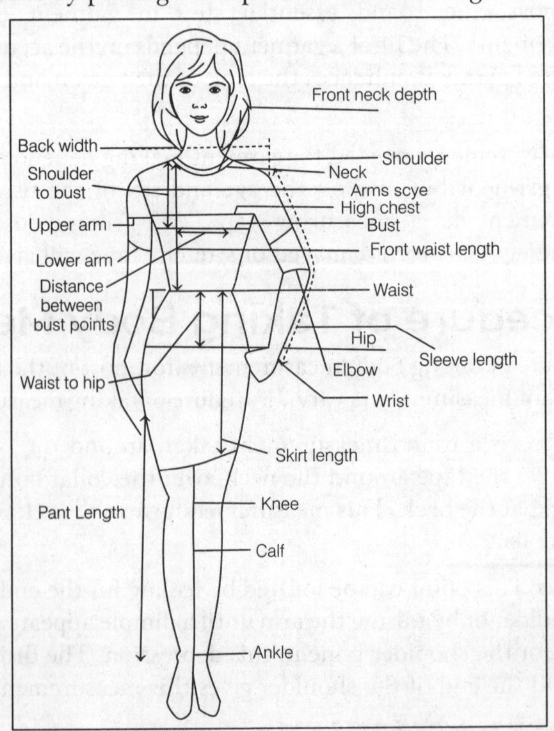

Measurement Labelling of a Girl

Need of Body Measurement

In order to make beautiful, attractive and supernatural apparel it is necessary to measure the body of the person properly.

If there is no proper measurement and stitching than also cloth will not look attractive. And this will also hamper the look and personality of a person.

While measuring the body measurement, it is necessary to take care of the personality of a person as it varies from person to person. As the personal characteristics of the person varies from being tall, short, fat or lean. Other than this, we have seen that someone's chest is wide, someone's narrow, someone's back is bent, someone's belly is out and someone's shoulders are tilted.

Therefore, it is clear that with the difference in body parts, the measurement of the cloth changes.

Points to be Consider While Taking Measurements

- A good quality measurement tape should be used for taking the body measurements. The long metal end of the tape is used for taking vertical measurements and the rounded metal end is used for taking horizontal measurements.
- Person giving the measurements should stand straight, but in a natural pose and preferably in front of a mirror. A well fitted garment should be worn while giving measurements.
- Another person is needed to take measurements. Basic lines of the body are to be taken into consideration while measuring body parts.
- A proper order and certain sequence should be followed in taking the measurements to make it more systematic.
- The amount of ease needed varies with the types of fabric used. More ease is needed for woven fabrics than knits.
- The accuracy of several measurements depends on this exact waistline location. Add to these measurements, the suggested amount of ease.
- Before body measurements are taken, a code or tape is fastened around the waist and left until all measurements have been completed.

Types of Figures

Our body/figure shape calculate our body shape, into one of seven most popular types. Naturally, not all women falling into one category are the same. Types of figures are :

Hourglass This body shape is balanced and harmonious. The bust and hips are proportional and well balanced and the waist is clearly defined.

Top Hourglass It is similar to the regular hourglass with a beautifully defined waist. Your bust is visibly larger than your hips.

Bottom Hourglass Just like the top hourglass, this body type has a clearly defined waist. Your bust is smaller than the hips.

Spoon If you are a spoon, your hips are much larger than your bust. Your hips have a shelf like appearance and you have a nicely defined waist.

Triangle Triangles have a slim upper body and wide hips. Their waist is not clearly accentuated.

Inverted Triangle Inverted triangle have a subtle waist and a proportionally larger upper body. Your bust and shoulder are quite wide and the hips are slim.

Rectangle This is a "boyish" body type your hips, waist and bust are about the same size. Your body is well proportioned and athletic in appearance.

Anthropometric Procedures

The term 'anthropometric' refers to comparative measurements of the human body. The anthropometric measurements commonly used as indices of growth and development for infants. It includes length, weight and head circumference. For anthropometric measurements to be valid, indices of growth status must be highly accurate, requiring precision in measuring technique.

The description of length, weight and head circumference measurement is given below :

Length Measurement

Measuring the length of the fabric according to the body measurement is very important. The measurement takes place once when the measuring tape was placed at the back of your neck and than bring down to the length where one wants the fabric to end.

Equipment

Use a length measuring device with a fixed headboard and a movable footboard that are perpendicular to the surface on which the child is lying. A fixed measuring tape, marked in millimetres or in 1/16 in segments should be attached to the surface with the zero end at the edge of the headboard.

Technique

Two people are required to measure length accurately :

Person A

- Hold the head with crown against the headboard so that the child can look straight upward.
- Make sure the trunk and pelvis are properly aligned with the measuring device.

Person B

- Straighten the child's legs and hold the ankles together with the toes pointed directly upward.
- Move the footboard firmly against the soles of the feet.
- Read the measurement to the nearest 0.1 cm (1/8 in).
- Repeat the measurement until two measurements agree within 0.2 cm (1/4 in).
- Record the numerical value and plot length for age on the appropriate growth chart.
- If the child is uncooperative and you cannot get an accurate measurement, record your best estimate on the growth chart and note the circumstances of the measurement.

Weight Measurement

It is important to measure the weight of the person for whom the cloth was made. This will take time to time checking of the body measurement.

Equipment

Use a beam scale with non-detachable weights or an equally accurate electronic scale. For infants and young children who are weighed lying down, use a pan type pediatric scale that is accurate within 10 grams or 1/2 ounces. Do not use spring type bathroom scales; with repeated use, they may not maintain the necessary degree of accuracy.

Technique

- Remove all clothing, including the diaper and place the infant in the center of the weighing surface.
- Read the measurement to the nearest 10 grams or 1/2 ounces.
- Repeat the measurement two to three times and after excluding those that are obviously wrong, average the values.
- Record the numerical value on the growth chart and plot weight for age and weight for length on the appropriate growth charts.

Note : It's not always possible to plot weight for length on small infants with lengths below 55 cm.

- If the infant moves excessively, an accurate measurement is unlikely; postpone the measurement for a few minutes.
- If the infant still does not keep still, skip the measurement unless you can make a reasonable estimate. If the weight you record on the growth chart is an estimate, note the circumstances on the growth chart.

Head Circumference Measurement

The measurement of head circumference is an important screening procedure for detecting abnormalities of head growth. Usually, abnormalities are caused by non-nutritional factors and slow head growth can be a result of severe under nutrition. Children with poor head growth frequently have poor linear growth as well.

Thus, knowledge of head size is very important in assessing possible nutritional factors contributing to short length or stature. Head circumference should be measured routinely.

Equipment

Use a flexible, non-stretchable measuring tape.

Technique

- Position the child standing or in a sitting position in the lap of the care giver.
- Place the lower edge of the measuring tape just above the child's eyebrows, above the ears and around the occipital prominence at the back of the head.
- Pull the tape snugly to compress the hair. The objective is to measure the maximal head circumference.
- Repeat the measurement twice or until two measurements agree to 0.1 cm (1/8 in).
- Record the numerical value immediately and plot on the growth chart.
- If the measurement appears abnormal when plotted, check the accuracy of plotting and recheck the measurement.

Equipments and Tools for Manufacturing

Sewing equipments and tools are needed for sewing which aid in construction of garments of good quality and appearance. The equipments or tools are broadly categorised into measuring, marking, cutting, general tools and pressing tools. A box with compartments is necessary to arrange these tools at one place.

Various types of tools are needed for the manufacturing of the garments.

Some of them are discussed below :

Measuring Tools

Measuring tools are essential for accurate sewing and they are as follows :

Measuring Tape It has a smooth surface tape that is clearly marked with increments of inches and centimeters on both sides. It is usually about 1/2 inch to 1/4 inch wide and 60 inch wide and 60 inches long and has 1/8 divisions. It has centimeter markings along other edge.

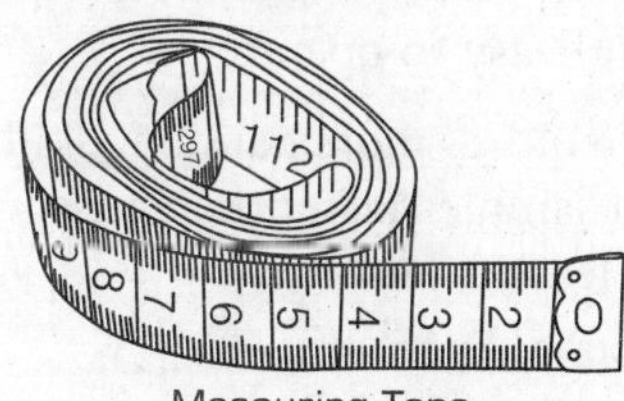

Measuring Tape

Rulers There are two types of rulers, one is a small ruler of 1 inch wide and 6 inches long, divided into 1/8" or 1/16" divisions on one side and centimeters on the other side, second one is of 2 inches wide and 18 inches long.

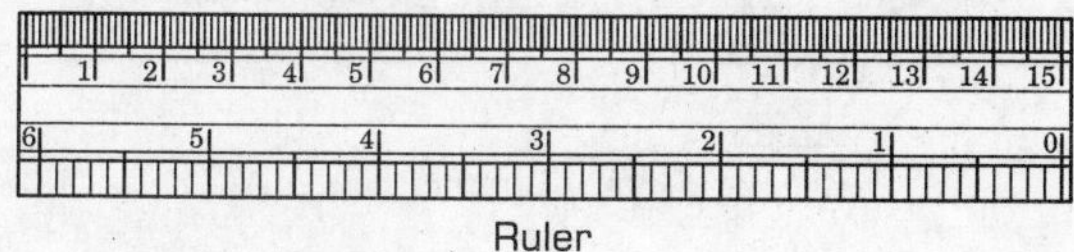

Ruler

Meter Scale/Yard Stick It may be of wooden, plastic or metal. It is available in 36 inches on 45 inches in length. They are useful for checking grain lines when fixing pattern pieces on material and for drawing long seam lines on fabrics or paper. It is also known as yard stick.

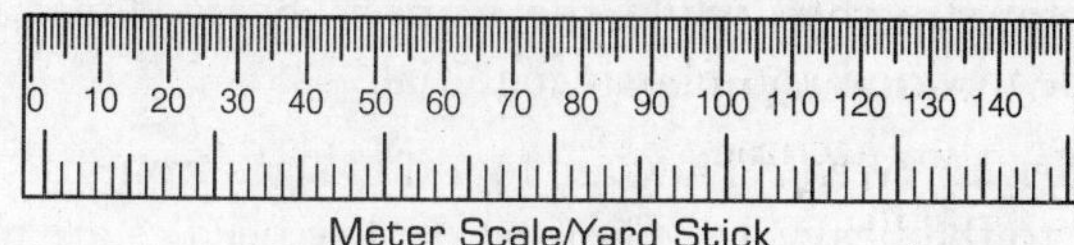

Meter Scale/Yard Stick

L-Scale It has arms or sides made of metal, giving it a L-shape; the long arm measures 24 inches and the short arm 14 inches. This has a perfect right angle corner and is used to draw lines at right angles at the time of drafting.

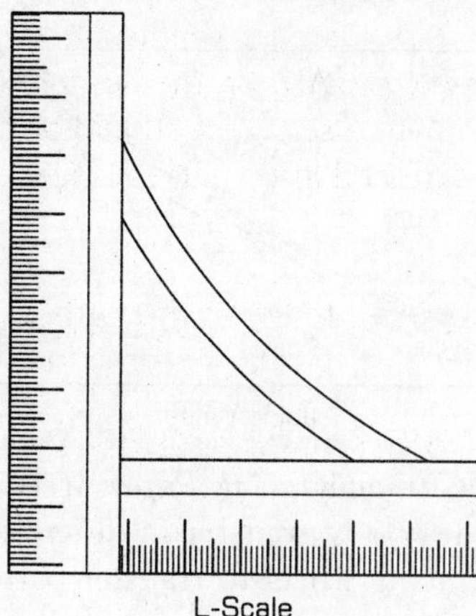

L-Scale

Hem Gauge It is a 6 inch gauge that can be made of cardboard or brought from a shop. It is used as a measuring guide for making width of the hems, pleats and seam allowances accurately. While measuring or making, use straight edge of the notch.

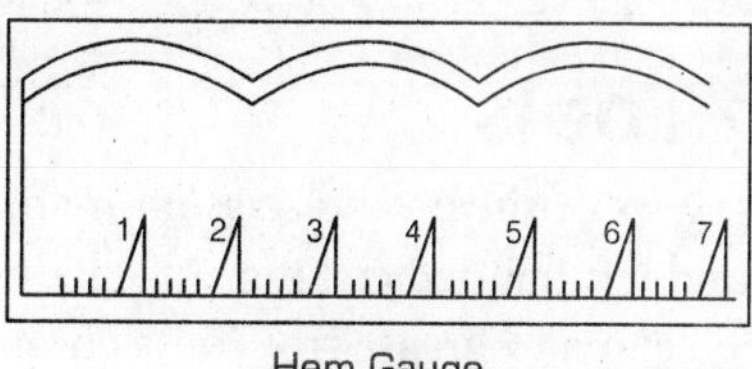

Hem Gauge

Hem Marker It is used for mark out a completely level hem line with chalk. It can be adjusted to any hem length. This is commonly used for professional hem marking.

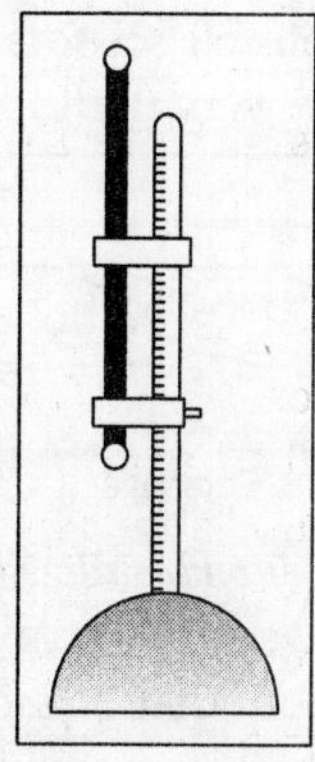

Hem Marker

Marking Tools

They are generally used for transferring the paper pattern onto the fabric.

Different types of marking tools are :

Tracing Wheel This is a sharp toothed wheel used with dress maker's carbon to transfer pattern markings to cloth. It transfers the pattern markings, including seams, darts and packet placements to the wrong side of the fabric. The small serrated edge tracing wheel is appropriate for most fabrics.

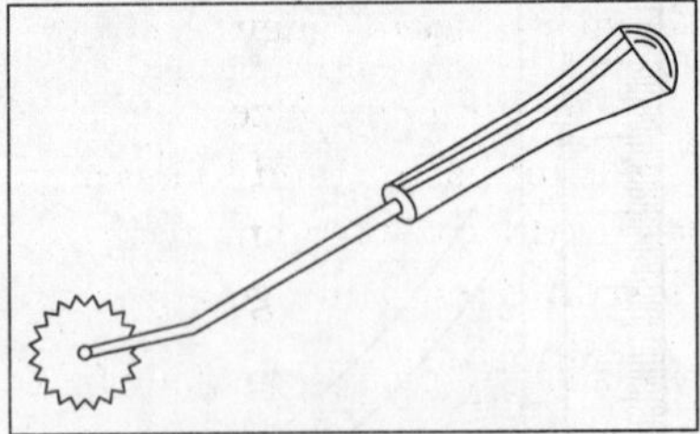
Tracing Wheel

Dress Maker's Carbon/Tracing Paper It is a wax coated paper on one side and is available in different colours. It is used with the tracing wheel to transfer pattern markings, such as lines, darts, pleats, etc., from paper patterns to the fabric being cut.

Tailor's Chalk It is made of wax or stone chalk. It is used to transfer seam lines and other pattern details to fabric. It is also used for marking fitting adjustments and hems. A wax chalk is acceptable only for woolen fabric.

Cutting Tools

The following types of shears and scissors are made for both right handed and left handed cutting. All cutting tools must be kept sharp, clean and grease free for accurate cuts.

Scissors They are 5 to 6 inches long. They are used for light cutting, trimming, clipping corners and cutting curves. These have round handles for both the blades. They are designed for shipping threads, trimming seams and for cutting holes. Sharp pointed scissors with blades and 1/2 inch to one inch long are very useful.

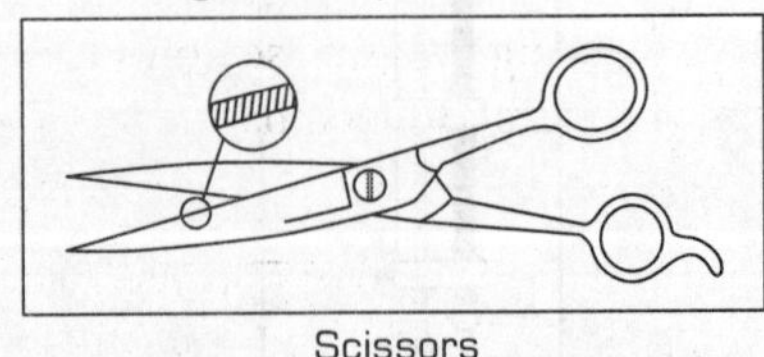
Scissors

Dress Maker's Shears/Bent Handle Shear They are 8 to10 inches long. They are used for cutting all types of fabrics. These are more satisfactory than scissors. Shears differ from scissors in that they have one small ring handle for the thumb and a large ring handle for the second, third and fourth fingers. One should protect the shear from rusting.

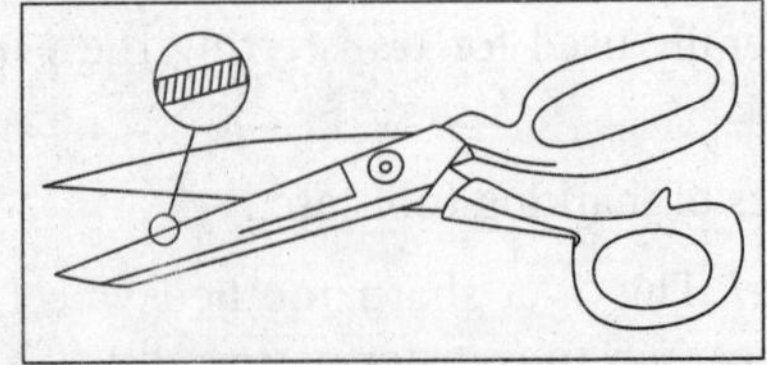
Dress Maker's Shear/Bent Handle Shear

Pinking Shears They are 9 to 10 inches long. They create a ravel resistant finish to raw edges of firmly woven fabrics when the seam allowance is left unfinished. They produce a notched cutting line which gives a neat appearance inside the garment.

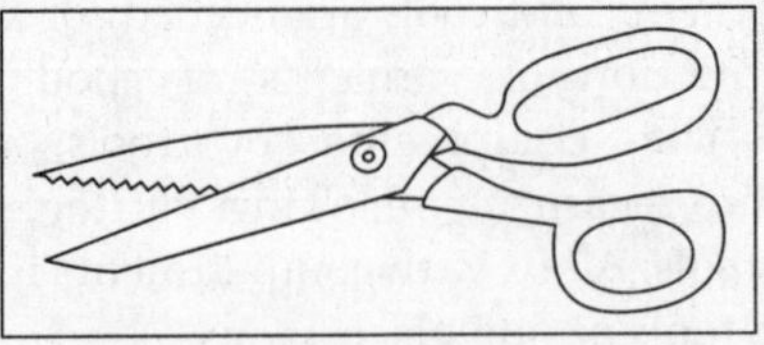
Pinking Shear

Buttonhole Scissors These can be adjusted so as to cut button holes in any size required. They are useful if one needs to make many button holes in a garment.

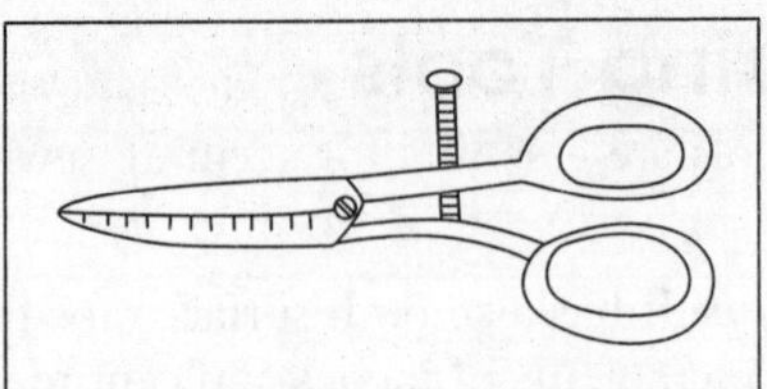
Buttonhole Scissor

Electric Scissors These are used in most sample rooms. They are ideal for cutting silk, nylon and soft fabrics. These are light in weight and easy to operate.

Rotary Cutter It requires more handling skill than shears. It cuts patterns and samples faster than scissors do. It cuts all fabrics as well as leather and vinyl.

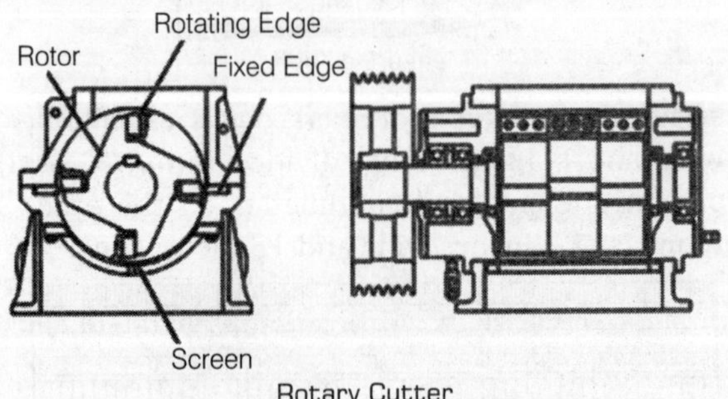

Rotary Cutter

Sewing Tools

These are used for hand and machine sewing. They are as follows :

Embroidery Frame This is a round frame used for keeping the fabric stretched while the work is being done. It is available in wood and plastic material.

Hand Sewing Needle They are found in sizes from the very fined 9 to the heavy 18. The best quality needles are made of hand ground steel. For hand sewing, medium length needles with a short oval eye is selected. Sharp and short needles are suitable for permanent stiching.

Sewing Machine Needles They are found in different sizes from the fine 9 to the heavy 18. The needles are made to fit the specific make and model of each sewing machine. The needle size should conform to the weight, thickness and kind of fabric.

Sewing Thread With the wide and ever increasing range of fabrics available in the market, it is important to know the right sewing thread for the various types of fabrics.

Both the thread and the garment should share the same characteristics, as they have to be laundered and ironed together, they should shrink and stretch together.

Needle Case It is a round case with assorted sizes of hand and machine needles.

Needle Threader It is a device made of thin wire which aids in threading machine needles and hand needles.

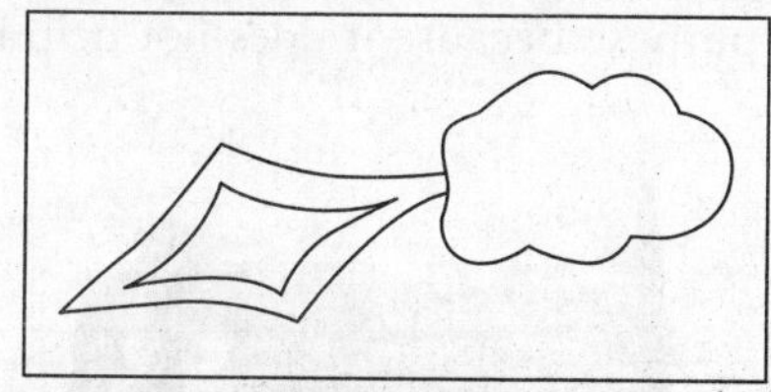

Needle Threader

Thimbles These are necessary for efficient and accurate hand sewing. A metal thimble should fit snugly on the middle finger of the needle holding hand.

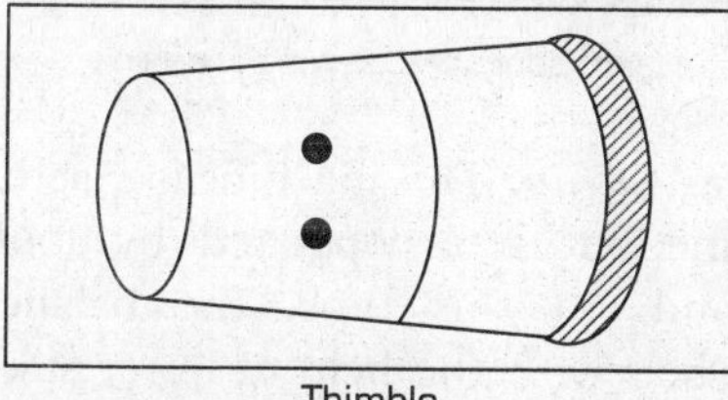

Thimble

Stiletto This is a sharp pointed instrument for punching holes in material. It is used for forming eyelets in belts and for embroidery work.

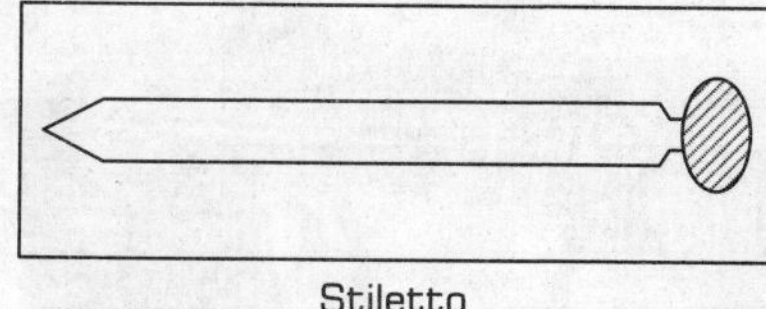

Stiletto

Bodkin This is a flat needle with blunt end and a large eye, used for threading ribbon or elastic through a tunnel.

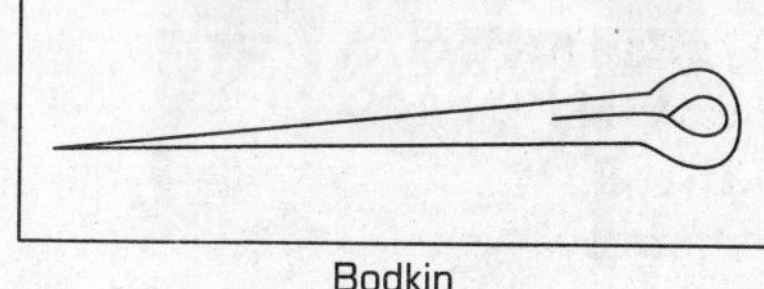

Bodkin

General Tools

These are the tools generally aid in cutting, construction and checking of the garments. They include :

Pins These come in different sizes for use in different fabrics. Use of pins for basting and fixing of pattern pieces onto fabric, makes work easier and more accurate. The right choice of pins is most essential for good workmanship.

Pin Cushion A small stuffed cushion made of wool or felt, to hold the pins while working near the table is. Pin cushion is made with an elastic strap so that it can fastened be to the wrist and can make work faster.

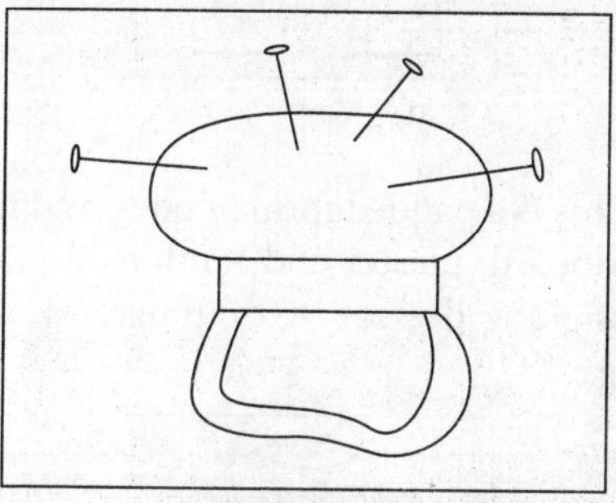

Pin Cushion

Seam Ripper This is useful for ripping out machine stiches. It has a handle and a bent point, which can be inserted into the stiches and pulled to break them.

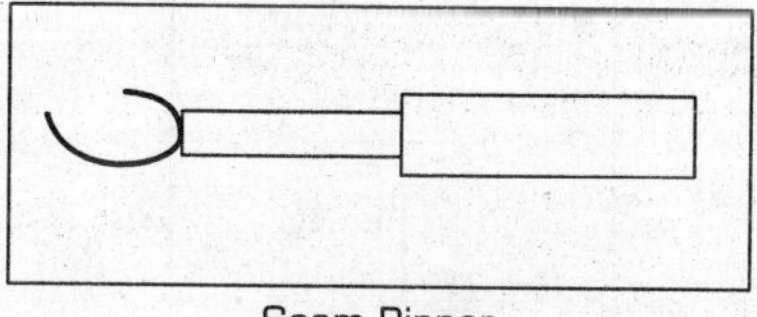

Seam Ripper

Orange Stick This is a long tool whose point can be inserted into the corners of collars and seams, so as to give a neat pointed appearance.

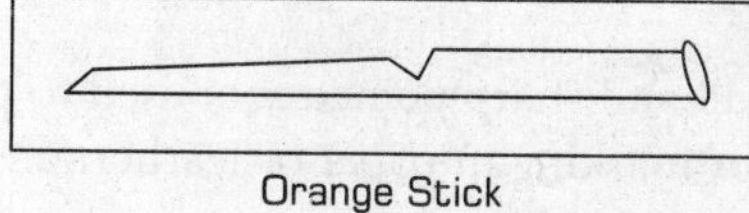

Orange Stick

Cutting Board/Table A table of 5 feet by 3 feet and height of 2 feet 6 inches is of convenient height and size for cutting and construction of garments.

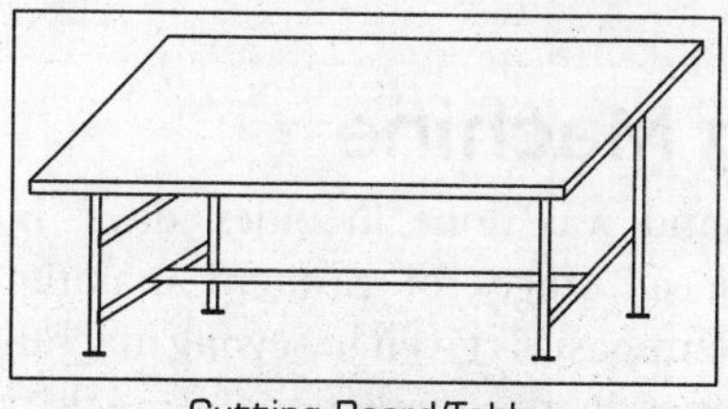

Cutting Board/Table

Mirror A full length mirror is useful for checking the fit and design of the garment on model.

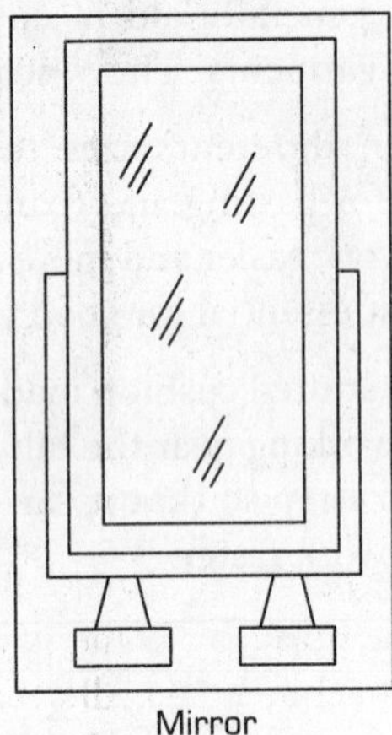
Mirror

Dress Form This is a padded form of body and may be made of wood, cardboard, plaster and reinforced plastic. This is useful for designing dresses by draping and also to check correct fitting.

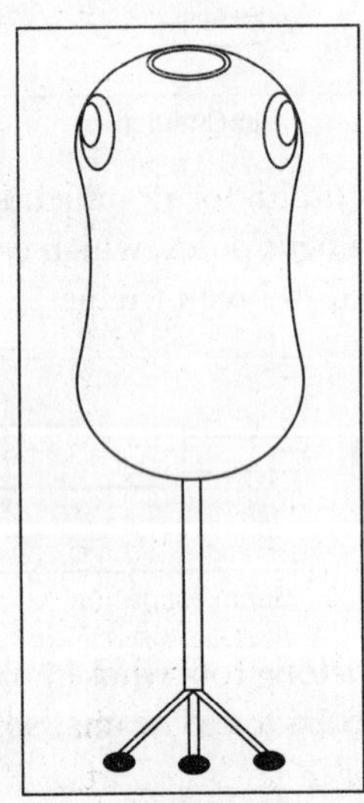
Dress Form

Awl It is a small and sharp poined tool used to punch small round holes for marking in paper or leather.

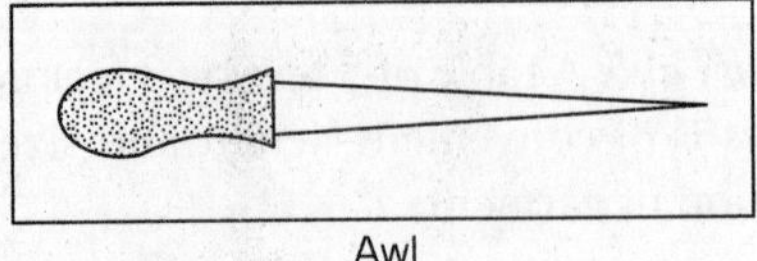
Awl

Sewing Machine

Sewing by hand was done in olden days, but it is not applicable for all stages of garment making. Therefore, considerable emphasis is given to sewing machine. There are several machines in the market today, each with its own desirable features and advantages.

Machines range from most basic, having only simple lock stitch to the electronic machines that use advanced computer technology having various functions. For example, piping, binding, ruffling, pleating, darning, hemming and even making button holes and attaching fasteners.

Types of Sewing Machines

Now, sewing machines are available in various models, such as domestic model, tailor model, industrial model, portable and cabinet models. They may be operated by hand, treadle or electronic motor.

Different types of sewing machines are :

Hand Operated Sewing Machine It is the simplest form of sewing machine which is operated by hand. A detachable handle provided to the flywheel is used to operate the machine. This machine is generally suitable for domestic purpose because it does not help in speeding up the work.

Hand Operated Sewing Machine

Treadle Sewing Machine This machine is exactly like a hand sewing machine but it is operated by foot, using an additional stand. In this type, the balance wheel is operated by a belt with the help of lower stand, which is driven by feet. This machine is suitable when there is no power supply.

Treadle Sewing Machine

Electric Sewing Machine This is the fastest sewing machine. One needs practice to handle it. The three types of electric sewing machines available are straight stitching with semi-automatic and automatic stiching machines. In an electric machine, the balance wheel comes to motion by a belt which is attached to an electric motor.

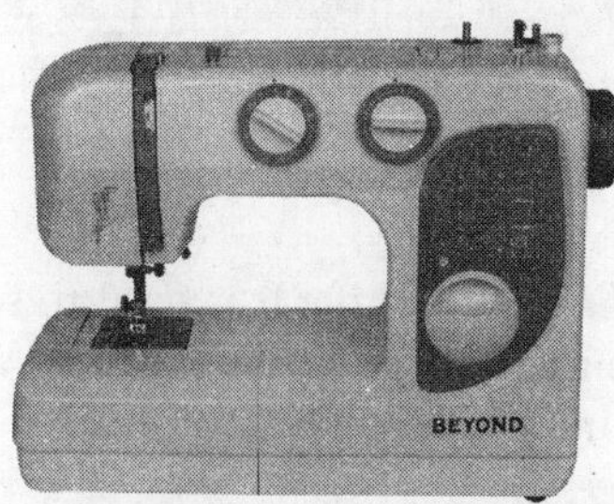

Electric Sewing Machin

Single Needle Lock Stitch Machine It makes lock stitches (stitch class 301). Lock stitches are formed with one needle thread and one bobbin thread.

It is a widely used sewing machine and used for sewing stitch class 301. Basic to computer controlled version is available in this machine category.

They are used for joining two or multiple fabric plies together. The machine is used to sew light weight, medium weight and heavy materials.

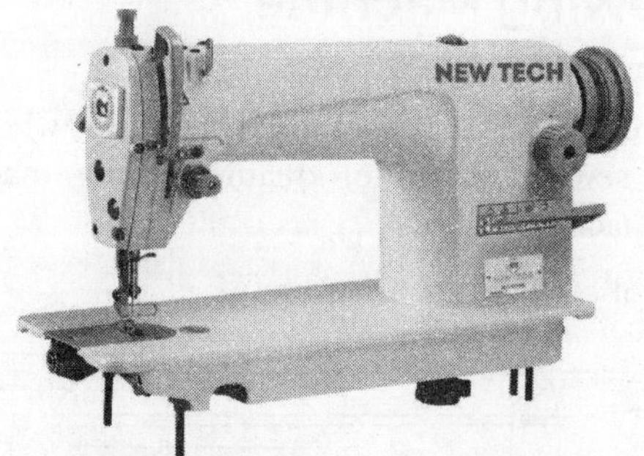

Single Needle Lock Stitch Machine

Overlock Sewing Machine Overlock machines are available in 3 threads, 4 threads and 5 threads over edge sewing. An overlock machine can form various types of stitches, like stitch class 503, stitch class 504 and stitch class 512. It is used for serging garment panels (for example, trouser panels serging) and for overedge stitch.

These types of machines are mostly used in knitted garment sewing for overedge stitch. For example, side seam stitch of a t-shirt is done using an overlock machine.

Overlock Sewing Machine

Flatlock Sewing Machine It is also known as cover stitch sewing machine. They normally come with 2-3 needles. For bottom cover stitch machine, 2 needle threads pass through the material and interloop with 1 looper thread with the stitch set on the underside of the seam. They form stitches like stitch class 406. They are available in two types i.e. Flat Bed and Cylinder Bed. They are used for hemming sleeve and bottom of the knits products. A cover stitch machine can be used in any part of the garment for decorative purpose.

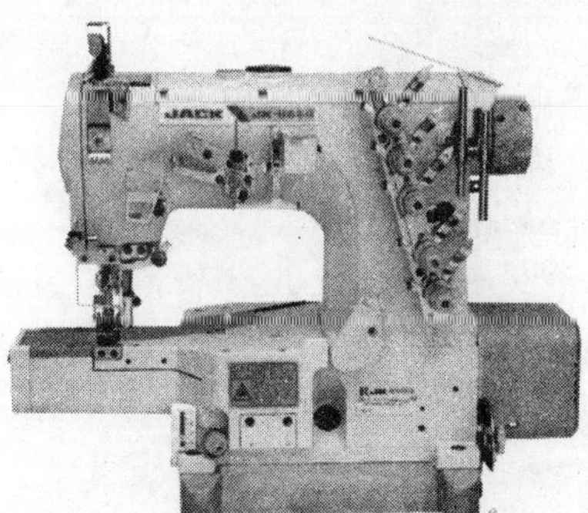

Flatlock Sewing Machine

Feed Off the Arm Machine It is used in making flat and felt seam. Two needle threads form the chain stitch. For example, the machine is used for sewing shirt side seams and under arms and for sewing jeans seam.

Feed Off the Arm Machine

Button Attaching Machine A special machine used only for stitching button in a garment. Different sizes of buttons can be attached in same machine by changing the settings.

Button Attaching Machine

Button Hole Machine It is used for making the button holes on garments. Button holes can be made with different stitch density, like in shirts, trousers, polo shirts, etc.

Button Hole Machine

Bartack Machine Bartack stitch is made to reinforce the seam and garment component, like in belt loop joining and at the bottom of side pocket, opening bartacking is done.

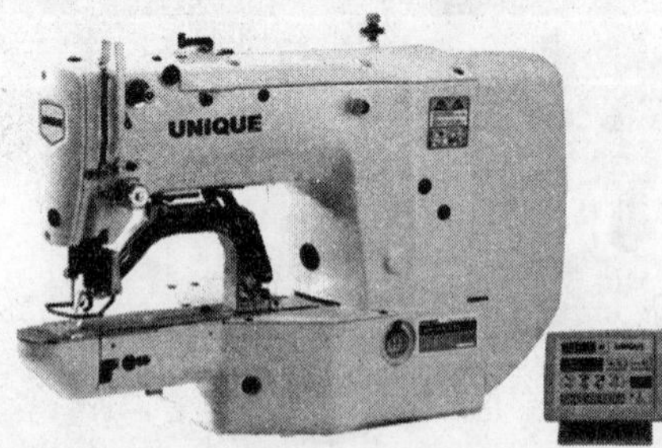

Bartack Machine

Zig-Zag Sewing Machine It is used for zig-zag stitching. It is used in bra manufacturing and jacket manu- facturing.

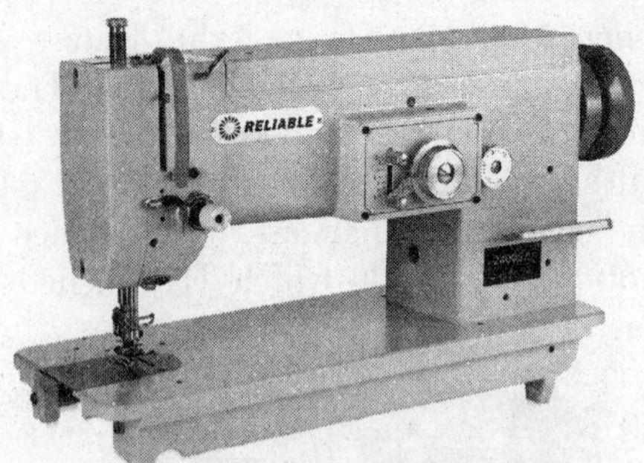

Zig-Zag Sewing Machine

Double Needle Lock Stitch Machine It is used to sew two stitch lines at a time on the garment part. This reduces stitching time where double stitch line is needed to sew.

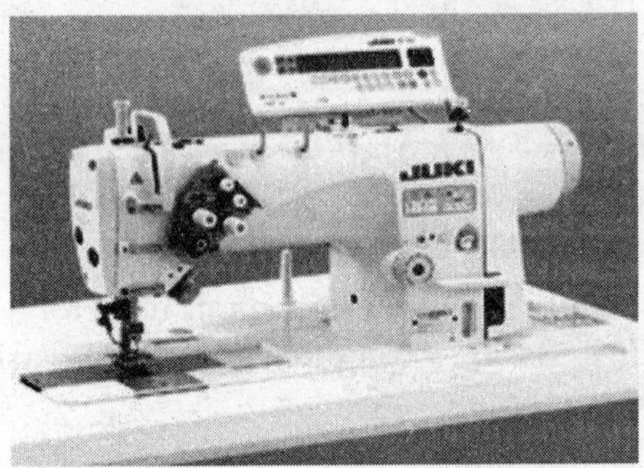

Double Needle Lock Stitch Machine

Parts of Sewing Machine and their Functions

The basic structure of sewing machine is the same, whether it is hand operated sewing machine, treadle sewing machine or electric sewing machine.

The basic parts of sewing machines are :

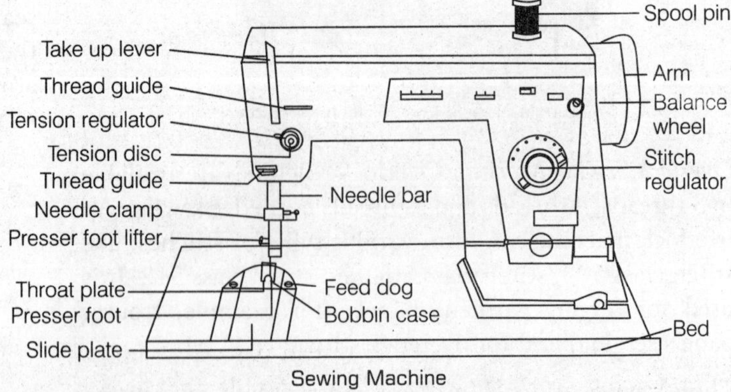

Sewing Machine

Some parts of sewing machine are discussed below :

Arm The horizontal upper part of the head, which has the mechanism for handling upper thread and driving the needle.

Bed Bed of machine is the base of the machine on which all attachments are fixed.

Balance Wheel It controls the operation of the machine. It is located on the right side of the machine. It is driven by hand or belt in the industrial machine. It controls the movement of the needle bar and drives the machine.

Bobbin Case It moves into position to catch the top thread and form the stitch as the needle is lowered into the bobbin chamber.

Clutch/Thumb Screw It is in the centre of the fly wheel and it engages and disengages the stitching mechanism.

Feed Dog It consists of a set of teeth fitted below the throat plate. It helps to move the cloth forward while sewing.

Throat Plate A cover which when removed gives access to the oiling points on the needle bar, presser bar and take up lever.

Needle Bar It is a steel rod to hold the needle at one end with the help of a clamp. Its main function is to give motion to the needle.

Needle Clamp A semi-circular disc with a hole to allow the needle to pass.

Presser Foot It is fixed to the presser bar to hold the cloth firmly in position when lowered.

Presser Foot Lifter A level attached to the presser bar for raising and lowering the presser foot.

Spool Pin It is fitted on the top of the arm to hold the reel.

Stitch Regulator It controls the length of the stitch. Some regulators can stitch in reverse.

Slide Plate A rectangular plate, which facilitates the removal of the bobbin case without lifting the machine.

Spool Pin for Bobbin Winding Spool of thread is placed on this at the time of bobbin winding.

Thread Guide It is a small hole made of spring wire through which thread runs directly to needle.

Tension Disc The two concave discs put together with the convex sides facing each other, compose the tension disc. The thread passes between the two. The tension of the thread is adjusted by a spring and nut which increases or decreases the pressure.

Take Up Lever It is a lever fitted to the body of the arm with a small hole through which the thread passes. Its up and down motion feeds the thread to the needle and tightens the loop formed by the shuttle and loosening the top thread to complete the stitch.

Pattern Making

Pattern making is an art of shaping a flat piece of fabric is drafted on a human figure/statue. It acts as a bridge between designing and production. It involves draping, drafting, flat pattern making techniques, pattern alteration, darts, etc. Their detailed description is given below :

Draping

Draping is the technique which means the way of fabric is draped in three dimensions. The method of draping includes stiching the garment by the use of loosely hanging material to create flowing effect. Even, it can create for a very impressive effect when finished appropriately. Draping needs ability and practice to do exact fitting, fall and fullness. Most of the designers choose to try out with the mode of fabric hangings, but also there are purposeable ways to determine drape. Draping technique is generally used in making garments, but can also be used to develop skirts and blouses.

Mechanism of Draping

Designers have to consider lot of aspects when they are draping the fabrics. The material and GSM of a fabric can significantly modify the way it drapes on a garment. The materials like chiffon, satin and silk are usually considered in the draped clothing. Some other materials can also be used as well. More inflexible fabrics are unsuitable for this draping effect.

However, most of the designers would have a preference to experiment with fabrics to check how they hang. There are some specific ways to check the fabric's draping mode. This can be either by identifying the thickness and stiffness of a fabric sample or the method of using a tool called a drape meter.

Drape meter is used to determine a drape co-efficient. It contains numbers from 0 to 100 in written format. For example, satin and muslin clothes have good draping property than twill hosieries.

Drafting

The following points should be kept in mind while drafting :

- Drafting should be done on a flat surface.
- Well sharped pencil is required.
- If wrong marking is done, it should be erased neatly.

- While making a draft, tailor's square provides accurate measurements at right angle. Marking of lines at right angle becomes easier. It should have smooth surface curves that can be drawn when it is the beginning, but later on these can be drawn by free hand.
- Drafting should be done on the wrong side of the material with the help of a tailor's chalk. Shrinkage has to do done before hand, otherwise extra allowances have to be given.
- Use smooth paper or fabric for drafting.
- Calculate the size of the paper accurately, according to requirements of the drafting/garment.
- Distinguish back and front with different types of lines.
- Draw lines neatly and make smooth curves.
- Always keep the fold of paper on left hand side if drafting is to be done on folded pack.
- If draft has been properly made by taking correct body measurements then no alterations in fitting are required.
- Draft of any size can be prepared, when one has got measurement of a person.
- Any type of design can be made, when basic draft is available.
- Wrong cutting of material can be avoided when a draft is available.
- Adaptation can be made when basic draft of any size has been prepared before hand.
- Draft has no allowance, but only ease. Hence, seam allowances are marked on the fabric and no chances of omitting them.
- The wastage of fabric can be avoided as all pieces of draft can be placed at odd places to save material.
- A draft can be used many a times that saves a time of calculation, every time.
- With the help of drafting, exact amount of material can be purchased.
- The requirement of cloth can be easily calculated when a draft has been made.

Flat Pattern Making Techniques

The flat pattern is a basic of industrial pattern drafting, commencing with the basic skirt and bodice and the various techniques, details, variations and the cutting techniques used for muslins and fabrics. Flat pattern work starts with a commercial basic pattern.

The pattern work consists of changing the basic pattern to create new designs. Flat pattern work is done on paper with a flat surface. It is often necessary to make the pattern up in fabric to get the full effect of the design that has been created. For dress designing, there are five basic pieces i.e. front blouse, back blouse, front skirt and back skirt and sleeve.

Procedure for securing a master pattern is as follows :

- A simple dress pattern, nearest to one's size is selected for the master pattern. It includes the five basic pieces, the front blouse, back blouse, front skirt, back skirt and the sleeves. The vertical dart at waistline makes good fitting and easy sewing. Dart may be from shoulder or underarm in the front blouse.
- The pattern is copied on plain paper and can be re-drawn, if needed fitting is done by altering the pattern by overlapping, spreading or slashing.
- Garment is cut out with 1 inch seam allowance in armhole and neckline. Ail the darts and silhouette seams are stitched to create the skirt, sleeves and blouse.
- The size of the darts and seam allowances can be changed to get the fit of the garment. For altering the length and width of basic pattern, thickness should also be considered.
- Fit of the garment is achieved by altering and correcting the pattern by repinning the circumferences. Concentration should be made on sleeves and armholes. The wristline, waist line and neckline should be made curved enough to fit naturally and comfortably.
- The basic 'dress maker' dart is extended, which tighten the garment slightly in width giving semi-casual effect.
- A ruler is used for drawing the skirt seam, underarm seam and darts. Notches are given in the armholes, sleeves and darts cut out and finally, the tracing of this foundation pattern is done.
- This muslin garment is same for depicting other seam locations or dart locations.
- The traced lines should be refined after each use of foundation pattern.
- For changing the details, the copies of frequently used patterns should be saved as basic blocks.

Pattern Alteration

Patterns are prepared according to standard measurement chart which are based on average sizes. After measuring the human body and adding needed ease, compare this measurement to pattern's measurement. Pattern adjustment or alteration is often necessary to achieve good fit in a garment. Once the fabric is cut, however, fitting adjustments are limited to existing darts and seam allowances. Before cutting the garment, check the pattern fit and alterations according to the correct body measurement that will eliminate many problems from fabric.

Therefore, fitting problems should be solved before the garment is cut by making needed changes in the pattern.

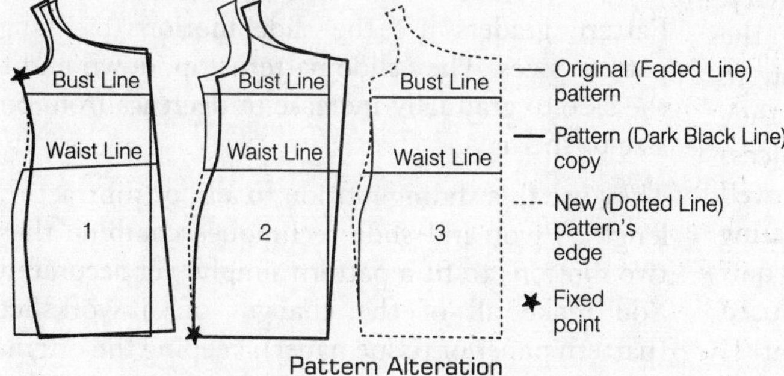

Pattern Alteration

A pattern can be altered and adjusted in three ways :

- By folding out excess fullness to make an area, smaller.
- By slashing and spreading to increase dimensions or slashing and overlapping to decrease dimensions.
- By re-drawing darts or seam lines.

Principles of Pattern Alteration

Some of the principles of pattern alteration are :

- A far as possible, make changes within the pattern by slashing and spreading or slashing and lapping. Patterns can also be altered by re-drawing the edges of the pattern. This is the method adopted for altering garments at the time of fitting. But, the first method is far the best in altering paper patterns.
- To preserve the original grain line, make all slashes and folds parallel or perpendicular to the grain line (to center front line, center back line, etc).
- Where there are darts, make changes between the tip of the dart and the outside edge.
- If an alteration in length is made along one edge of the pattern, take care to make an identical alteration in the adjoining edge. For example, if back shoulder seam is shortened, the front shoulder seam should also be shortened.

Darts

Darts help in shaping the fabric to fit the body and thus, provide comfort to the weaver. They provide fullness to natural body curves.

They are very rarely used for decorative purposes like providing a design line. The fitting, marking, stitching and pressing of darts should be done accurately.

To create new designs for garments, it is specially used for ladies garments. It saves fabric wastage and also use to remove excess fabric.

Darts are needed to turn two dimensional shapes into three dimensional shapes and to fit clothes closely to the body.

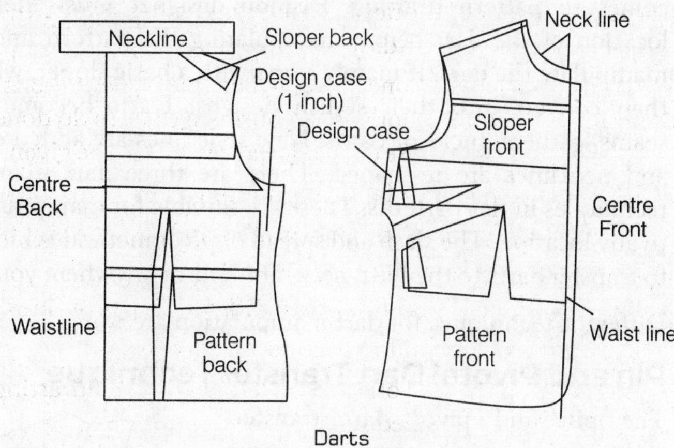

Darts

Different Dart Locations

Darts can be located in a number of different places on a bodice to alter its style.

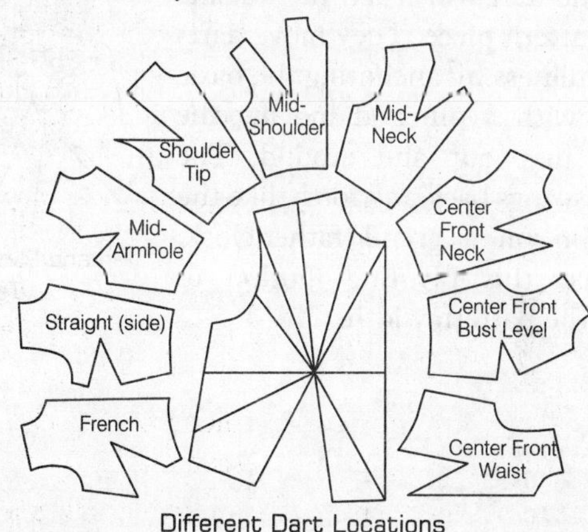

Different Dart Locations

This method is a transfer method and with experience, it is preferred. Few of them are explained below :

Mid Shoulder Dart It generally begins at a point slightly closer to the neck than half-way on the shoulder seam and slants slightly toward the centre front, ending on the point of the bust.

Side Straight Dart/Under the Arm It is placed two inches below the arms and point towards the bust.

Side Angled Dart (French Dart) It starts from the waistline to bust in an angled cut. This is a long curved dart. It is difficult to sew as you cannot fold and sew the dart.

Armhole Dart Slash a line to the high bust point from any point along the armhole. Fold all other darts into it.

Centre Front Neck Dart Slash a line to the high bust point and fold all other darts into it.

Dart Manipulation Techniques

Dart manipulation is one of the most important techniques, when it comes to pattern drafting. Fashion designer must identify the location of the dart before manipulating the pattern and how to manipulate the dart. It mainly starts with a basic sloper, which they then convert into their stylish designs. Darts become princess seams, gathers, tucks or cowls. New style lines are added or moved and necklines are re-shaped. There are three dart manipulating techniques in flat patterns. These are suitable for manipulating dart to any location. The slash and spread or pivot method is mostly used to transfer darts to the bust, neck, armhole or anywhere you want.

Different techniques for dart manipulation are :

Pin and Pivotal Dart Transfer Technique

The pin and pivot dart transfer technique requires tracing a new pattern from the original. The tracing starts from the one dart leg and continues from there to the new point where the dart will reach the outside of the pattern piece. They move darts or add fullness by anchoring the basic pattern with a pin and moving the pattern in , out and around. The pattern swings back and forth, like the pendulum on a grand father clock. They use this pivoting motion to change the pattern width.

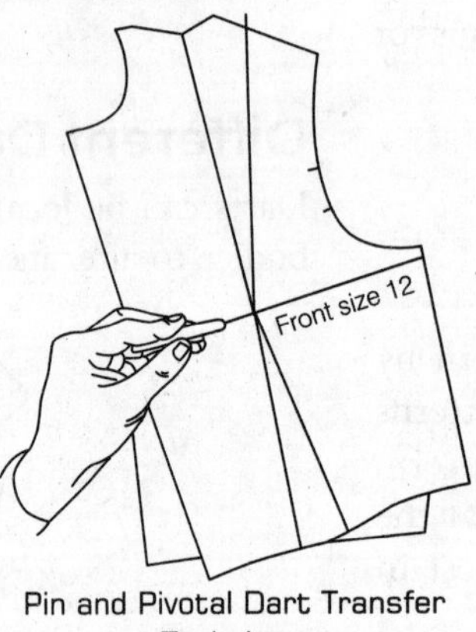

Pin and Pivotal Dart Transfer Technique

Slash Spread Dart Rotation and Overlap Technique

Pattern graders use the slide motion to change pattern sizes. They slide patterns up, down and to the side to gradually increase or decrease from one size to the next.

They use this sliding motion to add or subtract the length. Pivot and slide techniques combine these two motions to fit a pattern simply, yet accurately. You make all of the changes on a worksheet (pattern paper or tissue paper), keeping the original pattern intact i.e. no more cutting and taping.

By changing the pattern equally on both sides of the grain, the seam and the design lines are kept in proportion to the original pattern. Best of all, each change is easy to made.

Dart Equivalents Technique

Pleats or gathers in the fabric can be used for the same purpose as a normal stitched dart. These are called dart equivalents. Darts can also be worked into style lines.

The excess dart can be used to create a wide variety of other designs such as tucks, gathers, pleats and even cowls. Essentially, the dart or its equivalent is always present somewhere in the pattern. The dart or its equivalent will always radiate from the pivot point.

EXAM BASED QUESTIONS

1 Which among the following is the important step in garment construction?
(a) Choice of clothes
(b) Different varieties of fabrics
(c) Body measurements
(d) Fashion technology

2 What is/are the reason(s) which lead(s) to the perfect fit of a garment?
(a) Accuracy of body measurement
(b) Colour and type of fabric
(c) Equipment used for the construction of apparel
(d) All of the above

3 What is the most important tool for measurement?
(a) Tape (b) Scale
(c) Cod (d) Pencil

4 Why the measurement of neck is necessary?
(a) To measure shoulder's height
(b) To keep close fitting collar
(c) To look at the length of the cloth
(d) To use the fabric completely

5 What is the appropriate length of shoulder width?
(a) 9" below back neck (b) 7" below back neck
(c) 5" below front neck (d) 4" below back neck

6 Which among the following is not necessary for sleeve's measurements?
(a) Waist (b) Wrist
(c) Elbow (d) Arm

7 How can we measure the crotch length?
(a) From waistline, front to back
(b) Measure from waist to bottom
(c) Measure the front part of the waist
(d) Measure the back part of the waist

8 In how many types one can measure the body shape?
(a) Five (b) Nine (c) Seven (d) Eleven

9 Which is best defined as hour glass shape?
(a) Irregular body shape
(b) Balanced body shape
(c) Unpropotional hips and bust
(d) Undefined waist

10 What is/are the identifying feature(s) of triangle shape body?
(a) Larger bust and slim legs
(b) Boyish kind of body
(c) Slim upper body and wide hips
(d) Bust is smaller than hips

11 What does the term 'anthropometric' refers to?
(a) Comprehensive measurement of human soul
(b) Comparative measurement of human body
(c) Internal analysis of human body parts
(d) Comparison with different human bodies

12 What is/are the equipment(s) used for head circumference measurement?
(a) Non-flexible and non- stretchable pipe
(b) Measuring scale
(c) Flexible and non-stretchable measuring tape
(d) Beam scale with non-detachable weight

13 Which equipment is most commonly used for the construction of garments?
(a) Measuring equipment (b) Fixing equipment
(c) Sewing machine (d) Ruler scale

14 Which among the following is not a accurate tool for measurement?
(a) Iron (b) L-scale ruler
(c) Hem gauge (d) Meter scale

15 What is the usual measurement of the measuring tape?
(a) 1/2 inch to 1/7 inch (b) 1 inch to 1.5 inch
(c) 1/2 inch to 1/4 inch (d) None of these

16 What is the basic use of meter scale?
(a) Checking waist
(b) Looking at the length of the fabric
(c) Checking grain lines
(d) Measuring the height and shoulder of the person

17 Which scale makes the right angle?
(a) Meter scale (b) Measuring scale
(c) Normal ruler (d) L-scale

18 What is the basic use of marking tools?
(a) To make patterns on the paper
(b) To transfer the paper pattern on the farbic
(c) To make hemline chalk
(d) To mark the straight edge notch

19 Which among the following is the marking tool?
(a) Tracing wheel (b) Hem gauge
(c) Hem marker (d) L-scale

20 Which farbic is most suitable for tailor's chalk?
(a) Woolen fabric (b) Silk fabric
(c) Cotton fabric (d) Linen fabric

21 What is the average length of scissor?
(a) 10" long (b) 5" to 7" long
(c) 5" to 6" long (d) None of these

22 Which scissor cuts the leather with an ease?
(a) Electric scissor
(b) Buttonhole scissor
(c) Pinking shear
(d) Rotary cutter

23 What is use of embroidery frame?
(a) To make the round shape design
(b) To keep the fabric stretched
(c) To make colourful design
(d) To keep the fabric light weighted

24 Embroidery frame is made up of what?
(a) Wood (b) Plastic
(c) Both (a) and (b) (d) Neither (a) nor (b)

25 Which type of needles are suitable for permanent stiching?
(a) Oval shaped (b) Sharp and short
(c) Sharp and long (d) Thin and oval

26 Which among the following is not a general tool?
(a) L-scale (b) Pin cushion
(c) Pin (d) Orange stick

27 What is the need of full length mirror?
(a) To see the complete body shape
(b) To check the fit and design of the garment
(c) To make the paded form of body
(d) To make the cutting and construction of the garment for proper use

28 Which among the following is the type of sewing machine?
(a) Urban operated sewing machine
(b) Electronic sewing machine
(c) Peddle operated sewing machine
(d) Tailor operated sewing machine

29 Which type of sewing machine is suitable for domestic purpose?
(a) Hand operated (b) Treadle operated
(c) Electronic (d) All of these

30 Which type of sewing machine is operated by foot?
(a) Hand machine
(b) Treadle operated sewing machine
(c) Electronic machine
(d) None of the above

31 How the electronic machine works?
(a) Through the paddling of foot
(b) Balancing wheel through motion of the belt
(c) Both (a) and (b)
(d) Neither (a) nor (b)

32 Which is best defined as the bobbin winder?
(a) A simple mechanism to control the length of the stitch.
(b) A semi-circular disc with a hole to allow the needle to pass.
(c) The mechanism used for winding thread.
(d) This moves into position to catch the top thread.

33 What is the importance of perfect fit of the garment?
(a) Garment will look more colourful
(b) Garment will be more comfortable
(c) Garment's length will be perfect
(d) Garment will be of different fabric

34 Which is the most suitable technique which means the way of fabric hanging?
(a) Drafting (b) Alteration
(c) Flat pattern making (d) Draping

35 What do you mean by draping?
(a) Technique of fabric transformation
(b) Technique of fabric hanging
(c) Technique of painting the thread
(d) Technique of wearing the clothes

36 What is used to measure the drap co-efficiency?
(a) Threading machine (b) Dart
(c) Colour testing technique (d) Drape meter

37 What is the basic tool that is required for drafting?
(a) Pencil (b) Pen
(c) Scale (d) Tape

38 What do you mean by flat pattern?
(a) It is done on embroidery scale.
(b) It pattern is for domestic purpose.
(c) It pattern is basic "dress maker" technique.
(d) It pattern is done on paper with a flat surface.

39 How patterns are prepared?
(a) Through standard measurement chart
(b) Through paper and chart
(c) Re-drawn on fabric
(d) Through human body measurement

40 How many different locations of dart we have?
(a) 10 (b) 7
(c) 9 (d) 5

41 What is the basic purpose of dart?
(a) To make the body fitted cloth
(b) To make two dimensional shape into three dimensional shape
(c) To make garments suitable for women clothing
(d) None of the above

42 Match the following.

List I	List II
A. Measure around the fullest part of the thigh.	1. Thigh
B. Measure from the waist to the knee	2. Knee
C. Measure around the clalf muscle	3. Calf
D. Measure around the ankle	4. Ankle

Codes

	A	B	C	D		A	B	C	D
(a)	1	2	3	4	(b)	4	3	2	1
(c)	2	3	4	1	(d)	3	4	2	1

43 Match the following.

List I	List II
A. General tool	1. Stiletto
B. Sewing tool	2. Seam ripper
C. Measuring tool	3. Tracing wheel
D. Marking tool	4. Hem gauge

Codes

	A	B	C	D		A	B	C	D
(a)	1	2	3	4	(b)	4	1	2	3
(c)	2	1	4	3	(d)	4	3	2	1

44 Match the following.

List I	List II
A. At convenient height for cutting and construction of garments	1. Awl
B. To check the fit and design of the garment	2. Cutting board
C. This is a padded form of body made of wood	3. Mirror
D. It is a small pointed tool	4. Dress form

Codes

	A	B	C	D		A	B	C	D
(a)	1	2	3	4	(b)	4	3	2	1
(c)	2	3	1	4	(d)	2	3	4	1

45 Match the following.

List I	List II
A. Measuring tape	1. 24 inch
B. Ruler	2. 36 inch
C. Meter scale	3. 1/8" or 1/16"
D. L-scale	4. 1/2 inch to 1/4 inch

Codes

	A	B	C	D		A	B	C	D
(a)	1	2	3	4	(b)	2	3	4	1
(c)	4	3	2	1	(d)	2	4	1	3

46 Match tho following.

List I	List II
A. Round shape with assorted size	1. Thimbles
B. Device made of thin wire	2. Needle case
C. Necessary for accurate and efficient hand sewing	3. Bodkin
D. Flat needle with blunt end	4. Needle threader

Codes

	A	B	C	D		A	B	C	D
(a)	1	2	3	4	(b)	2	4	1	3
(c)	4	3	2	1	(d)	3	2	1	4

47 Match the following.

List I	List II
A. Bed	1. Gives motion to the needle
B. Arm	2. Fitted on top of the arm to hold the real
C. Spoil pin	3. Horizontal upper part of the head
D. Needle bar	4. Base of the machine

Codes

	A	B	C	D		A	B	C	D
(a)	1	2	3	4	(b)	1	3	2	4
(c)	4	1	2	3	(d)	4	3	2	1

48 Match the following.

List I	List II
A. This machine makes flat and felt seam	1. Button hole machine
B. Used for stiching button in a garment	2. Zig-zag sewing machine
C. Make button holes on garments	3. Feed off the arm
D. Used for zig-zag stiching	4. Button attaching machine

Codes

	A	B	C	D		A	B	C	D
(a)	1	2	3	4	(b)	4	3	2	1
(c)	3	4	1	2	(d)	3	4	2	1

49 What is the importance of well fitted garment?
1. Enhances the look of the person
2. Add value to the personality
3. Helps in the brand promotion
4. Gives life to new style

Codes
(a) 1 and 2 (b) 2 and 4
(c) 1, 2 and 4 (d) All of these

50 What are the factors on which the measurement of the garment depends?
1. Style of the garment 2. Type of the garment
3. Age of the user 4. Sex of the user

Codes
(a) 1 and 3 (b) 2 and 3
(c) 4 and 1 (d) All of these

51 Which among the following are the procedures for taking measurements?
1. Body measurement 2. Sleeves measurement
3. Shirt measurement 4. Pant measurement

Codes
(a) 1 and 4 (b) 2 and 3
(c) 1, 2 and 4 (d) All of these

52 Which among the following are the anthropometric procedures for measurement?
1. Length measurement
2. Head circumference measurement
3. Weight measurement
4. Waist measurement

Codes
(a) 1 and 2 (b) 2 and 4
(c) 1, 2 and 3 (d) All of these

53 What is the general categorisation of equipments for manufacturing garments?
1. Measuring tools 2. Marking tools
3. Cutting tools 4. Pressing tools

Codes
(a) 1 and 2 (b) 4 and 3
(c) 1, 2 and 3 (d) All of these

54 Which among the following is said to be the function of sewing machine?
1. Darting 2. Hemming
3. Binding 4. Piping

Codes
(a) 1 and 2 (b) 2 and 3
(c) 3 and 4 (d) All of these

55 Which among the following are the parts of sewing machine?
1. Bed 2. Hem gauge
3. Arm 4. L-scale

Codes
(a) 1 and 2 (b) 1 and 3 (c) 2 and 4 (d) 4 and 2

56 Which among the following influence the good fit?
1. Current fashion look
2. Hang and stretch of the fabric
3. Amount of ease preferred
4. Figure size and type

Codes
(a) 1 and 3 (b) 2 and 3
(c) All of these (d) None of these

Directions (Q. Nos. 57-64) *Below given are two statements, one labelled as Assertion (A) and other labelled as Reason (R). Following are the codes given below, select the correct code for the following.*

Codes
(a) Both A and R are true and R is the correct explanation of A
(b) Both A and R are true, but R is not the correct explanation of A
(c) A is true, but R is false
(d) A is false, but R is true

57 **Assertion** (A) The crucial step in garment construction is taking body measurement.
Reason (R) This enhances the body look and personality of a person.

58 **Assertion** (A) There are seven different types of body shapes.
Reason (R) Every person's body shape is different.

59 **Assertion** (A) Sewing machine have various models.
Reason (R) Sewing machine is not a machine for garment construction.

60 **Assertion** (A) If something is done wrong, it should be cutted while drafting.
Reason (R) Drafting should be done on flat surface.

61 **Assertion** (A) The crucial and essential step in garment construction is taking body measurement.
Reason (R) Garments enhances the look of the person.

62 **Assertion** (A) Anthropometric refers to comparative measurements of the human body.
Reason (R) This commonly used as indices of growth and development for infants.

63 **Assertion** (A) Marking tool generally used for transferring the paper pattern onto the fabric.
Reason (R) Hem is used for mark out a completely level hemline with chalk.

64 **Assertion** (A) Patters are prepared according to standard measurement chart based on average size.
Reason (R) Pattern alteration is not often used.

Directions (Q. Nos. 65-69) *Read the passage given below and answer the questions that follows.*

Body measurements are a pre-requisite to pattern construction. The size and fit of a garment depends upon the accuracy. At present, we are in transition by tape measure and computerised body scanning or using photographic systems. Manual measuring requires a high degree of skill and is time consuming.

The techniques of body scanning are constantly improving and will supersede manual methods in the future. Whichever method is used, the first consideration is to decide which measurements are required. From the data collected, the development of size charts for pattern grading and garment production begins.

Size chart formulation begins with the division of average body measurements artificially into categories to form a range of sizes. There are five stages in developing size charts for garments.

65 **...... are a pre-requisite the pattern construction.**
(a) Accuracy
(b) Body measurements
(c) Skills
(d) None of the above

66 **...... begins with the division of average body measurements artificially into categories to form a range of sizes.**
(a) Manual measuring
(b) Body scanning
(c) Size chart formulation
(d) None of the above

67 **How many stages are there in developing size charts for garments?**
(a) Four (b) Five
(c) Six (d) Three

67 **What is use of the data collected from measurement?**
(a) Used in development of size charts
(b) Use for beginning garment production
(c) Both (a) and (b)
(d) None of the above

67 **Which of the following technique is used taking measurement?**
(a) Tape measure
(b) Body scanning
(c) Measuring with photographic systems
(d) All of the above

PREVIOUS YEARS' QUESTIONS

July 2018

1 **For 'basting' operations in tailored men's wear and women's wear garments, which of the following stitch class is generally used in the garment industry?**
(a) Class 100 (b) Class 200
(c) Class 400 (d) Class 500

2 **Assertion** (A) Embroidery, sequins and applique form the structural design in a garment.
Reason (R) Structural design is the surface enrichment of the garment.
Codes
(a) Both A and R are true (b) Both A and R are false
(c) A is true, but R is false (d) A is false, but R is true

November 2017

3 **Assertion** (A) Applied design is the surface enrichment of the garment.
Reason (R) Applications of tucks and pleats are examples of applied design.
Codes
(a) Both A and R are true (b) Both A and R are false
(c) A is false, but R is true (d) A is true, but R is false

4 **Give the correct sequence of preparing a puff sleeve with band and its attachment to the garment.**
1. Gathering of cap line.
2. Stitching underarm seam of sleeve.
3. Finishing of band.
4. Flattering of band.
5. Gathering of lower underarm of sleeve.
6. Attaching the band.
7. Attaching sleeve in the armhole.

Codes
(a) 5, 6, 4, 2, 3, 1, 7 (b) 5, 1, 7, 6, 2, 3, 4
(c) 6, 2, 3, 4, 5, 1, 7 (d) 1, 2, 3, 4, 6, 7, 5

5 **Which of the following is not a sewing machine feed mechanism?**
(a) Drop feed (b) Differential bottom feed
(c) Unison feed (d) Spool feed

6 **Assertion** (A) Sewing machine needles with set points are used for knitted farbics.
Reason (R) Set points have less tendency to penetrate the lower twist knitting yarns and break them.
Codes
(a) Both A and R are true
(b) Both A and R are false
(c) A is true, but R is false
(d) A is false, but R is true

January 2017

7 **Which of the following is the theory of clothing?**
(a) Individuality (b) Conformity
(c) Tattooing (d) Modesty

8 **Assertion** (A) Collars, seams and texture, when put together create a structural design.
Reason (R) Structural design is the inherent part of the garment.
Codes
(a) A is true, but R is false
(b) A is false, but R is true
(c) Both A and R are true and R is the correct explanation of A
(d) Both A and R are true, but R is not the correct explanation of A

9 **Give the correct path for the upper thread in the sewing machine.**
1. Tension disc 2. Needle
3. Spool 4. Thread guide
5. Thread take up lever

Codes
(a) 2, 3, 4, 5, 1
(b) 1, 3, 2, 5, 4
(c) 3, 4, 1, 5, 2
(d) 4, 2, 3, 1, 5

10 **Assertion** (A) Anthropometric is a system of identification based upon measurement of selected portions of human frame.
Reason (R) Anthropometric deals with measurement of dimensions and proportions of human body.
Codes
(a) Both A and R are true
(b) Both A and R are false
(c) A is false, but R is true
(d) A is true, but R is false

11 **Give the correct sequence of cut order planning in a garment industry.**
1. Determining volume, size ratios for marker making and spreading.
2. Examining incoming orders and piece goods availability.
3. Developing instructions for optimum fabric utilisation.
4. Determining whether there are available markers or new markers have to be made.
5. Releasing orders for marker making, spreading and cutting.

Codes
(a) 1, 2, 3, 4, 5
(b) 3, 2, 1, 5, 4
(c) 4, 3, 2, 1, 5
(d) 2, 1, 4, 3, 5

July 2016

12 Give the correct sequence of draping front bodice block on the dress form.

1. Pinning the muslin at apex and centre front on dress form.
2. Pinning the muslin on horizontal balance line.
3. Pin side seam and armhole.
4. Blocking and marking the muslin.
5. Pinning the muslin at vertical balance line.
6. Pin waist line dart.
7. Drape the neckline and the shoulder dart.

Codes

(a) 7, 6, 4, 5, 1, 2, 3 (b) 4, 1, 2, 5, 6, 3, 7
(c) 7, 2, 3, 4, 5, 1, 6 (d) 1, 2, 3, 4, 5, 6, 7

13 Higher percentage of amorphous regions exhibit which of the following properties in a fibre.

1. Lower chemical resistance.
2. Stiff handle.
3. More absorbent.
4. Low inter-polymer forces of attraction.
5. Strong internal bonds.

Codes

(a) 1, 2 and 3 (b) 2, 3 and 4
(c) 3, 4 and 5 (d) 1, 3 and 4

14 **Assertion** (A) Majority of threads intended for use in machine sewing are constructed with (S) twist.

Reason (R) Thread with (Z) twist becomes untwisted by the action of machines and then fray and breaks.

Codes

(a) Both A and R are false (b) Both A and R are true
(c) A is true, but R is false (d) A is false, but R is true

December 2015

15 **Assertion** (A) Structural design is an integral part of the garment.

Reason (R) It comprises of applique, embroidery print, etc.

Codes

(a) Both A and R are false
(b) Both A and R are true
(c) A is true, but R is false
(d) A is false, but R is true

16 Give the correct sequence of cutting a garment.

1. Lay out plan.
2. Taking measurements.
3. Preparing of drafts.
4. Tracing the stitching lines.
5. Cutting the garment pieces.

Codes

(a) 2, 3, 4, 5, 1 (b) 2, 3, 1, 5, 4
(c) 1, 2, 3, 4, 5 (d) 5, 4, 3, 2, 1

June 2015

17 Which of the following are not dart equivalents?

1. Control seam 2. Ruffles
3. Frills 4. Gathers

Codes

(a) 1 and 2 (b) 2 and 3
(c) 3 and 4 (d) 1 and 4

18 Arrange the steps in the recommended sequence for designing an equipment based on anthropometric considerations.

1. Determine the principle applicable for the design of equipment.
2. Determine the body dimensions important in the design.
3. Define the population likely to use the equipment.
4. Add allowances, if necessary for special cases.
5. Decide the percentage of population to be accommodated.
6. Extract relevant values of the body dimensions from the anthropometric tables, appropriate for the population.

Codes

(a) 1, 2, 3, 4, 5, 6 (b) 2, 3, 1, 5, 6, 4
(c) 2, 1, 3, 5, 6, 4 (d) 2, 3, 1, 6, 4, 5

ANSWERS

Exam Based Questions

1 (c)	2 (a)	3 (a)	4 (b)	5 (d)	6 (a)	7 (a)	8 (c)	9 (b)	10 (c)
11 (b)	12 (c)	13 (c)	14 (a)	15 (c)	16 (c)	17 (d)	18 (b)	19 (a)	20 (a)
21 (c)	22 (d)	23 (b)	24 (c)	25 (b)	26 (a)	27 (b)	28 (b)	29 (a)	30 (b)
31 (b)	32 (c)	33 (b)	34 (d)	35 (b)	36 (d)	37 (a)	38 (d)	39 (a)	40 (c)
41 (b)	42 (a)	43 (c)	44 (d)	45 (c)	46 (b)	47 (d)	48 (c)	49 (a)	50 (d)
51 (c)	52 (c)	53 (d)	54 (d)	55 (b)	56 (c)	57 (b)	58 (a)	59 (c)	60 (a)
61 (a)	62 (a)	63 (b)	64 (c)	65 (b)	66 (c)	67 (b)	68 (c)	69 (d)	

Previous Years' Questions

1 (a)	2 (b)	3 (d)	4 (a)	5 (a)	6 (b)	7 (d)	8 (c)	9 (c)	10 (d)
11 (d)	12 (b)	13 (d)	14 (a)	15 (c)	16 (b)	17 (b)	18 (b)		

Apparel Manufacturing and Caring

Readymade apparel or garment manufacturing involves many processing steps, beginning with the idea or design concept and ending with a finished product. Apparel manufacturing process involves product design, fabric selection and inspection, pattern-making, grading, marking, spreading, cutting, banding, sewing, pressing or folding, finishing and detailing, dyeing and washing, etc. Caring and maintenance of clothing is also essential so that apparels can be used in long term.

In this Chapter

- Apparel Manufacturing
  - Techniques of Apparel Manufacturing
  - Process of Fabric to Apparel Manufacturing
  - Seam
  - Terminologies used in Appared Manufacturing
- Apparel Quality Testing
  - Importance of Apparel Testing
  - Defects of Fabric and Garments
- Care and Maintenance of Garments

Apparel Manufacturing

Apparel manufacturing is very lengthy and complex process. There are thousands of technical terms used in garment industry. Whole garment production process is not easy to keep in memory. If garment technologists can learn some important garment industry terminology than it will be easy to operate his duty.

The apparel manufacturing industry transforms fabrics produced by textile manufacturers into clothing and accessories. The apparel industry traditionally consists of production workers who performed the cutting and sewing functions in an assembly line. The industry remains labour intensive, despite advances in technology and workplace practices.

Techniques of Apparels Manufacturing

The commonly used apparel manufacturing techniques are :

Flexible Manufacturing Strategy This manufacturing strategy means the capability of quickly and efficiently producing a variety of styles in small production runs with no defects. The main advantage of implementing this strategy are its flexibility to operate to achieve the consumer's demands and the capacity to adapt swifty to changes in the garment market.

Value Added Manufacturing Strategy It is a quick response plan that concentrates on the managing of avoidable operations that does not improve the product value but instead leads to delays in production. The underlying principle of this technique is that every operation or task performed on a garment style should add value. Operations like material handling, souting, inspection, ware housing, etc., involve additional time, handling and workers; however it does not add product value.

Agile Manufacturing Strategy An agile manufacturing system is a system that is capable of operating profitably in a competitive environment of continually and unpredictably changing customer opportunities. This technique is used by manufacturing plant managers to improve operations capabilities. Agile is the dynamic ability of the firm to strategically use change as a vehicle to growth, with new products and to develop new competencies.

Mass Customisation Here, the strategy is to produce products that can be made to order rather than made to plan. Considering the complexity of many apparel products and the number of processes that a style may require, the equipment, skills, information and processes must be highly integrated.

Body scanning technology will be the basis of custom fit. Mass customisation reduces the risk associated in trying to anticipate consumer's demand months ahead of the point of sale to the ultimate consumer.

List of Machinery and their Functions in Apparel Industry

Name of Machine	Functions of Machine	Using Department
Fabrics inspection machine	Use to do fabrics inspection to check fabric's defects.	Fabrics inspection
Plotter printing machine	Print garments marker.	CAD
Cutting machine	Cut fabrics as per marker.	Cutting
Fusing machine	Fuse interlining	Fusing-Sewing
Embroidery machine	To set embroidery in garments	Embroidery
Sewing machine	Sew garments	Sewing
Thread trimmer machine	Thread trimming of garments uncut thread	Finishing
Thread sucking machine	Reduce loose and unnecessary thread from garments.	Finishing
Iron machine	Pressing garments to get good appearances.	Finishing
Pull test machine	To determine the pulling strength of any type of button.	Finishing
Metal detector machine	To get a metal-free final product in carton.	Packing and Finishing
Barcode scanning machine	Scan sticker and ticketing of garments.	Finishing
Heat seal joining machine	Set up heat seal label in garments.	Finishing
Case label printing machine	Print case label of garments carton.	Merchandising-Packing
Moisture checking machine	Find out moisture percentage of finished garments.	Packing
Digital Hygrometer	Determine RH% for every section.	All sections, specially warehouse
Air compressor machine	Produce compressed air for machine and maintenance department.	Utility section
Boiler machine	Generate hot steam for Iron machine.	Utility section
Generator	Produce electricity.	Utility section
Water pump	Pick water for factory.	Utility section

Process of Fabric to Apparel Manufacturing

Apparel production, also known as garment production is a process where fabric is being converted into garments. The apperal production is basically used when garments are manufactured in a factory. A factory produces bulk quality of garments for a style or design at a time. Prior to start production of an order factory needs to go through some activities which is known as pre-production.

Pre-production process includes sampling, costing, production planning, sourcing of raw material and production pattern making. Fabric cutting, printing, sewing, embroidery, thread trimming, washing, ironing, folding and packing are the production functions. The general steps involved in the process of fabric to apparal manufacturing are as follows:

Sampling Sampling is a process where factory develop garment samples according to buyer's specified design. This is also known as 'product development stage'. Samples are required at various stages to get approval from buyer on a particular design.

Costing A business is all about making profit. So correct costing of a product before order finalisation is very important. Costing of garment is the cumulative cost of raw materials, direct labours and direct and indirect overheads.

Production Planning After receiving the order, factory plans for raw material requirement for the order. Raw materials like fabrics, sewing threads, packing materials, hang tags and other accessories.

Cutting In this stage, fabrics are layered on a table layer by layer up to a certain height. Then by means of a cutting machine fabric are cut into garment shapes or pattern and separated from the layer. Fabric layering is possible both manual spreading and automated spreading. Cut parts are then numbered and bundled and send to sewing room.

Sewing or Stitching Garment panels are stitched together in sewing room by means of sewing machines. In sewing 2D, fabric patterns are converted in 3D forms. An operator run the machine and using sewing threads garment parts are joined together. Various types of sewing machines are available for sewing.

Thread Trimming After stitching, all hanging thread are cut by means of hand trimmer. Auto thread trimming machines are also available to perform this task. All loose threads inside a garment are removed as well.

Washing This process is performed when buyer want washing or special finishes to the garments. For light colour garment washing is carried out to remove dirt and stains though buyer does needed washed garment for orders.

Finishing Generally, this process includes checking of garment, measurement checking, ironing and spotting. After sewing of the garments, all pieces are checked by quality checker to ensure that garments are being made as per buyer quality standard. Checking normally done by visual appearance and measurement.

Packing and Folding Each pressed garment is then folded with tissue on card board. Folding varies product to product and also buyer to buyer. Hang tags, special tag and price stickers are attached with plastic thread. Folded and tagged garments are then packed into polybags.

Final Inspection and Dispatch Once garments are packed, before dispatching quality inspection of the garments is carried by buyer quality assurance department. Many times, a third party quality auditor is hired for this final inspection job.

Terminologies Used in Apparel Manufacturing

Terminologies used in apparel manufacturing are :

- **A-line** A garment with sloping sides, the widest part being at the hemline.
- **Alter** To change patterns so that it corresponds to body measurements.
- **Allowance** Extra fabric outside the seamline or within the garment to accommodate gathers, ease, tucks and pleats.
- **Applique** Decorative pieces of fabric applied by hand or machine.
- **Armhole** The opening in a garment for the arm.
- **Armscye** It is commonly known as armhole.
- **Backstitch** A small hand stitch that looks like machine stitching on the right side, but with stitches overlapping on the wrong side.
- **Bands** Strips of fabric, ribbon or bias applied to edges or set into garments to finish or decorate.
- **Bar** A group of cross threads used to stay the ends of a buttonhole.
- **Basque** A woman's tight-fitting dress-waist made separate from the skirt and having the waistline finish attached to the waist portion.
- **Basting** A long, loose temporary stitch made by hand or machine.
- **Bell Sleeve** A straight sleeve flaring at the bottom.
- **Bias** Any direction in the fabric which does not follow exactly the selvedge or weft yarns A true bias makes and angle of 45 across the lengthwise and widthwise grain. It has maximum stretch.
- **Binding** A bias strip of material used to enclose a raw edge as a finish or trim.
- **Bishop's Sleeve** A long, full sleeve gathered onto a narrow cuff.
- **Blend** A mixture of different fibers in one yarn or different yams in one fabric, each lending its own characteristics of the fabric.
- **Blind Stitch** A form of hemming made by catching only one thread of the outer fabric.
- **Braid** A woven novelty trim, finished at both edges.
- **Brides** The threads of warp or weft connecting parts of the pattern in lace.
- **Buckram** A stiff fabric made by impregnating a light-weight open cloth with adhesives and fillers.
- **Cap** The top part of a sleeve which is curved to fit the armhole.
- **Cap Sleeve** Extension of the shoulder and upper armhole to cover the top of the arm.
- **Casing** A hem with an opening so that ribbon or elastic may be drawn through.
- **Centre Front** The position of the pattern or garment at the exact the centre of the front section of the garment.
- **Clip** A small cut in the seam allowance of a garment which allows a comer or curved area to turn and lie flat.
- **Closing** A placket or any garment opening.
- **Construction** Basic seams that give shape to flat cloth lines.
- **Coordinates** A number of garments which match and can be worn together in different combinations.

- **Cord Piping** A cord which is encased in bias fabric and used to finish and decorate edges, waistlines, buttonholes and furnishings.
- **Cord Seam** A seam with a corded effect which is produced by turning both seam edges to one side and then stitching through the three thicknesses of material.
- **Costume** Dress belonging to a given country, time and class.
- **Count of Yarn** A number indicating the mass per unit length or the length per unit mass of a yam.
- **Dart** A fold of fabric stitched to a point at one end. Used to fit body curves.
- **Design Lines** Lines or seams that add design and make the garment to look different.
- **Drape** Soft folds of fabric controlled by pleats or gathers.
- **Draped** A style in which the fabric is gathered or folded into unpressed pleats to create a soft effect and provide shaping.
- **Dressform** A duplicate of the human form which is useful for fitting or draping a garment.
- **Ease** Extra measurement allowed for comfort. It is the difference between actual body measurement and the size of the garment. To work in excess material that has been allowed for comfort.
- **Edge Stitch** A line of stitching placed along an edge, usually decorative finish.
- **Edging** Narrow lace having one finished edge and the other. Usually scalloped or indented. Used for trimmings.
- **End** An individual strand of yarn.
- **Extension** Additional fabric jutting out beyond a seam or a centre line.
- **Eyelet** A small hole in a garment finished by hand or a metal ring to hold the prong of a buckle. Also for lacing with ribbon and cord.
- **Facing** A shaped or bias piece of self-fabric applied to a garment edge as a finish.
- **Fastenings** Hooks and eyes, press buttons and zippers used to fasten garments.
- **Fittings** Adjusting the pattern or garment to fit the individual figure.
- **Flared** A style which is much wider around the lower edge.
- **Flounce** Flared bands of fabric, sometimes gathered and used to decorate edges of garments or used in tiers to make a skirt.
- **Fly front** A closing which conceals buttons or zippers of trousers.
- **Fray** The threads which come out during the handling of fabric.
- **Gathering** One or two rows of stitching, either by hands or a machine, that is drawn up to form even fullness.
- **Gingham** Plain weave fabric constructed with colored woven check pattern.
- **Godets** A shaped or pleated section of material inserted into garments.
- **Gore** A skirt section that is shaping up to the hip level and then flared out to the hemline.
- **Grain** The direction of threads in a woven fabric. The lengthwise grain runs parallel to the selvedge and the cross-wise grain from selvedge to selvedge.
- **Grey Goods** Woven fabrics as they leave the loom before being bleached dyed or finished.
- **Gusset** A shaped piece of fabric inserted usually at the underarm of the garment to provide comfort.
- **Hand Finishing** The details sewn by hand to finish the garment.
- **Hem** The finish formed by folding back the raw edge of a garment to the wrong side.
- **Hemline** The line designating the finished length of a garment.
- **Knife Pleats** Series of pleats that turn in the same direction. They are usually equal in width and are pressed straight down to the hem.
- **Layout** The arrangement of pattern pieces on the material so as to ensure economical cutting.
- **Lining** A fabric used inside garments. Its edges may be attached to the garment at the seams with slip stitch or it may hang loosely from the neck or from the waist in the case of skirts.
- **Loop** A fastening which extends beyond the finished edge, used for closings with no overlap. Can be made of thread, cord or fabric.
- **Machine Basting** A temporary machine stitching using the longest machine stitch.
- **Marking** Transferring all necessary pattern lines or markings to the wrong side of the fabric.
- **Nap** The word means 'pile'. Pile fabrics should always be cut in one direction only.
- **Notch** A small V-shaped mark or cut, on seam allowance of the pattern pieces.
- **Opening** Term used interchangeably with closing.
- **Pile** Weave of a fabric with upright surface yams such as velvet or velveteen.
- **Pintucks** Tucks as fine as the width of a pin.
- Pinking Jagged cut finish for a raw edge.
- **Placket** A closing or opening in a garment.

- **Pleats** Folds of fabric used to control fullness.
- **Princess Line** Seam lines running from shoulder or armhole to the hem with no waist seam.
- **Pucker** To draw up into folds and wrinkles.
- **Puff sleeves** Short sleeves having fullness gathered into the armhole and into a band or binding at the lower edge.
- **Raglan** A style in which the armhole seams run up to the neckline giving a loose and comfortable fit.
- **Ravel** Vans drew out along the edge of the fabric.
- **Ribbon** An attractive woven fabric with a lustrous appearance, used for trimming and adornment.
- **Ricrac** A flat, woven braid made in the zigzag form.
- **Rip** To open a seam by pulling out or cutting the stitching.
- **Rolled Hem** A kind of hem used on sheer fabrics. The edge is rolled tightly between the thumb and forefingers of the left hand and hemming is done to hold the roll in place.
- **Ruffle** A band of fabric that is gathered or pleated and applied to an edge as a trimming.
- **Sag** The stretch that occurs in the bias grain of a garment after hanging or as the effect of strain on any part of a garment.
- **Scallop** An edge finish made up of a series of semicircles.
- **Smock** A straight garment with a gathered or smocked yoke.
- **Stay** A reinforcement of fabric or tape, to hold a part of a garment securely in position.
- **Stay Binding** A narrow, woven fabric generally used for the covering of seams and the strengthening of garments.
- **Stay Stitching** A row of stitching worked just inside the seam allowance and close to the stitching line in order to prevent areas of the bias or curve from stretching.
- **Straight** of goods A term used to designate the length wise in a fabric.
- **Tack** To fasten two fabric surfaces together loosely by running stitches.
- **Tailor's Tack** A stitch used to transfer pattern markings to the fabric.
- **Taper** To decrease width gradually and bring to a point.
- **Thread Count** The number of threads in a square inch of fabric.
- **Top Stitching** A line of stitching along the seam line on the right side of a garment, to add strength or design.
- **Trim** To cut off ragged edges or a part of a seam allowance to prevent it from being bulky and to give the seam a neat edge.
- **Trimming** An ornamental addition used on garments.
- **Tubing** A hollow cylinder of fabric used for button loops and decorative trim.
- **Tucks** Straight folds of fullness, evenly stitched.
- **Underlap** A part of a garment that extends or laps under another part.
- **Underlay** An additional piece of fabric placed under a section for the purpose of joining, as in a pleat or slot seam.
- **Weave** The pattern of interlacing of warp and weft yams in a wove fabric.
- **Wrap** The upper part of an opening which overlaps the underlayer.
- **Yardage** The amount of fabric needed to make a particular garment.
- **Yoke** Separately made shoulder piece of bodice or the top of a skirt.

Seam

Seam is the combination of stitches which make line to join two ply of fabric. It is used as functional purpose. Some time used as decorative purposes. Seams are widely used in modern mass-produced apparel, footwear, house hold textiles and sporting goods which are sewn by different industrial sewing machines.

Seam may be of hundred types and these types are classified into eight main classes.

Different Types of Seams in Sewing

Arrangement of fabric ends of the seam line is called seam type. They are classified into following types :

Seam Class 1 : Super Imposed Seam

Seam is achieved by two or more separate pieces of fabric sewing together. It is most commonly used. In this, the fabric ends are in same direction. The most basic superimposed seam is SSa. It has over 50 variations. This class seam can be sewn a variety of machine. E.g. lock stitch or overlock. It is mostly used in inside seam of shirt and pant.

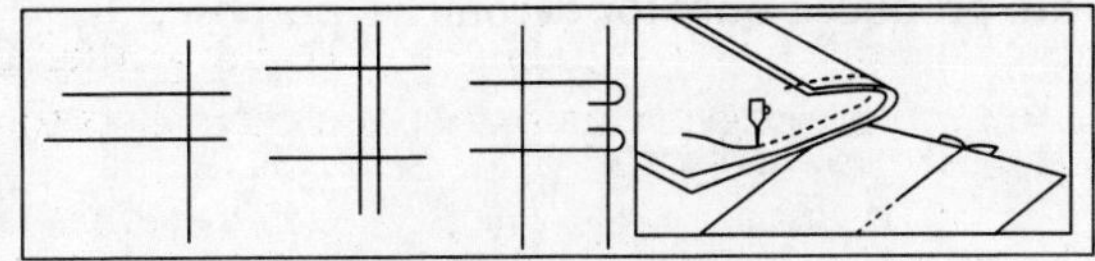

Super Imposed Seam

Seam Class 2 : Lapped Seam

This type of seam is achieved with two or more pieces of fabric overlapping each other. Two sewn ends of the fabric are in opposite direction. Mostly two needle chain stitch machine is used for this seam. Seam under this class is very strong.

It is used inside seam of jeans, dress, shirt, etc.

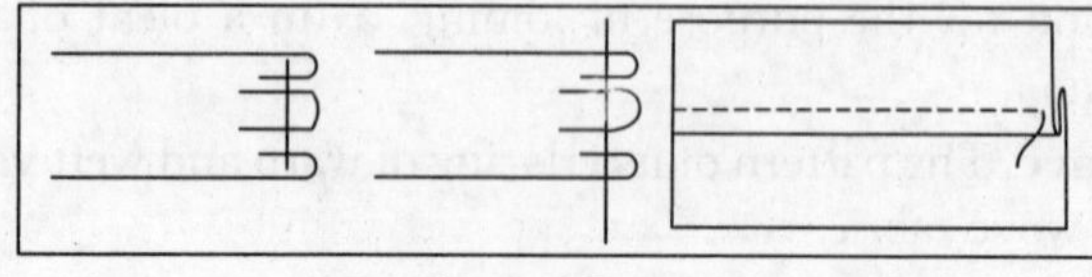

Lapped Seam

Seam Class 3 : Bound Seam

A bound seam is one piece of fabric encompassing the raw edge of another piece of fabric. The purpose of bound seam is to finish an edge of garment. It is sometimes used as decorative purpose's. There are 18 variations of bound seam.

It is used in neckline of a t-shirt, yoke joint in the shirt waist band, underwire etc.

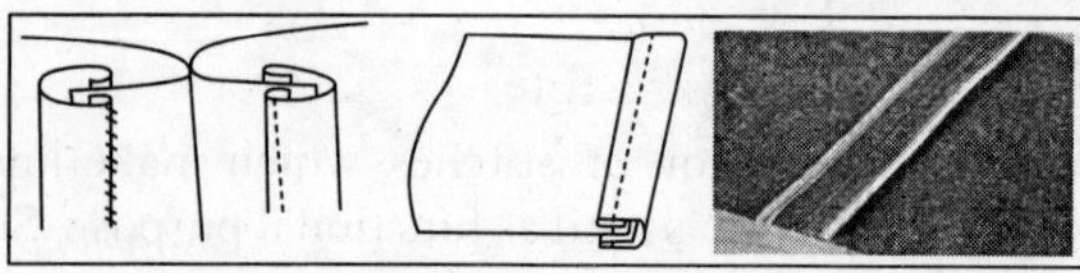

Bound Seam

Seam Class 4 : Flat Seam

Flat seam are constructed by having two pieces of fabric meet precisely of their edges. It's thickness is comparatively less. Zig-zag stitch may be produced in this seam. For this seam, edge should be cleaned before sewing to avoid trying.

It is intensively used in undergarments and in knit wear.

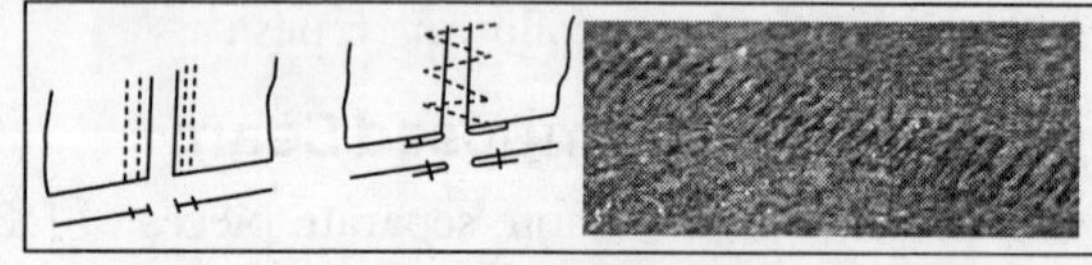

Flat Seam

Seam Class-5 : Decorative Seam

- This type of seam is made by making one or more adjacent stitch lines in one or more layer of fabric. Multi needle sewing machine is used for this seam. Seam under this class are produced only for decorative purpose.

It is used in pant or other dresses.

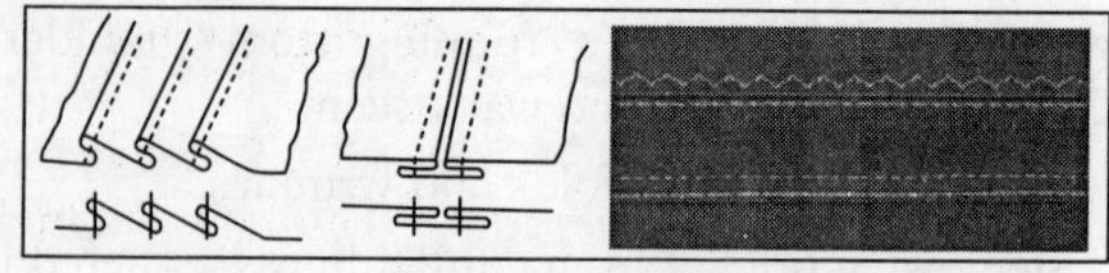

Decorative Seam

Seam Class-6 : Edge Neatening Seam

Seam under this class are produced in such a way so that the fabric ends from out area cannot come out during use. It can be used extensively. It can be made by over lock machine. It is mostly used in knitted garments and hemmings.

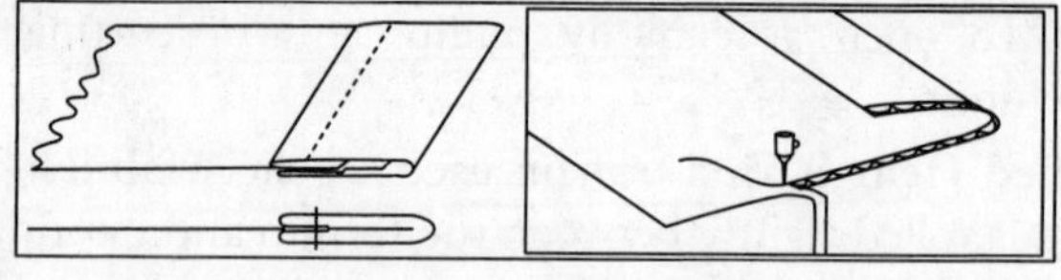

Edge Neatening Seam

Seam Class-7 : Attaching of Separate Items Seam

These are sometimes called applied seam because they are mainly used to a decorative material to an edge of seam such as lace-elastic. Similar to lapped (class-2) but the joined component is extended limited on both side from sewn line.

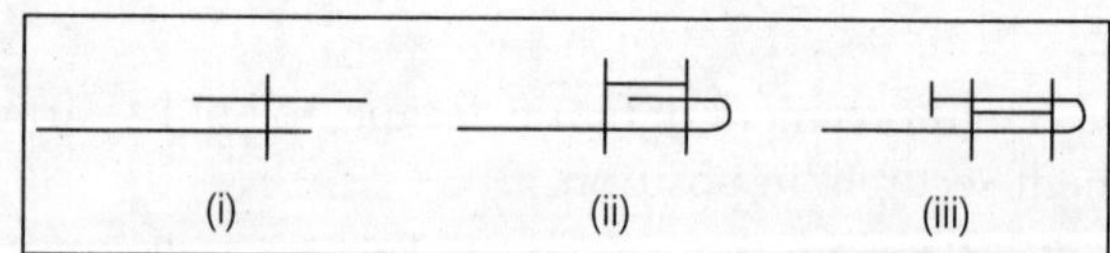

Attaching of Separate Items Seam

Seam Class-8 : Single Ply Construction Seam

- It this seam mainly one piece of fabric is used.
- This class is commonly used for waist belt and loop belt.
- The edges of fabric are sewn by folding in various ways.

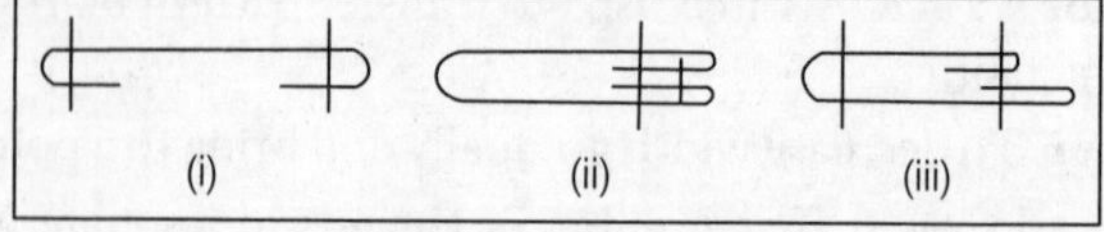

Single Ply Construction Seam

Apparel Quality Testing

Evaluation techniques are necessary for identifying accurate ingredients for producing textile goods. Testing is a valuable aid for textile production, distribution and consumption. During textiles testing, the variation of a fibre or fabric i.e. length, colour, fineness, threads per inch, cover factor, is detected properly.

Continuous test of the textiles results in an enhanced and efficient output of the production. By apparel testing, we can evaluate and ensure the quality of the garments to be used by the end users.

Importance of Apparel Testing

Textile and apparel testing is vital for fashion industry and conducted so that apparel manufacturers, clothing retailers and fashion wholesalers can evaluate and ensure the quality of the garments they manufacture and sell.

They ensure that it is safe to use by consumers and fit for the purpose, conforms to international or regional compliance, retain performance specification, quality standards, meets product liability, environmental and other current legislation, prevent recalls and promote repeat sales.

It is important for the manufacturers to learn and understand about fabric testing methods set by retailers and to stay compliant in regard to quality. If a clothing manufacturer does not know the retailer testing standard requirements that company may run into problems such as receiving a chargeback claim or returned merchandise.

Quality Standards

It is a document that has been prepared, approved and published by a recognised standards organisation and contains rules, requirements or procedures for an orderly approach to a specific activity. It may include product design requirements, test methods, classification, recommended practices and other considerations such as :

- Precision and Accuracy
- Types of Standards, Company Standard, Industry Standard, Government Standard. Full Consensus Standard, etc.
- Benefits of quality standards are:
  - It defines safety requirements intended to reduce the risk of accident.
  - It sets a level of performance for products.
  - They are a framework for quality processes.
  - It reduces cost and saves money.

Major organisations for quality standards

- AATCC (American Association of Textile Chemists and Colorists).
- ISO (International Organisation for Standardisation).
- ANSI (American National Standards Institute).
- ASQ (American Society for Quality).

The above organisations identify and define terms, develop consistent practices within the field for describing and evaluating materials and process. They encourage fair trade practices and develop technological advances to remain competitive in the world market and promote the textile industry.

Apparel Quality Testing Specifications

Apparel specification sheet is a technical document that contains the construction details of the product, a technical diagram/sketch of the apparel, measurements of the product. Here, fashion referred to the apparel and clothing products.

When the factory has a complete set of detailed instructions, the execution of accurate samples will improve the turn around time and simplify communication during each stage of manufacturing and quality control. Listed below are some of the essential information specification sheets should contain :

- Product sketch
- Fabric details
- PoM (Points of Measure)
- Print placement
- Embroidery placement
- Workmanship instructions
- Garment washing instructions
- Accessories details
- Label placement
- Comment section

Quality Parameters

Quality is of prime importance for every industry or business, to get increased sales and better name amongst consumers and fellow companies. For textile and apparel industry, product quality is calculated in terms of quality and standard of fibres, yarns, fabric construction, colours fastness, surface designs and final finished garments products. Some testing parameters are :

Tensile Strength It is the strength of fabric which denotes breaking force required to rupture fabric. It determines effective strength of specified width with assistance of adjacent yarns. Fabric assistance depends on type of fabric and construction variables.

Tearing Strength Tear force defined length from a cut in fabric when a sudden force is applied. This test is mainly applicable for woven fabrics not for knitted fabrics.

Seam Properties It is the property used to determine maximum force of sewn seams, when force is applied perpendicularly to seam. Test applies to standard seam applied to fabric samples or production seam as received.

Testing Quality of Fabric and Garment

Description of different tests used in the testing quality of fabric and garment are as follows:

Colour Fastness Test

There are different kinds of fastness tests. Some of them are as follows :

Crocking Through this method, transfer of colour of fabric/ garment is evaluated in dry and wet condition through crocking machine by using crock cloth and chromatic transference scale.

Colour Fastness to Light This is for evaluation of colour fading in sunlight. How much colour would fade in a specified condition of Sunlight?

Colour Fastness to Laundering This test is basically for the evaluation of fabric colour loss due to detergent solution and abrasive action equivalent to five home laundering. Minimum five wash guarantee is given by all the reputed fashion brand for their product.

Colour Fastness to Perspiration This is for determining the colour loss of fabric through perspiration. Three specimens of colour textile are soaked in simulated acid perspiration solution and allowed to dry slowly at a slightly elevated temperature in a circulating air oven for at least six hours.

Construction Test

Construction of fabric is based on yarn standard and weaving quality. Following two kinds of tests are important to know the construction and characteristics of fabrics :

Yarn Quality and Count Test Measurement of yarn thickness, plies and quality of yarn spinning and weave, comes under this test.

Weight Test Measurement of fabric mass per unit area / weight comes under this test.

Performance Test

Dimensional changes in fabrics and snagging resistance of fabrics come under this test.

Shrinkage/Dimensional Changes This is generic term for changes in length and width of fabric in a specified condition of wet processing. The changes are usually expressed in term of percentage compare to the original fabric. This test is important to know the dimensional changes of any kind of fabric while laundering at home in a given temperature, process and method.

Snagging Resistance of Fabrics Snagging is a common feature in woven and knitted fabrics and it is created when an object pulls, plucks, scratches and drags the yarns from its normal pattern.

Pilling Resistance Formation of pills and irregular surface due to rubbing is measured through this test.

Strength and Stretch Test

Following kinds of tests are normally done in this category :

Strength Test Determination of breaking force of woven textile fabrics in dry and wet both condition while clamping and pulling the fabrics in opposite direction. Force applied to tear the fabric is measured in this test. This is also called bursting strength test.

Stretch and Growth Test This test is recommended for the knitted fabrics. In specific condition and specific load, in length and width wise how much elongation happens in knitted fabrics.

Water Resistance/Rain Test

Any textile fabrics, which may or may not have been given the water repellent finish, need to go for this test. It measures the fabric's resistance from the probable rain penetration.

Subsidiary Test

Tests required to conduct main test, may call subsidiary test. Following may be considered as subsidiary test :

pH Test of Water or Any Solution Before Wet **Processing** This is a part of main test and before going to make any solution of chemical, water pH is tested for accuracy.

Colour Matching Test Through Colour Matching Cabinet This is a part of main test and use to see the result of colour loss after completion of any test comparison with original fabrics in different lights. Mainly five standards of lights are internationally recognised i.e., D65 (day light), CWF, Inc A, TL84 / TL83 and UV light.

Many of the tests, factory can do in-house and can save time and cost. All the tests and approvals are not required. Factory may do the essential and required test as according to buyer's standard or may make own standard of necessary test for maintaining quality parameter.

Defects of Fabrics and Garments

Fabric defect is any abnormality in the fabric that hinders its acceptability by the consumer. Fabric is produced with interlacement of warp and weft yarn or loop formation of yarn. During manufacturing of fabric, various types of defects occur in fabric. Some fabric faults are visible and some faults are invisible. The faults have a visible effect on a fabric, comprising all the disproportions within the structure of the textile material that interfere with its end use. If these faults are not detected early, i.e., during the manufacturing process, they can drastically affect the production process and the quality of the finished product.

Description of commonly found defects in fabrics and garments are given below:

Warp Direction Faults

Material defects in the warp direction occur in the threads and are defined as follows :

Thick or Thin End A warp thread that differs in diameter from the surrounding normal ends.

Tight or Slack End A warp thread or part of a warp thread, that is tighter or slacker than the surrounding normal ends.

Missing or Broken End The absence of a complete warp thread or part of a warp thread.

Broken Pattern Broken pattern is caused if warp yarn is broken when a pattern was being created during weaving.

Double End A thread or part of a thread in the warp, which has accidentally been doubled.

Defective Selvage Selvage having warp yarn under high tension may cause pucker or wavy surface resulting in defective selvage. Besides, selvage may be thick and thin and may possess broken ends, temple mark, etc. Defective selvage may make the whole fabric defective and fabric finishing difficult.

Warp Streak Streak running in warp direction. Group of yarns having different dye shades may result in warp streak. Testing for faults in the warp direction is conducted using a simple visual assessment of the imperfections in the fabric to decide which would be unacceptable in a garment.

The number or faults in the fabric are then counted and their lengths are measured. Faults are tolerated if the residual cloth width satisfies the terms of the contract.

Weft Direction Faults

Material defects in the weft direction also occur in the threads and are defined as follows :

Thick/Thin Pick A weft thread that differs in diameter from the corresponding normal picks.

Tight/Slack Pick A weft thread or part of a weft thread, that is tighter or slacker than the corresponding normal picks.

Loose Weft/Slough off/Snarl When a bunch or coil of yarn slips from the pirn during weaving then thick yarn bunches or coils appear on the fabric.

Missing Pick The unintentional omission of one complete pick across the full width of the cloth.

Broken Pick A pick that is inserted for only part of the cloth width.

Double Pick The thread or pieces of thread in the weft which form the woven structure but are accidentally doubled.

Trailer Weft Yarn that has been pulled inadvertently into the fabric during weaving. As with the assessment of faults in the warp direction, testing for faults in the weft direction is also conducted using a simple visual assessment of the imperfections in the fabric that would be deemed unacceptable in a garment, followed by a measurement of their lengths. In this case, however, no tolerance is permitted for faults detected using this method of control.

Stripes in the Warp

Stripes or streaks in the warp, which extend either for part of the warp direction or over its entire length and which show up as faults against the rest of the material, are considered being faults in the fabric.

A visual assessment of the fabric and the measurement of the length of the stripes are sufficient tests to decide whether the imperfections would be unacceptable in a garment. Stripe faults are tolerated if the residual cloth width meets the terms of the contract.

Bars in the Weft

Bars in the weft are defined as streaks, which occur over either the full or part of the length of the weft direction and which show up against the rest of the piece. Again, a visual assessment of the imperfections is used to decide whether they would be unacceptable in a garment.

The length of the bars is also measured if they occur in a sequence. No tolerance is permitted for faults detected using this method of control.

Knot/Slubs in the Warp/Weft Threads

Knot/slubs in some of the weft/warp threads are considered to be faults when they are visible to an experienced person and when they spoil the appearance of the fabric. This visual assessment is sufficient to test whether the faults would be unacceptable in a garment and no tolerance is permitted for faults detected using this method of control.

Faulty Mending and Burling, Tears, Holes and Stains

Faults caused by mending and burling, tears, holes and stains are defined as follows :

Faulty Mending Poor appearance of repair on the surface of the fabric.

Faulty Burling The presence of faults which have not been removed during burling.

Fabric Pieces Cut in Several Parts

Fabric is deemed faulty if it is cut across the whole width in two or more parts, the total being equal to the required length. Once it has been verified that the number of the separate parts together makes up the length ordered, no tolerance of this fault is permitted.

Crack/Open Set Mark

A higher pick density than the normal is referred to as open set mark while a lower pick density is referred to as crack. This kind of defect is mainly caused by the mechanical faults in the loom.

Care and Maintenance of Clothing

Textile products are complex products composed of many different parts of the conflicting instruction of fibres, yarns, fabric and wet processing within one fabric are often different to predict, when two or more fabrics are combine in a garment when we wear clothes they become dirty due to the dirt, grease, perspiration, etc.

Clothes look ugly if those are allowed to remain on the fabric. They also tend to loose their strength and stains can get fixed on the fabric. The dry dirt can be easily shaken off from the clothes, but greasy dirt requires a special treatment.

Processes of Laundering

Laundry work is undertaken by all housewives or home maker, some home maker have turned the job entirely to commercial laundries. The process and materials used in laundries, the fabrics are mainly responsible for detaining the strength of the clothes.

Laundering of clothes consists of two proceses :

- The process of removing dirt.
- The process of finishing them to retain the appearance of neatness as of a new fabric.

The process of removing dirt is greatly dependent on the soap and detergent and the method of cleaning employed. Soap we held for centuries as the chief substances that removes grease and dirt from fibres. Soap makes the penetration of water into the fabric easier. It helps to break down the surface tension or surface resistance of fabric and the soap solution will wet the fabric readily than plain water. The dirt in the fabric consists of grease and dirt particles. Thus, the fabric is made free from dust and grease.

Preparations before Laundering of Clothes

Following are the preparatory steps for laundering of clothes :

- Washing enlarges the teared part of the fabric. So, all teared parts should be mended prior to washing of the fabrics. Also, buttons should be replaced and eyelets should also be mended.
- Stains should be removed before washing the garments.
- White coloured clothes should be separated from the coloured ones.
- Sorting of the clothes for washing should also be done accordingly. Cottons, linens, silks and wools should be separated from each other.
- Also, heavily soiled clothes should be washed separately from less soiled clothes.
- Big articles like bed linen, table linen should be separated out from small articles and clothing of personal use.

Laundry Equipments

There are four kinds of laundry equipments. These are as follows :

Collecting Duity Articles Cupboard, Racks, Shelves, Buckets and Hangers.

Washing Sink, Basin, Bucket/Tub, Mugs, Brushes and Washing Machine.

Drying Indoor e.g. Rack
Outdoor e.g. Cloth line

Finishing Iron, Ironing board, etc.

Steps of Laundering Proccess

The process of laundering involves the following steps :

Steeping

The first step in laundering of clothes involves steeping of clothes in water, preferably in soapy water loose and soluble dirt can be easily removed by steeping or soaking of the clothes. Water soluble stains are removed, also the starch of previously laundering is also softened. Additional advantage of soaking/steeping of clothes are it economises time, labour and soap.

The length of time required for soaking depends on how dirty the clothes are. Warm water enhances the cleaning and dissolves the dirt more quickly. Soaking of the clothes for long-time leads to weakening of the fibres and dirt tends to get lodged more firmly.

Soaking of linen should be avoided in hot water as hot water will harden the protein matter of soiled linens and helps to fix the dirt. Rayon gets weakened by water, therefore, it should not be soaked and should be laundered as a very delicate fabric. Silks, woollens and non-fast coloured clothes should not be soaked.

Washing

Soft water is suitable for washing purpose. The temperature of water should be according to the type of fibres of the fabric, like hot water for cottons, warm for silk and lukewarm for woollens. The washing process involves the application of pressure or friction. Friction or pressure on coarse materials and strong cottons can be applied by scrubbing brushes or scrubbling boards. Washing of delicate fabrics requires kneading and squeezing by avoiding much friction. Dirty water should be drained off and is replaced.

Rinsing

Rinsing of clothes is done in plenty of clear, soft water after washing. Final rinsing in cold water helps in retaining the whiteness of the fabric. Final rinsing of silk clothes should be done in water to which a little methylated spirit or lime juice has been added, which helps in renewing and stiffening of silk and also brighten the colour.

Starching and Blueing

This may be combined as one process to save time and wasting of blue and starch. Blueing is done for white cottons and linens only and not for coloured clothes. Blue is tied up in a piece of muslin and squeezed into the starch solution still the required depth of blue is obtained. The water containing starch and blue should be stirred well to prevent blue from setting down as this may cause patches on the clothes.

The garment should be dipped well in this water, stirred and squeezed well, so that there is thorough penetration of starch and blue in the garment. Clothes can be kept clean and fresh for longer time through starching. Now, a days, liquid blue and liquid starches are also in use which are more convenient. Clothes of personal use are starched lightly, while articles of household use are heavily starched.

Hanging and Drying

Generally, used clothes lines for hanging and drying the clothes are made of cotton or hemp or wires made of galvanised copper or plastic, which may be either solid or twisted. The wire lines are more permanent than the cotton, hemp or plastic ones, but it should be wiped off before hanging to avoid stains on clothes.

Washing machines with dryers are major labour, time and space saving device. Drying white clothes in sunlight has an added advantage as sunlight bleaches clothes, freshens them and also this infects it. Hard wringing of clothes should be avoided specially of silks and wools. Shady place should be used for drying silks and coloured clothes.

Caring Factors in Laundering

While laundering, bleaching and boiling of the clothes can also be done to give fresh look to the clothes. Their description is given below :

Bleaching

Long storage and poor washing makes the clothes discoloured and thus, requires bleaching. It can be done by merely spreading the clothes in sunlight or by using chemical bleaching agents. The chemical bleaching agent can be used only for white coloured cottons and linen bleaching should be avoided on coloured and dyed fabrics.

Boiling

Very dirty clothes can be boiled upto 5-10 minutes to whiten, disinfect and freshen up. Long boiling has the tendency to yellow white fabrics. Thorough rinsing is required to remove the odour after boiling. The mires are more permanent, but must be wiped off with a damp cloth before being used and must be free from rust washed while cotton garments should be put in the Sun to dry, as Sunlight bleaches clothes.

Stiffening Agents

Repeated laundering of garments brings a loss in the glass, shine and pliability, starching or use of stiffening agents in the most common techniques to make the fabric firm and pliable with smooth and glossy finished. This finish not only emphasise appearance and feel, but also prevents direct contact of dirt with the fabric.

Stiffening agents are derived from nature either plants or animals and these are applied to clothes that have been washed or clean, starch is most commonly and widely used in stiffening agents. Best starch is one that can penetrate the fabric well to made it pliable, smooth and glossy.

When starch is heated with water, starch particles on the absorption of water in the presence of heat are ruptured and form a colloidal solution boiling or application of heat is necessary to that a smooth colloidal solution. It is during boiling that the hard surface covering the starch particle burst open allowing gelatimisation of them to form a gelly like solution.

These colloidal particles get bound to the fabric, forming a uniform coating. Starch as a stiffening agent is added only for cotton and linens, basically a thick starch solution is prepared and than diluted as per need. Thick cotton need light starch while thin fabric need heavy starch.

Types of Stiffening Agents

Some of the common starch used are :

Rice Starch This is basically a cold water starch. The grain of this starch are very small and make a viscous solution in water. This starch gelatinise easily in cold water and can penitent the cloth easily. It is suitable for almost all kind of fabrics.

Wheat Starch This is an uneconomical and expensive method. It is used where stiffeness and pliability of greater degree is desired. The germs of starch yeast in two sizes : large and small. It requires boiling to form a viscous solution.

Maize Starch It is a cheap starch and when with a rough surface. Though it forms a good viscous solution, it is not used by itself. Rather, it is mixed with other starch.

Tapioca Starch The roots of the Cassava plants are dried and powder finally. Refining process is long and complicated, but the final starch solution available is smooth and provides stiffening of good quality.

Potato Starch This starch is not very popular as fabric stiffening is concern as the grains are usually large. Potato and sweet potato are used for the manufacture of this starch. Finally, powder and boiled to form the solution of desired strength and viscosity.

Commercial Starch These are usually blanding of one or more kind of starch and inversably tinted with blue, green and cream colour. These are not favoured because colour use are of poor, inferior quality and hence, effect the final finish of the garment.

Dry Cleaning

It is the method of removing dirt from clothes without the use of water or soap. Although, nut cleaning is a cheaper method of laundering cloth, but this method is not suitable for all kinds of fibres and clothes. Fine rich fabric non -fast coloured and printed fabric furs etc., cannot be nut cleaning without loss in luster, shine colour and rich finish. Hence, these clothes are dry cleaned is based on the principle that most dirt is held by grease and any removal of grease ensures the removal of dirt held by it.

Instead of emulsification and saponification, the dirt is removal by a process of solvent action of certain chemicals and absorbent. This is an expensive method, but helps to maintain the original luster and colour (safe for water soluble dyes finishes) above all it minimise shrinkage of fabric. Dry cleaning agents employed in the method are solvents and absorbent.

Solvents

Petrol, benzine, methylated spirit, chloroform, carbon tetrachloride and mineral of grease solvent. These solvents are liquid and evaporate easily. The liquids form allows easy penetration into the fabric and has dissolve the grease and the dirt held along with it. Solvents are considered more suitable for highly soiled clothes.

The most common solvents used is non-flammable per-chloroethylene, a complete chlorinated hydrocarbon. Refined petrol is also commonly used but been highly inflammable in nature, there is the risk of fire. Benzine and methylated spirit are not favoured because of the risk of fire. Carbon tetra chloride, tri-chloroethylene are fire resistant, but the vapours given off during use, when inhaled can cause fainting and giddiness.

Absorbents

They are dry powders. These absorb the grease and along with it, the dirt and are then brushed out the fabric. Fuller's Earth, French chalk, talcum powders, salt, baked floor, powdered sulphur and bread cramp are some of the absorbents commonly used. Absorbents are greatly favoured for cleaning of heavily soiled part like cuffs and collar. They are suitable for cleaning of light coloured and white fabric, furs.

Stain Removal

Stain is a spot or mark of discolouration left on fabrics by the contact and absorption of someforeign substance. Some stains are easily removed but some may require special treatment.

They can be classified according to the substances that cause them :

Animal Stains They caused by blood, egg, milk juice etc. They contains protein matter and heat must be avoided, otherwise protein matter will be fixed and it will be difficult to remove.

Vegetable Stains They includes coffee, tea, cocoa, fruit and wine. These are acidi therefore, requires alkaline reagents to remove them.

Grease Stains They may be just grease spot or some calorie matter fixed with grease. In removing these, some grease solvents and absorbents is used CCl_4 and tri chloro ethane are non flammable and are used for removing grease. Petroleum ether, ethyl ether, benzene, petrol, acetone, methylated spirit are very effective for removal of grease, facts etc. They should the stored away from flame.

Washing

There are various cleaning operations that are done by water or water containing detergents, alkali or builders. It is used to convey information regarding the maximum washing temperature and the maximum washing process severity. Thus, while selecting the method of washing two main factors need to be considered.

- How dirty is the fabric?
- What kind of fabric it is? i.e. cotton, silk, wool, rayon, nylon and so on.

Principle and Objectives of Washing

Washing is a process which changes outer appearance, comfort, feel of the garment. Wash types usually depend on the product nature and usage. Based on consumer demand and fashion trends buyers fix washing type of any product. Garment wash here refers to garment pre-wash performed after production of garment's prior to using it for the consumers.

The main objectives of garment washing are as follows :

- To remove stiffness and roughness in some garments which aren't pre–washed.
- Different washing methods are being used to provide a different or customised appearance.
- Softness can be increased by addition of softeners.
- During manufacturing dirt, spot or oil mark may get added with the garment's which gets eliminated by washing process.
- To eliminate starch and chemicals which are used during fabric manufacturing and dying process.
- Due to washing, maximum shrinkage occurs, hence there is zero possibility of further shrinkage. As a result, there is no size or fitting problem in washed garments.

Ways of Washing

Friction Washing This method is suitable for washing strong fabrics like cotton. Friction can be applied as follows :

- **By Hand** This means rubbing vigorously with the hand. It is suitable for cleaning very soiled small articles like small garments, handkerchief, etc. It is economical in the use of soap.
- **With a Plastic Scrubbing Brush** With a scrubbing brush friction is applied by placing the dirty article flat on a hard surface. It is suitable for very soiled household articles made of strong fabric, for example, dusters.
- **Beating with a Stick** Large articles like bedsheets, etc., are washed by this method.

Suction Washing This method is used for articles like towels, etc., which are heavy and have a pile weave, on which a brush can not be used.

The article is placed in soap solution in a tub and the suction washer is pressed down on it and lifted repeatedly. The vacuum created by pressing losens the dirt particles.

Washing by Kneading and Squeezing This method is used for delicate fabrics like silk, woollens, rayon, etc. This method does not damage the fabric or change its shape as only gentle rubbing with hands is applied.

Washing by Machines Washing machine is a labour saving device especially useful for large institutions. Now a days, it is being used at home also.

The washing time varies with types of fabrics and amount of soiling. Woollens take less time than cottons to get cleaned. The instructions with the machine should be read carefully before using it.

Laundry Agents

There are only a few major types of laundry agents. These are :

- Detergents
- Bleaches
- Sour/Acid Agent
- Optical Brightener
- Alkali
- Antichlors
- Fabric Conditioner
- Starch

Detergents

Strictly speaking, the term detergent can be applied to any cleaning agent. Its usage is known generally restricted to those cleaning agents containing significant quantities of a group of chemicals known as surfactants. A number of other chemicals are frequently included to produce a detergent suitable for a specific use.

A good detergent will possess many or all of the following properties :

- Reduce the surface tension of water so that the cleaning solution can penetrate the soil and surface.
- Emulsify soil and lift it from a surface.
- Suspend soil in the cleaning solution
- Be soluble in cold water
- Be effective in hard water
- Be harmless to user and surface to be cleaned
- Rinse easily to leave no streaks or scum
- Be economical in use

Chemical Composition of Detergents

Detergents are formulated from the types of chemicals described in the following :

Anticorrosive Agents Inhibit the formation of water films on a surface. Chemical reactions resulting in corrosion are generally dependent on the presence of water. Perfumes and dyes are included to increase consumer acceptability but increase the risk of allergic reaction.

Builders These are alkaline chemicals that influence the effectiveness of cleaning agents. They sequester (combine with) calcium ions in hard water to form water-soluble salts, thus preventing the adverse effects of calcium. Enhance the emulsifying and dispersing properties of the detergent.

Sodium metasilicate and sodium carbonate are included in many liquid detergents and function in the second of the ways described Builders, in general, can have damaging effects on many surfaces e.g. chrome, aluminium, wool, silk, paints, wood and linoleum.

Bleaches These will break down by oxidation, stains which have not been removed from a surface by surfactants or builders. Sodium perborate, weak bleach is included in detergents intended for washing textile.

Bulking Agents e.g. Sodium sulphate, contribute to the volume of detergent powders.

Chelating Agents These are relatively complex chemicals which are included in many liquid detergents to sequester calcium ion. In simple terms, a combination of sodium carbonate or metasilicate and a chelating agent v ill have a similar effect to tripolyphosphatic alone. Tripol phosphate is not normally included in a liquid detergen because it tends to break down in alkaline solution. Chelati g agents are now frequently used as descaling agents, being a more acceptable alternative to strong acids.

Conditioning Agents These ensure that the granules in detergent powders are crisp, firm and dry.

Complex Phosphates These are included in many detergents powders and act in both of the ways described e.g. Sodium Tripolyphosphate.

Enzymes These are complex proteins that will break down organic substances e.g. blood stains, adhering to a surface. They are most effective at 30-50°C and are inactivated at temperatures above 60°C.

Foaming Agents These increase or stabilise the foam formed by a detergent. Foaming can be used to indicate surfactant activity, the level of foam is dependent on the amount of surfactant active in a cleaning solution. Alkalonamides derived from coconuts oil are frequently used for this purpose. Other foaming agents can be used to produce stable, relatively thick foams in which the other chemicals are dispersed. The foam will.stick to the non-horizontal surface and the cleaning chemicals.

Suspending Agent The role of the suspending agent in cleaning is to hold the dirt in suspension and prevent it from re-depositing onto the surface of the article. It plays a crucial role in the laundry agent due to the amount of time that the clothes rotate in the machine while the dirt is in suspension. The suspending agent is carboxylmethylcellulose.

Sequestering Agent These act along with the suspending agent to hold dirt in suspension. They assist by holding a greater amount of dirt in suspension thereby reducing the likelihood of re-deposition. They also have the additional ability to dissolve lime salts that are responsible for temporary hardness in water. Sodium polyphosphates act as sequestering agents.

Surface Active Agents or Surfactants These are chemicals, the molecules of which when dissolved in water possess a water-seeking (hydrophilic) end and a water repelling (hydrophobic) end. They may or may not carry a negative or positive electrical charge.

The molecules are dispersed through the water so that they reduce the surface tension of the water by overcoming the forces of attraction between the water molecules, thus allowing the water and surfactant molecules to penetrate the soil and surface. The hydrophobic ends of the surfactant molecules are attracted to the soil, surrounding particulate soil particles and lifting them from the surface while breaking and rolling up grease into small particles and lifting them from the surface.

The hydrophilic ends of the surfactant molecules point out from the soil particles into the surrounding water. As individual particles approach each other the hydrophilic parts of the surfactant molecules on different particles repel each other keeping the soil in suspension and preventing it from settling back onto the surface.

Water Softeners These are frequently comprised of complex phosphates e.g. Sodium hexametaphosphate because of their sequestering properties.

Whiteners These absorb ultraviolet light and transmit it as visible white light. The whiteness of a surface will normally depend on the amount of natural light reflected from it and received by the eye. Whiteners, therefore, increase the amount of light received by the eye.

Other Laundering Agents

Description of other laundering agents is given below :

Alkali

Alkali used in the wash process include :

- Washing Soda (Sodium Carbonate $Na_2CO_{310}H_2O$)
- Sodium Phosphate
- Sodium Hydroxide
- Sodium Metasilicate
- Borax ($Na_2B_4O_{170}H_2O$)
- Ammonium hydroxide (NH_4OH)

The role of the alkali in the wash process :

- Combines with calcium ions in hard water to form water-soluble salts, thus preventing the adverse effects of calcium.
- Enhance the emulsifying and dispersing properties of the detergents.

Bleaches

These are used on white articles only they remove colouring matter by their oxidising or reducing action. If not in liquid form, they should be dissolved in hot water in order to ensure that no powder residue remains in the washing machine which may affect later loads. The bleaches commonly used in the laundry process are sodium perborate and sodium hypochlorite (Javelle water).

Antichlors

These are agents used to neutralise the chlorine bleach and are essential particularly in the case of polyesters. The use of chlorinated bleaches has a tendency to leave yellow deposits.

Sour/Acid Agents

This is used only in industrial laundering in the final rinse, to neutralise any alkaline soap residues that may be present. It brings the pH of the linen articles to a level between 5 and 6.5, which is agreeable to the human skin and also gets rid of yellow or brown deposits caused by residue alkali. Acetic acid is used as the sour. In cases where there is a high iron content in the water, Oxalic acid is used which serves a dual purpose, by also getting rid of the reddish, iron deposits. If starch is being used, sour should be added 2 minutes before the starch to achieve a pH of 5.0 to 5.5. If a sizing agent is being used, the ideal pH is 7.0 to 8.0 so sour is generally not used.

Some common used sour/acid agents are :

Oxalic Acid Sold in white Crystals Used for removal of fruit stains, bleaching of brown stains after using potassium permanganate and tannin base of ink stains together with Hydrogen peroxide.

Salt of Lemon Salt of Sorrel Compound of Potassium Oxalate and Oxalic Acid referred as Potassium binoxalate. Used for neutralizing strong alkali.

Acetic Acid Removes excessive bluing agents and as a neutralising agents.

Oleie Acid

- Unsuitable for coloured fabrics.
- Produces soap when mixed with alkali.
- Used for grease and oil stain.

Fabric Conditioner/Softener

A fabric conditioner or softener has surface active agents like a detergent but they don't perform the function of cleaning. Fabric conditioners are based on cationic surface-active agents, carrying a positive charge and creates anti-static properties. A fabric conditioner is never used on loads where starch or sizing will be used.

The role of the fabric conditioner in laundering

Optical Brightener

This is an optical brightener/whitener, which is, in fact, a very fine dye, which gets bleached in course of time.lt has a fluorescent effect by reflecting the UV rays of the sun.The laundry blue in a powder form tends to accumulate in the weave of the fabric and causes it to turn grey and is no longer used in modern laundries.

Starch

This is a stiffening agent used to impart a better appearance to the fabric.The use of starch has declined due to the minimum-iron finishes on fabrics and garments and the reduced use of cotton in favour of man-made fibres. However, there are some articles that have a better feel and drape when starched and it is particularly essential for napkin folds.Since polyesters do not have the ability to absorb starch they are stiffened with sizing agents.

Types of Starch

- Hot-Water Starches
- Cold-Water Starches
- Gelatin
- Glue
- Synthetic Sizing

Storage Techniques

Whether you are looking to store baby clothes, winter clothing, or seasonal wardrobes, it's very important that you know how to store clothes in a storage unit the proper way. It may seem as easy as packing boxes with clothing and loading them into your unit, but it's a bit more complex than that. To maintain the quality of your clothing, you want to make sure it is stored properly.

This involves choosing the right storage containers, the right storage unit, and taking steps to avoid moisture and pests from ruining your clothes.

Below are some most important tips for how to store clothes in a storage unit :

Wash Everything Washing all the clothes before storing is crucial to maintain the longevity of the clothes. Unwashed clothing can produce, mold, mildew, and begin to smell if left long term. Even if clothes don't look or smell dirty, they may reveal stains over time. Residual perfumes, lotions, oil, or even sweat can sit in the fabric and turn clothing yellow. Food stains or clothes that have been starched can attract pests, which will ruin clothing.

Use Plastic Bins Many people use cardboard boxes or plastic bags to store clothes, as these are more cost-effective options, but these methods leave your clothing vulnerable to damage. Plastic bags can trap moisture and will lead to mold and mildew. Free used plastic boxes may seem appealing, but if they were previously used to hold food, they may contain bacteria or hidden pests. Cardboard boxes are also vulnerable to humidity and water damage.

Instead, plastic bins can be used that can be kept shut to keep clothing safe from all threats. These bins will keep items safe from pests, water, humidity, and dust. Bins should not be overpacked as there is no air flowing through to let items breathe. Transparent bins can be used to see items inside but if storage area is exposed to light, darker bins should be used to avoid fading of fabrics.

Create an Inventory System Creating an inventory system is crucial to keeping thing organised and allowing easy access items of clothing. There are few options to choose from when deciding on an inventory system :

- **Colour Coordinated Inventory** For this inventory system, you will colour code each box in your unit. Each colour should be linked to a specific type of clothing whether it be divided by family members, season, or item type. Keep a sheet to refer to that will indicate which colour coordinates with which items.
- **Labels** With this system, you will label each box. Something like "Mom's Winter Sweaters" will work well. This way, you can easily find the bin that has the item you are looking for. Make sure you are organised and specific while packing to help when you need to unpack.
- **Inventory List** The inventory list is the most extensive option. It can be combined with the other two options and will help you be certain about where your items are. On this list, you will write down every item in your bin. You should list the item, a brief description of it, and the size of the article of clothing. This can be taped onto the bin or live in an excel spreadsheet. It will allow you to know for certain the contents of your bins so that you don't waste time digging through them.

Never Vacuum Pack Vacuum packing may save a lot of space, but it's also very damaging to clothes. Packing clothing this way in long term can lead to permanent creasing and wrinkles. Natural fibres need to breathe, and by sucking all the air out of them, you are quickening the process of deterioration to your clothing. To avoid suffocating your items, lightly pack them into bins, keeping the heavier items on the bottom.

Keep Bugs Out Mothballs keeps bug out but tuese have awful. Some cedar chips can be used in clothes to deter pests. They work just as well as mothballs, but without pesticides that can be harmful to clothing. Storing with a responsible storage company that practices preventative pest control and does not allow food storage is another way to avoid pests in clothing.

Store in a Dry Dark, and Cool Place Store clothing in a dry, dark and cool environment. If the environment is bright, the light can cause fading in your fabrics. Many people choose to store their clothing in attics or garages, but these areas are susceptible to extreme temperature changes, which can damage clothing. The best option will be a climate-controlled storage unit. Climate-control units are kept at consistent humidity and temperature, providing you with a perfect environment for long-term clothing storage.

Use a Wardrobe Box For more delicate clothing, invest in a wardrobe box to hang clothing. Always avoid metal hangers, as they can cause the fabric to stretch. They may also rust in humid environments or rip clothes with their sharp edges. Instead, invest in wooden or padded hangers for your clothing. Do not cover wardrobe boxes with plastic. Instead, cover with a cotton sheet to protect them from dust and light.

Refold Every Few Years Storage unit should be visited every 1-2 years to refold clothing. This helps prevent permanent creasing and will also allow to check clothing. It should be checked and make sure there are no pests, dust, water damage, or stains developing.

Care Labels and Symbols

Care Labels and Symbols for Washing

Symbols	Washing Process
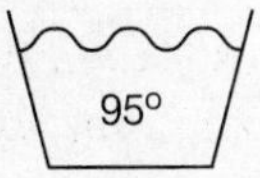 95°	Maximum temperature 95°C Mechanical action normal Normal rinsing Spinning normal
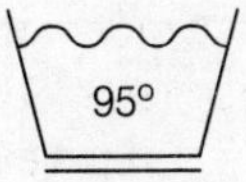 95°	Maximum temperature 95°C Mechanical action reduced Ringing at gradually decreasing temperature(cool down) Spinning reduced
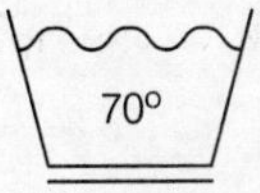 70°	Maximum temperature 70°C Mechanical action normal Normal rinsing Spinning normal
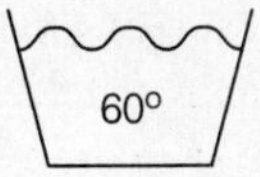 60°	Maximum temperature 60°C Mechanical action normal Normal rinsing Spinning normal
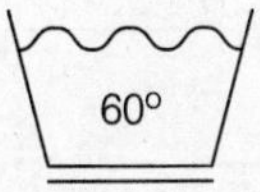 60°	Maximum temperature 60°C Mechanical action reduced Ringing at gradually decreasing temperature(cool down) Spinning reduced
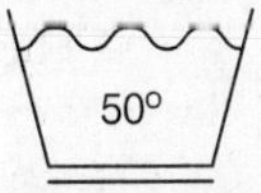 50°	Maximum temperature 50°C Mechanical action reduced Ringing at gradually decreasing temperature(cool down) Spinning reduced
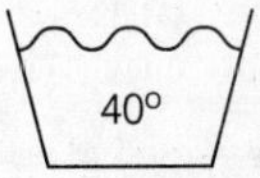 40°	Maximum temperature 40°C Mechanical action normal Normal rinsing Spinning normal
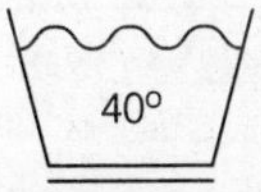 40°	Maximum temperature 40°C Mechanical action reduced Ringing at gradually decreasing temperature(cool down) Spinning reduced
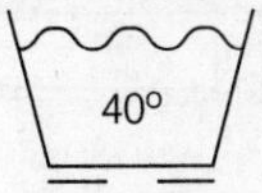 40°	Maximum temperature 40°C Mechanical action normal Normal rinsing Spinning normal Do nor wring by hand
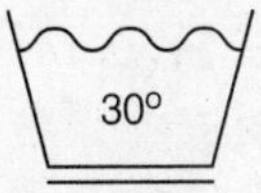 30°	Maximum temperature 30°C Mechanical action normal Normal rinsing Spinning normal
	Hand wash only Do not machine wash Maximum temperature 40°C Handle with care
	Do not wash Be cautious when treating in wet stage

Care Labels and Symbols for Chlorine Based Bleaching

Symbols	Chlorine Based Bleaching Process
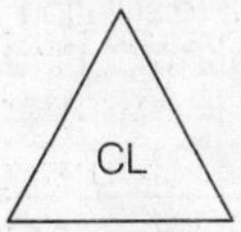 CL	Chlorine based bleaching allowed Only cold and dilute solution
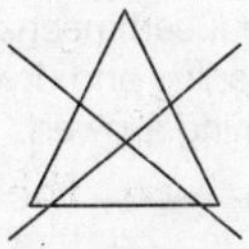	Do not use chlorine based bleach

Care Labels and Symbols for Ironing

Symbols	Ironing Process
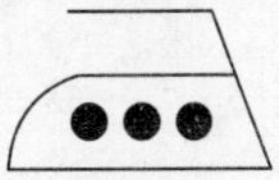	Iron at a maximum sole plate temperature of 200°C for cotton fabric
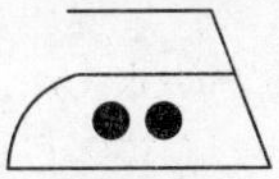	Iron at a maximum sole plate temperature of 150°C for polyester fabric.
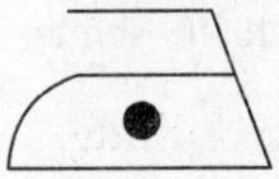	Iron at a maximum sole plate temperature of 110°C for silk fabric.
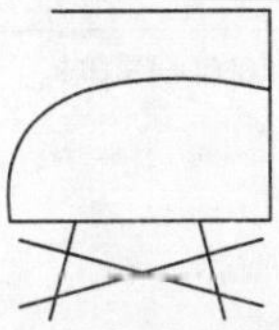	Steaming or steam treatment are not allowed.
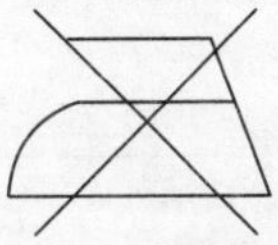	Do not iron

Care Lables and Symbol is for Professional Dry Cleaning

Symbols	Dry cleaning process
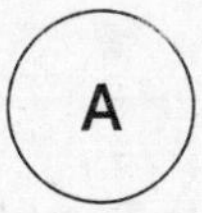 A	All solvents normally used for dry-cleaning.
 P	Any solvent except trichloroethylene normal cleaning procedures without restrictions.
 P	Dry cleaning in the solvent accordance with P Strict limitation on amount of water, reduced mechanical action, Low drying temp No self service cleaning allowed.

Symbols	Dry cleaning process
F	Petroleum Solvent, Liquid Silicone Dry cleaning in trifluoro trichloroethane white sprit (distillation temperature) between 150°C and 210°C. Flash point 38°C to 60°C. Normal cleansing procedures without restrictions
F	Dry cleaning in the solvent accordance with F Strict limitation on amount of water, Reduced mechanical action, Strict limitation during cleaning and drying temperature No self service cleaning allowed.
	Do not dry clean No stain removal with solvent.

Care Label and Symbols for Tumble Dry

Symbols	Process
	Tumble dry possible on high heat. Normal drying cycle.
	Tumble dry possible on medium heat 150°C Normal drying cycle.
	Tumble drying possible. Drying at low temperature setting 70°C
	Tumble dry possible on any heat.
	Tumble dry possible on no heat/air.
	Do not tumble dry.

Care Label and Symbols for Normal Air Dry-No Tumble Dry

Symbols	Process
	Drying symbol
	Line dry
	Dry flat
	Drip dry
	Dry in the shade
	Line dry in the shade
	Dry flat in shade
	Drip dry in shade

Care Label and Symbol for Professional Wet Cleaning

Symbols	Process
W	Professional wet cleaning process
W	Mild process
W	Very mild process
	Do not professionally wet clean

EXAM BASED QUESTIONS

1 What is the major function of textile manufacturing industry?
(a) Transform thread into cloth
(b) Transform fabric into clothing and accessories
(c) Transform your through weave
(d) Transform the fabric into sewing function.

2 Where the workers perform cutting and sewing function?
(a) Assembly line
(b) Production house
(c) Manufacturing department
(d) Labours cost

3 On which factor apparel manufacturing industry depends upon?
(a) Technology (b) Work place
(c) Labour-intensive (d) All of these

4 What do you mean by the term "alter"?
(a) To modify fabric as per size
(b) Changing cloth according to the age
(c) Decorative piece of fabric
(d) Change of pattern according to body measurement

5 What do you mean by "applique"?
(a) Decorative piece of fabric applied by hand or machine.
(b) Dress that belong to particular time and country.
(c) Thred that connects parts of the pattern in lace.
(d) A loose stitch made by hand on machine.

6 What is the term used for "Jagged cut finish for a raw edge"?
(a) Pintucks (b) Placket
(b) Pinking (d) Pleats

7 What is said to unfold and remove the wrinkler from the fabric?
(a) Notch (b) Pucker (c) Loop (d) Fray

8 What is the defination of the term "end"?
(a) A small V-shaped mark or cut.
(b) Pile which is cutted in one direction.
(c) Style which is wider on lower edge.
(d) An individual strand of yarn.

9 What do you mean by Hemline?
(a) A design of the fabric from the neck.
(b) A line designating the finished length of sleenes.
(c) Arrangement of pattern pieces on the material.
(d) A line designating the finished length of a garment.

10 What is said about the ornamental addition on the garment?
(a) Yoke (b) Tucks (c) Trimming (d) Ruffle

11 What is the term used for the stiches with semi-circles?
(a) Ravel (b) Scallop (c) Tack (d) Tubing

12 It is better to pack each article of clothing in polythene bags separately. It keeps away
(a) mildew (b) insects
(c) moths (d) All of these

13 The purpose of including brand names on apparel is to
(a) guarantee good quality
(b) meet textile product labelling laws
(c) influence consumer buying habits
(d) link the name to the logo

14 The BEST edge treatment for scarves or products made from sheer fabrics is a
(a) faced hem (b) folded hem
(c) rolled hem (d) shirttail hem

15

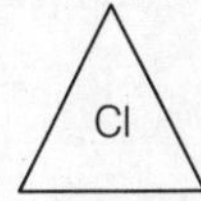

is indicative of
1. limited use
2. stain removal allowed
3. bleach with chlorine
4. information for commercial laundry

Select the correct answer using the codes given below
(a) 1, 2, 3 and 4 (b) 2, 3 and 4
(c) 3, 4 and 1 (d) None of these

16

This symbol on the label of a garment indicates
(a) delicate silk (b) delicate wool
(c) washing not advisable (d) All of these

17 A broken line of the tub means
(a) overflow with water
(b) overflow with soap
(c) special gentle treatment
(d) None of the above

18 A line underneath the wash tub indicates
(a) low water level (b) gentle wash
(c) less severe process (d) All of these

19

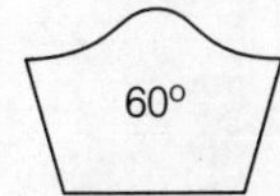

is the symbol for
(a) maximum temperature
(b) 60 minutes dipping
(c) 60 times rubbing
(d) None of the above

20 Shrinkage of cotton fabrics is reduced by the process called
(a) felting (b) mercerisation
(c) sanforisation (d) calendaring

21 Stain of adhesive tape can be removed by
(a) neutralise with vinegar
(b) harden with ice cube and rub off with fingers, then with perchlorate ethylene or other solvent
(c) neutralising with ammonia
(d) None of the above

22 The most widely used bleaches are
(a) chlorine bleaches
(b) hydrogen peroxide bleaches
(c) Both (a) and (b)
(d) None of the above

23 To remove stain of ...., sponge with oxalic acid and rinse well or spread salt, moisten with lemon juice and place in Sun.
(a) ink (b) egg (c) iron rust (d) lipstick

24

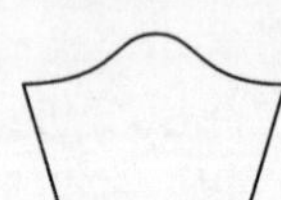

is the symbol for
(a) wash tub (b) mug
(c) bucket (d) None of these

25 Which of the following textile materials is not suitable to be washed with alkaline washing detergents?
(a) Linen (b) Cotton (c) Terylene (d) Wool

26 The substance which gives stiffness to clothes is/are
(a) borax (b) jewel in water
(c) gum water (d) All of these

27 The hardness of water can be removed by the
(a) magnesium (b) sodium carbonate
(c) sodium sulphate (d) ammonium

28 For washing rayon fabric, kneading and squeezing method is used because
(a) it is weaker when wet
(b) it is not very durable
(c) it has a very smooth surface
(d) it has a natural luster

29 Which of the following is least affected by mildew and moth?
(a) Vegetable fibres
(b) Animal fibres
(c) Regenerated cellulose fibres
(d) Synthetic fibres

30 Synthetic detergents are better for cleaning than soap because they
(a) need soft water
(b) clean well in hot water
(c) clean well in warm water
(d) do not precipitate in hard water

31 To prevent mildew, cotton fabrics should be preserved by
(a) keeping it in dry and ventilated place
(b) keeping it in warm place
(c) placing with other fabrics
(d) ironing

32 Woollen and silk garments are better washed in a warm neutral soap or detergent solution, because
(a) it is easy to do so
(b) there will be economy
(c) there will be no colour fading
(d) it will maintain shape or size

33 The brightness of silk garment can be maintained by the use of
(a) sulphuric acid (b) vinegar
(c) sodium hydroxide (d) boric acid

34 Javelle water is a
(a) blueing agent (b) finish
(c) bleaching agent (d) starch

35 Silk can be stiffened by
(a) Starch (b) cornflour
(c) gum arabic (d) rice water

36 Woollen materials are liable to be affected in washing for which of the following?
(a) Damage to stitch
(b) Loss of colour and fading
(c) Damage to surface structure
(d) Shrink and deform

37 Match the following.

List I	List II
A. A placket or any garment opening	1. Closing
B. A straight sleeve flauing at the bottom	2. Bell sleeve
C. Another word for armholes	3. Armscye
D. Decouative piece of fabric	4. Applique

Codes

	A	B	C	D		A	B	C	D
(a)	1	2	3	4	(b)	4	3	2	1
(c)	2	3	1	4	(d)	3	2	1	4

38 Which among the following are not the term used for apparel manufacturing?
1. Clip 2. Drape
3. Bias 4. L-shape

Codes
(a) 1 and 4 (b) 2 and 3
(c) 1, 2 and 3 (d) 2, 3 and 4

39 Which among the following are the types of sleeves?
1. Bell sleeves
2. Bishop's sleeves
3. Cap sleeves
4. Puff sleeves

Codes
(a) 1 and 3 (b) 2 and 4
(c) 1, 3 and 4 (d) All of these

40 **Which among the following are used for the fastening of the garment?**

1. Hooks and eyes
2. Zipper
3. Press button
4. Pile

Codes

(a) 1 and 2 (b) 2 and 3
(c) 1, 2 and 3 (d) All of these

41 **Match the following.**

	List I	List II
A.	A line of stich at the edge	1. Hem
B.	Finish formed back of the raw edge of a garment to wrong side.	2. Notch
C.	Small V shaped cut	3. Edge Stitch
D.	Temporary stitching	4. Machine Basting

Codes

	A	B	C	D		A	B	C	D
(a)	1	2	3	4	(b)	3	1	2	4
(c)	3	2	1	4	(d)	4	3	2	1

42 **Match the following.**

	List I	List II
A.	Brand name	1. Usually indicated by a super script R in a circle
B.	Quality marks	2. Temperature, time, washing medium and mechanical action
C.	Registered trademarks	3. Optional
D.	Factors important in washing or dry cleaning	4. Used by manufactures to advise the consumer or dry cleaning of special high quality products
E.	The provision of washing symbols	5. Product which may be supplied by different symbols, manufacturers confirm to certain written, qualities standards

Codes

	A	B	C	D	E		A	B	C	D	E
(a)	4	5	1	2	3	(b)	5	1	4	3	2
(c)	1	3	2	5	4	(d)	5	4	3	1	2

43 **For which item of clothing would this care label be most suitable?**

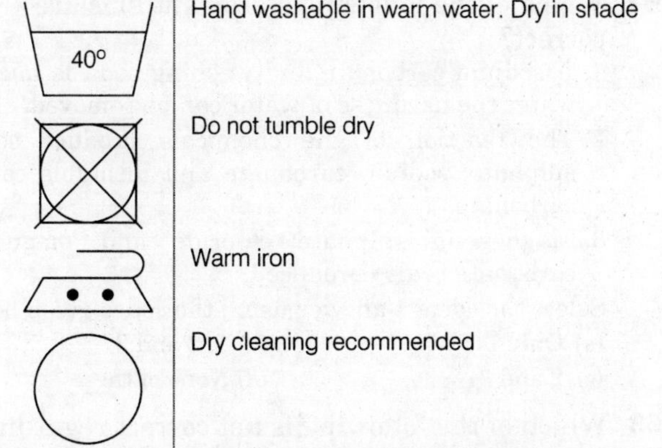

Select the correct answer using the codes given below

(a) Cotton sports shirt (b) Lycra bike shorts
(c) Nylon swim suit (d) Wool jumper

44 **Consider the following statements**

1. Rayon garments undergo progressive shrinkage, hence care has to be taken, while drying and ironing.
2. Direct dyes bleed while washing, therefore direct dyed fabrics are after treated with catonic agent.

Which of the statements given above is/are correct?

(a) Both 1 and 2 (b) Only 1
(c) Only 2 (d) None of these

45 **The chemical which used in dry cleaning is/are**

1. carbon tetrachloride, commercial dry cleaner powder.
2. petrol, benzine.
3. telcum powder, sulphur powder.
4. French chalk, fuller Earth.

Select the correct answer using the codes given below.

(a) Only 1 (b) 1 and 2
(c) 1, 2 and 3 (d) All of these

46 **Consider the following statements regarding the procedure for ironing of cotton and linen**

1. Iron first cuff collar and joints.
2. Iron on the outer side of the fabric.
3. Moisturise clothes.
4. Withstand high heat.

Which of the statements given above is/are correct?

(a) Only 1 (b) 1 and 2
(c) 1, 3 and 4 (d) All of these

47 **Silk clothes do not tolerate, alkali and heat because these fabrics is/are**

1. Nitrogenous
2. Animal organ

Select the correct answer using the codes given below.

(a) Only 1 (b) Only 2
(c) Both 1 and 2 (d) None of these

48 **While washing fabrics of protein fibres bleeding can be prevented by**

1. vinegar
2. common salt
3. washing soda
4. acetic acid

Select the correct answer using the codes given below.

(a) 1 and 2 (b) 2 and 3
(c) 3 and 4 (d) 1 and 4

49 **Choose the correct sequence of steps followed while dyeing.**

1. After treatment
2. Preparation of fabric
3. Preparation of dye-bath
4. Addition of exhaustion agents

Codes

(a) 1, 2, 3, 4 (b) 2, 3, 4, 1
(c) 3, 4, 1, 2 (d) 4, 1, 2, 3

50 **Consider the following statements**

1. Garments, which have warm should not be put away until they have been throughly aired.
2. Washable garments should be laundered frequently.

Which of the statements given above is/are correct?

(a) Only 1 (b) Only 2
(c) Both 1 and 2 (d) None of these

51 Consider the following statements
1. Soap are made by a chemical combination of an oil and alkali such as soda.
2. Carbolic soaps are sometimes used, when on antiseptic required.
3. High class soaps usually have a hard highly polished textured and are delicately coloured and scented.

Which of the statements given above is/are correct?
(a) Only 1 (b) 1 and 2
(c) 1, 2 and 3 (d) None of these

52 Which of the following statements are correct?
1. Stains should be removed before washing the garments.
2. White coloured clothes should be separated from the coloured ones.
3. Big articles like bed linen, table linen should be separated.

Select the correct answer using the codes given below
(a) 1 and 2 (b) 2 and 3
(c) 1 and 3 (d) 1, 2 and 3

53 The advantage of using soap in laundry is/are
1. greasy dirt coagulates.
2. water and soap solutions makes cleaning easier.
3. enters the fibres move readily.

Select the correct answer using the codes given below
(a) 1 and 2 (b) 2 and 3
(c) 1 and 3 (d) All of these

54 Starch can be made from which of the following?
1. Sago 2. Arrowroot
3. Maida 4. Rice

Select the correct answer using the codes given below
(a) 1, 2 and 3 (b) 2, 3 and 4
(c) 1, 3 and 4 (d) All of these

55 Emulsification of dirt means
1. water is discarded.
2. greasy gramuals from fabric enters into water.
3. alkali from soap alkaline solution.
4. action of water on soap.

Select the correct answer using the codes given below
(a) Only 1 (b) 1 and 2
(c) 1, 2 and 3 (d) All of these

56 Calendaring is a mechanical finishing process, which used to
1. smooth the surface.
2. provide various surface effects.
3. lift the fibres from the fabric to form a soft fibrous surface.

Which of the statement(s) given above is/are correct?
(a) 1 and 2 (b) 1 and 3
(c) 2 and 3 (d) All of these

57 The clothes to be stored need
1. dry condition 2. clean
3. mended 4. use of insecticides

Select the correct answer using the codes given below
(a) 1, 2, 3 and 4 (b) 1, 2 and 3
(c) 1 and 2 (d) 3 and 4

58 Which of the following statement(s) is/are correct?
1. The grades vanes according to the types of measurement circumference length or width.
2. Plaids are design of woven or printed colours bars intersecting at right angles which could be even or uneven.

Select the correct answer using the codes given below
(a) Only 2 (b) Only 1
(c) Only 2 (d) None of these

59 Consider the following statements
1. The soap available in the market use various ingredients in their preparation like colour perfume and oils.
2. Broadly, soaps can be divided into hard soap and soft soap categories.

Which of the statement(s) given above is/are correct?
(a) Only 1 (b) Only 2
(c) Both 1 and 2 (d) None of these

60 Which of the following statements is/are oxidising agent?
1. Potassium permangnet
2. Hydrogen peroxide
3. Sodium perborate
4. Sodium hypochlorite

Select the correct answer using the codes given below
(a) 1, 2, 3 and 4 (b) 1 and 2
(c) 1, 2 and 3 (d) 1, 3 and 4

61 The stains can be removed by
1. oxidising agents
2. reducing agent

Select the correct answer using the codes given below
(a) Only 1 (b) Only 2
(c) Both 1 and 2 (d) None of these

62 Which of the following statement(s) is/are correct?
1. If sodium carbonate and washing soda is mixed in water the hardness of water can be removed.
2. The reaction of the chemicals produce sodium sulphate, sodium carbonate and insoluble calcium carbonate.
3. Magnesium sulphate chloride and magnesium carbonate is also produced.

Select the correct answer using the codes given below
(a) Only 1 (b) 1, 2 and 3
(c) 2 and 3 (d) None of these

63 Which of the following is not correct regarding auality standard?
(a) Sets level of performance for products.
(b) Increases cost of apparel manufacturing.
(c) It sets framework for quality process.
(d) It defines safety requirements.

64 ...... sheet is a technical document that contains the detail of the product.

(a) Apparel specifications (b) Apparel standards
(c) Laundry agents (d) Qualification

65 Specification sheet should contain

1. product sketch 2. Label placement
3. print placement 4. comment Section

Codes

(a) 1, 2, 3 (b) 1 and 4
(c) 2 and 3 (d) 1, 2, 3, 4

66 ...... is the strength of fabric which denotes breaking force required to rupture fabric.

(a) Tearing strength (b) Seam properties
(c) Tensile strength (d) Property strength

67 Which of the following are laundry agents?

1. Alkali 2. Bleaches
3. Starch 4. Fabric Conditioner

Codes

(a) 1 and 2 (b) 2 and 3
(c) 3 and 4 (d) 1, 2, 3 and 4

68 Alkali wash include which of the following compounds?

1. Washing Soda 2. Whiteners
3. Suspending agents 4. Sodium Hydroxide

Codes

(a) 1 and 2 (b) 1, 2 and 3
(c) 1 and 4 (d) 1, 2, 3 and 4

69 ...... is a stiffening agent used to impart a better appearance of the fabric.

(a) Starch (b) Optical brightener
(c) Oleic acid (d) aceti acid

70 Which of the following storage techniques are used for care and maintenance of clothing?

1. Use Plastic Bins 2. Wash Everything
3. Never Vacuum pack 4. Use a Wardrobe box

Codes

(a) 1 and 2 (b) 1, 2, 3 and 4
(c) 1 and 3 (d) Only 4

Directions (Q.Nos. 71-80) *In the questions given below are two statements, labelled as Assertion (A) and the Reason (R). In the context of two statements, which one of the following is correct?*

Codes

(a) Both (A) and (R) are true and (R) is the correct explanation of (A)
(b) Both (A) and (R) are true but (R) is not the correct explanation of (A)
(c) (A) is true and (R) is false
(d) (A) is false, but (R) is true

71 **Assertion** (A) Petrol, benzine, methylated spirit chloroform, carbon tetrachloride and mineral of grease solvent.

Reason (R) These solvents are liquid and evaporate easily.

72 **Assertion** (A) Bleaches could be oxidising and reducing.

Reason (R) The most common variety includes chlorine bleaches and hydrogen peroxide.

73 **Assertion** (A) Dry cleaning uses a solvent as the liquid in which the fabric is placed.

Reason (R) When only dry cleaning solvents are used, there is mineral damage to most fabrics.

74 **Assertion** (A) Clothes need to be soaked in water before washing.

Reason (R) This has many advantages especially in the washing of cotton and linen, as it economises on time, labour and soap.

75 **Assertion** (A) Washing process involves the application of pressure or friction in the presence of soap or detergent.

Reason (R) Washing should be done in soft water.

76 **Assertion** (A) The method used for removing dirt and cleaning the clothes depend on nature of fabric and a kind of dirt.

Reason (R) The dirt that soil the fabric consist of the dust particle which are either on the surface of fabric.

77 **Assertion** (A) Soft water is suitable for washing purpose.

Reason (R) The temperature of water should be according to the type of fibres of the fabric, like hot water for cottons warm for silk and lukewarm for woollens.

78 **Assertion** (A) The washing process involves the application of pressure of friction. Friction or pressure on coarse materials and strong cottons can be applied by scrubbing.

Reason (R) Washing of dedicate fabrics requires kneading ad squeezing by overiding much friction.

79 **Assertion** (A) Rayon garments undergo progressive shrinkage.

Reason (R) Hence, care has to be taken while drying and ironing.

80 **Assertion** (A) Direct dyes bleed while washing.

Reason (R) Therefore direct dyed fabrics are after treated with cationic agent.

PREVIOUS YEARS' QUESTIONS

July 2018

1 **Assertion** (A) Embroidery, sequins and applique form the structural design in a Garment.

Reason (R) Structural design is the surface enrichment of the Garment.

Codes

(a) Both A and R are correct
(b) Both A and R are incorrect
(c) A is correct but R is incorrect
(d) A is incorrect but R is correct

2 **Assertion** (A) Acid dyes are suitable for wool and silk.

Reason (R) Acid dyes form iconic bonds with the hydroxy groups found in wool and silk.

Codes

(a) Both A and R are correct
(b) Both A and R are incorrect
(c) A is correct but R is incorrect
(d) A is incorrect but R is correct

November 2017

3 **Assertion** (A) Sewing machine needles with set points are used for Knitted fabrics.

Reason (R) Set points have less tendency to penetrate the lower twist Knitting yarns and break them.

Codes

(a) Both A and R are correct
(b) Both A and R are incorrect
(c) A is correct but R is incorrect
(d) A is incorrect but R is correct

4 **Assertion** (A) BARS are generally considered the best and most effective means of performance appraisal.

Reason (R) The advantage of this method is that scales are easy to administer and applicable to all.

Codes

(a) Both A and R are correct
(b) Both A and R are incorrect
(c) A is incorrect but R is correct
(d) A is incorrect but R is incorrect

5 **Assertion** (A) Water repellant finishes produce a fabric that resist wetting and the penetration of water.

Reason (R) Water repellant fabrics are coated with rubber and are not comfortable as wearing apparel.

Codes

(a) Both A and R are correct
(b) A is correct and R are incorrect
(c) A is incorrect and R is correct
(d) Both A and R are incorrect

6 Structural jamming pucker can be prevented by

1. Using chain stitch
2. Using thicker thread
3. Using thinner thread
4. Using lock stitch
5. Reinforcing the seam

Codes

(a) 1, 2, 3 (b) 1, 3 , 5
(c) 3, 4, 5 (d) 2, 3, 4

7 Which of the following fibres are stretch fibres?

1. Neoprene
2. Spandex
3. Sisal
4. Lyo cell

Codes

(a) 1 and 2 (b) 2 and 3
(c) 2 and 4 (d) 4 and 1

8 **Assertion** (A) Maintenance of fabrics made from low twisted yarns is easier for the consumer.

Reason (R) Low twisted yarns shed soil easily since there is less space between the fibres for soil to settle.

Codes

(a) A is correct but R is incorrect
(b) A is incorrect but R is correct
(c) Both A and R are incorrect
(d) Both A and R are correct

9 **Assertion** (A) Applied design is the surface enrichment of the garment.

Reason (R) Application of tucks and pleats are examples of applied design.

Codes

(a) Both A and R are correct
(b) Both A and R are incorrect
(c) A is incorrect but R is correct
(d) A is correct but R is incorrect

10 Which of the following fibres can be confirmed by performing microscopic test?

(a) Wool (b) Silk
(c) Nylon (d) Acrylic

January 2017

11 **Assertion** (A) The most suitable method of printing with disperse dyes is transfer printing.

Reasoning (R) Disperse dyes sublime when heated to high temperature.

Codes

(a) Both A and R are incorrect
(b) Both A and R are correct
(c) A is correct but R is incorrect
(d) A is incorrect but R is correct

12 **Assertion** (A) Threadless bonding and welding offers a tangible alternative solution to the sewing of micro-fiber textiles.

Reason (R) This technology has the ability to produce narrow lap seams which are less bulky.

Codes
(a) Both A and R are incorrect
(b) Both A and R are correct
(c) A is correct but R is incorrect
(d) A is incorrect but R is correct

13 Give the correct sequence of making woolen felts.
1. Layering of wool fibers
2. Cleaning, blending and carding of wool fibers
3. Beating, compressing and squeezing the web.
4. Application of heat and moisture.
5. Imparting required finish to the felt.
6. Scouring, rinsing and drying

Codes
(a) 1, 2, 3, 4, 6 and 5 (b) 2, 1, 4, 3, 5 and 6
(c) 3, 4, 2, 1, 5 and 6 (d) 2, 1, 4, 3, 6 and 5

14 **Assertion** (A) Collars, seams and texture when put together create structural design.

Reason (R) Structural design is inherent parts of the garment.

Codes
(a) A is correct but R is incorrect
(b) A is incorrect but R is correct
(c) Both A and R are correct and R is the correct explanation of A
(d) Both A and R are correct, but R is not the correct explanation of A

15 Which of the following fibres have good resiliency?
1. Wool 2. Polyester 3. Rayon 4. Cotton

Codes
(a) 1, 3 (b) 3, 4 (c) 1, 2 (d) 1, 4

16 Which of the following is the theory of clothing?
(a) Individuality (b) Conformity
(c) Tattooing (d) Modesty

17 Denier is the weight in gms of
(a) 9000 metres of yarns (b) 1000 metres of yarn
(c) 560 metres of yarn (d) 840 metres of yarn

July 2016

18 Give the correct sequence of making Ajrakh.
1. Application of gum
2. Dyeing in myrobalam
3. Washing of fabric
4. Application of black colour
5. Dyeing with indigo
6. Application of alum

Codes
(a) 2, 3, 1, 4, 5 and 6 (b) 1, 2, 3, 4, 5 and 6
(c) 3, 2, 1, 4, 6 and 5 (d) 6, 5, 4, 1, 2 and 3

19 Which of the following fibres when taken away from flame continue burning with an after glow?
1. Cotton 2. Rayon
3. Silk 4. Nylon

Codes
(a) 1 and 2 (b) 2 and 3
(c) 3 and 4 (d) 1 and 4

December 2015

20 Give the correct sequence of manufacturing wool.
1. Shearing 2. Carding
3. Combing 4. Carbonising
5. Grading

Codes
(a) 1, 4, 5, 3 and 2 (b) 2, 3, 4, 5 and 1
(c) 1, 5, 4, 2 and 3 (d) 4, 5, 2 and 1

21 Give the correct sequence of cutting a garment.
1. Lay out plan
2. Taking measurements
3. Preparing of drafts
4. Tracing the stitching lines
5. Cutting the garment pieces

Codes
(a) 2, 3, 4, 5 and 1 (b) 2, 3, 1, 5 and 4
(c) 1, 2, 3, 4 and 5 (d) 5, 4, 3, 2 and 1

22 Give the correct ful form of ASTM.
(a) All Standards for Testing Materials
(b) American Society for Textiles and Materials.
(c) American Society for Testing Materials
(d) Australian Standards for Testing Materials.

23 Which of the following is a theory of clothing?
(a) Adornment (b) Conformity
(c) Individuality (d) Custom

June 2015

24 **Assertion** (A) Foaming is always undesirable in dyeing.

Reason (R) It leads to uneven dyeing and excessive foam leads to overflow of dye solution and loss of dye.

Codes
(a) Both A and R are correct
(b) Both A and R are incorrect
(c) A is correct, but R is incorrect
(d) A is incorrect, but R is correct

25 **Assertion** (A) Cross dyeing can produce multi-coloured fabrics.

Reason (R) Two or more fibre types in a fabric accept a different types of dye.

Codes
(a) A is correct but R is incorrect
(b) A is incorrect but R is correct
(c) Both A and R are incorrect
(d) Both A and R are correct

26 Assertion (A) While washing woolen garments kneading and squeezing method is used.

Reason (R) Scaly structure of wool cause felting due to friction.

Codes

(a) Both A and R are incorrect
(b) Both A and R are correct and R is the correct explanation.
(c) A is correct but R is not the correct explanation
(d) A is incorrect but R is correct.

27 Organization responsible for preventing unfair or deceptive trade practices in textile and textile products is

(a) AATCC
(b) Federal Trade Commission (FTC)
(c) Textile Fibre Products Identification Act (TEPIA)
(d) ASTM

December 2014

28 Assertion (A) Wool recovers readily from crushing and creasing.

Reason (R) It has excellent elongation property.

Codes

(a) A is correct, R is incorrect
(b) A is incorrect, R is correct
(c) A and R both are correct, explanation is incorrect.
(d) A and R both are incorrect.

29 Pigment colours are used in solution dyeing of the following fibres.

1. Nylon 2. Silk
3. Wool 4. Rayon

Codes

(a) 1 and 2 (b) 2 and 3
(c) 4 and 3 (d) 1 and 4

30 In a high quality garment which of the following are key seams and locations where pattern matching is expected?

1. Center front and Center back
2. Raglan sleeve
3. Seams with darts
4. Side seams
5. Pockets and Pocket flaps

Codes

(a) 1, 4 and 5 (b) 2, 3 and 4
(c) 3, 4 and 5 (d) 1, 2 and 3

31 Give the correct sequence for preparing the fabric for draping.

1. Measure the dress form 2. Tear the fabric
3. Press the fabric 4. Block the fabric
5. Mark the fabric 6. Straighten the fabric

Codes

(a) 2, 3, 1, 5, 4, 6 (b) 3, 2, 1, 5, 4, 6
(c) 6, 1, 2, 4, 3, 5 (d) 5, 4, 6, 1, 2, 3

32 While washing cotton fabrics colour can be prevented from bleaching by using

(a) Vinegar
(b) Common salt
(c) Sodium Carbonate
(d) Lissapol

33 Give the correct full form of SASMIRA.

(a) Silk And Synthetic Mills and Research Association.
(b) Synthetic and Art Silk Mills and Research Association
(c) Silk And Art Silk Mills and Research Association.
(d) Standards And Specifications of Mills and Research Association

June 2014

34 AATCC stands for

(a) American Association of Textile Chemists and Colourists.
(b) All Associations of Textile Chemists and Colourists.
(c) Association of American Textiles, Colours and Chemists.
(d) Australian Association of Textiles Chemists and Colourists.

35 Match the following symbols used in process chart with the event.

List I (Symbols)	List II (Events)
A. ○	1. Operation cum-transportation
B. ▽	2. Delay
C. D	3. Temporary Storage
D. ⇐	4. Transport
E. □	5. Inspection
F. ⇐ in circle	6. Inspection cum operation
G. ○	7. Operation
	8. Storage
	9. Movement

Codes

	A	B	C	D	E	F	G
(a)	7	8	2	4	5	1	6
(b)	7	4	8	9	5	1	6
(c)	7	2	4	5	1	8	5
(d)	6	8	2	4	5	1	7

36 Match the methods of dyeing given in List I with their explanation given in List II.

List I	List II
A. Union dyeing	1. Perforated spools containing yearns are dyed.
B. Cross dyeing	2. Textile material is constantly fed in the dye range.
C. Batch dyeing	3. Exhaust dyeing
D. Package dyeing	4. 2 or more fibre types are dyed in the same dye bath in the same shade.
	5. Dyeing blends in the same dye bath with two or more shades.

Codes

	A	B	C	D
(a)	1	3	2	4
(b)	2	1	4	3
(c)	1	2	3	5
(d)	5	1	2	4

37 E-commerce is an emerging field in the apparel sector due to

1. Increase in technology.
2. Global network.
3. Government policies.
4. Economic effectivity and feasibility.

Codes

(a) 1 and 2 are correct
(b) 2 and 3 are correct
(c) 3 and 4 are correct
(d) All of the above are correct

38 The most popularly used textiles in olden times in Egypt 2500BC was

1. Jute
2. Wool
3. Linen
4. Cotton

Codes

(a) 1 and 4 (b) 3 and 2
(c) 3 and 4 (d) 1 and 3

ANSWERS

Exam Based Questions

1 *(b)*	2 *(a)*	3 *(c)*	4 *(a)*	5 *(a)*	6 *(b)*	7 *(b)*	8 *(d)*	9 *(d)*	10 *(c)*
11 *(b)*	12 *(d)*	13 *(c)*	14 *(c)*	15 *(b)*	16 *(d)*	17 *(c)*	18 *(d)*	19 *(a)*	20 *(c)*
21 *(b)*	22 *(c)*	23 *(c)*	24 *(a)*	25 *(d)*	26 *(c)*	27 *(b)*	28 *(a)*	29 *(d)*	30 *(d)*
31 *(a)*	32 *(d)*	33 *(b)*	34 *(c)*	35 *(a)*	36 *(d)*	37 *(a)*	38 *(c)*	39 *(d)*	40 *(c)*
41 *(b)*	42 *(a)*	43 *(d)*	44 *(a)*	45 *(d)*	46 *(d)*	47 *(c)*	48 *(d)*	49 *(b)*	50 *(c)*
51 *(c)*	52 *(d)*	53 *(d)*	54 *(d)*	55 *(d)*	56 *(b)*	57 *(a)*	58 *(a)*	59 *(c)*	60 *(a)*
61 *(c)*	62 *(b)*	63 *(b)*	64 *(a)*	65 *(d)*	66 *(c)*	67 *(d)*	68 *(c)*	69 *(a)*	70 *(b)*
71 *(a)*	72 *(b)*	73 *(b)*	74 *(b)*	75 *(a)*	76 *(b)*	77 *(a)*	78 *(b)*	79 *(a)*	80 *(c)*

Previous Years' Questions

1 *(b)*	2 *(c)*	3 *(b)*	4 *(b)*	5 *(b)*	6 *(b)*	7 *(a)*	8 *(c)*	9 *(d)*	10 *(a)*
11 *(b)*	12 *(b)*	13 *(d)*	14 *(c)*	15 *(c)*	16 *(d)*	17 *(a)*	18 *(b)*	19 *(b)*	20 *(c)*
21 *(b)*	22 *(c)*	23 *(a)*	24 *(a)*	25 *(d)*	26 *(b)*	27 *(b)*	28 *(c)*	29 *(d)*	30 *(a)*
31 *(c)*	32 *(b)*	33 *(h)*	34 *(a)*	35 *(a)*	36 *(a)*	37 *(d)*	38 *(c)*		

Fashion, Designing and Selection of Clothes

Appearance is the most important factor in our daily life style. In current society personal appearance, dressing and clothing does matter a lot. Wearing clothes also carries specific cultural and social meanings and in this process designs play an important role. Clothing can be divided into apparels and accessories. Design communicate on behalf of wearer. Therefore selection of designs for clothing is very important consideration.

Fashion

Fashion is the style that is most popular at a given time. The term fashion implies following three components :

Style It is any particular characteristic or look in apparel or accessories. Style may come and go in fashion, but a specific style always remains the same, whether it is in fashion or not.

Acceptance It implies that consumers must buy and wear a style to make it a fashion. It is said that there is no fashion, if nobody buys it. Acceptance by a large number of people makes a fashion important. Designers plan styles to appeal to certain consumer groups. It is then up to public whether to make the offered style into a fashion by accepting it.

Timeliness It indicates change of fashion time to time. Many people criticise the changeability of fashion, but if fashion never change, the public would not continue to buy clothing.

Factors Affecting Fashion

There are various fashion trends that lead to the development of fashion industry. Some among them are as follows :

Economic Factor The economic factors such as recession, depression, inflation or affluence either accelerates or retards fashion technology and on going trends. It has

In this Chapter

been observed that the economically progressive society is flourished by on going fashion trends as fashion is directly related to the individual's earnings.

Social Factor The geographical area, living styles and standards of education are also important social factors influencing fashion. The demand of fashion is governed by various organisations, different religions, different personalities and socialites and people of all stages of life.

Political Factor A number of political factors affect small businesses in the clothing industry. The industry has repeatedly been affected by issues such as worker's right and child labour laws.

Technological Factor The developments in field of textiles due to research work, innovative methods and mass production has greatly influenced fashion outcome. Various technological inventions, communication facilities and travelling also has great impact on fashion trends.

Fashion Cycles

Fashion cycle is related to periodically repeated styles which may be recycled to tally or in parts and is accepted as fashion. Fashion designers play an important role in up bringing fashion areas by altering the clothing styles or time periods. Also they perceive ideas from museums and costume collections of various civilisations or culture of historical importance. The recycling process of fashion or style statement induces changes in sleeves, collars, skirt or type of pant leg and not the complete style. The progression of fashion cycles is accompanied by slow and rapid movements.

It means that introduction of fashion may become popular or may fade away. It is the public, who may accept or reject any style statement presented as fashion cycle or fashion process.

The steps of fashion cycle are as follows :

Innovation The beginning of a fashion cycle is marked with the introduction of fashion, creation or innovative approach in styles. Creative fashion designers possesses the ability of sensing public demands in advance and introduce major fashion trends which are accepted by public. The high fashion trends introduced by fashion designers are usually influenced by economic, social, political and technological factors. These high fashion is usually purchased by fashion innovators.

Rise Adoption of the fashion style takes place at the rising state. At this stage the fashion innovators communicates the fashion styles to the socialites through shows and magazines and there are equal chances of acceptance or rejection of fashion at this stage. If the fashion is accepted, it rises, purchased and worn by fashion admirers.

Acceleration The fashion style takes an upward zoom or is accelerated at this stage. Various versions of the original design is circulated in the fashion market with mostly the simplified versions of original design.

General Acceptance The production of the style on a mass level is the sign of acceptance of the style and thus, is called a fashion. The fashion fundamentalists show strong interest in the durability, practicality and costing of the fashion. When an style is in demand, generally all stores and show-rooms have their stocks.

Decline The saturation point of consumer interest in any style is the decline of that style and thus, the fashion also declines. Consumer gets bored of the same style having possessed by everyone and therefore, consumer starts searching for new styles leaving that particular style taking a downward slump.

Obsolescence The obsolete style is no longer a fashion, The manufacturing and storage of that style comes to an end. Also, it is no longer in use with the consumer, also called the end of that particular fashion cycle.

Fashion Theories and Adoption

Theories of fashion adoption or distribution are concerned with how fashion moves through the various socio-economic levels of society. There are three primary theories of fashion adoption trickle down, trickle across and trickle up. However, no one theory is adequate to discuss fashion theory or explain how fashion moves through society.

In addition to these theories, there is an alternate populist model of fashion adoption, which applies to some situations that identify fashion distribution as moving through social groups rather than socio-economic classes. Their description is given below :

Trickle–Down Theory

This theory is coined by economist **Thorstein Veblem** in 1889, which assumes that fashion begins in the upper echelon of society. Style worn by the wealthy change, and those changes are gradually adopted by the middle and lower classes. When those styles have been assimilated by the lower classes, the wealthy, in turn change their style and attire. This theory assumes that the lower classes want to emulate the upper classes and is the oldest theory of fashion adoption.

Trickle Across Theory

This theory developed in the late 1950s by **Robinson** and **King**. This theory assumes that fashion moves across socio-economic levels relatively rapidly. Clothing styles do not trickle down but appear at all price points at approximately the same time.

Mass communications and popular media support the existence of this theory, providing pictures and details about new styles, as does the modern retail world. Many designers show similar styles in a variety of lines, ranging from high end designer clothing to lower and affordable pieces.

Trickle-up Theory

The trickle-up theory was developed by **John Maynard Keynes** (1883-1946). This theory of fashion adoption reflects changing styles and practices in fashion. According to the theory, styles may begin with youth or street fashion and move progressively up the fashion ladder until they are favoured and worn by older and wealthier consumers. Once the styles have been adopted by more traditional consumers, the street or youth culture may adopt a new style.

Populist Model

While the three primary theories of fashion adoption largely apply to socio-economic levels, the populist model, conceived by anthropologist. A social group, such as punks in 1970's London, for instance, may adopt a distinctive style and appearance shared throughout the group. The style serves to unify the group and identify individuals within the group, but is often unrelated to trends outside of the group. Individuals adopt the style to become and remain an identifiable member of that particular social group.

Fashion Forecasting

Fashion forecasting is a global career that focuses on upcoming trends. A fashion forecaster predicts the colours, fabrics, textures, materials, prints, graphics, footwear, street style and other styles that will be presented on the runway and in the stores for the upcoming seasons. The concept applies to not one, but all levels of the fashion industry including haute couture, ready to wear, mass market and street wear. Fashion forecasting is responsible for attractive consumers and helping retail businesses and designers to sell their brands. Today, fashion industry workers rely on the internet to retrieve information on new looks, hot colour, celebrity wardrobes and designer collections.

The fashion forecasting process includes the basic steps of understanding the vision of the business and profit of target customers, collecting information about available merchandise, preparing information, determining trends and choosing merchandise appropriate for the company and target customer.

Fashion forceasting can be long-term and short-term.

Long-Term Forecasting

Long term forecasting is the process of analysing and evaluating trends that can be identified by scanning a variety of sources for information. It is a fashion which lasts over two years. While scanning the market and the consumers, fashion forecasters must follow demographics of certain areas, both urban and suburban, as well as examine the impact on retail and its consumers due to the economy, political system, environment, and culture. Long term forecasting seeks to identify: major changes in international and domestic demographics, shifts in the fashion industry along with market structures, consumer expectations, values and impulsion to buy, new developments in technology and science, and shifts in economic, political and cultural alliances between certain countries. There are many specialised marketing consultants that focus on long-term forecasting and attend trade shows and other events that notify the industry on what is to come.

Short-Term Forecasting

Short-term forecasting focuses on current events both domestically and internationally as well as pop culture in order to identify possible trends that can be communicated to the customer through the seasonal colour palette, fabric, etc. It gives fashion a modern twist to a classic look that intrigues our eyes. Some important areas to follow when scanning the environment are current events, art, sports, science and technology.

Fashion Terminology

Term	Description
Basic Fashion	
Style	A particular design, shape or type of apparel item. It is best defined by the distinct features that create its overall appearance. e.g. A–line skirts, Bermuda shorts or Western Shirts.
Fashion	The prevailing type of clothing that is favoured by a large segment of the public at any given time.
Fad	Temporary, passing fashion. Around only for a short period of time.
Classic	Item of clothing that continues to be popular even though fashions change. e.g., The little black dress
Apparel	Refers to any men's, women's or children's clothing.
Garment	A particular article of apparel e.g. a dress, suit, coat or sweater.
Basic Sketching	
Silhouette	The shape of a clothing style. Formed by the width and length of the neckline, sleeves, waistline and pants or shirts.
Croquis	A rough, preliminary drawing or sketch.
Fit	It refers to how tight or loose a garment is on the person wearing it.

Term	Description
Bodice	The area above the waist in a garment.
Haute Couture	Literally means 'finest dressmaking' in French. Refers to the high fashion industry or fashion houses with a designer who creates original, individually designed fashions.
Ready to Wear Garments	Garments that are mass produced in factories. Garments that are mass produced in factories. Garments Garments that are mass produced in factories.
Body Shapes	
Tall and Thin	Almost all fabrics can be worn well by people with this build. Should avoid wearing tight, straight dresses, skirts or pants.
Tall and Heavy	Tend to look their best in garments with simple lines and little decoration. We should avoid loud prints, checks, plaids and stripes.
Short and Heavy	The best in garments providing the illusion of height. Vertical lines are preferable. One should avoid two-piece or two-coloured garments.
Large Upper Body	Dark, dull plain fabrics in simple, slim tailored tops. Should avoid wearing clingy, shiny fabrics or large, bright prints on top.
Large Lower Body	Garments including vertical lines pointing towards necklines as well as wide shoulder lines. Should avoid tight fitting pants or skirts, especially those with patch pockets, as well as shirts that end at the hipline.
Face Shapes	
Oval	Slightly narrow at the jaw line.
Rectangular	Long and slender Forehead and area below cheeckbones are of the same width.
Round	This face shape is fuller with a found hairline.
Square	If you have a strong jawline as well as a strong hairlines.
Heart	Wider and the forehead and temples with a narrow and delicate chin.
Triangular	Broaden chin and narrow forehead.

Designing

Designing means to map every part of any style in such a way that it will result in beautiful fabric. In such a design, not only the fitting is perfect but all the style lines are well formulated and should be fashionable. Keeping in view the changing fashion, various patterns are structured. Natural abilities, fashion sense and personal interest helps the designer to create a new and unique designs.

Elements of Design

The elements of design are flexible and should be interpreted within the context of current fashion. Elements of design are those components which an apparel designer employs in designing the garments.

A design can be defined as an arrangement of lines, shape, colours and texture that create a visual image. The principles of design are the guides that govern how elements are combined. The elements are therefore the raw materials in design that must be combined successfully.

Following are the elements of design :

Dot

It is known as basic element of point. It is the smallest unit suggesting its presence and location. The sizes of the dots also convey a message. The bigger the dot is, the more enlarged the surface appears, and vice versa. Hence, a thin figure should wear a dress of bigger dots to conceal the figure problem. Points joined and proceeding towards one side indicate direction. A chain of dots become a line.

There are various types of Dots.

- Irregularly space/uneven
- Regularly space/even
- Big dots
- Small dots
- Scattered dots

Various Pattern of Dots

Line

It is the distance between two points joined together. It is a chain of dots joined together indicating direction. Line is the simplest and most important of the design elements and is incorporated into the other elements. All lines have directions, length and width. Line is the basic requirement for almost all designs. It provides the visual dimensions of length and width.

When lines combine, space is enclosed and forms and shapes are defined. Lines offer a path of vision for the eyes when a person is wearing an object/outfit with lines creating various illusions. The arrangement of lines in clothing design can cause to appear a person look heavier or thinner than his actual size.

Types of Lines

Basically there are four types of lines. These are :

Vertical Lines These produce an illusion of added height to the outfit design by adding and contrasting coloured vertical bark in the centre or a centre panel added with a vertical line gives an added height to the outfit. These lines tend to make a short person look tall. Vertical lines on a dress are shown below :

A dress with vertical lines

Horizontal Lines These lines add width to the garment and decrease the apparent height e.g. a wide contrasting coloured belt shortens the height of the figure by cutting the garments into two segments, however the belt has the effect of slimming the waist line. The coloured belt will not shorten the height of the outfit well as the wearer. Horizontal lines on a dress are shown below :

A dress with horizontal lines

Diagonal Lines These lines can add or decrease the height of the wearer depending on their slope.

Long uninterrupted diagonals tilting almost vertically are the most lengthening and most dramatic of all lines. Diagonal lines on a dress are shown below :

A dress with diagonal lines

Curved Lines These lines are pensive by nature. Curved lines can be a full circle or may even appear almost straight. Curved lines are considered graceful and feminine and can be seen in the soft folds of material in a draped dress or a ruffled collar. Curved lines on a dress are shown below :

A dress with curved lines

Form and Shape

Any object have three dimensions like length, width and depth. The human body is a form and by viewing it analytically, its various perspectives are revealed. The human form changes visually with clothing, especially as fashion changes. Shape describes the outer dimensions or contour of an object.

Through clothing design, the shape of the human body is often revealed in a natural way, but sometimes even distorted. The shape of clothing in a human body, communicates silently, the message about the wearer. Every fashion period has a specific shape of garment. It has been observed that an easy fitting shape of the garment is easily accepted where as a tight fitting garment is generally short lived since it is suitable to only perfect figure types.

Shape is flat space closed by a line and in clothing, it is defined as a flat, two-dimensional area enclosed by a line. When both ends of a line meet to surround space, the line forms a shape. Shapes have both physical and psychological effects based on the lines surrounding them.

Space within the shapes and separating the shapes also has an effect. The word shape usually suggests geometric shapes and there are many shapes. Some of these are discussed below :

Rectangle Dresses of rectangle shape are long, straight, hanging in loose graceful folds, such as in Greek and Roman styles. For example, straight lines sheaths; tailored suits.

A dress with rectangle shape

Triangle Dresses of triangle shape are generally of Spanish styles, fitted bodies, bell-shaped and gently widening skirt.

A dress with triangle shape

Inverted Triangle Dresses of interverted triangle shape have wide shoulders, narrow skirt.

A dress with inverted triangle shape

Oval Dresses of oval shape are draped and softly molded. These are very feminine and decorative. These are good for well proportioned, ideal figure. These are suitable, especially for afternoon and evening wear.

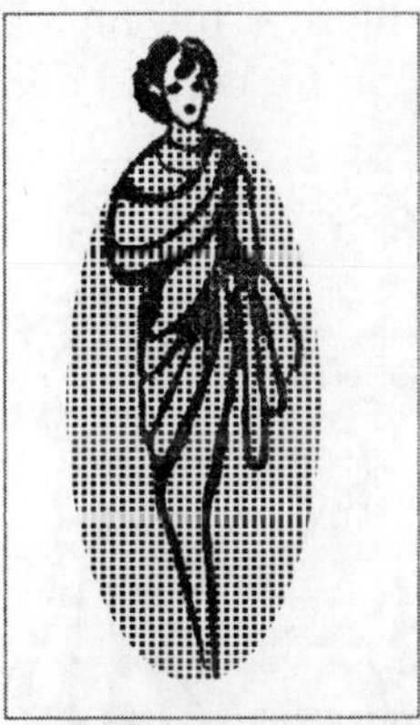

A dress with oval shape

Square Dresses of square shape have straight or boat shaped neckline, bony jackets. Generally this style is very good for the very thin figure, however, with proportions well planned and good design, can camouflage various figure irregularities.

A dress with square shape

Round Dresses of round shape consist of wide lined skirts, petal shapes, puffed sleeves. These are suitable for formal wear or afternoon frocks. This type of design is most attractive on the very young and the very thin figured women.

A dress with round shape

Hourglass Dresses of hourglass shape have wide shoulders, natural waist smooth fit over the hips and full skirt at bottom. These are suitable for tall and thin figure.

A dress with hourglass shape

Colour

Colour is the visual element. Colour carries aesthetic, visual, and commercial value. The colours present in rainbow are available colours of spectrum called VIBGYOR, i.e., Violet, Indigo, Blue, Green, Yellow, Orange and Red. But there are only three basic colours i.e Red, Yellow, Blue.

By mixing the three basic colours, secondary colours are obtained. Tertiary colours are obtained from secondary colours. When all colours of light are absorbed, it gives black colour whereas if all colours are reflected back from some surface, it gives white colour. Red and yellow makes orange, yellow and blue makes green whereas blue and red makes violet colours. Tertiary colours are made by mixing primary and secondary colours in equal colours.

A colour can have visual, physical and psychological effect. When we talk about principles of designing, or when we start off with a given design theme that first thing to occur to our minds is the colour and texture of the fabric.

Every season or now and then a colour emerges in the fashion scene which is decided by the leading manufacturers, exporters and textile experts of the fashion world. Also while choosing a colour one must be utmost careful as colour creates the first impression and hence can glorify or destroy ones appearance. Even simple silhouette may be enhanced by using effective colour schemes. Colour is the most exciting design element as it is the first thing noticed in a garment attracted by consumers.

Colour is the major deciding factor. Colour is a property of light, a sensation, which occurs when light enters eyes. Colour enables one to express themselves, to affect the feeling, and also reveal the personality of the wearer. Colour has the power to thrill and shock, irritate or soothe, attract or repel. A detailed study on colour will be dealt in later chapters. As texture is the feel, drape and degree of stiffness and softness of the fabric, it also creates a visual effect upon the wearer.

Texture

Texture is the element of design that describes surface appearance and feel understood by sight as well as by touch. It also means the appearance of the fabric. It is quality of roughness or smoothness, dullness or glossiness, stiffness or softness.

Some words to describe the texture of fabrics are: rough, smooth, dull, shiny, firm, crisp, fuzzy, bulky, etc. Texture is defined as tactile quality of a fabric. Hand refers to the tactile aspects of the fabric. Texture has the definite physical dimensions of weight, size, bulk and shape.

There are two types of textures-**structural texture**, which is created when fabrics or garments are manufactured, and **added visual textures**, which come when a design is printed onto the fabric surface. There are various components like fibres, yarns, fabrics and finishes that determine texture.

Determinants of Texture

Texture is determined by the arrangement of the component parts in fabric. These are the fibre, the yarn, the weave and the finish that make up a fabric.

Fibres Fibres are hairline strands that are made into yarns. Fibres of wool produce soft textures while that of linen, produce crisp textures. The short fuzzy fibres of cotton will produce a dull appearance due to the fuzz. The smooth and long filaments like silk fibres and synthetic fibres make fabrics that are shiny, smooth and cool touch fabrics.

Yarn Yarns produced from fibers that are twisted in different ways. A yarn which has a low twist will produce a shiny texture because the natural gloss of fiber is not lost in the twist, where as a highly twisted yarn gives a rough texture. Novelty yarns that are looped or coiled in manufacture of yarn create interesting surface contours too,

Fabric Fabric is constructed either by weaving, knitting, felting, bonding, crocheting or braiding techniques. Often this construction of the fabric determines the texture. A satin weave of loosely twisted yarns produces shiny textures whereas knits absorb light and are dull textured.

Finish Finish is given to fabric after it is constructed. Finishes like sizing gives stiffness, moireingadds shine and watermark design to the fabric, calendaring gives shine to the fabric, singeing makes the surface smooth and napping makes the fabric fuzzy.

Principles of Design

Designing is the process of combining known components in different ways to create new products or effects. An understanding of how the elements and principles work, and how to manipulate them, enables the designer to create different visual effects and to analyse and appreciate all art forms. Principles of design are guidelines for the use of the elements of design to create attractive garments, different forms of expression in an artistic manner. They are used for creating, discussing and evaluating garment designs on and off the individual/dress form. In order to arrange the elements of design well, principles like balance, proportion, emphasis and unity/harmony are essential.

Principles of design include :

- Harmony
- Balance
- Rhythm
- Emphasis
- Proportion

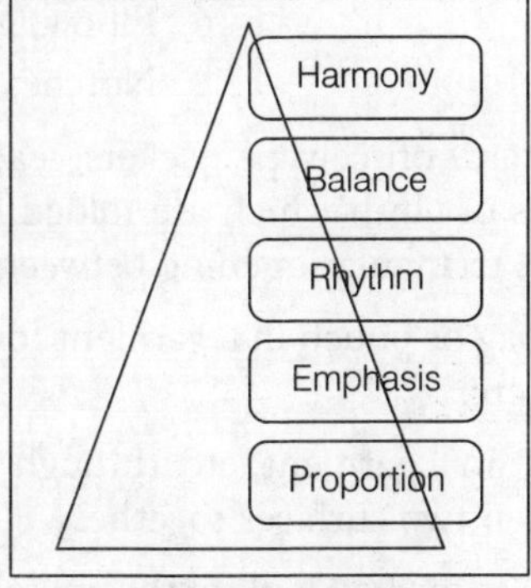

Principles of Design

Description of the principles of design is given below :

Harmony

When design elements and principles work together successfully they create harmony. Unity is also called harmony in design. It is a pleasing visual unity, the relationship among all parts within a whole design. When a design has unity, it gives an overall impression, a feeling of belongingness to the composition that attracts and holds the attention of the observer and gives a balanced look to the design.

Balance

Balance means pose, equilibrium, stability and security. The average human body is visually symmetrical which mean that the body seems to be same on each side of a central line. When important details or decorations are designed for a dress, they should be grouped in such a way that there seems to be equal interest or weight on each side of an imaginary center of the garment. When the design elements are in balance, a pleasing harmony is established. Balance in garments is produced by structural parts and by added decoration. Balance in clothing refers to a visual distribution of weight, from a central area.

Rhythm

Rhythm is an important principle of art created by repeated use of the design. It has a feeling of organised movement as the arrangement of the design elements makes the eye move easily over the apparel areas. Though repetition of pattern is required, it is not always very essential to obtain. Rhythm can be created in a garment with repetition, gradation, transition, opposition or radial arrangement of various parts of design and also the fabric design.

Emphasis

Emphasis involves the concentration of interest in the selected area of design when compared with other subordinated areas. Designers often create emphasis partially though the careful arrangement of line, texture and colours. There is some portion in every dress which is the centre of attraction. Emphasis is concentration of interest in one area called eye arresting area of a design that acts as the center of attention. It is the center of attention of an outfit. Without any such centre of interest, an outfit looks unplanned and monotonous too. When many focal points are created in a dress, a jumbled, confusing design results. So, it is best for instance, to leave the cuffs, hemline and other areas of a dress fairly plain if the neckline is being emphasised.

Some methods to lay emphasis include :

- Grouping of design units.
- Using of contrast of hues.
- By leading lines.
- A combination of any of the above elements.
- Repeating details such as tucks gathers, button, etc.
- Unusual shapes and textures.
- Applied design on a contrast background.

Proportion

Proportion is sometimes called scale. Proportion includes the relationship of height, width, depth and surrounding space of each design. When all the parts work well together, the garment is well proportioned. Good proportion refers to pleasing relationship between the sizes of various design details in a dress and between the garment itself and the design details. Unequal parts are more interesting than when all areas are exactly equal in size. Also, an odd number of parts, such as three, is more interesting than an even number such as two or four. Of course, fashions that make the body look distorted, or out of proportion, are sometimes referred as popular fads too. Proportion in relation to clothing design and to that of body conformation is important aspect to be considered to create a well-proportioned garment style. The given figure shows garment styles in different proportions. Note the interesting effects created by each of the proportions on the figure.

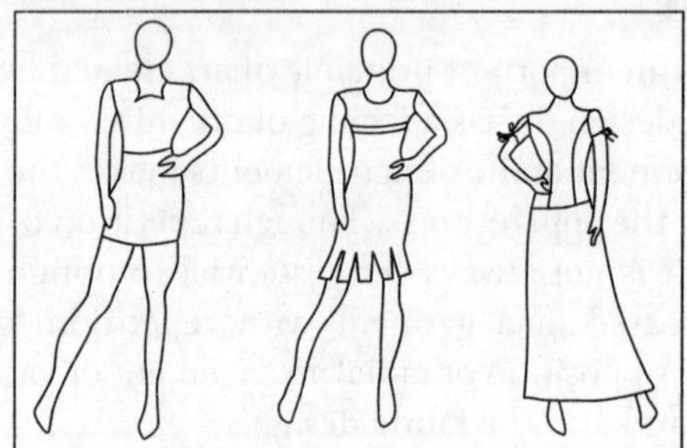

Proportion of Apparel

Types of Designs

There are two basic types of design, these are as follows :

Structural Design

The design is formed by stitching pieces together like collar, cuff, yoke, pleats, etc., requirements of structural design are :

- It should be suited to the purpose.
- It should be simple and well proportionate.
- It should be suited to the material, by which it is made and to the process that will be followed in making it.

Decorative Design

Decorative design is made after the dress is stitched e.g. by putting buttons, frills or lace, etc., through embroidering with different colours patch work or dying in different colours. For designing a dress, different lines, curves, colours and textures are used. These elements should be blended in such a way as to make the design beautiful. For this, knowledge of basic principles of art is essential. Elements of art are used on the basic of these principles only. These principles guide us about the proper use of various elements.

Parts of Garments

Garments are important because they reflect individual's culture, personality and preferences. People can use clothing to enhance personal appearance and protect the body from extreme temperatures and elements.

Parts of garments are :

Collars Most collars fall into one of three types i.e. flat collars, turn over or straight collar and stand up collars.

The first group encompasses flat collars, which turn away from the neckline and lie flat on the shoulder. This type of collar has the neckline cut to the same shape as the neckline of the garment itself. These collars should be cut with the straight of grain parallel to the centre back, an example is the peter pan collar. The turn over or straight collars are **like shirt collars** and collars with reverse. These stand up at the back for about half their depth and then fold over and fall down to cover the neckline seam. The neck edge of these collars is only very slightly curved. It is the joining of a straight edge to a curved one as well as the relation of the outer edge to the neck edge that causes the collar to rise and fall at the back neck edge *e.g.,* mandarin collars. These stand up and turn over. These collars should be cut either exactly on the bias or exactly on the straight of the grain.

Yoke A fitted part of a garment, especially around the neck, shoulders and chest or around the hips, to which a gathered, pleated, flared, or unfitted part is attached.

Sleeve Sleeve is a section of the garment that covers all part of arm. Sleeves can be of different designed like short, long, add width to the shoulder or minimise the shoulder. There are various parts of sleeves, some of them are given below :

1. Sleeve Cap
2. Cap Height
3. Bisceps Level
4. Sleeve Ease
5. Cap Ease
6. Elbow Level
7. Wrist Level
8. Notches

Lapel In standard office-type jackets, each of the two triangular pieces of cloth which are folded back below the throat, leaving a triangular opening between.

Pocket A small bag or pouch in a garment for carrying small articles, money etc.

Buttonhole A slit in a garment, etc, through which a button is passed to fasten two surfaces together.

Cuff These give a finished look to the end of a sleeve. They are had together with buttons or cuff links.

Part A triangular bold of fabric stitched to a point, to give garment a shape and bit it to the body.

Inseam Inside leg measurement from the crotch to the hem edge of the pants. Men's pants are often sold by inseam garments.

Pleats Folds of fabric that are unstitched and pressed in place. Typical places to find pleats are the back of shirts, pant blunts and skirts.

Application of Apparel Design

Apparel design is the art of applying design, aesthetics and natural beauty to clothing and its accessories. Designers conduct research on fashion trends and interpret them for their audience. Their specific designs are used by manufacturers.

This is the essence of a designer's role; however, there is variation within this that is determined by the buying and merchandising approach, and product quality; for example, budget retailers will use inexpensive fabrics to interpret trends, but high-end retailers will ensure that the best available fabrics are used.

Selection of Clothing for Different Age Groups

Clothes worn by an adult woman are definitely not the same as those worn by a college going girl. Similarly, men will prefer to wear light and comfortable clothes rather than fashionable ones. The description of selection of clothing by different age groups is given below :

Infant Wear

The clothing requirements from birth to 12 months of age are few. The major requirements of the newborn are for warmth, comfort and cleanliness.

Clothes should be soft and light as babies have tender and delicate skin. Since, they are sleeping most of the time, their clothes should be simple to put on and taken off easily. It is also important that they should be easy to maintain.

Cotton shirts that slip on or that have double breasted front opening with shapes are some easy wear style. The diapers should be made of absorbent and soft cotton material.

School Going Children

Children of this age group are in the growing style. They like the run about and play and are very active. Hence, their clothes must be made of strong and durable fabrics which can take a lot of wear and tear.

While selecting, do take care to see that there is adequate cloth inside the seams which can be opened up to fit rapidly growing children. The clothes must also be easy to launder as they get dirty frequently.

Latent Teen Years

This is the age when one starts going to college. Teenagers are very conscious about clothes and latest styles. They like to have variety in their clothes because they do not want to repeat the same dress every day.

For them, fitting and style are important, quality of clothes and construction is not often considered. It is advisable to select clothes which they can mix and match so that they can achieve variety with few clothes eg: few colours of churidars or salwars can be combined with few 'Kameez' which can go with all legwears.

Similarly, if a teenaged boy gets a couple of pair of jeans and a few T-shirts, he can combine them to achieve variety in his wardrobe.

Adults

Selection of clothes for adults depends to a large extent upon the type of work that a person is engaged in. A working woman will need clothes which are easy to launder and which do not need much ironing because she has very limited time. She will also prefer to wear clothes which do not easily wrinkle as she must look good till the end of the day.

Old Age

In the old age, the body becomes stiff, the eye sight becomes weak and energy level is considerably reduced. You must wear light material clothes in this age. The clothes they wear must be loose and comfortable rather than fashionable. These clothes should be front open and have large buttons and button holes.

Selection of Fabrics for Different End Uses

There are various types of fabric used for different things. Fabric used for curtains is different from the fabric used for apparel or the intimate garments. A particular type of fabric is used for a particular end use.

The difference in fabrics is due to difference in fabric properties that depends on fibre, yarn, fabric construction techniques and also the finishes given to the fabric.

Fabric selection is a crucial step because fabrics are designed for specific applications. A fabric manufactured for one purpose may not be adaptable for another use. Therefore, selecting the appropriate fabric is only the first step in providing serviceable fabrics for apparel manufacturing. Designers specify the fabric as part of their design concept.

Fabrics used in garment manufacturing can be categorised into two groups i.e. on the basis of **properties** and **characteristics**.

A property is a static physical dimension such as yards per pound, whereas characteristics is the reaction of the fabrics when a force is imposed upon it. Elongation, elasticity, shrinkage and seam strength are examples of characteristics.

Properties of Fabric

The properties required for the selection of fabric and their influence on selection of textiles and clothing is as follows :

Overall Thickness The thickness of a fabric is defined by the distance between the face and backside of the fabric. It is measured at a specific pressure using a fabric thickness guage. Thickness is important if the fabric needs to be sewn or cut by the manufacturer.

Overall Width The width of the fabric must be measured under standard conditions and is expressed in centimetres. Many factors can cause variation in the width measurement including moisture, tension and contractions during finishing. If the cloth's width changes, other parameters, such as area density and threads per centimetre will be affected.

Elasticity The ability of a strained material to recover to its original size and shape immediately after removal of stress that causes deformation.

Strength Fabric strength is the load per inch-width that a fabric can withstand before breaking.

Abrasion Resistance It is the ability of a fibre or fabric to withstand surface wear and rubbing. A high abrasion resistance is especially important for cords ropes that will be rubbing along a support or hold.

Characteristics or Features of Fabric Selection

There are three major categories of fabric characteristics that interest the apparel manufacturer. They are :

Style Characteristics These are those changes which affect the emotional appeal, the fabric imparts to the consumer. This is exemplified when a consumer handles a fabric and refers to the fabric such as stiff, soft, etc.

The three basic characteristics for style characteristics are :

- **Hand Characteristics** These are the changes of the fabric with hand manipulations, which exert tensile compression, molding or supporting forces on the fabric. The hand characteristics include some of the utility characteristics such as elongation, elasticity, flexibility, etc.
- **Tactile Characteristics** It refers to the changes in surface contour that result from a mechanical force exerted on or against the surface structure. Designers specify tactile characteristics with terms such as soft, coarse, rough, hard, smooth, sticky, oily and greasy.
- **Visual Characteristics** These are the changes in the colour values when either the fabric or light is moved.

Utility Characteristics These are the changes in the fit, comfort and wearing functions of the garment when the fabric engages a mechanical thermal, electrical or chemical force during the utilisation of the garment. The two major types of utility characteristics are transmission and transformation. Transmission characteristics include : Air permeability, heat transmission, light permeability, moisture transmission, etc. While, the transformation characteristics include shrinkage, crease resistance, colour fastness, dimensional stability, etc.

Durability Characteristics These are the capacities of fabric to maintain the style and utility characteristics during wear. It includes :

- Abrasive strength (measure of rubbing action)
- Tensile strength
- Launder-ability (measure of washing)
- Fire resistance
- Corrosive strength (measure of chemical action, acid or alkaline)
- Dry cleaning durability (measure of dry cleaning performance)

Thus, the properties and characteristics required for selecting the fabrics depend upon the method of construction. We can choose the fabrics according to the end use.

EXAM BASED QUESTIONS

1 What is fashion?

(a) Fashion is the get up of the clothes that are made from the fabric
(b) Fashion is the style that is most popular at a given time
(c) Fashion is associated with wearing clothes related to children clothing
(d) Fashion is popular accessories that are used to decorate home.

2 What makes fashion, a fashion?

(a) Production and supply should be well formulated
(b) When we see the fickleness in the wearing pattern of the people of different age group
(c) When a consumer buys and wears a style to make it a fashion
(d) When due to the fabric, the style changes with respect to age

3 What is the major significance of fashion?

(a) Fashion indicates change
(b) Fashion shows the long lasting nature of clothes
(c) Fashion is the stagnant position that is only suitable for particular time and position
(d) Fashion is all about forgetting the past fashion and concentrating on new

4 What do you mean by Apparel?

(a) Any temporary, passing fashion is apparel
(b) Thing that is responsible for the overall appearance of the personality
(c) Refers to any men's, women's or children's clothing
(d) All of the above

5 What is said to be the particular article of the apparel?

(a) Fashion (b) Garment
(c) Style (d) Classic

6 What is said about Bodice?

(a) Silhouette (b) Croquis
(c) Fit (d) Bodice

7 Which among the following have face shapes categorised?

(a) Oval (b) Heart
(c) Triangular (d) All of these

8 What is said about fashion cycle?

(a) It is timeliness of trend
(b) It is periodically repeated style
(c) It is same overall
(d) It does not give time for innovation.

9 Fashion designers have to take a lot of things into consideration when developing a new design. Which of the following statements is incorrect?

(a) Velvet has gloss and direction of pile. The most important consideration when using velvet is the direction of the pile
(b) The same colour scheme means, to use different intensity
(c) The use of bias cut can create the best draping effect
(d) Triad colour matching method is a strong, dramatic and fashionable colour combination

10 What marks the decline of fashion?

(a) Wrong fabric choice
(b) Wrong clothing style for wrong group
(c) Saturation point of consumer
(d) All of the above

11 Which among theme is not the fashion adoption theory?

(a) Trickle across (b) Trickle up
(c) Trickle through (d) Trickle down

12 Who was responsible for Trickle down theory?

(a) Marx (b) Weber
(c) Thorstein Veblen (d) Aristotle

13 What is the fashion trend in trickle down theory?

(a) Lower to middle class
(b) Middle to lower class
(c) Upper and middle on same platform
(d) Upper to middle and lower class

14 What is fashion forecasting?

(a) A global career that focuses on upcoming trends
(b) A fabric demand in the market
(c) Acceptability of cloth according to the cloth selection
(d) None of the above

15 Which of the following statements is not suitable for describing lines used in fashion design?

(a) You should use vertical line design at the front of bodices to increase 'vision height'
(b) You should use horizontal line design in puff sleeves to increase 'vision width'
(c) You should use diagonal line design in skirts to increase 'energetic feeling in vision'
(d) You should use curved line design hemlines to increase 'rhythm in vision'

16 Cuff where both ends flush with placket edges and cufflinks are used in this case

(a) Roll up cuff
(b) Lapped cuff
(c) French cuff
(d) Contoured cuff

17 A close fitting standing band which extends up from neckline and may be designed to meet at the CF which overlap or end somewhere between the shoulder and CF of the garment?

(a) Wing collar
(b) Bertha collar
(c) Mandrin collar
(d) Collar stand

18 A line from where fold comes over and divides collar into stand and outer collar section
(a) roll line (b) neck line
(c) rolled edge (d) collar edge

19 A pocket, which is stitched on garment piece as a patch?
(a) Welt pocket (b) Bound pocket
(c) Patch pocket (d) I seam pocket

20 Principles of design does not include
(a) colour (b) rhythm
(c) harmony (d) emphasis

21 For children's play clothes it is better to assure
(a) large pockets (b) comfort
(c) freedom of movements (d) absorbency

22 Ready-made garments are preferred to tailored garments, because of
(a) their colour fastness
(b) their durability
(c) their cost
(d) their ready availability

23 Fullness in garments can be achieved by the use of
(a) darts (b) pleats
(c) tucks (d) All of these

24 Sewing machine runs heavily due to
(a) lack of oiling and cleaning
(b) belt too loose
(c) more pressure on presser foot
(d) thread clogged in the shuttle

25 Point which forms the shape of pattern, without these points you cannot redraw your pattern and the point is called
(a) split point (b) cross mark
(c) cardinal point (d) zero point

26 A line where collar is joined to neck
(a) neck line (b) collar line
(c) roll line (d) None of these

27 Smoothing, shaping and rounding off angular lines is done by
(a) shaping (b) blending
(c) ironing (d) None of these

28 Which of the following statements is/are correct in men's tailoring?
(a) Ferepart is the front section of a jacket or coat
(b) Seat angle is the angle of the back fork line of trousers
(c) Button stand is the distance between the button line and the front edge of the garments
(d) All of the above

29 Which among the following are design elements?
(a) Dot (b) Texture
(c) Both a and b (d) Neither a nor b

30 How many times are classified in apparels?
(a) Seven (b) Eleven
(c) Three (d) Five

31 What makes an object three dimensional?
1. Length 2. Width
3. Height 4. Depth
Codes
(a) 1 and 2 (b) 2 and 4
(c) 1, 2 and 4 (d) All of these

32 Fabric part needle of a sewing machine includes
1. Set point needle
2. Ball point needle
Select the correct answer using the codes given below
(a) Both 1 and 2 (b) Only 1
(c) Only 2 (d) None of these

33 Arrange the correct threading sequence pattern of a sewing machine.
1. Needle
2. Spool
3. Thread take up lever
4. Tension discs
Codes
(a) 1, 2, 4 and 3 (b) 2, 4, 3 and 1
(c) 3, 1, 2 and 4 (d) 4, 3, 1 and 2

34 Which among the following is/are parts of a sewing machine?
1. Butt, shank, shoulder
2. Blade, long groove, short groove
3. Eye, point, scarf
4. Tip
Select the correct answer using the codes given below
(a) 1, 2, 3 and 4 (b) 1, 2 and 3
(c) 1 and 2 (d) 3 and 4

35 Sleeves most appropriate for infants garment are
1. Leg of mutton 2. Saddler
3. Kimono 4. Raglan
Select the correct answer using the codes given below
(a) 1 and 2 (b) 1 and 3
(c) 2 and 3 (d) 3 and 4

36 Arrange the correct sequence of cutting a sleeve pattern.
1. Marking the stitching line
2. Tracing the stitching line
3. Cutting the sleeve pattern
4. Marking the cutting line
Select the correct answer using the codes given below
(a) 2, 1, 4 and 3 (b) 1, 4, 3 and 2
(c) 3, 2, 1 and 4 (d) 4, 3, 2 and 1

37 Notch is a symbol used for marking
1. seam allowance
2. centre lines
3. identify parts
4. sleep cap, placements
Select the correct answer using the codes given below
(a) 1, 2, 3 and 4
(b) 1, 2 and 3
(c) 1 and 2
(d) 3 and 4

38 Match the following.

List I (Principles of Design)	List II (Description)
A. Harmony	1. Concentration of interests in the selected area of design when compared with other subordinated areas.
B. Emphasis	2. When a design has unity it holds the attention of the observer and gives a balanced look to the design.
C. Rhythm	3. A visual distribution of weight from a central area.
D. Balance	4. It can be created in a garment with repetition, gradation, transition or radical arrangement of design.
E. Proportion	5. It includes the relationship of height, width, depth and surrounding space of each design.

Codes

	A	B	C	D	E		A	B	C	D	E
(a)	1	2	3	4	5	(b)	2	1	4	3	5
(c)	3	4	5	1	2	(d)	5	3	2	4	1

39 Which among the following is said to be the component of fashion?

1. Style 2. Acceptance
3. Formation 4. Timeliness

Codes

(a) 1 and 2 (b) 3 and 4
(c) 1, 2 and 3 (d) 1, 2 and 4

40 What are the factors that influence fashion?

1. Economic factor 2. Social factor
3. Political factor 4. Technological factor

Codes

(a) Only 1 (b) 2 and 4
(c) All of these (d) None of these

41 Match the following.

List I	List II
A. Fab	1. Temporary and passing fashion
B. Classic	2. A particular article of apparel
C. Apparel	3. Style that continues even when fashion changes
D. Garment	4. Refers to men's, women's or children's clothing

Codes

	A	B	C	D		A	B	C	D
(a)	1	3	2	4	(b)	1	2	3	4
(c)	1	3	4	2	(d)	4	3	2	1

42 Match the following.

List I	List II
A. Silhouette	1. A rough preliminary drawing
B. Croquis	2. The area above the waist
C. Bodice	3. Finest dressmaking in French
D. Haute Couture	4. The shape of clothing style.

Codes

	A	B	C	D		A	B	C	D
(a)	1	2	3	4	(b)	4	3	1	2
(c)	1	3	2	4	(d)	4	1	2	3

43 What are the classifications on which fashion terminologies depend upon?

1. Basic terms 2. Sketching terms
3. Face shape 4. On the basis of wash

Codes

(a) 1 and 4 (b) 2 and 3 (c) 1, 2 and 3 (d) All of these

44 Which among the following presents the fashion cycle?

1. Innovation 2. Acceleration
3. Decline 4. Obsolescence

Codes

(a) Only 1 (b) Only 2
(c) 1, 2 and 4 (d) All of these

45 How can one determine texture?

1. Fibre 2. Yarn
3. Fabric 4. Finish

Codes

(a) 1 and 3 (b) 2 and 4
(c) 1, 2 and 4 (d) All of these

46 Which among the following come under principles of design?

1. Harmony 2. Evaluation
3. Rhythm 4. Finishing

Codes

(a) 1 and 2 (b) 3 and 4
(c) 1 and 3 (d) None of these

47 What are the core components of balance?

1. Pose 2. Equilibrium
3. Stability 4. Security

Codes

(a) Only 1 (b) 2 and 3
(c) 1, 2 and 3 (d) All of these

48 What are the different classification for clothes of different age group?

1. Infant 2. School going 3. Teenager
4. Adult 5. Old age

Codes

(a) 1 and 4 (b) 1, 3, 4 and 5
(c) 1, 3 and 5 (d) All of these

Directions (Q. Nos. 49-58) *In the questions given below are two statements labelled as Assertion A and Reason (R). In the context of the two statements, which one of the following is correct?*

Codes

(a) Both A and R are true and R is the correct explanation of A
(b) Both A and R are true, but R is not the correct explanation of A
(c) A is true, but R is false
(d) A is false, but R is true

49 **Assertion** (A) Rhythm can be created by the use of radiated lines.

Reason (R) The radiated lines are created by gathers. Eye can move easily fron one part to other on the small lines created by gathers. This movement creates rhythm.

50 Assertion (A) Harmony means a relationship of different portions of a dress.

Reason (R) Harmony is achieved through judicious use of colour, shape and texture to give a feeling of oneness.

51 Assertion (A) It has been observed that the economically progressive society is flourished by ongoing fashion trends as fashion is directly related to the individuals earnings.

Reason (R) The economic factors such as recession, depression, inflation or affluence either accelerates or retards fashion technology and on going trends.

52 Assertion (A) Adoption of the fashion styles takes place at the declining state.

Reason (R) If the fashion is accepted, adoption rises purchased and worn by fashion admirers.

53 Assertion (A) Style is first adopted by higher social state and trickles down to lower socio-economic levels.

Reason (R) On reaching the general acceptance state, that particular style losses its attraction.

54 Assertion (A) The effectiveness of merchandising activities is evaluated on the basis of consumer's acceptance.

Reason (R) Reports on current sales activities are formulated on daily, weekly and monthly basis.

55 Assertion (A) Acceptance by a large number to people makes a fashion important.

Reason (R) Designers plan styles to appeal to certain consumer groups.

56 Assertion (A) In the old age one should wear light material clothes.

Reason (R) In the old age, body becomes stiff and eye sight becomes weak and energy is low.

57 Assertion (A) Designing makes the products look beautiful.

Reason (R) In designing printing is done by the manufacturer.

58 Assertion (A) Long term forecasting is the process of analysing and evaluating trends.

Reason (R) Short term forecasting focuses on current events both domestically and internationally.

Directions (Q. Nos. 59-63) *Read the passage given below and answer the following questions.*

Clothing is something we all should wear in order to fit into society. The act of wearing clothing is a choice in some indigenous societies while in a more modern culture you could find yourself in trouble with the police if you choose not to wear clothes. Clothes are easily accessible and can be bought in most high street shops. Supermarkets are also beginning to sell clothes. Clothes are for keeping people warm or serving as protection from the strong burning sun. Certain items of clothing can be expensive, especially if it is made by a well known brand or is a particular design.

While clothing is affordable for most people, the price usually depends on the quality of the material used to make the item and its brand name. In most countries clothing is taxed, while food is not. This is probably because clothing can be considered as a luxury item, especially if it is of very good quality. The type of clothing that is worn usually depends on the occasion. People that attend a wedding usually wear formal clothes. Men often wear suits and women wear dresses. Formal and smart clothing is often worn in times of celebration. People often wear different clothing at work. Some jobs require people to wear a special uniform which should be worn by all employees.

A pilot, doctor or air hostess may be required to wear a uniform so that all the staff can be easily recognised. Other jobs are less strict and may allow people to wear casual clothes. Construction workers are usually asked to wear protective clothing, especially when the site is considered highly dangerous. People often choose to wear comfortable clothing inside their own home.

This choice of clothing may be very different to the clothing they would normally wear outside. Some people even stay in their bedclothes all day on the weekend when they plan to relax and not go anywhere. People often wear clothing which matches their current state of health or their age.

Pregnant women are likely to wear baggy clothes, while youths often wear tighter clothing to show their figure. Younger females often wear high heeled shoes while elderly people tend to wear more comfortable shoes which will allow them to walk with ease.

59 When can items of clothing be expensive?

(a) When they are from the supermarket.
(b) When they are taxed too much.
(c) When it is a well-known brand or design.
(d) When they are in the sale.

60 What kind of job requires workers to wear protective clothing?

(a) Pilots (b) Construction workers
(c) Doctors (d) Air hostess

61 How do some youths usually like to wear their clothes?

(a) Baggy (b) Tight (c) Short (d) Long

62 What type of clothing is worn in times of celebration?

(a) Formal (b) Casual
(c) Protective (d) Bedclothes

63 Who is more likely to wear baggy clothing?

(a) Youths (b) Workers
(c) Pregnant ladies (d) Elderly people

PREVIOUS YEARS' QUESTIONS

July 2018

1 **Assertion** (A) The grain in a woven fabric can be identified by the degree of stretch along the yarns.
Reason (R) Warp yarns stretch more in comparison to weft yarns.
Codes
(a) Both A and R are correct.
(b) Both A and R are incorrect.
(c) A is incorrect, but R is correct.
(d) A is correct, but R in incorrect.

2 **Assertion** (A) Embroidery, sequins and applique form the structural design in a Garment.
Reason (R) Structural design is the surface enrichment of the Garment.
Codes
(a) Both A and R are correct.
(b) Both A and R are incorrect.
(c) A is correct, but R is incorrect.
(d) A is incorrect, but R is correct.

November 2017

3 Match the following.

List I (Finishes)	**List II** (Purpose)
A. Singeing	1. Increases the lustre of the fabric
B. Scouring	2. Provides smooth surface
C. Tentering	3. Removal of desizing products, pectin and wax from wool
D. Calendering	4. Mechanical straightening process
	5. Burning of the raised fiber ends

Codes

	A	B	C	D		A	B	C	D
(a)	5	2	3	4	(b)	1	2	4	3
(c)	2	5	1	4	(d)	5	3	4	2

July 2016

4 Which of the following are examples of using diagonal line in clothing design?
(a) Raglon sleeve (b) Halter tops
(c) Fish darts (d) Box pleats

5 **Assertion** (A) Structural design is an integral part of the garment.
Reason (R) It comprises of applique, embroidery and print etc.
Codes
(a) Both A and R are incorrect.
(b) Both A and R are correct.
(c) A is correct, but R is incorrect.
(d) A is incorrect, but R is correct.

6 Which of the following factors favour fashion?
1. Leisure
2. An economy of abundance
3. Transportation and communication
4. Low income
5. Sumptuary laws
Code
(a) 1, 2, 3
(b) 2, 3, 4
(c) 3, 4, 1
(d) 4, 1, 2

7 **Assertion** (A) Cotton is the most appropriate fabric for infant wear.
Reason (R) Cotton is the most absorbent, washable and breathable fabric.
Codes
(a) Both A and R are correct.
(b) Both A and R are incorrect.
(c) A is correct, but R is incorrect.
(d) A is incorrect, but R is correct.

8 **Assertion** (A) Fabrics woven in leno weave are sheer but durable for its construction.
Reason (R) In leno weave, each filling yarn is encircled by 2 warp yarns twisted about each other.
Codes
(a) Both A and R are correct.
(b) Both A and R are incorrect.
(c) A is correct, but R is incorrect.
(d) A is incorrect, but R is correct.

ANSWERS

Exam Based Questions

1 (b)	2 (c)	3 (a)	4 (c)	5 (b)	6 (d)	7 (d)	8 (b)	9 (a)	10 (c)
11 (c)	12 (c)	13 (d)	14 (a)	15 (d)	16 (c)	17 (c)	18 (a)	19 (a)	20 (a)
21 (c)	22 (d)	23 (d)	24 (a)	25 (c)	26 (a)	27 (b)	28 (d)	29 (c)	30 (d)
31 (c)	32 (a)	33 (b)	34 (a)	35 (b)	36 (d)	37 (a)	38 (b)	39 (d)	40 (c)
41 (c)	42 (d)	43 (c)	44 (d)	45 (d)	46 (c)	47 (d)	48 (d)	49 (a)	50 (a)
51 (b)	52 (d)	53 (b)	54 (c)	55 (c)	56 (a)	57 (c)	58 (b)	59 (c)	60 (b)
61 (b)	62 (a)	63 (c)							

Previous Years' Questions

1 (d)	2 (b)	3 (d)	4 (c)	5 (c)	6 (a)	7 (a)	8 (a)

UNIT V

Concept and Functions of Management

Management is a universal phenomena. It is very popular and widely used term. It is a wide term under which individuals work together to achieve a common goal. For effective running of an organisation or an institution, it is necessary to have management knowledge which increases the effective utilisation of human and material resources.

Management

The term 'management' is not applied to housekeeping alone, but has a wide spectrum. **Koontz** (1971) had said that "there is perhaps no more important area of human activity than managing, for it the basic task of all managers, at all levels, in all kinds of activities is to design and maintain an environment in which individuals work together in groups can accomplish selected mission and objectives."

Management is both an art and science as it effectively utilising human and non-human resources to achieve positive results. The management implies as an art of creating such environment within any organisation or an institution within which people perform their role as individuals and yet cooperate with each other to achieve group goals or common goals. It also means optimising efficiency in effectively reaching the goals.

The term 'management' is coined from the French word '*menage*' meaning 'housekeeping'. Presently, society management has become a key social institution as it fulfils the social purpose. In simple words, management is using what a person have to get what he wants?

In this Chapter

In this, 'what a person have to get, refers to the 'resources' and 'what he wants' refers to the aim or goals. Basically, management is a process of making best utilisation of available resources in order to attain certain goal.

Definitions of Management

- According to **M P Follett**, "Management is the art of getting things done through people."
- According to **F W Taylor**, "Management is the art of knowing what you want to do and then seeing that they do it in the best and the cheapest may."
- According to **George R Terry**, "'Management is a distinct process consisting of planning, organising, actuating and controlling; utilising in each both science and art, and followed in order to accomplish pre-determined objectives."
- According to **Webster's New World College Dictionary** "management is the act, art, or manner of managing, or handling, controlling, directing, etc."

Concept of Management

The concept of management can be viewed from different viewpoints which are discussed :

As an Economic Resource From the perspectives of economists, management is a valuable resource of production which uses land, labour, capital and entrepreneurship to produce goods. The managers of the firm determine the productivity and profitability of a firm by making good decisions. It is observed that organisations run by poor managers always fail. So, possessing managerial skills is the dominant factor in economic growth.

As a Class It has to be viewed from the sociological view point which defines management as a group of organisation members that occupies the social position responsible for achieving the goal of the firm. From this view point the members of the organisations can be categorised into two classes i.e., managers and non-managers.

As a Discipline Management as a discipline is a part of social sciences and integrative in nature. It derives its theories from humanities and behavioural sciences. Its status as a discipline increases because it continuously discovers many aspects of business enterprises and also passes on the verified knowledge to the practitioners of managerial process.

Management can be considered as a process because it involves a number of functions, which are performed by managers. These functions comprises planning, organising, staffing, coordinating and controlling.

None of the managerial functions would produce the ultimate result in the absence of all other basic function. So, management can be considered as a continuous process.

As a System of Authority Since the essence of management is to direct, guide and control, it posseses authority. It denotes power relationships. Authority is the power to compel others to work and behave in a particular manner. Management cannot discharge its function without authority.

Due to changing pattern of management, like authoritarian, humanitarian, constitutional and democratic, the modern system of management is a synthesis of these four patterns of authority. Thus. authority is the foundation of management.

Approaches to Management

Approaches to management are as follows :

Traditional Approach

Frederick W Taylor's work was best represented by the traditional approach. His ideas were centred around the thought that everyone was primarily motivated by economic gain. He also believed that managers knew more about the jobs being performed than the workers who performed these jobs. He believed that if you paid enough to a person he/she could perform any job. He dismissed common motivators such as the job itself, co-workers, flexibility with their schedule, etc.

Human Relations Approach

Unlike the Traditional Approach, the Human Relations Approach is focused on the social environment of an organisation. It focuses on the role of the social processes and relationships. The Human Relations Approach understands that employees have strong social needs and that economic gain can't always fill that gap. This approach is more concerned with the employees' well-being at work than the financial compensation the employees get for working. Making an employee feel important is also a huge key to the Human Relations Approach.

To make an employee feel important, a manager doesn't need to go to extreme lengths to accomplish this. A simple thing like including employees in decision-making even if they don't have a huge say can make them feel very valued. The Human Relations Approach tells us that employees want to contribute and make real contributions to something. Human relationists will tell you that the illusion of contribution and participation is enough to motivate employees.

However, some employees need more than just an illusion of contribution and participation, but instead need to be actively involved in decision-making and feel like they truly are contributing to the group.

Managers need to figure out how to use all their human resources and encourage employees to participate. A way that managers can also make employees feel more involved is to create work teams that collaborate and make decisions.

Social System Approach

This approach says that management is a social system composed of people who work in cooperation. The relationships exist between the external and internal environment of organisation. According to this approach there should be harmony between the goals of organisation and goals of the group. This approach suggests that cooperation amongst the group is necessary.

Management of Time, Energy, Money and Space

For an organisation to perform effectively, management of time, energy, money and space is very essential.

Management of Time

It is rightly said "Time and Tides Wait for None." An individual should understand the value of time to succeed in all aspects of life. People who waste time are the ones who fail to create an identity of their own. It is very necessary for achieving the desired goal.

With the help of effective time management, one is able to finish more jobs/work with less effort. Suppose, if you are alloting a certain amount of time for each activity, you don't have to worry about the next thing that you will do. With time management, you become more organised and the things you do become more habitual than panic driven.

For better time management, develop the habit of using planners, organisers, table top calendars, etc. To manage the time effectively, prioritise the task as per the importance and urgency. The good time management allows you to accomplish more in shorter period of time, which leads to more free time. This lets you take the advantage of learning opportunities, lower your stress and helps you focus on more career success. Planning plays a pivotal role in effective time management. An individual needs to plan his/her day well in advance to make the best possible use of time. Planning gives an individual a sense of direction in the organisation or personal lives as it motivates a person to complete his/her task on time.

Importance of Time Management

Time is one resource that is available in equal amount for each and every member of the world. Every individual has twenty-four hours a day to complete his job and to achieve his goals. A basic awareness along with practice and perseverance are necessary for the proper utilisation of time. The value of time has to be learnt in the early years of life so that one does not fritter away time available, because a moment wasted is a moment lost forever. One must be always conscious of time available and time needed to carry out the various jobs. Planning, whether long-term or short-term, must allow time for one's routine jobs and leisure. Time is a useful resource not only for occupational activities but also for rest and leisure. Time allotted for occupational activities should include time for sleeping, eating, working and relaxing. The plan should not only include the quantity but also pinpoint when (which part of the 24 hours) it be utilised for achieving these goals.

Before one plans, one must be fully aware about the quantity of time each activity requires. For example, one needs 7-8 hours of sleep (at night) or an hour for gardening (in the evening), an hour for meals (afternoon and night), etc. Any time that can be spared or is available surplus after having undertaken all the occupational activities is termed as leisure. Leisure time activities enable the individual to relax and be refreshed to tackle occupational activities in a better way.

Leisure time activities could include socialising with friends and relatives; participating in social and cultural functions; organising and participating in games, sports, picnics, hikes, etc., indulging in social service; listening to music, reading, painting, drawing, embroidering, watching films, etc.

Planning the wise use of time not only enables one to achieve more but also reduces tension and worries. Plans made must be properly implemented to be effective. A time plan should enable one to use time available for achieving a maximum benefit.

The biggest advantage of drawing up a time plan means being aware of all problems in advance, thus overcoming delays and indecision later.

Energy Management

For sustaining individual growth and physical output energy is essential. Energy management is difficult and complex. The demand for energy will be less during beginning and contracting stage and more during expanding stage. Energy refers to the ability to do work. All activities of personal well-being and of the home's efficiency require energy to be carried out.

Whether it is standing, sitting, dusting, cooking, repairing, all need energy. It is of prime importance that one is not only aware of all energy resources available, but also learns to use them wisely to achieve the family goals. It is wiser to let a man push, pull and lift heavy articles in the home rather than a woman (who will be using more energy and time to do a similar job).

Energy for working is available from human and non-human sources. Energy from non-human sources is called fuel and is available in the form of wood, coal, oil, electricity, water and sun. Human energy or energy from human sources refers to the individual's ability to do work.

The amount of human energy available for work varies from person to person, as it is dependent upon the physical and mental state of a person and also related to heredity and family background of the individual undertaking the work.

Ways of Saving Energy

To conserve energy and to use it most effectively, one must carefully think and plan through the activity so that one can complete the task efficiently. Some of the ways to save our energy, while performing different activities are :

Break the Task into Smaller Activities Completing one task involves a number of tasks. For example, washing of clothes. So, now break this task of washing clothes into smaller activities involves separating different types of clothes, cotton coloured, white etc., dipping clothes in soap/detergent solution for some time; rubbing of soiled areas, etc. It also involves taking out soap/ detergent. Then these are to be squeezed and put out or hung for drying. Breaking one task into small tasks, saves energy.

Cut All Extra Movements and Combine Activities Sometimes, we see that some people do more of running around and do less work. For example, some guests arrive at home and you have to serve them water. You keep going to the kitchen and bring one glass of water at a time. Don't you think that a better option is to bring all the glasses in a tray and serve all the guests.

Money Management

Money is the pivotal resource which can be exchanged to buy material things, commodities and services. It can also be used for future use and thus gives a sense of security to the family. Among all the resources that are available to the family, the most important one is money. Money plays an important role in the life of man as an instrument through which he can satisfy his physical, material and mental needs. The income and expenditure pattern of the family decides the family's standard of living and its place in the society.

Money management is a skill that everyone must learn in life. Money management is the process of saving, investing, spending or otherwise overseeing the capital usage of an individual or group. It is a strategic technique to make money yields the highest interest output value for any amount spent. Spending money to satisfy cravings is a natural human phenomenon.

Money management is important as one can manage its money by knowing the assets and liabilities one has by overlooking long-term goals. When you manage money effectively you are better able to save for the future. It is aid in avoiding overspending. Money management can help use your monthly cost properly. Quite often we are overcharged but choose to ignore it. By sitting down and reviewing the cost of each of our expenses we may be able to save money.

The effective money management can help in bringing certain level of calm and a feeling of peace of mind. Money management can also help in keeping finances control.

The money management is also important for the family because it helps to feel more secure financially. It also helps in managing money properly for different household activities.

Space Management

Space is utilised by people to carry out various activities at home, outside the home and at workplace. You must have observed that a well-designed room gives a sense of spaciousness, while a non-managed room with similar dimensions, results in the cramped or cluttered look.

Space management involves planning of space, organising it as per the plan, implementing the plan in terms of its utilisation and evaluating it in terms of achieving functionality and aesthetic appeal. A well-managed space not only offers comfort while working but also appears attractive.

Space and Home

Sitting, sleeping, studying, cooking, bathing, washing, entertainment, etc., are the major activities to be carried out in the home. To conduct each of these activities and the actions that may follow them, usually specific areas are identified in the home.

Wherever there is space available, specified rooms are built to carry out such activities. Most urban middle Socio Economic Status (SES) homes are likely to have sitting room/area, bed room/rooms, kitchen, store room, bathroom and toilet, verandah/courtyard (optional).

Principles of Space Planning

Space must be planned for its maximum utilisation. Following principles should be kept in mind while assigning or designing work, areas in the house.

Aspect It indicates the arrangement of doors and windows in the external walls of a building which allows the occupants to enjoy the nature in the form of sunshine, breeze, scenery, etc.

Prospect It is the impression or impact that a house is likely to make on a person who looks at it from outside. Therefore, it includes the attainment of pleasing appearance using natural beauty, positioning of doors and windows and covering up of undesirable views.

Privacy It is one of the most important principle in space planning. Privacy requires consideration in two ways :

- **Internal Privacy** Privacy of one room from another is referred to as internal privacy. It is attained by careful planning in the house with respect to grouping, positioning of doors, provision of small corridor/lobby, etc. Internal privacy can be also be achieved by setting up screens and curtains. In some homes with large families, separate sitting area is provided for women, ensuring their privacy.
- **External Privacy** This means privacy of all parts of a house from the neighbouring buildings or houses, public streets and by ways. It can be a shade secured by carefully planning the entrance and covering it with a tree or creepers.

Grouping It implies the outlook of rooms with respect to their relative position with each other. For example, in a building, the dining area must be close to the kitchen and the kitchen must be away from the toilet.

Roominess It means the spacious effect a room gives to those who live in it. The available space should be made use of fully. For example, one can have built-in wall cupboard, shelves and storage area so that the floor of the room is left free for various activities. In addition, the size and shape of the room, the furniture arrangement as well as the colour scheme used have a bearing on its roominess. Well proportionate rectangular room looks spacious compared to a square room of similar dimensions. Light colours make a room looks more spacious than dark ones.

Furniture Requirements The rooms must be planned with due thought to the furniture to be placed there. Every room in a building should serve its purpose well. Care must be taken to place only required pieces of furniture while planning about space, one should take consideration of practical points like strength and stability of the structure, convenience and comfort for the family.

Motivating Factors of Management

The concept of motivation focuses on explaining what 'moves' behaviour. Infact, the term 'motivation' is derived from the Latin word 'movere' referring to 'movement of activity'. Most of our everyday explanation of behaviour is given in terms of motives.

Motivation is considered important because it helps to identify and satisfy the needs of human resources in the organisation and thereby help in improving their performance. It means incitement or inducement to act or move. It is the process of stimulating people to action, to accomplish desired goals. It depends upon satisfying needs of people.

There is a common saying that "Where there is a will there is a way". This indicates that to accomplish any task, the worker must be motivated and interested in doing it. For example, if a student is not interested in learning a task, even when other resources are available, she/he still may give excuses and not finish the task. We may pursue dance, painting, reading fiction, art and craft and other hobbies as per our motivation.

The motivating factors in the resource management are discussed below :

Values

They are the key to all motivating factors in human behaviour. Value as concept is vague and subjective although it is very important to an individual. Values grow out of human desire and interest. Values differ in culture. The family has the major responsibility for fostering value among the members.

The term 'value' signifies the meaning of worth that is attached to any object, principle or ideas. Values provide basis for judgement, discrimination and analysis and it is these qualities that make intelligent choices possible between alternatives. Thus, values are the fundamental forces that force or motivate human activities and endeavors. According to **Gross and Crandall** (1980), "A value is always important to the person who holds it. It is desirable and satisfying. It has the ability to develop in self-creative way and it tends to endure. It is a concept of the desirable, explicit or implicit which governs our choice of methods, modes or goals."

The following are the motivating values of human behaviour :

- Comfort
- Love
- Technological satisfaction
- Art
- Health Ambition
- Desire for knowledge
- Play
- Religion

Types of Values

The values can be classified as :

Intrinsic or Instrumental An intrinsic value is one that is important and desirable simply for its own sake. It is worthy of being sought for itself alone. Honesty, cooperation, creativity, beauty, discipline, respect, etc., are some of the intrinsic values in management.

On the other hand, instrumental values are ways of reaching intrinsic or end values, sometimes called goal values. Therefore, they form the basic values leading to another. Planning, skills, order and efficiency and technological satisfaction are examples of instrumental values. .

Factual and Normative Values The factual values are also called 'descriptive values'. Generally, they are based on people's preferences and desires. The normative values are ethical values, which carry the idea of right or wrong. Some examples of factual values are honesty, religion, loyalty and faithfulness.

Goals

Goals are the desires that individuals or families are willing to work for. They are more definite and clear than values because they are to be accomplished. They are tangible things, objects, ends or purposes. Goal is an objective or purpose to be attained. They are specific ways of realising the values that one holds. Goal is defined as an objective, condition or something you desire to achieve or attain at any given period of time.

Presently, your goals are to complete your course and to obtain higher degree so as to get job in your chosen field.

As each of these goals are achieved, new goals, will emerge leading to other higher goals in your life. Goals, like values, play an important role in your life. Values give meaning to your life. Goals on the other hand, point the direction of your path you want to follow. Thus, it can be said that values and goals are interrelated. Values are the vehicles and goals are the highways you use to attain your desired quality of life.

Types of Goals

Goal are classified under the following heads :

Individual Goals These are established by an individual for himself. These are based on his own value. For example, he puts in efforts for their achievement and receives satisfaction to himself and scoring 70% marks in the examination.

Group Goals These are established by the group. These are based on some of the common values and interests of the group members. For example, achievement of 100% result of the class at the higher secondary examination.

Achievement of Goals According to Duration

Throughout life, each individual and each family is always seeking some objectives. According to duration for achievement, goals are classified as short-term, intermediate and long-term goals.

These can be understood as :

Short-term Goals In short term goals, the period of attainment of goal is short. Example is to successfully complete the course of study. Since the achievement is anticipated in the near future, these goals usually involve a time period of six months or less.

Intermediate Goals Intermediate goals are nothing but the link connecting between short term and long term goals. They have definite characteristics and serve a purpose in your life time achievement. The time duration involved in intermediate goals is longer than short term goals. Achievement of these goals is measured in terms of several months or years. For example, to complete your graduation you will require few years.

Long Term Goals The duration of achieving this goal is long. Classification differs from the other two, in regard to the time period, the degree of specificity and the extent of active implementation involved in attainment. Long term goals are those you have set for yourself in the distant future. Long term goals may include one or more of the following:

- Getting a good job in chosen profession.
- Getting married.
- Owning home or farm.

Standards

Standard is a scale of measurement of values. According to **Nickell and Dorsey** (1970), "Standards are a set of measure of values stemming from our value patterns, determining the amount and kind of interest in something and the satisfaction we receive."

Standards serve as a measure or criterion for measurement of objects or ways of doing things. There are standards that apply to a single situation or area such as standard of food or dress or conduct. Standards set the limits one will accept in working towards a goal.

Classification of Standards

Gross and **Crandall** classify standards as conventional and flexible.

Conventional Standards Conventional standards are those that are traditional and accepted by the community at large or by a social group within it. To illustrate high standard of cleanliness, we can take an example of cleaning and dusting furniture twice a day. This can be standard of any family. If an unexpected guest arrives and there is dust visible, the homemaker is apt to say, "I did not dust today."

Flexible Standards Flexible standards can be changed to suit different situations; they give greater freedom of choice. Adjusting family standards to changing conditions is an example of the need to have flexibility in one's standards.

Motivation Theories of Management

There are many competing theories, which attempt to explain the nature of motivation. These theories are all, at least, partially true and all help to explain the behaviour of certain people at certain time. However, the search for a generalised theory of motivation at work appears a vain quest. Motivation varies over time and depending upon the circumstances.

Maslow's Need Hierarchy Theory

The most well known and pioneering theory of motivation is that of Abraham Maslow's Hierarchy of Needs. According to **Maslow's Hierarchy of Human Needs**, people are motivated by five basic needs. These needs are arranged in the order in which a person seeks to gratify them. These needs are :

Physiological Needs Food, clothing, shelter, etc.,

Need for Safety and Security Freedom from danger, job security, health-care. etc

Need to Belong Acceptance by the group, friendships, love cordial relationship, etc.

Need Forosteem Recognition by others, feeling of achievement self-respect, etc.

Need for Self-Actualisation Fulfillment of capacities.

The needs are arranged in order of importance under the assumption that a lower level need is satisfied before the next higher level need becomes a motivating factor. People try to satisfy their physiological needs first. When their basic needs are ensured, they seek security, belongingness, esteem and finally self-actualisation. When one need is satisfied, next higher level need emerges to take its place. People are always striving to satisfy the new needs that emerge.

Alderfer's ERG Theory
(Existence Relatedness and Growth)

Clayton Alderfer reorganised Maslow's Need Hierarchy into three levels of core needs as :

- Existence needs
- Relatedness needs
- Growth needs

Existence needs includes both physiological and safety needs; it corresponds to the lower order needs of Maslow's Theory.

Relatedness comprises love and belongingness needs.

Growth incorporates both esteem and self-actualisation needs. Relatedness and growth needs together comprise the higher order needs as set by **Maslow**.

ERG Theory argues like that of Maslow that satisfied lower order needs lead to the desire for satisfaction of higher order needs. But, Alderfer states that multiple needs can be operating as motivators at the same time. An employee frustrated in efforts to satisfy growth needs. For example, might be motivated to satisfy the lower level relatedness needs.

Herzberg's Two Factors/Hygiene Maintenance Theory

An eminent management theoretician and psychologist **Fredrick Herzberg** have developed two factor or Hygiene Maintenance Theory of Work Motivation. Herzberg's theory has made a significant contribution towards understanding human behaviour. This theory is widely accepted by managers confronted with the problem of human behaviour at workplace. According to Herzberg, satisfaction and dissatisfaction are two independent dimensions.

Motivators affect satisfaction and hygiene factors affect dissatisfaction. A manager has to decide whether he wants to motivate his subordinates and employees. If he wants to motivate them, he may increase the hygiene factors to remove dissatisfaction. Once dissatisfaction is removed from the minds of the subordinates, they can be motivated by increasing motivating factors. These motivating factors are known as satisfiers.

Decision-Making in Management

Management occurs when there is some problem to solve and some choice to make. The various steps in the management process are really a series of decisions, based upon our previous experiences. Therefore, decision-making is the heart of the management.

A decision can be defined as a course of action consciously chosen from the available alternatives for the purpose of desired result. So the role of decision-making in management involves knowing and actually applying essential information in problem situations of day to day life.

Thus, it is used to achieve goals and assessing standards. Management is a mental process which involves a series of decision-making.

Types of Decisions

All members of the family are generally involved in the decision-making process in home management. In solving various day to day problems in the home, families are constantly faced with situations requiring decisions and actions.

Various types of decisions are made in the family which are discussed as :

Individual Decisions It relates to personal problems and needs. Usually, these decisions are pertaining to an individual and decisions are made by the person concerned, For example, when a girl child has passed out from high school, she will think through different alternatives for her higher studies. She may go to the college or sit at home waiting for marriage or search for employment. She can choose the best alternative by her own. So in this case, this is her individual decision.

Individual decisions are more quickly made than group decisions. The decision-making of an individual moves round the values, goals and standards. Selection of household equipment or furniture and furnishings are some of the areas where personal or individual decisions are common. Deciding on the methods of saving and investments, types of insurance are the decision taken solely by the male head of the family in most homes.

Group Decision These decisions involve not only the different members of the family but sometimes extends to include relatives, friends and community. Although, some of the decisions in a family originate from individual but there are more decisions in the family which are concerned with the family as an organisation. Group decisions are made from the collective actions of several individuals of varying values, goals and standards. In this case, more alternatives are to be suggested.

Unproductive approaches are identified and eliminated, because the experience of many people acts as guiding points in the process of selecting the best alternative. The development of group decisions is a slower process. Sometimes, conflicts may arise in different situations. Generally, group decisions are taken in solving the problems of land and property divisions, decision of family finances, investments and community development programmes.

Habitual Decisions This type of decisions is the lowest level of decisions. Many routine decisions become habits based on established patterns of behaviour. Here, the decision and the course of action are combined to form a habit. So much thought and considerations are not involved in these decisions. They relate to day-to-day activity of cooking, cleaning, washing, looking after children going to office, etc.

If mother is busy; the other members of the family can finish her work. The choice is automatic because the criteria are well established and no fresh decisions are involved. Making of tea or coffee in the early morning is an example of habitual decision. In this decision, there is no need for choice of alternatives. Once it becomes a habitual choice, the action becomes quick and spontaneous.

Central Decisions A central decision is a very crucial decision in one's life, where he has to make careful deliberations and analysis before arriving at the final decision. There are other supporting decisions which would follow to complete the action of central decisions.

For example, a wife's employment after the retirement of the husband may be central decision for a family to get additional financial support. Building or purchasing of a house is also a central decision of the family. For each central decision many supporting decisions are to be made to complete the whole decision.

Economic Decisions It is based on allocation and exchange process relating to the use of resources. As we have multiple goals with limited resources, we are facing many problems for satisfying our unlimited wants. Most families are in a situation how to satisfy their wants with limited resources. Question may arise like which want to be satisfied first and which to be later on? For the proper allocation of resources, family makes many decisions daily. A family has to utilise the limited resources effectively to achieve goals.

Maximising the output and minimising the input of resources and getting maximum satisfaction can be possible by economic decisions of the family. Economic decisions are related to saving investment, expenditure and utilisation of human and non-human resources.

Technical Decisions Decisions that fall into this category are goal oriented. These decisions involve weighing of the alternatives.This means choosing the course of action that are sure to meet the desired goal. In case of health crisis in the families or emergencies, one might use this type of decision-making. Family decision-making is likely to be more complicated than decision-making by individuals, but decisions made by groups have the advantage of having been taken after much discussion and thought.

However, many decisions made in a family affect all the members of the family. Often, decisions taken by a single individual member affect not only that individual but also others in the family. In many families, husband and wife may jointly take certain decisions after discussion. In some cases, the opinions of children or other members of the family may be taken and may influence the final decision.

Functions of Management

The functions of management are :

Planning

Planning is very important for the success of management process. It is basically working out ways or course of action to achieve the goals. Planning can be habitual or conscious. Planning involves thinking through the possible ways of reaching a desired goal. It is the basis for successful managerial practices. Management was considered as synonym to planning. Every work starts with a plan. Efficient planning results in high grade or outcomes. In many ways, planning is the hardest function of management.

Planning is very important, as it guides actions of various members towards goal achievement. As every individual in a family has a personal as well as family goals. Goals are achieved by making plans. For better results, plans should be formulated with devotion and zeal. According to **Starch**, "Everyday experience in thinking occurs in planning of any kind." Planning is an essential directive factor for the fulfilment of family wants.

Planning is a series of decisions concerning sequences of action. It is essentially drawing up of a plan of action based on analysis of available opportunities and options to achieve certain objectives. Planning should always be future oriented. Every work is regarded as a unit and each part includes different activities to be performed in a proper perceptive to each other.

According to **WM Fox**, "Planning involves problem-solving which includes the step in decision-making like identifying the problem, obtaining information/ formulating courses of action, considering consequencies of each alternative and selecting the course of action, considering consequences of each alternative and selecting the course of action that seems best". Planning is the forecast of some future action. In order to develop a workable plan, one must identify and clarify the problem or goal.

Steps of Planning

The basic steps of planning are :

Recognition of the Problem It means that the problem which has to be solved should be recognised and a plan can be formulated to solve the problem. While planning, the importance should be given to the urgency of the problem, as proper planning will lead to better results.

Identification of Different Alternatives In order to solve the problem, various alternatives are to be sought. The identification of each alternative is important because pros and cons of each alternative will affect the final outcome of the planning.

Choose an Appropriate Alternative An appropriate or best suited alternative should be selected.

Prepare a Work Plan A work plan is prepared where the alternative solution is used. Implementation of the plan is very important for the successful result.

Acceptance of the Consequences After completion of the plan, one has to accept the consequences. Decision once taken, form a stable feature which cannot be changed early. So, one should accept the consequences as they are. This will lead to psychological satis faction.

Supervision

Supervision is one of the most important managment function in an organisation. In every organisation there is a provision for supervision. According to **R.C. Davis** "supervision is the function of assuring that the work is being done in accordance with plan and instruction.

Supervision is concerned with three main functions such as : direction, immediate guidance and control with a view to see that people are working according to plans, policies programmes instructions and time schedule. Supervision not only checks the misuse of time and resource but it helps in promoting working effciency by giving personal encouragment.

It means establishing one's wider vision above vision, supreme vision and seeing others work carefully. From the management point of view, supervision means overseeing the subordinates at work to ensure that work is being performed as required.

The utilisation of human resources can be done through the process of supervision. Supervision is an important function of the management process.

Controlling

Controlling is carrying out the plan. It calls for flexibility in thinking. It involves a careful observation of performance. It includes making changes when things seems to be getting off course. Regular checks make the plan more easy to carry out. Usually, people ignore the steps of controlling, but this step is very important in carrying out the plan.

During this step, many new decisions are required which may result in changes of the previous plans. For example, menus are planned for meals and certain food materials are not available during shopping due to some reasons, then fresh decision needs to be made at once to substitute the previous plan.

Also in case of building a house, the plans may be changed if necessary at the controlling step.

The controlling has different phases which are explained as :

Energising It means that any plan must be implemented by energising or initiating and sustaining the action. The individuals who are involved in doing a particular task must be energised in order to get results. Inspite of having a good plan, sometimes implementing the plan would become difficult. Here, the energising function would act as a catalyst.

Checking The second phase of controlling the plan of action is checking the progress of the plan. It is quick step-by-step appraisal of a plan in action. Seeking ways of checking plans in action vary with resources concerned and the people involved in the process. For example, to go to school on time one has to get the clothes, meals and books ready, which need checking of time at all stages.

Adjusting The third phase of controlling is adjusting the plan if there is need for fresh decision to be taken. This should be done taking into account the problem in hand and the resources available. Getting into action, keeping the resources mobile and knowledge of what is to be done are all important in this step. Controlling calls for leadership and joint action in the family.

Organising

All the plans made in a home each day need variety of activities and if these activities are to be carried out effectively, some form of organisation is essential. Organising consists of dividing and grouping of activities. Then they are assigned to all the members.

According to **Nickel** and **Dorsey**, "Organising is the process of establishing proper relationships among work, people and other resources and channeling authority and responsibility." The simple meaning of organising is to arrange things in an orderly manner. Organisation means dividing various activities and distributing them, so that goals can be easily achieved. It is influenced by the size of the family. Proper organisation and allocation of work ensure that all the household work gets done and no one is over taxed.

According to **G. Baker**, there are three levels of organisation as :

- First level is one person is organising a task. Sometimes this is called work simplification.
- Another level is one person arranging his own efforts for the completion of several tasks he needs to do. For example, A mother employed outside her home is likely to be organising at this level.
- In the third level, the manager arrange the efforts of others who are doing work in a pattern, so that one or more tasks can be completed. Parents who include their growing children in various homemaking tasks are organisinig at this level.

Evaluation

This is the final step of management process. It looks towards both the process of management and the results. Evaluation helps in judging the success and achievement of a plan of action. Its chief purpose is to see what has been achieved as a result of effective planning and controlling. This forms the guidelines and basis for future planning.

A considerable amount of evaluation is associated with controlling. It is through this process of evaluation that control is affected. Evaluation step is actually a review of what his already taken place, with an objective towards better management in future. For example, the home maker learns through experience about the effectiveness of a plan. It helps her to analyse how well the plan has been executed and how far it has been successful in achieving the goals.

The shortcomings and advantages are noted and may be considered in future planning due to this evaluation. Evaluation must be done in relation to goal or objective. Evaluation can be general or more detailed. The general evaluation might be casual and subjective. Without analysing the outcome thoroughly, a manager may recognise a job as good or bad in a given situation.

On the other hand, the detailed evaluation is of elaborate type. This means determining the degree of excellence of the managerial job of the home, one has to look into different aspects of management.

Family Life Cycle and Its Stages

The family cycle is a series of stages through which a family may pass over time. The life cycle for a family includes three major phases/stages which are discussed as follows :

Stage I : Beginning Stage

This is the stage of establishment of the family. It begins with the marriage of two adults and it continues until the first child is born. Here, both the partners get acquaint with each other with their family members, lifestyle, etc. At this stage, the resource utilisation is comparatively low.

During this stage, the partners try to formulate short term and long term goals and decide towards achieving these goals. At this stage, the three main concerns of the family are methods of dividing the family responsibilities, the establishment of a physical home and providing the other basic necessities for day-to-day family maintenance. At this stage, both (partners) should think of making provisions for the basic necessities for each other. The resources in the form of help by the members and relatives of both families are very important ın the establishing stage of the family life cycle.

Stage II : Expanding Family

This stage covers a longer period than first and third stages of family life cycle. It begins with the birth of first child and includes number of sub-stages and lastly ends with the last child leaving the home to settle down his family.

At this stage, the family pattern and lifestyles of the parents change due to arrival of children. The expenditure of energy, the work load and the efficiency are at the highest peak. Responsibilities towards children, their education and welfare increases, bringing about a great strain on the parents. During this stage, the size and composition of the family greatly influence their standard of living.

Stage III : Contracting Stage

It has three sub-stages such as the launching period during which the children leave the home, the financial recovery period and the period of retirement. These are as follows :

Vocational Adjustment The launching period begins when the first child completes its education and takes up an employment and last upto the lasts child becoming financially independent. During this period, financial assistance may be required for children for their new employment vocation or for their marriage and family settlement. In this sub-stage, parents will have new role as grand parents.

Financial Recovery The period of financial recovery starts for the parents when the children are settled independently and become self-sufficient. At this stage, parents will have enough money and time to travel and also have enough time for each other. This stage also calls for social and vocational adjustment as a pre-retirement planning.

Retirement The last stage of the family cycle is retirement. It is the stage when the person employed will retire from his occupation and starts living at home. The financial resources will be reduced and the lifestyle will change as there is ample leisure time. It is the time of adjustment to changes in physical, physiological and environmental conditions, changes in human relations and also sometimes changes in the health status. During this sub-stage, there may be managerial problems in availability of resources, use of time and also financial problems.

Family Life Cycle : Stages/Sub-Stages

Stages	Sub-Stages
Beginning	Period of establishment.
Expanding	Child bearing and pre-school elementary School, high School, college.
Contracting	Vocational adjustment, financial recovery, retirement.

Availability and Use of Resources

Resources are anything which we make use of while carrying out any activity. They help us in accomplishing our goals you may need more of a certain resource for a particular activity as compared to others. Every resource is important and useful.

Resources are used for specific objectives and aims which are :

Achievement of Goals It means to achieve better results and success in goal achievement one should utilise the available resources in a well-planned sequence.

Economy of Resource It means that every resource is very limited. Use of resources should be done very economically so that valuable and scarce resource can be conserved. For example, all families do not have same amount of resources, so one has to think before utilising the limited resources.

Desire to Gain Satisfaction It means the resources are utilised to achieve goals and to gain satisfaction. Resources are consumed not only because wants and goals are to be satisfied but primarily to increase the satisfaction level gained in the process.

Resources are Interrelated It means the use of one resource will definitely affect the use of the other. Thus, while using resources, we have to ensure that we utilise them in such a way that we get maximum benefit from their use, for this we have to identify all available resources.

Make use of only the right amount of resources substitute the less expensive resources for the more expensive ones. For instance, for the overall development of family members, all the members have to understands and cooperate in the management process, so that optimal use of resources can be achieved.

A family member develops skills and knowledge of relating to resource utilisation with this basis they plan their goals, individual as well as family. Parents help the family members to identify the available resources and encourage them the use, their interest and capability for gaining maximum success and happiness in life.

EXAM BASED QUESTIONS

1 Which of the following statement(s) is/are correct about management?

(a) Management is a universal phenomena.

(b) It is an umbrella term under which individual work together to achieve a common goal.

(c) It is an art and as well as science.

(d) All of the above

2 The term 'management' is coined from the .... word 'menage'.

(a) Greek (b) French

(c) Latin (d) Spanish

3 Who said "There is perhaps no more important area of humans activity than managing for it is the basic task of all managers, at all levels in all kinds of activities to design and maintain an environment in which individual work together in groups can accomplish selected mission and objectives."

(a) Koontz (b) MP Follett

(c) K. Kautilya (d) Donald M. Johnson

4 "Getting results through people" is the description of

(a) management (b) government

(c) training (d) controlling

5 "Resource management is the utilisation of resources to achieve one's goal, objective and to meet demand it involves knowing the quantitative and qualitative aspects." This has been stated by

(a) K Kautilya

(b) Rose, Randle Knoll

(c) Gross and Crandal

(d) Nickell and Dorsey

6 Which of the following is not a management approach?

(a) Classic (b) System approach

(c) Human relation (d) Double entry system

7 Indicate the region, separating one system from another, in the system approaches to management

(a) boundary (b) interface

(c) exchanger (d) divider

8 Who stated "Time with use is handled much like a material we can earn it, spend it?"

(a) Nickell and Dorsey

(b) Edward Eleven

(c) Hall ET

(d) Gross and Crandall

9 Who is the author of "Time for living"?

(a) George Soule (b) Binni Mandela

(c) Jacque Barzun (d) Hazel Kyrk

10 Time allotted for occupational activities should include ....

(a) sleeping (b) eating

(c) working (d) All of these

11 The demand for energy will be less during .... stage.

(a) beginning (b) contracting

(c) expanding (d) All of these

12 Money as a non-human resource can be in the form of

(a) wages (b) saving

(c) income or investment (d) All of these

13 Psychic income is ....

(a) a flow of satisfaction that arises out of everyday experiences.

(b) intangible

(c) subjective and is most important income in terms of quality of living

(d) All of the above

14 Family income can be categorised as

(a) money income (b) real income

(c) psychic income (d) All of these

15 The term 'motivation' is derived from the .... word 'movere'.

(a) Latin (b) French

(c) Greek (d) Hebrew

16 It is a concept of the desirable explicit or implicit, which governs our choice of methods, modes or goals or action?

(a) Standard (b) Values

(c) Goals (d) Demand

17 Who said with regard to spiritual values that the family is not only the best conveyor, but is the producer of values?

(a) Louis F Raths

(b) William E Englore andson

(c) Lawrence Frank

(d) Leonard Mayo

18 Who said, "In the absence of clearly defined values, effective appraisal of practices or decision is impossible"?

(a) Goodyear and Klohr (b) MacIver and Page

(c) P Eberman (d) Gross and Crandall

19 Who said, "Values are those deep-seated beliefs and desires that give direction to our life"?

(a) Goodyear and Klohr

(b) Mahendra Jain

(c) Gross and Crandall

(d) Nickell and Dorsey

20 Who stated "life is characterised by striving for goals"?
(a) Nickell and Dorsey (b) Lawrence Frank
(c) Goodyear and Klohr (d) Dewitt H Parker

21 The types of goals which are limited to the available resources or when the effectiveness of a decision ends, the goals are completed and they are known as
(a) values (b) short-term goals
(c) mean-end goals (d) long-term goals

22 One can assess the person's character, behaviour culture, etc, on the basis of
(a) goals (b) standards
(c) values (d) All of these

23 Family health, higher education and intellectual development of the members of the family are
(a) short-term goals (b) mean-send goals
(c) long-term goals (d) set goals

24 They are necessary for daily routine. They are plenty in number, but all are not equally important. What are 'they'?
(a) Standards (b) Goals
(c) Short-term goals (d) Long-term standards

25 "A value is a conception, explicit or implicit distinctive of an individual or characteristic or a group of the desirable standards, which influence the selection from the available models means of ends of action." This definition is given by
(a) Martin Luther (b) Clyde Kluck Hobin
(c) Nickell and Dorsey (d) Gross and Crandall

26 According to whose view points "Checking, evaluating and defining values periodically is crucial for effective management?
(a) Dr K Kautilya (b) Goodyear and Klohr
(c) P Eberman (d) Gross and Crandall

27 Intrinsic value is also called
(a) personal value (b) terminal value
(c) value orientation (d) None of these

28 Long-term and short-term goals are based on
(a) continuity (b) duration
(c) interdependence (d) All of these

29 It is a concept of the desirable explicit or implicit which governs our choices of methods, modes, or goals of action.
(a) Standard (b) Demand
(c) Values (d) Goals

30 .... values are those that stand alone and are important and desirable simply for their own sake.
(a) External (b) Instrumental
(c) Intrinsic (d) None of these

31 Values play major role in determining
(a) attitudes (b) standards
(c) goals (d) All of these

32 Objective standards are the earnest standards to identify that influence much of one's life as they are rigid standards.
(a) Object standards (b) Qualitative standards
(c) Quantitative standards (d) None of these

33 According to whom, "The making of decisions implies the existence of objective towards which decisions are oriented"?
(a) Dewey and Tufts (b) Thomas and Cook
(c) C A Bratton (d) D Woods, Thomas

34 "...... decision-making occurs over time ...... solution of most of the difficulties of predicting for either practical application or theoretical understanding will come only by full appreciation of the longitudinal dimension in consumer behaviour.
(a) N N Foote (b) N K Manohar
(c) Robert Tannenbaum (d) H A Simon

35 Individual decision refers
(a) to personal problems and needs
(b) decisions that are made by the person concerned
(c) decisions that are quickly made as compared to group decisions
(d) All of the above

36 ...... decision is very crucial decision in one's life where he has to make careful deliberations and analysis before arriving at the final decision.
(a) Central (b) Economic (c) Habitual (d) Group

37 Economic decisions are related to
(a) values (b) saving
(c) expenditure (d) Only (b) and (c)

38 "When a girl child has passed out from high school. She will think through different alternative for her higher studies. She may go to the college or sit at home for marriage or search for employment." Which type of decision is this?
(a) Technical (b) Group
(c) Individual (d) Habitual

39 "......... said that the hardest work of all is to think and decision-making is thinking."
(a) George Soule (b) Peter King
(c) Hazel Kyrk (d) Jacque Barzun

40 According to whom, "Income management may be defined as planning, controlling and evaluating the use of all types of income."
(a) Nickell and Dorsey (b) Gross and Crandall
(c) FD Roosevelt (d) Elizabeth E Hoyt

41 Who said, "Everyday experience in thinking occurs in planning of any kind ?"
(a) Starch (b) Peter king
(c) Nickell and Dorsey (d) Gross and Crandall

42 What does supervision mean?
(a) Establishing one's wider vision
(b) Establishing above vision
(c) Supreme vision
(d) All of the above

43 Identify the characteristics of general evaluation.
(a) Casual and subjective
(b) Outcomes not thoroughly analysed
(c) Elaborate type
(d) Only (a) and (b)

44 The steps of controlling include
(a) checking (b) adjustment
(c) incentive (d) All of these

45 The process of assessing the progress of a project based on pre-determined indicators and objectives of the programme is known as
(a) planning (b) implementation
(c) monitoring (d) evaluation

46 Planning of the family may be
(a) long-term planning (b) short-term planning
(c) strategic planning (d) Only (a) and (b)

47 The contracting stage has ...... sub-stages
(a) three (b) four (c) two (d) six

48 At the beginning stage of family life cycle ....
(a) the resource utilisation is comparatively low
(b) the partners tries to formulate short term and long-term goals
(c) both the partners get acquainted with each other
(d) All of the above

49 Effective management recognises the validity of
(a) resources (b) decision-making
(c) management process (d) values and standards

50 Resource management is the utilisation of resources to achieve one's goal, objective and to meet demand it involves knowing the quantitative and qualitative aspects. This has been stated by
(a) Rose, Randle Knoll (b) K. Kautilya
(c) Nickell and Dorsey (d) Gross and Crandall

51 Which of the following statements is/are correct?
(a) Management is a separate art or activity and can be learned by able people
(b) A woman has responsibility to develop her managerial skills
(c) Management development will result when managers believe in its importance, a manager can give commensurate authority and be held accountable for results
(d) All of the above

52 State which is/are true?
(a) Management process understanding helps in guiding research work for codifying existing knowledge and a useful guide to administrative behaviour.
(b) Instrumental value is a means of attaining other values or goals.
(c) Home management makes use of the findings of science and knowledge concerning all aspects of family life, economic, social, psychological, physical, spiritual and technological.
(d) All of the above

53 Which of the following statement(s) is/are correct with regard to the ways of saving energy?
(a) Break the task into smaller activities
(b) Take different tasks together
(c) Run around to do different activities
(d) Plan out your task in a haphzard manner

54 Which of the following statement(s) is/are correct with regard to the principles of space planning?
(a) Space must be planned for maximum utilisation
(b) While managing space internal and external privacy should be kept in mind
(c) While planning space, practical points like strength and stability should be kept in mind
(d) All of the above

55 Which of the following statement(s) is/are correct or incorrect?
(a) Group values come through prising, cherishing and choosing then in the use of resources.
(b) Homemaker needs clarification of aims and purpose, aspirations and values.
(c) In the absence of clearly defined values, effective appraisal of decision is impossible, value are some what unstable and always in the process of change.
(d) All of the above

56 Which one of the following is considered as the characteristic of goals?
(a) Goals are important for human life
(b) Wants of the family member are fulfilled by setting of goal
(c) Goals are changeable
(d) All of the above

57 Which of the following statements are correct with the origin and development of values?
1. Values originate from human desires and interests.
2. Interaction between individuals in environment and situations originate values.
3. It is human being who originates values and protects it.
4. Attitude of an individual is based on values.

Codes
(a) 1 and 2 (b) 2 and 3
(c) 1, 2 and 3 (d) 1, 2, 3 and 4

58 Which of the following statement(s) is/are correct?
(a) Short-term goals are used as a means of achieving other goals.
(b) As the years go by the family goals help direct and control the desire of the group and thus, shape the family's pattern of living.
(c) Clearly defined goals not only encourage the wise use of family resources, they also stimulate the cooperation.
(d) All of the above

59 Which of the following statement(s) is/are correct?
(a) Economic decision is based on exchange of resources.
(b) Technical decisions are goal-oriented.
(c) Central decisions are supporting decisions.
(d) All of these

60 Which of the following statement(s) is/are correct?
(a) Planning is the initiating process in a democratic society and any plan of education must correspond to the ideals of a democratic philosophy.
(b) Planning is retrospective. It looks forward to see how things take shape and materialise.
(c) At the end of the activity, planning looks backward to see how for the desired results have been attainable. and what limitations hindered their execution.
(d) All of the above

61 Which of the following statement(s) is/are correct?
(a) Controlling can be done by direction or by guidance.
(b) The book 'The Philosophy of Home Management' has been written by Lawrence K Frank.
(c) The book 'Values in Home Management' is written by William W Mackee.
(d) All of the above

62 Consider the following features about the expanding family stage and state the correct feature(s).
(a) It begins with the birth of a first child.
(b) At this stage, the family pattern and life styles of parents change due to arrival of children.
(c) At this stage, the expenditure of energy, the work load and the efficiency are at the highest peak.
(d) All of the above

63 Individual decisions are more quickly made then group decision and the quality of group decisions tends to be no higher than the contribution of the ablest member of the group." It is said by
(a) M P Follett (b) K Kautilya
(c) Jean M Steckle (d) Donald M Johnson

64 Which of the statement(s) is/are correct about Human Resource Approach ?
Statement I It tells us that employees want to contribute and make real contributions to something.
Statement II The approach is focused on social environment.
Codes
(a) Only statement I is correct
(b) Only statement II is correct
(c) Both the statements I and II are correct
(d) Neither statement I nor II is correct

65 Consider the following statements
Statement I Decision-making is the heart of management.
Statement II The role of decision-making in management involves knowing and actually applying essential information in problem situation.
Codes
(a) Only statement I is correct.
(b) Only statement II is correct.
(c) Both the statements, I and II are correct
(d) Neither statement I nor II is correct

66 Consider the following statements regarding levels of organisation.
Statement I Level I is related to organising a task.
Statement II Level II is when one person arranging through his own efforts for the completion of several tasks.
(a) Only statement I is correct
(b) Only statement II is correct
(c) Both the statements I and II are correct
(d) Neither statement I nor II is correct

67 Which of the following are long-term goals?
1. Economic stability 2. Good health
3. Discharging social responsibilities
4. House
Codes
(a) 1 and 2 (b) 1 and 4
(c) 1, 2, 3 and 4 (d) 1, 2 and 3

68 The motivating factors to make decisions and choice are
1. resources 2. values
3. goals 4. standards
Codes
(a) 1, 2 and 4 (b) 1, 2, and 3
(c) 2, 3 and 4 (d) 1, 3 and 4

69 Which of the following are characteristics of goals?
1. Goals keep on changing
2. Society affects goals
3. All goals are not of equal importance
4. Goal formation is a continuous process
Codes
(a) 1 and 4 (b) 1, 2 and 3
(c) 1 and 2 (d) All of these

70 The success of goal achievement depends upon
1. cooperation 2. able leadership
3. decision power 4. goal achievable
Codes
(a) 1 and 2 (b) 1 and 4
(c) 1, 3 and 4 (d) All of these

71 Which of the following are long-term goals?
1. Economic stability
2. Good health
3. Discharging social responsibilities
4. House
Codes
(a) All of these (b) 1 and 4
(c) 1 and 2 (d) 1, 2 and 3

72 The normal family goals is/are
1. all round development of family members.
2. cordial interpersonal relationships.
3. common aim.
4. discharge of responsibilities.
Codes
(a) 1 and 2 (b) 1 and 4
(c) 1, 2 and 3 (d) All of these

73 If I have a dollar bill L95484272A and I give it to you, you have it and I do not. Either you or I can have it but not both of us. This is an example of

1. more mental value
2. allocative value

Codes

(a) Only 1 (b) Only 2
(c) Both 1 and 2 (d) None of these

74 Playing is good for enjoyment, passing leisure time and helps to attain good health. It is an example of

1. intrinsic value
2. instruments value

Codes

(a) Only 1 (b) Only 2
(c) Both 1 and 2 (d) None of these

75 Which of the factor(s) effect use of resources?

1. Motivation
2. Capacity
3. Philosophy
4. Life cycle and family factors like heritage

Codes

(a) 1 and 2 (b) 1 and 4
(c) 1, 2, 3 and 4 (d) 1, 2 and 3

76 Decision-making is a process involving following in sequence.

1. Evaluate the alternatives
2. Identify the alternatives
3. Identify the problem
4. Make a decision
5. Evaluate the decision

Codes

(a) 4, 3, 5, 2 and 1 (b) 3, 1, 2, 5 and 4
(c) 3, 2, 1, 4 and 5 (d) 3, 4, 2, 1 and 5

77 Planning should be

1. flexible
2. adoptable
3. consistent
4. stable

Codes

(a) 1 and 2 (b) 1 and 4
(c) All of these (d) 1, 2 and 3

78 Planning is an intellectual activity, which needs knowledge of affairs and resources.

1. Sufficient reasoning
2. Insight and imagination
3. Professional skill
4. Specialised knowledge

Codes

(a) 1 and 2 (b) 1 and 4
(c) 1, 2 and 3 (d) All of these

79 Nickell and Dorsey has given six steps for income planning. Which of the following is/are his view point?

1. Clearly define and recognise one's goal.
2. Analyse all kinds of available income.
3. Analyse money income for short and long period of time.
4. Recognise the stages of the family.

Codes

(a) 1 and 2 (b) 1, 2, 3 and 4
(c) 1 and 4 (d) 1, 2 and 3

80 Give the correct sequence of managerial functions listed below.

1. Reporting
2. Staffing
3. Planning
4. Organising
5. Co-ordinating
6. Budgeting
7. Directing

Codes

(a) 3, 4, 2, 6, 7, 1, 5 (b) 3, 4, 2, 7, 5, 1, 6
(c) 2, 4, 6, 3, 1, 7, 5 (d) 5, 7, 4, 6, 2, 1, 3

81 Which of the following is/are correct about home management?

1. Decision-making
2. Dynamic
3. Administrative
4. Marital work

Codes

(a) 1, 3 and 4 (b) 1 and 2
(c) 1 and 4 (d) All of these

82 Components of implementing are

1. adjusting
2. facilitating
3. controlling
4. checking

Codes

(a) 1 and 3 (b) 2 and 4
(c) 2 and 3 (d) 3 and 4

83 Arrange the right sequence of home management process.

1. Energising
2. Evaluation
3. Planning
4. Adjusting
5. Checking

Codes

(a) 3, 1, 5, 4, 2 (b) 1, 2, 3, 4, 5
(c) 4, 2, 1, 3, 5 (d) 5, 4, 3, 2, 1

84 All the resources have similiarity which is are

1. They are limted.
2. All resources are useful.
3. Arrangement of resources is applicable to all.
4. Use of resource depends on the individual.

Codes

(a) 1 and 2 (b) 1 and 4
(c) 1, 2, 3, and 4 (d) 1, 2, and 3

85 The limitation of resources could be

1. quantitative
2. qualitative

Codes

(a) Only 1 (b) Only 2
(c) Both 1 and 2 (d) None of these

86 Which of the following is/are true?

(a) Management process understanding helps in guiding research work, for codifying existing knowledge and a useful guide to administrative behaviour.
(b) Instrumental value is a means of attaining other values or goals.
(c) Home management makes use of the findings of science and of knowledge concerning all aspects of family life, economic, social, psychological, physical, spiritual and technological, in a well managed home management is looked upon as a tool or process.
(d) All of the above

87 Select the correct pair from the following codes
(a) Standard—Traditional—Stable
(b) Standard—Traditional—Goals
(c) Standard—Traditional—Flexible
(d) Standard—Traditional—Values

88 Sources of value development in a person
1. culture
2. life experience
3. interpersonal relationship
4. religion

Codes
(a) 1 and 2 (b) 1 and 4
(c) 1, 2, 3 and 4 (d) 1, 2 and 3

89 Match the following.

List I	List II
A. Intelligence and enthusiasm	1. Motivating factors
B. Values, goals and standards	2. Home management process
C. Planning, controlling and evaluating	3. Homemaker
D. Higher education	4. Long-term goals

Codes

	A	B	C	D		A	B	C	D
(a)	3	1	2	4	(b)	4	2	1	3
(c)	1	4	3	2	(d)	4	3	1	2

90 Match the following.

List I	List II
A. Psychological needs	1. Fulfilment of capacities
B. Self-esteem needs	2. Freedom from danger, job security, health care, etc.
C. Self-actualisation needs	3. Recognition by others/feeling of achievement
D. Need for safety and security	4. Food, clothing and shelter

Codes

	A	B	C	D		A	B	C	D
(a)	4	3	1	2	(b)	2	3	1	4
(c)	1	2	3	4	(d)	4	3	2	1

91 Match the following.

List I	List II
A. Selecting an alternative	1. It needs relevant information to identify and define
B. Recognition of the problem	2. One needs to identify possible alternatives
C. Identifying the alternatives	3. The problem should be clearly selected from the possible alternatives
D. Accepting the consequences	4. It is important for making future decisions

Codes

	A	B	C	D		A	B	C	D
(a)	1	2	3	4	(b)	3	1	2	4
(c)	4	3	2	1	(d)	2	4	1	3

92 Which of the following are the basic steps involved in planning?
(a) Recognition of the problem
(b) Choosing an appropriate alternative
(c) Accepting the consequences
(d) All of the above

93 Arrange Maslow's Hierarchy of needs in the proper sequence.
1. Physiological
2. Social
3. Safety
4. Self-esteen
5. Self-actualisation

Codes
(a) 1,3,2,4,5 (b) 1,2,3,4,5
(c) 5,4,3,2,1 (d) 1,4,3,2,5

94 Conventional standards are those that are
(a) traditional
(b) accepted by an individual
(c) accepted by community or social group at large
(d) Only (a) and (c)

95 Which of the following are the sub-stages of the contracting stage?
(a) Vocational adjustment
(b) Financial recovery
(c) Retirement
(d) All of the above

Directions (Q. No. 96-106) *In the questions given below are two statements labelled as Assertion (A) and Reason (R). In the context of the two statements, which are of the following is correct.*

Codes
(a) Both A and R are correct and R is the correct explanation of A.
(b) A is correct, but R is not the correct explanation of A.
(c) A is correct, but R is not correct.
(d) A is in correct, but is correct.

96 **Assertion** (A) Management is a continuous process. It includes planning, controlling and evaluating in a specialised manner.
Reason (R) Management plays an important role in the development of human being in a family.

97 **Assertion** (A) Management process is a valuable key for the successful achievement of goals.
Reason (R) There are individual and family goals in every household. They need a method to achieve goals.

98 **Assertion** (A) Human life, health and happiness are values, but they are theoretical and not clear values are very important in man's social life.
Reason (R) Value is a belief that something is good and desirable.

99 **Assertion** (A) Goals are helpful in the development of personality's and well-planned goals will satisfy an individual's interests, attitudes desires and make the life successful.
Reason (R) Goals are changeable and change according to the change in need, interest and want.

100 **Assertion** (A) Standards are based on resources, values and goals that are stable.
Reason (R) Values and goals are based on hypothetical facts and are more stable.

101 **Assertion** (A) Manager is one, who guides and directs the work of other people. He is both a leader and a supervisor.

Reason (R) Planning, organisation, coordination, motivation, control and evaluation are works performed by a manager.

102 **Assertion** (A) Family environment depends on the efforts made by the housewife, is the creator of homely environment.

Reason (R) A housewife should have a knowledge of latest happeings.

103 **Assertion** (A) Values grow out of human interests.

Reason (R) Human behaviour is guided by the thoughts and emotional background.

104 **Assertion** (A) Control is the first and most important function of management.

Reason (R) It determines what is to be accomplished, evaluates performance, applies corrective measures and ensures achievements of plans.

105 **Assertion** (A) The quality of decision determine the quality of management.

Reason (R) Decision-making occurs when there is a problem to solve or some choice to make.

106 **Assertion** (A) Evaluation is an integral component of management system.

Reason (R) It facilitates information about day-to-day transaction how they compare goals and provide opportunity for correction.

Directions (Q. Nos. 107-111) *Read the passage carefully and answer the questions that follow.*

Lot of people believe that they cannot reach their dreams, travel to exotic location, land their dream jobs, finish their projects before the deadline, get enough sleep every night and spend enough time with loved ones because they don't have enough time. It's not limited time that's the problem, it's bad time management. It is important for a person to manage time effectively.

Effective time management is the effective use of your time that allows you to plan your days in such a way that you finish your work with less effort and make the most of the limited time you've got. It is essential for one to know the importance or benefits of time management in one's life. It helps your to achieve what you want. and faster. When you understand the importance of time management, you gain the motivation to stop sitting around and pursue your goals. As a result of this hard work and new found motivation, you reach your goals faster.

It helps you get more done, but in less time, and avoid more friction and problems. Properly managing time includes making a to-do list, allocating time to each item from your to-do list and then scheduling those tasks on your calendar. By doing so, you'll no longer be indecisive about what you have to do next and whether you'll have to finish everything you need to. It helps you clear your schedule for more leisure time and feel more energised. Considering that proper time management helps you finish your work faster, you'll find that you now have more free time as a consequence. More free time will mean you have more time to spend with your loved ones, practice a hobby or even go on a trip abroad, which will all result in you feeling more energised. It helps you fulfill more tasks in less time, and in turn, feel more fulfilled.

When you properly manage your time, you" ll enjoy the feeling of success a completed to-do list brings-you'll see how you can live up to your expectations and in turn feel a boost of self-confidence about your abilities. Effective time management helps you feel calmer and less stressed over time. But, poor time management increases our stress levels. It makes us feel frustrated and angry. It can actually ruin our finances. Poor time management makes one impatient towards or any other activity. It can have very real and very negative consequences for our lives and ultimately, our health and well-being.

107 **People with good time management often succeed because**

(a) they finish their project before the deadline
(b) they know how to make use of time for a particular activity assigned to them.
(c) they don't make big promises
(d) All of the above

108 **The properly managing time includes**

(a) making a do-to list
(b) allocating time to each item
(c) scheduling the task on calendar
(d) All of the above

109 **Which of the following statement(s) with regard to effective time management is/are correct.**

Statement I Effective time management helps you to get more work done, but in less time.

Statement II Effective time management is not needed in home management.

Codes

(a) Statement I is correct
(b) Statement II is correct
(c) Both the statements are correct
(d) Neither statements I nor II is correct

110 **If a person plans his/her time effectively it means he/she**

(a) plan their days in advance
(b) finish their work before deadline
(c) pursue for the goals set by them
(d) All of the above.

111 **The possible consequences of poor time management are**

(a) it increases stress level
(b) one feels frustrated and angry
(c) it can have negative consequences on our lives
(d) All of the above

PREVIOUS YEARS' QUESTIONS

July 2018

1 The principle of management that 'in union there is strength' is called as

(a) Scalar Chain (b) Equity to Gain
(c) Stability of Tenure (d) Esprit De Corps

2 Which of the following are the intrinsic values in management?

1. Cooperation
2. Technological satisfaction
3. Honesty 4. Creativity

Codes

(a) 1, 2, 3 (b) 2, 3, 4 (c) 1, 3, 4 (d) 1, 2, 4

3 Hidden Family Income is derived from a combination of

1. investment income 2. community income
3. employment benefit 4. psychic income

Codes

(a) 1, 2, 3 (b) 1, 3, 4
(c) 1, 2, 4 (d) 2, 3, 4

4 Assertion (A) Record keeping in money management helps to compare monthly expenditure with the spending plan.

Reason (R) Records show distribution of money after expenditure has been made.

Codes

(a) Both A and R are true
(b) A is true, but R is false
(c) A is false, but R is true
(d) Both A and R are false

5 Arrange in correct sequence the monitoring and evaluation process of a national nutrition programme.

1. Develop a structure for the analysis.
2. Determine key indicators for the evaluation and monitoring process.
3. Write up the findings and conclusions.
4. Identify patterns, trends and possible interpretations.
5. Collect information on the indicators.

Codes

(a) 2, 1, 4, 5, 3 (b) 2, 4, 1, 3, 5
(c) 5, 2, 1, 3, 4 (d) 2, 5, 1, 4, 3

November 2017

6 Arrange the following steps in making time plans in proper sequence.

1. Determine time sequence.
2. List all the items to be included grouping under flexible and inflexible activities.
3. Bring total estimated time needed and total available time into harmony.
4. Write out plan.
5. Set out as accurate an estimate for each task as is obtainable.

Codes

(a) 3, 4, 2, 1, 5 (b) 5, 1, 3, 2, 4
(c) 2, 5, 3, 1, 4 (d) 4, 3, 5, 2, 1

January 2017

7 Which of the following motivators are listed in Herzberg's Theory of Motivation?

1. Challenging work 2. Physiological need
3. Growth in job 4. Recognition

Codes

(a) 1, 2, 3 (b) 2, 3, 4 (c) 1, 3, 4 (d) 1, 2, 4

8 Arrange the following steps of planning in a sequence.

1. Preparation of derivative plans.
2. Determination of objectives.
3. The use of strategy.
4. Providing follow up to the proposed course of action.
5. Establishment of planning premises.
6. Timing and sequence of operations.
7. Selection of the operation plan.

Codes

(a) 1, 7, 6, 3, 4, 2, 5 (b) 2, 5, 7, 1, 6, 3, 4
(c) 3, 4, 7, 2, 1, 5, 6 (d) 4, 3, 1, 2, 6, 5, 7

July 2016

9 Arrange the steps in making time plans in the proper sequence.

1. Merge individual plan with other plans for coordination.
2. Determining time sequence.
3. List all items to be included.
4. Set down as accurate an estimate of time for each task.
5. Bring total estimated time needed and total available time into harmony.
6. Write out plan.

Codes

(a) 3, 4, 5, 2, 6, 1 (b) 1, 2, 3, 4, 5, 6
(c) 3, 2, 1, 6, 5, 4 (d) 3, 2, 4, 1, 6, 5

10 Arrange the following as per the Maslow's Theory of Hierarchy of Needs for Motivation.

1. Safety and security
2. Social needs friendship and family
3. Physiological needs - air and water
4. Self-actualisation - creativity and problem-solving
5. Self esteem - confidence and achievement

Codes

(a) 3, 2, 1, 4, 5 (b) 3, 1, 2, 5, 4
(c) 3, 1, 4, 5, 2 (d) 3, 2, 5, 4, 1

December 2015

11 **Assertion** (A) Management of time can be practiced to tackle peak loads.

Reason (R) Allocation of work to family members will be a helpful method.

Codes

(a) Both A and R are true
(b) Both A and R are false
(c) A is true, but R is false
(d) A is false, but R true

June 2015

12 Arrange in sequence the steps involved in the planning process of management.

1. Formulating possible course of action
2. Setting priorities.
3. Obtaining relevant information.
4. Organising.
5. Recognition of the fact that a problem exists.
6. Selecting the best course.

Codes

(a) 1, 2, 3, 4, 6, 5 (b) 5, 3, 1, 4, 2, 6
(c) 5, 3, 1, 2, 6, 4 (d) 5, 2, 4, 3, 1, 4

13 **Assertion** (A) Systemic evaluation enables to determine the effectiveness of any programme.

Reason (R) Information obtained through evaluation shows strengths and weaknesses of a programme.

Codes

(a) Both A and R are true (b) Both A and R are false
(c) A is true, but R is false (d) A is false, but R is true

June 2015

14 Arrange the steps involved in implementing a plan in the proper sequence.

1. Controlling
2. Checking
3. Activating
4. Adjusting
5. Facilitating

Codes

(a) 1, 2, 3, 4, 5 (b) 3, 1, 2, 4, 5
(c) 3, 1, 4, 2, 5 (d) 1, 3, 2, 4, 5

December 2014

15 Sequence the various functions of management in extension.

1. Planning
2. Directing
3. Coordinating
4. Reporting
5. Organising

Codes

(a) 1, 5, 2, 3, 4 (b) 1, 2, 3, 4, 5
(c) 5, 1, 2, 4, 3 (d) 1, 3, 5, 2, 4

16 **Assertion** (A) Planning permits the action or work to be seen as a whole.

Reason (R) Planning is essential to forecast future actions and it comprises of decision-making.

Codes

(a) A is true but R is false
(b) Both A and R are true
(c) Both A and R are false
(d) Both A and R are true, but R is not the correct explanation of A.

June 2014

17 Participating planning in community development employs

1. participatory learning
2. participatory rural appraisal
3. participatory action
4. passive participation

Codes

(a) 1, 2 and 4 (b) 1, 2, and 3
(c) 1 and 3 (d) 2 and 4

ANSWERS

Exam Based Questions

1 (d)	2 (b)	3 (a)	4 (a)	5 (b)	6 (d)	7 (a)	8 (a)	9 (a)	10 (d)
11 (a)	12 (d)	13 (d)	14 (d)	15 (a)	16 (b)	17 (d)	18 (c)	19 (a)	20 (c)
21 (c)	22 (b)	23 (c)	24 (b)	25 (b)	26 (b)	27 (a)	28 (d)	29 (c)	30 (c)
31 (a)	32 (c)	33 (d)	34 (a)	35 (d)	36 (a)	37 (d)	38 (c)	39 (d)	40 (a)
41 (a)	42 (d)	43 (d)	44 (d)	45 (c)	46 (d)	47 (a)	48 (d)	49 (a)	50 (a)
51 (d)	52 (d)	53 (a)	54 (d)	55 (d)	56 (c)	57 (c)	58 (d)	59 (d)	60 (d)
61 (d)	62 (d)	63 (d)	64 (a)	65 (c)	66 (c)	67 (c)	68 (c)	69 (d)	70 (d)
71 (a)	72 (b)	73 (b)	74 (c)	75 (c)	76 (c)	77 (c)	78 (d)	79 (b)	80 (b)
81 (a)	82 (c)	83 (b)	84 (d)	85 (d)	86 (d)	87 (a)	88 (c)	89 (a)	90 (a)
91 (b)	92 (d)	93 (a)	94 (d)	95 (d)	96 (b)	97 (a)	98 (b)	99 (b)	100 (c)
101 (a)	102 (a)	103 (b)	104 (b)	105 (b)	106 (a)	107 (d)	108 (d)	109 (a)	110 (d)
111 (d)									

Previous Years' Questions

1 (d)	2 (c)	3 (d)	4 (a)	5 (d)	6 (c)	7 (c)	8 (b)	9 (c)	10 (b)
11 (a)	12 (c)	13 (a)	14 (b)	15 (a)	16 (d)	17 (b)			

Resource and Resource Management

Human beings uses resources to satisfy their needs and comforts. They are of great economic importance for the development. The resources are limited, so it is essential to conserve and utilise them judiciously. In the present time, there is a need that the resources should be managed properly for the use of future generations.

Resources

Nature has bestowed human beings with various types of resources, which they are using for different purposes for fulfilling their requirements. One may need more of a certain resources for a particular activity as compared to another. Resources help us in accomplishing our goals. In simple words, resources can be defined as material asset or capital which can be used to fulfil our goals.

The resources have been defined by various authors as follows :

- According to **Moloch** and **Decan**, "resources as a means are available and recognised for their potential in meeting demands." They further define it as those things which have 'want satisfying power' and which are instrumental in reaching desired ends.
- According to **Gross** and **Crandall Knoll**, "resources are available means for reaching goals and meeting demands." According to them. "a resource means anything which is used for the attainment of goals, *e.g.*, time, energy, money, etc."
- According to **Betty B Swanson** "resources as tangible and intangible components which one uses to achieve goals, objectives and to meet demands."
- According to **Random House Dictionary** of the English language, "resource is a source of supply, support or aid, especially one holds in reserve and has the capability in dealing with a situation or in meeting difficulties."
- According to **Nickel et al** "resources are the assets that can be used to accomplish goals."

In this Chapter

- According to **Deacon** and **Firebaugh** "the resources are the supply reservoir for use in the system's specific action and are necessary in some form to solve every management problem."
- According to **Cambridge dictionary** "resource is a valuable possession or quality of a country, organisation or person."

Classification of Resources

The resources can be classified as human and non-human, individual and shared resources, natural and community resources. These are discussed as follows :

Human Resources

Human Resources are central to carrying out any activity. These resources can be developed through training and self-development. For example, knowledge regarding any field/task can be acquired, skill may be developed which may help you to develop aptitude. Human resources are less tangible and can be easily determined.

These resources are used for productive purposes. They originate internally and constitute the personal characteristics and attributes. These resources cannot be utilised independently of the individual. These resources are explained below in the form of table given below:

Human Resources

Name of Resources	Example
Time	A minute, an hour, a day, a week, a month, a year.
Energy	Energy required for doing any type of work, physical, mental, etc.
Interest	In your own work, studies, job, activity, learning, etc.
Skill	In doing any task, skillful work, etc.
Knowledge	Of your subject, knowledge required for particular thing/job/work or everything around.
Ability	In doing any particular thing.
Attitude	A way of feeling about some one, something nature.
Aptitude	A natural ability or tendency of doing certain things skillfully.
Capability	Having the necessary ability or quality to do so, ability to achieve whatever one has to do.

Non-Human Resources

They are not internal. In other words, non-human resources are those resources which are available to a person within his community, state and nation *e.g.,* recreational facilities, parks, health facilities and educational facilities. Non- human resources are follows :

Time and Energy Calculative method to conserve and utilise energy and time are aspect of non-human resources.

Money Medium of producing goods and services is money.

Community Facilities Community facilities are provided to the members of the society *e.g.,* transport facility, hospital, school, police, etc which are used by the community members. It is the basic unit of community.

Material Goods Material goods are used for the achievements of goals and procured by expending money *e.g.,* property, house, food, clothing and every comfort products, etc. Non-human resources could be better understood by the following tables

Non-Human or Material Resources

Money	Cash, in the form of wages, salary, yearly income, saving, investment, etc.
Material Goods	In the form of assets food gains, clothing, furniture furnishing rugs, carpets and everything available in our house. Like car, scooter, cycle, house, farm house, flat, plot, farm, etc.
Community Facilities	Educational, recreational facilities, etc.Tuition class, coaching class, schools, colleges, training centres, academy, tutorials, computer institutes, typing institutes, etc. Garden, park, picture hall, musical concerts, reading room, libraries, internet etc.

Individual and Shared Resources

The individual resources are those resources which are available to an individual for personal use only, e.g. your school bag, clothes, etc. On the other hand, the shared resources are those which are available to many members of the community/society.

Natural and Community Resources

The resources which are available in nature such as water mountain, etc. are natural resources. These resources are available to all of us. There are resources which are available to an individual as a member of community/society. These resources are generally provided by the government such as hospitals, roads, park, post office, etc. These resources may be human or non-human.

Characteristics of Resources

All the resources in the world have their own characteristics. The following are the characteristics of resources :

Usefulness Usefulness of resources are one of the most important characteristics of all the resources. All resources are useful, is more clear by this example "Money is an important resource which can be used in fulfiling needs of the family."

Resources can be Developed Redevelopment of resource by using mental abilities and collecting information regarding resources help homemaker to perform his activity in a good manner.

Limitedness Limited supply of resources makes it limited in nature, different resources vary in their limitation. Limitedness of resources are of two types i.e. qualitative and quantitative. Human resources are qualitatively limited, whereas non-human resources are quantitatively limited.

All Resources are Inter-related The resources are inter-related, it is one of the most essential characteristics because, use of one resource depends on the use of other resource. It is difficult to achieve good in the absence of one. For example, if a person decides to learn cooking in cookery class, the things required are combination of resources i.e., money, material, time and energy, skill, knowledge, interest, etc, so, it is clear that there is inter-relationship among all resources.

Use of Alternative Resources To get success in achieving goal a person has the quality to make best use of the resources or to know about the alternative use of resources because there is a wide variety of methods in which resources are used.

Quality of Life is Improved by the Resources Use of mental ability and careful planning help the home maker to gain satisfaction and it also improves the quality of life, when resources are consumed in a systematic way.

Managerial Process Applicable to All Resources Managerial process is applicable on resources to achieve the goals. The process of managerial involves three steps planning, controlling, implementation and evaluation. Managerial processes are applicable on both resources like energy, time, money and material goods.

Resources Conservation

The resource conservation may be defined as "the management for the benefit of all life including humankind of the biosphere so that it may lead sustainable benefit for the present generation while maintaining its potential to meet the needs and aspirations of the future generations."

It is important to note that due to the continuou. increase in population the demand for resources have also increased. This has created a situation, when in the coming year the non-renewable resources may come to an end. All resources are finite, none are unlimited. We need to utilise resources effectively and judiciously, therefore these resources should not be misused or wasted.

The conservation of resources is also important as with the growth of industry and technology, human beings have started utilising natural resources at a much larger scale. There is a need for some kind of balance between the population growth and the utilisation of natural resources. There is a dire need to conserve our resources worldwide for our own interest and for the use of future generations. Conservation is that aspect of management which ensures that the fullest sustainable advantage is derived from the living resource base and that activities are located and conducted that the resources base is maintained.

Objectives of Resources Conservation

Resource conservation has three main objectives which are as follows :

- To maintain essential ecological processes and life support system e.g., soil regeneration, the recycling of nutrients, etc.
- To ensure the sustainable utilisation of species and ecosystem such as wildlife, forests, etc.
- To preserve genetic diversity.
- The conservation of natural resources is the responsibility of every individual. Environment belongs to everyone of us so all of us has the responsibility to conserve it.

Factors Affecting Use of Resources

Resources which are very important for human being affects the use of resources in various ways which are discussed below in detail:

- *Firstly,* the size of income is correlated with the purchasing practices. Larger the money, income, higher will be the satisfaction of the family members. Thus, the size of income affects the use of all resources.
- *Secondly,* the socio-economic status which accounts for differences in family values, attitudes decision making and in expenditure pattern.

  In the modern urban areas, status is something which is achieved and not ascribed through birth. Status groups are classified as upper-upper class, low-upper class, lower middle class and lower-lower class.
- *Thirdly,* size and composition of the family also affect use of resources i.e., the family size, age and sex make up family composition that affect their resource usage.

  For example, if a large family attends to maintain the same level of consumption as that of a small family, it is clear that it will require more commodities and services like food, clothing, medical, etc.

  The availability of the resources like time and energy for use increases similar to the size of the family in the use of time, energy and other resources the composition of family assume importance.

  If a large family is made up of adolescents and adults, more human resources are available and extra demand on money resource may be expected. Thus, the composition of the family affects the availability and use of their resources.

- *Fourthly,* family heritage and cultural background of the family also affects the use of resources as the eating and spending, hobbies, their beliefs, festivals, superstitions, etc. All are governed by this factor. This directly influences the way family utilises its resources on various occasions of similar situations.
- *Fifthly,* the location of the family within any community in relation to shopping areas, schools, place of husband's work, etc. Affects the homemakers use of time, energy and other resources. For instance, families residing near the city, all the community facilities like market, school, parks, etc will be easily available to the family that may affect the use of resources such as time, energy and especially the money.

Time Management

Time is limited and irreversible. It is the resource which is always calculated and used accordingly. Time is measured in years, months, days, hours, minutes and seconds. Time is used after thoughtful practical consideration. If time not managed properly, it keeps slipping away inspite of our efforts to control it.

No matter how important and valuable an individual may be, one cannot stop time nor slow down or speed it up. To be successful it is essential to develop time management skills. Proper time management allows one to have adequate rest and recreation along with work.

Meaning of Time Management

Time management is the utilisation of time available, so that an individual can accomplish the individual and group goals. Time management means minimising the expenditure of time to complete a task without altering the quality of work and achieving a balance in use of work, rest and leisure time to achieve maximum satisfaction. The principles of time management are recognising importance of achieving a balance between work and leisure, considering the need of all family members while making time and activity, considering the time cost of various activities while making plans of action and minimising time cost of domestic activities.

A plan is prepared where in all the household activities are included. Allocation of time is made on the basis of the nature of work, i.e. heavy work, light work, liked and disliked work, etc.

Fixed time allotted is for performing every activity of work, like time fixed for lunch going to school or place of work, etc. All these activities are performed within the allotted time, because the body gets used to the time of work, like time to eat and sleep will force the person to eat or to sleep. The time needed to do a job depends on knowledge, practice and experience of an individual. This time can be improved by practice and by gaining extra knowledge about the work. Every family has individual and family goals. Family goals have to be adhered by family members for this every member has to devote some part of his personal time and routine to do the household activities. For this one has to adjust with time and his routine to cooperate and assist the other family members.

Importance of Time in Performing Different Activities

Time plays an important role in performing any type of work. In the catering field, where food has to be served at particular times the pressure build-up for staff in kitchen and service and clearing areas from time to time.

Philip E Atkinson (1981) has suggested that to collect data on time a diary or time log should be maintained in which details are recorded. These show how time was utilised by whom, what was the desirable result and any comment on the achievement in that time period against what were the objectives for the period . An analysis of the information recorded accurately will show the amount of time which may have been spent on :

- Doing other people's jobs because they are absent or incapable of handling their work load.
- Writing for ingredients, instruction equipment maintenance.
- Doing routine non-creative jobs such as feeding potatoes into a peeling or chipping machine.

Utility of Time Management

Time is one factor which is equally distributed to all people (24 hours a day) irrespective of their education background skills and nature of jobs. **Krishnan and Agnihotry** (1983) have aptly stated most of us spend the better part of our lives, not knowing where we want to go and the rest of our lives in extricating ourselves from a self-women web of confusion.

To maximise utility of time management need to :

- Set clear cut goals and plans out work sequences in detail.
- Trust colleagues and delegates work to subordinates.
- Get priorities right so, that the most important work is done first and the rest in descending order of importance. This ensures that work which cannot be completed would not matter very much at the end of the day or could easily be taken up first thing next morning without affecting the work of others.

- Schedule work among employees, so that their skills are best utilised.
- Develop an easy management style so, that people gain confidence in the plan of action laid out for them.

Therefore, it is possible to control time wasting activities and save this valuable resource for constructive, planned action and achievement.

Tools in Time Management

There are various important tools that help in managing time effectively. These are discussed below in detail :

Peak Load Period

This tool signifies the maximum load of work during a specified period of time such as early morning or dinner time. The peak load depends on the style of working and managerial activities. It is seen that all the urgent work compile in the morning hours e.g. bathing, washing, preparing breakfast, preparing lunch for office/school. So, the time management becomes very important in order to solve the problem of peak load problem.

To overcome this problem, some amount of preparations can be done in advance to lessen the load of work. To lighten the peak load work, the non-essential activities should be avoided and one should try to find new or innovative methods to conserve their time and energy.

Work Curve

This is the device constructed between time and work. It helps the person to balance work and time and to simplify the work load. The work curve provides the information with regard to housewife's capacity and tendency to do work. The work curve is not same for every individual. It is seen that some people are more active/energetic in the afternoon whereas other are found to be active in evenings so, it is important to make a separate work curve for one self and thus plan the routine.

Rest Period

According to this tool, the frequency and duration of rest period is very important. The rest period should not be too long or too short. For an individual, rest is very essential in order to keep the body in healthy condition. So, he/she can take rest in these ways such as:

- After doing mental work, a person should take atleast 2-3 minutes rest after one hour of mental work.
- If a person is involved in doing heavy or energy consuming work then he/she should take rest by lying down or having a sound sleep.
- One can get himself/herself relaxed or rest if one changes body posture and position of the body.
- An individual can also have rest period by dovetailing of work thereby means doing light work after a heavy work or shifting to the liked work after during disliked work.

So, the rest period can be defined as unproductive interruptions of working time.

Work Simplification

It refers to developing the easiest and most effective way to do the task and putting the new method into use. It is of accomplishing more work with a given amount of time and energy. A homemaker need to conserve her energy and simply to fit work time available to required work.

Work simplification needed for several purposes which are :

- It reduces frustration fatigue which arises due to lack of effectiveness in a job.
- Routine habits of work resulting in boredom can be reduced by work simplification.
- It can reduce time of a given operation.
- It helps in cut down of motion and improve type of motions on a specific task.
- It helps the person in performing activities in a simple and innovative method, which increases the interest of the work and save the time and energy. This conservation is done only by adopting work simplification technique.

Advantages of Work Simplification

Advantages of work simplification are :

- By adopting innovative new methods to perform the work a person should conserve time and energy.
- Work simplification and elimination of unnecessary activities can reduce the work load of the homemaker.
- By adding some innovative idea of task performing can reduce the monotony of daily routine.
- A homemaker can improve the peace and efficiency of work performance by evaluating the physical labour and introducing the task performed by involving the muscles in activities.
- Unsuitable body position due to constant working strain the muscles causing pain, sometimes pressure on one type of muscles for a long duration of time, affects the blood circulation and it also affects the nerves system.

Importance of Work Simplification

It is a scientific approach to study work processes with a view to simplifying the process such that the work process becomes more efficient and effective and thereby raises productivity and reduces wastage of labour effort, materials, space, time and energy in the process of producing a good or delivering a service.

Understanding the fundamental steps in your work processes will help you get those things done which you feel stressed out about. Work simplification helps you get there faster, cheaper and better.

Techniques of Work Simplification

Some of the techniques used for motion and time studies are the process chart, the pathway chart, the operation chart. Work simplification techniques are helpful for the homemaker to simplify her work load. A home manager should have proper knowledge about these techniques.

Techniques of work simplification are of two types :

1. Formal technique
2. Informal technique (Pen-Pencil technique)

Formal Technique

Formal technique helps the homemaker to study the performance of work in detail or in controlled laboratory atmosphere.

The following are some formal techniques :

Micro Motion Film Performance is analysed to see the motion picture camera in which activities are recorded. To get the final result, the worker is asked to introduce the necessary improvement which help to evaluate the result.

Memo-Motion Large operations or tasks are studied by applying the memo-motion picture. Analysis of the activity is done by seen 60-100 still pictures taken by the camera, generally meal preparation task are studied by this technique.

Cyclograph Method In cyclograph method, the motion of left and right hands, motion of wrist, motion of fingers, forearm, upper arm and shoulder is picturised.

Stop Watch Technique Stop watch technique method is used to improve the working procedure. Time Management Unit (TMU) is used to study the work its various actions activities, its parts involved. Every second record is maintained using a stop watch.

Informal Technique

This technique is also known as **Pen-Pencil technique.** Informal technique is generally used by the homemaker or house wife to simplify her work performing at home. It is easy to follow technique which are easily adopted by the house wife.

Informal technique involves following steps :

Process Chart In this technique, some signs and symbols are allotted to the movement of activity. It can be used to assess each and every step involved in work. These activities help, in performing a task in a simplified manner.

Some Signs and Symbols of Process Chart Activities

Sign/Symbol	Activity
○ (small circle)	Movement from one place to other
◯ (large circle)	Operation done
Ⓒ	Movement and operation done simultaneously
▭	Inspection for quality and quantity delay

Multiman Chart To study a task by a far person this chart is used. Similar symbol represents the activities as it represents in process chart that is why, it is also called identical chart.

Operation Chart It is quite similar to process chart. In operation chart, evaluation of activities are based on hand and finger activities, where as process chart is used to analyse the work in totality. Operation chart is made for one activity, where different parts of the work are performed in sequence.

Pathway Chart In this method, the room layout is specified by using the plan. In pathway method, plan is laid on the drawing board, the worker position is marked with the help of thread and pins. Place is marked by a pin and thread is around the pin when the worker is moved around or moved from one place to another.

Length of the thread is measured by removing the pins from the board after completing the work. Working pattern of the worker has introduced with some changes like shifting cabinet containing crockery and cutlery warer to the kitchen door.

Shifting, the other cabinet closer to the kitchen wall, now the worker asked to use the trolley to carry utensils. Worker's plan to move in Whater's sequence into kitchen is systematically planned.

Mundel's Classes of Change

For the simplification of work, Mundel has suggested following classes of change :

Class 1 : Changes in Body Motions and Positions

Routing in dishwashing requires that stacking can be done in such a manner as to anticipate ease in washing. Drying and storing the dishes. For example, putting away dishes with two hands instead of one, eliminating unnecessary motions such as useless pats while making a bed, using rhythmic motions in sweeping, long handled tools such as bath tub, brushes and dust pans promote correct postures, sitting instead of standing.

All these steps reduces the distance covered and the number of retracement, thus, implying changes in body motions and positions.

Class 2 : Changes in Equipments and Working Arrangements

In this replacing, the equipments or completely rearranging the kitchen from hand, equipments are replaced such as the vacuum cleaner replacing the broom, etc. Hence, in this changes occur in the work areas, changes in tools and equipment.

Class 3 : Changes in Production Sequence

Motion can be reduced by elimination, combination or change in order without using the wiping, draining the dishes or allowing them to air dry, it helps in a process to reduce the number of steps. For example, elimination of step mixing all the ingredients of cake at one time instead of separately creaming fat beating eggs and so on.

Tailing is also known as combining steps which may be done by setting the table for next meal immediately without putting washing dishes away from the proceeding meal.

Commutating is one of the another phase of change in sequence it is known as **saving device** because in this more time is saved than hand motion. It consists of doing several things at once.

Class 4 : Changes in Finished Product

If refers to new finished product. It may be better or worse sometimes more desirable or less desirable. For example, square biscuits instead of round ones cut with a biscuit cutter. Cutting 25 round biscuits requires a minimum of 25 motions, cutting the same number of squares requires first eight motions four vertical cuts and four horizontal ones with a knife.

Class 5 : Changes in Raw Material

In this raw material with which one starts is different. The finished product is not necessarily changed, although, it is likely to be.

For example, using Idli with instant mixer instead of making in a traditional way.

Fatigue and Its Management

Fatigue, means tiredness, exhaustion, describes a physical and/or mental state of being tired and weak, Fatigue is a symptom, rather than a sign.

A symptom is something the patient feels and describes, such as a headache or dizziness, while a sign is something the doctor can detect without talking to the patient, such as a rash.

Reasons for Fatigue

Following are the reasons for fatigue :

Internal Factors

- Attitude towards work
- No interest in work
- Emotional stress
- Suffering from a disease along work in a standing position for long period
- Lack of practical experience
- Psychological hindrance weakness due to some other reasons

External Factors

- Polluted air affecting the worker
- Storage space and arrangement of work area
- Insufficient light at work place
- Circumstance of doing work
- Heavy work, disliking unstable work place
- Excessive noise around work

Types of Fatigue

Fatigue are of two types :

1. Physiological fatigue
2. Psychological fatigue

Physiological Fatigue

In this, an individual reduces the capacity of working when muscular work is done and energy is consumed. Fatigue related to the feeling of unwillingness to continue the work, feeling of tiredness, feeling of weariness all such things happen due to lack of energy or interest.

Food eaten by the individual helps in supplying the energy and work done with interest will definitely give positive result.

Psychological Fatigue

Complexity of life increasing day-by-day, which increase the factor of psychological fatigue in a worker. Situations including prolonged activity and performance arises fatigue or tension and reduces the capacity of work.

Fatigue is a common symptom for various diseases but does not indicate disease by itself. Psychological fatigue is an erosion of enthusiasm caused by obstacles, roadblocks or added rules and constraints. Not to be confused with sleep-related brain deficiency (haziness or memory loss, *e.g.,* psychological fatigue is a diminution in emotional, spiritual, or attitudinal components of our skills, our contributions and our output.

Some possible explanations for fatigue include depression, anemia (low blood count), sleep disorders such as insomnia and hypothyroidism.

Psychological fatigue are of following two types :

Boredom Fatigue Disliked work and unhealthy environment leads to psychological fatigue or boredom. Boredom fatigue depends upon nature of work, personal taste, attitude towards work, family and pressure of work, etc.

Frustration Fatigue When goals are not achieved because of poor planning, controlling it leads to failure or unsuccess; it is called frustration fatigue and worker suffer from mental tension and frustration.

Measures to Avoid Fatigue

A fatigued worker will not be able to work energetically, so by following some of these methods one can reduce fatigue :

Long Hours of Work This is the main cuase of fatigue. The hours of work should be reduced to that optimum level where workers are able to keep up their working speed.

Rest Pauses They are of great importance in reducing fatigue as well as monotony. Rest pauses should be provided in such a way that workers feel relieved after working for some hours.

Improving Environmental Conditions A proper balance of temperature humidity and ventilation should be maintained to make the workplace comfortable and worth working so that fatigue is reduced.

Reduction of Noise It means undesirable noise will cause fatigue. It may also cause muscular tension lower noise levels increase productivity or workers by reducing fatigue.

Job Rotations Sometimes workers start feeling bore and tired while working repeatedly on the same job. If job rotation is provided, it will avoid boredom and fatigue.

Natural Resource Management

The natural resource management deals with managing the way in which people and natural landscape interact. It brings together land use planning, water management, biodiversity conservation and forestry. Natural resource management focuses on a scientific and technical understanding of resources and ecology and the life supporting capacity of those resources.

The natural resource management also has to manage different stakeholders and their interest such as policies geographical boundaries, economic implications, etc.

As regard to natural resource management, we will study about forest resource management, water resource management, land resource management, water harvesting, air management.

Management of Land Resource

Land resource management is the process of managing the use and development (in both urban and rural areas) of land resources. Land is finite resource. If land is managed properly and in accordance with natural cycles, resource renewal becomes infinite and scarcity disappears. Land resources are used for various purposes such as organic agriculture, reforestation, etc.

Management of Forest Resource

Today, a forest is any land managed for the diverse purpose of forestry. Forest provides a number of invisible environmental benefits, these include release of energy, preparation of leaf protein, conservation of soil erosion, operation of hydrological cycle and carbon dioxide, cycle control of humidity, control of wind flow, control of air pollution, mitigation of green house effect. Forests also safeguard the economy from flood, drought and natural calamity.

By adopting following measures, the management of forest can be carried out :

- No forest should be permitted to be worked without the government having approved the management plan. Which should be in a prescribed format and in keeping with National Forest Policy.
- Need to enhance the forest cover and productivity of the forest through application of scientific and technical output.
- The rights and concessions including grazing should always remain related to the carrying capacity of forests.
- The forest land or land with tree cover should not be treated merely as a resource readily available to be utilised for various projects and programmes.
- Forest management should take special care of the needs of wildlife conservation and forest management plan should include prescription for this purpose.
- There exists a symbiotic relationship between the tribal people and forest, so the primary task of all agencies responsible for forest management should provide protection to them.
- The community forestry and agro forestry should be promoted.
- Steps should be taken to prevent occurrence of forest fire.

Management of Air Resource

Air is a third critical resource for humans, plants, animals and all other organisms within a natural area. Air must be monitored in order to control and lower pollution levels, control smoke caused by wildland fires, and to monitor air quality.

The Forest Service monitors the effects of air pollution that may impair visibility, harm human health, injure trees and other plants, acidify or cause unnatural fertilisation of streams and lakes, leach nutrients from soils, and degrade cultural resources, like archaeological site and historical buildings.

Forest activities that can affect air quality such as prescribed burning, ski areas, and mining are also monitored to ensure compliance with air regulations for human health and to monitor possible impacts to natural resources.

Management of Water Resources

Water is indispensable for the sustenance of life on Earth. It is very much important for various purposes such as drinking, cooking, washing, industrial uses, generation of power, etc. In order to meet the increasing demand of population growth water is over utilised and polluted.

So affective and sustainable management of water resource is important for ensuring sustainable development. It is also important for maintaining ecological balance and for developmental activities of all kinds. To overcome the over utilisation of water and to provide safe water to all living organisms, water resource management is highly essential.

By management of water, we mean making best use of water resources available for human benefit. The process not only prevents its depletion and degradation but also takes appropriate steps for its development in view of the present and future needs.

Methods of Conserving Water

In the present scenario, due to scarcity of water, it is necessary that some methods need to devised for its conservation through adoption of proper water management. Some of the methods are discussed as :

- Awareness should be created among the people regarding the importance of water and its unnecessary wastage.
- There should be controlling measures to check flood and improper use of rain water.
- Qualitative degradation should be avoided.
- Steps should be taken for the harvesting and storage of roof top rainwater.
- There should be reclamation of waste water, storage of ground water transfer of surplus water.
- Pollution of water resources should be checked.
- There should be long range forecasting of rain.
- There should be adequate afforestation programmes. Through afforestation, the plants bind the soil and soil binds the water.
- There should be national and state level water harvesting perspective plan.

Management of Water Harvesting

Water harvesting means capturing rainwater, where it falls and captures the run off from catchment and streams, etc. It is direct rainwater collection. Water harvesting can be carried out in a number of ways such as :

- Capturing run off from roof tops
- Capturing run off from local catchments
- Capturing seasonal flood waters from local streams
- Conserving water through watershed management

In the present times, we depend entirely on such secondary sources of water. It is forgotten that rain is the ultimate source to feed all secondary sources (rivers, lakes and ground water) and remain ignorant of its values. Water harvesting means to understand the value of rain and to make the optimum use of rainwater at the place where it falls.

The management of water harvesting is important as rain is precious and vital natural resource. Primarily rain water harvesting is aimed at managing rainwater from the moment it falls and ensuring the most of it is used productively before it is returned to atmosphere. Thus, management of water harvesting means storage of rainwater in various structures by adopting traditional and modern practices.

To tackle the problem some of water harvesting techniques can be adopted such as :

- Increase ground water recharge
- Surface run off harvesting
- Roof top rain water harvesting
- Absorption of pit methods
- Percolation tanks
- Integrated tanks
- Recharge of ground water
- Storage of rain water on surface for future use
- Construction of trenches
- Recharge shafts

Thus, it can be said that water harvesting helps prevent flood due to excessive rain. It is considered as a very reliable way to conserve water.

Solid Waste Management

Since the beginning, humankind has been generating waste, be it the bones or another parts of animals they slaughter for their food or the wood they cut to make their carts. With the progress of civilisation, the waste generated became of a more complex in nature.

At the end of the 19th century, the industrial revolution saw rise of the world of consumers. Not only did the air get more and more polluted but the Earth itself became more polluted with the generation of non-biodegradable solid waste. The increase in population and urbanisation was also largely responsible for the increase in solid waste. The solid waste management is a term that is used to refer to the process of collecting and treating solid wastes. It also offers solution for recycling items that do not belong to garbage or trash.

The solid waste can be categorised in different ways such as :

- Household waste as municipal solid waste
- Agricultural waste
- Industrial waste
- Hazardous waste, bio-medical or hospital waste as infectious waste.

Municipal Solid Waste Management

Municipal Solid Waste Management (MSWM), a critical element towards sustainable metropolitan development, comprises segregation, storage, collection, relocation, carry-age, processing, and disposal of solid waste to minimise its adverse impact on environment. Unmanaged MSW becomes a factor for propagation of innumerable ailments.

In the developed countries, solid waste management (SWM) belongs to prominent thrust areas for pursuing research and economic and technological advancements have initiated responsiveness of stakeholders towards it. High population growth rates, rapidly varying waste characterisation and generation patterns, growing urbanisation and industrialisation in developing countries (Troschinetz and Mihelcic, 2009) are the important reasons for paying attention towards MSWM as more area is required to accommodate waste.

MSWM is one of the major environmental problems of Indian cities. India, being the third largest producer of waste, specially municipal solid waste in the world with 109, 589 tons of waste per day.

The Central Government in exercise of the powers conferred by sections 3, 6 and 25 of the Environment (Protection) Act, 1986 has notified Municipal Solid Wastes (Management and Handling) Rules, 2000. These rules shall apply to every Municipal authority responsible for collection, segregation, transportation, processing and disposal of municipal solid wastes in following sections.

Collection of Municipal Solid Wastes

Littering of municipal solid waste shall be prohibited in cities, towns, and urban areas notified by the Government. To prohibit littering, following steps shall be taken :

- Organising house to house collection of garbage through any of the methods, like containerised collection, community bin collection (central bin), collection at regular pre-informed timings and scheduling by using bell ringing/musical vehicle (without exceeding permissible noise levels).
- Collection of waste from slums and squatter areas/ localities including hotels/ restaurants/office complexes and commercial areas shall be devised in consultation with municipal authority.
- Wastes from slaughter houses, fruits and vegetable markets, which are biodegradable in nature, shall be managed to make use of such wastes.
- Bio-medical wastes and industrial wastes. Shall not be mixed with solid wastes as per rules specified separately for the purpose.

- Collected waste from residential and other areas shall be transferred to community bins or dhalaos by hand driven containerised carts.
- Horticultural and construction/demolition wastes/ debris shall be separately collected and disposed off following proper norms. Similarly, activities relating to dairies (milking of cows/buffaloes) shall be regulated in accordance with state laws.

Segregation of Municipal Solid Wastes

Municipal authority shall organise awareness programs for segregation of wastes and shall encourage recycling/reuse of segregated materials. Municipal authority shall undertake phased programmes to ensure that the community is fully involved in waste segregation.

Storage of Municipal Solid Wastes

Municipal authorities shall establish and maintain storage facilities in such a manner as not to create unhygienic/ insanitary conditions around it. Following criteria shall be taken into account while establishing and maintaining storage facilities :

- Storage facilities shall be created/ established by taking into account quantities of waste generation in a given area and the population density. A storage facility shall be so sited such that the user finds it easy to approach.
- Storage facilities to be set-up by Municipal authorities or by any other agency shall be so designed that waste stored is not exposed to open atmosphere and shall be aesthetically acceptable and user-friendly.
- Storage facilities or bins shall have 'easy to operate' design for handling, transfer and transportation of waste.
- Manual handling of waste shall be prohibited. If unavoidable due to constraints, manual handling shall be carried out under proper precaution with due care for safety of workers.

Transportation of Municipal Solid Waste

Vehicles used for transportation of wastes shall be covered. Wastes should not be visible to public, nor exposed to open environment. The following criteria shall be met :

- The storage facilities set-up by Municipal authorities shall be daily attended for clearing of wastes.
- Collection and transportation vehicles shall be so designed that multiple handling of wastes, prior to final disposal, is avoided.

Processing of Municipal Solid Wastes

Municipal authorities shall adopt suitable technology (or combination of such technologies) to make use of wastes so as to minimise burden on landfill. Following criteria shall be adopted :

- The biodegradable wastes not containing any toxic contaminants, shall be processed by composting, vermicomposting, anaerobic digestion or any other appropriate biological processing for stabilisation. It shall be ensured that compost shall be free from contamination due to heavy metals, pesticides or any other contaminants.
- Waste containing recoverable material shall follow the route of recycling.

Sustainable Development

Sustainable development is any form of positive change which does not erode the ecological and environmental balance upon which biosphere is dependent. It means improving the quality of life while living within the carrying capacity of supporting.

Sustainable development is formally defined by the **World Commission on Environment and Development** (WCED) as "development that meets the needs of the people today without compromising the ability of future generating to meet their own needs."

The concept of need goes beyond simply material needs and includes values, relationships, freedom to think, act and participate, all amounting to sustainable living morally and spiritually.

The definition given by the **Brundtland Commission** on sustainable development stated thus: "Humanity has the ability to make development sustainable–to ensure that it meets the needs of the present without compromising the ability of future generations to imply limits–not absolute limits but limitations imposed by the present state of technology and social organisation on environmental resources and by the ability, of biosphere to absorb the effects of human activities. But technology and social organisation can be managed and improved to make way for a new era of economic growth.

Sustainable development is not a fixed state of harmony, but rather a process of change in which the exploitation of resources, the direction of investments, the orientation of technological development and institutional change are made consistent with future as well as present needs.

Requirements of Sustainable Development

The sustainable development seeks to respond to five main requirements such as :

- Satisfaction of basic human needs.
- Achievements of equity and social justice.
- Integration of conservation and development.
- Maintenance of ecological integrity.
- Provision of social determination and cultural diversity.

Sustainable also means sustainable resource management, i.e. using resources in a sustainable way so that the rate of use can be less than the rate of regeneration. Sustainable development is the long term stability of the economy and environment and this is only achievable through the integration and acknowledgement of economic, environmental and social concerns throughout the decision making process.

Sustainable Development Goals

Twenty years after the Rio Summit the world leaders met in June 2012 at the UN Conference on Sustainable Development, the so-called Rio+20. The key takeaway was a document titled 'The Future We Want' in which the idea of a new agenda for the post-2015 era was posted.

World leaders committed to migrate from the Millennium Development Goals (MDGs) to the SDGs. An Open Working Group of nations was set-up, and the next three years saw negotiations leading to a 24-page document including 17 Sustainable Development Goals with 169 targets. The SDGs are to be achieved between January 2016 and 2030.

Sustainable Development Goals (SDGs) are international agreements of many countries under UN initiation that have certain goals and targets. Achieving these goals and targets of the SDG requires a broad and focused effort from various sectors including higher education.

The Sustainable Development Goals (SDGs), otherwise known as the Global Goals, are a universal call to action to end poverty, protect the planet and ensure that all people enjoy peace and prosperity. The goals are interconnected–often the key to success on one will involve tackling issues more commonly associated with another.

The seventeen SDGs goals are given in the table as follows :

Goals	Objectives	Descriptions
Goal 1	No Poverty	By 2030, eradicate extreme poverty for all people everywhere.
Goal 2	Zero Hunger	End hunger, achieve food security and improved nutrition by 2030.
Goal 3	Good Health and Well-being	Ensure healthy lives and promote well-being for all at all ages by 2030.
Goal 4	Quality Education	Ensure that all girls and boys complete free, equitable and quality primary and secondary education by 2030.
Goal 5	Gender Equality	To achieve gender equality and empower all women and girls.
Goal 6	Clean Water and Sanitation	Ensure availability and sustainable management of water and sanitation for all by 2030.
Goal 7	Affordable and Clean Energy	Ensure access to affordable, reliable, sustainable and modern energy for all by 2030.
Goal 8	Decent Work and Economic Growth	Promote sustained, inclusive and sustainable economic growth.
Goal 9	Industry, Innovation and Infrastructure	Build resilient infrastructure, promote inclusive and sustainable industrialisation and foster innovation by 2030.
Goal 10	Reduced Inequality	Reduce inequality within among countries by 2030.
Goal 11	Sustainable Cities and Communities	Make cities and human settlements inclusive, safe, resilient and sustainable.
Goal 12	Responsible Consumption and Production	Ensure sustainable consumption and production patterns.
Goal 13	Climate Action	Take urgent action to combat climate change and its impacts.
Goal 14	Life Below Water	Conserve and sustainably use the oceans, seas and marine resources for sustainable development.
Goal 15	Life on Land	Protect, restore and promote sustainable use of terrestrial.
Goal 16	Peace and Justice Strong Institutions	Promote peaceful and inclusive societies for sustainable development; provide access to justice for all.
Goal 17	Partnerships to achieve the Goal	Strengthen the means of implementation and revitalise the global partnership for sustainable development.

EXAM BASED QUESTIONS

1 Who said "resources as the assets that can be used to accomplish goals"?
(a) Deacon and Firebaugh (b) Crandall and Knoll
(c) Nickel et. al (d) Betty B Swanson

2 Resources can be classified as
(a) Human, Physical and Capital Resources
(b) Specific v/s General
(c) Human v/s Non-Human
(d) All of the above

3 Police protection, roads and temples, etc. are examples of
(a) Community Resources (b) World Society Resources
(c) Temporal Resources (d) National Resources

4 Pick the odd one among the characteristics of Resources
(a) Unlimited (b) Interchangeable
(c) Useful (d) Accessible

5 .... consists of a series of decision making up the process of using family resources to achieve family goals.
(a) Home management
(b) Business management
(c) Resource management
(d) Institutional management

6 "According to .... "the resources are the supply reservoir for use in the system's specific action and are necessary in some form to solve every management problem."
(a) K Kautilya (b) Deacon and Firebaugh
(c) Betty B Swanson (d) Rillian Gilberth

7 Food and owned house, car etc is example of
(a) material goods (b) non-human resources
(c) money (d) All of these

8 Community facilities as non-human resources include
(a) libraries (b) parks
(c) shopping facilities (d) All of these

9 Which among the following are the characteristics of resources?
(a) Limitedness
(b) Managerial process available
(c) Interrelated
(d) All of the above

10 Which of the following factors are responsible for affecting the use of resources?
(a) Socio-Economic Status
(b) Size and Composition of the family
(c) Location of the family
(d) All of the above

11 Peak load is
(a) time period where various activities are performed simultaneously.
(b) constructed between time and work.
(c) provides maximum satisfaction and efficiency in work.
(d) helps person to balance work and time and to simply the work load.

12 Which of the following statement(s) is/are correct with regard to work curve?
(a) It is constructed between time and work.
(b) It provides information about housewife's capacity and tendency to do work.
(c) Simplify the work load
(d) All of the above

13 Work is the conscious seeking of the simplest easiest and quickest method of doing work. This definition is given by
(a) Lillian Gilberth
(b) V V S Laxman
(c) Nickell and Dorsey
(d) Gross and Crandall

14 Work simplification is accomplishing more work with a given amount of time and energy or as reducing the amount of either or both to accomplish a given amount of work
(a) Norman C Landon
(b) Allan Donald
(c) Allan Mogenson
(d) Gross and Crandall

15 It is a chart which shows step-by-step description of the method used in doing a task
(a) Micromotion film (b) Process chart
(c) Operation chart (d) None of these

16 It is used in making a more detailed study of some particular parts of the process
(a) Cyclograph (b) Process chart
(c) Operation chart (d) None of these

17 In ...... method the room layout is specified using the plan.
(a) Process chart (b) Multiman chart
(c) Operation chart (d) Pathway chart

18 The internal factors responsible for fatigue are
(a) Excessive noise around work
(b) No interest in work
(c) Emotional stress
(d) Both b and c

19 The natural resource management issues are inherently complex as it involves
(a) the ecological cycle (b) climate
(c) hydrological cycle (d) All of these

20 **In view of the forest management, which of the following techniques can be adopted for conservation of forest?**
(a) There should be intensive and extensive social forestry.
(b) The community forestry and agro forestry should be neglected.
(c) Prevents the occurrence of forest fire.
(d) Both (a) and (c)

21 **Which of the following statement(s) is/are incorrect with regard to the conservation method?**
(a) Qualitative degradation should be avoided.
(b) Awareness programmes should be restricted to urban areas only.
(c) The village ponds should be revived.
(d) Controlling measures should be adopted to check flood.

22 **Which among the following organisations are responsible for water management?**
(a) Central Ground Water Board
(b) Central Water Commission for Surface Water
(c) Central and State Pollution Board
(d) All of the above

23 **Conservation methods to be adopted for water management include**
(a) Qualitative degradation should be avoided.
(b) Check pollution of water resources.
(c) Adequate afforestation programme.
(d) All of the above

24 **Which of the following is not a method for water conservation?**
(a) Rain water harvesting
(b) Ground water extraction
(c) Improving irrigation efficiency
(d) Avoiding water wastage

25 **In what different ways water harvesting can be undertaken?**
(a) Capturing runoff from rooftops.
(b) Capturing run off from local catchments.
(c) Conserving water through watershed management.
(d) All of the above

26 **The method of rainwater harvesting which can be adopted by individual house owner is**
(a) Construction of recharge trenches
(b) On channel storage of water
(c) Creation of new water bodies
(d) Rooftop rain water harvesting

27 **The steps taken by the government to prohibit littering in cities, towns and urban areas are**
(a) Bio-medical wastes and industrial wastes shall not be mixed with municipal solid waste.
(b) Waste (garbage, dry leaves, etc) shall not be burnt.
(c) Horticulture and construction, debris shall be separately collected and disposed off according to norms.
(d) All of the above

28 **"The sustainable development seeks to respond to broad requirement." Which are these?**
(a) Satisfaction of basic human needs
(b) Maintenance of ecological integrity
(c) achievement of equity and social justice
(d) All of the above

29 **Which solid waste disposal method is suitable to Indian conditions?**
(a) Land filling (b) Incineration
(c) Pulverisation (d) Composition

30 **Which of the following is correct regarding disposal of waste by land filling?**
(a) Economical method
(b) Preferred in low lying areas
(c) Foul gases are not produced
(d) Separation of different types of waste are not required

31 **...... is the cutting and tearing of municipal solid waste.**
(a) Land fills
(b) Shreddry
(c) Pulverisation
(d) Composting

32 **Which process improves efficiency of solid waste management?**
(a) Disposal (b) Collection
(c) Composting (d) Processing

33 **The idea of sustainable development was conceived in early**
(a) 1950 (b) 1960
(c) 1970 (d) 1980

34 **Which of the following statements is/are correct?**
(a) Both human and material resources are needed to solve the food management problems.
(b) The material resources, money, determine the types of food selected and the method of buying by the homemaker.
(c) The more the homemaker knows about the time required to do each task connected with food buying and preparation, the better will be the management of this resources.
(d) All of the above

35 **Which of the following statements is/are correct?**
(a) Despite resources being inter-related, the lack of a single resource may prove crucial to the attainment of a desired goal.
(b) All resources are useful and limited, otherwise management would not be necessary.
(c) Ellen H Richard was a home economist of beginning of 19th century.
(d) All of the above

36 **Consider the following statement(s) is/are correct about non-human resources.**

Statement I These are those resources which are available to a person within his community, state or nation.

Statement II These resources are used for productive purposes.
(a) Only Statement I is correct
(b) Only Statement II is correct
(c) Both the statements are correct
(d) Neither statements I nor II are correct

37 State which is/are true
(a) A study on work simplification in dish washing was made by Eva Goble.
(b) A good sitting posture of or work the weight is carried by the bony support of the skeleton thus relieving the muscles and nerves of all strain.
(c) The cyclograph is a photographic device used to study types of motion used in performing task. Micromotion film analysis is research techniques and applies best to tasks that can be easily filmed.
(d) All of the above

38 Consider the following statement regarding the storage of municipal solid waste is/are correct.
Statement I The storage facilities or bins shall have 'easy to operate design for handling, transfer and transportation of wastes.'
Statement II Manual handling of waste to be prohibited.
(a) Only statement I is correct
(b) Only statement II is correct
(c) Both the statements I and II are correct
(d) Neither statements I nor II are correct

39 Which of the following statements in relation to sustainable development is not true?
(a) Sustainable development is defined as the development that meets the need of present without compromising the ability of our future generations to meet their own needs.
(b) Sustainability has the main objective of purely focusing on the natural environment.
(c) Sustainable development of various countries and the entire world is the only solution left with mankind to survive for a longer period on Earth.
(d) Sustainable development not only considers the protection of the environment but also the maintenance of economic viability as well as social and ethical consideration.

40 Human resources at our disposal include
1. Skills 2. Knowledge
3. Energy 4. Meta Bolism
Select the correct answer using the codes given below
(a) 1, 2 and 3 (b) 1, 2, 3 and 4
(c) 1 and 2 (d) 1 and 4

41 The resources that individuals and families have at their disposal consist of
1. Tools 2. Assets
3. Capabilities 4. Ways and means they possess
Select the correct answer using the codes given below
(a) 1, 2 and 3 (b) 1, 2, 3 and 4
(c) 1 and 4 (d) 1 and 2

42 Which among the following is/are not basic characteristic(s) of all resources?
1. Usefulness 2. Unlimited
3. Inter-related 4. Substitution
Select the correct answer using the codes given below
(a) 1 and 2 (b) 1, 2 and 3
(c) Only 2 (d) 1, 2, 3 and 4

43 All the resources have similarity, such that
1. they are limited.
2. all resources are useful.
3. arrangement of resources is applicable to all.
4. use of resources depends on the individual.
Select the correct answer using the codes given below
(a) 1, 2 and 3 (b) 1, 2, 3 and 4
(c) 1 and 2 (d) 1 and 4

44 The aim of resources are to provide satisfaction of family members. Elizabeth Hoyt in her book 'consumption in our society' has stated which of the following with regard to resources?
1. Knowledge of alternate uses
2. Balancing choices among resources
3. Supplementing resources
4. Enhanced use and increase in skills
Select the correct answer using the codes given below
(a) 1 and 2 (b) 1 and 4
(c) All of these (d) 1, 2 and 3

45 The limitation of resources could be
1. qualitative 2. quantitative
Select the correct answer using the codes given below
(a) Only 1 (b) Only 2
(c) Both 1 and 2 (d) None of these

46 Satisfaction from resources can be enhanced by
1. balancing chances.
2. knowing alternative uses.
3. increasing supply of resources.
4. increasing utility and expanding appreciations.
Select the correct answer using the codes given below
(a) 1, 2, 3 and 4 (b) 1, 2 and 3
(c) 1 and 2 (d) 1 and 4

47 Which of the factor(s) effect the use of resources?
1. Motivation 2. Capacity
3. Philosophy
4. Life cycle and family factors like heritage.
Select the correct answer using the codes given below
(a) 1 and 2 (b) 1 and 4
(c) All of these (d) 1, 2 and 3

48 Internal factors of fatigue include
1. No interest in work
2. Emotional stress
3. Insufficient light at workplace
4. Lack of practical experience
Codes
(a) 1, 2 and 3 (b) 1, 2 and 4
(c) 1 and 2 (d) 1 and 3

49 Formal technique of work simplification is/are
1. Memo motion
2. Pathway chart
3. Micro motion film
4. Cyclograph method

Codes
(a) 1 and 2 (b) 2 and 4
(c) 1, 2 and 4 (d) 1, 2, 3 and 4

50 Work simplification can be grouped into 3 classes
1. Body position and motions sequence of work
2. Tools equipment and work arrangement
3. Product
4. Learning experience and group problem

Codes
(a) 1 and 2 (b) 1 and 4
(c) 1, 2, 3 and 4 (d) 1, 2 and 3

51 Mundel's classes of change includes
1. Changes in body motions and positions
2. Changes in equipment and working arrangements
3. Changes in production sequence
4. Changes in finished product
5. Changes in raw material

Codes
(a) 1, 2 and 3 (b) 1, 2, 3 and 4
(c) 1, 2, 3, 4 and 5 (d) Nono of these

52 Sustainable development consist of constituent parts.
1. Environmental sustainability
2. Economic sustainability
3. Socio political sustainability
4. Cultural sustainability
5. Low-economic sustainability

Codes
(a) 1, 3, 4 and 5 (b) 1, 2, 4 and 5
(c) 1, 2, 3 and 4 (d) 1, 3, 4 and 5

53 Consider the following statement(s) related to the sustainability?
1. It refers to a process that can be maintained indefinitely.
2. Natural resources must use in ways that do not create ecological debt by over exploiting the carrying and productive capacity of the Earth.
3. A minimum necessary condition for sustain ability is the maintenance of the total natural capital stock at or above the current level.

Codes
(a) Only 1 (b) Only 2
(c) Only 2 and 3 (d) 1, 2 and 3

54 Match the following.

List I	List II
A. Human Resources	1. Inter-related
B. Resources	2. Recurring
C. Routine decisions	3. Golden oblong
D. Proportion	4. Intangible

Codes

	A	B	C	D		A	B	C	D
(a)	4	1	2	3	(b)	4	1	3	2
(c)	1	2	3	4	(d)	2	4	1	3

55 Match the following.

List I	List II
A. Money	1. Includes recreation, health facilities
B. Material goods	2. School, colleges, training centres, etc.
C. Community facilities	3. Car, scooter, cycle, plot, farm
D. Educational facilities	4. Includes wages salary, saving investment

Codes

	A	B	C	D		A	B	C	D
(a)	4	3	1	2	(b)	1	2	3	4
(c)	4	3	2	1	(d)	2	1	4	3

56 Match the following.

List I (Sign/Symbol)	List II (Activities)
A. ○	1. Inspection of quality and quantity delay.
B. ◯	2. Movement and operations done simultaneously.
C. ©	3. Movement from one place to another.
D. □	4. Operation done.

Codes

	A	B	C	D		A	B	C	D
(a)	2	1	4	3	(b)	3	4	1	2
(c)	1	2	3	4	(d)	4	1	2	3

57 Match the following.

List I(SDGs)	List II (Description)
A. No poverty	1. Protect restore and promote sustainable use of terrestrial.
B. Life on land	2. Take action to combat climate change and its impact.
C. Climate Action	3. By 2030, eradicate extreme poverty.
D. Zero Hour	4. End hunger, achieve food security and improve nutrition by 2030.

Codes

	A	B	C	D		A	B	C	D
(a)	3	1	2	4	(b)	1	2	3	4
(c)	2	4	3	1	(d)	4	3	2	1

58 Match the following.

List I	List II
A. Process chart	1. It is similar to process chart.
B. Multiman chart	2. It helps pinpoint all movements that can be reduced or eliminated.
C. Operation chart	3. It is also called indentical chart.
D. Patway chart	4. In it some signs and symbols are alloted to the movement of actvity.

Codes

	A	B	C	D		A	B	C	D
(a)	1	2	3	4	(b)	4	3	2	1
(c)	4	3	1	2	(d)	2	4	3	1

Directions (Q. Nos. 59-65) *In the questions given below are two statements labelled as Assertion (A) and Reason (R). In the context of the two statements, which one of the following is correct codes.*

Codes

(a) Both A and R are correct and R is the correct explanation of A
(b) Both A and R are correct but R is not the correct explanation of A
(c) A is correct, but R is incorrect.
(d) A is incorrect, but R is correct

59 **Assertion** (A) Human resources are central to carrying out any activity.
Reason (R) These resources are used for productive purposes.

60 **Assertion** (A) Standing in a static posture is fatiguing.
Reason (R) Blood circulation is affected in the extremities while standing for work.

61 **Assertion** (A) General fatigue results from the stress of performing tedious and boring activities and this lacks personal satisfaction.
Reason (R) Strenuous and disliked activities when performed by workers this may lead to fatigue and stress and hence the worker is not satisfied.

62 **Assertion** (A) Work simplification helps the person in performing activities in a simple way.
Reason (R) It reduces frustration fatigue which arises due to lack of effectiveness in a job.

63 **Assertion** (A) Water harvesting is the activity of direct collection of rainwater.
Reason (R) The rainwater can be stored for direct use.

64 Assertion (A) Time balance as a management tool should be observed in work, rest entertainment.
Reason (R) It helps one to be mentally alert and emotionally balanced.

65 **Assertion** (A) Time management means minimising the expenditure of time to complete a task without altering the quality of work.
Reason (R) Time management hardly allows one to have adequate rest and recreation along with work.

Directions (Q. Nos. 66-70) *Read the following passage and answer the questions that follows.*

The concept of sustainable development formed the basis of the United Nations Conference on Environment and Development held in Rio de Janeiro in 1992. The summit marked the first international attempt to draw up action plans and strategies for moving towards a more sustainable pattern of development. It was attended by over 100 heads of state and representatives from 178 national governments. The Summit was also attended by representatives from a range of other organisations representing civil society. Sustainable development was the solution to the problems of environmental degradation discussed by the Brundtland Commission in the 1987 report 'Our Common Future'.

The remit of the Brundtland Report was to investigate the numerous concerns that had been raised in previous decades, namely, that human activity was having severe and negative impacts on the planet and that patterns of growth and development would be unsustainable if they continued unchecked.

Key works that highlighted this thinking included Rachel Carson's Silent Spring (1962) Garret Hardin's Tragedy of the Commons (1968), the Blueprint for Survival by the Ecologist magazine (1972) and the Club of Rome's Limits to Growth report (1972).

The concept of sustainable development received its first major international recognition in 1972 at the UN Conference on the Human Environment held in Stockholm. The term was not referred to explicitly, but nevertheless the international community agreed to the notion-now fundamental to sustainable development-that both development and the environment, hitherto addressed as separate issues, could be managed in a mutually beneficial way.

The World Summit on Sustainable Development was held in Johannesburg in 2002, attended by 191 national governments, UN agencies, multilateral financial institutions and other major groups to assess progress since Rio. The Johannesburg Summit delivered three key outcomes i.e. a political declaration, the Johannesburg Plan of Implementation, and a range of partnership initiatives. Key commitments included those on sustainable consumption and production, water and sanitation, and energy.

The Sustainable Development Goals (SDGs) are the blueprint to achieve a better and more sustainable future for all. They are a collection of 17 global goals set by the United Nations General Assembly in 2015 for the year 2030. The SDGs are part of Resolution 70/1 of the United Nations General Assembly, the 2030 Agenda.

66 **The term sustainable development was used by the Brundtland Commission in the year**
(a) 1987
(b) 1983
(c) 1985
(d) 1986

67 The United Nations 2005 World Summit Outcome Document refer to interdependent and mutually reinforcing pillars of sustainable development include
(a) economic development (b) social development
(c) environmental protection (d) All of the above

68 The concept of sustainable development received its first major international recognition in
(a) 1976 (b) 1972
(c) 1975 (d) 1970

69 The World Summit on Sustainable Development was held in ...... in 2002.
(a) Rio de Janeiro
(b) Johannesburg
(c) Geneva
(d) Auster dam

70 The sustainable development goals are collection of ...... goals.
(a) 10 (b) 12
(c) 17 (d) 20

PREVIOUS YEARS' QUESTIONS

July 2018

1 Hidden Family Income is derived from a combination of
1. Investment Income
2. Community Income
3. Employment Benefit
4. Psychic Income

Codes
(a) 1, 2 and 3 (b) 1, 3 and 4
(c) 1, 2 and 4 (d) 2, 3 and 1

2 **Assertion** (A) Work curve is an important tool for managing work force.
Reason (R) Work curve helps to study the changes in output of work over a period of time.
Codes
(a) A is correct but R is incorrect
(b) A is incorrect and R is correct
(c) Both A and R are correct
(d) Both A and R are incorrect

November 2017

3 **Assertion** (A) A family budget is a way of detailing expenses under different headings.
Reason (R) It helps the family to live within their income.
Codes
(a) A is correct, but R is incorrect
(b) A is incorrect, but R is correct
(c) Both A and R are correct
(d) Both A and R are incorrect

December 2015

4 Which of the following are the tangible tools used by managers to perform their functions efficiently?
1. Training
2. Staff appraisal
3. Communication skills
4. Inventory records
5. Organisation charts
6. Job descriptions

Select the correct answer using the codes given below
(a) 1, 2, 3 and 5 (b) 1, 3, 4 and 5
(c) 2, 3, 5 and 6 (d) 2, 4, 5 and 6

5 **Assertion** (A) Management of time can be practised to tackle peak loads.
Reason (R) Allocation of work to family members will be a helpful method.
Codes
(a) Both A and R are correct
(b) Both A and R are incorrect
(c) A is correct, but R is incorrect
(d) A is incorrect, but R is correct

6 Arrange in correct sequence the steps in Programme Planning.
1. Community needs assessment
2. Setting goals and objectives
3. Problem identification
4. Programme implementation
5. Selecting intervention
6. Monitoring and evaluation

Codes
(a) 3, 1, 2, 5, 4, 6 (b) 1, 3, 5, 2, 4, 6
(c) 3, 2, 4, 5, 1, 6 (d) 2, 3, 1, 5, 4, 6

June 2015

7 **Assertion** (A) Time and energy demands of employed women are same in different states of family cycle.
Reason (R) Energy management is more difficult and complex than time management irrespective of stages of family life cycle.
Codes
(a) A is correct and R is incorrect
(b) Both A and R are correct
(c) A is incorrect and R is correct
(d) Both A and R are incorrect

8 Assertion (A) Systemic Evaluation enables to determine the effectiveness of any programme.

Reason (R) Information obtained through evaluation shows strengths and weaknesses of a programme.

Codes

(a) Both A and R are correct
(b) Both A and R are incorrect
(c) A is correct and R is incorrect
(d) A is incorrect and R is correct

December 2014

9 Which of the following are intangible tools of management?

1. Leadership
2. Organisation chart
3. Communication
4. Work schedule
5. Decision-making

Select the correct answer using the codes given below

(a) 1, 2 and 4
(b) 1, 3 and 5
(c) 2, 3 and 5
(d) 2, 4 and 5

June 2014

10 Arrange in correct sequence the steps to be adopted for preparing a time and activity schedule.

1. Enlisting all the tasks performed in a day.
2. Estimate time spent for each task.
3. Classify tasks as flexible and inflexible.
4. Determine the sequential order.
5. Analyse the schedule.
6. Include meta plans for any extra time.
7. Prepare the final time and activity plan.

Codes

(a) 1, 3, 2, 4, 6, 5, 7
(b) 1, 3, 2, 5, 4, 6, 7
(c) 1, 5, 4, 3, 2, 6, 7
(d) 1, 3, 5, 2, 6, 4, 7

ANSWERS

Exam Based Questions

1 (c)	2 (d)	3 (a)	4 (a)	5 (a)	6 (b)	7 (d)	8 (d)	9 (d)	10 (d)
11 (a)	12 (d)	13 (c)	14 (d)	15 (b)	16 (c)	17 (d)	18 (b)	19 (d)	20 (d)
21 (b)	22 (d)	23 (d)	24 (b)	25 (d)	26 (d)	27 (d)	28 (d)	29 (d)	30 (c)
31 (b)	32 (d)	33 (d)	34 (d)	35 (d)	36 (a)	37 (d)	38 (c)	39 (b)	40 (a)
41 (b)	42 (d)	43 (b)	44 (c)	45 (c)	46 (a)	47 (c)	48 (b)	49 (c)	50 (d)
51 (c)	52 (c)	53 (d)	54 (a)	55 (a)	56 (b)	57 (a)	58 (c)	59 (a)	60 (b)
61 (c)	62 (b)	63 (a)	64 (a)	65 (b)	66 (a)	67 (d)	68 (b)	69 (b)	70 (c)

Previous Years' Questions

1 (d)	2 (c)	3 (c)	4 (d)	5 (a)	6 (a)	7 (c)	8 (a)	9 (b)	10 (b)

Money Management and Human Resource Management

Money is the most important source to live a healthy and prosperous life. It is difficult to sustain without money as it is the basic necessity. So, it is equally important for a person to master the skill of money management. In the present day, world Human Resource Management also plays a strategic role in managing people and workplace environment. HRM, can contribute greatly to the overall organisation's direction and the accomplishment of its goals and objectives.

Among all the resources that are available, the most important is money. Money plays a significant role in the life of a man. It is an instrument through which he can satisfy his physical, material and mental needs. In the context of the family money is important both psychologically and economically.

Coulborn defines money as "the means of valuation and of payment as both the unit of account and the generally accepted medium of exchange." Money can be the beauty of living, a support in misfortune, education of the children or security of old age. But, if there lack of wisdom, money can become a bone of contention and source of bitterness in the family. Therefore, money should be managed properly if a family strives for better living.

Money Management

The quality of living that can be exchanged for financial resources is dependent not only on how much income is available but more importantly in the regularities and stability of income. So, it is important to learn/know about the skill of managing money. By money management we mean the process of budgeting, saving, investment and spending taxes. Money management is an essential part of debt free life style. The money management is a broad term which involves and incorporates services and solutions across the entire investment industry. It is a strategic technique to make money yield the highest interest output for any amount spent.

In this Chapter

- *Money Management*
  - *Family Income*
  - *Budgeting*
  - *Control in Money Management*
  - *Household Account*
  - *Family Savings and Investment*
  - *Tax Implications*
- *Human Resource Management*
  - *Functions of Human Resource Management*
  - *Need for Human Resource Management*
  - *Human Resource Development*
  - *Manpower Planning*
  - *Training Need Assessment*
  - *Training Evaluation*

Family Income

Income is the inflow of money, goods and services. Family income is the income from all sources like salary of family members, rent and interest received from banks and savings from using skill of family members. The family income can be annual, monthly, weekly or daily income.

The income may be in the form of wages, salary, commissions, pensions, bonus, interest on cash, profit from business, royalties, rent from properties, charities, etc.

A family cannot lead a comfortable life without sufficient money so to learn about the family income and the types of family income is essential.

Types of Family Income

The types of family income can be divided into three categories such as :

Money Income

It is the purchasing power in rupees and paisa that goes into the family treasury in a given period of time. It comes to the family in the form of wages, salary, bonus, commission, rent, dividends, interest, retirement income, royalties and any other allowances to any member of the family. Money income is converted into goods and services, required for daily living and often a part is diverted into savings for delayed use or for investment purposes.

Real Income

It is defined by economists as means of flow of commodities and services available for satisfaction of human wants and needs over a given period of time. Real income is a flow of goods and services, it is not stagnant. It consists of goods and services which might or might not be available with money. For example, produce from your own land, services of a household. There is a time period involved– it may be a month or a year.

Real income is of two types i.e. Direct income and Indirect income.

Direct Income It consists of those goods and services available to the family members without the use of money, such as services rendered by family members, like cooking, laundering, stitching, maintaining kitchen garden, etc. A house which is fully paid for and community facilities like parks, roads, libraries also come under direct income.

Indirect Income Those material goods and services which are available to the family only after some means of exchange (ordinarily money) For example, use of money to buy good quality vegetables because it involves one's skill and ability to select.

Psychic Income

It is the satisfaction that results from the ownership and utilisation of goods and services. It can also be defined as the satisfaction derived from real income. It is difficult to quantify psychic income in terms of rupees. It is a form of hidden income. It is intangible and subjective and the most important in terms of quality of living.

Supplementation of Family Income

Family income supplementation is a weekly tax free payment available to married or unmarried employees with children. It gives extra financial support to people on low pay. In present times, where price index is rising everyday and demands are also increasing. One has to really work hard in order to improve his economic resources and to get all the material comfort. Additional income has to be generated for this and all the family members have to contribute in it.

Budgeting

Different families handle budgeting in different ways. Budgeting can help you and your family take the first step towards control your money. It can also help you to avoid debt. The key to budgeting is spend less than you earn. One way to start is to list what you earn, spend money on and owe. Budget is the most common planning device for the use of money. A budget is a plan for future expenditure. It represents the first step in the managerial process as applied to money.

Its success depends upon :

- its being realistic and flexible.
- suitability to the group for which it is prepared.
- quality of the control and evaluation steps which follow.

A family budget gives in detail the income and the expenditure of a family for a month or a year. It mentions all the sources of income during the period and also all the items of expenditure under different headings, such as food, clothing, housing, entertainment, travel, education, health and medicine and savings.

Steps Involved in Making Budget

For making budgets following steps are needed :

Listing of Commodities List the commodities and services needed by the family members throughout the proposed budget plan. Group that related goods and services such as food and related costs, household operations, income tax, personal allowances, education medical miscellaneous, provision for future.

Estimation of Cost Estimate the cost of the desired items totalling each classification and the budget as a whole. For example, if prices are showing an upward trend, sufficient margin should be allowed to cover such increases.

Estimate Total Expected Income It is helpful to list income under two headings. Such as assured and possible income. The budget should ensure that necessities are taken care from the assured income and not necessary items can be obtained from possible income.

Bring Expected Income and Expenditure into Balance To bring balance these are two ways i.e., one can either increase the income or cut expenditure.

Check Plans The plans are checked in the following ways :

- The needs of the family have been met.
- The budget allows for emergencies. A joint fund may be kept and for emergency period.
- Long-term goals of the family recognised.

Advantages of Planning Family Budget

Advantages of planning family budget are :

- Planning enables a family to take an overview of the use of their income.
- Amount allocated to various categories can be studied in relation to total income.
- The budget helps families use their income to first attain those goals which they consider most important. Spending without a plan frequently results in wastage of income.
- Family members are less likely to be swayed, as they can make rational decisions which are reflective of long term goals of the family.

Control in Money Management

After planning, controlling is the next step in money management. Control in money management is usually of two types: checking to see how well the plan is progressing and adjusting wherever necessary. Checking is important because it tells how one's plans are progressing and where adjustments are required.

There can be two kinds of checks namely mental and mechanical. Mental checks are generally established by breaking the allocation into units which can be related to actual expenditure. Whereas a mechanical check is one in which you set aside a certain amount of money in cash to be used for a particular item.

Household Account

Household accounts present data on disposable income, spending, savings, debt and financial assets of household. A household may be a person who makes provision for his/her own food and other essentials for living or may be the small group of people who share the same living accommodation, pool some or all of their income and wealth and consume certain types of goods and services collectively mainly housing and food.

Family Savings and Investment

Savings and investment are often used interchangeably but there is difference. By saving we mean the money you don't spend now but keep it for emergencies or for future purchases whereas investment is an asset or item acquired with a goal of generating income. It is the process of using your money. Investment can be stocks, bonds, mutual funds, etc.

Savings means keeping aside a part of your money or other resources for use in future or for further production. Savings are important for a family to take care of their future needs. Savings are also important for any economy to survive and grow as savings lead to capital formation and accumulation. This happens when savings are put to productive use by starting a business or depositing money in banks and financial institutions which mobilise public savings and use them for productive use.

Savings of a family depend on the ability to save and willingness to save. Ability to save depends on per capita income. Higher income families have a higher potential to save compared to low income families who have little to save after taking care of their basic needs. Willingness to save depends upon the long-term goals of the family and how willing they may be to sacrifice some luxuries in the present to take care of the future.

Saving money is not easy. It takes discipline, planning, cooperation and hard work on the part of family members. But saving money is very important for family security and happiness. Saving for saving's sake is futile. Savings have meaning only when the purpose is well-planned and understood by all family members and the money wisely invested for future use.

Investment implies using money for further production. If savings are put under the folds of a saree or kept hidden in a pitcher, it is not going to result in investment. So, saving have to be put to productive use in the economic sense to result in investment.

Investments in Type of Assets

Investment may be in two types of assets such as physical assets and financial assets.

Savings in Financial Assets It means money put into bank accounts post offices, or financial credit societies, in shares and securities, insurance policies, etc. The financial assets provide financial security to the family and are productive in economic terms.

Savings in Physical Assets It means using your savings to purchase land, property, house, gold, etc. Such a kind of investment is not productive in the economic sense of the term and does not result in capital formation. However, it usually has long-term positive returns.

Thus, the investment is the commitment of money that have been saved by deferring consumption and purchasing an asset, either real or financial with an expectation that it could yield some positive future returns. Investment is a sacrifice of current rupees for future rupees.

Principles of Sound Investments

The principles of sound investment consists of :

Safety of the Principal Amount It means the principal, has to be safe if it is to earn interest or dividends. The safety can be ensured by owning securities in both government and private sectors.

Reasonable Rate of Return In general, the higher, the rate of return on an investment, the greater the risk i.e. safety of principal and rate of return are inversely related. To some people, particularly those depending upon investments as their major source of income, regularity of income is more important than a higher but fluctuating return. This is determined by the selection of securities.

Therefore, before investing money one should compare the rate of interest and the associated risk under various schemes and options.

Liquidity It is the ability to convert the securities into cash without sacrificing value. The more liquid an investment is, the higher is its price, or in other words, the lower, the return to the investor. Hence, income and liquidity must be balanced.

Recognition of Effect of World Conditions Changes in business trends will affect both the amount of protection needed, the ease of providing it and the methods chosen to provide it. Considering the long-time business trends, a family must recognise the effect of their savings on the entire economy. Their willingness or unwillingness to invest in business enterprises at various stages in the cycle may well have an effect in reducing the extremeness of the cycle.

Easy Accessibility and Convenience While choosing an investment option for family funds, one must consider the knowledge required for its success. A family may choose an investment which might result in loss simply because they did not foresee the problems involved in the management of security or property acquired.

Investing in Needed Commodities The date on which an investment is to mature is important for a family that plans to have funds available for a known future need.

Therefore, while investing money, families should purchase securities of lengths and durations so that they mature close to the time of the envisaged need or needs, e.g. for the child's higher education.

Tax Efficiency Investments should be made in those instruments which lead to tax savings. A number of provisions in the Income Tax Act can be used to save taxes. Investment in insurance policies, Employees Provident Fund, PPF etc., have built-in tax rebates with a specific ceiling limit.

After Investment Service While selecting an investment instrument, customer care or customer service must be a critical decision-making factor. Good customer care includes easy encashability of securities, good communication network, timely dispatch of interest or dividend warrants, timely disbursal of the due amount after completion of investment period, keeping the customer posted about changes in the policies, interest rate etc. A customer-friendly company provides the needed support and protection to the investor as and when required.

Tax Implications

Implications of taxation is a critical concern in a country like India because there are number of problems.

Taxes are the main source of income for the government. Taxes imposed by the government (central and state) on sellers, purchasers, firms, companies and individuals. Different types of taxes collected by the government from general public and businessman, which is used for the economic welfare and development.

The taxes are divided into main categories i.e., direct and indirect. Different taxes are imposed by the central and state governments for different purposes such as to reduce the unequal distribution of income in societies, to raise the economy.

Human Resource Management

Human Resource Management (HRM) is a function within an organisation which focuses mainly on the recruitment of, management, and providing guidelines to the manpower in a company. It is a function of the company or organisation which deals with concerns that are related to the staff of the company in terms of hiring, compensation, performance, safety, wellness, benefits, motivation and training.

Human Resource Management is also a premeditated approach to manage people and the work culture. An efficient human resource management enables the workforce of an organisation to contribute efficiently and effectively towards the overall achievement of a company's goals and objectives. The traditional method of human resource management involved planned exploitation of staffs. This new function of human resource management involves HRM Metrics and measurements and strategic directions to display value.

Human Resource Management has an important role to play in equipping organisations to meet the challenges of an expanding and increasingly competitive sector. Increase in staff numbers, contractual diversification and changes in demographic profile which compel the HR managers to reconfigure the role and significance of Human Resource Management. All the functions of HRM are correlated with the core objectives of HRM. For example, personal objectives is sought to be realised through functions like remuneration, assessment, etc.

Definitions of Human Resource Management are :

- According to **Dale Yoder**, "Human Resource Management is the provision of leadership and direction of people in their working or employment relationship."
- According to **Mathis** and **Jackson**, "Human Resource Management is the effective use of Human resources and organisation through the management of people related activities."
- According to **Ricky W Griffin**, "Human Resource Management is the set of organizational activities directed at attracting, developing and maintaining an effective workforce."
- According to **Milkovich** and **Boudreau**, "Human Resource Management is a series of decision that affect the relationship between employee and employer: it affects many constituencies and is intended to influences the effectiveness of employee and employer.
- According to **Cambridge Dictionary**, "Human Resource Management is the activity of managing a company's employees; for example, by empolying new workers, training them, managing their employment records and helping them with problems.

Functions of Human Resource Management

Following functions of Human Resource Management are discussed below :

- Managerial Functions
- Operative Functions
- Advisory Functions

Managerial Functions

The Human Resource Manager is a part of the organisational management. So, he must perform the basic managerial functions of planning, organising, directing and controlling in relation to his department.

Planning It is necessary to determine the goals of the organisation and lay down policies and procedures to reach the goals. On the part of manager, it is necessary that he must plan ahead to get things done through the subordinates.

Organising Once the human resource manager has established objectives and developed plans and programs to reach them, he must design and develop organisation structure to carry out the various operations.

Directing The directing function is meant to guide and motivate the people to accomplish the personnel programs. The personnel manager can motivate the employees in an organisation through career planning, salary administration, ensuring employee morale, developing cordial relationships and provision of safety requirements and welfare of employees.

Controlling It is concerned with the regulation of activities in accordance with the plans, which in turn have been formulated on the basis of the objectives of the organisation.

Thus, controlling completes the cycle and leads back to planning. It involves the observation and comparison of results with the standards and correction of deviations that may occur.

Operative Functions

The operative functions are those tasks or duties which are specifically entrusted to the human resource or personnel department. These are concerned with employment, development, compensation, integration and maintenance of personnel of the organisation.

Advisory Functions

It means that human resource manager has specialised education and training in managing human resources. He is an expert in his area and so can give advise on matters relating to human resources of the organisation. He also offers advice to the heads of various departments on matters such as manpower planning, job analysis and design, recruitment and selection, placement, training, performance appraisal, etc.

Need for Human Resource Management

In an organisation, the human resource management is needed because of the following reasons listed below :

Create Organisational Commitment An improvement in efficiency and quality of work can come only when workers develop organisational commitment. HRM approach helps in creating a sense of pride for the organisation among the employees.

Meeting with Changing Environment Now-a-days there is a need to cope with new and changing situation. The operational efficiency of workers must cope up with a revolutionary change in the technology which necessitates a new approach to manpower.

Change in Political Philosophy It means that the political philosophy has also undergone a substantial change all over the world. The new approach is to develop human resources properly for making their better use.

Enhanced Pressure on Employees In the fast changing world due to the technological innovations there is a need for large number of trained and skillful personnel to cope up with new technology to meet the goals of the organisation this sometimes enhanced pressure on employees.

Meeting Research and Development Requirements Fresh initiatives and emphasis on research and development in the realm of industry also led to a new policy of human resource development to cope with the increasing demand for technically capable people. As a result of this, a need arose for a new approach to human resources.

Managing Disputes There are several issues in an organisation on which disputes may arise between the employees and the employers. You can say conflicts are almost inevitable.

In such a scenario, it is the human resource department which acts as a consultant and mediator to sort out those issues in an effective manner. They first hear the grievances of the employees. Then they come up with suitable solutions to sort them out. In other words, they take timely action and prevent things from going out of hands.

Thus, it can be said that any organisation, without a proper set up for HRM is bound to suffer from serious problems while managing its regular activities.

Human Resource Development

In 1970, **Leonard Nadler** published his book. Developing Human Resources', in which he coined the term 'Human Resource Development' (HRD). Human resource refers to the talents and energies of people that are available to an organisation as potential contributors to the creation and realisation of the organisation's mission, vision, values, and goals.

Development refers to a process of active learning from experience-leading to systematic and purposeful development of the whole person, body, mind, and spirit. Thus, HRD is the integrated use of training, organisational and career development efforts to improve individual, group, and organisational effectiveness.

Definitions of Human Resource Development are :

- According to **South Pacific Commission**, "human resource development is equipping people with relevant skills to have a healthy and satisfying life."
- According to **Watkins**, "human resource development is fostering long-term work related learning capacity at individual, group and organisational level."
- According to **American Society for Training and Development**, "Human Resource Development is the process of increasing the capacity of the human resource through development. Thus, it is the process of adding value to individuals, teams or an organisation as a human system.

Functions of Human Resource Development

The functions of Human Resource Development are as follows :

Training and Development It focuses on changing or improving the knowledge, skills and attitudes of individuals. Training involves providing employees the knowledge and skills needed for particular tasks.

Work System The work planning system ensures that attracted and retained human resources are utilised in the best possible way.

Self-renewal System It is not enough to develop individuals and teams in the organisations but occasional there is a need to review and rejuvenate the organisation itself.

Culture System Building a desired culture system is of paramount importance in today's changed scenario. It is very important to have cultural practices that facilitates, business/ enterprise.

Challenges of Human Resource Development

The human resource development faces various types of challenges, few common challenges are detailed as :

Values of Behaviour It means that HRD professionals have to adjust themselves to the emerging values as principle centric leadership is becoming trend in the world. Values like trust, credibility, timeliness and simpler rules are becoming important challenges.

Knowledge or Information Due to the enhancement of knowledge, the HRD professional have to understand the different philosophies e.g. philosophy related to leadership changes in organisations.

Knowledge of New Practices An HRD professionals has to be aware of the new practices adopted by the organisation around. He should know about the practices like dignity of individual, clear convince relationship with employees, customers and society.

Environment It is another challenge as an open environment is required for the success of an organisation. The organisational environment should have meritocracy, justice, fearlessness and accountability.

Culture and Attitude The countries over the world have different types of cultures, so the Human Resource Development have to face the cultural challenges in different countries or with employees belonging to the various countries.

Manpower Planning

Manpower planning is also known as human resource planning. It is a broad topic. Manpower planning is the process by which the organisation ensures that it has the right kind of people at right time, at right place and they are working effectively and efficiently and help the organisation in achieving overall objectives.

Manpower planning and human resource planning are synonymous. In the past, the phrase manpower planning was widely used but in present times the emphasis is on human resource planning.

The manpower planning has been defined variously by different authors as follows :

- According to **Gorden MacBeath**, manpower planning involves two stages.The first stage is concerned with the detailed "planning of manpower requirements for all types and levels of employees throughout the period of the plan," and the second stage is concerned with "planning of manpower supplies to provide the organisation with the right types of people from all sources to meet the planned requirements."
- According to **Vetter**, the process by which management determines how the organisation should move from its current manpower position to its desired manpower position. Through planning, management strives to have the right number and the right kinds of people, at the right places, at the right time, doing things which result in both the organisation and the individual receiving maximum long-run benefit.
- **Coleman** has defined human resource or manpower planning as "the process of determining manpower requirements and the means for meeting those requirements in order to carry out the integrated plan of the organisation."

Thus, Human Resource (HR) planning or manpower planning is the process by which the organisation ensures that it has the right kind of people, at right time, at right place and they are working effectively and efficiently and help the organisation in achieving the overall objective. It is a continuous process.

The manpower planning is important because it is helpful in finding out surplus/shortage of manpower. It is helpful in employee development. It serves the purpose of a planning and control technique. It gives an indication of the lead time available to select and retain the required additional manpower. It assesses future accommodation requirements.

Thus, manpower planning is admittedly an essential tool for proper acquiring utilisation and development of the human resource of an organisation.

Training Need Assessment

The training need assessment identifies individual's current level of competency, skill or knowledge in one or more areas and compares that competency level to the acquired competency established for their positions or other positions within the organisations. The difference between the current and required competencies can help determine the training needs. Rather than assure that all employees need trainers or even the same trainers. In this regard the management can make the informed decisions about the best ways to address competency gaps among individual employees specific job categories or group/teams.

Assessment can be conducted at any time but these are often done, after hiring, during performance reviews and when performance improvement is required for career plans, for succession planning, or when changes in an organisation also involves making necessary changes to employees jobs. So, it is beneficial to perform these assessments periodically to determine the training needs of an organisation, employees knowledge and skills and also training programme effectiveness.

Training Evaluation

The training evaluation is the process of examining a training programme. The training evaluation checks whether training has led the desired effect or not. It also ensures whether candidates are able to implement their learning in their respective workplace. Training evaluation usually includes a combination of methods and thus reframe our thinking about evaluation in that measurements aimed at different levels of system.

A properly designed methodologies of evaluation provide insight of the effectiveness of the training. It enables on organisation to monitor and modify the training programme.

Types of Training Evaluation

There are generally four kinds of standard training evaluation :

Formative Evaluation It may be defined as "any combination of measurements obtained and judgements made before or during the implementation of materials, methods, or programs to control, assure or improve the quality of program performance or delivery. Formative evaluation furnishes information for programme developers and implementers."

It helps to determine programme planning and implementation activities in terms of target population, program organisation and program location and timing.

Process Evaluation It focuses on procedures and actions being used to produce results. It answers question 'What did you do?' It monitors the quality of an event or project by different means working as an 'onlooker', the evaluator describes this process and measures the results in oral and written reports. It takes place during training delivery at the end of the event.

Outcome Evaluation It is a long-term undertaking. It answers the questions "What happened to the knowledge, attitude and behaviours of the intended population?"

Impact Evaluation It takes longer than outcome evaluation and one may never know for sure that project helped bring about the change impact through an accumulation of outcomes.

Methodologies of Training Evaluation

The methodologies to be adopted for training evaluation include :

Observation Under this method, direct observation takes place in order to assess the changed knowledge, skills and attitudes of the participants. During observation, the errors and mistakes in actual work situation are carefully observed.

Questionnaire They are the most common training evaluation method. These are used to gather information on a programme or session. They are an efficient way to gather large amounts of both quantitative and qualitative data about a training course. They need minimum time to administer. They can easily encompass a large number of participants.

Interviews Through interview, the participant's reaction on training can be obtained. Interviews are a way to collect useful data for training evaluation programme.

Self-diaries It helps the trainer to evalute the training programme by maintaining record in the diaries.

Self-recording or Specific Incident Through this methodology the information is collected about one's action and then accordingly changes can be made in knowing one's behaviour.

Surveys A survey is a part of a systematic and continual process of evaluating the effectiveness and value of a training programme. It helps in knowing exactly what information participants are struggling with and then accordingly solve their problems. It helps to determine to which extent training sessions were effective.

EXAM BASED QUESTIONS

1 The primary goal of money management is
(a) to maximise the return
(b) to minimise the risk
(c) to maximise the wealth of owners
(d) to maximise profit

2 Family income can be
(a) annual (b) monthly
(c) daily income (d) All of these

3 The family income can be in the form of
(a) wages (b) pensions
(c) bonus (d) All of these

4 Real income is of .... types.
(a) two (b) three (c) four (d) five

5 Real income ....
(a) is a flow of goods and services not stagnant
(b) consists of goods and services might or might not be available with money
(c) involves a time period
(d) All of the above

6 Direct income consists of
(a) those goods and services available to the family without the use of money
(b) those material goods and services which are available to the family only after some means of exchange
(c) a form of hidden income
(d) intangible

7 Investment is when you
(a) save money every month
(b) put money in piggy bank
(c) earn interest on your savings
(d) put money in bank locker

8 Psychic income means
(a) satisfaction (b) services
(c) money (d) goods

9 Expenditure of a family is influenced by
(a) size of the family
(b) status of the family
(c) locality in which the family lives
(d) All of the above

10 The success of the budget depends on
(a) its being realistic and flexible
(b) suitability to the group for which it is prepared
(c) quality of the control and evaluation
(d) All of the above

11 A family budget gives in
(a) detail the income of the family
(b) expenditure of the family
(c) it does not mention all sources of income
(d) Both (a) and (b)

12 Which of the following commodities and services are needed by the family members throughout the proposed budget plan?
(a) Food and related costs (b) Income tax
(c) Personal allowances (d) All of these

13 Which among the following are the advantages of planning family budget?
(a) Planning enables a family to take an overview of the use of their income
(b) Amounts allocated to various categories can be studied in relation to total income
(c) The planning helps families to use their income to first attain those goals which they consider most important
(d) All of the above

14 A budget is not
(a) a forecast
(b) a plan
(c) a part of strategic management process
(d) a qualitative statement

15 Which of the following is not onc of tho main purpose of budget?
(a) Planning and control
(b) The alignment of individual and corporate goals
(c) To enable a flexibility of approach to company policies
(d) To optimioe tho uoo of ocarce resources.

16 There are mainly......... kinds of checks in controlling money management.
(a) two (b) four
(c) three (d) six

17 Household accounts presents data on
(a) disposable income (b) Spendings
(c) financial assets (d) All of these

18 Choose the correct statement(s) with regard to savings
(a) Using money for further production.
(b) Keeping inside a part of money for future use.
(c) Savings are important for family security and happenings.
(d) All of the above

19 Which of the following are the functions of human resource management?
(a) Managerial (b) Operative
(c) Advisory (d) All of these

20 The basic purpose of human resource planning is to
(a) identify the human resource requirement
(b) match the HR requirements with HR availability
(c) identify the human resource ability
(d) All of the above

21 Personal resources include
(a) skills and time (b) abilities and time
(c) knowledge and skills (d) energy and money

22 Human resource management refers to
(a) all managerial activities
(b) concepts and techniques used in heading person at work
(c) the management of people in organisations
(d) the management techniques for controlling people at work.

23 Human resource management is mainly ...... in nature.
(a) proactive (b) reactive
(c) combative (d) None of these

24 Which of the following is the benefit of need assessment?
(a) Assessment makes training department more accountable.
(b) Higher training costs
(c) Loss of business
(d) Increased overtime working

25 Identify the managerial function out of the following functions.
(a) Procurement (b) Development
(c) Organising (d) Performance appraisal

26 The primary responsibility for human resource planning lies with
(a) HR Manager (b) General Manager
(c) Trade Union Leader (d) Line Manager

27 Which of the following is not an objective of Human Resource Management functions?
(a) Societal (b) Political
(c) Personal (d) Organisational

28 In which year did the term HRM emerge?
(a) 1970 (b) 1990 (c) 1980 (d) 1999

29 What are the various methods of training evaluation?
(a) Interview
(b) Self-recording of specific incident
(c) Questionnaire
(d) All of the above

30 "Human Resource Development is fostering long-term work related learning capacity at individual, group and organisational level." Who said this?
(a) Watkins (b) Leonard Nadler
(c) MC Farland (d) R C Davis

31 In 1970 .... published the book entitled "Developing Human Resources".
(a) EW Crandall (b) R P Devdas
(c) Leonard Nadler (d) Watkins

32 The principles of sound management include
(a) safety of the principal amount
(b) liquidity
(c) investing in needed commodities
(d) All of the above

33 Choose the correct statement(s)with regard to the advisory functions.
(a) Manager has specialised education in training and managing.
(b) He offers advice to the heads of different departments.
(c) He designs and develops organisation structure to carry out various operations.
(d) Both a and b

34 Which of the following options is not the factor that hinders with human resource planning process?
(a) Time horizons
(b) Unite the perspectives of line and staff managers
(c) Environmental Uncertainities
(d) Type and quality of forecasting information

35 The safety of the principal amount can be ensured by
(a) owing securities in both government and private sectors
(b) owing shares and bonds in different companies
(c) investing in companies in different geographical zones
(d) All of the above

36 Which of the following statement(s) is/are correct with regard to tax efficiency?
Statement I Investment should be made in those investments which lead to tax savings.
Statement II It is the most important factor of sound investing.
(a) Only statement I is correct
(b) Only statement II is correct
(c) Both the statements are correct
(d) Neither I nor II statements are correct

37 Which of the following characteristic(s) is/are helpful in manpower planning?
(a) Employee development
(b) Finding out the deficiencies in existing manpower
(c) Overall planning process of organisation
(d) All of the above

38 Consider the following statement(s) is/are correct with regard to money management.
Statement I Money management is an essential part of debt free life style.
Statement II It is a broad term involves incorporates services and solutions across the entire investment.
(a) Statement I is correct
(b) Statement II is correct
(c) Both the statements I and II are correct
(d) Neither statements I nor II are correct

39 Which of the following are needed for Human Resource Management?
1. Meeting with Changing Environment
2. Create Organisation Commitment
3. Managing Disputes

4. Meeting Research and Development Requirements.

Codes

(a) 1 and 4 (b) 1, 2, 3 and 4
(c) 1, 3 and 4 (d) 2 and 4

40 Rearrange the step in training programme.
1. What should be the level of training?
2. What principle of training?
3. Who are the trainees?
4. What methods and techniques?
5. Where to conduct the programme?
6. Who are the trainers?

(a) 3 6 4 1 2 5 (b) 1 2 3 4 5 6
(c) 6 5 4 3 2 1 (d) 5 6 3 4 1 2

41 Give the correct sequence of managerial functions.
1. Reporting 2. Staffing
3. Planning 4. Organising
5. Coordinating 6. Budgeting
7. Directing

Codes

(a) 3 4 2 7 5 1 6 (b) 3 4 2 5 6 1 7
(c) 7 6 5 4 3 2 1 (d) 6 7 4 5 2 1 3

42 The functions of Human Resource Development are
1. Training and Development
2. Operative
3. Culture System
4. Directing

Codes

(a) 1 and 4 (b) 1 and 3
(c) 1, 2 and 4 (d) 2, 3 and 4

43 Match the following.

List I (Functions)	List II (Characteristics)
A. Planning	1. guides and motivates the people to accomplish personal programmes
B. Organising	2. necessary to determine goals of organisation
C. Directing	3. means to develop organisation structure to carry out various operations
D. Controlling	4. concerned with the regulation of activities in accordance with plans.

Codes

	A	B	C	D		A	B	C	D
(a)	2	3	1	4	(b)	4	3	2	1
(c)	1	2	3	4	(d)	3	4	1	2

44 Match the following.

List I (Type of Evaluation)	List II (Characteristics)
A. Formative	1. determines whether or not the desired results of applying new skills achieved
B. Process	2. determines how the results of the training affect the strategic goal
C. Outcome	3. provides information about what occur during training
D. Impact	4. provides on going feedback

Codes

	A	B	C	D		A	B	C	D
(a)	1	2	3	4	(b)	4	3	1	2
(c)	2	4	1	3	(d)	4	3	2	1

Directions (Q. Nos 45-60) *In the questions given below are two statements labelled as Assertion (A) and Reason (R). In the context of the two statements which one of the following is correct?*

Codes

(a) Both A and R are correct and R is the correct explanation of A
(b) Both A and R are correct, but R is not the correct explanation A
(c) Both A and R are not correct
(d) A is incorrect while R is correct

45 **Assertion** (A) Money income is the pure purchasing power in rupees and paise that goes into the family treasury.
Reason (R) It comes to the family in the form of wages, salary etc.

46 **Assertion** (A) Real income is the flow of goods and services.
Reason (R) It is a form of hidden income

47 **Assertion** (A) A budget is the most common planning device for the use of money.
Reason (R) It is the first step in managerial process.

48 **Assertion** (A) A training need assessment identifies individual's current level of competency skills or knowledge.
Reason (R) It is beneficial to perform these assessment periodically.

49 **Assertion** (A) Training evaluation checks whether training has had the desired effect.
Reason (R) Training evaluation ensures whether candidates are able to implement their learning in their respective workplace.

50 **Assertion** (A) Formative evaluation determines programme planning and implementation activities.
Reason (R) In terms of target population, program organisation and program location and testing.

51 **Assertion** (A) Process evaluation is not the common type of training evaluation.
Reason (R) It takes place during training delivery at the beginning of the event.

52 **Assertion** (A) Outcome evaluation answers the question what did the participants do.
Reason (R) Outcome evaluation is the long-term standing.

53 **Assertion** (A) Formative evaluation does not furnish information for program developers and implementers.
Reason (R) It provides short loop feedback about the quality and implementation of programmes.

54 **Assertion** (A) Money plays a significant role in the life of man.

Reason (R) It is an instrument through which he can satisfy his physical, material and mental needs.

55 **Assertion** (A) Controlling is concerned with the regulation of activities is a not in accordance with the plans.

Reason (R) It involves the observation and comparisons of results.

56 **Assertion** (A) Human Resource Management is needed to create organisational commitment.

Reason (R) HRM is needed to cope with new changing situation.

57 **Assertion** (A) Manpower planning is the process by which the organisation ensures that it has the right kind of people.

Reason (R) It helps in employees development.

58 **Assertion** (A) Family income supplementation is a weekly tax free payment.

Reason (R) It is available to married or unmarried employees with children.

59 **Assertion** (A) A family budget does not give in detail the income and expenditure of a family for a month or a year.

Reason (R) It mentions the sources of income during the period.

60 **Assertion** (A) Saving is important for family.

Reason (R) It is kept for future use to satisfy needs.

PREVIOUS YEARS' QUESTIONS

July 2018

1 **Assertion** (A) The system is a set of inter-dependent subsystems that constitute a united whole.

Reason (R) The management of a family depends upon the components of the environments of these subsystems.

Codes

(a) A is correct and R is incorrect.
(b) A is incorrect and R is correct.
(c) Both A and R are correct.
(d) Both A and R are incorrect.

2 **Assertion** (A) Record keeping in money management helps to compare monthly expenditure with the spending plan.

Reason (R) Records show distribution of money after expenditure has been made.

Codes

(a) Both A and R are correct.
(b) A is correct and R is incorrect.
(c) A is incorrect and R is correct.
(d) Both A and R are incorrect.

November 2017

3 **Assertion** (A) A family budget is a way of detailing expenses under different headings.

Reason (R) It helps the family to live within their income.

Codes

(a) A is correct and R is incorrect.
(b) A is incorrect and R is correct.
(c) Both A and R are correct.
(d) Both A and R are incorrect.

January 2017

4 **Assertion** (A) Child budgeting must begin at the very level of Panchayats, the very basic unit of democratic functioning.

Reason (R) This will logically result in de-centralisation in implementation and monitoring of programmes for children.

Codes

(a) Both A and R are correct.
(b) Both A and R are incorrect.
(c) A is correct and R is incorrect.
(d) A is incorrect and R is correct.

5 **Assertion** (A) Organisation is an important tool for the managerial performance.

Reason (R) Lack of organisation gives rise to many defects in its structure.

Codes

(a) Both A and R are correct.
(b) A is correct but R is incorrect.
(c) A is incorrect but R is correct.
(d) Both A and R are incorrect.

July 2016

6 Identify the aspects that contribute to a family's hidden income

1. Community facilities
2. Consumer savings through bargaining
3. Mortgages
4. Employment benefits
5. Loans from banks

Codes

(a) 1, 2 and 4 (b) 1, 3 and 4
(c) 1, 3 and 5 (d) 1, 2 and 3

December 2015

7 **Assertion** (A) The challenge of management lies in the abundance of resources and being able to manage the most of the family goals.

Reason (R) Minimising inputs and maximising outputs are the essence of management.

Codes

(a) A is correct but R is incorrect.
(b) A is incorrect but R is correct.
(c) Both A and R are correct.
(d) Both A and R are incorrect.

June 2015

8 **Assertion** (A) Systemic evaluation enables to determine the effectiveness of any programme.

Reason (R) Information obtained through evaluation shows strengths and weaknesses of a programme.

Codes

(a) Both A and R are correct.
(b) Both A and R are incorrect.
(c) A is correct and R is incorrect.
(d) A is correct and R is incorrect.

June 2014

9 The managerial and the psychosocial sub-systems are part of the

(a) household environment
(b) near environment
(c) large environment
(d) internal environment

ANSWERS

Exam Based Questions

1 (c)	2 (d)	3 (d)	4 (a)	5 (d)	6 (a)	7 (c)	8 (a)	9 (d)	10 (d)
11 (d)	12 (d)	13 (d)	14 (a)	15 (c)	16 (a)	17 (d)	18 (d)	19 (d)	20 (d)
21 (d)	22 (c)	23 (a)	24 (a)	25 (c)	26 (b)	27 (b)	28 (a)	29 (d)	30 (a)
31 (c)	32 (d)	33 (d)	34 (b)	35 (d)	36 (a)	37 (d)	38 (c)	39 (b)	40 (a)
41 (a)	42 (b)	43 (a)	44 (b)	45 (a)	46 (b)	47 (a)	48 (b)	49 (a)	50 (a)
51 (b)	52 (b)	53 (d)	54 (a)	55 (d)	56 (b)	57 (b)	58 (a)	59 (d)	60 (a)

Previous Years' Questions

1 (c)	2 (a)	3 (c)	4 (a)	5 (a)	6 (b)	7 (b)	8 (a)	9 (a)

Consumer Issues and Entrepreneurship

Consumers are the basic economic entities of an economy. No country can disregard the interest of the consumers. But consumers' issues can come up whenever an individual purchases goods or services as a consumer. To protect consumers there are various protection laws for protecting consumers from unfair and dishonest trade practices by sellers. The entrepreneurship is both the study of how business is created as well as the actual process of starting a new business.

Consumer

Consumer is a person who buys goods or services to be used or consumed by himself/herself or by someone else on behalf of the buyer. In general, a consumer is a person who 'consumes'. The word consumer is derived from the Latin word 'consumer' which means 'to take up totally or to eat'. Consumer is an ultimate user of product or services. He is an individual who buys product or services for personal use and not for resale or reproduce. A consumer plays a vital role in the economic system of a nation. Without consumer demand, producers would lack one of the key motivations to produce, to sell to consumers. The consumer also forms part of chain distribution. "The consumer is one who consumes or uses any commodity or service available to him either from natural resources or through a market." Thus, consumers are end users of product or services.

Some definitions of consumers are as follows :

- The **International Dictionary Management** defines, "Consumers are purchasers of goods and services for immediate use and consumption."
- According to **Cambridge Dictionary**, "Consumer is a person who buys goods or services for their own use."
- According to **John F Kennedy**, "Consumer are the largest economic group, affecting and affected by almost every public and private economic decision. Yet they are the only important group whose views are often not heard."

In this Chapter

Role of Consumers

The consumers play a significant role in an economic system because it is the consumers who demand goods and services. When they do this, they make it so that other people can have jobs making the goods and services the consumers want. Consumers also play an important role in marketing process.

In every trade and commerce, the role of consumer is indispensable. The existence of consumers makes an economy grow and prosper. The profit which has been generated in the economy is because of the intelligent choices and purchases made by the consumers.

According to **Gandhiji**, "A customer is the most important visitor on our premises. He is not dependent on us. We are dependent on him. He is not an interruption to our work. He is the purpose of it. He is a part of it. We are not doing him favour by serving him. He is doing favour by giving us an opportunity to do so."

Thus, in an economy the consumers' role is very important.

Rights and Responsibilities of Consumer

There is no denying the fact that most of us always prefer knowing facts related to our rights to avail them. We often remain lazy in practising them by judging their values in the context of consumer responsibilities we owe.

Consumer Rights

Today, consumers face numerous problems due to growing competition in the market, misleading advertisements, availability of inferior quality of goods and services etc. So, the protection of consumers' interest is a matter of grave/ serious concern for the government and public bodies. In order to safeguard the interest of the consumers, government has recognised certain rights of the consumers.

The rights which are recognised by the government discussed below :

Right to Safety According to this right, consumers have the right to be protected against marketing of goods which are injurious to health and life. As a consumer, if you are conscious of this right, you can take precautions to prevent the injury or if injury is caused inspite of precaution. In this situation, you have a right to complain against the dealer and even claim situation, Suppose, as a consumer, if you purchase any medicine the pharmacy selling it can be held responsible if the medicine proves harmful.

Right to be Informed This right gives the consumer to be informed about the quality, purity, standard or grade and price of the goods available, so that consumer can make proper choice before buying any product or service. Also, where necessary, the consumer must be informed about the safety precautions to be taken while using the product to avoid loss or injury. For example, the consumer is using gas cylinder and if it starts leaking, the supplier must inform him to stop the flow of the gas with the help of the regulator, when it is not in use. This right gives the power to the consumers to have easy access to information which is necessary for the consumers.

Right to Choose This right ensures that every consumer has the right to choose the goods needed from a variety of similar goods. They should not be forced to select a product. A consumer should be convinced of the product e.g. T.V he is about to choose and should make a decision by himself. This also means consumer should have a variety of articles to choose from the products available in the market.

Monopolistic practices are not legal. It is seen that very often dealers and traders try to use pressure tactics to sell goods of poor quality. Consumers are also carried away by advertisement on the TV. These possibilities can be avoided if consumers are conscious of their rights.

Right to be Heard This right has three interpretations. Broadly speaking, this right means that firstly, consumers have a right to be consulted by the government and public bodies, when decisions and policies are made affecting consumers' interest. Secondly, consumers also have the right to be heard by manufacturers, dealers and advertisers about their opinion on production and marketing decisions. Thirdly, consumers have the right to be heard in legal proceedings in law courts dealing with consumer complaints.

Right to Seek Redressal The consumers through this right are assured that their complaints will receive due attention. It provides for due compensation to consumers, if they have suffered a loss or are put to inconvenience due to the fault of the supplier or manufacturers. We have a three-tier redressal according to the Consumer Protection Act, 1986. Suppose, if and when any consumer has a complaints or grievances due to unfair trade practices like charging higher price, selling of poor quality or unsafe products, lack of regularity in supply of services, etc. He/She has a right to get the defective goods replaced or money refunded by the seller or dealer. He/she can seek redressal legal remedies in the appropriate court of law.

Right to Education This right makes sure that the consumers in the country have informational programmes and materials which are easily accessible and would enable them to make purchasing decision which are better than before. This is the last right provided by the Consumer Protection Act, 1986. This right is essentially required to prevent market malpractices and exploitation of consumers, consumer awareness and education. For this purpose, consumer associations, educational institutions and government policy makers are expected to enable consumers to be informed and educated. These are as follows :

- The relevant laws which are aimed at preventing unfair trade practices.
- The ways in which dishonest traders and producers may try to manipulate market practices to deceive consumers.
- How consumers can protect their own interest.
- The procedure to be adopted by consumers while making complaints.

Consumer Responsibilities

There is a well-known saying that "there cannot be rights without responsibilities."

Consumer responsibilities refer to the responsibilities of having awareness of the quality and safety of goods and services while purchasing. The responsibility to collect information about products or services and to update with changing innovations taking place in the market. As a responsible consumer, he/she should keep few things in mind while purchasing them. Some of the consumer responsibilities are listed below :

Consumer should Use his Right It means consumers have many rights regarding goods and services. They must be aware of their rights while buying as under Consumer Protection Act. They have been granted various rights. These rights are right to safety, right to choose, right to be informed, right to representation, right to be heard and right to seek redressal, etc.

Cautious Consumer do not Buy Blindly As a consumer his/her responsibility is that he/she should make full use of their right while purchasing things. They should not blindly believe on the words of seller. In other words, while buying, consumer must get information regarding the quality, quantity, price and utility, etc., of goods and services.

Filing Complaint for the Redressal of Actual Grievances It is the responsibility of a consumer to approach the officer concerned, if there are some complaints about the goods purchased. He/She must file a complaint even for a small loss. This awareness among the consumers will make the seller more conscious to supply quality product. Whenever, consumer files a complaint it must be genuine. The consumer should not exaggerate the loss or defect of goods. It is also the responsibility of consumers to buy only goods with ISI, Agmark, FPO, etc., printed on them.

Proof of Transactions It means that every consumer should have the proof of purchase and documents relating to purchase of goods to be preserved. As for filing a complaint, a consumer needs the evidence of purchase otherwise, he may not be liable for compensation. For example, if you purchase a durable goods like TV, refrigerators or any other items, carry warranty/guarantee cards issued by the dealers. The card entitles the consumer to get the service for repair and replacement of parts free of cost during a certain period after purchase. As a consumer, he should always insist on cash memo for purchase of goods from seller.

Proof of Claim As regard this responsibility, the consumers are expected to bear in proper claim.

Beware of False Advertisement The advertisements often exaggerate the qualities or features of product or services. The consumer must compare the actual use of product with the use shown in advertisement. Whenever, there is any difference or discrepancy it must be brought to the notice of the sponsor of advertisement and exist to stop showing exaggerated qualities. Thus, it can be said that it is the responsibility of the consumer to recognise the truth of advertisements.

Proper Use of Products/Services Some consumers, particularly during the guarantee period, make rough use of the product, thinking that it will be replaced during guarantee period. This is not fair on their part. They should always use the product properly.

Consumer Behaviour

Human being differs from one another. It is not easy to predict the human behaviour. They differ in their taste, needs, wants and preferences. So, understanding consumer behaviour and 'knowing consumers' are not that simple. It is almost impossible to predict with surety, how consumers will behave in a given situation.

Consumer behaviour explains the reasons and logics that underlie purchasing decisions and consumption patterns. It explains the process through which buyers make decisions.

Consumer behaviour has been defined by different authors. Some are as follows :

- According to **Schiffman** and **Kanuk**, "It is the behaviour that consumers display in searching for purchasing, using, evaluating and disposing of product and services that they expect will satisfy their needs."
- According to **Loudon** and **Bitta**, "Consumer behaviour is the decision process and physical activity engaged in when evaluating, acquiring, using or disposing of goods and services."
- According to **Wells** and **Prensky**, "Consumer behaviour is the study of consumers as they exchange something of value for a products or services that satisfies their needs."

- According to **Engel, Blackwell** and **Miniard**, "Consumer behaviour involves those actions directly involved in obtaining, consuming and disposing of products and services including the decision processes that precede and follow these actions."
- According to **American Marketing Association**, "Consumer behaviour is the dynamic interaction of effect and cognition, behaviour and the environment by which human beings conduct the exchange aspects of their lives."

Importance of Studying Consumer Behaviour

The study of consumer behaviour is very important to understand what influences the buying decisions of the consumers and why does it so. To survive in the market, a firm has to constantly innovate and understand the latest consumer needs and tastes. So, it is important for the marketers to understand the buyer behaviour due to the following factors/reasons:

- It is significant for regulating consumption of goods and thereby maintain stability.
- It helps marketers to decide how to present their products such that they have maximum impact on consumers.
- It is useful in developing ways for more efficient utilisation of resources of marketing.
- Studying consumer behaviour is also vital in making decisions regarding sales promotion. It enables the producer to know what motive prompt consumer to make purchase and the same is utilised in promotional campaigns to awaken desire to purchase.
- Rapid introduction of new product with technological advancement has made the job of studying consumer behaviour more imperative.
- Consumers give more importance on environment friendly products. They are concerned about health, hygiene and fitness, so detailed study on upcoming group of consumers is essential for any firm.
- It is also important to study consumer behaviour as now a days there are highly diversified consumer preferences. In the market more choices are available to the consumer for choosing products.

Consumer Problems

Consumer is the most neglected person in the present scarcity ridden society. A firm or business cannot ignore its consumers, if it wants to flourish. But even after a lot of Acts and Rules, a number of problems are faced by the consumers, which are discussed below :

Lack of Information The main problem faced by the consumers is lack of information. The consumers even do not know the source of getting information.

Adulteration This is one such problem which is faced by the consumers in day-to-day purchase. Most of the time, consumers even after paying high price, do not get pure or quality goods e.g. ghee, milk, spices, cereals, etc. Such items are sold in the market with a guarantee of purity but are found to be adulterated when used. Consumers do not have any knowledge to judge the purity. The organisation usually supplies adulterated good for its profit maximisation.

Wrong Weights and Measures Consumers are cheated by traders and others with false weights and measures. in the unorganised market. Even in the organised markets, such as shopping malls, customers are cheated with wrong weight pasted on the packet. Spurious, under weights or stones are used in place of standard weights.

Sale of Sub-Standard Goods Sometimes seller sells sub-standard goods at higher price in place of standard goods. The sellers do so by claiming it of a superior quality and inflates its price e.g. selling furniture made up of inferior quality wood.

Irregular Supply It is one of the most common problems faced by consumers. It is because of shortage of goods. The organisations create artificial scarcity of necessary goods by hoarding these goods resulting in high prices.

Shortage of Standardised Products Most of the goods which are available in the market do not carry standardised markings. When a consumer goes to the market to buy an electronic iron, he finds a number of brands without standardised markings. Still these brands are very cheap. In such a situation, the consumer is not able to decide whether he should buy a cheaper and popular brand or less expensive standardised, expensive brand.

Illiteracy In urban and remote areas most of the consumers are illiterate and are not able to understand the policies of the organisation or government. Even they do not understand uses or misuses of products.

Attractive Packaging The packaged goods supplied in the market are not up to the mark. The packaging is very attractive and it attracts the attention of consumers. The packets may contain inferior goods thereby fooling consumers.

Problem of Duplicate Goods Consumers face a major problem of duplicate goods. Unethical producers duplicate popular brand names and thereby customers get cheated. For example, the products like medicines are duplicated by illegal producers.

No Proper Return for Money It is noticed many a times, consumers feel that they do not get proper return for the price they pay to buy the products. This may be due to inferior quality, less durability, adulteration, etc.

Poor After Sale Service The consumer after-sales service is very poor. Even the MNCs do not provide effective after sales service in the case of office equipment and consumer durables. Customers have to give constant reminders for after sales service. At many times, the customers have to get the equipment repaired or serviced by third party due to poor after-sales service.

Consumer Education and Empowerment

Consumer education plays a significant role in empowering consumers, so that consumers can safeguard oneself from being checked. As an empowered consumer, he will not hesitate to use his rights, if he/she is being cheated by seller or providing incorrect information with regard to the products or services.

Consumer Education

Consumer education is basically an education which brings about behavioural changes in a person, who goes to the market to buy anything. It aims to encourage individuals to analyse and make value based decisions at a personal level in terms of needs and wants.

Thorelli and Thorelli (1977) have argued that a free-market economy can only function effectively with the support of an educated customer."

Importance of Consumer Education

In the present day world, the consumer education is very important because it provides the public with the information, it needs on products and services. So, he can make well- informed decision on what it is purchasing and from whom it purchases.

It helps consumers understand their rights and become active participants in the buying process. Consumer education familiarises the consumer with various standards of standardisation and markings.

It also provides the consumer the complete information of marketing conditions such as different sources of purchasing a particular commodity, from where to get cheap and best goods, the shops providing additional facilities, and to latest products. All these information enable him to take right decision regarding shopping. Consumer education motivates consumers to provide feedback that can be used to improve the quality of goods and services.

Above all, it familiarises the consumers about the various acts enacted by the government from time to time. Consumer education helps the consumer in getting maximum satisfaction by proper utilisation of his money and leads a better living standards.

Consumer Empowerment

Consumer empowerment is a multifaceted concept which tells us about skills, capabilities, rights and abilities of the consumer to collect required information for making an informed and prudent choice. It also talks about the capacity of the market to provide legal and realistic mechanism to the consumers.

Consumer empowerment consists of two broad elements which interact to create the conditions for consumers to thrive. Firstly, the consumers have at their disposal to make better choice. This includes a certain state of mind (confidence and willingness to play active role), decision-making tools such as good information and the skills to use these tools to make effective decisions that secure positive outcome. Secondly, the institutions such as consumer protection and regulatory organisations that support consumers to shape markets.

Consumer Protection

Consumer protection means protecting the rights of consumers. It refers to the steps necessary to be taken or measures required to be accepted to protect consumers from business malpractices. Consumer protection also helps to protect fair trade competition and truthful information in a market economy. So, a Consumer Protection Act, 1986, came into force.

Consumer Protection Act, 1986

Consumer Protection Act, 1986 seeks to promote and protect the interest of consumers against deficiencies and defects in goods or services. It also seeks to secure the rights of a consumer against unfair or restrictive trade practices. The Consumer Protection Act, 1986 was passed in Lok Sabha on 9th December,1986 and Rajya Sabha on 10th December, 1986 and was signed by the President of India on 24th December, 1986. It was published in the Gazette of India in 26th December, 1986. The Act was the milestone in the consumer movement in the country. This revolutionsed consumer rights.

According to Consumer Protection Act, 1986 defined "An Act to provide for better protection of the interests of consumers and for that purpose to make provision for the establishment of consumer councils and other authorities for the settlement of consumer disputes and for matters connected herewith."

The Act is one of the most progressive and comprehensive piece of socio-benevolent legislation covering all goods and services. It provides for a separate three-tier quasi judicial consumer disputes redressal machinery, which are called consumer courts. These are set up at the national, state and district levels to provide simple, speedy and free redressal against consumers' complaints.

According to the act an aggrieved consumer can seek redressal against any defect in the goods purchased or deficiencies in services availed, including restrictive/unfair trade practices adopted by such manufacture of goods/services. The Act applies to all goods and services and covers all sectors be it private, public or cooperatives.

Consumer Organisation

One of the most important milestone in the consumer movement in the country has been the consumer organisation. Consumer organisation has been set up to achieve promote and protect consumer interests. A number of organisations have been set up in various parts of India. It is felt that neither it is possible to discipline all members of the business community through moral sanctions and a code of fair business practices nor can administrate orders and legislative provisions to ensure consumer protection without the active involvement of consumer organisation. Some of the organisations, which were /are active in helping consumers are discussed.

Consumer Organisations in India

Important consumer organisations working India are :

- The first organisation to really make an impact was the **Consumer Guidance Society of India** (CGSI) in Bombay. The organisation was started by nine housewives in 1966 with Mrs Leela Jog as its founder secretary. This organisation started testing and reporting the quality of items of daily use of food stuffs and handling consumers' complaints. The CGSI, had eight branches at different places carrying on publicity exhibitions and education. A magazine called 'Keemat' was published by this organisation in English.
- **Karnataka Consumer Services Society** (KCSS), a consumer organisation, which made an impact in making the cause of consumers known throughout the country. It was formed in 1970. The organisation organised seminars on consumer education in schools, and also represented on prevention of Food and Drug Adulteration Committee and Karnataka Food and Civil Supplies Corporation.
- **Visakha Consumer Council** (VCC) was started in 1975 in Visakhapatnam. The organisation made a significant contribution to the consumer movement.
- **Consumer Education and Research Centre** (CERC) was started in 1978 in Ahmedabad added a new dimension to the consumer movement. This organisation constantly used legal machinery to bring about charges and protect consumer rights. Its special focus and intervention was against the government and public corporations. The organisation started a project on comparative testing in Ahmedabad, where comparative testing, ranking and evaluation of consumer products were undertaken with the aim of publication of such findings for consumer education.
- To wage a war against exploitation by the traders, some organisations came up with the novel idea of buying quality products of everyday use at wholesale and selling, these to the consumers at much lower prices than that being sold by the merchants. These were **Akhil Bhartiya Grahak Panchayat** started in 1973 in Pune, **Mumbai Grahak Panchayat** in 1979 in Mumbai and **Grahak Panchayat** in 1979 in Jamshedpur.
- The nineties saw the fulfillment of efforts towards a unified approach. In 1990, the **Federation of Consumer Organisation** (FEDCOT) of Tamil Nadu was established to bring together as many consumer groups as possible in the state under one umbrella.
- **Confederation of India Consumer Organisation** (CICO), New Delhi was formed in 1991 and **Consumer Coordination Council** (CCC), New Delhi was formed in 1992.
- **Consumer Care Society** was established in the year 1994. If functioned as the voice of consumer in many forums. CCS is widely recognised as a premier Voluntary Organisation in Bengaluru (Karnataka).
- **Consortium of South India Consumer Organisation** (COSICO) is spread out in six states i.e. Karnataka, Tamil Nadu, Andhra, Telangana, Puducherry and Kerala. It is a Non-government not for profit organisation founded in 2007. It was formed with the idea to share work together and plan joint action in strengthening the consumer movements in these states.
- **Consumer Association of India** (CAI) is a membership based organisation. Its main objectives are to spread consumer awareness, empower consumers and teach them their responsibilities and rights as consumers. Its new division established in 2007 to help consumers by cyber crimes in collaboration with cyber society of India.
- **Voluntary Organisation in Interest of Consumer Education** (VOICE) It is a consumer protection group set up by teachers and students with the objective of promoting and strengthening consumer education in India. Its main mission is to empower consumer through comparative product testing and service evaluation. To educate consumers about good business practices in competitive market. To trigger a charge by sent sensitising stakeholders towards quality products and services.

Thus, it can be said, that these organisations collect data on different products and test them investigate problems of consumers, publish and distribute brochures and journals. They also organise consumer awareness, programmes file, complaint suits and write petitions on behalf of the consumer.

Consumer Cooperative

A consumer cooperative is a cooperative business owned by its customers for their mutual benefit. It is a form of enterprise that is oriented toward service rather than pecuniary profit. Consumers cooperatives often take the form of retail outlets and operated by their consumers.

The consumer cooperative provides quality goods and services at the lowest cost to the consumers/owners rather than to sell goods and services at the highest price above cost that the consumer is willing to pay. In practice consumer cooperative price goods and services at competitive rates. There are many types of consumers' cooperatives such as healthcare, insurance and housing, agricultural and utility cooperatives, wholesale cooperatives and retailers cooperatives.

Characteristics of Consumer Cooperatives

The characteristics of consumer cooperatives are :

- It is a voluntary association of persons and is registered under the Cooperative Societies Act, which extends certain privileges and grants certain exceptions to a registered society.
- The liability of members is limited to the extent of their contribution. The membership of a society running in cooperative lines is open to all major people (adults).
- Cooperative societies sell for cash and seldom allow credit facilities.
- The accounts are regularly audited by an auditor appointed by the Registrar of cooperative societies.
- The profit earned by the society is distributed among the members and also spent on general welfare measures.
- Consumer cooperative utilises the principles of democratic member control or one member/one vote.
- The prices of commodities sold by such societies are fixed.

Ways to Protect Consumers

Different alternative ways to protect consumers in the market place are given below:

Alternative Redressal

The alternative redressal is different from judicial process. In this the disputes are settled with the assistance of a neutral, third person generally of parties own choice. The person is generally familiar with the nature of the dispute. Here, the proceedings are informal without any procedural technicalities. It is expeditious, inexpensive and confidential. The decision-making process aims at substantial justice. The alternative redressal is a fast track system of dispensing justice. The purpose of alternative redressal is to provide more effective dispute resolution. It is taken up to resolve pending disputes as well as pre- litigation stage. The concerns for alternatives, including alternatives to courts as well as alternative in the court also represent a desire to move the justice system closer to the people and their problems, needs, perceptions and understandings. Thus, the alternative redressal has not only helped reduce cost and time taken for resolution of disputes but also in providing congenial atmosphere.

Standardisation

Standardisation is a framework of arguments to which all relevant parties in an industry or organisation must adhere, to ensure that all processes associated with the creation of a good or performance of a services are performed within a set guidelines.

This ensures that the end product has consistent quality. Standardisation can help maximise compatibility, interoperability, safety, repeatability or quality. Standardisation is a prime requisite for attaining quality.

Standard Marks

Another mechanism of consumer protection is through standardisation marks. Standard mark notes that each product bearing the mark meets the requirement of the standards applicable to the product. Quality and safety as defined in the applicable standards are ensured for the product bearing the standard mark.

The standard mark system grants the manufacturers a licence to mark a product with a standard mark symbol. It is important for the consumer to know about different standard marks and the products covered under them. A good label should contain information like name of product, branch name, trade mark manufacturers name and address country's standardisation marks such as Agmark, FPO, ISI, woolmark, Hall Mark, Red mark, etc.

Quality Control

According to **J A Stalin**, "Quality Control is used to connote all those activities which are directed for defining, controlling and maintaining quality." Quality Control (QC) is a process through which a business seeks to ensure that product quality is maintained or improved with either reduced or zero errors. Quality Control requires the business to create an environment in which both management and employees strive for perfection.

This is done by training personnel, creating benchmarks for product quality and testing products to check for statistically significant variations. A major aspect of Quality Control is the establishment of well-defined controls. These controls help standardise both production and reaction to quality issues.

Limiting room for error by specifying which production activities are to be completed by which personnel reduces the chance that employees will be involved in tasks for which they do not have adequate training. Quality Control involves testing of units and determining if they are within the specifications for the final product. The purpose of the testing is to determine any needs for corrective actions in the manufacturing process. Good Quality Control helps companies meet consumer demands for better products.

Buying Aids

Buying aids are those which guide consumers in selecting goods according to their requirements. Following are the buying aids help consumers in making purchase :

Labels and Price Lists Label informs the consumer about the quality and method of its usage. Label is engraved, printed or pasted on the packing (i.e. bottle, container, packets, etc.) of the product. Bureau of Indian Standard has fixed certain standards for a complete label.

Packing Packed products are safe in many ways. Packed product does not get spoiled. It is safe against breakage. There is no possibility of adulteration. There is no possibility of pilferage.

Advertisement Advertisement provides important information to the consumers regarding availability, quality and use of the product.

Consumer Forums and Consumer Societies

Through, consumer forums and consumer societies the consumer gets good quality of product at reasonable prices. Mostly these societies do not earn profit. Their overhead charges are comparatively less because the members render free services.

Food Laws

Food laws are very important to ensure that the consumer gets safe and nutritious food products.

Consumer Legislations

In India, a large number of legislations have been enacted over all these years to safeguard the interests of the consumers. The aim of these legislations was to control product supply, distribution, price and quality of a large number of goods and services.

Some important consumer legislations are as follows:

Contract Act, 1872

The Act binds people on their promises made in a contract. The Act also provides remedies available to parties in case of breach of contract.

Sale of Goods Act, 1930

The Act provides safeguard and relief to customers in case goods are not complying with the expressed conditions and warranty.

Drugs and Cosmetics Act, 1940

The Act regulates the import, manufacture and distribution of drugs in India. The primary objective of the Act is to ensure that the drugs and cosmetics sold in India are safe, effective and conform to state quality standards.

The Drugs and Cosmetics Rules, 1945 framed under the Act contain provisions for classification of drugs under given schedules and there are guidelines for the storage, sale, display and prescription of each schedule.

The Act defines the standards of quality for drugs and defines 'misbranding'. A drug is considered misbranded if it claims to be of more therapeutic value than it actually is. The manufacturer of such a drug may be asked to suspend manufacture of the drug, the Act also deals with fake and adulterated drugs.

Drugs and Magic Remedies (Objectionable Advertisements) Act, 1954

The Act controls advertising of drugs in India. It prohibits advertisement of drugs and remedies that claim to have magical properties and makes doing so a cognisable offence. The Act defines 'magic remedy' as any talisman, mantra, amulet or any other object, which is clamed to have miraculous powers to cure, diagnose, prevent or mitigate a disease in humans or animals. It also includes such devices that are claimed to have power to influence structure or function of an organ in humans or animals.

Essential Commodities Act, 1955

The Act empowers the government to regulate prices, production, supply, distribution etc., of essential commodities for maintaining or increasing their supplies and for securing their equitable distribution and availability at fair prices. Most of the powers under the Act have been delegated by the Central Government to the State Government with the direction that they shall exercise these powers.

Exercising powers under the Act, various Ministries/Departments of the Central Government and State Government/UT Administrations have issued Control Orders for regulating production, distribution, pricing etc; and trading of the commodities declared as essential to the public. At present seven commodities have been retained under the Essential Commodities Act, 1955 to protect the interests of the consumers which include farmers, general population and the families below the poverty line.

Food Safety and Standards Act, 2006

The Act envisages regulation of manufacture, storage, distribution, sale and import of food to ensure availability of safe and wholesome food for human consumption and for consumers connected therewith. The Food Safety and Standards Authority of India (FSSAI) has been established under this Act for laying down scientific standards for articles of foods and to regulate their manufacture, storage, distribution, sale and import to ensure availability of safe and wholesome food for human consumption. The Food Safety and Standards (FSS) Act, 2006 was operationalised with the notification of Food Safety and Standards Rules, 2011 and six regulations, w.e.f the 5th August, 2011.

The setting of food standards is undertaken through a number of Scientific Panels and the Scientific Committee of the FSSAI and final approval by the authority.

Legal Metrology Act, 2009

The Act has came into force on 1st April, 2011 and has repealed the Standards of Weights and Measures Act, 1976 and Standards of Weights and Measures (Enforcement) Act, 1985. The government ensures through the Act that all weights and measures used for trade or commerce or for protection of human health and safety are accurate and reliable so that users are guaranteed for correct weighment and measurement. Provisions of the Act also empower regulatory and enforcement actions for ensuring that the consumer gets the right quantity for which he has paid for.

Bureau of Indian Standards Act, 2016

The Bureau of India Standards (BIS) Act, 2016 establishes BIS as the National Standards Body of India. Besides containing provisions for establishing voluntary standards. The Act also contains provisions to bring under compulsory certification regime any article, process or service which it considered necessary from point of view of health, safety, environment, prevention of deceptive practices, security, etc.

Enabling provisions have also been made for making hallmarking of the precious metal articles mandatory. The Act allows multiple types of conformity assessment schemes, including Self Declaration of Conformity against any standard which provides simplified options to manufacturers to adhere to the standards and get certificate of conformity. It enables the Central Government to appoint any authority, in addition to the BIS, to verify the conformity. There have been some recent initiatives in upgrading legislations. A comprehensive upgradation of the existing Consumers Protection Act, 1986, by way of introduction of a new bill in the Parliament under consideration. The bill aimed at making consumer law more effective, functional and purposeful. Its important features are :

- Establishment of the Central Consumer Protection Authority (CCPA) to promote, protect and enforce the rights of consumers, to investigate and intervene when necessary to prevent consumer detriment arising from unfair trade practices and to take action against misleading advertisements.
- Provision for 'mediation' as an Alternate Dispute Resolution (ADR) mechanism which aims at giving legislative basis to resolution of consumer disputes through mediation, thus making the process less cumbersome, simple and quicker. This will be done under the aegis of the consumer fora.
- Several provisions aimed at simplifying the consumer dispute adjudication process in the consumer forum are envisaged. These include, among others, enhancing the pecuniary jurisdiction of the consumer disputes redressal agencies, increasing minimum number of members in the consumer forum to facilitate quick disposal of complaints, power to review their own orders by the state and district commission.
- Constitution of 'circuit bench' to facilitate quicker disposal of complaints, reforming the process for the appointment of the President and members of the district forum, enabling provisions for consumers to file complaints electronically and file complaints in consumer forum that have jurisdiction over the place of residence of the complainant, and deemed admissibility of complaints if the question of admissibility is not decided within the specified period of 21 days.

Entrepreneurship

Entrepreneurship is the capacity and willingness to develop, organise and manage a business venture alongwith any of its risk in order to make a profit. Entrepreneurship is a process of actions of an entrepreneur who is a person always in search of something new and exploits such ideas into gainful opportunities by accepting the risks and uncertainty with the enterprise. The word entrepreneur is derived from the French word *entreprendre* which means to, 'undertake.' This refers to those who undertake the risk of new enterprise. An enterprise is created by an entrepreneur. The process of creation is called 'entrepreneurship'.

According to **Oxford dictionary**, "Entrepreneurship is the activity of setting up a business or businesses, taking on financial risks in the hope of profit."

Entrepreneurship Process

Entrepreneurship process can be defined as the steps taken in order to establish a new enterprise. It is a step-by-step method, one has to follow to set up an enterprise.

These are as follows :

Preliminary Step Preliminary steps are the initial steps one has to follow for establishing a firm. At this stage, the entrepreneur should be able to make a decision that is going to affect the company.

Decision-making Decision-making steps can be defined as those steps or say the lessons learnt by an entrepreneur to make decisions efficiently.

Planning Planning is an assumption or prediction of business requirements and outcome in the future. It provides a space to review the best strategy to run the business by cutting expenses and maximising profit.

Implementation Step Implementation is the execution of plan. It is the action taken to implement the plan so that something actual happens.

Managerial Step Managerial duties are also very important for an entrepreneur as well as the organisation.

Entrepreneurship Barriers

Barrier to the development of entrepreneurship are :

- The lack of start-up financing programmes from loans, funds and public subsidies.
- High labour cost
- High taxes
- High competition
- Difficulties of access to new technologies
- Inability to conduct market research
- Non-availability of affordable technical and managerial consultancy.

Entrepreneurial Motivation

The entrepreneurial motivation is the process that activates and motivates the entrepreneur to exert higher level of efforts for the achievement of his/her entrepreneurial goals. In other words, entrepreneurial motivation refers to the forces or drive within an entrepreneurs that affect the direction, intensity and persistency of his/her voluntary behaviour as entrepreneur. So, a motivational entrepreneur will be willing to exert a particular level of effort/intensity for a certain period of time (persistent towards a particular goal.) The entrepreneurial motivating factors can be classified as– internal and external.

Internal Factors

These include the following factors :

- Desire to do something new
- Become independent
- Achieve what one wants to have in life
- Be recognised for one's contribution
- One's educational background
- One's occupational background and experience in the relevant field

External Factors

These include the following factors :

- Government assistance and support
- Availability of labour and raw material
- Encouragement from big business houses
- Promising demand for the product

Entrepreneurial Challenges

Every entrepreneur faces their own share of struggles or challenges. Such challenges provide great entrepreneurial lessons when one overcomes them. Some of the challenges which are faced by entrepreneurs are as follows :

Cash Flow Management Cash flow as we all know is an internal part of all business ventures. However, instances are not rare when entrepreneurs struggle with bill payment while waiting for bills to get cleared. Delayed invoicing is a major trigger of these challenges of entrepreneurs.

Time Management This is the biggest challenge faced by multi-tasking entrepreneurs who often fall short of time while accomplishing their objective.

Hiring of Employees In reality, entrepreneurs dread job interviews more than the procandidates as it is usually very time-consuming. Entrepreneurs need to review resumes, conduct interviews and filter out unqualified candidates for finding the ones who are best suited for the job. Once the screening process is completed, entrepreneurs need to negotiate on the salary aspect for rctaining, those candidates without bleeding the company's exchequer.

Choosing the Product Entrepreneurs are often unsure about the products and services they wish to sell. However, it is imperative to take the right pick which can determine the ultimate success and failure in a competitive scenario.

Delegation of Tasks The successful delegation comprises of building the right process apart from providing the resources and authority required for its enactment. However, finding the right resources and choosing the delegation drive can be a very complicated task.

Enterprise Setting

Starting an enterprise involves several steps :

Information Collection In this step one has to decide which enterprise one wants to set up. This begins by collecting information about the units already working in the field of concern.

Information Organisation Having collected information about the enterprise concern, the prospective entrepreneur needs to organise the same in an orderly and systematic manner to derive the meaning from them. It means it will help in assessing about the requirements to start an enterprise.

Acquiring Required Vocational Skills Here, one understands the need for upgrading one's vocational skills.

Financial Requirement It means to ascertain the financial requirement for setting up an enterprise. It is important because small entrepreneurs do not have their own funds. They depend on borrowed funds.

Market Assessment No business enterprise can be thought of without business. Planning for establishing an enterprise, the prospective entrepreneur needs to know who will buy his/her product.

Provision for Crisis This is most essential as for setting up a business enterprise is that one should always be prepared to manage in crisis situations. It is always useful to remain prepared for unexpected in terms of resources, policies, finances, natural calamities, etc.

Project Planning

Project planning is at the heart of the project life cycle, and tells everyone involved where you are going and how you are going to get there. The planning phase is that when the project is documented, the project deliverables and requirements are defined and the project schedule is created.

It involves creating a set of plans to help guide yours team through the implementation and closure phases of the project. They also help you to control staff and external suppliers to ensure that you deliver the project on time within budget and with schedule. The basic processes of project planning are :

Scope Planning Specifying the in-scope requirements for the project to facilitate creating the work breakdown structure.

Preparation of the Work Breakdown Structure Spelling out the breakdown of the project into tasks and sub-tasks.

Project Schedule Development Listing the entire schedule of the activities and detailing their sequence of implementation.

Resource Planning Indicating who will do, what work, at which time and if any special skills are needed to accomplish the project tasks.

Budget Planning Specifying the budgeted cost to be incurred at the completion of the project.

Procurement Planning Focusing on vendors outside your company and sub-contracting

Risk Management Planning for possible risks and considering optional contingency plans and mitigation strategies.

Quality Planning Assessing quality criteria to be used for the project

Communication Planning Designing the communication strategy with all project stakeholders.

Project Appraisal

Project appraisal is a consistent process of reviewing a given project and evaluating its content to approve or reject the projects. It is done through analysing the problem or need to be addressed by the projects, generating solutions/ options for solving the problem.

It is carried out by selecting the most feasible option, conducting a feasibility analysis of the option, creating a solution statement and identifying all people and organisations concerned with or affected by the project. It also sees its expected outcomes. So, project appraisal is done to know how much the company has invested on the project and in return how much it is gaining from it.

Enterprise Management

Enterprise management is a term used for modern example of ERP that allows business to manage vital day-to-day process of like inventory management accounting, human resources and customer relationship management. Enterprise management supports how various business units work by sharing information through shared database. Enterprise management is beneficial in number of ways such as :

Helps in Achieving Group Goals It arranges the factors of production, assembles and organises the resources, integrates the resources in effective manner to achieve goals.

Optimum Utilisation of Resources Management utilises all the physical and human resources productively. This leads to efficacy in management.

Reduces Cost It gets maximum results through minimum input by proper planning and by using minimum input and getting maximum output. This helps in cost reduction.

Establishes Sound Organisation To establish sound organisational structure is one of the objective of management which is in tune with objective of organisation and for fulfillment of this, it establishes effective authority and responsibility relationship.

Establishes Equilibrium It enables the organisation to survive in changing environment. It keeps in touch with the changing environment. With the change in external environment, the initial coordination of organisation must be changed. It is responsible for growth and survival of organisation.

Essentials for Prosperity of Society Efficient management leads to better economical production which helps in turn to increase the welfare of people. Organisation comes with new products and researches beneficial for society.

EXAM BASED QUESTIONS

1 A consumer is
(a) who buys goods or services to be consumed by himself/herself.
(b) a person who consumes.
(c) end user of product or services.
(d) All of the above

2 Consumer plays an important role
(a) in an economic system
(b) in every trade or commerce
(c) in the marketing process
(d) All of the above

3 Who said that "the consumers are the largest economic group affecting and affected by almost by every public and private economic decisions. Yet they are the only important group whose views are often not heard."
(a) John F Kennedy (b) Adam Smith
(c) Wells and Prensky (d) Loudon and Bitta

4 .... provides the adequate and accurate information about quality, quantity, purity, standard and the price of the goods and services.
(a) Right to Choose
(b) Right to be Heard
(c) Right to be Informed
(d) Right to Consumer Education

5 .... provides the consumer must be assured whenever possible access to a variety of goods and services at competitive prices.
(a) Right to Consumer Protection Act
(b) Right to Choose
(c) Right to Safety
(d) Right to be Heard

6 .... provides a safeguard for consumers against goods and services which are hazardous to health.
(a) Right to Safety (b) Right to be Informed
(c) Right to Choose (d) Right to be Heard

7 .... provides the consumer to approach the government and public bodies when decisions and policies are made, which can hamper consumers' interests.
(a) Right to Safety
(b) Right to Consumer Education
(c) Right to Consumer Protection Act
(d) Right to be Heard

8 .... provides a fair settlement of genuine grievances relating to the performance, grade, quality, etc. of goods and services.
(a) Right to Safety
(b) Right to Consumer Education
(c) Right to Consumer Protection Act
(d) Right to Choose

9 The consumer's right to be informed about the true benefits of a product has led to specific proposals regarding
(a) bulk price (b) unit price
(c) maximum retail price (d) pure price

10 .... provides consumer to choose the products available in the market judiciously.
(a) Right to Safety
(b) Right to Consumer Education
(c) Right to Choose
(d) Right to be Heard

11 The redressal of consumer grievances, the Consumer Protection Act is a
(a) one-tier enforcement
(b) two-tier enforcement
(c) three-tier enforcement
(d) four-tier enforcement

12 .... can sue in negligence for injury caused by a defective product.
(a) Good customer
(b) Bad customer
(c) Regular customer
(d) Diseased customer

13 Consumer disputes redressal agencies are working on three different levels i.e. National Commission, State Commission and ....
(a) District Court (b) Supreme Court
(c) Gram Panchayat (d) District Forum

14 The goods which satisfy human wants directly are called
(a) consumer's goods
(b) producer's goods
(c) public goods
(d) intermediate goods

15 Which of the following is a situation in which consumer behaviour occurs?
(a) Communications situation
(b) Purchase situation
(c) Usage situation
(d) All of the above

16 Who defined "Consumer behaviour as a study of consumers as they exchange something of value for products or services that satifies their needs?"
(a) Schiffman (b) Wells
(c) Prensky (d) Both (b) and (c)

17 In terms of consumer behaviour; culture, social class and reference group influence have been related to purchase and ....
(a) economic situations
(b) situational influences
(c) consumption decisions
(d) physiological influences

18 .... are the factors that have been shown to affect consumer behaviour.
(a) Brand name, quality, newness and complexity
(b) Advertising, marketing, product and price
(c) Outlets, strategies, concept and brand name
(d) Quality, advertising, product positioning and strategy

19 .... provides separate definitions of consumer for the purpose of goods and services.
(a) Consumer Protection Act, 1988
(b) Consumer Protection Act,1989
(c) Consumer Protection Act,1986
(d) Consumer Protection Act,2000

20 The Consumer Protection Act, 1986 enacted on
(a) 24th October, 1986
(b) 24th October, 1987
(c) 24th August, 1986
(d) 15th June, 1986

21 The Consumer Protection Act, 1986 extends to
(a) the whole India
(b) the whole India except Jammu and Kashmir
(c) the whole India except Nagaland's tribal area
(d) Both (b) and (c)

22 As per Section 2(1)(b) of Consumer Protection Act, 1986, 'complainant' means
(a) a consumer
(b) any consumer association, registered under the Companies Act, 1956
(c) the Central Government or any State Government,
(d) All of the above

23 In case of death of a consumer, who can prefer complaint under Section 2(1)(b) of Consumer Protection Act, 1986?
(a) His legal heir or representative
(b) State Government
(c) Consumer association, registered under the Companies Act, 1956
(d) No one can prefer complaint

24 Which Section of the Consumer Protection Act, 1986 states about 'the Central Consumer Protection Council'?
(a) Section 7 (b) Section 2
(c) Section 5 (d) Section 4

25 Who shall be the Chairman of the Central Consumer Protection Council?
(a) The Minister in charge of consumer affairs in the Central Government.
(b) The Minister in charge of consumer affairs in the State Government.
(c) The Prime Minister.
(d) The Speaker of the Lok Sabha.

26 What is the minimum age, to be appointed as the Member of Consumer Dispute Redressal Forum/Commission?
(a) 35 years (b) 40 years
(c) 25 years (d) 20 years

27 For appointing as a Member of the Consumer Dispute Redressal Forum/ Commission, at least .... experience in dealing with problems relating to economics, law, commerce, accountancy, industry, public affairs or administration is required.
(a) 15 years (b) 5 years
(c) 10 years (d) 7 years

28 The District Forum shall have jurisdiction to entertain complaints, where the value of the goods or services and the compensation claimed does not exceed .... rupees.
(a) 50 lakhs (b) 20 lakhs
(c) 10 lakhs (d) 5 lakhs

29 Six rights (1) Right to Safety, (2)Right to be Informed, (3) Right to Choose, (4) Right to be Heard, (5) Right to Seek Redressal and Right to Consumer Education were first seen by ....
(a) Philip Kotler (b) Nielson
(c) John F Kennedy (d) H R Bowen

30 If a consumer is not satisfied with District Forum. In how many days he can challenge the same and approach the State Commission?
(a) 20 days (b) 30 days
(c) 50 days (d) 70 days

31 .... is the problem, which is faced by consumers in day-to-day purchase.
(a) Lack of information
(b) Adulteration
(c) Wrong weights and measures
(d) Irregular supply

32 Consumer empowerment
(a) is a multifacted concept.
(b) tells about rights, skills and capabilities of consumers.
(c) talks about the capacity of market to provide legal and realistic mechanism to the consumers.
(d) All of the above

33 The consumer cooperative's chief characteristics is/are
(a) it is a voluntary association of persons.
(b) sell for cash and seldom allow for credit facilities.
(c) the accounts are regularly audited by an auditor. appointed by the registrar of cooperative societies.
(d) All of the above

34 Alternative redressal means
(a) a fast track system of dispensing justice.
(b) is different from judicial process.
(c) helps to reduce cost and time, taken for resolution of disputes.
(d) All of the above

35 Standardisation helps maximum
(a) safety (b) quality
(c) compatibility (d) All of these

36 **Who said that "Quality Control is used to connote all those activities which are directed for defining, controlling and maintaining the quality?"**
(a) John a Shubin (b) Adam Smith
(c) John F Kennedy (d) John Maynard Keynes

37 **The Essential Commodities Act, 1955 empowers government to**
(a) regulate prices (b) production
(c) distribution (d) All of these

38 **The entrepreneurial motivating factors can be classified as**
(a) internal factors
(b) external factors
(c) multiple factors
(d) Both (a) and (b)

39 **The external factors include**
(a) government assistance and support
(b) encouragement from big business houses
(c) promising demand for the product
(d) All of the above

40 **Which of the following is/are the entrepreneurial challenges faced by the consumers?**
(a) Choosing the product
(b) Time management
(c) Cash flow management
(d) All of the above

41 **The basic process of project planning includes**
(a) scope planning
(b) preparation of the work breakdown structure
(c) budget planning
(d) All of the above

42 **Quality planning means ....**
(a) assessing quality criteria to be used for the project.
(b) specifying the budgeted cost to be incurred at the completion of the project.
(c) focusing on vendors, outside the company.
(d) listing the entire schedule of the activities.

43 **The word entrepreneur' is derived from .... word 'entreprendre'.**
(a) French (b) Latin
(c) Greek (d) Chinese

44 **Entrepreneurial behaviour includes**
(a) solving problems (b) taking initiatives
(c) taking responsibility (d) All of these

45 **Entrepreneur's skills include:**
(a) creative problem- solving
(b) persuading
(c) negotiation
(d) All of the above

46 **The term 'entrepreneurs' was applied to business, initially by the French economist, in the 18th century.**
(a) Cantillon (b) Jan Tinbergen
(c) JSMill (d) None of these

47 **The entrepreneurial process comprised of each of the following except?**
(a) deciding to become an entrepreneur
(b) inventing a new product or process
(c) managing and growing the entrepreneurial firm
(d) moving from an idea of an entrepreneurial firm

48 **Basic problems of women entrepreneurs in India are**
(a) lack of education and skill
(b) male dominating society
(c) absence of listen bearing capacity
(d) All of the above

49 **From the following, types of entrepreneurs are**
(a) innovating entrepreneur (b) initiative entrepreneur
(c) drone entrepreneur (d) All of these

50 **Which one is not the barrier of entrepreneurship?**
(a) Lack of technical skills
(b) Political instability
(c) Not high competition
(d) Time pressure and distractions

51 **An entrepreneur is a/an**
(a) initiator (b) motivator
(c) visualizer (d) All of these

52 **Which of the following factors influence entrepreneurship?**
(a) Technical knowledge (b) Entrepreneurial training
(c) Local manpower (d) All of these

53 **........ is a voluntary and democratic association of human beings, based on equality of control, opportunity, distribution and mutuality for the promotion of their common interests as producers or consumers.**
(a) Organisation (b) Company
(c) Cooperation (d) Non-profit organisation

54 **Misleading advertisements, supply of inferior services, charging more than MRP, hoarding and black marketing, etc., lead to consumer exploitation called**
(a) defective product
(b) business malpractice
(c) diseased customer
(d) consumer protection

55 **As per Section 2(1)(c) of Consumer Protection Act, 1986, 'complaint' means any allegation in writing made by a complaint that**
1. An unfair trade practice or a restrictive trade practice.
2. The goods/services bought/ hired suffer from one or o:e defects/deficiencies.
3. .. trader or service provider has charged a price in excess of the price.
4. Goods/services which are hazardous or likely to be hazardous to life and safety of the public when used.

Codes
(a) 1, 2 and 3 (b) 1, 2 and 4
(c) 1, 3 and 3 (d) 1, 2, 3 and 4

56 **As per Section 2(1)(j) of Consumer Protection Act, 1986, 'manufacturer' means a person who**
1. makes or manufactures any goods or parts thereof
2. does not make or manufacture any goods, but assembles parts thereof made or manufactured by others.
3. puts or causes to be put his own mark on any goods made or manufactured by any other manufacturer.

Codes
(a) 1 and 2 (b) 1 and 3
(c) 2 and 3 (d) 1, 2 and 3

57 **Which of the following are the objectives of the Consumer Protection Council?**
1. The right to be protected against the marketing of goods and services, which are hazardous to life and property.
2. The right to be informed about the quality, quantity, potency, purity, standard and price of goods or services so as to protect the consumer against unfair trade practices.
3. The right to seek redressal against unfair trade practices or restrictive trade practices or unscrupulous exploitation of consumers.
4. The right to consumer education.

Codes
(a) 1, 2 and 4 (b) 1, 2 and 3
(c) 1, 3 and 4 (d) 1, 2, 3 and 4

58 **What are the qualifications to be appointed as the Member of the Consumer Dispute Redressal Forum/Commission?**
1. Not less than 35 years of age.
2. Possess a bachelor's degree from a recognised university.
3. Be persons of ability, integrity and good reputation

Codes
(a) 1 and 2 (b) 1 and 3
(c) 2 and 3 (d) 1, 2 and 3

59 **A person shall be disqualified for appointment as a Member of the Consumer Dispute Redressal forum/commission, if he/she**
1. has been convicted and sentenced to imprisonment for an offence which involves moral turpitude.
2. is an undischarged insolvent.
3. is of unsound mind and stands so declared by a competent court.
4. has been removed or dismissed from the service of the government or a body corporate owned or controlled by the government.
5. has such financial or other interest as is likely to affect prejudicially, the discharge by him of his functions as a member.

Codes
(a) 1 and 3 (b) 1, 2 and 4
(c) 2, 4 and 5 (d) All of these

60 **Match the following.**

List I	List II
A. Project schedule development	1. Specifying budgeted cost to be incurred at the completion of project.
B. Budget planning	2. Listing the entire schedule of activities.
C. Quality planning	3. Who will do what work at which time.
D. Resource planning	4. Assessing quality criteria used for project.

Codes

	A	B	C	D		A	B	C	D
(a)	2	1	4	3	(b)	4	3	2	1
(c)	1	2	3	4	(d)	2	4	1	3

61 **Match the following.**

List I (Rights)	List II (Features)
A. Right to Safety	1. Consumers should not be forced to select a product
B. Right to Education	2. Consumers to be informed about the quality, purity and standards of goods.
C. Right to be Informed	3. To make sure that the consumers have informational programmes enable them to make purchasing decisions.
D. Right to Choose	4. Ensures that Consumers have a way to demand justice from those who can harm them.

Codes

	A	B	C	D		A	B	C	D
(a)	4	3	2	1	(b)	4	1	2	3
(c)	1	2	3	4	(d)	3	2	1	4

62 **The consumer education is important because it**
(a) helps consumers to understand their rights.
(b) provides complete information of marketing conditions.
(c) familiarises the consumer with various standards and standardisation marks.
(d) All of the above

63 **Consider the following statements with regard to consumer organisations.**

Statement I They were important milestones in consumer movement.

Statement II They protect and promote interest of the consumers.

Codes
(a) statement I is correct
(b) statement II is correct
(c) Both the statements are correct
(d) Neither statement I nor II is correct

64 Which of the following are the characteristics of the Legal Metrology Act, 2009?

(a) Provides safeguard and relief to customers, in case goods are not complying with expressed conditions and warranty.
(b) Provides remedies to parties in case of breach of contract.
(c) Through the Act all weights and measures used for trade or for protection of human health and safety should be accurate and reliable.
(d) The Act allows for multiple types of conformity assessment schemes.

65 Consider the following statements about project appraisal.

Statement I Project appraisal is a consistent process of reviewing a project and evaluating its content.

Statement II It hardly helps in analysing the project.

Codes

(a) Only Statement I is correct
(b) Both the statements are correct
(c) Only Statement II is incorrect
(d) Neither statement I nor II is correct

66 Enterprise management

(a) allows business to manage vital day-to-day process.
(b) allows the organisation to survive in the changing environment.
(c) supports how various business units work by sharing information through data base.
(d) All of the above

Directions (Q. Nos. 67-80) *Below given are two statements, one labelled as Assertion (A) and other labelled as Reason (R). Following are the codes given below, select the correct code for the following.*

Codes

(a) Both A and R are true and R is the correct explanation of A
(b) Both A and R are true, but R is not the correct explanation of A
(c) Both A and R are false
(d) A is false, but R is true

67 **Assertion** (A) The Right to Safety, protect consumers against marketing goods.

Reason (R) The goods which are injurious to health and safety.

68 **Assertion** (A) A responsible consumer should be a cautious consumer while purchasing any item.

Reason (R) As a responsible consumer , he must file a complaint even for a small loss.

69 **Assertion** (A) The sellers do not cheat consumers with false weights and measures.

Reason (R) The consumers are cheated with false weights and measures in organised and unorganised market.

70 **Assertion** (A) Consumer education is basically an education which brings about behaviour changes in a person who goes to the market to buy things.

Reason (R) Consumer education familiarises the consumer with various standards of standardisation and marking.

71 **Assertion** (A) The Consumer Protection Act, 1986, seeks to protect the Rights of a Consumer against unfair or restrictive trade practices.

Reason (R) It was passed in Lok Sabha on 9th December, 1986.

72 **Assertion** (A) The Visakha Consumer Council was started in 1975 in Visakhapatnam in 1975.

Reason (R) This organisation made significant contribution to Consumer Movement.

73 **Assertion** (A) The cooperative societies sell for cash and seldom allow credit facilities.

Reason (R) The profit earned is distributed among the members.

74 **Assertion** (A) The alternative redressal dispute does not provide effective dispute resolution.

Reason (R) The alternative redressal is a fast track system dispensing justice.

75 **Assertion** (A) Good quality control helps companies to meet consumer demands for better products.

Reason (R) Quality control is a process through which a business seeks to ensure that product quality is maintained or improved with either reduced or zero errors.

76 **Assertion** (A) The consumers legislation have been enacted to safeguard the interest of the consumers.

Reason (R) The aim of consumers legislation is to control product supply, distribution price and quality of large number of goods and services.

77 **Assertion** (A) An enterprise is created by an entrepreneur.

Reason (R) The process of creation is called entrepreneurship.

78 **Assertion** (A) The first step of enterprise setting begins by information collecting about the units already working in the concerned field.

Reason (R) The information helps in assessing about the requirements to start an enterprise.

79 **Assertion** (A) The basic purpose of project planning is the development of project schedule.

Reason (R) This process of project planning involves listing the entire schedule of the activities and detailing their sequence of implementation.

80 **Assertion** (A) Enterprise management helps in achieving group goals.

Reasons (R) Enterprise management enables the organisation to survive in changing environment.

PREVIOUS YEARS' QUESTIONS

July 2018

1 A consumer passes through five stages in buying decision process. Arrange the sequence of decision- making steps in correct order.

1. Information search 2. Problem recognition
3. Purchase decision
4. Post purchase behaviour
5. Evaluation of alternatives

Codes

(a) 3, 4, 5, 2, 1 (b) 1, 3, 5, 4, 2
(c) 2, 1, 5, 3, 4 (d) 5, 4, 2, 3, 1

2 Match the following.

List I	List II
A. CERC	1. Flow of goods and services in the economy.
B. GNP	2. International Organisation for Consumer Protection.
C. CI	3. National Consumer Organisation.
D. OMBUDSMAN	4. Alternative Agency for Consumer Redressel.
E. District Forum	5. Journal for Consumer Education.
	6. Consumer Protection Act.

Codes

	A	B	C	D	E		A	B	C	D	E
(a)	4	2	3	5	6	(b)	3	1	2	4	6
(c)	1	5	3	2	4	(d)	2	3	4	6	1

November 2017

3 Problems connected with entrepreneurship development can be identified in the following domains.

1. Procuring of raw material
2. Marketing of products
3. Country of origin 4. Procuring of capital

Codes

(a) 1, 2 and 3 (b) 2, 3 and 4
(c) 1, 3 and 4 (d) 1, 2 and 4

January 2017

4 Which of the following are included in the list of voluntary consumer organisation?

1. PIL 2. CGSI
3. VOICE 4. CUTS

Codes

(a) 1, 2 and 4 (b) 1, 2 and 3
(c) 3, 4 and 1 (d) 2, 3 and 4

5 For an entrepreneur, the target market means

1. a group of customers, a venture reaches by accident.
2. all consumers, who will choose to purchase the venture's product.
3. a chain of discount stores.
4. a specific group of potential customers towards which a venture aims its marketing plan.

Codes

(a) 1 and 2 (b) 2 and 3
(c) 2 and 4 (d) 1 and 4

July 2015

6 Who is an entrepreneur?

1. Someone who invests time and money to start a business.
2. Someone who takes risk to make profit.
3. Someone who travels extensively.
4. Someone who makes a lot of money.

Select the correct answer using the codes given below.

(a) 1 and 2 (b) 2, 3 and 4
(c) 1, 2 and 4 (d) 3 and 4

ANSWERS

Exam Based Questions

1 (d)	2 (d)	3 (a)	4 (c)	5 (b)	6 (a)	7 (d)	8 (c)	9 (b)	10 (b)
11 (c)	12 (d)	13 (d)	14 (d)	15 (d)	16 (d)	17 (c)	18 (a)	19 (c)	20 (a)
21 (b)	22 (d)	23 (a)	24 (d)	25 (a)	26 (a)	27 (c)	28 (b)	29 (c)	30 (b)
31 (b)	32 (d)	33 (d)	34 (d)	35 (d)	36 (a)	37 (d)	38 (d)	39 (d)	40 (d)
41 (d)	42 (a)	43 (a)	44 (d)	45 (d)	46 (a)	47 (b)	48 (d)	49 (d)	50 (c)
51 (d)	52 (d)	53 (c)	54 (b)	55 (d)	56 (d)	57 (d)	58 (c)	59 (d)	60 (a)
61 (a)	62 (d)	63 (c)	64 (c)	65 (b)	66 (d)	67 (a)	68 (b)	69 (d)	70 (b)
71 (b)	72 (a)	73 (b)	74 (d)	75 (b)	76 (a)	77 (a)	78 (b)	79 (a)	80 (b)

Previous Years' Questions

1 (c)	2 (b)	3 (d)	4 (d)	5 (c)	6 (a)

UNIT VI

Housing and Environment

Housing is a basic need of an individual. It plays a vital role in the growth and development of the family, community and the country. Housing provides social status, feeling of independence and privacy. Housing has become a major economic issues of our time. Housing has direct impact on the environment that's why buildings should be designed while keeping environmental protection in wind.

House is the primary unit of human habitation. Buddha described housing as 'the root of happiness.' According to Buddhist Philosophy, without a home. human beings can't fully develop emotionally, intellectually and spiritually. Therefore, housing provides many kinds of services like shelter, security, comfort and a feeling of independence, privacy and social status.

Housing plays a prominent role in the economy of the country and it is an indicator of country's social progress. With the changing pattern of life style in the form of human settlement and climatic conditions, external forces of environment have an impact on the design aspects of housing. House is a synonym to dwelling residence, home abode logding, accommodation or housing.

Building Regulations

Building regulations refer to building code, a set of rules that specify the minimum acceptable level of safety for constructed objects. Planning permission is required to develop or modify land and buildings. The building's regulations are needed to get a green signal to start construction. You need to ensure that your house plan follows the building bylaws. These laws are a set of rules and regulations drawn up by the government of every country, to assure a systematic and disciplined growth of the town or city.

In this Chapter

Following these laws will ensure the maximum utilisation of available space and safety of the people living in and around the house. The building's rules and regulations are aimed to ensure adequate stability of the buildings, clean environment and adequate standard of healthy life.

Building bylaws are unique for every region. What may be applicable in a city, may not be possible in villages.

The building by laws apply to the buildings, where the building is newly erected bylaws shall apply to the design and construction of buildings, where the whole or any part of the building is demolished bylaws apply to any remaining part and to the work involved in demolition, where the occupancy of a building is changed bylaws apply to all parts of the building affected by the change.

Norms and Standards of Building Regulations

Before drawing up a blueprint for a home, study of building applicable in particular region is done. Given below is a list of general norms and standards :

Floor Area Ratio (FAR)

It means the quotient obtained by dividing the total covered area (plinth area) of all floors by the plot area i.e.

$$FAR = \frac{\text{Total area of all floors}}{\text{Plot area}}$$

If the quotient is 1.6, it means the total area of all the floors in a building cannot be more than 1.6 times the area of a plot. This prevents excessive pressure on the plot.

The FAR of every building will differ, depending upon its usage, type of construction, locality and its population, the width and traffic on the street infinite, parking facilities, water and drainage facilities and local fire fighting facilities.

Ground Coverage

It is the total area covered by the building on the ground floor. If you are constructing a basement, consider that it should not exceed the ground coverage area. Based on the restriction of height and FAR, the ground coverage can be adjusted to get maximum usage of the plot.

Setback

A building setback is the open space between building and the property boundary or lot line. One can construct the house, only upto the setback line. This again differs for different types of buildings. For example, a stand alone building must have more front open space than a row type building. The setback line is applicable not just in the front, but also around the entire building. The table given below shows the minimum requirement for a plot upto 50 sq m and above 50 sq m :

Minimum Requirement for different Components of Building

Components of Building	Minimum Requirement for Plots upto 50 sq m		Minimum Requirement for Plots Above 50 sq m	
Habitable Room	Area	7.50 sq m	Area	9.50 sq m
	Width	2.10 m	Width	2.40 m
	Height	2.75 m	Height	2.75 m
Kitchen	Area	3.30 sq m	Area	4.50 sq m
	Width	1.50 m	Width	1.50 m
	Height	2.75 m	Height	2.75 m
Pantry	Area	Not applicable	Area	3.00 sq m
	Width	Not applicable	Width	1.20 m
	Height	Not applicable	Height	2.20 m
Bathroom	Area	1.20 sq m	Area	1.80 sq m
	Width	1.00 m	Width	1.20 sq m
	Height	2.20 m	Height	2.20 m
WC (Water Closet)	Area	1.00 sq m	Area	1.10 sq m
	Width	0.90 m	Width	0.90 m
	Height	2.20 m	Height	2.20 m
Combined Bath and WC (Toilet)	Area	1.80 sq m	Area	2.80 sq m
	Width	1.00 m	Width	1.20 m
	Height	2.20 m	Height	2.20 m
Store	Area	No restriction	Area	No restriction
	Width	No restriction	Width	No restriction
	Height	2.20 m	Height	2.2 m
Projections	Permitted within the setbacks upto 0.75 m width		Permitted within the setbacks upto 0.75 m. width	
Garage	–	–	Area	14.85 sq m
			Width	2.75 m
			Length	5.40 m
			Height	2.40 m
Passage	–	–	Width	1.00 m
Doorways Habitable rooms	Width	0.80 m	Width	0.90 m
	Height	2.00 m	Height	2.20 m
For kitchen bath, WC, etc.	Width	0.75 m	Width	0.75 m
	Height	2.00 m	Height	2.00 m
Staircase	Width	0.75 m	Width	0.90 m
	No restrictioin for internal ladder			

Zoning

Zoning is utilisation of the available land to the right use and to the correct location of each zone, so that there will be no conflict. It is the legal regulation of the use of land. It is an application of the local body enforcement for the protection of public health, welfare and society.

It can be explained by the examples, such as the residential zone and the industrial zone, that can be properly segregated so that the dwellers are kept free from any nuisance from smoke, dirt, noise, etc. It is the best method of accomplishing best arrangement of different components of the city. In other words, land use is known as zoning.

Classification of Zones

For the purpose of development, the area under any planning authority is divided into the following zones, which are explained as :

Residential Zone Dwellings, boarding houses, house occupations, nursing homes, nursery schools, neighbourhood parks, bakeries, restaurants, community centers, marriage halls, religious buildings; public libraries, play ground, art galleries, post and telegraph and telephone, electric sub-stations, fire stations, pumping stations, petrol pumps; community halls, auditoria, shops and stores, petrol filling stations, cemeteries and burials, etc.

Commercial Zone Offices, banks, service industries, cinemas and theatres, shopping centers, showrooms, diagnostic centers and nursing homes, wholesale markets, etc.

Industrial Zone Light and heavy industries, cold storages, integrated industrial parks, service and special industries, etc.

Institutional Zone Public and semi-public zone public offices, private offices, state and central government offices, educational institutions, research institutions, colleges, school and university centres, hospitals, museums, radio broadcasting studios, correctional and mental institutions, bus stands, truck terminals, prisons, etc.

Rural and Agricultural Zone Agriculture, dairy farms, cattle raising, piggeries, nurseries, farm houses, horticulture, poultry farms, etc.

Recreational Zone Recreational parks, stadiums, water fronts and green belts, picnic spots, zoological and botanical gardens, lakes, water bodies, etc.

Special Reservations Zone Forestry, reserved forest, national parks, military and defence installations, airport, garbage dumps, etc.

Housing for Special Groups and Areas

The problem of housing is a global issue. The housing problem is more chronic in developing countries as compared to the developed countries. In India, the housing conditions are not upto the minimum level of quality of life and also, they are not similar, they differ from region to region and area to area. So, to provide housing for special groups and areas, the government of India has taken various constructive measures which are discussed as :

Integrated Subsidised Housing for Industrial Workers and Economically Weaker Sections It was meant to provide open developed plots or small two-roomed, single or multi-stored houses on rental basis subject to certain ceilings. The houses for industrial workers could be built by the State Housing Boards and local bodies. The central government provided a 50% loan and 50% subsidy to the State Government with a lesser subsidy for the employee housing.

Subsidised Housing for Plantation Workers In this, the planters are given 37.5% subsidy and 50% loan to the ceiling cost. It provided a subsidy of 25% loan upto, 65% for cooperative housing colonies. The Central Government gave assistance to 90% of the approved cost of the house. It was available to plantation workers through housing cooperations.

Village Housing It was for rural areas, initiated by Central Government. It was a part of the total rural reconstruction programmes. It was basically aimed at re-building or substantially improving houses in rural area. The landless agricultural labours are given house sites, either free of cost or at a nominal price.

Housing for Weavers/Basket Makers It was initiated by the Ministry of Textiles for various categories of artisans and handloom workers.

Housing for Coolies It was mainly for persons engaged in carrying head load at public places, like railway stations, bus terminal, markets, etc. The criteria adopted for selection of beneficiaries was that person having license to operate in public places, does not have house. The Central Government contributes 50% of the total cost of the actual tenement having 200 sq feet total plinth area with one room, kitchen, bathroom and latrine.

Housing for Fisherman It is evident that the socio-economic condition of the fisherman in India is very poor. So, the Central Ministry of Agriculture promoted housing for fishermans, residing both in rural and urban areas and for the low income community among fishermen. In addition to above, the central government has taken initiative to construct low cost houses for the poorest of the poor, belonging to Scheduled Castes, Scheduled Tribes and indentured labourers in rural areas.

It benefitted non SC/ST rural people, below poverty line by providing them grant in aid. The physically handicapped, widows, families of personnel from defence services/para military forces, killed in action, displaced person on account of development projects, nomadic, semi-nomadic and denotified tribes and families with displaced members, subject to the condition that these households belong to below poverty line category.

Housing Finance

Housing finance is a broad topic, the concept of which differs across continents, regions and countries, particularly in terms of the area it covers. The term 'housing finance' in a developed country may be different to what is understood by the term in a developing country.

The purpose of housing finance system is to provide the funds, which home buyers need to purchase their homes. In simple words, housing finance is what allows for the production and consumption of housing. It refers to the money we use to build and maintain the nation's housing stock. But, it also refers to the money we need to pay for it, in the form of rent, mortgage loans and re-payments.

India's National Housing Policy insists on providing more dwelling houses to the citizens. It is natural for the government to create institutions which can provide housing finance.

Types of Housing Finance

The different types of housing finance can be divided as :

Direct Housing Finance It refers to the finance provided by banks to individuals or groups of individuals.

Supplementary Housing Finance Finance provided for alternation/repairs.

Indirect Housing Finance Finance provided by way of term loans to housing to financial institutions, housing boards, other public housing agencies, etc.

Advantages of Housing Finance

The housing finance helps people in many ways which have proved to be quite advantageous. The advantages are detailed as :

- Among the financial services, housing finance creates employment both directly and indirectly.
- It helps in creation of more houses, which results in building up more infrastructure facilities like roads, electricity generation, etc.
- Factories or industrial establishments create townships by providing more housing facilities to their employees. Housing finance, thereby reduces congestion in urban areas.
- Non-conventional energy get popularised due to modern housing facilities, which is one of the major benefit of housing finance.
- Due to housing finance, there is a vertical expansion and re-building of dilapidated houses and re-modelling of the existing houses.

Methods of Housing Finance

Commercial banks and co-operative societies are providing housing finance. Life Insurance Corporation (LIC) is also in the race for providing housing finance.

While providing housing finance, the lender and borrower enter into an agreement, under the Transfer of Property Act, whereby the house to be constructed is mortgaged alongwith the land to the creditor, who is called mortgage. The borrower is the mortgagor and he cannot sell the house to any third party, until the loan is re-paid. In other words, the financing institution has a charge on the property of the borrower, until he repays the loan.

When the housing loan is re-paid, the mortgage is lifted and the ownership of the house is transferred to the owner. The owner has now an absolute right to transfer or sell to any party he likes. In the case of granting housing loan to existing houses for the purpose of rebuilding or expansion, the house will be mortgaged to the financing company, till the loan is re-paid.

In order to encourage more houses construction in India and to boost housing finance, the Income Tax Act provides concessions to the assesses.

Housing and Environment

Building material is any material which is used for construction purposes. Many naturally occuring substances, such as clay, sand, twigs and leaves have been used to construct buildings.

The materials available in our country to construct building are natural materials which include mud, stone, wood, lime, asbestos, etc. And the other are man-made materials, such as cement, brick, tiles, metal, glass and plastic. The building materials may further be divided into organic and inorganic building materials. The organic material consists of wood and bio-mass while, inorganic material consists of mud, cement, lime and gypsum.

The beauty, utility, economy, comfort and convenience of the houses generally depend to a large extent on the selection, use and care of the building materials. The cost of building materials alone works out to be more than 50% of the total cost of the house.

Following guidelines should be kept in mind while choosing building materials :

- The construction material should be of good quality.
- Saving in construction time by accelerating the pace of construction with suitable material/technique.
- Saving in cost of construction and improving affordability.

Impact of Building Material on Environment

Building material can have effect on environment. So, use eco-friendly materials which cause minimum damage to the environment and require minimum energy for manufacturing. Many of the materials used in the construction of buildings are produced in non-sustainable way.

The destruction and renovation of buildings, result in a large amount of waste include concrete, metals, glass, plastics, wood, asphalt, bricks, etc. This waste is often disposed off in either landfills.

Not only does this pollute the land and air, but the transportation required to remove such waste has a major impact on environment too. Thus, the attention need to be focused on judging the building materials and the construction materials, which of interest should be judiciously chosen.

Green Rating System

A green rating system is a tool that evaluates the performance of building and its impact on the environment. It comprises a pre-defined set of criteria, relating to the design, construction and operations of green buildings Over the world green buildings are providing multiple benefits.

They provide some of the most effective means for achieving a range of global goals, such as addressing climate change, creating sustainable development ties and driving economic growth.

The advantages of using green rating system are as follows :

- Environmental aspirations can be set.
- Environmental performance can be verified and can be demonstrated to third party.
- It results in a more efficient, durable and re-silient project.
- It provides economic benefits.

Energy Efficiency in Buildings

Energy efficiency buildings can be defined as buildings that are designed to provide a significant reduction of the energy need for heating and cooling, independently of the energy and of the equipments that will be chosen to heat or cool the building.

The energy efficiency of the buildings is the extent to which the energy consumption per square metre of floor area of the building measures upto established energy benchmarks for that particular type of building, under defined conditions.

Energy Efficiency Measures for Buildings

Energy efficiency measures for buildings are approaches through which the energy consumption of a building can be reduced while maintaining or improving the level of comfort in the building.

They can typically be categorised into the following :

Reducing Heating Demand Heating demand can be reduced by :

- limiting the exposed surface area of the building
- improving the insulation of the building's fabric
- reducing ventilation losses
- selecting efficient heating systems with effective controls

Reducing Cooling Demand Energy use in typical air-conditioned office buildings is approximately double that of naturally ventilated office buildings. The need for air-conditioning can be reduced by :

- controlling solar gains through glazing
- reducing internal heat gains
- making use of thermal mass and night ventilation to reduce peak temperatures
- providing effective natural ventilation
- reducing lighting loads and installing effective lighting controls

Reducing Energy Requirements for Ventilation When the cooling demand is sufficiently reduced by implementing the above measures, it may be possible to reduce heat gains so that air-conditioning is unnecessary and comfort conditions can be maintained through the use of natural ventilation.

The energy required for ventilation can be minimised by :

- a building design that maximises natural ventilation
- an effective window design
- use of mixed mode ventilation
- using efficient mechanical ventilation systems

Reducing Energy Use for Lighting This can be accomplished by :

- making maximum use of daylight while avoiding excessive solar heat gain.
- using task lighting to avoid excessive background luminance levels.

- installing energy efficient luminaries with a high light output to energy ratio.
- selecting lamps with a high luminous efficacy.
- providing effective controls that prevent lights being left on unnecessarily.

Reducing Energy Used for Heating Water This can be achieved by :

- installing time controls and setting them to correctly reflect the hours of hot water requirements.
- switching off electric heating elements (immersion) when hot water from the boiler is available.
- replacing any damaged or missing insulation from all hot water pipe work and cylinders, except where the pipes are providing useful heat into the space.

Reducing Consumption of Office Equipment and Appliances Office equipment is the fastest growing energy user in the business world, consuming 15% of the total electricity. As ventilation and air conditioning are major energy consumers themselves, it makes good business sense to ensure they are only used when absolutely necessary. Typical measures to reduce consumption which also apply to household appliances are :

- **Switching Off** It reduces the energy consumption and heat produced by equipment, which in turn lowers cooling costs.
- **Upgrading Existing Equipment** Some energy efficient appliances may cost more to buy but will help savings over the lifetime of the equipment.
- **Matching the Equipment to the Task** Bearing in mind current and predicted requirements and purchase equipment that meet these requirements.

Good Housekeeping and People Solutions The level of achievable energy savings from office equipment is down to everyday management by staff. A simple energy conservation programme for an organisation would consider the following :

- Setting-up an energy policy for the organisation
- Appointing an energy champion
- Involving staff
- Setting targets
- Using notices and reminders.

Energy Auditing

An energy auditing is an inspection survey and an analysis of energy flows for energy conservation in a building. It may include a process or system to reduce the amount of energy input into the system without negatively affecting the output.

An energy auditing is a detailed inventory of the energy performance of your home carried out by an auditor. The auditor assesses the energy performance of your home by examining the healing, hot water production, insulation, ventilation, etc. This makes it possible to identify any weak point in your home and give you personalised advice to help you rationalise your energy consumption. Energy audit helps in energy optimisation, pollution control, safety aspects and suggests the methods to improve the operating and maintenance practice of the system.

Energy auditing is an effective tool in defining and pursuing comprehensive energy management programmes. It has positive approach, aiming at continuous improvement in energy utilisation in contrast to financial auditing which stresses to maintain regularity.

Energy audit generally has three stages, such as :

Preparation It is a information gathering stage.

Survey Review and analysis of the building. In this stage, the review and analysis of the building are based on the information gathered, the operating parameters and condition of equipment, occupancy data, process involved and data collection.

Report Here, the data is analysed on which a report with recommendation is submitted.

Types of Energy Auditing

There are two basic types of energy auditing as :

Preliminary Auditing In this, readily available data is used to analyse the performance. The inspection takes a relatively short time and results are more generic, providing easy and low opportunity for energy efficiency.

General Auditing Here, a more detailed data and information are analysed which are recorded using specific sensors and meters. The inspection takes longer time and results are more specific providing accurate energy performance.

Indices of Indoor Comforts

The most important consideration to be kept in mind while designing a building is the extent to which it provides an environment that is comfortable for its occupants. Building exist to protect people. The quality of the indoor environment is important for the comfort, health and productivity of the people using buildings.

The thermal comfort is more than just pleasant conditions, it is a part of vital survival behaviour. A lack of thermal comfort causes stress among the building occupants. When they are too warm, people feel tired and when they are too cool people feel restless and tired.

So, providing comfort in building is really a challenging task because thermal comfort is not only influenced by temperature, but also by factors like relative humidity, air, velocity, environment radiation, etc.

Human comfort can also be affected by the quality of ventilation in a building. Ventilation is necessary for buildings to remove stale air and replace it with fresh air as well as to prevent over heating. Recently, new methods for indoor temperature control are being used. One of them is natural ventilation.

Comfort can also be influenced by the amount/type of noise in a building. Noise nuisance is excessive noise or disturbance that may have a negative effect on health or on the quality of life. For example, being able to hear occupants of neighbouring house through walls.

Energy as a Resource

Energy provides power to progress. We cannot grow without it. More the man is advancing towards modernity, more he is becoming dependent on energy. From the pre-historic period, when man first came to know about the use of fire, till today, it plays a prominent role in the economic and social development of mankind.

Sources of Energy

Sources of energy are :

Conventional Sources of Energy

Conventional sources of energy are the sources that are commonly in use, since long time. They can be exhausted due to over consumption. They pollute environment on a large scale and adds to global warming. All the non-renewable types of energies come under this category. Once it is used, its stock is depleted forever. e.g., coal, oil and natural gas. The energy produced from conventional sources are highly used for industrial and commercial purposes. It causes greenhouse effect and also affect climate change. It has serious health consequences. The preservation cost is very high as they need to be stored and then converted because they are sent through transmission lines and grid. This energy source has a limited resource and will run out sometime in future.

The different conventional sources of energy are :

Oil (Petroleum)

Oil is the lifeline of global economy. The identified deposits from which oil can be extracted profitably at present prices with current technology are known as oil resources. Thirteen countries of the world make up the Organisation of Petroleum Exporting Countries (OPEC), which have 67% of oil reserves.

About one-fourth of the oil reserves are located in Saudi Arabia. It is further estimated that the undiscovered oil will also be located in Middle East Thus, the world oil supplies and prices are likely to be controlled by OPE Cover a long period of time. United States of America is the world's largest consumer of oil using 30% of global total, whereas it has only 4% of the world's oil reserves.

Maximum use of oil is in transportation (63%), followed by industry (24%), residential and commercial buildings (8%) and electric utilities (8%). At the present rate of consumption, the world's crude oil reserves are estimated to be depleted in 40 years and there may be enough undiscovered oil lasting for another 40 years. Some analysts argue that rising oil prices will stimulate exploration and that the Earth's crust may contain more oil than is generally thought. Such oil even if it exists, lies about 10 kilometres or still more below the surface (twice the depth of wells known today). Some analysts strongly believe that at the current rate of use of crude oil, the following are expected :

- Saudi Arabia, with the largest known crude oil reserves, could supply all the world's needs for another 10 years.
- The estimated reserves under Alaska North slope (the largest reserve of North America) would meet US demand for just 3 years.
- All undiscovered deposits could-meet world demand for 30-40 years.

Coal

Coal is the most abundant conventional fossil fuel in the world. Identified world reserves of coal should last about 210 years at the current rate of usage and just 65 years, if the rate of usage increases by 2% per year. However the world unidentified coal reserves are projected to last about 900 years at current rate and 150 years, if usage rate increases by 2%.

About 68% of world's coal reserves and 85% of the estimated undiscovered coal deposits are located in USA, CIS (Commonwealth of Independent States) and China. About 55% of US coal reserves are found West of Mississippi River.

Natural Gas

About 40% of the world's natural gas reserves are in CIS countries. Other countries with natural gas reserves are Iran (14%), United States (5%), Qatar (4%), Saudi Arabia (3%) and Nigeria (3%). Geologists expect to find more natural gas, especially in unexplored LDCs (less developed countries). Most of the natural gas reserves are located in same area as crude oil.

Presently we are passing through the peak period of fossil age. The fossil age may last for a few more decades, as the reserves are getting depleted very fast. Probably, the next generation would witness a sharp depletion of oil and natural gas in their lifetime and alternate fuels will have to be developed.

Renewable Resources	Non-Renewable Resources
The renewable resources are present in the atmosphere of the earth.	The non-renewable resources are typically found in the underground layers of the Earth.
The renewable resources are replaced by nature itself in a very short period.	The non-renewable resources cannot be replaced by nature during the time of human life span.
These resources are abundant in nature.	The non-renewable resources are scarce resources and not available in abundant manner in nature.
These resources are obtained free of cost or at a very less cost in nature.	These rescources are very costly and not easily available.
They do not affect the environment of the earth and don't cause any climate changes in the atmosphere.	They seriously affect the environment and cause climate changes in the environment.

Non-Conventional Sources of Energy

Non-conventional sources of energy refers to the sources that are identified few decades ago. They cannot be exhausted. They are environment friendly sources, which does not cause pollution. They are used for domestic purposes and are less expensive. The non-conventional source of energy is non-replenishable or non-exhaustible form, which is obtained from the continuous or repetitive currents of energy occuring in the natural environment. These are called renewable sources of energy. The Government of India has established a separate department, under the Ministry of Energy called the Department of Non-Conventional Energy Sources for effective exploitation of non-conventional energy. The examples are solar energy, tidal energy, bio-energy and wind energy.

The different non-conventional sources of energy are :

Solar Energy It is the most readily available and free source of energy. It is produced through sunlight. Under this programme, solar photovoltaic cells are exposed to sunlight and in the form of electricity produced. Photovoltaic cells are those which convert sunlight energy into electricity. Under Solar Thermal Programme, solar energy is directly obtained. Sunlight is converted into thermal power. Solar energy is used for cooking, hot water, distillation of water, etc.

Tidal Energy It is produced by exploiting the tidal waves of the sea. Due to the absence of cost effective technology, this source has not yet been trapped.

Wind Energy The wind energy can be produced by harnessing wind power. It is used for operating water pumps for irrigation purposes. India has second place in wind energy generation.

Bio Energy Bio energy is obtained from organic matter. It is of two kinds, bio gas and bio mass. They can be understood as follows :

- **Biogas** It is an energy gas which is produced from the organic waste such as farm waste, shrubs, animals and human waste. It is a non-conventional source of energy. It has higher thermal efficiency in comparison to cowdung, coal and charcoal. It does not cause any pollution. It is the mixture of gases produced by the breakdown of organic matter in the absence of oxygen. Biogas is used for cooking, lighting and in generation of electricity. It is eco-friendly. The technology used to produce biogas is quite cheap.
- **Bio Mass** It is also a source of generating energy from plants and animals and includes crops, waste wood and trees. When biomass is burned, the chemical energy is released in the form of heat can generate electricity with steam turbine. The purpose of Biomass Programme is to encourage afforestation for energy, so that the fuel for the generation of energy based on gas technique could be obtained. 56 MW capacity for the generation of biomass energy has been installed.

Energy from Urban Waste Now, urban waste can be used for producing energy, as urban waste possess a big problem for disposal.

Energy Management

The term 'energy management' is used for saving or reducing the use of energy in business, public sector or government organisations and homes. It is the art of using optimum energy to maximise profits and minimise costs, thereby improving the economic competitiveness.

Energy management can also be defined as the science involving planning and controlling the supply and consumption of energy to improve productivity and comforts of the public and also to minimise the energy cost and pollution with conscious and effective use of energy. The energy should be used efficiently, economically and optimally. It is the best solution for direct and immediate reduction of energy consumption.

The main objectives of energy management are resource conservation, climate protection and cost savings. The central task of energy management is to reduce costs for the provision of energy in buildings and facilities without compromising work processes. Energy management deals with already existing resources and actual consumption. The simplest way to introduce energy management is the effective use of energy to maximise profits by minimising costs. Energy management could save upto 70% of the energy consumption in a typical building or plant.

National Efforts for Energy Conservation

Energy conservation refers to efforts made to reduce energy consumption. This can be achieved either by using the energy more efficiently or by reducing the amount of service used. Energy conservation is the part of the concept of eco-sufficiency.

For the conservation of energy, government has taken various initiatives/efforts which are discussed as :

Energy Conservation Act (2001) The Government of India considering the vast potential of energy savings and benefits of energy efficiency enacted the Energy Conservation Act (2001).

This act provided for the legal framework, institutional arrangements and a regulating mechanism at the central and state level to remark upon energy efficiency drive.

The five major provisions of Energy Conservation Act are :

- It is related to designated consumers.
- It is related to standard and labelling of appliances.
- It is related to energy conservation building codes.
- It is related to creation of institutional setup, Bureau of Energy Efficiency (BEE).
- It is related to establishment of Energy Conservation Fund.

The Energy Conservation Act became effective from March 2002 and BEE operationalised it from 1st March, 2002. The Act was amended in 2010 and the main amendments of the Act are given as :

- The Central Government may issue the energy savings certificate to the designated consumer, whose energy consumption is less than the prescribed norms and standards in accordance with the procedure as may be prescribed.
- The designated consumer whose energy consumption is more than the prescribed norms and standards shall be entitled to purchase the energy savings certificate to comply with the prescribed norms and standards.
- The Central Government may in consultation with the Bureau, prescribe the value of per metric ton of oil equivalent of energy consumed.
- Commercial buildings, which are having a connected load of 100 kW or contract demand of 120kVA and above come under the purview of Energy Conservation Building Code (ECBC) under EC Act.

Nation Programme for LED Based Home and Street Lighting This initiative was part of the government's effort to spread messages of energy efficiency in the country. LED bulbs have a very long life, almost 50% times more than ordinary bulbs and 8-10 times that of CFLs. So, they therefore provide energy and cost savings in the medium term. Under this Scheme, LED bulbs were distributed in a phased manner from March, 2015 onwards. The entire project of installing LED bulbs for domestic and street lighting in 100 cities was targeted for completion by March 2016.

Energy Conservation Building Code (ECBC) It was launched by Ministry of Power for new commercial buildings in 2007. It sets minimum energy standards for new commercial buildings. The ECBC in 2017 sets parameters for builders, designers and architects to integrate renewable energy sources in building design with the inclusion of passive design strategies.

National Mission for Enhanced Energy (NMEE), Under National Action Plan in Climate Change The National Mission for Enhanced Energy Efficiency aims to strengthen the market for energy efficiency by creating conductive, regulatory and policy regime. It is fostering innovative and sustainable business models to energy efficiency sector.

The NMEE has four initiatives to enhance energy efficiency intensive industries which are as follows :

- **Perform, Achieve and Trade Scheme** It is market based mechanism to enhance the cost effectiveness in improving energy efficiency.
- **Market Transformation for Energy Efficiency** For accelerating the shift to energy efficient appliances in designated sectors through innovate measures, so as to make the products more affordable.
- **Framework for Energy Efficient Economic Development** It is for the development of fiscal instruments to promote energy efficiency.
- **Energy Efficiency Financing Platform** It is for creation of mechanism that would help to meet finance demand in all sectors by capturing future energy savings.

School Education Program by Bureau of Energy Efficiency and NCERT Through this programme, students to be made aware with regard to efficient use of energy resources. In this regard, promotion of energy efficiency in schools is promoted through energy clubs. The BEE intends to prepare material on energy efficiency and conservation in science for classes 6 to 10.

EXAM BASED QUESTIONS

1 Who described housing as the root of happiness?
(a) Mahavir (b) Buddha
(c) Sri Aurobindo (d) Gandhiji

2 The building's rules and regulations are aimed to
(a) ensure adequate stability of the buildings.
(b) clean environment.
(c) adequate standard of healthy life.
(d) All of the above

3 The floor area ratio of every building differs depending upon its
(a) usage
(b) type of construction
(c) locality and its population
(d) All of the above

4 A .... is a set of rules that specify the standards for constructed objects, such as buildings and non-building structures.
(a) building code (b) building's by laws
(c) system (d) procedure

5 The ratio of the total floor area inclusive of all the floors to the area of the plot, on which building stands is known as
(a) ground coverage ratio (b) plot area
(c) floor area (d) build up area

6 Different types of housing finances include
(a) Direct finance (b) Supplementary finance
(c) Indirect finance (d) All of these

7 .... building is the open space between buildings and the property boundary. It differs for different types of buildings.
(a) Setback (b) Ground coverage
(c) Floor area ratio (d) Only (a) and (b)

8 Zoning is
(a) utilisation of available land for the right use
(b) legal regulation of the use of land
(c) the correct location of each zone
(d) All of the above

9 Which of the following is not a zone?
(a) Residential (b) Commercial
(c) Industrial (d) Electrical

10 According to the text, zoning ordinance regulate
(a) structural dimension (b) population density
(c) land use (d) All of these

11 Zoning must be enacted in accordance with the comprehensive plan and regulates development by district, throughout the city or country .
(a) True
(b) False
(c) Can't say
(d) Neither (a) nor (b)

12 Light and heavy industries, cold storages, integrated industrial parks, services and special industries, fall under which of the following mentioned zones?
(a) Re-creational zone (b) Industrial zone
(c) Commercial zone (d) Institutional zone

13 Housing is a chronic problem in .... countries.
(a) under developed (b) developed
(c) developing (d) Only (a) and (c)

14 Housing for coolies are
(a) mainly person engaged in carrying head load
(b) new at public places like railway stations
(c) initiated by Central Government
(d) All of the above

15 Green Rating System comprises a pre-defined set of criteria relating to
(a) design (b) construction
(c) operations (d) All of these

16 The building materials may be classified as
(a) natural (b) man-made
(c) organic and inorganic (d) All of these

17 The inorganic material consists of
(a) mud (b) brick
(c) lime (d) (a) and (c)

18 ...... is an apex financial institution for housing.
(a) RBI (b) SBI
(c) NHB (d) None of these

19 Who regulates the housing finance companies in India?
(a) Reserve Bank of India (b) National Housing Bank
(c) SBI (d) Government of India

20 Which of the following are the advantages of housing finance?
(a) It creates employment, both directly and indirectly
(b) It reduces congestion in urban areas
(c) It helps in creation of more houses
(d) All of the above

21 Which is the major energy source to meet the India's energy demand?
(a) Coal (b) Oil
(c) Natural gas (d) Lignite

22 Which one of the following forms of energy leads to least environmental pollution in the process of its harnessing and utilisation?
(a) Thermal energy (b) Geothermal energy
(c) Solar energy (d) Nuclear energy

23 Which of the following is a non-renewable resource?
(a) Coal (b) Forests (c) Water (d) Wildlife

24 **Which among the following is not a renewable source of energy?**
(a) Solar energy (b) Bio-mass energy
(c) Hydro-power (d) Geothermal energy

25 **Which of the following is a disadvantage of most of the renewable energy sources?**
(a) Highly polluting (b) High waste disposal cost
(c) Unreliable supply (d) High running cost

26 **Which among the following is not an adverse environmental impact of tidal power generation?**
(a) Interference with spawing and migration of fish.
(b) Pollution and health hazard in the estuary, due to blockage of flow of polluted water into the sea.
(c) Navigational hazard
(d) None of the above

27 **Both power and manure are provided by**
(a) nuclear plants (b) thermal plants
(c) bio gas plants (d) hydroelectric plants

28 **Common energy source in Indian villages is**
(a) electricity (b) coal
(c) Sun (d) wood and animal dung

29 **Steam reforming is currently the least expensive method of producing**
(a) coal (b) biogas
(c) hydrogen (d) natural gas

30 **Which energy of water is used to produce hydro electricity?**
(a) Potential energy (b) Kinetic energy
(c) Both (a) and (b) (d) None of these

31 **Which of the following is a disadvantage of renewable energy?**
(a) High pollution
(b) Available only in few places
(c) High running cost
(d) Unreliable supply

32 **In hydroelectric power, what is necessary for the production of power throughout the year?**
(a) Dams filled with water (b) High amount of air
(c) High intense sunlight (d) Nuclear power

33 **The main composition of bio gas is**
(a) methane (b) carbon dioxide
(c) nitrogen (d) hydrogen

34 **Which of the following is not under the Ministry of New and Renewable Energy?**
(a) Wind energy (b) Solar energy
(c) Tidal energy (d) Large hydro

35 **Which of the following is non-conventional source of energy?**
(a) Oil and petroleum (b) Solar energy
(c) Wind energy (d) Geo-thermal

36 **The term 'biomass' often refers to**
(a) inorganic matter (b) organic matter
(c) chemicals (d) ammonium compounds

37 **Biomass is useful to produce**
(a) chemicals (b) fibres
(c) bio-chemicals (d) transportation fuels

38 **........... is called as the bio gas.**
(a) Bio ethanol (b) Bio methane
(c) Bio diesel (d) Bio butanol

39 **Wind energy is harnessed as .... energy with the help of wind mill or turbine.**
(a) mechanical (b) solar
(c) electrical (d) heat

40 **The energy which is not derived from the Sun is**
(a) biomass (b) fossil fuel
(c) nuclear energy (d) geo-thermal energy

41 **Energy management is a key component of**
(a) environmental management
(b) carbon management
(c) nitrogen management
(d) water management

42 **The main objective of energy management is to**
(a) minimise energy cost
(b) minimise environmental effects
(c) maintain optimum energy procurement and utilisation
(d) All of the above

43 **In the given options, the non-commercial source of energy is**
(a) coal
(b) lignite
(c) firewood
(d) refined petroleum products

44 **Which Ministry is mainly responsible for research and development in renewable energy sources, such as wind power, small hydro, biogas and solar power?**
(a) Human Resource Development
(b) Agriculture and Farmers Welfare
(c) Ministry of New and Renewable Energy
(d) Health and Family Welfare

45 **Which Indian enterprise has the motto "Energy Forever"?**
(a) Indian Renewable Energy Development Agency
(b) Indian Non-Renewable Energy Development
(c) Indian Agricultural Development
(d) Indian Bio-Technology Development

46 **The most durable, long lasting and low maintenance metal used commonly for construction of household equipment is**
(a) aluminium (b) iron
(c) stainless steel (d) copper

47 **Which among the following is/are most energy efficient?**
(a) Incandescent bulb
(b) Fluorescent tubelight
(c) Compact fluorescent lamp
(d) All of the above

48 "The judicious and effective use of energy to maximise profits and enhance competitive positions." This can be the definition of
(a) energy conservation
(b) energy management
(c) energy policy
(d) energy audit

49 The objective of energy management includes
(a) minimising energy costs
(b) minimising waste
(c) minimising environmental degradation
(d) All of the above

50 .... gas is obtained from gobar gas plant by putting cow dung into plants.
(a) Bio gas
(b) Bio mass
(c) Bio energy
(d) Only (a) and (b)

51 Which of the following are the major provisions of energy conservation?
(a) Energy Conservation Building Code
(b) Standard and Labelling of Appliances
(c) Establishment of Energy Conservation Fund
(d) All of the above

52 The Energy Conservation Act was amended in the year
(a) 2006
(b) 2002
(c) 2010
(d) 2004

53 The buildings bylaws apply to the building where
(a) the building is newly erected
(b) the whole or any part of the building is demolished
(c) where the occupancy of the building is charged
(d) All of the above

54 Which is not an objective of building's bylaws?
(a) Allow disciplined and systematic growth of buildings and towns and prevent haphazard development.
(b) Protect safety of public against fire, house, health, hazards and structural failures.
(c) They provide health, safety and comfort to the people who live in buildings.
(d) Renovation of old buildings without any charge by the government.

55 Which is not a building bylaws characteristics?
(a) The rules must be specific, celar and the language of the rules should be grammatically correct.
(b) Terms used should be defined clearly, so that there must be one and only one meaning of the term.
(c) Due to some special conditions and requirements, some by laws differ from the by laws of other places.
(d) No modification is allowed if required.

56 Integrated subsidised housing, industrial workers and economically workers section are meant for which purpose?
(a) To provide open developed plots, two named single or multi-storied houses on rental basis, subject to certain ceilings.
(b) It provided a subsidy.
(c) It aimed at re-building or improving houses in rural areas.
(d) It was initiated by Ministry of Textiles.

57 Consider the statement(s), which is/are true with regard to Green Rating System.

Statement I It provides economic benefits.

Statement II Environmental aspirations can be set.

Codes
(a) Only statement I is true
(b) Only statement II is true
(c) Both the statements are true
(d) Neither statement I nor II is true

58 Which of the following statements(s) is/are incorrect about energy auditing?
(a) Energy auditing has four stages.
(b) Energy audit does not help in energy optimisation, pollution control
(c) In energy auditing, the auditor assesses the energy performance of your home.
(d) Only (a) and (b)

59 Consider the following statement(s).

Statement I The construction material should be of good quality.

Statement II Saving in cost of construction and improving affordability.

Which is/are true with regard to choosing building guidelines?
(a) Only Statement I is true
(b) Only Statement II is true
(c) Both statements are true
(d) Neither statement I nor II is true

60 Under which act, National Housing Bank was setup as an apex institute of housing finance in the country?
(a) National Housing Bank Act, 1986
(b) National Housing Bank Act, 1987
(c) National Housing Bank Act, 1988
(d) National Housing Bank Act, 1989

61 Consider the following statements.

Statement I It was basically to spread message of energy efficiency in the country.

Statement II LED bulbs have long life, almost 50 times more than ordinary bulbs.

The correct statement about National Programme based home and street lighting is/are
(a) Only statement I is correct
(b) Only statement II is correct
(c) Both the statements are correct
(d) Neither statement I nor II is correct

62 Consider the following statements regarding conventional sources of energy.
1. The conventional sources of energy are the fossil fuels which took millions of years for the formation of fossil fuels; hence they are limited and non-renewable.

2. Fossils are remains of organisms that lived in the past and fossil fuels are plants that got buried under the Earth and became rock over years.

Which of the above statement(s) is/are correct?

(a) Only 1 (b) Only 2
(c) Both 1 and 2 (d) Neither 1 nor 2

63 **Consider the following statements regarding the energy from biomass.**

1. Biomass is a plant matter produced as a result of photosynthesis and some of it can be burnt to provide heat. For example, wood and agricultural waste.
2. Biomass can also be used for power generation or converted into alcohol (liquid or methane gas) to be used as fuel.
3. Biomass is renewable energy and shall be available as long as plants grow on Earth.

Which of the above statement(s) is/are correct?

(a) Only 1 (b) Only 1 and 2
(c) Only 1 and 3 (d) All of these

64 **Consider the following statements regarding the promotion of solar energy in India.**

1. The Ministry of New and Renewable Energy (MNRE) have initiated schemes and incentives like subsidy, easy loan, concessional duty on raw material imports, excise duty exemption on certain devices/systems, etc to encourage and use of solar energy systems.
2. The Indian Renewable Energy Development Agency (IREDA) provides financial help for the purchases of PV (Photo Voltaic) systems.
3. Government is planning to setup 10 million square meter solar collector area by 2022.

Which of the above statement(s) is/are correct?

(a) Only 1 (b) Only 1 and 2
(c) Only 1 and 3 (d) All of these

65 **Consider the following statements regarding Bureau of Energy Efficiency (BEE) of India.**

1. Bureau of Energy Efficiency (BEE) is an agency of the Government of India, under the Ministry of Power, created in March 2002, under the provision of Energy Conservation Act.
2. The agency's function is to develop programmes which will increase the conservation and efficient uses of energy in India.
3. The government has proposed to make it mandatory or compulsory for appliances in India to have ratings by the BEE starting in January, 2010.

Which of the above statement(s) is/are correct?

(a) Only 1 (b) Only 1 and 2
(c) Only 1 and 3 (d) All of these

66 **Choose the correct statement (s) with regard to biomass.**

(a) It is a source of generating energy from plants and animals.
(b) The purpose of Bio Mass Programme is to encourage afforestation of energy.
(c) The waste can be produced for generating electricity.
(d) Only (a) and (b)

67 **Match the following.**

List I	List II
A. Solar energy	1. It is produced by exploiting tidal waves of the sea.
B. Tidal energy	2. It is used for operating water pumps for irrigation purposes.
C. Wind energy	3. The energy is obtained from organic matter.
D. Bio energy	4. It is most readily available free source of energy.

Codes

	A	B	C	D		A	B	C	D
(a)	4	1	2	3	(b)	1	2	3	4
(c)	4	1	3	2	(d)	4	3	2	1

Directions (Q. Nos. 68-83) *Following are the statements given below, one labelled as Assertion (A) and other labelled as Reason (R). Following are the codes given below, select the correct code for the following.*

Codes

(a) A is true, and R is correct explanation of A
(b) A is true, but R is false
(c) Both A and R are false
(d) A is true, but R is not the correct explanation of A

68 **Assertion** (A) House is the primary unit of habitation.

Reason (R) Housing plays an important role in the economy of the country.

69 **Assertion** (A) Zoning is the legal regulation of use of land.

Reason (R) It is an application of the local body enforcement for the protection of public health, welfare and society.

70 **Assertion** (A) A green rating system is a tool.

Reason (R) It is not helpful in evaluating the performance of building and its impact on environment.

71 **Assertion** (A) An energy auditing is an inspection survey.

Reason (R) It analysis the energy flow for energy conservation in a building.

72 **Assertion** (A) In preliminary auditing, readily available data is not used to analyse the performance.

Reason (R) The inspection takes relatively more time.

73 **Assertion** (A) Housing finance is what allows for the production and consumption of housing.

Reason (R) The purpose of Housing Finance System is to provide funds which home buyers need to purchase their homes.

74 **Assertion** (A) Conventional sources of energy are the sources that are commonly in use since long time.

Reason (R) Once it is used, its stock depleted forever.

75 **Assertion** (A) The wind energy is produced by exploiting the tidal waves of the sea.

Reason (R) India has second place in tidal energy generation.

76 **Assertion** (A) Energy management is an art and science of optimum use of energy.

Reason (R) It helps to maximise profits.

77 **Assertion** (A) The Energy Conservation Act (2001) considered the vast potential of energy savings and benefits of energy efficiency.

Reason (R) The Act provided for legal framework.

78 **Assertion** (A) The housing problem is more chronic in developing countries.

Reason (R) In India, the housing conditions are not upto the minimum level.

79 **Assertion** (A) In general auditing, a detailed data is analysed.

Reason (R) The inspection takes longer time, thus results are more specific.

80 **Assertion** (A) Direct finance is provided to purchase another house.

Reason (R) Finance is provided for alternation repairs.

81 **Assertion** (A) The energy produced from conventional sources are used for industrial and commercial purposes.

Reason (R) The preservation cost is very high.

82 **Assertion** (A) Energy for urban waste is utilised for producing energy.

Reason (R) The urban waste possess a big problem.

83 **Assertion** (A) Energy efficiency buildings can be defined as buildings that are designed to provide significant reduction of energy.

Reason (R) The energy efficiency of the building is the extent to which the energy consumption per sq meter of the floor area of the building measures upto establish energy benchmarks.

Directions (Q. Nos. 84-88) *Read the passage given below and answer the following questions.*

Energy conservation offers a practical means of achieving development goals. It enhances the international competitiveness of industry in world markets by reducing the cost of production. It optimises the use of capital resources by diverting lesser amount in conservation investments as against huge capital investment in power sector. It helps environment in the short run by reducing pollution and in the long run by reducing the scope of global climatic changes. In this regard, the government has taken various initiatives to save energy for future.

The Bureau of Energy Efficiency (BEE) initiated the standards and labelling programmes for equipments and appliances in 2006 to provide the consumer with an informed choice about the energy saving.

The energy efficiency labelling programs, under BEE are intended to reduce the energy consumption of appliance without diminishing the services it provides to consumers. This app is linked to the standards and labelling database. It provides the user with a platform to compare personalised energy saving devices across the same class and to get a real-time feedback from consumers so that they can make an informed purchase decision.

Apart from being a one-stop solution for customers, it's also a valuable tool for policy makers to access the accumulated data and analyse the feedback of the market at any given point of time. The Energy Conservation Building Code (ECBC) was launched by Ministry of Power for new commercial buildings in 2007.

It sets minimum energy standards for new commercial buildings, in order to promote a market pull for energy efficient buildings. Bureau of Energy Efficiency developed a Voluntary Star Rating Programme for buildings which are based on the actual performance of a building.

The updated version of ECBC came in 2017, which sets parameters for builders, designers and architects to integrate renewable energy sources in building design with the inclusion of passive design strategies. The code aims to optimise energy savings with the comfort levels for National Mission for Enhanced Energy Efficiency (NMEEE), under NAPCC.

The National Mission for Enhanced Energy Efficiency (NMEEE) is one of the eight missions, under the National Action Plan on Climate Change (NAPCC). NMEEE aims to strengthen the market for energy efficiency by creating conducive regulatory and policy regime and has envisaged fostering innovative and sustainable business models to the energy efficiency sector plants and prefers life cycle cost effectiveness to achieve energy neutrality in commercial buildings.

School Education Program by Bureau of Energy Efficiency and NCERT aims to make the next generation more aware regarding efficient use of energy resources. In this regard, promotion of energy efficiency in schools is being promoted through the establishment of energy clubs. Narendra Modi described the LED bulb as "Prakash Path", "Way to Light".

The initiative is a part of the Government of India's efforts to spread the message of energy efficiency in the country. UJALA Scheme aims to promote efficient use of energy at the residential level, enhance the awareness of consumers about the efficacy of using energy efficient appliances and aggregating demand to reduce the high initial costs, thus facilitating higher uptake of LED lights by residential users.

It may be noted that the scheme was initially labelled DELP (Domestic Efficient Lighting Program) and was re-launched as UJALA.

The Government of india launched the National Electric Mobility Mission Plan (NEMMP), 2020 in 2013. It aims to achieve national fuel security by promoting hybrid and electric vehicles in the country. There is an ambitious target to achieve 6-7 million sales of hybrid and electric vehicles year on year from 2020 onwards.

84 **The Energy Conservation Building Code was launched by**

(a) Ministry of Power for New Commercial Building
(b) Ministry of Human Resource Development
(c) Ministry of Petroleum and Natural Gas
(d) Ministry of Coal

85 **The National Mission for Enhanced Energy Efficiency aims**

(a) to strengthen the market for energy efficiency
(b) to reduce energy consumption of appliances
(c) to foster innovative and sustainable business models the energy efficiency sector
(d) Only (a) and (c)

86 **The Bureau of Energy Efficiency (BEE) initiated the standards and labelling programme for equipment and appliances in the year**

(a) 2005 (b) 2006
(c) 2004 (d) 2013

87 **The Star Rating Mobile App**

(a) is linked to the standards and labelling database
(b) is a valuable tool for policy makers
(c) provides users with a platform to compare personalised energy saving device
(d) All of the above

88 **Who described the LED bulb as "Prakash Path", "Way to Light"?**

(a) Prime Minister
(b) Minister of State
(c) Minister of Petroleum and Natural Gas
(d) Minister of Jal Shakti

ANSWERS

Exam Based Questions

1 (b)	2 (d)	3 (d)	4 (a)	5 (d)	6 (d)	7 (a)	8 (d)	9 (d)	10 (d)
11 (a)	12 (b)	13 (d)	14 (d)	15 (d)	16 (d)	17 (d)	18 (c)	19 (b)	20 (d)
21 (a)	22 (c)	23 (a)	24 (b)	25 (c)	26 (d)	27 (c)	28 (d)	29 (c)	30 (a)
31 (d)	32 (a)	33 (a)	34 (d)	35 (a)	36 (b)	37 (d)	38 (b)	39 (a)	40 (c)
41 (b)	42 (d)	43 (d)	44 (c)	45 (a)	46 (c)	47 (c)	48 (b)	49 (d)	50 (a)
51 (d)	52 (c)	53 (d)	54 (d)	55 (d)	56 (a)	57 (c)	58 (d)	59 (c)	60 (b)
61 (c)	62 (c)	63 (d)	64 (d)	65 (d)	66 (d)	67 (a)	68 (d)	69 (a)	70 (b)
71 (a)	72 (c)	73 (d)	74 (d)	75 (c)	76 (a)	77 (d)	78 (d)	79 (a)	80 (d)
81 (a)	82 (a)	83 (a)	84 (a)	85 (d)	86 (b)	87 (d)	88 (a)		

CHAPTER

21

Interior Design and Its Fundamentals

Interior design plays a big role in everyday life. Nowadays, it is an important technique that is given high attention all over the world. Interior design provides a soul to a house or space and makes a space more functional, pleasant and viable. Interior designing is a systematic arrangement of linen, forms, texture, colours, etc., to create beauty to interiors. Interior design is important due to the aesthetic value it possesses in a given space.

The desire to create a pleasant environment is as old as civilisation itself, the field of interior design is relatively new. It is the specialised branch of architecture or environmental design. Interior design is an organised way for any plan with some definite purpose. It is a systematic process of accomplishing some end. Interior design is an art and science of enhancing a healthier and more aesthetically pleasing environment for the people using space. Interior design introduces people to beauty, relaxation and modernism. It is an important technique that is given high attention all over the world, nowadays.

Thus, the interior designing helps the person (designer) to learn a lot about the space and how people can feel comfortable while being at a specific place and using its facilities.

In this Chapter

Design Fundamentals

Elements of art, principles of designs and principles of composition together are called design fundamentals. Their description is given below :

Elements of Art

A work of art can be analysed by considering a variety of aspects of its individuality. The aspects are often called elements of art.

The commonly used elements of art include line, shape, form, space, colour, texture and pattern, which are detailed below as :

Line

The lines are the marks that span a distance between two points or the path of a moving point. A line has a width, direction and length. Lines are sometimes called strokes when referring to line in digital art work.

Lines can be used to create shapes and forms as well as give a sense of depth and structure. Line is the foundation of drawing and is a powerful tool.

By using different types of lines, such as horizontal, vertical, curved, crooked, oblique, diagonal and radiating the lines, drastically change the psychology of an art work impacting the viewer greatly.

Space

It is one of the most important element of interior design. Space acts as a foundation on which the entire design is built. It is divided into two types i.e. two dimensional space and three dimensional space. Two dimensional space covers the floor includes length and width and three dimensional space, which forms the living space, includes width, length and height. A space that is filled with furniture/ decorative items is a positive space, whereas an empty space is a negative space.

Forms

It means shapes in general, an outline of any three dimensional objects in the space. Forms can be created by combining two or more shapes and can be accentuated with the help of other elements, such as texture, patterns and colours. A well-defined form establishes harmony and additional forms add balance to the space.

There are two types of forms as :

- Geometric Form (Man-made)
- Natural Form (Organic)

Forms can also be categorised as open and closed forms. The open forms are those that can be looked into, whereas closed forms are those that are enclosed by a closed surface.

Shapes

These are two dimensional, flat and only have height and width. Shape implies some degree of organisation in the thing. Physical shape is determined by the outward boundaries of an object.

The boundaries refer to the outer countour or outline. With shape, space is formless. Natural shapes are characterised by softness and irregularity while man-made are distinguished by hardness and appear regular and rectangular.

Texture

It mainly deals with surface and determines how a typical surface looks. Texture adds depth and interest into living space and defines the feel and consistency of a surface.

Texture is broadly divided into two types, namely visual texture and actual texture. Visual texture is where the texture is only visible, while actual texture is where the texture is both seen and felt.

Colours

Colours establish an aesthetic connection between objects and set the mood. Colours must be chosen based on the psychology and the mindset of the person who dwells the house. For example, red is an excellent choice for dinning room as it encourages appetite and green for bedroom as it is the colour of tranquility and health. Colours are broadly classified as primary and secondary and also sub-categorised into tertiary, complementary, analogous and monochromatic.

Pattern

It adds interest and life to interior design and work alongwith colours. Pattern could be of any shape and mostly comprises of attractive and repetitive designs. For example, Paisley is a design pattern which takes the shape of a droplet and vegetables are one of the most commonly used patterns on wall paints, pillow covers and other decorative surfaces.

Principles of Design

Principles of design play a very important role in the art of any type. There are five major principles of design, such as balance, proportion and scale, emphasis, harmony and rhythm. These are discussed below as :

Balance

It refers to the arranging or grouping of pattern around a centre in such a way which provides equal attraction on each side of the centre. Balance is of three types viz. formal, informal and optical or obvious. The formal balance is sometimes referred to as passive or static balance. Here, objects of equal interest and weight are placed at equal distance from a central point of interest.

The informal balance is also called asymmetrical balance. Here, the objects are not placed at equal distance, but placed such that they appear to be in equilibrium. Lighter or smaller objects are placed more closer to the central point, while heavier and bigger objects are placed farther away.

The optical or obvious balance is that when the objects are not identical in shape and colour. But, they are placed equidistant from the central point, as they have equal value of interest and attraction.

The shape, colour and texture also play an important role in balancing the pattern. A balanced arrangement provides a sense of restfulness and repose. Suppose, when planning for an internally balanced design a person has to consider many items, such as size and number of shapes or forms, grouped on either side of the centre. The distance from the centre or from the front back of the design or the way in which dark and light, bright or dull, warm and cool form of colours are used to give a proper feeling of balance. If the object is heavy, dark and bright, it should be placed near the center.

Proportion and Scale

These refer to the relationship of various parts of the design to one another and to the whole. It deals with the relationship in size, shape, colour, height, texture and pattern. Proportion involves the relationship of object to the space and even the relationship of object to the other parts of the object.

Proportion helps to bring beauty and attraction. The ratio for proportion was formed as 2 : 3, 3 : 5, 5 : 8, 8 : 13. On the other hand, scale refers to the size of objects i.e. small, big, medium, light, heavy in relation to the surroundings. Scale is the relationship between sizes within an object and those of other objects used with it.

Emphasis

It involves the principles of design, which leads to one's eyes, first to the most important part of the design and then to the other subordinating areas in the order of their importance. To use this principle successfully, one needs to know what to emphasise, how and how much to emphasise and where to place emphasis.

Background should have the least emphasis against which the objects are to be seen. There are various ways in which we may attract attention to the important part of a design. Some of these are by placing or grouping of objects, by the use of contrast of hue, value or intensity, by using decoration and by having sufficient plain background space around objects.

There should be simplicity and restraint in the amount to be emphasised. Here, the use of principle of ratio is essential in emphasis i.e. two parts and three parts plain space.

Harmony

It means unity of proper composition and feeling of togetherness. If all the principles of design have been properly used, then harmony results. Harmony has five aspects i.e. line and shape, size, texture, idea and colour. Harmony of line and shape can be achieved in table setting, like flower arrange: 'ent, etc.

When sizes which are too different are used together, they are inconsistent. When cool and warm colours have to be mixed, harmony can be achieved by reducing their brightness and lightness or darkness.

Rhythm

It is a movement marked by regular reoccurrence and periodicity. A sense of order, a quality of gracefulness, a feeling of easy and organised movement all lead to rhythm. It means an easy connected path along which the eye may travel in an easy manner. Rhythm is possible by the use of the following :

Repitition The repitition of lines, colours and shapes create interest and movement of the eye.

Radiation The radiating lines create rhythm.

Alteration The alteration is the placement of space between lines producing interesting rhythm.

Gradation The gradation brings gradual changes in colour, width, height, size and pattern that help to produce rhythm.

Principles of Composition

Composition means that one has arranged, distributed aligned and compiled design in a manner that not only looks good but is also highly functional and effective.

The term 'composition' is used to describe the arrangement of the visual elements in painting or other art work. It is how the elements of art and design-line, colour, shape, texture and form value.

Space are organised or composed according to the principles of art and design i.e. balance, contrast emphasis, pattern rhythm and other elements of composition to give the painting structure.

The principles of composition are general guidelines which apply to all art forms. The principles of composition include visual hierarchy, unity, contrast and contrast of line and movement.

Colour

Colour makes things look beautiful and happening. Without colours, everything in this world is dark and gloomy.

Colour plays an important role in our lives, they are a source of pleasure to everybody. Colours can change the moods, reduce or increase tensions, cause excitement and sometimes have soothing effect on a person.

Dimensions of Colour

The intensity of colours separate one from the other and may create colour dimensions.

The qualities or dimensions of colours include hue, value and chroma or intensity which are discussed below as :

Hue It is the descriptive name of the colours like red, orange and violet. Each hue represents family of colour. It also indicates warmth or coolness of the colour. Red colour is pure hue. It has many variations. Pink colour is a tint of red. Maroon is a shade of red. Pink and maroon colours are members of the red hue.

Value It indicates the lightness or darkness of a hue by the addition of white, grey or black. The grey scale is a guide for modifying the value of any colour. White added to hue creates a tint. Adding grey creates tone shade. The addition of white lightens or brightens and increase the value of colour. It also increases the reflection of light. The addition of black darkens and decreases the value, creating shades of the colour and also more of a visual weight.

Chroma or Intensity It is the third dimension of colour, which indicates the brightness or dullness of colours. It refers to the degree of colour intensity, strength, saturation or purity of a colour. The purity of colours refers to its freedom from white, black or grey.

Colour Wheel/Prang Colour System

The colour wheel or prang colour system are as follows :

Primary Colour All colours are created out of combinations of three primary colours i.e. red, yellow and blue. These are called primary colours because they are the elements use in making the pigment. They are the only hues in pigment that cannot be obtained by mixing other hues.

Secondary Colour They are obtained by combining the primary colours. We get the secondary colours like orange (yellow + red), green (blue + yellow) and purple (red + blue).

Tertiary/Immediate Colour These colours are obtained by mixing primary and secondary colours. The tertiary colours are yellow, blue and red much neutralised. The tertiary yellow resembles a smoky yellow, the blue is known as slate blue and tertiary red is the colour of old red brick.

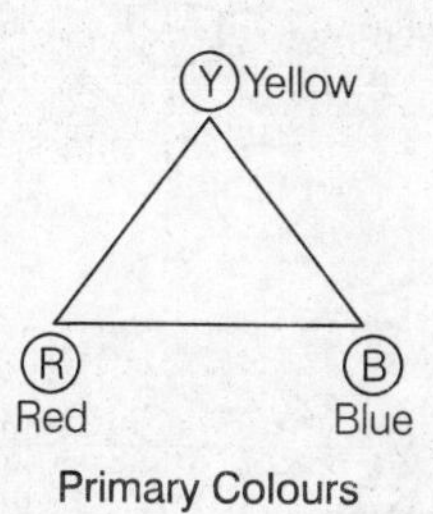

Primary Colours

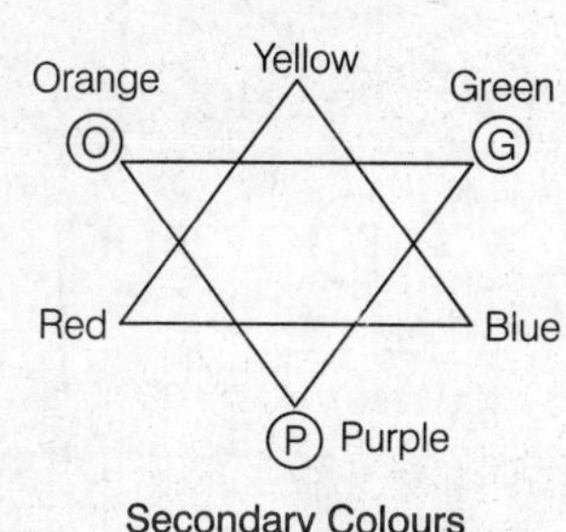

Secondary Colours

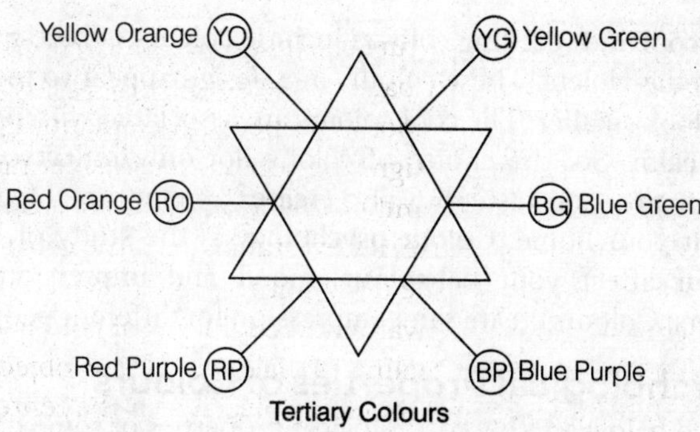

Tertiary Colours

By combining in this way, it is possible to make colour wheel of an infinite number of colours.

Psychological Effects of Colour

Colour creates mood and evoke emotions. Colours have different meanings and various emotional associations among the various people of the global community. The colour can create certain changes in our environment or in an object. This is because of the psychological perceptions of colours plus an association by experience of observation.

The exposure and experiences individual have with colours differ. So, the knowledge of colour is a powerful and creative tool. When creating an arrangement, the designer uses this knowledge as a tool to express his/her emotions and ideas.

To a professional interior designer, the psychological conscious and sub-conscious reactions to colours are tools with she creates a balance for objects and space from the colours available.

The colours have strong effect on emotions. Cool colours have quietening influence. On the other hand, warm colours have a cheerful effect which may increase stimulation and excitement. Colours, because of its emotional effect are largely responsible for atmosphere in the home. It is capable of smoothening or irritating or cheering, welcoming or repelling and charming or boring. For example, yellow has the effect of cheerful gaiety and optimism in the home. It gives effect of sunlight.

Cool colours carry an illusion of distance and thus, objects with cool colours seem to recede and on the other hand, warm colours seem to advance. The effect of colour is very important in interior decoration, since a square room can be made to appear oblong with receding or cool colours on three walls and an advancing or warm colour on one wall of the room. For example, white colour being the lightest of all is always used for painting the ceiling in order to create visual distance.

In furnishing a room, warm colours are used in smaller proportions and cool colours for larger areas. As warm colours advance, if not carefully used create restlessness, whereas cool colours recede.

The cool and receding colours include colours of blue-green and blue-violets. These colours in a design appear to recede and look smaller. The cool colours are associated with peace and calm. So, the choice of colour not only reflects your personality and taste, but also creates an emotional feeling about your home. Colour psychology is the study of how colour affect your behaviour, mood and impression on others. Colours create same impression for different people.

Psychological Properties of Colours

Listed below are the psychological properties of some of the commonly used colours as :

Orange It is quite a stimulating colour, related to action and vitality, but when used excessively it may induce restlessness.

Yellow This is a bright cheerful colour closely related to the Sun. Especially on dull grey days, it will cheer you up and makes you more mentally alert and enthusiastic. Too much and too bright yellow makes induce restlessness and freak you out.

Green Pure green and greyed out green induce coolness, tranquility and sedation. If mixed with a bit of yellow, it probably will induce biliousness.

Red It is very stimulating and excites the brain. It is also related with alertness, vitality and excitement and in a negative way with aggression and violence. A darker red colour invokes the feelings of richness (the "red pluche", royalty and the Church) and reverence. The brighter version has "amorous connotations".

Blue The psychological effect strongly depends on how the colour is used. Dark blue is connected to richness, royality and the Church, invoking feelings of calmness and sedation. However, if used indiscriminately, it can produce strong feelings of melancholia and uneasiness and can be quite depressing.

Purple When used in full or near-full chroma, purple is another colour inducing the impression of richness and reverence. The other side of the medal is instability and uneasiness, as some countries relate this colour to death. But, if you use it as a pastel tint, it is said that purple can trigger soft, romantic feelings; soothing and sedative.

Colour Schemes

There are many basis for choice of colours and colour schemes. One can select a pleasing combination of colours from a wallpaper or fabric, an oriental rug, a flower, a scene or even a picture in a magazine. It is advisable to let one colour predominate and limit the whole scheme to two or three colours, more colours with their values and shades.

While choosing colours, follow some rules such as :

- Always choose colour that please your personality.
- Colours chosen should be colourful and definite and not dull and wisty-wasty.
- Try out various colours combinations and then live with them and look at them frequently, before you actually start buying them.
- Ceilings may be white or natural or tinted with the colour of the wall of the room.
- Colours of walls should harmonise with furniture, draperies and carpets.

Types of Colour Schemes

In making colour schemes, the combinations of the following colours may be used effectively :

Monochromatic Colour Scheme

It can be varied in both value and intensity. This harmony is achieved by the use of different tints or shades of one hue or colour. It is a colour harmony of judicious and harmonious use of different values of single colour. This colour harmony is often termed as 'monotonous'. It is difficult to use. In this, usually, spaciousness and continuity are emphasised and the effect is quiet and peaceful e.g., peach, beige, brown and orange are tints and shades of colour.

Light Yellow	Yellow	Dark Yellow
Pink	Red	Maroon
Sky Blue	Blue	Navy Blue/ Royal Blue

Monochromatic Colour Scheme

Analogous Colour Scheme

The scheme uses colours that are close to each other on the colour wheel. They usually match well and create serene and comfortable designs. Analogous colour schemes are often found in nature and are harmonious and pleasing to the eye. Analogous colours are group of three colours with one being the dominant which tends to primary or secondry and a tertiary red, orange and red-orange.

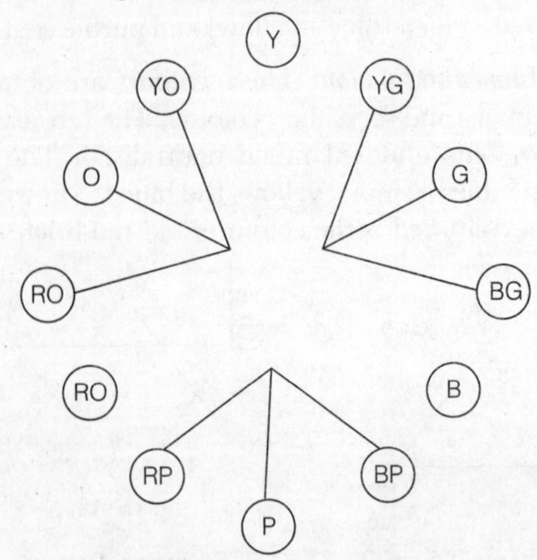

Analogous Colour Scheme

Complementary Colour Scheme

Single Complementary Colour Scheme Colours that are opposite on the colour circle are used in this scheme. It is stimulating type and well balanced. e.g. Red and green, blue and orange, etc.

Double Complementary Colour Scheme It is pairing of two or more complementary colours. Colours that are directly adjacent with their complements when used together form double complementary harmonies. e.g. Orange-blue and red orange-blue green.

Split Complementary Colour Scheme It is the combination of primary intermediate with the colours that are on either side of its complement. e.g. Yellow, red-violet and blue-violet.

Triad Colour Scheme Triad colour refers to any for hue that are equidistant from one another on the colour wheel. e.g. Yellow, red and blue, green, violet and orange, etc.

Tetrad Colour Scheme Tetrad colour schemes are any four hues from one another on the colour wheel. e.g. Yellow- orange, green, blue-violet and red.

Factors Affecting Use of Colours

Colour is a source of universal pleasure, everyone of us should have beautiful colours in our homes and learn to enjoy them. When an interior decorator visualises a colour's plan for a room, she should consider number of factors such as room, its size, shape and exposure, the mood style, current fashion, personal preferences, etc.

The use of colour helps to achieve the following effects :

Contrast Here, various colours are used as foils or background to flatter each other.

Blend In this, various shades and tint of one colour are used. e.g. One could use various shades and tint of the rug colour for the walls, upholstery and draperies.

Amount of Sunlight It is another aspect that affects the choice of colour, is the amount of sunlight that it receives. Room with too much light needs dark sub-dued colours. A wise choice of colour can help to change the warm or cool effects to provide feeling of comfort in the rooms.

Space Planning and Design : Housing Need and Importance

The space planning is a fundamental element of the interior design processes. It begins with an indepth analysis of how space is to be used. The designer then draws up a plan that defines the zones of the space and activities that will take place in those zones. The space plan will also define the circulation patterns that show how people will move throughout the space.

The space planning is a complex process. An effective space planning ensures optimal use of floor area without wasted space. A well-considered and designed space plan will allow one to make the best use of the floor area. An ideal space plan is one that can accommodate everything as well as gives you the desired comfort.

Thus, an ideal space planning can bring in a sense of balance between beauty and comfort. A space should be designed or planned in such a way that it should be visually appealing. The space planning must successfully reflect what you are looking for. An interior designer should make optimum use of space while planning.

Principles of Planning Spaces

Space planning is one of the most important element of interior design. It acts as a foundation on which the entire interior design is built. While planning space, few principles need to be considered which are as follows :

- Think about the structure of the room, what are the main focal points.
- Think about the space in terms of volume.
- Ensure that a circulation passageway through a room follow an easy and economic pathway from the door to all other main activity areas.
- Clutter close down space, so edit your clutter to avoid blocking both circulation and reducing the perceived size of the room.
- In large or long spaces, sub-divide different activity zones to give definite space to each part of the room.
- When furnishing small rooms blur the edges of the room, to break up the lines between floor and walls, draw furniture little away from the walls.
- Borrow space from outside ensuring an uninterrupted view of the outside world. You can also borrow space from adjoining rooms by using same flooring materials.
- In planning, space maintains balance and symmetry.

Types of House Plan

There are different types of house plans, some of them are discussed below as :

Simplex House Plan The building materials needed for simplex house plan include use of glass, steel, timbers and concrete. Geometry also plays an important role with the simplex house plan. Strong rectangular shapes and/or dramatic sweeping curves are identifying features of simplex house plan. Often times, both the bold right angles as well as spherical archs are incorporated in a simplex house plan. The clean lines, open floor plans and simple spaces are trademarks for simplex house plan.

Traditional House Plan This is the blend of old fashioned house plan with modern architecture, creativity or innovations. The traditional house plan have a wonderfully warm and familiar feel. Its exterior encompasses the entire range of siding options including brick, wood, stone, stucco. Interiors too are flexible enough to accommodate a broad range of traditional taste and design desired. Welcoming front porches, gracious dining and livingrooms as well as generously proportioned kitchens, family rooms and integrated garages are all that can be found in traditional houses.

Duplex House Plan This is meant for a single family which is built as a single dwelling with two separate units having one kitchen and dinning room. Duplex house plans gives a villa look and feel in same area.

Small House Plan The small house plans are intended to be economical to build. These are smartly built homes, flexible, cost efficient and energy saving home. The space saving strategy is the foremost concept in small house plans. These small house plans may be smaller in size, but are designed to live and feel comfortable.

Bungalow House Plan These house plans have their own luxury, utilisation of space, landscaping, etc. Bungalow make up in liveability what they lack in small house plans. It features an open living area with bedrooms, kitchens and bathrooms arranged for easy accessibility.

Economy in Construction

Construction is an important sector that contributes greatly in the economic growth of a nation. The construction industry is an investment led sector where government shows high interest. The construction activities affect nearly every aspect of the economy. When the economy is sluggish, the housing market takes a down turn. If construction companies are not building or building contracts hard to come by, it is usually indicative of slow economy.

In the construction, numerous clients like property builders, property developers, material suppliers and contractors are involved. The construction industry brings cost effective buildings, wherein all these clients play an active role to make the contract a success. Also, attractive construction of the infrastructure attracts many inward investors for business deals. Well constructed infrastructure creates a healthy environment to work in, thereby increasing productivity and flexibility of the labour force. Construction industry works with calculations and within the framework of carbon credits. Their input of resource is precise by implementing optimum use with minimum wastage.

Logistics also contribute greatly to construction. It teaches effective management of product transport, product handling, delivery of materials, storage, etc. Executing logistics on construction reduces cost by upto 2.5 percent. Over the past few years, the growth of construction has followed the trend of economic growth rate of the country. The construction industry is an important indicator of development, as it creates investment opportunities across various related sectors. It plays a powerful role in economic growth.

Planning for Different Income Groups

Planning for different income groups have been in practice for many years in India. In this regard, number of factors need to be considered for planning houses for low income groups, middle income groups and higher income groups.

Low Income Groups Planning low cost house design stick to the simple geometry that is not costly to build and that provides the maximal functionality without compromising comfort and quality. Calculate the overall cost. It means invest in quality building materials initially and save money on cheaper elements that can be easily replaced when necessary.

Also, you should consider using recycled materials that are not only cheaper, but also environment friendly and durable. Consider, space planning as the best low cost home design that revolves around lawfully planned space where none of the space is wasted, hence, providing maximal functionality at the minimal cost. Also, consider the floor area during low cost housing design. Square footage is a big contributor to the cost of the building. Reducing footprint and using space effectively is a great way of saving money for the overall cost and the maintenance without compromising much living space.

Middle Income Groups These are the people who are from an aspirational class. These groups make use of environment-friendly construction techniques and new technologies for construction, quality cost and suitable building materials.

Providing affordable houses including all the basic amenities. The carpet area should not exceed beyond 1200 sq. ft. The cost should be reasonable. Updation of provision of safety in construction, proper parking facilities, fire safety prevention, life safety and space efficient design.

Higher Income Groups The planning a house for higher income group people involves a good amount of budget. As in such type of houses, all the modern amenities are provided, so the planning needs to be done carefully. A designer needs to consider the availability of space, the rooms, kitchen, balconies, etc. In higher income group, carpet area of the houses is so large. In this case, the designer should try to make use of optimum utilisation of every room, open spaces, etc.

Furniture and Furnishing

Furniture is the most important factor that adds beauty and style to your home. Furniture brings about changes in the space and its functionality. The interior designers use furniture to establish a pleasing sense of order. On the other hand, furnishing refers to everything in a room including small paintings, flowers, etc. Furnishing include systematically providing furniture, curtains and other decorations in a room to enhance the aesthetic appeal of a home.

Historical Perspectives of Furniture and Furnishing

The concept of furniture first developed as early as 3100-2500 BC. People have made furniture since the Neolithic period. The excavation in Skara Brae, Ornkey, Scotland uncovered a settlement dating to 3215 BCE. Each house had evidence of stone furniture such as cupboards, beds and seating.

Development of furniture during different time periods is described below :

Ancient Greek Period The earliest Greek furniture was influenced by the boxy designs of Egypt but by the 4th and 5th BCE, the Greek designs became softer. Inlays and carvings were used. Stools were important pieces as was the couch which was used during the day for sitting and during night as bed. The earliest couches probably resembled Egyptian beds in structure and possibly in style.

Medieval Period In medieval times, many houses consisted of one large room, which was used for everything, so furnishing was limited to a table, some stools, a trunk or cabinet for storage and perhaps a bed. Medieval furniture was heavy with blocky legs. It was generally constructed from English oak. Folding chairs and stools, trestle tables with removable tops and beds with collapsible framework were usual.

Renaissance Period From the beginning of the renaissance in the early 15th century, there were changes in furniture forms that were to spread over Europe. Italian Renaissance furniture shows a strong architectural bias and the purpose of the piece, as in Roman furniture was subordinate to its form.

The furniture of the Italian Renaissance often restrained with beautiful, simple designs, carved in walnut. A type of chair called a 'Sagabello' was much favoured at this time in Italy. Chairs were high backed with cushion or upholstery. Tables were generally oblong, supported by columns, consoles (brackets) or terminal figures with a long central stretcher running from end to end.

The furniture of France was among the first to be influenced by the Italian Renaissance. The French furniture of the 16th Century was remarkably graceful and delicate, it was enriched with inlay of small plaques of figured marble and semi-precious stones, sometimes with inlay or marquetry of ivory, mother of pearl and different coloured wood's chairs were lighter in design. A specialised chair known as Caquetoire or Conversation Chair had a high narrow back and curved arms. The French furniture makers began to integrate their own styles into the furniture. As the Renaissance style spread to Netherlands and to England, less and less of the Italian influence was seen.

Different Styles of Furnitures

Egyptian Furniture It is primarily constructed using wood, but other materials were sometimes used such as leather and pieces were often adorned with gold, silver, ivory, ebony for decoration. The wood found in Egypt was not suitable for furniture, construction, so had to be imported from other places particularly Phoenicia. The earliest used seating furniture in the dynastic period was the stool.

Beds, stools, throne, chairs and boxes were chief forms of furniture. The beds may have been the earliest form, which were constructed of wood and consisted of simple framework supported on four legs. A flax cord, plaited, was lashed to the sides of the framework. The cords were woven together from opposite sides of the framework, a springy surface for the sleeper.

In the 18th dynasty (1567-1320 BCE), beds sloped up toward the head and a painted or carved wooden footboard prevented the sleeper from slipping down.

The footstools were made of wood. The royal footstool was painted with the figures of traditional enemies of Egypt, so that the pharaoh might symbolically treat his enemies under his feet. Carving of animals feet on straight chair legs were common. Tables, were almost unknown, a pottery or wooden stand supporting a flat basketwork tray held dishes for a meal and wooden stands held great pottery jars containing water or wine. Full chairs were much rare in early Egypt. Generally, the Egyptian furniture was light and easily transportable, its decoration was usually derived from religious symbols and stylistic change was very slow.

Roman Furniture It was based heavily on Greek furniture in style and construction. Roman furniture was contructed principally using wood, metal and stone with marble and limestone used for outside furniture. In Rome, the principal furniture forms were couches, chairs with and without arms, stools, tables, chest and boxes. Excellent evidence is found in mural paintings, relief carvings and literary descriptions.

Roman chairs were developed from Greek models. The arms chair was often of wickerwork, wood or stone. The couches were characterised by high back and sides. Tables with round and rectangular tops and three and four legs were common. Another type of smaller table was round or rectangular with only one central leg.

Rectangular footstools, sometimes with claw feet, were used with high chairs and couches. Pompeian walls painting show that plain, undecorated wooden tables and benches were used in kitchen and workshops. Similar to Greeks, Romans used tenons, dowels, nails and glue to join wooden pieces together and also practised veneering.

Jacobean Furniture An English style, Jacobean furniture was inspired by Elizabethan furniture. This style is very sturdy, large in size and made last. The furniture was generally square or rectangular and sat lower than previous styles. Furniture legs were narrower and many craftsmen created spiral turned legs to lighten appearance.

Baroque Style Furniture in Western Europe During 17th century, the Baroque style had a marked effect upon furniture design throughout Western Europe. Large wardrobes, cupboards and cabinets had twisted columns, broken pediments and heavy mouldings. In Baroque furniture, the details are related to the whole instead of a framework of unrelated surfaces. Each detail contributes to the harmonious movement of the overall design. The Baroque style was adopted in the 1620s. It was extended late into the 17th century, when the Germany and England began to develop it.

Early North American Furniture It dates to the early 20th Century in America. Furniture was more basic and made of necessity versus fancy artistic and detailed designs. The furniture consisted of basic dressers for storage. Simplistic chairs and stools were used for sitting. These were made of woods such as cherry or walnut as they were easily bent with steaming process.

Architectural Styles Furniture

Architectural style began in late 19th century. It was inspired by the churches. In planning and designing of furniture for the house, the architectural styles that were in use are detailed below as :

Biedermeir It is a furniture style of German derivation in the first half of the 19th century. The furniture is often plain and block like in form and borrows freely from many styles, particularly. French Empire, adding strength and comfort at the expense of grace and comfort.

Directoire It is a style of French furniture that spanned the end of French Revolution. Design for smaller scale and less ostentation.

Elizabethan It is a large furniture of severe form and style. It is characterised by heavy carvings as well as massive size.

Gothic It is a late medieval furniture. The heavy large pieces were generously carved in architectural motifs. Chest banded with decorative wrought iron large trestle tables, beds of estate and X frame chairs are the characteristics.

Baroque Furniture In this, furnishing and decoration reflected formal grandeur. Decorative motifs often boldly carved included beats from mythology, garlands of fruits and flowers and animal forms.

Mission It simple rectilinear furniture primarily of oak in which construction techniques are often exposed.

Rococo Style In 18th century, European furniture made of rich woods with elaborate scrollwork and curved forms.

Art 'NOUVEAU' This style is the new art of Europe developed about 1875 flowing nearly free from shapes from nature were carved and painted on furniture. An elongated slightly curved line that ends in a more abrupt, nearly whip like second curve is its most characteristic design.

Contemporary Trends in Furniture

The contemporary furniture trends refer to all modern or recent furniture design (from 1970 onwards) from all over the world. The aluminium and iron furniture are popular materials used in sleek and geometric contemporary designs.

Wall Finishes

As the name suggests 'wall finishes' is finish given to walls to enhance the interior or exterior look of the structure. Wall finishes have evolved from an aesthetic element meant to brighten and decorate a room to finish that serves as more of functional element. Wall finishes used for interiors are quite delicate and need maintenance. So, when selecting a wall finish it is important to get a feel for the entire space. The new contemporary trend has brought about a great deal of increase in the usage of various types of wall finishes.

The different types of wall finishes are given below as :

Cemented Plastered Finish It is prepared in the form of mortar with cement, sand and water in proper proportions and applied on masonry mutually to achieve a smooth finish or sand faced finish.

Plaster of Paris Finish It is a type of building material based on calcium sulphate hemihydrates. This is a smooth finish achieved by Plaster of Paris, generally applied on internal walls.

Gypsum Plaster Finish It is just like plaster of paris finish, but gypsum based material is used to prepare mortar. It is more durable and finer as compared to plaster of paris finish.

Cement Textured Finish It is a decorative finish, its mortar is prepared in cement based material. It is applied with sand faced plaster with a trowel and thereafter it is coloured with paint.

Marble Powder Finish It is a very smooth finish. It looks like marble flooring. This finish is obtained by mortar of marble powder, with cement and water. It is applied manually.

Designer Mirror Finish These are obtained by small pieces on walls to create mural like designs.

Coral Finish It is similar to plaster of paris finish and gypsum plaster finish. It is the name of type of plastering material. It gives a rough edgy finish.

Sand Textured Finish It is used to give fine texture to the wall. This type of wall finish is uncommon because its grains comes out.

Window and Window Treatments

Window originated from the term 'Vindauga' and it literally means 'wind eye'. In the early 13th century, the window was referred to as unglazed hole in the roof. A window is an opening in a wall or solid surface that allows the passage of light, if not closed or sealed air and sound. These are generally glazed or covered in some other transparent materials. Windows add to the decor of the room.

Types of Windows

There are several types of windows which are given as :

Single Windows It is the basic window with a single frame, it opens either inside or outside.

Double Hung Windows These are mostly the most common type of window. They open by sliding the bottom half of the window up or sliding the top half down. Double hung windows can be used to create movement in the home by opening the top portion of the windows on one side of the house and opening the lower portion of the window on the other side of the house.

Awning Windows These are also known as hopper windows. They are easy to clean and provide more security.

Rotating Windows These windows open by pivoting around a central point. They allow good ventilation, cleaning them is easy.

Fixed Pane Windows These do not open, it means they do not permit ventilation or easy cleaning, but their sealed edged protect against air infiltration.

Casement Windows These have hinged sash that swings in or out like a door comprising either side hung, a top hung or bottom hung.

Mullion Windows These consist of series of windows. Each window can be treated as a separate unit or unified into a single design.

Bay Windows These are three dimensional windows made by placing windows on the three walls that meet to form an alcove protruding outwards. They are generally large and give the room an illusion of spaciousness.

Ranch Windows These type of windows are high window set above eye level. They are provided basically to let the light in.

Window Treatments

Window treatments are used to control the degree to which windows perform their various functions. Window treatments are divided into three categories such as :

Hard Window Treatments These are made of hard materials like wood or vinyl such as shades, blinds and shutters.

Soft Window Treatments These are anything made of soft materials such as sheers, curtains, drapes and swags.

Layered Window Treatments A combination of both (hard and soft) is called a layered window treatment.

EXAM BASED QUESTIONS

1 **The interior design is**
(a) an organised way for any plan with some definite purpose.
(b) a systematic process of accomplishing some end.
(c) an art and a science of enhancing a healthier and more aesthetically pleasing environment for the people using space.
(d) All of the above

2 **The commonly used elements include**
(a) line (b) shape
(c) space (d) All of these

3 **The ……… lines express fluctuations of interest, uncertainty and indirected course.**
(a) curved (b) crooked (c) oblique (d) horizontal

4 **The proportion and scale**
(a) refers to the relationship of various parts of the design
(b) involves principle of design
(c) involves the relationship of object to the space
(d) Both (a) and (c)

5 **Rhythm is possible by the use of**
(a) repetition (b) radiation
(c) gradation (d) All of these

6 **Rhythm may carry the eye along smoothly flowing lines or it may force the attention abruptly here and there in order to convey the desired emotional affect.**
(a) variable rhythm
(b) oriented rhythm
(c) emphasis
(d) regular measured rhythm

7 **A progression of sizes is another technique to achieve rhythm. It is called**
(a) proportion (b) emphasis
(c) gradation (d) None of these

8 **It helps to create the interest to the most important things or spot in any arrangement. It is called**
(a) lines (b) emphasis
(c) rhythm (d) None of these

9 **If a pair of beautiful vases and an antique clock are put together in a place the beauty of both the things**
(a) lost (b) appearance
(c) neutralise (d) enchanced

10 **"However, common place one's life may be, it can be made bright and cheerful by the use of colour in the home." This is stated by**
(a) Rutt (b) Stella Saundaraja
(c) Crang and Rush (d) Mary Jean Alexander

11 **"Colour planning where feasible should be in terms of a whole unit, house apartment, factory and so on." This is stated by**
(a) Mary Jean Alexander (b) Rutt
(c) MJ Akbar (d) Crang and Rush

12 **"Colour is a quality of light, as seen by the eye, caused by light waves having different wave lengths." This is stated by**
(a) P Mehra
(b) Modern Century Encyclopedia
(c) Britanica
(d) Rutt

13 **"Unity or harmony is the expression of an agreeable combination of parts that produce a connected whole. When all other laws of design have been obeyed, unity is the inevitable result." This is stated by**
(a) Crang and Rush (b) Stella Saundaraja
(c) P Mehra (d) Rutt

14 **"Emphasis is the principle that directs us to have a centre of interest in any arrangement and a dominating idea, of colour form in any scheme." This is stated by**
(a) Ibid (b) Crang and Rush
(c) P Mehra (d) Rutt

15 **"Rhythm is disciplined movement marked by generally regular reoccurency of elements." This is stated by**
(a) Crang and Rush (b) HV Goldstein
(c) Mary Jean Alexander (d) S Saundararja

16 **"Balance is the relation of parts that creates a sense of repose and completion in a room." This is state by**
(a) HV Goldstein (b) Ibid
(c) Mary Jean Alexander (d) P Mehra

17 **"Balance is the principle of design that produces a feeling of rest and contentment." This is stated by**
(a) Ibid (b) K Alexander
(c) Crang and Rush (d) S Saundararja

18 **"Scale is the relationship of objects to each other and to people." This is stated by**
(a) Rutt (b) Friedman Pile Wilson
(c) Crang and Rush (d) Ibid

19 **"Good scale is the result of a pleasing relationship among the components of a space or room and between them and the whole." This is stated by**
(a) Alexander (b) Rutt
(c) S Saundararja (d) Ibid

20 "Proportion means the relationship of sizes or areas to one another or to a whole." This is stated by
(a) S Saundararja (b) Rutt
(c) Ibid (d) P Mehra

21 "Proportion is the law of relationships which demands that all space divisions be pleasingly related to each other and to the whole." This is the view of
(a) Rutt (b) Crang and Rush
(c) P Mehra (d) Ibid

22 "To make something in a way which exactly repeats the way such that a thing has been done, involves no design at all, but deciding to make changes, usually hoped to be improvements, is the act of a designer." This is stated by
(a) P Mehra (b) Friedman
(c) S Saundararaja (d) JF Pile

23 "The purpose of design is to make things beautiful" is stated by
(a) Wilson (b) Pile
(c) Friedman (d) All of these

24 A combination of vertical or horizontal and diagonal lines produce ……… form.
(a) square (b) triangle
(c) parallel (d) circle

25 Forms are closely related with
(a) rectangle (b) line
(c) circle (d) square

26 When black colour is added to any colour it is called
(a) chroma (b) tint
(c) shade (d) colour value

27 Colours known as primary colours are
(a) red and green (b) red, yellow and green
(c) red, blue and orange (d) red, green and blue

28 Colour Model is also called
(a) Colour System (b) Colour Space
(c) Colour Area (d) Both (a) and (b)

29 Overlapping of two primary colours forms a
(a) tertiary colour (b) mixed colour
(c) secondary colour (d) Both (a) and (b)

30 To form other colours like brown, peach, purple, etc., colours that are required are
(a) red, yellow and green (b) red, blue and orange
(c) green, blue and yellow (d) red, green and blue

31 When red and blue are combined together, they form
(a) yellow (b) magenta
(c) orange (d) purple

32 Amount of lightness or darkness in colour is
(a) complementary (b) hue
(c) value (d) dullness

33 Secondary colour made by mixing two primary colours is/are
(a) green (b) orange
(c) purple (d) All of these

34 Feel or appearance of any surface is
(a) texture (b) shape
(c) feel (d) line

35 Colours found opposite to each other on the colour wheel are
(a) complementary colours
(b) achromatic colours
(c) monochromatic colours
(d) analogous colours

36 The strength and weakness of any colour is called
(a) saturation (b) shade
(c) value (d) intensity

37 The simplex house plan includes the use of
(a) glass (b) steel
(c) timbers (d) All of these

38 ……… is an important sector that contributes greatly in the economic growth of a nation.
(a) Secondary (b) Construction
(c) Primary (d) Tertiary

39 In the construction, the numerous clients worked together are
(a) property builders (b) property developers
(c) material suppliers (d) All of these

40 What should be considered for planning for low income groups?
(a) Stick to simple geometry
(b) Calculate the overall cost
(c) Initially invest in quality building material
(d) All of the above

41 "An awareness of good design becomes a part of the individual and his character the way he feels, think and sees his world." This is stated by
(a) Ibid (b) Friedman
(c) Rutt (d) P Mehra

42 "An appreciation of beauty and good design must become an integral part of one's life entering each part of every day and each activity that takes place." This is according to
(a) Rutt (b) David B Van Dommelen
(c) OD Rush (d) Friedman

43 "Design is defined as any arrangement of line, form, colour, space, value and texture." This is stated by
(a) Friedman (b) Crang and Rush
(c) Stella Soundararaj (d) P Mehra

44 'Interior Design' has been written by
(a) Rutt
(b) Mary Jean Alexander
(c) P Mehra
(d) A Friedman, JF Pile and F Wilson

45 'A Text Book of House Hold Arts' is written by
(a) Boulby (b) P Mehra
(c) Stella Soundararaj (d) Rutt

46 'Designing Interior Environment' is written by
(a) OD Rush (b) Mary Jean Alexander
(c) Friedman (d) Ibid

47 'Designing and Decorating Interiors' is written by
(a) David B Van Dommelen (b) Friedman
(c) Mary Jean Alexander (d) Rutt

48 "Good design is not personal, but it is intended to be useful to people everywhere in the present and in the future." This is stated by
(a) Crang and Rush (b) Rutt
(c) Mery Jean Alexander (d) Friedman

49 Flow and movement which creates interests in design?
(a) Balance (b) Repetition
(c) Rhythm (d) Proportion

50 Furniture adds .... to your home.
(a) beauty and style
(b) space and its functionality
(c) pleasing sense of order
(d) enhance aesthetic appeal

51 The concept of furniture was first developed in
(a) 3200-3100 BC (b) 3100-2500 BC
(c) 1200-500 BC (d) 3300-1200 BC

52 The Egyptian furniture primarily constructed using
(a) metal (b) stone
(c) wood (d) iron

53 Which of the following statements is/are incorrect about the Roman furniture?
(a) Generally, the furniture was light and easily transportable.
(b) The principal furniture forms were couches, chairs with and without arms.
(c) The furniture was heavy with blocky legs.
(d) Both (a) and (c)

54 The Italian Renaissance Furniture showed
(a) strong architectural bias
(b) restrained with beautiful simple designs
(c) light, cheap and easily portable
(d) All of the above

55 The French Renaissance Furniture was
(a) panels were beautifully carved with graceful figures
(b) flemish scrolls were conspicuous
(c) solidly built with the structure of Gothic period
(d) All of the above

56 The Jacobean Furniture Style was
(a) very sturdy
(b) large in size
(c) generally square or rectangular
(d) All of the above

57 A bay window
(a) is three dimensional window
(b) is generally large
(c) gives the room an illusion of spaciousness
(d) All of the above

58 Which finish should be applied to wood to enhance its grain appearance?
(a) Wood stain (b) Varnish
(c) Latex (d) Shellac

59 Which paint finish is not used for ceiling?
(a) Textured finish (b) Roller finish
(c) Duco finish (d) None of these

60 Consider the following statements with regard to cement textured finish.
(a) It is a decorative finish
(b) Its mortar is prepared from cement based material
(c) It is applied with sand
(d) All of the above

61 State which is/are true.
(a) Curvilinear rhythm occurs naturally in flowering lines of arrangements of western, trumpet vine, nasturtiums, petunias or verbena.
(b) Rhythm in interior walls occurs in the relation of doors, windows and other architectural features.
(c) Radiating rhythm occurs in round or triangular flower arrangement where the lines radiate from one place.
(d) All of the above

62 State which is/are true.
(a) Form lines textures and colours should be harmonious.
(b) In seeking unity the room can never turn art to be dull and monotonous.
(c) One colour should dominate in quantity usually another colour should be secondary in quantity. The third colour least in quantity.
(d) All of the above

63 Which of the following statement(s) is/are correct?
(a) Radiating rhythm occurs in round or triangular flower arrangement where the lines radiate from one place.
(b) All types of rhythm are based on movement and repetition.
(c) Rhythm in interior walls occur in the relation of doors, windows and other architectural features.
(d) All of the above

64 Which of the following statement(s) is/are correct?
(a) Yellow and red are considered to be warm colours.
(b) A monochromatic colour scheme consists of using one colour is varying values or intensities.
(c) Complementary colours are directly opposite to each other on the colour wheel.
(d) All of the above

65 An example of tertiary colour scheme could be
(a) Red : Bluish Violet + Bluish Green
(b) Green : Red + Yellowish Orange
(c) Sun Orange : Yellowish Green + Bluish Green
(d) Reddish Violet : Bluish Violet + Yellowish Orange

66 **Which of the following analogous colour scheme makes using of following colours in a colour wheel?**
(a) Two or three colour adjacent to each other
(b) Two colour opposite to each other
(c) Three colours forming a triangle
(d) Half of colour wheel

67 **Which of the following statements is/are correct?**
(a) Space planning is a fundamental element of the interior design process.
(b) It is a complex process.
(c) Space planning can bring a sense of balance between beauty and comfort.
(d) All of the above

68 Consider the following statements with regard to texture.

Statement I It mainly deals with surfaces.

Statement II The texture is broadly divided into two types.

Codes
(a) Statement I is correct
(b) Statement II is correct
(c) Both the statements are correct
(d) Neither statement I nor II is correct

69 Consider the following statements with regard to traditional house plan.

Statement I These are the old fashioned house.

Statement II They are the blend of old fashioned house with modern architecture.

Codes
(a) Statement I is correct
(b) Statement II is correct
(c) Both the statements are correct
(d) Neither statement I nor II is correct

70 **Which of the following are the characteristics of Roman furniture?**
(a) It was based heavily on Greek furniture style
(b) It was principally constructed using wood, metal and stone
(c) Marbles and limestones were used for outside furniture
(d) All of the above

71 **Variable rhythm dominate in**
1. natural landscaping.
2. diagonal flower arrangement.
3. curvilinear flower arrangement.
4. oriental rugs.

(a) 1 and 2 (b) 1 and 4
(c) 1, 2, 3 and 4 (d) All of these

72 **Some ways of securing emphasis is/are**
1. by repeating a design or idea
2. by means of large or usual forms
3. focusing move light than elsewhere
4. unusual texture or bright colours

Codes
(a) 1 and 2 (b) 1 and 4
(c) 1, 2, 3 and 4 (d) 1, 2 and 3

73 **Accessories should be placed at the important parts in a room. Because they**
1. create focal centres
2. hold attention at points of interest
3. simplify design
4. unify design

Codes
(a) 1 and 2 (b) 1 and 4 (c) 1, 2, 3 and 4 (d) 1, 2 and 3

74 **Emphasis applies in several ways to the exterior of a house. Which of the options will create it?**
1. One large dominate block
2. Wings smaller
3. One surface material dominates
4. Wings lower than the main body

Codes
(a) 1 and 2 (b) 1 and 4
(c) 1, 2, 3 and 4 (d) 1, 2 and 3

75 **Rhythm occurs in**
1. regular repeated movement.
2. variable transitional movement.

Codes
(a) Only 1 (b) Only 2
(c) Both 1 and 2 (d) None of these

76 **According to Rutt, correct scale or consistency is size indispensable in**
1. garden design 2. exterior house design
3. interior design 4. furniture design

Codes
(a) 1 and 2 (b) 1 and 4
(c) 1, 2 and 3 (d) All of these

77 **Line movements create**
1. rhythm 2. confusion

Codes
(a) Only 1 (b) Only 2
(c) Both 1 and 2 (d) None of these

78 **How are colours classified? Indicate the correct sequence.**
1. Primary 2. Secondary
3. Quaternary 4. Tertiary
5. Intermediate

Codes
(a) 3, 5 and 4 (b) 1, 2 and 4
(c) 1, 2 and 5 (d) 5, 1 and 2

79 **Which of the following colours are cool colours?**
1. Bluish Green 2. Reddish Orange
3. Blue 4. Yellow Orange
5. Green

Codes
(a) 1, 2 and 3 (b) 2, 3 and 4
(c) 1, 3 and 5 (d) 3, 4 and 5

80 Arrange in correct sequence, the stage of an interior design process.

1. Bubble diagram 2. Schematic diagram
3. Detaileddrawing 4. Construction administration
5. Execution

Codes

(a) 2, 3, 1, 5, 4 (b) 2, 1, 3, 5, 4
(c) 1, 5, 3, 2, 4 (d) 1, 2, 3, 5, 4

81 Which among the following are neutral colours?

1. Black 2. Red 3. Green 4. White

Codes

(a) 1, 2 and 3 (b) 1 and 2
(c) 1 and 3 (d) 1 and 4

82 An intermediate colour is made by mixing

1. primary colour
2. its adjoining secondary colour
3. mixing complementary colour
4. by adding black or white

Codes

(a) All of these (b) 1, 2 and 3
(c) 1 and 2 (d) 1 and 4

83 Intensity or chroma in colour means

1. brightness 2. dullness
3. soft colour 4. hard colour

Codes

(a) 1, 3 and 4 (b) 1 and 4
(c) 1, 2 and 3 (d) 1 and 2

84 In interior decoration warm advancing colours should be kept

1. in background 2. in foreground

Codes

(a) Only 1 (b) Only 2
(c) Neither 1 nor 2 (d) None of these

85 Match the following.

List I	List II
A. Colours with predominance of blue	1. Warm
B. Yellowish green	2. Cool hues
C. Blue-green	3. Warm hues
D. Seem to advance	4. Are considered as cool
E. Seem to recede	5. Cool

Codes

	A	B	C	D	E		A	B	C	D	E
(a)	3	1	4	5	2	(b)	1	2	4	3	5
(c)	4	1	5	3	2	(d)	5	4	2	1	3

Directions (Q No. 86-95) *In the questions given below are two statements labelled as Assertion (A) and Reason (R). In the context of the two statements which one the following is correct?*

Codes

(a) A is true, but R is the correct explanation of A
(b) A is true, but R is not the correct explanation of A
(c) Both A and R are false
(d) A is true, but R is false

86 **Assertion** (A) Painting walls and ceilings with light colour, matt finish paint will reduce the size of the room.

Reason (R) The matt finish even though the colour is light will absorb the light by creating illusion of advancing effect.

87 **Assertion** (A) Interior design introduces people to beauty, relaxation and modernism.

Reason (R) It is an organised way for any plan with some definite purpose.

88 **Assertion** (A) The oblique lines convey a sense of reserve and restraint.

Reason (R) These lines add grace and flexibility.

89 **Assertion** (A) Space is one of the most important element of interior design.

Reason (R) Space acts as a foundation on which the entire design plan is built.

90 **Assertion** (A) Colour establish an aesthetic connection between objects and sets the mood.

Reason (R) It is broadly divided into two types.

91 **Assertion** (A) Harmony has four aspects.

Reason (R) Harmony means disunity of compositions.

92 **Assertion** (A) Chroma is the third dimension of colour which indicates brightness or dullness of colours.

Reason (R) It refers to strength, intensity, purity or saturation of a colour.

93 **Assertion** (A) The yellow colour is cheerful colour closely related to the Sun.

Reason (R) It is not connected to richness, royalty and invoke feeling of calmness.

94 **Assertion** (A) The single complementary colour scheme is pairing of two or more colours.

Reason (R) The triad scheme is the combination of primary colours.

95 **Assertion** (A) Double hung windows are common type of windows.

Reason (R) These are also known as hopper windows.

Directions (Q. Nos. 96-100) *Read the following passage and answer the questions that follow.*

Interior design is the process of shaping the experience of interior space, through the manipulation of spatial volume as well as surface treatment. Not to be confused with interior decoration, interior design draws on aspects of environmental psychology, architecture and product design in addition to traditional decoration.

Interior design provides a soul to a building or space and makes a space more functional, pleasant and livable. Interior design plays a big role in the everyday life. It introduces people to beauty, relaxation and modernism.

Space for residential and commercial places is shrinking due to rapid urbanisation. This anomalous situation calls for professional help to make the living and working space more comfortable, beautiful and practical. Earlier, it was the task of an architect to do the entire exteriors along with the interiors of a house, office or any other functionally useful edifice. Nowadays, people have become more and more particular about the designs and the layout of the living or working area. This has led to an increasing requirement for professionals in interior designing.

The popularity of interior designing as a discipline is not confined to urban cities, but it has rapidly spread to small town and cities across the nation.

This is largely because of the changing lifestyle of people and they want to customise their residence with the help of an expert who can understand their taste and preference. Interior design is a growing industry with good job prospects and a good salary.

Interior design is a multi-faceted profession that brings together technical expertise and a comprehensive understanding of design to enhance the function and quality of interior spaces. An interior designer can work in these fields: Architects: Architects plan and design houses, factories, office buildings and other structures. Art Director: Art directors are responsible for the visual style and images in magazines, newspapers, product packaging, movie and television productions.

Crafts and Fine Artists. Craft and fine artists use a variety of materials and techniques to create art for sale and exhibition. Craft artists create handmade objects, such as pottery, glassware, textiles and other objects that are designed to be functional.

Fine artists, including painters, sculptors and illustrators, create original works of art for their aesthetic value, rather than for a functional one. Fashion Designer: Fashion designers create original clothing, accessories and footwear. They sketch designs, select fabrics and patterns and give instructions on how to make the products they design. Floral Designers: Floral designers also called florists, cut and arrange live, dried and silk flowers and greenery to make decorative displays.

Graphic Designers: Graphic designers create visual concepts, using computer software or by hand, to communicate ideas that inspire, inform and captivate consumers. They develop the overall layout and production design for various applications such as advertisements, brochures, magazines and corporate reports.

Industrial Designers : Industrial designers develop the concepts for manufactured products, such as cars, home appliances and toys.

Landscape Architects: Landscape architects design parks and the outdoor spaces of campuses, recreational facilities, businesses, private homes and other open areas.

96 An interior design

(a) is a process of shaping the experience of interior space
(b) provides soul to a building
(c) makes space more functional and pleasant
(d) All of the above

97 Why there is a need for interior design?

(a) Space for residential and commercial places is shrinking.
(b) People have become more and more aware about the design and layout of the living area.
(c) The popularity of interior design is confined to metropolitan cities only.
(d) Both (a) and (b)

98 Interior design is considered as a multi-faceted because it

(a) brings technical expertise
(b) gives knowledge about comprehensive understanding of design
(c) helps an aspiring designer to pursue a career in different fields
(d) All of the above

99 Consider the following statements about fashion designer.

Statement I **Fresh designers create original clothing, accessories and footwear.**

Statement II **They sketch designs, select fabrics and patterns.**

Codes

(a) Statement I is true
(b) Statement II is true
(c) Both the statements are true
(d) Neither statement I nor II is true

100 Which of the following is not the characteristic of graphic designer?

(a) They create visual concepts using computer software.
(b) They design parks and outer spaces of campuses, recreational facilities, private homes and other open areas.
(c) They develop overall layout and production design for various applications such as magazines, advertisements, home appliances, etc.
(d) Both (a) and (b)

PREVIOUS YEARS' QUESTIONS

July 2018

1 Which of the following combination of colours on the Prang Colour Wheel make a complementary colour scheme?

1. Red and Blue
2. Blue and Orange
3. Red and Green
4. Yellow and Purple

Codes

(a) 1, 2 and 3
(b) 1, 2 and 4
(c) 1, 3 and 4
(d) 2, 3 and 4

2 Match the following.

List I	List II
A. Proportion	1. Furniture joint
B. Butt	2. Greek oblong
C. Glare	3. Colour dimension
D. Valve	4. Surface ornamentation
E. Pattern	5. Illumination
	6. Accessories

Codes

	A	B	C	D	E
(a)	2	1	5	3	4
(b)	3	2	4	6	1
(c)	1	4	6	3	2
(d)	6	5	3	1	2

November 2017

3 **Assertion** (A) Opposite of advancing colour is receding colours.

Reason (R) Those colours which are near to red are receding colours and those near to blue are advancing colours.

Codes

(a) Both A is true, but R is false
(b) Both A is false, but R is true
(d) Both A and R are false
(d) Both A and R are ture

June 2015

4 Match the following.

List I (Lines)	List II (Characteristics)
A. Vertical lines	1. Gracefulness
B. Horizontal lines	2. Movement
C. Curved lines	3. Rest
D. Diagonal lines	4. Activity
	5. Excitement

Codes

	A	B	C	D
(a)	3	5	2	4
(b)	4	3	1	2
(c)	1	2	4	3
(d)	2	4	3	5

December 2014

5 Which element of Art is used when shapes, colours and lines are repeated?

(a) Emphasis (b) Focal point
(c) Balance (d) Pattern

ANSWERS

Exam Based Questions

1 (d)	2 (d)	3 (b)	4 (d)	5 (d)	6 (c)	7 (c)	8 (b)	9 (a)	10 (b)
11 (a)	12 (b)	13 (a)	14 (d)	15 (c)	16 (c)	17 (c)	18 (b)	19 (a)	20 (a)
21 (b)	22 (b)	23 (d)	24 (b)	25 (b)	26 (c)	27 (d)	28 (d)	29 (c)	30 (d)
31 (b)	32 (c)	33 (d)	34 (a)	35 (a)	36 (d)	37 (d)	38 (b)	39 (d)	40 (d)
41 (a)	42 (b)	43 (c)	44 (d)	45 (c)	46 (b)	47 (a)	48 (d)	49 (c)	50 (a)
51 (b)	52 (c)	53 (d)	54 (d)	55 (d)	56 (d)	57 (d)	58 (c)	59 (a)	60 (d)
61 (d)	62 (d)	63 (d)	64 (d)	65 (c)	66 (a)	67 (d)	68 (c)	69 (a)	70 (d)
71 (a)	72 (c)	73 (c)	74 (c)	75 (c)	76 (c)	77 (c)	78 (b)	79 (c)	80 (d)
81 (d)	82 (c)	83 (d)	84 (b)	85 (c)	86 (a)	87 (b)	88 (d)	89 (a)	90 (b)
91 (c)	92 (b)	93 (d)	94 (c)	95 (d)	96 (d)	97 (d)	98 (d)	99 (c)	100 (d)

Previous Years' Questions

1 (d)	2 (a)	3 (a)	4 (c)	5 (d)

CHAPTER 22

Product Design and Ergonomics

Product design is all about manufacturing a product that will attract the customers and also provide value for them. It is a critical factor in organisational success. It is of great significance because it brings together three important issues, the concept, the package and the process. The ergonomics is also known as human factor engineering, is the science of refining the design of product to optimise them for human use.

In this Chapter

- Product Design
  - Diffusion of Innovation
- Ergonomics
  - Anthropometry
  - Man-Machine
  - Body Mechanics
  - Time Motion Study
  - Energy Studies

Product Design

Product design is commonly defined as a holistic approach of building a new product from start to finish. It is a technical field. The product design encompasses everything from doing market research, identifying problems, development designing, solutions and everything in between. It is the process of creating a new product for sale to the customer. The product design has many fields of application, such as medical devices, tableware, jewellery, food preservation appliances, sports and leisure, furniture etc.

There are some essential requirements for a good product design in order to achieve customer's satisfaction such as :

- The product should function correctly.
- It should have desired degree of reliability.
- It should have pleasant appearance. Colour and the surface finish play an important role in product design.
- Product design should be such that it is easy to achieve accessibility for services.
- It should possess desired degree of accuracy.
- It should be sufficiently rugged to withstand all but exceptionally rough handling.
- It should be of reasonable price to compete with other products in the market.

Product Design Thinking Process

Before understanding the product design thinking process it is important to understand the term design thinking. In simple terms, the design thinking is a methodology that aims to tackle highly complex problems. Design thinking process fosters an outside approach box, with great emphasis on creativity, innovation and the needs of the users. The design thinking process is all about outcomes. It provides a non-linear series of steps that one can follow to come up with innovation, actionable ideas/solutions. These should be desirable for users, viable for business and technology feasible.

The design thinking process has five stages which are discussed below :

Stage I : Empathise

In this stage, one has to gain an empathic understanding of the problem trying to solve. This involves consulting experts to find out more about the area of concern through observing, engaging and empathises with people to understand their experiences and motivations as well as immersing yourself in the physical environment.

This helps to gain you a deeper personal understanding of the issues involved. Empathy is crucial to human centred design process, such as design thinking. Empathy allows design thinkers to set-aside their own assumptions about the world in order to gain insight into users and their needs. At this stage a substantial amount of information is gathered.

Stage II : Define

The problem at this stage, you put together the information you have created during the empathise stage. This is where you analyse your observation and synthesise them in order to define the core problems that you identified. Define the problem as problem statement in a human centred manner.

The define stage will help the designers gather ideas to establish features, functions and any other elements that will allow them to solve the problems. At the very least allow users to resolve issues themselves with the minimum of difficulty. In the define stage, "you will start to progress to the third stage, ideate, by asking questions which can help you look for ideas and for solutions."

Stage III : Ideate

During the third stage of the design thinking process the designers are ready to start generating ideas. The ideation phase is a judgement free zone where the group is encouraged to venture away from the norm, to explore new angles and to think outside box. Throughout this stage of the decision thinking process you will continuously refer back to your problem statement.

Stage IV : Prototype

In the fourth stage of decision thinking process you will turn down your ideas from stage three into prototype. The prototype stage turn your ideas into something tangible which can be tested on real uses. It allows you to gather feedback before you go ahead and develop the whole product. This ensures that the final decision actually solves the user's problem. Thus, this is an experimental stage and the aim is to identify best possible solution for the problems identified during first three stages.

Stage V : Test

During the testing phase, you will observe your target users or representative users. You gather feedback on how your users felt. The testing phase quickly highlights any design flaws that need to be addressed. Even during this stage, the alterations and refinements are made in order to rule out problems' solutions and derive at deep understanding of the product and its users as possible.

Benefits of Design Thinking Process

The design thinking process has some benefits such as :

- It encourages creative problem solving. It pushes you to redefine the problem space and seek out the challenge that's really worth solving
- It brings multi-disciplinary teams together, breakdown silos and encourages people to collaborate and challenge their assumptions.
- It not only help designers to come up with ground breaking products, but it also fosters a culture of innovation and user centricity at every level of business.
- The design thinking process offers a proven competitive advantage.

Diffusion of Innovation

The diffusion of innovation is all about understanding trends and factoring in consumer tendency groups like influences, early adopters and laggards. The diffusion of innovation is a theory built on the premise that any commercial consumer market place has different types of customers, who vary on their enthusiasm for a particular product and for trying out that product.

The diffusion of innovation theory was developed by **EM Rogers** in 1962.

The economist have placed consumers into five different adopter categories when citing about diffusion of innovation.

These are as follows :

Innovators These are people who want to be the first to try the innovation. They are venturesome and interested in new ideas. These people are willing to take risks. They are often the first to develop new ideas.

Early adopters These are the people who represent opinion leaders. They enjoy leadership roles and embrace change opportunities. They are already aware of the need to change and very comfortable in adopting new ideas. They do not need information to convince them to change.

Early Majority These people are rarely leaders but they do adopt new ideas before the average person. They typically need to see evidence that the innovation works before they are willing to adopt it. Strategies to appeal to this population include success stories and the evidence of the innovation effectiveness.

Late Majority These people are skeptical of change and will only adopt an innovation after it has been tried by the majority. Strategies to appeal to this population include information on how many other people have tried the innovation and have adopted it successfully.

Laggards These people are bound by tradition and very conservative. They are very skeptical of change and are the hardest group to bring on board. Strategies to appeal to this population includes statistics fear appeals and pressure from people in the other adopter groups.

The diffusion of innovation explains the rate at which new ideas and technology spread. The diffusion of innovation theory is used extensively by marketers to understand the rate at which consumers are likely to adopt a new product or service.

In other words, for businesses looking to roll out new products, diffusion of innovation can help spell the difference between a successful product launch and a failed one. It allows the designers and marketers to examine, why it is that some inferior products are successful when some superior products are not.

The diffusion of innovation involves certain processes. These are discussed below :

Knowledge This is the stage at which the adopter is first exposed to the innovation itself. They do not have enough information to make a decision to purchase on and have not yet been sufficiently inspired to find out more. At this stage, marketers will be looking to increase awareness of the product and provide enough education that the prospective adopter move to the second stage

Persuasion This is the point at which the prospective adopter is open to the idea of purchase. They are actively seeking information which will inform their eventual decision. This is the stage at which marketers will be seeking to convey the benefits of the product in detail. There will be a conscious effort to sell the product to someone at this stage of the diffusion of innovation.

Decision At this stage eventually the adopter must make a decision. They will weigh up the pros and cons of adoption and either accept the innovation or reject it.

Implementation This stage is when the adopter makes a decision as to whether or not the product is actually useful to them. They may also seek out further information to either support the use of the product or to better understand the product in context. This phase suggests the designers and marketers alike need to consider the ownership process in detail.

Confirmation This is the stage at which the user evaluates their decisions and decides whether they will keep using the product or abandon use of the product. This phase can only be ended by abandonment otherwise it is continual. This phase will normally involve a personal examination of the product and also social one. The users will seek information from their peers, colleagues and friends etc.

Design Communication

Design communication is a mixed discipline between design and information development which is concerned with how media intervention such as printed, crafted communication with the people. The design communication must achieve a reaction or get customer to see a product in a genuine way to attract sales or get message across.

The design communication seeks to attract, inspire, create desires and motivate people to respond to messages. It is with a view making a favourable impact. This impact can be to the bottom line of the commissioning body, which can either to build a brand or move sales. The process of design communication involves strategic business thinking using market research, creativity and technical skills. It also involves the knowledge of colour page, layout, topography and creating visuals hierarchies.

Communication designers translate ideas and information through a variety of media. The talents lie not only in the traditional skills of the hand, but also in their ability to think strategically in design and marketing terms, in order to establish credibility and influence audiences through communication.

Ergonomic Considerations

Ergonomic consideration in design is defined as the relationship between man and machine and the application of anatomical, physiological and psychological principles to solve the problems arising from man-machine relationship. The ergonomic consideration into product machine, equipment component design as well as work environment takes into account both psychological and physical needs of the users helps to enhance user efficiency, satisfaction and productivity. The ergonomics can optimise both human performance and the use of technology for improved efficiencies and reduced costs.

Ergonomics

Ergonomics is the science which deals with relationship between man and his working environment. It takes care of factors governing the physical and mental strain.

Ergonomics is the study of how humans interact with man made objects. The word ergonomic is derived from the Greek word '*ergon*' meaing work and '*nomos*' meaning laws or usage. Ergonomics is relevant in many fields, it is commonly applied to workplace environment.

The **International Labour Organisation** (ILO) has defined ergonomics as "the application of human biological Science in conjunction with engineering sciences, to the worker and his working environment so as to attain maximum satisfaction for the work which at the same time enhances productivity."

The word ergonomics was independently used in 1949 by a British scientist **KR H Murrell**. The modern ergonomics contribute to the design and evaluation of work systems and products. In earlier times an engineer designed a machine or products, but now a days design is a team effort.

Significance of Ergonomics

The ergonomists generally has an important role to play at the conceptual phase and in detailed design as well as in prototyping and the evaluation of existing products and facilities.

Ergonomics needs to be considered in the design of virtually any product, system or environment. Failure to do so may lead to designs which do not fit the physical, psychological or sociological needs of the users, leading to ineffective, inefficient or unsafe designs, which are to be commercially successful. Ergonomics can be applied in all schemes of human activity, be it in offices, factories, shops etc.

Scope of Ergonomics

Some of the areas where ergonomics has been successfully applied are as :

- Design of furniture, seats, rests and steps for operators
- Design of tools jigs and fixtures
- Design in equipment, power and hand tools
- Improvement in working conditions and environments
- Computation of relaxation allowances for workers
- Selection training and placement of personnel
- Motivation to workers.

The fundamental themes of ergonomics such as user-centred design, user friendly inclusive design and usability have become buzzwords within the design industry. The ergonomics methods can be applied at the earliest stages of the design process, defining user needs and identifying opportunities for innovation.

Thus, the ergonomics aim is to ensure that the working situation is in harmony with the activities of the worker. It helps in developing most comfortable conditions related to climate, lighting, ventilation and noise level.

Areas of Study Under Ergonomics

Ergonomics is a wide concept. Areas of study under ergonomics are anthropometry, man-machine relationship, environmental relationships, factors affecting physiological cost of work, body mechanics, functional design of work place, time and motion study, energy studies, etc.

Their detailed description is given below :

Anthropometry

Anthropometry is the scientific study of the measurements and proportions of human body. **Alphouse Bertillon** is credited as the father of anthropometrics. It includes the measurement such as height, elbow, wrist, length etc., of human beings. The factors which affect the anthropometric measurements include gender, ethnicity, growth and development, ageing, social and occupation as well as clothing and personal equipment.

The word anthropometry is derived from the Greek words '*anthropas*' meaning man and '*metron*' means measure. Anthropometric data are used in ergonomics to specify the physical dimensions of workspaces, equipment, furniture and clothing so as to fit the task to man and also to ensure that physical mismatch between the dimensions of equipment and products and the corresponding user dimensions are avoided.

According to **Encyclopaedia of Britannica**, "anthropometry is a systematic collection of measurements of the human body." The human body dimensions vary a significant amount from one individual to the next by differences in shapes and sizes of various body parts. Anthropometry can be used to examine the different ways that engineers and scientists can measure the human body.

Anthropometry is significant to interior designer, as anthropometrics are tools which aid them to work out how high or how far an average male or female may reach in relative comfort.

These factors need to be considered when designing, joinery or cabinetry, furniture planning circulation spaces, work spaces accessible spaces and to generally make the user comfortable in their interior environment.

These anthropometric measurements are taken as per the average human being measurements and drawings are human being performing various functions and movements. Thus, anthropometry has special importance because of the emergence of complex work systems. Where knowledge of the physical dimensions of man with accuracy is important.

Man-Machine Relationship

Human factors are a system concerned with the relationship among human beings, work place or work environment and machines. All man-machine systems are produced with some objective in view.

There is another aspect of man-machine system which though not strictly a part of it, effects the system performance to a great extent. This is the system environment or what we call as working conditions. The proper integration of man and machine which is beneficial for human operator and enhances the overall system performance. There are certain characteristics of man-machine which are as follows :

- The man-machine consists of the man, the machine and system environment.
- It has specific inputs and outputs which are appropriately balanced.
- It is variable in size and complexity and is dynamic in performance.
- It is essentially artifical by nature and is specifically developed to fulfil some purpose or specific aims.
- The subsystem of man-machine interact with and effects the other parts.
- Environmental factors or system environment effects system performance.

The man-manchine becomes more efficient when inputs or outputs are adequately balanced.

Classification of Man-Machine

The man-machine can be classified depending upon the size and complexity into the following types :

Manual They are directed by man. They are flexible in nature and small in size. Simple tools and equipments are used and the efficiency is dependent upon the human factor. A large difference is possible in manual system as every worker may select various methods to do the same job.

Mechanical They are more complex and flexible in comparison to manual. The machine component is power driven and human activity is information processing, decision making and controlling , they are known as semi-automatic systems. They have components which are well-integrated. An automobile tool operated by driver or operator are good examples of this.

Automatic It is complex in which all functions are performed by automatic devices known as automatic system. Operational functions are sensing information, processing decision-making and action. It is completely inflexible in nature and cannot be adopted to uses other than the one for which it has to be designed.

The human element performs the job of monitoring, programming the function, maintenance and upkeep. An automobile telephone exchange, a digital computer and automatic screw cutting machines are examples of this.

Environmental Relationships

The environment can be termed as a man's closest surrounding which he can manipulate for his survival. If this surrounding is wrongly manipulated, it may lead to unsafe situations rising and making it difficult for man's survival. Hazards as a results of the poorly managed surrounding can hinder employeess productivity rate and lead to low morale. This makes the workplace environment crucial determinant of the employees performance , morale and productivity. The workplace entails an environment in which the worker performs his work, if there is effective workplace environment then results can be achieved as expected by management. Task performed in the workplace can be directly affected by the physical environment where the task is being performed.

The physical environment as an aspect of the workplace environment has direct impact on the human sense and can slow down change in interpersonal interactions and also productivity satisfaction level. Lighting and other factors such as ergonomic furniture has also been found to have positive influence on employees health and consequently on productivity.

The ambient features in office environment such as lighting, temperature, existence of windows and free air movements etc., influence employee's attitudes, behaviours, satisfaction, performance and productivity. If the working environment is congenial, performance shall be increased, absentism can be reduced with in turn increase employees performance and productivity.

Factors Affecting Psychological Cost of Work

According to an International Labour Organisation in their resolution 1975 stated that "work should not only respect worker's lives and health but also give them free time for rest and leisure."

Work is good for mental health, but a negative working environment can lead to physical and mental health problems.

The depression, stress of work, least managerial support, inflexible working hours jobs carrying higher personal risk than other employees, lack of team cohesion, all these factors have a great psychological effect on individuals, work and its productivity.

Bullying and psychological harassment are the commonly work related streses which the workers face. The relationship problem with superior is the most common reason for office stress. Another reason could be the relationship problem with colleagues.

Now a days families are struggling to cope with an increasingly complex world. Individuals are struggling to find the right balance between work and family responsibility. Domestic issues also affect work.

Thus, the unrealistic expectations especially in the time of corporate reorganisations which, sometime puts unhealthy and unreasonable pressure on the employee can be tremendous source of stress and suffering. Increased workload, intense pressure to perform at peak levels all the time for the same pay, leave the employee physically and emotionally drained.

Body Mechanics

Body mechanics refer to the principles of proper body alignment, balance and movement. It is the way we move as we go about in our daily lives.

Poor body mechanics is often the cause of spinal problems, when you do not sit or move properly. Most injuries in the workplace can be avoided by using good body mechanics, maintaining physical fitness and reducing stress.

The following simple principles can be employed in body mechanics to avoid injuries :

Posture Stand up straight, this ensures that your spine is in its anatomical position, not bent or strained in any way.

Base of Support Stand with your feet apart this ensures stability.

Standing Try to avoid standing in one position for prolonged time periods, change positions as often as you can. Not only does this relieve spinal stress, but also increases blood circulation and reduces muscle fatigue.

Lifting It is also a good body mechanics principle.

Symmetry It means using muscle on both sides of the body equally. Use symmetry as a principle of good body mechanics. Besides above principles also take care of the following postures. Try to use both sides of your body equally. Use a chair with good lower back support. Arrange your work area to reduce the amount of reaching and twisting. (To avoid fatigue, often shift the position.

Functional Design of Workplace

Functional design takes into consideration all of the adverse side effects of the inspired workplace trends and finds solutions that make the trends attainable for all generations. Functional design capitalises of the benefits of these trends and finds ways to introduce them in corporate environment. Functional design is no longer about providing companies with a space for head down work. But rather a space that balances human needs, flaws and desires to create an optional work environment.

A large part of functional design is planning space based on the work being done rather than the status of employee. In doing so, workspace floor plate is looked with one question in mind. This is "how can we make the efficient use of space." Designing for function results in a better use of the space and takes into consideration things like optimisation of natural light and creating a design that provides future change.

Time and Motion Study

Time and motion study is systematic osbervation, analysis and measurement of the separate steps in the performance of a specific job for the purpose of establishing a standard time for each performance and increasing productivity. It is also called motion and time study. Time and motion study can reduce and control costs, improve working conditions and environment and motivate people. Its basic purpose is to improve work and to reduce waste by motion analysis techniques, time study technique and uses of time standards.

A time and motion study is a business efficiency technique combining the time study work of **Frederick Winslow Taylor** with the motion study of **Frank** and **Lillian Gilberth**. After its first introduction, time study developed in the direction of establishing a standard times, while motion study evolved into a technique for improving work methods.

The two techniques became integrated and refined into widely accepted method applicable to the improvement and upgrading of work systems.

Time and motion studying was invented around 1885 by observing process of bricklaying in construction life. The simple yet effective observation, time and motion study was "the horizontal line consumes more time than vertical lines. " So just a minor change improves the motion in such a way that more and more construction can be done in less time. Another observation was to get all tool nearby that can will help to save potential time of gathering it for bricklaying purpose.

Time study and motion study are two aspects of work study, but there is difference between the two such as :

- Motion study involves the study of motions on operation while time study notes the time involved in carrying out each element of operation.
- Motion study reduce wastage of time and materials scrapping the unnecessary movements whereas the time study aims at fixing the standard time for carrying out a job.
- Time study is not suitable for workers, where quality is prime consideration. On the other hand motion study is suitable for all types of jobs.

Energy Studies

Extensive research studies help to analyse work methods that has helped to find better and easier ways to carry out tasks and save energy. The time and motion studies for a task calculate how long it takes, on an average to perform a certain tasks. The amount of energy required performing a task separately and together.

Unable one to assess its performance. To succeed in the long run, one needs the active and engaged participation of employees. This means unleashing energy that is within each one of them. By unleashing the energy of the employees and getting out of the way, you can create high energy workforce.

Energy is required to perform any task, energy requirement depends on the kind of the work, i.e. heavy work requires more energy where light work does not. According to studies, it is found that positive energy not only increases individual productivity but also mitigates the effect of stress. Increases employee engagement. Increases speed with which employees carry out tasks. It also increases job satisfaction. Energy is the fuel that makes great organisations run successfully. Every interaction with others at work big or small, short or lengthy has the potential to create or deplete vital energy.

EXAM BASED QUESTIONS

1 In the age of social media great products are defined by............ .
(a) quantity
(b) popularity
(c) great design
(d) Both (a) and (b)

2 The product design encompasses
(a) doing market research
(b) identifying problems
(c) development designing/solutions finding
(d) All of the above

3 The product design has many fields of application such as
(a) medical devices
(b) food preservation appliances
(c) sports and leisure
(d) All of the above

4 Which of the following is/are the characteristics of design thinking?
(a) Design thinking is a methodology
(b) It aims to tackle highly complex problem
(c) It has four stages
(d) Both (a) and (b)

5 The design thinking process has .... stages.
(a) two (b) four
(c) five (d) three

6 The design thinking process lays great emphasis on
(a) creativity (b) needs of the users
(c) innovation (d) All of these

7 Designs are periodically modified to
(a) improve product performance
(b) strive for zero-based rejection and waste
(c) make products easier and faster to manufacture
(d) All of the above

8 The expected qualities of a product are
(a) it satisfies the needs and expectations of the customer
(b) it has a pleasing appearance and handles well
(c) it has high reliability and functions safely over its intended life
(d) All of the above

9 The ultimate objective of the product is
(a) to provide a new look
(b) utilising existing manpower
(c) to monopolise the market
(d) All of the above

10 The stages of Design Thinking process are
(a) empathise
(b) define
(c) ideate
(d) All of the above

11 Which of the following statement(s) is/are true about empathise?
(a) At this stage one has to gain an empathic understanding of the problem.
(b) Empathy is crucial to human factor design process.
(c) A substantial amount of information is gathered.
(d) All of the above

12 Choose the incorrect statement with regard to the third stage (Ideate) of decision making
(a) In this stage you analyse your observations and synthesise them in order to define the core problem.
(b) The designers are ready to start generating ideas.
(c) It is a judgement free zone.
(d) The group is encouraged to venture a way from norm.

13 The define stage helps the designers to
(a) gather ideas
(b) establish features
(c) other elements that will allow them to solve problems.
(d) All of the above

14 Which of the following are the benefits of decision thinking process?
(a) It encourages creative problem solving.
(b) It brings multidisciplinary teams together.
(c) It fosters a culture of innovation.
(d) All of the above

15 Innovation is defined as
(a) the commercialisation of a new product or process
(b) the invention of a new product or process
(c) a new product or process idea
(d) the implementation of a new production method

16 Process innovation refers to
(a) the development of a new service
(b) the development of a new product
(c) the implementation of a new or improved production method
(d) the development of new products or services

17 The first discovery of a product or process through the use of imagination, ingenious thinking, and experimentation and the first proof that it will work is
(a) process innovation
(b) product innovation
(c) creative destruction
(d) invention

18 Innovation is a major factor in competition because it can
(a) be patented to protect the investment of the developers
(b) enable firms to make competitors' products obsolete
(c) guarantee the monopoly position of innovative firms
(d) reduce research and development costs for firms

19 The theory of diffusion of innovation is a theory built on the premise that
(a) any commercial consumers market place has different types of customers.
(b) the customers vary on their enthusiasm for a particular product.
(c) they try out the new product.
(d) All of the above

20 The process of diffusion of innovation are
(a) knowledge
(b) persuasion
(c) decision
(d) All of the above

21 The process of design communication involves
(a) strategic business thinking
(b) market research
(c) creativity
(d) All of the above

22 'Ergonomics' is related to human
(a) comfort
(b) safety
(c) Both (a) and (b)
(d) None of the above

23 The following subject (s) is/are related to 'Ergonomics'.
(a) Anthropology
(b) Physiology
(c) Psychology
(d) All of the above

24 In designing an efficient workspace, the left hand will cover
(a) maximum working area (b) normal working area
(c) minimal working area (d) None of these

25 Ergonomics has expanded as a discipline in its own right over the past 50 years and there is often overlap between what ergonomists and work psychologists do. Simply put, ergonomics has evolved to be concerned with
(a) adapting the person to the workplace
(b) design of whole systems of work
(c) design and development of equipment
(d) design of work equipment

26 Ergonomics is a body of knowledge concerned with
(a) human abilities
(b) design of tools, machines, systems, tasks, jobs, and environments
(c) Fitting the job or task to the person
(d) All of the above

27 The word ergonomic is derived from the .... word where Ergori means work and 'nomos' means law.
(a) Latin (b) Greek
(c) Sanskrit (d) Hebrew

28 Which international organisation has defined ergonomics "as the application of biological sciences in conjunction with engineering sciences to the workers and his working environment so as to attain maximum satisfaction for the work which at the same time enhances productivity?"
(a) International Labour Organisation (ILO).
(b) World Health Organisation
(c) International Monetary Fund
(d) World Trade Organisation

29 The word ergonomics was used independently in 1949 by........... scientist.
(a) American (b) Indian
(c) British (d) Chinese

30 The fundamental themes of ergonomics are
(a) user centred design
(b) user-Friendly
(c) inclusive design
(d) All of the above

31 Who is the father of anthropometrics?
(a) Alphonse Bertillon (b) Martens
(c) Carron (d) Spielberger

32 Anthropometry is the science that measures
(a) height, weight and size
(b) body fat and percentage
(c) grip strength range of motion and functional reach
(d) All of the above

33 Which of the following factors affect the anthropometric measurement?
(a) Growth and development
(b) Gender
(c) Ageing
(d) All of the above

34 Anthropometry is significant to interior designers because
(a) anthropometrics are the tools for them
(b) it aids to workout how far, how high are an average male of female may reach in relative comfort.
(c) Both (a) and (b)
(d) None of the above

35 The man-machine can be classified as
(a) manual (b) mechanical
(c) automatic (d) All of these

36 Functional design is
(a) smart design
(b) takes considerations of all adverse side effects
(c) planning space based on the work being done
(d) All of the above.

37 The time and motion study invented around ....
(a) 1886
(b) 1885
(c) 1901
(d) 1889

38 Time and motion study can help to
(a) reduce and control cost
(b) working conditions
(c) motivate people
(d) All of the above

39 The following factor(s) must be considered while selecting the work for method study
(a) economic considerations
(b) technical considerations
(c) human reactions
(d) All of the above

40 Work study is also recognised as
(a) Time study
(b) Motion study
(c) both (a) and (b)
(d) None of the above

41 Which of the following is not an aspect of Taylor's scientific management?
(a) Time and motion study
(b) Division of labour
(c) Using craft skills
(d) Separation of planning and doing

42 In which of the following situations would rational work design function best?
(a) A changeable environment where the specification of products needs to be changed often.
(b) A market where customers desire niche products with high levels of customisation.
(c) A stable environment where a standard, simple product is produced.
(d) Manufacture of luxury goods where craft skills are required.

43 Which of the following statement (s) is/are correct about fifth stage (test) of the decision thinking process?
Statement I At this stage one gathers feedback on how your users felt.
Statement II This stage quickly highlights any design flaws that needs to be looked.
(a) Statement I is correct
(b) Statement II is correct
(c) Both the statements (I and II) are correct
(d) Neither I nor II statement is correct

44 Which of the following statement (s) is/are correct about design communication?
Statements I Design communication is a mixed discipline between design and information development.
Statement II Design communication does not involve the knowledge of colour, page layout and creating visuals.
(a) Only statement I is correct
(b) Only statement II is correct
(c) Both the statements are correct
(d) Neither I nor II statement is correct

45 Consider the following statements (s) is/are correct with regard to anthropometry.
Statement I It is the scientific study of the measurements of human body.
Statement II The anthropometry data are not used in ergonomics.
(a) Only statement I correct
(b) Only statement II is correct
(c) Both the statements are correct
(d) Neither I nor II statement is correct

46 Choose the incorrect statement (s) with regard to the mechanical classification of man-machine.
Statement I They are essentially man directed
Statement II It is power driven.
(a) Statement I is incorrect
(b) Statement II is incorrect
(c) Both the statements are correct
(d) Both the statements are incorrect

47 Which of the following are the characteristics of man-machine.
(a) It has specific input and outputs which are appropriately balanced
(b) It is variable in size and complexity and is dynamic in performance
(c) It consists of the man, machine and system environment
(d) All of the above

48 Which of the following statements about ergonomics is correct?
(a) It can be applied on all schemes of human activity.
(b) It is commonly applied to workplace environment.
(c) It contributes to the design and evaluation of work systems and products.
(d) All of the above

49 Arrange the following stages of decision thinking process in correct sequence
1. Empathy 2. Define
3. Test 4. Prototype
5. Ideate
Codes
(a) 1, 2, 3, 4 and 5 (b) 1, 3, 2, 4 and 5
(c) 1, 2, 5, 4 and 3 (d) 5, 4, 3, 2 and 1

50 Match the following.

List I (Principles of Body mechanics to avoid injuries)	List II (Characteristics)
A. Posture	1. Using muscle on both sides of the body equally
B. Standing	2. Stand with your feet apart this ensures stability
C. Symmetry	3. Here try to avoid standing in one position for prolonged time
D. Base of support	4. Stand-up straight this ensures your spine is in its anatomical position not bent.

Codes

	A	B	C	D		A	B	C	D
(a)	1	2	3	4	(b)	4	3	2	1
(c)	4	3	1	2	(d)	1	4	3	2

Directions (Q. Nos. 51-65) *In the questions given below are two statements labelled as Assertion (A) and Reason (R). In the context of the two statements which one of the following is correct?*

Codes

(a) Assertion A is correct and R is the correct explanation of A
(b) Assertion A is correct, but R is not the correct explanation of A
(c) (A) is correct, but R is incorrect
(d) A is incorrect, but R is correct

51 Assertion (A) In the preset time product design is a critical factor in organisational success.

Reason (R) It sets the characteristic features and performances of the services or goods that consumers demand.

52 Assertion (A) The prototype stage turn your ideas into something tangible which can be tested in real users.

Reason (R) This is not an experimental stage.

53 Assertion (A) The diffusion of innovation explains the rate at which new ideas and technology spread.

Reason (R) It is used extensively by marketers.

54 Assertion (A) Design communication is not a mixed discipline.

Reason (R) The design communication seeks to attract, inspire, create desires and motivate people to respond to messages.

55 Assertion (A) Ergonomics is relevant in many fields.

Reason (R) It is commonly applied to workplace environment.

56 Assertion (A) the proper integration of man and machine is benefical for human operator and enhances the overall performance.

Reason (R) The man machine becomes more efficient When inputs and outputs are adequately balanced.

57 Assertion (A) The automatic classification in which all functions are performed manually.

Reason (R) The human element performs the job of monitoring, programming, function, maintenance and up keep.

58 Assertion (A) The environment can be termed as man's closest surroundings.

Reason (R) Human beings can manipulate for his survival.

59 Assertion (A) The congenial working environment can increase performance of the workers.

Reason (R) The physical environment as an aspect of the workplace environment has direct impact on the humans.

60 Assertion (A) A negative working environment leads to physical and mental health problems.

Reason (R) The workers should be provided congenial working environment to overcome problem of physical and mental health problems.

61 Assertion (A) Rapid technological changes reduce the quantity and intensity of physical energy.

Reason (R) It in turn increases mental burdens, this influences workers' attitudes and behaviour.

62 Assertion (A) Body mechanics means maintaining proper muscular and skeletal positioning during movement.

Reason (R) Poor body mechanics is after the cause of spinal problem.

63 Assertion (A) Time and motion study is a business efficiency technique.

Reason (R) It is a major part of scientific management.

64 Assertion (A) The motion study involves the study of motion on operation.

Reason (R) Motion study is not suitable for all types of jobs.

65 Assertion (A) The shift work is physically less stressful.

Reason (R) The work schedules are better organised and individual workers are helped by various means of social support.

Directions (Q, Nos. 66-70) *Read the passage below and answer the questions that follow based on your understanding of the passage.*

Every product that is manufactured by any organisation is supposed to have a distinguishing physical characteristic which will make it attractive to customers, this characteristic is known as a design.

Product design therefore is all about manufacturing a product that will attract the customer and also provides value for them. Since the design of a product is the first impression of a customer, has about a particular product.

There is therefore the need for organisations to design products that meet and exceed the customer's expectation product design, is a means of adding value to a product by ensuring that its layout is attractive to the customer.

Product design is all about trying to link customer needs to product attributes, therefore providing the customer with value. 'Good design satisfies' customers, and communicates the purpose of the product to its market.

The objective of a good product design is to satisfy the customer by meeting their actual needs or expectation.

This therefore enhances the competitiveness of the organisation; product design can be seen as starting and ending with' the customer.

The job of the product designers is to achieve designs that exceed customer's expectation. According to Schroeder product design is crucial to the survival of most firms. While a few firm experience little product change, most firm must continually revise their products.

Product design is seldom the responsibility of the operations function but operations is greatly affected by new product introduction and vice versa. Product design is a prerequisite for production. According to Chase et al.

The design of a product differs depending on the industry; for example for consumer products, understanding consumer preference, market testing and prospective product are very important activities. Companies that specialise in the design of products have highly developed processes to support the activities needed for an industry.

Nigel et al further states that good design also helps business connect strongly with their customers by anticipating their real needs, this in turn gives them the ability to set themselves apart in increasingly tough markets.

Product design should be made in such a way that it is within the budget of the organisation but at the same time meets expectations of the customers and consumers. Good product design attracts more customers thereby giving an organisation a hedge above other competitors in the market. It also brings together three important issues, the concept, the package and the process.

Good design makes a business grow by enhancing profitability and turnover because it transforms the needs of customers into the desired shape and value of the product demanded.

It makes life easy and comfortable for the customer by introducing products that are easy to use. Good product design is important in replacing obsolete designs.

A well designed product makes a great difference to a customers perception of the product, and certain factors influence the decision of a customer about the design of a particular product, these factors are the value attributes, they are the value perceived by a customer, these are what the customer considers before, making a decision to buy a product, these factors are; convenience, cost, technology quality, style/fashion.

66 Good design satisfies

(a) businessmen (b) customers
(c) management (d) Both (a) and (c)

67 The objective of good product design is

(a) to satisfy limited customers
(b) all the customers
(c) to satisfy all customers by meeting their needs
(d) to satisfy the company's personnel

68 According to .... product design is crucial to the survival of most firms.

(a) Schroeder (b) Taylor
(c) Chase etal (d) Nigel etal

69 Which of the following is a characteristic of good product design?

(a) It is important in replacing obsolete design
(b) It attracts more customers
(c) It makes a great difference to a customer's perception of the product
(d) All of the above

70 Which of the following are the important issues of the good product design?

(a) The concept (b) The package
(c) The process (d) All of these

PREVIOUS YEARS' QUESTIONS

November 2017

1 Which technique in time and motion studies consider movement of both the hands?
(a) Pathway chart
(b) Operation chart
(c) Process chart
(d) Chromocyclography

2 Arrange the following category of ' Adopter's as per the speed with which they adopt a new idea, practice or a technology as proposed by Evrett Rogers
1. Early majority
2. Laggards
3. Late majority
4. Early adopters
5. Innovators

Codes
(a) 4, 5, 1, 3 and 2
(b) 5, 4, 1, 3 and 2
(c) 4, 5, 3, 1 and 2
(d) 5, 1, 4, 3 and 2

June 2015

3 **Assertion** (A) The Man-Machine System (MMS) is most effective when input and output are appropriately balanced.

Reason (R) The Man-Machine System consists of only man and machine.

Codes
(a) A is correct and R is incorrect
(b) A is incorrect and R is correct
(c) Both A and R are correct
(d) Both A and R are incorrect

December 2015

4 Benefits of ergonomics include
1. safer jobs
2. increased efficiency and productivity
3. effective financial management
4. fewer injuries

Select the correct answer using the codes gives below
(a) 1, 3 and 4 (b) 1, 2 and 3
(c) 1, 2 and 4 (d) 1, 3 and 4

ANSWERS

Exam Based Questions

1 (c)	2 (d)	3 (d)	4 (d)	5 (c)	6 (d)	7 (d)	8 (d)	9 (c)	10 (d)
11 (d)	12 (a)	13 (d)	14 (d)	15 (a)	16 (c)	17 (b)	18 (d)	19 (d)	20 (d)
21 (a)	22 (c)	23 (d)	24 (a)	25 (b)	26 (d)	27 (b)	28 (a)	29 (c)	30 (d)
31 (a)	32 (d)	33 (d)	34 (c)	35 (d)	36 (d)	37 (b)	38 (d)	39 (d)	40 (c)
41 (c)	42 (c)	43 (c)	44 (a)	45 (a)	46 (a)	47 (d)	48 (d)	49 (c)	50 (c)
51 (a)	52 (c)	53 (b)	54 (d)	55 (b)	56 (a)	57 (d)	58 (a)	59 (b)	60 (a)
61 (a)	62 (b)	63 (b)	64 (c)	65 (a)	66 (b)	67 (c)	68 (a)	69 (d)	70 (d)

Previous Years' Questions

1 (b)	2 (b)	3 (b)	4 (c)

Human Growth and Development

Since the day of conception, human development starts from a zygote to an infant to child to adult, development takes place rapidly with time. Development is a life long process. It consists of physical, behavioural cognitive, emotional growth and change.

Growth and Development

Growth refers to the quantitative changes, which means increase in size and structure of the body as a whole. This includes, physical growth as well as the growth of size and structure of the internal organs and the brain as well. With the growth of the brain, the child has a greater capacity for learning, remembering and reasoning. The child grows mentally as well as physically.

In **Encyclopedia Britannica**, "growth is defined as an increase in size or the amount of an entity". It means growth involves all those structural and physiological changes that take place within individual during the process of maturation.

Hurlock has defined "growth as change in size, in proportion, disappearance of old features and acquisition of new ones".

Development refers to qualitative and quantitat've changes. Development may be defined as a progressive series of orderly change Progressive refers to the changes that are directional i.e they load forward rather than backward. Orderly refers that there is relationship between changes taking place and they are well-planned.

In **Webster's dictionary**, "development is defined as the series of changes which an organism undergoes in passing from an embryonic stage to maturity."

In **Encyclopedia Britannica** the term "development is defined as the progressive change in size, shape and function during the life of an organism by which its genetic potential are translated into functioning adult system."

In this Chapter

According to **Crow** and **Crow** "development is concerned with growth as well as those changes in behavior which results from environmental situation."

Principles of Growth and Development

The various principles of growth and development are as follows :

Development is Sequential Development occurs in an orderly manner and follows specific sequence. Direction of growth and development in human is of two types– Cephalocaudal sequence and Proximodistal sequence.

- **Cephalocaudal Sequence** Development starts from head and progresses toward feets. In womb, the head of foetus develops first then body and afterward legs develop.
- **Proximodistal Sequence** Development starts from centre to outside of the body. First the organs like heart and stomach develop, then shoulders and arms start to develop.

Development from General to Specific Response In any developmental change, the general changes take place before the specific change. This can be observed in the behaviour of infants and young children. The law applies to all forms of physical, mental, emotional, social areas as well. For example, a baby waves his arm in general response before he is capable of specific response such as reaching out for a specific object.

Development Proceeds at Different Rates Development is a continuous process. But it always proceeds at different rates for different organisms. For example, the feet, hand and nose reach maximum development by early adolescent. The lower part of face and shoulder in contrast develops more slowly.

Each Phase of Development has Predictable Characteristics Development has certain physical and mental, common and predictable characteristics. All children follow a similar developmental pattern with one stage leading to the next. For example, babies learn to stand before they learn to walk. Likewise, children learn to draw circles before drawing squares.

There are Individual Differences in Development Every individual is unique. Developmental process is same, but at the same time its pace is different in different individuals. Children who are fast in physical and mental development, their other developments also occur rapidly. The children who are mentally slow remain slow in other developmental aspects. Children of same age differ in the rate of their development.

Every Stage has its own Characteristics The developmental span has been divided into the various stages, which have their own special characteristics, e.g. prenatal period, post-natal period, adolescence. There are certain typical behaviour patterns in each and every stage, which are not found in other stages.

Every Child Passes through Each Stage of Development Due to the specific and systematic pattern of development the child passes through every stage. It never happens that the child jumps over a stage to reach another.

Every Child Reaches his Maximum Stage of Development Every child has a different rate of development, but reaches the optimum limit of his own development sooner or later. Some factors enhance development while certain factors hinder the process of development.

Different Stages of Human Development

At the time of birth, the child's body is in the initial stage of development. The baby is neither sufficiently strong nor fully mature. It goes through many stages to be fully developed.

Child's physical development takes place in the following ways :

Changes in Size These include physical changes in height, weight, circumference and internal organs. With the increase in age, the proportion of child's length increases. Thus, the body weight keeps increasing in same proportion.

Changes in Proportion The development of body parts is not in equal proportion. For example, the head develops faster than other organs when in womb but after birth, other organs develop faster than the brain. Proportional changes also affect mental, social and emotional development. As a result of which the actions of humans continue to be refined. For example, in infancy, self-centredness is found in the child. But as he grows and develops, he also learns to respect others.

Changes in Features During development, changes in features like changes in colour, form, gait can easily be seen. This include, loss of teeth and hair, clear speaking skills instead of babble and the ability to walk instead of crawling. Such changes are influenced by learning and maturity.

Changes in Motivation There is a noticeable change in motivation as a child moves from infancy to adulthood. Things that motivate children during childhood lose their attraction as they grow up. For example, a child may eat ice-cream or watch TV in exchange of studying but as they grow up they are motivated by social and economic factors.

Factors Affecting Human Development

Human development is equally affected by the heredity and environment. Some of these factors help in development while others act as a barriers. The most influential factors are as follows :

Nutrition Nutrition plays an important role in overall development of any animal. Since, infancy to adulthood, an individual must have good nutritional food to lead a healthy life. Good nutrition and healthy eating is also required for personality development. A balanced and nutritious diet helps in providing necessary mental and physical strength to the individual.

Family Support Families have the most profound impact in nurturing a child. They determine the ways in which child develops psychologically and socially. Whether raised by parents, grandparents or foster care, a child needs love and care to develop as healthy individual. If the family environment is peaceful and pleasant, then the children grow normally. On the other hand, families whose environment is stressed and toxic, the children may develop abnormal behaviour.

Gender The gender of the child is another major factor affecting the physical growth and development of a child. Boys and girls grow in different ways, especially nearing puberty. Boys tend to be taller and physically stronger than girls. Girls tend to mature faster during adolescent. Boys mature over longer period of time.

School The school in which the child studies, plays an important role in his development. When the child gets enough opportunities and gets full support from teammates, he or she develops properly. In contrast, child's development is hampered if the school does not give enough support and opportunities.

Cultural Environment Every country and society have its own cultural identify. According to this, the nurturing of future generation takes place. In other words, the development of every child is in accordance with their own culture. Thus, a child growing up in Western culture has an independent and free ideology.

Peer Group Getting into peer group is tough. Generally, initiative has to be taken by the child to fit into the group. He learns cues and responses which are appreciated by the peers. The process of integration is slow. The peer group consists of children from various backgrounds. Conflicts are easier to happen.

Community Many entities like a family, school, society bring about collective changes on individual belonging to the community.

Each community has its own tradition, history and culture influencing the development of an individual. For example, an Israelite can be easily distinguished from Japanese.

Theories of Human Development

The growth and development of human can be understood by the theories given by different psychologists. Given below are some of them :

Freud's Psychoanalytic Theory

Psychoanalysis was founded by **Sigmund Freud**. He has worked with Erikson to develop psychoanalytic theory of human development. Psychoanalytic Theory can be described by Id, Ego and Super Ego.

Id It is the original personality. Ego and super Ego become differentiated after this level. It consists of everything psychological that is inherited and that is present at birth. Freud called the Id as 'true psychic reality'. It represents the inner world (unconscious mind) devoid of knowledge of objective reality. It does not have grasp over reality or consequences.

Ego It helps in maintaining reality sense of an individual. It helps the individual to create a balance between pleasure and pain. The basic difference between Id and Ego is that Id knows only the need of mind. But Ego distinguishes between need of mind and the reality. The Ego is said to obey the reality principle.

Super Ego It develops around the age of 4 or 5. It is about morality. Super Ego is developed by family value and ideas of society. It is reinforced upon the child through rewards and punishment by parents. Super Ego replaces the pleasure needed by Id with perfection. As the child grows up, it is controlled by Id, Ego and Super Ego, but Ego leads the way. The personality is total of what the three of them decides it to be.

Freud's Psychosexual Theory of Development

According the Freud, childhood development takes place in stages. If the baby lacks proper nurturing and parenting during any of this stage, he/she gets fixated on that stage. There are five stages of development according to Freud. These are linked to different specific areas of body called Erogenous zone. These are given below :

Oral (0-1 year of age) Mouth is the pleasure centre for this stage. Freud believed this is why infants are born with sucking reflex. If the child's oral needs are not met, he/she may develop negative habits like nail biting or thumb sucking.

Anal (1-3 years of age) Children start to experiment during this stage with urine and faeces. They learn to control their bodily function. They are toilet trained at this state.

Phallic (3-6 years of age) According to Freud, the pre-schooler starts to struggle with sexual desire towards opposite sex parent (boy's to mother and girl's to father). For boys, this is called the oedipus complex. This is a boy's desire for his mother and urge to replace father. Father is seen as a rival competiting for mother's attention.

Latency (6-12 years of age) At this stage sexual instincts subside. The child begins to develop super ego. Children begin to behave in morally acceptable ways. They adopt the values by their parents and other important individual.

Genital (12+ years of age) During this stage, sexual impulses reemerges. If other stages have been successfully met, adolescent engage in appropriate sexual behaviour.

Erikson's Stages of Psychosocial Development

Erik Erikson (1902-1994) was a stage theorist who modified Freud's controversial psychosexual theory into an eight-stages psychosocial theory of development. According to the theory, successful completion of each stage results in a healthy personality.

Failure to successfully complete a stage can result in a reduced ability to complete further stages and therefore a more unhealthy personality and sense of self. These stages, however, can be resolved successfully at a later time.

Description of these stages are given below :

Trust vs. Mistrust From birth to 12 months of age, infants learn that adults can be trusted. This occurs when adults fulfil a child's basic needs for survival. Infants are dependent upon their caregivers.

So, caregivers who are responsive and sensitive to their infant's need to help their baby to develop a sense of trust. The baby will see the world as a safe, predictable place.

Autonomy vs. Shame and Doubt This stage occurs between the ages of 18 months to approximately 3 years. According to Erikson, children at this stage are focused on developing a sense of personal control over physical skills and a sense of independence. For example, we might observe a budding sense of autonomy in a 2- years-old girl who wants to choose her clothes and dress herself.

Initiative vs. Guilt Once children reach the pre-school stage (ages 3-6 years), they are capable of initiating activities and asserting control over their world through social interactions and play. Initiative occurs when parents allow a child to explore within limits and then support the child's choice. These children will develop self-confidence and feel a sense of purpose.

Industry vs. Inferiority During the elementary school stage (ages 6-12 years), children face the task of industry vs. inferiority. Children begin to compare themselves with their peers to see how they measure up. They either develop a sense of pride and accomplishment in their school works, sports, social activities, and family life, or they feel inferior and inadequate because they feel that they don't measure up.

Identity vs. Role Confusion This occurs during adolescence, from about 12-18 years. During this stage, adolescents search for a sense of self and personal identity, through an intense exploration of personal values, beliefs, and goals.

Intimacy vs. Isolation People in early adulthood (20s through early 40s) are concerned with Intimacy vs. Isolation. After we have developed a sense of self in adolescence, we are ready to share our life with others. However, if other stages have not been successfully resolved, young adults may have trouble in developing and maintaining successful relationships with others.

Generativity vs. Stagnation Generativity refers to 'making your mark' on the world through creating or nurturing things that will outlast an individual. People experience a need to create or nurture things that will outlast them, often creating positive changes that will benefit other people.

Ego Integrity vs. Despair From the mid-60s to the end of life, we are in the period of development known as late adulthood. Erikson's task at this stage is called Integrity vs. Despair. He said that people in late adulthood reflect on their lives and feel either a sense of satisfaction or a sense of failure.

Kohlberg's Stages of Moral Development

Kohlberg believed that moral development, like cognitive development, follows a series of stages. After presenting people with various moral dilemmas, Kohlberg reviewed people's responses and placed them in different stages of moral reasoning.

According to **Kohlberg**, "An individual progresses from the pre-conventional morality (before age of 9 years) to the conventional morality (early adolescence) towards attaining post-conventional morality."

The levels of moral development are as follows :

Level 1 : Pre-Conventional

Throughout the pre-conventional level, a child's sense of morality is externally controlled. Children accept and believe the rules of authority figures, such as parents and teachers. A child with pre-conventional morality has not yet adopted or internalised society's conventions regarding what is right or wrong, but instead focuses largely on external consequences that certain actions may bring.

The sub-stages of the pre-conventional level are :

Stage 1 Obedience and Punishment Orientation

Stage 2 Instrumental Orientation

Level 2 : Conventional

Throughout the conventional level, a child's sense of morality is tied to personal and societal relationships. Children continue to accept the rules of authority figures, but this is now due to their belief that this is necessary to ensure positive relationships and societal order.

Adherence to rules and conventions is somewhat rigid during these stages, and a rule's appropriateness or fairness is seldom questioned.

The sub-stages of conventional level are :

Stage 3 Good Boy, Nice Girl Orientation

Stage 4 Law and Order Orientation

Level 3 : Post-Conventional

Throughout the post-conventional level, a person's sense of morality is defined in terms of more abstract principles and values. People now believe that some laws are unjust and should be changed or eliminated. This level is marked by a growing realisation that individuals are separate entities from society and that individuals may disobey rules inconsistent with their own principles. Some theorists have speculated that many people may never reach on this level of abstract moral reasoning.

The sub-stages of post-conventional level are :

Stage 5 Social Contract Orientation

Stage 6 Universal-Ethical-Principle Orientation

Piaget's Stages of Cognitive Development

Jean Piaget is one of the most influential figures in the study of child development. He developed his cognitive developmental theory based on the idea that children actively construct knowledge as they explore and manipulate the world around them.

Piaget believed that as children grow and their brains develop, they move through four distinct stages that are characterised by differences in thought processing. Piaget's four stages correspond with the age of the children and these are the sensorimotor, preoperational, concrete operational and formal operational stages.

Sensorimotor Stage

The sensorimotor stage occurs from birth to 2 years. It is characterised by the idea that infants 'think' by manipulating the world around them. Children figure out ways to elicit responses by doing, like throwing an object to see what happens.

Between 5 and 8 months old, the child develops object permanence, which is the understanding that even if something is out of sight, it still exists. For example, a child learns that even though his mother leaves the room, she has not ceased to exist; similarly, a ball does not disappear because a bucket is placed over it.

Preoperational Stage

The preoperational stage occurs from 2 to 7years . During this stage, children can use symbols to represent words, images, and ideas, which is why children in this stage engage in pretend play. Language development and make-believe play begin during this stage. Logical thinking is still not present, so children cannot rationalise or understand more complex ideas.

Children at this stage are very egocentric, meaning they focus on themselves and how actions will impact on them, rather than others. They are not able to take on the perspective of others, and they think that everyone sees, thinks and feels just like they do.

Concrete Operational Stage

The concrete operational stage occurs from years 7 to 11years. It is characterised by the idea that children's reasoning become focused and logical. Children demonstrate a logical understanding of conservation principles, the ability to recognise that key properties of a substance do not change even as their physical appearance may be altered.

For example, a child who understands the principles of conservation will recognise that identical quantities of liquid will remain the same despite the size of the container in which they are poured.

Children who do not yet grasp conservation and logical thinking will believe that the taller or larger glass must contain more liquid.

Formal Operational Stage

The formal operational stage occurs from age 11 to adulthood. It is characterised by the idea that children develop the ability to think in abstract ways. This enables children to engage in the problem-solving method of developing a hypothesis and reasoning their way to plausible solutions. Children can think of abstract concepts and have the ability to combine various ideas to create new ones. By the end of this stage, children have developed logical and systematic thinking. They are capable of deductive reasoning, and can create hypothetical ideas to explain various concepts.

Theories of Human Behaviour

Thorndike's theory of Learning, Ivan Pavlov' theory of Classical Conditioning, Clark Hull's Theory of Human Behaviour and, BF Skinner's theory of Operant conditioning are popular theories of Human behaviour. Their description is given below :

Thorndike's Theory of Learning

Edward Lee Ted Thorndike developed learning theory that lead to the development of operant conditioning within behaviourism. Operant conditioning involves learning from the consequences of the behaviour.

Thorndike formulated the major laws of learning on the basis of his belief in connectionism. Connectionism is a learning theory which is based on the concept of bonds formed between **Stimulus** and **Response** i.e. natural connections between **Situations** (S) and **Responses** (R) are formed and strengthened. The stimulus affects the organism which responds to it. Thorndike presented the theory on laws of learning on the basis of his belief in connectionism.

The three major laws are :

- Law of Readiness
- Law of Exercise
- Law of Effect

Law of Readiness

"When a bond is ready to act, act gives satisfaction and not to act gives annoyance." If a person is ready to learn, he/she can learn quickly. The law of readiness describes those situations in which the person, who learns either invites the object of his/her learning or rejects it.

Readiness means a preparation of action. If a person is not prepared to learn, then learning cannot be instilled in him/her. The readiness creates a mental set for learning.

Law of Exercise

The second important law has two aspects. It is based on law of use and disuse. The law of use states, "When a modifiable connection is made between a situation and a response, that connection's strength is being increased." Similarly, the law of disuse states, "When a modifiable connection is not made between a situation and response over a length of time, the connection's strength is decreased."

The repeated application of an activity fixes it firmly in the mind. While on the other hand, the relation is weakened through continuous disuse.

According to Thorndike's S-R bond theory, the connections are strengthened with trial and practice. It is the experience that whenever any action is repeated, it becomes easy and prompt.

Law of Effect

The meaning of the law of effect is the effect of learning. Satisfying states lead to strengthening of connection, whereas dissatisfaction annoyance or pain leads to the weakening of the connection.

Success brings with it satisfaction and alongwith it a strengthening of the relation of the experiences. Failure increases dissatisfaction and the absence of the relation among the experiences weakens them. The success can be compared to reward and failure to punishment.

Ivan Pavlov's Theory of Classical Conditioning

First discovered by a Russian physiologist Ivan Pavlov (1849-1936), classical conditioning is a learning process governed by associations between an environmental stimulus and another stimulus which occurs naturally. All classical conditioned learning involves environmental interaction.

For learning to occur, there must also be a 'neutral stimulus' which is then followed by a naturally occurring reflex. For instance, Pavlov's dogs heard a tone (neutral stimulus) followed by salivating (naturally occurring reflex) in response to the arrival of food.

Once the sound of the neutral stimulus became linked to the stimulus present in the environment (food arriving), it soon became possible to induce salivating just by sounding the neutral stimulus.

The action of classical conditioning upon a subject is a three-phases process :

Phase 1 : Pre-Conditioned State

Classical conditioning demands a naturally occurring stimulus which will induce an automatic response. So at this stage, there is a **UCS (Unconditioned Stimulus)** linked to a **UCR (Unconditioned Response)** which occurs naturally.

Phase 2 : Conditioning State

Next, a neutral stimulus is repeatedly introduced alongside the UCS. Soon, the neutral stimulus becomes linked with the UCS. Once this starts to happen, the neutral stimulus is transformed into a CS (Conditioned Stimulus) because the subject has now become conditioned to respond to the CS as if it were the natural UCR.

Phase 3 : Post-Conditioning State

Once the UCS and the CS are connected, the CS alone will trigger a response. At this final stage, the response has now become a **CR (Conditioned Response)**. That means the subject has learned to produce the CR when triggered by the CS which was previously just a neutral signal.

The key elements of classical conditioning :

Acquisition It requires a neutral stimulus to become linked with an unconditioned stimulus. This must then be repeatedly reinforced to ensure strong learning takes place.

Extinction It is opposite of acquisition. It occurs when a conditioned response weakens or ceases to exist. For a conditioned response to be maintained, the unconditioned stimulus must be reintroduced occasionally to 'top up' the desired conditioned response.

Generalisation of Stimulus Once a conditioned response has been created, it can tend to emerge as a response to other stimuli which appear similar. For instance, if a particular bell tone is the conditioned stimulus, similar sounding bell tones can elicit the same response.

Clark Hull's Theory of Human Behaviour

Hull was one of the first theorists to attempt creating a grand theory designed to explain all behaviour. In his theory, Hull used the term drive to refer to the state of tension or arousal caused by biological or physiological needs.

Thirst, hunger, and the need for warmth are all examples of drive. A drive creates an unpleasant state, a tension that needs to be reduced. In order to reduce this state of tension, humans and animals seek out ways to fulfill these biological needs. We get a drink when we are thirsty. We eat when we are hungry. He suggested that humans and animals will then repeat any behaviour that reduces these drives.

Conditioning and Reinforcement

Hull believed that human behaviour could be explained by conditioning and reinforcement. The reduction of the drive acts as a reinforcement for that behaviour. This reinforcement increases the likelihood that the same behaviour will occur again in the future when the same need arises. In order to survive in its environment, an organism must behave in ways that meet these survival needs. Hull has explained that, "When survival is in jeopardy, the organism is in a state of need (when the biological requirements for survival are not being met) so the organism behaves in a fashion to reduce that need." In a Stimulus-Response (S-R)" relationship, when the stimulus and response are followed by a reduction in the need, it increases the likelihood that the same stimulus will elicit the same response again in the future.

BF Skinner's Theory of Operant Conditioning

BF Skinner believed that looking at the causes of an action and its consequences was the best way to understand behaviour. He termed this approach, which looked at the effects of the behaviour as operant conditioning. BF Skinner distinguished between two types of behaviour :

Respondent Behaviour This includes things which happen automatically and reflexively. For example, pulling your hand away from a hot stove. These are not learned behaviours, they simply occur automatically and involuntarily.

Operant Behaviour This includes things which require our conscious control. Though some may occur spontaneously or purposely, it is the consequences of such actions which then determine whether or not these actions recur in the future. Our actions upon our environment, and their consequences, play an important role in the learning process.

Reinforcement in Operant Conditioning

Reinforcement is any immediately subsequent event which increases or strengthens behaviour. There are two types of reinforcement :

Positive Reinforcers They are favourable outcomes presented after the behaviour. Positive reinforcement occurs when a behaviour is strengthened by praise or a reward.

Negative Reinforcers They are result in the removal of an unpleasant outcome as a direct consequence of a behaviour. Negative reinforcement grows stronger when something unpleasant is then immediately removed. The behaviour increases in response to each kind of reinforcement.

Child Development Stages

Growth and development stages of child are as follows :

Growth and Development During Prenatal Stage

With conception the story of prenatal development begins. The 38 weeks of pregnancy are divided into following periods :

- Conception
- Period of zygote(1-2 weeks)
- Period of embryo (3-8 weeks)
- Period of foetus (9-38 weeks)

Conception

Once every 28 days in between of women's menstural cycle an ovum is released from the ovary and is drawn in one of the two fallopian tubes. While the ovum travels, the spot on the ovary from which it was released, now called corpus luteum, secretes hormones that prepare the lining of the uterus to receive the fertilised ovum.

If pregnancy does not occur, the corpus luteum shrinks and the lining of uterus is discarded two weeks later with menstruation. The male produces sperms on an average of 300 million a day, but only 300-500 are able to reach the ovum.

Each sperm develops a tail to swim upstream in female reproductive tract through cervix (opening of the uterus) and into the fallopian tubes where the fertilisation takes place. Sperm lives upto six days, while ovum survives for only 1 day after being released into the fallopian tube.

Period of Zygote

Characteristics of this period are as follows :

- This period lasts about two weeks from fertilisation.
- By fourth day from conception 60 to 70 cells exist, forming a hollow, fluid filled ball called blastocyst.
- The cells on the inside called the embryonic disk, will become new organism and the outer cells called trophoblast, provides protective covering and nourishment.
- Implantation occurs between 7th and 9th day.
- Trophoblast forms a membrane called amnion, which encloses the zygote in amniotic fluid.
- The amnion helps to keep the temperature of the prenatal world constant and provides safety against jerks and movements.
- The yolk sac emerges, producing blood cells until the liver, spleen and bone marrow matures to take over this function.
- Trophoblast forms another protective membrane called the chorion surrounding the amnion, from which tiny hair like villi or blood vessels emerge.
- These villi burrow into the uterine wall and a special organ called the placenta starts to develop.
- Placenta helps in permitting food and oxygen to reach the organism and waste products to be carried away.
- A membrane forms that allows these substances to be exchanged, but prevents the blood of the mother and that of the embryo from mixing directly.
- Placenta is connected by the umbilical cord.
- The umbilical cord grows to the length of 1-3 feet and contains one large vein to deliver blood loaded with nutrients and two arteries, which removes waste products.

Period of Embryo

Following characters found the period of embryo :

- The embryonic disk from three layers of cells :

  Ectoderm which becomes the nervous system and skin.

  Mesoderm from which the muscles, skeleton, circulatory system and other internal organs will develop.

  Endoderm which becomes the digestive system, lungs, urinary tract and glands.
- The nervous system develops fastest.
- The ectoderm folds to form a neural tube or primitive spinal cord.
- The top of the neural tube swells to form a brain.
- The heart begins to pump blood and muscles, backbone, ribs and digestive tract appear.
- Changing body proportion causes the embryo's posture to become more upright.

Period of Foetus

Stages of the period of foetus :

- It is the longest prenatal period and the organism increases rapidly in size.
- The foetus can kick, bend its arms, open and close its hands and mouth and suck its thumb.
- A white cheese like substance called vernix covers the skin, protecting it from chapping.
- White, downy hair called lanugo also covers the entire body.
- Brain weight increases due to increased rate of glial cells which supports and feeds the neurons.
- Sex of the foetus can be detected through ultrasound.
- The age of viability occurs which is the point at which the baby can first survive, between 22 and 26 weeks.

- The foetus also receives antibodies from the mother's blood to protect against illnesses.
- Most foetus take upside-down position because of the shape of the uterus and also because the head is heavier than the feet.

Care during Pregnancy and Prenatal and Neonatal Development

A woman having a healthy pregnancy is one of the best ways to promote a healthy birth. Getting early and regular prenatal care improves the chances of a healthy pregnancy. A pregnant women should visit a doctor atleast once a month for the first eight months of pregnancy and once a week during the last month. She may need to go to consult her doctor more frequently in the first trimester because of the various problems she faces.

A pregnant woman must also focus on the following things during her pregnancy :

She should take nutritious diet, i.e. she must eat the right food. As it is only a healthy woman can give birth to a healthy child. During first three months of pregnancy, nausea and vomiting are quite common.

To combat this morning sickness she must eat a piece of dry toast or biscuit before she leaves the bed in the morning. She must eat a lot of fruits and raw salads and drinks plenty of fluids.

Medicines A pregnant woman must avoid taking medicines as far as possible. As the medicines may prove harmful. A pregnant woman must take a tetanus vaccination in the 7th and 8th months in order to prevent tetanus in the newborn child.

Clothes A pregnant woman must wear loose and comfortable clothes. Clothes which are tight at the abdomen interfere in the development of foetus.

Exercise The pregnant woman must remain active and continue with her normal daily work. She must also get adequate rest because the woman tends to get tired easily during this period.

Drugs The use of drugs, alcohol and smoking should be avoided during pregnancy as these can fatally harm the child.

The pregnant woman must also take care during prenatal and neonatal time. The prenatal, which is also known as antenatal care is type of preventive healthcare. Its goal is to provide regular check-ups that allow doctors or midwives to treat and prevent potential health problems throughout the course of the pregnancy and to prevent healthy lifestyles that benefit both mother and child.

During check-ups pregnant woman receives medical information over maternal physiological changes in pregnancy, biological changes and prenatal nutrition including prenatal vitamins.

The availability of routine prenatal care, including prenatal screening and diagnosis, has played a part in reducing the frequency of maternal death, miscarriages birth defects low birth weight, neonatal infections and other preventable health problems.

The prenatal development starts with fertilisation in the germinal stage of embryonic development and continues in foetal development until birth. Development happens quickly during prenatal period.

The neonatal care refers to that care given to the new born infant from the time of delivery through about the first month. Neonatal care is a type of care given to a baby when he/she is born premature or. He/She sick receives in a neonatal unit.

The neonatal period (birth to 1 month) is a time of extensive and ongoing system transition from uterine environment to external world. It includes the initial period after birth which is referred to as the prenatal period. It is a time when changes are very rapid.

In the neonatal stage is characterised that the head is larger than the trunk and legs shoulders of neonate are narrow, while the abdomen is large. Bones are soft and flexible mainly composed of cartilage. Neonates are extremely vulnerable to disease. There is lack of control over eye movement.

Growth and Development in Case of Infants

Infant development is most often divided into the following areas :

Physical Development

An infant's physical development begins at the head and then moves to other parts of the body. For example, sucking comes before sitting, which comes before walking.

Newborn to 2 months

- Can lift and turn their head when lying on their back.
- Hands are fisted, the arms are flexed.
- Neck is unable to support the head when the infant is pulled to a sitting position.
- Extends arms then bends and pulls them in toward body with a brief cry, often triggered by loud sounds or sudden movements.
- Infant closes hand and 'grips' your finger.
- Placing, leg extends when sole of foot is touched.

- Infant flexes the toes and forefoot.
- Rooting and sucking, turns head in search of nipple when cheek is touched and begins to suck when nipple touches lips.
- Stepping and walking, takes brisk steps when both feet are placed on a surface, with body supported.
- Left arm extends when infant gazes to the left, while right arm and leg flex inward and vice versa.

3 to 4 months

- Better eye-muscle control allows the infant to track objects.
- Begins to control hand and feet actions, but these movements are not fine-tuned. The infant may begin to use both hands, working together, to accomplish tasks.

  The infant is still unable to coordinate the grasp, but swipes at objects to bring them closer. Increased vision allows the infant to tell objects apart from backgrounds with very little contrast.
- Infant raises up (upper torso, shoulders, and head) with arms when lying face down (on tummy).
- Neck muscles are developed enough to allow the infant to sit with support, and keep head up.
- Primitive reflexes have either already disappeared, or are starting to disappear.

5 to 6 months

- Infant is able to sit alone, without support, for only moments at first, and then for up to 30 seconds or more.
- Infant begins to grasp blocks or cubes using the ulnar-palmar grasp technique (pressing the block into palm of hand while flexing or bending wrist in) but does not yet use thumb.
- Infant rolls from back to stomach. When on tummy, the infant can push up with arms to raise the shoulders and head and look around or reach for objects.

6 to 9 months

- Crawling may begin.
- Infant can walk while holding an adult's hand.
- Infant is able to sit steadily, without support, for long periods of time.
- Infant learns to sit down from a standing position.
- Infant may pull into and keep a standing position while holding onto furniture.

9 to 12 months

- Infant begins to balance while standing alone.
- Infant takes steps holding a hand; may take few steps alone.

Language Development

An infant's language develoment begins with crying. It is a very important way to communicate. By the baby's third day of life, mothers can tell their own baby's cry from that of other babies.

By the first month of life, most parents can tell if their baby's cry means hunger, pain or anger. Crying also causes a nursing mother's milk to letdown (fill the breast).

Description of infant's language development through different mouths is given below:

0 to 2 months

- Alert to voices
- Uses range of noises to signal needs, such as hunger or pain

2 to 4 months

- Coos

4 to 6 months

- Makes vowel sounds ('OO,' 'ah')

6 to 9 months

- Babbles
- Blows bubbles ('raspberries')
- Laughs

9 to 12 months

- Imitates some sounds
- Says 'Mama' and 'Dada', but not specifically for those parents.
- Responds to simple verbal commands, such as 'no'.

Cognitive Development

Cognitive development is the mental development in infants. New borns interact with their environment through reflexive behaviour.

Description of infant's cognitive development through different months is given below:

0 to 2 months

- Learns about things by feel, sound, sight and smell
- Begins repeating movements to help brain growth and memory

2 to 4 months

- Starts paying attention, watching and recognising faces.
- Recognises familiar people at a distance.
- Shows signs of boredom (fussiness) when doing one thing too long.
- Uses eyes and hands together and plans, such as seeing a toy and reaching for it.

4 to 6 months

- Is curious about things out of reach and looks at new things
- Explores things by putting them in mouth
- Recognises and responds to own name

6 to 9 months

- Practices turn-taking when "talking" with caregivers
- Starts testing cause and effect, such as seeing what happens when shaking a toy

9 to 12 months

- Finds hidden objects
- Looks at or points to a picture when you name it
- Bangs, throws and shakes things to see what happens
- Explores everyday objects, both in correct ways (using a cup to drink) and incorrect ways (puts a toy in a cup)
- Follows one-step directions
- Shakes head no and waves

Social Skills Development

Infants start to develop relationships with the people around them right from birth. Description of social skill development through

0 to 2 months

- Responds to calming actions such as rocking, singing, baby wearing, or baby massage
- Has short periods of wakefulness
- Follows parents with eyes (sees most clearly around 8 inches, or the distance between a mom's and baby's face during breastfeeding)

2 to 4 months

- Smiles and shows emotions-happiness and sadness
- Laughs and blows bubbles
- Self-calms by sucking on hands
- Loves human faces, maintains eye contact, and mimics facial gestures

4 to 6 months

- Learns which sounds and actions are most likely to get a desired response
- Follows moving objects with eyes

6 to 8 months

- Responds to name
- Plays peek-a-boo

8 to 10 months

- Shows separation anxiety

10 to 12 months

- Waves bye-bye
- Shows stranger anxiety

Growth and Development During Childhood

Childhood begins after infancy.This is a important stage of creation of child's body. At this stage, various habits, behaviours, desires and interests are created in the child.

Physical Development

Gross Motor (physical) skills are those which require whole body movement and which involve the large (core stabilising) muscles of the body to perform everyday functions, such as standing, walking, running, and sitting upright. It also includes eye-hand coordination skills such as ball skills (throwing, catching, and kicking).

Description of physical development through different years is given below :

2 to 3 years

Between 2 and 3 years, young children stop 'toddling,' or using the awkward, wide-legged robot-like stance that is the hallmark of new walkers. As they develop a smoother gait, they also develop the ability to run, jump, and hop. Children of this age can participate in throwing and catching games with larger balls. They can also push themselves around with their feet while sitting on a riding toy.

3 to 4 years

- Children who are 3 to 4 years old can climb upstairs using a method of bringing both feet together on each step before proceeding to the next step (in contrast, adults place one foot on each step in sequence). However, young children may still need some 'back-up' assistance to prevent falls in case, they become unsteady in this new skill.
- Children of this age will also be stumped when it's time to go back down the stairs; they tend to turn around and scoot down the stairs backwards. 3 to 4 years old can jump and hop higher as their legs muscles grow stronger. Many children can even hop on one foot for short periods of time.

4 to 5 years

- By 4 to 5 years, children can go up and down the stairs alone in the adult fashion (i.e., taking one step at a time). Their running continues to smooth out and increase in speed.
- Children of this age can also skip and add spin to their throws. They also have more control when riding their tricycles (or bicycles), and can drive them faster.

5 to 6 years

- During 5 to 6 years, young children continue to refine earlier skills. They are running even faster and can start to ride bicycles with training wheels for added stability. In addition, they can step sideways.
- Children of this age begin mastering new forms of physical play such as the jungle gym and begin to use the see-saw, slide, and swing on their own. They often start jumping rope, skating, hitting balls with bats, and so on. Many children of this age enjoy learning to play organised sports such as soccer, basketball, t-ball or swimming. In addition, 5 to 6 years old often like to participate in physical extracurricular activities such as karate, gymnastics, or dance. Children continue to refine and improve their gross motor skills through age 7 and beyond.

Mental Development

The factors that affect mental development include maturation, learning and education. The kind of nervous system the human child inherits is an important factor. It helps him to coordinate various activities and responses. It regulates the activity of all the organs. The brain, an important part of the nervous system, plays a more significant role in the mental development of the individual than any other part.

Description of mental development through different years is given below :

From birth to 3 Years

The child is born with all the sensory equipment that is needed for mental activity. By the age of 3, he shows the ability to fulfill his needs in a selective manner. There in lies his mental development. This is evident from other types of behaviour as well. He secures or tries to secure approval from his parents and others for the things he likes or does. The chiid's curiosity is another characteristic of mental development at this stage. Another evidence is the child's tendency to make believe. He lives in a world of fantasy and personifies the objects that are around him. He develops the ability to differentiate between himself and others.

From 3 to 6 Years

This period of the child's life is characterised by his ability to use symbols and words. He acquires a variety of sensory and perceptual experience and these experiences contribute a lot towards his mental development.

Later Childhood

This period is marked by the ability to acquire keen and accurate perception. With keen and accurate perception grows the process of conceptualisation. Mental development is also indicated in him growing interests. He begins to admire things and people around him. He begins to imitate the manners and behaviour of those people whom he admires.

Early Childhood Care and Education

The term early childhood education is very comprehensive. It encompasses all aspects related to or affecting a child. The focus of ECCE programme is mainly for 3 years old, who are in pre-school stage. Today, there is a universal demand for early childhood education in the whole world. In India, the programme was launched in the sixth plan as a distinct strategy to reduce dropout rates and rate of retention of children in school. The National Policy of Education (NPE 1986) has given a great deal of importance to ECCE.

Emphasising the holistic nature of early child programme. It has highlighted the need of community involvement in ECCE as well as the need to establish a linkage between Integrated Child Development Schemes (ICDS) and ECCE programmes at all levels.

ECCE programmes include a component of health, nutrition and pre-school education for ensuring all round development of the child. The policy has emphasised that all the ECCE programmes should be transacted through play way and activity approach. It has also cautioned against the dangers of using formal methods of teaching and introduction of 3Rs at this early stage.

It is a programme with a focus on the holistic development of the child. It prepares children for primary grades. ECCE is a programme which provides stimulating play environment for intellectual, language, social, emotional and physical development of the child. All together, it is a programme which indirectly promotes self-control and thereby inner discipline in children.

ECCE can make a positive difference in the lives of young children. The early childhood care and education are an arena of play and build a foundation for primary education.

Activities to Promote Holistic Development

Holistic development is an approach to learning that emphasises the importance of the physical, emotional and psychological well-being of children, particularly in early childhood. To promote the holistic development of the child few creative activities can be promoted in early childhood. It can be through stimulation of creative learning process. Some daily indoor and outdoor play activities will prove beneficial to the child's development.

The activities may also include puppet play, dramatic play, visits/nature walk, whole group activity, physical play, object play, small group activity and games with rules.

Influence of Family, Peers, School, Community and Culture on Personality Development

The environment that children grow up certainly has influence on what type of personality they develop.

Family The family has a very powerful effects on the developing child, impacting attitudes, beliefs, opportunities, habits and personality traits. If families are high conflict and the children are drawn into many arguments and disagreements, they are much likely to become withdrawn or have a personality that is conflict driven as they grow older. For a child with talent, the influence of the family can be determining factor as to whether the ability is developed to high level or not.

Peers Peers have the most obvious influence on a child's personality. By interacting with children of their own age. learn how to work cooperatively, collaborate with others. Peer interactions also foster communication skills.

The influence of peers provides an arena of learning and practising a variety of social skills including negotiation, persuasion, cooperation, compromise, emotional conflict and conflict resolution. It is seen that when children become members of a peer group gradually reduces the family influence on their attitudes, thinking and behaviour. Thus, peer relationships play an important role in shaping the behaviour of children, where they feel accepted and feel good about themselves.

School After family school is the second agent which profoundly affect shaping of personality. School affects personality in two ways-first it affects development of personality traits second it leads to self-confidence. Teacher's personality, classroom environment, discipline system and academic achievement all influence the child.

Children learn social traits of cooperation, adjustment and sharing. They develop realistic self-concept. The school in which one studies also influence an individual (child). Children schooled in different types of school may be intellectually, socially and emotionally different and manifest different behaviours.

Community The kind of community in which one lives has a decided influence upon ones personality. The communities that children grow up can have a profound effect on their personality.

Culture It is a broad term and includes in it all the customs, traditions, folks, fashions, etc. We all are part of one or other culture.

Therefore, culture's effect on personality is bound to take place. Different cultures have different child rearing practices. The culture can have positive and negative effects on child's development. The culture influences the manner one learns, lives and behaves.

The effect of culture on personality on the child is that who is born and bred in the same culture share common personality traits.

The cultural effect is most prominently seen in the way one welcomes and greet people. So, it can be said that culture plays an important role in shaping the personality development of the child.

EXAM BASED QUESTIONS

1 Which is the first stage of human development?
(a) Zygote (b) Infancy
(c) Adolescent (d) Adulthood

2 Growth refers to ...... changes.
(a) qualitative (b) quantitative
(c) Both (a) and (b) (d) None of these

3 Which is the specific sequence of human development?
(a) Cephalocaudal Sequence (b) Proximodistal Sequence
(c) Both (a) and (b) (d) None of these

4 Which of the following is correct sequence of development under proximodistal sequence?
(a) From head to toe (b) From toe to head
(c) From centre to outside (d) None of these

5 Baby waving his arm is a
(a) general response (b) specific response
(c) unconscious act (d) conscious act

6 Which of the following reaches maximum development by early adolescent?
(a) Feet (b) Hand (c) Nose (d) All of these

7 ...... has certain physical and mental, common and predictable character.
(a) Industrialisation (b) Fertilisation
(c) Development (d) None of these

8 Which of the following is not a developmental stage?
(a) Prenatal (b) Post natal
(c) Adolescence (d) Fusion

9 Sigmund Freud founded
(a) psychoanalysis (b) teacher education
(c) home science (d) library science

10 Which is the part of psychoanalysis theory?
(a) ID (b) EGO
(c) Super EGO (d) All of these

11 Ego helps in sense of
(a) reality (b) anger
(c) imagination (d) ignorance

12 At what age does Super EGO develop?
(a) 4-5 years (b) 6-7 years (c) 8-9 years (d) 10-12 years

13 Who gave psychosexual theory of development?
(a) Skinner (b) Pavlov (c) Freud (d) Erikson

14 Which is the pleasure centre for oral?
(a) Feet (b) Hand (c) Nose (d) Mouth

15 What is Oedipus complex?
(a) A boy's attraction for his mother
(b) A girl's attraction for her mother
(c) A boy's attraction for his father
(d) A girl's attraction for her father

16 When does sexual urge reemerge?
(a) 6-12 years of age (b) 12+ years of age
(c) 13-14 years of age (d) None of these

17 Which theory was given by Erikson?
(a) Psychosexual theory (b) Psychoanalysis theory
(c) Psychosocial theory (d) All of these

18 ...... occurs when adults meet a child's basic needs for survival.
(a) Autonomy vs Shame (b) Trust vs Mistrust
(c) Guilt vs Initiative (d) Intimacy vs Isolation

19 When do human undergoes role confusion?
(a) 12-18 years (b) 20-30 years
(c) 10-20 years (d) 18-28 years

20 Which is the level of Kohlberg's stages of moral development?
(a) Pre-conventional (b) Conventional
(c) Post-conventional (d) All of these

21 Which stage occurs at the age of 2 years according to Piaget?
(a) Sensorimotor stage
(b) Preoperational stage
(c) Concrete operational stage
(d) Formal operational

22 ...... begins during preoperational stage.
(a) Walking (b) Language development
(c) Crying (d) Tooth development

23 What physical change occur in babies?
(a) Increase in height
(b) Increase in weight
(c) Change in internal organ
(d) All of the above

24 The development of body parts are not in equal
(a) proportion (b) rate (c) time (d) change

25 Proportional changes affect ...... development.
(a) mental (b) social
(c) emotional (d) All of these

26 Changes in feature is affected by
(a) learning (b) maturity
(c) Both (a) and (b) (d) None of these

27 Human development is affected by
(a) heredity (b) environment
(c) Both (a) and (b) (d) None of these

28 Families have the most profound impact in ...... a child.
(a) spoiling (b) nurturing
(c) training (d) None of these

29 Boys and girls grow in different way during
(a) puberty (b) childhood
(c) adulthood (d) old age

30 What should a school provide to child?
(a) Support (b) Opportunity
(c) Both (a) and (b) (d) None of these

31 Every country and society have its own
(a) industries (b) cultural identify
(c) school (d) All of these

32 Why is conflict easy to happen in peer groups?
(a) Children are rude
(b) Children want to lead the group
(c) Children come from various backgrounds
(d) Children may not listen to each other

33 Which of the following is Thorndike's law?
(a) Law of readiness (b) Law of exercise
(c) Law of effect (d) All of these

34 Which theory did Ivan Pavlov give?
(a) Operant conditioning (b) Classical conditioning
(c) Psychoanalysis (d) Psychosocial

35 What are the key element of classical conditioning?
(a) Acquisition
(b) Extinction
(c) Generalisation of stimulus
(d) All of the above

36 Who was the first theorist to attempt grand theory to explain all behaviour?
(a) Clark Hull (b) Ivan Pavlov
(c) BF Skinner (d) Thorndike

37 Which is the type of behaviour by BF Skinner?
(a) Respondent behaviour (b) Operant behaviour
(c) Both (a) and (b) (d) None of these

38 From where does ovum is released?
(a) Follopian tube (b) Uterus
(c) Ovary (d) None of these

39 How long does period of zygote last after fertilisation?
(a) 3 weeks (b) 4 weeks
(c) 2 weeks (d) 1 month

40 ...... helps in permitting food and oxygen to the zygote.
(a) Placenta (b) Chorion
(c) Amniotic sac (d) Trophoblast

41 ...... layer of embryo becomes nervous system and skin.
(a) Trophoblast (b) Ectoderm
(c) Mesoderm (d) Endoderm

42 What is the white cheese like substance that covers the skin?
(a) Amniotic fluid (b) Lactoglobulin
(c) Vernix (d) All of these

43 .... is a reflex of toes fan outward and sole of foot is stroked.
(a) Babinski reflex (b) Moro reflex
(c) Central reflex (d) Short reflex

44 At what month do children learn to sit alone?
(a) 3 to 4 months (b) 5 to 6 months
(c) New born to 2 months (d) 7 to 12 months

45 What is the language development from 6 to 9 months?
(a) Coos (b) Laughs
(c) Babbles (d) Both (b) and (c)

46 At what month can the child recognise its own name?
(a) 4 to 6 months (b) 2 to 4 months
(c) 6 to 9 months (d) 9 to 12 months

47 .... skills are those which require whole body movement.
(a) Fine motor (b) Gross motor
(c) Reflex motor (d) Central motor

48 What are the factors affecting mental health?
(a) Maturation (b) Learning
(c) Education (d) All of these

49 ...... play an important role in mental development.
(a) Brain (b) CNS (c) PNS (d) Hormones

50 .... is a completely new situation for a child.
(a) Hospital (b) School
(c) Relative's house (d) All of these

51 The main purpose of studying development of children is to know and understand them better. Which of the following are correct in this regard?
1. To know what to expect from child.
2. To known the standards or norms of age groups.
3. To guide the children in different stages.
Select the correct answer using the codes given below:
(a) 2 and 3 (b) 1 and 2 (c) 1 and 3 (d) All of these

52 Which of the following statements are correct?
1. According to Erikson, the part of the body on which their attention is focused and the life tasks which preoccupy them, change radically from one stage to another.
2. A key word to describe children's thought by Piaget is 'unsystematic'.
3. Preoperational children tend to focus their attention only on the most compelling aspect of an event.
4. Perceptual constancy appears easily in infancy, but object, constancy develops relatively slow.
Select the correct answer using the codes given below:
(a) 1 and 4 (b) 1, 2 and 3 (c) 1 and 2 (d) All of these

53 Which of the following statement are correct?
1. Development psychology is the study of changes in behavioural and mental processes through life.
2. In the longitudinal method of study people are followed through their life spans.
3. In cross-sectional method of study, representative group who are at different stages in development are compared.
4. Environment influence interacts with maturation to determine the final form of the behaviour.

Select the correct answer using the codes given below:
(a) 1 and 2 (b) 1 and 4
(c) 1, 2 and 3 (d) All of these

54 The term egocentrism, as used by Piaget, meant that children
(a) are concerned only with getting what they want
(b) perceive the world from their own perspective
(c) think in a round about manner
(d) are concerned about their egos

55 Which of the statements given below is/are correct?
1. Childhood is the foundation period of life.
2. Development comes from maturation and learning.
3. Each developmental phase has a characteristic traits.

Select the correct answer using the codes given below:
(a) Only 1 (b) Only 2
(c) Only 3 (d) All of these

56 Maturation refers to ...... changes from conception to death.
1. neurophysiological changes
2. bio-chemical changes

Select the correct answer using the codes given below :
(c) Only 1 (b) Only 2
(c) Both 1 and 2 (d) None of these

57 Which of the following statements are correct?
1. During the period of the fetus actual growth and development is greater than during the period of embryo.
2. During the period of the embryo and fetus growth follows law of developmental direction.
3. Towards the end of the period of the fetus the amount of activity in the leg region is similar to that of the head region.
4. Muscles in the head region come under voluntary control first and those in the leg region later.

Select the correct answer using the codes given below:
(a) 1, 2, 3 and 4 (b) 1, 2 and 3
(c) 1 and 2 (d) 1 and 4

58 Which of the following is correct of sensitive periods on prenatal development?
(a) All major organ systems share the exact same sensitive period.
(b) Teratogens have the most serious effect on prenatal development immediately before a system's sensitive period.
(c) A sensitive period is the time when a system's basic structures are being formed.
(d) The sensitive period of limb development occurs several weeks before the limbs begin to formed.

59 Consider the following statements
1. Peer sociability is present in the first 2 years and is promoted by the early caregiver.
2. From interacting with sensitive adults, babies learn how to send and interpret emotional signals.
3. Children who promote positive peer exhanges, display more socially competent behaviour as pre-schoolers.

Which of the statements given above are correct?
(a) 1 and 2 (b) 3 and 4
(c) 2 and 3 (d) All of these

60 Which of the following statement(s) is/are correct?
1. The child who does not learn tasks at periods of readiness may have great difficulty learning them later.
2. Serious behaviour problems cause abruptly in adolescence, but trace their organ to maladjustment in the early years.
3. In the pattern of development, there is a marked correlation between physical and psychological development.
4. In the pattern of intellectual development, memory precedes reasoning with abstract reasoning following concrete reasoning.

Codes
(c) Only 1 (b) Only 2
(c) Both 1 and 2 (d) None of these

Directions (Q. Nos. 61-74) *In the questions given below are two statements labelled as Assertion (A) and Reason (R). In the context of the two statements, which one of the following incorrect?*

Codes
(a) Both A and R are true and R is the correct explanation of A
(b) Both A and R are true, but R is not the correct explanation of A
(c) A is true, but R is false
(d) A is false, but R is true

61 **Assertion** (A) Each child has his own characteristic rate of development.
Reason (R) We may expect same behaviour from all children of the same age.

62 **Assertion** (A) Ego deals with the real world. It is based on reality principle.
Reason (R) Ego searches for real objects to satisfy the need. The hungry person must get real food to satisfy the hunger.

63 **Assertion** (A) The Id is that structure of the mind that is present at birth.
Reason (R) Freud's believed that difficulty at any stage can cause a person to become fixated.

64 **Assertion** (A) Height or length of children below the age of 2 years should be measured with an infantometer.
Reason (R) An infantometer is used for children, who cannot stand properly.

65 **Assertion** (A) Energy requirements during lactation is higher than during pregnancy.
Reason (R) The turn over of iron is greater during lactation because of milk secretion.

66 Assertion (A) Growth of different body parts is differential.
Reason (R) During human growth muscles show minimum growth, while brain shows maximum growth.

67 Assertion (A) Schools, peers and neighbours all have an influence in the social development of the child.
Reason (R) Social development is a continuous process, which goes on from the birth of a child till death.

68 Assertion (A) Cognitive development refers to the ability of the child to think and find solution to the problems.
Reason (R) Cognitive development involves changes occurring in the mental ability of a child.

69 Assertion (A) Piaget believed that as children grow their brain develop and they move through four distinct stages.
Reason (R) Its four stages correspond with the age of children.

70 Assertion (A) During pregnancy the use of alcohol drugs, smoking should be avoided.
Reason (R) These can fatally harm the child.

71 Assertion (A) A neonatal care is give to a baby born premature.
Reason (R) The development starts with fertilisation in the germinal stage of embryonic development.

72 Assertion (A) The focus of ECCE programme is mainly on 3 years old children.
Reason (R) The ECCE programmes excludes the component of health, nutrition and pre-school education.

73 Assertion (A) A high conflicting family has adverse impact/influence on child's personality.
Reason (R) Such children have conflict driven personality when they grow older.

74 Assertion (A) The peers influence on child always have negative impact.
Reason (R) Children when become the member of peer group they gradually reduce their relationship with family members.

75 Match the following.

List I	List II
A. Development of the body from upper to lower portion	1. Proximodistal
B. Development of the body from centre to periphery	2. Cephalocodal
C Intrauterine life	3. Neonatal stage
D. New born baby	4. Period of feotus

Codes

	A	B	C	D
(a)	1	2	3	4
(b)	2	1	3	4
(c)	2	1	4	3
(d)	4	2	1	3

76 Match the following.

List I	List II
A. Sucking and eye blinking	1. Classical conditioning
B. Less than 2.5kg, of birth weight	2. Loneliness
C. Empty nest	3. Operant conditioning
D. Pairing of stimuli	4. Permanent reflex
	5. Small for date
	6. Broken homes

Codes

	A	B	C	D
(a)	5	2	6	3
(b)	6	5	2	3
(c)	2	4	6	1
(d)	4	5	2	1

77 Match the following.

List I	List II
A. Language development	1. Jealousy, fear, love
B. Emotional development	2. Words and sentences
C. Cognitive development	3. Motor skills
D. Childhood diseases	4. Influensa, chickenpox

Codes

	A	B	C	D
(a)	2	1	3	4
(b)	1	2	3	4
(c)	1	2	4	3
(d)	4	3	2	1

78 Match the following.

List I	List II
A. Formal operational	1. 0-2 years
B. Sensory motor	2. 2-7 years
C. Preoperational	3. 7-12 years
D. Concrete operational	4. 12-18 years

Codes

	A	B	C	D
(a)	4	1	2	3
(b)	3	2	4	1
(c)	4	2	1	3
(d)	3	4	1	2

79 Arrange the development tasks during early childhood period sequentially.
1. Learning to talk
2. Bladder control
3. Learning to walk
4. Learning gender difference
5. Distinguishing right and wrong
6. Getting ready to read

Codes
(a) 2, 1, 3, 6, 4, 5
(b) 5, 2, 3, 6, 1, 4
(c) 3, 1, 2, 4, 6, 5
(d) 1, 3, 4, 2, 5, 6

Directions (Q. Nos. 80-84) *Read the passage and give answer to following questions.*

At birth, the average baby's brain is about a quarter of the size of the average adult brain. Incredibly, it doubles in size in the first year. It keeps growing to about 80% of adult size by age 3 and 90% - nearly full grown - by age 5.

The brain is the command center of the human body. It receives signals from the body's sensory organs and output information to the muscles. It is responsible for all body functions.

A newborn baby has all of the brain cells (neurons) they'll have for the rest of their life, but it's the connections between these cells that really make the brain work. Brain connections enable us to move, think, communicate and do just about everything.

The early childhood years are crucial for making these connections. At least one million new neural connections (synapses) are made every second, more than at any other time in life.

Brain development builds on itself, as connections eventually link with each other in more complex ways. This enables the child to move and speak and think in more complex ways. The early years are the best opportunity for a child's brain to develop the connections they need to be healthy, capable, successful adults. The connections needed for many important, higher level abilities like motivation, self-regulation, problem-solving and communication are formed in these early years or not formed. It's much harder for these essential brain connections to be formed later in life.

Starting from birth, children develop brain connections through their everyday experiences. They are built through positive interactions with their parents and caregivers and by using their senses to interact with the world. A young child's daily experiences determine which brain connections develop and which will last for a lifetime.

The amount and quality of care, stimulation and interaction they receive in their early years make all the difference. A child's relationships with the adults in their life are the most important influences on their brain development. Loving relationships with responsive, dependable adults are essential to a child's healthy development.

These relationships begin at home, with parents and family, but also include child care providers, teachers and other members of the community. From birth, young children serve up invitations to engage with their parents and other adult caregivers. Babies do it by cooing, smiling and crying.

Toddlers communicate their needs and interests more directly. Each of these little invitations is an opportunity for the caregiver to be responsive to the child's needs.

80 **Which of the following staement(s) is/are correct about the brain of the human body?**

(a) It is the command centre of the human body.
(b) Brain connections enable us to move, think, communicate and do everything.
(c) It receives signals from the body's sensory organs and output information to the muscles.
(d) All of the above

81 **The growth of brain of a baby**

(a) at the birth is about the quarter of the size of adult brain.
(b) triples in size in the first year.
(c) keeps growing to about 80 percent of the adult size by the age of 5 years.
(d) grows 90% by the age of 12 years.

82 **Consider the following statement(s) is/are correct with regard to child's brain.**

Statement I Children develop brain connections through their everyday experiences.

Statement II A young child's daily experiences determine which brain connections develop and which will last for a lifetime.

(a) Statement I is correct
(b) Statement II is correct
(c) Both the statement I and II are correct
(d) Neither statement I nor statement II is correct

83 **Which among the following is essential for child's healthy development?**

(a) Loving relationship with adults
(b) The responsive adults
(c) Not responding for child's essential social and psychological needs
(d) Both (a) and (b)

84 **How do toddlers communicate?**

(a) They communicate their needs and interest more directly.
(b) They communicate through gestures.
(c) They do it by cooing, smiling or crying.
(d) All of the above

PREVIOUS YEARS' QUESTIONS

June 2018

1 **Match the stage in List I with achievement in List II.**

List I	List II
A. Sensory motor stage	1. Centration
B. Preoperational stage	2. Object permanence
C. Concrete operations	3. Test hypothesis
D. Formal operations	4. Conservation of numbers
	5. Formation

Codes

	A	B	C	D		A	B	C	D
(a)	2	1	4	3	(b)	4	2	1	3
(c)	3	4	2	5	(d)	2	1	4	5

2 **Assertion** (A) **The process of socialisation of children as girl's and boy's is called gendering.**

Reason (R) **Children internalise behaviours and roles as per the gendering processes.**

Codes

(a) A is correct and R is incorrect
(b) A is incorrect and R is correct
(c) Both A and R are correct
(d) Both A and R are incorrect

3 **Theorists that extended the work of psychoanalytic theorist Freud are**

1. Erik Erikson
2. Carl Jung
3. Urie Bronfenbrenner
4. Alfred Adler

Codes

(a) 2, 3 and 4 (b) 1, 2 and 4 (c) 1, 3 and 4 (d) 1, 2 and 3

4 **Which of these theorists contributed to behaviourism?**

1. Pavlov
2. Skinner
3. Watson
4. Voigt

Codes

(a) 2, 3 and 4 (b) 1, 3 and 4 (c) 1, 2 and 4 (d) 1, 2 and 3

November 2017

5 **According to Piaget, children's thinking during the preoperational period is characterised by**

1. centration
2. irreversibility
3. conservation
4. egocentrism

Codes

(a) 1, 2 and 3 (b) 1, 3 and 4
(c) 1, 2 and 4 (d) 2, 3 and 4

6 **Match the terms in List I with the development in List II.**

List I	List II
A. Period of the fetus	1. Body structure forms
B. Period of the zygote	2. External genitals formed
C. Neonatal period	3. Conservation
D. Period of embryo	4. Rooting reflex
	5. Implantation

Codes

	A	B	C	D		A	B	C	D
(a)	2	5	4	1	(b)	5	2	4	1
(c)	2	4	5	1	(d)	3	1	4	2

7 **Arrange in sequence the development of characteristics based on the psychoanalytic perspective.**

Codes

1. Sucking activities
2. Pleasure in genital stimulation
3. Toilet related activities
4. Acquires social values
5. Sexual impulses

Codes

(a) 1, 2, 3, 4, 5 (b) 1, 2, 4, 3, 5
(c) 1, 3, 2, 4, 5 (d) 1, 3, 4, 2, 5

8 **Arrange the following in the sequential order of moving from lower order thinking skills to the higher order thinking skills for 'learning'.**

1. Analysing
2. Evaluating
3. Remembering
4. Applying
5. Creating
6. Understanding

Codes

(a) 1, 2, 3, 4, 5, 6 (b) 2, 3, 4, 5, 6, 1
(c) 3, 6, 4, 1, 2, 5 (b) 3, 4, 6, 2, 1, 5

9 **The emergence of the following adaptive behaviours occur during the sensorimotor period between 8-12 months as given by Piaget.**

1. Goal directed behaviour
2. Object permanence
3. Intentionality
4. Deferred imitation

Codes

(a) 1, 2 and 3 (b) 1, 2 and 4
(c) 1, 3 and 4 (d) 2, 3 and 4

July 2016

10 **Arrange in order of psychosocial stage of development.**

1. Industry vs Diffusion
2. Initiative vs Guilt
3. Intimacy vs Isolation
4. Identity vs Identity Confusion

Codes

(a) 2, 4, 1, 3 (b) 1, 2, 3, 4
(c) 2, 1, 4, 4 (d) 1, 2, 4, 3

11 **Arrange in accordance with Kohlberg's stages of moral understanding.**

1. Instrumental purpose orientation.
2. Punishment and obedience orientation.
3. Social-order-maintaining orientation.
4. Good boy-good girl orientation.

Codes

(a) 2, 1, 4, 3 (b) 2, 4, 1, 3
(c) 1, 2, 4, 3 (d) 2, 1, 3, 4

December 2015

12 Arrange Kohlberg's stages of moral understanding in correct sequence.

1. Social order maintaining orientation
2. Punishment and obedience orientation
3. Good boy-good girl orientation
4. Social contract orientation
5. Instrumental purpose orientation

Codes

(a) 5, 3, 1, 2, 4 (b) 4, 2, 1, 5, 3
(c) 2, 5, 4, 3, 1 (d) 2, 5, 3, 1, 4

13 Some newborn reflexes are

1. moro 2. cooing
3. rooting 4. babinski
5. creeping

Select the correct answer using the codes given below:

(a) 1, 3 and 4
(b) 1, 2 and 3
(c) 2, 3 and 4
(d) 3, 4 and 5

14 **Assertion** (A) For an infant, cognitive development is expressed through perceptual and motor activity.

Reason (R) In Piaget's view, the development of knowledge involves the interplay of two processes, assimilation and accommodation.

Codes

(a) Both A and R are correct
(b) Both A and R are incorrect
(c) A is correct, but R is incorrect
(d) R is correct, but A is incorrect

ANSWERS

Exam Based Questions

1 (a)	2 (b)	3 (c)	4 (c)	5 (a)	6 (d)	7 (c)	8 (d)	9 (a)	10 (d)
11 (a)	12 (a)	13 (c)	14 (d)	15 (a)	16 (b)	17 (c)	18 (b)	19 (a)	20 (d)
21 (a)	22 (b)	23 (d)	24 (a)	25 (d)	26 (c)	27 (c)	28 (b)	29 (a)	30 (c)
31 (b)	32 (c)	33 (d)	34 (b)	35 (d)	36 (a)	37 (c)	38 (c)	39 (c)	40 (a)
41 (b)	42 (c)	43 (a)	44 (b)	45 (d)	46 (a)	47 (b)	48 (d)	49 (a)	50 (b)
51 (d)	52 (a)	53 (c)	54 (b)	55 (d)	56 (a)	57 (a)	58 (c)	59 (d)	60 (c)
61 (c)	62 (a)	63 (b)	64 (c)	65 (a)	66 (c)	67 (a)	68 (a)	69 (a)	70 (a)
71 (b)	72 (c)	73 (a)	74 (d)	75 (c)	76 (d)	77 (a)	78 (a)	79 (a)	80 (c)
81 (d)	82 (a)	83 (c)	84 (d)						

Previous Years' Questions

1 (a)	2 (c)	3 (b)	4 (d)	5 (c)	6 (a)	7 (c)	8 (c)	9 (a)	10 (c)
11 (a)	12 (d)	13 (a)	14 (a)						

CHAPTER 24

Stages of Human Development

Human development is a continuous process. It is divided into infancy, childhood, adolescence, adulthood and old age. In adolescence, physical, mental and sexual development take place. In adulthood, a person has to take up some responsibilities. By old age, the person reaches a stage of decline. Many types of physical and mental impairments occur at this stage. After this stage, a person becomes an adult.

In this Chapter

- Adolescence/Youth
- Adulthood
- Old Age

Adolescence/Youth

Adolescence is derived from Latin word 'adolescence' meaning 'to grow into maturing'. Adolescence is considered to be the transitional stage from childhood to adulthood. It generally occurs between 10 to 19 years of age. Children entering in adolescence, undergo many changes i.e. physical, intellectual, personality and social development.

Changes During Adolescence

Changes during the adolescence occur in the following three stages :

Early Adolescence (From age 10 to 13)

During this stage, children often start to grow more quickly. They also begin to experienced body changes. These include hair growth under the arms and near the genitals, breast development in females and enlargement of the testicles in males. Changes usually start a year or two, earlier in girls than boys. Many girls may start their period at around age 12, on average 2-3 years after the onset of breast development.

These body changes can inspire curiosity and anxiety in some. Especially, if they do not know what to expect or what is normal. Some children may also question their gender identity, at this time. The onset of puberty can be a difficult time for transgender children.

Early adolescents have concrete, black and white thinking. Things are right or wrong, great or terrible, without much room in between. It is normal at this stage for young people to center their thinking on themselves (called 'egocentrism'). As part of this, pre-teens and early teens are often self-conscious about their appearance. They feel that they are always being judged by their peers.

Pre-teens feel an increased need for privacy. They may start to explore ways of being independent from their family. In this process, they may push boundaries and may react strongly if parents or guardians reinforce limits.

Middle Adolescence (From age 14 to 17)

Physical changes from puberty continue to middle adolescence. Most males will have started their growth spurt and puberty related changes continue. They may have some voice cracking and their voices lower. Some develop acne. Physical changes may be nearly complete for females. Most of the girls now have regular periods.

At this age, many teens become interested in romantic and sexual relationships. They may question and explore their sexual identity, which may be stressful if they do not have support from peers, family or community.

Many middle adolescents have more arguments with their parents as they struggle for more independence. They may spend less time with family and more time with friends. They are very concerned about their appearance and peer pressure may peak at this age.

The brain continues to change and mature in this stage. There are still many differences between middle adolescence thinking and adult thinking. Much of this is because the frontal lobes are the last areas of the brain to mature. Thus, development is not complete until a person is well into their 20s. The frontal lobes play a big role in coordinating complex decision-making, impulse control and being able to consider multiple options and consequences.

Late Adolescence (From age 18 to 21)

Late adolescents generally have completed physical development and grown to their full adult height. They usually have more impulse control by now. Thus, better able to gauge risks and rewards accurately. Teens entering into early adulthood have a stronger sense of their own individuality now and can identify their own values.

They may become more focused on the future and base decisions on their hopes and ideals. Friendships and romantic relationships become more stable. They become more emotionally and physically separated from their family. However, many re-establish an 'adult' relationship with their parents, considering them more as equal. They ask for advice and discuss mature topics with parents.

Challenges Affecting Adolescents

The most challenging task for an adolescent is to choose his/her career. For a teenager, choosing the field of occupation is a difficult task. This is because the adolescent is unable to find balance between his interest, abilities and the oppurtunities available to him. His approach is idealistic, rather than realistic and practical. Thus, his decisions are immature.

Following are the challenges for adolescents :

Physical Challenges Adolescents face several challenges related to physical changes in their bodies . As during this phase, many early adolescents either gain or lose weight. If they are healthy then they need to make the right food choice without being prorpted by their parents. They are dealing with a body that is beginning to make their gender more evident.

Intellectual Challenges As children become adults, they are faced with new intellectual challenges. Their school work becomes more demanding. They are supervised less and need to learn to manage their time and school work on their own.

During childhood, we see things in concrete terms but in adolescence. We begin to understand more abstract concepts. The adolescents who get a job will need to learn the requirements for that work as well as skills that allow them to complete it successfully.

Social Challenges During adolescence, they begin to make more friends outside of that small circle (which they have with family members) and spend more time with those friends.

Moral Challenges Adolescents are faced with difficult moral dilemmas such as: Is it right to stand up to a bully? Do I have responsibility to help others? Am I mature enough for sexual relationship? Is physical violence ever justified? etc. Besides above challenges, adolescents also face some other challenges like delinquency, substance abuse uncertainity loneliness, self doubt and concerns about themselves and their future.

They also like to experience excitement, joy and feeling of competence as the overcome challenges. Thus, it can be said that adolescence is a difficult and frustrating time, so they should be helped to meet the challenges they are faced with through positive attitude/outlook.

Impact of Surrounding Environment and People on Adolescents

Parents, school, societal expectation, personal characteristics, media surround adolescents and affect their decisions, behaviour, career, etc.

Their description is given below :

Parents Parents play an important role in choosing the career of their children. The family environment affects the kind of job the child takes up in future. Parents expect from the child to become principal, magistrate, doctor, teacher or other reputable position. Thus, the child get motivated and choose the career according to his parent's wish.

School The experiences in school also affect the career of teenagers. The teacher recognises the interest, abilities and personal characteristics of children. They instill a notion of ambition in students. Many schools conduct vocational education and workshop. Career advisors are also employed in many schools. They help to put the students in right path of their career.

Societal Expectation Expectations from society also influence choice of adolescent's occupation. Some occupations leave strong impression on adolescent's mind. So, they choose the career path that requires a lot of hard work. This include doctor, engineer, carpenter, mechanic, pilot, etc. Sometimes, the child may opt for off beat profession due to personal interest.

Personal Characteristics Different professions require different abilities, skills and attitudes. Some occupations require creativity, speaking skills, painting skills, etc. So, the adolescent needs to be trained in special skills to meet the job's demand.

Media It attracts and motivates adolescent to take up various occupations.

Media, especially TV and internet inform the adolescent about the diverse options they have. Thus, the adolescents are inspired to live into new ventures.

Programmes to Promote Optimal Development in Adolescents

From the beginning of adolescence, the adolescence needs to be educated. Given below are the programmes for maximising adult's development :

Education for Physical Development Many physical changes take place in the body during adolescence. The school must make their body strong and fit. This can be done through :

- physical education
- physical exercises
- playing all types of sports

Education for Mental Development The nature of education should be in accordance with student's interest, trend, attitude and ability. This will maximise the mental development. The following topics should be given place in the education :

- Art, science, literature, geography, history, etc., should be in the course.
- Students should be taken to natural and historical places. This will increase their knowledge and solve their curiosity.
- To know the interest and fantasies of teenagers, debate, poetry writing and literary seminar should be organised.

Education for Social Relations Teenagers give great importance to their groups. Thus, the organisation of such group should be in a way that the teenager learns good social behaviour. This can be done by collective activities, sports and scouting.

Adulthood

Adulthood is the period in the human lifespan in which full physical and intellectual maturity have been attained. Adulthood is commonly thought of as beginning at age 20 or 21 years. Middle age, commencing at about 40 years, is followed by old age at about 60 years.

Characteristics of Adulthood

Adulthood is called the 'golden period of life'. It is a stable stage. An adult takes his own decisions, how to lead his life. The characteristics of puberty can be described as follows :

Physical Development in Adulthood By the time we reach early adulthood, our physical maturation is complete, although our height and weight may increase slightly. In early adulthood, our physical abilities are at their peak, including muscle strength, reaction time, sensory abilities and cardiac functioning.

Cognitive Development in Adulthood Cognitive changes are numerous during this period. Infact, research suggests that adult cognitive development is a complex, everchanging process. Early adulthood is a time of relativistic thinking, in which young people begin to become aware of more than simplistic views of right vs. wrong. They begin to look at ideas and concepts from multiple angles and understand that a question can have more than one right (or wrong) answer.

Relationships and Families in Adulthood Positive relationships have been found to contribute to a state of well-being among adults. An interpersonal relationship is built at this age. It is a strong, deep or close association or acquaintanceship between two or more people that may range from brief to enduring in duration. Like people, relationships change and grow; they may either improve or dissipate over time. The association between two people can be based on various factors including love, solidarity, business or any other context that requires two (or more) people to interact.

Changing Roles and Responsibilities in Early and Middle Adulthood

In every stage of life the roles and responsibilities continue to change not only because of the biological growth process but also because of our understanding and the way we interact with the environment. Certain roles and responsibilities taken up by people in the early and middle adulthood are discussed below :

Early Adulthood

An early adulthood can be a very busy time of life. It is the transition from free of responsibility to a stage full of responsibility. The stage of early adulthood is characterised by new roles.

There are establishing relationships, adjustments, learning how to manage households, preparing budget for family and also maintaining home properly. They rear children and manage household with children. They spend very less time with friends because their energies are consumed for family and work.

During this period, they also take many important decisions of life. At this stage of life one often tries to put efforts to make a better future and earn good status in society. Thus, the role in early adulthood are located in social life, adjustment with the family members and new arrivals in the family.

Middle Adulthood

During middle adulthood, lot of adjustments is needed within the family career and professional development. At this stage, people try to establish and maintain economic standard of living. They assist teenage children to become responsible and happy adults. They adjust to care for ageing parents and also making their life more comfortable.

During this stage, they often assume social and civic responsibility. They develop interest-oriented leisure time activities which were not taken care of during early adulthood.

They engage in taking stock of their lives to assess the extent to which they have realised their dreams. They help growing children to be responsible adults, relinquishing the central role in the live of grown children. They also play an important role in helping future generation. They act as caregivers for ageing parents and spouses.

Old Age

Old age, also called 'senescence' in human beings, is the final stage of the normal life span. Old age is frequently defined as 60 or 65 years of age or older.

Chronological age is a poor criteria to use in marking off the beginning of old age because there are such marked differences among individuals in the age. Due to better living conditions, health care, most men and women today do not show the mental and physical signs of ageing.

Old age is a period of decline. Decline comes partly from physical and partly from psychological factors. There is a change in body cells due to the Ageing process. Unfavourable attitude towards oneself and life in general can lead to decline or become depressed and disorganised. Motivation plays a very important role in decline.

There are individuals differences in the effects of ageing. People age differently because they have different hereditary endowment, different socio-economic and educational backgrounds and different patterns of living. The general rule is physical Ageing precedes mental ageing.

Old age is judged by different criteria . Age is judged in terms of physical appearance and activities. Thus, it one who has white hair is labelled as old. There are many who try to cover up their ageing symptoms to create an illusion that they are not yet old.

Physical and Psychological Changes in the Body with Ageing

All vital organs begin to lose some functions. These changes affect the functioning of all body systems.

The eyes, followed by the ears, begin to change early in mid-life. Most internal functions also decline with Ageing. Most bodily functions peak shortly before age 30 and then begin a gradual but continuous decline. Some organs are more likely to malfunction under stress than others. These organs include the heart and blood vessels, the urinary organs (such as the kidneys) and the brain.

Different parts of the body that change with ageing are :

Bones and Joints

Bones tend to become less dense. Moderate loss of bone density is termed as 'osteopenia' and severe loss of bone density (including occurrence of a fracture due to loss of bone density) is 'osteoporosis'. With osteoporosis, bones become weaker and more likely to break. In women, loss of bone density speeds up after menopause because less estrogen is produced.

Bones become less dense partly because they contain less calcium (which gives strength to bones). The amount of calcium decreases because the body absorbs less calcium from foods. Also, level of vitamin D, which helps the body to use calcium, decreases slightly.

The vertebrae become less dense and the cushions of tissue (disks) between them lose fluid and become thinner, making the spine shorter. The cartilage that lines joints tends to thin, partly because of the wear and tear of years of movements. Thus, older people become shorter. Damage to the cartilage, due to lifelong use of joints or repeated injury often leads to osteoarthritis. It is one of the most common disorder of later life.

Eyes

As people age, the following occur :

- The lens stiffens, making focusing on close objects harder.
- The lens becomes denser, making seeing in dim light harder.
- The pupil reacts more slowly to change in light.
- The lens yellows, changing the way colours are perceived.
- The number of nerve cells decrease, impairing depth perception.
- The eyes produce less fluid, making them feel dry.
- A change in vision is often the first undeniable sign of ageing.

Ears

Most changes in hearing are due to noise exposure than the ageing. Exposure to loud noise over time damages the ear's ability to hear. Nonetheless, some changes in hearing occur as people age, regardless of their exposure to loud noise. As people age, hearing high pitched sounds become more difficult. This change is considered as age-associated hearing loss (presbycusis). Words become harder to understand. As a result, older people may think that other people are mumbling. Gradually, hearing lower pitches also become more difficult. Many older people have more trouble in hearing in noisy places or in groups because of the background noise. Also earwax, which interferes with hearing, tends to accumulate more.

Mouth and Nose

As people age, taste buds on the tongue decrease number and sensitivity. This change affects tasting sweet and salt more than bitter and sour. The ability to smell diminishes because the lining of the nose becomes thinner and drier and the nerve endings in the nose deteriorate.

However, the change is slight, usually affecting only subtle smells. Because of these changes, many foods tend to taste bitter and foods with subtle smells may taste bland. The mouth tends to feel dry more often and partly because less saliva is produced. Dry mouth further reduces the ability to taste food. As people age, the gums recede slightly. Consequently, the lower parts of the teeth are exposed to food particles and bacteria. Also, tooth enamel tends to wear away. These changes, as well as a dry mouth, make the teeth more susceptible to decay and cavities (caries) and thus, make tooth loss more likely.

Skin

The skin tends to become thinner, less elastic, drier and finely wrinkled. Skin changes partly because collagen (a tough, fibrous tissue that makes skin strong) and elastin (which makes skin flexible) becomes chemically changed and less flexible. As a result, the skin tears more easily. The fat layer under the skin thins. This layer acts as a cushion for the skin and help is protection. The fat layer also helps to conserve body heat. When the layer thins, wrinkles are more likely to develop and tolerance for cold decreases. The number of nerve endings in the skin decreases. As a result, people become less sensitive to pain, temperature and pressure. Injuries become more likely.

Brain and Nervous System

The number of nerve cells in the brain typically decreases. However, the brain can partly compensate for this loss in several ways :

- As cells are lost, new connections are made between the remaining nerve cells.
- New nerve cells may form in some areas of the brain, even during old age.
- The brain has more cells than it needs to do most activities. This characteristic is called 'redundancy'. Levels of the chemical substances involved in sending messages in the brain tend to decrease, but some increase. Nerve cells may lose some of their receptors for thes chemical messages.

Blood flow to the brain decreases. Because of these age related changes, the brain may function slightly less well. Nerves may repair themselves more slowly and incompletely. Therefore, in older people with damaged nerves, sensation and strength may be decreased.

Heart and Blood Vessels

The heart and blood vessels become stiffer. The heart fills with blood more slowly. The stiffer arteries are less able to expand when more blood is pumped through them. Thus, blood pressure tends to increase. Differences between young and old hearts become apparent only when the heart has to work hard and pump more blood. For example, during exercise or an illness. An older heart cannot speed up as quickly or pump as fast or as much blood as a younger heart. Thus, older athletes are not able to perform as well as younger athletes. However, regular aerobic exercise can improve athletic performance in older people.

Lungs and Muscles for Breathing

Slightly less oxygen is absorbed from the air that is breathed in. The lungs become less elastic. Breathing at high altitudes (where there is less oxygen) may also be harder. The lungs become less able to fight with infection, partly because the cells that sweep debris containing micro organisms out of the airways are less able to do so. Cough, which also helps to clear the lungs, tends to be weaker.

Digestive System

Overall, the digestive system is less affected by ageing than most other parts of the body. Food is emptied from the stomach slightly more slowly and the stomach cannot hold as much food because it is less elastic.

The digestive tract may produce less lactose, an enzyme that the body needs to digest milk. As a result, older people are more likely to develop intolerance of dairy products (lactose intolerance). The liver may be slightly less able to remove to drugs and other substances from the body. So, the effects of drugs are last longer.

Kidneys and Urinary Tract

The kidneys tend to become smaller because the number of cells decreases. Less blood flows through the kidneys and at the age of 30, they begin to filter blood less well. As years pass, they may remove waste products from the blood less well.

They may excrete too much water and too little salt, making dehydration more likely. Nonetheless, they almost always function well enough to meet the body's needs.

Certain changes in the urinary tract may make controlling urination more difficult :

- The maximum volume of urine that the bladder can hold decreases. Thus, older people may need to urinate more often. The bladder muscles weaken. As a result, they cannot empty the bladder as well and more urine is left in the bladder after urination.
- Older people have more difficulty postponing urination. These changes are one reason that urinary incontinence (uncontrollable loss of urine) becomes more common as people age.

Endocrine System

The levels and activity of some hormones, produced by endocrine glands, decrease. Growth hormone levels decrease, leading to decreased muscle mass. Aldosterone levels decrease, making dehydration more likely. This hormone signals the body to retain salt and water.

Insulin, which helps to control the sugar level in blood is less effective. Less insulin may be produced. Insulin enables sugar to move from the blood into cells, where it can be converted into energy. The changes in insulin mean that the sugar level increases more after a large meal and takes longer to return to normal.

Immune System

The cells of the immune system act more slowly. These cells identify and destroy foreign substances, such as bacteria, other infecting microbes and probably cancer cells.

Psychological Changes and Care Needs

Most elderly people seems to be most vulnerable to psychological dysfunction when they experience change. The psychological changes involved are related to mental health, stress, work, retirement, restlessness fear of being lonely, anxiety, uncertainity, low-self esteem, feeling of inadequacy and depression which includes sleep disturbance, lack of interest, lack of energy, decreased concentration and memory loss.

Caring for Elderly People

It is seen that elderly people tend to look towards others to lean on and to care for them. Some effective care needs that can be adopted to help elderly people are :

- Help them to develop an attitude of flexibility so that they may adopt to the pressure and problems of old age.
- By increasing self-confidence, self-reliance developing healthy attitudes about their strengths and weaknesses.
- By encouraging them to participate in various social groups by joining clubs, building a social network of people of their own age group in their neighbourhood or else where. It would provide them greater opportunity to share life circumstances and find emotional expressions for their existing problems.
- By their involvement in granol parenting helps them to satisfy many of their personal and emotional needs.
- In present time to cope up with problem, many elderly people develop IT skills and make good use of social media.
- The older people need to be engaged in telling their life story, reminiscing or reviewing their life to help create self-esteem and confidence.
- By leading a disciplined life means giving the body enough time to rest, proper work, less tensions, proper nutrition and spirituality. This may help in coping with the problems of old age.

EXAM BASED QUESTIONS

1 Human development is a .... process.
(a) stagnant (b) continuous
(c) path breaking (d) fun

2 What are the stages of human development?
(a) Infancy (b) Old age
(c) Adulthood (d) All of these

3 What is the transitional stage between childhood and adulthood?
(a) Adolescence (b) Infancy
(c) Old age (d) None of these

4 At what age, does adolescence occur?
(a) 5-9 years (b) 10-19 years
(c) 6-12 years (d) 14-20 years

5 What kind of development takes place during adolescence?
(a) Physical (b) Behavioural
(c) Both (a) and (b) (d) None of these

6 When do the girls start their period?
(a) Around 12 years (b) Around 8 years
(c) Around 20 years (d) Around 25 years

7 Young people centre their thinking around themselves. This is called
(a) centralism (b) egocentrism
(c) egoistic (d) None of these

8 At what stage, the adolescent starts to have arguments with their parents?
(a) Early adolescent (b) Middle Adolescent
(c) Late adolescent (d) All of these

9 On what does the adolescents based their decisions?
(a) Hopes (b) Ideal
(c) Both (a) and (b) (d) None of these

10 Which is the most challenging task for an adolescent?
(a) To be in a peer group
(b) To be independent
(c) To choose his career
(d) To talk frankly with parents

11 What kind of approach do adolescents have?
(a) Idealistic (b) Realist
(c) practical (d) Optimistic

12 Parents expect from the child to become a
(a) principal (b) magistrate
(c) doctor (d) All of these

13 Teachers instill a notion of .... in students.
(a) fear (b) ambition
(c) hope (d) sadness

14 What are the initiatives taken by schools to guide the student in right career path?
(a) Conduct workshop
(b) Employ career advisor
(c) Conduct vocational education
(d) All of the above

15 Due to .... , adolescents choose career that requires a lot of hard work.
(a) social pressure (b) family expectation
(c) personal characteristic (d) None of these

16 ...... inform(s) to diverse career option they have.
(a) TV (b) Internet
(c) Both (a) and (b) (d) None of these

17 .... have the responsibility to make children's body strong and fit.
(a) Peers (b) Families
(c) Hospitals (d) Schools

18 How can the school make the teenager strong and fit?
(a) Through physical education
(b) Through physical exercise
(c) Both (a) and (b)
(d) None of the above

19 The nature of education should be according to student's
(a) interest (b) attitude
(c) ability (d) All of these

20 How can the interest of teenagers be known?
(a) By organising debate
(b) By filling up questionnaire
(c) By interviewing student
(d) All of the above

21 Teenagers give great importance to
(a) their parents (b) their siblings
(c) their groups (d) their teachers

22 At what age do adulthood start?
(a) 40 years (b) 20 years
(c) 50 years (d) 15 years

23 Which stage is called the 'golden period of life'?
(a) Adolescence (b) Adulthood
(c) Infancy (d) Old age

24 Which physical ability is high during adulthood?
(a) Muscle strength (b) Reaction time
(c) Cardiac functioning (d) All of these

25 Adulthood is a time of ...... thinking.
(a) relativistic (b) optimistic
(c) simplistic (d) All of these

26 How should adult be financially stable?
(a) By taking loans (b) By going to job
(c) Both (a) and (b) (d) None of these

27 What are the responsibilities of an adult?
(a) To get a job (b) To get married
(c) To raise children (d) All of these

28 Adults serve as a ...... to their children.
(a) role model (b) guide
(c) rival (d) None of these

29 Senescence is a term for
(a) infancy (b) preteen
(c) old age (d) adulthood

30 Old age is a period of
(a) decline (b) stability
(c) Both (a) and (b) (d) None of these

31 When does old age begin?
(a) 60 years (b) 40 years
(c) 25 years (d) 90 years

32 Why do people age differently?
(a) Hereditary endowment
(b) Socio-economic background
(c) Pattern of living
(d) All of the above

33 First sign of ageing involves
(a) change in digestive system
(b) change in psychology
(c) change in musculoskeletal system
(d) change in nervous system

34 Severe loss of bone density is known as
(a) arthritis (b) osteoporosis
(c) neuronal damage (d) osteopeania

35 How does food taste in old age?
(a) Bitter (b) Bland
(c) Both (a) and (b) (d) None of these

36 Which of the following statements is/are correct?
Statement I During old age, kidneys tend to become larger.
Statement II Less blood flows though kidneys during this age.
Codes
(a) Only I (b) Only II
(c) Both I and II (d) None of these

37 Which of the following statements is/are correct?
Statement I Growth hormone level decreases in old age.
Statement II Aldosterone level decreases causing dehydration.
Codes
(a) Only I (b) Only II
(c) Both I and II (d) None of these

38 Which of the following statements is/are correct?
Statement I Skin become thinner and wrinkled during old age.
Statement II Collagen and elastin change chemically.
Codes
(a) Only I (b) Only II
(c) Both I and II (d) None of these

39 Which of the following statements is/are correct?
Statement I Adults have to raise their children.
Statement II Adults can leave their children, whenever they want.
Codes
(a) Only I (b) Only II
(c) Both I and II (d) None of these

40 Which of the following statements is/are correct?
Statement I Adults have relationships with their partners only.
Statement II Relationships change and grow overtime.
Codes
(a) Only I (b) Only II
(c) Both I and II (d) None of these

41 Which of tho following statements is/are correct?
Statement I Teenagers are conscious about their appearance.
Statement II Teenagers have simple black and white thinking.
Codes
(a) Only I (b) Only II
(c) Both I and II (d) None of these

42 Match the following.

List I (Stages of Development)	List II (Ages)
A. Infancy	1. Above 60
B. Adolescence	2. 21-60
C. Adulthood	3. 0-9
D. Old age	4. 10-21

Codes

	A	B	C	D		A	B	C	D
(a)	3	4	2	1	(b)	1	4	3	2
(c)	2	1	4	3	(d)	3	2	1	4

43 Match the following.

List I (Organs)	List II (Changes)
A. Eyes	1. Nerve cell decreases
B. Ears	2. Lens stiffen
C. Brain	3. Blood filteration is slow
D. Heart	4. Presbycusis

Codes

	A	B	C	D		A	B	C	D
(a)	3	1	2	4	(b)	2	4	1	3
(c)	4	1	3	2	(d)	2	3	1	4

44 Write in correct sequence.

1. Adulthood	2. Infancy
3. Adolescence	4. Old age

Codes

(a) 3, 2, 1, 4 (b) 1, 3, 2, 4 (c) 2, 3, 1, 4 (d) 4, 1, 2, 3

45 Following are the stages of adulthood.

1. Marriage	2. Taking up job
3. Paying bills	4. Raising kids

Codes

(a) 1, 2, 3, 4 (b) 2, 3, 1, 4 (c) 4, 1, 2, 3 (d) 3, 2, 1, 4

Directions (Q. Nos. 46-55) *Below given are two statements, labelled as Assertion (A) and Reason (R). Following are the codes given below, select the correct code for the following.*

Codes

(a) Both A and R are true and R is the correct explanation of A
(b) A is true, but R is not the correct explanation of A
(c) A is true, but R is false
(d) A is false, but is true

46 **Assertion** (A) In ageing, power of intake of useful material and expelling of harmful materials out of the cells both decrease.

Reason (R) With age, elastin protein of connective tissue becomes less flexible, less permeable and insoluble.

47 **Assertion** (A) Old age is not an illness. It is continuation of life with decrease capacity for capacity for adaptation.

Reason (R) Cessation of mitosis is normal genetically programmed event.

48 **Assertion** (A) Adolescence in girls generally start one year prior to boys.

Reason (R) Adolescence starts earlier in India as compared to other countries.

49 **Assertion** (A) Adolescents frequently argue with their parents and peer groups.

Reason (R) Adolescents have highly intense emotions.

50 **Assertion** (A) Adolescents adopt old customs and conventions.

Reason (R) Adolescents examine everything in a scientific way.

51 **Assertion** (A) Adolescent goes through many physical changes.

Reason (R) Almost every body parts go through change during adolescence.

52 **Assertion** (A) Adulthood gives direction to individual's life.

Reason (R) Adults choose their career which act as foundation for rest of their life.

53 **Assertion** (A) Adulthood is a stage filled with passion and enthusiasm.

Reason (R) A person almost decides his life's goals through this stage.

54 **Assertion** (A) During old age, the persons are usually irritable and angry.

Reason (R) Nature change is quite significant during old age.

55 **Assertion** (A) It is tough to fight against diseases during old age.

Reason (R) There is lesser amount of B lymphocyte during this stage.

Directions (Q. Nos. 56-60) *Read the passage and answer the following questions.*

Puberty is the period during which growing boys and girls undergo the process of sexual maturation. Puberty involves a series of physical stages/steps that lead to the achievement of fertility and the development of the so called secondary sex characteristics, the physical features associated with adult males and females (such as the growth of pubic hair).

While puberty involves a series of biological or physical transformations, the process can also have an effect on the psychosocial and emotional development of the adolescent. The onset of puberty varies among individuals. Puberty usually occurs in girls between the ages of 10 to 14, while in boys it generally occurs later, between the ages of 12 to 16.

Doctors do not completely understand the timing of the onset of puberty; a number of factors likely determine its onset. One theory proposes that reaching a critical weight or body composition may play a important role in the onset of puberty. The increase in childhood obesity may be related to the overall earlier onset of puberty in the general population in recent years. Leptin, a hormone produced by fat cells (adipocytes) in the body, has been suggested as one possible mediator of the timing of puberty.

In research studies, animals deficient in leptin did not undergo puberty, but puberty began when leptin was administered to the animals. Further, girls with higher concentrations of the hormone leptin are known to have an increased percentage of body fat and an earlier onset of puberty than girls with lower levels of leptin. The concentration of leptin in the blood is known to increase just before puberty in both boys and girls.

Leptin, however, is likely only one of multiple influences on the hypothalamus, an area of the brain that releases a hormone known as Gonadotropin Releasing Hormone (GnRH), which in turn signals the pituitary gland to release Luteinizing Hormone (LH) and Follicle Stimulating Hormone (FSH). LH and FSH secretion by the pituitary gland is responsible for sexual development through regulation of the production of estrogen and testosterone.

Genetic factors are likely involved in the timing of puberty and the timing of puberty tends to 'run in families'. Additionally, a gene has been identified that appears to be critical for the normal development of puberty.

The gene, known as GPR54, encodes a protein that appears to have an effect on the secretion of GnRH by the hypothalamus. Individuals who do not have a functioning copy of this gene are not able to enter puberty normally.

56 Puberty is a period when girls and boys undergo
(a) emotional development
(b) physical development
(c) sexual maturation
(d) mental maturation

57 When does puberty occur in boys?
(a) 12-16 years (b) 10-11 years
(c) 20-25 years (d) 19-20 years

58 The increase in ...... may be related to early onset of puberty in recent years.
(a) knowledge (b) curiosity
(c) obesity (d) technology dependence

59 ..... is a hormone that affects the onset of puberty.
(a) Aldosterone (b) Leptin
(c) Prolactin (d) TSH

60 LH and FSH is released by...... gland.
(a) thyroid (b) adrenal
(c) pituitary (d) hypothalmus

PREVIOUS YEARS' QUESTIONS

July 2018

1 **Assertion** (A) When the elderly are not cared by their children, they develop early dementia.
Reason (R) Caring for the aged leads to a greater sense of well-being and this prevents onset of dementia.
Codes
(a) Both A and R are true (b) Both A and R are false
(c) A is true, but R is false (d) A is false, but R is true

July 2016

2 Match the following.

List I	List II
A. Object permanence	1. Adolescence
B. Animistic thinking	2. Preschoolers
C. Decentration	3. Infancy
D. Hypothetico deductive reasoning	4. Middle childhood
E. Rooting	5. Neonate
	6. Adulthood

Codes

	A	B	C	D	E		A	B	C	D	E
(a)	3	2	6	1	5	(b)	3	2	4	1	5
(c)	2	3	1	4	5	(d)	3	2	1	5	4

December 2015

3 Match the following.

List I	List II
A. Autonomy Vs. Shame and Doubt	1. Old age
B. Initiative Vs. Guilt	2. Birth -1 Year
C. Intimacy Vs. Isolation	3. 1-3 years
D. Generativity Vs. Stagnation	4. Young adult
E. Ego integrity Vs. Despair	5. 3-6 years
	6. Middle adulthood

Codes

	A	B	C	D	E		A	B	C	D	E
(a)	2	3	4	5	1	(b)	2	3	4	6	1
(c)	3	5	4	6	1	(d)	5	3	4	6	1

June 2015

4 **Assertion** (A) Ageing is associated with loss of lean body mass, bone mass and total body calcium.
Reason (R) High fat and low protein diets are recommended for elderly.
Codes
(a) A is true, but R is false (b) R is true, but A is false
(c) Both A and R are true (d) Both A and R are false

ANSWERS

Exam Based Questions

1 (b)	2 (d)	3 (a)	4 (b)	5 (c)	6 (a)	7 (b)	8 (b)	9 (c)	10 (c)
11 (a)	12 (d)	13 (b)	14 (d)	15 (a)	16 (c)	17 (d)	18 (c)	19 (d)	20 (a)
21 (c)	22 (b)	23 (b)	24 (d)	25 (a)	26 (c)	27 (d)	28 (a)	29 (c)	30 (a)
31 (a)	32 (d)	33 (c)	34 (b)	35 (c)	36 (c)	37 (c)	38 (b)	39 (a)	40 (d)
41 (b)	42 (b)	43 (a)	44 (a)	45 (a)	46 (b)	47 (c)	48 (c)	49 (a)	50 (b)
51 (c)	52 (a)	53 (b)	54 (c)	55 (b)	56 (c)	57 (a)	58 (c)	59 (b)	60 (c)

Previous Years' Questions

1 (b)	2 (d)	3 (c)	4 (a)

Developmental Problems and Disabilities of Children

Each child has individual strengths, personality and experiences, so particular disabilities will impact differently on individual children. The children with special needs require extra support and additional services, this would help them to develop positive attitude towards life. These children are an important segment of our society , so school and caregivers have a significant role in helping children with physical disabilities and special abilities.

People differ from each other due to their physical and mental qualities. This difference exists due to heredity and environmental factors. The child may become talented or disabled owing to these factors. Every child has its own needs. If the needs are not met, child will suffer. Thus, it is the responsibility of the society to provide for less fortunate children. If someone is lacking in physical, mental or socio-economic aspect, the society must find ways to uplift them. Thus, it is important to know about the children with special needs. Also, to study the children at risk.

In this Chapter

- Children with Special Needs
  - Physically Challenged Children
  - Mentally Handicapped Children
  - Care and Support for People with Special Need
  - Special Education
  - Teaching Strategies for Children with Learning Disabilities
  - Prevention of Disability
  - Rehabilitation
  - Problematic Children
- Children at Risk
  - Juvenile Crime
  - Prevention of Juvenile Crime

Children with Special Needs

The designation 'children with special needs' is for children who may have challenges which are more severe than the typical child and could possibly last a lifetime. Children with special needs may have been born with a syndrome, terminal illness, profound cognitive impairment, or serious psychiatric problems. These children will need extra support and additional services. They will have distinct goals and will need added guidance and help meeting academic, social, emotional and sometimes medical milestones. Physically and mentally challenged children are the children with special needs. Their description is given below :

Physically Challenged Children

Children having any type of physical defect, or deformity is called a physically disabled child. These defects can be due to congenital, abnormal delivery, illness or injury. Such children are mentally healthy. But due to physical deformity, they fail to adjust in normal life. As a consequence, the child might feel himself or herself as inferior.

Characteristics of Physically Challenged Children

There are many children who are born with physical disabilities. However, the disabilities do not have to limit their life or natural talents if they are supported and encouraged correctly. Their characteristics are :

Physical Limitations Physically handicapped children are all challenged with physical limitations to some degree. Many physically handicapped children suffer from a lack of coordination, weak muscles, stiff muscles, or no muscle strength at all. Rehabilitation and physical therapy can greatly assist physically handicap children in lessening and even resolving the handicap over time. All of the necessary equipment and safety measures should be taken in order to allow the child to be as mobile and independent as possible.

Emotional Challenges It is important for parents, family members, friends, and teachers to monitor a physically disabled child's emotional state. At times, physical limitations can lead to frustration, anger and sadness. The emotional outlook of the child is often directly impacted by the level of support and encouragement that is received from the people around him. It is important for physically disabled children to have people that they can talk to openly in order to discuss, understand, and resolve emotional issues. In some cases, it is beneficial for the child to see a therapist or enroll in a therapy programme with animals or physical activities that increase his confidence.

Learning Abilities Although some children with physical disabilities also have mental disabilities. Many children are mentally strong and just as capable as any other child. It is important that parents and teachers encourage physically handicapped children to excel in school and discover their individual talents and strengths. Parents and teachers must recognise the gifts of the child and not limit them mentally because of physical disabilities.

Causes of Physical Disability in Children

Following are the causes of physical disabilities in children :

Hereditary Problem Some hereditary problems are carried down to children. Thus, the child develops congenital disorders. These diseases include deafness, dwarfism, abnormal speaking skills, etc.

Diseases Diseases also prevent physical development. It can cause a variety of physical disabilities. These diseases can be inborn or occur post birth. They may cause defects to the organ e.g. leprosy, polio.

Environment Faulty environment affects the physicality of the child. If the child is brought up in an unhealthy environment (polluted environment, lack of nutritious food and improper upbringing, etc) he may develop physical disabilities. This may include malnutrition.

Accident Any kind of accident might occur at any time. This can harm the child physically. For example, bone fracture, excessive bleeding, burn, amputation, etc.

Effect of Physical Disability on Child

Physical disability affects the child on following different aspects :

Hampers Physical Development Due to being physically disabled development of physical skills are hindered. Thus, the child does not develop various kind of skills like other children.

Social Rejection A physically disable child is unable to socialise with normal children. Even if they want to be included in the group, they can't be due to their disability. For example, a child with polio cannot be included in sports team.

Lack of Proper Aptitude Development Physically challenged children are seen as helpless and weak. They are referred to as poor. Many a times they are seen as burden to their family. The society neglects them. Thus, the disable child does not develop confidence, hence a healthy personality.

Less Educational Achievement Achievement of physically challenged student is less than normal student. Some disabled students like blind and deaf require separate special schools.

Mentally Challenged Children

A child who is not mentally mature as the children of their age or is less intellectually developed is known as mentally challenged. These children are physically fit. But their intellectual capabilities are less. Their learning pace is either low or nill. They have difficulties in socially/adjusting.

Characteristics of Mentally Challenged Child

Bad Memory These kids have a short-term memory recall. However, when doing a task repeatedly, they can recall information without displaying any symptoms of mental retardation.

Slow Learning Curve Their ability to process new information is relatively low when compared to other kids. That does not mean they are incapable of learning. Some educationists are of the view that a slowing down of the instructions can help in better reception of the information.

Attention Deficiency They are unable to sustain their attention for too long on a single task. A good way of tackling this deficiency is by making them aware of the most crucial aspect of the work and then building their attention from there on.

Disinterest Due to repeated failures, some children don't trust their skills, even if they are correct. Over time they lose faith in their abilities and become disinterested in learning.

Independent Living One of the brighter side children with special needs can be trained in repetitive tasks which they can master over time. This can help them stay independent for a short duration of time and also prepare them for adulthood.

Inability to Restrain Emotions As children grow older, they can give measured responses when faced with unknown situations. Children with mental disabilities are unable to do this and may respond unpredictably, usually displaying aggression. Once the episode is over, they can sense that they have misbehaved and are capable of feeling like they are a burden.

Social Development Due to bizarre outbursts and poor language skills, they may be unable to have healthy social interactions.

Application of New Ideas They are unable to incorporate any newly acquired skills innovatively.

Causes of Mental Retardation in Children

Some of the reasons include :

Genetic Over 30% of mental retardation is attributed to genetics. These children are likely to suffer from problems such as down syndrome and fragile X syndrome.

Head Trauma A severe head injury can cause inflammation in the brain. This can change the mental state of the child and lead to difficulties in memory, attention and reasoning.

Pregnancy-Related Issues Pregnant women who do recreational drugs, smoke and drink alcohol can severely affect the brain development of the foetus.

Illness Children suffering from measles can develop encephalitis which causes mental retardation. Infants suffering from congenital hyperthyroidism are also at the risk of poor brain development.

Exposure to Toxic Materials Elements such as mercury, lead and cadmium are known to be linked with a reduction in intellectual growth.

Problems Faced by Mentally Challenged Children

There are different problems of mentally challenged children. Some of the common problems are :

- Difficulty in articulating a point
- Learning speech at a slower rate
- Misplacing objects
- Having trouble remembering things
- Poor academic performance
- Overall low intelligence
- Poor performance in IQ tests
- Particular attention required to learn simple skills
- Have trouble putting on clothes
- Behavioural symptoms such as :
  - Aggression
  - Depression
  - Anxiety
  - Impulsive
  - The tendency to inflict injury on self
  - Suicidal thoughts
  - Poor interpersonal relationships
  - Excessive dependency on parents
  - Unable to respond to situations in a measured manner
  - Low attention span

Care and Support for People with Special Need

The Constitution of India ensures equality, freedom, justice and dignity of all individuals and implicitly mandates an inclusive society for all, including persons with disabilities. The Constitution in the schedule of subjects lays direct responsibility of empowerment of disabled persons on the state governments. Therefore, the primary responsibility to empower the disabled rests with the state governments.

- Under Article 253 of the Constitution the Government of India enacted 'The Persons with Disabilities (Equal Opportunities, Protection of Rights and Full Participation) Act, 1995', in an effort to ensure equal opportunities for persons with disabilities and their full participation in nation-building.
- A multi-sectoral collaborative approach, involving all the appropriate governments, i.e. ministries of the Central Government, the State Governments, UTs, Central/State undertakings, local authorities and other appropriate authorities is being followed in the implementation of various provisions of the Act.
- India is a signatory to the 'Declaration on the Full Participation and Equality of People' with Disabilities in the Asia-Pacific Region. India is also a signatory to the Biwako Millennium Framework working towards an inclusive, barrier free and rights-based society.

India signed the UN Convention on Protection and Promotion of the Rights and Dignity of Persons with Disabilities on 30th March, 2007. India ratifies the UN Convention on 1st October, 2008.

- In order to give focused attention to policy issues and meaningful thrust to the activities aimed at welfare and empowerment of the Persons with Disabilities, a separate Department of Disability Affairs was carved out of the Ministry of Social Justice and Empowerment on 12th May 2012.

  The Department was renamed as Department of Empowerment of Persons with Disabilities (Divyangjan) on 8th December 2014. The Department deals with the following legislations governing different aspects of disability and welfare and empowerment of the Persons with Disabilities :

  - The Rehabilitation Council of India Act, 1992,
  - The Persons with Disabilities (Equal Opportunities, Protection of Rights and Full Participation) Act, 1995; and
  - The National Trust for the Welfare of Persons with Autism, Cerebral Palsy, Mental Retardation and Multiple Disabilities Act, 1999

Special Education

All the children with special needs must be enrolled in primary schools. After the assessment of their disabilities by a team of a doctor, a psychologist and a special educator, in schools, the child will be placed in appropriate educational settings. Children with mild and moderate disabilities of any kind may be integrated in normal schools, severe in special schools/ remedial schools, dropouts who have problems in availing benefits of normal schools can join open schools.

All the children with learning disabilities alone are first managed in the normal schools. Open and special schools also offer vocational courses also for children with disabilities. In India, mainly formal schools, special schools and open schools provide special education. Their description is given below :

Formal Schools The Ministry of Human Resource Development (Department of Secondary and Higher Education) has been implementing a scheme of 'Integrated Education for the Disabled Children' (IEDC) in formal schools since 1982.

The main objective of the scheme is to provide educational opportunities for the disabled children in normal schools so as to facilitate their retention in the school system. The disabled children who are placed in special schools should be considered for integration into common schools once they acquire the communication and daily living skills at a functional level.

Special Schools This is a programme of the Ministry of Social Justice and Empowerment. Children with severe multiple disabilities who have difficulty in coping with regular schools are referred to such special schools. Most of these special schools are located in urban areas and run by voluntary organisations.

A majority of them are residential schools and boarding-lodging and other services are provided free of cost. At present more than 3000 special schools for the disabled children are functioning across the country.

Out of them approximately 900 institutions are specialised for the hearing impaired, 400 for the visually impaired, 1000 for the mentally retarded and the remaining 700 are for the children with physical disabilities. 40 per cent disability of any such particular types is a benchmark for identification and certification for admission in these special schools.

National Institute of Open Schooling (NIOS) It is formerly known as National Open School (NOS) was established as an autonomous registered society in 1989 with the mission to provide education through an open learning system at the school stage as an alternative to the formal system.

It offers courses like the foundation course, notionally equivalent to class VIII level, secondary education and higher secondary courses and vocational courses. The NIOS also provides the programme of open basic education for Universal Elementary Education (UEE), which includes programme for the disabled children.

Teaching Strategies for Children with Learning Disabilities

Children with learning disabilities show greater learning when techniques like task analysis, peer teaching, cooperative learning, learning corners and multisensory approach are used.

The following strategies would be helpful to both the parents and teachers while teaching such children :

Strategies for Reading Skills

- Prepare the student by presenting new concepts and vocabulary
- Guide the student into reading a story by asking questions which bring up to purpose or goal of the reading
- Develop or strengthen skills relating to the material through drills or worksheet activities
- Assign work in order to apply the skills acquired during a lesson

- Read aloud to students regularly
- Devote a few minutes every day to sustained silent reading
- Use writing activities that provide opportunities for the teacher to model writing strategies and skills
- Include journal writing as part of the student's individualised educational programme
- Provide meaningful printed materials in the instructional setting (e.g. dictionaries, categorised lists of words
- Establish a network of communication with other teachers and thus using holistic techniques in working with such students
- Let the child reads aloud (oral reading). If the child makes mistakes can be easily identified by the teacher and corrected.
- Reading can be done with peers or with parents (paired reading). This will enhance the confidence of the child
- Reading in a group (choral reading). Here, they get both auditory and visual stimulus to correct themselves
- Use colour-coded textbooks (e.g. green equals start, red equals stop)
- Have a small group of class read aloud simultaneously

Strategies for Writing Skills

- A sufficient amount of time should be allocated for writing (e.g. four times per week) because students can learn and develop as writer only by writing.
- Expose students to a broad range of writing tasks. Students should participate in writing activities that present highly structured problem-solving situations as well as activities that involve self-selected and expressive writing.
- Create a social climate conducive to writing development. Teachers need to be encouraging in non-threatening environment and should try to develop a sense of community by promoting student sharing and collaboration.
- Integrate writing with subjects such as language and arts so as to stimulate the writing skills.
- Help students develop the processes central to effective writing. The composition process of writing can be divided into a series of discrete stages (e.g. prewrite, write and rewrite) and students can be taught appropriate task-specific and metacognitive strategies (e.g. self-instructional strategy training).
- Help students develop explicit knowledge about the characteristics of good writing.
- Students should be given exposure to the characteristics of various literary compositions either through reading or teacher presentation of writing or live models that incorporate a specific skill or style.
- Help students develop the skills and abilities to carry out more sophisticated composing processes.
- Assist students in the development of goals for improving their written products.
- Goal setting and having students evaluate their own writing according to specific criteria can help students accurately monitor and evaluate progress.
- Tape alphabets forms to the floor, have students walk or hop around the form. Have them reproduce the form with coloured yarn.
- Have students use a stick (broom handle) and their bodies to form the letters.
- Spray shaving cream can be used to form large letters. Paper provides a suitable surface.
- Have students use a torch light beam to trace letters on a chalkboard.
- Have student's form letters in wet fingerprint/paint/sand.
- Use coloured directional cues such as green arrows and red dots.
- Help students to form an association for a letter they have difficulty remembering.
- Have students orally describe their movements as the letter is being written. This provides auditory reinforcement.

Prevention of Disability

Disability can be prevented in three stages :

Primary Prevention Action taken prior to the onset of the disease/disability, which will remove the possibility that a disease/disability will occur.

Secondary Prevention Action, which halts the progress of the disease/disability at its incipient stage and prevents complications. The specific interventions are early diagnosis and adequate treatment.

Tertiary Prevention All measures available to reduce or limit impairments and disabilities and minimise suffering caused by existing disability. This phase is also called rehabilitation, which includes physical, psychosocial and vocational measures taken to restore the patient back to normal or near normal condition.

It is extremely important that the women undertake adequate and effective preventive measures during their pregnancy and immediate postnatal period and also for their children especially during the early childhood period, in order to significantly reduce the incidence of impairment and disabilities in them.

Care during Pregnancy

During the pregnancy, disability can be prevented by the following :

- Avoid hard physical work such as carrying heavy loads, especially in fields and other accident-prone activities such as walking on slippery ground or climbing stools and chairs.
- Avoid unnecessary drugs and medications. Even the normally considered safe drugs which are sold commonly can potentially cause serious defects in an unborn child.
- Avoid smoking, chewing tobacco, consuming alcohol and narcotics.
- Avoid X-rays and exposure to any kind of radiation.
- Avoid exposure to illnesses like measles, mumps, etc., especially during the first 3 months of pregnancy.
- Avoid sexual contact with a person having venereal disease.
- Take precautions against lead poisoning.

Care at the Time of Birth

At the time of birth, disability can be prevented by the following :

- Delivery must be conducted by trained personnel, preferably in a hospital where all facilities are available.
- If a baby does not cry immediately after birth, resuscitation measures should be undertaken at once.
- Babies born prematurely and with a low birth weight (<2.5 Kg) may need Neonatal Intensive Care.
- If the baby's head appears to be abnormally small or large then a physician should be consulted, preferably a pediatrician. The approximate head size for a male child at birth is 35 cm and for female child is 34.5 cm.
- To protect a child from infections, breast-feeding must be started immediately after birth. First milk (colostrum) must be fed to the baby and should not be thrown away, as it has antibodies which are protective.

Early Childhood Care

During early childhood, disability can be prevented by the following :

- Do not allow a child's temperature to rise above 101° F because of any reason. It can cause febrile seizures or convulsion.
- If a child gets a fit take him to doctor immediately.
- Every child should be immunised against infectious diseases as per the recommended schedule of immunisation.
- Do not allow a child to have too much contact with paint, newsprint ink, lead, etc., as they are toxic.
- Take precautions against head injury and other accidents.
- Ensure that the child gets a well-balanced diet and clean drinking water.
- Introduce additional foods of good quality and in sufficient quantity when the child is 4 -6 months old.
- Vitamin A deficiency and its consequences including night blindness can be easily prevented through the use of Vitamin A supplementation.
- Protect a child from Meningitis and Encephalitis by providing a hygienic environment which is free of overcrowding.
- Common salt must be iodised as a precaution against goiter and cretinism.
- Do not allow a child to use hairpins, matchsticks and pencils, to remove wax from the ears.
- Use ear protectors to reduce the exposure to high levels of noise, if children are living or working in a noisy environment.
- Do not slap a child over the face as this may, lead to injury of the eardrum and consequent hearing loss.

Rehabilitation

Physical medicine and rehabilitation also known as psychiatry or rehabilitation medicine, is defined as a branch of medicine that aims to enhance and restore functional ability and quality of life to those with physical impairments or disabilities.

A physician having completed training in this field is referred to as a physiatrist or rehabilitation medicine specialist. Physiatrists specialise in restoring optimal function to people with injuries to the muscles bones, tissues, and nervous system (such as stroke patients).

Rehabilitation of people with disabilities is a process aimed at enabling them to reach and maintain their optimal physical, sensory, intellectual, psychological and social functional levels. Rehabilitation provides disabled people with the tools they need to attain independence and self-determination.

The type of therapy and goals of therapy is different for different people. Rehabilitation often focuses on :

- Treatment of pain
- Physical therapy to help your strength, mobility and fitness
- Occupational therapy to help you with your daily activities
- Speech-language therapy to help with speaking, understanding, reading, writing and swallowing

Problematic Children

Problematic children do not have specific disability. They can belong to any family. When a normal child is unable to adjust to the society, they become problematic. This can happen during stress or when the requirements of child are not met. When the circumstances become tough, or the child is not getting proper love and care. The child becomes difficult to handle.

Types of Problematic Child

Psychologists have studied various children. Depending on these studies they have defined different types of problematic children. These include stealer, liar, stubborn, etc.

Psychiatric Problem These are the children whose mental needs are not met. This may be due to lack of nutrition, lack of adequate security or affection, feeling of inferiority, etc. When the mental requirements are unfulfilled, psychiatric problems arises. This may include bed wetting, thumb sucking, day dreaming, etc.

Emotionally Disturbed Child These children are stubborn and irritated. They are a challenge to society, schools and family. Anger, arrogance, making noise and being sad for no reason are the main symptoms. They need to be diagnosed as soon as possible. Otherwise their intelligence is hampered. Thus, they are unable to adjust in school. They behave indecently fight with other children, snatch their book, beat them up, etc.

Indisciplined Child These children are result of in appropriate family and social environment. The children do not receive proper love and care from family, school or society. Thus, the children become defiant and indisciplined. They develop an rebelling attitude towards the society. These children are destructive. Lying, stealing, harming, violating are some of their characteristics.

Common Problems with Children

Thumb sucking, bed wetting, nail biting, kleptomania are common problems with children. Their description is given below :

Thumb Sucking

Babies have natural rooting and sucking reflexes, which can cause them to put their thumbs or fingers into their mouths-sometimes even before birth. Because thumb sucking makes babies feel secure, some babies might eventually develop a habit of thumb sucking when they're in need of soothing or going to sleep. Many children stop sucking their thumbs on their own, often by age 6 or 7 months or between ages 2 and 4 but even a child who has stopped sucking his or her thumb might go back to the behaviour during times of stress. Reason for thumb sucking are :

- When a mother is not able to breakfast feed her baby. She may be feeding the baby from bowl, spoon, glass or bottle for some reason. Then the instinctive reaction of sucking of baby is not satisfied thus they suck the thumb.
- When the child does not get enough affection from his/her parents. Or the parent's behaviour is neglectful towards the child. The child reduces his mental stress by sucking his/her thumb.

Techniques to Stop Thumb Sucking

Sometimes paying no attention to thumb sucking is enough to stop the behaviour-especially if the child uses thumb sucking to get attention. If ignoring it isn't effective, try one of these techniques :

Use Positive Reinforcement When the child is not sucking thumb, praise the child or provide small rewards such as an extra bedtime story or a trip to the park. Setting attainable goals, such as no thumb sucking an hour before bed. Stickers can be placed on a calendar to record the days when the child successfully avoids thumb sucking.

Identify Triggers Many times child sucks his or her thumb in response to stress. Identifying the real issue and providing comfort in other ways can help. Such as with a hug or reassuring words. Child can also be given a pillow or stuffed animal to squeeze.

Offer Gentle Reminders If the child sucks his or her thumb without thought, rather than as a way to get attention. Gently reminding him or her to stop can help. Child should not be scolded or ridiculed.

Bedwetting

While bedwetting can be a symptom of an underlying disease, a large majority of children who wets the bed have no underlying disease that explains their bedwetting. In fact, an underlying condition is identified in only about 1% of children who routinely wet the bed. That does not mean that the child who wets the bed can control it or is doing it on purpose. Children who wet bed are not lazy, willful, or disobedient. Bedwetting is most often a developmental issue. Causes of bedwetting are :

- The child cannot yet hold urine for the entire night.
- The child does not waken when his or her bladder is full.
- The child produces a large amount of urine during the evening and night hours.
- The child has poor daytime toilet habits. Many children habitually ignore the urge to urinate and put off urinating as long as they possibly can. Parents usually are familiar with the leg crossing, face straining, squirming, squatting, and groin holding that children use to hold back urine.

Techniques to Stop Bedwetting

To stop bedwetting, doctors suggest following techniques :

Shift Times for Drinking Increase fluid intake earlier in the day and reduce it later in the day.

Schedule Bathroom Breaks Get your child on a regular urination schedule (every two to three hours) and right before bedtime.

Be Encouraging Make your child feel good about progress by consistently rewarding successes.

Eliminate Bladder Irritants At night, start by eliminating caffeine (such as chocolate milk and cocoa) and if this doesn't work, cut citrus juices, artificial flavourings, dyes (especially red) and sweeteners. Many parents don't realise that these all can irritate a child's bladder.

Avoid Thirst Overload If schools allow, give your child a water bottle so they can drink steadily all day. This avoids excessive thirst after school.

Consider if Constipation is a Factor Because the rectum is right behind the bladder, difficulties with constipation can present themselves as a bladder problem, especially at night. This affects about one-third of children who wet the bed, though children are unlikely to identify or share information about constipation.

Don't Wake Children up to Urinate Randomly waking up a child at night and asking him or her to urinate on demand isn't the answer, either - and will only lead to more sleeplessness and frustration.

Don't Resort to Punishment Getting angry at your child doesn't help him learn. The process doesn't need to involve conflict.

Nail Biting

About half of all kids and teens bite their nails. Many don't grow out of it, either. Sometimes, nail biting can be a sign of emotional or mental stress. It tends to show up in people who are nervous, anxious or feeling down. It's a way to cope with these feelings.

Causes of Nail Biting in Children

Children bite their nails due to various reasons such as anxiety, stress and boredom and comfort. Here are some of the most common reasons for child biting nails :

For Comfort Infants and toddlers suck their thumb as a self-soothing action which is a natural thing to do. It provides comfort when they are playing or being on their own. The nail biting is a modified form of thumb-sucking that develops as the kids grow. Hence, children and even teenagers bite their nails as it feels comforting.

Boredom Kids engage in nail biting when they are bored or doing something monotonous. It can also be seen when they are not involved in an activity and their hands are free; during watching TV or attending a class.

To Relieve Anxiety and Stress Situations at home or school that can cause stress or anxiety triggers nail biting in children. There are plenty of stressful situations that can cause them to get anxious such as :

- Fights between family members or parents
- Loss of a family member or a close relative
- Divorce
- Relocating to a new city or home
- Joining a new school
- Getting bullied by other kids
- Punishment
- Pressure to perform well in class or sports

Imitating Habits of Others Children pick up behaviours of others quickly. Nail biting is one such behaviour which is common, and when they see another sibling or a family member doing it, they imitate the habit.

Genetics There are chances that parent's habits get passed on to their children through the genes. If parent were a nail biter as a kid, chances are their children will be too.

Technique to Stop Nail Biting in a Child

Here are some effective home remedies for child nail biting :

Pacify Anxieties/Techniques If the child bites his nails more often when he is stressed or anxious about issues such as changing schools, moving to a different place or conflicts within the family. Then take time to talk to him. Find a good time when he is in the right mood and connect with him. Discuss the things he may be worried about.

Trim their Nails Regularly Trimming their nails is a good way to minimise the urge to bite nails. Clip and file their nails every week, so there are no rough edges that tempt them to bite.

Offer an Alternative Give them something else to release their anxiety and fidgeting. A stress ball is great for releasing anxiety. Squeezing and rolling it in their hands can give the children a better way to relax. Activities and projects that keep their hands busy are another good option. Arts and crafts along with stimulating their imagination relieve their stress. Outdoor activities, playtime and sports are also some of the best ways to release pent-up energy.

Make Them Aware of the Habit Habits such as nail biting are mostly unconscious. The child might not know at most times that they are doing it. Hence, get surprised when they are yelled at. Talk to the child about what causes them to bite the nail. Suggest secret ways to remind them of it when they do it. This is useful when done in a subtle way, especially in public where they can get embarrassed. A tap on the shoulder or a code word only the parent and child knows is a good start.

Reward Positive Behaviour When the child is making progress in the right direction by channeling their anxiety in healthier ways, appreciate and reward them. Taking them out for ice cream as a reward or buying them a new toy they have been wanting. Children are naturally inclined to please their parents and seek attention from them. Therefore, praising their mindfulness regarding their habits or building healthy ones encourages them to repeat those.

Kleptomania

Kleptomania refers to a compulsive stealing behaviour, belonging to the family of impulse-control disorders. Children with kleptomania experience strong impulses to steal objects. The impulse to steal is extremely strong and the child cannot resist it no matter how hard he or she tries. There is a loss of control and some children experience it as an automatic act. Before the act of stealing an extreme tension builds up in the mind and the body and when the act is carried out the child usually experiences pleasure and relief. The child usually carries out the stealing act alone and it is a carefully guarded secret. Children suffering from kleptomania develop uncomfortable feelings of shame, guilt and fear. They live in a dread of being caught and feel ashamed and guilty that they are indulging in a 'bad activity.'

Causes of Kleptomania

The causes of kleptomania have not been fully understood. An interaction of psychological, environmental and biological factors can lead to the condition.

Inside the Brain of a Kleptomaniac A decrease in the availability of neurotransmitter serotonin in the brain has been associated with a tendency toward risk taking behaviours. Serotonin regulates emotions and mood of a person. There may also be an increase in the level of dopamine which produces feelings of pleasure and reinforces the stealing.

Stolen Object as a Symbol for Something Else In many cases of kleptomania, although the stolen object initially seems very bizarre in course of psychological treatment it is known that the object stands as a symbol for something else. Usually, a child has some deep wishes which he or she is scared to acknowledge and suppresses. The stolen object fulfils these wishes in a symbolic and complicated manner.

Coping with Deprivation or Loss Children suffering from kleptomania have often experienced a real or imagined deprivation or loss and both the act of stealing and stolen object help them deny and cope with this painful sense. The stolen object has a deep symbolic significance in relation to the trauma.

Techniques to Stop Kleptomania

Techniques to stop kleptomania are:

- Parents should try to fulfill all the requirement of the child.
- Parents should not beat up the child. They should make the child understand about his bad behaviour calmly.
- If a child is interested in something and if he has stolen for that reason. Then the parents must make that thing available.

Children at Risk

Children at risk are those children who appear to be healthy, but they will have emotional or physical disability in the future. This can happen due to hunger, poverty, exploitation, or war. About 1.2 billion children under the age of 18 are at risk. Children at risk require basic facilities such as food, clothing, housing, parental support, health care and education. The children are generally exploited. They are expected to do task which are not meant for them. Child labourers, street children, ophans, children of destitutes fall under the category of children at risk. Their description is given below :

Child Labour

Child labour is a global issue that prevents children from fulfilling their potential. Child labour is a violation of children's rights the work can harm them mentally or physically, expose them to hazardous situations or stop them from going to school. But around the world, millions of children do work in child labour. They work in fields, in factories, down mines, as servants or maids, or selling goods in the street or at markets. Girls are more likely than boys to do domestic work, such as cleaning, making food and serving. The work that children can be forced to do might also be illegal-such as working with drug gangs or in prostitution. Many children may get no money for the work they do but they will get food and a place to sleep.

If they become sick or injured, most children will not get any money for missing work. All these forms of child labour can prevent a child from going to school and limit their opportunity to fulfil their potential. Many child labourers never go to school or drop out. Education is a proven strategy for reducing child labour. Lack of access to education keeps the cycle of exploitation, illiteracy and poverty going-limiting future options and forcing children to accept low-wage work as adults and to raise their own children in poverty. Children who have access to education can break the cycle of poverty at the root of child labour.

Street/backward Children

These children are homeless with their families. They may be displaced due to poverty or natural disasters or are refugees from areas of conflict. The family will move around frequently, taking their possessions with them. These children often work on the streets with other members of their families. Many other children have run away from home or an institution to escape psychological, physical or sexual abuse. They have no home except for the streets and may move from place to place, living in shelters and abandoned buildings.

Some street children may have very low-paid work such as shining shoes or selling goods on the streets. Some children may scavenge for food or beg. Others are exploited by gangs and criminals and end up selling drugs, stealing and in prostitution. Their situation and the need to earn money for survival will likely prevent them from being able to access schooling. It's common for street children to be in unsafe situations. They are frequently harassed or harmed by the police and often find themselves in conflict with the law. As a consequence many street children use drugs, including alcohol, cigarettes, heroin, cannabis and glue, to help them deal with the hardships they experience.

Orphans

A large number of children are deprived of parental protection because of death or desertion of one or both parents, inability of parents to take adequate care due to disease, alcoholism, poverty, etc., or abandonment which could be because of birth before marriage of the mother. Such children, who are actually in need of care and protection become victims of abuse and neglect by adults. Some of them take to rag picking, begging, petty crimes etc., for which they are punished in different ways.

Several of them are admitted in institutions in which they are encouraged to learn one or the other craft that would help them in making a living. Ideally, they are provided opportunities to improve their conduct. Orphaned and delinquent children suffer from inadequate attention, affection and concern of elders, pressure of being closely watched and monitored by adults in the institutions, few or no avenues for recreation and play, lack of opportunities for free expression of personal wishes. The children are alienated from society. This adds to their anguish and frustration. Children already suffering from lack of parental love and attention and made to encounter difficult situations in reformatory institutions develop a sense of being wronged and try to escape from them.

Children of Destitutes

These children have parents who work, but low wages and unstable employment leave their families struggling to make ends meet. Poverty can impede children's ability to learn and contribute to social, emotional and behavioural problems. Poverty also can contribute to poor health and mental health. Risks are greatest for children who experience poverty when they are young and/or experience deep and persistent poverty. Growing up in poverty can damage children's well-being and their future life chances. Children living in poverty are more likely to :

- Have poor physical health
- Experience mental health problems
- Have low sense of well-being
- Underachieve at school
- Have employment difficulties in adult life
- Experience social deprivation
- Feel unsafe
- Experience stigma and bullying at school

Offence Against Children

Child trafficking and child abuse are most common offence against children. Their description is given below :

Child Trafficking

- Child trafficking occurs when children are taken away from safety and exploited. Children who are trafficked are often forced into some form of work, used for sex or simply sold.
- Trafficking involves all part of the process from finding and recruiting children, to transporting and receiving them. Men, women and children all over the world are victims of trafficking, but children are particularly at risk.
- Child trafficking is linked to demand for cheap labour, especially where the working conditions are poor. Children may be forced into many dangerous and/or illegal situations, including slavery, domestic labour, sexual exploitation or prostitution, drug couriering and/or being turned into child soldiers.
- Children who are trafficked are exposed to many dangers such as working in hazardous environments. Many are also denied the chanc to reach their full potential because they don't get an education or have the freedom to make their own choices.
- In disasters, conflicts and other humanitarian emergencies, children can become separated from their families. Left without protection, they are easy prey for traffickers to exploit either by force or with false promises.

Child Abuse

Child abuse is not just physical violence directed at a child. It is any form of maltreatment by an adult, which is violent or threatening for the child. This includes neglect. When child abuse occurs in the home and the abuser is, for example, the child's parent or caregiver, this is a form of domestic violence. But children are sometimes abused by other adults on whom they are dependent, such as day nursery workers, teachers and sports coaches. Sometimes abuse is intentional, but not always. If parents or caregivers are no longer able to cope with caring for the child, this can result in dysfunctional behaviour and abuse.

There are five general types of child abuse :

- ***Physical Abuse*** All forms of physical violence.
- ***Emotional or Psychological Abuse*** An adult regularly berates the child, acts in a dismissive and hostile manner towards the child or intentionally scares the child.
- ***Physical Neglect*** The child does not receive the care and nurturing that it needs.
- ***Emotional or Psychological Neglect*** continuous lack of positive attention for the child. Ignoring the child's need for love, warmth and security. This category also covers cases in which children are witnesses to violence between their parents or caregivers.
- ***Sexual Abuse*** Sexual contact which an adult forces upon a child.

Juvenile Crime

A juvenile can be defined as a child who has not attained a certain age at which he can be held liable for his criminal acts like an adult person under the law of the country. He is a child who is alleged to have committed certain acts or omissions which are in violation of any law and are declared to be an offence.

Crimes such as theft, burglary, snatching which are not so serious in nature and crimes such as robbery, dacoity, murder and rape, etc., which are relatively serious are on the rise in whole of the country.

All types of these crimes are also being committed by children below the age of 18 years. Some of the most common causes which are associated with juvenile crimes are : Poverty; Drug Abuse; Anti-social Peer Group; Easy availability of firearms; Abusive parents; Singleparent child; Nuclear Family; Family Violence; Child sexual abuse and Role of Media. However, as far as India is concerned, it is poverty and the effect of media, especially the social media which make juveniles more inclined towards criminal activities.

Some of the definitions of juvenile crime are :

- According to **Clyde B Vedder** "juvenile crime refers to the anti-social acts of children and young people of under age. Such acts are specifically forbidden by law and require official action".
- According to **WH Sheldon**, "juvenile crime is a behaviour disappointing beyond reasonable expectation".
- According to **Cyril Bur**, "juvenile crime occurs when a child's antisocial tendencies appear so grave that he becomes a subject of official action".

Types of Juvenile Crime

Theft This includes shoplifting, stealing bikes and stealing from backpacks.

Burglary This includes entering a home or building with an intent to steal something.

Vandalism This includes graffiti, drawing on walls, keying cars and cutting tires.

Drug and Alcohol Offenses This includes the purchase and possession of alcohol or marijuana.

Weapons Possession This includes possession of a gun (even a BB gun), knives, brass knuckles, nunchucks and pepper spray.

Disorderly Conduct This includes nudity in public (such as flashing or mooning), cursing at an adult and starting fights in public.

Assault and Battery This includes verbal bullying or physical altercation such as pushing or hitting another person.

Traffic Violations These offenses include speeding, running red lights and not wearing a seat belt.

Trespassing This includes entering a vacant building and using another person's land without permission.

Fraud This includes sending spam emails in an attempt to obtain personal information, writing bad checks and impersonating another person for personal gain.

Unauthorised Use of a Motor Vehicle This includes driving without a license or using someone else's car without their permission.

Reason of Juvenile Crime

Juvenile crime can be attributed to two factors :

Inheritance Factor According to the child scholar Halley 15%-30% of crimes are due to genetic factor. Physical defects, structural formation and poor functioning of endocrine gland lead to criminal behaviour. Valentine a scholar, also said that heredity affects criminal tendencies.

Environmental/Social Factor The social factor and family environment have the most profound impact on child. Thus, the faulty environment leads to criminal behaviour in child.

Prevention of Juvenile Crime

Juvenile crime disrupts family and social peace. Thus, it becomes necessary for the family, school and society to work toward preventing juvenile crime.

Role of Family

Family Atmosphere For family happiness and peace, family atmosphere should be good. All the members should have love and mutual respect towards each other. A child feels safe in such an environment.

Fulfill the Necessities of Child If the basic necessities of child are not met, then the child becomes dissatisfied. A hungry child will steal. Thus, the parents should fulfill the child's need.

Behaviour Towards Children Parent's abusive and biased behaviour can lead to aggression in children. Therefore, the parents need to equally love all their children.

Taking Care of Child's Education Parents live with their child since beginning. They know child's interest and intellectual level. Thus, parents should arrange education that suits their child.

Role of School

Teacher Understands the Child The school teacher should understand the psychology of the child. The teacher should try to know when the child commits any mistake. The child should only be corrected when his/her mistake is appropriately identified. Punishing without knowing the reason will not help.

Teaching Method should be Interesting and Effective Teacher must use interesting teaching method. So that the child listens to them. A child lacks through concentration and may do mischief in class when not interested in subject.

Emphasis should be Laid on Moral Education A part of school time table should be set for moral education. This will help the child to distinguish between right and wrong.

Teachers should Maintain Contact with Parents To know about the problems faced by the child, the teacher and parents should maintain contact. This will help them to know child's interests, attitudes, temperament and adjustability.

Role of Society

Advisory Centres should be Arranged The government should set up child advisory centre for the prevention of juvenile crime. They should appoint psychologist and psychiatrists who can give parents advise about criminal behaviour.

More Parks and Garden should be Set Up Government should set up park and garden. Thus, the children can enjoy healthy recreation by playing there in free time.

Restricting Unethical Works Certain people in society indulge in unethical activities in order to earn money. This include selling drugs, running gambling stalls, prostitution, etc. The government should find these centre and try to eliminate them.

Child Reform House The government should keep child doing illegal work, begging, neglected helpless and orphan in the reform house. They should not be roaming in streets or markets. Reform houses have proper arrangement for sports, entertainment and education.

Rehabilitation For Juvenile in India

Rehabilitation of Juvenile in India started in 1850. Many organisation functions to provide rehabilitation as given below :

Probation House These probation houses were set up under Probation Act, 1958. Here, the first time juvenile offenders are kept. They are kept under the observation of probationary officers. The officer studies the mental instinct of the juvenile. He tries to put the juvenile in correct path of law by showing softness or sometimes punishing.

Children's Court In the year 1960, Children's Act was passed. Under this, cases of juvenile offender were heard in separate children's court. The environment of these courts is like home. There are no lawyers and no police officers stationed here. Most of the judges are female. They lovingly try to find out the reason for the crime. The court case is carried out in a way that the child does not get scared. If found guilty the child is sent to reform house.

Reform House When the juvenile offenders found guilty, they are sent to reform house as a punishment. The main motive of reform house is to improve the child. The juvenile is kept in reform house for 3 to 7 years. Here, children are given morality lesson, to build a good character. They are trained according to their abilities. So that they can get into occupation after serving their term. Currently reform houses are operational in various states of India. These reform houses train the juvenile so that they can become self-reliant.

EXAM BASED QUESTIONS

1 People differ from each other due to ..... qualities.
(a) physical (b) mental
(c) Both (a) and (b) (d) None of these

2 The difference in child exist due to ...... and environmental factor.
(a) heredity (b) parenting (c) schooling (d) social

3 Physical defects can be caused due to
(a) abnormal delivery (b) congenital
(c) injury (d) All of these

4 Physical limitation can lead to........
(a) mental retardation (b) frustrations
(c) narcism (d) None of these

5 Hereditary disabilities include
(a) deafness (b) dwarfism
(c) Both (a) and (b) (d) None of these

6 Faulty....... can affect the physicality of the child.
(a) environment (b) life skill
(c) etiquette (d) education

7 A physically disable child is unable to ...... with normal children.
(a) fight (b) socialise
(c) cry (d) None of these

8 Physically challenged children are seen as
(a) helpless (b) weak
(c) Both (a) and (b) (d) None of these

9 Mentally challenged children are not mature.... .
(a) physically (b) mentally
(c) emotionally (d) All of these

10 What are the characteristics of mentally challenged child?
(a) Bad Memory (b) Attention Deficiency
(c) Disinterest (d) All of these

11 Which one is a genetic mental disorder?
(a) Down syndrome (b) Phenylketonuria
(c) Scurvy (d) Rickets

12 Aggression, depression, and anxiety are ...... problem.
(a) personality (b) childhood
(c) behavioural (d) educational

13 The Persons with Disabilities Act was enacted on
(a) 1995 (b) 1994 (c) 1996 (d) 1993

14 Department of disability affairs was renamed to
(a) department of person with disability
(b) department of empowerment of person with disabilities
(c) department of empowerment
(d) All of the above

15 Which are the school options for children with disability?
(a) Formal School
(b) Special School
(c) National Institute for open schooling
(d) All of the above

16 A child's body temperature must not rise above
(a) 107° F (b) 110°F (c) 101°F (d) 112°F

17 A child becomes problematic due to
(a) lifestyle (b) stress (c) peer group (d) school

18 Psychiatric problem in children include
(a) bedwetting (b) thumb sucking
(c) day dreaming (d) All of these

19 .... is a challenge to society.
(a) Indisciplined child
(b) Psychiatric problematic child
(c) Emotionally disturbed child
(d) Teenager

20 Indisciplined child is result of inappropriate ..... environment.
(a) family (b) social
(c) Both (a) and (b) (d) None of these

21 When do the thumb sucking starts?
(a) Before birth (b) Since birth
(c) 2-3 months (d) 1-2 years

22 Child can be thumb sucking to
(a) rebel against parents (b) get attention
(c) as a part of addiction (d) All of these

23 Bedwetting is often a ...... issue.
(a) developmental (b) psychological
(c) chemical (d) hormonal

24 Which is the bladder irritants?
(a) Milk (b) Cocoa (c) Fruit (d) Vegetable

25 Nail biting can be a sign of
(a) emotional stress (b) mental stress
(c) Both (a) and (b) (d) None of these

26 A stress ball is a great option to release....... .
(a) anxiety (b) frustration
(c) endorphins (d) blood pressure

27 Kleptomania is the act of
(a) thumb sucking (b) group fighting
(c) nail biting (d) stealing

28 Decrease in .... hormone leads to risk taking behaviour.
(a) adrenaline (b) insulin
(c) serotonin (d) testosterone

29 Children at risk require basic facilities such as
(a) food (b) clothing
(c) parental support (d) All of these

30 The work that the child labour can be forced to do is
(a) legal (b) illegal
(c) satisfying (d) financially stable

31 Many children run away from home to avoid
(a) psychological abuse (b) sexual abuse
(c) Both (a) and (b) (d) None of these

32 Street children use .... to cope with hardship.
(a) drug (b) candy
(c) medicine (d) adult support

33 Common cause of juvenile crimes is
(a) poverty (b) drug abuse
(c) family violence (d) All of these

34 Who said 15%–30% of juvenile crimes are due to genetic factor?
(a) Halley (b) Golem (c) Charles (d) Erick

35 A child should feel .... in family environment.
(a) threatened (b) sad (c) safe (d) scared

36 Parents must equally .... all the children.
(a) cold (b) love (c) slap (d) hurt

37 What should the teacher understand about the child?
(a) Psychology (b) Biology
(c) Eating habits (d) Company he keeps

38 Student must be taught ....
(a) fighting (b) moral education
(c) karate (d) singing

39 Who can advise the parents about the criminal behaviour?
(a) Psychologist (b) Psychiatrist
(c) Both (a) and (b) (d) None of these

40 Government should stop people who indulge in .... activities.
(a) extracurricular (b) comical
(c) unethical (d) political

41 When was probation houses set up?
(a) 1958 (b) 1956 (c) 1957 (d) 1953

42 Children court were established under
(a) Probation Act (b) Rehabilitation Act
(c) Children Act (d) Teach India Act

43 Judges in children's court are
(a) male (b) female
(c) previous offender (d) Police officer

44 For how long juveniles are kept in reform house?
(a) 3-7 years (b) 5-10 years (c) 10-20 years (d) 20-15 years

45 Which of the following statement(s) is/are true?
1. Children bite their nails as it comforts them.
2. Children bite their nails when they are bored.
3. Slapping the children can help with nail biting.
4. Stopping nail biting is not required as it is not a major problem.

Codes
(a) Only 1 (b) Only 3
(c) Both 1 and 2 (d) None of these

46 Which of the following statement(s) is/are true?
1. According to Halley 15-30% of crime is due to environmental factor.
2. Faulty environment can lead to criminal behaviour in child.
3. Family plays an important role.
4. Juvenile criminals are born criminal.

Codes
(a) 1, 2, and 4 (b) 2 and 3
(c) 1 and 4 (d) None of these

47 Which of the following statements is/are true?
1. Child labour is a global issue.
2. Child labour trains the child for future opportunities.
3. Children live in street because they are homeless.
4. Street children living with their parents are safe.

Codes
(a) 1 and 3 (b) Only 4
(c) 2 and 3 (d) None of these

48 Which of the following statement(s) is/are true?
1. Physical disability does not affect the child.
2. A physically disable child can easily adjust to his environment.
3. Physically disable child are emotionally stable.
4. They are always mentally weak.

Codes
(a) 1, 2 and 3 (b) Only 2
(c) 2 and 3 (d) None of these

49 Which of the following statement(s) is/are true?
1. Thumb sucking makes child feel secure.
2. Thumb sucking relieves the child's stress.
3. Child abuse is necessary to discipline the child.
4. Parents can abuse the child any time.

Codes
(a) 1, 3 and 4 (b) Only 3
(c) 1 and 2 (d) None of these

50 Which of the following statement(s) is/are true?
1. Children could be abandoned by mother if born before marriage.
2. Future of orphan child is very bright.
3. Orphans may become rag picker.
4. Orphans are alienated from the society.

Codes
(a) 1, 3 and 4 (b) Only 2
(c) 2 and 3 (d) None of these

51 Which of the following statement(s) is/are true?
1. Family does not play any role in prevention of juvenile crime.
2. Teachers should understand the child to prevent juvenile crime.
3. Advisory centre should be arranged.
4. Unethical work leads to creativity.

Codes
(a) 3 and 4 (b) 2 and 3
(c) 1 and 3 (d) None of these

52 Which of the following statements is/are true?

1. People differ from each other due to hereditary and environmental factor.
2. A child may become skillful or disabled due to this factor.
3. A child should fulfill his own needs.
4. There is no requirement of studying people with special need.

Codes

(a) 2 and 3 (b) 2 and 4
(c) 1 and 2 (d) None of these

53 Match the following.

List I	List II
A. Rehabilitation of Juvenile in India	1. 1960
B. Probation Act	2. 3 to 7 year
C. Children Act	3. 1850
D. Reform House	4. 1958

Codes

	A	B	C	D		A	B	C	D
(a)	1	3	4	2	(b)	2	1	3	4
(c)	3	4	1	2	(d)	3	2	1	4

54 Match the following.

List I	List II
A. Child Labour	1. Children run away from home
B. Street Children	2. Children are sold
C. Orphan	3. Underage children work in a field
D. Child Trafficking	4. Both the parents leave the child

Codes

	A	B	C	D		A	B	C	D
(a)	3	1	4	2	(b)	1	3	2	4
(c)	4	3	1	2	(d)	2	1	3	4

Directions (Q. Nos. 55-64) *Given below are two statements, one labelled as Assertion (A) and the other labelled as Reason (R). Following are the codes given below choose the correct option.*

Codes

(a) Both A and R are true and R is the correct explanation of A
(b) Both A and R are true, but R is not the correct explanation of A
(c) A is true, R is False
(d) A is false, R is true

55 **Assertion** (A) Children having physical deformity are called physically disable.
Reason (R) Physical disability is caused by genetic factors only.

56 **Assertion** (A) Children may inherit some hereditary disorder.
Reason (R) Dwarfism is a hereditary disorder.

57 **Assertion** (A) IQ of mentally challenged child is more than normal children.
Reason (R) Children having IQ less than 70 are called mentally challenged.

58 **Assertion** (A) Mentally challenged child may be produced by aged parents.
Reason (R) If the age of parents are more than 40 the child may be mentally retarded.

59 **Assertion** (A) Mentally retarded kids must be adjusted to family.
Reason (R) Family and society must support mentally retarded child.

60 **Assertion** (A) Juvenile crimes are regularly committed in India.
Reason (R) Valentine said heredity affects criminal tendencies.

61 **Assertion** (A) Children Act was passed in 1960.
Reason (R) Juvenile offenders are heard in separate court.

62 **Assertion** (A) Mentally challenged children have bad memory.
Reason (R) Down syndrome can cause mental retardation.

63 **Assertion** (A) Problematic children do not have specific disability.
Reason (R) Family environment may cause a child to become problematic.

64 **Assertion** (A) Kleptomania refers to compulsive stealing behaviour.
Reason (R) Parents are the reason, why the child steals.

Directions (Q. Nos. 65-69) *Read the passage given below and answer the questions that follow.*

In India, the first legislation dealing with children in conflict with law or children committing crime was the Apprentices Act, 1850. It provided that children under the age of 15 years found to have committed petty offences will be bounded as apprentices. Thereafter, the Reformatory Schools Act, 1897 came into effect which provided that children up to the age of 15 years sentenced to imprisonment would be sent to reformatory cell. After the Independence, with an aim to provide care, protection, development and rehabilitation of neglected or delinquent juveniles, our Parliament enacted the Juvenile Justice Act, 1986. It was an Act which brought uniform system throughout the country.

Section 2(a) of the Act defined the term 'juvenile' as a "boy who has not attained the age of 16 years and a girl who has not attained the age of 18 years." Later on the Parliament enacted the Juvenile Justice (Care and Protection) Act, 2000 which raised the age bar to 18 years for both girl and boy. The Juvenile Justice (Care and Protection) Act, 2000 lays down that juvenile in conflict with law or juvenile offenders may be kept in an 'Observation Home' while children in need of care and protection need to be kept in a 'Children Home' during the pendency of proceedings before the competent authority.

A juvenile can be detained only for a maximum period of 3 years irrespective of the gravity of offence committed by him and he will be remanded to 'Special Home'. The Juvenile Justice (Care and Protection) Act, 2000 provides immunity to the child who is less than 18 years of age at the time of the commission of the alleged offence from trial through Criminal Court or any punishment under Criminal Law in view of Section 17 of the Act. The purpose of this new Act was to rehabilitate the child and assimilate him/her in mainstream society.

The rationale is that a child still has the possibility of getting reformed due to his/her tender age and lack of maturity and it is the responsibility of the state to protect and reform the child.

65 What is the theme of passage?
(a) Domestic violence (b) Child labour
(c) Juvenile crime (d) Child abuse

66 When was Apprentice Act enacted?
(a) 1845 (b) 1850 (c) 1855 (d) 1840

67 Under Apprentice Act children under ...... age will be bounded as apprentice.
(a) 15 (b) 16 (c) 14 (d) 17

68 Under Reformatory Act, children under 15 will be sent to...... .
(a) detention centre (b) reformatory cell
(c) prison (d) rehabilitation centre

69 A juvenile can be detained for maximum of ...... years.
(a) 3 (b) 4 (c) 5 (d) 2

PREVIOUS YEARS' QUESTIONS

July 2018

1 A resilient child is one who
(a) gives up easily on tasks of endurance.
(b) lacks emotional stability.
(c) suffers from various health problems.
(d) bounces back from circumstances that would harm most others.

January 2017

2 Arrange in sequence the processes that need to be undertaken to rehabilitate a child who is abandoned.
1. Initiate restoration process
2. File on FIR
3. Produce the child before CWC
4. Admit to children home
5. When child legally free place in adoption

Codes
(a) 2, 4, 3, 1, 5 (b) 1, 2, 3, 4, 5
(c) 2, 4, 3, 5, 1 (d) 2, 4, 1, 3, 5

3 Arrange in order of enactment of legislations from earliest to latest.
1. The Child Labour Act
2. The Immoral Traffic (Prevention) Act
3. Prevention of Child Sexual Offences Act
4. The Juvenile Justice (Care and Protection of Children Act)

Codes
(a) 3, 1, 2, 4 (b) 2, 4, 3, 1 (c) 1, 2, 3, 4 (d) 2, 1, 4, 3

June 2015

4 **Assertion** (A) Juveniles in conflict with law are children below 16 years of age who have committed a crime.
Reason (R) Children who are less than 16 years are considered innocent and pure and are given less punishment for their crime.

Codes
(a) A is correct and R is incorrect
(b) A and R are both incorrect
(c) A is correct, but R is not the correct explanation of A
(d) A and R are correct and R is the correct explanation of A

ANSWERS

Exam Based Questions

1 (c)	2 (a)	3 (d)	4 (b)	5 (c)	6 (a)	7 (b)	8 (c)	9 (b)	10 (d)
11 (a)	12 (c)	13 (a)	14 (b)	15 (d)	16 (c)	17 (b)	18 (d)	19 (c)	20 (c)
21 (a)	22 (b)	23 (a)	24 (b)	25 (c)	26 (a)	27 (d)	28 (c)	29 (d)	30 (b)
31 (c)	32 (a)	33 (d)	34 (a)	35 (c)	36 (b)	37 (a)	38 (b)	39 (c)	40 (c)
41 (a)	42 (c)	43 (b)	44 (a)	45 (c)	46 (b)	47 (a)	48 (d)	49 (c)	50 (a)
51 (b)	52 (c)	53 (c)	54 (a)	55 (c)	56 (a)	57 (d)	58 (a)	59 (a)	60 (b)
61 (a)	62 (b)	63 (a)	64 (c)	65 (c)	66 (b)	67 (a)	68 (b)	69 (a)	

Previous Years' Questions

1 (d)	2 (a)	3 (d)	4 (b)

UNIT VIII

Family Studies

Marriage and family are key structures in most societies. Marriage is one of the social institutions established to control and regulate the life of mankind. It is closely related with the institution of family. Family studies focuses on families the challenge one faces and how to meet challenges and improve their quality of life.

Family and marriage have a special place in social institution. Family studies researches are on how the individual grows and interacts within the family. These studies include incompatibility, domestic violence, conflict and resolution, disintegration, family crisis, etc. Under family studies various aspects and issues of family are studied like upbringing, sibling relationship, marriage relationship how family member interact with each other, how family deals with external situation etc.

Marriage establishes family, relations and forms long-term alliance between two families socially and economically. Marriage can be defined as "a socially sanctioned union between a man and a woman which is accomplished by culture specific rituals and ceremonies." The traditional Hindu family followed the joint family system, in which many generations continued to live together under one roof.

Dynamics of Marriage and Family Relationships

Marriage is the foundation of family and the basic building block of society. It is ideal for child-rearing and brings stability in human relationships. According to social science research and government surveys, there has been a change in the outlook towards marriage in recent years, due to the following reasons :

Changes in Patriarchal Rights Earlier the life-partners were selected by the eldest male member or patriarchal head of the family. Now, the consent of the boy and girl is essential.

Change in Nature/Purpose of Marriage Modern Hindus believe in 'life-long companionship' between husband and wife. Earlier, the main objective of a traditional Hindu marriage was 'dharma'.

In this Chapter

Deterioration in Relationships This situation is a result of the changing roles between husband and wife in modern society. The husband was the sole earner of the family and the wife looked after the children. Now, the women are gainfully employed, sometimes earning more than their husbands.

Rise in Instability Industrialisation, urbanisation and education have had a tremendous impact on the stability of marriage. Values like gender equality and individualism have changed the perception of women towards marriage. Their economic independence has led to higher incidences of divorce and separation.

Lack of Cooperation Globalisation has made the traditional Indian society more westernised. The modern Indian youth is egoistic and unwilling to compromise self-interests. They do not consider marriage as essential. Arranged marriages have consequently become less popular. In cities and urban areas eligible youngsters prefer to choose their own life partners.

Domestic Violence

Domestic violence can be physical or psychological, and it can affect anyone of any age, gender, race or sexual orientation. It may include behaviours meant to scare, physically harm, or control a partner. While every relationship is different, domestic violence generally involves an unequal power dynamic in which one partner tries to assert control over the other in a variety of ways.

Insults, threats, emotional abuse and sexual coercion all constitute domestic violence. Some perpetrators may even use children, pets, or other family members as emotional leverage to get the victim to do what they want. Victims experience diminished self-worth, anxiety, depression, and a general sense of helplessness that can take time and often professional help to overcome.

The legal definition of domestic violence is 'any abusive, violent, coercive, forceful or threatening act or word inflicted by one member of a family or household on another. Violence that involves abuse and harassment are mainly linked with power and exist in close relationships. Men commit domestic violence if they have low education, low self-esteem, are alcoholic with low economic status and exposed to domestic violence against their mothers.

Types of Domestic Violence

When most people think of domestic violence, they imagine a situation where the abusive partner physically hurts the victim. However, physical harm is only one form of abuse and there are various types of domestic violence; domestic violence can be physical, emotional, sexual, financial or psychological.

Physical Abuse Physical abuse is the most recognisable form of domestic violence. It involves the use of force against the victim, causing injury (a punch or a kick, stabbing, shooting, choking, slapping, forcing you to use drugs, etc.).

Emotional Abuse Emotional abuse involves the destruction of the victim's self-worth, and is brought about by persistent insult, humiliation or criticism. Emotional abuse can be a difficult type of domestic violence for many people to understand, since, on the surface, it appears to be quite common in unhealthy relationships. In most states, emotional abuse is not enough on its own to bring a domestic violence action unless the abuse is so persistent and so significant that the relationship can be labelled extremely coercive. Typically, evidence of emotional abuse is combined with other abuse (physical, financial, sexual, or psychological) to bring a domestic violence action.

Sexual Abuse Sexual abuse is a common form of domestic violence. It includes not only sexual assault and rape, but also harassment, such as unwelcome touching and other demeaning behaviours. Many victims don't realise how broadly sexual abuse is interpreted. For example, if you've ever been coerced into not using contraception (the pill, a condom, an IUD, etc.) or having an abortion, then you may have actually been sexually abused. This form of abuse is known as reproductive coercion.

Financial Abuse Of the types of domestic violence, financial abuse is perhaps the least obvious. Financial abuse may take on many forms, such as a husband preventing his wife from obtaining an education or a job outside the home. Financial abuse is extremely common, particularly when families have pooled their money into joint accounts (with one partner controlling) and where there's little or no family support system to help.

Financial abuse is simply another form of control, even though it is usually less obvious than physical or sexual abuse. Often, the victim is completely dependent on their partner for money. With no access to money except through the abusive partner, the victim is completely at the abusive partner's mercy. The abusive partner may withhold money for food, clothing, and more. If children are involved, this can overlap with neglect.

Psychological Abuse Psychological abuse is basically a term for intimidating, threatening or fear-causing behavior. This behaviour must be persistent and significant. A one-time event generally won't be enough to bring a domestic violence action.

Like emotional abuse, psychological abuse may not, on its own, be enough to bring a domestic violence action unless it's especially severe. A wide variety of behaviours fall under the umbrella of psychological abuse.

Some common examples include :

- Preventing the victim from talking to people unless they have 'permission';
- Preventing the victim from leaving the house;
- Threatening the victim with violence or
- Emotional blackmail for doing something the abusive partner doesn't agree with.

Reasons for Domestic Violence Against Women

Reasons for domestic violence against women are :

Male Dominance Men tend to control women in their family to show off their masculinity, and to ensure that women fulfill expected roles. Men react violently against women who challenge men's actions and supremacy.

Economic Dependence of Female on Male This kind of financial abuse occurs in majority of domestic violence cases. It is a tactic by which abusers gain power and control in a relationship.

Illiteracy Illiteracy among women is one of the major causes of domestic violence. Lack of education prevents women from earning, planning and managing their own finances and are therefore unable to extricate their families from the clutches of poverty.

Jealousy Towards Women Jealousy appears to be one of the major causes for domestic violence to take place. Jealousy is a complex emotion comprising various feelings and desires. Jealousy is more intense in younger people, who are more prone to violence as compared to older people.

Evil Social Customs Social customs like 'insufficient dowry' at the time of marriage results in innumerable domestic violence cases, very often resulting in bride-burning.

In our society, violence erupts intensely behind doors of homes, in which women are brutally tortured and beaten. The greed for dowry and desire for a male child are major factors of domestic violence against women in rural and urban areas.

Family Pressures Family pressures of observing the 'purdah' system (veiling and seclusion of women) restricts women in every aspect of life. Women who oppose observance of such practices, especially in rural areas, are often victims of domestic violence. Poor and low-status women must observe veiling while working in fields and on construction sites.

Intoxication Strong association has been found between consumption of alcohol (intoxication) and domestic violence. Intoxication directly affects cognitive and physical function of the body and results in reduction of self-control.

Lack of Action Against Perpetrator of Domestic Violence Several incidents of harassment and abuse are not reported because of the fear of shame or guilt, fear of not being believed or fear of disclosing the identify to the perpetrator. In such cases, no action is taken against the wrong-doer. Hence, such acts of domestic violence continue as no attempt at prevention takes place.

Complaint Against Domestic Violence

The helpline number for women is '181'. It provides a toll free (24 hours) telecom service for women, affected by domestic violence, seeking support.

Protection of Women from Domestic Violence Act, 2005 (PWDVA, 2005)

This Act was enacted to protect women from domestic violence. It was enforced on 26th October, 2006. This Act has provided, for the first time, the definition of 'domestic violence'. It is a civil law meant for protection orders and not to penalise criminally.

Salient features of the Domestic Violence Act, 2005 are :

- The Domestic Violence Act, 2005 seeks to ensure civil remedy to the victim of domestic violence.
- This Act seeks to cover those women who are or have been in relationship with the abuser where both parties lived together in a shared household and are related by consanguinity, marriage or relationship in the nature of marriage or adoption, in addition relationship with family members living together as a joint family are also included. Even those women who are sisters, mothers, widows, single women or living with them are entitled to get legal protection under the proposed Act.
- The Act provides for the woman's right to reside in the matrimonial or shared household, whether or not she has any title or rights in the household. This right is secured by a residence order which is passed by a court.
- The other relief envisaged under the Act is that of the power of the court to pass protection orders that prevent the abuser from aiding or committing an act of domestic violence or any other specified act, entering a workplace or any other place frequently visited by the abused, attempting to communicate with the abused. Isolating any assets used by both the parties and causing violence to the abused, her relatives and others who provide her assistance from the domestic violence.
- The Act provides for appointment of protection officers and NGOs to provide assistance to the woman with respect to medical examination, obtaining, legal aid, safe shelter.
- The Act allows woman's right to her stridhan.

- The Act provides for breach of protection order or interim protection order by the respondents as a cognisable and non-bailable offence punishable with imprisonment for a term which may extend to one year or with a fine which may extend to twenty thousand or with both. Similarly, non-compliance or discharge of duties by the protection officer is also sought to be made an offence under the Act.
- The act provides a simplified procedure to woman who faces domestic violence.

Marital Disharmony

Marital disharmony can be referred to as a strain in marriage interaction between a couple who are living together. Marriage is a basic form of long-term interpersonal social relationship. Conflict in such relationships is unavoidable. Negative interactions and behaviour are an obvious and natural outcome of communication and sharing lives together. A happy, successful marriage does not necessarily reflect absence of conflict. There is merely a higher level of positive behaviour in such marriages. Marital disharmony has become more evident in recent years due to some of the following reasons :

Opportunities for Women Access to higher level of education and entry into professional occupation by women has altered their traditional role within families.

Dual Career Couples High pressure jobs and responsibility at work-places are not compatible with household chores. Trying to create work and home life balance by women often result in disputes between couples and causing disharmony.

Childcare Women with greater financial independence now, have to still face the responsibility of childcare and rearing. This aspect poses a higher burden on women leading to stress and conflict.

Type of Marriage and Family Arranged marriages are now giving way to self-choice marriages. The choice of selecting a suitable partner rests with the females in many cases. Very often the extended family may or may not act as an active support system.

Children Higher marital disagreements have been reported among couples with young children. Motherhood often results in overload of domestic duties at home.

Financial Matters Couples were found to be in conflict when women earned more than their husbands. High financial status is a clear indicator of high self-worth. In such cases, the male partner is susceptible to stress, thereby leading to marital disharmony and conflict.

Marital Conflict

Marital conflict comprises events that involve bitterness, pride, anger and stubbornness and hinder direct and effective communication in a marriage. Conflict in marriage, mainly among urban couples can be handled in ways that can remove stress from their lives, to result in more satisfying relationships.

Resolution of Conflict

Some of the ways to resolve conflict are given below :

Spend Quality Time with One Another Quality of time spent with each other must be enhanced through positive communication and pursuits such as gardening, cooking together.

Respect One Another No matter how much income the other earns, there must be mutual respect for each other.

Curb the Ego Both partners should remove their ego when communicating with each other. They must understand that unity is strength. A positive commitment in their relationship will positively impact their performance in their respective work-places.

Avoid Disagreements Practise empathy and try to see the other partners view-point before exercising judgement. This will reduced disagreements and lead to more harmony in their relationship.

A study was carried out by Gottman, 1999 in which it was concluded that satisfaction in marital relationships depend more strongly on the kind of frequent interactions between married couples than the type of disagreements between them.

Parent Education

Parent Education is an opportunity for parents to discover their own strength and participate in their child's cognitive, literacy and developmental growth. Many studies have shown a link between parental involvement and a child's success in school.

Children whose parents are involved in their school have better grades, fewer behavioural problems and are more sociable (National Centre for Family Literacy, 2003). There are four components of family literacy and parent education is one of them.

According to Family Literacy Programmes, the education of children and parents is interdependent. The Adult Education and Family Literacy Act, reflects this dual goals and encourages adults to become full partners in the educational development of their children.

Positive Parenting

Positive parenting is an approach built on mutual respect. Parenting built on mutual respect means we handle our children as individuals and not as our own property. Positive parenting focuses on teaching your child the who, what, when, and why of a situation. Positive parenting is focused on developing a strong, deeply committed relationship between parent and child based on communication and mutual respect. Positive parenting means training children toward self-control.

There are three major components of positive parenting :

- Rules and consequences are laid out, discussed often and followed.
- Parents focus on helping children internalise discipline, children rather than obey orders based on fear of punishment in order to develop self-discipline.
- Parents use active listening to understand children's thoughts. This allows parents to correct misunderstanding or mistaken link of logic.

Positive parenting allows children to be treated with respect. It is about nurturing the relationship between parent and child. Positive parenting teaches discipline that builds children's self-esteem, while at the same time correcting their misbehaviour. Positive parenting is the continual relationship of a parent and a child that includes caring, teaching, leading communicating and providing for the needs of a child consistently and unconditionally.

Community Education

Community education, also known as community based education or community learning and development, is an organisation's programmes. In order to promote learning and social development, work with individuals and groups in their communities using a range of formal and informal methods.

Community education encompasses all those occupations and approaches that are concerned with running education and development programmes within local communities. Rather than within educational institutions such as schools, colleges and universities. Community education has three basic components such as life long learning opportunities, community involvement in schools and efficient use of resources, and is based on set of ten broad principles. These principles are :

Self-determination Community residents have a right and a responsibility to be involved in assessing community needs and identifying community resources that can be used to address those needs.

Self-help People are best served by their leaders when their capacity to help themselves is acknowledged and developed. When people assume responsibility for their own-well being, they achieve some degree of independence.

Leadership Development Training local leader in problem-solving, decision-making and group-process skills is essential to community improvement efforts.

Life Long Learning Education is a continuous process, everyone in the community shares the responsibility of educating all members of the community. The learning opportunities should be available to residents of all ages.

Institutional Responsiveness The public institutions exist to serve the public, they are obligated to develop programmes and services that address constantly changing public needs and interests.

Integrated Delivery of Services Organisation and agencies that operate for the public good can best use their limited resources to meet their own goals and serve the public by collaborating with organisations and agencies with similar goals and purposes.

Maximum Use of Resources The physical, financial and human resources of community should be fully available and rationally inter connected if the diverse needs and interests of the community are to be met.

Localisation Community services, programmes and volunteer opportunities close to people's homes have the greater potential for high levels of public participation.

Inclusiveness Community programmes, activities and services should involve the broadest possible cross-section of community residents with distinction.

Access to Public Information Public information should be shared across agency and organisation. Thus, community education advocates and supports the creation of innovative programmes and collaboration between all members of the community. It is for the purpose of advancing community learning and sustainability.

Family Disorganisation

Any non-harmonious functioning within a family results in family disorganisation. It includes both tension between husband and wife; and between parents and children. Tension between couples is a major cause for families to break-up as the conjugal relationship creates a bond uniting the family in any society. When this bond is broken, the family also breaks-up. This break-up can be of several types such as separation, divorce, physical violence or use of abusive language.

Memoria (1960) has listed six dimensions of family disorganisation :

(i) Disappearance of common objective. Family aims have been replaced by individual aims.
(ii) All cooperative efforts cease
(iii) Mutual services are withered.
(iv) The relationship of husband and wife is no longer coordinated.
(v) The status of the family in its external relations to other social groups is changed.
(vi) An attitude of indifference exists between the couple.

Single Parent Families

The family is in transition and the traditional picture of two parents and children is fading away as more marriages are breaking down at an alarming rate. The number of single parent families is rising rapidly. Some of the reasons for this are as follows :

- People are getting more materialistic.
- Mothers prefer to gain financial independence by seeking employment and working less at home.
- Urbanisation and industrialisation have brought about socio-psychological changes in attitudes and values of people.
- Tragedy in the family leading to death of one parent also results in single parent families.
- Divorce or abandonment by one parent.
- In Western countries, many independent youngers choose to become single parents out of wedlock either by adopting or accepting surrogacy motherhood.

Family Studies

Family studies in an area of psychological study and research that sees how individuals change and grow and how those changes interact within the family matrix. Under it, family in crisis, family therapy and initiative for child development are studied. Their description is given below :

Family in Crisis

Meaning of crises is a time of intense difficulty. A family crisis, therefore, occurs when changes take place within the family as result of the following occurrences :

- Relocation of family
- Divorce
- Illness or accident.
- Loss of job/employment
- Death of family member

A family is a semi-closed system in which the role of each member is clearly defined. Consequently, change in the member or position affects the other's role and position.

Family Therapy

This includes counselling to family members resolve conflicts and improve communication either in groups or on a one-to-one basis. This kind of therapy is carried out by a psychotherapist, who helps the client to solve the psychological problems faced by him/her.

Psychotherapists aim at changing the maladaptive behaviours, decreasing personal distress and helping the client to adapt better to her/his environment. Inadequate marital, occupational and social adjustment require major changes to be made in an individual's personal environment. Some of the changes, a psychotherapist can bring about in a client, are of the following kinds :

- Reinforcing client to strive for betterment
- Modifying habits
- Changing thinking pattern by increasing self-awareness
- Releasing or lessening emotional stress
- Improving communication and inter-personal relationship
- To become aware of one's choices in life
- To relate to one's environment more positively and creatively
- To help in strengthening decision-making skills

Child Development

Child development refers to the process through which human beings grow and mature from infancy to about seventeen years of age. This includes physical, cognitive and social growth.

Initiatives for Child Development

Some popular initiatives for child development are :

- Integrated Child Development Services, ICDS (1975)
- Balika Samridhi Yojana, BSY (1997)
- Child-line Service (1988-99)
- National Charter for Children (2003)
- Integrated Child Protection Scheme, ICPS (2009)
- National Policy for Children (2013)
- Sukanya Samridhi Yojana, SSY (2015)
- National Nutrition Mission, NNM (2017-18)
- Poshan Abhiyaan (2018)

EXAM BASED QUESTIONS

1 **Which one of the following characterised the traditional Hindu family?**
(a) Nuclear family
(b) Joint family
(c) Sole member
(d) Only elders living together

2 **Which one of the following can be considered building block of society?**
(a) Live in relationship (b) Marriage
(c) Family (d) Joint family system

3 **Which was the main objective of a traditional Hindu marriage?**
(a) Life long companionship (b) Dharma
(c) Patriarchal patronage (d) Stability

4 **Which one of the following has changed the face of Indian marriage?**
(a) Youngsters
(b) Globalisation and Westernisation
(c) Elders in the family
(d) Egoistic attitude

5 **Which one of the following is the most likely reason for men to commit domestic violence?**
(a) High education (b) High self-esteem
(c) Low self-esteem (d) High moral values

6 **Which one is an objective of the Domestic Violence Act, 2005?**
(a) Woman gives up right to reside with husband
(b) Woman has right to reside in shared house with husband
(c) Woman cannot have right to her 'stridhan'
(d) Husband can enter workplace of woman

7 **Which of the following evil social customs causes domestic violence against women?**
(a) Sufficient dowry (b) Insufficient dowry
(c) Desire for a female child (d) Non-purdah system

8 **Which helpline number can be reached to lodge a complaint against domestic violence?**
(a) 161 (b) 171
(c) 181 (d) 100

9 **When was PWDV Act enforced?**
(a) 25th October, 2006
(b) 26th October, 2006
(c) 25th October, 2005
(d) 24th October, 2006

10 **Marital conflict comprises events that are**
(a) happy (b) reconciling
(c) bitter and angry (d) compromising

11 **With whom is the responsibility of childcare?**
(a) Father (b) Mother
(c) Paternal grandmother (d) Paternal grandfather

12 **How can conflict be resolved among couples?**
(a) By living apart
(b) By spending quality time with one another
(c) By displaying ego
(d) Having argument with each other

13 **What is the relationship between parental involvement and child's success in academics?**
(a) Child fails miserably
(b) Child is successful at school
(c) Child has behavioural problems
(d) Child has learning disability

14 **Positive parenting helps in which of the following ways?**
(a) Under-development of child
(b) Growth and development of child
(c) Failure in class
(d) Unsuccessful in academics

15 **Which of the following principles related to the community education is/are correct?**
(a) Leadership development
(b) Maximum utilisation of available resources
(c) Access to public information to be shared across agency and organisation
(d) All of the above

16 **What is the meaning of family disorganisation?**
(a) Lack of proper organisation
(b) Weakness in conjugal bonding in couples
(c) Healthy friendship between couples
(d) Stability in conjugal bonding

17 **According to Memoria (1960) which one is a part of family disorganisation dimension?**
(a) lack of cooperation among couples
(b) presence of common objective
(c) strong coordination between spouses
(d) sympathy for each other

18 **What are single parent families?**
(a) Where both parents look after children
(b) Where only mother cares for children
(c) Where only father cares for children
(d) Where either parent cares for children

19 **Crisis in family results due to which one of the following reasons?**
(a) Family stability
(b) Family harmony
(c) Death of a family member
(d) No change within a family

20 **Family Therapy is carried out by**
(a) a counsellor
(b) a doctor
(c) a psychologist
(d) a psychotherapist

21 What is maximum age limit for Sukanya Samridhi Yojana?
(a) 11 years (b) 10 years
(c) 12 years (d) 9 years

22 Which of the following schemes was started in Rajasthan?
(a) Balika Samridhi Yojana
(b) Mukhyamantri Rajshri Yojana
(c) Sukanya Samridhi Yojana
(d) Beti Bacchao, Beti Padhao

23 Which of the following schemes is given to families below poverty line in Jharkhand?
(a) Mukhyamantri Laadli Yojana
(b) Beti Bacchao, Beti Padhao
(c) Balika Samridhi Yojana
(d) Sukanya Samridhi Yojana

24 Which one of the following is applicable in Uttarakhand?
(a) Nanda Devi Kanya Yojana
(b) Mukhyamantri Kanya Suraksha Yojana
(c) CBSE Scholarship Scheme
(d) Beti Bacchao, Beti Padhao

25 Which of the following is not the duty of the protection officer according to protection of women from Domestic Act Violence 2005?
(a) Ensuring that aggrieved person is provided legal aid under legal services Authorities Act, 1987.
(b) Make domestic incident report.
(c) Assist the magistrate in the discharge of her/his functions under the Act.
(d) Coordinate between the services provided by concerned ministries and NGOs.

26 Which of the following are the basic components of community education?
(a) Lifelong learning
(b) Opportunities
(c) Community Involvement
(d) All of the above

27 Which of the following are the components of positive parenting?
(a) Rules and consequences are laid out, discussed often and followed.
(b) Parents focus on helping children.
(c) Parents use active listening to children's thoughts.
(d) All of the above

28 Which parenting style can be characterised as: Parents place value on obedience and favour punitive punishment in order to exert control over their children?
(a) Indulgent (b) Authoritarian
(c) Authoritative (d) Permissive

29 Which parenting style can be characterised as: Parents nurture their children, but prefer to allow them to much freedom of expression?
(a) Authoritarian (b) Indulgent
(c) Restrictive (d) Permissive

30 Integrated Child Development services scheme implemented with the aim of holistic development of children upto .... years.
(a) four (b) five (c) six (d) ten

31 Which of the following are the major objectives of Beti Bachoo-Beti Padao Yojana?
(a) Ensuring survival and protection of girl child.
(b) Ensuring vocational training of a girl child.
(c) Ensuring education and participation of the girl child.
(d) Both (a) and (c)

32 Integrated child protection was launched in the year.
(a) 2009-2010 (b) 2011-2012
(c) 2013-2014 (d) 2014-2015

33 Poshan Abhiyaan has been launched on 8th March, 2018 by the Prime Minister to address malnutrition through convergence, use of technology and targeted approach. In which of the following places it was launched?
(a) Panipat (b) Jhunjhunu
(c) Varanasi (d) Meerut

34 The National Charter for children 2003 was adopted on ....
(a) 9th February, 2004
(b) 12th March, 2004
(c) 15th February, 2004
(d) 20th February, 2004

35 Long-term alliance between two families is an outcome of
1. marriage
2. a socially sanctioned union
3. live in relationship
4. observance of culture specific rituals
5. separation

Codes
(a) 1, 2, 5 (b) 1, 2, 4
(c) 3, 2, 1 (d) 4, 3, 5

36 Benefits of marriage include
1. foundation of family
2. unstable relations
3. lack of specific ceremonies
4. strong support system
5. social and economic bonding between families

Codes
(a) 1, 2, 5 (b) 2, 3, 4 (c) 1, 4, 5 (d) 2, 4, 5

37 A change in the outlook of marriage is mainly due to
1. rise in economic status of youngsters.
2. a shift in the objective of traditional marriage.
3. patriarchal head of family.
4. rise in stability of married couples.
5. falling trend in arranged marriage.

Codes
(a) 2, 3, 5 (b) 1, 2, 5 (c) 2, 3, 4 (d) 1, 2, 4

38 Which of the following actions comprise domestic violence?
1. Non-abusive language
2. Threatening act
3. Abusive language
4. Pain inflicted by an outsider
5. Coercive action by a family member

Codes
(a) 1, 2, 5 (b) 2, 3, 5 (c) 1, 2, 4 (d) 2, 3, 4

39 The Domestic Violence Act, 2005 provides for which of the following?
1. Seeks to ensure civil remedy to the victim.
2. No protection is provided to the victim.
3. Woman can claim right to her 'stridhan'.
4. A woman loses right to reside with her husband.
5. State provides protection officers for victim.

Codes
(a) 2, 1, 5 (b) 1, 3, 5 (c) 2, 3, 4 (d) 1, 3, 4

40 Women are victims of domestic violence because of which of the following reasons?
1. Lower education level in men
2. Intoxication of males
3. Low moral values
4. High morality
5. Higher economic status of men

Codes
(a) 1, 2, 3 (b) 2, 3, 4 (c) 1, 2, 4 (d) 2, 3, 5

41 Observance of 'purdah' system includes which of the following ?
1. Sit with men
2. Secluded from men
3. Use veil before men to cover their face
4. Prevalent in villages
5. It is not observed at all

Codes
(a) 2, 3, 4 (b) 2, 3, 5 (c) 1, 5, 3 (d) 1, 4, 5

42 Intoxication is associated with which of the following?
1. Helps in cognitive development
2. Deteriorates physical functioning of body
3. Reduces self-control
4. Unable to think rationally
5. Results in employment and progress

Codes
(a) 2, 3, 4 (b) 1, 5, 4
(c) 1, 3, 5 (d) 2, 3, 5

43 Acts of domestic violence are not reported due to which of the following reasons?
1. Fear of disclosing identity of perpetrator
2. Fear of shame
3. Fear of not being believed
4. Action already taken against wrong-doer
5. Prevention of violence

Codes
(a) 1, 2, 3 (b) 3, 4, 5 (c) 1, 2, 4 (d) 2, 3, 5

44 Following are the provisions of PWDVA
1. Civil law
2. Non-protection of women
3. It does not penalise criminally
4. It was enforced on 26th October, 2006
5. It does not define domestic violence

Codes
(a) 1, 3, 4 (b) 1, 3, 5 (c) 2, 3, 4 (d) 1, 2, 4

45 Which of the following factors are responsible for marital disharmony?
1. Conflict in relationship
2. Pride in partners
3. Lack of effective communication between partners.
4. A happy and successful relationship
5. A relationship based on mutual harmony

Codes
(a) 1, 2, 3 (b) 3, 4, 5 (c) 1, 2, 4 (d) 3, 4, 1

46 The implication of dual career couples is
1. maintaining work-life balance
2. both partners in employment
3. only one partner in employment
4. disrupts home-life
5. difficulty in rearing off-springs

Codes
(a) 2, 4, 5 (b) 1, 3, 4 (c) 2, 4, 1 (d) 1, 2, 5

47 Which of the following can be attributed to resolution of conflict in marriages?
1. Avoidance of disagreement
2. Practise empathy
3. Curbing of ego
4. Disrespecting one another
5. Increase in misunderstanding

Codes
(a) 1, 2, 3 (b) 2, 3, 4 (c) 1, 2, 5 (d) 2, 3, 5

48 Which of the following are salient features of study by Gottman?
1. It was carried out in 1999.
2. The study was based on resolution of marital conflict.
3. Satisfaction is due to frequent interactions.
4. Lack of mutual respect.
5. Study was based on type of agreements between couples.

Codes
(a) 1, 2, 3 (b) 3, 4, 5 (c) 1, 2, 4 (d) 1, 3, 5

49 Which of the following are salient features of Parent Education?
1. Non-involvement of parents leads to better grades in children.
2. Involvement of parents leads to better grades of children.
3. Education of children and parents is interdependent.
4. Parents do not care for their child's cognitive development.
5. The Adult Education and Family Literacy Act reflects dual goal.

Codes

(a) 2, 3, 5 (b) 2, 3, 4
(c) 1, 2, 3 (d) 1, 2, 5

50 Which of the following are salient features of family disorganisation?

1. Stating of six dimensions by Memoria (1960)
2. Individual aims replaced by common objective
3. High level of cooperation between partners
4. Lack of coordination between partners
5. High level of indifference

Codes

(a) 1, 4, 5 (b) 1, 2, 3
(c) 3, 4, 5 (d) 1, 2, 5

51 Which of the following correctly define single parent families?

1. The family is in transitional phase
2. Occurrence of tragedy within family
3. People love single parent families
4. Divorce or abandonment by one parent
5. It depicts a picture of both parents with two child norm.

Codes

(a) 1, 2, 4 (b) 1, 2, 5
(c) 2, 3, 5 (d) 2, 3, 1

52 'Family in Crisis' involves

1. gaining suitable employment
2. harmony and progress within family
3. death of family member
4. family relocating
5. loss of job

Codes

(a) 3, 4, 5 (b) 3, 4, 1
(c) 2, 3, 4 (d) 2, 4, 5

53 Family Therapy involves

1. counselling for resolving marital conflict
2. normally carried out by a psychotherapist.
3. improves effectiveness in communication
4. unable to resolve conflicts within family
5. unable to overcome personal distress

Codes

(a) 1, 2, 3 (b) 1, 2, 5
(c) 2, 3, 4 (d) 1, 5, 3

54 What changes can a psychotherapist bring about?

1. Strengthen an individual's decision-making skills
2. Negatively relate to one's environment
3. Disrupting communication
4. Lessening emotional stress
5. Change in attitudes and habits of individual

Codes

(a) 1, 4, 5 (b) 3, 4, 5
(c) 2, 3, 4 (d) 1, 2, 3

55 Salient features of Child Development include

1. infancy to eighteen years of age
2. infancy to seventeen years of age
3. physical growth only
4. physical, cognitive and social growth
5. many schemes to benefit girl-child

Codes

(a) 2, 4, 5 (b) 1, 2, 3
(c) 2, 3, 5 (d) 1, 3, 5

56 Salient features of MRY

1. Mukhyamantri Rajshri Yojana
2. It is applicable to state of Rajasthan
3. It is for benefit of all children
4. It is for benefit of girl child only
5. Mukhyamantri Laadli Yojana

Codes

(a) 1, 2, 4 (b) 2, 3, 5
(c) 1, 2, 5 (d) 1, 2, 3

Directions (Q. Nos. 57-77) *In the questions given below, two statements are labelled as Assertion (A) and Reason (R). In the context of the two statements, which one of the following is correct.*

(a) Both A and R are true and R is the correct explanation of A.
(b) Both A and R are true, but R is not the correct explanation of A.
(c) A is true, but R is false.
(d) A is false, but R is true.

57 **Assertion** (A) Family disorganisation is more frequent these days.

Reason (R) Family disorganisation is seen more in village than town.

58 **Assertion** (A) Early 20th century saw rapid development in the field of industrialisation.

Reason (R) Disorganisation of family is due to industrialisation as well.

59 **Assertion** (A) An educated mother inspires her child to get educated.

Reason (R) Thus the child is motivated to study.

60 **Assertion** (A) Violence is broad term that included anger, harming etc.

Reason (R) Physical and psychological torture is part of domestic violence.

61 **Assertion** (A) As per Hindu Marriage Act, 1955, Marriage is a legal act.

Reason (R) Traditionally, Hindu marriage was a religious act.

62 **Assertion** (A) Fights and argument in marriage may lead to marital disharmony.

Reason (R) Marital disharmona may lead to divorce.

63 **Assertion** (A) Marital disharmony is caused due to financial problem.

Reason (R) Marital disharmony forces the husband and wife to separate.

64 **Assertion** (A) Marital disharmony can be resolved by communication.

Reason (R) Marital disharmony can not be resolved.

65 **Assertion** (A) The pace of overall development of society is determined by status of women and children.

Reason (R) Thus govt. take special effort to safeguard them.

66 **Assertion** (A) Single parents have lots of stressor.

Reason (R) Absence of spouse doesn't let the family to lead a normal life.

67 **Assertion** (A) Marriage is a socially sanctioned union between man and woman.

Reason (R) The joint family system thrived under the traditional family.

68 **Assertion** (A) Marriage is the basic building block of society.

Reason (R) The foundation of family is marriage.

69 **Assertion** (A) The modern Indian youth no longer believes in arranged marriage.

Reason (R) Globalisation has had a tremendous impact on youth making them westernised.

70 **Assertion** (A) Low self-esteem drives male partners to indulge in domestic violence.

Reason (R) Such men crave power and control over their female counterparts.

71 **Assertion** (A) Women become a viction of domestic violence perpetrated by their husbands or in-laws.

Reason (R) There is no remedy to such acts of domestic violence.

72 **Assertion** (A) Jealousy is one of the major causes of domestic violence.

Reason (R) Jealousy is an intense emotion in the youth, who are more prone to violence.

73 **Assertion** (A) Sufficient dowry results in innumerable domestic violence cases.

Reason (R) The greed for dowry is an evil social custom.

74 **Assertion** (A) It is essential for poor and low status women to observe 'purdah'.

Reason (R) 'Purdah' system restricts women in every aspect of life.

75 **Assertion** (A) A happy, successful marriage reflects absence of conflict.

Reason (R) A higher level of positive behaviour exists in happy marriages.

76 **Assertion** (A) Ego between partners is one of the major causes of marital confict.

Reason (R) Woman wants to crush ego of her husband to gain control and vice-versa.

77 **Assertion** (A) A child's mind is highly fertile can be moulded in any way.

Reason (R) Parents must ensure right development of their children.

78 Match the following.

List I	List II
A. Marriage	1. Dharma
B. Joint family	2. Patriarchal head
C. Eldest male Family member	3. Generations living together
D. Old tradition	4. Institution

Codes

	A	B	C	D		A	B	C	D
(a)	3	1	4	2	(b)	4	3	2	1
(c)	4	1	2	3	(d)	2	1	4	3

79 Match the following.

List I	List II
A. Westernisation	1. 2005
B. Domestic violence	2. Retrievable
C. Stridhan	3. Close relationships
D. Domestic violence Act	4. Globalisation

Codes

	A	B	C	D		A	B	C	D
(a)	2	1	4	3	(b)	4	3	2	1
(c)	2	4	3	1	(d)	3	4	1	2

80 Match the following.

List I	List II
A. Domestic violence	1. Veiling
B. Insufficient dowry	2. Alcoholism
C. Intoxication	3. Evil social custom
D. Purdah	4. Physical abuse

Codes

	A	B	C	D		A	B	C	D
(a)	2	4	3	1	(b)	4	3	2	1
(c)	3	4	2	1	(d)	2	1	4	3

81 Match the following.

List I	List II
A. PWDVA	1. 1999
B. Helpline	2. 1960
C. Gottman	3. 181
D. Memoria	4. 2005

Codes

	A	B	C	D		A	B	C	D
(a)	3	4	2	1	(b)	4	3	1	2
(c)	1	3	4	2	(d)	2	1	3	4

82 Match the following.

List I	List II
A. Cognitive development	1. Memoria
B. Community education	2. Divorce
C. Family disorganisation	3. A cripps
D. Single parent	4. Parental involvement

Codes

	A	B	C	D		A	B	C	D
(a)	2	3	4	1	(b)	4	3	1	2
(c)	3	4	1	2	(d)	2	1	3	4

83 Match the following.

List I	List II
A. Psychotherapist	1. Modified
B. Effective	2. One to one basis
C. Habits	3. Released
D. Emotional stress	4. Communication

Codes

	A	B	C	D		A	B	C	D
(a)	2	1	4	3	(b)	2	4	1	3
(c)	4	1	3	2	(d)	2	3	4	1

84 Match the following.

List I	List II
A. SSY	1. Mukhyamantri Kanya Suraksha Yojana
B. MRY	2. Mukhyamantri Laadli Yojana
C. MLY	3. Mukhyamantri Rajshri Yojana
D. MKS	4. Sukanya Samridhi Yojana

Codes

	A	B	C	D		A	B	C	D
(a)	1	3	4	2	(b)	4	3	2	1
(c)	2	1	4	3	(d)	3	4	2	1

85 Match the following.

List I	List II
A. National Charter for Children	1. 1988-99
B. Child Line Service	2. 2013
C. National Policy for Children	3. 2009
D. Integrated Child Protection Scheme	4. 2003

Codes

	A	B	C	D		A	B	C	D
(a)	2	4	1	3	(b)	4	1	2	3
(c)	3	4	2	1	(d)	2	3	4	1

Directions (Q. Nos. 86-90) *Read the passage and answer the question given.*

Domestic violence, social and legal concept that, in the broadest sense, refers to any abuse—including physical, emotional, sexual, or financial—between intimate partners, often living in the same household.

Males may also be victims of domestic violence, although instances are both less common and less severe. However, such occurrences are also less likely to be reported, because of the fear of ridicule and the lack of support services made available to male abuse victims. Perpetrators of domestic violence come from all socioeconomic, cultural, and educational backgrounds. The stresses of poverty and the abuse of such substances as alcohol and drugs contribute to the problem.

Frequently there is no workable solution for female victims of domestic violence. For some victims the unrelenting cycle of violence produces diminished self-esteem, helplessness, depression, and exaggerated feelings of imprisonment, even the belief that they deserve abuse. More material obstacles stand in the way of most victims.

Many are financially dependent on their abusers and since many abuse victims are mothers, they particularly fear being unable to support their children if they leave a violent partner. Many fear reporting the crime because the police can offer no reliable protection against retaliation.

One of the worst problems is that typical abusers often become most violent and vengeful precisely when women try to leave.

The 1967 training manual for the International Association of Chiefs of Police stated that arrests in instances of domestic violence were to be made only as a "last resort". The revived women's movement of the 1970s brought the issue of domestic violence into the open. Feminists encouraged battered women to speak up and to refuse to accept blame for their victimisation.

Women's organisations pressured police to treat domestic violence as they would treat any other assault. Established battered women's shelters where victims and their children could find safety, help, counselling, and legal advice. The increased visibility of these campaigns raised public awareness of the issue.

In 1994, US Congress passed the Violence Against Women Act. Bill Clinton established the Violence Against Women Office in the department of Justice; this office attempts to aid and coordinate the work of federal, state, and local agencies on issue of domestic violence.

86 The perpetrators of domestic violence come from which of the following?
(a) Socio-economic backgrounds
(b) Cultural backgrounds
(c) Educational backgrounds
(d) All of the above

87 What is the theme of passage?
(a) Single Parent (b) Domestic abuse
(c) Marital Disharmony (d) None of these

88 Domestic violence may cause
(a) low self esteem (b) helplessness
(c) depression (d) All of these

89 The ...... raised public awareness of the domestic abuse.
(a) campaigns (b) advertisement
(c) street play (d) revolt

90 Violence against Women Act was passed in
(a) 2005 (b) 1994
(c) 1985 (d) 1975

PREVIOUS YEARS' QUESTIONS

July 2018

1 **Arrange the following legislations in the chronological order of their implementation.**

1. Medical Termination of Pregnancy Act
2. Dowry Prohibition Act
3. Pre-conception and Pre-natal Diagnostics Techniques Act
4. Hindu Marriage Act
5. Protection of women from Domestic Violence Act
6. The sexual harassment of women at workplace (Prevention, Prohibition and Redressal Act)

Codes

(a) 6, 3, 4, 2, 5, 1 (b) 4, 2, 1, 3, 5, 6
(c) 4, 3, 2, 1, 5, 6 (d) 6, 5, 4, 3, 2, 1

Novemeber 2017

2 **Assertion** (A) 'Singlehood' as a trend has risen considerably in recent years.

Reason (R) Women with high status careers, later marriage and high divorce rate have contributed to remaining single.

Codes

(a) Both A and R are correct
(b) Both A and R are incorrect
(c) A is correct, but R is incorrect
(d) A is incorrect, but R in correct

January 2017

3 **Match the programmes given in List I with the year of their inception given in List II.**

List I	List II
A. ICDS	1. 2015
B. Swach Bharat Abhiyan	2. 1975
C. Sarva Shiksha Abhiyan	3. 2001
D. Beti Bachao Beti Padhao	4. 2010
	5. 2014

Codes

	A	B	C	D
(a)	2	5	3	4
(b)	2	5	3	1
(c)	2	4	3	1
(d)	2	4	5	1

June 2015

4 **Assertion** (A) A family functions as a system.

Reason (R) It is a set of parts coordinated to accomplish a set of goals.

Codes

(a) Both A and R are correct
(b) Both A and R are incorrect
(c) A is correct, but R is incorrect
(d) A is incorrect, but R is correct

ANSWERS

Exam Based Questions

1 (b)	2 (b)	3 (b)	4 (b)	5 (c)	6 (b)	7 (b)	8 (c)	9 (b)	10 (c)
11 (b)	12 (b)	13 (b)	14 (b)	15 (d)	16 (b)	17 (a)	18 (d)	19 (c)	20 (d)
21 (b)	22 (b)	23 (a)	24 (a)	25 (d)	26 (d)	27 (d)	28 (b)	29 (d)	30 (c)
31 (d)	32 (a)	33 (b)	34 (a)	35 (b)	36 (c)	37 (b)	38 (b)	39 (b)	40 (a)
41 (a)	42 (a)	43 (a)	44 (a)	45 (a)	46 (a)	47 (a)	48 (a)	49 (a)	50 (a)
51 (a)	52 (a)	53 (a)	54 (a)	55 (a)	56 (a)	57 (b)	58 (b)	59 (a)	60 (b)
61 (b)	62 (a)	63 (d)	64 (c)	65 (a)	66 (a)	67 (b)	68 (a)	69 (a)	70 (a)
71 (c)	72 (a)	73 (d)	74 (b)	75 (d)	76 (a)	77 (a)	78 (b)	79 (b)	80 (b)
81 (b)	82 (b)	83 (b)	84 (b)	85 (b)	86 (d)	87 (b)	88 (d)	89 (a)	90 (b)

Previous Years' Questions

1 (b)	2 (b)	3 (b)	4 (a)

Family Welfare, Human Rights and Guidance

Family welfare simply refers to welfare of a family. The Family Welfare Programme seeks to promote the small family norm through voluntary choice. Human rights are part of Family Welfare Programme as they help to get along with each other and live in peace. Guidance and counselling help individuals to solve their problems by finding out solutions.

Family Welfare

Among the various social institutions, family is the primary basic institution of mankind. The progress of a country can be measured by the state of families and their standard of living. Family welfare involves improve living standard of a family and quality of life of its people. For improving the quality of life of the people, it was felt necessary to adopt small family norm as a way of life. Thus, the Family Welfare Programme was implemented by the government as involuntary programme. It is an integral part of overall national policy of growth covering health, maternity and child care, family welfare, women's rights and nutrition.

Family Welfare Programme was started in the year 1951. In 1977, the Government of India redesignated the National Family Planning programme as the National Family Welfare Programme and also changed the name of the ministry of 'Health and Family Planning' to 'Ministry of Health and Family Welfare.' It is a reflection of the government's anxiety to promote Family Planning through the total welfare of the family.

The Family Welfare Programme in India is recognised as a priority area and is being implemented as a 100% centrally sponsored programme.

In this Chapter

Approaches Toward Family Welfare

Approaches toward family welfare are discussed below :

Clinical Approach

During the First and Second Five Year Plan, Clinical Approach was adopted toward family welfare and family planning programmes in India. Under this approach facilities for provision of services were created. The first five year plan emphasised field research with a view to identify values, norms, customs and beliefs concerning child bearing. As India was the first country in the world to adopt family planning as a nation wide programme there was no model that she could follow. The only model available for this purpose was the one used by Planned Parenthood organisations in the West which setup family planning clinics. The people who needed family planning were expected to take advantage of this. But, there were certain limitations to this approach as this approach was not considered suitable for a developing country like India. So, another approach 'Extension Approach' to family planning was soon realised.

Extension Approach

In 1963, Lt. Col B.L. Raina in his report of historic importance, highlighted the need to strengthen the Extension Approach. This approach involves the adoption of an Educational Approach to bring about changes in the knowledge, attitudes and behaviour of the people in regard to family planning.

This approach involves the acceptance of the principle that "The power, inherent in a group itself to bring about changes in deeply rooted practices; is greater than the influence of individual instruction by outsiders".

This approach calls for actively working with the people for whom the programme is meant. The approach envisaged expansion of services facilities along with spread of message of small family norm.

Integrated Approach

Today, this approach has assumed importance but it was adopted way back during second Five Year Plan period. The approach clarifies that the "Family Planning Service is likely to succeed if the clinics are associated with '**maternity and child health**' work or with centres which provide medical aid and welfare services."

The rationale for such integration is that when infant and child mortality rates are high, as in India, parents cannot be expected to limit the size of their families unless they have some confidence that the children they already have will survive to adulthood. Such confidence can be created only by providing preventive and curative medical services for children. At present, the special schemes under the Family Planning Programme include the following Maternal and Child Health Programmes :

- Immunisation of infants and pre-school age children against DPT.
- Immunisation of expectant mothers against tetanus.
- Prophylax is against nutritional anaemia among mothers and children.
- Prophylaxis against blindness caused in children by vitamin 'A' deficiency.

Another aspect of the Integrated Approach is the Post Partum Programme, which is restricted only to hospitals, where women are enrolled either for delivery or for abortion. An extension of the Integrated Approach was the introduction of the Child Survival and Safe Motherhood (CSSM) Programme in 1992-93.

Camp Approach

The idea of holding mass vasectomy camp was introduced in a big way in 1971-72 of the 2.19 million vasectomies in 1971-72, about 61 percent were performed in mass vasectomy camps. In 1972-73, 3.12 million vasectomies were performed in such camps.

This approach however had limitations. First, setting up of vasectomy camp involved tremendous organisation and anti-departmental co-operation and co-ordination, which was at the cost of other developmental programmes.

Reproductive Health Approach

It applies two things. The first is that people are able to have a satisfying and safe sex life and second is that they have the capacity to reproduce and the freedom to decide its frequency.

As one of the nations adopting the International Conference on Population and Development (ICPD) Programme of Action, India took steps to incorporate this Programme in the national context. The package of essential reproductive and child health services include the following :

- Services for the prevention and management of unwanted pregnancy.
- The promotion of safe motherhood and child survival.
- Nutritional services for vulnerable groups.
- Services for the prevention and management of reproductive tract infections and sexually transmitted infections.
- Reproductive health services for adolescents.

- Reproductive and Child Health (RCH) approach not only suggests a package of integrated services, but also an emphasis on individual needs rather than on demographic goals. The RCH approach also implies providing client centered quality services.
- Policy Commission was released on December 2018. In this report, direction for family welfare has been given.

Family Welfare Programme

Various schemes under Family Welfare Programme by Indian Government are :

National Family Welfare Programme India launched the National Family Welfare Programme in 1951 with the objective of reducing the birth rate to the extent necessary to stabilise the population at a level consistent with the requirement of the National Economy. The Family Welfare Programme in India is recognised as a priority area and is being implemented as a 100% centrally sponsored programme.

Sterilisation Beds Scheme A scheme for reservation of sterilisation beds in hospital run by government, local bodies and voluntary organisations was introduced as early as in the year 1964 in order to provide immediate facilities for tubectomy operations in hospitals where such cases could not be admitted due to lack of beds, etc. But later with the introduction of the **postpartum** programme, some of the beds were transferred for this programme and thereafter, the beds were only sanctioned to hospitals run by local bodies and voluntary organisations. Post Partum Programme has been initiated to help women to stop closely spaced pregnancies or unwanted pregnancies.

Urban Family Welfare Schemes This scheme was introduced following the recommendation of the Krishnan Committee in 1983. The main focus was to provide services through setting up of health posts mainly in slum areas. The services provided are mainly outreach of RCH services, preventive services. First Aid and referral services including distribution of contraceptives.

Reproductive and Child Health Programme The Reproductive and Child Health Programme was launched in October 1997 incorporating new approach to population and development issues, as exposed in the International Conference in Population and Development held at Cairo in 1994.

The programme integrated and strengthened in services/interventions under the Child Survival and Safe Motherhood Programme and Family Planning Services and added to the basket of services, new areas on Reproductive Tract/Sexually Transmitted Infections (RTI/STI) etc.

National Population Policy The National Population Policy, 2000 affirms the commitment of government towards voluntary and informed choice and consent of citizens while availing of reproductive healthcare services and continuation of the target free approach in administering family planning services.

National Rural Health Mission The National Rural Health Mission (2005-12) seeks to provide effective healthcare to rural population throughout the country with special focus on 18 states, which have weak public health indicators and/or weak infrastructure. The mission aims at effective integration of health concerns with determinants of health like sanitation and hygiene, nutrition and safe drinking water through a district plan for health.

Challenges of Family Welfare Programme

The family welfare programme in India has been recognised as a priority area. The family welfare programmes are successful to a great extent, but it has still a long way to go because of varied challenges. Some of the challenges are discussed as :

- The widespread illiteracy particularly in the rural areas creates hurdles in the path of implementation of family welfare programmes. Due to widespread illiteracy and lack of consciousness a good number of population does not realise the importance of family planning measures and also of small family norms.
- The poverty in India is also a serious hurdle in the ways of implementing family welfare measures. Poor people prefer more children in the family. They have misconceptions that greater number of children would become an asset in their old age. They also think that increasing number of children are expected to support the increasing income for the family.
- Fatalism prevails upon the sizeable section of people of India. They consider the birth of the child as a gift of god and accept the birth as a chance and not by choice. They do not accept the importance of family welfare programme.
- The country is facing the problem of shortage of trained staff for the implementation of family welfare programmes.
- The family welfare programme and the movement of population control has failed to cover the entire areas of the country due to lack of finance. In order to spread the message of family welfare programme and also to implement the programme sufficient fund is required. But the required amount of fund is not available for the implementation of the programme.

- There is also a lack of motivation on the part of family welfare programme staff to motivate the people for adopting family planning or birth control devices so as to accept the small family norms.
- The family welfare programme is suffering from lack of publicity. Although 70% of the total population of the country are living in the rural areas. But there are gaps in imparting knowledge and information related to family welfare programmes mainly in rural areas.
- There has been 17.7% increase in population in the decade (2001-11). Increase in population leads to poverty, unemployment, discrimination, health problem etc.
- The birth rate by 2017 is 19 and death rate is 7.3 This needs to be improved.

Role in National Development

Family welfare plays a significant role in national development in the following ways :

- Family welfare programme is not only about family planning. It also works towards financially uplifting the family. This creates financial security in the nation.
- Family welfare programme works towards providing better health care to the mother and the child. This leads to a healthier family and developed nation.
- Family welfare programme controls birth rate, mortality rate, morbidity rate and etc. Thus, controlling the population rate.
- Family welfare programme fights against the gender inequality. This leads to an aware nation.
- Family welfare programme leads to an educated India.

Human Rights

Every person is entitled to certain fundamental rights, simply by the fact of being human. These are called 'human rights'. They are 'rights' because they are things you are allowed to be, to do or to have.

According to **United Nations** "Human rights are rights inherent to all human beings, regardless of reace, sex, nationality, ethnicity, language, religion or any other status."

These rights are there for our protection against people who might want to harm or hurt us. They are also there to help us to get along with each other and live in peace.

Many people know something about their rights. Generally they know they have the right to food and a safe place to stay. They know they have a right to be paid for the work they do. But there are many other rights. When human rights are not well known by people, abuses such as discrimination, intolerance, injustice, oppression and slavery can arise.

Types of Human Rights

The Universal Declaration of Human Rights has guaranteed a number of rights which can be classified as follows :

Social or Civil Human Rights All human beings are entitled to :

- The right to life, liberty and security of persons
- Right to freedom from slavery and servitude
- Right to freedom from torture or cruel, inhuman or degrading treatment or punishment
- Right to freedom from arbitrary interference with privacy, family, home or correspondence
- Right to marry and have family and right to property.

Political Human Rights To take part in the political process, all human beings are provided with some rights such as :

- Right to nationality
- Right to equality before law and equal protection by law
- Right to judicial remedies, fair trial and freedom from arbitrary arrest, detention or exile
- Right to freedom of thought, expression, belief, faith, conscience and religion
- Right to freedom of peaceful assembly and association
- Right to take part in government affairs and equal access to public service
- Right to equal suffrage
- Right to freedom of movement and right of asylum etc.

Economic Human Rights To ensure the economic interest of the human being,United Nations Organisation (UNO) also provides certain economic rights, such as :

- Right to social security
- Right to work and the right to equal pay for equal work
- Right to form trade unions
- Right to rest and leisure
- Right to food, health and adequate standard of living.

Cultural Human Rights For the protection of the various types of cultures, traditions and customs of the human being, the declaration of human rights also provides certain rights, such as:

- Right to participate in the cultural life of the community,
- Right to enjoy the art and to share in the scientific advancement and its benefits

- Right to the protection of the moral and material interests resulting from any scientific, literary and artistic production of which the individual is the author
- Right to a social and international order in which the human rights as provided in the universal declaration can be fully realised.

Rights of Children

In the history of human rights, the rights of children are the most certified. The United Nations Convention on the Rights of the Child (UNCRC) defines "child rights as the minimum entitlements and freedoms that should be afforded to every citizen below the age of 18 regardless of race, national origin, colour, gender, language, religion, opinions, origin, wealth, birth status, disability, or other characteristics".

These rights encompass freedom of children and their civil rights, family environment, necessary healthcare and welfare, education, leisure and cultural activities and special protection measures. The UNCRC outlines the fundamental human rights that should be provided to children in four broad categories that suitably cover all civil, political, social, economic and cultural rights of every child.

These categories are given below :

Right to Survival

- Right to be born
- Right to minimum standards of food, shelter and clothing
- Right to live with dignity
- Right to health care, to safe drinking water, nutritious food, a clean and safe environment, and information to help them stay healthy.

Right to Protection

- Right to be protected from all sorts of violence
- Right to be protected from neglect
- Right to be protected from physical and sexual abuse
- Right to be protected from dangerous drugs

Right to Participation

- Right to freedom of opinion
- Right to freedom of expression
- Right to freedom of association
- Right to information
- Right to participate in any decision making that involves him/her directly or indirectly

Right to Development

- Right to education
- Right to learn
- Right to relax and play
- Right to all forms of development-emotional, mental and physical

Rights of Women

The rights available to women (ladies) in India can be classified into two categories, namely as constitutional rights and legal rights. The constitutional rights are those which are provided in the various provisions of the Constitution.

The legal rights, on the other hand, are those which are provided in the various laws (acts) of the Parliament and the State Legislatures.

Constitutional Rights to Women in India

The rights and safeguards enshrined in the Constitution for women in India are listed below :

- The state shall not discriminate against any citizen of India on the ground of sex.
- The state is empowered to make any special provision for women. In other words, this provision enables the state to make affirmative discrimination in favour of women.
- No citizen shall be discriminated against or be ineligible for any employment or office under the state on the ground of sex.
- Traffic in human beings and forced labour is prohibited.
- The state to secure for men and women equally the right to an adequate means of livelihood.
- The state to secure equal pay for equal work for both Indian men and women.
- The state is required to ensure that the health and strength of women workers are not abused and that they are not forced by economic necessity to enter avocations unsuitable for their strength.
- The state shall make provisions for securing just and humane conditions of work and maternity relief.
- It shall be the duty of every citizen of India to renounce practices derogatory to the dignity of women.
- One-third of the total number of seats to be filled by direct election in every Panchayat shall be reserved for women.
- One-third of the total number of offices of Chairpersons in the Panchayats at each level shall be reserved for women.
- One-third of the total number of seats to be filled by direct election in every Municipality shall be reserved for women.
- The offices of Chairpersons in the Municipalities shall be reserved for women in such manner as the State Legislature may provide.

Legal Rights to Women

The following legislations contain several rights and safeguards for women :

- Indian Penal Code(1860) contains provisions to protect Indian women from dowry death, rape, kidnapping, cruelty and other offences.
- Immoral Traffic (Prevention) Act (1956) is the first legislation for prevention of trafficking for commercial sexual exploitation. In other words, it prevents trafficking of women and girls for the purpose of prostitution as a means of living.
- Dowry Prohibition Act (1961) prohibits the giving or taking of dowry at or before or any time after the marriage from women.
- Maternity Benefit Act (1961) regulates the employment of women at workplace for the period before and after child-birth. It also provides for maternity benefit and certain other benefits.
- Medical Termination of Pregnancy Act (1971) provides for the termination of certain pregnancies by registered medical practitioners on humanitarian and medical grounds.
- Code of Criminal Procedure (1973) has certain safeguards for women like arrest of woman by female police and so on. A woman cannot be arrested after sunset and before sumrise with few exceptions.
- Equal Remuneration Act (1976) provides for payment of equal salary to both men and women workers for same work or work of a similar nature. It also prevents discrimination on the ground of sex, against women in recruitment and service conditions.
- Family Courts Act (1984) provides for the establishment of Family Courts for speedy settlement of family disputes.
- Indecent Representation of Women (Prohibition) Act (1986) prohibits indecent representation of women through advertisements or in publications, writings, paintings, figures or in any other manner.
- Commission of Sati (Prevention) Act (1987) provides for the more effective prevention of the sati and its glorification on women.
- National Commission for Women Act (1990) provided for the establishment of a National Commission for Women to study and monitor all matters relating to the Constitutional and legal rights and safeguards of women.
- Pre-Conception and Pre-Natal Diagnostic Techniques (Prohibition of Sex Selection) Act (1994) prohibits sex selection before or after conception and prevents the misuse of pre-natal diagnostic techniques for sex determination leading to female foeticide.
- Protection of Women from Domestic Violence Act (2005) is a legislative measure to protect women in India from all forms of domestic violence. It also covers women who have been/are in a relationship with the abuser and are subjected to violence of any kind–physical, sexual, mental, verbal or emotional.
- Sexual Harassment of Women at workplace (Prevention, Prohibition and Redressal) Act (2013) provides protection to women from sexual harassment at all workplaces both in public and private sector, whether organised or unorganised.

Status of Women

Women have completely transformed in the modern day, the urban woman especially has changed from being a mere homemaker to the modern day multitasking woman, handling responsibilities without fear. She has taken on the world with confidence. Women of today handle their duties and chores at home, manage a career outside their homes, nurture their children and balance their family lives with their professions. This is the scene in most of the urban households today.

The modern day woman is independent, takes right decisions boldly, stands up for her rights and walks a path of success. This is the scene in the developing economy of today. Women are well educated, they have crossed horizons, and their presence can be felt in many male dominated areas.

Women have been sent on many space missions. Women have risen as journalists, politicians, doctors, engineers, lawyers, actors and in many other professional spheres. Women of today choose the right career paths that determine their future and thus we see them excelling in every walk of life.

But this is just one side of the story. Women in downtrodden regions and rural backgrounds still have to compete a lot in terms of their urban counterparts. Not that the rural women are backward in any aspect, but the change and transformation that the urban woman sees, is definitely a little slower to the rural women. Women, be it from urban or rural backgrounds, still face harassment and humiliation in domestic as well as professional circles. However high they reach in their lives, women are still made to feel helpless when men put out unhealthy treatments and behave badly in front of them.

Women can be seen in rackets of prostitution, as call girls, as dance bar girls etc., that focuses on the other side of society. Women may come from socially challenging situations, they may be part of difficult situations and they may cease to have any kind of support from their families.

Reasons unknown, they may be provoked to earn a livelihood out of immoral practices which makes women vulnerable and want to join easy, but wrong routes of earning money. This is another side of the story. As such women have achieved great feats and laurels, but there always exists a sad part of the story which we cannot move away from.

The necessity of the day is a strong legislation and most importantly, education and empowerment of women that will take them away from being part of these dark areas of the country.

Gender Roles

Gender roles in society means how we're expected to act, speak, dress, groom, and conduct ourselves based upon our assigned sex. For example, girls and women are generally expected to dress in typically feminine ways and be polite, accommodating, and nurturing. Men are generally expected to be strong, aggressive, and bold. Every society, ethnic group, and culture has gender role expectations, but they can be very different from group to group. They can also change in the same society over time. A stereotype is a widely accepted judgement or bias about a person or group–even though it's overly simplified and not always accurate. Stereotypes about gender can cause unequal and unfair treatment because of a person's gender. This is called sexism.

Example of gender stereotyping are the failure to criminalise marital rape based on societal perception of women as the sexual property of men, and the failure to effectively investigate, prosecute and sentence sexual violence against women based on, e.g., the stereotype that women should protect themselves from sexual violence by dressing and behaving modestly.

Gender stereotypes compounded and intersecting with other stereotypes have a disproportionate negative impact on certain groups of women, such as women from minority or indigenous groups, women with disabilities, women from lower caste groups or with lower economic status, migrant women, etc. Wrongful gender stereotyping is a frequent cause of discrimination against women and a contributing factor in violations of a vast array of rights such as the right to health, adequate standard of living, education, marriage and family relations, work, freedom of expression, freedom of movement, political participation and representation, effective remedy, and freedom from gender-based violence.

There are four basic kinds of gender stereotypes :

Personality traits For example, women are often expected to be accommodating and emotional, while men are usually expected to be self-confident and aggressive.

Domestic behaviours For example, some people expect that women will take care of the children, cook, and clean the home, while men will take care of finances, work on the car, and do the home repairs.

Occupations Some people are quick to assume that teachers and nurses are women, and that pilots, doctors, and engineers are men.

Physical appearance For example, women are expected to be thin and graceful, while men are expected to be tall and muscular. Men and women are also expected to dress and groom in ways that are stereotypical to their gender (men wearing pants and short hairstyles, women wearing dresses and make-up.

Guidance and Counselling

Guidance and counselling are two interrelated concepts. Their description is given below :

Guidance

According to **Brewer** "Guidance is a process through which individuals are able to solve their problems and pursue a path suited to their abilities and aspirations."

According to **McBaniel** "Guidance is a facilitative service, which provides aids to pupils and staff :

- To help pupils determine the courses most appropriate to their needs and abilities
- To find instructors who will be more sympathetic to their individual requirements and seek out activities which will help them to realise their presentation".

According to **Hamrin** and **Erikson** "Guidance is an aspect of educational programme which is concerned especially with helping the pupil to become adjusted to his present situation and to plan his future in line with his interests, abilities and social needs." So, we can say that guidance is a process which helps every individual to help himself, to recognise and use his own inner potentials, to set goals, to work out his own problems of development. It is a continuous process needed at every stage of life.

Principles of Guidance

There are 14 significant principles of guidance. They are :

- Every aspect of person's complex personality pattern constitutes a significant factor of his total displayed attitudes and form of behaviour. Guidance service which is aimed at bringing about desirable adjustments in any particular area of experience must take into account, the all round development of the individual.

- Although all human beings are similar in many respect, individual difference must be recognised and considered in any effort aimed at providing help or guidance to a particular child.
  - The functions of the guidance is to help a person
  - Formulate and accept stimulating, worthwhile and attainable goals of behaviour
- Apply the goals to conduct his behaviour.
- Existing social, economic and politic unrest is giving rise to many maladaptive factors that require the cooperation of experienced and thoroughly trained guidance workers and the individuals with the problem.
- Guidance should be regarded as a continuing process of service to an individual from young childhood through adulthood.
- Guidance service should not be limited to the few who give observable evidence of its need, but should be extended to the person of all ages who can benefit there from either directly or indirectly.
- Curriculum materials and teaching procedure should evidence a guidance point of view.
- Parents and teachers have guidance appointed responsibilities.
- To administer guidance intelligently and with as thorough knowledge of the individual as is possible , programs of individual evaluation should be conducted and accurate consultative records of progress should made accessible to guidance workers.
- An organised guidance programme should be flexible according to the individual and social needs.
- The responsibilities for administration of guidance programme should be centered in a personally qualified and adequately trained person, working cooperatively with his assistance and other community welfare and guidance agencies.
- Periodical appraisal should be made for existing guidance programmes.
- Guidance touches every phase of an individual's life pattern.
- Specific guidance problems on any age level should be referred to persons who are trained to deal with particular areas of adjustment.

Counselling

According to **Krumbotz**, "Counselling is an effort to help client engage in those types of behaviour which will lead to a resolution of the client's problems."

According to **Burks** and **Steffire**, "Counselling denotes a professional relationship between a trained counselor and a Client."

Thus, counselling is an interactive learning process in which the counsellor helps the individuals or families or group to understand the causs of difficulties faced by them and guides them to sort out issues and reach at decisions. The approach in counselling is holistic addressing social, cultural, economic and emotional issues.

Difference between Guidance and Counselling

The differences between guidance and counselling are :

- Guidance is mainly preventive and developmental whereas counselling is remedial as well as preventive and developmental.
- Intellectual attitudes are the raw material of guidance but emotional rather than pure intellectual attitude are the raw materials of counselling process.
- In guidance decision-making is operable at intellectual level, whereas in counselling it operates at emotional level.
- In educational context, counselling service is one among various services offered by guidance programme.

Guidance and Counselling Across Life Span

Guidance and counselling is an evolving process. To achieve high records, students need to be guided at various stages. This include:

Guidance at Primary Stage

- Guiding children to have a good start at school.
- Assisting in judicial planning.
- Increase the interest of child in study via games.
- Help the child to prepare for senior classes.
- Controlling the child's anger. Instilling moral values in child.

Guidance at Secondary Stage

- Help in solving social pressure on adolescent.
- Instill leadership qualities
- Direct the adolescent toward studies
- Develop a feeling of belonging in adolescent.

Guidance in Higher Secondary Level

- Help choosing the career option according to their interest.
- Solve queries regarding sexuality.
- Assisting in choosing to pursue higher studies.

Guidance and Counselling For Caregiver

Caregiving is a very challenging responsibility that requires a significant investment of time, energy and emotion. Caregivers may often underestimate the challenges involved in the same and may be left with no time for self-care. This in turn may have an adverse impact on their health and well-being. In order to care effectively, caregivers must prioritise their own health and well-being. A first step in doing so can be the acknowledgement of their own physical and psychological needs.

A few simple things that can be helpful in ensuring the well-being of caregivers are as follows :

Psychoeducate themselves Read up about patient's diagnosis which will help develop a more empathetic understanding of their experience.

Don't Judge Yourself when faced with frustration, remember that it is alright to feel so and do not blame yourself.

Seek Assistance from Others When the caregivers feel that they can't handle a particular issue or situation, they should feel free to ask for assistance from others in the extended social network. Identify people who are supportive and talk to them during times of distress. Support system can be your family members, loved ones, relatives, friends or even a colleague, who seem helpful and reliable.

Delegate responsibility Don't force yourself to do things that you are not able to do just because you are supposed to dedicate yourself to it.

Engage in Enjoyable Activities No matter how busy the caregiver is, they should take time out to eat, relax and rest even if for short periods. They should understand their own emotional and psychological needs. They can de-stress by engaging in enjoyable activities, hobbies, meditation etc.

Health and Well-Being Across Life Span Development

Health for all people, all over the world, is an important part of sustainable development. Over the years, significant efforts have been made in increasing life expectancy and reducing some of the common elements responsible for child and maternal mortality. Still much is to be done in order to counteract occurrences of HIV/AIDS, Malaria and T.B. We have made immense progress globally in finding new vaccines, treatments and technologies for healthcare, but universal affordable access to healthcare remains a challenge.

Importance of Health and Well-Being

Feeling of well-being is fundamental to the overall health of individuals enabling them to successfully overcome difficulties and achieve what they want out of life. Wellness or well-being is an overall balance of several factors; physical, social, spiritual, emotional and intellectual.

Good health and wellness of people is important as disease and burdens family, their resources and public resources as well. Protection from disease, therefore is not only fundamental to survival but it also provides opportunities for everyone and strengthens economic growth and prosperity.

Addressing the Issue of Health and Well-Being

The community all over the globe has committed itself to eradicate disease, strengthen treatment and healthcare and address emerging health issues. Everybody has realised that poor health constitutes suffering and deprivation of the most fundamental kind. Over the years, significant strides have been made in increasing life expectancy and reducing some of the common killers associated with child and maternal mortality.

A Holistic Approach to better health will require ensuring universal access to healthcare and making medicines and vaccines affordable. It also calls for a renewed focus on mental health issues. Suicide is the second leading cause of death globally between the age 19 to 25 and finally health and well-being are closely linked with the quality of our environment.

Health and Well-being in Sustainable Development

Health and well-being is discussed in the Goal 3 of the 17 Sustainable Development Goals. Goal 3 of sustainable development aims to substantially reduce the numbers of death and illnesses caused by air, water, soil pollution and contamination.

Targets for Goals 3 are :

- By 2030, reduce the global maternal mortality ratio to less than 70 per 1,00,000 live births.
- By 2030, bring to an end preventable death of new borns and children under 5 years of age, with all countries aiming to reduce neonatal mortality to atleast as low as 12 per 1,000 live births and under 5 mortality to at least as low as 25 per 1,000 live births.
- By 2030, end the epidemics of AIDS, T.B., Malaria and neglected tropical diseases and Combat Hepatitis, water-borne diseases and other communicable diseases.
- Strengthen the prevention and treatment of substance abuse, including narcotic drug abuse and harmful use of alcohol.
- By 2030, ensure universal access to sexual and reproductive healthcare services, including family planning, information and education and integration of reproductive health into national strategies and programmes.

Status of India in Health and Well-being

The following points state the status of India in health and well-being are :

- India has made some progress in reducing its Under-Five Mortality Rate which declined 125 per 1000 live births in 1990-91 to 39 per 1000 live births in 2018-19.
- India has also made significant strides in reducing the prevalence of HIV and AIDS across different types of high-risk categories, with adult prevalence reducing from 0.45% in 2002 to 0.27% in 2011. However, a quarter of global tuberculosis cases occur in India where nearly 2.1 million people live with disease and an estimated 423000 die annually as a result.
- According to press release by National Health Mission, India has made progress in many areas of health which earlier used to be a menace.
- India achieved biggest success in bringing down Malaria cases and deaths by 49.09%. It is now leading with its initiatives against Malaria among the other Malaria endemic countries.

EXAM BASED QUESTIONS

1 Progress of a country can be measured by the state of the ..... .
(a) women (b) children
(c) families (d) men

2 What does family welfare programme includes?
(a) Family planning (b) Maternity and child care
(c) Women's right (d) All of the above

3 When was family planning association of India established?
(a) 1939 (b) 1949 (c) 1959 (d) 1948

4 India was the .... country to adopt family planning programme.
(a) first (b) second
(c) third (d) fourth

5 Which one of the following is the main target of Family Welfare Programmes?
(a) Couples in the fertile age
(b) Children below 12 years
(c) Women after fertile age
(d) Male after fertile age

6 Which organisation works as an administrative unit for implementation of Family Welfare Programme in all districts of the state and functioning at State Head Quarter?
(a) The District Family Welfare Bureau
(b) The National Family Welfare Bureau
(c) The State Family Welfare Bureau
(d) The International Family Welfare Bureau

7 The Clinical Approach of family welfare included
(a) clinics were setup at different places
(b) facilities for provision of services were created
(c) planned parenthood organisations were followed
(d) All of the above

8 The Extension Approach of family welfare involves
(a) involvement of group and individuals
(b) adoption of an Educational Approach to bring about the changes
(c) spread of message of small family norm
(d) All of the above

9 Providing preventive and curative medical services for children comes under which approach?
(a) Clinical Approach (b) Integrated Approach
(c) Camp Approach (d) None of these

10 In which year, idea of holding mass vasectomy camps was introduced?
(a) 1960 (b) 1972
(c) 1980 (d) 1967

11 The Reproductive Health Approach focusses on
(a) services to prevent and manage unwanted pregnancy
(b) promotion of safe motherhood and child survival
(c) emphasis on individual needs rather than on demographic goals
(d) All of the above

12 What did government enacted in 1977?
(a) Pollution Scheme
(b) Population Scheme
(c) Family Planning Act
(d) Upliftment of Women Scheme

13 How much did Indian government aims to spend under 9th Five Year Plan?
(a) 1 lakh (b) 2 lakh
(c) 2 Arab (d) 1 Arab

14 10th, 11th and 12th Five Year Plans consist of
(a) population control
(b) care of mother and child
(c) Both (a) and (b)
(d) None of the above

15 When was National Family Welfare Programme launched?
(a) 1941 (b) 1951 (c) 1931 (d) 1961

16 Which scheme was introduced following the recommendation of Krishnan Committee?
(a) Urban Family Welfare Scheme
(b) National Rural Health Mission
(c) National Population Policy
(d) All of the above

17 Reason for failure of Family Planning programme includes
(a) male child preference (b) religious fundamentalist
(c) political apathy (d) All of these

18 Condom is made up of
(a) rubber (b) plastic (c) latex (d) urea

19 Birth control pills contains
(a) estrogen (b) progestin
(c) Both (a)and (b) (d) None of these

20 Ortho Evra is a type of
(a) progestin injection (b) skin patch
(c) diaphragm (d) vaginal ring

21 IUD can be kept for how long?
(a) 5 to 10 years (b) 1 to 5 years
(c) 3 to 9 years (d) 5 to 10 months

22 Increase in population leads to
(a) poverty (b) unemployment
(c) discrimination (d) All of these

23 What was the birth rate in 2013?
(a) 22.4 (b) 21.4
(c) 20.4 (d) 23.4

24 Family Welfare Programme controls
(a) population rate (b) pollution rate
(c) GDP (d) None of these

25 According to Civil Human right, all human beings are entitled to
(a) right to life (b) right to liberty
(c) right to security (d) All of these

26 United Nations Convention on the Right of Child is also known as
(a) UNCRC (b) UNRC
(c) UNCORC (d) UNCR

27 Child Rights are for the citizen below the age of
(a) 20 years (b) 19 years
(c) 18 years (d) 16 years

28 Which are the basic rights of a child?
(a) Right to Survival (b) Right to Protection
(c) Right to Development (d) All of these

29 Rights of women in India can be divided in which categories?
(a) Constitutional (b) Legal
(c) Both (a)and(b) (d) None of these

30 When was protection of women from Domestic Violence Act launched?
(a) 2005 (b) 2003
(c) 2006 (d) 2004

31 Which act aims to prevent prostitution?
(a) Indecent Representation of Women act
(b) Immoral Traffic Act
(c) Commission of Sati Act
(d) Anti prostitution Act

32 The Urban women is now a .... women.
(a) multitasking (b) fearful
(c) aggressive (d) docile

33 Women can still be seen in the
(a) prostitution (b) dance bar
(c) Both (a) and (b) (d) None of these

34 According to gender roles, girls are supposed to be
(a) aggressive (b) polite
(c) strong (d) bold

35 Which are the basic kind of gender stereotypes?
(a) Personality Traits (b) Domestic behaviour
(c) Occupation (d) All of these

36 Wrongful gender stereotypes have lead to failure to criminalise...... .
(a) prostitution (b) marital rape
(c) dowry (d) trafficking

37 Who gave the definition, "Guidance is a process through which an individual is able to solve their problems and pursue a path suited to their abilities and aspiration?"
(a) Brewer (b) Mc Baniel
(c) Hamrin (d) Erikson

38 Guidance is mainly .... and developmental.
(a) remedial (b) preventive
(c) raw (d) boosting up

39 The function of ..... is to help a person.
(a) parent (b) coworker
(c) guidance (d) scientist

40 Guidance and Counselling is a ...... process.
(a) evolving (b) deteriorating
(c) slow (d) growing

41 What is the function of guidance at secondary step?
(a) Solving social pressure
(b) Instill leadership qualities
(c) Directing toward studies
(d) All of the above

42 Caregiving requires investment of
(a) time (b) energy
(c) Both(a) and (b) (d) None of these

43 Life expectancy of people has increased due to
(a) efforts made by governments at different levels
(b) efforts of doctors
(c) advancement in medical technology
(d) Only (a) and (c)

44 Well-being is an .... of several factors.
(a) over all balance
(b) result
(c) quality
(d) achievement

45 A Holistic Approach to better health will comprise of
(a) ensuring universal access to healthcare
(b) affordable vaccines and medicines
(c) talented doctors
(d) Only (a) and (b)

46 In India, malaria cases and deaths have been brought down by
(a) 70% (b) 49.09%
(c) 51.04% (d) 60%

47 Well-being according to WHO is a state of complete physical .... and social well-being and not merely the absence of .... or infirmity.
(a) intellectual, emotions
(b) mental, disease
(c) emotional, energy
(d) spiritual, stamina

48 Choose the correct statement

1. Family is the primary basic institution of mankind.
2. Joint family is encouraged by Family Welfare Programme.
3. Progress of a country can be measured by state of family and their state of living.
4. Government has taken no step for family welfare.

Codes

(a) 1 and 2 (b) 1 and 3
(c) 2 and 4 (d) 4 and 1

49 Choose the correct statement

1. Family Welfare Programme is run under Ministry of Health and Family Welfare.
2. Both mother and child are taken care of under Family Welfare Programme.
3. Family planning was introduced in first Five Year Plan.
4. First Population Scheme was announced in 1975.

Codes

(a) 1 and 2 (b) 2 and 4
(c) 2, 3 and 4 (d) 1, 2, 3 and 4

50 Choose the correct statement

1. Contraceptives are both natural and artificial.
2. Contraceptive pills contain estrogen.
3. Contraceptive help in getting pregnant.
4. IUD is a kind of contraceptive.

Codes

(a) 1 and 2 (b) 1, 2 and 4
(c) 2 and 3 (d) 2, 3 and 4

51 Guidance at secondary stage includes

1. Instill leadership qualities
2. Direct the adolescent toward studies
3. Help the student in choosing curriculum
4. Develop a feeling of belonging.

Codes

(a) 1, 3 and 4 (b) 2, 3 and 4
(c) 1, 2 and 4 (d) 1, 2, 3 and 4

52 Choose the correct statement

1. Hormonal contraceptive include pills and injection.
2. Women need to have hormonal pills regularly to prevent pregnancy.
3. Permanent contraceptive include vasectomy and tubectomy
4. Vasectomy is easier than tubectomy.

Codes

(a) Only 2 (b) 1 and 3
(c) 1, 2 and 4 (d) 1, 2, 3 and 4

53 Challenges of Family Welfare Programme include

1. Increase in population
2. Decrease in GDP
3. Barrier of religion
4. Less awareness of programme

Codes

(a) 1 and 4 (b) 2 and 3
(c) Only 1 (d) Only 3

54 Arrange in the sequence of enactment

1. Department of Family Planning
2. Policy Commission
3. Family Planning Association of India
4. Population Scheme

Codes

(a) 1, 3, 4 and 2 (b) 3, 1, 4 and 2
(c) 2, 3, 4 and 1 (d) 1, 2, 4 and 3

Directions (Q. Nos. 55-65) *Given below are two statements, one labelled as Assertion (A) and other labelled as Reason (R). Following are the codes given below. Choose the correct option.*

Codes

(a) Both A and R are true and R is correct reason for A
(b) Both A and R are true, but R is not the correct reason for A
(c) A is true, but R is false
(d) A is false, but R is true

55 **Assertion** (A) Family Planning Association of India was established in 1952.

Reason (R) Good health is a way to long life.

56 **Assertion** (A) Guidance includes multiple service programmes.

Reason (R) Guidance is not a result, it is a process

57 **Assertion** (A) Guidance is a continuous process which doesn't end on specific stage of life.

Reason (R) Every person may requires guidance at some point of life.

58 **Assertion** (A) Human rights are important for mental peace of an human.

Reason (R) Human right and mental peace are closely related.

59 **Assertion** (A) Family Welfare Programme is about family planning only

Reason (R) Contraceptives are used to prevent unwanted pregnancies.

60 **Assertion** (A) Counselling is the advice given to help out an individual.

Reason (R) Counselling comes under guidance.

61 **Assertion** (A) Rights of women include prohibition of trafficking.

Reason (R) Rights of women include equality among the citizen of India on the ground of sex.

62 **Assertion** (A) Women has taken over the world with confidence.

Reason (R) Urban women are well educated which have caused liberation.

63 **Assertion** (A) Health all over the world is an important part of sustainable development.

Reason (R) Child and maternal mortality need to be improved.

64 **Assertion** (A) Any disease burdens family and their resources and public resources as well.
Reason (R) Medication for treatment of any disease is quite expensive.

65 **Assertion** (A) Goal 3 calls for reducing behavioural and environmental health risk factors.
Reason (R) EU has made significant progress in almost all health related spheres.

66 Match the following.

List I (Approaches)	List II (Year)
A. Family Planning Association of India.	1. 2018
B. Department of Family Planning.	2. 1977
C. Population Scheme	3. 1949
D. Policy Commission	4. 1966

Codes

	A	B	C	D		A	B	C	D
(a)	1	3	2	4	(b)	3	4	2	1
(c)	2	3	1	4	(d)	1	4	3	2

67 Match the following.

List I	List II
A. Right of Life	1. Article 19
B. Right to Education	2. Article 28
C. Right to Growth	3. Article 14
D. Right to Participate	4. Article 21
	5. Article 6
	6. Article 12

Codes

	A	B	C	D		A	B	C	D
(a)	1	2	6	4	(b)	5	1	6	3
(c)	5	1	2	6	(d)	3	2	1	5

68 Match the following.

List I (Legal Rights)	List II (Year)
A. Immoral Traffic Act	1. 1961
B. Commission of Sati	2. 1956
C. Dowry Probition	3. 1984
D. Family Courts Act	4. 1987

Codes

	A	B	C	D		A	B	C	D
(a)	2	4	1	3	(b)	3	1	2	4
(c)	1	4	3	2	(d)	2	1	3	4

69 Match the following.

List I (Category of Rights)	List II (Rights)
A. Right to Survival	1. Right to freedom of opinion
B. Right to Protection	2. Right to education
C. Right to Participation	3. Right to be protected from all sort of violence
D. Right to Development	4. Right to be born

Codes

	A	B	C	D
(a)	1	3	4	2
(b)	3	4	2	1
(c)	4	1	2	3
(d)	4	3	1	2

70 Match the following.

List I	List II
A. Diaphragm	1. Ortho Eura
B. Progestin injection	2. Rubber Cup
C. Skin patch	3. Nuva Ring
D. Vaginal Ring	4. Depo Provera

Codes

	A	B	C	D
(a)	2	4	1	3
(b)	1	3	2	4
(c)	3	1	2	4
(d)	4	2	1	3

Directions (Q. Nos. 71-75) *Read the passage and answer the following questions.*

Tamil Nadu is the first Indian State to recognise the basic relevance of family planning to national planning. It was given national awards for outstanding work in family planning for every year except 1964 from 1961 to 1967, and from 1973 to 1976.

Family planning activity was initiated in large maternity hospitals as a postpartum programme. The Medical Termination of Pregnancy Act was first implemented in Tamil Nadu. 141 institutions have been certified for the operation.

An oral pill Programme is being implemented in all the rural and Urban Family Welfare Centres including the hospitals. The Family Welfare Programme has been fully integrated with the Maternal and Child Health (MCH) programme which has created confidence among people that their children will be protected from health hazards. The MCH Schemes are conducted through Primary Health Care (PHC) centres, Urban Family Welfare centres, MCH centres, hospitals, and dispensaries.

Dais are trained to improve the techniques of midwifery and aid delivery in a hygienic manner. Dais can also use 'their influence in the local community to further family planning. It is proposed to establish additional subcentres in selected districts to average 1/centre/5000 population. The government continues to sponsor and fund equipment, facilities, and infrastructure to facilitate sterilisation operations in Primary Health Centers.

71 What is the basic theme of the passage?
(a) Family Planning in Tamil Nadu
(b) Family Planning in Maharashtra
(c) Child Care in Tamil Nadu
(d) Child Care in Maharashtra

72 Which act was first implemented in Tamil Nadu?
(a) Dowry Act
(b) Medical Termination of Pregnancy Act
(c) Commission of Sati Act
(d) All of the above

73 How many institutes have been employed for Medical Termination of Pregnancy?
(a) 131 (b) 121 (c) 141 (d) 151

74 ...... Programme is being implemented in all the rural and Urban Family Welfare Centres.
(a) Oral Pill (b) Contraceptive
(c) Health (d) Tobacco free

75 ...... are trained to provide services of midwife.
(a) Angangwadi workers (b) Dais
(c) Nurses (d) None of these

PREVIOUS YEARS' QUESTIONS

June 2018

1 Arrange the following legislations in the chronological order of their implementation.
1. Medical Termination of Pregnancy Act.
2. Dowry Prohibition Act
3. Pre-conception and Pre-natal Diagnostics Techniques Act
4. Hindu Marriage Act
5. Protection of women from Domestic Violence Act
6. The sexual harassment of women at workplace (Prevention, Prohibition and Redressal Act).

Codes
(a) 6, 3, 4, 2, 5 and 1 (b) 4, 2, 1, 3, 5 and 6
(c) 4, 3, 2, 1, 5 and 6 (d) 6, 5, 4, 3, 2 and 1

December 2015

2 **Assertion** (A) Research in reproductive health describes women's disadvantaged position and lack of reproductive rights.
Reason (R) Notions of masculinity and feminity are outcomes of social construction which shape sexuality and reproductive rights.

Codes
(a) Both A and R are incorrect
(b) Both A and R are correct
(c) A is correct, but R is incorrect
(d) R is correct, but A is incorrect

ANSWERS

Exam Based Questions

1 (a)	2 (d)	3 (b)	4 (a)	5 (a)	6 (c)	7 (b)	8 (d)	9 (b)	10 (b)
11 (d)	12 (b)	13 (c)	14 (c)	15 (b)	16 (a)	17 (d)	18 (c)	19 (c)	20 (b)
21 (a)	22 (d)	23 (b)	24 (a)	25 (d)	26 (a)	27 (c)	28 (d)	29 (c)	30 (a)
31 (b)	32 (a)	33 (c)	34 (b)	35 (d)	36 (b)	37 (a)	38 (b)	39 (c)	40 (a)
41 (d)	42 (c)	43 (d)	44 (a)	45 (d)	46 (b)	47 (b)	48 (b)	49 (d)	50 (b)
51 (c)	52 (d)	53 (a)	54 (b)	55 (d)	56 (b)	57 (a)	58 (b)	59 (d)	60 (c)
61 (b)	62 (a)	63 (c)	64 (a)	65 (b)	66 (c)	67 (a)	68 (a)	69 (d)	70 (a)
71 (a)	72 (b)	73 (c)	74 (a)	75 (b)					

Previous Years' Questions

1 (b)	2 (b)

UNIT IX

Basics of Communication and Its Theories

A large portion of our lives is spent communicating with others. Sharing your thoughts and understanding of another person's feelings are essential skill for functioning in any society in the world. Communication works with the necessary pieces of information which is send by sender and received by the receiver.

Communication is the practise that provides the most important aid for the development and modernisation of India. It helps to attain higher level of excellence by establishing a link between two entities. Studying about communication process helps you in coordinating, counselling, evaluating and supervising various processes of life.

Communication

Communication is the process of understanding and passing information from one person to another. The word Communication originates from the word *Communis*, which means common. So, communication is an act by which a person shares the knowledge, feelings, ideas, information, etc., in ways such that each gains a common understanding of the meaning, intent and use of the message. Communication is a process of social interaction. Communication is an exchange of information, knowledge, ideas or feelings taking place between two individuals.

In a face-to-face situation communication is not a mere exchange of information, but something more, because in such a situation alongwith the information one passes, the gestures, expression, language, the manner of expression and tone all of these combined together, create a sort of impact on both.

It is the process of transmitting meaning between individuals. It is vital for the progress of society. Early man communicated through symbols and gestures and later on the spoken word, in the form of language, which was used for communication. As technology developed, written words and other media were used in addition to the symbols, gestures and spoken words. Every symbol and the gesture had a meaning and have an important place in the communication process.

In this Chapter

Definitions of Communication

Some definitions related to communication are given below :

- According to **Schramm**, "Communication occurs when two corresponding systems coupled together through one or more non-corresponding systems, which assumes identical status as a result of a single transfer along the chain, to establish commonness."
- According to **Loomis** and **Beegle**, "The process by which information, decisions and directions passess through a social system and the ways in which knowledge, opinions and attitudes are formed or modified."
- According to **Leagans**, "It is a process by which two or more people exchange ideas, facts, feelings or impressions in ways that each gains a common understanding of the message." In essence, it is the act of getting a sender and a receiver turned together for a particular message or series of messages.
- According to **Leland Brown**, "Communication is the transmission and interchange of facts, ideas, feelings or courses of action."
- According to **Coleman and Marsh**, "All educational and action programmes in agriculture are communication."
- According to **Louis A**, "Communication is the sum of all the things one person does, when he wants to create understanding in the mind of another. It involves a systematic and continuous process of telling, listening and understanding."
- According to **American College Dictionary**, "Communication is the imparting or interchange of thoughts, opinions or information by speech, writing or signs."

Nature of Communication

The nature of communication represents the important role inside personal existence, family member's existence, cultural existence, company existence and may others. The nature of communication is discussed below :

- Communication has both the elements of Science and Art.
- Communication can be pervaded in every area of human existence.
- Communication comes about by means of bringing a selected method e.g. media. This media should be composed of verbal and non-verbal media.
- Communication is the sum of all things that one person does, when he wants to create an understanding in the mind of another.
- Communication involves a systematic and continuous process of speaking, listening and understanding.
- Communication is a process, to be done through the words, letters, symbols or messages. It is a way by which the members of an organisation share their meanings, ideas and understanding with each other.

Characteristics of Communication

Characteristics of communication are given below :

Two or More Persons It is the important characteristic of communication. Atleast two persons are there for communication because no single individual can have an exchange of ideas with himself. A listener must receive one's ideas. Therefore, there must be atleast two persons-the sender of information and the receiver to receive the information.

Exchange of Ideas Communication cannot be possible in the absence of exchange of ideas. Process of communication required an exchange of ideas, orders, feelings, etc., among two or more persons.

Mutual Understanding Here, the understanding of information is more important than to carry it. Receiver should receive the information in the same way in which it is being given.

Direct and Indirect Communication It is not necessary that receiver and sender should be face-to-face with each other in the indirect communication. It can be possible through other means of communication like phone, internet etc., Whereas in direct communication sender and receiver have face-to-face conversation.

Continuous Process It is an endless process, as is the case with business where the manager continuously assigns work to his subordinates, tries to know the progress of the work and gives directions.

Use of Words As Well As Symbols There are many ways of communication, like the written, the oral and symbolic. In symbolic we communicate through symbols for instance the ringing of bell for closing a school or a college, saying something by the movement of neck, etc.

Principles of Communication

The following are the principles of communication :

Effectiveness of Policies Policies and programmes of the enterprise need effective communication to be executed. Effective communication of policies and programmes gives way to progress of enterprise. Effectiveness of the policies can be judged from its success, which indirectly depends on effective communication stem.

Human Relations Mutual understanding is possible through communication. Therefore, communication make use of other medium or media to help and promote human relations.

Avoid Errors The purpose of communication is to avoid errors or mistakes or misunderstanding in different walk of life.

Persuasion The process of convincing and motivating others to get the things done is called as persuasion, which is achieved by good communication.

Dialogue The exchange of ideas is done through dialogues, which are the backbone of communication.

Empathy Effective communication includes effective speech, which is helpful in understanding others feelings.

Improved Efficiency and Productivity The efficiency of employees improves with effective system of communication, productivity goes up and cost of production shows a decline trend if the communication is effective and workers have good understanding.

Conveying the Right Message The purpose of communication is to convey the right message to the right person. If the message conveyed is well understood and accepted, the receiver is able to carryout the message effectively.

Coordination Communication plays an important role in coordinating activities involved in running a business, which is an important and necessary activity of management.

Development of Managerial Skills Communication is a learning process. Fact, information, ideas, enrich the knowledge of the executive.

Elements of Communication

An efficient information carrier transmits content to the audience through appropriate channels in successful communication. Elements of communication are as follows :

Sender

In order to be the good reporter, it is necessary to know the nature of the elements in order to fulfil the objective and make proper logical arrangement. The source of the communication process is the communicator. It can also be said as the starting point. It can have various names and form in the system such as: source, sender, informant, communicator, speaker, etc. It is very difficult to present an objective truth and influence people through own saying. The communication duty is to fulfil the social responsibilities. His presentation not only transmits facts, ideas, information, etc., but also motivates people to move towards change.

The communicator should be a balanced personality. He should have a wide knowledge of his subject, an understanding of diverse communication mediums, prudent decision-making ability and the biggest thing should be interest and honesty towards his work.

The communicator should be tolerant, kind, polite, friendly and selfless. Such a person can think about public welfare and disseminate correct information. Credibility to the communicator has established many newspapers, radios and television programmes and audiences, listeners and readers have been seen to be eager for them.

In all the great leaders or social reformers of the world, it has been found that they were excellent communicators, because they were reliable among people and people were easily drawn towards them.

There was enthusiasm, impulse, boldness, dynamism and clarity of voice. It is important to understand the people's sentiments.

Therefore, they gave importance to sympathy. People used to get their feelings in their words, find solutions to their problems with their words and get solutions, so people were attracted towards them. Any communicator can gain credibility towards the communicator only by bringing allegiance to his duty.

Communication is a planned process. For this reason, a well planned or pre-planned programme is important. As stated, the communicator or sender is the source point of this process. Being the originator of a communication subject has to make many important decisions before stating the communication process, which are as follows :

- Selection of Messages
- Selection of Communication Channel
- Treatment of Message
- Selection of Receiver

Message

Under the communication process, the first task of a communicator is to choose the message or its content. This work usually starts on the mental plane i.e. deep thinking which is very necessary.

After this we must look into the content of the message as it should be important, useful, contemporary and relevant. It should also have the ability to attract as many people as possible.

For example, most of the farmers in the country cultivate wheat and rice. Therefore, things related to these food grains will prove useful for a large group. But it is important to follow the complete plantation process.

Similarly, when plants are big, there should be discussion of maintenance, spraying of pesticides, etc., and storage during harvesting. When it is the season of rice cultivation, it will be useful and interesting to talk about rice farming and attract people.

For example, if housewives are informed about making various cauliflower dishes, pickles, etc., during the cabbage season, they can take advantage of the information provided. In summer or rainy season the discussion of cabbage will not prove to be unusable and housewives will not take interest in communication. The communicator should keep in mind that the information given is beneficial to the people. These benefits can be direct or indirect, enlightening. Everyone has the greed for profit, even if the message is a customer.

Communication Medium

Communication medium are the formula or links that connect the communicator and the receiver. The communication message is transmitted through them. Medium can be media, bulletin, radio, television, microphone, film, e-mail, etc., these are all diffusion teaching methods.

In fact, dissemination methods are also a communication medium. They can be properly used only, if they are used properly, given the relevance of the message and the educational level of the facilitation. Correct selection of these is also necessary for their effective results. Media plays an important role in effective communication. The communicator can use many mediums simultaneously from the point of view of need, utility and influence, if he has so much desires. Successful use of communication mediums requires attention to the following points :

- Suitability
- Availability
- Economical
- Appropriate Selection
- Use of Multiple Media

Receiver

Receiver is said to be the fourth element of class of community communication. It can also be called the last point, because it is the goal of the communicator. Under Prasar Shiksha, the recipients are often pramanas, young male and female leaders.

They are called to be the receptacles, listener or spectator. The success of the communication process is based on the role of recipient. The applicability of the message is proved only when the recipient displays positive behaviour towards the communicated message.

Models of Communication

Models of communication are conceptual models used to explain the human communication process. The first major model for communication was developed in 1948 by **Claude Elwood Shannon** and published with an introduction by **Warren weaver.**

Models of communication showing process of communication are given below ;

Dance's Helix Model

The process of giving, receiving or exchanging ideas, information, signals or messages through appropriate media, which enables an individual or group to persude. To express emotion and to seek and give information is called communication.

A Dance's Helix Model for communication process, proposed by **France Dance**, shows communication as a dynamic and non-linear process.

Communication Model

Communication takes place when the sender selects a certain message and gives it a special treatment for transmission over a selected channel to a receiver, who interprets and message before taking the desired action.

This model has following steps :

Sender It is the person or apparatus that puts the process into operation. The sender may be the extension worker/teacher in a meeting or in front of a radio microphone. He decides what message to send, how to treat it.

Message This is the 'information package' the technical know how to improve framing, live stock, home, village sanitation, health, etc., of the people. It may be a signal as on poster or complete information through a pamphlet about the 'package of practices' instructions, blue print, etc.

Treatment of Message It refers to the ways, in which the message in handled before it is placed on the channel. Its purpose to make the message clear, understandable and realistic to the audience.

Channel It is the avenue of communication i.e. in a telegram the wire, over which the message is sent, in a radio talk. It is the radio station, the newspaper in which our message appears.

Receiver The receiver may be a single person when we write a letter, it may be a group of people, who read the message or the masses who listen to the radio or see television. The more homogeneous the audience is, the greater are the changes of effective communication.

Functions of Communication

Functions of communication are as follow :

Teaching Function To teach and educate workers about safety on the work place/job, requirement of complete communication process is needed. Such communication is needed to avert risks, accidents, etc. at the work place.

Orientation Function Communication plays an important role in acquainting the employees of an organisation with their superiors and other co-workers and also with the organisational rules and regulations, objectives and policies.

Directing Function To issue directions by the top management or managers to lower level, communication is necessary. This communication may be either in writing or in oral form.

Informing Function To inform the individual or group about the subject matter is an important function of communication in an organisation. The policies of the organisation is informed to the lower level of workers *via* middle level of workers by the top officials.

Decision-Making Function Communication helps in making decisions whether in written or verbal forms. Necessary information is provided to every worker of an organisation for efficient and effective work done.

Influencing Function Influencing others or being influenced involves a complete communication process. This also includes motivational factors, which helps the individual within the working environment, within the organisation and within individual itself.

Evaluation Function An adequate and effective communication process is required for effective evaluation of work done.

Types of Communication

Types of communication are classified on the basis of relationship element, purpose style, direction, etc. The types of communication on this basis are discussed below :

On the Basis of Relationship Element

On the basis of relationship element, communication can be classified as :

- Verbal and Non-verbal Communication
- Interpersonal and Intrapersonal Communication
- Small Group versus Mass Communication

Verbal and Non-Verbal Communication

The forms of verbal communication are speaking and writing. As we try to communicate we verbalise our messages. We can say that, we use language in verbal communication. Whether you speak or write, you are generally thinking about words and sentences and the most effective way to put them together.

Verbal communication is of basic importance to everyone because it is the main way, we engage in social relationships. Non-verbal communication deals with all the body language activities to communicate the range of emotions like disgust, affection, smile, frawn, grimace, shrug, applaud, raising hands, denching fists, folding arms, waving good bye, etc.

We all do a lot of communication without using words, which encompasses the importance of eye contact and physical gestures. Those all comes under non-verbal communication.

Interpersonal and Intrapersonal Communication

Interpersonal communication takes atleast two persons to start the process. It is the communication between or among the persons. Interpersonal communication can take place face-to-face, one on one or it can involve groups, both large and small. It can be formal or informal personal or impersonal.

Intrapersonal communication takes place within a single person or we can say that the person is engaged in self-communication. This involves formulating or encoding a message within one self, which is also called as the process of thinking. It is impossible to communicate with someone else without first communicating within yourself.

Small Group Versus Mass Communication

The small group communication is the simplest type of communication, in which one person attempts to communicate with another. Interaction can be easily accomplished in smaller communication environments because the potential exists for return message (feed back) to be sent very quickly from the message-receiver to the message-senders. Examples are communication between friends, communication between professor and students, etc.

The extension of group communication is done through mass communication, which involves television, radio, cinema, internet, books, journals and newspapers and other electronic media.

The less expensive and easy to access community media at direct and personal level, which communicate much more effectively is the traditional community media like the folk traditions.

On the Basis of Purpose and Style

On the basis of purpose and style, types of communication can be divided in two forms. They are :

Formal Communication

A formal communication is deliberately established by upper level of management for day-to-day transmission of official information.

There are six types of formal communication :

Chain Network In this communication, the information and message flow only up or down in hierarchical chain of command.

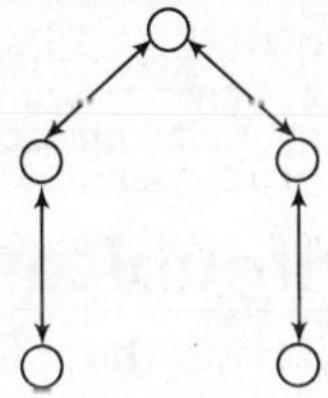

Chain Network

Star Network Under this communication, the information and message flow among the group members through a leader.

In other words, the group members do not communicate with each other directly, but rely on the leader.

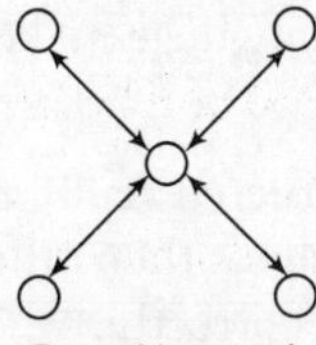

Star Network

Circle Network In this communication, the group members interact with the adjoining member only.

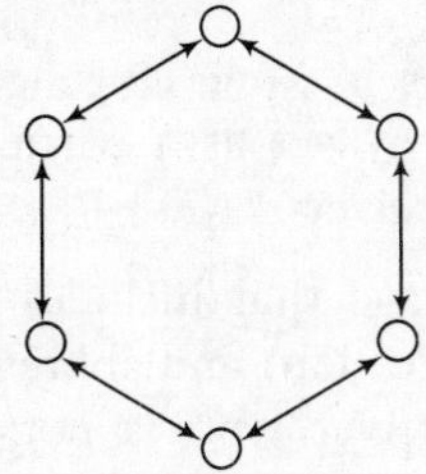

Circle Network

All Channel Network Under this communication, all members of a group actively communicate with each other freely. It is most decentralised type of formal communication.

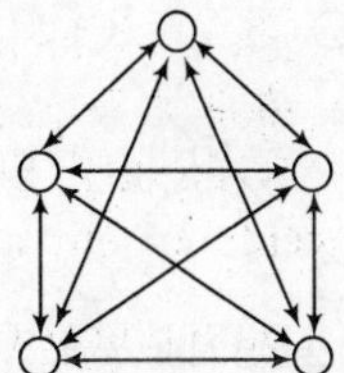

All-Channel Network

Inverted-V Network Under this communication, a subordinate communicates with his immediate superior as well as second superior.

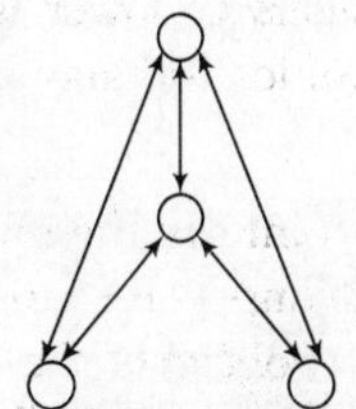

Inverted-V Network

γ-Network Under this communication, two subordinates through the hierarchical chain, communicate with the superior. In turn, the superior communicates with two superiors who are senior to him.

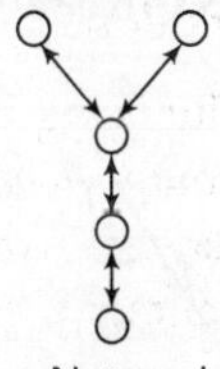

γ-Network

Informal Communication

An informal communication is an unofficial channel and is the result of the operations of social forces at the work place. It mainly addresses the social needs of the employees. It is also known as the **Grapevine** and supplements formal communication.

Keith Davis has investigated the phenomena of grapevine.

There are four types of grapevine networks :

Single Strand Network Under this communication, the information passes from one to one, that is one member communicates to another member who in turn communicates to another member and so on.

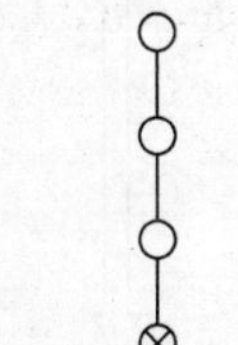

Single Strand Network

Gossip Network Under this communication, the member communicates non-selectively, i.e. a member having information passes it on to everyone he meets.

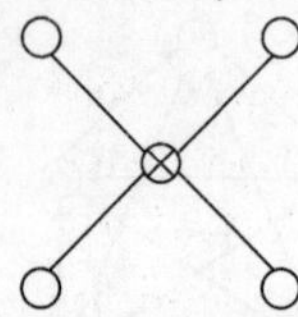

Gossip Network

Probability Network Under this communication, information passes according to the law of probability, i.e. one member communicates randomly with others who in turn communicate to some others.

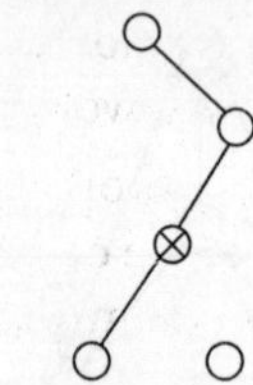

Probability Network

Cluster Network Under this communication, the information passes selectively, i.e. one member communicates with only those members whom he trusts. In turn, they pass it on to some other selected members. It is most popular type of grapevine communication and widely prevalent in organisation.

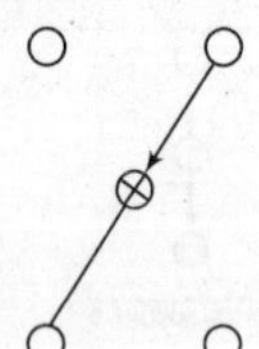

Cluster Network

On the Basis of Direction

Communication flows through the networks in an organisation which may be of three types i.e. horizontal, vertical and diagonal.

Vertical Communication

This is basically a formal communication, where communication is most dominated. This follows the hierarchical chain of command. The verticle direction of communication can be upward (bottom up) and downward (top down).

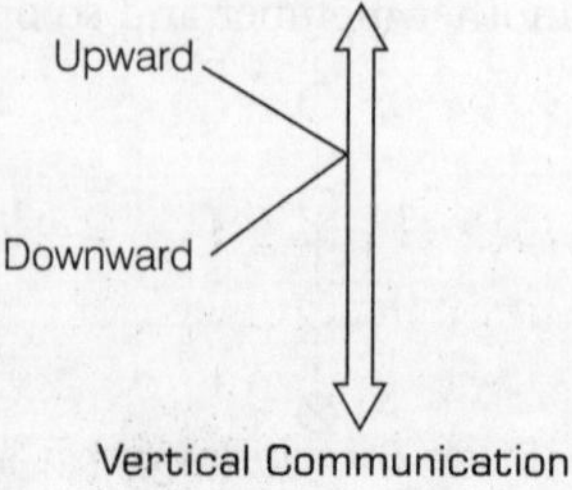

Vertical Communication

Horizontal or Lateral Communication

It is the communication where people can communicate their colleagues and peers at same level in hierarchical chain of command.

It is necessary for smooth coordination. It may be combined of both formal and informal.

It is beneficial when organisations are very large.

This leads to a successful interactive interpersonal communication.

Horizontal Communication

Diagonal Communication

It is free flow of communication hence, no barrier of hierarchy. It encourages the bonding between superior and subordinate as well as among the colleagues.

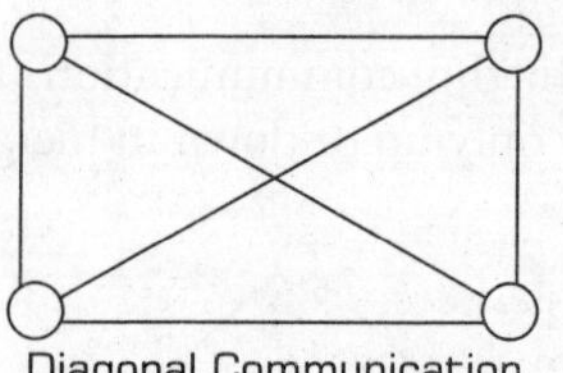

Diagonal Communication

Barriers of Communication

Barriers of communication are those factors which produce obstacles in the way of reaching message to the receiver.

Accordingly, following are the barriers of communication :

Language or Linguistic Barriers

Language means using words or deliver something to the receiver. It includes both verbal and non-verbal communication. Through the following points, we can understand easily, how language makes barriers to effective communication.

If the language is constructed badly or faulty or there are mistakes in the message, then the receiver will find difficulty to understand correctly.

There are certain assumptions underlying a communication. If the receiver is not clear about these assumptions, the purpose of the communication would be lost.

When communicating in same language, the terminology used in a message may act as a barrier if it is not fully understood by the receivers.

For example, a message that includes a lot of specialist jargon (technical expression) and abbreviations will not be understood by a receiver who is not familiar with the terminology used.

If a message written in one language and translated into another language, then, it is highly important that the translation should be free from errors or omissions. Therefore, the receiver can easily understand.

Semantic Barriers

The semantic barriers refers to the misunderstanding between the sender and receiver arising due to the different meaning of words, and other symbols used in the communication. The semantic barriers usually arise when the information is not in the simple language and contains those words or symbols that have multiple meanings.

Psychological or Emotional Barriers

Following are psychological or emotional barriers to the effective communication :

- Some people have the tendency to form a judgement before listening to the entire message.
- If the receiver is pre-occupied with other matters then he can not properly listen to or attend to a message.
- When communication passes through several levels or channels, each transmission, may cause some distortion by omission or fault. Thus, poor retention of information has been received by the receiver.
- When emotions are strong, it is difficult to know the frame of mind of other person or group. Emotional attitudes of both, the communicators as well as the receivers obstruct free flow of transmission and understanding of messages.
- The attitude of a person to interprete the messages in accordance with his self-concept, also affects communication. The communicator responds favourably to those messages that reinforce his self-concept. He also rejects those messages that are perceived to be threat to his self-image.

Organisational Barriers

Following are the organisational barriers to effective communication :

- If an organisation does not believe in free flow of information to the lower levels or in any particular direction, then, there will be problems of understanding within the organisation.
- The rules and regulations may restrict or circumscribe the flow of information.
- The hierarchical consciousness comes in the way of effective communication in the upward direction.
- If there are no adequate facilities for communications, there will be difficulties in ensuring effective communication.
- Noise causes disturbance, distortion, confusion and interference in an organisation for transmission of messages.

Personal Barriers or Status Barriers

Following are the personal barriers to effective communication :

- In the event of unfavourable attitude of supervisors towards their subordinates in an organisation, consequently there would arise a barrier.
- Lack of trust or confidence in subordinates, when the supervisors are not communicative enough with their subordinates.
- A superior may give only selected information to his subordinates, as to maintain status differences. It leads to lack of coordination between them.
- Subordinates, usually, tend to convey only those things which the superiors would appreciate.
- Supervisors, due to overwork or otherwise, express inability to listen or in some cases employees may have lack of enthusiasm to communicate freely with their supervisors.

Physical Barriers

Following are the physical barriers to the effective communication :

- Use of medium with which the recipient is unfamiliar, it may lead to communication barrier.
- Environmental stress such as high temperature, poor ventilation, etc., leads to barrier in the organisation or at any places.
- Subjective stress includes sleeplessness, ill-health, effects of drugs, mood swings, etc., also affect the communication.
- Surrounding area such as traffic noise, music, loudspeaker, etc., create some disturbance while communication takes place between two parties.

Mechanical Barriers

Following are the mechanical barriers to communication :

- In the absence of communication facilities, there is difficulty in reaching of a message to the destination.
- Channel noise, that includes any disturbance in physical transmission of a message, makes barrier to effective communication.
  For example, disturbances in radio transmission, blurredness on TV screens, inaudibility in telephone devices and so on.

Perception in Communication

The way people perceive information around them is unique or varies from person to person. It is based on number of factors that people are born with and gain experience throughout their lives.

Perception is how people make sense of the messages they encounter in their daily lives. With the help of perception, you will be able to clear up any communication misunderstandings before they happen.

Present feelings of the person can also affect the perception regarding the people you are communicating with. Their mood at the time of communication can affect the way they perceive the message.

Your mood whether positive or negative can affect the understanding and interpretation of the information during communication.

Perception Process

Perception and communication are linked with each other. While communicating with others, perception follows a three-step process :

- Selection
- Organisation
- Interpretation

In selection people select the information than organise the information during organisation and in final stage people assign meaning to the information they have selected and organised accordingly that is interpretation.

Types of Perception

There are four main factors that affect now perception varies between people like physiology, past experiences, culture and present feelings.

Perception and Physiology A person's physiology is one of the factors that affect how they perceive messages and includes aspects like age, gender, physical appearance and physical characteristics.

Perception and Past Experiences A person's past experience plays a big role in shaping their perception of communication. This is more clear in a business environment because it will affect the purchasing behaviour of the customers like whether or not your customers want to buy from you.

Perception and Culture Perception can be varies due to their culture. People from the same nation, social group or geographical group often share the same social customs and values. This plays major role in the communication.

Persuasion in Communication

Persuasion basically means trying to influence the way someone thinks or behaves. There are all kinds of different ways to persuade someone to do something. The ad is using an appeal to emotion. The students at the debate club are doing something different. Instead of appealing to emotion, they're trying to persuade each other with logical arguments that use facts and evidences. The purpose of persuasion is to convince, motivate or move readers toward a certain point or opinion.

Rational Model of Persuasion

The rational model of persuasion is based on the idea that people behave in predictable ways based on their beliefs and values. Beliefs and values are based on what the person knows about the world. So for example, if someone knows that wearing a seatbelt saves lives and if he or she values their own life, they probably believe that they should wear a seatbelt. Based on their beliefs and values, they will probably behave in a rational way and wear their seatbelt in the car.

The rational model can be complicated. For example, most of us believe that a salad is healthier than pizza, but lots and lots of people every day go into restaurants and order pizza instead of salads. What gives? One possible answer is that those people have conflicting values and beliefs. They might believe that salad is healthier, but they might also believe that pizza is more delicious. They might value health, but they might also value pleasure.

A person with complicated beliefs and values might sometimes order a salad and sometimes order a pizza. When it comes to the important things in life, a lot of us have complicated and conflicting beliefs and values, and we don't necessarily act in simple ways. So, the rational model of persuasion can be complicated. But it's still a useful tool for understanding why people think and act the way they do and what you can do to change their mind or change their behaviour or both.

In the rational model, people's behaviour is based on their beliefs and values. Their beliefs and values are based on what they know (or think they know!) about the world. So, if you want to change their behaviour you'd have to change their beliefs and/or values.

Empathy in Communication

Empathy is important for good communication. Empathy means the ability to imagine how another person is feeling and so understand his/her mood. It is the capacity to place oneself in another's position. It encompasses a broad range of emotional states.

Following suggestions for being empathetic as you communicate your ideas :

- Successful communication is a two-way process. Sender must send their ideas in such a way that others can understand and receiver must listen to others to understand how the message is received.
- Present your ideas in a organised form, it must be clear to you. You should be confident that your ideas will be understood and accepted by others.

- Present your ideas to others in a form that highlights their benefits. Strive to understand the needs and expectations of others for effective communication.
- Use the communication style which is comfortable and familiar to your listener.

Communication System or Process

Claude Shannon and **Warren Weaver** developed the most widely used model of communication process.

This model consists of eight components :

Source The source is the initiator of communication, who wants to transmit his ideas, thoughts, needs, intentions or other pieces of information to another person.

Encoding It is a process in which the ideas to be conveyed, are translated into a code or set of symbols or some other formate of expression.

Message It is the actual physical product from the source-encoding. It represents the meaning which the source wants to convey.

Channel It is the medium through which the message transmits. It is the connecting link between the sender and the receiver.

Decoding It is the process which translates the message into a form that can be understood by the receiver.

Receiver It is the person to whom the message is directed (conveyed).

Feedback It is the response from the receiver which enables the sender (source) to determine whether the message was received and understood as originally intended.

Noise It includes those factors in each of the components of communication that reduces the accuracy of the message.

Thus, it can occur at any stage in the communication process.

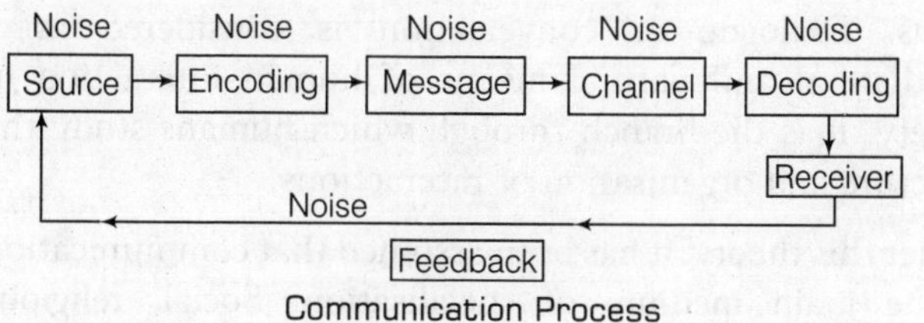

Communication Process

Culture and Communication

Culture is the basic life value of a society. Other civilisations of culture, colloquial, living style, conduct, behaviour, customers, etc., are included. The basis of Indian culture is considered to be 'Vasudhaiva kutumbakam', which is accepted by the whole world at present. With the expansion of communication, the world is currently confined. You can sit in any corner of the country and observe culture, living and society in any part of the world.

In ancient times, when the means of communication were not developed, the technique of printing was not there, however the process of communication was going on, at that time the communication process was carried out through oral communication i.e. personal communication.

Communication is considered as the carrier of culture. The media always play an important role in advancing and strengthening the culture. On the positive side, culture and communication are said to be complementary to each, such as radio transmits all aspects of Indian culture to its listeners.

News, ideas, music, programmes, etc., are good examples of this like radio, television and films have promoted traditional cultures. The cultural programmes of India are seen not only by the people of India but also by people from outside countries.

Taking things from negative side, the media has hurt our culture in some way or other. Change is always cherished by India through media. People's costumes, interests, lifestyles, food and drink have a direct impact on communication, as a result people's lives have changed.

Levels (Settings) of Communication Transaction

Communication between two people occurs on numerous levels simultaneously, each with its nuances and complexities. These levels of communication are verbal, physical, auditory, emotional and energetic.

Verbal Level of Communication

Although this is perhaps the most apparent level of human communication, people can spend a lifetime trying to master it. This level includes our selection of words based on an understanding of meaning between the speaker and the listener. There are multiple definitions for most words, and few of us hold the exact same meaning for each word. Different words evoke different images, memories, and meaning for different people. Communicate effectively, select the "right" words and usage for the context of the conversation.

Physical Level of Communication

To communicate effectively on the physical level, its helpful to physically align with others, connecting with them in form and movement. It also helps to be mindful of your posture, facial expressions, and hand gestures.

Auditory Level of Communication

To communicate effectively on the auditory level, become aware of various auditory cues, speaking to others in a manner more akin to their own ways (another form of "matching and mirroring"). The sound of our voice, including the tone, range, volume, and speed affects how our messages are received and interpreted by others.

Emotional Level of Communication

To communicate effectively on the emotional level, become aware of your emotional state, learning to pause and release negative emotions before attempting to connect with others. Words delivered with pride, anger or fear are rarely well received. The speaker's emotions put the recipient in a particular state of mind and influence how the listener interprets what is said.

Energetic Level of Communication

To communicate more effectively, hold the highest intention for the other person's wellbeing. This requires a unique level of mindfulness generally cultivated through compassion practices. When we are centered in a state of mastery, we are more likely to access this psychic dimension that holds great treasures of insights into others, helping us communicate with greater ease.

Also called the psychic level, this level of communication encompasses a vast range of unseen factors including a person's level of consciousness, the frequency or harmonics of the message, and other subtle energies.

Bringing All the Levels of Communication Together

These levels of communication are interdependent, as each level affects the other. For example, our emotional state affects our body language and our overall field influences our emotional state. When we see the complexities inherent in human communication, we can be made more patient in our speech and more compassionate towards others and ourselves.

Process of Listening

Listening is an active process by which we make sense of, assess, and respond to what we hear. Active listening is a particular communication technique that requires the listener to provide feedback on what he or she hears to the speaker.

The listening process involves five stages, i.e. receiving, understanding, evaluating, remembering, and responding.

Receiving It is the international focus on hearing a speaker's message, which happens when we filter out other sources so that we can isolate the message and avoid the confusing mixture of incoming stimuli. At this stage, we are still only hearing the message.

Understanding Here, we attempt to learn the meaning of the message, which is not always easy. For one thing, if a speaker does not enunciate clearly, it may be difficult to tell what the message was.

Remembering It begins with listening, if you can't remember something that was said, you might not have been listening effectively. Even when you are listening attentively, some messages are more difficult than others to understand and remember.

Evaluating The fourth stage in the listening process is evaluating, or judging the value of the message. Evaluation of the message can vary widely from one listener to another. People are more likely to evaluate a message positively if the speaker speaks clearly, presents ideas logically, and gives reasons to support the points made.

Responding Sometimes referred to as feedback is the fifth and final stage of the listening process. It's the stage at which you indicate your involvement. Almost anything you do at this stage can be interpreted as feedback.

Communication Theories

Human Interaction Theory, Mass Communication Theory and Message Design Theory are prominent communication theories. Their description is given below :

Human Interaction Theory

Communication plays an important role in forming interpersonal relationships. It is an exchange of knowledge, ideas, information or experience of two or more people in which people speak, write, dance, sing, express their feelings by presenting themselves.

Human communication takes place in both written and oral forms. Dialogue or conversation is considered as a multilateral and natural means of human interaction in society. It is the branch through which humans study the structure and organisation of interactions.

Under this theory, it has been assumed that communication is the main medium of socialisation. Social, religious and cultural traditions reach from generation to generation through communication. This social gathering is an important means of bonding, coordination and harmony.

Mass Communication Theory

There are five types of services that are prescribed under the Mass Communication Principle. They are monitoring, correlation, communication, entertainment and organisation. While talking about mass communication theory **Laswell** and **C. Wrights**' names are much prominent.

In an article published in the year 1948, 'In the Structure and Function of Communication of Society', Laswell has discussed about the functional principles of communication. After this, in the year 1960, in the article 'Functional Analysis and Mass Communication' published in a magazine called 'Public Opinion' in the year 1960.

Under this principle, the mass media carries out many tasks for the society. This theory shows that every person has a strong desire at some level. Under the same desire, they use mass media to fulfil different objectives. It is believed that mass media works like an important part of our society.

Message Design Theory

This theory is used to generate message and explain about the message in detail. The main fact of the message design model is that when a situation is complicated, different people make it clear. This principle gives importance to the clear expression of one's thoughts and feelings. According to this theory, there should be clarity in information. If two meanings come out from reading the information, then there is a possibility of confusion, due to which the meaning of the message is lost.

According to the Management Association of America, there are many things necessary to clarify information, such as being self-evident about ideas before expressing them, properly, understanding its purpose before clarifying ideas, consulting other colleagues about it and avoiding misinterpretation while giving ideas language. The messages to be delivered should not be too large or too small to be understood by anyone.

EXAM BASED QUESTIONS

1 The English word 'communication' is derived from the words
(a) communis and communicare
(b) communist and commune
(c) communism and communalism
(d) communion and commonsense

2 What do you mean by communication?
(a) Communication is transfering and conveying through thoughts, views, emotions or information through specific signals and symbols.
(b) Communication is done through radio, TV, cinema.
(c) Communication is telephone, telegram, fax, radio.
(d) None of the above

3 Which of the following statements is/are correct?
(a) Communication does not generally imply intimacy nor does constant gazing into each others eyes.
(b) Only the ones, who have our trust and have proved themselves are allowed to cross the barriers of an intimate relationship.
(c) In European cultures, it is considered bad manners and bad communication to get too close
(d) All of the above

4 Which of the following statements is/are correct?
(a) Gossip group and other traditional groups come together either regularly or occasionally for sharing information.
(b) In group communication particularly where the group is large, deception and pretence cannot be detected immediately.
(c) In interpersonal communication, feedback is instantaneous, is not so in group communication.
(d) All of the above

5 What is the main feature of communication?
(a) Communication is the transmission of information.
(b) Communication is the transmission of meaning.
(c) Both (a) and (b)
(d) None of the above

6 Which of the following is/are the feature (s) of efficient and effective communication?
(a) Less expenditure of money
(b) Minimised time
(c) Both (a) and (b)
(d) None of the above

7 Which of the following is the most fundamental component of manager's job?
(a) Directing (b) Testing
(c) Communicating (d) Managing

8 What are the factors that influence the choice of communication partner?
(a) Proximity, secrecy dissonance
(b) Utility, loneliness, proximity
(c) Secrecy, dissonance, deception
(d) Dissimilarity, dissonance, deviance

9 What is experienced by every communicator?
(a) Manipulated emotions (b) Anticipatory excitement
(c) The issue of homophiles (d) Status dislocation

10 What the factor that affects every type of communication?
(a) Reception (b) Transmission
(c) Context (d) Non-regulation

11 Which one of the following is correct?
(a) Communication is not a mere transmission, it aims at understanding.
(b) Efficient communication minimises time and cost involved in the exchange process.
(c) Communication is a process involving a sender who sends a message a channel through which a message is transmitted and a receiver.
(d) All of the above

12 Imagine you are working in an educational institution where people are of equal status. Which method of communication is best suited and normally employed in such a context ?
(a) Horizontal Communication
(b) Vertical Communication
(c) Corporate Communication
(d) Cross Communication

13 In the classroom, the teacher sends the message either as words or images. The students are really
(a) encoder (b) decoder
(c) agitator (d) All of these

14 In the process of communication which one of the following is in the chronological order?
(a) Communicator, Medium, Receiver, Effect, Message
(b) Medium, Communicator, Message, Receiver, Effect
(c) Communicator, Message, Medium, Receiver, Effect
(d) Message, Communicator, Medium, Receiver, Effect

15 The sender of information expresses his idea into words, symbols or signs to convey the message. This is known as
(a) decoding (b) encoding
(c) communication channel (d) None of these

16 In circular communication the encoder become a decoder when there is
(a) noise (b) audience
(c) criticality (d) feedback

17 Which of the following can hamper the process of communication?
(a) Channel (b) Encoder (c) Noise (d) Pollution

18 The process of communication runs through
(a) a sender (b) a receiver (c) a channel (d) All of these

19 In the communication process, to encode means to
(a) block a pathway between the sender and receiver message
(b) translate ideas into a code
(c) speak to large group of people
(d) interpret a code

20 Which of the following stages of communication process includes the conversion of symbols into a meaningful information?
(a) Encoding (b) Decoding
(c) Receiving (d) Channelising

21 Which of three components are part of human communication process?
(a) Message, Noise, Feedback
(b) Feedback, Message, Critiquing
(c) Message, Recording, Feedback
(d) Noise, Feedback, Jargon

22 Which of the following is/are the stage(s) of communication process?
(a) Encoding (b) Decoding
(c) Both (a) and (b) (d) None of these

23 A teacher decides to form six groups of students and assigns a sub-theme to each group for discussion and reporting. Which kind of communication model will best describe his/her strategy in this regard?
(a) Transactional model (b) Linear model
(c) Horizontal model (d) Interactional model

24 Which of the following is also known as Circular Model of Communication?
(a) Transactional Model of Communication
(b) Linear Model of Communication
(c) Interactional Model of Communication
(d) None of the above

25 The 'Linear Model' was founded by
(a) Aristotle (b) Shannon (c) Weaver (d) All of these

26 Who supported the Interactional Model of Communication?
(a) Aristotle (b) David Berlo
(c) Weaver (d) Wilbur Schramm

27 When interpersonal communication occurs?
(a) When intimate converssation takes place.
(b) An individual converses with people they have no interest in knowing.
(c) An individual interacts with another person as a unique individual.
(d) Three or more people are communicating with each other at the same time.

28 In interpersonal communication, ethics
(a) increase barriers to understand
(b) are not a consideration
(c) stand in the way of honesty
(d) are important.

29 What is the other name for interpersonal communication?
(a) Mass communication
(b) Face-to-face public communication
(c) Eyadic communication
(d) Virtual reality

30 It is the process of communication resulting in the acceptance with conviction of the communicated proposition in the absence of logically adequate grounds for its acceptance. It is
(a) identification (b) imitation
(c) suggestion (d) None of these

31 What is the help provided by intrapersonal communication?
(a) To known what others are thinking
(b) Learn about oneself
(c) Communicate with the general public
(d) To become a talented public speaker

32 Organisational communication can be equated with
(a) interprasonal communication
(b) interpersonal communication
(c) group communication
(d) mass communication

33 The type of communication best suited to add an audience is
(a) interpersonal communication
(b) group communication
(c) cosmopolite communication
(d) mass communication

34 The degree of directness and intimacy in group communication depends upon
(a) place of meeting
(b) size of the group
(c) group leader
(d) relationship between members

35 In the field of communication, the word 'mass' in mass communication is used to refer to
(a) common people
(b) large number of people
(c) Both (a) and (b)
(d) None of the above

36 Which of the following is/are basic components of mass communication?
(a) Mass audiences (b) Mass messages
(c) Mass media (d) All of these

37 Formal communication can move
(a) upward (b) downward
(c) horizontal (d) All of these

38 The mode of communication that involves a single source transmitting information to a large number of receivers simultaneously, is called
(a) group communication
(b) mass communication
(c) intrapersonal communication
(d) interpersonal communication

39 Which of the following communication is official?
(a) Formal (b) Informal (c) Vertical (d) Sectoral

40 Formal communication usually flows in
(a) four direction (b) three direction
(c) six direction (d) nine direction

41 Which of the following communication is unofficial?
(a) Formal (b) Informal (c) Vertical (d) Sectoral

42 Which of the following is the commonest grapevine chain in orgainisations?
(a) Single strand chain (b) Gossip chain
(c) Probability chain (d) Cluster chain

43 Which of the following is not true about the grapevine?
(a) It is somewhere between 75% and 95% as accurate.
(b) It is found in almost all organisations.
(c) Managers usually welcome its existence.
(d) It is faster at conveying information than an organisation's formal communication system.

44 Any idea, practice or product and which individual perceives to be new, it is called
(a) different (b) innovation
(c) adoption (d) inclusion

45 The three components of message are
(a) code, content, treatment
(b) warmth , gestures, treatment
(c) words, skills, codes
(d) presentation, content, gestures

46 What are the barriers to effective communication?
(a) Moralising, being judgemental and comments of consolation
(b) Dialogue, summary and self-review
(c) Use of simple words, cool reaction and defensive attitude
(d) Personal statements, eye contact and simple narration

47 A jargon means
(a) a specialised language of a particular group of people
(b) techniques of good writing
(c) a special article written by an editor
(d) None of the above

48 Which of the following is not a barrier to effective communication associated with the media and channel?
(a) Noise
(b) Information overland
(c) Space proxemics
(d) In appropriateness of media or channel

49 Which of the following is described in the text as a contextual factor that can impact effectiveness of communication in an organisation?
(a) Organisational structure (b) Organisation culture
(c) Technology (d) All of these

50 Which of the following set of statements are correct for describing the human communication process?
1. Non-verbal communication can stimulate ideas.
2. Communication is a learnt ability.
3. Communication is not a universal panacea.
4. Communication cannot break down.
5. More communication means more effective learning by students.
6. Value of what is learnt through classroom communication is not an issue for students.

Select the correct answer from the codes given below
(a) 1, 2, 3 and 4 (b) 1, 4, 5 and 6
(c) 1, 3, 5 and 6 (d) 2, 4, 5 and 6

51 What causes a lot of relevant information to be lost?
(a) Volume of information
(b) Timing of information
(c) Accuracy of information
(d) Flow of information

52 How human interaction takes place?
(a) Written form (b) Oral form
(c) Both (a) and (b) (d) Only (b)

53 Which among them is not the service of mass communication?
(a) Monitoring (b) Correlation
(c) Entertainment (d) Performance

54 What is/are the key feature(s) of message design theory?
(a) Generate and explain message
(b) Organise and plan message
(c) Understand message
(d) All of the above

55 The communication threshold follows which of the following?
1. Non-communicative behaviour
2. Communicative behaviour
3. A combination of communicative and non-communicative behaviour
4. Storage of the need state in the perceptual field for later action.

Select the correct answer using the codes given below
(a) 1 and 2 (b) 1 and 4
(c) 1, 2 and 3 (d) All of these

56 State the true option according to the statements given. Fundamental principle of perception includes
(a) perception is organised and has structure.
(b) perception is selective.
(c) perception depends upon receivers characteristics.
(d) All of the above

57 Buddhism has four social emotions that should guide interpersonal communication.
1. Metta (loving kindness)
2. Karuna (compassion)
3. Murdita (sympathetic joy)
4. Upekkha (equanimity)

Select the correct answer using the codes given below
(a) 1 and 2 (b) 1 and 4
(c) 1, 2, 3 and 4 (d) 1, 2 and 3

58 In which of the following orders does a person spend his time communicating?
1. Listening 2. Speaking
3. Reading 4. Writing

Codes
(a) 1, 2, 4 and 3 (b) 2, 3, 1 and 4
(c) 1, 2, 3 and 4 (d) 4, 3, 2 and 1

59 Consider the following statements
1. The information which a communicator wishes his audience to receive, understand and accept is action.
2. Non-verbal sign communicate feelings, preferences and likings and either to support or to contracted verbal communication.

Which of the statements given above is/are correct?
(a) Only 1 (b) Only 2
(c) Both 1 and 2 (d) None of these

60 Consider the following statements
1. Upward communication is non-directive in nature from down below, to give feedback, to inform about progress or problems, seeking approvals.
2. Professional discussions rarely go beyond intimate stage.

Which of the statements given above is/are correct?
(a) Only 1 (b) Only 2
(c) Both 1 and 2 (d) None of these

61 Arrange the following in correct order of communication.
1. Message 2. Sender
3. Decoder 4. Encoder
5. Receiver

Codes
(a) 2, 1, 4, 3, 5 (b) 1, 2, 4, 3, 5
(c) 2, 1, 4, 5, 3 (d) 4, 2, 3, 1, 5

62 In the communication process, the sender may
1. speak 2. write
3. draw 4. act

Select the correct answer using the codes given below
(a) 1 and 2 (b) 1 and 4
(c) 1, 2 and 3 (d) All of these

63 Which of the following help the communicator about the opinion holders?
1. Intelligence backgrounds
2. Social atmosphere attitude
3. Receptiveness, temperament
4. Capabilities

Select the correct answer using the codes given below
(a) 1 and 2 (b) 1, 2, 3 and 4
(c) 1, 2 and 3 (d) 1 and 4

64 Face-to-face communication between two persons
1. highest form of communication
2. persuasive and influential
3. interplay of words and gestures
4. involve all five senses

Select the correct answer using the codes given below
(a) 1 and 2 (b) 1, 2, 3 and 4
(c) 1, 2 and 3 (d) 1 and 4

Directions (Q. Nos. 65-70) *In the questions given below are two statements labelled as Assertion (A) and Reason (R). In the context of the two statements which one of the following is correct ?*

(a) Both A and R are true and R is the correct explanation of A.
(b) Both A and R are true, but R is not the correct explanation of A.
(c) A is true, but R is false.
(d) A is false, but R is true.

65 **Assertion** (A) A language is the expression of the thoughts and experiences of a people in term of their cultural environment.

Reason (R) Language facilitates understanding, but there are times when it can be a barrier communication.

66 **Assertion** (A) Functional strategies are a set short-term plans related to the over all realisation of the forms of grand strategy.

Reason (R) The success of any strategy depends upon how well the strategist can adopt his resources to an identifiable opportunity.

67 **Assertion** (A) Communication is the sum of all the things one person does, when he wants to create understanding in the mind of another.

Reason (R) It involves a systematic and continuous process of telling, listening and understanding

68 **Assertion** (A) The purpose of communication is to avoid errors or mistakes or misunderstanding indifferent walk of life.

Reason (R) Mutual understanding is possible through communication.

69 **Assertion** (A) Communication is the transmission and interchange of facts, ideas, feelings or course of action.

Reason (R) Communicants of different backgrounds are able to establish communication more easily.

70 **Assertion** (A) Formal communication tends to be fast and flexible.

Reason (R) Formal communication is a systematic and orderly flow of information.

Directions (Q. Nos. 71-75) *Read the passage given below and answer the questions that follows.*

In an organisation communication facilitates the flow of information and understanding between different people and departments through different media using all the channels and networks. This flow of information is vital for managerial effectiveness and devision making in general and for human resource manager in particular.

Communication thus helps understand people better removing misunderstanding and creating clarity of thoughts and expression. It also educates people. It bridges the gap between individuals and groups through flow of information and understanding between them. Information is the most vital aspect for communication. Information is the most vital aspect for communication. It is the information which is transmitted, studied, analysed, interpreted and stored.

Communication that occurs for carrying out operations of the organisation is known as internal operational communication. Internal members of the organisation such as workers, managers, board of directors, member of trade unions, etc are the participants of internal communication. In modern time, many organisations provide intranet facility for internal electronic communication. Communication with external parties or groups is known as external operational communication. External parties include customers, suppliers, government agencies, regulatory authority, local community, special interest group and the general public.

71 **In an organisation ...... facilitates the flow of information and understanding between different people.**

(a) Media (b) Network
(c) Communication (d) Resources

72 **Communication helps to remove misunderstanding and creating clarity of ...... and expression.**

(a) Throughts (b) Networks
(c) Information (d) None of these

73 **...... is the most vital aspect for communication.**

(a) Interpretation (b) Information
(c) Analysis (d) Understanding

74 **Which of the following are the parties involved in internal operational communication?**

(a) Members of trade unions (b) Board of Directors
(c) Workers (d) All of these

75 **Communication between a manager of a company and a regulatory authority is known as**

(a) Organisation Communication
(b) External Communication
(c) Internal Communication
(d) None of the above

PREVIOUS YEARS' QUESTIONS

July 2018

1 **Our 'self-concept' which influences our communication behaviour is developed due to the following factors**

1. cultural traditions 2. self-evaluation
3. social roles 4. social organisation

Codes

(a) 1, 2 and 4 (b) 2, 3 and 4
(c) 1, 2 and 3 (d) 1, 3 and 4

2 **A Whats App chat between two friends can be an example of the following**

1. formal communication
2. informal communication
3. dyadic communication
4. interpersonal communication

Codes

(a) 1, 2 and 3 (b) 2, 3 and 4 (c) 1, 3 and 4 (4) 1, 2 and 4

3 **Advantages of written communication are**

1. serve as an evidence 2. reduce ambiguity
3. enable authority 4. enable uniformity

Codes

(a) 1, 2 and 3 (b) 2, 3 and 4
(c) 1, 3 and 4 (d) 1, 2 and 4

November 2017

4 **Assertion** **(A) Intrapersonal communication takes place between two people.**

Reason **(R) Intrapersonal communication takes place whenever we evaluate and react to internal and external stimuli.**

Codes

(a) A is correct, but R is incorrect.
(b) A is incorrect, but R is correct.
(c) Both A and R are correct.
(d) Both A and R are incorrect.

5 **Arrange interpersonal distances in communication from least to maximum.**

1. Social 2. Personal
3. Public 4. Intimate

Codes

(a) 1, 2, 4, 3 (b) 1, 2, 3, 4 (c) 1, 2, 1, 3 (d) 1, 4, 3, 2

6 Aspects of non-verbal communication are

1. body language 2. facial expressions
3. posture 4. rigour of repetition

Codes

(a) 1, 2 and 3 (b) 2, 3 and 4
(b) 1, 2 and 4 (d) 1, 3 and 4

7 **Assertion** (A) Building interpersonal competence is a complicated process.

Reason (R) It involves reading people's reactions and feelings even when people don't express them in words.

Codes

(a) A is correct, but R is incorrect.
(b) A is incorrect, but R is correct.
(c) Both A and R are correct.
(d) Both A and Rare incorrect.

8 Arrange the following steps of the communication process as per the Shramm's first model of communication.

1. Source 2. Signal
3. Encoder 4. Decoder
5. Destination

Codes

(a) 1, 2, 3, 4, 5 (b) 1, 3, 2, 4, 5
(c) 1, 4, 3, 2, 5 (d) 1, 4, 3, 5, 2

9 'Distrust' between a sender and a receiver in communication is a type of

(a) mechanical barrier
(b) language or semantic barrier
(c) socio-psychological barrier
(d) organisation barrier

10 The following are important aspects of using para language in communication.

1. Verbal expression 2. Seating arrangement
3. Use of artefacts 4. Use of colour

Codes

(a) 1, 2 and 3 (b) 2, 3 and 4
(c) 1, 3 and 4 (d) 1, 2 and 4

11 A good communicator begins his/her presentation with a

(a) non-sequitur (b) repetitive phrase
(c) ice breaker (d) complex question

January 2017

12 Arrange the elements of the communication process as per the Shannon's and Weaver's model.

1. Destination 2. Transmitter
3. Signal 4. Receiver 5. Source

Codes

(a) 5, 3, 2, 4 and 1 (b) 5, 2, 4, 3 and 1
(c) 5, 2, 3, 4 and 1 (d) 5, 4, 3, 2 and 1

13 The qualities of a receiver, which influence face to face communication are

1. positive attitude 2. active listening skills
3. channel vehicle 4. decoding skills

Codes

(a) 1, 2 and 3 (b) 2, 3 and 4
(c) 2, 3, 4, and 1 (d) 4, 3, 2 and 1

14 The selection of a channel for communication is based on

1. availability 2. organisational hierarchy
3. cost 4. frequency of use

Codes

(a) 1, 2, and 3 (b) 2, 3 and 4
(c) 1, 3 and 4 (d) 1, 2, 3 and 4

15 Individual reflection, contemplation and meditation are the chief functions of the following type of communication.

(a) Intrapersonal communication
(b) Interpersonal communication
(c) Dyadic communication
(d) Intracultural communication

16 As per the Aristotle's model of communication, the three dimensions of persuasive speech are

(a) Ethos, Empathy, Mathos (b) Ethos,Logos, Pathos
(c) Empathy,Chaos, Pathos (d) Logos, Ethos, Laos

July 2016

17 Match the concepts used in communication given under List I with their related term or form given under List II.

List I	List II
A. Mass communication	1. Instruction and control
B. Downward communication	2. Body language
C. Informal communication	3. Delayed feedback
D. Non-verbal communication	4. Grapevine
	5. Empathy

Codes

	A	B	C	D		A	B	C	D
(a)	3	1	2	4	(b)	3	1	4	2
(c)	2	1	5	4	(d)	5	1	2	3

18 The psychological barriers in communication can be

1. stage-fright 2. day-dreaming
3. fidelity 4. entropy

Codes

(a) 1 and 2 (b) 2 and 3 (c) 3 and 4 (d) 1 and 4

19 The communication model "who says, what, in which channel, to whom, with what effect" was proposed by

(a) Aristotle (b) Lasswell
(c) Shannon and Weaver (d) David Berlo

July 2015

20 The term 'Grapevine' is also known as

(a) downward communication
(b) upward communication
(c) informal communication
(d) horizontal communication

June 2015

21 Match the following

List I (Elements of communication process)	List II (Characteristics)
A. Communicator	1. Needs
B. Message	2. Availability
C. Channel	3. Relative advantage
D. Receiver	4. Credibility
	5. Fidelity

Codes

	A	B	C	D		A	B	C	D
(a)	4	2	1	3	(b)	4	3	2	1
(c)	4	1	2	3	(d)	4	5	1	2

22 Match the following.

List I (Functions of communication)	List II (Intended results)
A. To play	1. Guidance
B. To help	2. Skill building
C. To learn	3. Agreement
D. To relate	4. Judgement
	5. Gratification

Codes

	A	B	C	D		A	B	C	D
(a)	4	3	2	5	(b)	4	2	5	3
(c)	5	1	2	3	(d)	4	3	2	1

23 Which one of the following models uses only three elements to explain the process of communication?

(a) Westley and Machlean's Model
(b) Berlo's Model
(c) Leagan's Model
(d) Aristotle's Model

24 Extension uses which of the following as a tool to motivate people to change their behaviour?

(a) Social work (b) Communication
(c) Diagnosis (d) Analysis

25 In communication, the language is

(a) the verbal code (b) intrapersonal
(c) the symbolic code (d) the non-verbal

December 2015

26 **Assertion** (A) Each person in the communication process is both an encoder and a decoder.

Reason (R) Communication often involves an action-reaction interdependence.

Codes

(a) Both A and R are incorrect.
(b) Both A and R are correct and R is the correct explanation of A.
(c) Both A and R are correct, but R is not the correct explanation of A.
(d) A is incorrect, but R is correct.

27 **Assertion** (A) Communication Accommodation Theory highlights that the speakers adjust their speaking style to their listeners, to gain social approvals.

Reason (R) We are gatekeepers in interpersonal communication as we have the power to omit or hold back the information.

Codes

(a) A is correct, but R is incorrect.
(b) A is incorrect, but R is correct.
(c) Both A and R are correct.
(d) Both A and R are incorrect.

28 Users who use media for their own ends are identified as

(a) passive audience (b) active audience
(c) positive audience (d) negative audience

ANSWERS

Exam Based Questions

1 (a)	2 (a)	3 (d)	4 (d)	5 (c)	6 (c)	7 (c)	8 (b)	9 (b)	10 (c)
11 (b)	12 (a)	13 (b)	14 (c)	15 (b)	16 (d)	17 (c)	18 (d)	19 (b)	20 (b)
21 (a)	22 (c)	23 (a)	24 (a)	25 (d)	26 (d)	27 (c)	28 (d)	29 (c)	30 (c)
31 (b)	32 (c)	33 (d)	34 (b)	35 (b)	36 (d)	37 (d)	38 (b)	39 (a)	40 (c)
41 (b)	42 (d)	43 (c)	44 (b)	45 (a)	46 (a)	47 (a)	48 (b)	49 (d)	50 (a)
51 (a)	52 (c)	53 (d)	54 (a)	55 (d)	56 (d)	57 (c)	58 (c)	59 (b)	60 (a)
61 (a)	62 (d)	63 (c)	64 (c)	65 (a)	66 (a)	67 (b)	68 (b)	69 (c)	70 (a)
71 (c)	72 (a)	73 (b)	74 (d)	75 (b)					

Previous Years' Questions

1 (c)	2 (b)	3 (d)	4 (b)	5 (c)	6 (a)	7 (c)	8 (b)	9 (c)	10 (b)
11 (c)	12 (c)	13 (c)	14 (c)	15 (a)	16 (b)	17 (b)	18 (a)	19 (b)	20 (b)
21 (b)	22 (c)	23 (c)	24 (b)	25 (d)	26 (b)	27 (c)	28 (b)		

Developmental Communication

Communication plays a vital role in building of the nation and in its development and also contribute significantly in bringing about social change. The traditional and modern methods of communication help in achieving these goals irrespective of the approaches of communication.

Development and communication are mainly concerned with the human beings and society. Development is a process of change for creation of a new man having control over his environment and lifestyle.

Developmental communication is an instrument for interpretations and application of human and material resources. Communication is a tool and resource for development. Development communication does not mean development of technology or gross national product. It focuses on imparting new ideas, developing the attitudes and teaching skills required for the development of the human beings and nation as a whole.

Therefore, it is communication for planned change. Television and radio have been proved to be the best communication for creating awareness and interest among the audience regarding new idea or message. It is purposive communication for planned change and aims at enhancing human development and their potential.

This helps in reduction of unemployment and poverty. Its main aim and goal is to bring about social change. It is purposive, goal directed, educated and always associated with some programme for desirable planned change. The success of development communication is based on the needs of the audience, availability and access of mass media and communication network.

In this Chapter

- *Development*
- *Development Communication*
- *Diffusion and Communication*
- *Innovation and Communication*
- *Mass Media and Communication*
- *Social Marketing and Communication*
- *Need and Importance of Communication in Development*

Development

It is the process that creates growth, progress, positive change or the addition of physical, economic, environmental, social and demographic components. Its purpose is to raise the level and quality of life of the population, creation and expansion of employment opportunities without damaging the resources of the environment.

According to **Amartya Sen**, "development is a tool enabling people to reach the highest level of their ability through granting freedom of action i.e., freedom of economic, social and family actions."

Theories of Development

Theories of development are as follows :

Development Theory

Development theory is a collection of theories about how desirable change in society is best achieved. Such theories draw on a variety of social science disciplines and approaches. In this article, multiple theories are discussed, as are recent developments with regard to these theories. Depending on which theory that is being looked at, there are different explanations to the process of development and their inequalities.

Modernisation Theory

It is used to analyse the processes in which modernisation in societies takes place. This theory looks at the aspects of countries that are beneficial and constitute obstacles for economic development. Scientists from various research disciplines have contributed to modernisation theory.

Sociological and Anthropological Modernisation Theory

The earliest principles of modernisation theory can be derived from the idea of progress, which stated that people can develop and change their society themselves.

This theory also states that technological advancements and economic changes can lead to changes in moral and cultural values. It described how social order is maintained in society and ways in which primitive societies can make the transition to more advanced societies.

Dependency Theory

It is essentially a follow up to structuralist thinking, and shares many of its core ideas. Whereas structuralists did not consider that development would be possible at all unless a strategy of delinking and rigorous was pursued, dependency thinking could allow development with external links with the developed parts of the globe. However, this kind of development is considered to be "dependent development".

Dependency thinking starts from the notion that resources flow from the periphery of poor and underdeveloped states to a 'Core' of wealthy countries which leads to accumulation of wealth in the rich states at the expense of the poor states. Dependency theory states that not all societies progress through similar stages of development.

Models of Development

When many countries from Asia, Africa and Latin America gained independence from colonial rule after World War II, the main challenges before them were poverty, malnutrition, unemployment, illiteracy and lack of basic facilities.

These developing nations argued that the reason for their backwardness is due to the negligence of the colonial rule and draining the resources of the country for their own advantage.

Therefore, to overcome their backwardness, the discussion of developmental model becomes important. Although, some development models were already in place like capitalist model, the communist model and the mixed model was adopted after the World War II.

Following are the different models of development :

Capitalist Model This model is adopted in Western developed nations. It is also called the 'paradigm of developed nations'. Under the capitalist model all the means of production are privately owned. Production is not planned by the government, but handled by private enterprises. The state organises summons for the development of society at different levels and members.

Socialist Model This model has been seen in communist countries of Eastern Europe. It was adopted by the communist nations after the Russian Revolution with Russia taking the first place. In this, all the productive assets of the country are owned by the entire society and government is the only business enterprise, which practically handles all aspects of economic activities.

Mixed Model This model is the mixture of both capitalist and socialist model. This model have three coordinates market, private sector and public sector. This kind of model is adopted by India for their growth. India implemented a series of Five Year Plan for development after independence. In this model, it is hoped that a multi-pronged strategy will increase the wealth of the country, eradicate poverty and reduce economic inequality. But this model faced various criticism in the last decade.

Indicators and Measures of Development

In order to understand the development of a country, we need to understand their social, economic and educational sectors. Thus, for understanding development, they include various signals like expectancy rate, death rate, sex ratio, literacy, national language, per capital income, level of unemployment, etc., which we see on various informative indexes. Various types of indexes are realised by the United Nations to measure the economic, social and educational development of the world. These indexes include Human Development Index, Gender Inequality Index, Multidimensional Poverty Index, Technological Achievement Index, etc. Other international organisations as well formulate such kind of indexes. The growth index is most important in terms of indicators and measurements of growth.

Indicators of Economic Development

The following points highlight the four key indicators of economic development :

Per Capita Income The most important indicator of economic under-development is low per capita income. Statistical studies show low income countries are much poorer than advanced countries like the USA. **Prof Samuelson** states that "standard comparisons are distorted by the use of official exchange rates to compare living standards." However, some economists have expressed the view that one cannot treat a country as developed only because its per capita income is as high as that of USA or Switzerland. **Joan Robinson** states that, "For several of the Arab States, Gross National Product (GNP) per capita suddenly jumped to levels which exceed that of the richest Western States. Yet, in these countries some of the poorest and least developed communities in the world are found."

Poverty The second important indicator of economic underdevelopment is poverty. Not only per capita income is low but there is inequality in the distribution of income. Many people in least developed countries which do not get the minimum level of income necessary for a minimum calorie intake are said to be living below the poverty line. In India, it is 25%. It is easier to describe poverty than to measure it.

Social and Health Indicators There are certain social and health indicators of economic backwardness. These show the effects of poverty in poor countries. Life expectancy at birth is low, but rate of infant mortality is high. The percentage of illiterate people in total population is high and educational attainment by most people is modest. This reflects low levels of investment in human capital.

Occupational Pattern Another important indicator of economic backwardness is occupational pattern. It is widely believed that the countries in which most of national output or national income is derived from the primary sector (i.e. agriculture, forestry, animal husbandary, mining, etc.) are underdeveloped. In India, 70% of total population depends on agriculture directly or indirectly. According to **Misua** and **Puri**, "Most of the poor countries are essentially agricultural and even if some industries have been established in these countries, their impact is yet to be felt on the socio-economic life of the people."

Measures of Economic Development

There are various measures to consider while measuring economic development. Some of these are discussed below :

Quality of Life and Expectancy When the basic facilities like water, electricity and housing are available to anyone than the quality of life is considered as good in that nation. Here, the measuring factor is the needs of the people. These needs are basic needs like access to health, sanitation, education, nutrition, etc. The main factor for this is the Infant Mortality Rate. This is the death rate of a child who is less than a year old. While life expectancy is the average life of the population that lives in that area.

Real Gross National Product (GNP) GNP as well as GDP are the measuring factors for economic development of a nation. Increase in both of these ensures the larger availability of goods and services in that country. If this supports the standard of living of the people than it increases the economic conditions of the nation. Whenever the GDP is calculated for the current prices, there may be an increase due to price rise. But this does not mean that the availability of goods and services have increased.

Human Development Index (HDI) It includes several factors like long and healthy living, the welfare of the people, etc. This index also includes the standard of living of the people, literacy rate and Purchasing Power Parity (PPP) in terms of real income.

Gender Related Development Index (GDI) This is used to measure gender inequalities by measuring three basic dimensions of human development. They are education, health and economic resources. Education is measured by calculating expectancy years for schooling of males and females. While the health measures the male and female life expectancy during the time of birth. Economic resources are measured by the income earned by males as well as females.

Poverty Index It is also called multi-dimensional poverty index which helps in identifying various factors. These factors include health, standard of living and education. Based on the availability of these factors each person is termed as poor and non-poor.

Development Communication

Development communication is a continuous manufacturing process with a wide scope. This includes education, population and health communication, scientific and technological communication, environmental communication, etc. Efforts are made to energise the development works by paying attention to all aspects of development reports, explanations, opinions and evaluations, etc.

Communication emerged as a major branch of mass communication after World War II. Communication experts conducted central research on the subject of development communication for social, political and economic prosperity and showed interest in changing human life and create better environment and conditions for the people around. Its purpose is to remove the backwardness of the society, to create new ideas and new technology.

This is the reason why development communication was considered a strong force in 21st century.

Definitions of Development Communication

According to various scholars, definition of development communication are as follows :

According to **Naura C Cubell**, "Development communication seeks to accelerate social changes and reduce poverty. Its purpose is to elevate the individual and society."

According to **Gelcote and Steve**, "It is a form of liberal communication aimed to counter injustice and oppression. It is sometimes used for one type of marketing and public opinion research."

According to **World Bank**, "Development communication is the integration of strategic communication into development projects based on a clear potential for indigenous realities."

Role of Development Communication

Development communication can be said to have two primary roles :

Transforming Role Development communication can be used for transforming by bringing in social change in a way that it inspires the people to aim for a higher quality of life. Here, communication acts as an instrument to achieve these objectives.

Socialising Role Development communication also tries to maintain the established values of the society by playing a socialising role. Development communication tries to build and atmosphere so the planned or proposed changes may be brought about while keeping the social fabric of the society intact.

Approaches of Development Communication

There are various approaches to handle development communication which are not exclusive to each other. The main approaches can be understood as :

Diffusion/Entension Approach The focus of this approach is largely on the adoptation of technological and social innovations by bringing in new ideas , services and products.

Diffusion of both material and social innovations is necessary for development. Material innovations refers to economic and technological innovations and social innovations pertain to social needs and structures.

Mass Media Approach A well-defined developed mass media and interpersonal communication infrastructure is necessary for development communication. It is necessary that these infrastructures should be accessible to the people, both physically and socially. The content of the messages should be balanced. It should be both rural and urban oriented and should cater masses in both sectors. The messages should be need-based and they should appeal to the audience.

Development Support Communication Approach In this approach, communication strives not only to inform and educate, but also to motivate people and secure public participation in the growth and process of change. An awareness of development plans is an essential stage in the public cooperation for national development.

Institutional Approach This approach focuses on education for development. The emphasis is on literacy, universal education, adult education, formal and informal education. There is emphasis on need-based training and development-oriented programmes conducive to development.

Integrated Approach This approach to development communication emphasises the need to avoid duplication and waste in development efforts. The balance in the spread of information facilities must be maintained both for rural and urban, backward and prosperous areas.

Localised Approach It is also known as community based communication system. This approach may be evolved to ensure greater participation of local people in planning and production of communication material which is community based.

Planned Strategy Approach The success of development communication depends on team approach i.e the coordination between the communication agencies (extension workers, radio, TV, Press etc.) and development agencies.

Diffusion and Communication

Roger defines diffusion as "The process in which an innovation is communicated through certain channels over time among the members of a social system." There are four key elements in formulation of diffusion process: Innovation, Communication, Time and Social System.

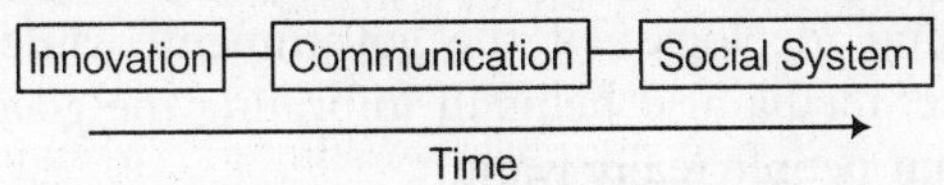

Diffusion of innovation includes both spontaneous spread of new ideas and a planned method of propagating a new idea.

Innovation and Communication

Rogers defines innovation as, "An idea, practice or object that has perceived as new by an individual or other unit of adoption." First time knowledge about a well-established practice can be perceived as 'new' and an innovation, for that particular group of individuals.

As **Rogers** said, "newness can be expressed in terms of knowledge, persuasion or a decision to adopt". It is incorrect to assume that all innovations are beneficial and that all innovations are equally adopted.

The main characteristics of an innovation that significantly affect its adoption or (rejection) are :

- Relative advantage
- Compatibility
- Complexity
- Trial-ability
- Observability

Mass Media and Communication

The word media comes from the plural of the Latin word 'medium' and it is a collective noun refers to TV, Radio, Newspapers, Magazines, Films, the International Network (Internet), etc. The media can be examined either in terms of broadcast media or print media. Media and society are closely related to each other. With the advancement in technological area, our society has also observed the expansion in the thoughts and ideas of people. Mass media has become an integral part of our society as we are just a click away from any information that is available on the internet.

This could happen due to various media units of the country. Therefore, mass media is also known as the Fourth Estate of Pillar of a Democratic Nation.

Media has become the most authentic source of information for people. It helps in bringing considerable changes in the existing laws as per the prevailing social conditions, by playing the role of intermediary between the government and the mass.

Many journalists and writers gave the following definitions about mass media such as :

According to **Denis McQuail**, "Media is the mechanism of change of society."

According to **Rashmi Bohra**, "Media is the mirror of society."

According to **R K Majumdar**, "Media is the medium through which the society is educated."

Objectives of Mass Media

The main objective of mass media is to provide knowledge, educate and entertain people. The important objectives of mass media are given below :

- To provide information about different aspects of human life. For example, education, government policies, programmes and so on.
- To convey cultural and educational programmes.
- To entertain people.
- To create public awareness.
- To establish international relations.
- Establish social contact and linkage.
- Also help in facing disaster and calamity and so on.

Characteristics of Mass Media Communication

There are four major distinctive features of mass media communication :

Distance The sender and the receiver are the two major components of a communication system. There is, however, a gap or a break between the sender and the receiver.

The senders in this case are the makers of the media text, do not have a direct access to the feedback of the audience. This means that one of the characteristics of mass communication is that it is a one way process. For the producers of the information, the audience is imaginary as well as stereotype.

They need to shape their information accordingly. Not just the audience, but they also have to base their ideas on a conceptual of presumed thought.

Technology The next feature of mass communication is the use of specialised technologies. For example, the internet profoundly affects the one way system of communication. The specialised technologies have also made transfer of messages in their physical forms with the means of photographs, films, tape recordings, etc. Such ways of storing information has also led to historical durability.

Scale The next characteristic is that the mass media messages are capable of extending itself globally. Selling of the syndicated rights to the world media helps the media institutions to gain profit.

Commodity The above characteristics have led to the emergence of media as a modern commodity or an industry. Thus, it is highly influenced by the market forces. Media, thus have become the centre of life both socially and culturally.

Functions of Mass Media

Mass media undertakes several functions in a societal set-up. Some of these are given below :

Providing Information The most important and foremost role of mass media is to provide information about different aspects of human life. For example, education, government policies, programme summits and so on. Its main function in a democratic country is to create awareness among the masses. Thus, mass media plays a great role in this respect.

Providing Entertainment Mass media plays an important role in providing entertainment on a larger extent. Open as movies, stories (published), music, videos, photographs, internet, podcasts are used by the media to entertain and enthrall audience. Mass media is a great source for the audiences, seeking the emotional release.

Socialising People Mass media connects people in the world. Through mass media, the world has become a 'Global Village'. Now, people can share their thoughts, opinions and views freely on social networking sites, like Twitter, Whatsapp, Facebook and so on.

Work as Responsible Source Mass media works as a responsible source in the society. The media keeps watch on the government and others in power. Local news stations often have a segment in which they investigate problems for people. Entire, hour long news shows are devoted to exposes, which are stories designed to expose wrong doings. Government officials, who engage in bad behaviour know that, they will be on every news show and newspaper in the country, if they are caught.

Providing Political Forum The media also provides a forum to the political leaders belonging to different parties and ideologies. This function of the media becomes very active and important at the time of campaigns during elections.

In this, candidates belonging to various parties often broadcast advertisements and debates on television. It is only through these mediums that voters learn about the candidates as well as the issues raised by them.

Being the Common Carrier Mass media plays a great role in exchanging news and information as well. Media acts in a dual manner. On one side, the people learn about the policies and ideologies of the government; while on the other side, media also helps in informing the government about what people really want.

Effects of Mass Media

The effects of mass media can be seen through the following points :

Positive Effects

- Mass media informs the public about government policies and programmes and how these programmes can be useful to them. This helps the people voice their feelings and helps the government to make necessary changes in their policies or programmes.
- It can bring in positive social changes.
- It can entertain people.
- It can act as an agent of change in development.
- It can help the political and democratic processes of a country.
- It has brought people of the world closer to each other.
- It can educate the public and promote trade and industry through advertisements.

Negative Effects

- The traditional culture of country is adversely affected by mass media.
- Entertainment has become the main component of mass media. This affects the primary objectives of media to inform and educate people.
- Mass media promotes violence. Studies have proved that violence shown on television and cinema, have negative effects on children.
- It also promotes the desire in people to buy and own products that are advertised through the media, but which may not be essential for them.

Social Marketing and Communication

Social marketing objective is to influence the social behaviours but not to benefit the marketer, but to benefit the target market and the society.

While demarketing is an effort aimed at discouraging the consumer to demand the product which a firm cannot produce in available product, or does not want to provide in a certain places where the cost of distribution is high and allow only a too little profit.

Therefore, in the following section, it will discuss the importance of social marketing and demarketing to the current environment.

Develop a Strategic Vision The first point in the list of importance of marketing communication is that it helps the management of the company and marketing managers develop a strategic vision about leveraging on the various marketing opportunities and platforms and device the plans that make the company come up with the new and innovative methods to promote the offerings to the customers.

Create Brand Awareness The concept of branding is totally related to the promoting of the objectives and vision of the brand and company as a whole. But understanding the importance of marketing communication helps in the creating and providing the required impetus to the brand awareness in an indirect manner.

As the strategy and the creative artworks of the marketing communication starts with leverages on the strong legacy of the brand followed by the features and unique selling propositions of the products and services.

Enlightens the Investor Community Its continuation to the above point and harping on the importance of marketing communication, yet another benefit to the company is that it enlightens the investor community about the strengths core values, fundamentals, visions, approaches and objectives of the company along with its competitive advantages, unique selling propositions and the features and attributes of the products and services offered to the target market.

Boosts Profits As the thumb rule of business strategy states that the marketing and sales department work as the backbone of each other and when they both join forces, the profit of the company are on an all-time high owing to the increased sales and market share as compared to the competitors in the market as the marketing communication in the market as the marketing communication is strategic, innovative and creative in nature plus is well aligned with the overall business objectives of the company.

Come Up With Innovative Marketing and Promotional Ideas Understanding the importance of marketing communication helps the management and the marketing department to try and come up with the innovative marketing and promotional ideas that do not only convey the brand messages in an inventive fashion, but also gives the brand edge to creativity as compared to their competitors in the market.

Need and Importance of Communication in Development

Initially communication for development was vertical, one-way and top-down in its approach. Feedback was not only delayed but also not necessary, as people's views were not considered.

But today communication is circular and participatory. So, its need and importance are increasing day-by-day.

Human Empowerment To empower is to give somebody more control over his/her own life or the situation he/she finds himself/herself. Empowerment liberates and, therefore, gives people the access to the resources for which they had no access.

Consensus Building Human society is so heterogeneous and varied that no single issue of public importance goes without eliciting divergent views and arguments. Development projects as an all important aspect of human life always generate this different views and opinions in the society.

Capacity Building Capacity building means creating locally the human capital needed for the development of a particular society. One major way of achieving this is through education and training.

Transmission of Culture Culture as people's way of life cannot be useful to be development if the norms, values, local wisdom, technology, etc., cannot be transferred from one generation to the other.

This is called "cultural transmission". Communication plays a very important role in this transmission. Cultural and traditional wisdom is usually communicated verbally and non-verbally from one generation to another.

Journalism in Developmental Communication

According to **Wilbur Schramn**, "the role of media in development can be divided into three parts."

To Inform 'Information is power'. For the development of the society, correct social, political and economic influence is very important. Media helps the people to be aware about and develop a consensus upon important national and international development issues. It also helps them understand the various obstacles in the process of development.

To Instruct Mass literacy is an essential criteria to development. This is possible by imbibing basic skills among the people . Mass media plays an important role in this. Mass media can instruct people and educate them. Projects like SITE and Gyan Darshan are few such examples where media is used to instruct people, educate them and teach them basic skills. These basic skills help people to develop their standard of living.

To Participate All development activities are based primarily on people's participation. Voluntary and continuous participation of the citizen of the country is necessary for continued development. Debate and discussions help people to know about the current issues, participate in development programme and bring about a change in the society. Schramn has laid a lot of emphasis on Content, Feedback and Multiplier effect of mass media while discussing the role of mass media in development.

Writing for Development

Written communication involves any type of interaction that makes use of the written word. Communicating through writing is essential in the modern world and is becoming ever more so as we participate in what is now commonly called the information age. Its various ways of contribution to development are given below :

Print Media

Print media is one of the oldest and basic forms of communication. It includes newspapers, weeklies, magazines, monthlies, banners and graphics, posters and other forms of printed material. The contribution of print media in providing information is remarkable. Even after the advent of electronic media, the print media has not lost its charm or relevance. Print media has the advantage of making a longer impact on the minds of the reader, with more in-depth reporting and analysis. Magazines and newspapers are the dominant traditional print media used in advertising. Brochures, flyers and other collateral pieces also are sometimes referred to as print collateral.

Radio

This is a good source of communication of ideas to the rural people especially in a country like India. It carries news bulletins and special programmes for rural people, house wives and children. It is a good source of dissemination of agricultural information to farmers.

All India Radio broadcasts in all major Indian language and even in dialects. It can become a true local mass medium with locally relevant news on health, farming, trading and other news of day-to-day household value. Radio is a spoken means of communication.

The broadcaster has to get and hold the attention of the audience, otherwise the message is lost. Radio is a very fast medium. It is popular, pleasing, even exciting. However, it cannot be used to convey heavy, detailed knowledge. It can be used for announcement of meetings, demonstrations, etc. Radio can reach more people more quickly than any other means of communication. It can disseminate timely and urgent information and is relatively cheap.

It can reach illiterates and builds enthusiasm and maintains interest. Some severe limitations to the use of radio are: broadcasting facilities are available only in limited places, recorded time assigned to extension is limited, frequently losses out in competition with entertainment, difficult to check on results, requires a special technique, not enough sets in rural areas and influence is limited to people, who can listen intelligently.

Television

It is one of the most popular method of communication. It attracts the number of audience or group of people at a time. These groups of people may be literate or illiterate and people from different socio-economic groups.

It is an audio-visual medium, brings us into contact with events in an exciting and clarifying way. It stimulates and reinforces ideas, beliefs and thoughts. It has more flexibility and mobility in its coverage due to audio-visual presentation.

Television not only informs and educates, but also inspires and motivates. The moving images of television catch the attention of the viewers. Television can transmit not only words, but pictures as well.

The significance of TV as a medium of mass communication has universally been realised and recognised. Television is described as a powerful medium by many people, but effectiveness of television may depend on many factors like infrastructure practicability of recommendations and follow up the programmes.

Internet

The process of networking is said to be done by Internet. It works through the telephone lines that are installed at various places in the world through which the two computers get connected with each other. At present, any type of information and research can be obtained through Internet.

Importance of Internet

The importance of Internet are as follows :

- It is a major centre of business. Items are sold and brought by 'internet'. Information about the stock market is known through Internet.
- Money is bought through Internet to buy goods.
- Today, all the functions of the bank are being done by computer. Major banking companies are also providing withdrawal and payment facilities through Internet.
- As a result, large transactions are taking place through the Internet. It has amazing power and ability to connect and contact people easily.

Internet Communication Platforms

Some of the popular communication platforms on the internet are :

Facebook It is an American online social media which was launched on 4th February, 2004, by Mark Zuckerberg. It is operated by Facebook Inc which is based in Menlo Park, California. Facebook can be accessed from devices with Internet connectivity.

To become a facebook user one has to create an account on facebook and after registering users may join common-interest user groups organised by workplace, school hobbies and so on. It can also be used by companies for advertising their products.

Instagram It is a social networking service where people can create their accounts and can share their photos and videos. It was launched by **Kevin Systrom** and **Mike Krieger** in 2010. It is owned by Facebook Inc. company.

Twitter It is an American online news and social networking service which can be used by any person by creating an account. Twitter was created in March 2006 by **Jack Dorsey, Noah Glass, Biz Stone and Evan Williams**. On this social networking site users can post and interact with messages known as 'tweets'. Before 2017 tweets were restricted to 140 characters, but from November 2017, this limit was doubled for all languages except Chinese, Japanese and Korean.

YouTube YouTube, LLC is a video-sharing website where anyone can upload, view rate and share, add to favourites, report, comment on videos and subscribe to other users. It was created by Chad Hurley, Steve Chen and Jawed Karim in 2005. The headquarters of YouTube is in San Bruno, California, America. In 2006, Google bought this site.

Whatsapp Whatsapp was founded by Jan Koum and Brian Acton in 2009. It is a freeware and cross-platform messaging application which can be accessed by anyone who has a smartphone. It is an alternative to SMS. It is owned by Facebook. The users of Whatsapp can send text messages, voice calls, video calls, images, documents and user location to each other.

Blog It is the short form of 'Weblog' which was coined by **Jorn Barger** on 17th December, 1997. The term 'Blog' was coined by Peter Merholz in 1999. Initially, some online journals were published which consisted of links of news, other information and about the details of bloggers.

These were known as 'Blogs' and the writers who used to write these blogs were known as 'Bloggers.' Gradually, blogs became popular but to write these blogs, bloggers needed to have knowledge about the computer programming languages like HTML language.

But after seeing possibilities some websites provided free and easy equipments to write these blogs where bloggers did not need to know about the computer programming languages. Blogs can be written about any aspect of life and in any language of the world. Blog became more famous from the time when an American soldier wrote about his experience during the war when America attacked on Afghanistan.

EXAM BASED QUESTIONS

1 What is the major concern of developmental communication?
(a) Development of social media
(b) Development of human beings and society
(c) Development of communication network
(d) Reduction in unemployment and poverty

2 Which among the following is/are the best tool(s) for development of communication?
(a) Television (b) Radio
(c) Both (a) and (b) (d) Neither (a) nor (b)

3 What is the aim of developmental communication?
(a) To change human life
(b) To enhance the personality of a person
(c) To preserve the environment
(d) To create new ideas and technology

4 Which era marked as the development of communication technology?
(a) 1950's (b) Early 1970s
(c) 1990's (d) 21st Century

5 Who said that, "Developmental communication seeks to accelerate social changes and reduce poverty"?
(a) Naura Charles (b) Steven Cubell
(c) Naura C-Cubell (d) None of these

6 What is defined as Gelcote and Steve Theory of Communication?
(a) Communication is an environmental ethical issue.
(b) Communication is a form of liberal development.
(c) Communication is strategic in nature.
(d) Communication is the way of enhancing marketing.

7 What are the two primary role of development communication?
(a) Transforming role (b) Socialising role
(c) Only (a) (d) Both (a) and (b)

8 What is the key feature of transforming role?
(a) It helps in the development of the child.
(b) It transforms the personality of the person.
(c) It inspires the higher quality of life.
(d) It keeps in the interest of the person.

9 What is the other name of extension approach?
(a) Diffusion (b) Intention
(c) Infusion (d) Interaction

10 How diffusion approach contribute to the development?
(a) Diffusion of cultures are important
(b) Diffusion of material and social innovation
(c) Diffusion of developmental theories
(d) Diffusion of communication structure

11 Which model is called as the "paradigm of developed nations"?
(a) Capitalist model (b) Mixed model
(c) Social model (d) Democratic model

12 Which model is seen in the communist country?
(a) Capitalist model (b) Socialist model
(c) Mixed model (d) None of these

13 What are the three coordinates of mixed model?
(a) Public, private and social
(b) Market, social and religion
(c) Market, public and private
(d) None of the above

14 Which plan shows the mixed model in India?
(a) Swaach Bharat Yojana (b) Five Year Plan
(c) Planning Commission (d) All of these

15 Which among the following is not the development indication?
(a) Sex ratio (b) Marriage ratio
(c) National language (d) Per Capital Income

16 What is/are the factor(s) that indicate(s) the growth and development of any country?
(a) Economic (b) Social
(c) Education (d) All of these

17 Which Index is most important for measuring growth of a country?
(a) Human Development Index
(b) Technological Achievement Index
(c) Growth Index
(d) Achievement Index

18 Which among the following are the key elements of diffusion?
(a) Invention, communication, innovation, and time
(b) Innovation, diffusion, production and communication
(c) Communication, planning, ploting and time
(d) Innovation, communication, time and social system

19 What is/are involved in the diffusion process?
(a) Spontaneous spread of new ideas
(b) Planned method of propagating a new idea
(c) Only (a)
(d) Both (a) and (b)

20 What is said to be innovation?
(a) Innovation is developing something new by discovery or through adoptation.
(b) Innovation is giving away the technological idea.
(c) Innovation is the change in knowledge.
(d) None of the above.

21 What is/are the main characteristic(s) of innovation?
(a) Compatibility (b) Complexity
(c) Observability (d) All of these

22 **Media is known as**
(a) first estate (b) second estate
(c) third estate (d) fourth estate

23 **Who said that "Media is the mechanism of change of society"?**
(a) Rashmi Bohra (b) Denis McQuail
(c) RK Majumdar (d) None of these

24 **Which of the following clearly defines the function of mass media?**
(a) Providing information
(b) Work as a responsible source
(c) Providing a political forum
(d) All of the above

25 **Which of the following is/are type(s) of social media?**
(a) Instagram (b) Blog (c) You Tube (d) All of these

26 **Facebook was launched in which year?**
(a) 1972 (b) 1980 (c) 1999 (d) 2004

27 **Instagram was launched in**
(a) 2001 (b) 2010 (c) 2005 (d) 2013

28 **Which of the following is/are true about mass media?**
(a) It can act as an agent of change in development.
(b) It has brought people of the world closer to each other.
(c) It can bring in positive social changes.
(d) All of the above

29 **Which of the following statements is/are correct?**
(a) TV and Radio entertain and inform people
(b) TV and Radio are used by the government to project mostly their point of view and build public relations
(c) Illiterates follow, what they see or listen on TV or Radio
(d) All of the above

30 **Media have a role and a function in society, which could be**
(a) maintain the consensus (b) reinforce
(c) stabilise (d) All of these

31 **Radio experiments in the use of radio for promoting literacy and education was conducted as early as**
(a)1930s (b) 1940s (c) 1900s (d) 1920s

32 **Which of the following statement(s) is/are correct?**
(a) Radio is a useful tool for extension work in rural areas.
(b) Radiò is a device with whole mass can be contacted at a time, efficiently and economically.
(c) Evening time is the best time for broadcasts for the rural people.
(d) All of the above

33 **Which of the following statements is/are correct?**
(a) Radio provides the communicator with the opportunity to reach local communities and audiences segmented by age.
(b) Radio is low cost medium.
(c) Posters are miniature bill-board whose main advantages are lower cost and greater flexibility of placement.
(d) All of the above

34 **Which among the following is most important for social marketing?**
(a) Development of strategic vision
(b) Creating brand awareness
(c) Promoting brand
(d) Fund raising

35 **Why branding is important for a company?**
(a) Providing financial assets to the company
(b) Promoting the objective and vision of a company
(c) Promoting competitive environment
(d) Informing about company USP

36 **What is the role of journalism?**
(a) To create (b) To develop
(c) To produce (d) To instruct

37 **According to Journalism, what is said about information?**
(a) Information is creativity
(b) Information is power
(c) Information is development
(d) Information is transforming

38 **Which projects market as the instructors for communication development?**
(a) SITE (b) Gyan Darshan
(c) Both (a) and (c) (d) Both (a) and (b)

39 **What is most necessary aspect of development?**
(a) Innovation (b) Diffusion
(c) Participation (d) Mass media

40 **Match the following.**

List I	List II
A. Slide	1. Non-projected visual aid
B. Radio	2. Projected audio-visual aid
C. Chart	3. Audio aid
D. Video	4. Projected visual aid

Codes

	A	B	C	D		A	B	C	D
(a)	4	3	1	2	(b)	4	1	2	3
(c)	1	3	2	4	(d)	3	4	1	2

41 **Match the following.**

List I	List II
A. The role of communication	1. It is a link between experts, scientists, bureaucrats and receiver at grassroot level
B. Development communication	2. It is mediator between the technical experts and their target groups
C. Aim at creating environment for transactional communication and constructive interaction	3. Wilber Schramm
D. Mass media has potential to inform	4. Development communicator
E. Mass media	5. Agent of social change

Codes

	A	B	C	D	E		A	B	C	D	E
(a)	4	3	1	5	2	(b)	5	4	3	2	1
(c)	2	1	4	3	5	(d)	5	1	2	3	4

42 Which of the following are the objectives of mass media?
1. To provide information
2. To convey cultural and educational programme
3. To entertain people
4. To establish social contact and linkage

Codes
(a) 1 and 2 (b) 2, 3 and 4
(c) 2 and 3 (d) All of these

43 In forming his attitude, the individual evaluates the innovation in some identifiable characteristics like
1. relative advantage
2. compatibility, complexity
3. trial use potential
4. observability

Select the correct answer using the codes given below
(a) 1, 2 and 3 (b) 1, 2, 3 and 4
(c) 1 and 4 (d) 1 and 2

44 Those who recognise an innovation early show the characteristics.
1. Higher social status.
2. Greater exposure to mass media, exposure to inter-personal channels of communication.
3. Greater social participation.
4. More cosmopolitan.

Select the correct answer using the codes given below
(a) 1 and 2 (b) 1 and 4
(c) 1, 2 and 3 (d) All of these

45 Which approaches are good in communicating messages to the community?
1. Participatory approach
2. Training and visit approach
3. Commodity specialised approach
4. Direct approach by the community

Select the correct answer using the codes given below
(a) 1, 2 and 3 (b) 1, 2 and 4 (c) 1 and 4 (d) 2, 3 and 4

46 Development supporting communication focuses on grassroot level development and participation using small media like
1. flashcards, slides 2. video, falk media
3. personal contacts 4. meetings

Select the correct answer using the codes given below
(a) 1, 2 and 3 (b) 1, 2, 3 and 4
(c) 1 and 4 (d) 2 and 4

47 Consider the following statements
1. Harold Lasswell Model is most effective communication model that identifies the sources message, content, channel, audience., etc.
2. Professor BC Roy was the author of "Communication and Social Development of India."

Which of the statements given above is/are correct?
(a) Only 1 (b) Only 2
(b) Both 1 and 2 (d) None of these

48 The degree to which the result of an innovation are visible to others.
1. Observability 2. Communicability
3. Trial 4. Complexity

Select the correct answer using the codes given below
(a) 1 and 4 (b) 1 and 2 (c) 3 and 4 (d) 2 and 4

49 Radio is a means of........ the material for other audio-visual aids.
1. correcting 2. modernising
3. supplementing 4. vitalising

Codes
(a) 1 and 2 (b) 2 and 4
(c) 1, 3 and 4 (d) All of these

50 Which of the following are applicable to mass communication?
1. Indirect 2. Impersonal
3. One way
4. Lack means of immediate feedback

Select the correct answer using the codes given below
(a) 1, 2, 3 and 4 (b) 1, 2 and 3
(c) 1, 3 and 4 (d) 2 and 4

51 Which two approaches are good in communication messages to the community?
1. Participatory Approach
2. Training and Visit Approach
3. Commodity Specialised Approach
4. Direct approach by the community

Select the correct answer using the codes given below
(a) 1 and 2 (b) 2 and 4
(c) 1 and 4 (d) 3 and 4

52 Television is medium with its own psychological and emotional appeal and able to transcend barriers of
1. time 2. place
3. discipline 4. personalities

Select the correct answer using the codes given below
(a) 1, 2, 3 and 4 (b) 1, 2 and 4
(c) 1 and 2 (d) 2 and 4

53 The group which are taken into account for communication are
1. cultural groups 2. social groups
3. family groups 4. reference groups

Select the correct answer using the codes given below
(a) 1 and 2 (b) 1 and 4
(c) 1, 2 and 3 (d) All of these

54 Arrange the sequence of the given media of communication by the years they were started.
1. Televisioin 2. Radio
3. Films 4. Print

Codes
(a) 4, 3, 2, 1 (b) 3, 4, 1, 2
(c) 2, 3, 4, 1 (d) 1, 2, 3, 4

55 Which are used for mass contact methods?

1. Personal calls
2. Circular letter
3. Radio and television
4. Tours

Select the correct answer using the codes given below

(a) 1, 2 and 3 (b) 2, 3 and 4
(c) 2 and 3 (d) 1 and 4

56 Match the following.

List I	List II
A. Jargon of communication	1. Communication skills
B. Sender, Message, Receiver	2. Types of communication
C. Abilities to encode and decode message	3. Barrier to communication
D. Verbal and non-verbal	4. Elements of communication process

Codes

	A	B	C	D		A	B	C	D
(a)	3	4	1	2	(b)	2	4	3	1
(c)	1	2	3	4	(d)	4	3	2	1

57 Match the following.

List I	List II
A. Objective of communication	1. Clear in mind of the speaker
B. Idea	2. Coordination
C. Dialogue	3. Movement of arts
D. Non-verbal communication	4. Backbone of communication

Codes

	A	B	C	D		A	B	C	D
(a)	1	2	3	4	(b)	3	4	1	2
(c)	2	1	4	3	(d)	1	2	4	3

58 Match the following.

List I	List II
A. Verbal communication	1. Communication between Friends
B. Human relation	2. Mass media
C. Agents of modernisation	3. Objective of communication
D. Small group communication	4. Writing

Codes

	A	B	C	D		A	B	C	D
(a)	4	1	2	3	(b)	2	1	4	3
(c)	1	2	4	3	(d)	1	2	3	4

Directions (Q. No. 59-64) *In the questions given below are two statements labelled as Assertion (A) and Reason (R). In the context of the two statements, which one of the following is correct?*

Codes

(a) Both A and R are true and R is the correct explanation of A.
(b) Both A and R are true, but R is not the correct explanation of A.
(c) A is true, but R is false.
(d) A is false, but R is true.

59 **Assertion** (A) Most of the poor countries are agricultural and their impact is yet to be felt on the socio-economic life of the people.

Reason (R) The occupational pattern of the country affects the economic development.

60 **Assertion** (A) Development communication refers to the use of communication for future development.

Reason (R) It is an information technology based on modern method of communication with wide networking.

61 **Assertion** (A) The process of networking is done by Internet.

Reason (R) Internet is able to connect two computers.

62 **Assertion** (A) Communication plays a vital role in building nation.

Reason (R) Development and communication are concerned with human and society.

63 **Assertion** (A) Transformation takes place in development communication.

Reason (R) This works as an instrument for a change.

64 **Assertion** (A) Development can be measured through indicators.

Reason (R) Measurement indicators are Gender Inequality, Index, Human Development Index.

Directions (Q. Nos. 65-69) *Read the passage and answer the following questions.*

In New Media Arts, Minimalism is a way of expressing an idea and is an inescapable theme in modem day social concerns as well as art. As its name suggests, Minimalism means using limited material to create a desired effect.

A minimalist artist will typically use a limited palette of colours and have a simplified geometric design, as in the works of David Smith, which can be seen at the Gagosian Gallery in New York City. Minimalist sculpture on the other hand is greatly focused on the materials.

While many claim that Minimalism is a movement specific to geometric representations, it extends in the modern day far outside this relatively narrow constraint. The Influences of Minimalism are deep and meaningful. "It is not necessary for a work to have lots of things to look at, to compare, to analyse, one by one and to contemplate. The thing as a whole and its qualities as a whole is what is interesting."

What philosophical and social implications does Minimalism have in the 21st century? It would be necessary to see where it originates.

The term itself now common parlance, first appeared in the New York of 1929 when David Burlyuk used it in a catalogue for an exhibition at the Dudensing Gallery of John Graham's paintings as described on the Worldwide Art Resources web page Art History: Minimalism, but was largely unheard outside the small world of art and design circles until the late 20th century. Even today, its definition is difficult as it covers such diverse genres.

Minimalism still exists despite the fact that it is pronounced dead from time to time. Kyle Gann in 1998 for instance declared that the term, as far as music was concerned was confined to a particular American group of composers and that critics declared the movement to be dead by 1978. Gann explains how the minimalist music of composer, Philip Glass was condemned as being a dumbing down of music for a public incapable of understanding anything more complicated.

Minimalism is not only recognisable, but visible on many fronts. The style once considered to be subversive has over time become acceptable, in part because it is so widespread in society at all levels.

The word has become part of the modern day lingua franca, as mass culture has taken as its own what was once dismissed and seen only as a target for ridicule, from the repetition of 'broken-record music' to the bald simplicity of monochrome canvasses by artists, such as David Smith and monolithic sculptures, such as 'Accession II' by minimalist sculptor, Eva Hesse.

"Make it pure and simple" - this brief sentence could have served as the motto for Minimalism, an art movement that really began in the 1960s, although there were some earlier manifestations. The movement has been variously described as minimalist and ABC art.

The concept behind the movement was propounded by the critic, Clement Greenberg, who had a powerful influence over many of the artists and designers of his era. As early as 1939, although he does not use the term 'Minimalism' he stated, when describing modern abstract art: "The excitement of their art seems to lie most of all in its pure preoccupation with the invention and arrangement of spaces, surfaces, shapes, colours, etc., to the exclusion of whatever is not necessarily implicated in these factors." Greenberg urged artists to emphasise the 'objecthood' or actuality of their works whether a canvas in the case of a painter, or a cube in the case of a sculptor.

With Minimalism, the former gestural qualities and illusionism of art were no longer important. The emphasis was supposed to be on shape and materials, and these were to be as pure, plain and simple as possible.

65 The passage describes "Minimalism" as all of the following EXCEPT

1. an inescapabqle theme in modern day social concerns.
2. recognisable and visible on many fronts.

Select the correct answer using the codes given below

(a) Only 1 (b) Only 2
(c) Both 1 and 2 (d) Neither 1 nor 2

66 It can be reasonably inferred from the passage that regarding Minimalism, art critic, Clement Greenberg, felt

(a) skeptical about modern influences on the pure medium
(b) critical of the usage of unnecessary elements
(c) enthusiastic about the purity of the art form
(d) supportive of older artists willing to try a new art form

67 As it is used paragraph, the word 'parlance' most nearly means

1. jargon 2. knowledge 3. place

Select the correct answer using the codes given below

(a) 1 and 2 (b) 2 and 3
(c) Only (d) All of these

68 The main function of the first paragraph in this article is to

(a) demonstrate the sway Mimimalism had on David Smith's works at the Gagosian Gallery is New York city
(b) define Minimalism and introduce the concept of its far-reaching influence
(c) outline Minimalism's onset and progress through modern day media
(d) introduce the topic of Minimalism as an art form

69 In the passage, Brian Eno and Philip Glass were credited as advocating Minimalism through

(a) monochromatic canvases
(c) the crafts movement
(b) monolithic sculpture
(d) new age music

PREVIOUS YEARS' QUESTIONS

November 2017

1 Match the following approaches used in communication for development given in List I with their description given in List II.

List I	List II
A. Community Mobilisation	1. Two way communication
B. Interpersonal communication	2. To motivate partners and people
C. Social marketing	3. Ensures public opinion for a cause
D. Advocacy	4. Promotion of social goals
	5. Promotion of institutions

Codes

	A	B	C	D
(a)	3	1	4	5
(b)	2	1	4	3
(c)	4	1	5	2
(d)	3	1	5	2

2 Which one of the following is not a form of feedback in mass communication?

(a) Letter to the editor
(b) Live phone-ins
(c) News headlines
(d) TRPs

January 2017

3 Match the desirable qualities of the elements of communication given in List I with the name of the element given in List II.

List I	List II
A. Simplicity	1. Communicator
B. Empathy	2. Message
C. Penetration	3. Channel
D. Immediacy	4. Receiver
	5. Feedback

Codes

	A	B	C	D		A	B	C	D
(a)	3	2	4	5	(b)	3	1	4	5
(c)	2	3	1	5	(d)	2	1	3	5

4 **Assertion** (A) Mass communication is a transactional process.

Reason (R) In most of the mass communication situations, the communicator and the audience are in asynchronous relationship.

Codes

(a) A is correct, but R is incorrect
(b) A is incorrect, but R is correct
(c) Both A and R are correct
(d) Both A and R are incorrect

5 Arrange the first seven steps to develop a social marketing plan as given by Philip Kotler.

1. Conduct a situation analysis
2. Identify the competition and target market barriers
3. Develop a strategic marketing mix (4Ps)
4. Describe the plan background, purpose and focus'.
5. Set objectives and goals
6. Craft a desired positioning
7. Select target markets

Codes

(a) 1, 2, 3, 4, 5, 6, 7
(b) 1, 2, 5, 7, 3, 1, 4
(c) 4, 1, 5, 6, 7, 3, 2
(d) 1, 7, 5, 2, 6, 3, 4

June 2015

6 Effective development communication is influenced by which of the following factors?

1. Dissemination of information
2. Use of the information by users
3. Location of the users
4. Size of the audience

Select the correct answer using the codes given below

(a) 1 and 2 (b) 2 and 3
(c) 3 and 4 (d) 1 and 4

7 Development communication is

1. resource for development.
2. precursor for social change.
3. an approach for charity.
4. a component of Press Information Bureau.

Select the correct answer using the codes given below

(a) 2, 3 and 4 (b) 1, 2 and 3
(c) 1 and 2 (d) 1, 3 and 4

December 2015

8 Match the following.

List I (Communication Initiatives)	List II (Issues They Address)
A. Beti Bachao Andolan	1. Girl child education
B. Red Ribbon Express	2. Credit for micro-enterprises
C. Navdanya	3. Anti-domestic violence
D. Mudra Yojana	4. HIV/AIDS awareness
	5. Eco-feminism

Codes

	A	B	C	D
(a)	3	4	5	2
(b)	3	2	1	5
(c)	3	4	2	1
(d)	3	4	2	5

9 Match the following.

List I (Concepts used in Communication and Extension)	List II (Proponents)
A. Media are magic multipliers	1. Robert Chambers
B. Passing of traditional society	2. Wilbur Schramm
C. Participatory learning and action	3. Marshall McLuhan
D. World is a global village	4. Daniel Lerner
	5. Paul Leagans

Codes

	A	B	C	D		A	B	C	D
(a)	1	2	3	5	(b)	2	4	1	3
(c)	3	4	1	2	(d)	4	5	3	2

10 Public relations is a strategic communication process that

1. builds mutually beneficial relationship between the organisations and their public.
2. practices managing of the spread of information between an individual or an organisation and the public.
3. is an exclusive function of corporate organisations.
4. is not practised by government organisations.

Select the correct answer using the codes given below

(a) 1 and 4 (b) 2 and 4

(c) 2 and 3 (d) 1 and 2

ANSWERS

Exam Based Questions

1 (b)	2 (c)	3 (d)	4 (d)	5 (c)	6 (b)	7 (d)	8 (a)	9 (a)	10 (b)
11 (a)	12 (b)	13 (c)	14 (b)	15 (b)	16 (d)	17 (c)	18 (d)	19 (d)	20 (a)
21 (d)	22 (d)	23 (b)	24 (d)	25 (d)	26 (d)	27 (b)	28 (d)	29 (d)	30 (d)
31 (a)	32 (d)	33 (d)	34 (a)	35 (b)	36 (d)	37 (b)	38 (d)	39 (c)	40 (a)
41 (c)	42 (d)	43 (a)	44 (d)	45 (b)	46 (b)	47 (a)	48 (b)	49 (d)	50 (a)
51 (c)	52 (a)	53 (d)	54 (a)	55 (b)	56 (a)	57 (c)	58 (a)	59 (d)	60 (c)
61 (a)	62 (b)	63 (a)	64 (a)	65 (b)	66 (c)	67 (c)	68 (b)	69 (d)	

Previous Years' Questions

1 (b)	2 (c)	3 (d)	4 (b)	5 (d)	6 (a)	7 (c)	8 (a)	9 (a)	10 (d)

Concerns of Development Communication and Role of Media in Development

Communication can play important role in promoting human development. Communication skills and technology are vital to stimulate people's awareness, participation and capabilities, but at present are often underutilised. Policies are needed that encourage effective planning and implementation of communication programmes.

Development Communication

Development is the basis of social change, while communication is the basis of the pace of the development. There is an interrelation between communication and development. The information of business structure in people works to increase the speed of the communication.

According to **Dr. Dipankar**, "Plans for development are not as important as awareness among the important people, whose most effective medium is communication."

Developmental communication facilitates the social development. This is to improve the standard of living of all sections of farmers, women, youth, workers, etc. This type of communication is enhanced with the help of various ways of communication. Communication has an important role in the work being done for development.

The aim of development communication is to make people aware of development programs and to ensure their participation because the development process is meaningful only when the participation of people in it, is in the process of development communication.

There should be the participation of all i.e. poor, weak, women and other people of the society.

Concerns of Development Communication

The concerns or important issues of development communication have changed into a global village as a result of the current world communication revolution. Communication media has played an important role in the process of change. As the pace of human development is advancing, so are the means of communication.

Due to this role and responsibility, communication is also increasing continuously. Even today, gender, health, environment, sustainability, human rights, population, literacy, rural development and tribal development are important issues all over the world which need to be discussed and created in the society. Their description is given below :

Gender

Gender means the birth of a woman and man with specific genitals. The child is identified by its gender. When they show their feminity and masculinity it is called gender role. It is necessary to have special and specific mental qualities for any specific gender role.

Gender Inequality

The study of gender inequality has a become an international issue. Due to the rising inequality between men and women, it has taken social form.

Masculinity and feminity are the biological facts, if any inequality is combined with this fact, it is called gender inequality. Social identity of a person is based on gender.

This expectation is based on the idea that qualities, behaviours, traits, needs and roles are natural for men, while for women their gender identity and social roles as masculine and feminine in each society are determined through socialisation.

From 80s, the news of female exploitation began to find place in newspapers and TV channels. The meaning of domestic violence is no longer the violent activities going on inside the nation, but the exploitation of women is happening in homes.

It's been a long time, yet the female exploitation is same in the developed nations. According to UNESCO report in 2009, the women are still been shown by the media as a sex symbol, a strict administrator or a highly ambitious politician. This shows that 75 years more are required for the development.

All over the world it is common in the media to show about the women 'abuse.' The Delhi rape scandal created a stir throughout the country which is possible through media only. Incomplete, false news are captured in various media sources like Facebook, Youtube, etc.

Health

Health is a state of physical, mental and social well-being. Initially, health meant simply the ability of the body to function smoothly. A new concept of health came in the year 1980 where health is considered as an important resource for the development. Today, a person is healthy if he/she is enjoying good physical, mental, social, spiritual and cognitive health.

Today, maintaining good health is a big challenge because in the material age people are constantly living life as a race. In such a situation, development communication can play an important role to bring health awareness among the people. Academically, health communication is a discipline within communication studies. Health communication may variously seek to :

- A person who is physically unfit, cannot take care of the family. Similarly, if a person is facing mental stress and is unable to handle his feelings, he cannot build and promote good relationships with the family. And even lead an excessive human resource and human development.
- Communication can play a major role in keeping a person healthy and contribute well to the development of human resources. Through the means of communication, such as radio, television, newspapers, magazines, etc., people can be informed how to follow a healthy diet plan for good health.
- Information about exercise, meditation, etc, is given through development communication. Various health-related plans and programmes; such as National Health Scheme, Ayushman Bharat, Pradhan Mantri Swasthya Bima Yojana, etc. can be successful only when the importance of communication can reach to the common public.
- Under this, radio, television, newspapers and magazines are playing the leading role. Nowadays, people also share important things related to health awareness on social media. Today, yoga is playing the most important role in human good health. People watch and adopt live yoga programmes on television.

Environment

Communication and environment are interdependent relationships between humans and the environment. In fact, human is a part of nature and it is the responsibility of human beings for the welfare of nature and humanity.

Due to exploitation of nature global warming has become a global issue all over the world today. Collective efforts are needed to deal with its threat.

The role of communication/media is also very important in this context. Environmental protection plays a remarkable role in bringing a wider consciousness in environmental protection, environmental management, environmental awareness and environmental education.

The role of the public in the formulation and planning of environmental policies can be effective only if they are informed about environmental issues from time to time. Media/communication is expected to convey the environmental events, news and information on global, regional and national level to the public in such a way that they can analyse the facts and form their opinion.

Printed communication, electronic communication and traditional communication have important roles under communication in environmental protection.

Sustainability

Sustainable development is possible on.y through communication. Infact, communication is an important link between the apex national and international governments and organisations and the general public. Sustainable development is a process under which natural resources are consumed in such a way that not only the present needs of human beings are met, but also the needs of generations to come.

The emphasis is on protecting the natural environment and proper utilisation of resources. In fact, any activity that continues without harmonising with natural resources, ecology and environment results in unbalanced development.

Concept of Sustainability

The term'sustainable development' was first used in 1970 in the 'Cocoyok Declaration on Environment and Development'. According to the **Cocoyok Declaration,** "The process of development that provides optimal satisfaction without environmental destruction is sustainable development."

In the year 1985, a scholar named **Dassman** presented a model for the execution of economic development works under which ecological sustainability, basic need and self reliance should be taken as the basis of these three and progress of development works.

Report presented by the **World Commission on Environment and Development** (WCED) in the year 1987 says that "Sustainable development is development that meets the needs of the present without compromising the ability of future generations to meet their own needs."

Characteristics of Sustainability

The following are the characteristics of sustainable development :

- Emphasis on conservation of natural resources and development of capacity in society.
- Availability of equal economic, social and political opportunities for all individuals.
- Equality in resource utilisation, economic policies, technological development and population development, which will promote the possibilities of human development in the present and future.
- Development of production potential.
- Successful management of issue resources in order to satisfy the changing needs of humans.
- Conservation of natural resources and environmental quality.

Human Rights

It is the main function and responsibility of communication to deliver the right information to the general public at the right time so that they can make their own decisions and protect their human rights. Similarly, the National Human Rights Commission and the State Human Rights Commission and various organisations related to human rights also play their respective roles. These organisations take responsibility to play a real role in all their relationships with the public and with proper information.

Talking about the present context of human rights, the basic form of communication media comes as an advocate of human rights and its basic objective is to make people around the world aware of their rights. The media has tried to develop a new culture in the present context, which we can also call a culture of empowerment.

Today, due to communication tools/media, a lot of sensitive human rights issues have come up. In fact, development communication is very important to protect human rights.

Although, newspapers are mostly published in police custody and prison activities and deaths in the name of human rights abuses, human rights abuses are still not getting the space it deserves.

Sometimes, it is seen that the means of communication on the issue of human rights cause confusion in the society. Social media is also responsible for this to some extent.

Today, electronic media remains a matter of concern for human rights news than newspapers. The scope of human rights is very wide. Even today, people with communication / media do not have detailed information about it.

Population

The famous economist **Malthus** has written that it cannot be possible to increase production at the speed at which the flow of population increases, so it is the duty of all people not to allow unnecessary population growth in their society.

According to **S. Chandrasekhar**, "India's prosperity will depend on slowing down the pace of increasing population." Indeed, population growth remains a major challenge for the economy and society today. Therefore, it needs to be controlled in which communication is playing the most important role.

In fact, either the resources should be generated according to the population or otherwise the population should be limited according to the means. It is necessary to balance the two.

If the population is unbalanced and the population grows in comparison to resources, its reward is visible in the form of sickness, premature death, poverty, unemployment, crime and illiteracy, which affect the socio-economic development of the country.

According to the World Population Prospects of the United Nations, in 2027, India will overtake China to become the world's largest populous country.

According to the 2011 census, India's population is about 121.05 crore, of which the male population is 51.47% and female population 48.53%. Even today, India is struggling with challenges like infant sex ratio and maternal mortality. In this context, literacy and awareness campaigns need to be conducted in which communication can play a leading role.

Literacy

If the media continues to strive to connect the general public with literacy, then the pace of development of the country will accelerate. India is a country of villages. Here, illiteracy is a major problem, because of this problem there are many other problems such as population growth, unemployment and disease causes epidemics, pollution, stress, adultery, etc.

The rural population, who are under the curse of illiteracy, are wandering in the darkness of ignorance. They are victims of social, economic and political exploitation, which is bound to block their cultural progress and spiritual progress. Illiteracy leads to loss of total production and increased dependence on others.

According to **Mahatma Gandhi**, "The illiteracy of crores of people is a stigma and a curse for India." According to the 2011 census, the literacy rate in India is 73%, of which rural literacy is 67.8% and urban literacy is 84. 1%, male literacy is 80.9% across India, while female literacy is 64.6%. This data suggests that rural literacy and female literacy are still low today, which needs to be increased. Communication is playing an important role. Radio and television also increased in rural areas. They have been successful to a great extent in changing the mindset of the common man. Electronic communication has revolutionised.

Now, the focus of people is towards literacy and rural development, literacy and unemployment, literacy and environment and literacy and agriculture has started to be known, through the medium of letters, magazines and common media. People are beginning to understand the importance of literacy.

Today, due to awareness of communication and literacy in agricultural production developed. We protect ourselves by being alert from the prior notice of floods and storms.

Control over social ugliness has also started. Electronic communication is also very useful for housewives. From the care of pregnant women to the upbringing of children, all the information is found sitting at home. The benefits of cleaning, cooking and keeping it covered are conveyed. There is also another aspect of the role of communication in literacy. Electronic media creates a fascination for young men and women in the glare of cities. Modern fashion gets a boost. Inflammation advertisements are given to create attraction among consumers.

Due to some effects, we should not be indifferent to the benefits of communication, we must keep the common people literate and aware through the medium of communication. In this context, a channel 'Doordarshan' can be ensured for literacy.

Various literacy related programmes, such as Saakshar Bharat Programme, Prime Minister Rural Digital Literacy Campaign, Right to Education, etc., have been implemented.

Communication has the most important role in the success of all because communication is a link between the government and the general public, which creates awareness among the people.

Rural and Tribal Development

Communication media has created many programs for the development of rural and tribal areas. Infact, the communication medium connecting the city and the village plays an important role. Many serials are made in such a way, which are still associated with rural and tribal surroundings and culture.

In this, social issues are raised, educational programs are made in relation to the political process. Awareness is also created by making election programmes. Development communication also brings out many problems of rural and tribal society.

But, there is still a need to take the communication to a remote village. Right now, much improvement and communication is needed in the field of agriculture. Rapid development is not possible without communicating technologies.

In 1975, the Kheda Communication Project surveyed several villages. Similarly, reader survey is also done in cities and villages.

Operation Research has a wider role in this. Now, India too is changing fast and communication/media has to put its picture in front of the whole world. The role of mass media has greatly increased, especially in the field of television and it is working through many projects in the fields of agriculture, health, entertainment, education, development and information.

In this regard, there are many programmes like Integrated Rural Development Programme, National Employment Programme, Rural Landless Employment Guarantee Programme, etc.

Advocacy in Communication

Advocacy means to communicate effectively, it emphasises the interests, desires, needs and rights of any one initiative, policy, programme or individual or group. Advocacy is needed at all national, state, district and local community levels for spreading awareness and proper implementation of policy.

Facilitative support activities can take place in a variety of ways and may include interaction among individuals, meeting, workshop, media campaign, public interaction, etc.

A good advocator side supporter has the following qualities :

- He should know enough about the relevant field or issue.
- The party supporter should have sufficient knowledge about the system of campaign and in the socio-cultural environment.
- He should understand the nature and need of the target audience.
- The program motivates the target audience to participate in the discussion.
- Listen carefully to the problem of the targeted people.
- The supporter should not become aggressive and critical. He should always be positive and humble.

Importance of Advocacy

Advocacy is very important, as it can affect the following points :

- Formulation of policies and methods by the government.
- Consideration of the impact of their activities by business and other organisations.
- To support the preparation of options for their interest by individuals, groups and communities.
- Initiating differences by individuals and communities for the promotion of their interests.
- It can be used to highlight problems and gaps in a particular service.

Steps for Planning the Advocacy Campaign

Advocacy is a process of a dynamic and multi-faceted nature. Party support works as a guide which can be used for awareness generation. The following are the steps in planning a party support campaign :

- Identifying the party support issue
- Collecting information / analysing the situation
- Identifying goals, impacts and resources
- Message creation
- Building support and working with partners
- Real and effective implementation / action planning
- To inspect and evaluate
- Setting goals and objectives

Strengthening Advocacy Using Media / Communication

- Supporting TV channels, print media, audio and video channels and internet, magazines / journals to form a strong alliance for supporting social issues.
- Making media campaign an integral part of editorial policy. Apart from this, to make the reporters regularly sensitive to social issues like HIV / AIDS, drug abuse and the status of women in internal meetings.
- Updates on need, status, awareness, availability, accessibility, quality of service delivery and community participation in programmes such as Beti Bachao, Beti Padhao, Jago Grahak Jago, Pulse Polio, etc., in print media, TV and radio (especially, FM radio based in cities), starting a weekly column with information.
- Using brand ambassadors to highlight the issue for better impact and coverage. Strengthening of side support campaigns can also be done through ICT based training. This can be done using traditional and new communication.

Behaviour Change due to Communication

Behaviour change communication is a means to understand the desired change in the behaviour of a target group and brings about a change in behaviour which serves as a link between the two. With the knowledge and skills gained through behaviour change communication programs, students can directly connect with the government's major programs related to health, nutrition, education and other fields. It is also beneficial for students and teachers, those looking for social work in the corporate sector, officers directly connected with civil services and the aspirants of these services, so that they can play an important role in bringing a change in the society.

Concept of Behavioural Change

Human behaviour is multi-dimensional and complex. Although some generalisations can be made, most individuals have their own different opinions about situations and even more, their own reactions. Apart from this, there are different types of individuals within the groups and each group is different from the other.

Considerable research has been done to understand and shed some light on the behaviour of individuals. Thus, the theories that have been formulated after research help to get a better insight about human behaviour and to form interactions that orient behaviour towards a positive direction.

Models of Behaviour Change

Individuals are the basic unit of behaviour change in behaviour change models. In this, individuals can be reached at any level whether they are in groups, in any organisation, community or nation. Proponents have an important role in human behaviour change. Important issues related to development are raised by them. For this, various means of communication are assisted by making pamphlets, booklets, videos and posters. Apart from this, the mass media is sent to the general public through the use of print and electronic media.

Health Confidence Model

In this model, we try to understand health behaviour in the context of individual decisions. The initial attempt is made. It is hereby proposed that any possibility of an individual adopting a prescribed health behaviour recurrence is the person's attitude of danger to his/her personal health and his/her belief that the proposed behaviour will reduce this risk. This model has been widely used in compliance studies in the context of health.

According to **Kirsch** and **Joseph** (1989), this model has four components i.e. personal hypersensitivity to negative health status, perceived severity of the situation, behavioural significance and action disruption. All of these combined create a situation where a person's readiness to act, i.e. by being helpful in situations, the work is started and the behaviour may change.

Rojnstok included (1974) has been presented to suggest that the necessary means expression (signal) to the occurrence of a job. Some people considered patience and self-capability as an important elements for behaviour change.

Theories of Behavioural Change

Behavioural change theories are attempts to explain why behaviours change. These theories cite environmental, personal and behavioural characteristics as the major factors in behavioural determination. Theories of change are more process-oriented and generally aimed at changing a given behaviour.

Thus, from this perspective, understanding and changing behaviour are two separate but complementary lines of scientific investigation :

Self-efficacy Self-efficacy is an individual's impression of their own ability to perform a demanding or challenging task such as facing an exam or undergoing surgery . This impression is based upon factors like the individual's prior success in the task or in related tasks, the individual's physiological state, and outside sources of persuasion.

Learning theories and behaviour analytic theories of change Behaviourists such as B F Skinner state that complex behaviour is learned gradually through the modification of simpler behaviours. Limitation and reinforcement play important roles in these theories, which state that individuals learn by duplicating behaviours they observe in others and that rewards are essential to ensuring the repetition of desirable bahaviour.

Social Learning and Social Cognitive Theory According to the social learning theory, behavioural change is determined by environmental, personal, and behavioural elements. Each factor affects each of the others. An individual's behaviour may change the environment as well as the way the individual thinks or feels. Social learning theory focuses on the reciprocal interactions between these factors, which are hypothesised to determine behavioural change.

Theory of Reasoned Action The Theory of Reasoned Action assumes that individuals consider a behaviour's consequences before performing the particular behaviour. As a result, intention is an important factor in determining behaviour and behavioural change.

Theory of Planned Behaviour It emphasises the role of intention in behaviour performance but is intended to cover cases in which a person is not in control of all factors affecting the actual performance of a behaviour. As a result, the new theory states that the incidence of actual behaviour performance is proportional to the amount of control an individual possesses over the behaviour and the strength of the individual's intention in performing the behaviour.

Trans-theoretical or stages of Change Model It states that there are five stages towards behaviour change. The five stages, between which individuals may transition before achieving complete change, are precontemplation, contemplation, preparation for action, action and maintenance.

Education Behavioural change theories can be used as guides in developing effective teaching method. Since the goal of education is behavioural change, the understanding of behaviour afforded by behavioural change theories provides insight into the formulation of effective teaching methods that tap into the mechanisms of behavioural change.

Criminology Empirical studies in criminology support behavioural change theories. At the same time, the general theories of behavioural change suggest possible explanations to criminal behaviour and methods of correcting deviant behaviour.

Energy Recent years have seen an increased interest in energy consumption reduction based on behavioural change, be it for reasons of climate change mitigation or energy security. The application of behavioural change theories in the field of energy consumption behaviour yields interesting insights.

Approaches, Applications and Challenges

Strategic approaches of advocacy and behaviour change communication are :

Advocacy Advocacy operates at the political, social and individual levels and works to mobilise resources and political and social commitment for social change or policy change. Resources can include political will and leadership as well as money to fund the implementation of policies or programs.

Advocacy aims to create an enabling environment at any level, including the community level to ask for greater resources, encourage allocating resources equitably and remove barriers to policy implementation.

Community-Based Media Community-based media reach communities through locally-established outlets. Such outlets include local radio stations and community newsletters/newspapers as well as activities such as rallies, public meetings etc.

Community Mobilisation Community mobilisation is a capacity-building process through which community individuals, groups or organisations plan, carry out and evaluate activities on a participatory and sustained basis to improve their lives, either on their own initiative or stimulated by others. A successful community mobilisation effort not only works to solve problems at the community level but also aims to increase the capacity of a community to successfully identify and address its own needs.

Counselling Counselling is based on one-to-one communication and is often done with a trusted and influential communicator such as a counsellor, teacher or health provider.

Distance Learning Distance learning provides a learning platform that does not require attendance at a specific location. Rather, the students access the course content either through a radio or via the internet and interact with their teacher and fellow classmates through letters, telephone calls, internet sites etc.

Information and Communication Technology ICT is the fastest growing and evolving approach, with an increasing reach throughout the world. This approach includes digital media such as web sites, e-mails, chat rooms, virtual learning and e Toolkits.

Interpersonal Communication (IPC)/ Peer Communi cation Interpersonal and peer communication are based on one-to-one communication. This could be parent-child communication, peer-to-peer communica- tion or communication with a community leader or religious leader.

Mass Media Mass media can reach large audiences effectively through the formats of radio, television and newspaper.

Social Mobilisation Social mobilisation brings relevant sectors such as organisations, policy makers, networks and communities together to raise awareness, empower individuals and groups for action, and work towards creating an enabling environment and effecting positive behaviour or social change.

Support Media/Mid-Media Mid-Media's reach is less than that of mass media and includes posters, brochures and billboards.

Applications of Advocacy and Behaviour Change Communication

Advocacy and behaviour change communication has proven effective in several health areas, such as increasing the use of family planning methods, reducing the spread of malaria and other infectious diseases, and improving newborn and maternal health.

Advocacy and behaviour change communication is an effective tool for dealing with many community and group related problems. It has been adopted as an effective strategy for community mobilisation, health and environment education and various public outreach programs.

Enhanced knowledge has facilitated the design of communications programs to reduce the risk of HIV transmission and AIDS. A wide variety of health promotion strategies use communication as either an educational or norm-forming strategy.

In addition, specific strategies must be designed for high-risk groups such as women, young people, injecting drug abusers, HIV positive groups.

Challenges of Advocacy and Behaviour Change and Communication

The use of persuasive mass communication techniques by public relations and advertising practitioners, rather than abating in influence as early theorists hoped because of more widespread education, is an increasing component of both private and government communication.

This implies social utility in addition to the negative connotations often attached to commercial propaganda. The whole topic of advocacy remains a volatile point of debate, particularly if one sees media playing less an agenda setting role than one as a legitimate target audience for institutional communicators seeking entry into the various constituencies making up the public mind.

In an information environment, persuasion serves a public interest when it assists social utility, but there has been no "Macro-ethical" consistency by practitioners.

The lack of a single common framework is ultimately influences the outcome of public policymaking and the reputation of public relations, as demonstrated by the challenges.

Traditional, Modern and New Media for Development

Media has played an important role in development and development communication. Role of traditional, modern and new media is discussed below :

Traditional Communication

Communication is an important mass media for development. It plays an important role in the development of human civilisation. It is a process in which one person exchange feelings and thoughts on the basis of reciprocity with another person. It is a double flow, which carries the communicator on one side and its message on the other, where one is recipient and other is its response. Traditional media has always been in vogue for development in India. Traditional means of communication include folk performances, drama, hymns, Ramlila, Krishnalila, Kirtan, Khel 'Tamasha' etc.

Religious and historical thoughts are the varied means of traditional means of communication. In this way, their relation is particularly related to the values and morals of human life. Therefore, they have a profound effect on the heart and mind of the people. This is the reason that these traditional media have played a very crucial role in development.

Modern Communication Tools

Modern tools are important means of communication for development. Modern communication mediums have played important roles in the development of India. Newspapers, computers, magazines, radio, television etc., are the modern communication mediums.

- At present, scientists have achieved amazing successes in the field of communication. After the invention of this, new dimensions are being established in this field everyday.
- The benefits of the use of e-mail or the benefits of it in the communication world have earned amazing successes. You can also setup contact in every corner of the world. The most important thing is that the cost involved in this is also very low.
- In addition, the fax machine will send the messages written on paper to the person sitting far away with the help of telephone lines. It can be sent in few seconds. E-mail can be considered an advanced form of fax only.
- To be connected to the media in some form or the other is becoming a necessity of modern human. Through mobile, radio, television, internet, etc. one wants to keep an eye on the news of the world all the time.

- Today, newspapers, magazines, radio and television have become the major and popular medium of mass media worldwide. Out of these, the spread of newspapers and magazines are the highest, but in the villages and remote areas, where there is no electricity even today, radio is the only medium of most popular for mass communication.
- Thus, media is influencing in every sphere of modern society. Even, it is fully capable of influencing the culture. Presently, due to media, the influence of Western culture is being seen on the Indian youth.

New Media for Development

New media has been a major contributor to the field of development. New media refers to the media that has developed in contemporary times. In this social media, mobile phones, etc., are included. The popularity of social media as a new form of media is growing fastly in present times. The increasing use of the Internet gave new media a new height. New media like Youtube, Blog, Facebook, News Portal and Twitter has waved its glory. Social media showed the courage to bring the news of the mainstream which was hidden by the media. Thus, the new media transcended the traditional and modern media to play an important role in development.

Various Communication Mediums

There is a development of various media from ancient to modern times which we have seen in India. Following is the description of some of communication mediums:

Traditional Folk Songs and Dances

This have been prevalent in India since immemorial time. Folk songs and dances are performed here on festivals, marriages and other special events. Nautanki, Swang, Kavian, Lavani, Bhand, Bhajan, Ramlila, Krishnalila, Qawwali, Sohar, Harikatha, Kirtan, Garba, Chaiti, Holi, Alha-Udal, Tamasha, Jhumar, Ghoomar, etc. are prominent among them. All these are still very popular today. Folk songs are sung and folk dances are performed by local people on occasions such as weddings, festivals, etc.

The greatest feature of traditional folk songs and dances is their connection to contemporary subjects. In this, not only religious and historical stories are presented, but social and economic conditions are also demonstrated. Various commentaries are also commented on the day to day events and family relations.

Through Sohar, Jhoomar and Ghoomar, the relationship of husband-wife, mother-in-law and sister-in-law, sister in law and brother-in-law, brother-in-law and daughter-in-law, etc., are exposed. Therefore, they are a good medium for moral education, they have a profound effect on the mind of the public.

Theatre

Theatre is a dramatic art of communication. Through theatre we experience something from our own world. Theatre is the medium of mass education as it can reach a wide segment of the society. It is capable of communicating information and increasing awareness about human rights, positive health issues to specific target audience. Actor or performer and audience are the primary and unique elements in theatre. According to **Brook**, "the only thing that all forms of theatre have in common is the need for audience". The sole purpose of communication is to influence people and persuade them into any particular way of thinking or acting. The persuasive function of communication is extremely important for inducing people into changing their behaviour in any particular desirable direction. Through repeated use of messages over long period of time theatre, can persuade its audience in the formation of certain attitudes and behaviour patterns.

As a form of communication and as an interpersonal medium of the moment, theatre brings about intellectual challenges for its viewers, turning them into a public that interpret the performance based on their own social and individual experiences.

Puppetry

Puppet is also an important tool in the means of teaching folk form of communication in puppet arts. Nowadays, efforts are being made to educate people through puppet display in Prasar teaching, health discussion, agricultural education, etc. India is the country where the art of puppetry was originated. Where previously only songs and historical songs were presented through it. Nowadays, puppet performance has taken a very modern and wide form. It has become a very powerful medium of modern education. The Ministry of Health has successfully conveyed the message of family planning to the public through puppets.

There are many types of puppets, such as hand puppets, thread puppets, rod puppets, shadow puppets, paper mash puppets, fiber puppets , plastic puppets, etc. Puppet makers usually perform the work of puppets. The broadcaster should pay special attention to local problems and situations while using puppet as a teaching method, only then the performance becomes interesting and the audience is able to assimilate it. Instead of giving a direct message in this, one should try to teach recreationally. Through the puppet, the teacher can present many subjects like superstition, social evils and adult education in a breathtaking manner. The successful performance of a puppet game depends heavily on the speaker of the presenter. The presentation of the content must be in clear-witted words. The expressions of the puppet were presented correctly only through words and advertisement.

Film

Film communication is a very modern and popular method of teaching. The role of films has been very important and positive in changing the outlook of the person. Everyone has acknowledged its contribution to social change. The facts presented by the films have unique ability to attract attention.

So, the audience participates in it with interest. Both literate and illiterate people take advantage of films. Films are also screened through projectors. The projector shows films of 35 mm, 16 mm or 8 mm size.

Movies shown in commercial theatres are of 35 mm. Films of 8 mm are performed in small groups or rooms. Movies are very beneficial due to visual and audio learning tools. Seeing the character of films, people consider them as their counterparts and disarm them. Hence, films are established as a strong medium of communication teaching. It directly or indirectly disseminated the teaching message.

While choosing films for rural audiences, the broadcaster should keep in mind many things. The films should be in simple language. Also, the presentation of the subject in an interesting manner is also important. The broadcasters should be aware that the level of films shown should be in accordance with the intellectual and educational level of the villagers.

Advertising

Advertising is a type of communication that persuades and encourages people to take a particular action. Advertisements also shows the advantages, features and values of a certain product. There is a relationship between advertising and communication because firms con not advertise without communicating.

Advertising insects itself in the daily lives of most people. It has a subtle and soft way of persuading people. It manipulates consumer cultures. Advertisements should be age appropriate because they have a wide market. For an advertisement to be effective, it must be credible i.e. should be truthful and believable for the people.

Information and Communication Technology For Development

- Information and Communication Technology (ICT) is considered as a subset of Information Technology (IT).
- It refers to the technology used for telecommunications, broadcast media, audio-visual processing and transmission system network based control. The technology used to collect, store, improve, send and transmit information is called Information and Communication Technology(ICT).
- ICT includes all the tools, which are used for operation of information and communication including computers and networks, hardware and necessary software.
- According to the **United Nations Development "Program**, Information and communication technology is related to the handling of information; it is a group of various tools, services and applications, which are mainly used in the production, distribution and exchange of information."

The following are the various components of ICT :

- Computer hardware technology includes micro-computers, servers, mainframe computers, as well as input, output and storage devices.
- Computer software technology includes operating system, Database Management System (DBMS), server and commercial and commercial software.
- Telecommunication and network technology includes wired or wireless based software, network security and information cryptography to connect with the medium of telecommunications, processors and the internet.
- Human resources include system administrator and network administrator.

Administrator Use of ICT

In various fields, ICT has become an integral part of our life. It has benefited the common man in every sphere of life. Some of these areas are as follows :

In the Field of Education There is no time limit on a person to get education. Through ICT, education can be attained by attending class at anytime and at anywhere. Teachers can create interactive classes that influence each other and make the lesson less interesting. Teacher through the use of graphics, video and animation can explain complex concepts in a very simple way. Learning tools can be accessed very easily. Children's progress can be mapped as an electronic journal, which will help teachers and students to identify strong and weak points.

In the Field of Health ICT helps in improving the safety and security of diseases, updating in latest technology, knowledge on population health and statistics. This also helps to reduce and eliminate ICT diseases in healthcare research. This helps in finding possible prevention measures. ICT is used in the hospital for electronic storage of medical data. It helps in retrieving information easily. Even the use of ICT has reduced the cost of treatment.

In the Field of Governance, Better effective public service delivery through ICT access to government information and services. The internet provides an opportunity to the government to present public services and provide information and policies more efficiently.

ICT helps to give better response to customers and effective management. The widespread use of ICT has provided the government an opportunity to present services and information in an efficient manner.

Community Radio

Community radio is a form of local radio. It is also called mass radio, democratic radio or local radio. This radio is used to become a voice for a particular community. They are limited to a small geographical area. Community radios are broadcasts from low power transmitters covering 20 to 30 km. Community radio unlike public service broadcasting, brings small communities closer to each other.

Focuses on the day to day needs of the common man and helps in fulfilling local aspirations. In many countries, community radio has played an important role in informing the poor and empower them by giving expression to their needs. Keeping the above objectives in mind, the government announced a policy of giving community radio licenses to educational institutions in December, 2002.

After this, many voluntary organisations sought to expand this policy, so that the civic community can participate more in social development. The governments rethink this policy and make it more liberal in December, 2006 and many organisations running without profit have been brought under its purview.

These organisations include civic committees, voluntary organisations, agricultural universities of the states, institutions falling under the Indian Council of Agricultural Research, Krishi Vigyan Kendras, registered societies, autonomous institutions and public trusts.

This scheme can become a powerful medium of rural empowerment, especially if it focuses on the marginalised communities of society, such as dalits, rural women and disabled people. This led to rural development, agriculture, health, nutritious food, education and panchayati raj. The dissemination of information on issues can help in promoting development and the government can reach the beneficiaries of various programs more effectively.

Participatory Video

Participatory video is a form of participatory media in which a group or community creates their own film. The idea behind this is that making a video is easy and accessible and is a great way of bringing people together to explore issues, voice concerns or simply to be creative and tell stories. It is therefore, primarily about process, though high quality and accessible films can be created using these methods if that is a desired outcome.

This process can be very empowering, enabling a group or community to take their own action to solve their own problems, and also to communicate their needs and ideas to decision-makers and/or other groups and communities. As such, participatory video can be highly effective tool to engage and mobilise marginalised people, and to help them to implement their own forms of sustainable development based on local needs.

Social Media and Mobile Phones

Social media is basically exchange of information through a computer, tablet or smart phone. Smart phone is a type of personal computer. There are many websites and apps under social media such as Facebook, WhatsApp, Instagram, Telegram, etc. which are continuously increasing the field of social media.

Social media and mobile phones are complementary to each other, because people use social media mostly through their mobile phones. Social media is becoming the largest medium of communication today and is rapidly gaining popularity. Social media enables people to share their ideas, content, information, news, etc. with each other very fast.

Social media and mobile phones are a collection of websites, applications and other platforms that help us exchange information and to participate in social networking. Social media is not limited to blogging and sharing of pictures, but it also provides us with very strong tools. This is because the impact of social media is far and wide and it can create or even spoil someone's image.

Today, social media and mobile phones contribute to the social development of the society and also helps in growing many businesses. Today, they play an important role in providing public awareness in society towards any socio-political issue. It is being used more in developed countries as well as in developing countries.

At the same time, there are negative aspects of social media and mobile phones as it helps in cheating during the exam, hurting the student's ability and performance. This has also increased the possibility of privacy violations, as well as cyber crimes like hacking, phishing, questioning it. Due to excessive use of social media, people are starting to get away from family and society. This adversely affects their physical and mental health.

Thus, it can be said that each subject has both positive and negative aspects i.e. social media and mobile phones too. Given the importance of communication, its positive aspect should be adopted. According to the statistics of the Telecom and Regulatory Authority of India, teledensity of India is continuously increasing, in which mobile phone is at the top, which indicates its importance.

Organisations/Agencies for the Development Communication

NGOs, international agencies and Corporates, national Corporates, etc; are the organisations agencies for development communication their description is given below :

Mass Communication by NGOs

Non Governmental Organisations or NGOs are voluntary groups of individuals or organisations, usually not affiliated with any government. These organisations are formed to provide services or to advocate a public policy.

The term was first coined in 1945 with the formation of the United Nations (UN). NGOs are found to be active in various fields including humanitarian issues, education, health care, public policy, human rights, environment, etc.

The NGOs with their initiatives and campaigns achieve their objectives that differ not only in their activities, but also in forms. The different form of activities differ in various parts of the world. NGOs seek to achieve a large scale change promoted directly through influence of the political system by using their campaigns.

For campaigning, NGOs need an efficient group of members to keep their supporters informed and motivated. They plan and host their demonstrations and events to keep their cause in media and to gain mass supporters. They do this to gain media attention and influence policy changer. The defining activity of a campaign is generally the demonstration on social issues, such as human rights, women's rights and education of children. They work to advocate, to defend and to promote a specific issue.

A few notable NGOs with important mass campaigns are given below :

Help Age India It was founded in the year 1960 by Dr. Sarvapalli **Radhakrishnan**, **Jackson Cole** and **Samson Daniel**. It is secular, non-profit and non governmental organisation. It is registered as national level voluntary organisation. The NGO is working towards cause and care of disadvantaged older persons. It helps in improving their quality of life. Help age advocates for different elder needs, such as quality healthcare, universal pension, action against elder abuse and many more at national, state and societal level with state and central governments. It works hand in hand with senior citizens associations, understanding elder needs working with and for them. It advocates for elder friendly policies and their implementation.

Child Rights and You (CRY) This organisation was founded in 1979 by **Rippan Kapoor**. Using photography as a advocacy tool for child rights in India, it calls for all photographers to participate in their mass campaigns with an aim that highlights quality education and allows all to participate in the campaign.

Give Foundation It is an online donation-non-profit organisation of India. 'Give India' or 'Give Foundation' uses its campaigns to raise funds and further donates it to those who need it. It, organises various activities in its mass campaigns, with an aim of charity. For example, the Standard Chartered Mumbai Marathon and the Vodafone Delhi Half Marathon.

Goonj.. a Voice, An Effort Another important NGO known for its various campaigns is 'Goonj.' It was founded in the year 1999 by **Anshu Gupta**. It is known for disaster relief, humanitarian aid and community development. Its campaigns include events like Ek Jodi Kapda, Joy of Exchange and Share the Language of Love that aims at development for rural areas.

The Akshaya Patra Foundation This foundation is running its famous school lunch programme. It was founded in the year 2000 by **Madhu Pandit Dasa**. It aims at reducing classroom hunger and education of children. Its 'Go Green' initiative focuses at the production of organic waste that can produce biogas.

Smile Foundation It was founded in the year 2002 by **Santanu Mishra**. This foundation is committed for the welfare of the deprived children or children born to the less fortunate parents.

It introduces various mass campaigns that lead to fulfil the basic minimum education, health status and towards inculcating a good character. With such missions and goals, the foundation has been assisting a number of development initiatives undertaken by NGOs.

Sammaan Foundation It was founded in the year 2007 by **Irfan Alam**. With an aim of empowering all vulnerable sections of our country, this NGO has introduced various campaigns that help the downtroddens. Better healthcare, sustainable livelihood, financial inclusion and leadership skills development are the basic concerns of this NGO.

Mass Campaigns by International Agencies and Corporates

Today, almost every agency/corporation be it national or international, uses mass campaign to promote a cause. Brands increasingly use a social purpose to guide marketing communications. A term 'commercial marketing' comes in such campaigns. It is a set of activities carried out by a commercial enterprise designed to influence the common masses. Over a long run, it has evolved to make significant contributions to social changes and development.

Their credibility and marketing expertise, reach and access to key influences, make them unique in the process that drives change around social norms. Social marketing or doing social good then becomes as central as selling a service or a product. Marketing is an example of how companies seek to develop and integrate to social change. It aims to influence behaviours that benefit individuals and communities for the greater social good.

The goal is to deliver competition, sensitive and segmented social change programs that are effective, efficient, equitable and sustainable. In its pursuit to bring out a change through campaigns all agencies or corporates apply a customer-oriented approach.

Some international agencies and corporates are :

Yoplait It is headquartered at Boulogne Billancourt, France. It is an international 'Yogurt' brand which decided to use advertisements to bring out a change for the cause of women.

HP (Hewlett-Packard) It was founded on 1st January, 1939. It is headquartered at Palo Alto, California. It always sustainability and social impact in its DNA. Its campaign also focuses on sustained development besides social well-being.

Airbnb It was founded in August, 2008. It is headquartered at San Francisco. Using the mode of video advertisement, an interesting campaign was introduced by 'Airbnb' which focuses to make the society better. It hits upon the cause of discrimination to bring out a change in the ideology of its viewers.

P&G (Procter and Gamble) It was founded in 1837. It is headquartered at Gincinnati, Ohio. Issues related to gender, sexuality and poverty have been central to P& G. Already known for its mass campaigns, P&G portrays a more diverse and progressive image to bring out a social change.

National Corporates

A few important national corporates are as follow :

Tata Group It was founded in 1868 by **Jamsetji Tata**. The Tata Group conglomerate in India carries out various projects that aim at community improvement and poverty alleviation programs. Through self help groups, it is engaged in women empowerment activities and other social welfare programs. It has initiated several healthcare as well as educational programs.

Ultratech Cement The biggest cement company of India is involved in social work across 407 villages aiming to create sustainability and self-change.

Mahindra and Mahindra It focuses on providing educational programmes that bring about a change and development. Mahindra and Mahindra promotes its campaigns in the remotest areas to meet its objectives.

Mass Campaigns by Government of India

Development communication is an essential feature of the Indian situation. With the growing population, the efforts by the government are increasing. Within this perspective of development communication, our government started relying on two approaches.

The first approach focused on mass media that targeted larger populations and large scale actions, while the second approach promoted grassroot communications, small-scale projects and light media. Both the approaches coexist today to advertise and increase the effectiveness of the mass campaigns introduced by the Government of India. The mass campaigns initiated by our government covered all health, social, economic and other aspects for the growth and development of our nation.

Some of these campaigns are discussed below :

Make In India It was launched on 25th September, 2014. It encourages local Indian products and also focuses to boost entrepreneurship in India. Its aim is to create more job opportunities, skill enhancement and better infrastructure that would make business an easy process.

Swachh Bharat Abhiyan The 'Clean India Campaign' launched by the Government of India in 2014 focused on the construction of proper sanitation and promoting sanitation programmes in the rural areas. Alongwith this, it further aimed at maintaining cleanliness on the streets and roads to present a clean and a better India.

Beti Bachao, Beti Padhao One of the most prominent and popular campaigns introduced by the Government of India is the 'Beti Bachao, Beti Padhao Campaign', launched in 2015. It aimed at improving the conditions of females in the society. Females faced social discrimination in the society. It severed two purposes. It not only encouraged the birth of a girl child, but also her education. The government, in support of this campaign, also initiated another campaign that urged fathers to take a selfie with their daughters.

Accessible India Campaign (Sugamya Bharat Abhiyan) It is a nationwide campaign thataims to make barrier free environment for persons with disabilities all over the country for leading a safe and dignified life. The campaign is implemented by Ministry of Social Justice and empowerment and is in line with the UN Convention on the Rights of Persons with Disabilities (UNCPRO) to which India is a signatory. It was launched in July 2018.

EXAM BASED QUESTIONS

1 What is the characteristic of development?
(a) Development leads to communication
(b) Development is the basis of social change
(c) Development is the cultural barrier
(d) Development is an instant process

2 How communication is related to development?
(a) Both are indifferent
(b) Both are correlative
(c) Both are interrelated
(d) Both are different

3 If any information need to spread to mass, which medium is most suitable?
(a) Organising fairs and conferences
(b) Organising debates on the television
(c) Through road shows
(d) Through mass communicative mediums

4 Which of the following is/are the aspect(s) of development communication?
(a) Modernisation (b) Transformational
(c) Socialising (d) Both (b) and (c)

5 Development communication creates a space for .... in society.
(a) change (b) mass campaigns
(c) reform (d) development

6 Which of the following statement(s) is/are correct?
(a) Gossip groups are micro-groups.
(b) Modern mass media are processed and not be mistaken for the phenomenon of communication itself.
(c) Modern mass media are produced and distributed like other consumer and industrial products on a mass scale.
(d) All of the above

7 What do you mean by gender?
(a) Women and men with specific genitals
(b) Male and female candidates
(c) Calling according to the age and colour
(d) Depends on the role which one plays in society

8 What do you mean by domestic violence?
(a) It is work international discrimination against women.
(b) It is a nationwide discrimination against women professions.
(c) It is the exploitation of women happening in homes.
(d) All of the above

9 What do one mean by 'being healthy'?
(a) Health is the best means for communication.
(b) Health is the state of physical, social and mental well-being
(c) Health means doing body functions smoothly
(d) None of the above

10 Which among these is / are health related plan(s)?
(a) National Health Scheme
(b) Ayushman Bharat
(c) Pradhan Mantri Swasthya Bima Yojana
(d) All of the above

11 Which type of communication mean(s) is/ are used for providing environmental protection?
(a) Printed communication
(b) Electronic communication
(c) Traditional communication
(d) All of the above

12 Which of the following statements is/are correct?
(a) Today, Doordarshan devotes atleast 10% of its telecast time to educational or enrichment programmes for farmers, school children, youth and other groups.
(b) Television was introduced in India by the Nehru government with the primary aim of exploring the medium for distance education.
(c) Mahatma Gandhi spoke just once over radio and was able to mobilise the masses.
(d) All of the above

13 The purpose of using a poster is to
(a) arouse interest
(b) motivate
(c) create awareness
(d) create understanding

14 Which is true, as regards with puppet play?
(a) A simple puppet play can be presented through glove puppets in an open area.
(b) One or two kerosene lamps will be enough for the evening presentation for a small group.
(c) The players can sit at the back and the audience can sit in front.
(d) All of the above

15 Folk media is often packed with
(a) spontaneity (b) boisterousness
(c) humour (d) All of these

16 The folk or traditional arts of India from ancient times been used for .... purposes.
(a) socio-political
(b) religious
(c) moral
(d) All of the above

17 Which media would be ideal to attract the attention of children to sell chocolates to them?
(a) Radio
(b) Newspapers
(c) TV (advertisements)
(d) Leaflets

18 Which of the following statements is/are correct?
(a) Rapport in folk media is immediate and direct, the barriers of communication almost not exist.
(b) The Keertan, Alha and various street theatre are examples of audience participation.
(c) Folk media cater to small audiences at a time, but impact is at much deeper level.
(d) All of the above

19 Puppetry becomes a valuable .... only if the message to be communicated is developed in dramatic terms.
(a) visual aid (b) art
(c) drama (d) guzzet

20 Studies show that folk traditions are uniformly popular regardless of the .... standing of any community.
(a) education (b) financial
(c) social (d) All of these

21 A single printed sheet of paper of small size, containing preliminrary information relating to a topic is known as
(a) newsletter (b) bulletin
(c) leaflet (d) folder

22 "The complex of values, ideas, attitudes and other meaningful symbols created by man to shape human behaviour and the artifacts of that behaviour as they are transmitted from one generation of the next" is known as
(a) character (b) culture
(c) adaptation (d) civilisation

23 One study estimates the existence of about 7000 street theatre group in different parts of the country with the largest number in
(a) Tamil Nadu (b) Kerala
(c) West Bengal (d) Andhra Pradesh

24 Puppet's history tells us that nearly .... years ago in ancient India, the only form of theatre was the puppet theatre.
(a) 500 (b) 1000
(c) 1500 (d) 2000

25 Folk forms of the local region have been utilised both by voluntary social action groups and by government supported literacy campaigns in the state of
(a) Maharashtra (b) Kerala
(c) Andhra Pradesh (d) All of these

26 The term 'NGOs' was first coined in
(a) 1947 (b) 1948
(c) 1945 (d) 1950

27 Which of the following is not used by the NGOs in their mass campaigns?
(a) Television (b) Radio
(c) Newspaper (d) Pamphlets

28 .... is an essential activity organised by NGOs.
(a) Demonstration (b) Television shows
(c) Radio jingles (d) None of these

29 The Akshaya Patra Foundation initiated the
(a) Vodafone Delhi Marathon
(b) Swachh Bharat Abhiyan
(c) Go Green
(d) Photography Contest

30 ...... brand uses the social campaign as guide.
(a) The CSR team
(b) The marketing communication
(c) Consumer report
(d) All of the above

31 Which term defines the campaigns initiated by the NGOs?
(a) Corporatisation
(b) Commercial marketing
(c) Corporate Social Responsibility
(d) All of the above

32 Which of the following theory is not related to advocacy and behaviour change communication:
(a) Self-efficacy (b) Education
(c) Criminology (d) Illusion

33 .... practice corporates social responsibility.
(a) Corporates
(b) Governments
(c) Non-governmental organisation
(d) Corporate citizens

34 The 'Corporate Social Responsibility' allows the company to ....
(a) their products (b) create an impact
(c) initiate social change (d) None of these

35 Which campaign supports twin motives regarding women empowerment?
(a) Swachh Bharat Abhiyan (b) Beti Padhao
(c) Beti Bachao (d) Both (b) and (c)

36 .... can be highly effective tool to engage and mobilise marginalised people.
(a) Human Rights (b) Participatory video
(c) Television (d) Radio

37 Which of the following is the strategic approach of advocacy and behaviour change communication?
(a) Counselling (b) Health
(c) Individual (d) Group

38 Making the puppets developing a story, format a science concept and then presenting in the form of puppet play to a small group shows
1. Active involvement 2. Interaction
3. Withdrawal 4. Disinterest
Select the correct answer using the codes given below.
(a) 1 and 2 (b) 1 and 4
(c) 1, 2 and 3 (d) All of these

39 Only usually comes across the art of puppetry used mostly in the presentation of historical or mythological stories. This medium can be effectively used to bring out some basic facts and scientific aspect on
1. cleanliness
2. nutrition
3. educational topics

Select the correct answer using the codes given below.
(a) 1, 2 and 3 (b) 1 and 2
(c) 2 and 3 (d) Only 2

40 Which are used for mass contact methods?
1. Personal calls
2. Circular letter
3. Radio and Television
4. Tours

Select the correct answer using the codes given below.
(a) 1, 2 and 3 (b) 2, 3 and 4
(c) 2 and 3 (d) 1 and 4

41 The Indian folk forms have a generous mix of
1. dialogue and dance 2. song and clowning
3. moralising 4. prayer

Select the correct answer using the codes given below.
(a) 1, 2, 3 and 4 (b) 1, 2 and 3
(c) 2 and 3 (d) 3 and 4

42 Comments on current events can be introduced into the traditional folk media form of
1. tamasha 2. jatra
3. keertana 4. bhavai

Select the correct answer using the codes given below.
(a) 1, 2, 3 and 4 (b) 1, 2 and 3
(c) 3 and 4 (d) 2 and 4

43 Arrange the following teaching learning methods in the order of learner's ability.
1. A video show
2. Laboratory method
3. Demonstration
4. Radio talk

Codes
(a) 1, 2, 3 and 4 (b) 2, 3, 4 and 1
(c) 3, 2, 1 and 4 (d) 4, 1, 3 and 2

44 Match the following.

List I	List II
A. The very diversity of folk tradition.	1. During Telangana Movement.
B. Mass opinion created by 'Barra Katha'.	2. Use them as vehicles for communication, a popular folks form in Andhra Pradesh.
C. Folk media and personal contact.	3. Personal contact, demonstration, interaction.
D. Three important aspects of folk media.	4. Utilised to communicate
E. Radio advertisement.	5. Based on folk tones promoting agricultural products.

Codes

	A	B	C	D	E
(a)	2	3	5	4	1
(b)	5	2	3	1	4
(c)	2	1	4	3	5
(d)	5	4	3	1	2

45 Match the following.

List I	List II
A. Advantage of mass media in campaigns.	1. Inconvenient backups.
B. Failure of campaigns.	2. To reach mass audience effectively.
C. Use of mass media campaigns.	3. Both advantageous and disadvantageous.
D. Campaigns revelations.	4. Examined on the basis of recall.

Codes

	A	B	C	D
(a)	1	2	3	4
(b)	2	1	3	4
(c)	1	3	2	4
(d)	3	4	1	2

46 Match the following.

List I	List II
A. Poverty was equivalent to under development.	1. Accessible in every village.
B. Downwards hierarchy	2. Old paradigm.
C. Mass communication	3. Government to public.
D. Radio	4. Important role in development.

Codes

	A	B	C	D
(a)	2	4	1	3
(b)	3	2	4	1
(c)	1	2	3	4
(d)	2	3	4	1

47 Match the following.

List I	List II
A. Video	1. Audio aid
B. Slide	2. Projected audio-visual aid
C. Chart	3. Projected visual aid
D. Tape recorder	4. Non-projected visual aid
	5. Multimedia aid

Codes

	A	B	C	D
(a)	5	4	2	3
(b)	2	3	4	1
(c)	5	1	3	2
(d)	3	2	4	1

48 Match the following

List I	List II
A. CD ROM	1. Interactive multimedia
B. Video conferencing	2. Folk media
C. Satellite technology	3. Computer stored media
D. Mime and puppetry	4. Global networking media

Codes

	A	B	C	D
(a)	2	4	3	1
(b)	3	1	4	2
(c)	1	3	2	4
(d)	4	2	1	3

49 Match the following.

List I	List II
A. Puppets	1. Graphic aid
B. Charts	2. Electronic
C. Computer	3. Traditional
D. Print	4. Mass media

Codes

	A	B	C	D		A	B	C	D
(a)	2	3	4	1	(b)	4	1	3	2
(c)	3	1	2	4	(d)	1	2	3	4

Directions (Q. Nos. 50-60) *Below given are two statements, labelled as Assertion (A) and Reason (R). Following are the codes given below, select the correct code for the following.*

Codes

(a) Both A and R are true, and R is the correct explanation of A
(b) Both A and R are true, but R is not the correct explanation of A
(c) A is true, but R is false
(d) A is false, but R is true

50 **Assertion** (A) Posters used as audio-visual aids, compel attention and motivate action.
Reason (R) Posters help in communicating as they present abstract information in a graphic way.

51 **Assertion** (A) Campaigning, which is an educational extension activity helps to mobilise and solve the problems of a community.
Reason (R) It is done to seek emotional participation of the community for adopting new practices.

52 **Assertion** (A) Aristotle's Model of Communication emphasised the audience role in communication chain.
Reason (R) This model is more focussed on public speaking than inter-personal communication.

53 **Assertion** (A) Communication is effective, if it flows freely in a communication loop between the sender and receiver.
Reason (R) Free flow means uninterrupted transmission of the message through an appropriate medium, correct decoding of the message by receiver and appropriate feedback from them.

54 **Assertion** (A) Indian and international corporates are increasingly investing in areas of development.
Reason (R) The concept of the corporate social responsibility has taken the internet by storm.

55 **Assertion** (A) Development communication is not an essential component in the Indian Constitution.
Reason (R) The mass campaigns initiated by the Government of India aim at growth and development.

56 **Assertion** (A) Media has played a very important role in conveying social messages to individuals and to make them aware of all the conditions.
Reason (R) Today, media is not that much responsible to carry out this constructive role without any profit.

57 **Assertion** (A) A campaign is an intense educational activity for motivating and mobilising a community to action, to solve a problem or satisfy a need urgently felt by it.
Reason (R) A campaign is done to induce emotional participation of the community to create a favourable psychological climate for adoption of new practices.

58 **Assertion** (A) The mass media docs not play major roles in the campaigns of development through communication.
Reason (R) The unilinear models of communication were less effective while the bi-directional tends to make message more effective.

59 **Assertion** (A) All types of puppets used for educational purposes should be of prominent colour and appropriate size.
Reason (R) Being attractive, puppets motivate learners.

60 **Assertion** (A) Media plays a significant role in the society and its influence on the individual has been growing with time.
Reason (R) The media cannot be avoided anywhere in the society, today.

Directions (Q. Nos 61-65) *Read the passage and answer the questions that follows.*

Information Technology (IT) is the application of computers and internet to store, retrieve, transmit, and manipulate information, often in the context of a business or other enterprise.

IT is considered a subset of information and communications technology (ICT) and has evolved according to the needs. It is worthwhile noting that the term IT is commonly used as a synonym for computers and computer networks, but it also encompasses other information distribution technologies such as television and telephones.

Several industries are associated with information technology, including computer hardware, software, electronics, semiconductors, internet, telecom equipment, engineering, healthcare, e-commerce, and computer services.

Thanks to the continuous development of computers, the original computing systems became minicomputers and later personal computers took the lead. Nowadays, mobile phones are dethroning the personal computer and computing is evolving faster to become disembodied more like a cloud, becoming accessible more easily whenever needed. Information technology has transformed people and companies and has allowed digital technology to influence society and economy alike. It has, in this sense, shaped societies and adapted itself to people's needs. If you want a brief history of Information Technology, here is one.

Humans were the first "computers". Then, machines were invented to carry out the computational tasks. Now these machines have given way to new form of information technology. Information has become disembodied accessible from anywhere through cloud technology. Recent advances in IT is the consequence of the development in computing systems.

Humans have been storing, retrieving, manipulating, and communicating information since the Sumerians in Mesopotamia developed writing in about 3000 BC, but the term information technology in its modern sense first appeared in a 1958 article published in the Harvard Business Review; authors Harold J.

Leavitt and Thomas L. Whisler commented that "the new technology does not yet have a single established name. We shall call it information technology (IT)." Their definition consists of three categories: techniques for processing, the application of statistical and mathematical methods to decision-making, and the simulation of higher-order thinking through computer programs.

61 Information technology is changing principally because of
(a) the changing needs
(b) new technological advances
(c) new softwares
(d) All of the above

62 According to the author, the first computers were
(a) calculators
(b) humans
(c) printers
(d) None of the above

63 Development of information technology is the result of
(a) advances in computing systems
(b) development of machinery in general
(c) invention of semiconductors
(d) All of the above

64 Computing systems are taking the form of clouds means
(a) computers have become smaller
(b) computing power are becoming disembodied.
(c) computers have become portable
(d) All of the above

65 The idea of modern Information Technology was propounded by
(a) Harold J. Leavitt (b) Thomas L. Whisler
(c) Both (a) and (b) (d) None of these

PREVIOUS YEARS' QUESTIONS

November 2017

1 **Assertion** (A) Studies have also shown that bilingual children achieve higher scores than monolingual on a number of tests of cognitive theory.

Reason (R) Bilingualism trains children to focus their attention on the relevant variables in the context, particularly that is ambiguous or contradictory.

Codes
(a) Both A and R are correct
(b) Both A and R are incorrect
(c) A is correct and R is incorrect
(d) A is incorrect and R is correct

2 Match the following approaches used in communication for development given in List I with their description given in List II.

List I	List II
A. Community Mobilisation	1. Two way communication
B. Interpersonal Communication	2. To motivate partners and people
C. Social Marketing	3. Ensures public opinion for a cause
D. Advocacy	4. Promotion of social goals
	5. Promotion of institutions

Codes

	A	B	C	D
(a)	3	1	4	5
(b)	2	1	4	3
(c)	4	1	5	2
(d)	3	1	5	2

3 Arrange interpersonal distances in communication from least to maximum.
1. Social 2. Personal
3. Public 4. Intimate

Codes
(a) 1, 2, 4, 3 (b) 1, 2, 3, 4
(c) 4, 2, 1, 3 (d) 4, 1, 2, 3

December 2015

4 Techniques used in behaviour modification which involve reinforcement contingent on a particular response.
(a) Analytical therapy (b) Cognitive therapy
(c) Classical conditioning (d) Operant conditioning

June 2015

5 Development communication is
1. resource for development
2. precursor for social change
3. an approach for charity
4. a component of press information bureau

Codes
(a) 3, 2 and 4 (b) 1, 2 and 3
(c) 1 and 2 (d) 4, 1 and 3

6 Effective development Communication is influenced by which of the following factors?
1. Dissemination of information
2. Use of the information by users
3. Location of the users
4. Size of the audience

Codes
(a) 1 and 2 (b) 2 and 3
(c) 3 and 4 (d) 1 and 4

December 2014

7 **Assertion** (A) Learning obtained through transformation of experiences into knowledge is referred to as experiential learning.

Reason (R) A well designed educational programme tries to influence the cognitive, affective and psychomotor domains of human behaviour.

Codes
(a) A is correct and R is incorrect
(b) A is incorrect and R is correct
(c) Both A and R are correct
(d) Both A and R are incorrect

8 **Assertion** (A) In order to make development programmes effective, the approach and procedure must be culturally appropriate.

Reason (R) Culture is passed on from one generation to the next through communication.

Codes
(a) Both A and R are incorrect
(b) A is correct, R is incorrect
(c) A is incorrect, R is correct
(d) Both A and R are correct, but R is not the correct explanation of A

9 Participatory communication can be ensured, through the use of following.
1. Community Radio 2. Participatory Video
3. Street Theatre 4. Public Speeches

Codes
(a) 1, 2, 3 and 4 are correct (b) 1, 2 and 3 are correct
(c) 1, 2 and 4 are correct (d) 1 and 2 are correct

10 The communication process is always
1. systematic 2. intentional
3. interactional 4. functional

Codes
(a) 1 and 2 are correct (b) 2 and 3 are correct
(c) 3 and 4 are correct (d) 1 and 4 are correct

11 In mass communication, PSA stands for
(a) Public Service Assessment
(b) Public Service Announcement
(c) Public Service Access
(d) Public Service Account

ANSWERS

Exam Based Questions

1 (b)	2 (c)	3 (d)	4 (d)	5 (b)	6 (d)	7 (a)	8 (c)	9 (b)	10 (d)
11 (d)	12 (d)	13 (c)	14 (d)	15 (d)	16 (d)	17 (c)	18 (d)	19 (a)	20 (d)
21 (a)	22 (b)	23 (c)	24 (d)	25 (d)	26 (c)	27 (d)	28 (a)	29 (c)	30 (b)
31 (b)	32 (d)	33 (d)	34 (b)	35 (d)	36 (b)	37 (a)	38 (a)	39 (a)	40 (b)
41 (a)	42 (a)	43 (c)	44 (c)	45 (b)	46 (d)	47 (b)	48 (b)	49 (c)	50 (a)
51 (b)	52 (b)	53 (a)	54 (a)	55 (d)	56 (c)	57 (a)	58 (b)	59 (a)	60 (c)
61 (a)	62 (b)	63 (a)	64 (b)	65 (c)					

Previous Years' Questions

1 (a)	2 (b)	3 (c)	4 (d)	5 (c)	6 (a)	7 (c)	8 (d)	9 (b)	10 (d)
11 (b)									

Extension Education, Methods and Materials

Extension education deals with practical items and knowledge and information about it. It is useful for rural people for solving their day to day problems especially agricultural related. In extension education diverse methods and materials are employed to deliver the content effectively.

Extension Education

"Education is a social process. Education is growth. Education is not preparation for life, Education is life, itself."

Education is usually referring to formal education institutions delivering a planned curriculum leading to degree or diploma before entering into the workforce. Education is the process of bringing desirable change into the behaviour of human beings. If education needs to be effective, it should result in changes in all the behavioural components. Extension education is usually referring to planned educational programmes, designed to meet the needs of people in the workforce.

According to **Paul Leagans**, "Extension education is an applied social sciences consisting of relevant context derived from physical, biological and social sciences and in its own process synthesised into a body of knowledge, concepts, principles and procedures oriented to provide non-credit of school education largely for adults."

Areas of Extension Education

The areas of extension education are :

Agricultural Extension It means extending knowledge to workers.

Veterinary and Animal Husbandary Extension It means extending knowledge about managing, feeding, care of animals and birds, breeding, etc.

Agricultural Engineering Extension Extending knowledge about agricultural machinery, such as tractors and pumps, the levelling of land, water use, soil conservation, etc.

In this Chapter

- *Extension Education*
  - *Areas of Extension Education*
  - *Genesis (Origin) of Extension Education*
  - *Philosophy and Principles of Extension Education Programme Development*
- *Instructional Methods and Materials*

Home Science Extension Extending technical knowledge to wives or ladies in urban and rural areas on food, child care, home decoration, kitchen, gardening, etc.

Industry Extension Extending knowledge on the managing and running of industries.

Genesis of Extension Education

The word 'extension' is derived from the Latin root 'ex' meaning 'out' and 'tension' meaning 'stretching'. The word 'extension' signifies 'out of school system of education'. It combines both adult education and informal education.

Extension education as a practice has a long history. The extension dates back to times when human civilisation started farming. There are evidences which suugest that people were sharing information on better methods of agricultural practices at that time. An example is Mesopotamian civilisation. Extension evolved in different forms with different purposes over time. The extension education evolved into a formalised public services and was undertaken by government with the objective of improving the abilities of rural people to adopt new technologies and new practices. The modern history was related to the birth of more or less organised form of extension education. For instance, the outbreak of potato blight in Europe led to the development of extension service.

Origin of Extension Education in Various Countries

The origin of the term 'extension education' was **first introduced in 1873 by Cambridge University** in England to describe a particular system dedicated to the disseminating of knowledge to rural people where they lived and worked. The first practical steps were taken in 1867-68, when James Stuart gave lectures to women's associations and working men's in North of England. In 1871, James Stuart approached the authorities in the Cambridge University to organise centres for extension lectures under university's supervision.

In 1873, Cambridge formally adopted this system and was followed by London University in 1876 and Oxford University in 1878. By 1880, the work was being referred to as the 'Extension Movement'. The university extended its work in the areas beyond its campus. **James Stuart** is often considered as the **Father of University of Extension.**

The growth and success of extension work in Britain influenced similar activity elsewhere, especially in the United States.

The out of college lectures in many states of the US became a established practice by the 1880s. During the first two decades of this century, extramural work of the land grant colleges, concerned serving the needs of the farmers.

The extension is now seen as a form of adult education in which teachers were the staff members of the university. For many years, this was mainly an activity of college of agriculture, which employed extension agents, later on these agents started serving other sub-sectors of development in addition to agriculture and allied activities.

In China, the first extension was established in 1924, in Wujiang, the country, Anhui Province followed by the establishment of an agricultural research station. In 1929, regulation of agro extension, which was first law of extension was enacted in the form of **Central Agro Extension**. During 1950s, when the People Republic of China came into being the agricultural technology extension system was well setup.

Origin of Extension Education in India

The extension education in India aimed at the integrated development of rural, remote and underdeveloped areas of the country is of relatively recent origin (1952-53). Its administrative set up had begun for agricultural development in India, as the outcome of several reforms and efforts made over years. It had its beginning in 1860 and basically started with the focus on agricultural development. K N Singh is known as the 'Father of Extension Education in India'.

Stages of Extension Education in India

The development and growth of extension education and extension system can mainly be divided into four stages as :

Stage I Pre-Independence Era.

Stage II Post Independence Era.

Stage III Community Development and Extension Services.

Stage IV Intensive Agricultural Development.

These stages can be understood as :

Stage I Pre-Independence Era

During this stage, various efforts were made towards rural development in different parts of the country by individuals and organisations. These are discussed below :

Ideal Village Project Sir Daniel Hamilton, in 1903 began a project in Sundaram Village near Chennai. Under this programme in 1903, Cooperative Deposit Institute was setup. Alongwith the savings, the programme of health, literacy and small industry was setup. In this planning, the was emphasis was on specialised training for unemployed young farmers to make them self-dependent.

Shriniketan Project Shri Rabindranath Tagore started this project for village development with the help of Shri L M Hurst (Sociologist). He thought that if some villages were developed, the other villages also will be inspired and the programme of village development will spread all over the country.

Shriniketan Village Welfare Institute was established in 1920. It had the objectives to increase the knowledge of rural people to help rural people in establishing cottage industry to inspire people to follow new technology, to create a feeling of cooperation, to arrange facility of health and education and to create the feeling of rural leadership.

Gurgaon Project It was started by **F L Brayne** in 1920. He began this project for rural upliftment in the Gurgaon district which became famous as 'Gurgaon Project'. The main objectives of this project were to increase crop production, to control extra expenditure to improve health, to develop the feeling of women education and home development work.

Sevagram **Gandhiji** began a welfare project known as 'Sevagram' established his ashram in Vardha in 1920. The main objective of this programme was to prevent the economic and social suppression of the people and to create the feeling of patriotism among them.

For fulfilling this objective, Gandhiji made a programme known as 'Gandhian Constructive Programme'. The main objectives of this project were to introduce health programme, the programme of women welfare, the programme of sanitation in the village, primary and adult education programme, programme of social harmony and to popularise the mother tongue and other national dialects.

Marthendam Project This project of rural development was started in the village 'Marthendam' near Trivandrum of Kerala State by **Dr. Spencer Hatch** in 1928. The objectives of this project were :

- To develop the sentiments of people or to create the feeling of progress in their mind. If people are inspired for progressing, then people can be motivated for these development works.
- To develop the people mentally strong as this would help in thinking, understanding and the capacity of taking decision.
- To develop people physically strong because physically weak person cannot work well.
- To develop person socially, because all the activities of a person is determined by the society and so the development of their society is essential.
- To give economic advantage to people, because he will not work if he has no hope of economic benefits.

Baroda Village Reconstruction Project This project was started by **B T Krishnamachari** in Baroda in 1932. The objectives of the project were to spread education and industrialisation to develop necessary factors for the progress of agriculture, to extend adult education and to use the school teachers of village in the extension of programme.

Indian Village Service It began in the village 'Agosoli', Aligarh (UP) in 1945, under the guidance of **Dr W H Wisher**. The main objectives were to educate the rural people in such a manner so that people could self-diagnose their problems. To inspire people to help them in development works. To provide a good chance to the citizens and other individuals to cooperate in the rural development work. To guide them for making other planning of development successful. These were health programme, Home Science programme, the programme of education and the development of cottage industry.

Fikra Vikas Yojana It began in 1946 by the Government of Madras for the development of villages at Fikra Level. The objectives of the projects were all round development of rural people, to develop the committees of Panchayat and cooperatives, to develop animal husbandary, farming and irrigation facilities and to introduce khadi and cottage industry.

Stage II Post-Independence Era

In the post-independence era the major focus has been on increasing the agricultural production. The projects/ campaign during this stage are discussed below :

Grow More Food Campaign It was started in 1947. The main aim of this project was to increase agricultural production. Under this campaign, new seeds and chemical fertilisers were provided to the farmers.

Etawah Pilot Project This pilot project in rural planning and development, played a key role in reorganising the setup of 'Etawah Project' in 1948-52. This project can be regarded as the forerunner of Community Development Projects in India. **Albert Mayer** of USA was the originator of this project. In this project, major emphasis was given on increasing agricultural production by the use of green manure, better seeds, agricultural implements, adult education and reactivation of saline soils. In this, the extension workers were known as colleagues. The objectives of this project were :

- To see what degree of productivity and social improvement as well as initiative, self-confidence and cooperation can be extended.
- To see the extent of improvement possible in an average district.
- To see how quickly the results could be achieved.

- To ascertain the permanency and applicability of results to other areas.
- To build up a sense of community living.
- To build up a spirit of self help in the villagers.

Nilokheri Project Shri S K Dey in 1948, prepared this project for the purpose of providing residence for 700 immigrants from Pakistan. The objectives of this project were to arrange professional training and provide occupation for the people on the basis of their experience, to make people self-dependent in all fields of life and to eliminate the middle man system. Rehabilitation of displaced person from Pakistan. Self-sufficiency for the township in all the essential requirements of life.

Stage III Community Development and National Extension Service

The development under this period/stage is broadly discussed under two heads–Community Development and National Extension Service.

Community Development Project

The Government of India introduced a new scheme on 2nd October, 1952. It was designed to promote better living for the whole community with the active participation of the community. It is technically aided and locally organised self-help activity for the development of the community. Its objective was the all round development of rural community, the extension of new scientific knowledge, increase agricultural production, development of small and medium irrigation projects, increase adult education and primary education.

It seeks to create new administrative machinery suited to the manifold needs of the village. It is pre-eminently people oriented. It promoted self-confidence among the rural population.

This programme was instrumental in raising the standard of living of the ruralities and in reconstructing the rural India. Community thinking and collective action were encouraged through people's institutions like the Panchayats, Cooperative Societies, Vikas Mandals, etc.

The programme had short and long-term objectives.

The short-term objectives were :

- To increase agricultural production both quantitatively and qualitatively.
- To solve problem of rural unemployment.
- To bring development in the sphere of primary education, public health and recreation.
- To encourage people for setting up cottage industries and indigenous handicrafts.

Long-term objectives were :

- The holistic development of rural life through optimum utilisation of physical and human resources.
- To provide all sorts of facilities available in a welfare state to ruralities.
- To increase agricultural production.
- To provide required educational facilities for children and an adult education programme.
- To impart vocational training in the field of tailoring, embroidery, carpentry, etc.

Thus, the community development emerged out of the experiments made at Etawah and Gorakhpur under inspiration of **Albert Mayer**. The programme proved to be a great success in India.

National Extension Services (NES)

The Government of India decided to expand the coverage of the programme to other parts of the country with somewhat less intensive approach than Community Development (CD) project. This programme was named as National Extension Service (NES) initiated on 2nd October, 1953. The idea behind NES was to cover whole country by 1960. Basic idea of CD and NES was the same and the operational unit in both CD and NES was development block.

The activities under NES were less intensive than those of CD. Both were complementary, interwoven and were run concurrently. NES was viewed as the permanent set up for extension in the country and was intended to cover the whole country with an organisation for agriculture and rural development. NES was thought of as the agency of CD as the method to bring about socio-economic transformation of the rural people.

Stage IV Technological and Infrastructure Development

In this era, Technological and Infrastructure Development have been intensified efforts for the development of extension focus gradually shifted from purely agricultural and community development to technological development to social justice to infrastructure development. Government of India launched various programmes discussed below :

Intensive Agricultural District Programme (IADP) The government started this programme in 1960. The central idea behind the programme was that "Increased agricultural production leads to economic growth which in turn brings the welfare of the society." Intensive efforts for production were undertaken with the combination of all the technological improvements and concentration of manpower and resources in selected areas.

The IADP is popularly known as package programme, because of the collective and simultaneous application of all improved practices viz., improved seeds, irrigation, fertilisers, plant protection, implements, storage facilities, marketing facilities, etc.

Intensive Agricultural Area Programme (IAAP) It was started in March 1964. The main objective was to bring progressive increase in production of major crops in selected areas by intensive and coordinator use of various aids.

Small Farmers Development Agency (SFDA) The SFDA (1970-71) and Marginal Farmers and Agricultural Labourers Scheme (1971-72) were started by the Government of India. The SFDA programme was intended to help the small farmers in their farm production. On the other hand, the objective of the MFAL programme was designed to improve the conditions of weaker sections and to generate greater employment opportunities.

Integrated Tribal Development Agency (ITDA) It was specially designed to develop tribal areas and tribal people. This was initiated in 1971-72. Its objectives were to sensitise administration to the basic problems of the tribes and to enforce the existing laws concerning debt relief, poverty alleviation and protection of tribal lands.

Training and Visit System (1974) It was a 'reorganised agricultural extension system' popularly known as 'Training and Visit System' was developed by the World Bank expert **Daniel Benor**. He was instrumental in introducing this innovation (new concept) in agricultural extension.

In India, this system was evolved on the basis of experience gained in the areas of Andhra Pradesh, Madhya Pradesh and Rajasthan under the World Bank assistance. The main objective of this system was to remove short comings in the existing agricultural extension system. This system has given the country a new vision bringing farm scientists and field extension functionaries closer with sole intentions of improving production and income of farmers.

National Agriculture Extension Project (NAEP) It was initiated in 1983. The main objective was to bridge the gap between the research system with that of extension system, so that the transfer of technology takes place at a much faster rate, resulting in higher production and prosperity in the rural sector in general and agricultural sector in particular.

Institute-Village Linkage Programme It was initiated in 1995-96 by the Indian Agricultural Research Institute, New Delhi in four villages. It provides opportunities to scientists to test or demonstrate new technologies on farmer's fields and direct feedback from farmers. Application of new technologies tested under different production systems such as small farms, green revolution farms and commercial farms.

Agricultural Human Resource Development Programme It was World Bank Aided Project, launched in 1995. It was meant for financially assisting the Indian agricultural education sector. It aimed at improving the quality and relevance of higher agricultural education through in-service training programmes and effective management of agricultural human resources.

National Agricultural Technology Project (NATP) It was started in 1998 by the Ministry of Agriculture, Government of India. NATP was intended to shift the balance of technology generation, assessment and dissemination programmes towards greater location-specify needed for the future. The basic premise of NATP was that research and extension programmes should be farmer centered and demand driven.

National Agricultural Innovation Project (2006) It was introduced to assist farmers in the changing contexts. Its overall objective was to alleviate the accelerated and sustainable transformation of Indian agriculture in support of poverty easing and income generation.

Mahatma Gandhi National Rural Employment Guarantee Act (MGNREGA), 2005-2009. It was enacted by Legislative on 25th August, 2005 and the scheme was launched in 2006. It was initially called the 'National Rural Employment Guarantee Act'. The Act was introduced with the aim of improving the purchasing power of people, semi or unskilled people living in rural India, whether they are below the poverty line or not. The scheme provides a legal guarantee for 100 days in every financial year to adult members of any rural household willing to do public work related to unskilled manual work at the statutory minimum wages of ₹100 per day. Thus, MGNREGA aims to achieve twin objectives of rural development and employment.

The Government of India in 2010-11 initiated the programme "Bringing Green Revolution to Eastern India". It was to improve agriculture productivity in this region.

National Mission on Agriculture Extension and Technology (NMAET) It was introduced by the Government of India in 2014-15, in order to take a holistic view of extension by making the system farmer driver and increase accountability by restructuring and strengthening agriculture extension programmes. It was to enable the delivery of technology and to improve agronomic practices of farmers.

In recent years, the National Agriculture Market (*e*-NAM) was introduced. It provides *e*-marketing platform at national level and support creation of infrastructure to enable *e*-marketing.

Objectives of Extension Education

The objectives are expression of the ends towards which our efforts are directed. The objectives of the extension education are as follows :

- To develop the rural people economically, socially and culturally by means of education.
- To assist people to discover and analyse their problems, their felt and unfelt needs.
- To develop leadership among people and help them in organising groups to solve their problems.
- To disseminate information based on research and/or practical experience, in such a way that the people would accept it and put it into actual practice.
- To assist people in mobilising and utilising the resources which they have and which they need from outside.
- To promote better social, natural, recreational, intellectual and spiritual life among the people.
- To open up new opportunities for rural people so that they may develop all their talents and leadership.
- To train rural people, youth for development works.
- To build rural citizens, independent in their thinking, constructive in their outlook, capable, efficient and self-reliant.
- To change the attitudes and practices of the people with whom the work is done.
- To provide knowledge to the rural people about the improved practices in a convincing manner. And also to help them to take decisions within their specific local conditions.
- Its aim is to teach a person how to think and to teach people to determine accurately their own needs so that they can find solution to their own problems. This helps them to acquire knowledge and develop conviction.

Philosophy of Extension Education

Philosophy in the original and wider sense is the pursuit of wisdom or knowledge of things and their causes, both theoretical and practical. It is also defined as moral wisdom. Philosophy is an attempt to answer ultimate questions critically after investigating all that makes such questions puzzling and after realising the vagueness and confusion that underlie our ordinary ideas. The philosophy of extension education has been described and interpreted in different ways by different authors and a clear picture cannot be drawn due to the very complexity of its nature. Views of various authors about philosophy of extension education are :

Kelsey and ***Hearne*** (1955) They stated that the philosophy of extension work is based on the importance of the individual in the promotion of progress for rural people and for the nation. Extension educators work with the people to help them to develop themselves and achieve superior personal well-being. Together, they establish specific objectives, expressed in terms of everyday life, which lead them in the direction of overall objectives.

According to them, some will make progress in one direction while others will do so in another direction. Progress varies with individual's needs, interests and abilities. Through this process, the whole community improves, as a result of cooperative participation and leadership development.

Ensminger According to him, the philosophy of extension can be expressed in the following lines :

- Extension is education for all village people.
- Extension is changing the attitudes, knowledge and skills of the people.
- Extension is "helping people to help themselves".
- Extension is working with men and women, young people, boys and girls to answer their needs and wants.
- Extension is teaching people what to want and ways to satisfy their wants.
- Extension is 'learning by doing' and 'seeing is believing'.
- Extension is developing of individuals, their leaders, their society and their world as a whole.
- Extension is working together to expand the welfare and happiness of people.
- Extension is working in harmony with the culture of the people.
- Extension is a two way channel.
- Extension is a living relationship, respect and trust for each other.
- Extension is a continuous, educational process.

Dahama He gave the following points as the philosophy of extension :

- People are the greatest resources.
- Self-help.
- It is a cooperative effort.
- It has its foundation in democracy.
- Voluntary, cooperative participation in programmes.
- It is based on creating interest by seeing and doing.
- Persuasion and education of the people.
- It is a never ending process.

Mildred Horton He has described four principles which make the philosophy of extension education, they are :

- The individual is supreme in a democracy.
- The home is the fundamental unit in a civilisation.
- The family is the first training group of the human race.
- The foundation of any permanent civilisation must rest on the partnership of man and land.

Rudramurthy He has linked the philosophy of extension work with the Vedas, the Upanishads, the Gita as well as the orthodox and unorthodox schools of philosophy. This is based on the concept of man and the values which are worthy of human pursuit.

Principles of Extension Education

Before taking up the discussion of the principles of extension, it will be worthwhile to examine what is meant by the word 'principle.' A principle is a statement of policy to guide decision and action in a consistent manner.

Its meaning will be clear when we try to understand the sequence of generalisation. When something is put forth as a point of view or an assumption and its proof is not known, it is called a hypothesis. When a hypothesis is put to a test and the point of view or the assumptions, turn out to be acceptable, it is called a theory. When a theory is put to several rigorous tests under different settings by different individuals and the findings are found to be in substantial agreement then it is given the name of a principle. Thus, a principle is a universal truth that has been observed and found to be true under varying conditions and circumstances. A principle is a fundamental truth and a settled rule of action.

Some important principles of extension education are as follows :

Relative Sequence of Extension Principle

Generally, the principles of extension are relative and not necessarily fixed in importance or sequence. However, it is also true that all the principles are important. It may also be relevant to point out that it is never possible to prepare a complete and final list of the extension principles. The principles discussed below are those which are either fundamental in nature or widely accepted in literature on the subject.

Principle of Interests and Needs

To be effective, extension work must begin with the interests and needs of the people. Many a times, the interests of the rural people are not the interests of the extension worker. Even though, he sees the needs of the people better than they do themselves, he must begin with the interests and needs as they (the people) see them. In this way, only can the extension agency mould the needs and interests of the people into realistic needs. Needs that can satisfy the individuals, groups, community and national interests, needs that can be fulfilled with the available resources and the needs that should be fulfilled first.

Grassroot Principle of Organisation

For extension work to be effective and real, it has to be a synthesis of democracy obtained at the level of the family and more particularly at the village level. Things must spring from below and spread like grass. At the same time, modern science calls for an advanced stage of organisation and a wiser coordination of thinking and action that is feasible in a single family or a single village. A higher level of living means wider specialisation in a village. This calls for the corresponding organisations of different professions and a vocations. These will have to be woven together at the level of the enlarged family at the village community level.

The Panchayats, as social institutions, have also to be established at the block and the district levels. Thus, the establishment of the three-tier system, namely Village Panchayat, Block Samiti and Zila Parishad, followed by State Legislatures and Parliament satisfies the grassroot principle of organisation in the extension.

Principle of Cultural Changes

This principle can be summed up in the words of **Earl Moncur** "As each culture is unique and each particular situation within which a change is occurring or is to be made, is unique, it is not possible to lay down prescription for what to identify and to describe the process which occurs, so that each particular individual or team charged with responsibility for planning, execution or adjusting to some type of change, may be able to act in terms of the process."

Principle of Cultural Differences

In order to make extension programmes effective, the approach and procedure must be suited to the culture of the people who are taught. Different cultures require different approaches. A blueprint of work designed for one part of the globe cannot be applied effectively to another part, mainly because of the cultural differences. These differences can be perceived in the way of life of the people, their attitudes, values, loyalties, habits and customs.

Principle of Cooperation and Participation

In an attempt to involve a great number of persons in achieving desired common ends, there seems to be no acceptable alternative but to let them choose the ends and then aiding them to organise their self-help efforts successfully to do the things they want to do.

Most members of the village community will willingly cooperate in carrying out a project which they helped to decide to undertake. It has been the experience of many countries that people become dynamic if they are permitted to take decisions concerning their own affairs, exercise responsibilities and helped to carry out projects in their own villages.

Principle of Applied Science and Democratic Approach

Applied agricultural science is not a one way process. The problems of the people are taken to the scientists who do the experimentation necessary to find out the solutions. The extension worker translates the scientific findings of the laboratories in such a way that the farm families can voluntarily adopt them to satisfy their own needs.

Principle of Warning by Doing

In extension work, farmers should be encouraged to learn new things by doing and by direct participation. The motive for improvement must come from the people and they must practice the new ideas by actually doing them. It is learning by doing, which is most effective in changing people's behaviour and developing the confidence to use the new methods in future.

Principle of Trained Specialists

It is very difficult for a multi-purpose extension worker to keep himself with all the latest findings of research in all the branches of science he has to deal with in his day-to-day activity. Trained specialists have to be provided, who keep themselves in touch with their respective research institutes. They should extend to the extension worker, meaningful terms, the latest scientific developments which have scope for adoption in particular areas.

Adaptability Principle in the Use of Extension Teaching Methods

No single extension teaching method is effective under all situations. Reading material is for those who can read, radio programmes for those who have radios, meetings for those who can attend, demonstrations of recommended practices are for those who can come to the farms where the demonstrations of recommended practices are laid. Farm and home visits are, by far, the most valuable, but they take up considerable time. New situations also arise where a special combination of method is necessary.

Principle of Leadership

A good rule in extension work is "Never do anything yourself that you can get someone to do for you." This calls for the development of local voluntary leadership.

The involvement of leaders in extension programmes is the one single factor that determines the success or failure of those programmes. Local leaders are the guardians of local thought and action and can be trained and developed to best serve as interpreters of new ideas to the villagers.

Whole Family Principle

The family is the primary unit of any society. All the members of the family have to be developed equally by involving all of them.

This is because of the following reasons :

- The extension programme effects all members of the family.
- The family members have great influence in decision-making.
- It creates mutual understanding.
- It aids in money managements.
- It balances farm and family needs.
- It educates the younger members.
- It provides an activity outlet for all.
- It verifies related aspects, such as the social, economic and cultural aspects of the family.
- It assures family service to the community and society.

Principle of Satisfaction

Satisfaction of the people is very essential in extension work. Unless, the people are satisfied with the end product of any programme, it is not going to be able to run. In democratic societies, people cannot be made to move like machines. They must continue to act out of their own conviction and that is possible only when they drive full satisfaction through adoption of innovations well suited to their needs and resources.

Importance of Principles in Extension Work

It is usually believed that the knowledge of the principles is of no value to an extension worker. These principles are considered to be of academic interest for the students taking advance courses in extension. **Leagans**, however, holds out clearly on the need for a sound knowledge of the principles for the extension workers.

He points out that without this knowledge extension workers either keep on labouring under some handicaps or make grave mistakes, particularly in the initial stages, further if an extension worker aspires to become an administrator or a supervisor, it will be all the more necessary for him to possess a complete knowledge of the principles of extension.

Extension/Instructional Methods and Materials

The instructional methods are kinds of instructional ways or activities used to guide the facilitation of learning in each phase of the instruction process. The instruction methods are the 'how to' in the delivery of training.

These are the methods of imparting new knowledge and skill to the rural people by drawing their attention towards technologies, thereby arousing their interest and helping them to have a successful experience of new. The extension methods can be classified as :

Interpersonal or Individual Contact

In this method, face-to face or person to person contact between the rural people and extension workers is held. It is a very effective in teaching. It provides first hand information about the village problems, ongoing activities and it establishes confidence in the worker. An extension worker can provide individual approach through personal visits and personal letters. The quantum of feedback available is very high, but slow communication.

Small Group Methods

In the small group methods, there are two or more people. Here, the extension worker is required to know the type of group he is approaching. Through this method, a number of people can be reached even if the material and staffing provision of the extension service is limited. There are definite time savings. It permits more participation by group (clients) people. Techniques of group dynamics can be used to accelerate the spread of information and increase the willingness of the clients (people/villagers) to make decisions.

Through this method, the group as a whole is prepared to accept a higher risk than an individual and the potential for superior performance of groups. And teams compared to individuals can be activated for extension purposes group extension motivates clients (farmers/villagers) to move from interest stage to trial stage of learning. Small group methods include demonstration, training leaders, group panel discussions, extension group circles, symposiums, group interviews, dialogues, workshops, field days, field tours/trips, etc.

Large Group Methods

The methods to be adopted for large group (masses). Through this method, the information can be conveyed to a large number of people at a time. In this method, the masses are approached through films, slides film strips, flash cards, radio talks, charts, diagrams, circular letters, etc.

The audio-visual material plays an important role in making teaching and learning process (formal or non-formal) more interesting, effective and permanent. It is essential know about the need and importance of audio-visual materials.

Audio-Visual Materials

The audio-visual materials help the extension worker to approach and contact the masses. This is more useful for making people aware of the new agricultural technology quickly. When agent is communicating with a group of farmers, its impact and effectiveness can be greatly increased by the use of suitable audio-visual materials.

Need and Importance of Audio-Visual Materials

When selected and used properly, audio-visual materials can help in the following ways :

- The interest of the audience can be maintained if the agent varies the mode of presentation. It is difficult to concentrate for long on what someone is saying, but if the agent refers to a wall chart or illustrates a point with some slides, his audience attention can be maintained.
- Processes and concepts are difficult to express in words, but a simple chart or diagram can make the process clear.
- The audio-visual materials help in gaining knowledge of the latest technology, software application and visual communication skills with the ability to demonstrate the skill in using technology. It help develops continuity of thought this is especially true of motion pictures.
- The audio-visual materials make the teaching and learning process more interesting, effective and permanent.
- They help bringing the world to the people or audience in classrooms/workshops.
- They stimulate motivation and help learners.
- They help to make teaching realistic.
- They help to attract attention of audience.
- They help to convey the meaning clearly.

Planning of Audio-Visual Materials

The planning for audio-visual materials should suit the age level and other characteristics of learner. It should be interesting and motivating. While planning, they should be the true representative of real things. When planning for materials, as far as possible locally available material should be used and one should carefully visualise the use of teaching aids before their actual presentation. The adequate care should be taken to handle the aids.

While planning of audio-visual materials, agents should keep in mind that what is to be communicated and why it is important to communicate. Outline the subject matter point by point. Visualise the key points in the outline. A rehearsing should be done to make a smooth presentation. It should be properly balanced.

The properly planned audio-visual materials can impact a large number of audience in an effective manner. For example, the pictures can have a more immediate impact on one's emotions than words. For example, photographs of a heavy crop are likely to arouse interest more effectively than details of yields read out by an extension agent.

A real object is often the most effective aid. It enables the audience to understand exactly what the extension agent is talking about. The effects of decisions and actions that farmers might take can be shown. For explaining the procedure, a simple flow chart or diagram can be used and make the process clearer.

Classification of Audio-Visual Materials

The audio-visual materials are an effective means of communication. A new sophisticated mass communication technology capable of producing sound and pictures is widely used. The audio-visual materials are mostly used in teaching and conferences.

The audio-visual materials have relevance for distance communication. Audio technique is a tool to give effect and impression to effective communication, have the qualities of seeing and hearing.

Audio Materials

The audio materials/aids can be classified as :

Radio

It is a good source of communication of ideas to the rural people, especially in a country like India. It carries news bulletins and special programmes for rural people, house wives and children. It is a good source of dissemination of agricultural information to farmers. 'All India Radio' broadcasts in all major Indian languages and even in dialects.

It can become a true local mass medium with locally relevant news on health, farming, trading and other news of day-to-day household value. It is a spoken means of communication. The broadcaster has to get and hold the attention of the audience, otherwise the message is lost. It is a very fast medium. It is popular, pleasing and even exciting. However, it cannot be used to convey heavy, detailed knowledge.

It can be used for announcement of meetings, demonstration, etc. Radio can reach more people more quickly than any other means of communication. It can disseminate timely and urgent information and is relatively cheap. It can reach illiterates and build enthusiasm and maintain interest.

Some severe limitations to the use of radio are :

- Broadcasting facilities are available only in limited places.
- Recorded time assigned to extension is limited.
- Frequently losses out in competition with entertainment.
- Difficult to check on results.
- Requires a special technique.
- Not enough sets in rural areas.
- Influence is limited to people, who can listen intelligently.

Tape Recorder

It is a sound recording and reproduction device that records and plays back sounds usually using magnetic tape for storage. It is suitable for extension work in meetings, training programmes, campaigns, recording radio programmes, etc. It facilitates on-the-spot recording of sound.

It helps in duplication and dissemination of sound. Recorded tape can be immediately played back without any processing. It has low operational cost, as the same tape may be used again.

Public Address System

A public address system amplifies sound so that it is audible to a large audience, over a distance. It consists of three segments, viz., microphone, amplifier and speaker.

The microphone converts sounds into electrical waves which are fed into an amplifier. The amplified electric current is fed into a speaker to convert into sound waves, and the magnified sound is heard through speakers. It is very useful in meetings and campaigns to disseminate information.

Telephone

The telephone allows people to talk to each other, from distant places. It provides for instant interpersonal communication, in which the communicator and the person who is communicated to change roles while giving and getting information. This improves speed of communication and involves considerable saving of time, money, and labour.

Though, usually, only two persons can communicate at a time through a telephone, the system serves many people in a given area if a speaker is attached to it, like.

Digital Audio Player

A digital audio player has the primary function of storing, organising and playing audio files. Some digital audio players are also referred to as portable media players as they have image-viewing andlor video-playing support.

Visual Aids

The following are the visual materials/aids :

Chalkboard or Blackboard

The chalkboard is probably the simplest, cheapest, most convenient, and widely used non projected visual aid in extension teaching. A black wooden board is mostly used, hence, it is also known as blackboard.

However, ground glass, roll-up materials, coloured in black, olive green, or blue may also be used. For extension teaching under field conditions, inward folding wooden boards or roll-up materials are convenient. The chalkboard is suitable for use in lectures, training programmes, group meetings, etc.

White Board

Modern classrooms are equipped with boards, also called marker boards or multipurpose boards. They can be used for more than one purpose. They are preferred around computers. They require special erasable markers. A felt eraser is required to erase the surface soon after use. Markers are available in different colours.

Interactive White Board

An interactive white board is a large interactive display that connects to a computer and projector. A projector projects the computer's desktop onto the board's surface, where users control the computer using a pen, finger, or other device. The board is typically mounted to a wall, or on a floor stand.

Bulletin Board

A bulletin board displays message. It is a surface on which bulletins, news, information, announcements, of specific or general interest can be displayed. Bulletin boards are of different sizes with provisions to hold pins, books exhibits and other materials. The message on the bulletin board may be in the form of words, graphs, charts, photographs, illustrations, publications, etc.

Pictures and Photographs

A picture is a representation made by drawing, painting, or photography which gives an accurate idea of an object. A good picture may tell a story without using a single word. Pictures may be in black and white. or in colour. Colour pictures and enlarged photographs have more appeal. For extension photography, a good quality 35 mm single-lens reflex camera with some essential attachments like a flash gun, lens hood, filters, close-up lens, etc are useful.

Rope Board

Rope, wire, heavy string can be used to create a background for pictures or exhibit materials. The rope can be stretched from floor to ceiling. Pictures mounted on cardboard or three dimensional objects can be taped in place. A heavy wire screen can also be used as a background.

Flannel Board and Flannel Graph

A flannel board is a visual aid in which messages are written or drawn on thick paper and presented step-by-step by the extension worker to the audience to synchronize with the talk. The board is a flannel covered flat surface. Flannel is stretched and then glued to a piece of plywood or heavy cardboard.

Flash Cards

Flash cards are brief visual messages on poster board cards flashed (turned over at short intervals) before the audience to emphasize important points in a presentation. Flash cards are held like a pack of cards and are flashed to the audience, one at a time, in a sequence, along with the talk

Posters

A poster is displayed in a public place with the purpose of creating awareness amongst the people. A poster is generally seen from a distance and the person glancing at it seldom has the time or inclination to stop and read.

The job of the poster is to stop the persons in hurry give message to them. Poster may contain a written message, diagram, map, picture, or a cartoon. A few hand drawn posters may be used in extension training programme, group meeting, etc. Printed posters may be used in large numbers in campaigns, exhibitions, etc.

Charts

A chart is a symbolised visual aid with pictures of relationships and changes used to tabulate a large mass of information, or show a progression. Charts can help communicate difficult, often dull subject matter in an interesting and effective way.

They make facts and figures clear and interesting, show or compare changes, show the size and placement of parts. They are also helpful in presenting abstract ideas in visual form.

Slides

A slide is a transparent mounted picture which is projected by focusing light through it. The projection may be made on a screen or on a white wall. Slides of 35mm films, mounted on individual cardboard or plastic frames are common, and are extensively used in extension work during training programmes, seminars, workshops, group meetings, campaigns, exhibitions, etc.

Overhead Projector

The overhead projector projects the picture over the head of the speaker on the screen. Drawings, diagrams, letterings, etc., are made on transparent sheets and are put on the glass platform of the overhead projector, through which a strong light is passed.

The rays of light are made to converge with a lens, and are reflected by a mirror held at an angle on the screen at the back. Overhead projection is used in training programmes, group meeting, seminar, symposium, workshop, etc.

Handheld Projector

The handheld projector is also known as a pocket projector, or a mobile projector, or a pico-projector. It is an emerging technology that applies the use of a projector in a handheld device.

It is a response to the emergence of compact portable devices such as mobile phones, personal digital assistants and digital cameras, which have sufficient storage capacity to handle presentation materials with an attached display screen. A handheld projector has the ability to project a clear image, regardless of the physical characteristics of the viewing surface

Diagrams

It is able to illustrate a process or an object, which cannot be brought to a classroom or meeting. We can draw a picture of any specimen like goat, cow, building plan, sketch of a machine, etc. A diagram is a visual symbol made with the help of lines and geometrical forms and pictorial elements to explain mostly a process or part of something.

Facsimile

It is a mechanical media that makes an exact copy. Facsimile transmits through telephone lines, exact copies of blueprints, layouts and other visual materials. It is increasingly being used to transmit exact copies between distant places.

Flip Chart

It is like an album of drawings, pictures and charts. It is an aid and assists an extension worker or a teacher to tell a story. Its advantages are that it is handy, can be carried easily and can be prepared with few simple tools.

Flip chart can be prepared as follows :

- Decide the topic.
- Collect relevant facts and select important points.
- Make rough visuals, make drawings simple, use colours for drawings or use bold photographs.
- Use stencils to draw lines or to make sprayed pictures.
- Make two holes on the upper side and tie a string, which hangs loose and can help in hanging it on a stand or a black board.
- The script describing the pictures or sketches should be written on the back side of the previous page or on a separate sheet from which to talk while using the illustrations and reherse well before presentation.

Audio-Visual Aids

Audio-visual materials/aids are :

Motion Pictures

Motion pictures are extremely useful in motivating and teaching any learner. Yet educational films are not being widely used by extension educators in many development sub sectors. The reasons usually given are:

- The expense of films and projectors.
- Non availability of suitable films.
- Transportation and maintenance of films and projectors.
- Dominance of entertainment over educative function of films.
- Lack of skills, on the part of extension workers, to operate projectors.

Video Projector

A video projector is also known as a Digital Projector, now popular for many applications for extension and development. All video projectors use a very bright light to project the image. Projected image size is important because the total amount of light does not change - as size increases, brightness decreases. They are widely used with, or without a connection to an interactive white board for presentations, training, demonstrations, etc.

Television

It is one of the most popular method of communication. It attracts the number of audience or group of people at a time. These groups of people may be literate or illiterate and people from different socio-economic groups. It is an audio-visual medium, brings us into contact with events in an exciting and clarifying way.

It stimulates and reinforces ideas, beliefs and thoughts. It has more flexibility and mobility in its coverage due to audio-visual presentation. Television not only informs and educates, but also inspires and motivates. The moving images of television catch the attention of the viewers. Television can transmit not only words, but pictures as well.

The significance of TV as a medium of mass communication has universally been realised and recognised. Television is described as a powerful medium by many people, but effectiveness of television may depend on many factors like infrastructure practicability of recommendations and follow up the programmes.

Multimedia and Computer Based Media

It is a combination of more than one media. It can include several forms of media such as audio, text, still images, animation, graphics, video, film, etc. Multimedia in a present context generally implies to computer based media.

Interactive video is one form of computer based media. In this access to information can be done easily. For example, through information kiosks, a lot of developmental information is being accessed in remote and rural areas.

Mobile Phone

It is also known as cellular phone. It is a device that can make and receive telephone calls over a radio link while moving around a wide geographic area.

Cell Phone Operated Mobile Audio Communication and Conference System(COMBACCS). COMBACCS can help community members at different locations build relationships and understanding.

Short Message Service (SMS) and Wireless Application Protocol (WAP) enabled cell phones with cameras can be effective in offering 'always available extension' between experts and people.

Preparation and Field Testing of Audio-Visual Materials

- The audio-visual materials should be prepared with locally available material.
- It should be cost-effective and relevant to the needs of the target group.
- It should be simple, easy to understand and which can help in motivating the learners. Above all should himself inspect the audio-visual material in all its respect.
- Field testing plays an important role in the preparation of a plan.
- In this, the data are collected from the people/group in order to know about their problems, the techniques used by them, their income and the geographical conditions.
- Through field testing, the information is gathered with regard to people's values and their problems. Fielded testing also enables one to know about the planning and execution of the programmes taken earlier.
- It helps in comparing the new plans and programmes with old plans and then accordingly incorporate new ideas and plans in the new scheme.
- It also helps in knowing about the problems of a particular area/people.

Use and Evaluation of Audio-Visual Materials

- When the materials have been used as part of the instructional process, the materials themselves should be evaluated for their relevancy, practicability and usefulness.
- The evaluation should be continuous (comprehensive) and also summative. The teaching objectives must cover the type of behaviour change, information gained change in attitudes and learning skills.
- The audio-visual materials have really met the needs of the target audience. For a fair evaluation, the agents should see whether his use of audio-visual material has really helped him in his field work or changed his attitude and style of work.
- The agents should review basic information and decide which part needs to be updated.
- The evaluation should focus how fully each objective have been achieved by the use of audio-visual materials and the reasons for any lack of progress. The evaluation becomes effective if the follow up is throughly considered by the agents. This would give an opportunity to further improve the weakness of the material while using.
- The agents should see that the material is well planned and of quality, meeting the needs of the target group. Whether small or large use upto date material, it should be easily portable and also the confidentiality of the material.

EXAM BASED QUESTIONS

1 From which word, the word 'extension' is derived?
(a) Latin (b) Greek (c) Hebrew (d) Chinese

2 The areas of extension education can be divided into
(a) agricultural extension
(b) home science extension
(c) agricultural engineering extension
(d) All of the above

3 Who is the father of extension education?
(a) O P Dahama (b) Mildred Horton
(c) J P Leagans (d) Kelsey and Hearne

4 Who defined extension education as "An educational process to provide knowledge to rural people about the improved practices in a convincing manner and help them to take decisions within their specific local conditions?"
(a) D Ensminger (b) Kelsey and Hearne
(c) V C Sanoria (d) O P Dahama

5 An extension education is basically
(a) need oriented
(b) local resource based
(c) problem solution oriented system
(d) All of the above

6 Home science extension is
(a) extending technical knowledge to wives or ladies in urban and rural areas.
(b) extending knowledge about agricultural machinery.
(c) extending knowledge on the managing and running of industries.
(d) All of the above

7 "Extension is a communication intervention to use resources strategically to manipulate seemingly casual factors in a social process as considered desirable by the intervening party." It is stated by
(a) JAC Brown (b) Rolling
(c) Dr. G Shivarudrappa (d) None of these

8 Who stated, "Extension is an ongoing process of giving useful information to people and helping them acquire knowledge, skill and attitude to utilise the information?"
(a) Dr. G Shivarudrappa (b) Rolling
(c) Swanson Clear (d) None of these

9 Extension education is understood as
(a) education meant to spread knowledge among villagers.
(b) a programme for educating the farmers.
(c) extending educational opportunities to the deprived.
(d) extending new knowledge to the doorstep of those who need it.

10 Ever since, its commencement in 1952, the scope of extension education has been concerned with upto 1955
(a) agricultural education (b) home science education
(c) rural education (d) women empowerment

11 Which one of the following can be considered as the relation between extension and communication?
(a) Extension worker needs to convey the changes to the community by communicating effectively.
(b) Extension is extending help, communication is not necessary for extension.
(c) To create good environment in education, communication is necessary.
(d) Communication is not an integral part of extension.

12 Pre-colonial African tradition did not have school's children learnt by living and doing, this type of education can be considered as an
(a) informal education (b) extension education
(c) formal education (d) distance education

13 Which one of the following is not an objective of the extension of home science?
(a) Increased productivity
(b) Increased people participation
(c) Generate better employment
(d) No community involvement

14 Extension worker solves the major and minor problems of the community, the problem may be related to health, education, employment, etc., so, he can be considered as a
(a) doctor (b) educationist
(c) physician (d) multi-tasker

15 To promote all round development of all individuals in the home, is one of the broad objectives of
(a) home science extension (b) informal education
(c) formal education (d) education extension

16 Highly institutionalised, chronologically graded and hierarchically structured education system is termed as
(a) formal education (b) informal education
(c) home science extension (d) adult education

17 Any organised, systematic, educational activity carried outside the framework of the sub-groups of the population, can be called as
(a) extension education (b) non-formal education
(c) home science education (d) mass education

18 Extension education as a discipline has its historical roots in
(a) India (b) USA
(c) UK (d) Sri Lanka

19 The origin of the term 'education' was first introduced in ...... by Cambridge university in England.
(a) 1875 (b) 1873 (c) 1864 (d) 1901

20 The first state Agricultural University was established in 1906 on the pattern of Land Grant College in the US. Which was that university?
(a) Pantnagar University
(b) Punjab Agricultural University
(c) Haryana Agricultural University
(d) Bihar Agricultural University

21 With whose help Rabindranath Tagore started the project 'Shriniketan'?
(a) Sir Daniel Hamilton (b) B T Krishnamachari
(c) L M Hurst (d) S K Dey

22 The Gurgaon Project started by F L Brayne in the year ....
(a) 1925 (b) 1930
(c) 1920 (d) 1940

23 Who initiated the Marthendam Project?
(a) Dr. Spencer Hatch (b) S K Dey
(c) Daniel Benor (d) Paul Leagans

24 Which among the following project was started in 1932?
(a) Baroda Village Reconstruction Project
(b) Gurgaon Project
(c) Nilokheri Project
(d) Etawah Project

25 Which among the following philosopher has linked the philosophy of extension work with the Vedas, the Upanishads, the Gita as well as the Orthodox and Morthodox School of Philosophy?
(a) Mildred Horton (b) Rudramurthy
(c) Srinivasa Ramanujan (d) Kelsey and Hearne

26 Charts are utilised
(a) for development of an aspect
(b) for classification
(c) to show relationship
(d) All of the above

27 Charts try to explain
(a) symbolise matter (b) express of a product
(c) how of events (d) All of these

28 Which one of the following is not a modern information technology?
(a) Pageant (b) Video conferencing
(c) Facsimile (d) Teletext

29 The purpose of using a poster is to
(a) arouse interest (b) motivate
(c) create awareness (d) create understanding

30 Media have a role and a function in society, which could be
(a) maintain the consensus (b) reinforce
(c) stabilise (d) All of these

31 Radio experiments in the use of radio for promoting literacy and education was conducted as early as
(a) 1930s (b) 1940s (c) 1900s (d) 1920s

32 The role of coordination in a satellite programme is
(a) crucial (b) difficult
(c) time consuming (d) expensive

33 Learning through satellite is basically learning by
(a) unitation (b) seeing
(c) guidance (d) None of these

34 Who is known as the 'Father of Indian Cinema'?
(a) Torney (b) JF Madan
(c) Dada Saheb Phalke (d) Natraj Mudaliar

35 Which media would be ideal to attract the attention of children to sell chocolates to them?
(a) Radio (b) Newspapers
(c) TV (advertisements) (d) Leaflets

36 Who believes that mass media are primarily moulders of society as well as reflections of it?
(a) Denis Mcquail (b) George Gerbner
(c) Harold Lasswell (d) Wilbur Schramm

37 An advertisement that looks like an article or feature is a
(a) advertorial (b) billboard
(c) display (d) campaign

38 A publication that is half the size of the standard newspaper page, is flashy as well as heavily illustrated is called a
(a) tabloid (b) broadsheet
(c) leaflet (d) brochure

39 The three dimensional recognisable limitation of an object is known as
(a) mock-ups (b) film
(c) specimen (d) poster

40 Which of the following is/are the characteristic(s) of Ideal Village Project?
(a) It was initiated by Sir Daniel Hamilton in 1903.
(b) Under this programme, Cooperative Deposit Schemes were set up.
(c) The emphasis was on specialised training for unemployed young farmers.
(d) All of the above

41 Which of the following statements is/are correct about Gurgaon Project?

Statement I The project was for the rural upliftment in the district Gurgaon.

Statement II It was started to develop the feeling of women education and home development work.

(a) Only statement I is correct
(b) Only statement II is correct
(c) Both the statements I and II are correct
(d) Neither statement I nor II is correct

42 The Sevagram Project started by Gandhiji in 1920 in Vardha with the aim
(a) to promote primary and adult education programme.
(b) to popularise mother tongue and other national dialects.
(c) to create the feeling of rural leadership.
(d) Both (a) and (b)

43 Which of the following statements regarding Nilokheri Project is incorrect?
(a) The project was started by Dr. W H Wisher.
(b) To develop the committees of Panchayats and cooperatives.
(c) To eliminate the middle man system.
(d) Both (a) and (b)

44 What were the short-term objectives of the Community Development Programme started in 1952?
(a) To increase agricultural production both qualitatively and quantitatively.
(b) To encourage cottage industries and indigenous industries.
(c) To solve problem of rural unemployment.
(d) All of the above

45 Which of the following agricultural programmes is popularly known as 'Package Programme'?
(a) Intensive Agricultural Area Programme
(b) Intensive Agricultural District Project
(c) Training and Visit System
(d) National Agricultural Extension Project

46 What were the main objectives of National Agriculture Extension Project?
(a) To remove shortcoming in the existing agricultural system.
(b) To bridge the gap between research system with that of extension system.
(c) To test or demonstrate new technologies on farmer's fields.
(d) The research and extension programme should be farmer centered.

47 Which among the following is/are the objectives of extension education?
(a) To assist people in mobilising and utilising the resources which they have and which they need from outside.
(b) To build rural people independent of their thinking.
(c) To train rural people, youth for development works.
(d) All of the above

48 According to Esminger, the philosophy of extension can be expressed as
(a) extension is helping people to help themselves.
(b) extension is 'learning by doing' and 'seeing is believing'.
(c) extension is a two way channel.
(d) All of the above

49 The principle of trained specialist implies
(a) who keep themselves in touch with their respective research institute.
(b) extend to the extension worker the latest scientific developments.
(c) serve as interpreter of new ideas to the villagers.
(d) Both (a) and (b)

50 Which of the following statements is/are correct?
(a) Gossip groups are micro-groups.
(b) Modern mass media are procession and mist.
(c) Modern mass media are produced and distributed like other consumer and industrial products on a mass scale.
(d) All of the above

51 Which of the following statements is/are correct?
(a) Radio is a useful tool for extension work in rural areas.
(b) Radio is a device with whole mass can be contacted at a time, efficiently and economically.
(c) Evening time is the best time for broadcasts for the rural people.
(d) All of the above

52 Which of the following statements is/are correct?
(a) Radio provides the communicator with the opportunity to reach local communities and audiences segmented by age.
(b) Radio is a low cost medium.
(c) Posters are miniature billboard whose main advantages are lower cost and greater flexibility of placement.
(d) All of the above

53 Which of the following statements is/are correct?
(a) Today, 'Doordarshan' devotes atleast 10% of its telecast time to educational or enrichment programmes for farmers, school's children, youth and other groups.
(b) Televisions was introduced in India by the Nehru Government with the primary aim of exploring the medium for distance education.
(c) Mahatma Gandhi spoke just once over radio and was able to mobilise the masses.
(d) All of the above

54 Choose the correct statements regarding interpersonal method.
(a) It provides first hand information about the village problems.
(b) It is not very effective.
(c) The quantum of feedback available is very high.
(d) Both (a) and (c)

55 What factors need to be considered while planning audio-visual materials?
(a) Use locally available material.
(b) It should be interesting and motivating.
(c) Visualise the teaching aids before their actual presentation.
(d) All of the above

56 Which of the following principles regarding extension education was not given by Mildred Horton?
(a) It is never ending process.
(b) The individual is supreme in a democracy.
(c) The home is the fundamental unit in a civilisation.
(d) The individual is not supreme in a democracy.

57 **A flip chart**
(a) is an aid to assist an extension worker or teacher to tell a story.
(b) is handy and can be carried away early.
(c) can be prepared with few simple tools.
(d) All of the above

58 **Shriniketan Project was started with the objective**
(a) to increase the knowledge of rural people
(b) to help rural people in establishing cottage industry
(c) to inspire people to follow new technology
(d) All of the above

59 **Which of the following are the hindrances in extension work?**
1. Faulty communication.
2. Faulty programme planning.
3. Inability to involve the local leaders.
4. Lack of motivation of the people.

Select the correct answer using the codes given below
(a) 1 and 2 (b) 2 and 3
(c) 1, 2 and 3 (d) All of these

60 **Which of the following are considered as the characteristics of the home science extension?**
1. It is action oriented.
2. It is a need-based programme.
3. It is voluntary.

Select the correct answer using the codes given below
(a) 1 and 2 (b) 2 and 3
(c) 1, 2 and 3 (d) None of these

61 **The use of knowledge and abilities acquired through non-formal education can be evaluated in terms of**
1. personal development.
2. involvement in community.
3. competency in doing similar work.
4. increased employment opportunities.

Select the correct answer using the codes given below
(a) 1, 2 and 3 (b) 2, 3 and 4
(c) 2, 4 and 1 (d) 1, 3 and 4

62 **Write the steps of extension educational process in sequence.**
1. Objectives 2. Teaching
3. Evaluation 4. Situation
5. Reconsideration

Codes
(a) 4, 1, 2, 3 and 5 (b) 4, 1, 2, 5 and 3
(c) 5, 3, 4, 2 and 1 (d) 3, 2, 1, 4 and 5

63 **Which of the following are the objectives of home science extension education?**
1. To bring about change in knowledge, skill and attitude.
2. To make people aware that kitchen, gardening and small scale industries are a profitable professions.
3. To bring out the talent, leadership and efficiency of rural people.
4. To bring the scientist closes to the formers.

Select the correct answer using the codes given below
(a) 1 and 2 (b) 2 and 3
(c) 1, 2 and 3 (d) All of these

64 **Charts can be**
1. pictorial 2. organisation, flow chart
3. suspense chart 4. strip tease chart

Codes
(a) 1 and 2 (b) 1 and 4
(c) 1, 2, 3 and 4 (d) 1, 2 and 3

65 **The advantage of flip charts includes**
1. handy
2. easy to carry
3. easy to prepare
4. size "15 to 20" approx

Codes
(a) 1 and 2 (b) 1 and 4
(c) 1, 2, 3 and 4 (d) 1, 2 and 3

66 **Charts are being used to teach**
1. reading 2. working
3. maths tables 4. practicals

Codes
(a) 1 and 2 (b) 1 and 4
(c) 1, 2, 3 and 4 (d) 1, 2 and 3

67 **Which are used for mass contact methods?**
1. Personal calls 2. Circular letter
3. Radio and television 4. Tours

Select the correct answer using the codes given below
(a) 1, 2 and 3 (b) 2, 3 and 4
(c) 2 and 3 (d) 1 and 4

68 **Television is a medium with its own psychological and emotional appeal and able to transcend barriers of**
1. time 2. place
3. discipline 4. personalities

Select the correct answer using the codes given below
(a) 1, 2, 3 and 4 (b) 1, 2 and 4
(c) 1 and 2 (d) 2 and 4

69 **Development supporting communication focuses on grassroot level development and participation using small media like**
1. flashcords, slides
2. video, folk media
3. personal contact
4. meetings

Select the correct answer using the codes given below
(a) 1, 2 and 3 (b) 1, 2, 3 and 4
(c) 1 and 4 (d) 2 and 4

70 **Arrange the sequence of the given media of communication by the years, they were started.**
1. Television 2. Radio
3. Films 4. Print

Codes
(a) 4, 3, 2, 1 (b) 3, 4, 1, 2
(c) 2, 3, 4, 1 (d) 1, 2, 3, 4

71 **Satellite Educational Programme has much less to offer you if you believe in**
1. learning by doing
2. learning by personal exploration.
3. learning by role.
4. learning by conditioning.

Select the correct answer using the codes given below
(a) 1 and 2 (b) 1 and 4
(c) 1, 2 and 3 (d) All of these

72 **Arrange the following teaching learning methods in the order of learner's ability.**
1. A video show 2. Laboratory method
3. Demonstration 4. Radio talk

Codes
(a) 1, 2, 3 and 4 (b) 2, 3, 4 and 1
(c) 3, 2, 1 and 4 (d) 4, 1, 3 and 2

73 **Match the following.**

List I	List II
A. 2 D	1. Field visit
B. 3 D	2. Poster
C. Projected aid	3. Models
D. Non-projected aid	4. Films
	5. Bulletin boards

Codes

	A	B	C	D		A	B	C	D
(a)	2	3	4	1	(b)	2	3	1	4
(c)	2	3	5	4	(d)	2	3	4	5

74 **Match the following.**

List I	List II
A. Video	1. Audio aid
B. Slide	2. Projected audio-visual aid
C. Chart	3. Projected visual aid
D. Tape recorder	4. Non-projected visual aid
	5. Multimedia aid

Codes

	A	B	C	D		A	B	C	D
(a)	5	4	2	3	(b)	2	3	4	1
(c)	5	1	3	2	(d)	3	2	4	1

75 **Match the following.**

List I	List II
A. Overhead projector	1. Slides
B. LCD projector	2. Films
C. Slide projector	3. Flannel
D. Motion picture projector	4. Transparency sheet
	5. Power point

Codes

	A	B	C	D		A	B	C	D
(a)	4	5	1	2	(b)	3	1	5	4
(c)	2	5	1	3	(d)	1	3	4	5

76 **Match the following.**

List I	List II
A. Puppets	1. Graphic aid
B. Charts	2. Electronic
C. Computer	3. Traditional
D. Print	4. Mass media

Codes

	A	B	C	D		A	B	C	D
(a)	2	3	4	1	(b)	4	1	3	2
(c)	3	1	2	4	(d)	1	2	3	4

77 **Match the following.**

List I	List II
A. Slide	1. Non-projected visual aid
B. Radio	2. Projected audio-visual aid
C. Chart	3. Audio aid
D. Video	4. Projected visual aid

Codes

	A	B	C	D		A	B	C	D
(a)	4	3	1	2	(b)	4	1	2	3
(c)	1	3	2	4	(d)	3	4	1	2

78 **Match the following.**

List I	List II
A. Intensive Agriculture District Programme	1 1970-71
B. Small Farmers Development Agency	2. 2006
C. National Agriculture Extension Project	3. 1960
D. National Agriculture Innovation Project	4. 1983

Codes

	A	B	C	D		A	B	C	D
(a)	1	2	3	4	(b)	3	1	4	2
(c)	4	2	1	3	(d)	2	3	1	4

Directions (Q. Nos. 79-96) *Below given are two statements, one labelled as Assertion (A) and other labelled as Reason (R). Following are the codes given below. Select the correct code for the following.*

Codes
(a) Both A and R are true and R is the correct explanation of A
(b) Both A and R are true, but R is not the correct explanation of A
(c) A is true, but R is false
(d) A is false, but R is true

79 **Assertion** (A) The success of an extension programme depends on the involvement of the leader in the programme.
Reason (R) An active mass following and participation makes any programme success.

80 **Assertion** (A) Good communication is an integral part of extension activity.
Reason (R) It is important for the extension worker to be a good communicator.

81 **Assertion** (A) An extension worker should familiarise himself with the local norms, belie, language, dress and eating habit of the community he is going to work with.

Reason (R) Programmes should be implemented by extension worker without giving prominence to religion or caste.

82 **Assertion** (A) Extension education is not free with hindrances in extension work.

Reason (R) Lack of prioritisation of needs of the people is one of the needs of extension education.

83 **Assertion** (A) The traditional media gets neglected because of their low prestige rating.

Reason (R) This is because of the mass media, which gets higher prestige due to its interpersonal networks, newness and attractiveness.

84 **Assertion** (A) Three persons sitting at different places can have a common talk through audio/video conferencing.

Reason (R) Internet and electronic media facilitate the contact amongst different persons at a time.

85 **Assertion** (A) The effectiveness of audio-visuals rely upon the skill of the user.

Reason (R) The audio-visual materials are selected on the basis of the criteria used for teaching and learning.

86 **Assertion** (A) Effective communication is a combination of seeing, learning and doing.

Reason (R) Exclusive uses audio-visual materials make learning experience complete.

87 **Assertion** (A) Posters used as audio-visual aids compel attention and motivate action.

Reason (R) Posters help in communicating as they present abstract information in a graphic way.

88 **Assertion** (A) 'The Grow More Food Campaign's aim was to increase agricultural production.

Reason (R) It can be regarded as the forerunner of Community Development Programme.

89 **Assertion** (A) The basic premise of National Agricultural Technology Project was that research and extension programme should be farmer centered and demand driven.

Reason (R) It was enacted by legislation.

90 **Assertion** (A) The Principle of Cooperation and Participation involves many persons.

Reason (R) The involvement of people determines the success or failure of the programme.

91 **Assertion** (A) The small group method is useful in approaching to number of people.

Reason (R) The extension worker in small group use the techniques of group dynamic to accelerate the speed of information.

92 **Assertion** (A) A chart is a pictorial presentation in the form of table or diagram.

Reason (R) A chart shows non-numerical relationship.

93 **Assertion** (A) Magnetic boards are similar to flannel boards.

Reason (R) It is a mechanical media that makes an exact copy.

94 **Assertion** (A) Shriniketan Project helped to increase knowledge of rural people.

Reason (R) It helped to develop the feeling of women education and home development.

95 **Assertion** (A) Television is one of the popular method of communication.

Reason (R) It has more flexibility and mobility in its coverage due to audio-visual presentation.

96 **Assertion** (A) The evaluation of audio-visual materials should focus fully on each objective to be achieved.

Reason (R) The evaluation should be continuous.

Directions (Q. Nos. 97-101) *Read the passage and answer the following questions.*

The role of extension worker is of vital importance because they are like a teacher, philosopher, leader, guide and colleague for the community and on the basis of his special qualities, he is able to carry on developmental programme successfully. It is undoubtedly true to say that the success and failure of development programmes depend upon the qualities of extension worker.

By extension worker, we mean a man who is the last chain of extension organisation, who while living in the midst of the community, propagates his programmes.

The roles of extension worker are as follows : To introduce villagers to new ideas and to bring change in their behaviour. But, he cannot be successful in this work unless he himself is aware of new technologies. Only after having full and complete knowledge about latest techniques/ technologies, he will be able to impress the people.

He should have burning desire to know his subject and problems and requirements of people, so that the research work of research institutions can be brought to the people and problem of the people could be brought to the research institutions for analysis and inspection and again their results can be brought to the people. It is correct to say that the extension worker should play the role of teacher as well as that of a student.

Extension worker lives alone in the village and he has to provide appropriate solution to the problems of the people. Therefore, extension worker should be capable of taking prompt action and providing explicit solution.

Extension worker should be tactful and try to derive relevant benefits from the experiences, problems and resources of the people in order to gain their trust and become reliable person for them. Extension worker should have foresightedness to know which type of work will bring, what kind of result and what will be its impact on the people. He should also know which work should be given priority in order to achieve long lasting benefit.

Extension worker should have sympathetic attitude. If he is capable of listening to the problems of people sympathetically and able to solve them then undoubtedly people will respect and honour him.

He should perform his duties and should not exert his rights. Extension worker's personality should be able to attract people easily. Extension worker should be courageous enough to tackle difficult conditions and situations. The extension worker should develop his personality in such a way as not get easily hurt by opposition.

Firm Determination Extension Worker should have firm determination so that he can do his work inspite of all hurdles, which come in his way. If he lacks in determination then he will be unable to generate faith among people. Extension worker should not hesitate to do social work and labour work, of any kind.

This way he himself will do less work but the environment created is essential for the progress of development work in which development programme will progress rapidly. In this way, dignity of labour will be enhanced among people. The extension worker has to perform certain responsibilities.

To Create Motivation and Feeling By motivating rural people for the development of programmes so that they themselves may become anxious to improve their standard of living and make new programmes and implement them for their upliftment.

- Knowledge of local felt needs.
- Precedence of instant needs.
- To create self-belief in rural people cooperation.

Emphasis on Self-Dependence Our villages were self-dependent before British rule. Their needs like food, clothing and housing were fulfilled in villages itself, but now they have to go outside to fulfill their basic needs and still they are unable to earn enough for themselves.

- To develop the close relations between research centre and agricultural farm.
- Full use of present local resources.
- Plan for all round development of the society. Some extension workers are more professional than others because of these qualities like come easily while to others, they have empathy, credibility, humility, commitment, listening, observation and encouragement.

97 The role of extension worker is important because he is like a

(a) teacher (b) philosopher
(c) leader (d) All of these

98 The success and failure of Extension Development Programme depends on

(a) community
(b) extension workers
(c) leaders
(d) state government

99 Which of these is/are the role(s) of extension worker?

(a) To introduce villagers about new ideas.
(b) Should have burning desire towards his subject and problems of the people.
(c) He should have tact to deal with people.
(d) All of the above

100 Which of the following statements is/are correct about the duties of extension worker?

Statement I The extension worker should take his duties highly.

Statement II He should create self-belief among the people.

(a) Only statement I is correct
(b) Only statement II is correct
(c) Both the statements are correct
(d) Neither statement I nor II is correct

101 By 'extension worker' we mean

(a) who is the last chain of extension organisation
(b) lives in the midst of community
(c) propagates his programme
(d) All of the above

PREVIOUS YEARS' QUESTIONS

July 2018

1 Match the names of the proponents of the extension and development initiatives given in List I with the project/scheme they are associated with given in List II.

List I	List II
A. Albert Mayer	1. Sriniketan Project
B. Rabindranath Tagore	2. Sevagram Project
C. F L Bryan	3. Marthandam Project
D. M K Gandhi	4. Etawah Project
E. Spencer Hatch	5. Gurgaon Project
	6. Servants of India Project

Codes

	A	B	C	D	E
(a)	5	4	2	1	3
(b)	4	2	6	1	3
(c)	4	6	3	2	1
(d)	4	1	5	2	3

January 2017

2 Assertion (A) Extension workers have to be sensitive to the cultural changes taking place in the communities, they work with.

Reason (R) Outsiders do not realise that villages change often because there is little outward change as compared with urban areas.

Codes

(a) A is true, but R is false (b) A is false, but R is true

(c) Both A and R are true (d) Both A and R are false

November 2017

3 Which one of the following is not a form of feedback in mass communication?

(a) Letter to the Editor (b) Live Phone-ins

(c) News Headlines (d) TRPs

4 An interactive PLA tool to collect data for planning an extension programme is

(a) sociometry (b) seasonal diagramming

(c) scatter diagramming (d) sequencing

5 Arrange interpersonal distances in communication from least to maximum.

1. Social 2. Personal

3. Public 4. Intimate

Codes

(a) 1, 2, 4, 3 (b) 1, 2, 3, 4

(c) 4, 2, 1, 3 (d) 4, 1, 2, 3

July 2016

6 Arrange the following steps used by an extension professional for bringing a positive change in people's behaviour.

1. Attention 2. Satisfaction

3. Desire 4. Action

5. Conviction

Codes

(a) 1, 5, 4, 3, 2 (b) 1, 2, 3, 4, 5

(c) 1, 3, 4, 5, 2 (d) 1, 3, 5, 4, 2

June 2015

7 Non-formal Education Processes and Programmes should in the long-run lead to

1. creating awareness among individuals and society.
2. enriching human potential.
3. increasing functional relevance of learning.
4. increasing the autocratic action.

Select the correct answer using the codes given below

(a) 1, 2 and 4 (b) 1, 2 and 3

(c) 2, 3 and 4 (d) 1, 3 and 4

ANSWERS

Exam Based Questions

1 (a)	2 (d)	3 (c)	4 (d)	5 (d)	6 (a)	7 (a)	8 (d)	9 (d)	10 (b)
11 (b)	12 (a)	13 (b)	14 (b)	15 (a)	16 (c)	17 (d)	18 (c)	19 (b)	20 (a)
21 (c)	22 (c)	23 (a)	24 (a)	25 (b)	26 (d)	27 (c)	28 (a)	29 (c)	30 (d)
31 (a)	32 (c)	33 (c)	34 (c)	35 (c)	36 (a)	37 (a)	38 (a)	39 (c)	40 (d)
41 (c)	42 (d)	43 (d)	44 (d)	45 (b)	46 (a)	47 (d)	48 (d)	49 (d)	50 (d)
51 (d)	52 (d)	53 (d)	54 (d)	55 (d)	56 (a)	57 (d)	58 (d)	59 (a)	60 (d)
61 (a)	62 (b)	63 (b)	64 (c)	65 (d)	66 (a)	67 (b)	68 (a)	69 (a)	70 (a)
71 (a)	72 (c)	73 (b)	74 (b)	75 (a)	76 (c)	77 (a)	78 (c)	79 (a)	80 (d)
81 (a)	82 (a)	83 (a)	84 (c)	85 (b)	86 (a)	87 (c)	88 (c)	89 (c)	90 (c)
91 (a)	92 (a)	93 (c)	94 (c)	95 (a)	96 (b)	97 (d)	98 (b)	99 (c)	100 (b)
101 (d)									

Previous Years' Questions

1 (d)	2 (c)	3 (c)	4 (b)	5 (c)	6 (d)	7 (c)

CHAPTER 32

Programme Management and Curriculum Development

In today's fast changing and competitive world the programme management is very important because it is an essential vehicle of organisational change. It is helpful in managing any programme from the initial stage till the end. The curriculum development is a planned, purposeful, progressive and systematic process to create positive improvements in the education system.

In this Chapter

- Programme Management
- Non-Formal Education
- Curriculum Development
- Planning for Extension Education and Development Activities

Programme Management

Programme management is the process of managing several related projects, often with the intention of improving an organisation's performance. It also involves linking in with the business change functions within the business area affected to ensure that the changes are properly implemented. As with project management, planning work and task is a key part of programme management, but the work is more closely aligned to the organisation's ongoing strategy, rather than specific deliverables. It often provides a layer of governance above specific projects and ensure that they are run effectively. Programme management is extensively helpful in managing any programme from beginning till the end.

Different aspects of programme management are :

Governance Defining the programme roles and responsibilities as well as the processes and metrics to assess its progress.

Management Planning the projects and the overall programme, ensuring that regular reviews are undertaken and that stakeholders are engaged.

Financial Management Cost of managing the programme needs to be tracked and controls need to be put in place.

Infrastructure Developing a programme plan based on the specific projects, resources, timescales and controls for the overall programme.

Approaches to Programme Management

Management framework offer a governance structure and provides guidelines for adapting it to specific programmes. The programme manager plans the programme and allocates resources across its projects. He also manages the programme risk and the dependencies between projects as well as overall progress, resolving any issues. On larger programmes, a programme manager may be supported by a risk manager, benefits manager or communication manager.

Programme managers must have strong leadership, communication and interpersonal skills. So programme management sees the overall management of the interrelated projects that make up the programme.

Needs Assessment of Programme Management

Needs assessment is a phrase that relates to the assessment of the resources necessary to complete a task or project. It is used in project management to establish what time, financial commitment and staff will be required to bring a project to fruition.

Needs assessment and project management go hand in hand, with project managers carrying out this process to make the objectives of a project into a reality. Carrying out accurate assessment of the resources needed for a given project will help to prevent problems from arising later, as well as providing a basis to estimate the budget needed for the project. The needs assessment process should ensure that once the project commences, those involved have access to everything they need to reach the project goals and objectives. Without properly analysing needs of resources in carrying out project, many problems will arise in future and due to that completing project becomes difficult. Needs of resources have to be analysed properly so that they do not create problems in future programme completion.

Needs assessment can be done by doing needs assessment survey i.e. asking a group of people what they see as the most important needs of that group or community. The result of the survey then guides future action.

The survey can be informal or formal. However, true needs assessment survey have some common characteristics like :

- Have a pre-set list of questions to be answered.
- Have a pre-determined sample of the number and types of people to answer these questions.
- Analyse the results of a survey.

Situation Analysis in Programme Management

The next step of our programme management is situation analysis. Now, the programme managers analyse all the possible situations which may come in way of successful project completion. In social science, situation analysis is also called SWOT analysis i.e. Strength, Weakness, Opportunities and Threats analysis. This analysis allows the manager to identify areas that need improvement.

The first step in situation analysis is to clearly identify objective of the project. After this, identify all the task required to fulfill the objective. Next identify the potential risk that may come in way of objective. Situation analysis is one of the most important stage of programme management It not just help in programme completion but also helps in achieving success in any programme, whether professional or personal.

While doing situation analysis, we find answer of the questions like, what are the benefits of completing the project, has the project manager handled similar situations in the past, is the budget sufficient, does the organisation have talented staff, what are the potential drawbacks of the project. Situation analysis is often referred to as the **'3Cs analysis'** i.e analysis of Company, Competitors and Customers. Situation analysis may counter some of the challenges such as: information may appear confusing, strength and opportunities lack distinguishing factors, factors listed may be opinion instead of facts, you may lack prioritisation with your analysis.

Situation analysis is a one method which not only helps in programme management but also helps in preventing the organisation from upcoming threats while doing situation analysis of all the programme.

Planning in Programme Management

Planning is a vital part of the programme management process. A plan is basically a route-map from programme start to finish. Planning describes what needs to be done, how work will be done, when the work will be done, how much did it cost. Planning is as first and foremost managerial function which provides the base for other functions of the management i.e. organising, staffing, etc.

It focuses on the goals of the organisation, identifying alternate course of action and deciding the appropriate action plan. Planning is required at all the levels of the organisation. Although, the scope of planning varies at different levels and departments.

In the process of planning, we take a sneak peek of the future it encompasses looking into the future, to analyse and predict it so that the organisation can face future challenges effectively. Planning is concerned with setting objectives, targets and formulating plan to accomplish them. It helps managers analyse the present condition to identify the ways of attaining the desired position in future.

Organisation in Programme Management

Organisation is one of the major functions of the management. In layman terms, one can look at organising an activity to eliminate chaos and introduce a systematic functioning in the enterprise. In a nutshell, an organisation can be defined as a process that defines the resources as well as allocate them, coordinates human efforts and integrates both in order to achieve the desired goals.

Steps in the Process of Organisation

- The organisational work commences with the division of work into manageable activities. The idea behind is to share the burden of work.
- The next step involves the distribution of work among the employees.
- The responsibility of looking after the functioning of each department is given to an individual.

Therefore, organisation helps in smooth transition in accordance with the dynamic business environment.

Implementation in Programme Management

Implementation is about making a programme work effective. Implementation is more than a contributing factor in setting initiatives up for success. Research shows that the quality of implementation plays a significant part in bringing about outcomes. If a programme is implemented poorly or even moderately well, its goals are unlikely to be achieved, or the result will be less significant.

Effectively implemented programmes stand a better chance of achieving intended outcomes and producing positive results for children. Programme implementation helps in successfully executing the plan which we had made during initial stages.

Implementation is the most crucial stage of complete programmes. It is one such stage where programme managers had to be extra cautious while doing so.

Monitoring in Programme Management

Monitoring of a programme or intervention involves the collection of routine data that measures progress toward achieving programme objectives. It is used to track changes in programme outputs and performance overtime. It provides regular feedback and early indications of progress.

Monitoring is a continuous process that occurs throughout the life of a programme. To be most effective, monitoring should be planned at the design state of a programme, with all the resources that will be required calculated and allocated in advance.

To complete a project well, just implementing a pre-planned programme is not sufficient but the programme manager needs to have a continous check on each and every part of a programme. Manytimes a programme is started with full enthusiasm but with passage of time the energy starts declining and completion of goal becomes difficult.

The periodic tracking of any activity's process by systematically gathering and analysing data and information is called monitoring.

Monitoring should be conducted at every stage of the programme, with data collected, analysed, and used on a continuous basis.

Evaluation in Programme Management

Evaluation is usually conducted at the end of a programme. However, they should be planned at the start because they rely on data collected throughout the programme with baseline data being especially important. While doing evaluations, the programme manager should leave all biasness and should do monitoring in proper manner.

Programme evaluation is a systematic method for collecting, analysing, using information to answer questions about projects, policies and programmes, particularly about their effectiveness and efficiency. In both the public and private sectors, stakeholders often want to know whether the programmes, they are funding, implementing, voting for, receiving or objecting to are producing the intended effect. While programme evaluation first focuses around this definition, important considerations often include how much the programme costs per participant, now the programme could be improved, whether the programme is worth while, whether there are better alternatives, if there are unintended outcomes, and whether the programme goals are appropriate and useful.

The process of evaluation is considered to be a relatively recent phenomenon. However, planned social evaluation has been documented as dating as far back as 2200BC.

Evaluation became particularly relevant in the US in 1960's during the period of great society social programmes associated with the Kennedy and Johnson administrations. For judging the success and failure of a programme, evaluation is the last and most important component of programme management.

Measures of Evaluation

Six steps that help a programme to keep it on a right track for continuous evaluations are :

Define your Stakeholders Your stakeholders are supporters, implementers, recipients, decision makers related to your programme. Getting them involved early on will helps to clarify goals and objectives of the programme you will evaluate.

Describe the Programme Taking the time to articulate what your programme does and what you want to accomplish is essential to establish evaluation plan.

Focus the Design of Evaluation Focus on processes, means, activities, outputs etc. Focus on outcomes or how will you achieve your goal. You may also choose to evaluate both process and outcomes.

Gather Evidence Qualitative and Quantitative data are the two main forms of data you may collect. Qualitative data offers descriptive information that capture experience, behaviour, opinion, value, feeling, knowledge, sensory response or observable phenomena. Three commonly used methods for gathering qualitative evaluation data are: individual interview, focus group and case study etc. Qualitative methods refer to information that may be measured by numbers or tallies. Method for collecting qualitative data includes counting system, surveys, and questionnaires.

Draw Conclusions Data comparisons show trends, gaps, strength, weakness. Compare evaluation data with targets set for the programme against standards established by your stakeholders or funders, or make comparison with other programmes.

Present Findings and Ensure Use It is important that all the work you put into programme evaluations gets used for quality improvement. The improvements are done to ensure its use.

Curriculum Development

Curriculum development is defined as planned, a purposeful, progressive and systematic process to create positive improvements in the educational system. Now the question arises, why there is a need to develop new curriculum. Simply, there are changes or developments happening around the world, the school curricula are affected. There is a need to update them to address the society's needs.

During the ancient times, people taught their children and trained them in catching fish or hunting animals for the sake of food. So, people had no formal education during that time, but their children learned and acquired the knowledge and skills for survival.

So, during that time, they already had a curriculum refers to a kind of curriculum that other educators call as, the Saber-Tooth curriculum. This type of curriculum refers to a kind of curriculum that existed during the ancient times in which the purpose of teaching was for survival.

However, when the effects of discoveries and inventions became inevitable, ancient people's way of life had changed for the better. As a result, education became formal, and curriculum development evolved as systematic, planned, purposeful and progressive, even today.

The scope of curriculum development is very broad because it is not only about the school, learners, teachers etc. It is about the development of society in general. It plays very important role in improving the economy of the country.

Need and Importance of Curriculum Development

Curriculum development is a purposeful activity. It is undertaken to design or redesign for the realisation of certain specific educational objectives. The curriculum is the heart of the student and college.

The curriculum should be reviewed and revised on a regular basis so that it is able to serve the changing needs of both students and society. Curriculum development provides written curricular goals which are nothing but intended student development outcomes.

In a curriculum, educational activities are carefully ordered in developmental sequence. This sequence helps to form a well planned curriculum based on intended goals. It also helps in suggesting suitable teaching learning strategies, teaching methods, instructional material etc.

Scope of Curriculum Development

Curriculum development has a broad scope because it is not only about the school, the learners, and the teachers. It is also about the development of society in general. In today's knowledge economy, curriculum development plays a vital role in improving the economy of a country.

It also provides answers or solutions to the world's pressing conditions and problems, such as environment, politics, socio-economics, and other issues of poverty, climate change, and sustainable environment. There must be a chain of developmental process to develop a society.

First, the school curriculum, particularly in higher education, must be developed to preserve the country's national identity and to ensure its economy's growth and stability. Thus, the president of a country must have a clear vision for his people and the country as well.

If universities have curricular programmes that are innovative and in demand in the local or global markets, many students even from foreign countries will enroll. A higher number of enrollees mean higher income on the part of the universities. As a result, if the income is big, it can be used for teachers' promotion, scholarship and remuneration.

The country's economy can improve the people's way of life through curriculum development and to develop it, curriculum experts or specialists should work hand in hand with law makers such as senators and congressmen, the local govt. officials, governors, mayors, among others.

Hence, community development matters a lot in setting the direction of change in an organisation, not only at micro but also at macro level.

Planning of Curriculum Development

Curriculum development is a term used to describe the purposeful, deliberate and systematic organisation of curriculum within a class. In other words, it is a way for teachers to plan instruction. When teachers design curriculum, they identify what will be done, who will do it, and what schedule to follow.

Teachers design each curriculum with a specific educational purpose in mind. The ultimate goal is to improve student's learning, but there are other reasons to employ curriculum design as well. For example, designing a curriculum for middle school students with both elementary and high school curricula in mind helps to make sure that learning goals are aligned and complement each other from one stage to the next.

If a middle school curriculum is designed without taking prior knowledge from elementary school or future learning in high school into account can create real problems.

Types of Curriculum Development

There are three basic types of curriculum design :

Subject-Centred Curriculum Design Subject–centred curriculum design revolves around a particular subject matter or discipline. For example, a subject-centred curriculum may focus on math or biology.

This type of curriculum design tends to focus on the subject rather than the individual. It describes what need to be studied and how it should be studied.

Core curriculum is an example of a subject–centred design which can be standardised across schools, states, and the country as a whole. In standardised core curricula, teachers are provided a pre-determined list of things that they need to teach their students, along with specific examples of how these things should be taught.

The primary drawback of subject–centred curriculum design is that it is not student-centred. In particular, this form of curriculum design is constructed without taking into account the specific learning styles of the students. This can cause problem with student engagement and motivation and may even cause students to fall behind in class.

Learner-Centred Curriculum Design In contrast, learner-centred curriculum design takes each individual needs, interests, and goals into consideration. Learner-centred curriculum design is meant to empower learners and allow them to shape their education through choices. Instructional plan in a learner-centred curriculum are differentiated, giving students the opportunity to choose assignments, learning experience or activities. This can motivate students and help them stay engaged in the material that they are learning.

The drawback to this form of curriculum design is that it is labour intensive. Developing differentiated instruction puts pressure on the teacher to create instructions and find materials that are conducive to each students's learning needs.

Teachers may not have the time or may lack the experience or skills to create such a plan. Learner-centred curriculum design also requires that teachers balance student wants and interests with student's needs and required outcomes, which is not an easy balance to obtain.

Problem–Centred Curriculum Design Alike learner-centered curriculum design, problem-centred curriculum design is also a form of student–centred design. Problem- centred curricula focus on teaching students how to look at a problem and come up with a solution to the problem. Students are thus exposed to real life issues, which help them develop skills that are transferable to the real world.

Problem-centred curriculum design increases the relevance of the curriculum and allows students to be creative and innovative as they are learning. The drawback to this form of curriculum design is that it does not always take learning style into consideration. The skills acquired during solving issues help an individual in real world problem solving also.

Curriculum Development Steps

The following curriculum development steps can help educators manage each stage of the curriculum design process :

Identify the Needs of Stakeholders This can be done through analysis of needs, which involves the collection and analysis of data related to the learner. This data might include what learners already know and what they need to know to be proficient in a particular area or skill. It may also include information about learner perceptions, strengths and weakness.

Create a Clear List of Learning Goals and Outcomes This will help you to focus on the intended purpose of the curriculum and allow you to plan instruction that can achieve the desired results. Learning goals are the things teachers want students to achieve in the course.

Identify Constraints Constraints will impact your curriculum design. For example, time is a common constraint that must be considered. There are only so many hours, days, weeks or months in term. If there is not enough time to deliver all of the instructions that have been planned, it will impact learning outcomes.

Consider Creating a Curriculum Map It can help to evaluate the instruction in a proper sequence. Curriculum mapping provides visual diagrams or indexes of a curriculum.

Analysing the visual representation of the curriculum is a good way to quickly and easily identify potential gaps, redundancies or alignment issues in the sequencing of instruction. Curriculum map can be created on paper or with software programmes or online services designed specifically for this purpose.

Identify the Instructional Methods It will be used throughout the course and consider how they will work with student learning styles. If the instructional methods are not conducive to the curriculum, the instructional design or the curriculum design will need to be altered accordingly.

Establish Evaluation Methods Methods will be used at the end and during the school year to assess learners, instructors and the curriculum. Evaluation will help you determine if the curriculum design is working or if it is failing.

Examples of things that should be evaluated include the strengths and weaknesses of the curriculum and achievement rates related to learning outcomes. Remember that curriculum design is not a one-step process: Continuous improvement is necessary.

Making alterations to the design part ensure that learning outcomes attain a certain level of proficiency.

Planning for Extension Education and Development Activities

Extension education assists in the development of the individual as well as all categories of the constituents of society. As **Lewis Jones** says, "Invention of extension teaching was so original, so far in advance of conventional educational practice, that it has been little understood or even noticed by the main body of education."

Extension education is defined as an educational process to provide knowledge to the rural people about the improved practices in a convincing manner and to help them to take decisions within their specific local conditions. Extension is an education and its purpose is to change the attitude and practices of the people with whom the work is done.

Planning of extension education should be based on existing facts rather than imaginations. Therefore, the ability of a programmer to programme effectively requires; an in-depth knowledge of the nature and function of planning; skills in formulating procedure, skills in identifying problems and needs, ability to decide the objectives and goals, skills in formulating means of course of action and skills in involving key leaders in the planning process.

In view of these, it is a well known fact that effective programme planning is an intellectual activity that involves the study and use of facts and principles to attain objectives.

The activities that can be taken up are as follows :

- Sensitisation cum-awareness generation.
- On and off campus training
- Capacity building programmes
- On farm trials/frontline demonstrations
- Model training courses
- Vocational training
- Skill development and entrepreneurial promotion
- Dissemination through videsfilms
- Organising farm visits
- Participation in state/region/national agricultural fairs
- Organising farmers visits

Role of Extension Education in Development

- Extension education helps farmers by providing information, encourage them to adopt innovations, helps the people to improve conditions, builds confidence through action.
- Extension education helps in welfare of students by providing proper teaching aids to teacher, maintaining democratic atmosphere in the class etc.
- Extension education also helps workers in their work by evaluating one's own progress from time to time, by providing information of latest developments, providing skills, etc.

Bloom's Taxonomy of Educational Objectives and Learning

Bloom's Taxonomy refers to a classification of the different learning objectives that educators set for students. The Taxonomy was first presented in 1956 through the publication "The Taxonomy of Educational Objectives, The Classification of Educational Goals, Handbook 1 : Cognitive Domain".

The three domains of educational activities or learning according to bloom are :

- **Cognitive** Mental skills (knowledge)
- **Affective** Growth in feelings or emotional areas (Attitude or self)
- **Psychomotor** Manual or physical skills (skills).

The domains are further subdivided, starting from the simplest behaviour to the most complex. The cognitive domain emphasises upon intellectual outcomes. The major idea of taxonomy is that what educators want students to know (encompassed in statements of educational objectives) can be arranged in a hierarchy from less to more complex.

The educational objectives describe the goals toward which the education process is directed the learning that is to result from instruction.

Bloom's taxonomy is a **set of three hierarchical models** used to classify educational learning objectives into levels of complexity and specificity. The three lists cover the learning objectives are cognitive, affective and psycho motor domains.

Bloom's Taxonomy is named after **Benjamin Bloom** who chaired the committee of educators that devised the taxonomy. Goals are important to establish in a pedagogical interchange so that teachers and students alike understand the purpose of that interchange.

Having an organised set of objectives help teachers to plan and deliver appropriate instructions, design valid assessment task and strategies. It ensure that instructions and assessment are aligned with the objectives, plan lessons, evaluate the complexity of assignments, design curriculum maps, develop online courses, plan-project based learning and self-assessment.

Levels of Bloom's Taxonomy

Level 1: **To Remember** For example, memorise a poem, recall state capitals, remember math formulas.

Levels 2 **To Understand** For example, organise the animal kingdom based on a given framework, illustrate the difference between a rectangle and a square, summarise the plot of a simple story.

Level 3 **To Apply** For example, use a formula to solve a problem, select a design to meet a purpose, reconstruct the passage of a new law through a given system.

Level 4 **To analyse** For example, identify the parts of democracy, explain how the steps of the scientific process work together, identify why a machine is not working.

Level 5 **To Evaluate** For example, make a judgement regarding an ethical dilemma, interpret the significance of a given law of Physics, illustrate the relative value of a technological innovation in a specific setting.

Level 6 **To Create** For example, design a new solution to the old problem that honors the previous failures, date the least useful arguments in a persuasive essay, write a poem based on a given theme and tone.

Non-Formal Education

Non-formal Education (NFE) includes various structured learning situations which don't either have the level of curriculum, syllabus, accreditation and certification associated with formal learning, but have more structure than that associated with informal learning, which typically take place naturally and spontaneously as part of other activities.

For example, swimming sessions for toddlers, community based sports programmes, programmes developed by organisations such as boy scouts, the girl guides etc. The aim of Non-formal learning is to increase skills and knowledge, as well as to experience the emotional rewards associated with increased love for a subject.

Historical Perspectives of Non-Formal Education

Traditionally, formal learning takes place in a school or university and has a greater value placed upon it than informal learning, such as learning within the work place. This concept of formal learning being the socio-cultural accepted norm for learning.

It was first challenged by **Scribner** and **Cole** in 1973, who claimed most things in life are better learnt through informal processes, citing language learning as an example. Organisation for Economic Cooperation and Development (OECD) declared life long learning strategies in 1996. This includes 23 countries from 5 continents, who have sought to clarify and validate all forms of learning including formal, non-formal and informal.

Concept of Non-Formal Education

Non-Formal learning activities are frequently based on private initiatives by NGO's. Non-formal education had relevance to the needs of disadvantage groups, concern with specific categories of person, focus on clearly defined purpose, flexibility in organisation and methods, goals completion. It provides functional literacy and continuing education for adults and youths who have not had a formal education or did not complete their primary education.

Non-formal learning results from daily life activities related to work, family or leisure. It is not structured and does not lead to certification.

The term informal and non-formal appeared interchangeable, each being primarily defined in opposition to the dominant formal education system. Non-formal learning is a purposive but voluntary learnings that takes place in various learning environments and complements formal education.

Theories of Non-Formal Education

Education plays an important role in development. School education is important to provide adoptable learning opportunities and new skills and knowledge to a large percentage of people who are beyond the reach of formal education. Non-formal education began to gain popularity in the late 1960's and early 1970's. Today non-formal education is seen as a concept of recurrent and lifelong learning. It is popular among the adults specially the women as it increases women's participation in both private and public activities i.e. in household decision making and as active citizens in the community affairs and national development. Today, we see migration of people from villages to the cities, in such situation non-formal education can help people in acquiring new skills according to the needs of occupation, time and place. As regard theories of non-formal education is constructions views learner as active participants in the construction of their own knowledge. Knowledge is not static entity that can be passed from one person to the others. Learners learn through their personal interactions.

The teacher's role is to design the appropriate learning environment and material that fosters the construction of individual's learning. Socio-cultural approaches such as the learner–centered approaches will be implemented in non-formal education.

Approaches of Non-Formal Education

The non-formal education includes the following approaches :

Advocacy Approach According to this NFE is viewed as a complementary or addition on to formal education including all education and training outside of the system.

Ideological Appraoch It views NFE as a totally opposing stream recovering from the negative of formal education.

Empiricist Approach It views NFE as an equivalent with formal education and therefore amenable to the same tests and critique.

Pragmatic Approach It views NFE and formal education as an ends of continuum with many positions in between. An educational programme is hot either formal or non-formal rather it has elements of both.

Additive Approach According to this approach non-formal education programmes are generally to take action, carrying out some reforms in the formal school, mostly of a patch work character which do not make any significant impact on its weakness and initiating a few programmes of non-formal education in addition. The non-formal education being learner centred also uses participatory innovative approach.

Scope of Non-Formal Education

Non-formal education is beneficial in a number of ways. There are activities that encourage young people to choose their own programme and projects that are important because they offer the youth the flexibility and freedom to explore their emerging interest.

Non-formal learning has experimental learning activities that foster the development of skills and knowledge. This helps in building the confidence and abilities among the youth of today.

It also helps in development of personal relationships not only among the youth but also among the adults. It helps in developing skills among the young people as they learn to interact with peers outside the class and with adults in the community.

There have been created many online free courses and programmes, for example, massive open online courses that received recognition among various social groups in many countries of the world.

Non-formal education is constantly changing and showing positive prospects for future development. In the future, non-formal education is expected to be similar to formal education. As for technological development, it will probably affect both formal and non-formal education significantly as it can help to facilitate the process of building the organisations.

The major advantage of non-formal education is flexible schooling and participatory education. Flexible schooling helps to increase reach of education to everyone. As the world is changing fast, we need education for self development.

Methods Used in Non-Formal Education

Teaching method is a medium through which the teacher speaks to the students and establish contact with people in various ways. Interest and aspirations are aroused, so that they can learn new methods. The greatest feature of informal learning is that people learn by working.

Here the meaning of teaching method is to inform people about new things, to motivate them to adopt those methods and information. Discussions, work in pairs, tries, small and big groups, daily evaluations, etc, help in non-formal education dissemination. There are number of methods found effective in non-formal education, which are demonstration, workshop, illustrative talk, group discussion, presentation etc.

Their description is as follows :

Demonstration It may be effective method of showing how something works, what it is composed of, and why it is important. Learners become involved with the subject because they are looking at specific things which hold their attention. It helps to visualise a process that might be difficult to understand completely only through verbal description.

Workshop Workshop method is effective for development of certain skills, such as making clothes, wall hangings, etc. This method insures the participation of both instructors and learners.

Illustrative Talk This method facilitates transfer of knowledge from an instructor to learners through oral explanation.

Group Discussion It is a technique which helps to acquire all skills, knowledge and understandings. Ideal group discussion is the participation of group members in the discussion of some topic. It encourages people to take an initiative as they feel part of decision-making process.

Presentation There are various forms which fall under this category. This method arouse the interest of learners to participate. It also provides the opportunity to present emotional subject matter in an impersonal manner. In short, a combination of various methods help break the formality and makes learning easier.

While choosing a method it is important to remember that involving student in the process strengthen knowledge retention. So non-formal learning can be done by various methods and it is not restricted on classroom learning method.

Material used in Non-Formal Education

Non-Formal education is that type of formal education which enriches human and environmental potential. It is diversified in content and method. In today's era of digital revolution, there are many resources which helps an individual to attain such education. For example, Radio, Television, Smartphone,

Youtube etc. Social Networking giant Facebook has over 600 million users around the world, making it a first part of call for studying in touch with friends both new and old.

Microblogging site like Twitter has gone from strength to strength over the last couple of years, with many people now so addicted to it that they use it for breaking news and communicating with friends. Hence, such social media resources help in non-formal education dissemination.

Challenges of Implementation and Evalution

The biggest problem associated with non-formal education is of certification. As it is provided not in any school or college but during a person's life time. So, it lacks in certification. But this challenge can be overcome by authorities if they consider education acquired in any form, whether formal or informal.

Issues to be Addressed in Non-formal Education

While non-formal education offers additional possibilities for the learning process, it is often criticised for such disadvantages as :

- Lack of an accurate definition and clear conceptual framework.
- Inability to implement the goals of non-formal education into the learning process.
- Lack of change in the implementation of non-formal learning.
- Limited academic contribution to educational development

Adult and Lifelong Education

Adult education is different from formal education, which we get in schools and colleges, because some background factors influence this action. Of these, mainly moral values and attitude affect the adult. In addition, prominence and openness are not found in a adult interest which are found in the teenager brain.

As a result, adult stay confined in a limited range and the main thing is the extreme loss of confidence in them towards learning new things. Due to all these reasons teaching anything to adult becomes difficult. Hence, an adult does not complete the learning goal as far it should be :

- To provide a positive personality to the modern society, it is necessary that every person living in the society is educated, so that the society could understand his place.
- At the same time, a person should continue to develop skills and abilities, to wisely utilise its skills in fulfilling its socio-political duties. In the words of **Paul Freire**, "The goal of literacy is to bring people better understand their environment and progress their development."

Due to its practical nature and utility, adult learning is also called functional learning. Not only this person, but his environment also envisages all-round development. Now each of the society member starts to perform his work better. If he is oriented towards better economic situations, not just he, but also his family, society and even the country in which he stays, moves towards development. In this way, adult education plays important role in development of country also. Lifetime or lifelong education fulfill the learning needs of all the people, build a service-oriented society and promotes people's all-round development. It is a continuous process, which educates people through various means.

If the person is ready to learn all the ways then the age limit is not a constraint, because the changes that occur as a result of learning not only change the attitude and philosophy, but also bring change in its efficiency. The knowledge we gain during learning helps us in immediate time and future. This is the reason, learning becomes successful only if students are not audience but partner in the process of learning. Due to focused learning, the learner has freedom to choose the subject they want to learn.

According to educationalist and sociologist, **CS Kundu** "Adult education is a teaching system, which helps adults in tackling the problems of life in successful manner."

Prof **Wright** and **Heywood** discuss about those people who have not attended the schools. According to them, "adult education arranges the gradual and orderly activities for appropriate class and through this personal and community problems can be solved."

Historical Perspective of Adult and life one Education

The history of adult education in India is very old. **Wood** in 1854 AD attracted people's attention towards illiteracy of Indians. He suggested that people should be taught through native language only. He also emphasised that education given should be of public utility. We should also provide literacy to those who are unable to have elementary education. In schools, nowadays adult education programmes started running successfully. Besides this, schools were opened in many jails and teaching of prisoners was arranged. The adult education programme started in the year 1978. It mainly contained literacy, functionality and consciousness.

University Grants Commission (UGC) also started adult education programme in colleges. UGC decided to integrate adult and public education under one name.

Concept of Adult and Lifelong Education

From a psychological point of view, it is accepted that learning is a mental process, which is expressed by behaviour. Put into practice by learning, changes are based on experience and help in adjustment. The learning process is continuous. From the date of birth of a person, till his death learning continues.

In other words, learning action starts from childhood and reaches old age, till then we learn many things about our culture, simplicity and environment. Those people who are unable to cope with changes happening around, remains unsuccessful throughout life.

Prof. Tynby has rightly said that "any civilisation can only last as long as it respond to challenges faced during that time. Changes, processes, reactions and learning sequence go through life. Also the lifetime use of educational processes ensure maximum personal development."

Scope of Adult and Lifelong Education

Generally the purpose of education is to acquire school-teaching certificate, which helps in getting jobs. Most of the subjects taught in school are not utilised by a normal student in lifetime and some people after getting jobs are separated by the process of learning and education, but the aim of adult education is different, which applies to a teacher and students both.

It is necessary for adult education to be creative and purposeful, because for adults titles, degree or certificates are of no use. Job or work is important for them, to achieve proficiency in the same, they are oriented towards adult education.

The scope of adult and lifelong education is very comprehensive. Social education covers all these topics that are not touched by education in general at school. The topics like family planning can be discussed with adults who have a mature understanding.

Moreover, it aims at giving a new orientation to the outlook of adults to suit the dynamic world. The growth grooves of each individual are different from those of others. The education harmonises an opportunity to those who have not been able to grow properly or completely earlier.

The scope of adult and lifelong education continues to widen as modernisation, technology and globalisation bring about new ideas and inventions that touch on the life of the adult.

Theories of Adult and Lifelong Education

Theories of adult and lifelong education are :

Theory of Lindeman

Eduard C. Lindeman was the first expert who gave a systematic account of adult education. In this theory of education, education is regarded as a lifelong process. He pointed out that due to the constant development and change of social life and the surrounding environment, knowledge and information are in a cycle of constant transmission, supplement and update, which requires people to keep learning to adapt to the changes in the outside world.

At the same time, he believes that adult learners should not only learn for the needs of work and survival, but also have the opportunity to enrich themselves. He insists that adult education is an inspiring life-changing tool. Adult education should not only help people improve their skills and abilities in work, but also guide people to find happiness outside work. Otherwise,

Lindeman also proposed that the most valuable resource for adult learners is the learner's experience. He believes that the purpose of adult education is to give meaning to all kinds of experience. Experience can enhance learner's autonomous learning and cognitive ability. In addition, Lindeman believes that adult education is an important means of improving society. The basic function of adult education is to promote the physical and mental development of adult learners.

He argues that adult education is a powerful tool for social activities. Through adult education, the personal code of conduct and cultural knowledge of adult learners should be improved to gradually improve the social atmosphere and order.

Theory of Knowles

Malcolm Knowles introduced a central theory of adult learning in the 1970. He attempted to develop adult education and learning by popularising the notion of androgogy. His theory of androgogy helps adults use their experiences to create new learning from previous understandings.

The education of adults should recognise the experience of learners and use that experience as a resource for teaching and learning. Learners have to be self-directed, motivated volunteers of learning cannot be forced. Thus, it is important to equip learners with motivation and skills for lifelong learning. Learners should be engaged in informal learning. Activities where they share and learn by doing.

Approaches of Adult and Lifelong Education

Approaches of adult and lifelong education are :

Integrated Approach The general aims of the Integrated Approach for Adult Education Programme is to incorporate relevant life skills, vocational training and entrepreneurial trainning in the regular adult education programmes targeting women and young people.

Specific objectives are to :

- improve the relevance of existing adult education programmes
- improve the quality of existing adult education programmes
- contribute to the empowerment of women
- contribute to poverty reduction

Target Oriented Approach Target oriented approach to adult illiteracy was recommended for the first time by the Education Commission (1964-66). It formed the basis for National Adult Education Programme (NAEP) which was latter renamed Adult Education Programme (AEP).

Humanist Approach According to this the learning in adulthood must include learning by the whole person not just cognitive learning.

Behaviourist Approach This approach centres on the acts of reinforcing good behaviour and changing bad behaviours. It is most commonly used adult learning approach in professional development.

The adult education got strong support in the third world countries. It not only fulfill basic needs of man but also social, emphasis on community, cultural, democratic and national aspirations.

Method and Material used in Adult and Lifelong Education

As the world is changing, the needs and aspirations of the society is also changing. To adjust oneself in such an environment every individual should try to move according to demand of the time. Hence, education is not just limited to college days but it is a ongoing process which only end with person's life. In this global era, social media is playing a big role in educating people of any age.

The learning apps, channels on youtube are some of the example. Social media is a boon for adult and lifelong education. It helps in easy and cheap dissemination of knowledge throughout the world.

Teaching Methods Used in Adults and Life Long Education

The selection of teaching method from one or a combination of the categories is dependent upon the intended outcome and the maturity (readiness level) of the learners from knowledge and skill perspective. Some of the methods are discussed below :

One-way Communication Methods This method is most appropriate in situations where the objective is primarily focussed on transmitting information from one or more sources to a group of adult learners.

In this, the intended audience would be assumed to have limited background information regarding the subject and would receive the greatest benefit by simply expanding their knowledge through the acquisition of new information. Teaching methods used in one-way communication are as follows :

- **Lecture/Presentation** The information is presented orally with minimal amount of learner participation. This teaching method is an efficient means of communicating factual (Realistic) information in a limited amount of time. This method is also useful when the material is not readily available in other forms.
- **Subject Expert** An Expert provides awareness and new information regarding the subject concerned. The primary reason of using a subject expert is to assist learning by providing experiences of the subject or information that is not available in other forms.
- **Computer-Aided Instruction** This is an interactive instructional technique in which a computer and a specialised computer programme is used to present instructional material, monitor learning progress and select additional instructional material based on learner's need and progress.

Two-way (Interactive) Communication Methods Due to an expanded knowledge base, utilisation of two-way communication methods may be employed to facilitate an exchange or dialogue between the information source and the adult learners. Teaching methods using two-way communication are as follows :

- **Group Discussion** The entire group of learners participates in a discussion for the purpose of sharing information regarding issues problems or question of the subject matter and analysing and evaluating the information to arrive at some general conclusions.
- **Role-Play** A group of learners act out a situation or an incident to represent a common human relationship program. Role-plays are useful in adding relevance and meaning to the subject matter by introducing learners to common human-relations problems.

- **Case Study** A detailed analysis focuses on a particular problem or issue of an individual, group or organisation. Case studies can serve several purposes. They can be useful in generating discussion of an issue to provide relevance and meaning to the subject matter and they are useful in introducing and leading learners into defining a problem that needs to be solved.

Laboratory** (Skill Development) **Methods This method is used in learning situations where the objective is to gain or acquire knowledge and skill in the performance of a psychomotor task. This method is also useful in situations where observation of an application, practice or skill is desired.

Teaching methods for Laboratory are as follows :

- **Demonstration** This method is useful in illustrating and explaining in an orderly and detailed way, how to perform specific skills and procedures. It keeps the learners interested by involving them in the demonstration.
- **Tour/Field Trip** Through this the learners travel to specific locations to learn the specified objective. Field trips are usually to one site while tours may involve visiting several sites.

Challenges of Implementation and Evaluation

- As social media has no accountability, we cannot judge the reliability of education programmes on social media. Many a time false information is circulated through such platforms. Hence, the accountability of social media is a biggest challenge for adult and lifelong education.
- One more challenge which is stopping the spread of lifelong education is the connectivity of optical fibre in rural areas. Till today, many villages of India do not have basic necessity such as electricity. In such an scenario, net connectivity is another major challenge to adult and lifelong education.

Issues to be Addressed in Adult and Lifelong Education

Adult and lifelong education helps an individual to update with upcoming information. But there are some issues which need to be addressed, so that the benefit of such method of education is available to everyone. Issues like of internet connectivity to all, accountability of study material on social media, certification of study done throughout life etc. India is the only country having such a large no of youth population in the world. So, to bear fruit of this demographic dividend, issues faced by adult and lifelong education should be resolved as early as possible, so that these individual help in nation development.

EXAM BASED QUESTIONS

1 ...... is the process of managing several related projects.
(a) Project
(b) Process
(c) Project Management
(d) Project Cycle

2 Which of the following are aspects of programme management?
(a) Staff (b) Governance
(c) Education (d) Project

3 Which of the following is/are the responsibility of the project manager?
(a) Budgeting and cost control
(b) Allocating resources
(c) Tracking project expenditure
(d) All of the above

4 .... relates to the assessment of the resources necessary to complete a task.
(a) Situation analysis
(b) Needs assessment
(c) Planning
(d) Organisation

5 Which of the following are characteristics of needs assessment survey?
(a) Managers need to ask pre-set list of questions
(b) Authorities to give suggestions to the manager
(c) People had to vote on question asked by manager
(d) Posters show the survey results

6 What is the full form of SWOT analysis?
(a) Situation, Warning, Opportunity, Threat
(b) Strength, Wealth, Outing, Treasury
(c) Strength, Wealth, Office, Time
(d) Strength, Weakness, Opportunity, Threat

7 **Which of the following is the component of 3C Analysis?**
(a) Care (b) Cost (c) Customer (d) Challenge

8 **........ is a method which not only helps sin programme management but also helps in preventing the organisation from threat.**
(a) Situation analysis (b) Need assessment
(c) Monitoring (d) Evaluation

9 **Who said, "If you give me six hours to chop down a tree, I will spend the first four hours sharpening the axe."**
(a) Donald Trump (b) Barack Obama
(c) George Bush (d) Abraham Lincoln

10 **Organisation establishes relationship between**
(a) People, Money, Time
(b) People, Work, Resources
(c) Management, Money, Customer
(d) People, Work, Management

11 **An organisation is a**
(a) random group of people.
(b) people standing at a bus stand.
(c) group of people with a particular purpose.
(d) people gathered to watch football match.

12 **A good monitoring system helps to answer which of the following questions?**
(a) Is the project progress according to schedule?
(b) Have periodic benchmark been met?
(c) Is the project under or over achieving output targets?
(d) All of the above

13 **Project Monitoring is necessary to**
(a) increase speed of the project.
(b) decrease speed of the project.
(c) check each and every part of the programme.
(d) complain to the authorities.

14 **Periodic tracking of any activity's process by systematically gathering and analysing data is called**
(a) evaluation (b) monitoring
(c) content gathering (d) grievance redressal

15 **Evaluations are usually conducted at**
(a) beginning of the programme
(b) end of the programme
(c) in between the programme
(d) after need assessment

16 **........ is a systematic method for collecting, analysing, using information to answer questions about projects.**
(a) Evaluation (b) Monitoring
(c) Content gathering (d) Grievance redressal

17 **Which of the following are the commonly used method for evaluating qualitative data?**
(a) Individual interview (b) Focus group
(c) Case study (d) All of these

18 **........ is defined as planned and systematic process to create positive improvement in educational system.**
(a) Comprehensive evaluation
(b) Curriculum development
(c) Co-curricular activities
(d) Comparison

19 **The curriculum is updated due to**
(a) weather change (b) disaster
(c) changing needs of time (d) globalisation

20 **Scope of curriculum is about**
(a) school (b) learners
(c) teachers (d) All of these

21 **Curriculum development helps in**
(a) suggesting suitable teaching learning strategies
(b) teaching methods enhancement
(c) teaching resources planning
(d) All of the above

22 **Curriculum plays vital role in**
(a) health of the people (b) student's career
(c) electricity issue (d) sanitation of an area

23 **How many types of curriculum design are there?**
(a) One (b) Two (c) Three (d) Four

24 **Which of the following is a type of curriculum design?**
(a) Subject –Centred design (b) Learner–Centred design
(c) Problem–Centred design (d) All of the above

25 **........ type of curriculum design revolves around a particular subject matter.**
(a) Problem-Centred design (b) Learner–Centred design
(c) Subject–Centred design (d) Syllabus–Centred design

26 **Which of the following is student–centred curriculum design?**
(a) Subject–Centred (b) Learner–Centred
(c) Syllabus–Centred (d) Teacher–Centred

27 **The drawback of subject–centred curriculum design is that**
(a) it is student-centred.
(b) it is not student-centred.
(c) it is not completing syllabus on time.
(d) it is ahead of time.

28 **Which of the following are the characteristic of extension education?**
(a) Emphasis on theoretically significant empirical research.
(b) Interest in inter-dependence phenomena
(c) Inter-disciplinary relevance
(d) All of the above

29 **The aim of extension education is to bring**
(a) flexibility in education
(b) revolution
(c) disaster
(d) innovation in education

30 Bloom's Taxonomy is a set of .... models.
(a) one (b) two (c) three (d) four

31 The purpose of Bloom's Taxonomy is to
(a) determine age.
(b) check education level.
(c) develop new innovation model.
(d) classify learning objectives.

32 Bloom's Taxonomy is named after
(a) Herald Jem (b) Adam Bloom
(c) Benjamin Bloom (d) Charles Babbage

33 The aim of Non-Formal education is to
(a) increase skills and knowledge
(b) do innovation
(c) monitor students
(d) revise curriculum

34 The concept of formal learning was first challenged by
(a) Scribner and Cole (b) Herman and Dahl
(c) Stephen and Rowling (d) Charles and George

35 Non-Formal education are according to
(a) needs of disadvantage groups
(b) focus on clearly defined purpose
(c) flexibility in organisation
(d) All of the above

36 By what other name is adult education also known?
(a) Evasive education (b) Remedial education
(c) Focused learning (d) School teaching

37 Which elements should be required in adult education?
(a) Being functional and purposeful
(b) Social and mental attitude
(c) Custom and cultural understanding
(d) Being alert and effective

38 Adult education programme was put in which five year plan?
(a) First plan (b) Second plan
(c) Fifth plan (d) Sixth plan

39 Which commission decided to integrate adult education programme under one name?
(a) Secondary Education Commission
(b) Unversity Grants Commission
(c) Kothari Commission
(d) Muthiar Commission

40 Which among the following does not affect the motivation towards adult education?
(a) Life goals
(b) Interest and desires
(c) Social motivation
(d) Saving and planning

41 .... does not have significance in adult life.
(a) Time (b) Money
(c) Degree or certificate (d) Job

42 Wood in .... attracted people's attention towards illiteracy in India.
(a) 1896 AD (b) 1854 AD
(c) 1949 AD (d) 1868 AD

43 The adult education programme started in the year.........
(a) 1976 (b) 1972 (c) 1974 (d) 1978

44 Learning is a .... process.
(a) social (b) mental
(c) entertainment (d) funny

45 Initially many schools for adult education opened in
(a) Delhi (b) Bombay
(c) Manipur (d) Sri Lanka

46 Following are the phrases of Project Management. Arrange them in order.
1. Evaluation 2. Monitoring
3. Need assessment 4. Situation analysis
5. Planning 6. Organisation
Codes
(a) 1, 2, 6, 5, 3, 4 (b) 3, 4, 5, 6, 2, 1
(c) 2, 1, 5, 6, 3, 4 (d) 4, 3, 6, 5, 1, 2

47 Arrange the following steps of situation analysis.
1. Clearly identify objective of the project
2. Identify all task required to fulfill the objective
3. Identify the benefit of objective
4. Identify the Potential risks
Codes
(a) 1, 2, 3, 4 (b) 1, 4, 2, 3 (c) 1, 2, 4, 3 (d) 2, 3, 4, 1

48 Arrange the following according to curriculum development steps
1. Identify constraints
2. Create a curriculum map
3. Create a list of learning goals
4. Identify the needs of stakeholders
Codes
(a) 4, 3, 1, 2 (b) 4, 1, 2, 3
(c) 1, 2, 3, 4 (d) 4, 2, 3, 1

49 Write the steps of extension educational process in sequence.
1. Define objective 2. Reconsider
3. Analyse the situation 4. Evaluation
5. Teaching
Codes
(a) 1, 3, 5, 4, 2 (b) 2, 3, 1, 4, 5
(c) 1, 4, 2, 3, 5 (d) 1, 3, 5, 2, 4

50 The correct sequence of curriculum planning is
1. Tentative curriculum.
2. Consideration of curriculum needs.
3. Evaluation of tentative curriculum.
4. Plot testing of tentative curriculum.
Codes
(a) 1, 2, 3, 4 (b) 2, 1, 4, 3
(c) 2, 1, 3, 4 (d) 3, 1, 2, 4

51 **Arrange the following levels of bloom's Taxonomy.**
1. To apply 2. To create
3. To understand 4. To Remember

Codes
(a) 4, 3, 1, 2 (b) 4, 2, 3, 1 (c) 4, 2, 1, 3 (d) 1, 2, 3, 4

52 **Arrange the following in a sequence to evaluate a programme.**
1. Gather evidence 2. Design evaluations
3. Describe the programme 4. Define stakeholders

Codes
(a) 1, 2, 3, 4 (b) 2, 3, 4, 1 (c) 4, 1, 2, 3 (d) 4, 3, 2, 1

53 **Which of the following is student centred curriculum design?**
1. Subject-Centered 2. Learner-Centered
3. Problem-Centered 4. Teacher–Centered

Codes
(a) 1 and 2 (b) 2 and 3 (c) 3 and 4 (d) 4 and 1

54 **What is the intention behind programme management?**
1. Managing several related projects
2. Improving an organisation performance
3. Doing social work

Codes
(a) Only 1 (b) 1 and 2
(c) 1, 2 and 3 (d) None of these

55 **Which of the following is related to programme management?**
1. Planning 2. Organisation
3. Evaluation 4. Entertainment

Codes
(a) Only 1 (b) Only 2 (c) 1, 2 and 3 (d) 3 and 4

56 **Which of the following is a process related to management?**
1. A business 2. A human action
3. A social action 4. A physical verb
5. A geographical verb

Codes
(a) 1, 2 and 3 (b) 2, 3 and 4
(c) 3, 4 and 5 (d) 1, 4 and 5

57 **Which among the following are management functions?**
1. Planning 2. Organisation
3. Coordination 4. Control
5. Interest 6. Exploration

Codes
(a) 1, 2 and 5 (b) 2, 3 and 6
(c) 3, 4 and 5 (d) 1, 2, 3 and 4

58 **Experienced and skilled extension education workers can teach people by creating situations like**
1. can provide opportunity to people.
2. can bring changes in mind of people by having conversation.
3. can teach by scolding people.
4. can teach by bribing people.
5. can teach according to needs of the persons.

Codes
(a) 1, 2 and 5 (b) 1, 3 and 4 (c) 2, 3 and 5 (d) 1, 4 and 5

59 **The following are the characteristic of informal education.**
1. It does not contain Pre-scheduled courses.
2. It has both theory and experiment.
3. Teaching work is need and problem-oriented.
4. It is very important to follow the rules.

Codes
(a) 1 and 2 (b) 2 and 3 (c) 1 and 3 (d) 3 and 4

60 **Which of the following are characteristic related to informal education?**
1. The learner does not get any degree in informal education.
2. Students are taught by the local instructors
3. In Informal education there is no formal curriculum.
4. In Informal education learners are highly motivated to learn.

Codes
(a) 1, 2 and 3 (b) 1, 3 and 4
(c) 1 and 2 (d) 1, 2, 3 and 4

61 **Which of the following is a non-formal education assessment challenge?**
1. Missing Performance Record
2. Lack of Time
3. Lack of Scientific Method
4. Lack of Monitoring by teacher or students

Codes
(a) 1, 3 and 4 (b) 1, 2 and 4
(c) 2, 3 and 1 (d) 1, 2 and 3 and 4

62 **Which of the following is not a feature of formal education?**
1. Flexible Timing
2. Assured Course
3. Getting degree after Course
4. No-pre defined curriculum

Codes
(a) 1 and 2 (b) 1 and 3
(c) 1, 2 and 4 (d) 1 and 4

63 **Curriculum is all the learning which is planned and guided by the school, whether, it is carried on in groups or individually, inside or outside the school. According to this definition, what are the inter-related components?**
1. Curriculum objective 2. Curriculum evaluation
3. Knowledge 4. Learning experience

Codes
(a) 1, 2 and 3 (b) 1, 2, 3 and 4
(c) 1 and 2 (d) 1 and 4

64 **It is a challenge to attract adults for education and change their performance system because**
1. they suffer from prejudice
2. they have work efficiency
3. they have personal achievements

4. their perception of knowledge varies
5. their perception mainly works

Codes
(a) 1, 2, 3 and 5 (b) 1, 2, 3 and 4
(c) 1, 2, 4 and 5 (d) 2, 3, 4 and 5

65 **Which of the following are correct facts related to adult education programmes?**
1. The actual inauguration of the Technology education programmes took place in 1978.
2. Adult education is a form of informal education.
3. Include inspection or testing in the learning process of adults.

Codes
(a) 1 and 2 (b) 2 and 3 (c) 1, 2 and 3 (d) 3 and 1

66 **Which of the following statements indicate the characteristic of adult education?**
1. The purpose of teaching for elders is the success of adult education.
2. Degree or certificate does not have special significance in their life.
3. Teaching starts from alphabet study.

Codes
(a) 1 and 2 (b) 2 and 3 (c) 3 and 1 (d) 1, 2 and 3

Directions (Q. Nos. 67-84) *In the questions given below are two statements labelled Assertion (A) and Reason (R). In the context of the two statements, which one of the following is correct?*

Codes
(a) A is true, but R is false.
(b) R is true, but A is false.
(c) Both A and R are true and R is correct explanation of A.
(d) Both A and R are true, but R is not correct explanation of A.

67 **Assertion** (A) Extension education is considered as out-of-school education.
Reason (R) Its aim is that people solve their own problem by themselves.

68 **Assertion** (A) An organisation is not a random group of people.
Reason (R) An organisation is a group of people having common belief, ideas etc.

69 **Assertion** (A) Curriculum development is a systematic process to create improvement in education system.
Reason (R) Curriculum development is needed because of changing world requirements.

70 **Assertion** (A) Extension education is a multi-disciplinary education.
Reason (R) It included adult education and non-formal education.

71 **Assertion** (A) Until the stated goals are achieved, management process goes on.
Reason (R) management is a continuous process.

72 **Assertion** (A) A manager must have specific knowledge for programme management.
Reason (R) Plan is necessary before starting any work.

73 **Assertion** (A) Extension education is considered a continuous process.
Reason (R) It is aimed to bring change in attitude and behaviour of people with whom your work.

74 **Assertion** (A) Teachers should have an organised set of objectives.
Reason (R) It helps in delivering appropriate instructions to students.

75 **Assertion** (A) Bloom's Taxonomy helps in defining educational objectives and learnings.
Reason (R) As it helps to classify educational objectives into levels of complexity.

76 **Assertion** (A) Formal learning takes place in school.
Reason (R) Non-formal learning can be done anywhere.

77 **Assertion** (A) Education is a continuous process which educates people through various means.
Reason (R) The lifelong education fulfils learning needs of people, builds service oriented society and promotes all round development of the people.

78 **Assertion** (A) Under the adult education programme, measures were taken to make them literate only.
Reason (R) Under this, people get information related to growth, child development etc.

79 **Assertion** (A) Demonstration is an effective method of showing how something works.
Reason (R) This method helps to visualise a process that might be difficult to understand completely through verbal description.

80 **Assertion** (A) Only developing and developed countries focus towards adult education.
Reason (R) Developed countries have reached their climax.

81 **Assertion** (A) After Independence, many libraries were established for expansion of adult education.
Reason (R) National Fundamental Education Center established in the year 1956.

82 **Assertion** (A) First programme on the adult education included in first five year plan.
Reason (R) It is not included in second five year plan.

83 **Assertion** (A) Least developed countries like Bhutan and Nepal started adult education programme.
Reason (R) Developed countries focus on adult education.

84 **Assertion** (A) India is the fastest emerging economy in the world.

Reason (R) Education is given 10% of India's GDP.

85 Match the following.

List I	List II
A. Governance	1. Developing a programme plan
B. Management	2. Managing cost of programme
C. Financial Management	3. Defining the programme roles
D. Infrastructure	4. Planning the overall programme

Codes

	A	B	C	D		A	B	C	D
(a)	4	3	1	2	(b)	1	3	2	4
(c)	2	1	4	3	(d)	3	4	2	1

86 Match the following.

List I	List II
A. Programme Management	1. Assessing needs of the programme
B. Needs Assessment	2. Judging the result of programme
C. Situation Analysis	3. Managing overall programme
D. Evaluation	4. Analysing situations

Codes

	A	B	C	D		A	B	C	D
(a)	1	2	3	4	(b)	4	3	2	1
(c)	3	1	4	2	(d)	2	4	3	1

87 Match the following.

List I	List II
A. Define Stakeholders	1. Collect all the information
B. Gather Data	2. Presenting short summary
C. Drawing Conclusions	3. Analysing the results
D. Evaluation	4. Defining supporters, implementers, decision makers etc.

Codes

	A	B	C	D		A	B	C	D
(a)	4	2	3	1	(b)	4	1	2	3
(c)	1	2	4	3	(d)	1	2	3	4

88 Match the following.

List I	List II
A. Subject-Centered design	1. Focuses on individual problems
B. Learner-Centered design	2. Focues on method of teaching
C. Problem-Centered design	3. Focues on individual students
	4. Focuses on particular subject

Codes

	A	B	C		A	B	C
(a)	4	3	1	(b)	4	2	3
(c)	1	2	3	(d)	1	2	4

89 Match the following.

List I	List II
A. Formal Education	1. Flexible Teaching
B. Non-Formal Education	2. Pre-defined Curriculum
C. Adult Education	3. Learners are immature

Codes

	A	B	C		A	B	C
(a)	1	2	3	(b)	2	3	1
(c)	3	2	1	(d)	2	1	3

Directions (Q. Nos. 90-94) *Read the passage and answer the questions that follows.*

Curriculum Development is vital part of education system. On 31st May, the draft National Education Policy (NEP) developed by a committee chaired by K Kasturirangan was shared by the Ministry of Human Resource Development (MHRD) for public comment. A comprehensive education policy for India is on the anvil for the first time since 1986. Many fundamentals of education are normative or are founded in human psychology.

Changes on these are naturally gradual. But the transformative changes on almost all other matters in India and the world since 1986, and the fact that every aspect of education in India today demands urgent action, calls for such a comprehensive national policy as a priority. This piece and a few subsequent ones will offer glimpses of the policy. This article is sort of a teaser or trailer. There are eight highlights of the NEP below. These are selected to offer a sense of some key aspects of the document. But no such selection can give an adequate picture of the comprehensive and well-integrated document that it is.

One, early childhood care and education High-quality early childhood care and education will be provided for all children between the ages of 3 and 6 by 2025. This will be done within institutions such as school and anganwadi, which would have a mandate to take care of the overall well-being of the child-nutritional, health, and education.

These institutions will also provide similar support to families for children younger than three years of age within their homes. The criticality of brain development in the early years has become clear in the past few decades; this policy will result in a massive positive multiplier effect on society. **Two, ensuring foundational literacy and numeracy** Every student will start achieving age-appropriate foundational literacy and numeracy by 2025. A slew of programmes and measures are articulated for this purpose.

This is aimed at the basic issue facing our education system today of students not being able to read, write and do elementary math.

Three, transformed curricular and pedagogical structure for school education The curriculum and pedagogical structures will be designed anew to be appropriate and effective, based on children's cognitive and socio-emotional development. The curriculum will be integrated and flexible with equal emphasis on all subjects and fields.

There will be no separation of curricular, co-curricular or extra-curricular areas-with all in a single category of equal importance. Vocational and academic streams will be integrated and offered to all students. Examination systems will be radically changed to assess real learning, make them stress-free, and aim for improvement instead of the passing of judgements.

90 Early childhood care and education is target for which of the following age group?
(a) 2-5 yrs (b) 6-12 yrs
(c) 4-8 yrs (d) 3-6 yrs

91 Which of the following statements is true?
(a) Changes in education are gradual
(b) Fundamental of education are descriptive
(c) Fundamental are founded in human psychology
(d) All of the above

92 On which date the draft National Education Policy shared by HRD Ministry?
(a) 31st June
(b) 31st May
(c) 31st August
(d) 31st July

93 Which among the following is included in NEP?
(a) Comprehensive and continuous evaluation
(b) Co-curricular activities
(c) Early childhood care and education
(d) Teacher education

94 The target of achieving foundational literacy and numeracy by
(a) 2022 (b) 2025
(c) 2030 (d) 2020

PREVIOUS YEARS' QUESTIONS

June 2015

1 Non-formal Education Processes and Programmes should, in the long-run lead to
1. creating awareness among individuals and society.
2. enriching human potential.
3. increasing functional relevance of learning.
4. increasing the autocratic action.

Select the correct answer using the codes given below
(a) 1, 2 and 4 (b) 1, 2 and 3
(c) 2, 3 and 4 (d) 1, 3 and 4

2 The functional literacy programmes aim at enabling illiterate adults to acquire basic skills in
1. reading 2. writing 3. arithmetic
4. vocation 5 organisation

Select the correct answer using the codes given below
(a) 1, 2, 3 and 4 (b) 2, 3, 4 and 5
(c) 1, 3, 4 and 5 (d) 1, 2, 3, and 5

June 2014

3 The programme for promoting functional literacy among adults is
(a) Sarva Shiksha Abhiyan
(b) Sarva Shiksha Abhiyan Programme
(c) National Literacy Mission
(d) National Literacy Motivation Programme

ANSWERS

Exam Based Questions

1 (c)	2 (b)	3 (d)	4 (b)	5 (a)	6 (d)	7 (c)	8 (a)	9 (d)	10 (b)
11 (c)	12 (d)	13 (c)	14 (b)	15 (b)	16 (a)	17 (d)	18 (b)	19 (c)	20 (d)
21 (d)	22 (b)	23 (c)	24 (d)	25 (c)	26 (b)	27 (b)	28 (d)	29 (a)	30 (c)
31 (d)	32 (c)	33 (a)	34 (a)	35 (d)	36 (c)	37 (a)	38 (d)	39 (b)	40 (a)
41 (c)	42 (b)	43 (d)	44 (b)	45 (b)	46 (b)	47 (d)	48 (a)	49 (d)	50 (b)
51 (a)	52 (d)	53 (b)	54 (b)	55 (c)	56 (a)	57 (d)	58 (a)	59 (c)	60 (b)
61 (d)	62 (d)	63 (b)	64 (b)	65 (c)	66 (d)	67 (d)	68 (c)	69 (d)	70 (c)
71 (c)	72 (d)	73 (b)	74 (c)	75 (c)	76 (d)	77 (d)	78 (b)	79 (c)	80 (b)
81 (d)	82 (b)	83 (b)	84 (a)	85 (d)	86 (c)	87 (b)	88 (a)	89 (d)	90 (d)
91 (b)	92 (b)	93 (c)	94 (b)						

Previous Years' Questions

1 (a)	2 (a)	3 (c)

Human Resource and Community Development

Development is not only about economic growth or the building of infrastructure in a country, it is a way to improve the quality of life of human beings. Human Resource Development is important as it is an investment in one's employees that will ultimately result in stronger and more efficient workforce. Community development is also important for the society as members of the community come together to take collective actions and also generate solutions to common problems.

Human Resource Development

Human Resource Development is a new concept, which is used at both individual and macro levels. At the individual level, it means the development of the personnel and at the macro level, it means the development of an entire nation.

The aim of Human Resource Development is to utilise human labour, including the development of manpower. Manpower means all types of organised and unorganised workers, employers, supervisors, managers and staff. Today, the meaning of human resource development is becoming widespread. Human resource development is one such method in which work is available for all the classes and people working at all levels. Planned actions are taken with a view to make full use of their power.

The following points highlight importance of Human Resource Development :

- It prepares the personnel to meet the challenges of present work.
- It saves the worker from being unattached and untouched towards organisation and work.

In this Chapter

- It leads to development of creative abilities and talent in the personnel.
- It helps in overall quality management.
- It develops personnel and overall morale and is responsible for establishing emotion, cooperative attitude and good interpersonal relationship.

Training for Development of Human Resources

Training provides specific qualifications to the employee according to work. In other words, training is a process by which a persons'ability, efficiency and skill is increased. According to **Philppo**, "Training is to increase specific qualification of an employee."

Benefits of training are :

- Increases employee's efficiency and productivity.
- Improves methodology.
- Maximum and rational use of plants, tools, machines and raw materials.
- Employees do not require much supervision.
- Low work cost.

Objectives of Training

To Develop Work Related Knowledge The aim of training programme is to increase knowledge and skill. Skill not just means physical work but also include interpersonal relation, skills, supervision, etc.

Dissemination of Information Some training programmes are aimed to disseminate information, which has no relation to particular work.

Changes in Perception Some training programmes aimed towards changing perception of people. For example, supervisor and manager's perceptions towards employees, etc.

To Increase the Efficiency of the Workforce Training programmes help to teach workers about work, which results in increasing the efficiency of the workers.

In a nutshell, it can be said that training help employees to make full use of their skills.

Methods of Training

The various training methods are as follows:

On the Job Method of Training It is the most effective training where the workers are given training at the place of work. It means they learn in the actual working environment which means they are learning while doing. This type of training is cheaper and less time-consuming as it involves learning the skills that can be learnt in a short span of time.

It involves :

- **Understudy** Here the superior gives training to his subordinate as his understudy or assistant. It helps the subordinate to prepare for the superior's job in case superior leaves the organisation.
- **Coaching** Here supervisor gives knowledge to his subordinate. This type of training is given in case where the superior has enough time to give coaching to the subordinate.
- **Job rotation** It means changing the position of the employee from time to time to help them to learn different skills, to develop all round workers. But there should be no frequent changes in the job of the employees as they must be given sufficient time to acquire the full knowledge of the job. This kind of training is suitable for higher level employees.

Off the Job Method of Training It means the employees get the training for a specific period but not at the work place rather away from the work place. It means they are free from the tension of work while training. The different types of off the job training are :

- **Case Study** Under this method trainees are given a problem or a case study which is more or less related to their job. Then they analyse the problem and give solutions which are discussed in the classroom. Then the instructor helps them to reach at a common solution.
- **Lecture Cum Discussion Method** This is also called class room training. The special lectures can be given by the top executive of the organisation or by the specialist in a particular field. The person is generally expert in the particular field. The trainees generally had the notebooks to note down the important points said by the expert.

  This method can also be used for the new entrant in the organisation or to deliver the message to large group in that case the cost per trainee is less. But only in case of lecture method alone the learners are passive, there is only one way communication between them so lecture method can be combined with discussion method. Where the trainees take part in the discussion and give the feedback to the expert.
- **Conference Training** In this kind of training there is a group meeting in which different persons present their view relating to a particular topic. The members learn from the others and respect the others viewpoint. The proceedings of the conference are conducted by the chairman who is responsible for summing up the conference.

Vestibule Method of Training It means training in classroom for semi skilled jobs. By this method, large number of employees can be trained at the same time for same type of work. The emphasis on learning is given rather than the production. The attempt is made to create the similar type of working conditions as actual. It is generally given to clerks, typists etc., but this kind of training is expensive as it requires duplicate machines to learn the skill.

Skill Development and Capacity Building

A nation can develop only if youths of that nation are skilled, efficient and get employment in terms of skill and capacity. Infact, the biggest capital of a nation is human resource, but development of human resource is a biggest challenge, especially in India. Through skill development and capacity building, the goal of human resource development can be achieved.

Skill development and capacity building in the context of human resource development complement each other.

These are discussed below as :

- India's biggest capital is its young population. So, he/she has to make it working capital only by the medium of skill development. According to World Bank data, there is a shortage of skilled craftsmen in India. About 30 crores people in the country are either completely or partially unemployed. Out of 49 crore working population, only 3 crore people work in organised sector. Remaining 46 crore work in unorganised sector.
- Every year the education system of our country pushes one crore new youths into the work, while truth is that 80% of them have no professional qualifications or skills. It means to say that if India gives its workable population right and efficient business education, then like China, India will also have immense working human labour.
- In India, only 0.1% is spent on vocational education. National Sample Survey also considers that only 2% of the youth in the age group of 15 to 29 years receives institutional vocational training; whereas it is 96% in South Korea.
- There is a huge need to provide employment for the people both at home and abroad. Providing employment to people had multiplier effect as purchasing power increases, production increases. Therefore, strengthen the whole economy.

Government's Initiatives for Skill Development

It was proposed in the 12th Five Year Plan to create 5 crore new opportunities in non-agricultural sector. The Ministry of Skill Development and Entrepreneurship was established in this context. Many programmes were organised. These programmes are as follows :

Skill Development Programmes For the economic and social development of any country, skill and knowledge are the driving force. In the current scenerio, these emerging programmes are ahead in tackling the challenge, which has achieved high level of skill development.

In 2010, government launched National Skill Development Mission. Under this mission, there are some institutions such as :

National Skill Development Corporation This is a Non-Profit Organisation (NGO) established under the Companies Act, 1956. This corporation is funded by the National Skill Development Fund.

National Skill Development Agency It was established on 6th June, 2013 by merging National Skill Development Council, National Skill Development Coordination Board and Prime Minister office related to skill development. It is an autonomous body and the main function is to evaluate and suggest skill development projects.

National Skill Development Trust It was incorporated as a trust under the Act 1882. The objective of the trust is to provide funds for the skill development.

Entrepreneurship Development

Entrepreneurship is a willingness to take risks, desire for income and reputation, use technology and methodology for the purpose of economic development. It is the cornerstone of industrial, economic and social progress. It is only through the entrepreneurship that we can get rid of the problems of poverty, unemployment and income inequality. Thus, entrepreneurship works to connect society and business.

Characteristics of entrepreneurship are :

- The basic nature of entrepreneurship is innovation.
- Risk bearing is a core feature of entrepreneurship.
- It is a knowledge-based web.
- It is not limited to economic institutions but is necessary in every sphere of human life.

Enterpreneurship Development Programme

Entrepreneurship development programme is a comprehensive programme, which helps in developing entrepreneurial abilities. The skills that are required to run business successfully is developed among the people through this programme. It also guides the individuals on how to start business and effective ways to sustain it successfully. The entrepreneurship development programme has certain objectives which are as follows :

- To identify and train entrepreneurs.
- To analyse the environment related to the right project.
- To develop new entrepreneurship opportunities.
- To find support and motivation from the government.
- To create a sense of say-employment.
- To improve the managerial capabilities of entrepreneurs.

Leading Institutions of Entrepreneurship Development Programme are :

- National Small Industries Extension Training Institute, Hyderabad.
- National Institute of Entrepreneurship and Small Business Development, Noida.
- Indian Institute of Entrepreneurship, Guwahati.

Community Development

Community development consists two words *i.e.*, 'community' and 'development'. Community means those who live in specific areas and whose benefits are common, whereas development means progress, protection of groups of people, independence, dignity, etc. It includes both concepts of social and economic development. Community development is such a process by which the combined efforts of people and government authorities can change the economic and cultural conditions of communities.

The aim of community development is to improve the quality of life of people. It is based on social justice and mutual respect in the society. Hence, it can be said that community development is a process in which community manpower is used along with efforts of government and non-government organisations to enhance community's economic, social and cultural status.

Fundamental Elements of Community Development

The study of community development shows that it has four basic elements, which are as follows :

- Plan the programme, keeping in mind the needs of the community.
- Participation and initiative of villagers in development work.
- Assistance in the form of means and material.
- Reconciliation of various experts to assists the community.

Perspectives of Community Development

- To ensure socio-economic development of the entire community.
- To improve the health and prosperity of the whole community.
- To encourage community efforts.
- To enhance personnel dignity.
- To create community awareness.
- To address community issues.

Approaches to Community Development

Following are the approaches used in community development :

Asset Based Approach It is based on capabilities and available resources.

External Agent Approach The appointment of an external agent for the development of community program is the best approach. He convinces the people through his personal skills and experience and motivate them to work for the development of community. He identifies various problems and seek suitable solutions for it. He organises the people, discuss the situation, arrange meetings, forms committees and village councils to highlight the hinders in the development procedures. The External Agent Approach is also known as Managerial Approach.

Multiple Approach In this approach, the community development experts try to provide various facilities including health, education, sanitation, recreation etc., to control causative factors in the way of community development.

The basic philosophy of this approach is to convert centuries into decades. In this approach, some members are selected from the whole community. They try to make a combined policy for the improvement and betterment of the people. This approach is also called Representative Approach because these people work in community as representatives of the whole locality.

Inner Resource Approach In this approach, the local people are encouraged and motivated to use their resources for the improvement of the areas. These people are guided by the representatives of the community through different programmes working internally.

They arrange meetings, discussions and give suggestions to the community, so that the people should motivate to improve the living standard of the whole community by using their internal resources. This approach of community development is also called the Participatory Approach because the people actually take part in the progress and promotion process.

Therefore, Community Development Approach should be collaborative and inclusive, in which the weak and deprived should be included in community development programme.

Community Organisation

Community has special importance in life of a person. Everybody is a member of some or the other community. This community is a human group which is not formally organised. Infact, this human group lives together and enjoy all happiness together. Individuals in a community lives together in a small geographical area. All their biological and mental requirements are fulfilled in this community itself.

Generally, community organisation aims to solve problems of the community by coordination.

Community organisation establishes relationship between the needs and resources available in an area and also resolve the difficulties and the problems that arise in the process.

According to **Dunham**, "Community organisation is to bring adjustment in geographical area for the purpose of community welfare."

Stoop describes community organisation as :

- It is needed for those direct and inclusive processes of social work which are meant to serve the purpose of social welfare.
- It is used by the sociologist to enlighten the structure of community.
- It describes the work of business people and civilised citizens for community welfare.

Hence, community organisation is a dynamic, comprehensive and influential process. The resources of community organisation includes their employees, physical equipment, law, leadership, etc.

Leadership Development

Leadership development aspect of a community organisation is an important part of self-development and effective functioning. A successful organisation stand out from an unsuccessful organisation, as successful organisation has effective leadership. Leadership aims to handle or organise people properly. Under any circumstances, when a person tries to influence the behaviour of another group, then he actually tries to play the role of a leader. In this way, at some point or the other, every person is in a leadership position.

Characteristics of an Influential Leader

An influential leader has the following characteristics :

Skill and Creativity Both qualities help to present new ideas, not just for problem-solving but to create new ideas for understanding any issue.

Acceptance Any group wants a leader who is exactly similar to their chosen leader, even if their leader is appointed by some other authority.

Self-Confident Leader not only build confidence in people, but also reassure them about power.

Neutral The leadership always work with a fair and clean heart. He never try to discriminate the rights of the people. The leader knows very well that if he is neutral to everyone, then his strictness is also acceptable.

Support Structure for Community Development

The main objective of community development is poverty alleviation and elimination of illiteracy, to improve health and quality of life of rural people.

Earlier, the number of support structure was very limited, only administrative organisations were responsible.

Today, following act as the support structure for community development :

- Panchayati Raj Institutions
- Non-Government Organisations
- Community-Based Organisations

Panchayati Raj Institutions (PRIs)

The biggest challenge of democratic countries is how to increase participation of people in every decision, so that they can decide the path of their own development. In order to promote this objective, decentralisation is necessary. Panchayati Raj Institutions are the most important in solving the problems of the villages. Panchayati Raj in India Signifies the system of rural, local and self-governments. Father of Local Self-Government, **Lord Ripon** (1880-1884) considered the Father of Local Self-Government in India. He passed a proposal in 1882 for local governance.

He made the following provisions :

- The local board was given the means of work and income.
- District boards were formed.
- Permission for government intervention should be limited to review of works only.
- By 1935, efforts were made to make those institutions more stable.

Gandhiji always advocated for Gram Swaraj. Therefore, the Constituent Assembly under the directive principles of Article 40 gave powers to the state to form Gram Panchayat. For this, the Ministry of Panchayati Raj and Community Development at the center was formed.

Panchayat Raj in India signifies the system of rural, local and self-governments. In India, the Panchayati Raj functions as a system of governance in which Gram Panchayats are the basic unit of local administration. The system has three level. Gram Panchayat (Village Level) Mandal Parishad or Block Samiti or Panchayat Samiti (Block Level) and Zila Parishad (District level).

In the structure, the Village Panchayat is the lowest unit. It is a statutory body covering one or more villages with an average population varying between population and an average area of about 6 square miles. It is a body of elected representatives.

The Panchayat Samiti forms the middle level of the Panchayati Raj Institutions. It acts as a link between Panchayats and Zila Parishad. Zila Parishad stands at the apex of the three-tier structure of the Panchayati Raj System. It consists of the representatives of the Panchayat Samiti, all the members of state legislatures and the Parliament representing a part or whole of the district.

Amendment for the Panchayti Raj Institutions are :

- The Amendment Phase began with the 64th Amendment Bill (1989) which was introduced by Rajiv Gandhi seeking to strengthen the PRIs but the Bill was not passed in the Rajya Sabha.
- The Constitution (74th Amendment) Bill (a combined bill for the PRIs and municipalities) was introduced in 1990, but was never taken up for discussion.
- It was during the Prime Ministership of P. V. Narasimha Rao that a comprehensive amendment was introduced in the form of the Constitution 72nd Amendment Bill in September, 1991.
- 73rd and 74th Constitutional Amendments were passed by Parliament in December 1992. Through these amendments, Local Self-Governance was introduced in rural and urban India.
- The Acts came into force as the Constitution (73rd Amendment) Act, 1992 on 24th April, 1993 and the Constitution (74th Amendment) Act, 1992 on 1st June, 1993.

Non-Government Organisations (NGOs)

NGOs also play important role in community development. At present modern democratic states have to do many tasks, so states cannot alone uplift the weaker sections of the society. So, states take the help of many voluntary organisations and NGOs.

The states give them financial grant for upliftment of weaker sections. There are also voluntary organisations which do not get financial support from the government. NGOs do remarkable work for the welfare of people.

NGOs are those organisations which serve social services. Their purpose is the welfare of backward, under developed sections of the society. The number of voluntary organisations in India is increasing continuously about 2 million in India. As the name suggests, it is not created by the government.

Process of Creation of NGOs

NGOs had their own formal organisations. They also had to follow some rules and regulations. Operators of NGOs must first submit the name of their organisation, organisation's objective and service area to the registrar of the area office.

Atleast 11 members are required to form an institution. Out of the 11 members, 7 form an executive committee.

Generally, the following five are fundamental components for any NGO :

- General Assembly
- Management Committee
- Officer
- Statutory Consultant
- Purchasing Committee

All the above five organs are involved in achieving the goal of the organisation, so that welfare of the people can be done.

Types of NGOs

NGOs are classified based on direction and cooperation as :

- Charity or Charitable Organisation
- Service Organisation
- Participation Organisation
- Empowering Organisation
- The philanthropic or charitable organisations are pre-dominantly religious and inspired by religious feelings, so they try to do philanthropic work.
- Service organisations grant to weaker sections while participating organisations try to resolve problems.

Empowering organisations try to provide such facilities to the people so that they can make towards self-reliance. In World Bank terminology, NGO has been divided into two classes :

- Operational Organisation
- Support Organisation

As far as operational organisation is concerned, plans are to be formulated and implemented. Whereas support organisation is concerned with increasing awareness and knowledge.

Functions of NGOs

The following functions of NGOs work in the current scenario :

- To develop national level institutions on matters of rural interest.
- To strengthen existing institutions through research and development.
- To identify and finance development activities.
- To undertake rehabilitation projects based on local conditions and culture.
- To provide social justice to poor people.
- To enhance traditional skills of people and develop managerial expertise in them.

Community Based Organisations

Community based organisations are based on local communities. These are voluntary in nature and their formal structure is not simple. Their membership play an important role in any development work. These are small and informal organisations which aim to provide service to local communities.

The community based organisations has the following functions :

- They help to find means to achieve goals.
- They help in organising programmes for community welfare.
- They also clarify to its members the roles and duties.
- They emphasis on public problems of caste, poverty, etc.
- They inform members about useful methods and arts and help in goal setting for welfare of the people.

People's Participation in Community Development

The United Nations has considered people participation to be important in the management of community development. They believe that communal development is the process where all members of the community come together to solve problems. The participation of people brings transparency in development work. People's participation was vital for the solution to problems like poverty, social backwardness, low level of education, etc.

In today's era, e-governance has given a lot of strength to people's participation. To include citizens in the participation process, it is necessary to have trust between government and citizens. The government and the citizens need to be committed to ensure inclusive development. Considering the importance of public participation in community development, various scholars highlighted the benefits of it.

In regard to people's participation, different definitions has been given by various scholars which are as follows :

- According to **Mumtaz**, "Participation means all those activities through which citizens take part in the conduct of administration."
- According to **Stacion**, "Participation is interference in administration work by citizens."
- According to **V Subrahmanyam**, "The success of any development programme is relying on people's participation."

Types of People's Participation

People's participation in governance and administration is a bi-lateral activity. Full participation of government agencies as well as citizens is mandatory to get positive result by such participation. According to the Second Administrative Reforms Commission, the following types of people's participation can be there :

Citizens Seeking Information Citizens participate in governance to have access to information.

Citizens Giving Suggestions to Government About their problems and solutions.

To Demand for Better Services The aim of people's participation is to ensure that government organisations better serve the people's demands.

To Ensure Answerability of Service Providers and Government Agencies by People To ensure efficiency and equity, it is necessary that citizens raise their complaints in a systematic way.

Active Participation of Citizens in Decision-Making This result in better plans and policies.

Public Participation in Administration According to Prof. SN Mishra, there are five ways of public participation in administration :

Participation in Decision-Making Process Citizens offer ideas, express their interest in choosing one of the options.

Participation in Implementation of Ideas Citizens by giving donations and required assistance can play a role in effective implementation of decisions.

Participation in Evaluation People's opinion is useful in project evaluation.

Participation in Receiving Benefits Various schemes run by the government through which various types of benefits are distributed to the public.

Participation Related to Rural Development for Promotion and Education People participation can help in educating peoples and creating awareness about importance of education.

Stakeholders' Role in Community Development

A stakeholder is a person who is involved in community development. He affects the working procedure of the government. He plays a major role in maintaining communal development. Without involving stakeholder, any type of organisation is unable to function. Under the system of governance, stakeholders are seen in internal and external forms. Managers, employees and dependent people are included in the internal stakeholder, whereas government and others are included in external stakeholders.

Stakeholders play the following role in community development :

- They are organised and dynamic for the socio-economic development of the poor.
- They disseminate information about various schemes and programmes.
- They function at the lower level of the administration.
- They pave the way for local development using local resources and thus, makes communities self-sufficient.
- They assist the administration in identifying the target group.

Participatory Learning and Action (PLA)

PLA is a qualitative research, which is used to describe the state of a community, its active participation and knowing its activism in community development. It is widely used in works involving local communities. Its main objective is to assess community participation.

Originally, the PLA was formerly called Participatory Village. It became popular during 1980s. It is used in both village and city area. It is used to design, monitor, assess and evaluate project cycle.

PLA can also be seen in different forms, first, as a philosophy, in which the relationship between the community, researcher and the programme maker was seen.

Second, as interactive tools and approaches, in an action plan, it impacts the community.

PLA can also be seen in empowering the person with knowledge, life situation and help in planning and making others effective i.e. its philosophy reflects community status, decision-making, etc., by which a person resolves his problems and achieves the result.

Methods and Techniques of PLA

Participatory Learning and Action (PLA) is an approach for learning about and engaging with communities. It combines an ever growing tool kit of participatory and visual methods with natural interviewing techniques and is intended to facilitate a process of collective analysis and learning. There are many methods and techniques of PLA, some of them are :

Assignments (Theoretical and Practical) Ask participants to practice new roles and new skills e.g. ask a different person to act as a chairperson or fill in record book. Set assignments to find out the current market prices for something. As an exercise, work out the likely demand for a product e.g. chickens in a village for one year.

Brainstorming Ask members to think of any ideas that come to mind. List all the ideas without evaluation. The quantity, not the quality, is what matters. Ideas can be discussed later for practicality. Sometimes, unlikely or seemingly ridiculous ideas lead to a more practical ideas which would otherwise not have been considered.

Case Studies Discuss an imaginary or real situation from the village (e.g. a successful group of marketing women) to encourage discussion on marketing strategies. Use the case study to ask questions about an activity, the group is working on.

Community Surveys Survey individuals in the community for their knowledge or opinions. Ask a number of people who represent the audience you are thinking about. For example, if you are trying to find out the extent of demand for wooden chairs in the village, ask a number of people i.e., men, women, village elders, school teachers, etc. If you want to know which people are poor, ask several people about their jobs, houses and standard of living and if they think they are above or below average for the village.

Consultation with Specialists Carry out an interview with a specialist or knowledgeable person on an issue for which you need more information e.g. for chicken-raising, contact your local extension agent. For a health issue, contact your local health centre.

Critical Incident Use problem situations to analyse advantages and disadvantages and possible solutions to a given situation. Pictures or drawings will help. For example, "A group has saved up a lot of money enough to build a chicken house and start up a chicken raising activity. Just before they go to buy the materials, the treasurer tells them all the money has been burnt. What should they do?" Hold a discussion on the issue.

Describing Visual Images Choose a photograph or drawing with a clear, relevant message. Before displaying the image, ask three volunteers to leave the room. Discuss with the other participants how to describe the picture. Ask person A to return and listen to a description of the image (without seeing it). Let person A tell B and B tell C. Ask C to draw the picture. Discuss. Use this to highlight how messages become distorted when passed from one person to another.

Field Visits and Excursions These can be combined with observation and interviewing. Arrange a visit to a place of relevance to the group e.g. if they want to start a carpentry activity, arrange a trip to a carpentry business in another village (but far enough away so they would not compete if the activity becomes successful). A visit to another group successfully running an activity can be very useful in building members,s confidence.

Folk Songs Ask people to sing local traditional songs and explain them. You will learn a lot about values, practices and local terminology.

Participatory Discussion First, give five sticks to each participant and then starts a discussion. Everybody who speaks has to give away one of her/his stick. No one cannot speak without sticks. Discuss subjects such as dominance, shyness and importance of participation.

Participatory Discussion It is used in combination with other methods. Gather the members in small or large groups and discuss a topic of interest. Provoke reactions by using open questions: What do you see here? Why do you think it happens, etc.

Development Programmmes in India

Development programmes in India are implemented for rural and urban development, tribals, in nutrition, health, education, skill development, woman development, wage and self-employment, sanitation and infrastructure. Their description is given below :

Schemes/Programmes Related to Rural Development

After achieving Independence, emphasis was laid on rural development programmes. Economic Planning was started in the year 1951 by First Prime Minister of India. In this order, on 2nd October, 1952 Communal Development for the development of rural areas started. Several works were started with the aim of promoting agricultural operations in India. India being an agrarian economy, about 70-75% people were dependent on agriculture. So for slow growth special emphasis was laid on agro-based schemes.

Various types of schemes started to promote rural development. The details of which are as follows :

Shyama Prasad Mukherji Rurban Mission (SPMRM)

The SPMRM is a new initiative of the Modi government that aims to setup 300 rural clusters by 2020. It was formally launched on 16th August, 2015 by the Union Cabinet. PM Narendra Modi launched this scheme as National Rurban Mission on 22nd February, 2016.

The scheme of Providing Urban Amenities in Rural Areas (PUARA) is merged with Shyama Prasad Mukherjee Rurban Mission (SPMRM). It is based on the example of Gujarat that has demonstrated successfully the Rurban Development Model of Urbanisation of the rural areas, through which people living in the rural areas can get efficient civic infrastructure and associate services. It was proposed in the budget speech of 2014-15.

The Rurban Mission has some benefits which are as follows :

- Under this scheme, the facilities of cities will be given to villages. Electricity, water, roads and health facilities will be provided to villages.
- The villages will be developed on the line of the cluster.
- Population in a cluster will be 21,000 to 50,000.
- 30% of total expenditure on Center Gap Funding will be from Budget.

Pradhan Mantri Grameen Awas Yojana

It was launched in 2015. The old name of the scheme was Indira Awas Yojana. The main aim of the scheme is to construct 1 Crore Pucca Houses in rural areas in next 3 years by providing financial assistance. Under this scheme, following financial benefits will be given according to the location :

- Plain Areas – ₹ 1,20,000
- Hilly Areas – ₹ 1,30,000
- Along with this financial assistance, every beneficiary will be offered 90 to 95 days employment under MNREGA.
- A sum of ₹ 12,000 will also be offered to construct toilets.
- Financial asistance will be transferred directly to bank or post office accounts of beneficiary.
- The minimum space for the house has been set at 25 square metre.

Under this scheme, the government is committed to provide housing for all by 2022. This effort has been a part of a larger strategy of the Ministry's poverty eradication effort, supporting the development of an environmentally sound habitat with adequate provisions for incremental expansion and improvement.

Deen Dayal Upadhyay Gram Jyoti Yojana

It was launched on 25th July, 2015. It replaced the existing Rajiv Gandhi Grameen Vidyutikaran Yojana (RGGVY). It is one of the flagship programmes and will facilitate 24 × 7 supply of power to each rural household across the country by 2022. It will help in providing round the clock power to rural households and adequate power to agricultural consumers. The main aim of the scheme is to strengthen sub-transmission and distribution network to prevent power losses. Also strengthening of micro grid and off grid distribution network of rural electrification. The Ministry of Power has launched a app GARV II to provide real time data of all six lakh villages in the country. The app envisaged to ensure transparency in the implementation of rural electrification programme.

Sansad Adarsh Gram Yojana

It is a rural development and cleanliness programme broadly focusing upon the development in the villages, which includes social development, cultural development and spread motivation among the people on social mobilisation of the village community.

The programme was launched by the Prime Minister on the birth anniversary of **Jayprakash Narayan** on 11th October, 2014. Under it, each member of Parliament will take the responsibility of developing physical and institutional infrastructure in one village by 2016 and two more by 2019 make the model villages. Prime Minister Narendra Modi adopted Jayapur village under this scheme.

National Rural Livelihood Mission

It was started on 3rd June, 2011. The **Swarnajayanti Grameen Swarozgar Yojana** (SGSY) has been restructured and launched as the **National Rural Livelihood Mission** (NRLM). It was recently renamed as **Ajeevika**. Aajeevika is being implemented in mission mode.

The key features of Ajeevika are as follows :

- It will ensure that atleast one member (preferably a woman) from each identified poor rural household is brought under a Self Help Group (SHG). NRLM focuses on setting up and strengthening of institutions of the poor in partnership mode.
- Poor will be provided with the adequate skills to manage their institutions and existing livelihoods.
- NRLM would work towards universal financial inclusion.
- Funding would be in the ratio of 75:25 between Centre and States (90:10 for North-East and special category states).
- It was implemented in phases to reach all districts of the country by the end of 12th Plan.

Mahatma Gandhi National Rural Employment Guarantee Act (MGNREGA)

The National Rural Employment Guarantee Act (NREGA) was enacted in 2005. It was implemented in three phases, starting with 200 districts. On 2nd February, 2006 to cover the whole country by 2008.

On 2nd October, 2009, it was renamed as Mahatma Gandhi National Rural Employment Guarantee Act (MGNREGA). India's rural employment guarantee programme MGNREGA has been ranked as the world's largest public work programme. Rank is based on the report of World Bank Group titled as 'The State of Social Safety Nets 2015'.

Under this scheme, dams, irrigation channels, check dams, ponds, wells and aanganwdi assets are also created.

Features of MGNREGA

The features of MGNREGA are as follows :

- It seeks to provide at least 100 days (150 days for tribals) of guaranteed wage employment in one financial year to at least one adult member of every rural household who volunteers to do unskilled manual work.
- At least 33% of the beneficiaries are to be women. Aadhar is mandatory for MGNREGA.
- Originally, it promised a wage rate of ₹ 100 per day. From January 2011, wages have been linked to increase with Consumer Price Index for Agricultural Labour (CPI-AL) for each state. It focuses on works related to water conservation, drought proofing, land development, flood control, rural connectivity through all weather roads, etc.
- It provides time bound employment guarantee and wage payment within 15 days.
- A 60:40 wage to material ratio has to be maintained to ensure greater employment generation. No contractor or machinery is allowed for any work.
- Panchayats have been given an important role through preparation of perspective plan, approval of shelf of projects and execution of works at least to the extent of 50% in terms of cost.

Sampoorna Grameen Rozgar Yojana

To provide a greater thrust to additional wage employment, infrastructural development and food security in the rural areas, this scheme was on 15th August, 2001 launching of an ambitious new scheme with an annual outlay of ₹ 10,000 crore. Jawahar Rozgar Yojana has been merged with this scheme.

Accordingly, the Ministry of Rural Development reviewed the hitherto schemes—the Employment Assurance Scheme (EAS) (the only additional wage employment scheme for rural areas), the Jawahar Gram Samridhi Yojana (JGSY) (a rural infrastructure development scheme) and by merging them into one scheme, launched the new scheme as the Sampoorna Grameen Rozgar Yojana (SGRY) w.e.f. 25th September, 2001. This scheme was merged with MGNREGA in 2008.

Pradhan Mantri Gram Sadak Yojana

It was launched on 25th December, 2000, as a Fully Funded Centrally Sponsored Scheme to provide all weather road connectivity in rural areas of the country.

The programme envisages connecting all habitations with a population of 500 persons and above in the plain areas and 250 persons and above in hill states, the tribal and the desert areas. The government has revised its target year for completion of Phase I of PMGSY, a rural road scheme, to 2019 from 2022.

Under PMGSY III Scheme, it is proposed to consolidate 125000 km road length in the states at an estimated cost of ₹ 80,250 crore. It involves consolidation through routes and major rural links connecting habitations to Gramin Agricultural Markets, Higher Secondary Schools and hospitals. Under this, the funds to be shared in the ratio of 60 : 40 between the centre and for all the states except for North Eastern and Himalayan states.

Swarnajayanti Gram Swarozgar Yojana (SGSY)

This scheme was launched in April 1999, after restructuring the Integrated Rural Development Programme (IRDP) and allied programmes. It is a self-employment programme for the rural poor. The objective of SGSY is to bring Assisted *Swarozgaris* above the poverty line by providing them income generating assets through bank credit and government subsidy. The allocation of funds under SGSY is on the basis of existing BPL families in the districts. The scheme was merged with MGNREGA in 2008. It replaced Development of Women and Children in Rural Areas (DWCRA), Ganga Kalyan Yojana (1997), Million Wells Scheme (1989) and Supply Improved Tools Kits to Rural Artisans (1992).

Pradhan Mantri Rozgar Yojana

15th August, 1993, the Prime Minister of India announced on a scheme for giving self-employment opportunities to one million educated unemployed youth in the country during the 8th Plan Period.

This scheme is known as Pradhan Mantri Rozgar Yojana. Officially, the scheme was started on 2nd October, 1993 in the country.

Twenty Point Programme

TPP was initially launched by the Government of India in the year 1975 and restructured in 1982, 1986 and finally restructured in 2006. The restructured programme, known as Twenty Point Programme (TPP) 2006, became operational w.e.f. 1st April, 2007.

The schemes covered under the programme are as follows :

- Poverty Eradication
- Power to People
- Support to Farmers
- Labour Welfare
- Food Security
- Housing for All
- Clean Drinking Water
- Health for All
- Education for All
- Welfare of Scheduled Castes, Scheduled Tribes, Minorities and OBCs
- Woman Welfare
- Child Welfare
- Youth Development
- Improvement of Slums
- Environment Protection and Afforestation
- Social Security
- Rural Roads
- Energisation of Rural Area
- Development of Backward Areas
- IT enabled e-Governance

Urban Development Programmes in India

According to 2011 Census, 31.12% of population in India lives in urban area. For the development of urban area, many schemes are started by the government. Some of them are :

Heritage City Development and Augmentation Yojana (HRIDAY)

National Heritage City Development and Augmentation Yojana was launched on 21st January, 2015. Union Government has launched a Heritage City Development and Augmentation Yojana (HRIDAY) scheme to preserve and rejuvenate the rich cultural heritage of the country. Union Government's ambitious ₹ 500 crore HRIDAY project was launched by Urban Development Minister Venkaiah Naidu in New Delhi.

In the initial phase, 12 heritage cities have been identified which will be rejuvenated and developed under HRIDAY. The 12 cities are—Amritsar, Varanasi, Gaya, Puri, Ajmer, Mathura, Dwarka, Badami, Velankanni, Kanchipuram, Warangal and Amaravati.

The aims of HRIDAY are as follows :

- It aims to bring urban planning, economic growth and heritage conservation together for heritage cities.
- It also seeks beautification in an inclusive and integrated manner with foucs on cleanliness, livelihoods, skills, safety, security, accessibility and faster service delivery of heritage cities.
- Heritage Management Plan (HMP) will be prepared for the identified cities which will outline heritage resources and develop policies to guide their conservation, restoration, future use and development.
- It will seek to improve last mile connectivity heritage sites by documentation, conservation of areas, providing more facilities for women, senior citizens and differently abled citizens. HRIDAY will be dovetailed with the Tourism Ministry's Pilgrimage Rejuvenation and Spiritual Augmentation Drive (PRASAD) scheme which has an outlay of ₹ 100 crore for augmentation of infrastructure at pilgrimage sites across the country.

Atal Mission for Rejuvenation and Urban Transformation (AMRUT)

The Narendra Modi Government has renewed the 10 year old Jawaharlal Nehru National Urban Renewal Mission (JNNURM) in 2015 and named it after the first BJP Prime Minister. The renewed scheme is known as **Atal Mission for Rejuvenation and Urban Transformation** (AMRUT).

AMRUT for 500 Tier-2 and Tier-3 cities was also launched alongwith Smart City Project. For AMRUT as well, states have been asked to recommend cities which can be included under this scheme. Uttar Pradesh leads the pack, as it can nominate 64 cities under this project. Under this scheme, Central Government will provide 30% of the overall cost, if the city has a population of more than 10 lakh; and 50% if under 10 lakh.

The total outlay for AMRUT is Rs 50,000 crore for five years (2015-2020). It is a centrally sponsored scheme.

Pradhan Mantri Awas Yojana, 2022

It is a new integrated national housing mission launched in 2015 by merging UPA flagship scheme and Rajiv Awas Yojana. The third project is the 'Housing for All by 2022' scheme, wherein more than 2 crore homes would be built across all the urban locations in the next seven years. The Cabinet, headed by Prime Minister, accepted the recommendations of an Inter-Ministerial Committee to approve a substantial increase in interest relief on loan for the urban poor to promote affordable homes. The Committee recommended to increase interest subvention to 6.5% on housing loan for economically weaker sections of the society. Women, SC/STs and people from Economically Weaker Section (EWS) would be the main beneficiaries of this urban housing project.

There are four components of the National Urban Housing Mission :

- Re-development Plan of Slums.
- Affordable housing through Credit Linked Subsidy Scheme.
- Affordable housing in partnership with private and public sectors.
- Subsidy for individual beneficiary led construction or enhancement of houses.

Interest Subsidy Scheme for Housing and Urban Poor (ISHUP)

This scheme was launched on 26th December, 2008. Under this scheme, interest subsidy of 5% per annum is proposed to be provided to commercial lenders for lending to the EWS (Economically Weak Section) and LIG (Low Income Group) segments of urban areas.

The interest subsidy is expected to leverage market funds to flow into housing for the poor. The Interest Subsidy Scheme for Housing and Urban Poor (ISHUP) seeks to supplement the efforts of the government through the Jawaharlal Nehru National Urban Rural Mission (JNNURM) to comprehensively address the housing shortage.

Jawaharlal Nehru National Urban Renewal Mission

It was launched on 3rd December, 2005 with the objective of reforms-driven and fast track development of cities across the country, with focus on bringing about efficiency in urban infrastructure, service delivery mechanisms, community participation and accountability of urban-local bodies and parastatal agencies towards citizens.

Swarna Jayanti Shahari Rozgar Yojana

The scheme was started on 1st December, 1997. It provides gainful employment to the urban unemployed and under employed poors by encouraging self-employment ventures undertaken by the urban poors and also by providing wage employment and utilising their labour for construction of socially and economically useful public assets.

The scheme is being implemented on a cost sharing basis between the Centre and the States in the ratio of 75 : 25. It has been revamped w.e.f. April 2009.

The revamped scheme has five components :

- Urban Self-Employment Programme (USEP)
- Urban Woman Self-Help Programme (UWSHP)
- Skill Training for Employment Promotion amongst Urban Poor (STEP-UP)
- Urban Wage Employment Programme (UWEP)
- Urban Community Development Network (UCDN)

Development Programme for Tribal Groups

Vanbandhu Kalyan Yojana It was started to promote welfare of tribal people. Under this scheme, ₹ 1000 crore are reimbursed by central government in 2014-15.

Under this scheme, the government is providing livelihood, skill development, clean and safe drinking water to the people, etc. Such schemes are contributing for the welfare of tribal people in tribal areas. An online monitoring system has been started since 2017.

Adivasi Mahila Sashakti Karan Yojana (AMSY) Under this Scheme Scheduled tribes women can undertake any income generation activity. Loans upto 90 percent for scheme costing upto ₹ 1 lakh are provided at a concessional rate of interest.

Micro-credit Scheme for Self-Help Groups In this scheme the corporation provides loans upto ₹ 50,000 per member and ₹ 5 lakhs per Self-Help Group.

Adivasi Shiksha RrinnYojana Under this Scheme financial assistance upto ₹ 5.00 lakh is provided at a concessional rate to ST students for pursing professional/technical education including Ph-D in India.

Mechanism for marketing of Minor Forest Produce It was introduced to provide much needed safety net and support to people belonging to Scheduled Tribes and other traditional forest dwellers whose very livelihood depend on collection and selling of minor forest produce.

Nutrition Related Schemes

Nutrition related schemes are :

Food Safety Mission

This is a nutritional scheme of the people, which was started in the year 2013. Its main objective is to provide food security to 67% of the population of the country. The food is given to the people under the public distribution system.

National Nutrition Mission (NNM)

Central government has launched Rashtriya Poshan Mission/Kuposhan Mukt Bharat Scheme in Rajasthan on 8 March, 2018. Subsequently, NNM will tackle the problems of under-nutrition, anaemia, low birth weight and stunting. Accordingly, children (between 6 months to 3 years), pregnant women and lactating mothers (till six months after birth) can take ration at their home. NNM Scheme is going to benefit around 10 crore people across country.

Health Related Schemes

Following are health related schemes :

Ayushman Bharat Scheme

It is Centrally Sponsored Health Insurance Scheme of Ministry of Health and Family Welfare (MoHFW). It aims to target over 10 crore families belonging to poor and vulnerable population based on Socio Economic and Caste Census 2011 (SECC) database. It will cover ₹ 5 lakh family per year, taking care of almost all secondary care and teritiary care procedures. There will be no limitation on family size and age in the scheme. The insurance scheme was approved by Union Cabinet in March 2018.

Under this scheme, the government has set a target of setting up 12,500 Ayush centres across the country. Under this scheme, the beneficiaries are entitled to cashless medical care in government and private hospitals upto ₹ 5 lakh.

Kilkari Project

The government will launch Kilkari (literally, baby's noise), a mobile voice message service in 2015. It delivers weekly messages to families about pregnancy, family planning, nutrition, childbirth and maternal and child care. The Bill and Melinda Gates Foundation has provided the mobile phone application for Kilkari and mobile academy; the latter is a 240-minute free training module for ASHAs. In the first phase, the Kilkari application is expected to benefit 1.84 crore pregnant women/ newborns in Jharkhand, Odisha, UP, Uttarakhand and in some districts of Madhya Pradesh and Rajasthan.

Nand Ghar Yojana

The Centre launched the country's first Modernised Anganwadi Centre at Hasanpur village in Sonipat, on 24th June, 2015. Its aim is to make Anganwadi a Community Centre for children and mothers and provided with solar-power system to make them stand alone and television for teaching purpose.

Government plans to build 4000 such modern centres in coming years. Anganwadi Centres are the focal points for implementing Integrated Child Development Scheme.

The 'Nand Ghar' to act as a focal area for immunisation, gender sensitisation and maternal care. It also aims to enhance the learning environment through an e-learning module and skill enhancement programme for women.

National Ayush Mission (NAM)

The Union Cabinet on 15th September, 2014 approved the launching of National AYUSH Mission (NAM). This mission is aimed at addressing the gaps in health services particularly in vulnerable and far-off areas of India. The government in March 1995 had created the Department of Indian Systems of Medicine and Homeopathy (ISM & H). It was re-named as Department of Ayurveda, Yoga and Naturopathy, Unani, Siddha and Homeopathy (AYUSH) in November 2013.

The Union Cabinet's approval for continuation of the National Ayush Mission from April 2017-2020 March with an outlay of ₹ 2400 crore for over 3 years period to provide cost effective Ayush Services.

Mission Indradhanush

The Union Ministry of Health and Family Welfare on 25th December, 2014 launched 'Mission Indradhanush' to achieve full immunisation coverage for all children by 2020. The mission aims to cover all those children who are either unvaccinated or are partially vaccinated against seven vaccine preventable diseases including diphtheria, whooping cough, tetanus, polio, tuberculosis, measles and hepatitis-B. Under the programme, 201 high focus districts in the country having nearly 50% of all unvaccinated or partially vaccinated children have been identified and will be covered in the first phase of the mission.

National Urban Health Mission (NUHM)

A National Urban Health Mission (NUHM) was launched as a new sub-mission in May 2013, under the over-arching National Health Mission (NHM). Under the scheme, the following proposals have been approved :

- One Urban Primary Health Centre (U-PHC) for every fifty to sixty thousand population.
- One Urban Community Health Centre (U-CHC) for five to six U-PHCs in big cities.
- One Auxiliary Nursing Midwife (ANM) for 10,000 population.
- One Accredited Social Health Activist (ASHA community link worker) for 200 to 500 households.

The estimated cost of NUHM for 5 years period is ₹ 22,507 crore with the Central Government share of ₹ 16,955 crore. Centre-State funding pattern will be 75:25 except for Northern-Eastern states and other special states of Jammu and Kashmir, Himachal Pradesh and Uttarakhand for whom the funding pattern will be 90:10.

The scheme is further extended in march 2018 to continue until March 2020. There will be use of ICT in NUHM.

National Rural Health Mission (NRHM)

NRHM is an Indian Health Programme launched in 2013 for improving healthcare delivery across rural India, initially, the mission, mooted for 7 years (2005-2012). It is run by the Ministry of Health. The scheme proposes a number of new mechanisms for healthcare delivery including training for local residents as Accredited Social Health Activist (ASHA) and the Janani Suraksha Yojana (Motherhood Protection Programme). The Union Cabinet in its meeting, held in April 2012, has already approved the continuation of the National Rural Health Mission (NRHM) and the other sub-missions under NHM till 31st March, 2017.

The mission has a special focus on 18 states i.e., Arunachal Pradesh, Assam, Bihar, Chhattisgarh, Himachal Pradesh, Jharkhand, Jammu and Kashmir, Manipur, Mizoram, Meghalaya, Madhya Pradesh, Nagaland, Odisha, Rajasthan, Sikkim, Tripura, Uttarakhand and Uttar Pradesh.

The scheme seeks to drive towards 90% full immunisation coverage of India and sustain the same by the year 2020. The WHO, UNICEF, Rotary International and other be donor partners for the scheme.

Education Related Programmes

Major programmes have been conducted in the field of education, which are :

Atal Innovation mission (AIM)

The Atal Innovation Mission (AIM) is a flagship initiative setup by the NITI Aayog in July, 2018 to promote innovation and entrepreneurship across the country.

Its objective is to serve as a platform for promotion of world class innovation hubs, grand challenges, start-up businesses and other self-employment activities, particularly in technology driven areas. The other sections of AIM are the Atal Tinkering Lab and Atal Incubation entre.

The vision of Atal Tinkering Lab initiative is to cultivate millions of children in India as 'Neoteric Innovators. Under this scheme, about 8878 schools have been selected and 3020 schools have been given the ATL grant in aid for establishment of ATL.

Global Initiative on Academic Network (GIAN)

On 30th November, 2015, the former Union Minister of Human Resource Development Mrs. Smriti Irani launched the Global Initiative on Academic Network (GIAN) at IIT Gandhi Nagar (IITGN), Gujarat, India. GIAN aims at tapping the talent pool of scientists and entrepreneurs to engage with the institutes of higher education in India to augment the country's existing academic resources, accelerated the pace of quality reforms, and further strengthen India's scientific and technological capabilities.

Nai Manzil Scheme

The 'Nai Manzil' scheme has been launched for the first time in Patna by the Ministry of Minority Affairs on 8th August, 2015. Under the scheme, girls from minority communities will be imparted three month skill development training in seven identified sectors relevant to the region. It is a bridge course to fill the academic and skill development gaps of the Madarsa passouts with their mainstream counterparts. It will be introduced in all Madarsas in phased manner.

The Scheme is intended to cover people in between 17-35 age group from all minority communities as well as Madrasa students. This Scheme will provide avenues for continuing higher education and also open up employment opportunities in organised sector. The scheme has been approved with a cost of ₹ 650 crore for five years.

Pandit Madan Mohan Malviya National Mission on Teacher and Teaching

Under the 12th Five Year Plan, the Government of India has launched Pandit Madan Mohan Malviya National Mission on Teacher and Teaching (PMMMNMTT) on 25th December, 2014. With an outlay of and ₹ 900 crore and the scheme has been approved for continuation till March 2020.

This mission envisages to address comprehensively all issues related to teachers, teaching, professional development, assessment and evaluation methodology and effective pedagogy.

Under PMMMNMTT, in-service training programes for more than 1,00,000 college and university teachers have been organised. Also, newly appointed teachers are now required to undergo six months pedagogical training so they can develop a good rapport with students and also improves quality of teaching.

Saakshar Bharat Mission

Saakshar Bharat Mission was launched on 8th September, 2009 as a centrally sponsored scheme. It aims to recast India's National Literacy Mission to focus on literacy of women, which is expected to increase the literate population by 70 million adults, including 60 million women. It is a scheme from Department of School Education, Ministry of Human Resource Development, Government of India.

Schemes Related to Skill Development

'Skill India' is a campaign launched by Prime Minister Narendra Modi on 15th July, 2015 with an aim to train over 40 crore people in India in different skills by 2022. Some of the schemes are :

Pradhan Mantri Kaushal Vikas Yojana (PMKVY)

It is a demand-driven, reward-based skill training scheme. PMKVY is formed to provide skill training to class 10 and 12 dropout youths across the country. Under the scheme, besides assessing and certifying 10 lakh youth for the skills they already possess, around 24 lakh youth will be skilled over the next year.

Owing to its successful implementation, the Union Cabinet approved the scheme for four years. (2016-2020).

The important characteristics of PMKVY are as follows :

- It will cover 24 lakh persons and skill training would be based on the National Skill Qualification Framework (NSQF) and industry-led standards.
- It will be implemented by the Union Ministry of Skill Development and Entrepreneurship through the National Skill Development Corporation (NSDC) training partners. In addition, Central and State Government affiliated training providers would also be used for training purposes.
- Skill training would be on the basis of skill gap studies conducted by the NSDC for the period 2013-17.
- Focus of the training would be on improved curricula, better pedagogy and better trained instructors.
- Training would include soft skills, personal grooming, behavioural change for cleanliness and good work ethics.
- A Monetary Reward will be given to trainees on assessment and certification by third party assessment bodies. The average monetary reward would be around ₹ 8000 per trainee. It should be noted that the target for skilling would be associated with the recent programmes such as Make in India, Digital India, Swachh Bharat Abhiyan and National Solar Mission.

Upgradation of Skills and Training in Ancestral Arts/Crafts for Development (USTAD) Scheme

Upgradation of Skills and Training in Ancestral Arts/Crafts for Development (USTAD) was launched on 14th May, 2015, which aims at upgrading and promoting the skills of artisans from the minority community. It was launched in from Varanasi in order to improve degrading conditions of world famous Banarasi Saree Weavers who belong to minority communities. The programme is linked to the 'Make in India' campaign and termed as close to the Prime Minister's heart.

It seeks to help weavers and artisans connect with buyers all over the world. A portal dedicated to the programme was also launched to help artisans to log in and get connected to potential buyers all over world. Under this scheme, 16,200 trainees have been sanction to Project Implementing Agencies (PIA) during 2016-17 for training 34 traditional arts and crafts.

National Policy for Skill Development and Entrepreneurship, 2015

It is the second such policy on skill development, since Independence and intended to replace the National Policy on Skill Development (NPSD), 2009 by adding entrepreneurship to the policy framework.

The vision of the policy is to create an ecosystem of empowerment by skilling on a large scale at speed with high standards and to promote a culture of innovation-based entrepreneurship which can generate wealth and employment so as to ensure sustainable livelihoods for all citizens.

National Skill Development Mission

The mission is intended to operationalise the National Policy on Skill Development (NPSD) and Entrepreneurship, 2015. It has seven sub-missions under it that are monitored by a governing council under the Chairmanship of Prime Minister. The mission seeks to provide the institutional capacity to train a minimum of 300 million skilled people by the year 2022. The mission will have seven sub-missions under its purview.

Pandit Deen Dayal Upadhyay Shramev Jayate Karyakram

The Government of India has launched the programme on 16th October, 2014. The programme is being implemented by the Ministry of Labour.

Five other projects have been launched under this scheme :

Shram Suvidha Portal That would allot Labour Identification Number (LIN) to nearly 6 lakhs units and allow them to file online compliance for 16 out of labour laws.

Universal Account Numbers It enables 4.17 crore employees to have their Provident Fund Account portable, hassle-free and universally accessible.

Random Inspection Scheme Utilising technology to eliminate human discretion in selection of units for Inspection, and uploading of inspection reports within 72 hours of inspection mandatory.

Apprentice Protsahan Yojana It will support manufacturing units mainly and other establishments by reimbursing 50% of the stipend paid to apprentices during first two years of their training.

Revamped Rashtriya Swasthya Yojana Introducing a 'Smart Card', for the workers in the unorganised sector seeded with details of two more social security schemes.

Women's Related Developmental Schemes

Schemes related to the development of women are :

'Beti Bachao Beti Padhao' Scheme

Prime Minister Narendra Modi launched 'Beti Bachao Beti Padhao' programme in Haryana on 22nd January, 2015. It is a key scheme that aims to address the dipping child sex ratio and empower the girl child in India. According to the Census-2011, the number of females per 1000 males in Haryana stands at 879.

Bollywood actress Madhuri Dixit is the 'Brand Ambassador' of this ambitious campaign. Central Government has provided initial corpus of ₹ 100 crore for this scheme. The Ministry of Women and Child Development (MWCD) is the nodal agency for the implementation of the scheme.

- Mukhyamantri Kanya Vivah Yojana (Bihar)
- Sukanya Yojana (Maharashtra)
- Nandadevi Kanya Yojana (Uttarakhand)
- Kanya Vidya Dhan Yojana (Uttar Pradesh)
- The Union Government organised a three state field level campaign on 'Beti Bachao Beti Padao' scheme in the first week of January, 2019.

Sukanya Samridhi Yojana

Sukanya Samridhi Yojana under Beti Bachao Beti Padhao (BBBP) campaign began in Panipat (Haryana), on 22nd January, 2015.

This scheme encompasses all the girls besides their economic strata can open Sukanya Samridhi Account in Post Offices and in the Banks.

The features of Sukanya Samridhi Yojana are as follows :

- The girl child must be under the age of 10 years to open account and a minimum of ₹ 1000 and maximum of ₹ 1,50,000 can be deposited annually.
- Interest of 9.1% will be accrued to these accounts.
- When the girl child attains the age of 18 years, she would become eligible to operate the account herself.
- Under the scheme, for higher education, the girl child can withdraw 50% of the money after reaching age of 18 years.
- In this scheme , until November 2017, more than 1.26 crore accounts heve been opened across the country in the name of girl child securing an amount of ₹ 19.83 crore.

Accredited Social Health Activists (ASHAS)

ASHAs are community health workers instituted by the Government of India's Ministry of Health and Family Welfare (MoHFW) as a part of the National Rural Health Mission (NRHM). The mission begun in 2005, full implementation was targeted for 2012. Once fully implemented, there would be an ASHA in every village of India, a target that translates into 2,50,000 ASHAs in 10 states. ASHAs are local women trained to act as health educators and promoters in their communities.

Swadhar Scheme

The Swadhar Scheme was launched by the Union Ministry of Women and Child Development in 2002 for rehabilitation of women in difficult circumstances. The scheme provides shelter, food, clothing and care to the marginalised women/girls who are in need. The beneficiaries include widows deserted by their families and relatives, women prisoners released from jail and without family support, women survivors of natural disasters, women victims of terrorist/extremist violence, etc.

The implementing agencies are mainly NGOs. An Evaluation Study conducted through Centre for Market Research and Social Development to assess the performance of the scheme observed that the scheme is successful for which it was formulated/ implemented.

Schemes Related to Wage and Self-Employment

The Schemes for encouraging self-employment are as follows :

Stand Up India

On 5th April, 2016 to encourage self-employment in womens, scheduled caste and scheduled tribe, the Prime Minister started Stand Up India. Under this to promote self-employment, every individual can get between 10 lakh to 1 crore. The condition is that the beneficiary should be more than 18 years of age. All commercial banks provide loans for this, the minimum return period has been fixed to 7 years, plus the rate of interest is also minimum. The Start Up India Vision 2024 document aims at facilitating setting up of 50,000 new start ups in the country by 2024 and creating direct and indirect employment opportunities.

Roshini Scheme

It started in the year 2013, to provide education and self-employment to scheduled caste and scheduled tribe in Naxal area. For this, six districts of Odisha and Jharkhand, five districts of Chhattisgarh, two districts of Bihar and Andhra Pradesh, one district of Uttar Pradesh, Madhya Pradesh and Maharashtra are choosen.

Under this, 18 to 35 years of youths are choosen for training and after training they are provided loan for self-employment. It also ensures 50% participation of women. In this scheme, the contribution of centre and states is 75:25.

Schemes Related to Sanitation and Infrastructure

Swachh Bharat Abhiyaan and Smart Cities Mission are prominent sanitation and infrastructural programmes. Their description is given below :

Swachh Bharat Abhiyan

On 2nd October, 2014, Prime Minister Narendra Modi started Swachh Bharat Abhiyan. The programme was started to provide toilets, solid and liquid waste management, etc. Ministry of Drinking Water and Sanitation started this scheme.

The previous name of this scheme is 'Nirmal Bharat Abhiyan'. The campaign aims to achieve the vision of a Clean India by 2nd October, 2019. For Swachh Bharat Abhiyan Honble Prime Minister Narendra Modi has been conferred the Goal keeper Award by the Bill and Melinda Gates Foundation.

Smart Cities Mission

It was launched on 25th June, 2016. It is a major urban renewal programme launched by the government to develop and upgrade living conditions and infrastructure in selected 100 cities all over the country.

The main focus of the project is the area based development of cities by transforming existing areas through redevelopment. It also includes development of greenfield areas.

EXAM BASED QUESTIONS

1 How did a person become proficient under human resource?
(a) Bodily active (b) Mentally active
(c) Knowledge of technology (d) All of these

2 At what level is human resource development used?
(a) Individual (b) Macro
(c) Both (a) and (b) (d) None of these

3 According to whom, developing skill in a employee for specific work is training?
(a) Milet (b) Simon
(c) Flippo (d) Banard

4 Which of the following is a process by which an individual's ability and efficiency can be increased?
(a) Training (b) Recruitment
(c) Both (a) and (b) (d) None of these

5 Which of the following is a not a consequence of training?
(a) Improvement in functioning
(b) Decreased morale
(c) Reduction in work cost
(d) Increase in productivity

6 In which training method the workers are given training at the place of work?
(a) Vestibule method of training
(b) On the job method of training
(c) Conference training
(d) Off the job method of training

7 The goals of human resource development can be achieved through ....
(a) skill development
(b) capacity building
(c) individual efforts
(d) Both (a) and (b)

8 Which of the following is the largest asset of any nation?
(a) Economic resource (b) Human resource
(c) Cultural resource (d) None of these

9 About, how many people work in organised sector in India?
(a) 7 crore (b) 3 crore
(c) 4 crore (d) 5 crore

10 Approximately, what percentage of people in India have no professional qualification?
(a) 60% (b) 70%
(c) 80% (d) 90%

11 In India, about what percentage of GDP is spent on vocational education?
(a) 0.1% (b) 0.2%
(c) 0.3% (d) 0.4%

12 In which Five Year Plan, 5 crore new job opportunities were offered in non-agricultural sector.
(a) 10th (b) 11th
(c) 12th (d) 5th

13 In which year, central government started National Skill Development Mission?
(a) 2010 (b) 2012
(c) 2014 (d) 2016

14 National Skill Development Corporation started in
(a) 1952 (b) 1956 (c) 1978 (d) 1984

15 Which of the following institutions were included under the National Skill Development Mission launched by the Government of India in 2010?
(a) National Skill Development Corporation
(b) National Skill Development Agency
(c) National Skill Development Trust
(d) All of the above

16 Which among the following are the objectives of entrepreneurship developments programme?
(a) To identify and train entrepreneurs.
(b) To improve the managerial capabilities of entrepreneurs.
(c) To analyse the environment related to the project.
(d) All of these

17 In which of the following Community Development approach the local people are encouraged and motivated to use their resources for the improvement of the areas?
(a) Asset Based Approach
(b) External Agent Approach
(c) Inner Resource Approach
(d) Multiple Approach.

18 Which of the following essential characteristics are needed for an influential leader?
(a) Skill and creativity
(b) Neutral
(c) Self-Confident
(d) All of the above

19 Which of these are not the functions of NGOs?
(a) To undertake rehabilitation projects based on local conditions and culture.
(b) To identify finance development activities.
(c) To ignore social justice to poor people.
(d) To develop national level institutions on matters of rural interest.

20 Who said "Participation is interference in administration work by citizens".
(a) Mumtaz (b) Stacion
(c) Subrahmanyam (d) Stoop

21 Meaning of community development is
(a) economic development
(b) social development
(c) cultural development
(d) full development

22 According to whom Community organisation is the process of adjusting and maintaining social welfare in a geographic area."
(a) Lindemann (b) Dunham
(c) Patit (d) Jackson

23 Types of community based organisations are
(a) formal organisations (b) informal organisations
(c) Both (a) and (b) (d) None of these

24 Who is the father of local-self government in India?
(a) Lord Liton (b) Lord Ripon
(c) Lord Conrwallis (d) Lord William Bentick

25 Which committee established by government in 1957 recommended three tier Panchayati Raj System?
(a) Balwant Rai Mehta Committee
(b) Ashok Mehta Committee
(c) GVK Rao Committe
(d) PK Thungon Committee

26 Which Article of the Constitution gave powers to the state to form Gram Panchayat?
(a) Article 29 (b) Article 39
(c) Article 49 (d) Article 40

27 73rd Constitutional Amendment Act gave power for
(a) laying strong and vibrant Panchayati Raj Institutions in the country.
(b) providing employment in rural areas.
(c) providing skills to women.
(d) giving home to homeless.

28 Which Article of the Constitution provide for creation of Gram Sabha?
(a) Article 243 (b) Article 248
(c) Article 243(A) (d) Article 248 (A)

29 If the Zila Parishad is dissolved before time, then in how many days it is necessary to have an internal election?
(a) 6 months (b) 1 years
(c) 5 years (d) 1 month

30 How many members are required to form a NGO?
(a) 7 (b) 9
(c) 11 (d) 15

31 According to World Bank, in how many categories NGOs are divided?
(a) 2 (b) 3 (c) 4 (d) 5

32 Community based organisations are ...... in nature.
(a) voluntary (b) statutory
(c) Both (a) and (b) (d) None of these

33 What is the meaning of people participation in community development?
(a) Participation in problem-solving
(b) Participation in management
(c) Both (a) and (b)
(d) None of the above

34 Which of the following are the benefits of people participation?
(a) Skill development (b) Efficiency in work
(c) Development of people (d) All of these

35 For strengthening people participation, which of the following quality is necessary?
(a) Trust (b) Will power
(c) Inclusiveness (d) All of these

36 According to the second administrative reforms commission, the types of people's participation are
(a) suggesting citizens
(b) citizens active in decision-making
(c) citizens seeking better service
(d) All of the above

37 In which areas does participation prove effective?
(a) In decision-making (b) In evaluation
(c) In raising voice (d) All of these

38 Which of the following benefits are not found in people's participation?
(a) Control over corruption
(b) Extension of development
(c) Lack of responsiveness
(d) Development of public awareness

39 Which of the following are seen as stakeholder of community development?
(a) Children (b) Women
(c) Farmer (d) All of these

40 Which of the following are not included under the category of internal stakeholder?
(a) Manager (b) Employee
(c) Poor people (d) Government agencies

41 Stakeholders initiative towards community development help people
(a) socially (b) politically
(c) economically (d) All of these

42 What is the main use of participatory learning and action?
(a) To know the situation of community
(b) To know participation in community development
(c) To calculate income of people
(d) Only (a) and (b)

43 PLA was originally called
(a) civil service (b) participatory village
(c) rural tool (d) agency

44 PLA is used for
(a) monitoring (b) evaluation
(c) designing (d) All of these

45 Which of the following are method(s) of PLA?
(a) Case study (b) Community survey
(c) Assignment (d) All of these

46 On 2nd October, 1952 which scheme was launched for development of rural area?
(a) Community development (b) Social welfare
(c) Rural development (d) Affordable housing

47 How many percentage of people are engaged in agriculture in India?
(a) 40% (b) 50%
(c) 60% (d) 70%

48 Which of the following organisation helps in community development?
(a) Press Council of Agriculture
(b) Farming Technology Centre
(c) Agriculture University
(d) All of the above

49 Deendayal Upadhyay Gram Jyoti Yojana started on
(a) 25th July, 2015 (b) 1st January, 2016
(c) 13th April, 2017 (d) 2nd October, 2018

50 On whose birthday, launched Sansad Gram Yojana?
(a) Jawaharlal Nehru
(b) Mahatma Gandhi
(c) Jai Prakash Narayan
(d) Shyama Prasad Mukherjee

51 Under which mission, the objective of building 300 village cluster by 2020 was decided?
(a) Sansad Adarsh Gram Yojana
(b) Shyama Prasad Mukherjee Rurban Mission
(c) Pradhan Mantri Adarsh Gram Yojana
(d) Twenty Point Programme

52 For the development of rural area, which among the following was not included in Twenty Point Programme?
(a) Poverty in rural area
(b) Health For All
(c) Extension of education
(d) Urban development

53 Under the National Grameen Awas Mission, how much amount was decided for the villagers?
(a) 1 Lakh (b) 1.1 Lakh
(c) 2 Lakh (d) 1.5 Lakh

54 Under MGNREGA, how many days of guaranteed wage employment was provided for tribal people?
(a) 100 days (b) 150 days
(c) 200 days (d) 250 days

55 For the development of Smart Cities, which state will get maximum number of cities included in 100 Smart cities?
(a) Madhya Pradesh (b) Odisha
(c) Uttar Pradesh (d) Chattisgarh

56 Sampoorna Grameen Rozgar Yojana aims to
(a) provide time bound employment.
(b) provide self-employment to rural poor.
(c) provide additional wage employment, infrastructural development.
(d) provide self-employment to Scheduled Castes and Scheduled Tribes in naxal area.

57 .... Yojana was launched by the Union Government on 21st January, 2015
(a) Heritage City Development and Augmentation Yojana.
(b) Pradhan Mantri Rozgar Yojana.
(c) Swarna Jayanti Shahari Rozgar Yojana.
(d) Sukanya Samridhi Yojana.

58 Swarna Jayanti Shahri Rozgar Yojana was launched on
(a) 5 December, 1997
(b) 1 December, 1997
(c) 2 November, 1997
(d) 10 November, 1997

59 The objectives of Atal Innovation Mission is
(a) to promote innovation and entrepreneurship across the country.
(b) to serve as a platform of world class innovations hubs, grand challenges start up business, and self-employment.
(c) to promote a culture of innovation.
(d) Both (a) and (b)

60 Which of the following other projects have been launched under Pandit Deen Dayal Upadhyay Shramev Jayate Karyakram launched on 16th October, 2014.
(a) Shram Suvidha Portal
(b) Universal Account Number
(c) Random Inspection Scheme
(d) All of the above

61 The main objective of Food Security Mission is to provide food to ...... population.
(a) 27% (b) 37%
(c) 57% (d) 67%

62 Under the Ayushman Bharat Scheme, how many families will benefit from the scheme?
(a) 5 crore (b) 10 crore
(c) 12 crore (d) 15 crore

63 The 'Kilkari' application is expected to benefit ...... pregnant women/new borns.
(a) 1.72 crore (b) 1.84 crore
(c) 1.86 crore (d) 1.9 crore

64 The aim of Kilkari scheme is to
(a) provide information related to health
(b) provide training
(c) Both (a) and (b)
(d) None of the above

65 **Under Mission Indradhanush, the target of achieving full immunisation is**

(a) 2020 (b) 2022
(c) 2024 (d) 2030

66 **'Beti Bachao Beti Padhao' scheme was launched in**

(a) Sonipat (b) Panipat
(c) Gorakhpur (d) Varanasi

67 **Under the Sukanya Samridhi Yojana, the maximum limit for deposition per annum is**

(a) 1 lakh (b) 1.5 lakh
(c) 5 lakh (d) 10 lakh

68 **The beneficiary of Stand Up India scheme are**

(a) women (b) SCs
(c) STs (d) All of these

69 **Roshini Scheme is launched for**

(a) rural area
(b) urban area
(c) tribal area
(d) naxal area

70 **Swachh Bharat Abhiyan was launched on**

(a) 15th August, 2014
(b) 26th January, 2015
(c) 14th November, 2014
(d) 2nd October, 2014

71 **Match the following.**

List I (Schemes)	List II (Years)
A. National Skill Development Mission	1. 2013
B. MGNREGA	2. 2002
C. Roshini	3. 2015
D. Swadhar	4. 2005

Codes

	A	B	C	D		A	B	C	D
(a)	1	2	3	4	(b)	4	3	2	1
(c)	2	1	4	3	(d)	3	4	1	2

72 **Match the following.**

List I	List II
A. Asset Based Approach	1. People are motivated to use local resources.
B. External Agent Approach	2. People work as representatives of the whole community.
C. Multiple Approach	3. Best approach for community development programme.
D. Inner Resource Approach	4. Based on capabilities and available resources.

Codes

	A	B	C	D		A	B	C	D
(a)	1	2	3	4	(b)	2	3	4	1
(c)	4	3	2	1	(d)	4	2	1	3

73 **Match the following.**

List I	List II
A. Nai Manzil Scheme	1. 2000
B. Van Bandhu Kalyan Yojana	2. 2008
C. Pradhan Mantri Gram Sadak Yojana	3. 2015
D. Interest Subsidy Scheme for Housing and Urban poor	4. 2014-15

Codes

	A	B	C	D		A	B	C	D
(a)	3	4	1	2	(b)	1	2	3	4
(c)	4	3	2	1	(d)	1	4	2	3

74 **Match the following.**

List I	List II
A. National Small Industries Extension Training Institute	1. Rajasthan
B. National Institute of Entrepreneurship and Small Business Development	2. Guwahati
C. Indian Institute of Entrepreneurship	3. Noida
D. Entrepreneurship and Management Development	4. Hyderabad

Codes

	A	B	C	D		A	B	C	D
(a)	1	2	3	4	(b)	4	3	2	1
(c)	4	1	2	3	(d)	3	2	1	4

75 **Match the following.**

List I	List II
A. Shyama Prasad Mukherjee Rurban Mission	1. 16th August, 2015
B. Pradhan Mantri Gram Sadak Yojana	2. 25th December, 2000
C. Deendayal Upadhyaya Antyodaya Yojana	3. 25th September, 2014
D. Ayushman Bharat	4. 23rd September, 2018

Codes

	A	B	C	D		A	B	C	D
(a)	1	2	3	4	(b)	2	1	3	4
(c)	3	1	4	2	(d)	4	3	2	1

76 **Match the following.**

List I	List II
A. National Nutrition Mission	1. Immunisation
B. Food Security Mission	2. Providing food
C. Indradhanush Mission	3. Reducing stunting
D. Kilkari Project	4. Weekly message about family planning

Codes

	A	B	C	D
(a)	4	3	2	1
(b)	3	2	1	4
(c)	1	2	3	4
(d)	2	1	4	3

77 **Who among the following are included in people's participation?**
1. Information seeking people
2. Solution giving people
3. Better services demanding people
4. Participating in decision-making

Codes
(a) 1 and 2 (b) 2, 3 and 4
(c) 1,2, 3 and 4 (d) Only 3

78 **Which among the following is included in National Nutrition Mission?**
1. Below 6 years children
2. Pregnant women
3. Lactating mothers
4. Teenage girls

Codes
(a) Only 1 (b) 2 and 3
(c) 1 and 4 (d) 1, 2, 3 and 4

79 **Under Mission Indradhanush, which disease(s) is/are covered under it.**
1. Dipethilia 2. Cough
3. Polio 4. AIDS
5. Cancer

Codes
(a) Only 1 (b) 1 and 2
(c) 4 and 5 (d) 1, 2 and 3

80 **Which of the following statement is not correct about employment?**
(a) Child labour is not allowed in India.
(b) MGNREGA is a big scheme in India.
(c) Wage is same throughout India.
(d) According to 7th Pay Commission, ₹ 18000 is the minimum monthly salary.

81 **Which of the following is/are correct under Stand Up India?**
1. It encourages employment of SC,s STs and Women.
2. It aims to provide loan of ₹ 10 lakh to 1 crore to the people.
3. It started on 5th April, 2016.

Codes
(a) Only 3 (b) Only 2
(c) 1 and 2 (d) 1, 2 and 3

82 **Arrange the following committees in correct order.**
1. Balwant Rai Mehta Committee
2. PK Thungon Committee
3. GVK Rao Committee
4. Ashok Mehta Committee

Codes
(a) 2, 4, 3, 1 (b) 1, 2, 3, 4
(c) 4, 2, 3, 1 (d) 1, 4, 3, 2

83 **Arrange the following in correct order.**
1. Deen Dayal Upadhyay Gram Jyoti Yojana
2. Sansad Adarsh Gram Yojana
3. Shyama Prasad Mukherji Rurban Mission
4. Pradhan Mantri Gram Sadak Yojana

Codes
(a) 1, 2, 3, 4 (b) 2, 1, 3, 4 (c) 2, 3, 4, 1 (d) 4, 2, 3, 1

84 **Arrange the following in correct order.**
1. Heritage City Development and Augmentation Yojana
2. Jawaharlal Nehru National Urban Renewal Mission (JNNURM)
3. Swarna Jayanti Shahari Rozgar Yojana

Codes
(a) 1, 3, 2 (b) 1, 2, 3 (c) 3, 2, 1 (d) 3, 1, 2

85 **Arrange the following in correct order.**
1. National Nutrition Mission
2. Food Security Mission
3. National Rural Health Mission
4. National Ayush Mission

Codes
(a) 4, 3, 2, 1 (b) 1, 2, 3, 4 (c) 3, 2, 1, 4 (d) 2, 3, 4, 1

86 **Arrange the following in correct order.**
1. Global initiative of academic network planning.
2. Atal Innovation Mission.
3. Saakshar Bharat Mission.
4. Ustad Scheme.

Codes
(a) 1, 2, 3, 4 (b) 3, 1, 4, 2
(c) 3, 2, 1, 4 (d) 2, 1, 3, 4

87 **Arrange the following in correct order.**
1. Beti Bachao Beti Padhao Scheme
2. Stand Up India
3. Roshini scheme

Codes
(a) 2, 1, 3 (b) 1, 2, 3 (c) 3, 1, 2 (d) 2, 3, 1

88 **Objective of training is**
1. faith towards organisation
2. skill development
3. increase motivation
4. disseminate finformation

Codes
(a) 1, 3 and 4 (b) 2, 3 and 4
(c) 1, 2 and 3 (d) 1, 2, 3 and 4

89 **Principle of leadership are**
1. Specific Goal target 2. Humanistic Aproach
3. Personalised Principle 4. Path Oriented Approach

Codes
(a) 1, 2 and 4 (b) 2, 3 and 4
(c) 1, 3 and 4 (d) 1, 2, 3 and 4

90 **For Panchyati Raj institutions, it is important**
1. decentralisation of government
2. support of people
3. centralisation of government
4. financial resources

Codes
(a) 1, 2 and 3 (b) 1, 3 and 4
(c) 1, 2 and 4 (d) 1 and 4

Directions *(Q. Nos. 91-104) Below given are two statements, labelled as Assertion (A) and Reason (R). Choose the correct code for the following.*

Codes

(a) Both A and R are true and R is the correct explanation of A.
(b) Both A and R are true, but R is not the correct explanation of A.
(c) A is true, but R is false.
(d) A is false, but R is ture.

91 **Assertion** (A) The aim of human resource development is to utilise human skills.

Reason (R) Humans are the biggest resource for any nation.

92 **Assertion** (A) Training is in interest of both the employee and the organisation.

Reason (R) Expenditure incurred on training is appropriate, not wastage.

93 **Assertion** (A) To provide training to the employees, the prevailing system is functional.

Reason (R) Under this system, training is imparted while working.

94 **Assertion** (A) The biggest capital of any nation is human resource.

Reason (R) Without skill development, human resource is not possible.

95 **Assertion** (A) For any country to develop, skill and knowledge are important.

Reason (R) Skill India Programme started in 2008.

96 **Assertion** (A) The meaning of community development is development of people.

Reason (R) Development only means economic development.

97 **Assertion** (A) The biggest problem of community development is people's participation.

Reason (R) Until the people of a community do not help in problem solution, the community development is not possible.

98 **Assertion** (A) The rights and duties in a formal organisation is clear.

Reason (R) Formal organisation are not backed by the government.

99 **Assertion** (A) A successful organisation has effective leadership.

Reason (R) Leadership is a great quality.

100 **Assertion** (A) For community development, government organises development programmes.

Reason (R) People's participation can make Community Development Programme successful.

101 **Assertion** (A) Originally, Panchayati Raj started on 2nd October, 1954 in Rajasthan.

Reason (R) This is part of government centralisation policy.

102 **Assertion** (A) Zila Parishad comprises of people choosen by Panchayat members.

Reason (R) All the people of Gram Sabha choose their Chairman.

103 **Assertion** (A) NGO had their own formal organisation.

Reason (R) Minimum 11 people minimum are needed for making an NGO.

104 **Assertion** (A) People's participation brings transparency in work.

Reason (R) People's participation helps in changing opinion of the people.

Directions *(Q. Nos. 105-109) Read the passage carefully and answer the questions given below.*

The Guardian in 2013 cited one question that the entrance examination paper for a trainee programme at Merrill Lynch in 1972 had: "When you meet a woman, what interests you most about her?" The correct answer was beauty.

Those who thought intelligence, were given low marks. Of course there was, no question on what interests one the most when meeting a man. This is gender discrimination at its worst in the financial sector. Do we see this in 21st century India?

There is no gender discrimination in the Indian financial sector, whether at the organisational level or in choice of consumers. Then, why did the Ex-Finance Minister P. Chidambaram want to setup a bank exclusively for women customers and run by women?

One reason could be political. Women as a gender are not a separate constituency yet in India. There are urban women, rural women, wealthy women and poor women but women as a gender are not a vote bank. This is a relatively low cost experiment to create that.

Beyond politics, as a symbol of women's empowerment, this is not a laughing matter or an idea to ridicule, but translating this into success is not a easy job. There are quite a few cooperative banks in India that give loans to women borrowers.

Globally too, there aren't too many instances of banks run by women, for women. Tanzania has one such example. In 1999, a group of women entrepreneurs mooted the idea of a women's bank to then President Benjamin William Mkapa and it took eight years for the Women's Bank Public Ltd Co to setup, with the government holding 97% equity stake and private entities the rest and on the day the bank was launched, 110 women opened accounts. It focuses on low-income earners, small businesses and small and medium enterprises and men can also open accounts in this bank based in Dar s Salaam.

Ahead of Tanzania, Pakistan had setup First Women Bank Ltd. Late Prime Minister Benazir Bhutto was instrumental in establishing this to meet the needs of women entrepreneurs.

It commenced business in December 1989, with five leading public sector banks. i.e., National Bank of Pakistan, Habib Bank Ltd, Muslim Commercial Bank Ltd, United Bank Ltd and Allied Bank Ltd, holding 90% stake and the government the rest. After 23 years of existence, the bank has about 60,000 women customers, handled by 600 employees spread over 41 branches over 24 locations.

In India, the Self-Help Groups (SHGs) and Micro-Finance Movements have been driven by women. Such groups are an intermediary between the banking system and borrowers.

Banks and Micro-Finance Institutions are comfortable dealing with women borrowers as they are more responsible and disciplined in their approach in paying back the money. A woman's bank will not become successful in India if it focuses only on banking.

If our government is serious about this project, it must see that this bank goes beyond taking deposits and giving loans and becomes a vehicle for changing attitudes about women and their money, taking care of other things such as education, vocational training, etc and help in empowering women by educating them about self-finance.

At a parallel level, we also need to address two structural issues i.e. women must have right to property (otherwise they can't offer collateral for a loan) and get adequately involved in formal economy through jobs and entrepreneurship. Professional urban women do not need a bank of their own but rural women, particularly in those pockets of India which are fraught with casteism and gender discrimination, will find in it an oasis.

105 What is the another opinion about the announcement made by the Finance Minister to setup a Women's Bank in India?

(a) The author is critical about the motive behind it but believes that it has potential of really helping out women if certain issues are taken care of by the government.

(b) The author is totally critical of the idea and thinks that it was announced only with an eye on the large voter bank of women keeping in mind the forthcoming elections.

(c) The author is supportive of the idea from the start and even suggests that certain changes in the implementation which will take care of structural mistakes in the plan.

(d) The author thinks that Indian women face gender discrimination in the financial sector and thus, having a Women's Bank is a welcome change which supports their needs.

106 Which of the following is definitely true according to the passage?

(a) Globally, micro-finance initiatives are run by women

(b) In India, men as a gender are a vote bank.

(c) Women Cooperative Organisations are very successful all over India.

(d) In 1972, the Organisation Merril Lynch was working in the financial sectors.

107 Which of the following statement (s) is/are true about Women Bank in Tanzania?

(a) A group of women entrepreneurs mooted the idea of Women Bank to then President Benjamin William Mkapa.

(b) It was opened in 1988.

(c) Men can also open an account in this bank. It focuses on low income earners, small business and small and medium enterprise.

(d) Both (a) and (c)

108 Choose the statement(s) which is/are correct with regard to Women Bank in Pakistan.

Statement I Late Prime Minister Benazir Bhutto was instrumental in setting up of first Women Bank in Pakistan.

Statement II It commenced business in 1989 with five leading public sector banks.

(a) Only statement I is correct.

(b) Both the statements are correct.

(c) Only statement II is correct.

(d) Neither statement I nor statement II is correct.

109 In India the Self-Help Groups and micro finance movements have been driven by

(a) public sector (b) private sector

(c) women (d) Both (a) and (b)

PREVIOUS YEARS' QUESTIONS

December 2015

1 Arrange the following Development Programmes in the chronological order of their inception.

1. Integrated Child Development Scheme
2. District Primary Education Programme
3. Mahatma Gandhi National Rural Employment Guarantee Scheme
4. Swacch Bharat Abhiyan
5. National Literacy Mission

Codes

(a) 1, 2, 3, 5, 4 (b) 1, 5, 2, 3, 4
(c) 3, 4, 1, 2, 5 (d) 1, 5, 3, 2, 4

June 2015

2 Arrange the following milestone in National development in the chronological order.

1. National Rural Livelihood Mission
2. Right of Education Act
3. Right to Information Act
4. National Rural Employment Gurantee Scheme
5. Swach Bharat Abhiyan

Codes

(a) 1, 2, 3, 4, 5 (b) 3, 4, 2, 1, 5
(c) 2, 3, 1, 4, 5 (d) 3, 5, 1, 2, 4

December 2014

3 **Assertion** (A) Pradhan Mantri Jan Dhan Yojna is a radical step in development strategy.
Reason (R) Comprehensive Financial inclusion is important for building economic capabilities of the people.

Codes

(a) Both A and R are true
(b) Both A and R are false
(c) A is true, but R is false
(d) A is false, but R is correct

June 2014

4 Arrange the following Development Programmes according to their year of inception in descending order.

1. Community Development Programme.
2. Integrated Child Development Services.
3. Mahatma Gandhi National Rural Employment Guarantee Scheme.
4. National Rural Health Mission.

Codes

(a) 1, 2, 3, 4
(b) 1, 2, 4, 3
(c) 4, 3, 2, 1
(d) 2, 3, 4, 1

5 **Assertion** (A) Gram Sabha is the lowest range of decentralized governance.
Reason (R) Panchayati Raj Institutions are responsible for planning and execution of development programmes at the village level.

Codes

(a) Both A and R are false
(b) A is true, but R is false
(c) Both A and R are true
(d) A is false, but R is true

ANSWERS

Exam Based Questions

1 (d)	2 (c)	3 (c)	4 (a)	5 (b)	6 (b)	7 (b)	8 (b)	9 (b)	10 (c)
11 (a)	12 (c)	13 (a)	14 (b)	15 (d)	16 (d)	17 (c)	18 (d)	19 (c)	20 (b)
21 (d)	22 (b)	23 (c)	24 (b)	25 (a)	26 (d)	27 (a)	28 (c)	29 (a)	30 (c)
31 (a)	32 (a)	33 (c)	34 (d)	35 (d)	36 (d)	37 (d)	38 (c)	39 (d)	40 (d)
41 (d)	42 (d)	43 (b)	44 (d)	45 (d)	46 (a)	47 (d)	48 (d)	49 (a)	50 (c)
51 (b)	52 (d)	53 (b)	54 (b)	55 (c)	56 (c)	57 (a)	58 (b)	59 (d)	60 (d)
61 (d)	62 (b)	63 (b)	64 (c)	65 (a)	66 (b)	67 (b)	68 (d)	69 (d)	70 (d)
71 (a)	72 (c)	73 (a)	74 (b)	75 (a)	76 (b)	77 (c)	78 (d)	79 (c)	80 (c)
81 (d)	82 (d)	83 (b)	84 (c)	85 (a)	86 (b)	87 (c)	88 (d)	89 (a)	90 (d)
91 (b)	92 (b)	93 (a)	94 (b)	95 (c)	96 (c)	97 (b)	98 (c)	99 (b)	100 (b)
101 (b)	102 (a)	103 (b)	104 (a)	105 (b)	106 (c)	107 (d)	108 (b)	109 (c)	

Previous Years' Questions

1 (b)	2 (b)	3 (a)	4 (c)	5 (c)

Research Methods

Researching is the basic human activity, which leads to growth and development of human life. In order to carry research, a good research design plays a key role. Research design is a catalogue of the various phases and facts relating to the formulation of a research efforts.

Concept of Research

Research is the journey of knowledge which refers to systematic search for pertaining information regarding an answer to questions or a solution to a problem. The term 'Research' is a combination of two words 'Re' and 'search'.

Re means again and again; search means to find out something.

It can be defined as the careful, diligent and exhaustive investigation of a specific subject matter, its aim is the advancement of mankind's knowledge.

Research includes a wide variety of activities, the physical scientist in his laboratory, the artists studying in the museum, the archaeologists digging in the ruins, the sociologist observing pattern of marital interaction, management teams competing through computerised business etc.

Research in common term refers to a search for knowledge. One can also define research as a scientific and systematic search for pertinent information on a specific topic. In fact, advanced research is an art of scientific investigation. According to the **Advanced Learner's Dictionary of Current English** "Research is a careful investigation or inquiry specially through, search for new facts in any branch of knowledge." Some people consider research as a movement, a movement from the known to the unknown.

Definitions of Research

- According to **Clifford Woody**, "Research comprises defining and redefining problems, formulating hypothesis or suggested solutions; collecting, organising and evaluating data; making deductions and reaching conclusions and at last carefully testing the conclusions to determine whether, they fit the formulating hypothesis."
- According to **CC Crawford** "Research is simply a systematic and refined technique of thinking, employing specialised tools, instruments and procedures in order to obtain a more adequate solution of a problem than would be possible under ordinary means."

In this Chapter

- According to **Francis Bacon** "Research is a power of suspending judgement with patience of mediating with pleasures of asserting with caution, of correcting with readiness of arranging though with scrupulous plan."

Objectives of Research

Objectives of research are as follow :

- To portray accurately the characteristics of a particular individual situation or a group.
- To gain familiarity with a phenomenon or to achieve new insights into it.
- To test a hypothesis of a casual relationship between variables.
- To determine the frequency with which something occurs or with which it is associated with something else.
- To investigator a subject.
- To collect data regarding the problem.
- To conduct logical and objective study.
- To conduct a systematic enquiry of the subject.
- For carefully recording, reporting and presenting the facts.

Characteristics of Research

A research has following characteristics :

- It demands a clear statement of the problem.
- It requires a plan (it is not aimlessly 'looking' for something in the hope that you will come across a solution).
- It builds on existing data, using both positive and negative findings.
- New data should be collected as required and be organised in such a way that they answer the research questions.

Need of Research

Research is required in major spheres of life. This can be understood keeping in view the following points :

- Research is for those students, who have to write a master or PhD thesis, research may mean a way to attain a high position in the social structure.
- People are professionals in research methodology, research may mean a source of livelihood.
- To philosophers and thinkers, research may mean the outlet for new ideas and insights.
- To literary men and women, research may mean the development of new ideas and insights.
- The intellectuals research may mean the generalisations of new theories.
- Thus, research is the foundation of knoweldge for the sake of knowledge and an important source of providing guidelines for solving different business, governmental and social problems.

Scope of Research

In the age of science and technology, where new concepts and applications are searched continuously, it is necessary to know the scope of research. These are :

- It strives to be objective and logical.
- It is based on observable experience or empirical evidence.
- It is characterised by patient and unhurried activity.
- It demands accurate observations, reservations and descriptions.
- It is directed towards the solution of the problem.
- It is carefully recorded and reported.
- It required expertise.
- It involves gathering new data from primary or first hand sources or using existing data for new purpose.

Qualities of Good Research

Some features which are as follows :

Good Research is Systematic Specified steps all taken in a specified sequence with the well defined set of rules. Systematic characteristic reject the use of guessing and arriving at conclusions.

Good Research is Logical Logical reasoning and logical process are great value in carrying out research.

Logical reasoning makes research more meaningful in comparison to decision-making.

Good Research is Empirical One or more aspect of research is related to real situation and deals with concrete data that give research result an external validity.

Ethics in Research

Research that involves human subjects or participants, raises unique and complex ethical, legal, social and political issues.

It refers to a diverse set of values, norms and institutional regulations that help constitute and regulate scientific activity.

Following are the objectives of ethics in research :

- To protect human participants
- To ensure that research is conducted in a way that serves interests of individuals, groups and society as a whole.
- To examine specific research activities and projects for their ethical soundness, looking at issues such as the management of risk, protection of confidentiality and the process of informed consent.

Relevance of Research Methods

A fundamental understanding of research methodology will help you read about and correctly interpret the results of research in any field.

Relevance of research methods is in following fields :

Evaluating Research Reports One goal of it is to help you learn how to evaluate scientific research reports. We will examine how scientists develop ideas and test them, how they measure, analyse and interpret the data they collect.

Thus, the most important skill you can gain from the study of research methods is the ability to distinguish good research from bad research.

Conducting Research Research methods are used to help you learn how to conduct research.

Thinking Critically About Research Thinking critically is important to conduct sound research and to determine the value of research.

Significance of Research

This can also be understood keeping in view the following points :

- To those students, who are to write a master of PhD thesis, research may mean a careerism or a way to attain a high position in the social structure.
- To professionals in research methodology, research may mean a source of livelihood.
- To philosophers and thinkers' research may mean the outlet for new ideas and insights.
- To literary men and women, research may mean the development of new ideas and insights.
- To analysis and intellectuals, research may mean the generalisations of new theories.
- Thus, research is the foundation of knowledge for the sake of knowledge and an important source of providing guidelines for solving different business, governmental and social problems.

Fundamental Issues in Research Methods

Research methodology involves specific techniques that are adopted in research process to collect, assemble and evaluate data. It defines those tools that are used to gather relevant information in a specific research study.

But, there are certain fundamental issues in research methods as follows :

Formulation of Research Aims and Objectives Sometimes we might have formulated research aims and objectives too broadly. The formulation of research aims and objectives could be narrowed so that level of focus of the study could be increased.

Implementation of Data Collection Method Because we do not have an extensive experience in primary data collection, there is a great chance that the nature of implementation of data collection method is flawed.

Sample Size Sample size depends on the nature of the research problem. If sample size is too small, statistical tests would not be able to identify significant relationships within data set. The importance of sample size is greater in quantitative studies compared to qualitative studies.

Lack of Previous Studies in the Research Area Literature review is an important part of any research, because it helps to identify the scope of works that have been done so far in research area. Literature review findings are used as the foundation for the researcher to be built upon to achieve her research objectives.

Scope of Discussions We can include this point as a limitation of your research regardless of the choice of the research area.

Because we don't have many years of experience of conducing researches and producing academic papers of such a large size individually, the scope and depth of discussions in your paper is compromised in many levels compared to the works of experienced scholars.

Self-reported Data It can contain several potential sources of bias that we should be alert. These biases become apparent if they are incongruent with data from other sources.

These are :

- Selective memory
- Telescoping
- Attribution
- Exaggeration

Lack of Available and /or Reliable Data Lack of data or of reliable data will likely require you to limit the scope of your analysis, the size of your sample, or it can be a significant obstacle in finding a trend and a meanigful relationship.

Measure Used to Collect the Data Sometimes it is the case that, after completing your interpretation of the findings, you discover that the way in which you gathered data inhibited your ability to conduct a thorough analysis of the results.

Variables in Research

Variables are said to be the characteristics of the sample or the population that we intend to measure. Thus, age of the reader is a variable, so is gender, educational level or mother tongue.

Selection of Variables

Variable selection is intended to select the 'best' subset of predictors.

- To explain the data in the simplest way -redundant predictors should be removed. The principle of occam's Razor states that among several plausible explanations for a phenomenon, the simplest is best. Applied to regression analysis, this implies that the smallest model that fits the data is best.
- Unnecessary predictors will add noise to the estimation of other quantities that we are interested in. Degrees of freedom will be wasted.
- Collinearity is caused by having too many variables trying to do the same job.
- Cost: if the model is to be used for prediction , we can save time and/or money by not measuring redundant predictors.

Prior to Variable Selection

- Identify out liers and influential points-may exclude them at least temporarily.
- Add in any transformations of the variables that seem appropriate.

Types of Variables

Variables are of two kinds :

Dependent and Independent Variables

Variables are related to the concept, which take on different quantitative values. Examples of variables are income, height, weight.

On the basis of the presence or absence of the concurring attributes, quantitative phenomena are quantified. Continuous variables are the phenomena, which can take on quantitatively different values even in decimal points. All variableness are not continuous. Discrete variables or non-continuous variables can only be expressed in integeral values.

Extraneous Variable

Independent variables that effect the dependent variables, but not related to the purpose of study are called extraneous variables. Independent and dependent variables are more clearly understand by this example in a research to test the hypothesis that there is relationship between adolescence gains in social studies achievement and their self-concepts.

In this example self concept refers to independent variables and social studies refers to dependent variables. It is termed as an extraneous variable because it is not related to the purpose of the study undertaken by the researcher and intelligence will affect the social studies achievement.

As a result of extraneous variables, whatever effect is noticed on dependent variables is technically described as an experimental error. A study not to have extraneous variable or variables, but must have independent variables.

Types of Research

There are various types of research some of them are discussed below :

Qualitative Research

Qualitative research is a broad term that encompasses a variety of approaches to interpretative research and investigate methodologies describes as ethnographic, naturalistic, anthropological field or participant observer research. It focus upon human behaviour for better understanding about the world around them.

So, the emphasis given by qualitative researcher in their studies involves an examination of the perspectives of the people or group e.g. their ideas, attitudes, motives and intention. The researchers study things in their natural setting, attempting to make sense of or to interpret, phenomena in terms of the meaning people bring to them.

There are three most common characteristics as follows :

- Participant observation
- In-depth interview
- Focus groups

Although, it investigate on social norms, human behaviour (i.e. ideas, attitudes, motives and intentions). So, the research documents constructed the meaning of social reality by contextual dependence.

Thus, qualitative research is naturalistic, ethnographic and participatory in its approach. Ontological, epistemological and methodological framework together constitute the paradigm.

This is also termed as interpretative framework and is guided by a set of beliefs and feelings about the world and how it should be understood and studied. Ontology deals with what kind of being is the human being?

Or what is the nature of reality? Epistemology is the theory of knowledge and studies the relationship between the inquirer and the known. Ontology and epistemology in context to social science research has been discussed in the earlier chapter.

Historical Research

Research about events that occurred in the past e.g. study of corporal punishment in the 19th century. History is not a collection of facts about the past whose primary value is to improve one's skills, while playing trivia games; it is an interpretation of the past based on the weight of the available evidence.

There are many types of historical research, empirical or descriptive historiography assures that recorded facts are paramount and that readers and academics consumers share their concern about accuracy.

Social historiography is empirical in nature; its well disciplined focus says on social categories and the behavioural tendencies of group. Cultural historiography curtail our fixation on facts as objective reality and to begin serious discussions about the influence of social constructions, including the overriding role of culture, on historical events as subjective experience. In post modern historiography, traditional textual research methods are subjected to intense intellectual scrutiny in an attempt to uncover more explanation of power relations and the multiplicity of social and political behaviours.

Quantitative Research

Quantitative research is explaining phenomenon by collecting numerical data that are analysed using mathematically based methods. It shapes in different ways as discovery of a new theory; development of existing theory. Research in the best outcome of consensus curiosity. It is based on a critical interpretation of empirical observation.

Qualities of quantitative research are :

- Quantitative research is deductive.
- It is carried out after completing the task of theory construction.
- In quantitative research, the researcher defines the concepts before initiating the research.
- Quantitative researchers use mathematical models, inferential statistics and graph.
- It provides a tool for scientific analysis and solution for various business problems.
- Quantitative method research enable proper use of resources and provides statistical comparison between various groups.

Survey Research

It uses scientific sampling and questionnaire design to measure characteristics of the population. In survey research, each person in the population has a known probability of being sampled. In it, a researcher develops a survey instrument and research objectives. In a survey research, data is collected by direct method. Data should be primary and obtained by direct observation or from original and reliable sources. The term survey comes from words sure and veer. Sure means over and veer means see, which means to see a particular thing from high place. A survey is a way to collect information directly from people in a systematic, standaridised way.

Descriptive Research

It is a research method that describes the characteristics of the population or phenomenon that is being studied. This methodology focuses more on the "what" of the research subject rather than the "why" of the research subject. Thus, it does not make accurate predictions, and does not determine cause and effect.

It is a quantitative research method that attempts to collect quantifiable information to be used for statistical analysis of the population sample. It is a popular market research tool that allows the collect and describe the nature of the demographic segment. In descriptive research, none of the variables are influenced in any way because it uses observational method to conduct the research. Hence, the nature of the variables or **their behaviour is not** in the **hands** of the researcher. Descriptive research method is generally a cross-sectional study where different sections belonging to the same group are studied.

Analytical Research

The analytical research usually concerns itself with cause-effect relationships. In analytical research, the researchers use facts or informations which are already available and analyse these to make a critical evaluation of the material. In analytical research, the researchers try to test hypothesis and specify their interpretations.

Some of the examples of analytical research are as follows :

- To search measures to reduce the number of complaints made by customers.
- To search measures to reduce the absentee rate among employees of a company.

Action Research

Action research is a reflective process of progressive problem-solving led by individuals working with others in teams or as part of a "community of practice" to improve the way they address issues and solve problems.

Action research can also be undertaken by larger organisations or institutions, assisted or guided by professional researchers, with the aim of improving their strategies, practices and knowledge of the environments within which they practice.

Kurt Lewin , then a professor at MIT, first coined the term "action research" in about 1944, and it appears in his 1946 paper "Action Research and Minority Problems." In that paper, he described action research as "a comparative research in the conditions and effects of various forms of social action and research leading to social action" that uses "a spiral of steps , each of which is composed of a circle of planning, action and fact-finding about the result of the action."

Research Design

Research design refers to the task of defining the research problem by preparing the design of research project, taking decisions regarding when, how, where, what steps are taking for consuming a research design. Collection and analysis of a data in a way that aims to combine relevance to the research purpose is known as research design.

Some of the well known definitions are following :

- It is a conceptual framework under whose umbrella research will be conducted.
- It is a design for collection of measurement and analysis of data.
- It is a decision matrix which looks into the aspects of SWH (what, which,where and how).
- It can also be defined as collection and interpretation of data, which leads of efficient conduct of research procedure.

Principles of Good Research Design

The following are the main features of a good research design :

Simplicity It should be simple and understandable.

Economical It must be economical, cost effective and less time consuming.

Reliability It should give the smallest experimental error.

Work Ability It must be workable, pragmatic and practicable.

Flexibility It must be flexible enough to permit the consideration of many different aspects of research.

Accuracy It must lead to accurate result.

Purpose of Research Design

The three main purpose of research design are :

Exploration

- To satisfy the researcher's curiosity and desire for better understanding.
- To test the feasibility of undertaking a more extensive study.
- To develop the methods to be employed in any subsequent study.

Description

- Describe situations and events through scientific observation.
- In descriptive studies, the research design must be rigid and not flexible.
- Descriptive studies answer questions of what, where, when and how.

Experimental

- To find out the cause-effect relationship of the phenomena under study.
- It aims at testing the casual hypothesis.

The procedure followed under this research design help in drawing interference about the causality.

The following are the other purposes of research design :

- Proper care should be taken, while preparing the research design otherwise the error may upset the project.
- Research design has a great bearing on the reliability of the result.
- Making research as effective as possible use of maximal information with minimal expenditure of effort, time and money.
- Planning of the method to be adopted for collecting the relevant data are necessary for research design.
- For all type of research one single design can not be serve.
- A design may be quite suitable in one case, but cannot be suitable for some other problem.
- Availability of staff, keeping in view the objective of research and technique used for analysis are most essential for research design.
- Criteria for formulating a research design as control of variance are discussed.
- For accurate assessment of cause and effect relationship between independent and dependent variables permits a plan study, which provide by the purpose of research design.
- A good research design deals with the classic controlled experiment.

Steps in Research Design

A research design is a plan of action, collecting and analysing data in an economic, efficient and relevant manner.

In all the research designs, the following steps are followed :

Selection and Definition of Problem The problem selected for study should be defined clearly in operational terms, so that research knows positively what facts he is looking for and what is relevant to the study.

Source of Data Once the problem is selected it is the duty of the researcher to state clearly the various sources of information such as library, personal document, field work, a particular residential group, etc.

Nature of Study The research design should be expressed in relation to the nature of study to be undertaken. The choice of the statistical, experimental or comparative type of study should be made at this stage so that the following steps in planning may have relevance to the proposed problem.

Object of Study Whether the design aims at theoretical understanding or a welfare notion, it must be explicit at this point.

Temporal Context The geographical limit of the design should also be referred to at this stage.

Dimension The selection of an adequate and representative sample is necessary in any research.

Technique of Data Collection Suitable technique has to be adopted for collection of required data. Once the collection of data is complete, analysis, coding and presentation of the report follows.

Sampling and Sampling Techniques

A sample is a segment or a portion of a larger group called population. A researcher may use probability sampling in cases where the valuation's purpose is to generalise the whole group and non-probability samples where the purpose of evaluation is to learn about individuals or cases for some purpose other than generalising the populations.

Sampling is concerned with the selection of a subset of individuals from within a statistical population to estimate characteristics of the whole population. Acceptance sampling is used to determine, if a production lot of material meets the governing specifications.

Two advantages of sampling are that the cost is lower and data collection is faster than measuring the entire population. Each observation measures one or more properties (such as weight location, colour) of observable bodies distinguished as independent objects or individuals.

The statistical procedure of drawing a sample from the population is called sampling. When field study are undertaken in practical life, considerations of time and cost almost invariably lead to a selection of respondents selection of only a few items. The respondents selection should be as representative of the total population as possible in order to produce a miniature crosss-section.

The selected respondents constitute what is technically called a sample and the selection process is called sampling technique. The survey, so conducted is known as sample survey. A hypothesis forms the way for collecting the various types of data to proceed with the research. There is a vast pool of information through which a researcher may have to plunge to collect the data required. In these situations, researcher has to use different sampling methods such as random systematic or stratified depending upon his requirement.

Sampling Procedure

Sampling procedure involves following stages:

Survey Objectives The sample survey starts with the specification of the objectives. All other steps-like target population, sampling frame, selection of the sampling method etc., are designed according to survey objectives.

Questionnaire Design According to the objectives of the survey, it is required to design a questionnaire, particularly when the sample survey is conducted at a large scale involving a number of investigators.

Defining the Target Population To draw the samples from a population. It is necessary to know the target population. The target population is also referred as the universe. The target population is the group about which we wish to generalise or make inferences from the sample.

Identifying Sampling Frame The sampling frame is the actual operational definition of target population. If the target population or actual operation is excluded, it is called sampling frame error.

Selecting Sampling Procedure Selection of appropriate sampling procedure is necessary in sampling process.

Survey Data Processing After selection of sampling procedure and its unit, the next step is data collection and processing. Checking the incomplete questionnaires and editing or cross-checking the responses.

Analysis of Data In view of researcher requirements, researcher analyse the data by using various statistical tools.

Types of Sampling

There are two types of sampling i.e. Probability and Non-Probability Sampling.

Probability Sampling

In probability sampling, each element of the population has a known, non-zero chance of being included in the sample. Random sampling ensures the law of statistical regularity which states that if on an average the sample choosen is a random one, the sample will have the same composition and characteristics as the universe.

In brief, random sampling or non-probability sampling gives :

- Equal probability to each element getting into the sample.
- All choices are independent of one another.

It includes—simple random sampling, systematic sampling and stratified sampling, cluster sampling.

Their description is given below :

Simple Random Sampling

Each and every individual in a population has an equal chance of being included in the sample and that the selection of one individual is in no way dependent upon the selection of another person.

The two popularly used methods in random sampling are :

- Draw of lottery
- A random number table

Systematic Random Sampling

It uses a list of all members of the population in its sampling frame. Instead of using random numbers to select the sample elements the researcher applies a skip interval to the list to produce a sample of the required size.

$$\text{Skip interval} = \frac{\text{Number of elements in the population}}{\text{The required sample size}}$$

$$K = \frac{N}{n}$$

K = Skip interval,
N = Universe size,
n = Sample size

Stratified Random Sampling

If the population from which a sample is to be drawn does not constitute a homogeneous group, then stratified sampling technique is applied, so as to obtain a representative sample. In this technique, the population is stratified into a number of non-overlapping sub-populations or strata and sample items are selected from each stratum.

If the items selected from each stratum is based on simple random sampling the entire procedure, first stratification and then simple random sampling, is known as stratified random sampling.

There are two types of stratified sample :

Proportionate Stratified Sample A proportionate stratified sample selects the number of elements from each stratum, so that the stratum sample size $(n_1, n_2 \ldots n_k)$ is proportional to their respective stratum population size $(N_1, N_2 \ldots N_K)$.

For example, A selected village may have households of SC (10%), ST (5%), OBCs (45%) other (30%), Minority (10%). A village sample of 100 may constitute the households of various castes in the above proportion, so that the sample may contain all important characteristics of village population.

Disproportionate Stratified Sample A disproportionate stratified sample selects the number of elements from each stratum, so that the stratum sample size is not proportional to the stratum population size.

The most common reason for selecting this type of sample is to study a relatively rare, but important sub-population, such as younger patients suffering from heart disease.

Cluster Sampling

It involves grouping the population and then selecting the groups or the cluster rather than individual elements for inclusion in the sample.

Various types of cluster sampling are as follows :

Area Sampling It is quite close to cluster sampling and is often talked about when the total geographical area of interest happens to be big one. Under area sampling, we first divide the total area into a number of smaller non overlapping areas, generally called geographical clusters, then a number of these smaller areas are randomly selected and all units in these small areas are included in the sample.

Area sampling is specially helpful where we do not have the list of the population concerned. It also makes the field interviewing more efficient since the interviewer can do many interviews at each location.

Multi-stage Sampling This is further development of the idea of cluster sampling. This technique is meant for big inquiries extending to a considerably large geographical area like an entire country. Under multi-stage sampling, the first stage may be to select large primary sampling units such as states, then districts, then towns and finally certain families within towns.

Sequential Sampling This is somewhat a complex sample design where the ultimate size of the sample is not fixed in advance, but is determined according to mathematical decisions on the basis of information yielded as survey progresses. This design is usually adopted under acceptance of sampling plan in the context of statistical quality control.

Data Collection

Data collection is the process of gathering and measuring information on variables of interest, in an established systematic procedure that enables one to answer stated research questions, test hypotheses and evaluate outcomes.

The techniques of data collection begin when research problem is defined. For collecting data, social scientists use a number of different data collection strategies.

Types of Data

There are two types of data :

Primary Data

Primary data are those data that are collected for the specific problem. It is collected as fresh and for the first time. On every occasion, the primary data are collected, new data are added to the existing store of social knowledge.

There are several methods of collecting primary data, particularly in surveys and descriptive researches such as observation method, interview method questionnaires, etc. Their description is given below :

Observation

It is most commonly used method in studies relating to behavioural sciences. It becomes the method of data collection for the researcher when it serves a formulated research purpose, systematically planned recorded and subjected to check and controls on validity and reliability.

In observation method, the information is sought by way of investigator's own direct observation without asking from respondent.

While using this method, the researcher should keep in mind many things like what should be observed, how the observations should be recorded. How the accuracy of observations can be ensured.

It has two types :

Structured Observation In this observation method, careful definition of the units to be observed, the style of recording the observed information, standardised conditions of observation and selection of pertinent data of observation is included.

Unstructured Observation When observation is made without consideration of careful definition of the units to be observed, the style of recording the observed information. Standardised conditions of observation and selection of pertinent data is called unstructured observation.

Questionnaires

A questionnaire consists of a large number of questions arranged under different heading. These questions are sent to the respondent and the questionnaire is filled by the researcher or by the respondents themselves. These responses are then subjected to analysis and the results obtained. Thus, questionnaire is a research instrument consisting of a series of questions and other prompts for the purpose of gathering information from respondents. The questionnaire, was invented by **Sir Francis Galton.**

Questionnaire serves four basic purpose :

- Collect the appropriate data.
- Make data comparable and amenable to analysis.
- Minimise bias in formulating and asking questions.
- To make questions engaging and varied.

Types of Questionnaires

There are various types of questionnaires depending on the type of survey undertaken :

Structured Questionnaires In structured questionnaires the respondent has to tick mark the most suitable answer. In most questionnaires, the responses to most questions are exhaustive and in it if a respondent don't want to give a response in the questionnaire, there is a column indicating any other response, specify.

Unstructured Questionnaires In this, the questions are open ended and answers are not given or predetermined. Hence, respondents are free to give answer whatever he would like to these question. Since, there is flexibility to add one's own thoughts and feelings, these questionnaires elicit very factual, truthful and descriptive response .

Semi-Structured Questionnaires These types of questionnaires have a mixed approach. In this, some questions are structured and some are not structured. There is generally a mixed approach. It allows for the exploration of patterns and trends and provide a measure of respondent's opinion, attitudes, feelings and perception about issues of particular concern to the evaluator.

Interviews

Interviews are one of the most widely used method of gathering data in sociology that involves the presentation of real-verbal stimuli and reply in terms of oral-verbal responses (precisely, it is a form of verbal discourse). It is a test of a candidate by which interviewer gets an opportunity to collect information about the candidate. There are different methods of interview: oral, written, psychoanalytic, intellectual, all sorts of tests are used for the selection procedure.

Types of Interviews

There are different types of interviews which are as follows :

Structured Interview In this interview, the interviewer asks the pre-drafted questions. Interviewer cannot change the question nor their sequence. No freedom is given to add new question or delete any question.

Unstructured Interview In this interview, the interviewer asks on spot drafted question primarily based on interviewer's conscience. Interviewer's have full autonomy to ask questions.

It permits the interviewee to give responses freely or it may restrict free responses. It helps to know the areas to be covered and it also provides guidelines for smooth conduct of interview session. It is also called in-depth interview.

Traditional Face-to-Face Interview In this interview, the interviewer maintains eye contact, listen and respond once a question has been asked.

Panel/Committee Interview A panel involves a number of interviewers. The composition of this panel could include- The supervisor, The manager, A union representative, A human resources officer; A employment equity officer, Employees from the department that is hiring. In this interview, the interviewer's maintain eye contact with interviewee's, but also seek eye contact with other members of the panel as interviewee gives response.

Behavioural Interview In this interview, the interviewer's try to establish relation between past behavioural actions and then predict the future actions. If the interviewer's asks behavioural-oriented questions, they are no longer asking hypothetical questions but are now asking questions that must be based on facts.

Case Interview In this interview, the interviewers are looking for how interviewee apply their knowledge and skills to real-life situation. Speak and reason aloud so interviewers have a full understanding of interviewee's thought process.

Group Interview It is usually designed to uncover the leadership potential of prospective managers and employees, who will be dealing with customers.

In this interview, the interviewer see how interviewee interacts with others and how interviewee use their knowledge and reason to influence others.

Stress Interview The form of interview is more common in sales position and is very rare in contemporary scenario. It is usually a deliberate attempt to see how interviewee's handle themself under pressure.

Telephonic Interview This type of interview is conducted on phone and is best suited for market type of survey poll etc. It is a faster and cheaper method for obtaining information.

The Directed Interview This form of interview is impersonal and seek to reveal facts, that involves the interviewer's using an outline and asking specific questions within a certain time frame.

Secondary Data

Secondary data are those data which have already been collected by someone else and already been passed through the statistical process. Any type of primary data can serve as secondary data. When the researcher utilises secondary data, then he has to look into various sources from where the data, then he has to look into various sources from where he can obtain them. Secondary data may either be published data or unpublished data.

Published data are available in

- various publications of foreign governments or of international bodies and their subsidiary organisations.
- technical and trade journal.
- books, magazines and newspapers.
- reports and publications of various associations connected with business and industry, banks stock exchanges etc.

In using secondary data, researcher must be very careful.

Characteristics of Secondary Data

Secondary data should possess following characteristics :

Reliability of Data

It refers to the consistency of a measure. A test is considered reliable, if we get the same result repeatedly. e.g. If a test is designed to measure a trait, then each time the test is administered to a subject the results should be approximately the same. Unfortunately, it is impossible to calculate reliability exactly, but there are several different ways to estimate reliability.

Some of these are :

Test-Retest Reliability To test-retest reliability, the test is administered twice at two different points in time. This kind of reliability is used to assess the consistency of a test across time. This type of reliability assumes that there will be no charge in the quality or construct being measured. Test-retest reliability is best used for things that are stable over time, such as intelligence. Generally, reliability will be higher when little time has passed between tests.

Inter-Rater Reliability This type of reliability is assessed by having two or more independent judges score the test. The scores are then compared to determine the consistency of the raters estimates. One way to test inter-rate reliability is to have each rater assign each test item a score.

Parallel Forms Reliability It is gauged by comparing two different tests that were created using the same content. This is accomplished by creating a large pool of test items that measure the same quality and then randomly dividing the items into two separate tests. The two tests should then be administered to the same subjects at the same time.

Internal Consistency Reliability This form of reliability is used to judge the consistency of results across items on the same test. Essentially, comparing test items that measure the same construct to determine the tests internal consistency. When a researcher sees a question that seems very similar to another test question, it may indicate that the questions are being used to gauge reliability. Because the two questions are similar and designed to measure the same thing, the test taker should answer both questions the same, which would indicate that the test has internal consistency.

Validity of Data

It is the extent to which a test measures what it claims to measure. It is vital for a test to be valid in order for the results to be accurately applied and interpreted. Validity is not determine by a single statistic, but by a body of research that demonstrates the relationship between the test and the behaviour it is intended to measure. There are three types of validity:

Content Validity When a test has content validity the items on the test represent the entire range of possible items the test should cover. Individual test questions may be drawn from a large pool of items that cover a broad range of topics. In some instances, where a test measures a trait that is difficult to define, an expert judge may rate each item's relevance. Because each judge is basing their rating on opinion, two independent judges rate the test separately. Items that are rated as strongly relevant by both judges will be included in the final test.

Criterion Related Validity A test is said to have criterion related validity when the test is demonstrated to be effective in predicting criterion or indicators of a construct.

There are two different types of criterion validity :

Concurrent Validity It occurs when the criterion measures are obtained at the same time as the test scores. This indicates the extent to which the test scores accurately estimate an individual's current state with regards to the criterion. For example, on a test that measures levels of depression the test would be said to have concurrent validity, if it measured the current levels of depression experienced by the test taker.

Predictive Validity It occurs when the criterion measures are obtained at a time after the test. For example, tests with predictive validity such as career or aptitude tests, which are helpful in determining who is likely to succeed or fail in certain subjects or occupations.

Construct Validity A test has construct validity, if it demonstrates an association between the test scores and the prediction of a theoretical trait. Intelligence tests are one example of measurement instruments that should have construct validity.

Coding and Tabulation of Data

For presenting data in a proper ways, its coding and tabulation is done. Both of these are discussed below :

Coding

Coding refers to the process of assigning numerals or other symbols to answer so that responses can be put into a limited number of categories or classes. Such classes should be appropriate to the research problem under consideration.

They must also possess the characteristic of exhaustiveness and also that of mutual exclusively which means that a specific answer can be placed in one and only one cell in a given category set.

Coding is necessary for efficient analysis and through it several replies may be reduced to a small number of classes which contains the critical information required for analysis. Coding decisions should usually be taken at the designing stage of the questionnaire.

Tabulation

When a mass data has been assembled, it becomes necessary for the researcher to arrange the same in some kind of concise and logical order. This procedure is referred to as tabulation.

Thus, tabulation is the process of summarising raw data and displaying the same in compact form for further analysis. In order sense, tabulation is an orderly arrangement of data in columns and rows.

Tabulation is essential because of the following reasons :

- It conserves space and reduces explanatory and descriptive statement to a minimise.
- It facilitates the process of comparison.

Measurement and Ranking of Data

Measurement and ranking of data is essential for the proper conclusion of data. Their description is given below :

Measurement

The assignment of symbols to events according to a set of rules. Four scales of measurement for measuring dependent variables are :

Nominal Scale The numbers are assigned as labels in nominal measurement , they have no specific numerical value or meaning. It is the lowest measurement level.

Ordinal Scale When the terms in question can be rank ordered (intervals between ranks may not be ordered) (e.g. Ist, 2nd, 3rd place at a track meet-no information about how far apart the winners were).

Interval Scale When the terms in question can be rank orderd and equal intervals separate them, but there is no zero point (e.g. temperatures in °C, when at 0°C temperature doesn't cease to exist but interval of 1°C is constant).

Ratio Scale While going one step further ; ratio scale assumes the presence of a zero point (e.g. measurement of sound in decibels, zero means no sound and intervals are strict).

Nominal and ordinal scales are for discrete data- data in which each item is a separate , whole unit-number of individuals or species, members of particular groups species, types of car , round or square , heavy or light, etc.)

Interval and ratio scales are for continuous data-data for points along a scale that , at least theoretically, could be subdivided temperature, weight, lengths , units of time, etc.

Incremental progress	Measure property	Mathematical operators	Advanced operations	Central tendency
Nominal	Classification, membership	=, ≠	Grouping	Mode
Ordinal	Comparisons, level	>, <	Sorting	Median
Interval	Difference, affinity	+, −	Yardstick	Mean, Deviation
Ratio	Magnitude, amount	×, /	Ratio	Geometric mean, coefficient of variation

Ranking

A ranking is a relationship between a set of items such that, for any two items, the first is either 'ranked higher than', 'ranked lower than' or 'ranked equal to' the second. In mathematics, this is known as a weak order or total preorder of objects.

It is not necessarily a total order of objects because two different objects can have the same ranking. The ranking themselves are totally ordered. For example, materials are totally preordered by hardness, while degrees of hardness are totally ordered. If two items are the same in rank it is considered a tie. By reducing detailed measures to a sequence of ordinal numbers, rankings make it possible to evaluate complex information according to certain criteria.

Thus, for example, an internet search engine may rank the pages it finds according to an estimation of their relevance, making it possible for the user quickly to select the pages they are likely want to see.

Strategies for assigning rankings are :

1. Standard competition ranking
2. Modified competition ranking
3. Dense ranking
4. Ordinal ranking
5. Fractional ranking

Descriptive and Inferential Statistical Methods

The word 'statistics' can be defined in two different ways. In **singular sense**, statistics refers to **statistical methods**. In **plural sense**, statistics is used to refer the data.

The science of statistics is broadly studied under the following two statistics :

- Descriptive Statistics
- Inferential Statistics

Descriptive Statistics

Descriptive statistics refers to the analysis of data that helps in describing, presenting or summarising data in a meaningful way or in such a way that patterns might emerge from the data. However, descriptive statistics do not allow to make conclusions beyond the data we have analysed or reach conclusions regarding any hypothesis we might have made. Descriptive analysis enables a researcher to present the data in a more meaningful way and provides tool for simpler interpretation of the data.

The descriptive analysis is the branch of statistics, which deals with descriptions of obtained data. The descriptive statistics include classification, tabulation, diagrammatic and graphical representation of data, measures of central tendency and variability. These measures enable the researcher to know about the tendency of the data or scores, which further enhance the ease in description of the phenomenon.

Such single estimate of the series of data which summarises the distribution are known as parameters of the distribution.

Basically, descriptive statistics involves two operations :

- Organisation of data
- Summarisation of data

Organisation of Data

There are four major statistical techniques for organising the data. These are :

- Classification
- Tabulation
- Graphical Representation of Data
- Diagrammatical presentation

Classification

The arrangement of data in groups according to similarities is known as classification. A classification is a summary of the frequency of individual scores or ranges of scores for a variable. In classification, raw data are organised as a frequency distribution.

Frequency Distribution

Frequency distribution shows the number of cases following within a given class interval or range of scores. A frequency distribution is a table that shows each score as obtained by a group of individuals and how frequently each scores occurred.

Types of Frequency Distribution

Types of frequency distribution are :

Relative Frequency Distribution A relative frequency distribution is a distribution that indicates the proportion of the total number of cases observed at each score value or internal of score value.

Cumulative Frequency Distribution A cumulative frequency corresponding to a class interval is the sum of frequencies for that class and of all classes prior to that class.

Cumulative Relative Frequency Distribution A cumulative relative frequency distribution is one in which the entry of any score of class interval expresses that score's cumulative frequency as a proportion of the total number of cases.

Frequency Distribution with Grouped Data and Ungrouped Data

Grouped Frequency Distribution If there is a wide range of score value in the data, then it is difficult to get a clear picture of such series of data. In this case, grouped frequency distribution should be constructed to have a clear picture of the data. A group frequency distribution is a table that organises data into classes.

It shows the number of observations from the data set that fall into each of the class.

Ungrouped Frequency Distribution An ungrouped frequency distribution may be constructed by listing all score values either from highest to lowest or lowest to highest and placing a tally mark (/) besides each scores every time it occurs. The frequency of occurrence of each score is denoted by 'f'.

Construction of Frequency Distribution

To prepare a frequency distribution, it is essential to determine the following :

The Range of the given Data The difference between the highest and lowest scores.

The Number of Class Intervals There is no hard and fast rule regarding the number of classes into which data should be grouped. If there are very few scores, it is useless to have a large number of class intervals. Ordinarily, the number of classes should be between 5 to 30.

Limits of each Class Interval Another factor used in determining the number of classes is the size/ width or range of the class which is known as 'class interval' and is denoted by 'i'. Class interval should be of uniform width resulting in the same size classes of frequency distribution. The width of the class should be a whole number and conveniently divisible by 2, 3, 5, 10 or 20 etc. There are three methods for describing the class limits for distribution :

Exclusive Method In this method, the classes are so formed that the upper limit of one class becomes the lower limit of the next class. In this classification, it is presumed that score equal to the upper limit of the class is exclusive, i.e., a score of 40 will be included in the class of 40 to 50 and not in the class of 30 to 40 (30-40, 40-50, 50-60).

Inclusive Method In this method, the classes are so formed that the upper limit of one class does not become the lower limit of the next class. This classification includes scores, which are equal to the upper limit of the class. Inclusive method is preferred when measurements are given in whole numbers (30-39,40-49, 50-59).

True or Actual Class Method Mathematically, a score is an internal when it extends from 0.5 units below to 0.5 units above the face value of the score on a continuum. These class limits are known as true or actual class limits. (29.5 to 39.5, 39.5 to 49.5), etc.

Tabulation

Tabulation is the process of presenting the classified data in the form of a table. A table is a systematic arrangement of classified data in rows and columns with appropriate headings and sub-headings.

The main component of a table has been depicted in the figure below :

TITLE :				
Sub Head	**Caption**			
Sub Entries	**Column Head I**		**Column Head II**	
	Sub Head	Sub Head	Sub Head	Sub Head
	Main Body of the Table			
Total				

Footnotes(s):

Source :

Sub : Stands for brief and self explanatory headings for rows.

Graphical Representation of Data

The information contained in a frequency distribution is depicted in graphic and /or diagrammatic forms in such a way that it provides a systematic way of 'looking at' and understanding of data.

A graph is created on two mutually perpendicular lines called X-axis and Y-axis on which appropriate scales are indicated. The horizontal line is called the abscissa and vertical line as the ordinate. The commonly used graphs are Histogram, Frequency Polygon, Frequency curve and Cumulative Frequency Curve.

Histogram

The histogram consists of series of rectangles, with its width equal to the class interval of the variable on horizontal axis and the corresponding frequency on the vertical axis as its height. In this type of distribution, the upper limit of a class is the lower limit of the following class.

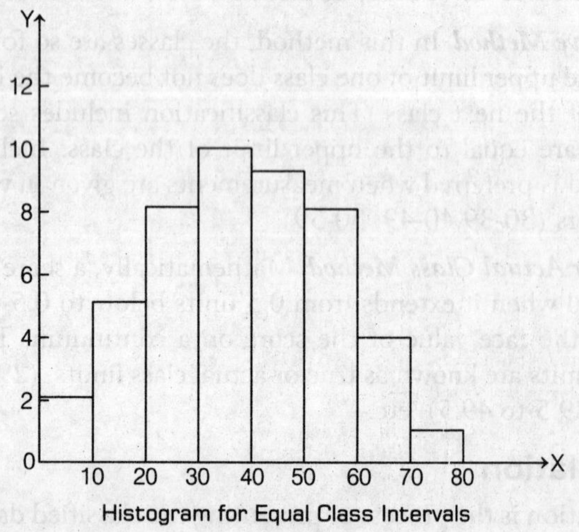

Histogram for Equal Class Intervals

Frequency Polygon

Polygon is a diagrammatic presentation of data which is constructed by joining the mid points of rectangles in a diagram. However, a polygon can also be constructed without constructing a histogram.

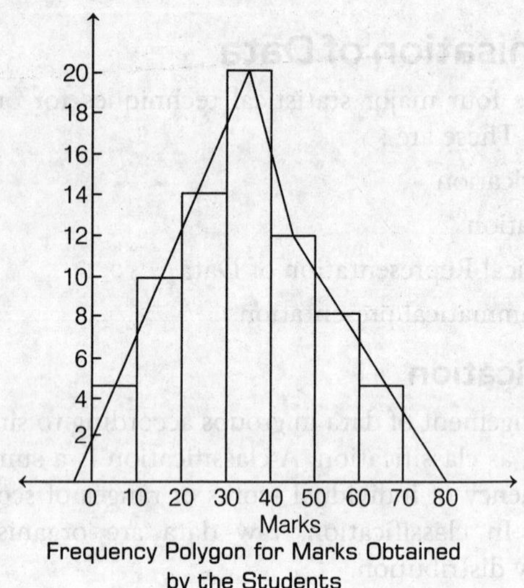

Frequency Polygon for Marks Obtained by the Students

Frequency Curve

A frequency curve is a smooth free hand curve drawn through frequency polygon.

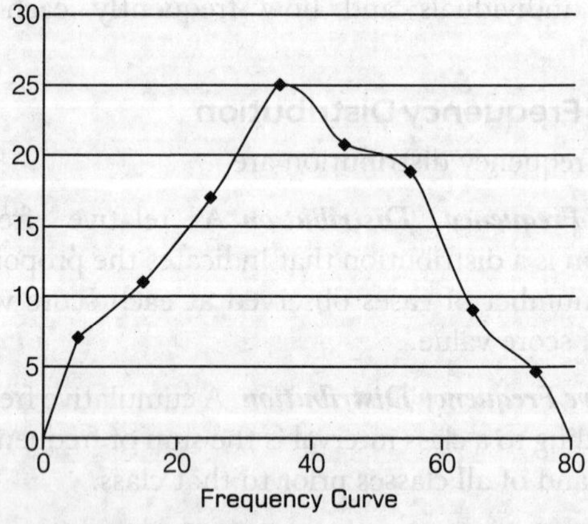

Frequency Curve

Cumulative Frequency Ogive

Cumulative frequency curve or ogive is the curve which is constructed by plotting cumulative frequency data on the graph paper in the form of a smooth curve.

A cumulative frequency can be constructed in two ways :

Less Than Ogive Less than ogives are plotted against the upper class boundaries of the respective classes. It is an increasing curve having slopes upwards from left to right.

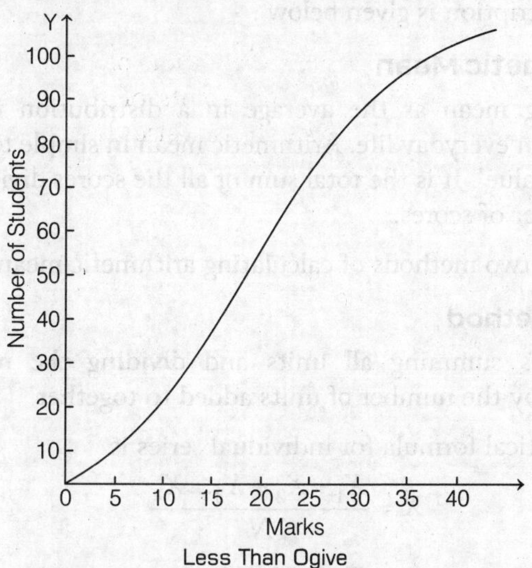

Less Than Ogive

More Than Ogive In more than ogive, the cumulative frequencies are plotted against the lower class boundaries of the respective class. It is decreasing curve and slopes downwards from left to right.

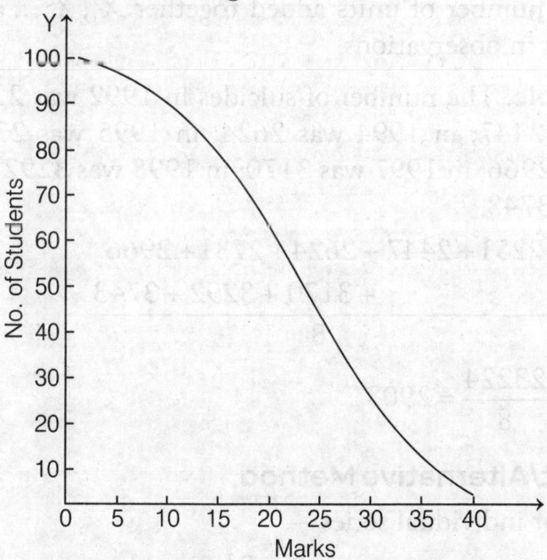

More Than Ogive Cumulative frequencies for marks Obtained by students in the class

Diagrammatic Representation of Data

A diagram is a visual form for the presentation of statistical data. Diagrammatic representation is only for the presentation of the data in visual form, whereas graphic representation of the data can be used for further analysis. There are different forms of diagrams:

- Bar Diagram
- Sub-Divided Bar Diagram
- Multiple Bar Diagram
- Pie Diagram
- Pictogram

Bar Diagram

It is used for categorical data. Bar diagram is drawn from the frequency distribution table representing the variable on the horizontal axis and the frequency on the vertical axis. The height of each bar will be corresponding to the frequency or value of the variable.

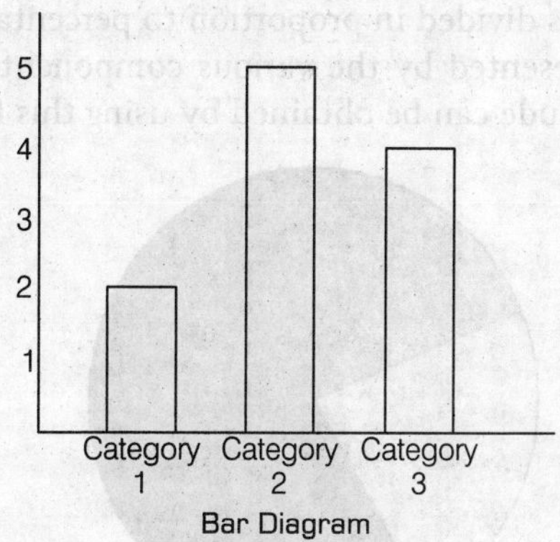

Bar Diagram

Sub-Divided Bar Diagram

Sub-divided bar diagram or component bar diagram is used to represent sub-classification. In this, representation corresponding to each sub-category of data the bar is divided and shaded. There will be as many shades as there will be sub-portion in a group of data. The portion of the bar occupied by each sub-class reflects its proportion in total.

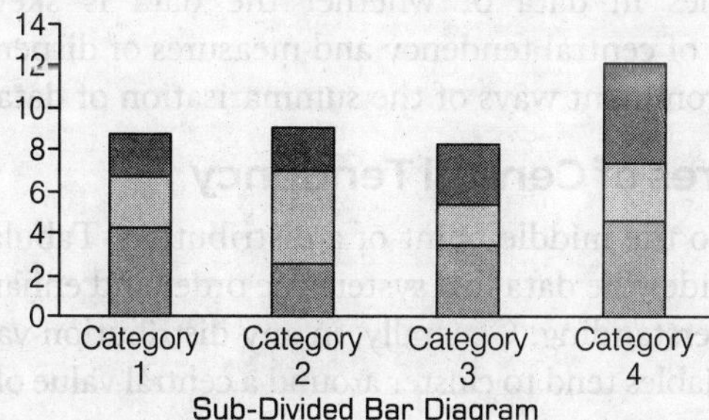

Sub-Divided Bar Diagram

Multiple Bar Diagram

It is used to depict two or more sets of interrelated variables or phenomena when compare is to be shown in between them.

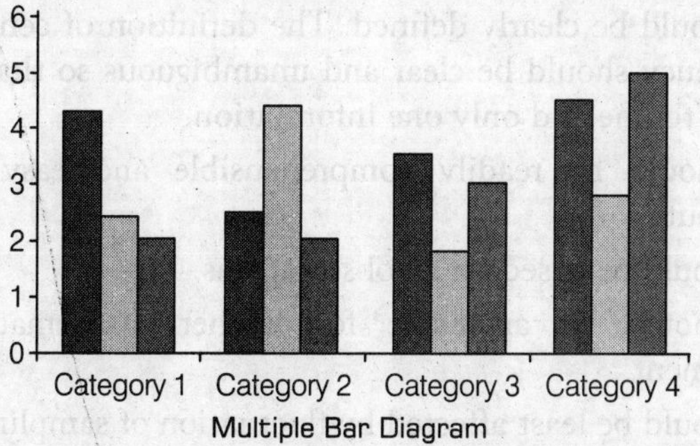

Multiple Bar Diagram

Pie Diagram

It is also known as 'angular diagram.' A pie chart or diagram is a circle divided into component sectors corresponding to the frequencies of the variables in the distribution. Each sector is proportional to the frequency of the variable in the group. A circle represents 360°. So, 360° angles is divided in proportion to percentages. The degrees represented by the various component parts of given magnitude can be obtained by using this formula.

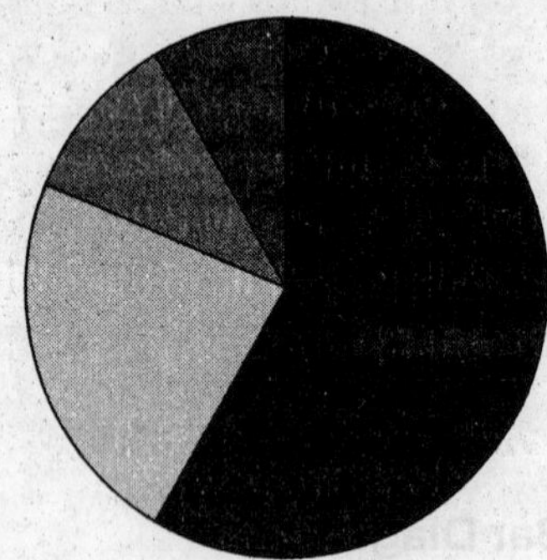

Pie Diagram

Summarisation of Data

Summarisation of data summarise and provide information about the sample data. It tells where the average lies in data or whether the data is skewed. Measures of central tendency and measures of dispersion are the prominent ways of the summarisation of data.

Measures of Central Tendency

It refers to the middle point of a distribution. Tabulated data provides the data in a systematic order and enhances their understanding. Generally, in any distribution values of the variables tend to cluster around a central value of the distribution.

This tendency of the distribution is known as central tendency and measures devised to consider this tendency is known as measures of central tendency. A good measure of central tendency has following characteristics :

- It should be clearly defined. The definition of central tendency should be clear and unambiguous so that it leads to one and only one information.
- It should be readily comprehensible and easy to compute.
- It should be based on all observations.
- It should be amenable for further mathematical treatment.
- It should be least affected by fluctuation of sampling.
- Measures of Central Tendency is calculated through mean, median and mode.

Their description is given below :

1. Arithmetic Mean

Describing mean as the average in a distribution is very common in everyday life. Arithmetic mean in simple terms is 'average value'. It is the total sum of all the scores divided by the number of scores.

There are two methods of calculating arithmetic mean :

Direct Method

It requires summing all units and dividing the number obtained by the number of units added to together.

Mathematical formula for individual series is

$$\overline{X} = \frac{X_1 + X_2 + X_3 \ldots X_n}{N}$$

(Individual series or ungrouped data)

or $$\overline{X} = \frac{\Sigma X}{N}$$

where, $\overline{X}$ is Mean,

N is total number of units added together $X_1, X_2 \ldots$ are the given units in observations.

For example, The number of suicides in 1992 was 2251; in 1993 was 2447; in 1994 was 2624; in 1995 was 2731; in 1996 was 2966; in 1997 was 3170; in 1998 was 3292 and in 1999 was 3743.

$$\text{Thus, } \overline{X} = \frac{2251 + 2447 + 2624 + 2731 + 2966 + 3170 + 3292 + 3743}{8}$$

$$= \frac{23224}{8} = 2903$$

Short Cut/Alternative Method

Formula for individual series

$$\overline{X} = A \pm \frac{\Sigma d}{N}$$

where, $\overline{X}$ is Mean

A is Assumed Mean

d is Deviation of x from A

N is Number of scores

For example, The total number of cricket matches played by India in last 7 years is as follows :

2000:23, 1999:43; 1998:40; 1997:39; 1996:32; 1995:12 and 1994:25.

By arranging these figures in a table form we can take an assumed mean and also calculate deviations from assumed mean.

One Day Cricket Matches Played by India

Years	Number of one day matches played (X)	Deviation from assumed means i.e., $d = X - A$
1994	25	−7
1995	12	−20
1996	A = 32	0
1997	39	+7
1998	40	+8
1999	43	+11
2000	23	−9
		$\Sigma d = -10$

$$\overline{X} = A + \frac{\Sigma d}{N} = 32 + \frac{-10}{7}$$

$$= 32 - 1.43 = 30.57$$

Formula for grouped data $\overline{X} = \frac{\Sigma fx}{N}$

where, $N = \Sigma f$ = the sum of all the frequencies

x = Class mark or mid value

Advantages and Disadvantages of Arithmetic Mean

Advantages	Disadvantages
It makes information so simple that even a common man understands its meaning.	It is difficult to assume arithmetic mean merely by seeing the frequencies of the units.
Its calculations are easy.	It cannot be used for qualitative analysis.
It takes into consideration all the scores in distribution.	If the frequency of anyone unit is missing, mean cannot be calculated.
It is not necessary that given units may be orderly ranked.	Mean is usually outside the given units.
Means of different distributions are useful for comparative purposes.	It is not useful in calculating unit.

2. Median

It is a middle value in a series of values that divides distribution into two equal parts. i.e. half the value lies above the median and half below it.

For ungrouped data (i.e. individual series), the median is obtained by locating the middle score.

For Individual Series

Arrange the N values of the given variable in ascending (or descending) order of magnitudes.

Case I When N is odd

$$\text{Median} = \text{Size of} \left(\frac{N+1}{2}\right)^{\text{th}} \text{term}$$

Case II When N is even

$$\text{Median} = \frac{\left(\frac{N}{2}\right)^{\text{th}} \text{term} + \left(\frac{N}{2}+1\right)^{\text{th}} \text{term}}{2}$$

where N is the number of items.

For Continuous Series

For grouped data with intervals

$$\text{Median} = l_1 + \frac{l_2 - l_1}{f} \times \left(\frac{n}{2} - c\right)$$

or

$$= l_1 + \frac{i}{f} \times \left(\frac{n}{2} - c\right)$$

where, $i = l_2 - l_1$

l_1 = Lower limit of the median group

l_2 = Upper limit of the median group

f = Frequency of the median group

n = Sum of frequencies $= \Sigma f$

c = Cumulative frequency of the group prior to the median group

Advantages and Disadvantages of Median

Advantages	Disadvantages
It can be calculated in all distributions.	It is not used in the context of qualitative phenomena e.g. Intelligent quality of individuals.
It can be ascertained even with the extreme items.	It cannot be used where items are assigned with weights.
It is very useful in quantitative analysis.	It cannot be applied for the analysis of natural phenomena.

3. Mode

It is the most frequent value or score in the distribution. i.e. It is the score with the highest number of points on the score scale. It can be represented as :

$$\text{Mode} = L + \frac{f_1 - f_0}{2f_1 - f_0 - f_2} \times i$$

where,

L = Lower limit of the modal class

f_1 = Frequency of the modal class

f_0 = Frequency of the class preceding the modal class

f_2 = Frequency of the class succeeding the modal class

i = Class interval of modal class

Empirical Relation Between Mean, Median and Mode

Mode = 3 Median − 2 Mean

Advantages and Disadvantages of Mode

Advantages	Disadvantages
It is easy to calculate and understand.	It is not rigidly defined.
It is not all affected by extreme observations and as such is preferred to arithmetic mean while dealing with extreme observations.	It is not based on all the observations of the series.
It can be conveniently obtained in the case of open and classes which do not pose any problems here.	It is affected to a greater extent by the fluctuations of sampling.

Measure of Dispersion

These are the ways of summarising a group of data by describing how spread out the scores are. Averages do not tell us about how the scores or measurements are arranged in relation to center.

It is possible that two sets of data with equal mean and median may differ in terms of their variability. Therefore, measure of dispersion refers to the measures of the variations of observations from each other (or from the mean). Some of the measures of dispersion have been discussed below :

1. Range

Range is the most simplest measure of dispersion. It is designated by 'R'. The range is defined as the difference between the largest score and the smallest score in the distribution. It gives the two extreme values of the variable. A larger value of range indicates greater dispersion while a smaller value indicates lesser dispersion among the scores.

In {4, 6, 9, 3, 7}, the lowest value is 3 and the highest value is 9, so the range is $9 - 3 = 6$.

2. Average Deviation

The average deviation is a part of several indices of variability that is used by statisticians to characterise the dispersion among the measures in a given population.

The average deviation of a set of scores is calculated by computing the mean and then specific distance between each score and that mean without regard to whether the score is above or below the mean. It is also called as average absolute deviation. Below mentioned is the formula to calculate the average deviation :

$$\text{Average Deviation} = \sum_{i=1}^{n} |x - \bar{x}|$$

where,

$x =$ Observation

$\bar{x} =$ Mean

$n =$ Number of Observations

3. Standard Deviation

Standard deviation is the most stable index of variability. In standard deviation, instead of the actual values of the deviations we consider the squares of deviations and the outcome is known as variance.

Further, the square root of this variance is known as standard deviation and designated as 'SD'. Thus, standard deviation is the square root of the mean of the squared deviations of the individual observations from the mean.

If all the scores have an identical value in a sample, the SD will be zero. Standard deviation is represented by Greek letter sigma (σ).

The formula to calculate the average deviation is :

$$SD = \sigma = \frac{\sqrt{\Sigma\,[x - (\bar{x})]^2}}{n}$$

where, $x =$ Items given

$(\bar{x}) =$ Mean

$n =$ Total number of items

4. Skewness and Kurtosis

There are two other important characteristics of frequency distribution that provide useful information about its nature. They are known as skewness and kurtosis.

Skewness Skewness is the degree of asymmetry of the distribution. In some frequency distributions, scores are more concentrated at one end of the scale. Such a distribution is called a skewed distribution.

Thus, skewness refers to the extent to which a distribution of data points is concentrated at one end or the other. Skewness and variability are usually related, the more the skewness the greater is the variability.

Kurtosis The term 'kurtosis' refers to the 'peakedness' or 'flatness' of a frequency distribution curve when compared with normal distribution curve. The kurtosis of a distribution is the curvedness or peakedness of the graph. If a distribution is more peaked than normal, it is said to be leptokurtic.

This kind of peakedness implies a thin distribution. On the other hand, if a distribution is more flat than the normal distribution it is known as platykurtic distribution. A normal curve is known as mesokurtic.

Advantages of Descriptive Statistics

The advantages of descriptive statistics are as follows :

- It is essential for arranging and displaying data.
- It forms the basis of rigorous data analysis.
- It is easier to work with, interpret and discuss the raw data.
- It helps in examining the tendencies, variability and normality of a data set.
- It can be rendered both graphically and numerically.
- It forms the basis for more advanced statistical methods.

Disadvantages of Descriptive Statistics

The disadvantages of descriptive statistics has been listed below :

- It can be misused, misinterpreted and incomplete.
- It can be of limited use when samples and populations are small.
- It offers little information about causes and effects.
- It can be dangerous if not analysed completely.
- There is a risk of distorting data or losing important data.

Inferential Statistics

Inferential statistics deals with drawing of conclusions about large group of individuals (population) on the basis of observation of a few participants from among them or about the events which are yet to occur on the basis of past events.

It provides tools to compute the probabilities of future behaviour of the subjects. There are two types of inferential procedures i.e., Estimation and hypothesis testing. Their description is given below :

Estimation

In estimation, inference is made about the population characteristics on the basis of what is discovered about the sample. There may be sampling variations because of chance fluctuations, variations in sampling techniques, and other sampling errors. Estimation about population characteristics may be influenced by such factors.

Therefore, in estimation the important point is that to what extent our estimate is close to true value. A good statistical estimator should have the characteristics like unbiased and accuracy.

Point Estimation

In statistics, point estimation involves the use of sample data to calculate a single value (known as a point estimate, since it identifies a point in some parameter space) which is to serve as a 'best guess' or 'best estimate' of an unknown population parameter (e.g., the population mean). Point estimation is estimating the value of a parameter as a single point. For example, population mean $(\mu) = 45.0$ from the value of statistics $\bar{x} = 45.0$.

Interval Estimation

Interval estimation refers to the use of sample data to calculate an interval of plausible values of an unknown population parameter. A confidence interval is a range of scores that is expected to contain the value of μ. The lower and upper scores that determine the interval are called confidence limits. A level of confidence can be attached to this estimate so that the researcher can be 95% or 99% confidence level that encompasses the population mean.

Hypothesis Testing

A statistical hypothesis is defined as the statement which may or may not be true about the population parameter or about the probability distribution of the parameter that a researcher wish to validate on the basis of sample information.

Most of the times, inferences are drawn from experiments performed on random samples and it is then generalised over the entire population. However, the observed results might have come due to chance factor.

The probability of chance occurrence of the observed results is examined by the **null hypothesis** (H_0). Null hypothesis is a statement of no difference. The other way to state the null hypothesis is that the two samples came from the same population. Here, we assume that the population is normally distributed and both the groups have equal means and standard deviations.

Since, the null hypothesis is a testable proposition, there is a counter proposition to it known as **alternative hypothesis** and denoted by H_1. In contrast to null hypothesis, the alternative hypothesis (H_1) proposes that :

- The two samples belong to different populations.
- Their means are estimates of two different parametric means of the respective population.
- There is significant difference between their sample means.

The alternative hypothesis is not directly tested statistically, rather its acceptance or rejection is determined by the rejection or retention of the null hypothesis.

The probability '*p*' of the null hypothesis being correct is assessed by a statistical test. If probability '*p*' is too low, H_0 is rejected and H_1 is accepted. It is inferred that the observed difference is significant. If probability '*p*' is high, H_0 is accepted and it is inferred that the difference is due to the chance factor and not due to the variable factor.

Level of Significance

The level of significance ($p<.05$) is that probability of chance occurrence of observed results up to and below which the probability 'p' of the null hypothesis being correct is considered too low and the results of the experiments are considered significant ($p \leq$).

On the other hand, if p exceeds, the null hypothesis (H_0) cannot be rejected because the probability of it being correct is considered quite high and in such case, observed results are not considered significant ($p>$).

The selection of level of significance depends on the choice of the researcher. Generally, level of significance is taken to be 5% or 1%, i.e. = .05 or = .01.

If null hypothesis is rejected at .05 level, it means that the results are considered significant so long as the probability 'p' of getting it by mere chance of random sampling works out to be 0.05 or less ($p< .05$).

In other words, the results are considered significant if out of 100 such trials only 5 or less number of the times the observed results may arise from the accidental choice in the particular sample by random sampling.

One-tail and Two-tail Test

Depending upon the statement in alternative hypothesis (H_1), either one-tail or two-tail test is chosen for knowing the statistical significance. A one-tail test is a directional test. It is formulated to find the significance of both the magnitude and the direction (algebraic sign) of the observed difference between two statistics.

Thus, in two-tailed tests researcher is interested in testing whether one sample mean is significantly higher (alternatively lower) than the other sample mean.

Errors in Hypothesis Testing

In hypothesis testing, there would be no errors in decision-making as long as a null hypothesis is rejected when it is false and also a null hypothesis is accepted when it is true. But, the decision to accept or reject the null hypothesis is based on sample data. There is no testing procedure that will ensure absolutely correct decision on the basis of sampled data. There are two types of errors regarding decision to accept or to reject a null hypothesis :

Type I Error

When the null hypothesis is true, a decision to reject it is an error and this kind of error is known as 'Type I error' in statistics. The probability of making a Type I error is denoted by 'α' (read as alpha).

The null hypothesis is rejected if the probability 'p' of its being correct does not exceed the 'p'. The higher the chosen level of 'p' for considering the null hypothesis, the greater is the probability of Type I error.

Type II Error

When null hypothesis is false, a decision to accept it is known as 'Type II error'. The probability of making a Type II error is denoted by 'β' (read as beta). The lower the chosen level of significance 'p' for rejecting the null hypothesis, the higher is the probability of the Type II error.

With a lowering of 'p', the rejection region as well as the probability of the Type I error declines and the acceptance region (l-p) widens correspondingly.

The goodness of a statistical test is measured by the probability of making a Type I or Type II error. For a fixed sample size n, *a'* and β are so related that reduction in one causes increase in the other. Therefore, simultaneous reductions in *a'* and β are not possible. If n is increased, it is possible to decrease both *a'* and β.

Power of Test

The probability of committing Type II error is designated by (β). Therefore, 1-β is the probability of rejecting null hypothesis when it is false. This probability is known as the power of a statistical test. It measures how well the test is working. The probability of Type II error depends upon the true value of the population parameter and sample size n.

Procedure for Testing a Hypothesis

Step 1 Setup a null hypothesis suitable to the problem.

Step 2 Define the alternative hypothesis.

Step 3 Calculate the suitable test statistically.

Step 4 Define the degrees of freedom for the test situation.

Step 5 Find the probability level 'p' corresponding to the calculated value of the test statistics and its degree of freedom.

Step 6 Reject or accept the null hypothesis on the basis of tabulated value and calculated value at practical probability level.

There are some situations in which inferential statistics is carried out to test the hypothesis and draw conclusion about the population.

For example, test of hypothesis about a population mean (Z-test), testing hypothesis about a population mean (small sample 't'-test).

Parametric and Non-Parametric Tests

Parametric tests are assumptions based on statistical distribution in data. On the other hand, non-parametric tests do not rely on such distribution.

Parametric Test

The parametric test is the hypothesis test which provides generalisations for making statements about the mean of the parent population. A **t-test** is based on student's t–statistics, which is often used in this regard.

The t-test statistics rests on the underlying assumption that there is the normal distribution of variable and the mean is known or assumed to be known. The population variance is calculated for the sample. It is assumed that the variables of interest, in the population are measured on the interval scale.

Assumptions of Parametric Test

Parametric tests, like 't' and 'f' tests may be used for analysing the data which satisfy the following conditions :

- The population from which the sample have been drawn should be normally distributed. Normal distributions refer to frequency distribution following a normal curve, which is infinite at both the ends.
- The variables involved must have been measured at interval or ratio scale.
- Variable and its types characteristic that can have different values.

Parametric Tests Used for Inference

Student's t-test, Analysis of Variance (ANOVA) and z-test are the parametric tests used for inference :

Student's t-test

It was developed by **Prof WS Gosset** in **1908**, who published statistical papers under the pen name of **Student**. Thus, the test is known as Student's t-test.

Student's t-test finds its applicability when :

- samples are small.
- population variances are not known.

Advantages of Student's t-test are :

- Two means of small independent samples.
- Sample mean and population mean.
- Two proportions of small independent samples.

Assumptions made in the use of t-test are :

- Samples are randomly selected.
- Data utilised is quantitative.
- Variable follows normal distribution.
- Sample variances are mostly same in both the groups under the study.
- Samples are small, mostly lower than 30.

Types of 't'-test

A t-test compares the difference between two means of different groups to determine whether that difference is statistically significant. Different types of t-test are :

One Sample t-test

It is used when mean of a single group of observations is compared with a specified value. In one sample t-test, we know the population mean. We draw a random sample from the population and then compare the sample mean and make a statistical decision as to whether or not the sample mean is different from the population.

Formula for one sample t-test; $t = \dfrac{\overline{X} - \mu}{S/\sqrt{n}}$

where, $\overline{X}$ = Sample mean

μ = Population mean

$S/\sqrt{n}$ = Standard error $S^2 = \dfrac{\Sigma (X - \overline{X})^2}{n-1}$

where, X = Element of sample

$\overline{X}$ = Sample mean

$n - 1$ = Degrees of freedom

Two Sample t-test

Two sample t-test can be both unpaired and paired :

Unpaired Two Sample t-test It is used when two means are compared. Unpaired two sample t-test is used when two independent random samples come from the normal populations having unknown or same variation. In this, we test the null hypothesis, that the two population means are same, i.e. $\mu_1 = \mu_2$ against an appropriate one sided or two sided alternative hypothesis.

Assumptions of unpaired two sample t-test are :

- The samples are random and independent of each other.
- The distribution of dependent variable is normal.
- The variance is equal in both the group.

Formula $t = \dfrac{\text{Mean 1} - \text{Mean 2}}{\text{SE (Mean 1} - \text{Mean 2)}}$

where, SE(Mean 1 – Mean 2) = $S\sqrt{(1/n_1 + 1/n_2)}$

$$S = \frac{(n_1 - 1)S_1^2 + (n_2 - 1)S_2^2}{(n_1 + n_2 - 2)}$$

where, S_1^2 and S_2^2 are respectively called Standard Deviations of first and second group.

Paired Two Sample t-test It is used when we have paired data of observations from one sample only, when individuals give a pair of observation.

Assumptions of paired two sample t-text are :

- The outcome variable should be continuous.
- The difference between pre and post measurement should be normally distributed.

Formula $t = \dfrac{\bar{d}}{SD / \sqrt{n}}$

where, d = Difference between x_1 and x_2

$\bar{d}$ = Average of d

SD = Standard deviation for the difference.

n = Sample size.

Analysis of Variance (ANOVA)

It was given by **Sir Ronald Fisher.** The principle aim of this statistical model is to explain the variation in measurements.

The statistical model involving a test of significance of the difference in mean values of the variable between the two groups is the student's t-test. If there are more than two groups, the appropriate statistical model is **Analysis of Variance** (ANOVA).

Assumptions of ANOVA of variance are :

- Sample population can be easily approximated to normal distribution.
- All populations have same standard deviation.
- Individuals in population are selected randomly.
- Samples are independent.

Calculation

ANOVA compares variance by means of a simple ratio, called F ratio.

$$F = \frac{\text{Variance between groups}}{\text{Variance within groups}}$$

The resulting F statistics is then compared with critical value of F (critic), obtained from F tables in much the same way as done with't'. If the calculated value exceeds the critical value for the appropriate level of as the null hypothesis is rejected.

One Way and Two Way ANOVA

- ANOVA can be One Way ANOVA or Two Way ANOVA.
- If the various experimental groups differ in terms of only one factor at a time, One Way ANOVA is used.
- If various groups differ in terms of two or more factors at a time, then a Two Way ANOVA is used.

Z-test

It is used for testing significance difference between two means ($n > 30$). Assumptions of z-test are :

- The sample must be randomly selected.
- Data must be quantitative.
- Samples should be larger than 30.
- Data should follow normal distribution.
- Sample variance should be almost the same in both the groups of study.
- If the SD of the population is known, a Z-test can be applied even for the samples smaller than 30.

Formula for Z Proportionality Test

It is used for testing the significant difference between two proportions i.e.

$$z = \frac{P_1 - P_2}{SE(P_1 - P_2)}$$

where, P_1 = Proportion rate for first population.

P_2 = Proportion rate for second population.

and $SE(P_1 - P_2)$ is defined as SE of difference.

Advantages of Parametric Test

Advantages of parametric test are :

Don't Require Data One of the biggest and best advantage of using parametric test is first of all that you don't need much data that could be converted in some order or format of ranks. The process of conversion is something that appears in rank format and in order to be able to use a parametric test, regularly you will end up with a severe loss in precision.

Quite Easy to Calculate Them Another big advantage of using parametric test is the fact that you can calculate everything so easily. In short, you will be able to find software much quicker so that you can calculate them fast and quick. Apart from parametric test, there is one more test known as non-parametric test, where the distributions are quite different and they are actually not all that easy when it comes to testing such questions that are focused related to the means and shapes of such distributions.

Provides All the Necessary Information One of the biggest advantage of parametric test is that it gives you real information regarding the population which is in terms of the confidence intervals as well as the parameters.

Other Benefits of Parametric Test It can perform quite well when they have been spread over and each group happens to be different. While these non-parametric tests don't really assume that the data follows a regular distribution, they do tend to have other ideas and assumptions which can become very difficult to meet.

Disadvantages of Parametric Test

Disadvantages of parametric tests are :

They aren't valid Parametric test is not valid when it comes to small data sets. The requirement that the populations are not still valid on the small sets of data, the requirement that the populations which are under study have the same kind of variance and the need for such variables are being tested and have been measured at the same scale of intervals.

The size of sample is always very big Another disadvantage of parametric test is that the size of the sample is always very big, something you will not find among non-parametric test. That makes it a little difficult to carry out the whole test.

What you are studying here shall be represented through the medium itself The best reason why you should be using a non-parametric test is that it is n't ever mentioned, especially not enough. Infact, it can also do a usual test with some non-normal data and that doesn't mean in any way that your mean would be the best way to measure if the tendency is the centre of the data. For example, if you look at the centre of any skewed spread out or distribution such as income which could be measured using the median where at least 50% of the whole median is above and the rest is below. In that case you can think add some billionaires to the sample, the mean will increase greatly even if the income doesn't show a sign of change.

You have ranked data as well as out liners and you just can't remove Typical parametric test will only be able to assess data that is continuous and the result will be affected by the outliners at the same time. The non-parametric test may also handle the ordinal data, ranked data will not in any way be affected by the outliners.

Non-Parametric Test

The non-parametric test is defined as the hypothesis test which is not based on underlying assumptions, i.e. it does not require population's distribution to be denoted by specific parameters. The test is mainly based on differences in medians. Hence, it is alternately known as the distribution free test.

The test assumes that the variables are measured on a nominal or ordinal level. It is used when the independent variables are non-parametric. Non-parametric test is not based on the assumption of normal distribution of population. Therefore, it is also known as distribution free test. It is not bound to be used with interval scale data or normally distributed data. The data with non-continuity is to be tackled with such statistics. In the samples, where it is difficult to maintain the assumption of normal distribution, non-parametric test is used for analysis.

The samples with small number of items are treated with non-parametric test because of the absence of normal distribution. These can be used even for nominal data along with the ordinal data. Some of the usual non-parametric tests include Chi square, Spearman's rank difference method of correlation, Kendall's rank difference method and Mann-Whitney U-test.

Assumptions of Non-Parametric Test

Assumptions of non-parametric test are as follows :

- We face many situations, where we cannot meet the assumptions and conditions, and thus we cannot use parametric statistical procedures. In such situation, we are bound to apply non-parametric.
- If our sample is in the form of nominal or ordinal scale and the distribution of sample is not normally distributed and also the sample size is very small; it is always advisable to make use of the non-parametric test for comparing samples and to make inferences or test the significance or trustworthiness of the computed statistics.

  In other words, the use of non-parametric test is recommended in the following situations :
  - Where sample size is quite small. If the size of the sample is as small as N = 5 or N = 6, the only alternative is to make use of non-parametric test.
  - When assumption like normality of the distribution of scores in the population are doubtful, we use non-parametric test.
  - When the measurement of data is available either in the form of ordinal or nominal scales or when the data can be expressed in the form of ranks or in the shape of (+) signs or (–) signs and classification like "good-bad", etc., we use non-parametric test.

Non-Parametric Test Used for Inference

The most frequently used non-parametric test for drawing statistical inferences in case of unrelated or independent samples are as follows :

- Chi square test
- Median test
- Mann-Whitney U-test

Chi Square (χ^2) Test

The chi square test is applied only to dis rete data. The data that are counted rather than measured. It is a test of independence and is used to estimate the likelihood that some factor other than chance accounts for the observed relationship. The chi square test is not a measure of the degree of relationship between the variables under study. The Chi square test merely evaluates the probability that the observed relationship results from chance.

The basic assumption, as in case of other statistical significance, is that the sample observations have been randomly selected.

The formula for chi-square ($x^2 = \chi^2$) test is :

$$x^2 = \chi^2 \ \Sigma[(f_o - f_e)^2 / f_e]$$

in which $f_\circ$ = frequency of occurrence of observed or experimentally determined facts.

f_e = expected frequency of occurrence.

Median Test

The median test is used for testing whether two independent samples differ in central tendencies. It gives information as to whether it is likely that two independent samples have been drawn from populations with the same median.

It is particularly useful when even the measurements for the two samples are expressed in an ordinal scale. In using the median test, we first calculate the combined median for all measures (scores) in both samples.

Then both sets of scores at the combined median are dichotomised and the data are set in a 2 × 2 table with two rows, one containing below median and the other row containing above median. On the column side we have two columns, one containing the sample 1 and the other column containing sample 2.

Mann-Whitney U-test

The Mann-Whitney U-test is more useful than the median test. It is one of the most useful alternative to the parametric t-test when the parametric assumptions cannot be met and when the measurements are expressed in ordinal scale values.

Advantages of Non-Parametric Test

Few advantages of using non-parametric test are as follows :

- It can be used to analyse categorical (nominal scaling) data, rank (ordinal scaling) data and interval (ratio scaling) data.
- Generally, it is easy to apply and quick to compute when sample size is small.
- It requires few assumptions but are very useful when the scale of measurement is weaker than required for parametric methods. Hence, it is widely used and yield a more general broad-based conclusion.
- It provides an approximate solution to an exact problem whereas parametric test provides an exact solution to an approximate problem.
- It provides solution to the problems that do not require to make the assumption that a population is distributed normally or in any specific shape.

Disadvantages of Non-Parametric Test

Few major disadvantages of non-parametric test are as follows :

- It should not be used when all the assumptions of the parametric test can be met. However, it is equally powerful when assumptions are met, when assumptions are not met it may be more powerful.
- It requires more manual computational time when sample size gets larger.
- Table values for non-parametric test are not as readily available as of parametric test.
- Usually, it is not as widely used and not well known as parametric test.

Differences Between Parametric and Non-Parametric Tests

Basis for Comparison	Parametric Test	Non-Parametric Test
Meaning	A statistical test, in which specific assumptions are made about the population parameter is known as parametric test.	A statistical test used in the case of non-parametric independent variables, is called non-parametric test.
Basis of test statistics	Distribution	Arbitrary
Measurement level	Interval or ratio	Nominal or ordinal
Measure of central tendency	Mean	Median
Information about population	Completely known	Unavailable
Applicability	Variables	Variables and attributes
Correlation test	Pearson	Spearman

Correlation

Statistically, correlation refers to a quantifiable relationship between two variables. Furthermore, it is a measure of the strength and direction of that relationship. Two measures for every subject in the group are required.

Two quantities are said to be correlated in the following cases :

- How much the two variables are correlated is determined by the degree of correlation.
- The degree of relationship is measured through the correlation analysis. This is called correlation coefficient.
- Two independent variables are never correlated because they will have nothing for interpreting.
- The degree of correlation will always vary from −1 to + 1 i.e., from perfectly negative to perfectly positive and zero degree means no correlation at all.

There are four things, which could be determined by correlation :

- Whether a relationship exists between variables i.e., measurement of relation.
- Whether correlation is positive or negative.
- Whether the degree of correlation is significant or not.
- Establishment of cause and effect relationships between variables.

Types of Correlation

Different types of correlation are :

Positive and Negative Correlation

- If both the variables are varying in the same direction i.e.if intelligence is high, adjustability is also high and vice-versa, the correlation is said to be postive, which is denoted by (+) sign.
- On the other hand, if values of two variables move in different directions, so that with the increase in the value of one, the other value decreases and vice-versa, the correlation is said to be negative. It is denoted by (–) sign.
- On the other hand zero coefficient of correlation, shows no relationship between the variables.

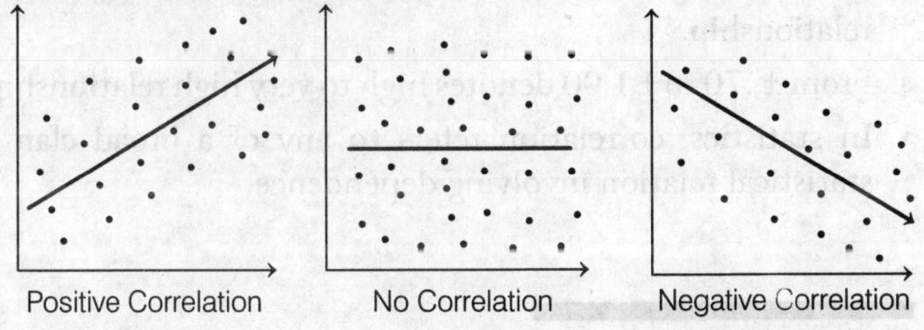

Simple, Partial and Multiple Correlation

These distinction in correlation is based on the number of variables studied :

- When only two variables are taken into consideration, it is simple correlation.
- In partial correlation, more than two variables are considered with only two variables to be influencing each other. Here, the effects of other variables are kept constant.
- In multiple correlation, three or more variables are studied simultaneously.

Linear and Non-Linear Correlation

When the variations in the values of two variables are in a constant ratio, correlation is said to be linear. Here, relationship will be maintained at a constant rate till the end.

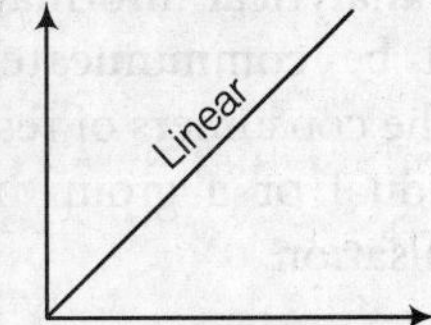

e.g.,

Variable X	2	4	6	8	10
Variable Y	5	10	15	20	25

On the other hand, if percentage change in X and Y are not constant all the time, it is further fluctuating, the relationship is said to be non-linear or curvi-linear.

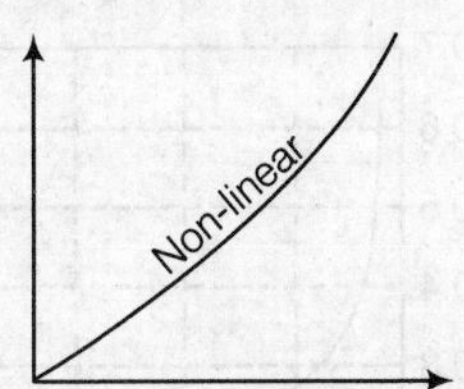

e.g.,

Variable X	2	4	6	8	10
Variable Y	5	8	12	17	24

Methods of Studying Correlation

These are as follows :

- Scatter diagram
- Correlation graph
- Product moment coefficient of correlation
- Rank difference correlation method
- Coefficient of concurrent deviation
- Method of least square.

Uses of Correlation

These are as follows :

- To evaluate the degree of reliability and validity of psychological tests and inventories.
- In the technique of factor analysis.
- To make predictions.
- In the technique of path analysis.

Methods of Correlation

- Product moment method or Pearson coefficient of correlation.
- Rank order coefficient of correlation.

Product Moment Method of Coefficient

Product moment method or Pearson's coefficient is as follows :

- It is used where relation between two variables is linear.
- In some situations, the data for two variables X and Y are expressed in interval or ratio level of measurement and the distribution is linear.

Product moment means that the mean of the product of the mean adjusted random variables, hence the modifier product moment in the name.

It is a measure of the strength and direction of the linear relationship between two variables that is defined as the (sample) covariance of the variables divided by product of their standard deviations.

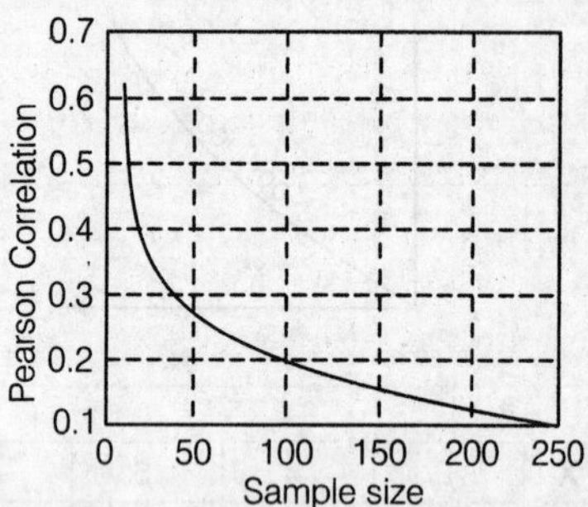

A graph showing the minimum of Pearson's correlation coefficient that is significantly different from zero at 0.05 level, for given sample size

There are two methods of Pearson's coefficient of correlation, which are as follows :

(i) For mean method, the correlation coefficient is given by

$$\pi = \frac{\Sigma (x-\bar{x})(y-\bar{y})}{\sqrt{\Sigma (x-\bar{x})^2}\sqrt{\Sigma (y-\bar{y})^2}}$$

(ii) For assumed mean method, the correlation coefficient is given by

$$\pi = \frac{\Sigma d_x d_y - \frac{\Sigma d_x d_y}{N}}{\sqrt{\Sigma d_x^2 - \frac{(\Sigma d_x)^2}{N}}\sqrt{\Sigma d_y^2 - \frac{(\Sigma d_y)^2}{N}}}$$

where, $d_x = x - A_1$ and $d_y = y - A_2$. Here A_1 and A_2 are assumed mean of x and y respectively.

- From the above examples, we see the if value of $\Sigma\, xy$ is very high in relation to $\Sigma x^2\ \Sigma y^2$, then correlation will be high and vice-versa. Moreover, if value of $\Sigma\, xy$ is in negative, negative coefficient of correlation will be there.
- Degree of π only shows the degree of variations on the two series.

Rank Order Coefficient of Correlation

It is used when we do not have data in the form of score, where rank of the individual is given. Nominal or ordinal range of scale, it is used if relationship of two variables is differ and then relation between the variables is found with the help of rho(ρ).

There are problems, in which the relationship among the measurement made is non-linear and cannot be described by product moment coefficient of correlation. In this case, rank order method is used.

It can be represented as :

$$\rho = 1 - \frac{6\Sigma d^2}{n(n^2-1)}$$

where,

d = Difference in the ranks of two variables

n = Number of pairs

ρ = Coefficient of correlation by rank order method.

This formula is also known as Spearman's rank correlation coefficient.

Significance of Correlation Coefficient

- From ± .00 to ± .20 denoted different or negligible relationship.
- From ± . 20 to ± .40 denotes how correlation presents, but slightly correlated.
- From ± . 40 to ± .70 denotes substantial or marked relationship.
- From ± .70 to ± 1.00 denotes high to very high relationship.
- In statistics, correlation refers to any of a broad clan of statistical relation involving dependence.

Scientific Report Writing

After collecting and analysing the data, the researcher has to accomplish the task of drawing inferences followed by report writing. This has to be done very carefully, otherwise misleading conclusions may be drawn and the whole purpose of doing research may get vitiated. It is only through interpretation that the researcher can expose relations and processes that underlie his findings.

In case of hypothesis testing studies, if hypothesis are tested and upheld several times the researcher may arrive at generalisations. But in case, the researcher had no hypothesis to start with researcher would try to explain his findings on the basis of some theory.

This may at times result in new questions, leading to further researches. All this analytical information and consequential inference may will be communicated, preferably through research report, to the consumers of research results, who may be either an individual or a group of individuals or some public/private organisation.

Presentation of Data

The presentation of the data means as to what the research report should contain in a comprehensive layout form.

- Preliminary Pages
- Main Text
- End Matter

Preliminary Pages

In its preliminary pages, the report should carry a little and date followed by acknowledgement in the form of preface or forward. Then, there should be a table of contents followed by test of tables and illustrations so that the decision-maker or anybody interested in reading the report can easily locate the required information in the report.

Main Text

The main text provides the complete outline of the research report along with all details. Title of the research study is repeated at the top of the first page of the main text and then follows the other details on pages numbered consecutively, beginning with the second page. Each main section of the report should begin on a new page.

The main text of the report should have the following sections :

Introduction

The purpose of introduction is to introduce the research project to the reader. It should contain a clear statement of the objectives of research. A brief summary of other relevant research may also be stated, so that the present study can be seen in that context.

The hypothesis of study, if any and the definitions of the major concepts employed in the study should be explicitly stated in the introduction of the report. The methodology adopted in conducting the study must be fully explained. The scientific reader would like to know in details about such things. How was the study carried out? What was the basic design? If the study was an experimental one, then what were the experimental manipulations? If the data were collected by means of questionnaires or interviews then exactly what questions were asked?

If measurements were based on observation then what instructions were given to the observer. Who were the subjects? How many were there? How were they selected? All these questions are crucial for estimating the probable limits of generalisability of the findings.

The statistical analysis adopted must also be clearly stated. In addition, the scope of the study should be stated. The various limitations under which the research project was completed must also be narrated.

Statement of Findings and Recommendations

The research report must contain a statement of findings and recommendations in non-technical language, so that it can be easily understood by all concerned. If the findings happen to be extensive at this point they should be put in the summarised form.

Result

A detailed presentation of the findings of the study with supporting data in the form of tables and charts together with a validation of results, is the next step in writing the main text of the report. This generally comprises the main body of the report, extending over several chapters. The result section of the report contain statistical summarise and reductions of the data rather than the raw data. All the results should be presented in logical sequence and spitted into readily identifiable sections.

Implications of the Results

Toward the end of the main text the researcher should again put down the results of this research clearly and precisely. Researcher should state the implications that flow from the results of the study.

Such implications may have three aspects as stated below :

- A statement of the inferences drawn from the present study which may be expected to apply in similar circumstances.
- The conditions of the present study which limit the extent of legitimate generalisation of the inferences drawn from the study.
- The relevant questions that still remain unanswered or new questions raised by the study along with suggestions for the kind of research that would provide answers for them. It is considered a good practice to finish the report with a short conclusion which summarises and recapitulates the main points of the study. The conclusion drawn from the study should be clearly related to the hypothesis that were stated in the introductory section.

Summary

It has become customary to conclude the research report with a very brief summary resting in brief the research problem the methodology the major findings and the major conclusions drawn from the research results.

End Matter

If the end of the report appendices should be enlisted in respect of all technical data such as questionnaires, sample information mathematical derivations and the like ones. Bibliography of sources consulted should be given. Index should invariably be given at the end of the report. The value of index lies in the fact that it works as a guide to the reader for the contents in the report.

Interpretation and Discussion of Data

Interpretation refers to the task of drawing inferences from the collected facts after an analytical and experimental study. Infact, it is search for broader meaning of research findings.

The task of interpretation has two major aspects viz

- The effort to establish continuity in research through linking the results of a given study with those of another.
- The establishment of some explanatory concepts. "In one sense, interpretation is concerned with relationship within the collected data, partially overlapping analysis. Interpretation also extends beyond the data of the study to include the results of other research theory and hypothesis.

Thus, "interpretation is the device through which the factors that seem to explain what has been observed by researcher in the course of the study can be better understood and it also provides a theoretical conception, which can serve as a guide for further researches."

Interpretation is essential for the simple reason that the usefulness and utility of research findings lie in proper interpretation. It is being considered a basic component of research process because of the following reasons :

- It is through interpretation that the researcher can understand the abstract principle that works beneath his findings. Through this, he can link up his findings with those of other studies, having the same abstract principle and theory can predict about the concrete world of events. Fresh inquiries can test the predictions later on. This way the continuity in research can be maintained.
- Interpretation leads to the establishment of explanatory concepts that can serve as a guide for future research studies, it opens new avenue of intellectual adventure and stimulates the quest for more knowledge.
- Researcher can better appreciate only through interpretation why this findings are what they are and can make others to understand the real significance of his research findings.
- The interpretation of the findings of exploratory research study often results into hypothesis for experimental research and as such interpretation is involved in the transition from exploratory to experimental research. Since, an exploratory study does not have a hypothesis to start with the findings of such a study have to be interpreted on a post-factum basis in which case the interpretation is technically described as post-factum interpretation.

Techniques of Interpretation

The task of interpretation is not an easy job, rather it requires a great skill and dexterity on the part of researcher. Interpretation is an art that one learns through practice and experience. The researcher or may, at times, seek the guidance from experts for accomplishing the task of interpretation.

The technique of interpretation often involves the following steps :

- Researcher must give reasonable explanations of the relations, which he has found and he must interpret the lines of relationship in terms of the underlying processes and must try to find out the thread of uniformity that lies under the surface layer of his diversified research findings. In fact, this is the technique of how generalisation should be done and concepts be formulated.
- Extraneous information, if collected during the study must be considered while interpreting the final results of research study, for it may prove to be a key factor in understanding the problem under consideration.
- It is advisable, before embarking upon final interpretation to consult someone having insight into the study and who is frank and honest and will not hesitate to point out omissions and errors in logical argumentation. Such a consultation will result in correct interpretation and thus, will enhance the utility of research result.
- Researcher must accomplish the task of interpretation only after considering all relevant factors affecting the problem to avoid false generalisation. He must be in no hurry while interpreting results, for quite often the conclusions.

EXAM BASED QUESTIONS

1 Research is
(a) searching again and again.
(b) finding solution to any problem.
(c) working in a scientific way to search for truth of any problem.
(d) None of the above

2 Who said this definition?
"Research is a power of suspending judgement with patience of mediating with pleasures of asserting with caution of correcting with readiness of arranging through surplus plan."
(a) Francis Bacon (b) Auguste Comte
(c) Clifford Woddy (d) Crawford

3 Which of the following is the objective of research?
(a) To gain familiarity with phenomena and achieve new insight into it.
(b) To determine the frequency with which something occurs.
(c) Both (a) and (b)
(d) All of the above

4 Which of the following is not a characteristic of research?
(a) Research is systematic
(b) Research is not a process
(c) Research is problem oriented
(d) Research is not passive

5 Research can be conducted by a person who
(a) has studied research methodology.
(b) holds a postgraduate degree.
(c) possesses thinking and reasoning ability.
(d) is a hard worker.

6 Which of the following statement(s) is/are true?
(a) In research, objectives can be worded in question form
(b) In research, objectives can be worded in statement form
(c) Objectives are to be stated in Chapter I of the thesis
(d) All of the above

7 By which of the following mean objective facts cannot be secured or established by a researcher?
(a) By observation and experiment.
(b) By research.
(c) By objective analysis of data.
(d) From material collected on the basis of oath and affirmation.

8 The depth of any research can be judged by
(a) title of the research.
(b) objectives of the research.
(c) total expenditure on the research.
(d) duration of the research.

9 The issue of 'research ethics' may be considered pertinent at which stage of research?
(a) At the stage of problem formulation and its definition.
(b) At the stage of defining the population of research.
(c) At the stage of data collection and interpretation.
(d) At the stage of reporting the findings.

10 Which of the following research designs will be appropriate for studying voting behaviour of urban middle class population?
(a) Exploratory
(b) Descriptive
(c) Experimental
(d) None of the above

11 Which of the following is/are the characteristic(s) of an authentic research?
(a) Validity
(b) Credibility
(c) Objectivity
(d) All of the above

12 A good piece of research is a product of
(a) collective scholarship
(b) a good library
(c) a penetrating and analytical mind
(d) a touch of genius

13 What is 'research design'?
(a) A way of conducting research that is not grounded in theory.
(b) The choice between using qualitative or quantitative methods.
(c) The style in which you present your research finding e.g. graph.
(d) A framework for every stage of the collection and analysis of data.

14 Which of the following is associated with descriptive design?
(a) Analysis of demographic trends
(b) Impact assessment of development intervention
(c) Casual explanation of violence against women
(d) Cross cultural study

15 In which research design, hypothesis is not necessarily required?
(a) Descriptive
(b) Experimental
(c) Diagnostic
(d) Exploratory

16 A study in which quantitative and qualitative data are collected at the same time is a
(a) concurrent mixed method design.
(b) mixed method design.
(c) sequential mixed method design.
(d) cross sectional mixed method design.

17 Why does validity pose a problem for qualitative research?
(a) Because there isn't any quantitative data on which to assess validity.
(b) Because validity is only an issue in quantitative research.
(c) Because the measurement of validity implies that there is something fixed which can be measured.
(d) Because the validity of interview cannot be measured.

18 Which is one of the main ethical problem associated with conducting a secondary analysis of qualitative data?
(a) The participants may not have given informed consent to the reuse of their data.
(b) It involves deceiving respondents about the nature of the research.
(c) The secondary analyst must adopt a convert role and is at risk of going native.
(d) Respondents are likely to experience physical harm as a result of the process.

19 An interest in qualitative methods has increased in terms of analysis of
(a) categorisations.
(b) laboratory experiments.
(c) language based data.
(d) interest in qualitative is actually on the decline.

20 Qualitative research methods can be thought of as
(a) a preliminary stage in the research which can contribute to the development of adequate quantification.
(b) a stark alternative to quantitative research.
(c) parallel with the physical sciences.
(d) methods used to search for the nature of reality.

21 Which of the following is not a contrast between quantitative and qualitative research?
(a) Distance vs proximity of researcher to participants.
(b) Generalisation vs contextual understanding.
(c) Hard, reliable data vs rich, deep data.
(d) Interpretivist vs feminist.

22 Research, in which the researcher uses both qualitative and quantitative research within a stage or across two of the stages in the research process is known as
(a) action research
(b) basic research
(c) quantitative research
(d) mixed model research

23 Research carried out in order to improve social situation for the betterment of individuals or social group or an organisation is called
(a) survey research
(b) action research
(c) qualitative research
(d) None of the above

24 Who first used Survey Method in Social Science research?
(a) Charles Booth (b) William J Goode
(c) CA Moser (d) Jahoda

25 Historical research is different from experimental research in the process of
(a) replication
(b) the formulation of hypothesis
(c) hypothesis testing
(d) All of the above

26 "This research is a process of critical inquiry into past events." The statement indicates towards which type of research?
(a) Correlational research
(b) Explanatory research
(c) Historical research
(d) Ex-post facto research

27 "To find out solutions for the betterment of tribal community in India" is an example of which research?
(a) Historical research (b) Correlational research
(c) Explanatory research (d) None of these

28 "To search measures to reduce the absentee rate among employees of company" is an example of which type of research?
(a) Correlational (b) Analytical
(c) Explanatory (d) Ex-post Facto

29 Which of the following is classified in the category of development research?
(a) Philosophical research (b) Action research
(c) Descriptive research (d) All of these

30 Which research is primarily concerned with finding out 'what is' or 'what was'?
(a) Explanatory research
(b) Correlational research
(c) Descriptive research
(d) None of the above

31 In which of the following research 'manipulation' is always a part of it?
(a) Historical research
(b) Fundamental research
(c) Descriptive research
(d) Experimental research

32 Which type of research concerns itself with cause effect relationships?
(a) Ex-Post Facto (b) Analytical
(c) Correlational (d) Explanatory

33 Which among the following is a tentative proposition, the authenticity of which is yet to be ascertained?
(a) Index (b) Hypothesis
(c) Introduction (d) Conclusion

34 A good hypothesis should be
(a) formulated in such a way that it can be tested by the data
(b) precise, specific and consistent with most known facts
(c) of limited scope and should not have global significance
(d) All of the above

35 Which of the following type of research, hypothesis is a pre-requisite?
(a) Biographical study
(b) Experimental study
(c) Interpretative research
(d) Critical research

36 Hypothesis cannot be stated in
(a) declarative terms
(b) null and question form terms
(c) general terms
(d) directional terms

37 A hypothesis that suggests no relationship among the variables selected under study is called
(a) conflict hypothesis (b) comfort hypothesis
(c) null hypothesis (d) contrary hypothesis

38 Which error is committed when the hypothesis is true, but out tests rejects it?
(a) Type I (b) Type II
(c) Both (a) and (b) (d) None of these

39 A statement of relationship between variables to be tested is known as
(a) research question (b) hypothesis
(c) objective of the study (d) problem of the study

40 A relationship in which change in one variable always induce change in another variable is known as
(a) positive correlation
(b) linear correlation
(c) unfounding relation
(d) cause and effect relationship

41 What is the opposite of a variable?
(a) A constant
(b) An extraneous variable
(c) A dependent variable
(d) A data set

42 Attributes of objects, events or things which can be measured are called
(a) data (b) qualitative measures
(c) variables (d) None of these

43 A researcher divides his population into certain groups and fixes the size of the sample from each group. It is called
(a) cluster sample
(b) stratified sample
(c) quota sample
(d) All of the above

44 Generalised conclusion on the basis of a sample is technically known as
(a) statistical inference of external validity of the research.
(b) parameter inference.
(c) data analysis and interpretation.
(d) All of the above

45 Which of the following is a non-probability sample?
(a) Simple random sample (b) Quota sample
(c) Purposive sample (d) Both (a) and (c)

46 Area (cluster) sampling technique is used when
(a) population is heterogeneous.
(b) population is scattered and large size of the sample is to be drawn.
(c) long survey is needed.
(d) Both (a) and (c)

47 If the sample drawn does not specify and condition about the parameter of the population, it is called
(a) selected statistics
(b) distribution free statistics
(c) census
(d) None of the above

48 Picking up small variable units and making a general prediction upon their study is called
(a) sample (b) census
(c) primary data (d) secondary data

49 All causes non-sampling errors except
(a) faulty tools of measurement
(b) inadequate sample
(c) non-response
(d) defect in data collection

50 Which type of sampling method is ideally suited, where there is no knowledge about population?
(a) Conventional Sampling Method
(b) Purposive Sampling Method
(c) Quota Sampling Method
(d) Snowball Sampling Method

51 In which of the following sampling methods, equal number of units are selected from each substratum regardless of their strength in the population and sub-population?
(a) Simple random sampling
(b) Stratified random sampling
(c) Proportionate stratified random sampling
(d) Disproportionate stratified random sampling

52 To obtain entirely reliable knowledge of the exact value of a parameter, observations must be made on
(a) all the elements in a single stratum of the stratified population.
(b) a stratified sample of the population.
(c) a complete census of the population.
(d) a simple random sampling of the population.

53 **To study the public opinion which sampling method is used?**
(a) Quota sampling (b) Random sampling
(c) Cluster sampling (d) Systematic sampling

54 **Seeing a very big rally, it was reported that JD will win the election, the conclusion was based on**
(a) random sampling (b) cluster sampling
(c) purposive sampling (d) systematic sampling

55 **The pre-condition to qualify a sample as a random one is**
(a) the researcher must pretest the subject.
(b) the researcher must conduct pilot study.
(c) at least 100 respondents must be selected from a given population.
(d) every member of the population must have an equal chance of being selected.

56 **In order to qualify as a random sample, ...**
(a) the researcher must pretest the subject.
(b) the researcher must conduct pilot study.
(c) at least hundred people must be selected.
(d) every member of the population must have an equal chance of being selected.

57 **The most important feature of a good sample is**
(a) smaller quantity
(b) big quantity
(c) correct representativeness
(d) None of the above

58 **In observation method participant observers, can collect material from a group to a large extent if he/she acts**
(a) emotionally (b) passively
(c) objectively (d) subjectively

59 **Which method is more suitable for collecting data from non-literate communities?**
(a) Questionnaire (b) Observation
(c) Both (a) and (b) (d) None of these

60 **Sometimes mailed questionnaire is preferable to interview method because**
(a) face to face contact is possible
(b) people immediately return it
(c) illiterates can also be covered
(d) it works out cheaper and easy

61 **Use of an interview method by a social researcher is expensive because it cove**
(a) more group of an area
(b) a few group of an areas
(c) more group of different areas
(d) a group of different areas

62 **While conducting a social survey, the questionnaire technique is not applicable if**
(a) there is widespread literacy
(b) the area to be covered is vast
(c) there is male illiteracy
(d) there is over population

63 **Which method has limitation that cannot be used among illiterates?**
(a) Participant observation
(b) Non-participant observation
(c) Questionnaire
(d) Interview

64 **Where informants are literate and are spread over a vast area, the most suitable method of collecting data is**
(a) direct personal interview
(b) mailed questionnaire method
(c) interview by investigator
(d) All of the above

65 **Which among the following method is less expensive?**
(a) Case study (b) Making questionnaire
(c) Interview (d) Questionnaire

66 **The first step for making a statistical investigation is**
(a) organisation (b) collection of data
(c) samples (d) None of these

67 **Direct personal interviews constitute**
(a) primary data (b) secondary data
(c) tertiary data (d) None of these

68 **Which of the following assumption would be correct from a statistical point of view?**
(a) Errors of observation will have frequencies that cannot approximate the normal probability curve.
(b) Linear magnitudes have measured frequencies closely following the normal probability curve.
(c) Measures of physical and mental traits cannot be accepted to follow the normal, probability curve.
(d) Linear magnitudes are measured frequencies that are always skewed.

69 **A researcher selects only 10 members as a sample from the total population of 5000 and considers it good because**
(a) he was guided by his supervisor.
(b) he was a good researcher.
(c) the population was homogeneous.
(d) All of the above

70 **The population census will have the primary data from**
(a) registrar general and census commissioner
(b) gram panchayats
(c) municipalities
(d) None of the above

71 **Some of the sources of secondary data are**
(a) internal records of a firm's sales, production, etc.
(b) the data obtained by a firm in a survey conducted by it.
(c) confidential records of the government.
(d) report and publications of central and state government.

72 A schedules is a list of questions which will be answered in an interview by
(a) an interviewer (b) a respondent
(c) a surveyor (d) a researcher

73 An interviewer can collect good material when the relationship between the interviewer and the interviewee is
(a) indifferent (b) uninterested
(c) cordial (d) ethical

74 A researcher wants to study the future of the Congress I in India. For the study, which tool is most appropriate for him/her?
(a) Questionnaire (b) Interview
(c) Schedule (d) Rating scale

75 An observation uninfluenced by personal bias is said to be
(a) functional (b) critical (c) objective (d) subjective

76 'Observation' means to see things
(a) with a purpose
(b) with many purposes
(c) without a purpose
(d) for important discussion

77 The two type of observation are
(a) spontaneous and controlled
(b) formal and informal
(c) open ended and closed ended
(d) None of the above

78 The reaction of a child when scolded can be studied under controlled conditions by applying the technique of
(a) observation (b) interview
(c) questionnaire (d) field survey

79 While writing research report, a researcher
(a) must arrange it in a logical, tropical and chronological order.
(b) must not use the numerical figures in numbers in the beginning of sentences.
(c) must compare his/her results with those of the other studies.
(d) All of the above

80 The review of the related study is important while undertaking a research because
(a) it avoids repetition and duplication.
(b) it helps in understanding the gaps.
(c) it helps the researcher not to draw illogical conclusions.
(d) All of the above

81 The report should mention
(a) sampling method (b) size of sample
(c) criteria for selection (d) All of these

82 What is the purpose of the report?
(a) Dissipation of knowledge
(b) Broadcasting of generalisation
(c) Widest use in public
(d) All of the above

83 Field study is a method of research, in which the observations are taken in the
(a) natural setup (b) observed setup
(c) laboratories (d) fields

84 The report is not
(a) tangible evidence of a research project
(b) a basis for decision-making
(c) a research proposal
(d) future secondary data

85 Introduction of a report includes
(a) concise and clear cut statement as to the nature of the study.
(b) aims of the study.
(c) scope of the study.
(d) All of the above

86 Good research reports will always
(a) provide respondent names and addresses.
(b) focus on addressing the research objectives.
(c) provide results that may be irrelevant.
(d) focus on the Harvard style.

87 Research reports are the product of slow, accurate and inductive work. The usual step(s) involved in writing report is/are
(a) logical analysis of the subject
(b) preparation of the outline
(c) Both (a) and (b)
(d) None of the above

88 Which of the following is not one of the seven major parts to the research report?
(a) Results (b) Abstract
(c) Method (d) Footnotes

89 Which of the following statements is not true in the context of participatory research?
(a) Its sole purpose is production of knowledge
(b) It recognises knowledge as power
(c) It emphasises on people as experts
(d) It is a collective process of enquiry

90 The most appropriate statistical test for analysing qualitative data is
(a) 'T'-test (b) 'Z'- test
(c) Chi-square (d) ANOVA

91 F-test is used
(a) when there are more than 2 groups
(b) to check accuracy of data
(c) to check design of experiment
(d) when analysis of variance is needed

92 Coefficient of correlation is a measure of
(a) relative position (b) dispersion
(c) relationship (d) central tendency

93 The following measure of central tendency and dispersion are used in ANOVA
(a) Mean and standard deviation
(b) Mean and variance
(c) Mean and standard error
(d) Median and standard deviation

94 **The correlation between two variables is said to be perfectly positive. If the value is equal to**
(a) 0 (b) – 1 (c) + 1 (d) 0.1

95 **Type I error is committed, when**
(a) null hypothesis is true and it is rejected
(b) null hypothesis is true and it is accepted
(c) null hypothesis is false and it is accepted
(d) null hypothesis is false and it is accepted

96 **The most appropriate statistical test for analysing quantitative data is**
(a) chi-square (b) sign test
(c) t-test (d) median test

97 **Which of the following is the most reliable measure of central tendency?**
(a) Median (b) Mode
(c) Mean (d) None of these

98 **Which of the following is not an average?**
(a) Mean (b) Median
(c) Mode (d) Standard deviation

99 **Which of the following is a measure of the variation of the items in a distribution?**
(a) Mean (b) Median
(c) Dispersion (d) None of these

100 **The simplest method of studying dispersion is**
(a) range (b) standard deviation
(c) mean deviation (d) central tendency

101 **Type I error is made when**
(a) True null hypothesis is rejected
(b) True null hypothesis is accepted
(c) False null hypothesis is rejected
(d) False null hypothesis is accepted

102 **Mode is**
(a) least frequent value
(b) middle most value
(c) most frequent value
(d) represents majority out of total frequency

103 **If all the items in a distribution are multiplied by a value X, the arithmetic mean () of the next series will be**
(a) $\overline{X} \cdot X$ (b) $\overline{X} + \frac{X}{N}$ (c) $\overline{X} + \frac{N}{X}$ (d) $\overline{X} - X$

104 **The mean of 9 items is 16. One more value is added, the mean is now 17. The value of the 10th item is**
(a) 24 (b) 27 (c) 26 (d) 25

105 **An extreme item or a lowest item will always have a bearing upon**
(a) mean (b) median
(c) mode (d) None of these

106 **The arithmetic mean of the direct 100 natural numbers is**
(a) 55.2 (b) 60.1 (c) 25.7 (d) 50.5

107 **The sum of the derivations of the items from mean is always**
(a) 1 (b) zero (c) 2 (d) 6

108 **The average comes down to 56.25. The total marks secured by these students were**
(a) 20 (b) 40 (c) 60 (d) zero

109 **It r is 0.5, $\Sigma xy = 120$, σ of $y = 8$ and $\Sigma x^2 = 90$, the value of n will be**
(a) 15 (b) 12
(c) 10 (d) 5

110 **The correlation between two variable is said to be perfectly negative. If the value is equal to**
(a) + 1 (b) – 1 (c) 0.5 (d) – 0.5

111 **Which average is affected most by extreme observations?**
(a) Median (b) Mode
(c) Arithmetic mean (d) Geometric mean

112 **Area (cluster) sampling technique is used when**
(a) population is scattered and large size of the sample is to be drawn
(b) population is heterogeneous
(c) long survey is needed
(d) Both (a) and (c)

113 **The method of ranking was formerly known as the method of**
(a) order of merits (b) constant intervals
(c) sequential order (d) order of steps

114 **Which scale represents the lowest level of measurement and imparts the least information?**
(a) Nominal scale (b) Ratio scale
(c) Ordinal scale (d) Interval scale

115 **Which scale has an absolute zero at the point of origin?**
(a) Nominal scale (b) Ratio scale
(c) Ordinal scale (d) Interval scale

116 **Match the following.**

List I	List II
A. Research design formulated for discovering new facts	1. Descriptive research design
B. Some specific variables are studied	2. Diagnostic research design
C. It refers to the exact nature and scope of the problem under investigation and then suggest remedies against it	3. Experimental research design
D. Events are observed about which a prediction is to be made in respect of both experimental and controlled group	4. Exploratory research design

Codes

	A	B	C	D		A	B	C	D
(a)	1	4	2	3	(b)	4	1	2	3
(c)	4	3	1	2	(d)	1	3	4	2

117 **Match the following.**

List I	List II
A. Technical report	1. Tables
B. Reference	2. Data
C. Result and discussion	3. Author index
D. Popular report	4. Results

Codes

	A	B	C	D		A	B	C	D
(a)	1	2	3	4	(b)	2	3	1	4
(c)	2	4	1	3	(d)	1	3	4	2

118 **Match the following.**

List I	List II
A. Figures	1. Layout of the research report
B. Aims	2. Result of data
C. Main text	3. Technical report
D. Data	4. Report should contain

Codes

	A	B	C	D		A	B	C	D
(a)	2	1	3	4	(b)	3	4	1	5
(c)	2	4	1	3	(d)	1	2	3	4

119 **There are two sets given below Set I specifies the types of research, while Set II indicates their characteristics.**
Match the two and give your answer by selecting the appropriate codes.

List I (Research Types)	List II (Characteristics)
A. Fundamental Research	1. Finding out the extent of perceived impact of an intervention.
B. Applied Research	2. Developing an effective explanation through use of interventions.
C. Action Research	3. Improving an existing situation through use of interventions
D. Evaluative Research	4. Exploring the possibility of a theory for use in various situations.
	5. Enriching technological resources.

Codes

	A	B	C	D		A	B	C	D
(a)	1	2	3	4	(b)	2	3	4	1
(c)	2	4	3	1	(d)	5	4	3	2

120 **In the two sets given below, Set-I specifies the methods of research while Set-II describes the critical feature associated with a method of research. Match the two and select from the code to indicate your answer.**

List I (Research Methods)	List II (Critical Features Associated)
A. Experimental method	1. Generalising to the population from a large sample.
B. Ex post facto method	2. Establishing the patterns of events which have happened, through primary and secondary sources.
C. Historical method	3. Studying shared behaviour patterns.
D. Ethnographic method	4. Establishing cause and effect through control.
	5. Probing into the casual factors from the observed effects.

Codes

	A	B	C	D		A	B	C	D
(a)	4	5	2	3	(b)	2	3	4	5
(c)	2	1	4	3	(d)	1	2	3	4

121 **Below are given two sets-research methods (Set-I) and data collection tools (Set-II). Match the two sets and indicate your answer by selecting the correct code.**

List I (Research Methods)	List II (Data Collection Tools)
A. Experimental method	1. Using primary and secondary sources
B. Ex post-facto method	2. Questionnaire
C. Descriptive survey method	3. Standardised tests
D. Historical method	4. Typical characteristic tests

Codes

	A	B	C	D		A	B	C	D
(a)	2	1	3	4	(b)	2	3	1	4
(c)	3	4	2	1	(d)	2	4	3	1

122 **What is the correct sequence of the below given steps of flow chart for conducting a research project?**

1. Formulation of hypothesis
2. Review of literature and concepts
3. Identification and conceptualisation of problem
4. Conclusion and generalisation

Select the correct answer from the codes given below

(a) 1, 3, 2 and 4 **(b) 2, 3, 4 and 1**
(c) 3, 2, 1 and 4 **(d) 4, 1, 3 and 2**

123 **Choose the correct sequence in writing a research proposal.**

1. Review of literature **2. Introduction**
3. Bibliography **4. Objectives**
5. Methodology **6. Analysis of data**

Codes

(a) 2, 4, 1, 5, 6, 3 **(b) 1, 2, 4, 3, 5, 6**
(c) 2, 1, 4, 3, 5, 6 **(d) 4, 2, 1, 5, 6, 3**

124 **The most importance methodological challenges of a survey methodologist include making decisions on how to?**

1. Identity and select potential sample members.
2. Evaluate and test question.
3. Select the mode for posing questions and collecting responses.
4. Check data field for accuracy and internal consistency.

Select the correct answer using the codes given below
(a) 1 and 2
(b) 2 and 3
(c) 3 and 4
(d) All of the above

125 **In any research one should**

1. know more and more about less and less in certain specific sub areas.
2. not try out anything windily, but wait until a sudden flash appears in his mind.
3. know everything in the area without bothering to learn the details if any.

Select the correct answer using the codes given below
(a) 1 and 2 (b) 1 and 3
(c) 2 and 3 (d) All of these

126 **Consider the following statements**

1. Interpretation leads to the establishment of explanatory concepts that can serve as a guide for future research studies. It opens new avenue of intellectual adventure and stimulates the quest for more knowledge.
2. They can better explain only through interpretation why this findings are, what they are and can make others to understand the real significance of his research findings.

Which of the statements given above is/are correct?
(a) Both 1 and 2 (b) Only 1
(c) Only 2 (d) None of these

127 **Consider the following statements**

1. The purpose of research is not well served unless the findings are made known to others.
2. Writing report is the last step in a research study requires a set of skills.

Which of the statement(s) given above is/are correct?
(a) Only 2 (b) Only 1
(c) Both 1 and 2 (d) None of these

128 **Arrange the following in correct sequence of the steps in the process of research designing**

1. review of literature.
2. organise and draft the research design.
3. select area and subjects. 4. formulate problem.

Codes
(a) 1, 2, 3, 4 (b) 3, 1, 2, 4
(c) 2, 3, 4, 1 (d) 4, 1, 3, 2

129 **Survey study aims at**

1. knowing facts about the existing situation.
2. comparing the present status with the standard norms.
3. criticisig the existing situation.
4. identifying the means of improving the existing situation.

Select the correct answer using the codes given below
(a) 1 and 2 (b) 2 and 3
(c) 1, 2 and 3 (d) All of these

130 **Consider the following statements**

1. Researcher can better appreciate only through interpretation why this findings are, what they are and can make others to understand the real significance of his research finding.
2. Research report is considered a major component of the research study for the research task remains incomplete, till the report has been presented and written.

Which of the statement(s) given above is/are correct?
(a) Only 1 (b) Only 2
(c) Both 1 and 2 (d) None of these

131 **Research reports should be reviewed in the light of**

1. investigator bias
2. cultural context
3. method dological factor

Select the correct answer using the codes given below
(a) 1 and 3 (b) Only 1
(c) Only 3 (d) All of these

132 **Consider the following statements.**

1. Research design will help identifying the importance of each step in the whole scheme of things.
2. The design help in making the research know as to why is he studying the issue and what type of data will be needed, how data will be found.
3. A research design will always helps us in knowing successive stages.
4. Design will also help in finding out what total time the study is likely to take and what time each step in the study is likely to consume.

Which of the statement(s) given above is/are correct?
(a) 1 and 2 (b) 2 and 3
(c) 1, 2 and 3 (d) All of these

133 **Bibliography given in a research report**

1. makes the report authentic.
2. helps those interested in further research and in studying the problem from another angle.

Which of the statement(s) given above is/are correct?
(a) Only 1 (b) Only 2
(c) Both 1 and 2 (d) None of these

134 **Consider the following statements.**

1. A research problems is feasible only when it is new and adds something to knowledge and also a researchable.
2. While writing research report, a researcher must arrange it in logical, tropical and chronological order.

Which of the statement(s) given above is/are correct?
(a) Only 1
(b) Only 2
(c) Both 1 and 2
(d) None of these

135 A good hypothesis should be

1. precise specific and consistent with most facts.
2. of limited scope and should not have global significance.
3. formulated in such a way that it can be tested by the data.

Select the correct answer using the codes given below :

(a) 1 and 2 (b) 2 and 3
(c) 1 and 3 (d) All of these

136 Match the following.

List I	List II
A. $\overline{X}$	1. Correlation coefficient
B. r	2. Probability
C. Σ	3. Chi-square
D. P	4. Mean
	5. Sum of

Codes

	A	B	C	D		A	B	C	D
(a)	4	1	5	2	(b)	5	1	3	2
(c)	4	2	5	1	(c)	1	2	3	4

137 Arrange in the correct sequence from the lowest to the highest scale of measurement.

1. Interval scale 2. Ordinal scale
3. Ratio scale 4. Nominal scale

Codes

(a) 4, 2, 1, 3 (b) 1, 2, 4, 3
(c) 2, 1, 3, 4 (d) 2, 4, 3, 1

138 Match the following.

List I	List II
A. T-test	1. Testing difference in means of more than two groups
B. F-test	2. Data is in frequencies
C. Chi-square	3. Bivariate distribution
D. Pearson's	4. Testing mean against population mean

Codes

	A	B	C	D		A	B	C	D
(a)	3	4	2	1	(b)	4	1	2	3
(c)	1	2	3	4	(d)	4	3	2	1

139 The variance is

1. directly proportional to the average squared difference between all pairs of observations.
2. smallest when calculated from the mean.
3. denoted by symbol σ.
4. described as the dispersion of the distribution.

Which of the statements given above is/are correct?

(a) 1, 2 and 4 (b) 1, 2 and 3
(c) 2, 3 and 4 (d) All of these

140 Given the series below

X	18	19	20	21	22	23	24	25
F	5	6	7	8	9	8	9	5

The mode is

(a) 20 (b) 23
(c) 22 (d) 21

141 Which aspects should investigator examine in using secondary data ?

1. Suitability 2. Adequacy
3. Reliability 4. Interest

Select the correct answer using the codes given below.

(a) 1 and 2 (b) 3 and 4
(c) 1, 2 and 3 (d) All of these

Directions (Q.Nos. 142-154) *In the questions given below are two statements labelled as Assertion (A) and Reason (R) In the context of the two statements, which one of the following is correct?*

Codes

(a) Both A and R are true, R is the correct explanation of A
(b) Both A and R are true, but R is not the correct explanation of A
(c) A is true, R is false
(d) A is false, R is true

142 **Assertion** (A) The report must provide a ready availability of the findings.

Reason (R) Readers are often interested in acquiring a quick knowledge of the main finding.

143 **Assertion** (A) The purpose of introduction is to introduce the research project to the reader.

Reason (R) Research report should contain a clear statement of the objectives of research.

144 **Assertion** (A) There are very definite and set rules which should be followed in the actual preparation of the research report or paper.

Reason (R) The criteria of format should be decided as soon as the materials for the research paper have been assembled.

145 **Assertion** (A) After collecting and analysing the data, the researcher has to accomplish the task of drawing inferences followed by report writing.

Reason (R) This has to be done very carefully otherwise misleading conclusions may be drawn and the whole purpose of doing research may get vitiated.

146 **Assertion** (A) Interpretation refers to the task of drawing inferences from the collected facts after an analytical and experimental study.

Reason (R) Interpretation is a search for broad meaning of research findings.

147 **Assertion** (A) Interrelation is essential for the simple reason that the usefulness and utility of research findings their when interpretation.

Reason (R) It is through interpretation that the researcher care understand the absent principle that works beneath his findings.

148 **Assertion** (A) Writing of report is last step in research study and requires a set of skills.

Reason (R) This task should be accomplished by the researcher with utmost care, he may seek the assistance and guidance of experts for the purpose.

149 **Assertion** (A) In a report, the essential data should be separated from the non-essential one and only the former one should be included in the report.

Reason (R) If all the available data is included in the report that will become not only boring, but will also make the report bulky.

150 **Assertion** (A) Critical analysis of a research report is valuable for researcher.

Reason (R) Through a critical analysis, the researcher gains some insight into the nature of a research problem, methods used and conclusions drawn.

151 **Assertion** (A) A good research report should neither be too voluminous nor too concise.

Reason (R) A short report may not contain all the essential data and relevant facts whereas a bulky report may discoverage the readers.

152 **Assertion** (A) A research design is a plan of the proposed research work.

Reason (R) A research design represents a comprise dictated by mainly practical considerations.

153 **Assertion** (A) A research design should be based on, more or less, on methodology.

Reason (R) It is prepared once the topic and problem for research have been selected and formulated.

154 **Assertion** (A) All research studies must begin with formulation of hypothesis.

Reason (R) Hypothesis will help the researcher to make generalisations about the population.

Directions (Q. Nos. 155-159) *Read this passage given below and answer the questions that follow.*

The hypothesis that is being tested can be used to predict the way the data should point. The hypothesis may state that the experimental group will perform better than the control group.

By confronting the hypothesis with the dependent variable values of the two groups, the experimenter can determine whether the, hypothesis accurately predicted the results.

But it is difficult to tell, simply by looking at unorganised data, whether the (dependent variable) values for one group are higher or lower than the values for the second group. Therefore, the data must be organised numerically to yield numbers that will provide an answer.

For example, we may complete average scores and find that the experimental group has a higher mean (say, 100) than the control group (say, 99). Although there is a difference between the groups, it is very, small and we must ask whether it is 'real' or only a 'chance' difference. If we conduct the experiment again, would we obtain similar results?

If it is a 'real', reliable difference the experimental group should obtain a higher mean than the control group almost every time the experiment is repeated. If there is no reliable difference between the two groups, we would expect to find each group receiving the higher score half of the time.

To tell whether the difference between the two groups in a single, experiment is reliable, rather than simply due to random fluctuations (chance), the experimenter resorts to a statistical test. The particular statistical tests used will be determined by the type of data obtained and the design of the experiment.

On the basis of such tests, it can be determined whether the difference between me to groups is likely to be 'real' (statistically reliable) or merely 'accidental' (due only to chance). If the difference between the dependent variable values of the groups is statistically reliable, the difference is very probably not due to random fluctuation. It is therefore concluded that the independent variable is effective in influencing the dependant variable (promoting that the extraneous variables have been properly controlled).

155 **Based on the passage, which one of the following is the correct hypothesis?**

(a) Performance of experimental group will be less than control group.
(b) There will be no difference in the performance of experimental and control groups.
(c) Performance of experimental group will be better than control group.
(d) Performance of control group will be better than experimental group.

156 **Statistical tests could be used, if the data are**

(a) unorganised
(b) organised
(c) normal
(d) variable

157 The reliable difference between two groups could be obtained, if we use
(a) norms
(b) validity
(c) statistical test
(d) reliability

158 Statistically reliable difference is known as
(a) chance difference
(b) hypothesised difference
(c) random difference
(d) real difference

159 Arrange the following concepts in which they appeared in the passage.
1. Reliable difference
2. Hypothesis
3. Statistical test
4. Random fluctuation

Codes
(a) 3 4 2 1
(b) 2 1 3 4
(c) 1 2 3 4
(d) 4 3 1 2

ANSWERS

Exam Based Questions

1 *(c)*	2 *(a)*	3 *(d)*	4 *(c)*	5 *(c)*	6 *(b)*	7 *(d)*	8 *(b)*	9 *(d)*	10 *(b)*
11 *(d)*	12 *(c)*	13 *(d)*	14 *(a)*	15 *(a)*	16 *(a)*	17 *(c)*	18 *(a)*	19 *(c)*	20 *(a)*
21 *(d)*	22 *(d)*	23 *(b)*	24 *(a)*	25 *(b)*	26 *(c)*	27 *(a)*	28 *(b)*	29 *(d)*	30 *(c)*
31 *(c)*	32 *(b)*	33 *(b)*	34 *(d)*	35 *(b)*	36 *(c)*	37 *(c)*	38 *(a)*	39 *(b)*	40 *(d)*
41 *(a)*	42 *(c)*	43 *(b)*	44 *(a)*	45 *(d)*	46 *(d)*	47 *(b)*	48 *(a)*	49 *(b)*	50 *(d)*
51 *(d)*	52 *(b)*	53 *(a)*	54 *(b)*	55 *(d)*	56 *(d)*	57 *(c)*	58 *(c)*	59 *(b)*	60 *(d)*
61 *(b)*	62 *(c)*	63 *(c)*	64 *(c)*	65 *(b)*	66 *(b)*	67 *(a)*	68 *(b)*	69 *(c)*	70 *(a)*
71 *(d)*	72 *(b)*	73 *(c)*	74 *(a)*	75 *(c)*	76 *(b)*	77 *(d)*	78 *(a)*	79 *(d)*	80 *(d)*
81 *(d)*	82 *(d)*	83 *(a)*	84 *(c)*	85 *(d)*	86 *(b)*	87 *(c)*	88 *(d)*	89 *(c)*	90 *(c)*
91 *(d)*	92 *(c)*	93 *(b)*	94 *(c)*	95 *(a)*	96 *(a)*	97 *(c)*	98 *(a)*	99 *(c)*	100 *(a)*
101 *(a)*	102 *(c)*	103 *(a)*	104 *(c)*	105 *(a)*	106 *(b)*	107 *(b)*	108 *(d)*	109 *(c)*	110 *(b)*
111 *(c)*	112 *(d)*	113 *(a)*	114 *(a)*	115 *(b)*	116 *(b)*	117 *(b)*	118 *(c)*	119 *(c)*	120 *(a)*
121 *(b)*	122 *(c)*	123 *(a)*	124 *(d)*	125 *(c)*	126 *(d)*	127 *(c)*	128 *(c)*	129 *(c)*	130 *(c)*
131 *(c)*	132 *(d)*	133 *(c)*	134 *(c)*	135 *(d)*	136 *(a)*	137 *(a)*	138 *(b)*	139 *(a)*	140 *(c)*
141 *(c)*	142 *(a)*	143 *(b)*	144 *(b)*	145 *(b)*	146 *(c)*	147 *(a)*	148 *(b)*	149 *(c)*	150 *(a)*
151 *(d)*	152 *(b)*	153 *(a)*	154 *(b)*	155 *(c)*	156 *(b)*	157 *(c)*	158 *(d)*	159 *(b)*	

NTA

UGC

NET/JRF/SET

MODEL PAPERS

(1-3)

Home Science (Paper-II)

Model Paper-1

General Instructions

1. There are total one hundred questions in this paper. Each question carries 2 marks.
2. All questions are compulsory.

1 Who regulates the housing finance companies in India?
(a) Reserve Bank of India (b) National Housing Bank
(c) SBI (d) Government of India

2 What is the etymological meaning of the word 'Ikat'?
(a) It is derived from the word 'Magikat' which means thread.
(b) It is derived from the word 'Kagikat' which means knot.
(c) It is derived from the word 'Magikat' which means bind or knot.
(d) It means coloured thread.

3 Poshan Abhiyaan has been launched on 8th March, 2018 by the Prime Minister to address malnutrition through convergence, use of technology and targeted approach. In which of the following places it was launched?
(a) Panipat (b) Jhunjhunu
(c) Varanasi (d) Meerut

4 What is used to measure the drap co-efficiency?
(a) Threading machine (b) Dart
(c) Colour testing technique (d) Drape meter

5 The Consumer Protection Act, 1986 enacted on
(a) 24th October, 1986 (b) 24th October, 1987
(c) 24th August, 1986 (d) 15th June, 1986

6 What does 'GSM' stands for?
(a) Graphic Per Square Metre
(b) Gram Per Sequencial Metre
(c) Gram Per Square Metre
(d) Gram Per Metre Square

7 Household accounts presents data on
(a) disposable income
(b) spendings
(c) financial assets
(d) All of the above

8 ……… is performed on pattern requiring a solid ground, usually dark shades and extremely tight registration of peg objects to the background.
(a) Block printing
(b) Discharge printing
(c) Carpet printing
(d) Stencil printing

9 Who said, "Values are those deep-seated beliefs and desires that give direction to our life"?
(a) Goodyear. and Klohr (b) Mahendra Jain
(c) Gross and Crandall (d) Nickell and Dorsey

10 1 nanometre = ... cm.
(a) 10^{-9} (b) 10^{-8}
(c) 10^{-7} (d) 10^{-6}

11 According to World Bank, in how many categories NGOs are divided?
(a) 2 (b) 3
(c) 4 (d) 5

12 "Good scale is the result of a pleasing relationship among the components of a space or room and between them and the whole". This is stated by
(a) Alexander (b) Rutt
(c) S Saundararja (d) Ibid

13 Polyester dissolved in
(a) hot phenol (b) meta cresol
(c) conc HCL (d) formic acid

14 Which food should be avoided by lactating mother?
(a) Chocolate (b) Citrus fruits
(c) Both (a) and (b) (d) None of these

15 Which scheme was introduced following the recommendation of Krishnan Committee?
(a) Urban Family Welfare Scheme
(b) National Rural Health Mission
(c) National Population Policy
(d) All of the above

16 The first discovery of a product or process through the use of imagination, ingenious thinking, and experimentation and the first proof that it will work is
(a) process innovation (b) product innovation
(c) creative destruction (d) invention

17 Kleptomania is the act of
(a) thumb sucking (b) group fighting
(c) nail biting (d) stealing

18 Folk media is often packed with
(a) spontaneity (b) boisterousness
(c) humour (d) All of these

19 Breast feeding prolongs the period of natural immunity to viral infections(s) like
(a) mumps and measles
(b) roliv
(c) some kinds of pneumonia and diarrheas
(d) All of the above

20 .... does not have significance in adult life.
(a) Time (b) Money
(c) Degree or certificate (d) Job

21 Choose the correct statement(s) with regard to savings
(a) Using money for further production.
(b) Keeping inside a part of money for future use.
(c) Savings are important for family security and happenings.
(d) All of the above

22 Fruits and vegetables get their characteristic colour from
(a) pigment (b) sunshine
(c) sugar (d) osmosis

23 How many women constitute basic unit of DWCRA?
(a) 5-10 (b) 2-4
(c) 10-15 (d) 15-25

24 Which media would be ideal to attract the attention of children to sell chocolates to them?
(a) Radio (b) Newspapers
(c) TV (advertisements) (d) Leaflets

25 The methods used to test water repellency of fabric are
(a) static absorption test
(b) dynamic absorption test
(c) bundesmann test
(d) All of the above

26 Which is a method of assessing dietary intake by listing all food consumed in previous 24-hours period?
(a) Pre-eating habit (b) 24 hours recall
(c) 24 hours diary (d) None of these

27 Scurvy is caused by deficiency of which vitamin?
(a) Vitamin D (b) Vitamin E
(c) Vitamin C (d) Vitamin K

28 What is the meaning of 'Codex Alimentarius'?
(a) A system of codes
(b) Food code
(c) Food standards
(d) A document published by ISO

29 Lodging properties use food and beverage service for all but which of the following marketing purposes?
(a) Creating new business opportunities.
(b) Creating a desired public image.
(c) Increasing operating profitability.
(d) Attracting desired business.

30 A stress ball is a great option to release ....
(a) anxiety (b) frustration
(c) endorphins (d) blood pressure

31 Which is level of Kohlberg's stages of moral development?
(a) Pre-conventional (b) Conventional
(c) Post-conventional (d) All of these

32 Which saree is said to be the most expensive?
(a) Jamdani (b) Kani
(c) Kanjeevaram (d) Pashmina

33 Extension education as a discipline has its historical roots in
(a) India (b) USA
(c) UK (d) Sri Lanka

34 Who developed the process of canning?
(a) Nicolas Appert (b) Louis Pasteur
(c) Norman Borlaug (d) Walter Hesse

35 "Scale is the relationship of objects to each other and to people." This is stated by
(a) Rutt (b) Friedman Pile Wilson
(c) Crang and Rush (d) Ibid

36 Where informants are literate and are spread over a vast area the most suitable method of collecting data is
(a) direct personal interview
(b) mailed questionnaire method
(c) interview by investigator
(d) All of the above

37 Food suppliers are often called
(a) Peddlers (b) Purveyors
(c) Providers (d) Distributors

38 First sign of ageing involves
(a) change in digestive system
(b) change in psychology
(c) change in musculoskeletal system
(d) change in nervous system

39 Which food bacteria should be avoided by pregnant lady?
(a) Listeria (b) E-coli
(c) Bacillus (d) Vibrio

40 What is the minimum age, to be appointed as the Member of Consumer Dispute Redressal Forum/Commission?
(a) 35 years (b) 40 years
(c) 25 years (d) 20 years

41 Wood in .... attracted people's attention towards illiteracy in India.
(a) 1896 AD (b) 1854 AD
(c) 1949 AD (d) 1868 AD

42 Reason for failure of Family Planning programme includes
(a) male child preference
(b) religious fundamentalist
(c) political apathy
(d) All of the above

43 RDI is based on
(a) sex (b) age
(c) body size (d) All of these

44 When was National Family Welfare Programme launched?
(a) 1941 (b) 1951
(c) 1931 (d) 1961

45 The time and motion study invented around
(a) 1886 (b) 1885
(c) 1901 (d) 1889

46 What is the main focus of DWCRA?
(a) Meeting of basic needs
(b) Empowerment of women
(c) Sustainable living
(d) None of the above

47 Which Article of the Constitution provide for creation of Gram Sabha?
(a) Article 243 (b) Article 248
(c) Article 243 (A) (d) Article 248 (A)

48 An observation uninfluenced by personal bias is said to be
(a) functional (b) critical
(c) objective (d) subjective

49 Monoglycerides and diglycerides are used as .... in a variety of foods.
(a) emulsifiers (b) calories
(c) flavours (d) colours

50 Who shall be the Chairman of the Central Consumer Protection Council?
(a) The Minister in charge of consumer affairs in the Central Government.
(b) The Minister in charge of consumer affairs in the State Government.
(c) The Prime Minister.
(d) The Speaker of the Lok Sabha.

51 A close fitting standing band which extends up from neckline and may be designed to meet at the CF which overlap or end somewhere between the shoulder and CF of the garment?
(a) Wing collar (b) Bertha collar
(c) Mandrin collar (d) Collar stand

52 What is the weight of pre-term baby?
(a) Less than 2500 g
(b) 2500-3000 g
(c) 3000g-4000 g
(d) More than 2500 g

53 Which of the following is also known as Circular Model of Communication?
(a) Transactional Model of Communication.
(b) Linear Model of Communication
(c) Interactional Model of Communication
(d) None of the above

54 The word ergonomics was used independently in 1949 by .... scientist.
(a) American (b) Indian
(c) British (d) Chinese

55 Who said, "In the absence of clearly defined values, effective appraisal of practices or decision is impossible"?
(a) Goodyear and Klohr
(b) MacIver and Page
(c) P Eberman
(d) Gross and Crandall

56 Match the following.

List I	List II
A. Research design formulated for discovering new facts.	1. Descriptive research design.
B. Some specific variables are studied.	2. Diagnostic research design.
C. It refers to the exact nature and scope of the problem under investigation and then suggest remedies against it.	3. Experimental research design.
D. Events are observed about which a prediction is to be made in respect of both experimental and controlled group.	4. Exploratory research design.

Codes

	A	B	C	D		A	B	C	D
(a)	1	4	2	3	(b)	4	1	2	3
(c)	4	3	1	2	(d)	1	3	4	2

57 Match the following.

List I	List II
A. Verbal communication	1. Communication between Friends
B. Human relation	2. Mass media
C. Agents of modernisation	3. Objective of communication
D. Small group communication	4. Writing

Codes

	A	B	C	D		A	B	C	D
(a)	4	1	2	3	(b)	2	1	4	3
(c)	1	2	4	3	(d)	1	2	3	4

58 Match the following.

List I	List II
A. Formal operational	1. 0-2 years
B. Sensory motor	2. 2-7 years
C. Preoperational	3. 7-12 years
D. Concrete operational	4. 12-18 years

Codes

	A	B	C	D		A	B	C	D
(a)	4	1	2	3	(b)	3	2	4	1
(c)	4	2	1	3	(d)	3	4	1	2

59 Match the following.

List I	List II
A. Phytochemicals	1. Cereal group
B. Pathogens	2. Minerals
C. Millets	3. Vitamin E
D. Oilseeds	4. Disease producing
	5. Flavones

Codes

	A	B	C	D		A	B	C	D
(a)	2	3	4	1	(b)	3	4	1	2
(c)	4	1	2	5	(d)	5	4	1	2

60 Match the following.

List I (Functions)	List II (Characteristics)
A. Planning	1. guides and motivates the people to accomplish personal programmes.
B. Organising	2. necessary to determine goals of organisation.
C. Directing	3. means to develop organisation structure to carry out various operations.
D. Controlling	4. concerned with the regulation of activities in accordance with plans.

Codes

	A	B	C	D		A	B	C	D
(a)	2	3	1	4	(b)	4	3	2	1
(c)	1	2	3	4	(d)	3	4	1	2

61 Match the following.

List I (Food Standards)	List II (Descriptions)
A. The PFA standard	1. Concerned with physical and chemical characteristics of food, both natural and acquired during processing.
B. The FPO standard	2. Lay down the minimum standards for all types of foods.
C. The AGMARK standards	3. Indicates conformity to laid down standards.
D. Indian standards	4. Concerned with the standards required for maintaining quality of fruits, vegetables and any products manufactured from them.

Codes

	A	B	C	D		A	B	C	D
(a)	3	2	4	1	(b)	1	2	3	4
(c)	2	4	1	3	(d)	4	3	2	1

62 Match the following.

List I	List II
A. Staining	1. Glass and metallic fibres, provide lustre and textural interest
B. Mineral fibres	2. Formally called artificial silk, soft, drapable, high lustre, less expensive than silk
C. Rayon	3. The stain seeps into the woods, still can see the grain of the wood
D. FFE	4. Fixtures, furnishings and equipment
E. Hand	5. A term used to describe the feel of a fabric to the touch

Codes

	A	B	C	D	E
(a)	1	2	3	4	5
(b)	5	4	3	2	1
(c)	3	1	2	4	5
(d)	3	2	1	4	5

63 Match the following.

List I (Principles of Body mechanics to avoid injuries)	List II (Characteristics)
A. Posture	1. Using muscle on both sides of the body equally
B. Standing	2. Stand with your feet apart this ensures stability
C. Symmetry	3. Here try to avoid standing in one position for prolonged time
D. Base of support	4. Stand-up straight this ensures your spine is in its anatomical position not bent

Codes

	A	B	C	D		A	B	C	D
(a)	1	2	3	4	(b)	4	3	2	1
(c)	4	3	1	2	(d)	1	4	3	2

64 Match the following.

List I	List II
A. Knits	1. Open work
B. Wovens	2. Web structure
C. Felt	3. Warps and wefts
D. Lace	4. Wales and courses

Codes

	A	B	C	D		A	B	C	D
(a)	1	4	3	2	(b)	2	1	4	3
(c)	3	2	1	4	(d)	4	3	2	1

65 Match the following.

List I (Rights)	List II (Features)
A. Right to Safety	1. Consumers should not be forced to select a product.
B. Right to Education	2. Consumers to be informed about the quality, purity and standards of goods.
C. Right to be Informed	3. To make sure that the consumers have informational programmes enable them to make purchasing decisions.
D. Right to Choose	4. Ensures that Consumers have a way to demand justice from those who can harm them.

Codes

	A	B	C	D		A	B	C	D
(a)	4	3	2	1	(b)	4	1	2	3
(c)	1	2	3	4	(d)	3	2	1	4

66 Match the following.

List I	List II
A. Product oriented	1. Routine test
B. Consumer oriented	2. Triangle test
C. Difference test	3. Affective
D. Objected evaluation	4. Analytical

Codes

	A	B	C	D		A	B	C	D
(a)	4	3	2	1	(b)	4	1	2	3
(c)	3	1	2	4	(d)	3	4	1	2

67 Match the following.

List I	List II
A. Simple and lightly embroidered for everyday use	1. Mochi Bharat
B. Kutch embroidery done by mochis	2. Abhla Bharat
C. Embroidery executed with untwisted silk	3. Soof Bharat
D. Use of mirror work	4. Phulkari

Codes

	A	B	C	D		A	B	C	D
(a)	1	2	3	4	(b)	4	1	3	2
(c)	4	3	2	1	(d)	1	2	4	3

68 Match the following.

List I (SDGs)	List II (Description)
A. No poverty	1. Protect restore and promote sustainable use of terrestrial.
B. Life on land	2. Take action to combat climate change and its impact.
C. Climate Action	3. By 2030, eradicate extreme poverty.
D. Zero Hour	4. End hunger, achieve food security and improve nutrition by 2030.

Codes

	A	B	C	D		A	B	C	D
(a)	3	1	2	4	(b)	1	2	3	4
(c)	2	4	3	1	(d)	4	3	2	1

69 Match the following.

List I	List II
A. Jargon of communication	1. Communication skills
B. Sender, Message Receiver	2. Types of communication
C. Abilities to encode and decode message	3. Barrier to communication
D. Verbal and non-verbal	4. Elements of communication process

Codes

	A	B	C	D		A	B	C	D
(a)	3	4	1	2	(b)	2	4	3	1
(c)	1	2	3	4	(d)	4	3	2	1

70 Match the following.

List I	List II
A. National Nutrition Mission	1. Immunisation
B. Food Security Mission	2. Providing food
C. Indradhanush Mission	3. Reducing stunting
D. Kilkari Project	4. Weekly message about family planning

Codes

	A	B	C	D		A	B	C	D
(a)	4	3	2	1	(b)	3	2	1	4
(c)	1	2	3	4	(d)	2	1	4	3

Directions (Q. Nos. 71-80) Given below are two statements, one labelled as Assertion (A) and the other labelled as Reason (R). Following are the codes given below. Choose the correct code.

Codes

(a) Both A and R are true and R is the correct explanation of A
(b) Both A and R are true but R is not the correct explanation of A
(c) A is true, but R is false
(d) A is false, but R is true

71 **Assertion** (A) It is tough to fight against diseases during old age.
Reason (R) There is lesser amount of B lymphocyte during this stage.

72 **Assertion** (A) The International Conference on Primary Health Care held at Alma Ata USSR, 1978.
Reason (R) It focused universal attention on the concept of primary health care as the most effective means of achieving an acceptable level of health for maximum number of people in the community.

73 **Assertion** (A) Interpretation refers to the task of drawing inferences from the collected facts after an analytical and experimental study.
Reason (R) Interpretation is a search for broad meaning of research findings.

74 **Assertion** (A) 'Package safety' is an important function of food packaging.
Reason (R) There must be adverse reactions between the food and its package.

75 **Assertion** (A) Nutritional awareness can be promoted by organising seminars.
Reason (R) Professionals can also help in nutritional awareness.

76 **Assertion** (A) Problematic children do not have specific disability.
Reason (R) Family environment may cause a child to become problematic.

77 **Assertion** (A) Nutrient requirements differ with the size and age of individual.
Reason (R) A person of specified age and size is labelled as reference.

78 **Assertion** (A) Under the adult education programme, measures were taken to make them literate only.

Reason (R) Under this, people get information related to growth, child development etc.

79 **Assertion** (A) A happy, successful marriage reflects absence of conflict.

Reason (R) A higher level of positive behaviour exists in happy marriages.

80 **Assertion** (A) Rayon garments under go progressive shrinkage.

Reason (R) Hence, care has to be taken, while drying and ironing.

81 Arrange in order of sequence the principles of HACCP.
1. Identify critical control points
2. Record keeping
3. Verification
4. Conduct a hazard analysis
5. Establish critical limits

Codes

(a) 4, 1, 5, 3, 2 (b) 4, 3, 2, 1, 5
(c) 4, 1, 5, 3, 1 (d) 1, 5, 4, 2, 3

82 Arrange the following in correct sequence in preparation of fabric for clothing construction.
1. Blocking 2. Shrinking
3. Pressing 4. Straightening

Codes

(a) 1, 2, 3, 4 (b) 2, 4, 1, 3
(c) 4, 1, 2, 3 (d) 3, 4, 1, 2

83 Choose the correct sequence of steps followed while dyeing.
1. After treatment
2. Preparation of fabric
3. Preparation of dye-bath
4. Addition of exhaustion agents

Codes

(a) 1, 2, 3, 4 (b) 2, 3, 4, 1
(c) 3, 4, 1, 2 (d) 4, 1, 2, 3

84 Arrange the following in correct sequence.
1. Juices are secreted from digestive organs glands.
2. Food intake from the mouth.
3. Enzymes break down the food.
4. Food passes through oesophagus.

Codes

(a) 1, 2, 3, 4 (b) 2, 3, 1, 4
(c) 2, 1, 4, 3 (d) 2, 4, 1, 3

85 Choose the correct sequence in writing a research proposal.
1. Review of literature 2. Introduction
3. Bibliography 4. Objectives
5. Methodology 6. Analysis of data

Codes

(a) 2, 4, 1, 5, 6, 3 (b) 1, 2, 4, 3, 5, 6
(c) 2, 1, 4, 3, 5, 6 (d) 4, 2, 1, 5, 6, 3

86 Arrange in the right sequence the steps taken in planning a physical facility for food service unit.
1. Planning team 2. Menu analysis
3. Architectural features 4. Prospectus
5. Budget 6. Feasibility study

Codes

(a) 1, 2, 4, 3, 6, 5 (b) 1, 6, 3, 4, 5, 2
(c) 4, 1, 6, 2, 3, 5 (d) 6, 5, 4, 3, 2, 1

87 Arrange Maslow's Hierarchy of needs in the proper sequence.
1. Physiological 2. Social
3. Safety 4. Self-esteen
5. Self-actualisation

Codes

(a) 1, 3, 2, 4, 5 (b) 1, 2, 3, 4, 5
(c) 5, 4, 3, 2, 1 (d) 1, 4, 3, 2, 5

88 Arrange the following stages of decision thinking process in correct sequece.
1. Empathy 2. Define
3. Test 4. Prototype
5. Ideate

Codes

(a) 1, 2, 3, 4 and 5 (b) 1, 3, 2, 4 and 5
(c) 1, 2, 5, 4 and 3 (d) 5, 4, 3, 2 and 1

89 Consider the following statements.
1. UNICEF is trying to help working male.
2. UNICEF has immunised children against 6 major childhood disease.

(a) Only 1 (b) Only 2
(c) Both 1 and 2 (d) None of these

90 The properties of silk which makes it a queen of the fibres include
1. smoothness 2. soft lustre
3. resiliency 4. cost

Select the correct answer using the codes given below

(a) 1 and 2 (b) 3 and 4
(c) 1, 2 and 3 (d) All of these

91 According to Rutt, correct scale or consistency is size indispensable in
1. garden design
2. exterior house design
3. interior design
4. furniture design

Codes

(a) 1 and 2 (b) 1 and 4
(c) 1, 2 and 3 (d) All of these

92 Which of the following pairs is/are correctly matched?
1. Food technology Study of food
2. Food processing Sorting
3. Functional property Calorie
4. Phytochemicals Animal origin

Codes

(a) Only 3 (b) Only 2
(c) None of these (d) All of these

93 Which among the following are not the term used for apparel manufacturing?
1. Clip 2. Drape
3. Bias 4. L-shape

Codes

(a) 1 and 4 (b) 2 and 3
(c) 1, 2 and 3 (d) 2, 3 and 4

94 Which of the following statement(s) is/are correct?
1. The child who does not learn tasks at periods of readiness may have great difficulty learning them later.
2. Serious behaviour problems cause abruptly in adolescence, but trace their organ to maladjustment in the early years.
3. In the pattern of development, there is a marked correlation between physical and psychological development.

4. In the pattern of intellectual development, memory precedes reasoning with abstract reasoning following concrete reasoning.

Codes

(a) Only 1 (b) Only 2
(c) Both 1 and 2 (d) None of these

95 Development supporting communication focuses on grassroot level development and participation using small media like

1. flashcards, slides 2. video, folk media
3. personal contact 4. meetings

Select the correct answer using the codes given below.

(a) 1, 2 and 3 (b) 2 and 4
(c) 1 and 4 (d) 1, 2, 3 and 4

Directions (Q. Nos 96-100) Read the passage and answer the questions that follows

Information Technology (IT) is the application of computers and internet to store, retrieve, transmit, and manipulate information, often in the context of a business or other enterprise. IT is considered a subset of information and communications technology (ICT) and has evolved according to the needs. It is worthwhile noting that the term IT is commonly used as a synonym for computers and computer networks, but it also encompasses other information distribution technologies such as television and telephones. Several industries are associated with information technology, including computer hardware, software, electronics, semiconductors, internet, telecom equipment, engineering, healthcare, e-commerce, and computer services.

Thanks to the continuous development of computers, the original computing systems became minicomputers and later personal computers took the lead. Nowadays, mobile phones are dethroning the personal computer and computing is evolving faster to become disembodied more like a cloud, becoming accessible more easily whenever needed.

Information technology has transformed people and companies and has allowed digital technology to influence society and economy alike. It has, in this sense, shaped societies and adapted itself to people's needs. If you want a brief history of Information Technology, here is one. Human were the first "computers". Then, machines were invented to carry out the computational tasks. Now these machines have given way to new form of information technology. Information has become disembodied accessible from anywhere through cloud technology. Recent advances in IT is the consequence of the development in computing systems.

Humans have been storing, retrieving, manipulating, and communicating information since the Sumerians in Mesopotamia developed writing in about 3000 BC, but the term information technology in its modern sense first appeared in a 1958 article published in the Harvard Business Review; authors Harold J.

Leavitt and Thomas L. Whisler commented that "the new technology does not yet have a single established name. We shall call it information technology (IT)". Their definition consists of three categories: techniques for processing, the application of statistical and mathematical methods to decision-making and the simulation of higher-order thinking through computer programs.

96 Which of the following industries is associated with Information Technology?

(a) Semi conductors (b) Engineering
(c) E-commerce (d) All of these

97 Information technology is changing principally because of

(a) the changing needs
(b) new technological advances
(c) new softwares
(d) All of the above

98 According to the author, the first computers were

(a) Calculators (b) humans
(c) printers (d) None of these

99 Development of information technology is the result of

(a) advances in computing systems
(b) development of machinery in general
(c) invention of semiconductors
(d) All of the above

100 Computing systems are taking the form of clouds means

(a) computers have become smaller
(b) computing power are becoming disembodied.
(c) computers have become portable
(d) All of the above

ANSWERS

1 (b)	2 (c)	3 (b)	4 (d)	5 (a)	6 (c)	7 (d)	8 (b)	9 (a)	10 (c)
11 (a)	12 (a)	13 (a)	14 (c)	15 (a)	16 (b)	17 (d)	18 (d)	19 (d)	20 (c)
21 (d)	22 (a)	23 (c)	24 (c)	25 (d)	26 (b)	27 (c)	28 (b)	29 (c)	30 (a)
31 (d)	32 (c)	33 (c)	34 (a)	35 (b)	36 (c)	37 (b)	38 (c)	39 (a)	40 (a)
41 (b)	42 (d)	43 (d)	44 (b)	45 (b)	46 (b)	47 (c)	48 (c)	49 (a)	50 (a)
51 (c)	52 (a)	53 (a)	54 (c)	55 (c)	56 (b)	57 (a)	58 (a)	59 (d)	60 (a)
61 (b)	62 (d)	63 (c)	64 (d)	65 (a)	66 (a)	67 (b)	68 (a)	69 (a)	70 (b)
71 (b)	72 (b)	73 (c)	74 (c)	75 (a)	76 (a)	77 (b)	78 (b)	79 (d)	80 (d)
81 (a)	82 (c)	83 (b)	84 (d)	85 (a)	86 (c)	87 (a)	88 (c)	89 (b)	90 (d)
91 (c)	92 (d)	93 (c)	94 (c)	95 (a)	96 (d)	97 (a)	98 (b)	99 (a)	100 (b)

Home Science (Paper-II)

Model Paper-2

General Instructions

1. There are total one hundred questions in this paper. Each question carries 2 marks.
2. All questions are compulsory.

---

1 Novelty yarns are used for decoration. Examples of novelty yarns include
(a) raschel, tricot and lace
(b) woollen, staple and boucle
(c) slub, boucle and core spun
(d) None of the above

2 The National Charter for children 2003 was adopted on ....
(a) 9th February, 2004 (b) 12th March, 2004
(c) 15th February, 2004 (d) 20th February, 2-004

3 The causal agent of human disease botulism can be classified under
(a) bacterial toxin (b) viral toxin
(c) mycotoxin (d) chemical toxin

4 ..... is an apex financial institution for housing.
(a) RBI (b) SBI
(c) NHB (d) None of these

5 The term 'Nanotechnology' was coined by
(a) Richard Feynman (b) Edward Jennings
(c) Norio Taniguchi (d) Albert Einstein

6 On whose birthday, launched Sansad Gram Yojana?
(a) Jawaharlal Nehru
(b) Mahatma Gandhi
(c) Jai Prakash Narayan
(d) Shyama Prasad Mukherjee

7 10th, 11th and 12th Five Year Plans consist of
(a) population control
(b) care of mother and child
(c) Both (a) and (b)
(d) None of the above

8 Niacin deficiency causes
(a) pellagra (b) scurvy
(c) osteoporosis (d) beri-beri

9 The folk or traditional arts of India from ancient times been used for .... purposes.
(a) socio-political
(b) religious
(c) moral
(d) All of the above

10 Which among the following method is less expensive?
(a) Case study
(b) Making questionnaire
(c) Interview
(d) Questionnaire

11 What procedure do diet counsellor follow to help individual to make dietary changes?
(a) Provides information (b) Educational support
(e) Follow-up (d) All of these

12 "Balance is the principle of design that produces a feeling of rest and contentment." This is stated by
(a) Ibid (b) K Alexander
(c) Crang and Rush (d) S Saundararja

13 Integrated child protection was launched in the year.
(a) 2009-2010 (b) 2011-2012
(c) 2013-2014 (d) 2014-2015

14 Adulthood is a time of .... thinking.
(a) relativistic
(b) optimistic
(c) simplistic
(d) All of the above

15 What is the basic purpose of dart?
(a) To make the body fitted cloth.
(b) To make two dimensional shape into three dimensional shape.
(c) To make garments suitable for women clothing.
(d) None of the above

16 The 'Linear Model' was founded by
(a) Aristotle (b) Shannon
(c) Weaver (d) All of these

17 When do human undergoes role confusion?
(a) 12-18 years (b) 20-30 years
(c) 10-20 years (d) 18-28 years

18 Which among the following does not affect the motivation towards adult education?
(a) Life goals (b) Interest and desires
(c) Social motivation (d) Saving and planning

19 Who supported the Interactional Model of Communication?
(a) Aristotle (b) David Berlo
(c) Weaver (d) Wilbur Schramm

20 Decrease in .... hormone leads to risk taking behaviour.
(a) adrenaline (b) insulin
(c) serotonin (d) testosterone

21 What is Oedipus complex?
(a) A boy's attraction for his mother
(b) A girl's attraction for her mother
(c) A boy's attraction for his father
(d) A girl's attraction for her father

22 Under which act, National Housing Bank was setup as an apex institute of housing finance in the country?
(a) National Housing Bank Act, 1986
(b) National Housing Bank Act, 1987
(c) National Housing Bank Act, 1988
(d) National Housing Bank Act, 1989

23 Under which mission, the objective of building 300 village cluster by 2020 was decided?
(a) Sansad Adarsh Gram Yojana
(b) Shyama Prasad Mukherjee Rurban Mission
(c) Pradhan Mantri Adarsh Gram Yojana
(d) Twenty Point Programme

24 Who defined extension education as "An educational process to provide knowledge to rural people about the improved practices in a convincing manner and help them to take decisions within their specific local conditions?"
(a) D Ensminger (b) Kelsey and Hearne
(c) V C Sanoria (d) O P Dahama

25 When was ICDS launched?
(a) 1965 (b) 1975 (c) 1985 (d) 1995

26 Extension worker solves the major and minor problems of the community, the problem may be related to health, education, employment, etc., so, he can be considered as a
(a) doctor (b) educationist
(c) physician (d) multi-tasker

27 High calories diet have concentrated amount of ....
(a) carbohydrate (b) protein
(c) salt (d) vitamin

28 These stiff plastics soften in hot water and are molded before they cool and stiffen.
(a) plaster bandage (b) thermo plastics
(c) fibre glass (d) sculptural arts coatings

29 Deendayal Upadhyay Gram Jyoti Yojana started on
(a) 25th July, 2015 (b) 1st January, 2016
(c) 13th April, 2017 (d) 2nd Octbber, 2018

30 What are the approaches by DWCRA?
(a) Provide income generating assets
(b) Make rural women understand role of hygiene
(c) Organising women into groups
(d) All of the above

31 What is 'Carryover Principle'?
(a) Additives added in raw materials are not present in final products.
(b) Antioxidant added to oil is present in all oil based products made from it.
(c) Both (a) and (b)
(d) Neither (a) nor (b)

32 Low sodium diet means
(a) salt free diet
(b) moderate salt restriction
(c) Both (a) and (b)
(d) None of the above

33 Which of the following marks is compulsory for Indian F and V products?
(a) FPO (b) ECOMARK (c) VOCO (d) GFSI

34 What is the feature of twist yarn?
(a) Low strength (b) High strength
(c) Medium strength (d) None of these

35 Subsidised pricing is followed in
(a) restaurant (b) fast food unit
(c) air catering (d) industrial canteen

36 In terms of additives, ... include both natural and synthetic colourants.
(a) flavours (b) colours
(c) gums (d) sweeteners

37 How many amino acids are essential amino acids?
(a) 7 (b) 5 (c) 8 (d) 6

38 How much body fat is required by adolescence girl to maintain regular ovulation?
(a) 23% (b) 22% (c) 20% (d) 25%

39 Which of the following international bodies is concerned with 'Quality Management'?
(a) CAC (b) ISO
(c) WTO (d) HACCP

40 Which of the following acts as co-enzyme?
(a) Thiamine (b) Riboflavin
(c) Both (a) and (b) (d) None of these

41 Match the following.

List I	List II
A. Nephrosis	1. Pancreas
B. Diabetes	2. Kidney
C. Arteriosclerosis	3. Intestine
D. Coeliac disease	4. Blood vessels
	5. Heart

Codes

	A	B	C	D		A	B	C	D
(a)	3	5	2	4	(b)	1	2	3	4
(c)	2	1	5	3	(d)	2	1	4	3

42 Match the following.

List I	List II
A. Manmade fibres	1. Accept dyes and finishes more readily
B. High lustre. low lustre	2. May be pure white
C. Fibres with good moisture regain	3. Rayon and cotton
D. Low wet strength, high wet strength	4. The percentage of return from elongation to the original length
E. Elastic recovery	5. Silk and cotton

Codes

	A	B	C	D	E
(a)	4	1	2	3	5
(b)	5	4	3	1	2
(c)	2	5	1	3	4
(d)	1	2	5	4	3

43 Match the following.

List I	List II
A. Measure around the fullest part of the thigh.	1. Thigh
B. Measure from the waist to the knee	2. Knee
C. Measure around the claf muscle	3. Calf
D. Measure around the ankle	4. Ankle

Codes

	A	B	C	D
(a)	1	2	3	4
(b)	4	3	2	1
(c)	2	3	4	1
(d)	3	4	2	1

44 Match the following.

List I	List II
A. Psychological needs	1. Fulfilment of capacities
B. Self-esteem needs	2. Freedom from danger, job security, health care, etc.
C. Self-actualisation needs	3. Recognition by others/feeling of achievement
D. Need for safety and security	4. Food, clothing and shelter

Codes

	A	B	C	D
(a)	4	3	1	2
(b)	2	3	1	4
(c)	1	2	3	4
(d)	4	3	2	1

45 Match the following.

List I	List II
A. Solar energy	1. It is produced by exploiting tidal waves of the sea.
B. Tidal energy	2. It is used for operating water pumps for irrigation purposes.
C. Wind energy	3. The energy is obtained from organic matter.
D. Bio energy	4. It is most readily available free source of energy.

Codes

	A	B	C	D
(a)	4	1	2	3
(b)	1	2	3	4
(c)	4	1	3	2
(d)	4	3	2	1

46 Match the following.

List I	List II
A. Rehabilitation of Juvenile in India	1. 1960
B. Probation Act	2. 3 to 7 year
C. Children Act	3. 1850
D. Reform House	4. 1958

Codes

	A	B	C	D
(a)	1	3	4	2
(b)	2	1	3	4
(c)	3	4	1	2
(d)	3	2	1	4

47 Match the following.

List I	List II
A. Shyama Prasad Mukherjee Rurban Mission	1. 16th August, 2015
B. Pradhan Mantri Gram Sadak Yojana	2. 25th December, 2000
C. Deendayal Upadhyaya Antyodaya Yojana	3. 25th September, 2014
D. Ayushman Bharat	4. 23rd September, 2018

Codes

	A	B	C	D
(a)	1	2	3	4
(b)	2	1	3	4
(c)	3	1	4	2
(d)	4	3	2	1

48 Match the following.

List I	List II
A. Project schedule development	1. Specifying budgeted cost to be incurred at the completion of project.
B. Budget planning	2. Listing the entire schedule of activities.
C. Quality planning	3. Who will do what work at which time.
D. Resource planning	4. Assessing quality criteria used for project.

Codes

	A	B	C	D
(a)	2	1	4	3
(b)	4	3	2	1
(c)	1	2	3	4
(d)	2	4	1	3

49 Match the following.

List I	List II
A. Process chart	1. It is similar to process chart.
B. Multiman chart	2. It helps pinpoint all movements that can be reduced or eliminated.
C. Operation chart	3. It is also called indentical chart.
D. Patway chart	4. In it some signs and symbols are alloted to the movement of activity.

Codes

	A	B	C	D
(a)	1	2	3	4
(b)	4	3	2	1
(c)	4	3	1	2
(d)	2	4	3	1

50 Match the following.

List I	List II
A. Puppets	1. Graphic aid
B. Charts	2. Electronic
C. Computer	3. Traditional
D. Print	4. Mass media

Codes

	A	B	C	D		A	B	C	D
(a)	2	3	4	1	(b)	4	1	3	2
(c)	3	1	2	4	(d)	1	2	3	4

51 Match the following.

List I	List II
A. Coal Wilhelm Scheele	1. Father of nanotechnology
B. Richard Feynman	2. Isolation of malic acid from apples
C. Food Chemistry	3. Scientific approach to food
D. JG Wallerius	4. Single grain experiment

Codes

	A	B	C	D		A	B	C	D
(a)	2	4	1	3	(b)	2	1	4	3
(c)	3	4	2	1	(d)	4	1	3	2

52 Match the following.

List I (Organs)	List II (Changes)
A. Eyes	1. Nerve cell decreases
B. Ears	2. Lens stiffen
C. Brain	3. Blood filteration is slow
D. Heart	4. Presbycusis

Codes

	A	B	C	D		A	B	C	D
(a)	3	1	2	4	(b)	2	4	1	3
(c)	4	1	3	2	(d)	2	3	1	4

53 Match the following.

List I	List II
A. A placket or any garment opening	1. Closing
B. A straight sleeve flauing at the bottom	2. Bell sleeve
C. Another word for armholes	3. Armscye
D. Decouative piece of fabric	4. Applique

Codes

	A	B	C	D
(a)	1	2	3	4
(b)	4	3	2	1
(c)	2	3	1	4
(d)	3	2	1	4

54 Match the following.

List I	List II
A. Xerophthalmia	1. Iodine deficiency
B. Anaemia	2. Vitamin C Deficiency
C. Scurvy	3. Vitamin A Deficiency
D. Goitre	4. Iron Deficiency

Codes

	A	B	C	D		A	B	C	D
(a)	4	1	2	3	(b)	3	4	2	1
(c)	2	3	1	4	(d)	4	1	3	2

55 Match the following.

List I	List II
A. Yeast	1. Fermentation
B. Moulds	2. Mycotoxin
C. AIDS	3. HIV
D. Fungi	4. Damp places

Codes

	A	B	C	D		A	B	C	D
(a)	2	1	4	3	(b)	2	3	4	1
(c)	3	4	1	2	(d)	3	1	2	4

56 Match the following.

List I	List II
A. Plain weave	1. A weave with three sets of yarn warp 60 inch to weft.
B. Basket weave	2. Weft interlaced wit warp to form diagonal ridges in fabric.
C. Triaxial weave	3. Simplest and least expensive weave.
D. Twill weave	4. Variation of plain weave of 2 weft 2 warp.

Codes

	A	B	C	D		A	B	C	D
(a)	1	2	3	4	(b)	2	3	4	1
(c)	3	4	1	2	(d)	4	1	2	3

57 Match the following.

List I	List II
A. Diaphragm	1. Ortho Eura
B. Progestin injection	2. Rubber Cup
C. Skin patch	3. Nuva Ring
D. Vaginal Ring	4. Depo Provera

Codes

	A	B	C	D		A	B	C	D
(a)	2	4	1	3	(b)	1	3	2	4
(c)	3	1	2	4	(d)	4	2	1	3

58 Match the following.

List I	List II
A. Community nutrition	1. Water is the most important nutrient
B. Sports nutrition	2. Prevention of malnutrition
C. Nutrition in emergencies	3. Develops healthy eating habit

Codes

	A	B	C		A	B	C
(a)	3	2	1	(b)	1	2	3
(c)	3	1	2	(d)	1	3	2

59 Match the following.

List I	List II
A. Energy giving	1. Proteins
B. Regulation and maintenance	2. Vitamins and minerals
C. Body building	3. Carbohydrates
D. Protective food	4. Water

Codes

	A	B	C	D		A	B	C	D
(a)	1	2	4	3	(b)	3	4	1	2
(c)	2	3	4	1	(d)	4	1	3	2

60 Match the following.

List I	List II
A. Sucking and eye blinking	1. Classical conditioning
B. Less than 2.5kg, of birth weight	2. Loneliness
C. Empty nest	3. Operant conditioning
D. Pairing of stimuli	4. Permanent reflex
	5. Small for date
	6. Broken homes

Codes

	A	B	C	D		A	B	C	D
(a)	5	2	6	3	(b)	6	5	2	3
(c)	2	4	6	1	(d)	4	5	2	1

***Directions** (Q. Nos. 61-75) Given below are two statements, one labelled as Assertion (A) and the other labelled as Reason (R). Following are the codes given below. Choose the correct code.*

Codes

(a) Both A and R are true and R is the correct explanation of A
(b) Both A and R are true but R is not the correct explanation of A
(c) A is true, but R is false
(d) A is false, but R is true

61 **Assertion** (A) The shrinkage test may be carried out either by immersion of the fabric in water for a specified period or by subjecting it to washing treatment at various temperatures.

Reason (R) The extent of shrinkage of fabric depends on fabric weave, tension during weaving and finishing treatment given to the fabric.

62 **Assertion** (A) The congenial working environment can increase performance of the workers.

Reason (R) The physical environment as an aspect of the workplace environment has direct impact on the humans.

63 **Assertion** (A) A functional property of food is determined by physical, chemical and organoleptic properties. .

Reason (R) Organoleptic properties are not associated with the senses of taste, sight, smell and touch.

64 **Assertion** (A) Enterprise management helps in achieving group goals.

Reasons (R) Enterprise management enables the organisation to survive in changing environment.

65 **Assertion** (A) Water harvesting is the activity of direct collection of rainwater.

Reason (R) The rainwater can be stored for direct use.

66 **Assertion** (A) Ego between partners is one of the major causes of marital confict.

Reason (R) Woman wants to crush ego of her husband to gain control and Vice-versa.

67 **Assertion** (A) Adoption of the fashion styles takes place at the declining state.

Reason (R) If the fashion is accepted, adoption rises purchased and worn by fashion admirers.

68 **Assertion** (A) Interrelation is essential for the simple reason that the usefulness and utility of research findings their when interpretation.

Reason (R) It is through interpretation that the researcher care understand the absent principle that works beneath his findings.

69 **Assertion** (A) Women has taken over the world with confidence.

Reason (R) Urban women are well educated which have caused liberation.

70 **Assertion** (A) Tie and dye is an ancient method of pattern-making on cloth.

Reason (R) Tie and dye is an ancient method of pattern-making cloth .

71 **Assertion** (A) In preliminary auditing, readily available data is not used to analyse the performance.

Reason (R) The inspection takes relatively more time.

72 **Assertion** (A) Functional strategies are a set short-term plans related to the over all realisation of the forms of grand strategy.

Reason (R) The success of any strategy depends upon how well the strategist can adopt his resources to an identifiable opportunity.

73 **Assertion** (A) Inspection of a fabric for appearance and hand is always the first step in fibre identification.

Reason (R) Manufactured fibres can be made into fabrics that ensemble natural fibre fabrics.

74 **Assertion** (A) Education is a continuous process which educates people through various means.

Reason (R) The lifelong education fulfils learning needs of people, builds service oriented society and promotes all round development of the people.

75 **Assertion** (A) Mentally challenged children have bad memory.

Reason (R) Down syndrome can cause mental retardation.

76 Arrange in correct sequence, the stage of an interior design process.

1. Bubble diagram
2. Schematic diagram
3. Detaileddrawing
4. Construction administration
5. Execution

Codes

(a) 2, 3, 1, 5, 4 (b) 2, 1, 3, 5, 4
(c) 1, 5, 3, 2, 4 (d) 1, 2, 3, 5, 4

77 Arrange the development tasks during early childhood period sequentially.

1. Learning to talk
2. Bladder control
3. Learning to walk
4. Learning gender difference
5. Distinguishing right and wrong
6. Getting ready to read

Codes

(a) 2, 1, 3, 6, 4, 5 (b) 5, 2, 3, 6, 1, 4
(c) 3, 1, 2, 4, 6, 5 (d) 1, 3, 4, 2, 5, 6

78 In the process of communication which one of the following is in the chronological order?
(a) Communicator, Medium, Receiver, Effect, Message
(b) Medium, Communicator, Message, Receiver, Effect
(c) Communicator, Message, Medium, Receiver, Effect
(d) Message, Communicator, Medium, Receiver, Effect

79 Arrange in correct sequence the processes involved in food technology.
1. Preservation
2. Selection
3. Use of safe food
4. Distribution
5. Packaging

Codes
(a) 5, 2, 1, 3, 4 (b) 4, 3, 2, 1, 5
(c) 1, 2, 3, 5, 4 (d) 2, 1, 5, 4, 3

80 Arrange the sequence of the given media of communication by the years, they were started.
1. Television
2. Radio
3. Films
4. Print

Codes
(a) 4, 3, 2, 1 (b) 3, 4, 1, 2
(c) 2, 3, 4, 1 (d) 1, 2, 3, 4

81 Write in correct sequence.
1. Adulthood
2. Infancy
3. Adolescence
4. Old age

Codes
(a) 3, 2, l, 4 (b) 1, 3, 2, 4
(c) 2, 3, 1, 4 (d) 4, 1, 2, 3

82 Arrange the sequence of the given media of communication by the years they were started.
1. Television
2. Radio
3. Films
4. Print

Codes
(a) 4, 3, 2, 1 (b) 3, 4, 1, 2 (c) 2, 3, 4, 1 (d) 1, 2, 3, 4

83 What is the correct sequence of the below given steps of flow chart for conducting a research project?
1. Formulation of hypothesis
2. Review of literature and concepts
3. Identification and conceptualisation of problem
4. Conclusion and generalisation

Select the correct answer from the codes given below.
(a) 1, 3, 2 and 4 (b) 2, 3, 4 and 1
(c) 3, 2, 1 and 4 (d) 4, 1, 3 and 2

84 Arrange in the sequence of enactment.
1. Department of Family Planning
2. Policy Commission
3. Family Planning Association of India
4. Population Scheme

Codes
(a) 1, 3, 4-and 2 (b) 3, 1, 4 and 2
(c) 2, 3, 4 and 1 (d) 1, 2, 4 and 3

85 The correct sequence of curriculum planning is
1. tentative curriculum.
2. consideration of curriculum needs.
3. evaluation of tentative curriculum.
4. plot testing of tentative curriculum.

Codes
(a) 1, 2, 3, 4 (b) 2, 1, 4, 3
(c) 2, 1, 3, 4 (d) 3, 1, 2, 4

86 Arrange the following in correct order.
1. Beti Bachao Beti Padhao Scheme
2. Stand Up India
3. Roshini scheme

Codes
(a) 2, 1, 3 (b) 1, 2, 3
(c) 3, 1, 2 (d) 2, 3, 1

87 Give the correct sequence of managerial functions.
1. Reporting
2. Staffing
3. Planning
4. Organising
5. Coordinating
6. Budgeting
7. Directing

Codes
(a) 3, 4, 2, 7, 5, 1, 6 (b) 3, 4, 2, 5, 6, 1, 7
(c) 7, 6, 5, 4, 3, 2, 1 (d) 6, 7, 4, 5, 2, 1, 3

88 Which aspects should investigator examine in using secondary data?
1. Suitability
2. Adequacy
3. Reliability
4. Interest

Select the correct answer using the codes given below.
(a) 1 and 2 (b) 3 and 4
(c) 1, 2 and 3 (d) All of these

89 Which of the following is not a feature of formal education?
1. Flexible Timing
2. Assured Course
3. Getting degree after Course
4. No pre defined curriculum

Codes
(a) 1 and 2 (b) 1 and 3
(c) 1, 2 and 4 (d) 1 and 4

90 Which are used for mass contact methods?
1. Personal calls
2. Circular letter
3. Radio and television
4. Tours

Select the correct answer using the codes given below.
(a) 1, 2 and 3 (b) 1, 2, 3 and 4
(c) 2 and 3 (d) 1 and 4

91 Which of the following are part of High Pressure Processing (HPP)?
1. Help in new development of product.
2. A new processing method.
3. A cold pasteurisation technique.
4. It is part of traditional thermal and chemical treatment.

Codes
(a) 1, 2, 4 (b) 1, 2, 3
(c) 1, 3, 4 (d) 2, 3, 4

92 Consider the following statements.
1. A balanced diet should have maximum amount of carbohydrates and fats.
2. A balanced diet should have adequate amount of roughage.

Which of the statement(s) given above is/are correct?
(a) Only 1 (b) Only 2
(c) Both 1 and 2 (d) Neither 1 nor 2

93 Face-to-face communication between two persons
1. highest form of communication
2. persuasive and influential
3. interplay of words and gestures
4. involve all five senses

Select the correct answer using the codes given below.
(a) 1 and 2 (b) 1 and 4
(c) 1, 2 and 3 (d) 1, 2, 3 and 4

94 Bibliography given in a research report
1. makes the report authentic.
2. helps those interested in further research and in studying the problem from another angle.

Which of the statement(s) given above is/are correct?
(a) Only 1 (b) Only 2.
(c) Both 1 and 2 (d) None of these

95 Following are the provisions of PWDVA.
1. Civil law
2. Non-protection of women
3. It does not penalise criminally
4. It was enforced on 26th October, 2006
5. It does not define domestic violence

Codes
(a) 1, 3, 4 (b) 1, 3, 5
(c) 2, 3, 4 (d) 1, 2, 4

Directions (Q. Nos. 96-100) Read this passage given below and answer the questions that follow.

The hypothesis that is being tested can be used to predict the way the data should point. The hypothesis may state that the experimental group will perform better than the control group. By confronting the hypothesis with the dependent variable values of the two groups, the experimenter can determine whether the; hypothesis accurately predicted the results.

But it is difficult to tell, simply by looking at unorganised data, whether the (dependent variable) values for one group are higher or lower than the values for the second group. Therefore, the data must be organised numerically to yield numbers that will provide an answer.

For example, we may complete average scores and find that the experimental group has a higher mean (say, 100) than the control group (say, 99). Although, there is a difference between the groups, it is very, small and we must ask whether it is 'real' or only a 'chance' difference. If we conduct the experiment again, would we obtain similar results?

If it is a 'real', reliable difference the experimental group should obtain a higher mean than the control group almost every time the experiment is repeated. If there is no reliable difference between the two groups, we would expect to find each group receiving the higher score half of the time. To tell whether the difference between the two groups in a single, experiment is reliable, rather than simply due to random fluctuations (chance), the experimenter resorts to a statistical test. The particular statistical tests used will be determined by the type of data obtained and the design of the experiment. On the basis of such tests, it can be determined whether the difference between me to groups is likely to be 'real' (statistically reliable) or merely 'accidental' (due only to chance). If the difference between the dependent variable values of the groups is statistically reliable, the difference is very probably not due to random fluctuation. It is therefore concluded that the independent variable is effective in influencing the dependant variable (promoting that the extraneous variables have been properly controlled).

96 Based on the passage, which one of the following is the correct hypothesis?
(a) Performance of experimental group will be less than control group.
(b) There will be no difference in the performance of experimental and control groups.
(c) Performance of experimental group will be better than control group.
(d) Performance of control group will be better than experimental group.

97 Statistical tests could be used, if the data are
(a) unorganised (b) organised
(c) normal (d) variable

98 The reliable difference between two groups could be obtained, if we use
(a) norms (b) validity
(c) statistical test (d) reliability

99 Statistically reliable difference is known as
(a) chance difference (b) hypothesised difference
(c) random difference (d) real difference

100 Arrange the following concepts in which they appeared in the passage.
1. Reliable difference 2. Hypothesis
3. Statistical test 4. Random fluctuation

Codes
(a) 3, 4, 2, 1 (b) 2, 1, 3, 4
(c) 1, 2, 3, 4 (d) 4, 3, 1, 2

ANSWERS

1 (c)	2 (a)	3 (a)	4 (c)	5 (c)	6 (c)	7 (c)	8 (a)	9 (d)	10 (b)
11 (d)	12 (c)	13 (a)	14 (d)	15 (b)	16 (d)	17 (a)	18 (a)	19 (d)	20 (c)
21 (a)	22 (b)	23 (b)	24 (d)	25 (b)	26 (b)	27 (a)	28 (b)	29 (a)	30 (d)
31 (b)	32 (c)	33 (a)	34 (a)	35 (d)	36 (b)	37 (c)	38 (b)	39 (b)	40 (c)
41 (d)	42 (c)	43 (a)	44 (a)	45 (a)	46 (c)	47 (a)	48 (a)	49 (c)	50 (c)
51 (b)	52 (a)	53 (a)	54 (d)	55 (b)	56 (c)	57 (a)	58 (c)	59 (b)	60 (d)
61 (a)	62 (b)	63 (c)	64 (b)	65 (a)	66 (a)	67 (d)	68 (a)	69 (a)	70 (c)
71 (c)	72 (a)	73 (b)	74 (d)	75 (b)	76 (d)	77 (a)	78 (c)	79 (d)	80 (a)
81 (a)	82 (a)	83 (c)	84 (b)	85 (b)	86 (c)	87 (a)	88 (c)	89 (d)	90 (b)
91 (b)	92 (b)	93 (c)	94 (c)	95 (a)	96 (c)	97 (b)	98 (c)	99 (d)	100 (b)

Home Science (Paper-II)

Model Paper-3

General Instructions

1. There are total one hundred questions in this paper. Each question carries 2 marks.
2. All questions are compulsory.

---

1 What is the role of vitamin K?
(a) Anti-oxidant (b) Anti-inflamatory
(c) Clotting of blood (d) Formation of bone

2 Ownership of product is transferred from the supplier to the food and beverage operation when the receiving employee signs the
(a) delivery notice (b) daily receiving report
(c) purchase order
(d) standard purchase specification sheet

3 Which of the following marks was introduced in 1991 to identify biodegradable products?
(a) ISO (b) ECOMARK (c) FSSAI (d) SQF

4 Which vitamin is essential for vision?
(a) Vitamin D (b) Vitamin A (c) Vitamin E (d) Vitamin K

5 Which stage occurs at the age of 2 years according to Piaget?
(a) Sensorimotor stage (b) Preoperational stage
(c) Concrete operational stage (d) Formal operational

6 Which of the following statement(s) is/are incorrect?
(a) A poor diet during pregnancy is a major cause of the high death rate of woman 'and infant.
(b) Haemoglobin blood content of non-pregnant woman is about 13 to 14.l.
(c) A pregnant woman must eat 2 times a day.
(d) None of the above

7 In relation to the purchasing function, the term quality refers to
(a) highest price (b) popularity of a menu item
(c) suitability for intended use (d) greatest value

8 .... begins during preoperational stage.
(a) Walking (b) Language development
(c) Crying (d) Tooth development

9 Vitamin D helps in absorption of
(a) calcium (b) phosphorus
(c) Both (a) and (b) (d) None of these

10 Who stated "Time with use is handled much like a material we can earn it, spend it?"
(a) Nickell and Dorsey (b) Edward Eleven
(c) Hall ET (d) Gross and Crandall

11 To help make the receiving function secure and efficient, the physical transfer of food and beverage products to the storage area should be the responsibility of
(a) supplier delivery personnel
(b) assigned staff from the property
(c) the food and beverage controller
(d) None of the above

12 Who is the author of "Time for living"?
(a) George Soule (b) Binni Mandela
(c) Jacque Barzun (d) Hazel Kyrk

13 What is the fashion trend in trickle down theory?
(a) Lower to middle class
(b) Middle to lower class
(c) Upper and middle on same platform
(d) Upper to middle and lower class

14 What is said about the ornamental addition on the garment?
(a) Yoke (b) Tucks (c) Trimming (d) Ruffle

15 What is fashion forecasting?
(a) A global career that focuses on upcoming trends
(b) A fabric demand in the market
(c) Acceptability or cloth according to the cloth selection
(d) None of the above

16

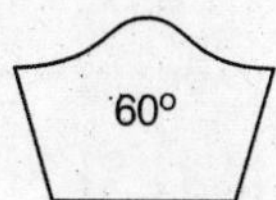

is the symbol for
(a) maximum temperature (b) 60 minutes dipping
(c) 60 times rubbing (d) None of these

17 What is use of embroidery frame?
(a) To make the round shape design
(b) To keep the fabric stretched
(c) To make colourful design
(d) To keep the fabric light weighted

18 What is the term used for the stiches with semi-circles?
(a) Ravel (b) Scallop (c) Tack (d) Tubing

19 What is zoning sampling technique?
(a) Method for selecting samples from raw cotton, wool or other fibres
(b) Method of doing quality control
(c) Method of handling bulk material
(d) Method of placing bulk fibres on the place

20 A broken line of the tub means
(a) overflow with water (b) overflow with soap
(c) special gentle treatment (d) None of these

21 Which farbic is most suitable for tailor's chalk?
(a) Woolen fabric (b) Silk fabric
(c) Cotton fabric (d) Linen fabric

22 Why core sampling technique is used?
(a) To make best fibre
(b) To assess the proportion of foreign matter
(c) To expand the raw material
(d) To press the fibre from tubes

23 What is the pattern of 'Lehariya print'?
(a) Mirrors (b) Fine dots
(c) Tiney boxes (d) Diagonal lines

24 Which of the following have low satiety value?
(a) Fat (b) Protein
(c) Carbohydrate (d) All of these

25 A line underneath the wash tub indicates
(a) low water level (b) gentle wash
(c) less severe process (d) All of these

26 How many administrative areas are under a district?
(a) 7 (b) 6 (c) 8 (d) 5

27 Why does protein provide satiety value?
(a) It takes long time to digest in alimentary canal
(b) It is tasty to eat
(c) It get stored in tissues
(d) None of the above

28 Which technique is widely used for both fibre and yarn?
(a) Stratified sampling (b) Cluster sampling
(c) Random sampling (d) None of these

29 Which among the following is the textile of Rajasthan?
(a) Bandhej (b) Bandhani (c) Zaukan (d) Zardozi

30 What is the global prevalence of obesity in adult men and women?
(a) 11% of men; 15% of women (b) 6% of men; 20% of women
(c) 27% of men; 34% of women (d) 45% of men; 36% of women

31 Which of the following textile properties are most desirable for Olympic swim wear?
(a) Absorption and reduced drag
(b) Comfort and durability
(c) Maximum stretch and durability
(d) Maximum stretch and reduced drag

32 What are the regions where finest 'Bandhej' is produced?
(a) Bikaner (b) Sikar (c) Both (a) and (b) (d) Only (b)

33 What is the average length of scissor?
(a) 10″ long (b) 5″ to 7″
(c) 5″ to 6″ long (d) None of these

34 Series of loops that intersect horizontally in a fabric are called as
(a) courses (b) wales (c) warp (d) weft

35 Which scissor cuts the leather with an ease?
(a) Electric scissor (b) Buttonhole scissor
(c) Pinking shear (d) Rotary cutter

36 Which among the following is/are most energy efficient?
(a) Incandescent bulb (b) Fluorescent tubelight
(c) Compact fluorescent lamp (d) All of these

37 According to the text, zoning ordinance regulate
(a) structural dimension (b) population density
(c) land use (d) All of these

38 Functional design is
(a) smart design
(b) takes considerations on all adverse side effects
(c) planning space based of the work being done
(d) All of the above

39 Zoning just be enacted in accordance with the comprehensive plan and regulates development by district, throughout the city or country.
(a) True (b) False
(c) Can't say (d) Neither (a) nor (b)

40 Standardisation helps maximum
(a) safety (b) quality
(c) compatibility (d) All of these

41 Match the following.

List I	List II
A. Clear liquid diet	1. Rest, drugs and fuid diet
B. Acute cholecystitis	2. Triples this birth weight end of 10-12 months
C. Infant	3. Septic throat
D. Staphylococci causes	4. Replaces the fluids lost by the body preventing dehydration

Codes

	A	B	C	D		A	B	C	D
(a)	4	3	2	1	(b)	2	4	1	3
(c)	4	1	2	3	(d)	1	3	4	2

42 Match the following.

List I	List II
A. Colours with predominance of blue	1. Warm
B. Yellowish green	2. Cool hues
C. Blue-green	3. Warm hues
D. Seem to advance	4. Are considered as cool
E. Seem to recede	5. Cool

Codes

	A	B	C	D	E		A	B	C	D	E
(a)	3	1	4	5	2	(b)	1	2	4	3	5
(c)	4	1	5	3	2	(d)	5	4	2	1	3

43 Match the following.

List I	List II
A. Dates	1. Potassium
B. Mango	2. Calcium
C. Ragi	3. Vitamin A
D. Mushroom	4. Iron
E. Banana	5. Protein

Codes

	A	B	C	D	E		A	B	C	D	E
(a)	2	3	1	4	5	(b)	1	2	4	3	5
(c)	4	3	2	5	1	(d)	3	2	1	4	5

44 Match the following.

List I	List II
A. For infants, children and pregnant and nursing mothers.	1. Significant amount of thiamine.
B. 70% of the calories in a diet.	2. Can be from carbohydrates.
C. Par-boiled rices.	3. Supply about 217 of total protein from animal foods.
D. The allowance for calories protein B complex.	4. Good supplementary value to cereal diet.
E. Pulse protein is rich in lysine.	5. Increased or decreased depending on body weight.

Codes

	A	B	C	D	E		A	B	C	D	E
(a)	3	2	5	1	4	(b)	3	2	1	5	4
(c)	4	5	2	3	1	(d)	3	2	1	4	5

45 Match the following.

List I	List II
A. Cognitive development	1. Memoria
B. Community education	2. Divorce
C. Family disorganisation	3. A cripps
D. Single parent	4. Parental involvement

Codes

	A	B	C	D		A	B	C	D
(a)	2	3	4	1	(b)	4	3	1	2
(c)	3	4	1	2	(d)	2	1	3	4

46 Match the following.

List I	List II
A. Child Labour	1. Children run away from home
B. Street Children	2. Children are sold
C. Orphan	3. Underage children work in a field
D. Child Trafficking	4. Both the parents leave the child

Codes

	A	B	C	D		A	B	C	D
(a)	3	1	4	2	(b)	1	3	2	4
(c)	4	3	1	2	(d)	2	1	3	4

47 Match the following.

List I	List II
A. Carbohydrates	1. Rigidity to bones
B. Amino acids	2. Synthesis of proteins
C. Phosphorous	3. Building block of proteins
D. Potassium	4. Facilitates excretion

Codes

	A	B	C	D		A	B	C	D
(a)	4	3	1	2	(b)	1	3	2	4
(c)	3	2	4	1	(d)	2	4	3	1

48 Match the following.

List I	List II
A. Sieve analysis	1. Pycnometer
B. Fluid flow	2. Image processing
C. Porosity	3. Particle diameter
D. Volume	4. Size of sample

Codes

	A	B	C	D		A	B	C	D
(a)	3	4	1	2	(b)	2	1	4	3
(c)	3	1	2	4	(d)	2	1	3	4

49 Match the following.

List I	List II
A. Banaras brocades	1. Kanchipuram
B. Jamdani	2. Varanasi
C. Kanjeevaram	3. Gwalior
D. Chanderi	4. West Bengal

Codes

	A	B	C	D		A	B	C	D
(a)	1	2	3	4	(b)	2	3	4	1
(c)	4	1	2	3	(d)	2	4	1	3

50 Match the following.

List I	List II
A. Cyclic menu	1. Menu of the day
B. A-La-carte menu	2. Set menu
C. Table d' hote menu	3. Choice of dishes
D. Dujour menu	4. Menu rotated at definite interval

Codes

	A	B	C	D		A	B	C	D
(a)	4	3	2	1	(b)	1	2	3	4
(c)	2	1	3	4	(d)	3	4	2	1

51 Match the following.

List I	List II
A. DWCRA	1 Integrated child development service
B. ICDS	2. Development of women and children in rural area.
C. CFTRI	3. Special nutrition programme
D. SNP	4. Central food technological research institute

Codes

	A	B	C	D		A	B	C	D
(a)	2	1	4	3	(b)	1	2	4	3
(c)	2	1	3	4	(d)	4	3	1	2

52 Match the following.

List I	List II
A. Subject-Centered design	1. Focuses on individual problems
B. Learner-centered design	2. Focuses on method of teaching
C. Problem-Centered design	3. Focuses on individual students
	4. Focuses on particular subject

Codes

	A	B	C		A	B	C
(a)	4	3	1	(b)	4	2	3
(c)	1	2	3	(d)	1	2	4

53 Match the following.

List I	List II
A. Silk-worm	1. The basic building block of fabric
B. Acetate	2. Made by reacting hydrocarbonic acid with dihydric alcohol
C. Fibre	3. Artificial wool
D. Dupont	4. Caterpiller
E. Polyester	5. Manufacturer of synthetic fibres

Codes

	A	B	C	D	E		A	B	C	D	E
(a)	1	2	3	4	5	(b)	3	4	2	5	1
(c)	4	3	1	5	2	(d)	2	1	5	4	3

54 Match the following.

List I	List II
A. Slide	1. Non-projected visual aid
B. Radio	2. Projected audio-visual aid
C. Chart	3. Audio aid
D. Video	4. Projected visual aid

Codes

	A	B	C	D		A	B	C	D
(a)	4	3	1	2	(b)	4	1	2	3
(c)	1	3	2	4	(d)	3	4	1	2

55 Match the following.

List I (Legal Rights)	List II (Year)
A. Immoral Traffic Act	1. 1961
B. Commission of Sati	2. 1956
C. Dowry Probition	3. 1984
D. Family Courts Act	4. 1987

Codes

	A	B	C	D		A	B	C	D
(a)	2	4	1	3	(b)	3	1	2	4
(c)	1	4	3	2	(d)	2	1	3	4

56 Match the following.

List I	List II
A. Convulsions in infants	1. Inadequate intake of Vitamin B_6.
B. Milk effective in preventing pellagra	2. Because of its richness in trypto phanm.
C. Vitamin B_6	3. Pyridoxal, pyridoxamine and pyridoxine.
D. Vitamin B_6 is required	4. For conversion of tryptophan to nicotinic acid and metabolism of essential fatty acids.
E. Niacin equivalent	5. In the assessment of the value of a food stuff as a source of nicotinic acid, take into account the tryptophan content.

Codes

	A	B	C	D	E		A	B	C	D	E
(a)	1	2	3	4	5	(b)	5	4	3	2	1
(c)	4	5	2	3	1	(d)	1	3	2	4	5

57 Match the following.

List I	List II
A. PWDVA	1. 1999
B. Helpline	2. 1960
C. Gottman	3. 181
D. Memoria	4. 2005

Codes

	A	B	C	D		A	B	C	D
(a)	3	4	2	1	(b)	4	3	1	2
(c)	1	3	4	2	(d)	2	1	3	4

58 Match the following.

List I	List II
A. Formal Education	1. Flexible Teaching
B. Non-Formal Education	2. Pre-defined Curriculum
C. Adult-Education	3. Learners are immature

Codes

	A	B	C		A	B	C
(a)	1	2	3	(b)	2	3	1
(c)	3	2	1	(d)	2	1	3

59 Match the following.

List I	List II
A. Language development	1. Jealousy, fear, love
B. Emotional development	2. Words and sentences
C. Cognitive development	3. Motor skills
D. Childhood diseases	4. Influensa, chickenpox

Codes

	A	B	C	D		A	B	C	D
(a)	2	1	3	4	(b)	1	2	3	4
(c)	1	2	4	3	(d)	4	3	2	1

60 Match the following.

List I	List II
A. Intelligence and enthusiasm	1. Motivating factors
B. Values, goals and standards	2. Home management process
C. Planning, controlling and evaluating	3. Homemaker
D. Higher education	4. Long-term goals.

Codes

	A	B	C	D		A	B	C	D
(a)	3	1	2	4	(b)	4	2	1	3
(c)	1	4	3	2	(d)	4	3	1	2

61 Match the following.

List I	List II
A. General tool	1. Stiletto
B. Sewing tool	2. Seam ripper
C. Measuring tool	3. Tracing wheel
D. Marking tool	4. Hem gauge

Codes

	A	B	C	D		A	B	C	D
(a)	1	2	3	4	(b)	4	1	2	3
(c)	2	1	4	3	(d)	4	3	2	1

62 Match the following.

List I (Stages of Development)	List II (Ages)
A. Infancy	1. Above 60
B. Adolescence	2. 21-60
C. Adulthood	3. 0-9
D. Old age	4. 10-21

Codes

	A	B	C	D		A	B	C	D
(a)	3	4	2	1	(b)	1	4	3	2
(c)	2	1	4	3	(d)	3	2	1	4

Directions **(Q. Nos. 63-80)** ***Given below are two statements, one labelled as Assertion (A) and the other labelled as Reason (R). Following are the codes given below. Choose the correct codes.***

Codes

(a) Both A and R are true and R is the correct explanation of A
(b) Both A and R are true but R is not the correct explanation of A
(c) A is true, but R is false
(d) A is false, but R is true

63 **Assertion** (A) Shriniketan Project helped to increase knowledge of rural people.
Reason (R) It helped to develop the feeling of women education and home development.

64 **Assertion** (A) Twist is defined as the spiral disposition of the components of the yarn and is generally expressed as the number of turns per unit length (turns per inch - tpi or turns per metres-tpm).
Reason (R) Yarn strength and yarn appearance is not affected by yarn twist.

65 **Assertion** (A) Petrol, benzine, methylated spirit chloroform, carbon tetrachloride and mineral of grease solvent.
Reason (R) These solvents are liquid and evaporate easily.

66 **Assertion** (A) Acute Renal failure means the kidneys have failed suddenly.
Reason (R) Various toxins or severe blood loss or trauma affect kidney functioning.

67 **Assertion** (A) Community Nutrition Programme may fail due to inadequate funding.
Reason (R) Community Nutrition Programme is a programme led by General Public.

68 **Assertion** (A) Work simplification helps the person in performing activities in a simple way.
Reason (R) It reduces frustration fatigue which arises due to lack of effectiveness m a Job.

69 **Assertion** (A) The basal metabolic rate decreases gradually, once adulthood is attained.
Reason (R) Energy degree rise in temperature results in 12% increases in the BMR.

70 **Assertion** (A) Bandhani is tie dye textile technique.
Reason (R) This technique pre-determines the areas on the fabric which are tied tightly With thread to protect from the colour.

71 **Assertion** (A) Balwadi Nutrition Programme was launched by Central Social Welfare Board.
Reason (R) The programme aims to help adolescent girls.

72 **Assertion** (A) An energy auditing is an inspection survey.
Reason (R) It analysis the energy flow for energy conservation in building.

73 **Assertion** (A) Food scientists specialists have incorporated various tests to evaluate quality of food.
Reason (R) These tests only check the physical properties of food like shape, size and colour.

74 **Assertion** (A) Obesity and heart disease result in excessive energy intake and reduced physical activity.
Reason (R) Sedentary life style and availability of high energy density foods lead to degenerative disease.

75 **Assertion** (A) Magnetic boards are similar to flannel boards.
Reason (R) It is a mechanical media that make an exact copy.

76 **Assertion** (A) Health all over the world is an important part of sustainable development.
Reason (R) Child and maternal mortality need to be improved.

77 **Assertion** (A) Scientific and technological advancement has greatly improved quality and safety standards in food production.
Reason (R) Use of computers has contributed tremendously for standardising operations.

78 **Assertion** (A) Kleptomania refers to compulsive stealing behaviour.
Reason (R) Parents are the reason, why the child steals.

79 **Assertion** (A) Newspapers are not a good way to spread nutritional awareness.
Reason (R) Nutrition should not be taught at school level.

80 **Assertion** (A) The basic purpose of project planning is the development of project schedule.
Reason (R) This process of project planning involves listing the entire schedule of the activities and detailing their sequence of implementation.

81 Give the correct sequence of managerial functions listed below.
1. Reporting 2. Staffing 3. Planning
4. Organising 5. Co-ordinating 6. Budgeting
7. Directing

Codes
(a) 3, 4, 2, 6, 7, 1, 5 (b) 3, 4, 2, 7, 5, 1, 6
(c) 2, 4, 6, 3, 1, 7, 5 (d) 5, 7, 4, 6, 2, 1, 3

82 Arrange the following in the sequence.
1. Distribute total amount of calorie required, decided between meals.
2. Check day's inclusion of specific food groups in the amount decided.
3. Identify the individual and his/her specific requirements.
4. Decide number of meals to be consumed.

Codes
(a) 3, 4, 1, 2 (b) 3, 1, 4, 2 (c) 1, 2, 3, 4 (d) 2, 3, 1, 4

83 Arrange the following in correct order.
1. Global initiative of academic network planning.
2. Atal Innovation Mission.
3. Saakshar Bharat Mission. 4. Ustad Scheme.

Codes
(a) 1, 2, 3, 4 (b) 3, 1, 4, 2 (c) 3, 2, 1, 4 (d) 2, 1, 3, 4

84 Following are the phrases of Project Management. Arrange them in order.
1. Evaluation 2. Monitoring
3. Need assessment 4. Situation analysis
5. Planning 6. Organisation

Codes
(a) 1, 2, 6, 5, 3, 4 (b) 3, 4, 5, 6, 2, 1 (c) 2, 1, 5, 6, 3, 4 (d) 4, 3, 6, 5, 1, 2

85 Arrange the following works of 'Food Chemistry' in increasing years of occurrence.
1. 'Elements of Agricultural Chemistry' was published.
2. Isolation of malic acid from apples.
3. Formation of Society of Public Analysts.
4. Establishment of Food Chemistry Division by Institute of Food Technologists.

Codes
(a) 4, 3, 1, 2 (b) 2, 1, 3, 4 (c) 3, 1, 2, 4 (d) 1, 2, 3, 4

86 Arrange the correct sequence of cutting a sleeve pattern.
1. Marking the stitching line 2. Tracing the stitching line
3. Cutting the sleeve pattern 4. Marking the cutting line
Select the correct answer using the codes given below.
(a) 2, 1, 4 and 3 (b) 1, 4, 3 and 2 (c) 3, 2, 1 and 4 (d) 4, 3, 2 and 1

87 Arrange the correct sequence of weaving operations.
1. Drawing 2. Looming and Weaving
3. Warp and Weft Winding 4. Denting
5. Warping and Sizing

Codes
(a) 5, 4, 1, 3, 2 (b) 3, 5, 1, 4, 2 (c) 1, 4, 5, 2, 3 (d) 1, 4, 2, 3, 5

88 Arrange the following in correct order.
1. Deen Dayal Upadhyay Gram Jyoti Yojana
2. Sansad Adarsh Gram Yojana
3. Shyama Prasad Mukherji Rurban Mission
4. Pradhan Mantri Gram Sadak Yojana

Codes
(a) 1, 2, 3, 4 (b) 2, 1, 3, 4 (c) 2, 3, 4, 1 (d) 4, 2, 3, 1

89 Arrange the following in correct order.
1. National Nutrition Mission
2. Food Security Mission
3. National Rural Health Mission
4. National Ayush Mission

Codes
(a) 4, 3, 2, 1 (b) 1, 2, 3, 4 (c) 3, 2, 1, 4 (d) 2, 3, 4, 1

90 Write the steps of extension educational process in sequence.
1. Define objective 2. Reconsider
3. Analyse the situation 4. Evaluation
5. Teaching

Codes
(a) 1, 3, 5, 4, 2 (b) 2, 3, 1, 4, 5 (c) 1, 4, 2, 3, 5 (d) 1, 3, 5, 2, 4

91 Arrange the right sequence of home management process.
1. Energising 2. Evaluation
3. Planning 4. Adjusting
5. Checking

Codes
(a) 3, 1, 5, 4, 2 (b) 1, 2, 3, 4, 5
(c) 4, 2, I, 3, 5 (d) 5, 4, 3, 2, 1

92 Arrange the correct sequence of weaving process.
1. Shedding 2. icking 3. Take up 4. Beating

Codes
(a) 2, 1, 3, 4 (b) 4, 3, 2, 1
(c) 2, 3, 4, 1 (d) 1, 2, 3, 4

93 Arrange the correct threading sequence pattern of a sewing machine.
1. Needle 2. Spool
3. Thread take up lever 4. Tension discs

Codes
(a) 1, 2, 4 and 3 (b) 2, 4,3 and 1
(c) 3, 1, 2 and 4 (d) 4, 3, 1 and 2

94 Arrange the following according to curriculum development steps.
1. Identify constraints 2. Create a curriculum map
3. Create a list of learning goals
4. Identify the needs of stakeholders

Codes
(a) 4, 3, 1, 2 (b) 4, 1, 2, 3
(c) 1, 2, 3, 4 (d) 4, 2, 3, 1

95 Arrange the correct sequence in weaving a fabric.
1. Shedding 2. Picking 3. Let off 4. Beat up

Codes
(a) 1, 4, 3, 2 (b) 2, 3, 4, 1
(c) 3, 1, 2, 4 (d) 4, 2, 1, 3

Directions (Q. Nos. 96-100) ***Read the passage and answer the following questions.***

Diet therapy is a branch of dietetics concerned with the use of food for therapeutic purpose. Diet therapy is a broad term used for the practical application of nutrition as a preventive or corrective treatment of a disease. It concerns with recovery from illness by giving good diet and prevention of disease. It may involve the modification of the existing dietary life style to promote optimum health. For example, a dietitian or a nutrition counsellor may prescribe a diet therapy to an obese person to improve health. The therapy may involve including foods (such as fats, sugars etc.) that may make the condition worse. Basically the therapy promotes a balanced selection of foods vital for good health. The principles of diet therapy are to : maintain good nutritional status correct deficiencies or disease, if any provide rest to the body help metabolise the nutrients and make changes in body weight, when necessary. Diet therapy may include prescribing specialised dietary regimes or meal plans. The specialised diet regimens or meal plans are called therapeutic diets. Therapeutic diet refers to a meal plan that controls the intake of certain food or nutrients. They are adaptation of the normal, regular diet.

96 Diet therapy is concerned with
(a) use of food for pleasure
(b) use of food for complete relaxation
(c) use of food for recovery from illness and prevention of illness
(d) All of tho above

97 The phrase 'optimum health' means
(a) more focus on mental health.
(b) more focus on emotional health.
(C) ability to adapt and manage life experiences and challenges.
(d) None of the above

98 Some principles of diet therapy are
(a) correct deficiencies or diseases if any
(b) help in reducing weight
(c) maintain good nutritional status
(d) Both (a) and (c)

99 The therapeutic diet refers to
(a) a diet which controls intake of certain foods or nutrients.
(b) liquid diet
(c) protein diet
(d) only soft diet

100 What will be a suitable title of the given passage?
(a) Optimum health, need of the day
(b) Diet therapy and its uses
(c) Nutrition and meal plan
(d) Prevention of diseases

ANSWERS

1 (c)	2 (a)	3 (b)	4 (b)	5 (a)	6 (c)	7 (c)	8 (b)	9 (c)	10 (a)
11 (b)	12 (a)	13 (d)	14 (c)	15 (a)	16 (a)	17 (b)	18 (b)	19 (a)	20 (c)
21 (a)	22 (b)	23 (d)	24 (c)	25 (d)	26 (b)	27 (a)	28 (c)	29 (a)	30 (a)
31 (c)	32 (c)	33 (c)	34 (d)	35 (d)	36 (c)	37 (d)	38 (d)	39 (a)	40 (d)
41 (c)	42 (c)	43 (c)	44 (b)	45 (b)	46 (a)	47 (a)	48 (a)	49 (c)	50 (b)
51 (a)	52 (a)	53 (c)	54 (a)	55 (a)	56 (a)	57 (b)	58 (d)	59 (a)	60 (a)
61 (c)	62 (b)	63 (c)	64 (c)	65 (a)	66 (b)	67 (c)	68 (b)	69 (b)	70 (a)
71 (c)	72 (a)	73 (b)	74 (c)	75 (c)	76 (c)	77 (b)	78 (c)	79 (b)	80 (a)
81 (b)	82 (a)	83 (b)	84 (b)	85 (b)	86 (d)	87 (b)	88 (b)	89 (a)	90 (d)
91 (b)	92 (d)	93 (b)	94 (a)	95 (b)	96 (d)	97 (c)	98 (d)	99 (a)	100 (b)